Volume II (I-Z)   Mrs. M. Grieve

A MODERN HERBAL

The Medicinal, Culinary, Cosmetic and
Economic Properties, Cultivation and Folk-Lore
of Herbs, Grasses, Fungi, Shrubs & Trees
with Their Modern Scientific Uses

STONE BASIN
BOOKS

ISBN: 978-1-62654-221-1

LIST OF PLATES

FLORENTINE IRIS
Iris Florentina

POISON IVY
Rhus Toxicodendron

ICELAND MOSS. *See* MOSS

IGNATIUS BEANS (*POISON*)

Strychnos Ignatii (BERG.)
N.O. Loganiaceæ

> *Synonyms.* Faba Ignatic. Ignatia amara (Linn.)
> *Part Used.* Ripe dried seeds
> *Habitat.* Philippine Islands

¶ *Description.* A large woody climbing shrub, introduced into Cochin China, and highly esteemed there as a medicine. It attracted the attention of the Jesuits, hence its name. In commerce the beans are about one full inch long; ovate, a dull blacky brown colour, very hard and horny, covered in patches with silvery adpressed hairs; endosperm translucent, enclosing an irregular cavity with an oblong embryo; no odour; taste extremely bitter. Each fruit contains about twelve to twenty seeds embedded in the pulp from which they have to be separated.

¶ *Constituents.* The beans have the same properties as Nux Vomica, but contain more strychnine, also brucine, a volatile principle extractive, gum, resin, colouring matter, a fixed oil, and bassorin; they contain no albumen or starch.

¶ *Medicinal Action and Uses.* Tonic and stimulant in action like Nux Vomica, which, being cheaper, is nearly always used as a substitute. Old writers lauded these beans as a remedy against cholera. They are useful in certain forms of heart trouble, but must be used with the greatest caution, as they are a very active and powerful poison.

¶ *Antidotes.* Same as for strychnine, chloroform, belladonna, aconite, tobacco, chloral hydrate 1 drachm doses, morphia.

¶ *Preparations and Dosages.* Tincture of Ignatia, 5 to 20 minims. Alkaline Tincture of Ignatia (*syn.* Goute Ameres de Beaume), 5 to 20 minims.

INDIAN HEMP. *See* HEMP

INDIAN PHYSIC

Gillenia trifoliata (MŒNCH.)
N.O. Rosaceæ

> *Synonyms.* Bowman's Root. American Ipecacuanha. Gillenia. Indian Hippo. Spiræa trifoliata. Spiræa stipulata
> *Part Used.* Root-bark
> *Habitat.* Eastern United States

¶ *Description.* A perennial herb, indigenous to the United States, its irregular, brownish root gives rise to several stems 2 or 3 feet in height, and has depending from it many long, thin fibres. The leaves and leaflets are of various shapes, and the white, reddish-tinged flowers grow in a few loose, terminal panicles.

The dried root is reddish brown, the bark being easily removed and pulverized. Within, it is light, ligneous, and comparatively inert. The bitterness of the bark is extracted by alcohol, or by water at 212° F., to which a red colour is given.

It grows well in the author's garden, in slightly moist, rich soil, not in the full blaze of the mid-day sun.

¶ *Constituents.* The roots have been found to contain gum, starch, gallotannic acid, fatty matter, wax, resin, lignin, albumen, salts and colouring matter.

Gillenin was obtained by W. B. Stanhope by exhausting coarsely powdered bark with alcohol, evaporating the resulting red tincture to the consistency of an extract, dissolving this in cold water, filtering, evaporating, and finally drying on glass.

Half a grain caused nausea and retching.

Two glucosides were found, Gillein, from the ethereal extract, and Gilleenin, from the aqueous infusion.

¶ *Medicinal Action and Uses.* Tonic, emetic, slightly diaphoretic, cathartic, and expectorant. The American Indians and early colonists knew the uses of the roots, the action of which resembles Ipecacuanha.

Recommended in dyspepsia, dropsy, rheumatism, chronic costiveness, and whenever an emetic is required. It is safe and reliable.

¶ *Dosages.* Of powdered root, as an emetic, 20 to 30 grains. In dyspepsia, as a tonic, 2 to 4 grains. As a sudorific, in cold water, 6 grains at intervals of two or three hours. It may be combined with opium. Frequent large doses of the infusion cause vomiting and purging.

¶ *Other Species.*
Gillenia stipulata, taller and more bushy, with fewer flowers and roots more like those of Ipecac; grows as far west as Kansas.

It is, equally with *G. trifoliata*, the source of Gillenia.

See MEADOWSWEET, HARDHACK.

INDIGO

Indigofera tinctoria
N.O. Leguminosæ

Synonyms. Pigmentum Indicum
Part Used. The plant
Habitat. India; cultivated in sub-tropical countries

¶ *Description*. A blue dyestuff is obtained from the various species of Indigofera. It does not exist ready formed, but is produced during fermentation from another agent existing in the plant. This is called Indocan, and is yellow, amorphous, of a nauseous bitter taste with an acid reaction; readily soluble in water, alcohol and ether.

¶ *Medicinal Action and Uses*. Indigo was at one time much used in medicine, but now is rarely employed. It is said to produce nausea and vomiting.

It is a very well-known and highly important dye, millions of pounds being exported from India annually.

An artificial product, Indigotine, is manufactured chemically and used as a substitute.

INDIGO (WILD)

Baptisia tinctoria (R. BR.)
N.O. Leguminosæ

Synonyms. Baptisia. Horse-fly Weed. Rattlebush. Indigo-weed. Sophora tinctoria (Linn.). Podalyria tinctoria (Michx.)
Parts Used. Root, bark, leaves
Habitat. Dry hilly woods from Canada to Carolina

¶ *Description*. An herbaceous perennial which takes its name from the Greek *Bapto* (to dye); has a black woody root, yellowish internally with many rootlets; stem about 3 feet high, smooth, glabrous, round, and branched; leaves, small, subsessile, alternate and palmately trifoliate; leaflets rounded at| end; calyx four-cleft; flowers, yellow, blooming August and September, in small loose terminal racemes. Legume short, bluish-black seeds, subreniform.
¶ *Constituents*. The root is non-odorous and of a nauseous acrid taste, containing gum, albumen, starch, a yellowish resin and a crystalline substance.
¶ *Medicinal Action and Uses*. Used internally in form of decoction or syrup in scarlatina, typhus, and in all cases where there is a tendency to putrescency; it is purgative, emetic, stimulant, astringent, and antiseptic; principally used for its antiseptic qualities.
¶ *Dosage*. Of the decoction, 1 tablespoonful. Fluid extract, ¼ to ½ drachm. Baptisin, 1 to 3 grains.

IPECACUANHA

Psychotria Ipecacuanha (STOKES)
N.O. Rubiaceæ

Synonym. Cephælis Ipecacuanha
Part Used. Root
Habitat. The root used in medicine under this name is that of a small, shrubby plant about a foot high, belonging to the order Rubiaceæ, which is found in most parts of Brazil, growing in clumps or patches, in moist, shady woods.

The drug is chiefly collected in the interior, in the province of Matto Grosso and near the German colony of Philadelphia, north of Rio de Janeiro. It is also found in New Granada and in Bolivia.

¶ *Description*. The plant has a slender stem, which grows partly underground and is often procumbent at the base, the lower portion being knotted.

Fibrous rootlets are given off from the knots, and some of them develop an abnormally thick bark, in which much starch is deposited.

The thickened rootlets alone are collected and dried for medicinal use, since the active constituents of the drug are found chiefly in the bark.

Ipecacuanha roots are collected, chiefly by the Indians, during the months of January and February, when the plant is in flower and are prepared by separation from the stem, cleaning and hanging in bundles to dry in the sun.

The drug is known in commerce as Brazilian or Rio Ipecacuanha.
¶ *History*. The name of the plant is the Portuguese form of the native word, *i-pe-kaa-guéne*, which is said to mean 'road-side sick-making plant.'

In an account of Brazil, written by a Portuguese friar who had resided in that country from about 1570 to 1600, mention is made of three remedies for the bloody flux, one of which is called Igpecaya, or Pigaya, which is probably this root.

Although in common use in Brazil, Ipecacuanha was not employed in Europe prior to the year 1672, when a traveller named Legros brought a quantity of the root to Paris from South America. In 1680, a merchant of Paris named Garnier became possessed of 150 lb. of Ipecacuanha, and informed his assistant and the physician Helvetius of its usefulness in treating dysentery.

Helvetius prescribed the new drug, and it formed the basis of a patent medicine for dysentery. Trials were made of the composition, and Helvetius was granted by Louis XIV the sole right of vending the remedy. A few years after, the secret was bought from him by the French Government for 1,000 louis d'or and the formula was made public in 1688.

The botanical source of Ipecacuanha was the subject of much dispute, until it was finally settled by Gomez, a physician of the Portuguese Navy, who brought authentic specimens from Brazil to Lisbon in 1800.

Ipecacuanha occurs in commerce as slender and somewhat tortuous closely annulated pieces, which seldom exceed 6 inches in length and $\frac{1}{4}$ inch in thickness. It varies in colour from very dark brown to dark red, the latter colour being partly due to adhering particles of earth. Difference in colour may also be due to difference of age or mode of drying. The bark is constricted at short intervals, so as to give the root the appearance of a number of discs somewhat irregularly strung together. The constrictions are sometimes quite shallow in Brazilian or Rio Ipecacuanha, though they may penetrate nearly to the wood. The root is hard and breaks with a very short fracture, the fractured surface exhibiting a thick, dark grey bark or cortex, with a horny, resinous or starchy appearance and a hard, wiry centre – small dense wood, in which no distinct pores or pith can be discerned; when examined with a lens though it is radiate.

The drug has a bitter taste, but only a slight, rather musty odour.

It is generally mixed with more or less of the slender subterranean stem, which has only a very thin bark, surrounding a ring of wood which encloses a distinct pith, and is thus easily distinguished from the root. The activity of the drug resides chiefly in the cortical portion, hence the presence of the stem diminishes its value.

The variety imported from Colombia and known as Cartagena Ipecacuanha, the product of *Psychotria acuminata*, differs only in its larger size and in being less conspicuously annulated, the constrictions of the bark assuming the form of narrow merging ridges.

¶ *Substitutes*. In addition to the Cartagena Ipecacuanha, various other roots have been offered as substitutes, but all differ considerably.

East Indian Ipecacuanha, from *Cryptocarpus spiralis*, exhibits a typically monocotyledous structure in transverse section, scattered bundles running the pith, and a white starchy bark.

The name *poaya* is applied in Brazil to emetic roots of several genera belonging to the natural orders Rubiaceæ, Violaceæ and Polygalaceæ, and hence several roots have from time to time been sent over to England as Ipecacuanha, but none of them possess the ringed or annulated appearance of the true drug. Of these, the root of *Ionidium Ipecacuanha*, *Richardsonia scabra* and *P. emetica* are those which have most frequently been exported from Brazil or Colombia.

Undulated Ipecacuanha, from *R. scabra*, is only lightly annulated, the wood is porous and the starchy bark often has a violet colour.

Lesser Striated Ipecacuanha from another species of *Richardsonia* is dark purplish brown in colour, longitudinally wrinkled, not annulated, and has porous wood.

Greater Striated Ipecacuanha from *P. emetica*, known as *Black or Peruvian Ipecacuanha*, closely resembles the preceding, but contains no starch and has dense wood. It grows in Peru and New Grenada, and in earlier days was for a long time considered as the source of the new drug, but is much less active.

White Ipecacuanha, from *I. Ipecacuanha* is greyish-white, or yellowish in colour and is also free from starch. This likewise was for long believed to be the plant which produces the genuine drug. It is a member of the order Violaceæ. The root is almost insipid and inodorous and is used in Brazil as an emetic, though it has been considered doubtful whether it possesses any well-defined properties.

The roots of several species of *Borreria*, as *B. ferruginia* and *B. Poaya*, are also used in Brazil as substitutes for Ipecacuanha.

¶ *Constituents*. The chief constituents of Ipecacuanha root are the alkaloids Emetine, Cephaelin and Psychotrine, of which the bark may contain from 1·5 to 2 per cent., of which about 72 per cent. consists of Emetine and 26 per cent. of Cephaelin, while only 2 per cent. consists of Psychotrine.

Emetine, to which Ipecacuanha owes its properties and which, with the exception of traces, occurs only in the cortical portion of the root, is an amorphous white powder, but it forms crystalline salts. It has a bitter taste, no odour and turns yellow when exposed to air and light.

Other constituents are a crystalline saponin-like glucoside, an amorphous, bitter gluco-side, which is a modification of tannin, and is known as Ipecacuanhic acid, choline, resin, pectin, starch, sugar, calcium oxalate, odorous, fatty matter and a disagreeable-smelling volatile oil.

Cartagena Ipecacuanha contains 2 to 3 per cent. more alkaloidal matter than the Brazilian drug, but a smaller proportion of Emetine, Cephaelin being the alkaloid present in largest quantities.

East Indian Ipecacuanha and White Ipecacuanha contain minute quantities of emetic principles, which differ from the alkaloids of true Ipecacuanha, but the Undulated and Striated Ipecacuanha contain Emetine.

¶ *Medicinal Action and Uses.* In large doses, Ipecacuanha root is emetic; in smaller doses, diaphoretic and expectorant, and in still smaller, stimulating to the stomach, intestines and liver, exciting appetite and facilitating digestion.

The dose of the powdered root is $\frac{1}{4}$ to 2 grains when an expectorant action is desired (it is frequently used in the treatment of bronchitis and laryngitis, combined with other drugs, aiding in the expulsion of the morbid product), and from 15 to 30 grains when given as an emetic, which is one of its most valuable functions.

The Pharmacopœias contain a very large number of preparations of Ipecacuanha, most of which are standardized.

Ipecacuanha has been known for more than a century to benefit amœbic (or tropical) dysentery, and is regarded as the specific treatment, but the administration of the drug by mouth was limited by its action as an emetic. Sir Leonard Rogers showed in 1912 that subcutaneous injections of the alkaloid Emetine, the chief active principle present in Ipecacuanha usually produced a rapid cure in cases of amœbic dysentery. The toxic action of Emetine on the heart must be watched. A preparation from which the Emetine has been removed, known as de-emetized Ipecacuanha, is also in use for cases of dysentery.

IRISES

The Iris belongs to a family of plants that is justly popular in this country for its many varieties of handsome garden blooms, beautifying the borders in spring and early summer.

The plant is named after the rainbow goddess, 'Iris,' from the beauty and variety of colours in the flowers of the genus.

From ancient times the stately Iris stood as a symbol of power and majesty – it was dedi-

The great value of the drug in dysentery and its rapid increase in price from an average of 2s. 9½d. per lb. in 1850 to about 8s. 9d. per lb. in 1870, led to attempts to acclimatize the plant in India, but without much commercial success, owing to the difficulty of finding suitable places for its cultivation and to its slowness of growth. It is grown to a limited extent in the Malay States, at Johore, near Singapore. In December, 1915, the Brazil root was valued at 24s. per lb. and the Johore root at 20s. per lb. At the same time, Cartagena root sold for 16s. per lb. It would probably pay to grow this plant more extensively in the British Colonies.

The diaphoretic properties are employed in the *Pulvis Ipecacuanhæa compositus*, or Dover's Powder, which contains 1 part of Ipecacuanha powder and 1 part of Opium in 10.

When applied to the skin, Ipecacuanha powder acts as a powerful irritant, even to the extent of causing pustulations.

When inhaled, it causes sneezing and a mild inflammation of the nasal mucous membrane.

Toxic doses cause gastro-enteritis, cardiac failure, dilation of the blood-vessels, severe bronchitis and pulmonary inflammation.

¶ *Preparations and Dosages.* Powdered root, 5 to 30 grains. Fluid extract, B.P., 2 to 20 drops. Comp. Tinct. (Dover's), U.S.P., 8 drops. Wine, B.P., 10 drops to 6 drachms. Syrup, U.S.P., $\frac{1}{4}$ to 4 drachms. Dover's Powder, B.P., 5 to 15 grains.

Other plants possessing emetic properties to a greater or less degree, to which the name of Ipecacuanha has been popularly applied are: American Ipec., *Gillenia stipulacea*; Wild Ipec., *Euphorbia Ipecacuanha*; Guinea Ipec., *Bœrhavia decumbens*; Venezuela Ipec., *Sarcostemma glaucum*; Ipecacuanha des Allemands, *Vincetoxicum officinale*, and the Bastard Ipecacuanha, *Asclepias cuirassavica*, of the West Indies. This plant is used by the negroes as an emetic and the root is purgative; the juice of the plant, made into a syrup, is said to be a powerful anthelmintic, and as such is given to children in the West Indies.

N.O. Iridaceæ

cated to Juno and was the origin of the sceptre, the Egyptians placing it on the brow of the Sphinx and on the sceptre of their kings, the three leaves of its blossoms typifying faith, wisdom and valour.

Cultivation has produced a great number of varieties, both among the bulbous or Spanish Iris (*Iris xiphium*) and the herbaceous, or Flag Irises, which have fleshy, creeping root-stocks or rhizomes. Among the latter, many have a considerable reputation for their medicinal virtues; in all the species belonging to this genus, the roots being more or less acrid, are possessed of cathartic and emetic properties. The chief economic use of the Iris at the present time is for the production of Orris Root (*Rhizoma Iridis*), which is derived from *I. Germanica*, *I. pallida* and *I. Florentina*, collected indiscriminately in Italy from these three species, well-known and very beautiful ornamental plants, natives of the eastern Mediterranean region, extending into Northern India and Northern Africa, and largely cultivated for their rhizomes in Southern Europe, mostly on the mountain slopes.

I. pseudacorus, *I. fœtidissima* and *I. tuberosa* are the European species that have been employed in medicine, though their use has much declined, but the American species, *I. versicolor*, produces a drug official in the United States Pharmacopœia.

Only two of these Irises are naturally wild plants in this country, *I. pseudacorus* (the Yellow Flag) and *I. fœtidissima* (the Stinking Iris). *I. tuberosa* (the Snakeshead Iris), which has cathartic properties, is occasionally but very rarely found in Cornwall and South Devon, but it is not native, and where it occurs it is considered a garden escape.

I. Germanica and other Flag Irises are cultivated in this country for their beautiful flowers, but no attempts have been made to supply the market with the rhizomes.

In ancient Greece and Rome, Orris Root was largely used in perfumery, and Macedonia, Elis and Corinth were famous for their unguents of Iris.

Theophrastus and Dioscorides were well acquainted with Orris Root; Dioscorides and Pliny remark that the best comes from Illyricum (the modern Dalmatia). Probably *I. Germanica* is the Illyrian Iris of the ancients, as it is plentiful there and *I. Florentina* and *I. pallida* do not occur. The latter were probably introduced into Northern Italy in the early Middle Ages. The ancient arms of Florence – a white Lily or Iris on a red shield – seem to indicate that the city was famed for the growth of these plants. A writer of the thirteenth century, Petrus de Crescentiro of Bologna, mentions the cultivation of the White, as well as of the Purple Iris, and states at what season the root should be collected for medicinal use.

IRIS GERMANICA (Linn.), Blue Flower de Luce, German Iris, is a handsome plant with sword-like leaves of a bluish-green colour, narrow and flat, the largest of all the species. The flower-stems are 2 to 3 feet high, the flowers, which bloom in May and June, are large and deep blue, or purplish-blue in colour. The three bending petals, or falls, are of a faint purple, inclining to blue, with purple veins running lengthwise; the beard on them is yellow and the three erect petals or standards are bright blue, with faint purple stripes. The flowers have an agreeable scent, reminiscent of orange blossoms. The creeping root-stocks are thick and fleshy, spreading over the surface of the ground and of a brownish colour.

¶ *Habitat.* The plant is a native of Southern Europe, very frequent in Italy, apart from its cultivation there, and is also cultivated in Morocco. In England, this German Flag or Flag Iris is by far the commonest of the family in gardens and justly deserves its popularity, for it will grow and flower well in the most unpromising situations and will bear with apparent equanimity hardships that few other plants would endure without loss of vitality. It is not moisture-loving – ordinary border soil, well cultivated, suits it well and the heavy clay soils are more or less inimical to its growth. If the best results are to be obtained, deep and rich beds should be prepared for these Irises, for they will well repay liberal treatment by the production of larger and more numerous flowers. Although they may be moved at any time of the year, April is the best month. They will not flower the same year, but they will during the summer, if attended to, become sufficiently strong to bloom freely the succeeding year. Winter is the worst time to move them, as in heavy soil, the plants often remain dormant without forming a single root-fibre until the spring. But they are easily increased in spring by dividing the root-stocks and replanting and watering into rich soil.

The German Iris, or Flag Iris of the nurseryman as it now exists, is a compound of many species and more varieties, as hybridization has been extensively carried on for many years.

¶ *Medicinal Action and Uses.* The juice of the fresh roots of this Iris, bruised with wine, has been employed as a strong purge of great efficiency in dropsy, old physic writers stating that if the dropsy can be cured by the hand of man, this root will effect it. The juice is also sometimes used as a cosmetic and for the removal of freckles from the skin.

IRIS PALLIDA (Lamarck) has sweet-scented flowers of a delicate, pale blue. It is a native of the Eastern Mediterranean countries and grows very freely in Italy. It yields, with *I. Germanica*, the bulk of the drug.

IRIS FLORENTINA (Linn.), called by our old writers White Flower de Luce, or Flower de Luce of Florence, has large, white flowers tinged with pale lavender and a bright yellow beard on the falls. Less commonly, a purple form occurs, of smaller growth.

¶ *Medicinal Action and Uses*. The fresh root, like that of *I. Germanica*, is a powerful cathartic, and for this reason its juice has been employed in dropsy.

It is chiefly used in the dry state, being said to be good for complaints of the lungs, for coughs and hoarseness, but is now more valued for the pleasantness of its violet-like perfume than for any other use.

Fresh roots have an earthy smell, the characteristic violet odour is gradually developed during the drying process and does not attain its maximum for at least two years, and even intensifies after that time. The essential oil may, therefore, be included in the class of so-called 'ferment-oils.'

The rhizomes of *I. Germanica*, *I. pallida* and *I. Florentina* so closely resemble one another that they are not easily distinguished. Contractions occur at intervals of about two inches, indicating the limit of a year's growth in each case.

When fresh, the rhizomes are extremely acrid and when chewed excite a pungent taste in the mouth, which continues some hours. This acridity is almost entirely dissipated when dried, the taste then being slightly bitter and the smell agreeable, closely approaching that of violets, though in the fresh state the rhizomes are practically odourless. The loss of acridity appears to be due to the disappearance of a volatile acrid principle on drying the rhizome.

All three species of Iris from which Orris root is derived were already cultivated in England in the time of Gerard, though not on a commercial scale.

¶ *Collection*. In Tuscany and other parts of Italy, large districts are given over to the cultivation of these three Irises. They are also cultivated, but only to a slight degree, in other parts of Europe, in Morocco and in India.

The planting of the Orris root in Tuscany – locally known as 'giaggiolo' – is a matter of great importance. When the Iris begins to grow, the ground is carefully and systematically weeded, this being chiefly done by women, who traverse the rows of the plants barefoot, hoeing up the weeds; whole families of peasants work together at this, and in the subsequent collection, trimming and drying of the roots.

The Orris plant takes two or even three years to arrive at maturity, only a somewhat sparse growth being attained during the second year: the flowers are very fine, but the roots are as yet immature. In the third year of its growth, the plant attains almost the height of a man. The full beauty of the flowers lasts during May and June, in July they fade and wither and the glory of the plantation is over.

The product of a good harvest at a large Orris plantation at San Polo, in the hilly region midway between Florence and Siena in Tuscany, is about a million kilogrammes of fresh roots (about 1,000 tons), yielding after peeling and drying, roughly 300 tons of dry root.

Orris root, in the decorticated, dried condition, is imported into England in large casks, mainly from Leghorn, Trieste and Mogador.

There are several varieties of Orris in commerce, differing chiefly in colour and the care with which they have been peeled. The finest is Florentine Orris, from *I. Florentina*, which is carefully peeled, nearly white, plump and very fragrant, irregular in shape, bearing small marks where the rootlets have been removed. Veronese Orris, from *I. Germanica*, is usually somewhat compressed and elongated, less suddenly tapering than the Florentine root, less carefully peeled, yellowish in colour, and somewhat wrinkled and has not the fine fragrance of the Florentine Orris.

Morocco or Mogadore Orris, also obtained from *I. Germanica*, bears particles of reddish-brown cork, is darker in colour generally and less fragrant; the pieces are also smaller, flatter, more shrunken and often bear the shrivelled remains of leaves at the apex. This variety is sometimes bleached with sulphur dioxide. It is altogether inferior to both the foregoing varieties. Bombay Orris is also of small size, dark-coloured and of inferior fragrance.

¶ *Constituents*. The chief constituent of Orris root is the oil of Orris (0·1 to 0·2 per cent.), a yellowish-white to yellow mass, containing about 85 per cent. of odourless myristic acid, which appears to be liberated from a fat present in the rhizome during the process of steam distillation. Oil of Orris is known commercially as Orris Butter.

Other constituents are fat, resin, a large quantity of starch, mucilage, bitter extractive and a glucoside named Iridin, which is not to be confused with the powdered extracti Iridin or Irisin, prepared from the rhizome of the American plant *I. versicolor*, by precipitating a tincture of the drug with water and mixing the precipitate with an equal weight of powdered liquorice root, or other absorbent powder.

The odorous constituent of oil of Orris is a liquid ketone named Irone, to which the violet-like odour is due (though it is not absolutely identical with oil of Violets obtained from the natural flower), and it is the presence of this principle in the rhizome that has long led to the employment of powdered Orris root in the preparation of Violet powders, which owe very little of their scent to the real Violet perfume. It was first isolated by the eminent chemist Tiemann and formed the basis of his researches on artificial Violet perfume, and in 1893 he succeeded in preparing an allied body, which was termed Ionone and which had an odour even more like that of Violets than had Irone, and is now largely manufactured for the perfumery trade in making toilet waters and handkerchief extracts. The discovery of Ionone, which costs about one-eighth of the natural oil of Violets, has popularized Violet perfume to an enormous extent: most of the cheaper Violet perfumes on the market contain no trace of true Violet, but are made entirely with the artificial Ionone.

Otto of Orris is a golden-yellow oily liquid, which contains the odorous principles of the concrete oil of the rhizome without the solid, fatty inodorous constituents.

The important industry of Orris root still requires the light of scientific research to be thrown upon the life history of the plant to determine the conditions under which the largest percentage of the volatile oil can be developed.

¶ *Medicinal Action and Uses*. Orris Root is rarely employed in *medicine* at the present time.

The fresh root possesses diuretic, emetic and cathartic properties. If given in large doses, it will occasion nausea, vomiting, purging and colic.

The drug was formerly employed in the treatment of bronchitis and chronic diarrhœa, and was considered a useful remedy in dropsy. The internal dose is stated to be from 5 to 15 grains.

The starch of the rhizome was formerly reckoned medicinal.

The dried powder is said to act as a good snuff, useful to excite sneezing to relieve cases of congested headache.

Pieces of the dried root are occasionally chewed for the purpose of overcoming a disagreeable breath.

The principal use of the dried root is, however, in *perfumery*, in sachet powders and to flavour dentifrices, toothpowders and cachous.

Oil of Orris, obtained by distilling powdered Orris root with steam, has an intense and extremely delicate odour of the fresh Violet and commands a high price. It is used commercially in the preparation of the finest scents and is also blended with artificial Violet perfumes, the odour of which it renders more subtle. Orris has the power of strengthening the odour of other fragrant bodies and is used as a fixative in perfumery.

Powdered Orris root is sometimes put into rinsing water in laundries and imparts a refreshing and fragrant scent to the linen.

Orris root, mixed with Anise, was used in England as a perfume for linen as early as 1480, under which date it is mentioned in the Wardrobe accounts of Edward IV.

One of the most interesting of the MS. still-room books of the later seventeenth century is *Mary Doggett: Her Book of Receipts*, 1682. In it we find 'A perfume for a sweet bagg,' as follows:

'Take half a pound of Cypress Roots, a pound of *Orris*, 3 quarter of a pound of Calamus, 3 Orange stick with Cloves, 2 ounces of Benjamin, 3 quarters of a pound of Rhodium, a pound of Coriander seed, and an ounce of Storax and 4 pecks of Damask Rose leaves, a peck of dryed sweet Marjerum, a pretty stick of Juniper shaved very thin, some lemon pele dryed and a stick of Brasill; let all these be powdered very grosely for ye first year and immediately put into your baggs; the next year pound and work it and it will be very good again.'

Dr. Rhind (*History of the Vegetable Kingdom*, 1868) states that Orris gives the peculiar flavour to artificial brandies made in this country, and the root is much used in Russia to flavour a drink made of honey and ginger which is sold in the streets.

The larger and finer roots are often turned into pretty forms to be used for ornamental purposes, rosary beads, etc., and long pieces of Verona Orris are often shaped for infants' use when teething. The less handsome rhizomes, as well as the chips, are distilled.

Lyte says 'the Iris is knowen of the clothworkers and drapers, for with these rootes they use to trimme their clothes to make them sweete and pleasant.' This was probably the 'swete clothe' so celebrated in the reign of Elizabeth.

IRIS PSEUDACORUS (LINN.)

N.O. Iridaceæ

Synonyms. Iris Aquatica. Iris lutia. Yellow Flag. Yellow Iris. Fleur de Luce. Dragon Flower. Myrtle Flower. Fliggers. Flaggon. Segg. Sheggs. Daggers. Jacob's Sword. Gladyne. Meklin. Levers. Livers. Shalder

Part Used. Root

Of all British wild plants, none can rival in stately beauty this native representative of the Irises, one of the most distinguished plants in the marginal vegetation of watery places, not only in this country, being universally distributed in Great Britain and growing also in

Ireland, but also throughout Europe, North Africa and Siberia.

It is found on river-banks, by the side of lakes, ponds, etc., in ditches and hedges, but any moist, shady place will suit it, and it is quite worthy of a place in our gardens.

Propagation is effected in autumn or spring, by division of the root-stocks. It should not, however, be allowed to grow where cattle feed.

¶ *Description.* From the thick, creeping rhizome, brownish on the outside, reddish and spongy within, which pushes through the moist ground parallel to the surface, many rootlets pass downwards. From above it, rise the broad, flat, sword-shaped, stalkless leaves, bound several together into a sheath at the base. The lower, radical leaves are 2 to 3 feet tall, the upper leaves much shorter, embracing the flower-stalk, which is round and seldom rises as high as the outer leaves. On the top of the stem are the beautiful, very conspicuous, deep yellow flowers, two or three together, the buds being very large and pointed. The mature flowers consist of three large, drooping, yellow petal-like sepals (the falls) with brownish mottled markings on their upper surfaces, inside which are the three petalloid stigmas, also yellow, which arch gracefully over the stamens, forming a rain-protecting roof for the pollen, as in all the Irises. The honey is contained in canals on the inner side, towards the base of the small, erect petals and out of these it exudes and lies round the ovary in the heart of the flower. The Yellow Iris is adapted to receive two kinds of insect visitors, the Bumble Bee (*Bombus*), and the Honey Bee (*Apis mellifica*), and also the long-tongued Hover-Fly (*Rhingia rostrata*), which in seeking the honey, push through the outer perianth segments and the style, the anther being between, dusting its back with the pollen.

After fertilization, the floral leaves fade and drop away from the top of the capsule, which increases in size. When ripe, the capsule opens above and allows the smooth, flattened seeds, when blown by the wind, to fall some distance away.

This Iris is in bloom from May to July.

Locally, the plant is often called 'Segg,' 'Skeggs' or 'Cegg,' all of which names come down from Anglo-Saxon days, 'Segg' being the Anglo-Saxon for a small sword, an obvious allusion to the shape of its leaves. The names 'Daggers' and 'Jacob's Sword' have a similar allusion, and 'Yellow Saggen,' 'Seag,' 'Seggin' are variations of Seg. In the days of Chaucer, it was called Gladyne. To the popular mind in early days, the fluttering segment of the perianth suggested the waving of a flag, hence the origin of the names 'Yellow Flag,' 'Water Flag' and 'Sword Flag,' and corruptions of the name such as 'Flaggon,' 'Flaggon's' and perhaps 'Fliggers,' the latter stated to be applied to it from the motion of its leaves by the slightest breeze. The strange name 'Cheiper' is explained 'because children make a shrill noise with its leaves,' and 'Cucumbers' refers to the seed-vessels, which when green resemble young cucumbers.

Culpepper calls it 'Myrtle Flag or Myrtle Grass.'

It is also called the Flower de Luce, or Fleur de Lys, being the origin of the heraldic emblem of the Kings of France. The legend is that early in the sixth century, the Frankish King Clovis, faced with defeat in battle, was induced to pray for victory to the god of his Christian wife, Clothilde. He conquered and became a Christian and thereupon replaced the three toads on his banner by three Irises, the Iris being the Virgin's flower. Six hundred years later, it was adopted by Louis VII of France as his heraldic bearings in his Crusade against the Saracens, and it is said that it then became known as Fleur de Louis, corrupted into Fleur de Luce and then into Fleur de Lys or Lis, though another theory for the name is that it was not named Fleur de Lys from Louis, but from the river Lys, on the borders of Flanders, where it was peculiarly abundant.

Its specific name, *Pseudacorus*, refers to its similarity to another plant, *pseudo* being the Greek for false, while *acorus* is the generic name of the Sweet Sedge (*Acorus calamus*), with which it is supposed to have been confused, the plants when not in flower resembling it and growing in the same situations. The Sweet Sedge, however, has an aromatic scent, while *Iris Pseudacorus* is odourless.

The Romans called the plant *consecratix*, from its being used in purifications, and Pliny mentions certain ceremonies used in digging up the plant.

¶ *Medicinal Action and Uses.* The Yellow Flag rhizome was formerly much employed as a medicine, acting as a very powerful cathartic, but from its extremely acrid nature is now seldom used. An infusion of it has been found to be effective in checking diarrhœa, and it is reputed of value in dysmenorrhœa and leucorrhœa.

It was formerly held in the highest esteem, the juice of the root being considered a cure for obstinate coughs, 'evil spleens,' convulsions, dropsies and serpents' bites, and as Gerard also says, 'doth mightilie and vehementlie draw forth choler.' Gerard recommended it as a cosmetic, saying:

'The root, boiled soft, with a few drops of rosewater upon it, laid plaisterwise upon the face of man or woman, doth in two daies at the most take away the blacknesse and blewnesse of any stroke or bruise,'

though he adds as a warning that if the skin

'be very tender and delicate, it shall be needful that ye lay a piece of silke, sindall or a piece of fine lawne betweene the plaister and the skinne for otherwise in such tender bodies it often causeth heat and inflammation.'

He recommends

'an oil made of the roots and flowers of the Iris, made in the same way as oil of roses and lilies. It is used to rub in the sinews and joints to strengthen them, and is good for cramp.'

Parkinson, of all the varieties, most esteems 'for his excellent beautie and raretie the great Turkie Flower de luce.'

'And for a sweet powder to lay among linnen and garments and to make sweet waters to wash hand-gloves or other things to perfume them' the roots of the sweet-smelling Flag.

The acrid juice snuffed up the nostrils excites violent sneezing, and on the authority of Dr. Thornton, 'in this way it has cured complaints of the head of long standing in a marvellous way.' The root powdered was also used as snuff.

The old authorities praised it as a cure for toothache, a slice of the rhizome rubbed against the aching tooth or held in the mouth between the teeth, being supposed to cause the pain to disappear at once.

The root was also an ingredient in an antidote to poison. Withering (*Arrangement of Plants*) mentions it as having cured swine bitten by a mad dog.

Culpepper (1652) says that the distilled water of the whole herb is a sovereign remedy for weak eyes, either applied on a wet bandage, or dropped into the eye, and that an ointment made of the flowers is very good for ulcers or swellings.

A French chemist, early last century, discovered that the seeds, when ripe, freed from the friable skin which envelops them, produces a beverage similar to coffee and even much superior to it in flavour, but they must be well roasted before using.

The flowers afford a beautiful yellow dye, and the root, with sulphate of iron, a good black dye.

The acrid properties are entirely dissipated by drying, after which it acts only as an astringent, so powerful from the amount of tannin contained, that it has been used in the place of Galls in the making of ink.

IRIS LENAX

N.O. Iridaceæ

Synonym. Iris Minor
Habitat. The hillsides of Oregon

A tincture of the whole plant, or of the bulbous stems, is given in bilious vomiting, and is recommended for depression.

The Indians use the fibres of this plant for making ropes.

IRIS VERSICOLOR (LINN.)

N.O. Iridaceæ

Synonyms. Blue Flag. Poison Flag. Flag Lily. Liver Lily. Snake Lily. Dragon Flower. Dagger Flower. Water Flag
Part Used. Root

Iris Versicolor (Linn.) is a perennial herb, found abundantly in swamps and low grounds throughout eastern and central North America, common in Canada, as well as in the United States, liking a loamy or peaty soil. It is not a native of Europe.

It grows 2 to 3 feet high, with narrow, sword-shaped leaves, and from May to July produces large, handsome flowers, blue, except for the yellow and whitish markings at the base of the sepals.

¶ *Description*. Blue Flag Rhizome has annual joints, 2 or more inches long, about ¼ inch in diameter, cylindrical in the lower half, becoming compressed towards the crown, where the cup-shaped stem-scar is seen, when dry, and numerous rings, formed of leaf scars are apparent above and scars of rootlets below. It is dark brown externally and longitudinally wrinkled. The fracture is short, purplish, the vascular bundles scattered through the central column. The rootlets are long, slender and simple. The rhizome has a very slight but peculiar odour, and a pungent, acrid and nauseous taste.

Owing to the similarity of name, and the appearance before blooming, this flag is sometimes mistaken by American children for Sweet Flag or Calamus, which grows in the same localities, often with disastrous results.

Of the 100 species of true Iris, twenty-two inhabit the United States, but only one, *Iris*

Missouriensis, much resembles this species (the rhizome of which yields an official American drug), or has a rhizome likely to be mistaken for it.

When *cultivated*, the American Blue Flag succeeds best in heavy, rich, moist soil. If planted in August or September, it can be harvested at the end of October the following year. The yield per acre is 3 to 4 tons of the rhizome.

¶ *Constituents*. The rhizome contains starch, gum, tannin, volatile oil, 25 per cent. of acrid, resinous matter, isophthalic acid, traces of salicylic acid and possibly an alkaloid, though a number of substances contained are still unidentified. It owes its medicinal virtues to an oleoresin.

Distilled with water, the fresh rhizome yields an opalescent distillate, from which is separated a white, camphoraceous substance with a faint odour. The oil possesses the taste and smell, but only partly the medicinal activity of the drug.

¶ *Medicinal Action and Uses*. The root is an official drug of the United States Pharmacopœia and is the source of the Iridin or Irisin of commerce, a powdered extractive, bitter, nauseous and acrid, with diuretic and aperient properties.

Iridin acts powerfully on the liver, but, from its milder action on the bowels, is preferable to podophyllin.

The fresh Iris is quite acrid and if employed internally produces nausea, vomiting, purging and colicky pains. The dried root is less acrid and is employed as an emetic, diuretic and cathartic. The oleoresin in the root is purgative to the liver, and useful in bilious sickness in small doses.

It is chiefly used for its alterative properties, being a useful purgative in disorders of the liver and duodenum, and is an ingredient of many compounds for purifying the blood. It acts as a stimulant to the liver and intestinal glands and is used in constipation and biliousness, and is believed by some to be a hepatic stimulant second only to podophyllin, but if given in full doses it may occasion considerable nausea and severe prostration.

Its chief use is for syphilis and some forms of low-grade scrofula and skin affection. It is also valuable in dropsy.

It is said to have been used by the southern North American Indians as a cathartic and emetic.

The flowers afford a fine blue infusion, which serves as a test for acids and alkalies.

¶ *Preparations and Dosages*. Powdered root, as a cathartic, 20 grains. Irisin, 1 to 3 grains. Solid extract, 10 to 15 grains. Fluid extract, ½ to 1 drachm. Tincture, 1 to 3 drachms.

IRISH MOSS. *See* MOSS

ISPAGHUL. *See* PLANTAIN

IVY, AMERICAN. *See* VIRGINIA CREEPER

IVY, COMMON

Hedera Helix (LINN.)
N.O. Araliaceæ

Parts Used. Leaves, berries

Habitat. The plant is found over the greater part of Europe and Northern and Central Asia, and is said to have been particularly abundant at Nyssa, the fabled home of Bacchus in his youth. There are many varieties, but only two accepted species, i.e. *Hedera Helix* and the Australian species, which is confined to the southern Continent

This well-known evergreen climber, with its dark-green, glossy, angular leaves is too familiar to need detailed description. It climbs by means of curious fibres resembling roots, which shoot out from every part of the stem, and are furnished with small disks at the end, which adapt themselves to the roughness of the bark or wall against which the plant grows and to which it clings firmly. These fibres on meeting with soil or deep crevices become true roots, obtaining nourishment for the plant, but when dilated at the extremity, they merely serve to attach the stems and do not absorb nourishment from the substance to which they adhere. The Ivy is therefore liable to injure the trees around which it twines by abstracting the juices of the stem.

When it attains the summit of a tree or wall, it grows out in a bushy form, and the leaves instead of being five-lobed and angular, as they are below, become ovate, with entire margins. Ivy only produces flowers when the branches get above their support, the flowering branches being bushy and projecting a foot or two from the climbing stems, with flowers at the end of every shoot.

Professor Henslow has an interesting note on the Ivy and its shoots, in his *Floral Rambles in Highways and Byways*:

'The shoots turn to the darker side, as may be seen when Ivy reaches the top of a wall, from *both* sides; wherever the sun may be the shoots lie flat upon the top. The roots themselves only come out from the darker side of the shoots, so that both of these acquired habits have their purposes. When the Ivy is going to flower, the shoots *now* turn to the light and stand out freely into the air; moreover the form of the leaf changes from a fine-pointed one to a much smaller oval type. As the shoot now has to support itself, if a section be made and compared with one of the same diameter which is supported by the adhesive roots, it will be found that it has put on more wood with less pith, than in that of the supported stem. It at once, so to speak, *feels* the strain and makes wood sufficient to meet it.'

The form of Ivy which creeps over the ground on banks and in woods, etc., never blossoms. The branches root into the soil, but they are of the ordinary kind deriving nourishment from it. On endeavouring to train this kind on a wall, it was found to have practically lost the power of climbing; for it kept continually falling away from the wall instead of adhering to it; just as cucumbers refuse to climb by their tendrils, if the stem and branches are supported artificially.

The flowers of Common Ivy are small, in clusters of nearly globular umbels and of a yellowish-green, with five broad and short petals and five stamens. They seldom open before the latter end of October, and often continue to expand till late in December. Though they have little or no scent, they yield abundance of nectar and afford food to bees late in the autumn, when they can get no other.

The berries, which do not become ripe till the following spring, provide many birds, especially wood pigeons, thrushes and blackbirds with food during severe winters. When ripe, they are about the size of a pea, black or deep purple, smooth and succulent, and contain two to five seeds. They have a bitter and nauseous taste, and when rubbed, an aromatic and slightly resinous odour.

¶ *History.* Ivy was in high esteem among the ancients. Its leaves formed the poet's crown, as well as the wreath of Bacchus, to whom the plant was dedicated, probably because of the practice of binding the brow with Ivy leaves to prevent intoxication, a quality formerly attributed to the plant. We are told by old writers that the effects of intoxication by wine are removed if a handful of Ivy leaves are bruised and gently boiled in wine and drunk.

It is the Common Ivy that is alluded to in the Idylls of Theocritus, but the Golden Ivy of Virgil is supposed to be the yellow-berried variety (*Hedera Chrysocarpa*), now so rare.

The Greek priests presented a wreath of Ivy to newly-married persons, and the Ivy has throughout the ages been regarded as the emblem of fidelity. The custom of decorating houses and churches with Ivy at Christmas was forbidden by one of the early Councils of the Church, on account of its pagan associations, but the custom still remains.

An Ivy leaf is the badge of the Gordons.

The Roman agricultural writers much recommended Ivy leaves as cattle food, but they are not relished by cows, though sheep and deer will sometimes eat them in the winter. The broad leaves being evergreen afford shelter to birds in the winter, and many prefer Ivy to other shrubs, in which to build their nests.

The wood when it attains a sufficient size is employed by turners in Southern Europe, but being very soft is seldom used in England except for whetting the knives of leather-dressers. It is very porous, and the ancients thought it had the property of separating wine from water by filtration, an error arising from the fact that wood absorbs the colour of the liquid in its passage through the pores. On the Continent it has sometimes been used in thin slices as a filter.

In former days, English taverns bore over their doors the sign of an Ivy bush, to indicate the excellence of the liquor supplied within: hence the saying 'Good wine needs no bush.'

The medicinal virtues of Ivy are little regarded nowadays. Its great value is as an ornamental covering for unsightly buildings, and it is said to be the only plant which does not make walls damp. It acts as a curtain, the leaves from the way they fall, forming a sort of armour and holding and absorbing the rain and moisture.

Ivy is very hardy; not only are the leaves seldom injured by frost, but they suffer little from smoke, or from the vitiated air of manufacturing towns. The plant lives to a great age, its stems become woody and often attain a considerable size – Ivy trunks of a foot in diameter are often to be seen where the plant has for many years climbed undisturbed over rocks and ruins.

The spring months are the best times for planting.

¶ *Medicinal Action and Uses*. Robinson tells us that a drachm of the flowers decocted in wine restrains dysentery, and that the yellow berries are good for those who spit blood and against the jaundice.

Culpepper says of the Ivy: 'It is an enemy to the nerves and sinews taken *inwardly*, but most excellent *outwardly*.'

To remove sunburn it is recommended to smear the face with tender Ivy twigs boiled in butter; according to the old English *Leechbook of Bald*.

IVY, GROUND

Glechoma Hederacea (LINN.)
N.O. Labiatæ

Synonyms. Nepeta Glechoma (Benth.). Alehoof. Gill-go-over-the-Ground. Haymaids. Tun-hoof. Hedgemaids. Lizzy-run-up-the-Hedge. Gill-go-by-the-Hedge. Cats-foot. Robin-run-in-the-Hedge
Part Used. Herb

¶ *Description*. Ground Ivy is one of the commonest plants, flourishing upon sunny hedge banks and waste ground in all parts of Great Britain. The root is perennial, throwing out long, trailing, unbranched square stems, which root at intervals and bear numerous, kidney-shaped leaves of a dark green tint, somewhat downy with many-celled hairs, and having regular, rounded indentations on the margins. The leaves are stalked and opposite to one another, the undersides paler and dotted with glands.

The flowers are placed three or four together in the axils of the upper leaves, which often have a purplish tint and are two-lipped, of a bright purplish blue, with small white spots on the lower lip, or more rarely white or pink and open early in April. The plant continues in blossom through the greater part of the summer and autumn.

Its popular name is attributed to the resemblance borne by its foliage to that of the true Ivy.

It varies in size, as well as the degree of colour in the flower, according to its situation and remains green not only in summer, but, like the true Ivy, at all times of the year, even throughout winter, unless the frost is very severe.

Green (*Universal Herbal*, 1832) tells us that Ground Ivy expels the plants which grow near it, and in consequence impoverishes pastures. Cattle seem in general to avoid it, though Linnæus says that sheep eat it; horses are not fond of it, and goats and swine refuse it. It is thought to be injurious to those horses that eat much of it, though the expressed juice, mixed with a little wine and applied morning and evening, has been said to destroy the white specks which frequently form on their eyes.

The whole plant possesses a balsamic odour and an aromatic, bitter taste, due to its particular volatile oil, contained in the glands on the under surface of the leaves. It was one of the principal plants used by the early Saxons to clarify their beers, before hops had been introduced, the leaves being steeped in the hot liquor. Hence the names it has also borne: Alehoof and Tunhoof. It not only improved the flavour and keeping qualities of the beer, but rendered it clearer. Until the reign of Henry VIII it was in general use for this purpose.

The plant also acquired the name of Gill from the French *guiller* (to ferment beer), but as Gill also meant 'a girl,' it came also to be called 'Hedgemaids.'

Some hairy tumours may often be seen in the autumn on the leaves of Ground Ivy, caused by the puncture of the *Cynips glechomæ*, from which these galls spring. They have a strong flavour of the plant and are sometimes eaten by the peasantry of France.

¶ *Part Used Medicinally*. The whole herb, gathered early in May, when most of the flowers are still quite fresh.

¶ *Medicinal Action and Uses*. Diuretic, astringent, tonic and gently stimulant. Useful in kidney diseases and for indigestion.

From early days, Ground Ivy has been endowed with singular curative virtues, and is one of the most popular remedies for coughs and nervous headaches. It has even been extolled before all other vegetable medicines for the cure of consumption.

An excellent cooling beverage, known in the country as Gill Tea, is made from this plant, 1 oz. of the herb being infused with a pint of boiling water, sweetened with honey, sugar or liquorice, and drunk when cool in wineglassful doses, three or four times a day. This used to be a favourite remedy with the poor for coughs of long standing, being much used in consumption. Ground Ivy was at one time one of the cries of London for making a tea to purify the blood. It is a wholesome drink and is still considered serviceable in pectoral complaints and in cases of weakness of the digestive organs, being stimulating and tonic, though it has long been discarded from the *Materia Medica* as an official plant, in favour of others of greater certainty of action. As a medicine useful in pulmonary complaints, where a tonic for the kidneys is required, it would appear to possess peculiar suitability, and is well adapted to all kidney complaints.

A fluid extract is also prepared, the dose being from ½ to 1 drachm. It has a bitter and acrid taste and a strong and aromatic odour.

The expressed juice of the fresh herb is diaphoretic, diuretic and somewhat astringent; snuffed up the nose, it has been considered curative of headache when all other remedies have failed. A snuff made from the dried leaves of Ground Ivy will render marked relief against a dull, congestive headache of the passive kind.

The expressed juice may also be advantageously used for bruises and 'black eyes.' It is also employed as an antiscorbutic, for which it has a long-standing reputation. Combined with Yarrow or Chamomile Flowers it is said to make an excellent poultice for abscesses, gatherings and tumours.

In America, painters used the Ground Ivy as a preventive of, and remedy for lead colic, a wineglassful of the freshly-made infusion being taken frequently.

The infusion is also used with advantage as a wash for sore and weak eyes.

Gerard says:

'it is commended against the humming noise and ringing sound of the ears, being put into them, and for them that are hard of hearing. Matthiolus writeth that the juice being tempered with Verdergrease is good against fistulas and hollow ulcers. Dioscorides teacheth that "half a dram of the leaves being drunk in foure ounces and a half of faire water for 40 or 50 days together is a remedy against sciatica or ache in the huckle-bone."

Galen hath attributed all the virtues to the flowers. Ground Ivy, Celandine and Daisies, of each a like quantity, stamped, strained and a little sugar and rose-water put thereto, and dropt into the eyes, takes away all manner of inflammation, etc., yea, although the sight were well-nigh gone. It is proved to be the best medicine in the world. The women of our Northern parts, especially Wales and Cheshire, do turn Herbe-Ale-hoof into their ale – but the reason I know not. It also purgeth the head from rheumatic humours flowing from the brain.'

Culpepper, repeating much that Gerard has already related of the virtues of Ground Ivy, adds that it is

'a singular herb for all inward wounds, ulcerated lungs and other parts, either by itself or boiled with other like herbs; and being drank, in a short time it easeth all griping pains, windy and choleric humours in the stomach, spleen, etc., helps the yellow jaundice by opening the stoppings of the gall and liver, and melancholy by opening the stoppings of the spleen; the decoction of it in wine drank for some time together procureth ease in sciatica or hip gout; as also the gout in the hands, knees or feet; if you put to the decoction some honey and a little burnt alum, it is excellent to gargle any sore mouth or throat, and to wash sores and ulcers; it speedily heals green wounds, being bruised and bound thereto.'

He concludes his account of the herb by saying:

'It is good to tun up with new drink, for it will clarify it in a night that it will be the fitter to be drank the next morning; or if any drink be thick with removing or any other accident, it will do the like in a few hours.'

(POISON)
IVY, POISON

Rhus Toxicodendron (LINN.)
N.O. Anacardiaceæ

Synonyms. Poison Oak. Poison Vine
Part Used. Leaves
Habitat. The American Poison Ivy is one of the species of Sumachs, an attractive group of plants widely distributed in Europe, Asia and North America, varying much in habit from low bushes to moderately-sized trees, and many of them familiar denizens of our gardens, for the sake of their ornamental foliage, which mostly assume beautiful tints in autumn, some of the varieties also bearing showy fruits. It grows in thickets and low grounds in North America, where it is quite common

Its sap is of an extremely poisonous character, and in many persons the slightest contact with the leaves causes a rash of a most distressing character, the hands and arms and sometimes the whole body becoming greatly swollen from simply touching or carrying a branch of the plant, the swelling being accompanied with intolerable pain and inflammation,

ending in ulceration. Some persons, however, are able to handle the plant with impunity. It has been sometimes known as *Ampelopsis Hoggii,* and under this name has occasionally been introduced with other climbers, but it has nothing to do with the group of Vines known under the name of *Ampelopsis,* and its presence in our gardens should be avoided.

¶ *Description*. The root is reddish and branching; the leaves rather large, three-parted (which will readily distinguish it from the five-parted *Ampelopsis*). The central leaflet has a longer stalk, the lateral ones are almost stalkless. The leaflets are entire when young, but when full-grown they are variously indented, downy beneath, thin and about 4 inches long. They abound with an acrid juice, which darkens when exposed to air, and when applied to the skin produces the inflammation and swelling referred to. When dry, the leaves are papery and brittle, sometimes with black spots of exuded juice turned black on drying. The flowers are in loose, slender clusters or panicles, in the axils of the leaves and are small, some perfect, others unisexual, and are greenish or yellowish-white in colour. They blossom in June, and are followed by clusters of small, globular, dun-coloured, berry-like fruit.

There are almost as many antidotes for the inflammation caused by Poison Ivy as for the bites of the rattlesnake. Alkaline lotions, especially carbonate of soda, alum and hyposulphite of soda, are all recommended, and the patient is advised to moisten the skin constantly with the agent in solution. A hot solution of potassium permanganate applied locally is also recommended as a cure, also solutions of lead and ammonia. *Rhus venenata* has similar poisonous qualities.

¶ *Part Used Medicinally*. The fresh leaves, from which a fluid extract is prepared.

¶ *Constituents*. The activity of the drug was formerly ascribed to a fixed oil, Toxicodendrol, but has been attributed more recently to a yellow resin, to which the name Toxicodendrin is applied.

¶ *Medicinal Action and Uses*. Irritant, rubefacient, stimulant, narcotic.

R. *Toxicodendron* was introduced into England first in 1640, but not used as a medicine till 1798, when Du Fressoy, a physician at Valenciennes, had brought to his notice a young man, who had been cured of a herpetic eruption on his wrist of six years' standing, on being accidentally poisoned by this plant. He thereupon commenced the use of the plant in the treatment of obstinate herpetic eruptions and in palsy, many cases yielding well to the drug. Since then it has rapidly gained a place in general practice, meeting with some success in the treatment of paralysis, acute rheumatism and articular stiffness, and in various forms of chronic and obstinate eruptive diseases.

It is not official in the British Pharmacopœia, but was formerly official in the United States Pharmacopœia. It is in extensive use by homœopathists for rheumatism, ringworm and other skin disorders, and is considered by them one of the most useful remedies in a great majority of cases of Nettlerash, especially if caused by some natural predisposition of constitution, in which the eruption is due to the use of some particular food.

The fluid extract, prepared from the fresh leaves, is mostly given in the form of a tincture, in doses of 5 to 30 drops. In small doses it is an excellent sedative to the nervous system, but must be given with care, as internally it may cause gastric intestinal irritation, drowsiness, stupor and delirium.

It has been recommended in cases of incontinence of urine. For this, the bark of the root of *R. aromatica* is also employed very successfully, an infusion of 1 oz. to a pint of boiling water being taken in wineglassful doses.

The fluid extract of *R. Toxicodendron* can be used as a vesicant or blister producer, like cantharides, mezeron, and oil of Mustard.

The best preparation is a concentrated alcoholic tincture made from the green plant in the strength of 1 in 4. The dose of 25 per cent. tincture is given in 1 to 5 drops three times a day. A solid extract is not used owing to the extreme volatility of the active principles of the crude drug.

Its milky juice is also used as an indelible ink for marking linen, and as an ingredient of liquid dressings or varnishes for finishing boots or shoes, though *R. venenata* is more extensively used for the latter purpose.

See SUMACHS.

JABORANDI

Pilocarpus Jaborandi (HOLMES.)
N.O. Rutaceæ

Synonyms. Arruda do Mato. Arruda brava. Jamguarandi. Juarandi
Part Used. Dried leaflets
Habitat. Brazil

¶ *Description*. There is divergence of opinion among recognized authorities as to the origin of the drug known as Jaborandi. Not only is the name applied to plants of quite different species in South America, but various shrubs are recognized as official in some countries that are classed as inferior substitutes in others.

Until 1914 *Pilocarpus Jaborandi* only was regarded as official in the British Pharmacopœia, but in the edition of that year it was omitted. In the United States *P. Jaborandi* is recognized as Pernambuco Jaborandi, and *P. microphyllus* as Maranham Jaborandi. Pernambuco Jaborandi was at first referred to *P. pennatifolius*, the leaves of which are now rarely found in commerce, and some writers describe this as being probably the true source of the drug. The uncertainty appears to be due to the fact that the fruit of the different species is not known to botanists, the drug being only introduced into Europe in 1847.

The names of Jaborandi, Iaborandi, and Jamborandi are applied to sundry pungent plants of the Rutaceæ and Piperaceæ orders, and especially to *Piper Jaborandi*.

The shrub grows from 4 to 5 feet high; the bark is smooth and greyish; the flowers are thick, small, and reddish-purple in colour, springing from rather thick, separate stalks about ¼ inch long. The leaves are large, compound, pinnate with an odd terminal leaflet, with two to four pairs of leaflets.

They are chiefly exported from Ceara and Pernambuco, and only the leaflets are officinal, though they arrive mixed with petioles and small fruits. The colour is brownish-green, the margin entire, with a notch cut out at the blunt tip of the leaf, which except in the case of the terminal leaflet, is unequal at the base. They are hairless, leathery, with large oil-glands, from 2½ to 4 inches long, and when crushed have a slightly aromatic odour. The taste is bitter and aromatic, becoming pungent. The powder is dark green or greenish brown.

¶ *Constituents*. A volatile oil, containing dipentene and other hydrocarbons, tannic acid, a peculiar volatile acid, and potassium chloride. The principal constituents are the three alkaloids, Pilocarpine (not found in all species), Isopilocarpine and Pilocarpidine.

Pilocarpine, only in the proportion of 0·5 per cent., is found as a soft, viscous mass yielding crystalline salts, freely soluble in alcohol, ether, and chloroform, and only slightly soluble in water. The nitrate should melt at 1·78° C. It is a white, crystalline powder, soluble in 95 per cent. alcohol, and giving a yellowish solution with strong sulphuric acid.

Various hypodermic solutions are prepared from it.

Hydrochlorate of Pilocarpine is official in the United States, and in some European Pharmacopœias.

¶ *Medicinal Action and Uses*. The crude drug is rarely used, its virtues being due to the alkaloid, Pilocarpine. It is antagonistic to atropine, stimulating the nerve-endings paralysed by that drug, and contracting the pupil of the eye. Its principal use is as a powerful and rapid diaphoretic, the quantity of sweat brought out by a single dose being as much as 9 to 15 oz. It induces also free salivation and excites most gland secretions, some regarding it as a galactagogue.

Jaborine, of which there is a small quantity in the leaves, resembles atropine, and is antagonistic to pilocarpine, so that an impure pilocarpine may vary largely in effect.

Jaborandi may irritate the stomach and cause vomiting and nausea, as may pilocarpine, even when given as a subcutaneous injection, but these symptoms yield to morphine.

It is useful in psoriasis, prurigo, deafness depending on syphilitic disease of the labyrinth, baldness, chronic catarrh, catarrhal jaundice, tonsillitis, and particularly dropsy. Probably it is most popularly known in preparations for the hair. In small doses it quenches thirst in fever or chronic renal diseases.

It is contra-indicated in fatty heart or pleurisy.

¶ *Dosages*. Of Powdered leaves, 5 to 60 grains. Of Pilocarpine, ⅒ to ¼ grain. Of Pilocarpine Nitrate, ⅒ to ¼ grain. Of Fluid extract, B.P., 10 to 30 drops. Of Tincture, B.P., ½ to 1 drachm.

¶ *Poisons with Antidotes*. An overdose may cause flushing, profuse sweating and salivation, nausea, rapid pulse, contracted pupils, diarrhœa, and even fatal pulmonary œdema. The stomach should be emptied and a full dose of atropine given.

¶ *Other Species*.

P. microphyllus, with smaller and more yellowish leaves, is regarded as identical in constituents in the United States.

P. pennatifolius, or *P. pinnatus* or *P. simplex*, inhabits Southern Brazil and Paraguay. The leaves are paler than the official ones, and contain little alkaloid. They are sometimes known as 'Paraguay Jaborandi.'

P. Selloamus, a variety of the above, with fleshier leaflets, yields Rio Janeiro Jaborandi. It was formerly official in the United States.

P. trachylophus, with smaller leaves, gives Ceara Jaborandi. It grows in Northern Brazil.

P. spicatus, giving Aracati Jaborandi, has simple lanceolate leaves said to have a high percentage of alkaloid.

P. racemosus of the West Indies, including a good percentage of alkaloids, yields Guadeloupe Jaborandi.

¶ *Substitutes*. Logwood leaves have been substitutes for Paraquay Jaborandi under the name of 'Feuilles de Bois d'inde.'

Leaves of *Tunatea decipiens*, or *Swartzia decipiens* are often mixed in parcels of *P. microphyllus*.

445

JACOB'S LADDER

Polemonium cœruleum (LINN.)
N.O. Polemoniaceæ

Synonyms. Greek Valerian. Charity
Part Used. Herb
Habitat. This species is found wild in bushy places and by the side of streams, apparently indigenous, from Stafford and Derby northwards to the Cheviots, but doubtedly indigenous elsewhere, and when found in Scotland and Ireland, only an escape from gardens

The Greek Valerian (*Polemonium cœruleum*, Linn.) is not a Valerian at all, but belongs to the natural order Polemoniaceæ, the family of the Phloxes. Cats are, however, nearly as fond of the smell of this plant as of the true Valerian, and will frequently roll on it and injure it, and hence, perhaps, it has been popularly termed Valerian. It does not possess any of the medicinal qualities of the Valerians, and has nothing in common with them except in the shape of the leaves.

It is a common garden plant, with showy, blue flowers, and is called 'Jacob's Ladder,' from its successive pairs of leaflets. The name of the genus, *Polemonium*, is somewhat obscure – it is apparently derived from the Greek *polemos* (war), but its application is unexplained.

¶ *Description.* The plant is bright green and smooth, the upper portion generally clothed with short, gland-tipped hairs. The perennial root-stock is short and creeping, the stem 18 inches to 3 feet high, hollow and angular; the leaves, with very numerous pairs of entire leaflets, $\frac{1}{2}$ to 1 inch long. The flowers are very numerous, terminating the stem of branches, slightly drooping, the corollas $\frac{3}{4}$ to 1 inch across, deep blue, with short tubes and five broad, spreading segments. The stamens, inserted at the throat of the tube, have yellow anthers.

A handsome form, frequent in gardens, has variegated leaves and white flowers.

¶ *Medicinal Action and Uses.* Culpepper says of it:

'It is under Mercury, and is alexipharmic, sudorific, and cephalic, and useful in malignant fevers and pestilential distempers; it helps in nervous complaints, headaches, trembling, palpitations of the heart, vapours, etc. It is good in hysteric cases, and epilepsies have been cured by the use of this herb.'

He tells us also, 'it is planted in gardens, and is found wild in some parts of Yorkshire.'

P. reptans (Linn.) (Abscess Root), known also as FALSE JACOB'S LADDER, is used in herbal medicine for its diaphoretic, astringent and expectorant qualities; an infusion of the root being considered useful in coughs, colds, and bronchial and lung complaints, producing copious perspiration; has been considered to have similar diaphoretic and astringent action to Jacob's Ladder.

See ABSCESS ROOT.

JALAP. *See* BINDWEED

JAMAICA DOGWOOD. *See* DOGWOOD

JAMBUL

Eugenia Jambolana (LANK.)
N.O. Myrtaceæ

Synonyms. Jambul. Jamum. Rose Apple. Java Plum. Syzygium Jumbolana
Part Used. Seeds, bark
Habitat. India, East Indies, Queensland

¶ *Description.* A tree from 20 to 30 feet high, with long narrow peach-like leaves; flowers a greeny-yellow colour, in terminal bunches, blooming in July; the fruit about the size of a hen's egg, varying from white to red and rose colour, in scent and taste like a ripe apricot. It was cultivated in England by Miller in 1768. The bark is dense and hard, pinky or reddy-brown colour, with a thick corky substance, whitish grey mottled, often ridged; the inner surface has a silky lustre; freshly fractured it shows a colour varying from fawn to a pinky purple, abruptly shortly fibrous; seeds are oval, $\frac{1}{2}$ inch long and $\frac{1}{5}$ inch round, hard, heavy, blacky-grey colour, almost tasteless.

¶ *Constituents.* Essential oil, chlorophyll, fat, resin, gallic and tannic acids, albumen and in their seed ellagic acid.

¶ *Medicinal Action and Uses.* In India Jambul has long been used as a carminative in diarrhœa; stomachic and astringent. The fresh seeds have been found most effective in diabetes, as they quickly reduce sugar in the urine; also very beneficial in glycosuria. No poisoning or other harmful effects have been reported from its use.

¶ *Preparations and Dosages.* Van Morden advises: Fluid extract, $\frac{1}{2}$ fluid ounce should be taken in 8 oz. hot water 1 hour before breakfast and before going to bed. Fluid extract, 1 to 2 drachms. Powdered seeds, 5 to 30 grains.

JASMINES

The Jasmine, or Jessamine (the name derived from the Persian *Yasmin*), belongs botanically to the genus *Jasminum*, of the natural order Oleaceæ, which contains about 150 species, mostly natives of the warmer regions of the Old World. About forty of these are cultivated in our gardens.

¶ *Description.* Their leaves are mostly ternate or pinnate; the flowers, usually white or yellow, with a tubular, five- or eight-cleft calyx, a cylindrical corolla-tube, with a spreading limb, two stamens enclosed in the corolla-tube and a two-celled ovary.

¶ *Habitat.* The COMMON WHITE JASMINE (*Jasminum officinale*), one of the best known and most highly esteemed of British hardy ligneous climbers, is a native of Northern India and Persia, introduced about the middle of the sixteenth century. In the centre and south of Europe it is thoroughly acclimatized.

Although it grows to the height of 12 and sometimes 20 feet, its stem is feeble and requires support. Its leaves are opposite, pinnate and dark green, the leaflets are in three pairs, with an odd one and are pointed, the terminal one larger with a tapering point. The fragrant flowers bloom from June to October; and as they are found chiefly on the young shoots, the plant should only be pruned in the autumn.

Varieties with golden and silver-edged leaves and one with double flowers are known.

¶ *Medicinal Action and Uses.* The roots of several species of *Jasminum* have had various ill-defined uses in medicine – that of *J. officinale* is mentioned by Millspaugh (*American Medicinal Plants*) as 'a proven plant' in the homœopathic sense, though he adds: 'the authority for the use of which I am unable to determine.'

The Dispensatory of the U.S.A. cites the case of a child, in 1861, being poisoned by the fruit of Jasmin,

'probably that of the common White species, *J. officinale*, the symptoms being coma, widely dilated pupil, snoring respiration, with cold, pale surface; slow, feeble pulse, followed by violent convulsions, with rigidity of muscle about head and throat.'

A palatable syrup can be prepared from the flowers. A preparation of the flowers has been employed medicinally. Green, in his *Universal Herbal* (1832), recommends :

'as an excellent medicine in coughs, hoarsenesses and other disorders of the breast, an infusion of five or six ounces of them picked clean from the leaves, in a quart of boiling water, being strained off and boiled in a syrup,

N.O. Oleaceæ and Jasminaceæ

with the addition of a sufficient quantity of honey.'

The SPANISH or CATALONIAN JASMINE (*J. grandiflorum*), a native of the north-west Himalayas, and cultivated in the Old and New World, is very like *J. officinale*, but differs in the size of the leaflets; the branches are shorter and stouter and the flowers very much larger and reddish beneath.

This is the Jasmine of the perfumery trade, one of the flowers most valued by perfumers, and grown at Grasse. Its delicate, sweet odour is so peculiar that it is without comparison one of the most distinct of all natural odours, and until quite recent years, it was believed that it was the only scent that could not be made artificially. A synthetic Otto of Jasmine now exists, however, its composition following more or less closely the constitution of the natural oil, containing benzyl acetate, a benzyl ester found in the natural oil of Jasmine, but the true perfume of Jasmine is not, however, exactly reproducible by any combination of chemical compounds or other natural products thus far known, and a proportion of the natural otto must be added to the mixture of synthetic substances to make the product satisfactory.

This Jasmine is very extensively cultivated at Cannes and Grasse. It is not grown on its own roots, but grafted on to two-year-old plants of *J. officinale*, an erect bush about 3 feet high being obtained, requiring no supports. The plants are set in rows, fully exposed to the sun, in a fresh, open soil, well sheltered from north winds, as they are very susceptible to cold and readily damaged by frost. They come into full bearing the second year after grafting. The blossoms, which are very large and intensely fragrant, are produced from July till the end of October, but those of August and September are the most odoriferous, the normal harvest being generally in full swing about the middle of August. The flowers open every morning at six o'clock and are culled after sunrise, as the morning dew would injure their fragrance. An acre of land will yield about 500 lb. weight of Jasmine blossoms.

A fungus, *Agaricus melleus*, is a plague of the Jasmine fields, attacking the roots of the grafted plants. When this mushroom has invaded a plantation, it is most difficult to combat, and the plants often have to be rooted out, causing much loss. It is not possible to grow Jasmine twice in succession on the same site, and the crop is replaced by roses or olives.

The perfume is extracted by the process

known as *enfleurage*, i.e. absorption by a fatty body, such as purified lard or olive oil. Jasmine flowers contain, when picked, only a portion of the perfume which they are capable of yielding, so fresh oil is developed by the flowers as the solvent removes what was originally present.

Square glass trays, framed with wood about 3 inches deep, are spread over with grease about ½ inch thick, in which ridges are made to facilitate absorption, and sprinkled with freshly-gathered flowers, which are renewed every morning during the whole time the plant remains in blossom. The trays are piled up in stacks to prevent the evaporation of the aroma and finally the pomade is scraped off the glass, melted at as low a temperature as possible and strained.

When oil is employed as the absorbent, coarse cotton cloths previously saturated with the finest olive oil are laid on wire-gauze frames, and are repeatedly covered in the same manner with fresh flowers. They are then squeezed under a press, yielding what is termed *huile antique au jasmin*. Three pounds of flowers will perfume 1 lb. of grease. This is extracted by maceration in 1 pint of rectified spirit to form the 'Extract.'

A small amount of Jasmine oil is prepared by extracting the blossoms with petroleum spirit and evaporating the solvent at a low temperature, but this treatment by killing the flower at once, stops the process of scent formation, so that the yield of oil is only one-fifth (some say one-ninth) of that extracted by fats in the enfleurage process. The Jasmine oil obtained by extraction with volatile solvents is a pale-brown liquid with a pleasant odour, which is quite distinct, however, from that of Jasmine pomade.

¶ *Constituents.* The essential oil of *J. grandi-florum* contains methyl anthranilate, indol, benzyl alcohol, benzyl acetate, and the terpenes linalol and linalyl acetate.

As essential oil is distilled from Jasmine in Tunis and Algeria, but its high price prevents its being used to any extent.

The East Indian oil of Jasmine is a compound, largely contaminated with sandal-wood-oil.

Syrup of Jasmine is made by placing in a jar alternate layers of the flowers and sugar, covering the whole with wet cloths and standing it in a cool place. The perfume is absorbed by the sugar, which is converted into a very palatable syrup.

The ZAMBAK, or ARABIAN JASMINE (*J. Sambac*), is an evergreen white-flowered climber, 6 or 8 feet high, introduced into Britain in the latter part of the seventeenth century. Two varieties introduced somewhat later are respectively three-leaved and double-flowered, and these, as well as that with normal flowers, bloom throughout the greater part of the year.

The Hindus string the flowers together as neck garlands for honoured guests. The flowers of one of the double varieties are held sacred to Vishnu and are used as votive offerings in Hindu religious ceremonies.

At Ghazipur, a town on the Ganges, Jasmine, there called *Chameli*, is used mainly for making perfumed hair oils by a process of enfleurage. The odour is absorbed in sesame seeds. The seeds are prepared by washing and rubbing, and when decorticated are dried. The prepared seeds and flowers are placed in alternate layers and allowed to remain for twelve to fourteen hours. The seeds are then separated from the flowers and repeatedly treated in the same way with fresh flowers. The spent flowers are used over and over again with fresh till seeds, these latter giving oil of an inferior quality. The oil obtained from seeds treated with fresh flowers only is the best. The perfumed seeds are pressed in an ordinary wooden country press borne by bullocks. The method is crude, wasteful, tedious and dirty. Some Otto of Jasmine is also made at Ghazipur.

In Borneo it is the custom among the women to roll up Jasmine blossoms in their well-oiled hair at night.

¶ *Medicinal Action and Uses.* An oil obtained by boiling the *leaves* of this Eastern Jasmine is used to anoint the head for complaints of the eye, and an oil obtained from the *roots* is used medicinally to arrest the secretion of milk.

In China JASMINUM PANICULATUM is cultivated. It is an erect shrub, valued for its flowers and known as *Sien-hing-hwa*, the flowers being used with those of *J. Sambac*, *Sambac-mo-le-hwa*, in the proportion of 10 lb. of the former to 30 lb. of the latter for scenting tea, 40 lb. of the mixture being required for 100 lb. of tea.

In Catalonia and in Turkey, the wood of the Jasmine is made into long, slender pipe-stems.

JASMINUM ANGUSTIFOLIUM, an Indian species, found in the Coromandel forest and introduced into Britain during the present century, is a beautiful evergreen climber, 10 to 12 feet high, its leaves of a bright shining green, its large, terminal flowers, white with a faint tinge of red, fragrant and in bloom throughout the year. Its bitter root, ground and mixed with the powdered root of *Acorus calamus*, the Sweet Sedge, is in India considered a valuable external application for ringworm.

In Cochin-China, a decoction of the leaves and branches of JASMINUM NERVOSUM is taken as a blood-purifier. The very bitter leaves of JASMINUM FLORIBUNDUM (called in Abyssinia, *Habbez-zelim*), mixed with kousso, is considered a powerful anthelmintic, especially for tapeworm; the leaves and branches are added to some fermented liquors to increase their intoxicating quality.

The distinguishing characters of the TRUE YELLOW JASMINE (*J. odoratissimum*), a native of the Canary Islands and Madeira, consist principally in the alternate, obtuse, ternate leaves, the three-flowered terminal peduncles and the five-cleft yellow corolla, with obtuse segments. The flowers have the advantage, when dry, of retaining their natural perfume, which is suggestive of a mixture of Jasmine, jonquil and orange-blossom.

Among other hardy species commonly cultivated in gardens are the low ITALIAN YELLOW-FLOWERED JASMINE (*J. humile*), an East Indian species, introduced into the south of Europe and now found wild there – an erect shrub, 3 or 4 feet high, with angular branches alternate and mostly ternate leaves, blossoming from June to September; JASMINUM FRUTICANS (Linn.) (*J. frutescens*, Gueldermeister), a native of Southern Europe and the Mediterranean region, a hardy, evergreen shrub, 10 to 12 feet high, with weak, slender stems, requiring support and bearing yellow, odourless flowers from spring to autumn, and JASMINUM NUDIFLORUM (Roth.) (*J. pubescens*, Willd.), of China, which bears its bright yellow flowers in winter before the leaves appear. It thrives in almost any situation and grows rapidly. The important medicinal plant known in America as the 'Carolina Jasmin' (*Gelsemium nitidum*) is not a true Jasmine, though often called 'Yellow Jasmine.' A more correct name for it is 'False Jasmine.'

The rhizome of *J. fruticans* is sometimes collected in the place of *Gelsemium*, but may be distinguished by the cells of the pith, which are thin-walled and full of starch, while those of *Gelsemium* are thick-walled and empty. *See* GELSEMIUM.

From the leaves of *J. fruticans*, the glucoside Jasminin has been isolated, and from the shoots of *J. nudiflorum*, the glucoside, Jasminiflorin.

Other plants called 'Jasmine,' but not related to it, are:

(i) The so-called American Jasmine (*Quamoclit coccinea*).

(ii) The Red Jasmine (*Plumiera rubra*), a shrubby tree, native to Central America, with delicately-scented flowers, which have obtained for it this name. Another member of the genus, *P. alba*, is known as the Frangipani plant, its scent having been characterized as 'the eternal perfume.'

(iii) The Cape Jasmine (*Gardenia florida*), with a strong, pleasant fragrance similar to that of Jasmine, much employed for 'buttonholes' and in wreaths, and in China, under the name of *Pak-Semahwa*, for scenting tea. Another Chinese species, *G. grandiflora*, is employed in dyeing the yellow robes of the mandarins. The fruit of *G. campanulata*, a species growing in the forests of Chittagong, is said to be used by the natives as acathartic and anthelmintic.

(iv) The Ground Jasmine (*Passerina stelleri*) is like the *Gardenia*, also a native of the Cape.

The WILD JASMINE or WHITE JASMINE OF JAMAICA (called there, 'Jamaica Wild Coffee'), with very fragrant white flowers, is a species of *Pavetta*. The Pavettas are shrubs inhabiting the tropical regions. The root of *P. Indica* is bitter and is employed as a purgative by the Hindus, the leaves being also used medicinally and for manuring; knife handles being made from the roots.

The leaves of the Indian Night Jasmine (*Nyctanthes arbortristis* – N.O. Jasminaceæ) are used in homœopathic medicine to make a tincture for rheumatism, sciatica and bilious fevers. – EDITOR.

JEQUIRITY. *See* INDIAN LIQUORICE

JEWELWEED

Impatiens aurea (MUHL.)
Impatiens biflora (WALT.)
N.O. Geraniaceæ

Synonyms. Wild Balsam. Balsam-weed. Impatiens pallida. Pale-touch-me-not. Spotted-touch-me-not. Slipperweed. Silverweed. Wild Lady's Slipper. Speckled Jewels. Wild Celandine. Quick-in-the-hand

Part Used. Herb

Habitat. Members of the genus *Impatiens* are found widely distributed in the north temperate zone and in South Africa, but the majority are natives of the mountains of tropical Asia and Africa

The flowers, purple, yellow, pink and white, sometimes a showy scarlet, are spurred and irregular in form and are borne in the leaf axils.

The name *Impatiens* is derived from the fact that the seed-pod, when ripe, discharges the seeds by the elastic separation and uncoiling of the valves.

Under the name of Jewelweed the herbage of *Impatiens aurea* and of *I. biflora* are largely employed in domestic practice and by homœopaths and eclectics.

¶ *Description*. The plants are tall and branching, tender and delicate succulent annuals, with swollen joints, growing in lowlying, damp, rather rich soil, beside streams and in similar damp localities.

They are smooth and somewhat glaucous, the stems somewhat translucent, the foliage showing a brilliant silvery surface when immersed in water, which will not adhere to the surface.

The leaves are thin, ovate oval, more or less toothed, of a tender green colour.

The slipper-shaped, yellow flowers, in bloom from July to September, have long recurved tails, those of the first-named species being of a uniform pale-yellow, those of the second species, orange-yellow, crowded with dark spots, hence its common name of Spotted-touch-me-not. The oblong capsules of both species when ripe explode under the slightest disturbance, scattering the seeds widely. Most of the popular names refer to this peculiarity, others to the shape of the flowers.

¶ *Medicinal Action and Uses*. The herbs have an acrid, burning taste and act strongly as emetics, cathartics and diuretics, but are considered dangerous, their use having been termed 'wholly questionable.'

¶ *Constituents*. The chemical constituents are not known, though the leaves apparently contain tannin, which causes them to be employed as an outward application for piles, proving an excellent remedy, the freshly gathered plants being boiled in lard and an ointment made of them.

The fresh juice of the herb appears to relieve cutaneous irritation of various kinds, especially that due to *Rhus* poisoning.

A yellow dye has been made from the flowers.

¶ *Other Species*.
The only species of *Impatiens* found wild in Europe is *I. Noli-me-tangere*, an annual, succulent herb about a foot high, with yellow flowers, in bloom in July and August, the lateral petals spotted with red (by cultivation, changing often to pale yellow and purplish).

This is our native 'Touch-me-not' or 'Quick-in-hand.' Although uncommon, it is to be found wild in moist mountainous districts in North Wales, Lancashire and Westmorland and occasionally in moist, shady places and by the banks of rivulets in other counties.

The plant will grow in cultivation, delighting in a moist soil and partially-shaded situations; the seeds being sown in autumn, soon after they are ripe. When once established, the plant will scatter its own seeds.

The whole plant is rather acrid, so that no animal except the goat will touch it.

It was formerly considered to have diuretic and vulnerary properties and was given to relieve hæmorrhoids and strangury.

Boerhaave, the famous Dutch physician (1668–1738), considered it poisonous.

I. balsamin a, the Common Balsam of gardens, a well-known annual, is a native of India, China and Japan. It is one of the showiest of summer and autumn flowers and of comparatively easy cultivation.

In the East, the natives use the prepared juice for dyeing their nails red.

I. Roylei, a tall, hardy, succulent annual, with rose-purple flowers, a Himalayan species, is common in England as a self-sown garden plant or garden escape.

I. Sultani, a handsome plant, with scarlet flowers, a native of Zanzibar, is easily grown in a greenhouse throughout the summer, but requires warmth in winter.

I. Cornuta, the 'Horned Balsam,' has long nectaries to its flowers, the spurs being three times as long as the corollas. In Ceylon it is called the 'Swallow-leaf.'

The whole plant is fragrant and in Cochin-China, where it is a common garden weed, a decoction of the leaves is used as a hairwash, imparting a very sweet odour.

The 'Balsam Apple' is not related to the *Impatiens*, but is the fruit of *Momordica balsamina*.

JOHN'S BREAD

Ceratonia siliqua (LINN.)
N.O. Leguminosæ

Synonyms. Locust Pods. Carob. Algaroba (Spain). Bharout (Arabia). Sugar Pods
Part Used. Fruit
Habitat. Southern Europe, Africa and Asia – bordering on the Mediterranean

¶ *Description*. There was a tradition that this tree was the food of St. John in the wilderness, and the name is derived from the legend.

It is very common in the south of Spain, where it forms a small branching tree about 30 feet high, the wood of which has a pretty pinkish hue. Leaves pinnate in two or three pairs of oval blunt-topped leaflets, leathery texture, and colour shiny dark green. Flowers in small red racemes followed by flat pods 6 to 12 inches long and fully 1 inch wide, ¼ inch thick, a shiny dark browny purple colour. They do not split open when ripe; they contain a number of seeds in a line along the centre of the pods, each seed in a separate cell of fleshy pulp. This tree is much cultivated in dry parts because its long roots can grow deep enough in the ground to find moisture. The pods contain a large amount of mucilage and saccharine matter of pleasant flavour, and are largely employed for feeding all sorts of animals, and in time of scarcity for human consumption. In 1811 and 1812 they formed the principal food of the British cavalry during the War; they have been imported in considerable quantities for cattle food, though they do not contain much nutritive property, the saccharine matter being carbonaceous, or heat-giving, the seeds alone being nitrogenous. These seeds are so small and hard they often escape mastication.

¶ *Constituents.* Similar to Cassia pods, it is not known to what constituents its laxative properties are due.

¶ *Medicinal Action and Uses.* Years ago the seeds were sold at a high price by chemists, as singers imagined they cleared the voice. By fermentation and distillation they give an agreeable spirit, which retains the flavour of the pod. The seeds were once used by jewellers as the original carat weight. Johannisbrod, so greatly esteemed in Germany, is made from the pulp of the Syrian *Ceratonia siliqua.* The fruit of John's Bread have similar constituents to those of Cassia pods and are also laxative and demulcent, with an odour somewhat like valerian.

¶ *Dosage.* Same as for Cassia pulp and pods.

JUJUBE BERRIES

Zizyphus vulgaris (LAMK.)
N.O. Rhamnaceæ

Synonyms. Zizyphus sativa. Brustbeeren. Judendornbeeren. Rhamnus Zizyphus
Part Used. Fruit
Habitat. Southern Europe

¶ *Habitat.* Originally a native of Syria, *Zizyphus vulgaris* was introduced into Italy in the reign of Augustus, and is now naturalized in Provence, and particularly in the islands of Hyères, where the berries are largely collected when ripe, and dried in the sun.

The trees average 25 feet in height and are covered with a rough, brown bark. They have many branches, with annual thorny branchlets bearing alternate, oval-oblong leaves of a clear green colour, with three to five strongly-marked, longitudinous veins. The small flowers are pale yellow and solitary. The fruit is a blood-red drupe, the size and shape of an olive, sweet, and mucilaginous in taste, slightly astringent. The pulp becomes softer and sweeter in drying, and the taste more like wine. They have pointed, oblong stones.

¶ *Constituents.* A full analysis has not yet been made, but the berries are valued for their mucilage and sugar.

¶ *Medicinal Action and Uses.* The Jujube is classed with the raisin, date, and fig as a pectoral fruit, being nutritive and demulcent. It is eaten both fresh and dried.

A syrup and a *tisane* were formerly made from it, but the berries are now little used in medicine.

Jujube paste, or 'Pâte de Jujubes,' is made of gum-arabic and sugar. It may be dissolved in a decoction of jujubes and evaporated, but is considered as good a demulcent without their addition. It is frequently merely mixed with orange-flower water.

A decoction of the *roots* has been used in fevers.

An astringent decoction of leaves and branchlets is made in large quantities in Algeria, and seems likely to replace the cachou.

¶ *Other Species.*
Z. Lotos, sometimes also called *Z. sativa,* of Northern Africa and *Z. Jujuba* of the East Indies possess similar properties, and are used in their respective countries. *Z. Lotos* is thought to have been one of the sources of the famous sweet fruits from which the ancient Lotophagi took their name, the liqueur prepared from which caused those who partook of it to forget even their native countries in its enjoyment. The Arabs call it *Seedra.* In Arabia a kind of bread is made of them by exposing them to the sun for a few days and then pounding them in a wooden mortar to separate the stones. The meal is mixed with water and formed into cakes which after drying in the sun resemble sweet gingerbread.

Z. Baclei is said to be used in the same way in Africa, and also for making a beverage.

Z. Jujuba is largely cultivated by the Chinese, in many varieties as a dessert fruit, some being called Chinese Dates, and it is also one of the main sources of stick-lac.

Z. Œnoplia of India has edible fruits, and the bark is esteemed as a vulnerary.

In Cochin-China the berries of *Z. agrestis* are eaten.

In Senegal the fruits of *Z. Barelei* are slightly styptic, and the negroes use the roots for gonorrhœa. It is probably the same species that is used there in venereal diseases.

A decoction of the dried leaves of *Z. Napeca* is said to be used for washing ulcers in Arabia.

Z. spina Christi, or *Rhamnus spina Christi*, of Ethiopia, is said to be the source of the crown of thorns placed on the Saviour's head. The Arabs call it *Nabka*.

JUNIPER BERRIES

Juniperus communis (LINN.)
N.O. Coniferæ

Synonyms. Genévrier. Ginepro. Enebro. Gemeiner Wachholder
Parts Used. The ripe, carefully dried fruits, leaves
Habitat. Europe. North Africa. North Asia. North America

¶ *Habitat.* The Juniper is a small shrub, 4 to 6 feet high, widely distributed throughout the Northern Hemisphere. It occurs freely on the slopes of the chalk downs near London, and on heathy, siliceous soils where a little lime occurs. It is a common shrub where bands of limestone occur, as on some of the Scotch mountains and on the limestone hills in the Lake district.

The *berries* are used for the production of the volatile oil which is a prime ingredient in Geneva or Hollands Gin, upon which its flavour and diuretic properties depend.

¶ *History.* Although these valuable berries are produced from a native shrub, the berries of commerce are chiefly collected from plants cultivated in Hungary. The oil distilled on the Continent, principally in Hungary, is chiefly from freshly-picked berries. It has, hitherto, not been possible to produce the oil competitively with Southern Europe because of the relative cheapness of labour and the vast tracts of land over which the trees grow wild. But the rise in the price of foreign oil of Juniper berries since the outbreak of war has directed attention to the possible extended production of the oil either in Great Britain or her northern colonies. Sunny slopes are likely to be the best places to cultivate the shrub for the berries. The yield of oil, however, varies considerably in different years.

There is a wide difference in the chemical and physical characters of the oil distilled on the Continent from fresh and that in England from imported berries, which in transit to this country have become partially dried.

Commercial oil of Juniper is obtained chiefly from the ripe fruit and is stated to be in all essential qualities superior to the oil of Juniper from the full-grown, unripe, green berries used medicinally, which occurs as a colourless or pale greenish-yellow, limpid liquid, possessing a peculiar terebinthic odour when fresh, and a balsamic, burning, somewhat bitter taste.

Juniper berries take two or three years to ripen, so that blue and green berries occur on the same plant. Only the blue, ripe berries are here picked. When collected in baskets or sacks, they are laid out on shelves to dry a little, during which process they lose some of the blue bloom and develop the blackish colour seen in commerce.

There is a considerable demand on the Continent for an aqueous extract of the berries called *Roob*, or Rob of Juniper, and the distilled oil is in this case a by-product, the berries being first crushed and macerated with water and then distilled with water and the residue in the still evaporated to a soft consistence. Much of the oil met with in commerce is obtained as a by-product in the manufacture of gin and similar products.

In Sweden a beer is made that is regarded as a healthy drink. In hot countries the tree yields by incision a gum or varnish.

¶ *Constituents.* The principal constituent is the volatile oil, with resin, sugar, gum, water, lignin, wax and salines. The oil is most abundant just before the perfect ripeness and darkening of the fruit, when it changes to resin. The quantity varies from 2·34 to 0·31 per cent. *Juniper Camphor* is also present, its melting-point being 1·65° to 1·66° C.

Adulteration by oil of Turpentine can be recognized by the lowering of the specific gravity.

The tar is soluble in Turpentine oil, but not in 95 per cent. acetic acid.

Junol is the trade name of a hydro-alcoholic extract.

¶ *Medicinal Action and Uses.* Oil of Juniper is given as a diuretic, stomachic, and carminative in indigestion, flatulence, and diseases of the kidney and bladder. The oil mixed with lard is also used in veterinary practice as an application to exposed wounds and prevents irritation from flies.

Spirit of Juniper has properties resembling Oil of Turpentine: it is employed as a stimulating diuretic in cardiac and hepatic dropsy.

JUNIPER
Juniperus Communis

AFRICAN KINO
Pterocarpus Marsupium

LAUREL
Laurus Nobilis

CHERRY LAUREL
Prunus Laurocerasus

The fruit is readily eaten by most animals, especially sheep, and is said to prevent and cure dropsy in the latter.

The chief use of Juniper is as an adjuvant to diuretics in dropsy depending on heart, liver or kidney disease. It imparts a violet odour to the urine, and large doses may cause irritation to the passages. An infusion of 1 oz. to 1 pint of boiling water may be taken in the course of twenty-four hours.

In France the berries have been used in chest complaints and in leucorrhœa, blenorrhœa, scrofula, etc. They are not given in substance.

The oil is a local stimulant.

¶ *Dosage.* Oil of Berries, B.P., 1 to 5 drops. Oil of Wood, 1 to 5 drops. Fluid extract, ½ to 1 fluid drachm. Spirit of Juniper, B.P. and U.S.P., 20 to 60 minims. Oil, 2 to 10 minims. Elixir of Potassium Acetate and Juniper as a diaphoretic, 4 fluid drachms. Comp. Spirit, U.S.P., 2 drachms. Solid extract, 5 to 15 grains.

¶ *Other Species.*

Gum Juniper is a name of Sandarac, the resinous product of *Thuja articulata* or *Callitris quadrivalvis.*

From dry distillation of the branches and heartwood of *Juniperus oxycedrus*, the Prickly Cedar or Medlar Tree, a large shrub, 10 to 12 feet high, with brownish-black berries the size of a hazel nut, native of the south of France, and occasionally from that of *J. communis*, is obtained the tarry, empyreumatic oil known as Cade Oil, or Juniper Tar Oil, used in the treatment of the cutaneous diseases of animals in France and other Continental countries, and for most of the purposes of Oil of Turpentine. It is a ready solvent for chemical drugs and is used externally for chronic eczema as oil, ointment, and soap.

J. virginiana, the American Juniper of Bermuda, known also as Red Cedar and Pencil Cedar, is only an ornamental tree in Britain, introduced in 1864, and growing 40 to 50 feet high. The smallness of the stem and slowness of growth render it unsuitable for planting here with a view to profit, but in America it is much used for cabinet-making, turnery, etc. The interior wood is of a reddish colour and highly valued on account of its great durability, being suitable for exposure to all weather. The highly-coloured and fragrant heartwood is largely used in the manufacture of the wood coverings of black-lead pencils, and also for pails, tubs, and various household utensils subjected to wettings. Boxes made of the wood are useful for the preservation of woollens and furs, it being an excellent insectifuge on account of the oil contained in it.

Red Cedar Oil is an article of commerce, obtained from the wood by distillation from the chips and waste wood, from 15,000 to 20,000 lb. of oil being annually produced in the United States. It is used in the preparation of insecticides and also in making liniments and other medicinal preparations and perfumed soaps. It is used generally in perfumery and was formerly one of the principal constituents of the popular Extract of White Rose.

The *berries* in decoction are diaphoretic and emmenagogue, like those of Common Juniper, and the *leaves* have diuretic properties.

KAMALA

Mallotus Philippinensis (MUELL.)
N.O. Euphorbiaceæ

Synonyms. Glandulæ Rotteleræ. Kamcela. Spoonwood. Röttlera tinctoria
Parts Used. Glands and hairs covering the fruits
Habitat. India, at the foot of the Madras hills, Malay Archipelago, Orissa, Bengal, Bombay, Abyssinia, Southern Arabia, China, Australia

¶ *Description.* A very common small Indian tree, named after the Rev. Dr. Röttler, the naturalist, who died in 1836. It is 20 to 30 feet high, trunk 3 or 4 feet in diameter, branches slender with pale bark, the younger ones covered with dense ferruginous tomentosum; leaves alternate, articulate petioles, 1 to 2 inches long; rusty tomentose, blade 3 to 6 inches long, ovate with two obscure glands at base, entire, coriaceous, upper surface glabrous, veins very prominent on under surface, flowers diœcious. Males three together in the axils of small bracts arranged in longer much-branched axillary branches to the females, both densely covered with ferrugineous tomentosum, flowering November to January. From the surface of the trilobed capsules of the plant, which are about the size of peas, a red mealy powder is obtained; this consists of minute glands and hairs coloured brick or madder red, nearly odourless and tasteless; it is much used by the Hindu silk dyers, who obtain from it by boiling in carbonate of soda, a durable flame colour of great beauty. The capsules are ripe February and March, when the red powder is brushed off and collected for sale; no other preparation is necessary to preserve it.

¶ *Constituents.* Rottlerin, yellow and red resins, wax, and a yellow crystalline substance, tannic acid, gum, and volatile oil.

¶ *Medicinal Action and Uses.* The root of the tree is used in dyeing, and for cutaneous eruptions, also used by the Arabs internally for leprosy and in solution to remove freckles and pustules. In this country it has been successfully used for an eruption in children known as wildfire, the powder is rubbed over the affected part with moist lint. Its greatest use, however, is in the use of tapeworm, being safer and more certain than other cures; the worm is passed whole and generally dead. The dose of Kamala for a robust person is 3 drachms, but only half that quantity for anyone of enfeebled health; the fluid extract is milder and acts with more certainty.

Kamala acts quickly and actively as a purgative, and often causes much griping and nausea, but seldom vomiting. It may be given in water mucilage or syrup; the worm is usually expelled at the third or fourth stool; if it fails to act, the dose is repeated after four hours, or a dose of castor oil is given. Kamala is largely used in India externally for cutaneous troubles, and is most effective for scabies. It has been successfully employed in herpetic ringworm (a disease very prevalent there), and as a tænifuge it has been used with good results, on the Continent, combined with Kousso and known as Kama-kosin.

Kamala is insoluble in cold water and boiling water has little effect on it. The resin is the most active constituent, and is dissolved by ether, chloroform, alcohol or benzol. When exposed to a flame it explodes with a flash resembling Lycopodium.

¶ *Preparations and Dosages.* Powdered Kamala, 2 to 4 drachms. Fluid extract, 2 to 4 drachms.

¶ *Adulterations.* Kamala is often grossly adulterated; its quality can be judged by throwing a little on the surface of water, when the adulterants, such as sand, ferric oxide, etc., will sink, and the pure drug float; stalks and leaves can be easily sifted out. Dyed starch is detected by microscope, also ground safflower by same means.

¶ *Other Species.* (N.O. Leguminosæ.)

Flemingia congesta, under the name of wurrus (contains a substance similar to Kamala), is a large shrub growing in India and Africa, gives a dull dark purplish powder and consists of single not grouped hairs and glands, the glands being in tiers not radiating; wurrus contains two resins, one dark and the other orange brown, an orange red crystalline substance, flemingin and homoflemingin, principles which while resembling Kamala are not identical with it, but largely used in India as a dye, giving silk a lovely golden colour.

Rottlera Schimfeeri, the bark of which has anthelmintic properties.

KAVA KAVA

Piper Methysticum (FORST.)
N.O. Piperaceæ

Synonyms. Ava. Intoxicating Pepper. Ava Pepper
Part Used. The peeled, dried and divided rhizome
Habitat. Polynesia, Sandwich Islands, South Sea Islands. Official in the Australian Colonies

¶ *Description.* An indigenous shrub several feet high, leaves cordate, acuminate, with very short axillary spikes of flowers; stem dichotomous, spotted. The natives prepare a fermented liquor from the upper portion of the rhizome and base of the stems; it is narcotic and stimulant and is drunk before important religious rites. The root of the plant, chewed and mixed with the saliva, gives a hot intoxicating juice; it is mixed with pure water or the water of the coco-nut. Its continued use in large doses causes inflammation of the body and eyes, resulting in leprous ulcers; the skin becomes parched and peels off in scales. Commercial Kava rhizome is in whitish or grey-brown roughly wedge-shaped fragments from which the periderm is cut off about 2 inches thick; the transverse section usually shows a dense central pith, surrounded by a clean ring of vascular bundles, narrow and radiating, separated by broadish light-coloured medullary rays. Fracture starchy, faint pleasant odour, taste bitter, pungent, aromatic; it yields not more than 8 per cent. of ash.

¶ *Constituents.* Oil cells often contain a greenish-yellow resin, termed kawine; it is strongly aromatic and acrid; the plant contains a second resin less active than the first, a volatile oil and an alkaloid, Kavaine Methysticcum yangonin, and abundance of starch.

¶ *Medicinal Action and Uses.* The effect on the nerve centres is at first stimulating, then depressing, ending with paralysis of the respiratory centre. The irritant action and insolubility of the resin has lessened its use as a local anæsthetic, but for over 125 years Kava root has been found valuable in the treatment of gonorrhœa both acute and chronic, vaginitis, leucorrhœa, nocturnal incontinence and other ailments of the genito-urinary tract. It resembles pepper in local action. A 20 per cent. oil of Kava resin in oil of Sandalwood, called gonosan, is used internally for gonorrhœa. Being a local anæsthetic it relieves pain and has an aphrodisiac effect; it has also an antiseptic effect on the urine. The capsules contain 0·3 gram; two to four can be given several times per day. As Kava is a strong diuretic it is useful for gout, rheumatism, bronchial and other ailments, resulting from heart trouble.

¶ *Dosages.* Fluid extract, ½ to 1 drachm. Powdered root, 1 drachm. Solid extract, 1 to 15 grains.

KIDNEYWORT

Cotyledon Umbilicus
N.O. Crassulaceæ

Synonyms. Wall Pennywort. Penny Pies. Wall Pennyroyal

The Kidneywort or Navelwort (*Cotyledon Umbilicus*) is a remarkably succulent plant, mostly to be found on moist rocks and walls in the high-lying districts in the west of England.

The whole plant is a pale bright green and very smooth. The rootstock from which it springs is a small, roundish tuber, varying according to the size of the plant, from the dimension of a small pea to that of a large nut. The leaves, most of which grow directly from the rootstock, are in shape somewhat like those of the garden Nasturtium, being circular, their stalks, 2 to 6 inches long, springing from about the centre of their under-surfaces, an arrangement that is termed botanically *peltate.* The succulent blades of the leaves are about 1 to 3 inches across, slightly concave, having a depression in the centre, where joined to the foot-stalk; and from this feature the generic name, *Cotyledon,* has been given, derived from the Greek *cotyle* (a cup). Some of the English names of the plant, Wall Pennywort, Wall Pennyroyal and Penny Pies, are references to the round form of the leaf suggesting a coin.

At the end of May or early in June, stout reddish flowering stems arise, decumbent for a greater or less distance at the base, but then growing very erect to the height of 6 to 18 inches or more. They bear leaves which pass by intermediate gradation from those of a round peltate form to a shortly stalked, wedge-shaped one, and are terminated by a long raceme, or spike, of numerous, pendulous, bell-shaped, yellow-green flowers, with corollas about half an inch long. The calyx is small and, like the corolla, is five-cleft. The plant is in blossom from June to August, and the leaves often remain green most of the winter.

The juice and extract of the Kidneywort had an old reputation for epilepsy, especially among herb doctors in the west of England, where it is most frequently found; its use as a remedy in epilepsy was revived last century even in regular practice, but it has obtained no permanent reputation as a remedy.

It is applied by the peasantry in Wales to the eyes as a remedy in some diseases. The leaves, bruised to a pulp and applied as a poultice, are said to cure piles, and are also recommended as an application for slight burns or scalds. A decoction of the leaves is considered cooling and diuretic, and the juice when taken inwardly to be excellent for inflammation of the liver and spleen.

Culpepper tells us that

'the juice or distilled water being drunk is very effectual for all inflammations, to cool a fainting stomach, a hot liver or the bowels; the herb, juice or distilled water outwardly applied healeth pimples, St. Anthony's Fire (erysipelas) and other outward heats.'

He also recommends the juice or distilled water for ulcerated kidneys, gravel and stone, and an ointment made with it for 'painful piles' and pains of the gout and sciatia. In addition,

'it heals kibes or chilblains if they be bathed with the juice or anointed with ointment made hereof and some of the skin of the leaf upon them: it is used in green wounds to stay the blood and to heal them quickly.'

See STONECROPS.

KINOS

Pterocarpus marsupium
Pterocarpus erinaceus
Butea frondosa
N.O. Leguminosæ

Kino is the inspissated juice of the Bastard Teak (*Pterocarpus marsupium*) obtained from incisions made in the trunk. The term Kino is also applied to the juice of other plants inspissated without artificial heat. The varieties commonly distinguished are:

MALABAR or EAST INDIAN KINO obtained from *P. marsupium.*

AFRICAN or GAMBIA KINO from *P. erinaceus.*

BUTEA, BENGAL, or PALAS KINO from *Butea frondosa.*

BOTANY BAY, AUSTRALIAN or EUCALYPTUS KINO from different species of Eucalyptus.

WEST INDIAN or JAMAICA KINO from *Coccoloba uvifera*.

SOUTH AMERICAN or CARACAS KINO, which is identified with Columbian Kino and is believed to be obtained from the same plant that yields the West Indian Kino.

In the British Pharmacopœia Malabar or West Indian Kino is the only one recognized, and this is found in small, brittle glistening pieces, reddish-black in colour. They are odourless with a very astringent taste and stick to the teeth when chewed and make the saliva bright red.

Kino is almost entirely soluble in alcohol and entirely in ether and partly in water.

Chemically it closely resembles catechu, and is very like it in action, but it is less astringent and therefore less effective.

The Indian Pharmacopœia recognizes this kind and also Bengal Kino are recognized, and in the United States other kinds are official as well as these two.

¶ *Medicinal Action and Uses*. Astringent. Used whenever tannin is indicated. Internally in diarrhœa, dysentery, and pyrosis. Externally as a gargle and as an injection for leucorrhœa.

¶ *Preparations and Dosages*. Powdered gum, 5 to 20 grains. Comp. powder, B.P., 5 to 20 grains. Tincture, B.P. and U.S.P., ½ to 1 drachm.

See EUCALYPTUS.

KNAPWEED, BLACK

Centaurea nigra (LINN.)
N.O. Compositæ

Centaurea nigra, the Black Knapweed, is a perennial, with an unwinged, erect stem, 6 inches to 3 feet high, generally freely branched in the upper part. The leaves are very variable, both in breadth and degrees of division, the upper ones narrow and generally with entire margins, but the lower ones lobed, or at any rate with some coarse teeth. The whole plant is dull green, rather rough with small hairs, the stems, like the preceding species, very tough. The flowers are without the spreading outer rays of the Greater Knapweed, the florets being all tubular, which makes the black fringes to the bracts of the involucre most noticeable, hence the name of the species. The florets are of a less bright purple in colour.

KNAPWEED, GREATER

Centaurea Scabiosa
N.O. Compositæ

Synonyms. Hardhead. Ironhead. Hard Irons. Churls Head. Logger Head. Horse Knops. Matte Felon. Mat Fellon. Bottleweed. Bullweed. Cowede. Boltsede
Parts Used. Root, seeds
Habitat. Frequent in the borders of fields and in waste places, being not uncommon in England, where it is abundant on chalk soil, but rare in Scotland

¶ *Description*. The plant is a perennial, the rootstock thick and woody in old plants. The stem is 1 to 3 feet high, generally branched, very tough. The leaves, which are firm in texture, are very variable in the degree of division, but generally deeply cut into, the segments again deeply notched. The lower leaves are very large, often a foot or even more in length, making a striking-looking rosette on the ground, from which the flowering stems arise. The whole plant is a dull green, sparingly hairy. It flowers in July and August. The flowers are terminal, somewhat similar to those of the Cornflower in general shape, though larger. All the florets are of the same colour, a rich purplish-crimson, the outer ray ones with the limb divided nearly to the base into narrow, strap-shaped segments. The flower-head is hard and solid, a mass of bracts lapping over each other like tiles, each having a central green portion and a black fringe-like edge. In some districts the plant is called from these almost round heads, 'Hardhead,' and the ordinary English name, Knapweed, is based on the same idea, *Knap*, being a form of *Knop*, or *Knob*.

This larger species of Knapweed was in olden times called 'Matte Felon,' from its use in curing felons or whitlows. As early as 1440 we find it called 'Maude Felone,' or 'Boltsede.'

This species is very common and generally distributed in pastures, borders of fields and roadsides throughout Britain, and flowers from early June till well into September. Both species of Knapweed may readily be distinguished from Thistles by the absence of spines and prickles.

¶ *Medicinal Action and Uses*. The Knapweed was once in great repute as a vulnerary. It was included in the fourteenth-century ointment, *Save*, for wounds and for the pestilence, and was also used with pepper for loss of appetite.

The root and seeds are used. Its diuretic, diaphoretic and tonic properties are recognized.

It is good for catarrh, taken in decoction, and is also made into ointment for outward application for wounds and bruises, sores, etc.

KNAPWORT HARSHWEED

Synonym. Brown Radiant Knapweed

Centaurea Jacea, known to old writers as Knapwort Harshweed, its modern name being the Brown Radiant Knapweed, is a rare species.

It was also applied as a vulnerary and was used internally. Culpepper describes it as a mild astringent, 'helpful against coughs, asthma, and difficulty of breathing, and good for diseases of the head and nerves,' and tells us that 'outwardly the bruised herb is famous for taking away black and blue marks out of the skin.'

The botanical name of the species, *scabiosa,* signifying the Scabious-like Knapweed, is

Culpepper tells us: 'it is of special use for soreness of throat, swelling of the uvula and jaws, and very good to stay bleeding at the nose and mouth.'

Centaurea Jacea

given this species of *Centaurea* from its resemblance in general size, form of leaf and other features to the Scabious, another common plant also found in the chalk district, which obtains its name from the Latin word *scabies,* an irritating roughness of the skin, for which it has been employed as a remedy.

The medicinal qualities of the Greater Knapweed are similar to those of the Black Knapweed, a smaller variety, which is more generally collected for medicinal use, perhaps because more common.

See CENTAURY, GENTIAN, THISTLES

KNOTGRASS

Polyganum aviculare (LINN.)
N.O. Polygonaceæ

Synonyms. Knotgrass. Centinode. Ninety-knot. Nine-joints. Allseed. Bird's Tongue. Sparrow Tongue. Red Robin. Armstrong. Cowgrass. Hogweed. Pigweed. Pigrush. Swynel Grass. Swine's Grass

Part Used. Whole herb

Habitat. The entire globe

The Knotgrass is abundant everywhere, a common weed in arable land, on waste ground and by the roadside.

¶ *Description.* The root is annual, branched and somewhat woody, taking strong hold of the earth; the stems, ½ to 6 feet in length, much branched, seldom erect, usually of straggling habit, often quite prostrate and widely spreading. The leaves, alternate and often stalkless, are variable, narrow, lance-shaped or oval, ½ to 1½ inch long, issuing from the sheaths of the stipules or ochreæ, which are membraneous, white, shining, torn, red at the base and two-lobed. The flowers are minute, in clusters of two to three, in the axils of the stem, barely ⅛ in. long, usually pinkish, sometimes red, green, or dull whitish. In contrast to the other Polygonums, there is little or no honey or scent, so that the flowers are very rarely visited by insects and pollinate themselves by the incurving of the three inner stamens on to the styles. The remaining five stamens alternate with the perianth segments and bend outwards, thus ensuring cross-pollination in addition, should any insect visit the flower.

The plant varies greatly in size. When it grows singly in a favourable soil and clear of other vegetation, it will often cover a circle of a yard or more in diameter, the stems being almost prostrate on the ground and leaves

broad and large; but when growing crowded by other plants the stalks become more upright and all the parts are generally smaller.

The stems are smooth, with swollen joints, hence the common names, Nine-joints, Ninety-knots, etc., and when gathered it generally snaps at one of the joints.

It begins flowering in May and continues till September or October. Cleistogamic flowers (which do not open at all and in which therefore self-pollination is necessarily effected) are found under the ochrea, and this species is said also to possess subterranean cleistogamic flowers.

The specific name, *aviculare,* is from the Latin *aviculus,* a diminutive of *avis* (a bird), great numbers of our smaller birds feeding on its seeds. The seeds are useful for every purpose in which those of the allied Buckwheat are employed and are produced in great numbers, hence its local name – Allseed.

Some of the older herbals call it Bird's Tongue or Sparrow Tongue, these names arising from the shape of its little, pointed leaves. Its minute reddish flowers gained it the name of Red Robin. From the difficulty of pulling it up, it was called Armstrong, and from the fact that cattle and swine eat it readily, we find it called Cowgrass and Hogweed, Pigweed or Pigrush. Gerard tells us:

'It is given to swine with good successe when they are sicke and will not eat their meate, whereupon the country people so call it Swine's Grass and Swine's Skir. In the Grete Herball (1516) it is called Swynel Grass.'

Shakespeare (*Midsummer Night's Dream*) speaks of this plant as 'the hindering Knotgrass,' referring to the belief that its decoction was efficacious in retarding the growth of children and the young of domestic animals.

The larvæ of Geometer moths will eat the plant as a substitute for their usual food.

¶ *Medicinal Action and Uses*. The plant has astringent properties, rendering an infusion of it useful in diarrhœa, bleeding piles and all hæmorrhages; it was formerly employed considerably as a vulnerary and styptic.

It has also diuretic properties, for which it has found employment in strangury and as an expellant of stone, the dose recommended in old herbals being 1 drachm of the herb, powdered in wine, taken twice a day.

The decoction was also administered to kill worms.

The fresh juice has been found effectual to stay bleeding of the nose, squirted up the nose and applied to the temples, and made into an ointment it has proved an excellent remedy for sores.

Salmon stated:

'Knotgrass is peculiar against spilling of blood, strangury and other kidney affections, cools inflammations, heals wounds and cleanses and heals old filthy ulcers. The *Essence* for tertians and quartan. The *decoction* for colick; the *Balsam* strengthens weak joints, comforts the nerves and tendons, and is prevalent against the gout, being duly and rightly applied morning and evening.'

The fruit is emetic and purgative.

¶ *Other Species*.

P. Arifoleum, or Sickle-grass, Halbert-leaved Tear-thumb, Hactate Knotgrass. An infusion is a powerful diuretic, to be drunk freely in all urinary affections.

The Russian Knotgrass (*Polygonum erectum*, Linn.) possesses similar astringent properties, and an infusion of this herb is used in diarrhœa and children's summer complaints.

The Alpine Knotweed (*P. viviparum*, Linn.), a small perennial, only 4 to 8 inches high, found in British mountain alpine pastures, is peculiar in that its slender, spike-like raceme of white or pinkish flowers bears in its lower portion, in place of flowers, little red bulbs (as in certain species of *Lilium* and *Alium*), on which the plant depends for its propagation, its fruit rarely maturing.

This species is found in North America, being there the one nearest related to the Bistort, whose properties it shares.

See BISTORT.

KNOTGRASS, RUSSIAN

Polygonum erectum (LINN.)
N.O. Polygonacea

Synonym. Erect Knotgrass
Part Used. Whole herb
Habitat. British America, and Western and Middle States

¶ *Description*. This perennial herb was discovered in North America in 1790, but up to date it has not been largely utilized. It is a variety of the English one – *Polygonum aviculare*, and has similar properties. It has an upright smooth branched stem and grows from 1 to 3 feet high. Leaves are smooth, broadly obvate, rather obtuse – 1 to 2 inches long – and about half as broad – either sessile or petiolate. Flowers bloom June to September in bunches at axils of the leaves.

¶ *Medicinal Action and Uses*. It is highly astringent as an infusion or decoction; useful in diarrhœa as an injection and in children's summer complaints; also as a good gargle and a valuable remedy for inflammatory diseases of the tissues.

KOLA NUTS

Kola vera (SCHUM.)
N.O. Sterculiaceæ

Synonyms. Cola acuminata. Sterculia acuminata. Kola Seeds. Gurru Nuts. Bissy Nuts. Cola Seeds. Guru Nut
Part Used. Seeds
Habitat. Sierra Leone, North Ashanti near the sources of the Nile; cultivated in tropical Western Africa, West Indies, Brazil, Java

¶ *Description*. This tree grows about 40 feet high, has yellow flowers, spotted with purple; leaves 6 to 8 inches long, pointed at both ends.

The seeds are extensively used as a condiment by the natives of Western and Central tropical Africa, also by the negroes of the West Indies and Brazil, who introduced the trees to these countries.

In Western Africa these trees are usually

found growing near the sea-coast, and a big trade is carried on with the nuts by the natives of the interior – Cola being eaten by them as far as Fezzan and Tripoli. A small piece is chewed before each meal to promote digestion; it is also thought to improve the flavour of anything eaten after it and even to render putrid water palatable; the powder is applied to cuts.

There are several kinds of Cola seeds derived from different species, but the *Cola vera* are most generally used and preferred for medicinal purposes. Those from West Africa and West Indies supply the commercial drug. *C. acuminata*, or Gurru Nuts, are employed in the same way as *C. vera*; they are from a tree growing in Cameron and Congo, not esteemed so highly, but much in use as a caffeine stimulant; 600 tons are said to be sent yearly to Brazil for the negroes' use, who also employ the seeds of *S. Chica* and *S. Striata*. The Kola of commerce consists of the separated cotyledons of the kernel of the seed; when fresh it is nearly white, on drying it undergoes a fermentative change, turning reddish brown and losing much of its astringency. The dried cotyledons vary in size from 1 to 2 inches, are irregular in shape but roughly plano-convex, exterior reddy brown, interior paler, easily cut, showing a uniform section, odourless and almost tasteless. Large quantities of the fresh seeds are employed in Africa on account of their sustaining properties, where they form an important article of inland commerce.

¶ *Constituents.* The different varieties of nuts give a greater or lesser percentage of caffeine, which is only found in the fresh state. The seeds are said to contain a glucoside, Kolanin, but this substance appears to be a mixture of Kola red and caffeine. The seeds also contain starch, fatty matter, sugar, a fat decomposing enzyme acting on various oils.

¶ *Medicinal Action and Uses.* The properties of Kola are the same as caffeine, modified only by the astringents present. Fresh Kola Nuts have stimulant action apart from the caffeine content, but as they appear in European commerce, their action is indistinguishable from that of other caffeine drugs and Kola red is inert. Kola is also a valuable nervine, heart tonic, and a good general tonic.

¶ *Adulterations.* Male Kola (not to be confused with Kola) is the fruit of a small tree, Garcinia Kola, and contains no caffeine. The fruit is oblong, from 2 to 3 inches long and 1 inch broad; it is trigonal in section, reddish brown with nutmeg-like markings. Taste, bitter and astringent. Under microscope shows resinous masses, surrounded by cells full of starch. The seeds of *Lucuma Mammosa* are sometimes found mixed with Kola Nuts, but are easily detected by their strong smell of prussic acid. *Hertiera Litorales* seeds are also sometimes found mixed with Kola Nuts.

C. Ballayi (cornu) seeds are also used, but these are easily distinguished as the seeds have six cotyledons and contain little caffeine.

¶ *Preparations.* Fluid extract of Kola, 10 to 40 drops. Solid extract alc., 2 to 8 grains.

KOUSSO

Hagenia Abyssinica (WILLD.)
Brayera anthelmintica (KUNTH.)
N.O. Rosaceæ

Synonyms. Banksia Abyssinica. Kooso. Kusso. Kosso. Cossoo. Cusso.
Parts Used. Herb, unripe fruit, and the dried panicles of the pistillate flowers
Habitat. North-Eastern Africa, and cultivated in Abyssinia; official in United States of America

¶ *Description.* The tree is named after Dr. K. G. Hagen of Königsberg, a German botanist (*d.* 1829), and also after A. Brayera, a French physician in Constantinople, who wrote a monograph on the tree in 1823. It is a beautiful tree growing about 20 feet high, at an elevation of 3,000 to 8,000 feet. The flowers are unisexual, small, of a greenish colour, becoming purple. The dried flowers have a slight balsamic odour, and the taste is bitter and acrid; the female flowers are chiefly collected, although not exclusively so. 'Loose Kousso,' i.e. flowers stripped from their panicles, sometimes come into the market, often with some staminate flowers among it. These are much less active, easily distinguished by their greeny colour, fertile stamens and outer hairy sepals, whereas the female flowers are a dark reddish colour. As a medicine it is very apt to be adulterated, owing to its high price; therefore it is advisable to buy it in its unpowdered state.

¶ *Constituents.* A volatile oil, a bitter acrid resin, tannic acid, and a bitter principle called A Kosin and B Kosin, which is found in Kousso, but thought to be decomposition products. The principle constituent of Kousso is Koso-toxin, a yellow amorphous body, possibly closely allied to filicia acid, and Rottlerin; other inactive colourless bodies are crystalline Protokosin and Kosidin.

¶ *Medicinal Action and Uses.* Purgative and anthelmintic; the Abyssinians are greatly troubled with tapeworm, and Kousso is used by them to expel the worms. One dose is said to be effective in destroying both kinds of tapeworms, the *tænia solium* and *bothriocephalus latus*; but as it possesses little cathartic power the subsequent administration of a purgative is generally necessary to bring away the destroyed ectozoon. The dose of the flowers when powdered is from 4 to 5½ drachms, macerated in 3 gills of lukewarm water for 15 minutes; the unstrained infusion is taken in two or three doses following each other, freely drinking lemon-juice or tamarind water before and after the doses. It is

advisable to fast twenty-four or forty-eight hours before taking the drug. The operation is usually safe, effective, and quick, merely causing sometimes a slight nausea, but it has never failed to expel the worm. Occasionally emesis takes place or diuresis, and collapse follows, but cases of this sort are extremely rare. It is said in Abyssinia that honey gathered from beehives immediately the Kousso plants have flowered is very effective in teaspoonful doses as a tænicide, its effect being to poison the worms.

¶ *Dosage.* Infusion of ½ oz. to 1 pint of boiling water is taken in 4 oz. doses, and repeated at short intervals. Fluid extract, 2 to 4 drachms.

LABRADOR TEA

Ledum latifolium (JACQ.)
N.O. Ericaceæ

Synonyms. St. James's Tea. Ledum Grœnlandicum
Parts Used. Leaves and tops
Habitat. Greenland, Labrador, Nova Scotia, Hudson's Bay

¶ *Description.* This evergreen shrub grows to a height of 4 to 5 feet, with irregular, woolly branches. The leaves are alternate, entire, elliptical or oblong, 1 to 2 inches long, the upper side smooth and woolly underneath, with the edges rolled back. The large, white, five-petalled flowers grow in flattened terminal clusters, opening in June and July. The plant grows in cold bogs and mountain woods. It is taller, more regularly formed, and has larger leaves than *L. palustre*. During the American War of Independence the leaves were much used instead of tea-leaves. They should be collected before flowering time, and the tops when the flowers begin to open.

Bees are much attracted by the flowers, but animals do not browse on the plants, which are said to be slightly poisonous.

Strewed among clothes, the leaves will keep away moths, and in Lapland the branches are placed among grain to keep away mice.

In Russia the leaves are used for tanning leather.

¶ *Constituents.* There has been found in the leaves tannin, gallic acid, a bitter substance, wax, resin, and salts.

¶ *Medicinal Action and Uses.* The leaves are tonic, diaphoretic, and pectoral, having a

pleasant odour and rather spicy taste. They yield their virtues to hot water or to alcohol. It is useful in coughs, dyspepsia, and irritation of the membranes of the chest. An infusion has been used to soothe irritation in infectious, feverish eruptions, in dysentery, leprosy, itch, etc. The strong decoction, as a wash, will kill lice. The leaves are also used in malignant and inflamed sore throat.

¶ *Dosage.* Of infusion, 2 to 4 fluid ounces, three to four times a day. Overdoses may cause violent headache and symptoms of intoxication.

¶ *Other Species.*

L. PALUSTRE (Marsh Tea, Marsh Cistus, Wild Rosemary, Wild Rosmarin, Rosmarinus[1] Sylvestris, Porsch, Sumpfporsch, Finne Thé) grows in swamps and wet places of northern Europe, Asia, and America, and on the mountains of southern districts. The leaves are reputed to be more powerful than those of *L. latifolium*, and to have in addition some narcotic properties, being used in Germany to make beer more intoxicating. The leaves contain a volatile oil, including *ledum camphor*, a stearopten, with valeric and volatile acids, ericolin, and ericinol. The tannin is called leditannic acid.

(POISON)
LABURNUM

Cytisus Laburnam (LINN.)
N.O. Leguminosæ

Synonym. Yellow Laburnum
Part Used. Seeds

The Laburnum, indigenous to the higher mountains of Europe, is cultivated throughout the civilized world for its flowers, which appear early in the spring, in rich, pendent, yellow clusters.

All parts of the plant are probably poisonous and children should be warned never to touch the black seeds which contain this highly poisonous alkaloid, as cases of poisoning after eating the seeds have been frequent.

[1] This species is used in Homœopathy. – EDITOR.

The Laburnum is a native of the mountains of France, Switzerland, and southern Germany, where it attains the height of 20 feet and upwards. It was introduced into England previously to 1597, at which time Gerard appears to have grown it in his garden under the names of Anagyris, Laburnum, and Bean Trefoil.

The heart-wood is of a dark colour, and though of a coarse grain it is very hard and durable, will take a polish, and may be stained to resemble ebony. It is much in demand among turners, and is wrought into a variety of articles which require strength and smoothness.

Cytisus purpurascens (Fr. *C. d'Adam*), the PURPLE LABURNUM, is a hybrid between *C. Laburnum* and *C. purpureus*. It was originated in Paris in 1828, by M. Adam, and has since been much cultivated in England. A curious result of hybridizing appears in this variety occasionally. The branches below the graft produce the ordinary yellow Laburnum flowers of large size; those above often exhibit a small purple Laburnum flower, as well as reddish flowers intermediate between the two in size and colour. Occasionally, the same cluster has some flowers yellow and some purple (Balfour).

Laburnum trees should not be allowed to overhang a field used as a pasture, for when cattle and horses have browsed on the foliage and pods, the results have proved deadly.

Symptoms of poisoning by Laburnum root or seeds are intense sleepiness, vomiting, convulsive movements, coma, slight frothing at the mouth and unequally dilated pupils. In some cases, diarrhœa is very severe and at times the convulsions are markedly tetanic.

In an article on the use of insecticides against lice, by A. Bacot, Entomologist to the Lister Institute of Preventive Medicine, in the *British Medical Journal* of September 30, 1916, the writer records the results of experiments with various reputedly insecticidal substances, but mainly with Cytisine, the alkaloid obtained from the seeds of the Gorse and Laburnum, the physiological properties of which resemble those of Nicotine. He found that while Cytisine is quite satisfactory from an experimental point of view, its use is contraindicated, because the degree of concentration required is such as to entail risk of absorption over a wide area of the body, with almost certain toxic consequences.

¶ *Constituents*. Cytisine was discovered in 1863 by Husemann and Marme, as one of the poisonous alkaloids present in the seeds of the Laburnum. It is a white, crystalline solid, of a bitter, somewhat caustic taste, with a very poisonous action. It has been recommended in whooping cough and asthma.

The same alkaloid has been isolated from the seeds of several leguminous plants. Plugge, in 1895, stated that he found it in eight species of the genus *Cytisus*, two of the genus *Genista*, two of the genus *Sophara*, two of the genus *Baptisia*, in *Anagyris fœtida*, and in other plants. He considered the Ulexine of Gerrard from *Ulex Europæa* (Linn.) to be identical with Cytisine.

LACHNANTHES

Lachnanthes tinctoria (ELL.)
N.O. Hæmodoraceæ

Synonyms. Gyrotheca capitata. Gyrotheca tinctoria. Wool Flower. Red Root. Paint Root. Spirit Weed

Parts Used. Root, herb

Habitat. The drug Lachnanthes is prepared from the entire plant, but especially from the rhizome and roots of *Lachnanthes tinctoria*, a plant indigenous to the United States of America, growing in sandy swamps along the Atlantic coast, from Florida to New Jersey and Rhode Island, and also found in Cuba, blossoming from June to September, according to locality

It was introduced into England as a greenhouse plant in 1812 and then propagated from seed

¶ *Description*. The plant is a perennial herb, $1\frac{1}{2}$ to 2 feet high, the upper portion white-woolly, hence one of its local names: Wool-flower. The rhizome is about 1 inch in length and of nearly equal thickness, and bears a large number of long, coarse, somewhat waxy, deep-red roots, yielding a red dye, to which its popular names of Paintroot and Redroot are due.

The leaves are mostly borne in basal rosettes and are somewhat succulent, $\frac{1}{4}$ to $\frac{3}{4}$ inch wide and reduced to bracts on the upper part of the stem. The flowers are in a close, woolly cyme, the ovary inferior, the perianth six-parted, the sepals narrower than the petals, the stamens three, alternately with the petals, on long filaments; the style is solitary, thread-like, its stigma slightly lobed; the fruit, a three-celled, many seeded, rounded capsule.

¶ *Constituents*. The root yields a fine red dye and a little resin, but so far no analysis determining the nature of its specific constituents has been made: they are, however, quite active, producing a peculiar form of cerebral stimulation or narcosis.

The drug has a somewhat acrid taste, but no odour.

¶ *Medicinal Action and Uses.*

'The root,' says Millspaugh, 'was esteemed an invigorating tonic by the American aborigines, especially by the Seminole tribe, who use it, it is said, to cause brilliancy and fluency of speech. A tincture of the root has been recommended in typhus and typhoid fevers, pneumonia, severe forms of brain disease, rheumatic wry-neck and laryngeal cough.'

Apart from its narcotic uses among the Indians, it has been used in the United States for dyeing purposes.

The drug is employed for various nervous disorders. A homœopathic tincture is prepared from the whole fresh plant, while flowering. Doses varying from a few drops of the tincture to a drachm, cause mental exhilaration, followed by ill-humour, vertigo and headache.

Fluid extract, 1 to 5 drops.

Although the drug is not related to the Solanaceæ, the effects of overdoses are said to resemble those of poisoning by Belladonna and other solanaceous drugs.

In the countries where it grows, there is a legend that the Paintroot plant is fatally poisonous to white pigs, but not injurious to black ones. Darwin, on the authority of Professor I. J. Wyman, cites the strange effect on albino pigs after eating the roots of this plant. In Virginia, where it grows abundantly, Professor Wyman noticed that all the pigs in this district were black, and upon inquiring of the farmers he found that all the white pigs born in a litter were destroyed, because they could not be reared to maturity. The roots of *Lachnanthes*, when eaten by white pigs, caused their bones to turn to a pink colour and their hoofs to fall off, but the black pigs, it was said, could eat the same plant with impunity. Heusinger has shown that white sheep and pigs are injured by the ingestion of certain plants, while the pigmented species may eat them without harm.

LADIES' BEDSTRAW. *See* BEDSTRAW

LADY'S MANTLE

Alchemilla vulgaris (LINN.)
N.O. Rosaceæ

Synonyms. Lion's Foot. Bear's Foot. Nine Hooks. Leontopodium. Stellaria
(*French*) Pied-de-lion
(*German*) Frauenmantle

Parts Used. Herb, root

Habitat. The Lady's Mantle and the Parsley Piert, two small, inconspicuous plants, have considerable reputation as herbal remedies. They both belong to the genus *Alchemilla* of the great order Rosaceæ, most of the members of which are natives of the American Andes, only a few being found in Europe, North America and Northern and Western Asia. In Britain, we have only three species, *Alchemilla vulgaris*, the Common Lady's Mantle, *A. arvensis*, the Field Lady's Mantle or Parsley Piert, and *A. alpina*, less frequent and only found in mountainous districts.

The Common Lady's Mantle is generally distributed over Britain, but more especially in the colder districts and on high-lying ground, being found up to an altitude of 3,600 feet in the Scotch Highlands. It is not uncommon in moist, hilly pastures and by streams, except in the south-east of England, and is abundant in Yorkshire, especially in the Dales. It is indeed essentially a plant of the north, freely found beyond the Arctic circle in Europe, Asia and also in Greenland and Labrador, and only on high mountain ranges, such as the Himalayas, if found in southern latitudes

The plant is of graceful growth and though only a foot high and green throughout – flowers, stem and leaves alike, and therefore inconspicuous – the rich form of its foliage and the beautiful shape of its clustering blossoms make it worthy of notice.

¶ *Description.* The rootstock is perennial – black, stout and short – and from it rises the slender erect stem. The whole plant is clothed with soft hairs. The lower, radical leaves, large and handsome, 6 to 8 inches in diameter, are borne on slender stalks, 6 to 18 inches long and are somewhat kidney-shaped in general outline, with their margins cut into seven or mostly nine broad, but shallow lobes, finely toothed at the edges, from which it has obtained one of its local names: 'Nine Hooks.' The upper leaves are similar and either stalkless, or on quite short footstalks and are all actually notched and toothed. A noticeable feature is the leaf-like stipules, also toothed, which embrace the stem.

The flowers, which are in bloom from

June to August, are numerous and small, only about ⅛ inch in diameter, yellow-green in colour, in loose, divided clusters at the end of the freely-branching flower-stems, each on a short stalk, or pedicle. There are no petals, the calyx is four-cleft, with four conspicuous little bracteoles that have the appearance of outer and alternate segments of the calyx. There are four stamens, inserted on the mouth of the calyx, their filaments jointed.

The rootstock is astringent and edible and the leaves are eaten by sheep and cattle.

The common name, Lady's Mantle (in its German form, *Frauenmantle*), was first bestowed on it by the sixteenth-century botanist, Jerome Bock, always known by the Latinized version of his name: Tragus. It appears under this name in his famous *History of Plants*, published in 1532, and Linnæus adopted it. In the Middle Ages, this plant had been associated, like so many flowers, with the Virgin Mary (hence it is Lady's Mantle, not Ladies' Mantle), the lobes of the leaves being supposed to resemble the scalloped edges of a mantle. In mediæval Latin we also find it called *Leontopodium* (lion's foot), probably from its spreading root-leaves, and this has become in modern French, *Pied-de-lion*. We occasionally find the same idea expressed in two English local names, 'Lion's foot' and 'Bear's foot.' It has also been called 'Stellaria,' from the radiating character of its lower leaves, but this belongs more properly to quite another group of plants, with star-like blossoms of pure white.

A yellow fungus sometimes attacks the plant known as *Uromyces alchemillæ*, and has the curious effect of causing abnormal length of the leaf-stalk and rendering the blade of the leaf smaller and of a paler green colour; this fungus produces the same effect in other plants.

The generic name *Alchemilla* is derived from the Arabic word, *Alkemelych* (alchemy), and was bestowed on it, according to some old writers, because of the wonder-working powers of the plant. Others held that the alchemical virtues lay in the subtle influence the foliage imparted to the dewdrops that lay in its furrowed leaves and in the little cup formed by its joined stipules, these dewdrops constituting part of many mystic potions.

¶ *Part Used Medicinally.* The whole herb, gathered in June and July when in flower and when the leaves are at their best, and dried.

The root is sometimes also employed, generally fresh.

¶ *Medicinal Action and Uses.* The Lady's Mantle has astringent and styptic properties, on account of the tannin it contains. It is 'of a very drying and binding character' as the old herbalists expressed it, and was formerly considered one of the best vulneraries or wound herbs.

Culpepper says of it:

'Lady's Mantle is very proper for inflamed wounds and to stay bleeding, vomitings, fluxes of all sorts, bruises by falls and ruptures. It is one of the most singular wound herbs and therefore highly prized and praised, used in all wounds inward and outward, to drink a decoction thereof and wash the wounds therewith, or dip tents therein and put them into the wounds which wonderfully drieth up all humidity of the sores and abateth all inflammations thereof. It quickly healeth green wounds, not suffering any corruption to remain behind and cureth old sores, though fistulous and hollow.'

In modern herbal treatment, it is employed as a cure for excessive menstruation and is taken internally as an infusion (1 oz. of the dried herb to 1 pint of boiling water) in teacupful doses as required and the same infusion is also employed as an injection.

A strong decoction of the fresh root, by some considered the most valuable part of the plant, has also been recommended as excellent to stop all bleedings, and the root dried and reduced to powder is considered to answer the same purpose and to be good for violent purgings.

In Sweden, a tincture of the leaves has been given in cases of spasmodic or convulsive diseases, and an old authority states that if placed under the pillow at night, the herb will promote quiet sleep.

Fluid extract, dose, ½ to 1 drachm.

Horses and sheep like the plant, and it has therefore been suggested as a profitable fodder plant, but the idea has proved unpractical. Grazing animals will not eat the leaves till the moisture in them is dissipated.

¶ *Other Species.*

Alchemilla alpine, a mountain variety, found on the banks of Scotch rivulets. The leaves are deeply divided into five oblong leaflets and are thickly covered with lustrous silky hairs. A form of this plant in which the leaflets are connate for one-third of their length is known as *A. conjuncta*.

See PARSLEY PIERT

LADY'S SLIPPER. *See* AMERICAN VALERIAN

LADY'S TRESSES[1]

Spiranthes autumnalis (ORICH.)
N.O. Spiranthideœ

Part Used. Tuberous root

Habitat. Dry, hilly fields all over Europe – towards the Caucasus

¶ *Description.* This orchis takes its name from *speira* (a 'spiral') and *anthos* (a flower), in allusion to the spiral arrangement of the flowers. Rootstock produces every season two or three oblong tubers and a tuft of spreading, radical, ovate leaves about 1 inch long, a flowering stem 6 or 8 inches high by the side of the tuft of leaves. Blooms in autumn, flowers a greenish-white, smelling like almonds, in a close spiral spike about 2 inches long, diverging horizontally to one side – with the bracts erect on opposite side, in appearance not unlike lilies of the valley.

¶ *Medicinal Action and Uses.* Formerly used as an aphrodisiac.

A tincture of the root is used in homœopathy for skin affections, painful breasts, pain in the kidneys and eye complaints.

¶ *Other Species.*

Spiranthes diuretica, used in Chile in cases of ischury.

LARCH. *See* PINES

LARKSPUR, FIELD

Delphinium Consolida
N.O. Ranunculacæ

Synonyms. Lark's Heel. Lark's Toe. Lark's Claw. Knight's Spur

Part Used. Seed

Habitat. Europe

The Field Larkspur grows wild in cornfields throughout Europe. Though a doubtful native, it is found occasionally in England in considerable quantities in sandy or chalky cornfields, especially in Cambridgeshire.

¶ *Description.* It is an annual, with upright, round stems a foot high or more, pubescent and divided into alternate, dividing branches. The leaves are alternate, the lower ones with petioles ½ inch long, the upper ones sessile, or nearly so. The plant closely resembles some of the species commonly cultivated in gardens.

The flowers are in short racemes, pink, purple or blue, followed by glabrous follicles containing black, flattened seeds with acute edges and pitted surfaces. The seeds are poisonous, have an acrid and bitter taste, but are inodorous.

The active principle of the plant – Delphinine – is the same as in Stavesacre and is an irritant poison. Children should be warned against putting any part of this plant, or of its garden representatives, into their mouths. The seeds are especially dangerous, and cause vomiting and purging if eaten.

¶ *Medicinal Action and Uses.* As in Stavesacre, the part used medicinally is the seed, a tincture of which in like manner acts as a parasiticide and insecticide, being used to destroy lice and nits in the hair.[2]

The tincture, given in 10-drop doses, gradually increased, is also employed in spasmodic asthma and dropsy.

The expressed juice of the leaves is considered good as an application to bleeding piles, and a conserve made of the flowers was formerly held to be an excellent medicine for children when subject to violent purging.

The juice of the flowers and an infusion of the whole plant was also prescribed against colic.

The expressed juice of the petals with the addition of a little alum makes a good blue ink.

The name Delphinium, from *Delphin* (a dolphin), was given to this genus because the buds were held to resemble a dolphin. Shakespeare mentions the plant under the name of Lark's Heel.

The name Consolida refers to the plant's power of consolidating wounds.

See STAVESACRE

LAUREL (BAY)

Laurus nobilis (LINN.)
N.O. Lauraceæ

Synonyms. Sweet Bay. True Laurel. Bay. Laurier d'Apollon. Roman Laurel. Noble Laurel. Lorbeer. Laurier Sauce. Daphne

Parts Used. Leaves, fruit, oil

Habitat. Shores of the Mediterranean

¶ *Description.* The Sweet Bay is a small tree, growing in Britain to a height of about 25 feet, but in warmer climates reaching as much as 60 feet. The smooth bark may be olive-green or of a reddish hue. The luxurious, evergreen leaves are alternate,

---

[1] Lady's Tresses grow on the Sussex downs near Amberley. – EDITOR.

[2] During the Great War, when the men in the trenches took the trouble to use it, the results were said to be quite successful. – EDITOR.

with short stalks, lanceolate, 3 to 4 inches long, the margin smooth and wavy. They are thick, smooth, and of a shining, dark green colour. The flowers are small, yellow and unisexual, and grow in small clusters. The shrub has been cultivated in Britain since the sixteenth century. It is the source of the ancients' crowns and wreaths for heroes and poets, and the modern term of 'bachelor,' given for degrees, is probably derived from *bacca-laureus*, or laurel-berry, through the French *bachelier*.

The Delphic priestesses are said to have made use of the leaves. It grows well under the shade of other trees if they are not too close, and is useful in evergreen plantations. The leaves are much used in cookery for flavouring. They are often packed with stick liquorice or dried figs. They are used fresh, and may be gathered all the year round.

The volatile oil is sometimes used in perfumery.

The dried, black, aromatic *berries* come from Provence, Spain, Italy and Morocco. They are ovoid, and the kernel of the seed is loose.

The *wood* is sweet-scented, and is used for marqueterie work.

Onguent de Laurier is prepared from the oil with *axonge* and the colouring and scenting principles of the leaves and fruit.

¶ *Constituents*. A greenish-yellow volatile oil is yielded by distillation from the leaves which contains a high percentage of oxygenated compounds. The berries contain both fixed and volatile oils, the former, known as *Oil of Bays*, includes *laurostearine*, the ether of *lauric acid*. *Laurin* can be extracted by alcohol.

A frequent substitute for the expressed oil is said to be lard-coloured with chlorophyll or indigo and turmeric, scented with the berries. Boiling alcohol, which dissolves the true oil, will detect this.

The volatile oil contains pinene, geraniol, eugenol, cineol, etc.

¶ *Medicinal Action and Uses*. Leaves, berries and oil have excitant and narcotic properties. The leaves are also regarded as a diaphoretic and in large doses as an emetic.

Except as a stimulant in veterinary practice the leaves and fruit are very rarely used internally. They were formerly employed in hysteria, amenorrhœa, flatulent colic, etc. The berries have been used to promote abortion.

Oil of Bays is used externally for sprains, bruises, etc., and sometimes dropped into the ears to relieve pain. The leaves were formerly infused and taken as tea, and the powder or infusion of the berries was taken to remove obstructions, to create appetite, or as an emmenagogue. Four or five moderate doses were said to cure the ague. The berries were formerly used in several French carminative preparations.

The following products are often mistaken for those of *Laurus nobilis*.

The fruits of *Cocculus Indicus* or *Anamirta paniculata*. They are odourless and kidney-shaped.

The oil of *Pimenta Acris*, from which *bay rum* is distilled in the West Indies, and which is also called oil of bay.

The leaves of *Prunus Laurocerasus*, or Cherry Laurel, to which the name of Laurel is now always applied. The margin of these short, strong serrations at intervals. Caution should be observed in distinguishing these, owing to their poisonous properties.

LAUREL, CHERRY

Prunus Laurocerasus (LINN.)
N.O. Rosaceæ

Synonyms. Laurocerasifolia. Cherry-Bay. Common Laurel. Laurier-armande. Laurier aux Crèmes. Laurier-cérise

Part Used. Fresh leaves

Habitat. A native of Asia Minor. Largely cultivated in Europe

¶ *Description*. This small, evergreen tree, growing to 20 feet in height, has spreading, slender branches, smooth, shining, and pale green. The leaves are thick, alternate, on short, thick stalks, oblong-ovate, from 5 to 7 inches long, growing narrower at each end, and with a slightly serrate margin. The dark green upper surface is smooth and shining and the under one much paler, dull, and the midrib very prominent. There are glandular depressions and hairs near the base.

The five-petalled, small white flowers grow in erect, oblong racemes. The fruit resembles black cherries, but grows in clusters like grapes. The leaves are without odour except when bruised and added to water, when they have the ratafia or almond odour of prussic acid. The taste is bitter, aromatic, and astringent.

The shrubs were introduced into Europe about 1580, and shortly afterwards into England.

The leaves are used for flavouring, but should be used with great care, owing to the risk of poisoning.

Cherry-Laurel Water has been used in Paris fraudulently to imitate the cordial called Kirsch.

The most active essence is reserved for perfumery.

There is difference of opinion as to the best season for gathering the leaves. Drying destroys the active principle.

The bruised leaves, like those of peach or almond, when rubbed within any vessel will remove the odour left by oil of cloves, balsam of copaiba, etc., if the grease has first been cleaned away with alcohol.

¶ *Constituents.* The leaves yield a volatile oil in the proportion of 40·5 grains to 1 lb. of leaves. This resembles oil of bitter almonds, and in Europe is sometimes sold for it, as flavouring, but the glucoside decomposes more slowly than crystallized amygdalin, and is liable to hold hydrocyanic acid, when it becomes poisonous. This glucoside was called Laurocerasin, or Amorphous amygdalin, and now Prulaurasin.

With emulsin and water, prulaurasin is de-composed, and yields benzaldehyde, hydrocyanic acid, and dextrose.

Cherry Laurel Water (Aqua Laurocerasi), according to the British Pharmacopœia, is prepared as follows:

'One pound of fresh leaves of cherry-laurel, 2½ pints of water. Chop the leaves, crush them in a mortar, and macerate them in the water for 24 hours; then distil 1 pint of liquid; shake the product, filter through paper, and preserve it in a stoppered bottle.'

In America, oil of Bitter Almonds is often substituted, owing to the variability of the above.

¶ *Medicinal Action and Uses.* The water is a sedative narcotic, identical in its properties, to a diluted solution of hydrocyanic acid, but of uncertain strength.

¶ *Dosage.* Water, B.P., ½ to 2 drachms. Used for asthma, coughs, indigestion and dyspepsia, 1 drop of sulphuric acid added to a pint of Cherry Laurel Water will keep it unchanged for a year.

(POISON)
LAUREL, MOUNTAIN

Kalmia latifolia (LINN.)
N.O. Ericaceæ

Synonyms. Broad-leafed Laurel. Calico Bush. Spoon Wood. Ledum Floribus Bullates. Cistus Chamærhodendros

Part Used. Leaves

Habitat. New Brunswick, Florida, Ohio, Louisiana, New Hampshire, Massachusetts, Alleghany Mountains

¶ *Description.* A beautiful evergreen shrub from 4 to 20 feet. When in full flower it forms dense thickets, the stems are always crooked, the bark rough. It was called Kalmia by Linnæus in honour of Peter Kalm, a Swedish professor. The hard wood is used in the manufacture of various useful articles. Leaves ovate, lanceolate, acute on each end, on petioles 2 to 3 inches long. Flowers numerous, delicately tinted a lovely shade of pink; these are very showy, clammy, interminal, viscid, pubescent, simple or compound heads, branches opposite, flowering in June and July. The flowers yield a honey said to be deleterious. The leaves, shoots and berries are dangerous to cattle, and when eaten by Canadian pheasants communicate the poison to those who feed on the birds. The fruit is a dry capsule, seeds minute and numerous.

¶ *Constituents.* Leaves possess narcotic poisoning properties and contain tannic acid, gum, fatty matter, chlorophyll, a substance resembling mannite, wax extractive, albumen, an acrid principle, Aglucoside-arbutin, yellow calcium iron.

¶ *Medicinal Action and Uses.* Indians are said to use the expressed juice of the leaves or a strong decoction of them to commit suicide. The leaves are the official part; powdered leaves are used as a local remedy in some forms of skin diseases, and are a most efficient agent in syphilis, fevers, jaundice, neuralgia and inflammation, but great care should be exercised in their use. Whisky is the best antidote to poisoning from this plant. An ointment for skin diseases is made by stewing the leaves in pure lard in an earthenware vessel in a hot oven. Taken internally it is a sedative and astringent in active hæmorrhages, diarrhœa and flux. It has a splendid effect and will be found useful in overcoming obstinate chronic irritation of the mucous surface. In the lower animals an injection produces great salivation, lachrymation, emesis, convulsions and later paralysis of the extremities and la'joured respiration. It is supposed, but not proved, that the poisonous principle of this plant is Andromedotoxin.

¶ *Preparations and Dosages.* A saturated tincture of the leaves taken when plant is in flower, is the best form of administration, given in doses of 10 to 20 drops every two or three hours. Decoction, ½ to 1 fluid ounce of powdered leaves from 10 to 30 grains. Salve made from juice of the plant is an efficient local application for rheumatism.

¶ *Other Species.*

Kalmia augustifolia (Sheep's Laurel or Lambkill, or Narrow-leaved Laurel, so called because it poisons sheep, which feed on its leaves), this species is said to be the best for medicinal use. A decoction of its leaves, 1 oz. to 1 quart of water reduced to a pint, is used by the negroes as a wash for ulcerations between the toes. A poisonous glucoside is found in the leaves of this species called asebotoxin, and also in *K. latifolia.*

K. Glauca, or Swamp Laurel, has similar properties.

LAVENDERS   N.O. Labiatæ

Habitat. Lavender is a shrubby plant indigenous to the mountainous regions of the countries bordering the western half of the Mediterranean, and cultivated extensively for its aromatic flowers in various parts of France, in Italy and in England and even as far north as Norway. It is also now being grown as a perfume plant in Australia.

The fragrant oil to which the odour of Lavender flowers is due is a valuable article of commerce, much used in perfumery, and to a lesser extent in medicine. The fine aromatic smell is found in all parts of the shrub, but the essential oil is only produced from the flowers and flower-stalks. Besides being grown for the production of this oil, Lavender is widely sold in the fresh state as 'bunched Lavender,' and as 'dried Lavender,' the flowers are used powdered, for sachet making and also for pot-pourri, etc., so that the plant is a considerable source of profit.

Various species of Lavender are used in the preparation of the commercial essential oil, but the largest proportion is obtained from the flowers of *Lavandula vera*, the narrow-leaved form, which grows abundantly in sunny, stony localities in the Mediterranean countries, but nowhere to such perfection as in England.[1] English Lavender is much more aromatic and has a far greater delicacy of odour than the French, and the oil fetches ten times the price. The principal English Lavender plantations are at Carshalton and Wallington in Surrey, Hitchin in Herts, Long Melford in Suffolk, Market Deeping (Lincs) and in Kent, near Canterbury. Mitcham in Surrey used to be the centre of the Lavender-growing industry, but with the extension of London the famous Lavender plantations of Mitcham and surrounding districts have been largely displaced by buildings, and during the War the cultivation of Lavender was still further diminished to give place to food crops, so that in 1920 not more than ten acres under Lavender cultivation could be stated to be found in the whole of Surrey, though some of the oil is still distilled in the neighbourhood, and the finest products continue to be described as 'Mitcham Lavender Oil.'

¶ *Description.* ENGLISH LAVENDER (*Lavandula vera*), the common narrow-leaved variety, grows 1 to 3 feet high (in gardens, occasionally somewhat taller), with a short, but irregular, crooked, much-branched stem, covered with a yellowish-grey bark, which comes off in flakes, and very numerous, erect, straight, broom-like, slender, bluntly-quadrangular branches, finely pubescent, with stellate hairs. The leaves are opposite, sessile, entire, linear, blunt; when young, white with dense stellate hairs on both surfaces; their margins strongly revolute; when full grown, 1½ inch long, green with scattered hairs above, smoothly or finely downy beneath, and the margins only slightly revolute. The flowers are produced in terminating, blunt spikes from the young shoots, on long stems. The spikes are composed of whorls or rings of flowers, each composed of from six to ten flowers, the lower whorls more distant from one another. The flowers themselves are very shortly stalked, three to five together in the axils of rhomboidal, brown, thin, dry bracts. The calyx is tubular and ribbed, with thirteen veins, purple-grey in colour, five-toothed (one tooth being longer than the others) and hairy; shining oil glands amongst the hairs are visible with a lens. The majority of the oil yielded by the flowers is contained in the glands on the calyx. The two-lipped corolla is of a beautiful bluish-violet colour.

French Lavender oil is distilled from two distinct plants, found in the mountain districts of Southern France, both included under the name of *L. officinalis* by the sixteenth-century botanists, and *L. vera* by De Candolle. The French botanist Jordan has separated them under the name of *L. delphinensis*, the Lavender of Dauphine, and *L. fragrans*. The oils from the two plants are very similar, but the former yields oils with the higher percentage of esters.

[1] The Editor has often come across fields of French Lavender in bloom and the scent has been poor compared with English Lavender grown under the worst conditions. – EDITOR.

¶ *Description*. The SPIKE LAVENDER (*L. spica*, D.C., or *latifolia*, Vill.) is a coarser, broad-leaved variety of the Lavender shrub, also found in the mountain districts of France and Spain, though preferring alluvial ground which has been brought down by water from higher levels. In this country it cannot so easily be cultivated in the open as the common Lavender, to which it has a very close similarity, but from which it can be distinguished by the inflorescence, which is more compressed, by the bracts in the axils of which the flowers are placed being much narrower and by the leaves which are broader and spatula shaped. The flowers yield three times as much of the essential oil – known as Spike oil – as can be got from our narrow-leaved plant, but it is of a second-rate quality, less fragrant than that of the true Lavender, its odour resembling a mixture of the oils of Lavender and Rosemary.

Parkinson in his *Garden of Pleasure* says the *L. spica* 'is often called the Lesser Lavender or minor, and is called by some, Nardus Italica.' Some believe that this is the Spikenard mentioned in the Bible.

¶ *History*. Dr. Fernie, in *Herbal Simples*, says:

'By the Greeks the name Nardus is given to Lavender, from Naarda, a city of Syria near the Euphrates, and many persons call the plant "Nard." St. Mark mentions this as Spikenard, a thing of great value. . . . In Pliny's time, blossoms of the Nardus sold for a hundred Roman denarii (or £3 2s. 6d.) the pound. This Lavender or Nardus was called Asarum by the Romans, because it was not used in garlands or chaplets. It was formerly believed that the asp, a dangerous kind of viper, made Lavender its habitual place of abode, so that the plant had to be approached with great caution.'

L. SPICA and L. FRAGRANS often form hybrids, known as 'Bastard Lavender,' which grow in the mountain districts of France and Spain. Great care is necessary to avoid admixture in the still during distillation of Lavender, as Spike and the hybrids both injure the quality of the essential oil of true Lavender.

'White Lavender,' which is sometimes found in the Alps at extreme altitudes, is considered to be a form of *L. delphinensis*, the white flowers being a case of albinism. Attempts to propagate this form in this country rarely meet with much success.

¶ *Description*. Another species of LAVENDER, *L. Stœchas*, known also as French Lavender, forms a pretty little shrub, with narrow leaves and very small, dark violet flowers, terminated with a tuft of bright-coloured leaflets, which makes it very attractive. It is an inhabitant of the coast, but only occurs on sand or other crystalline rocks, and never on limestone. It is very abundant on the islands of Hyères, which the Ancient Romans called the 'Stœchades,' after this plant. This was probably the Lavender so extensively used in classical times by the Romans and the Libyans, as a perfume for the bath (whence probably the plant derived its name – from the Latin, *lavare*, to wash). It is plentiful in Spain and Portugal and is only used as a rule for strewing the floors of churches and houses on festive occasions, or to make bonfires on St. John's Day, when evil spirits are supposed to be abroad, a custom formerly observed in England with native plants. The odour is more akin to Rosemary than to ordinary Lavender. The flowers of this species were used medicinally in England until about the middle of the eighteenth century, the plant being called by our old authors, 'Sticadore.' It was one of the ingredients of the 'Four Thieves' Vinegar' famous in the Middle Ages. It is not used for distillation, though in France and Spain, the country people, in a simple manner extract an oil, used for dressing wounds, by hanging the flowers downwards in a closed bottle in the sunshine. The Arabs make use of the flowers as an expectorant and anti-spasmodic.

The Dwarf Lavender is more compact than the other forms and has flowers of a deeper colour. It makes a neat edging in the fruit or kitchen garden, where the larger forms might be in the way, and the flowers, borne abundantly, are useful for cutting.

All the forms of Lavender are much visited by bees and prove a good source of honey.

Lavender was familiar to Shakespeare, but was probably not a common plant in his time, for though it is mentioned by Spencer as 'The Lavender still gray' and by Gerard as growing in his garden, it is not mentioned by Bacon in his list of sweet-smelling plants. It is now found in every garden, but we first hear of it being cultivated in England about 1568. It must soon have become a favourite, however, for among the long familiar garden-plants which the Pilgrim Fathers took with them to their new home in America, we find the names of Lavender, Rosemary and Southernwood, though John Josselyn, in his *Herbal*, says that 'Lavender Cotton groweth pretty well,' but that 'Lavender is not for the Climate.'

Parkinson has much to say about Lavender:

'Of Sage and of Lavender, both the purple

and the rare white (there is a kinde hereof that beareth white flowers and somewhat broader leaves, but it is very rare and seene but in few places with us, because it is more tender and will not so well endure our cold Winters).'

'Lavender,' he says, 'is almost wholly spent with us, for to perfume linnen, apparell, gloves and leather and the dryed flowers to comfort and dry up the moisture of a cold braine.'

'This is usually put among other hot herbs, either into bathes, ointment or other things that are used for cold causes. The seed also is much used for worms.'

Lavender is of 'especiall good use for all griefes and paines of the head and brain,' it is now almost solely grown for the extraction of its essential oil, which is largely employed in perfumery.

Of French Lavender he says:

'The whole plant is somewhat sweete, but nothing so much as Lavender. It groweth in the Islands Staechades which are over against Marselles and in Arabia also: we keep it with great care in our Gardens. It flowreth the next yeare after it is sowne, in the end of May, which is a moneth before any Lavender.'

Lavender was one of the old street cries, and white lavender is said to have grown in the garden of Queen Henrietta Maria.

¶ *Cultivation*. Lavender is of fairly easy culture in almost any friable, garden soil. It grows best on light soil – sand or gravel – in a dry, open and sunny position. Loam over chalk also suits it. It requires good drainage and freedom from damp in winter.

The plant flourishes best on a warm, well-drained loam with a slope to the south or south-west. A loam that is too rich is detrimental to the oil yield, as excessive nourishment tends to the growth of leaf. Protection against summer gales by a copse on the south-west is also of considerable value, as these gales may do great damage to the crop by causing the tall flower-spikes to break away at their junction with the stem. Lavender also is liable to injury by frost and low-lying situations and those prone to become weather-bound in winter are to be avoided.

The founding of a Lavender plantation for the purpose of oil production is an enterprise which requires very careful consideration. The land should first be carefully cleaned of weeds in the autumn; these should be burnt, and the ashes distributed over the ground, together with some ordinary wood ashes if obtainable. The soil should then be prepared by 'trenching in' a quantity of short straw and stable refuse, but not much rich dung, and should lie fallow until the following spring, when any weeds remaining should be dealt with as before and the whole ploughed over. Towards late spring, the young plants should be dibbed in in rows running from north to south. Some growers plant out in rows 2 feet apart, leaving a foot between each plant. Another mode of planting favoured is to plant out 18 inches apart each way and when these plants have occupied the ground for one year, each intervening plant and those of every other row are taken out, leaving the land planted 36 inches by 36 inches, the wide spaces being judged to allow the plant full growth for flower-bearing, room for cutting flowers and for keeping the ground quite clear of weeds. The plants removed are utilized for planting up fresh ground, each being divided into about three.

The crop may be grown from seed, sown in April, but is mainly propagated by cuttings and layerings. It may also be propagated by division of roots. Cuttings of the young wood, or small branches, with a root or heel, pulled off the large plants, may be inserted in free, sandy soil, under hand-lights in August and September, and planted out during the following spring. The 'cuttings' are taken by pulling the small branches down with a quick movement, when they become detached with the desired 'heel' at their base. Cuttings root freely in April, also, in the open, protection being given in cold weather. They should be of young growths. A certain amount of watering will be required in dry weather until the cuttings are thoroughly established.

Young plants should as far as possible be kept from flowering during the first year by clipping, so that the strength of the plant is thrown into the lateral shoots to make it bushy and compact. A full picking is usually obtained from the second to the fifth year. After the third year, the bushes are apt to become straggly. They can be pruned in March and care should be taken to always have young plants ready to follow on, to take the place of exhausted, over-straggly bushes. In commercial practice, the bushes are seldom retained after their fifth year. It follows, therefore, that in order to keep up a continuous supply of bushes in their prime, planting and grubbing must, on an established plantation, be done every year. Most growers plant say a fifth portion of the ultimate area of Lavender aimed at in the first instance and this is repeated each year until the fifth year, when the area first planted is grubbed immediately after flowering, the old plants burnt, the ashes put upon the ground, and the land ploughed and manured and left fallow until the following spring, when re-stocking can commence.

At Mitcham, Lavender was grown for even six years in succession by judiciously removing worn plants and inserting young ones. Severe frost will often kill rows of plants and their place must be renewed.

During the last few years, plants have been subject to Lavender disease, caused by the fungus, *Phoma lavandulæ*; this causes a heavy loss, as the disease spreads rapidly. It can be eradicated, however, by eliminating and burning the infested plants. English Lavender is more robust in habit than the French plant.

A parasitic plant, *Cuscuta epithymum*, one of the Dodders, will attack and destroy the fine Lavenders, *delphinensis* and *fragrans*, but does not affect the less valuable 'Bastard' Lavender, which eventually survives by itself.

Insect pests are principally small caterpillars and similar animals, which feed upon the leaves of the plant.

¶ *Harvesting*. The bulk of the flowers are used for the distillation of the volatile oil, which is commonly distilled from the flower-stalks and flowers together, the spikes being cut with a small hook about 6 to 9 inches below the flowers, at the end of July or August, according to season. It will be necessary to provide a small distilling plant on the grower's premises, unless arrangements can be made for the distillation of the crop at a local distillery.

Cutting for distilling takes place generally about a week later than for market; the blooms must all be fully developed, because the oil at this time contains the maximum amount of esters.

Harvesting should be carried out rapidly – the cutting managed in a week if possible – so long as the weather is dry and there is no wind, the morning and evening of a fine day being particularly favourable to the flower gathering, on account of the fact that a certain amount of the ester portion of the oil is dissipated by a hot sun, as is easily seen by the fact that the Lavender plantations, and all fields of aromatic plants, are most highly perfumed about mid-day. Further, if there is any wind, the mid-day is the time when it will be hottest and most saturated with moisture, thus easily taking up the more volatile and more soluble particles of the essential oil. Very cold weather prevents the development of esters and rain is fatal for harvesting. If rain or fog appears, cutting should cease and not be resumed till the sun shines again. The cut Lavender should be laid on clean dry mats and covered from sun scorch immediately. There must be no moisture in the stook, neither must it be dried up by wind or sun. The mats will be rolled up in the cool of the evening before the dew is falling and carted to the still. For some purposes, the stalks are shortened to about 6 inches before stilling, but, generally, the whole of the contents of the mat are placed carefully in the still right away.

If more flowers are cut than can be dealt with quickly in the still, the flowers should be stored in a closed shed so as to prevent them drying and losing a portion of the essential oil. Every effort should be taken to prevent the slightest fermentation of the flowers before distillation. Fermentation means a smaller yield and a poorer quality of oil.

In making the most refined Lavender oil, the blossoms are carefully stripped off the stalk previous to distillation and distilled alone, but this is necessarily a more expensive way of proceeding. The oil in the stalks has a much coarser odour. The British Pharmacopœia directs that Lavender oil for medicinal use should be thus distilled from the flowers after they have been separated from their stalks, and the oil distilled in Britain is alone official, as it is very superior to foreign oil of Lavender.

¶ *Distillation*. The stills usually employed by growers are of simple construction, any fault in the distillate being subsequently rectified by fractional distillation. The stills are constructed of copper, and generally built to take a charge of about 5 cwt. of flowers at a time. It is important to avoid burning, and the practice is to provide the stills with two chambers, with a perforated false bottom between, the lower chamber being filled with water which should be as soft as possible. Distillation is conducted by boiling the water beneath the charge with steam brought from a boiler to a coil, the top of which must be at least 1 foot beneath the bottom of the charge chamber. The oil-flow from the condenser must be watched for, and complete distillation of the charge usually takes about six hours from commencement of the flow.

The yield of the oil is apt to vary considerably from season to season, as the age of the bushes and the weather will affect both the quantity and quality of the product. The amount of sunlight in the weeks before distillation has a great influence: the best oil is obtained after a hot, droughty season, heavy rains detract from the yield.

An acre of Lavender in its prime would in a favourable year yield from 15 to 20 lb. of oil, but taking the whole of the area planted as described above, an average yield of 12 lb. to the area would be a fair estimate.

The distillate should be left for several months to become quite clear and transparent before it is offered for sale.

At Hitchin, it has been calculated that 60 lb. of good flowers will yield on the average 16 fluid ounces of oil.

Growers not doing their own distilling, but preparing the flowers dry for market, should spread the stalks out in the open, on trays or sieves, in a cool, shady position, out of the sun, so that they may dry slowly. The trays should be raised a few feet from the ground, to ensure a warm current of air, and the stems must not be allowed to touch, or the flowers will be spoilt by the moist heat engendered. They must be taken indoors before there is any risk of them getting damp either by dew or showers. When dry, they should be stored in a dry place and made up into bundles. The flowers may also be stripped from the stalks and dried by a moderate heat. They have a greyish-blue colour when dried.

¶ Constituents. The principal constituent of Lavender is the volatile oil, of which the dried flowers contain from 1·5 to 3 per cent. fresh flowers yielding about 0·5 per cent. It is pale yellow, yellowish-green or nearly colourless, with the fragrant odour of the flowers and a pungent, bitter taste. The chief constituents of the oil are linalool and its acetic ester, linalyl acetate, which is also the characteristic ingredient of oil of bergamot and is present in English oil of Lavender to the extent of 7 to 10 per cent. Other constituents of the oil are cineol (in English oil, only a trace in French oils), pinene, limonene, geraniol, borneol and some tannin. Lavender oil is soluble in all proportions of alcohol.

It is principally to the esters that Lavender oil owes its delicate perfume. In the oil there are two esters which practically control the odour, of these the principal is linalyl acetate, the second is linalyl butyrate, and Lavender oil nowadays is very largely valued by chemical analysis, involving a determination of the esters. Many things influence the ester value of Lavender oil. In the first place, the preponderance of one or other of the varieties of Lavender used for distillation makes an appreciable difference; in cultivated material, the use of artificial manures not only increases the ester value of the oil, but also increases the yield. The gathering of the flowers when fully expanded and their rapid transport to the stills has considerable influence and the rapid distillation by steam shows a very marked advantage over water distillation. The proportion of esters in Lavender also depends on the period of de-velopment of the flower. In June, the esters are found disseminated throughout all the green parts of the plant. From this time onwards, as the plants develop, the esters commence to concentrate in the flowering spikes: the accumulation of oil in these spikes can be distinctly seen by the naked eye in brilliant sunshine, the tiny oil globules shining like little diamonds. The delicacy is completed by the concentration of the esters during the following month; in an ordinary year, the maximum odour is developed by the end of July. About the middle of August, the perfume commences to deteriorate. Oil distilled from the earliest flowers is pale and contains a higher proportion of the more valuable esters; oil distilled from the later flowers has a preponderance of the less valuable esters and is darker in colour. It is evident from these facts that the correct time of gathering is directly flowering is at the full, and English Lavender is always entirely harvested in under a week, and the flowers are distilled on the spot.

¶ Medicinal Action and Uses. Lavender was used in earlier days as a condiment and for flavouring dishes 'to comfort the stomach.' Gerard speaks of Conserves of Lavender being served at table.

It has aromatic, carminative and nervine properties. Though largely used in perfumery, it is now not much employed internally, except as a flavouring agent, occurring occasionally in pharmacy to cover disagreeable odours in ointments and other compounds.

Red Lavender lozenges are employed both as a mild stimulant and for their pleasant taste.

The essential oil, or a spirit of Lavender made from it, proves admirably restorative and tonic against faintness, palpitations of a nervous sort, weak giddiness, spasms and colic. It is agreeable to the taste and smell, provokes appetite, raises the spirits and dispels flatulence. The dose is from 1 to 4 drops on sugar or in a spoonful or two of milk.

A few drops of the essence of Lavender in a hot footbath has a marked influence in relieving fatigue. Outwardly applied, it relieves toothache, neuralgia, sprains, and rheumatism. In hysteria, palsy and similar disorders of debility and lack of nerve power, Lavender will act as a powerful stimulant.

'It profiteth them much,' says Gerard, 'that have the palsy if they be washed with the distilled water from the Lavender flowers, or are annointed with the oil made from the flowers and olive oil in such manner as oil of roses is used.'

Culpepper says that

'a decoction made with the flowers of Lavender, Horehound, Fennel and Asparagus root, and a little Cinnamon, is very profitably used to help the falling-sickness (epilepsy) and the giddiness or turning of the brain.'

Salmon in his *Herbal* (1710) says that

'it is good also against the bitings of serpents, mad-dogs and other venomous creature, being given inwardly and applied poultice-wise to the parts wounded. The spirituous tincture of the dried leaves or seeds, if prudently given, cures hysterick fits though vehement and of long standing.'

In some cases of mental depression and delusions, oil of Lavender proves of real service, and a few drops rubbed on the temple will cure nervous headache.

Compound Tincture of Lavender, sold under the name of Lavender drops, besides being a useful colouring and flavouring for mixtures, is still largely used for faintness. This tincture of red Lavender is a popular medicinal cordial, and is composed of the oils of Lavender and Rosmary, with cinnamon bark, nutmeg and red sandle wood, macerated in spirit of wine for seven days. A teaspoonful may be taken as a dose in a little water after an indigestible meal, repeating after half an hour if needed.

It has been officially recognized in the successive British Pharmacopœia for over 200 years. In the eighteenth century, this preparation was known as 'palsy drops' and as 'red hartshorn.' The formula which first appeared in the London Pharmacopœia at the end of the seventeenth century was a complicated one. It contained nearly thirty ingredients, and was prepared by distilling the fresh flowers of lavender, sage, rosemary, betony, cowslips, lily of the valley, etc., with French brandy; in the distillate such spices as cinnamon, nutmeg, mace, cardamoms were digested for twenty-four hours, and then musk, ambergris, saffron, red roses and red sanders-wood were tied in a bag and suspended in the spirit to perfume and colour it. The popularity of this remedy for two hundred and fifty years may be understood by referring to the statements made concerning its virtues when it was first made official. It was said to be useful

'against the Falling-sickness, and all cold Distempers of the Head, Womb, Stomach and Nerves; against the Apoplexy, Palsy, Convulsions, Megrim, Vertigo, Loss of Memory, Dimness of Sight, Melancholy, Swooning Fits and Barrenness in Women. It was given in canary, or the Syrup of the Juice of Black-cherries, or in Florence wine. Country people may take it in milk or fair water sweetened with sugar. . . . It is an excellent but costly medicine.'

In the London Pharmacopœia of 1746 a very drastic change was made in the recipe and practically no change has been made since that time.

A tea brewed from Lavender tops, made in moderate strength, is excellent to relieve headache from fatigue and exhaustion, giving the same relief as the application of Lavender water to the temples. An infusion taken too freely, will, however, cause griping and colic, and Lavender oil in too large doses is a narcotic poison and causes death by convulsions.

'The chymical oil drawn from Lavender,' to quote Culpepper, 'usually called Oil of Spike, is of so fierce and piercing a quality, that it is cautiously to be used, some few drops being sufficient to be given with other things, either for inward or outward griefs.'

Lavender oil is found of service when rubbed externally for stimulating paralysed limbs. Mixed with ¼ spirit of turpentine or spirit of wine it made the famous Oleum Spicæ, formerly much celebrated for curing old sprains and stiff joints. Fomentations with Lavender in bags, applied hot, will speedily relieve local pains.

A distilled water made from Lavender has been used as a gargle and for hoarseness and loss of voice.

Its use in the swabbing of wounds obtained further proof during the War, and the French Academy of Medicine is giving attention to the oil for this and other antiseptic surgical purposes. The oil is successfully used in the treatment of sores, varicose ulcers, burns and scalds. In France, it is a regular thing for most households to keep a bottle of Essence of Lavender as a domestic remedy against bruises, bites and trivial aches and pains, both external and internal.

Lavender oil is also used in veterinary practice, being very efficacious in killing lice and other parasites on animals. Its germicidal properties are very pronounced. In the south-east of France it is considered a useful vermifuge.

The oil is used in the embalming of corpses to a steadily increasing extent.

¶ *Preparations and Dosages*. Fluid extract, ½ to 1 drachm. Compound Tincture, B.P., and U.S.P., ½ to 1 drachm. Oil, 1 to 3 drops. Spirit, B.P. and U.S.P., 5 to 30 drops.

Adulteration of Lavender Oil. French oils containing less than 30 per cent. of esters are very often mixed with Spike or Bastard Lavender oils. Formerly adulteration used to be with oil of Turpentine, often mixed with coco-nut oil, but this has given place to various artificial esters prepared chemically, which are practically odourless and only added to make the oil appear to have a higher ester percentage than it really has. Recently, crude mixtures of Lavender oil with Petit-grain oil have been noticed on the market.

Spanish Lavender Oil, distilled in Spain and sold largely to England as Lavender oil, is not a genuine Lavender oil at all, but an oil practically free from esters, having the general character of Spike Lavender oil. The production of this oil now reaches about 40,000 kilos per annum.

Spike Lavender Oil is of a penetrating, camphoraceous odour and is never worth more than about one-fifth of the value of genuine Lavender oil. The oil is used in veterinary practice in considerable quantities, as a prophylactic in cases of incipient paralysis. It is also employed (together with that from *L. Stœchas*) in the manufacture of certain types of fine varnishes and lacquers, with oil of turpentine, and used by painters on porcelain. It is used to a very great extent in cheap perfumery and for scenting soaps, especially in England and the United States. The annual production of Spike Lavender oil in France is about 25,000 kilos.

This oil of Latifolia or Spica is said to admirably promote the growth of the hair when weakly or falling off. A decoction – Spike Water – can be made from the plant.

Dried Lavender flowers are still greatly used to perfume linen, their powerful, aromatic odour acting also as a preventative to the attacks of moths and other insects. In America, they find very considerable employment for disinfecting hotrooms and keeping away flies and mosquitoes, who do not like the scent. Oil of Lavender, on cotton-wool, tied in a little bag or in a perforated ball hung in the room, is said to keep it free from all flies.

Not only are insects averse to the smell of Lavender, so that oil of Lavender rubbed on the skin will prevent midge and mosquito bites, but it is said on good authority that the lions and tigers in our Zoological Gardens are powerfully affected by the scent of Lavender Water, and will become docile under its influence.

The flowers and leaves were formerly em-ployed as a sternutatory and probably still enter into the composition of some snuffs.

In the East, especially in Turkey and Egypt, they are used, as of old, for perfuming the bath.

The 'straw,' completely freed from the flowers, is sold and used as litter and also for making ointment. If burnt, for deodorizing purposes, the stalks diffuse a powerful, but agreeable odour.

Lavender Water can easily be prepared at home. Into a quart bottle are put 1 oz. essential oil of Lavender, one drop of Musk and 1¼ pint spirits of wine. These three ingredients are well mixed together by shaking. The mixture is left to settle, shaken again in a few days, then poured into little perfume bottles fitted with air-tight stoppers. This is another recipe from an old family book:

'Put into a bottle half a pint of spirit of wine and two drachms of oil of lavender. Mix it with rose-water, five ounces, orange-flower water, two ounces, also two drachms of musk and six ounces of distilled water.'

This is stated to be 'a pleasant and efficacious cordial and very useful in languor and weakness of the nerves, lowness of spirits, faintings, etc.'

Another recipe is to mix 2 oz. of refined essence of Lavender with ¼ pint of good brandy. This Lavender Water is so strong that it must be diluted with water before it is used.

Lavender Vinegar. A refreshing toilet preparation is made by mixing 6 parts of Rose-water, 1 part of spirits of Lavender and 2 parts of Orleans vinegar.

It can also be prepared from freshly-gathered flower-tops. These are dried, placed in a stoppered bottle and steeped for a week in Orleans vinegar. Every day the bottle must be shaken, and at the end of the week the liquid is drained off and filtered through white blotting paper.

Another delicious and aromatic toilet vinegar is made as follows: Dry a good quantity of rose leaves, lavender flowers and jasmine flowers. Weigh them, and to every 4 oz. of rose leaves allow 1 oz. each of lavender and jasmine. Mix them well together, pour over them 2 pints of white vinegar, and shake well, then add ½ pint of rose-water and shake again. Stand aside for ten days, then strain and bottle.

LAVENDER COTTON

Santolina Chamæcyparissus (LINN.)
N.O. Compositæ

Synonym. Santolina
Part Used. Herb

Lavender Cotton (also sometimes called French Lavender, like *L. Stœchas*) is botanically known as *Santolina Chamæcy-parissus*. It is not a true Lavender at all, but has yellow, clustered buttons of composite flowers and finely-cut, grey, rather disagree-

473

ably-scented leaves, whose odour somewhat resembles Chamomile. It is used as a vermifuge for children. This plant was once also esteemed for its stimulant properties, and the twigs have been used for placing amongst linen, etc., to keep away moths. All the species of *Santolina* have a strong resemblance to one another, except *S. fragrantissima*, which differs in having the flowerheads in flat inflorescences termed corymbs, the flowers all being at the same level, instead of singly at the apex of the twigs.

The Arabs are said to use the juice of this plant for bathing the eyes. Culpepper tells us that Lavender Cotton 'resists poison, putrefaction and heals the biting of venomous beasts.' It is now chiefly used as an edging to borders, spreading like a silvery carpet close to the ground.

A perfume oil is also extracted from it.

LAVENDER, SEA, AMERICAN

Statice Caroliniana (WALT.)
N.O. Plumbaginaceæ

Synonyms. Statice Limonium. Ink Root. Sea Lavender. Marsh Rosemary
Part Used. Root
Habitat. America, Europe and England. A perennial maritime plant with a large, fleshy, fusiform, brownish-red root; limnal leaves in tufts – obovate, entire, obtuse, mucronate, smooth, and on long foot-stalks. Flowers, pale bluish-purple. Fruit an oblong utricle, one-seeded, enclosed in calyx, usually called Marsh Rosemary. It is common in the salt marshes of the Atlantic shore. Flowers August to October

¶ *Part Used* is the root. This is large, heavy, blackish, inodorous, with a bitter, saltish and very astringent taste.

¶ *Constituents.* Volatile oil, resin, gum, albumen, tannic acid, caoutchouc, extractive and colouring matter, woody fibre, and various salts. It has long been in use as a domestic remedy for diarrhœa, dysentery, etc., but is only used as an astringent tonic after the acute stage has passed. It is also very useful as a gargle or wash in ulcerations of mouth and throat, scarlatina, anguinosa, etc. The powdered root is applied to old ulcers, or made with a soothing ointment for piles. As an injection the decoction is very useful in chronic gonorrhœa, gleet, leucorrhœa, prolapsus of womb and anus, and in some ophthalmic affections. It can otherwise be used where astringents are indicated and may be applicable to all cases where kino and catechu are given. It is said to be a valuable remedy for internal and local use in cynanche maligna. Decoction is 1 ounce of powdered root to 1 pint, in wineglassful doses.

LEMON

Citrus Limonum (RISSO.)
N.O. Rutaceæ

Synonyms. Citrus medica. Citrus Limonum. Citronnier. Neemoo. Leemoo. Limoun. Limone
Parts Used. Rind, juice, oil
Habitat. Indigenous to Northern India. Widely cultivated in Mediterranean countries

¶ *Description.* The name *Limonum* is derived from the Arabic *Limun* or *Limu*, which in its turn probably comes from the Sanscrit *Nimbuka*. There are several varieties of *Citrus medica*, only differing in the character of their fruits. The principal ones are the lemon, citron or cedrat, and lime. The Bergamot is also closely related. The trees reached Europe by way of Persia or Media and were grown first in Greece and then in Italy in the second century.

The Lemon is a small, straggling tree about 11 feet high, irregularly branched, the bark varying in colour from clear grey on the trunk, green on the younger branches to a purplish colour on the twigs. The evergreen leaves are ovate-oval, about two inches long, the margin serrate with sharp spines in the axils of the stalks. The solitary, five-petalled flowers, white inside and tinged with deep pink outside, grow on stems in the axils. The well-known fruit is an ovoid berry, about three inches long, nipple-shaped at the end, smooth, bright yellow, indented over the oil-glands, having an acid, pale-yellow pulp. About forty-seven varieties are said to have been developed during the centuries of cultivation.

The finest fruits arrive wrapped separately in paper, cases of the Messina lemons containing 360, and of Murcia lemons 200. Those from Naples and Malaga are thought to be less fine. Inferior fruits, preserved in salt water, are packed in barrels. It is stated that they can be kept fresh for months if dipped in melted paraffin or varnished with shellac dissolved in alcohol.

The peel, *Limonis Cortex*, is white and spongy inside, varying much in thickness, and the yellow outer layer, formerly called the *flavedo*, has a fragrant odour and aromatic, bitter taste. Only the fresh rind is official.

SPIKE LAVENDER
Lavandula Spica

LEMON
Citrus Limonum

WILD LETTUCE
Lactuca Virosa

LIQUORICE
Glycyrrhiza Glabra

Candied lemon peel may be prepared by boiling the peel in syrup and then exposing it to the air until the sugar is crystallized.

The juice, *L. succus*, is largely imported as a source of citric acid, but is mixed with that of lime and bergamot. It does not keep well, and several methods are tried for preserving it, such as covering it with a layer of almond oil, mixing with alcohol and filtering, or adding sulphur dioxide, but none appear to be very satisfactory. The juice should be pressed fresh for pharmaceutical purposes, the amount of citric acid being greatest in December and January and least in August.

In Sicily, the pulp left after the production of the volatile oil is pressed for juice in large quantities and the solid matter left is used as cattle food.

The oil, *Oleum Limonis*, is more fragrant and valuable if obtained by expression than by distillation. It is usually prepared in Sicily and Calabria, and sometimes at Nice and Mentone, where the 'Essence de Citron distillée' is prepared by rubbing fresh lemons on a coarse, tin grater, and distilling the grated peel with water. The better 'Essence de Citron au zeste' is prepared with the aid of a saucer-shaped, pewter dish with a pouring lip at one side and a closed funnel sunk from the middle. In the bottom are sharp, strong brass pins on which the peel is rubbed. This vessel is called an *écuelle à piquer*, but a machine called *scorzetta* is gradually coming into use.

The method of expression in Sicily is that of squeezing large slices of peel against sponges fixed in the hand, the sponges when soaked being wrung into an earthen bowl with a spout, in which the oil separates from the watery liquid. The peel is afterwards pickled in brine and sold to manufacturers for candying.

The roots and wood are cut in winter. The latter takes a beautiful polish and is nicely veined.

The dried flowers and leaves are used in pharmacy in France.

The Lemon is widely used in cookery and confectionery. A thousand lemons yield between 1 and 2 lb. of oil. The immature fruit yields less and the quality is inferior.

Messina alone exported 155,000 kilos of oil in 1919.

¶ *Constituents. Lemon Peel* yields its virtues to alcohol, water, or wine. It contains an essential oil and a bitter principle. Crystals of the glucoside Hesperidin are deposited by the evaporation of the white, pulpy portion boiled in water. Diluted acids decompose it into Hesperitin and glucose.

Lemon Juice contains from 6·7 to 8·6 per cent. of citric acid. It is officially described as 'a slightly turbid yellowish liquor, possessing a sharp, acid taste and grateful odour.'

It contains also sugar, gum, and a very little potash. An imitation lemon juice has been made by dissolving tartaric acid in water, adding sulphuric acid and flavouring with oil of Lemon. It is useless therapeutically.

Oil of Lemon is dextrogyre. It contains 7 to 8 per cent. of *citral*, an aldehyde yielding geraniol upon reduction, a small amount of pinene and citronellal, etc. It is stated that citral, citronellal, and an ester of geraniol are all necessary for the true odour.

The oil is not very active, and is used chiefly for flavouring.

¶ *Medicinal Action and Uses.* Lemon juice is probably the best of all antiscorbutics, being almost a specific in scurvy. English ships are required by law to carry sufficient lemon or limejuice for every seaman to have an ounce daily after being ten days at sea. Its value in this direction has been stated to be due to its vitamines.

It is valuable as a cooling drink in fevers, and for allaying thirst. When unobtainable, a solution of 8 drachms of crystallized citric acid in 16 oz. of water, flavoured with oil of lemon, may be substituted.

The juice may be used in diaphoretic and diuretic draughts. It is highly recommended in acute rheumatism, and is sometimes given to counteract narcotic poisons, especially opium.

Locally, it is a good astringent, whether as a gargle in sore throat, in pruritis of the scrotum, in uterine hæmorrhage after delivery, or as a lotion in sunburn. It is said to be the best cure for severe, obstinate hiccough, and is helpful in jaundice and hysterical palpitation of the heart. The decoction has been found to be a good antiperiodic, useful as a substitute for quinine in malarial conditions, or for reducing the temperature in typhoid.

It is probable that the lemon is the most valuable of all fruit for preserving health.

The *oil*, externally, is a strong rubefacient, and taken internally in small doses has stimulating and carminative properties.

Preparations of the rind are used as an aromatic addition to tonics, and also the syrup of the fresh peel, and the juice.

¶ *Preparations and Dosages.* Fresh juice (for rheumatism), 4 to 6 fluid ounces. Oil, B.P., 3 to 5 minims. Juice, B.P., ½ to 4 drachms. Tincture, B.P. and U.S.P., ½ to 1 drachm. Syrup, B.P., ½ to 4 drachms.

¶ *Substitutes and Adulterations.* The most dangerous adulterant of the oil is *citrene*, the terpene left after extracting citral from oil of lemon which has been used in making terpeneless oil.

Fixed oils, alcohol, and purified oil of turpentine are sometimes found, the last causing a terebinthinate odour if evaporated from heated paper.

The pure oil should show scarcely any *pinene*.

Artificial lemon juice should not be used as an antiscorbutic.

¶·*Other Species.*

Lime juice, the product of *C. medica acida*, is recognized by the National Formulary under the name of *Succus Citri*.

Cedrat Lemon, or *C. medica cedra*, yields the essential oils of citron and cedra used in perfumery.

Lippia citriodora, yielding verbena oil, is commonly known as Lemon Verbena.

Java Lemon is *C. Javanica*. Median Lemon is a variety of *C. medica*. Pear Lemon is a variety of *C. Limetta*. Pearl Lemon is *C. margarita*. Sweet Lemon is *C. Lumia*. Water Lemon is *Passiflora laurifolia*. Wild Lemon or Ground Lemon is *Podophyllum peltatum*. Lemon Yellow is the name of Chrome Yellow, a neutral lead-chromate.

LETTUCE, WILD

Lactuca virosa (LINN.)
N.O. Compositæ

Synonyms. Lactucarium. Strong-scented Lettuce. Green Endive. Lettuce Opium. Laitue vireuse. Acrid Lettuce

Parts Used. The dried milk-juice (Lactuarium), the leaves

Habitat. Western and Southern Europe, including Britain

¶ *Description.* The name *lactuca* is derived from the classical Latin name for the milky juice, *virosa*, or 'poisonous.'

It is a biennial herb growing to a maximum height of 6 feet. The erect stem, springing from a brown tap-root, is smooth and pale green, sometimes spotted with purple. There are a few prickles on the lower part and short horizontal branches above. The numerous, large, radical leaves are from 6 to 18 inches long, entire, and obovate-oblong. The stem leaves are scanty, alternate, and small, clasping the stem with two small lobes. The heads are numerous and shortly-stalked, the pale-yellow corolla being strap-shaped. The rough, black fruit is oval, with a broad wing along the edge, and prolonged above into a long, white beak carrying silvery tufts of hair. The whole plant is rich in a milky juice that flows freely from any wound. This has a bitter taste and a narcotic odour. When dry, it hardens, turns brown, and is known as lactucarium.

¶ *Habitat.* The Wild Lettuce grows on banks and waste places, flowering in July and August. It is cultivated in Austria, France, Germany and Scotland. Collectors cut the heads of the plants and scrape the juice into china vessels several times daily until it is exhausted. By slightly warming and tapping, it is turned out of its cup mould, is cut into quarters and dried.

In the United States, after importation from Germany via England it is said to be used as an adulterant for opium. It is usually found in irregular, reddish-brown lumps the size of a large pea, frequently mouldy on the outside. In the United States the German and French *lactucarium* is considered inferior to the British product.

All lettuces possess some of this narcotic juice, *Lactuca virosa* having the most, and the others in the following order: *L. scariola*, or Prickly Lettuce, *L. altissima*, *L. Canadensis*, or Wild Lettuce of America, and *L. sativa*, or Garden Lettuce. Cultivation has lessened the narcotic properties of the last, but it is still used for making a lotion for the skin useful in sunburn and roughness. The Ancients held the lettuce in high esteem for its cooling and refreshing properties. The Emperor Augustus attributed his recovery from a dangerous illness to it; built an altar to it, and erected a statue in its honour.

Lactucarium is not easily powdered, and is only slightly soluble in boiling water, though it softens and becomes plastic.

Thridace, or the inspissated juice of *L. capitata*, is now regarded as inert.

A mild oil, used in cooking, is said to be obtained from the seeds in Egypt.

¶ *Constituents.* *L. virosa* has been found to contain lactucic acid, lactucopicrin, 50 to 60 per cent. lactucerin (lactucone) and lactucin. Lactucarium treated with boiling water and filtered is clear, but on cooling the filtrate becomes turbid. It is not coloured blue by iodine test solution. The usual constituents of latex are albumen, mannite, and caoutchouc.

The fresh juice reddens litmus paper.

¶ *Medicinal Action and Uses.* The drug resembles a feeble opium without its tendency to upset the digestive system. It is used to a small extent as a sedative and narcotic.

Dissolved in wine it is said to be a good anodyne.

Dr. Collins stated that twenty-three out of twenty-four cases of dropsy were cured by taking doses of 18 grains to 3 drachms of extract in twenty-four hours. It is used in Germany in this complaint, but combined with more active drugs. It is said to be also a mild diaphoretic and diuretic, easing colic, inducing sleep and allaying cough.

Water distilled from lettuce (*eau de laitre*) is used in France as a mild sedative in doses of 2 to 4 oz., and the fresh leaves boiled in water are sometimes used as a cataplasm.

Moderate doses given to the lower animals act as a narcotic poison, an injection having even caused death.

¶ *Dosages*. Of powder, 10 to 20 grains or more. Of tincture, 30 to 60 drops. Of alcoholic extract, 1 to 5 grains. Of Lactucarium, 5 to 20 grains. Of fluid extract leaves, ¼ to 1 drachm. Of syrup, U.S.P., 2 drachms. Tincture, U.S.P., 30 drops.

LIFE EVERLASTING (PEARL-FLOWERED)

Antennaria Margaritaceum
N.O. Compositæ

Synonyms. American Everlasting. Cudweed
Parts Used. Leaves, flowers, stalks
Habitat. North America, Kamschatka and in English gardens. Grows wild in Essex, near Bocking, and in Wales. Cultivated in Whin's Cottage garden by the writer

¶ *Medicinal Action and Uses*. Anodyne, astringent, pectoral, useful in diarrhœa, dysentery, pulmonary affections, as a poultice for sprains, bruises, boils, painful swellings. Said to produce sleep. When hops have failed, applied externally to the head, a decoction of the flowers and stalks used in America as a fomentation for pained and bruised limbs, and for bronchitis.

Leaves linear, lanceolate, acuminate; alternate stalk branched at top; corymbs fastigiate; root perennial, creeping, spreading, becoming almost a troublesome weed; stalks very downy, and white flowering branches form a flat broad bunch, each branch with numerous crowded heads, on short branched downy peduncles, the middle ones sessile; calyx scales bluntly ovate and white, but not downy, flowers July to September. Easily propagated by creeping roots. The plant is slightly fragrant.

See CATSFOOT, CUDWEED, GNAPHALIUM, WHITE BALSAM.

LIFE ROOT. *See* GROUNDSEL

LILACS (WHITE AND MAUVE)

Syringa vulgaris
N.O. Oleaceæ

Synonym. Common Lilac
Parts Used. Leaves, fruit
Habitat. Persia, mountainous regions of Eastern Europe

¶ *Description*. A shrub or small tree up to 20 feet in height producing a crowd of erect stems, occasionally a trunk over 2 feet in girth, clothed with spirally arranged flakes of bark. Shoots and leaves smooth, leaves heart-shape or ovate, 2 to 6 inches long, from ¾ to almost as much wide near the base; stalk ¾ to 1½ inch long. Panicles pyramidal, 6 to 8 inches long, usually in pairs from the terminal buds; flowers fragrant; corolla tube ⅓ to ½ inch long; lobes concave; calyx and flower-stalks have gland tipped down; seed vessels smooth, ⅜ inch long, beaked.

Introduced to Britain during time of Henry VIII, mentioned in an inventory taken at Norwich by Oliver Cromwell.

Syringa Baccifera is a synonym of *Mitchella repens* or Partridge Berry and *must not be confused* with *S. vulgaris*.

¶ *Medicinal Action and Uses*. Used as a vermifuge in America and as a tonic anti-periodic and febrifuge; may be used as a substitute for aloes and in the treatment of malaria.

LILIES

N.O. Liliaceæ

The Lilies belong to a genus consisting of less than 100 known species, occurring in all parts of the Northern Hemisphere. They are mostly found growing in fairly good soil in association with shrubs and other plants which shade their roots and help to keep the bulbs cool and in a uniform state as regards moisture.

¶ *Cultivation*. With some exceptions, Lilies grown as garden plants in this country are fairly hardy, especially if planted deep enough and in doubtful cases given protection with ashes or dry litter. The majority of Lilies require a soil fairly rich in humus or vegetable mould, and if it is desirable to plant Lilies in poor soil or in chalky districts, an area must be dug out 2 feet deep and filled in with kitchen garden soil mixed with fibrous loam and sand. Plant the bulbs fully 3 inches deep in most cases and surround them with an envelope of sand ½ inch thick; this allows excessive moisture to pass away freely; it acts also as a guard against the attacks of slugs and, by reason of its sterility, as a barrier against the spread of such fungoid diseases as may infest the surrounding soil and which would be likely to destroy the bulbs if they gained access to them. The bulbs of all Lilies root quicker and with greater freedom if a few pieces of peat are placed beneath them when planted. Many cases of failure can be traced to the condition of the soil, as the bulbs rot during winter owing to the presence of stagnant moisture: it is useless to plant Lilies in very poor ground or in any position which is waterlogged in winter. In their native countries they enjoy more sunshine in their growing season than we usually get and wet at the root during winter often proves fatal to many of them. When growing, however, all Lilies require plenty of moisture. If they are neglected in this respect they will not produce the glorious spikes of flowers they are capable of; moreover, a Lily once drought-stricken or in any way seriously checked in growth so as to produce debility, rarely recovers its health. Disappointment with Lilies is due often also to late planting, but if good home-grown bulbs of the different kinds are planted before the end of September, to give them time to make their natural autumn growth, they should, in suitable soil, flower well the next year.

A large number of varieties produce two distinct sets of root – those from the base of the bulb and others from the base of the stem, above the bulb. These are termed 'stem-rooting.'

In planting Lily bulbs, two points are essential to bear in mind: (1) Does the species relish lime or detest it? (2) Is it a stem-rooter, demanding in consequence to be deeply planted, or is it provided with basal roots only, requiring less depth in planting?

Lilium candidum, L. Martagon and *L. tigrinum* succeed in well-drained sandy loam and may with advantage be planted in the herbaceous border, all except *candidum* being planted at least 6 to 8 inches in depth.

The best manure for all Lilies is wood ash, provided it has been carefully stored in a dry place, because its virtue consists in the potash it contains, which a single shower suffices to dissolve and wash to waste. The ash of twigs and leaves contains a larger percentage of potash than that of large branches and logs.

¶ *Propagation.* Lilies are propagated by means of division or offsets, which as such increase freely, but increase by seed and bulb-scales are the more usual methods.

L. tigrinum and some others produce little bulbs in the axils of the leaves, which form a ready means of increase and only need growing on under suitable conditions to produce flowering bulbs. *L. candidum* produces plenty of small bulbs around the parent bulb and thus affords a ready means of increase. For those that do not produce seeds or offsets readily, propagation by bulb-scales is resorted to, each healthy scale being capable of producing a new bulb at its base. The scales are pulled off and inserted in pans and boxes of sandy soil and stood in cold frames, when in about six months small bulbs are produced at the base of the scales.

All Lilies that do not afford a ready means of increase by bulbils or division, or bulb-scales should be grown by seeds, which is the only way to attain success in this country with many of them. Imported bulbs as a rule only grow for one or two years and then die; although immense consignments of beautiful Asiatic species of Lilies are annually imported, less than 50 per cent. of them survive to a second season, flowering, if at all, only once from nutriment stored within the bulb, the cause being probably want of care in raising and packing the bulb and the fact, also, that the great majority of bulbs on arrival are found to be infested with mites or fungus.

Lilies grown from seed take from two to six years to produce flowers. When raising from seed, a regular rotation should be maintained by sowing a quantity of seed each year. Many Lilies germinate exceedingly well in cold frames when sown in March, April or May. When the young seedlings have made their second or third leaf, they may be planted outdoors in a sheltered border during the spring, to get well-established before winter, the less hardy ones being grown in frames.

The mould *Botrytis cinerea*, which attacks so many garden plants, often attacks Lilies, especially *L. candidum*: it is usually the foliage that is attacked. On the first signs, the plants should be sprayed with a solution of sulphide of potassium, using an ounce to a gallon of warm water (temperature 100° to 120° F.), at the same time removing any affected leaves and burning them. If a little soft soap is dissolved with the mixture, it adheres much better to the foliage and is not so easily washed off by rain. In bad cases, the bulbs may be affected, in which case they should be thoroughly dusted with flowers of sulphur. Cut off and burn the diseased stems, lift the bulbs, place them in a large paper bag containing flowers of sulphur, give a good shaking to work the sulphur well into the scales and then replant in a fresh site. This precaution has often proved successful in warding off a subsequent attack of the disease.

The disease is a more or less mysterious one: it often appears in a virulent form in one garden, whereas in a neighbouring one the plants may be quite free from it. Once it finds foothold in the soil of a garden it remains there, potent for evil whenever the atmospheric conditions are favourable. In dull, chilly, damp summers, the disease becomes epidemic, and does widespread harm to many plants besides Lilies. The sun is the most powerful antidote against the fungus, which is spread by spores too minute for the eye to see.

It is often said that white Lilies in cottage gardens are exempt from attacks of the disease, but in an epidemic they are spared no more than are those in manor gardens. Spraying the foliage with a solution of potassium sulphide helps to keep the disease in check, but it is not a cure; no absolute remedy has yet been discovered, and those who plant this lily must not expect to have it in full beauty every year. This country has relied too much on other nations for its supply of bulbs in the past, and quantities of infected bulbs of *L. candidum* are imported annually from Central and Southern France, where *la Toile* – as the French call *B. cinerea* – has even more of a grip than it has here; and the rapid spread of the disease may well be due in some measure to that tainted source. All the bulbs needed in Great Britain could be grown here. The wild Grecian form of *L. candidum* seems more resistant to *Botrytis* than the cultivated forms.

Lilies are on the whole singularly free from insect and other pests, though wood-lice sometimes prove troublesome. On some soils, slugs are the chief menace; the grey slug attacks the stem and leaves, but the black slug is the more insidious, as it attacks the bulbs and working underground is difficult to deal with. The best means of keeping slugs in check are good cultivation and trapping. One mode of trapping that is much recommended is to place on the ground in the evening boards smeared on their under-sides with a mixture of flour and stale beer. Examine the boards every morning and destroy the catch. Dry bran also catches many. Coarse, clean sand and small sifted cinders placed round the bulbs will also ward off attacks.

Mice will eat bulbs, especially *L. tigrinum*, and the edible Lilies of Japan.

In China, the dried scales of *L. japonicum* are considered nourishing and useful in diseases of the chest, as a substitute for Salep, the product of Orchis tubers.

L. Martagon (Linn.), the PURPLE TURK'S CAP LILY, is occasionally found growing wild in this country, but is rare, though it has been met with on chalk hills and in woody places in the south of England. It is, however, much cultivated, and is the hardiest of all Lilies, doing well in full sunshine, or in partial shade. It is a lime-lover, very easy to cultivate, usually increases very freely, and is easily raised from seed. It is strong-growing, but very graceful, producing twenty to thirty light spotted, purple flowers, on a tall stem, having reflexed petals, forming a sort of turban, the stamens appearing like a tuft of feathers at the top. The flowers give off their scent at night.

The Martagon group of Lilies, the form of whose flowers has led to their being called Turk's Cap, comprises many of our best known garden species whose habitats are in widely distant portions of the globe. From America have been introduced the so-called Swamp Lilies, *L. pardalinum*, the Panther Lily, *L. canadense* and *L. superbum*. *L. Hansoni* hails from Japan, and these with the Martagons proper carry their leaves in whorls, while in the best known of the remaining species the leaves are scattered on the stem. Of these may be mentioned the scarlet Turk's Cap (*L. chalcedonicum*) from Greece; *L. pyrenaicum* (straw-coloured) from the Pyrenees; *L. monadelphum* from the Caucasus; *L. pomponium verum* (yellow) from Italy.

The old Martagon is the commonest European species, being distributed throughout the whole of the southern and central portions of the Continent. It was mentioned by Gerard in his list of garden plants in 1596, and, though now out of favour, owing to its dull purple colour, has remained in cultivation, especially in cottage plots, ever since. Though interesting for its old associations, it is now superseded by the more striking forms. Although the purple Martagon bulbs are eaten in their native countries, they are too local here to be reckoned as one of our esculent herbs.

LILY, CROWN IMPERIAL

Fritillaria imperialis (LINN.)
N.O. Liliaceæ

Fritillaria imperialis (Linn.), the Crown Imperial Lily of Persia, is said to be there cultivated as a food plant, its bulb possessing poisonous properties when raw, but being wholesome when cooked.

There are two kinds of this handsome plant, associated with the earliest type of English gardens. They bear a circle of pendulous flowers – one blooms pure lemon yellow, the other deep orange red – and have a crown of foliage above them. The same name is given to this Lily in all European languages.

The bulbs have a fœtid odour, described as being like that of a fox, and are powerfully acrid and poisonous. Even honey from the flowers is said to be emetic.

Imperialine was isolated by Fragner in 1888, on extracting the bulbs with chloroform. This alkaloid and its salts are intensely bitter and are heart poisons.

No medicinal use is made of the plant.
See FRITILLARY.

LILY-OF-THE-VALLEY

Convallaria magalis (LINN.)
N.O. Liliaceæ

Synonyms. May Lily. Convallaria. Our Lady's Tears. Convall-lily. Lily Constancy. Ladder-to-Heaven. Jacob's Ladder. Male Lily

Parts Used. Flowers, leaves, whole herb

Habitat. It is a native of Europe, being distributed also over North America and Northern Asia, but in England it is very local as a wild flower. In certain districts it is to be found in abundance, but in many parts it is quite unknown. It is rare in Scotland and doubtfully native and only naturalized in Ireland. It grows mostly in the dryer parts of woods – especially ash woods – often forming extensive patches, and is by no means peculiar to valleys, though both the English and botanical names imply that it is so.

Culpepper reports that in his time these little Lilies grew plentifully on Hampstead Heath, but Green, writing about 100 years ago, tells us that 'since the trees on Hampstead Heath, near London, have been destroyed, it has been but sparingly found there.'

The Lily-of-the-Valley, with its broad leaves and fragrant little, nodding, white, bell-shaped flowers, is familiar to everyone.

¶ *Description.* In early spring days, the creeping rhizome, or underground stem, sends up quill-like shoots emerging from a scaly sheath. As they lengthen and uncoil, they are seen to consist of two leaves, their stalks sheathing one within the other, rising directly from the rhizome on long, narrowing foot-stalks, one leaf often larger than the other. The plain, oval blades, with somewhat concave surfaces, are deeply ribbed and slant a little backwards, thus catching the rain and conducting it by means of the curling-in base of the leaf, as though in a spout, straight down the foot-stalk to the root. At the back of the leaves, lightly enclosed at the base in the same scaly sheath, is the flower-stalk, quite bare of leaves itself and bearing at its summit a number of buds, greenish when young, each on a very short stalk, which become of the purest white, and as they open turn downwards, the flowers hanging, like a pearl of fairy bells, each bell with the edges turned back with six small scallops. The six little stamens are fastened inside the top of the bell, and in the centre hangs the ovary. There is no free honey in the little flowers, but a sweet, juicy sap is stored in a tissue round the base of the ovary and proves a great attraction to bees, who also visit the flower to collect its pollen and who play an important part in the fertilization of the flowers.

By September, the flowers have developed into scarlet berries, each berry containing vermilion flesh round a pale, hard seed. Though the plant produces fruit freely under cultivation, its propagation is mainly effected by its quickly-creeping underground stem, and in the wild state its fruit rarely comes to maturity. Its specific name, *Majalis*, or *Maialis*, signifies 'that which belongs to May,' and the old astrological books place the plant under the dominion of Mercury, since Maia, the daughter of Atlas, was the mother of Mercury or Hermes.

There is an old Sussex legend that St. Leonard fought against a great dragon in the woods near Horsham, only vanquishing it after a mortal combat lasting many hours, during which he received grievous wounds, but wherever his blood fell, Lilies-of-the-Valley sprang up to commemorate the desperate fight, and these woods, which bear the name of St. Leonard's Forest to this day, are still thickly carpeted with them.

Legend says that the fragrance of the Lily-of-the-Valley draws the nightingale from hedge and bush, and leads him to choose his mate in the recesses of the glade.

The Lily-of-the-Valley is one of the British-grown plants included in the Pharmacopœia, and its medicinal virtues have been tested by very long experience. Although not in such general use as the Foxglove, it is still prescribed by physicians with success. Its use dates back to ancient times, for Apuleius in his *Herbal* written in the fourth century, declares it was found by Apollo and given by him to Æsculapius, the leech.

In recent years it has been largely employed in experiments relating to the forcing of plants by means of anæsthetics such as chloroform and ether. It has been found that the winter buds, placed in the vapour of chloroform for a few hours and then planted, break into leaf and flower considerably before others not tested in this manner, the resulting plants being, moreover, exceptionally fine.

The leaves yield a green dye, with lime water.

¶ *Cultivation.* Lily-of-the-Valley is fairly easy to cultivate, preferring well-drained, rich, sandy loam, in moist situations.

Plant towards the end of September. The ground for Lily-of-the-Valley should be thoroughly stirred to a depth of 15 inches, early in September, laying it up rough for a few weeks, then breaking it down and adding some rotten manure, or if that cannot be obtained, some kind of artificial manure must be used, but this is better applied later on, hoeing it in just as growth appears. Plant the crowns about 6 inches apart and work fine, rich soil, with some leaf mould if possible, in between. Leave at least 9 inches between the rows. Keep the crowns well below the surface and above all plant firmly.

In some soils the plants will last longer in the best form than in others, but should be transplanted about every fourth year and in light, porous soils it may be necessary to do so every third year. Periodic transplanting, deep culture and liberal feeding produce fine blooms. Autumn is the best time for remaking beds, which are best done in entirely fresh soil. Cut the roots from the old bed out into tufts 6 inches or 9 inches square, and divide into pieces 3 inches square. Replant the tufts the original 6 inches apart. It is best to prepare the entire beds before replanting. Replanted by October, the crowns will be well settled in by winter rains, and the quality of the spikes will show a marked difference in early spring.

¶ *Parts Used Medicinally.* The whole plant, collected when in flower and dried, and also the root, herb and flowers separately. The inflorescence is said to be the most active part of the herb, and is preferred on that account, being the part usually employed.

The flowers are dried on the scape or flower-stalk, the whole stalk being cut before the lowermost flowers are faded. A good price is obtainable for the flowers, and in Lincolnshire, Derbyshire, Westmorland and other counties, where the plant grows freely wild, they would pay for collecting. During the process of drying, the white flowers assume a brownish-yellow tinge, and the fragrant odour almost entirely disappears, being replaced by a somewhat narcotic scent; the taste of the flowers is bitter.

If Lily-of-the-Valley flowers are thrown into oil of sweet almonds or olive oil, they impart to it their sweet smell, but to become really fragrant the infusion has to be repeated a dozen times with the same oil, using fresh flowers for each infusion.

¶ *Constituents.* The chief constituents of Lily-of-the-Valley are two glucosides, Convallamarin, the active principle, a white crystalline powder, readily soluble in water and in alcohol, but only slightly in ether, which acts upon the heart like Digitalin, and has also diuretic action, and Convallarin, which is crystalline in prisms, soluble in alcohol, slightly soluble in water and has a purgative action. There are also present a trace of volatile oil, tannin, salts, etc.

¶ *Medicinal Action and Uses.* Lily-of-the-Valley is valued as a cardiac tonic and diuretic. The action of the drug closely resembles that of Digitalis, though it is less powerful; it is used as a substitute and strongly recommended in valvular heart disease, also in cases of cardiac debility and dropsy. It slows the disturbed action of a weak, irritable heart, whilst at the same time increasing its power. It is a perfectly safe remedy. No harm has been known to occur from taking it in full and frequent doses, it being preferable in this respect to Digitalis, which is apt to accumulate in the blood with poisonous results.

It proved most useful in cases of poisonous gassing of our men at the Front.

It is generally administered in the form of a tincture. The infusion of $\frac{1}{2}$ oz. of herb to 1 pint of boiling water is also taken in tablespoonful doses. Fluid extracts are likewise prepared from the rhizome, whole plant and flowers and the flowers have been used in powdered form.

A decoction of the flowers is said to be useful in removing obstructions in the urinary canal, and it has been also recommended as a substitute for aloes, on account of its purgative quality.

¶ *Preparations and Dosages*. Fluid extract, herb, 10 to 30 drops. Fluid extract, whole plant, 10 to 30 drops. Fluid extract, flowers, ¼ to 1 drachm.

Russian peasants have long employed the Lily-of-the-Valley for certain forms of dropsy proceeding from a faulty heart.

Special virtues were once thought to be possessed by water distilled from the flowers, which was known as *Aqua aurea* (Golden Water), and was deemed worthy to be preserved in vessels of gold and silver. Coles (1657) gives directions for its preparation:

'Take the flowers and steep them in New Wine for the space of a month; which being finished, take them out again and distil the wine three times over in a Limbeck. The wine is more precious than gold, for if any one that is troubled with apoplexy drink thereof with six grains of Pepper and a little Lavender water they shall not need to fear it that moneth.'

Dodoens (1560) pointed out how this water 'doth strengthen the Memorie and comforteth the Harte,' and about the same time, Joachim Camerarius,[1] a renowned physician of Nuremberg, gave a similar prescription, which Gerard quotes, saying that

'a Glasse being filled with the flowers of May Lilies and set in an Ant Hill with the mouth close stopped for a month's space and then taken out, ye shall find a liquor in the glasse which being outwardly applied helps the gout very much.'

This spirit was also considered excellent as an embrocation for sprains, as well as for rheumatism.

We are told by old writers that a decoction of the bruised root, boiled in wine, is good for pestilential fevers, and that bread made of barley meal mixed with the juice is an excellent cure for dropsy, also that an ointment of the root and lard is good for ulcers and heals burns and scalds without leaving a scar.

Culpepper said of the Lily-of-the-Valley:

'It without doubt strengthens the brain and renovates a weak memory. The distilled water dropped into the eyes helps inflammations thereof. The spirit of the flowers, distilled in wine, restoreth lost speech, helps the palsy, and is exceedingly good in the apoplexy, comforteth the heart and vital spirits.'

The powdered flowers have been said to excite sneezing, proving serviceable in the relief of headache and earache; but to some sick people the scent of the flowers has proved harmful.

In some parts of Germany, a wine is still prepared from the flowers, mixed with raisins.

LILY, MADONNA

Lilium candidum (LINN.)
N.O. Liliaceæ

Synonym. White Lily
Part Used. The bulb
Habitat. Mediterranean countries

¶ *History*. When found in Palestine, *Lilium candidum* is sometimes pointed out as the 'Lily of the Field,' but this more probably was *L. chalcedonicum*, the brilliantly scarlet Martagon Lily, which is specially abundant about the Lake of Gennesaret on the plains of Galilee. The *Shushan*, or Lily of Scripture, had probably a very broad meaning and might refer to any striking blossom.

This white Lily was a popular favourite with the ancient Greeks and Romans. In the early days of Christianity it was dedicated by the Church to the Madonna (hence its popular name), probably because its delicate whiteness was considered a symbol of purity. It is employed on the 2nd July, in connection with the celebration of the Visitation of the Blessed Virgin.

It has been cultivated in this country for over three centuries, and no cottage garden was considered complete without this old favourite. Gerard, the famous apothecary, botanist and gardener of that period, says, 'Our English white lilie groweth in most gardens of England.'

It produces stiff, erect stems, 3 to 5 feet high, clothed with lance-shaped leaves. The flowers appear in June, flowering into July, and have a strong, sweet, penetrating perfume, so powerful as to be even annoying to some people. The honey is secreted in long grooves at the base of the white, floral leaves. There are several varieties, that with black stems, var. *peregrinum*, being the best for the garden.

¶ *Cultivation*. The Madonna Lily, when it is immune from disease, to which it is very prone, has a vigorous constitution, being so hardy that frost does not injure it. It will thrive in almost any soil and situation and is

---

[1] [Culpepper says it was *Gerard* who said this.–EDITOR.]

easily cultivated. Though it will do well in ordinary garden soil – especially in raised beds – one of the chief causes of disease is planting in low, badly-drained soil. It produces the finest flowers when growing in a rich, deep, moist loam, where its roots remain undisturbed for years. It is a lime-lover and failures to grow it can often be ascribed to absence of lime in the soil. No plant dislikes removal or digging near the roots more than this lily. This really is the secret of its thriving so well in cottage gardens. It should, therefore, be assigned a home where it can be left, so to speak, to the care of itself (if grown from the horticultural point of view), when it will flower and flourish for a number of years, but the bulbs should be dug up and replanted as soon as they show signs of deteriorating. So long as the plants continue to thrive, it is not advisable to disturb them, for cases have been known where they failed entirely after being transplanted, although they were in a perfect condition previous to shifting them, and they should never be moved more frequently than once in three years.

Planting or replanting should not be delayed beyond the end of August. The bulbs should not be planted more than 4 inches deep and not less than 6 inches apart, as the plants grow tall and spread very fast, being increased by offsets, which the bulbs send out in such plenty, as to make it necessary to take them off every other, or at most every third year, to prevent them weakening the principal bulb. The time for removing them, to ensure flowering next year, is the end of July to August, soon after the stalks decay.

Besides wood ash, an annual top dressing of decayed manure and a dusting of bonemeal in autumn have been found most beneficial to this Lily.

The bulbs are collected in August, and used both dry and fresh. Each bulb is composed of imbricated, fleshy scales, lanceolate and curved, about 1½ inch long and rather less than an inch broad at the widest part. It is odourless, with a slightly bitter and disagreeable taste. The scales should be stripped off separately for drying, and spread on shelves in a warm room for about ten days, then finished off by artificial heat.

The flowers of the Lily were formerly considered anti-epileptic and anodyne: a distilled water was employed as a cosmetic, and oil of Lilies was supposed to possess anodyne and nervine powers. But their odorous matter, though very powerful, is totally dissipated in drying and entirely carried off in distillation, either with spirit or water, so no essential oil can be obtained from them in this manner.

The petals communicate their fragrance to almond and olive oil, and also to lard, and have thus been employed in the past by perfumers.

¶ *Uses.* The *bulb*, only, is now employed for medicinal purposes, having highly demulcent and also somewhat astringent properties.

Bulbs are collected in August, and used both dried and fresh.

Each bulb is composed of imbricated, fleshy scales, lanceolate and curved, about 1½ inch long and rather less than ⅓ inch broad in the centre. It is without odour, but has a peculiar, disagreeable, somewhat bitter and mucilaginous taste.

To dry the scales, strip them off separately and spread them on shelves in a kitchen or other warm room for about ten days, then finish off more quickly in greater heat over a stove or gas fire, or in oven when the fire has just gone out.

The bulb contains a great deal of mucilage and a small proportion of an acrid principle, but the latter it loses by drying, roasting, or boiling; when cooked, the bulb is viscid, pulpy, sweet and sugary and is eaten by many people in the East. The Japanese are said to specially esteem the bulb of this species served with white sauce.

¶ *Medicinal Action and Uses.* Demulcent, astringent. Owing to their highly mucilaginous properties, the bulbs are chiefly employed externally, boiled in milk or water, as emollient cataplasms for tumours, ulcers and external inflammation and have been much used for this purpose in popular practice. The fresh bulb, bruised and applied to hard tumours, softens and ripens them sooner than any other application.

Made into an ointment, the bulbs take away corns and remove the pain and inflammation arising from burns and scalds, which they cure without leaving any scar.

The ointment also had the reputation of being an excellent application to contracted tendons. Gerard tells us:

'The root of the Garden Lily stamped with honey gleweth together sinewes that be cut asunder. It bringeth the hairs again upon places which have been burned or scalded, if it be mingled with oil or grease. . . The root of a white Lily, stamped and strained with wine, and given to drink for two or three days together, expelleth the poison of the pestilence.'

In the fresh state, the bulb is also said to have been employed with advantage in dropsy, for Culpepper (1652), besides confirming the uses of the Lily bulb which

Gerard gives, tells us 'the juice of it being tempered with barley meal baked is an excellent cure for the dropsy.'

Combined with Life Root (*Senecio aureus*), it is recommended in modern herbal practice for healing female complaints generally.

¶ *Dosage.* Of infusion, in water or milk, 3 tablespoonsful.

Country people sometimes steep the fresh blooms in spirit and use the liquid as a lotion for bruises in the same manner as *Arnica* or *Calendula*.

The bulbs of several other species of Lilies besides those of *L. candidum* are eaten, as those of *L. Kamschatcense*, *L. Martagon*, the Turk's Cap, and *L. Pomponium*, the Turban or Yellow Martagon, in Siberia. The Chinese and Japanese eat regularly the bulbs of *L. tigrinum*, the Tiger Lily and the Golden-rayed Lily of Japan, *L. auratum*.

LILY, TIGER

Lilium tigrinum
N.O. Liliaceæ

Parts Used. Leaves, stalks, flowers, collected when the plant is in full maturity
Habitat. China and Japan

¶ *Description.* The plant flowers in July and August; the bloom is orange colour and spotted. The upper leaves cordate and oval. It does not ripen seed in this country, but is propagated from the bulbils produced in the axils of the leaves which should yield flowering bulbs in three years from the time of planting.

¶ *Medicinal Action and Uses.* A tincture is made from the fresh plant and has proved of great value in uterine-neuralgia, congestion and irritation, also in the nausea and vomiting of pregnancy.

It relieves the bearing down pain accompanying uterine prolapse.

It is an important remedy in ovarian neuralgia. Poisoning by the pollen of the plant has produced vomiting, drowsiness and purging.

¶ *Dosage.* ⅛ to 5 drops of the tincture.

LILY, WHITE POND

Nymphæa odorata (SOLAND)
N.O. Nymphæaceæ

Synonyms. Sweet Water Lily. Sweet-scented Water Lily. Water Nymph. Large White Water Lily
Part Used. The fresh root
Habitat. Sluggish streams, ponds and marshes, in most parts of the United States, near the coast

¶ *Description.* Perennial aquatic herb, grows to the surface of the water from a thick horizontal root-stock, stem absent, flowers growing on long peduncles and the leaves on separate petioles. Stipules deltoid or nearly reniform, emarginate; leaves always floating orbicular, smooth, and shining, dark green above, wine-colour beneath. Flowers large white, showy and fragrant, often 6 inches in diameter; sepals four elliptical scaphoid, nearly free; petals numerous; stamens indefinite; ovary large globular, depressed, eighteen to twenty-four-celled. Fruit a depressed globular, fleshy body; seeds oblong, stipulate. The flowers open as the sun rises, after a few hours gradually closing, being entirely closed during the midday heat and at night.

¶ *Constituents.* The roots contain tannin, gallic acid and mucilage, starch, gum, resin, sugar, ammonia, tartaric acid, fecula, etc.

¶ *Medicinal Action and Uses.* The root is astringent, demulcent, anodyne, and anti-scrofulous, used in dysentery, diarrhœa, gonorrhœa, and leucorrhœa externally. The leaves and roots have been used in form of poultice to boils, tumours, scrofulous ulcers and inflamed skin; the infusion is used as a gargle for ulcers in the mouth and throat.

¶ *Dosage.* The powdered root, ¼ drachm. Infusion up to 2 fluid ounces.

The virtues of the root are quickly imparted to water.

A poultice of leaves and roots relieves boils, tumours, ulcers, and inflamed skin. A complete cure of uterine cancer by a decoction and a vaginal injection is recorded.

The dose of the powdered root is ¼ drachm in milk or sweetened water; but the best form is an infusion of 1 oz. in a pint of boiling water, macerated for thirty minutes, of which 2 to 4 fluid ounces may be given three or four times a day.

The EUROPEAN YELLOW POND-LILY (*Nuphar Advena* or *Nuphar luteum* – Spatterdock or Frog-lily) may be used as a substitute. It contains much nuphar-tannic acid.

LIME FRUIT

Citrus acida (ROXB.)
N.O. Rutaceæ

Synonyms. Citrus acris. Limettæ Fructus
Parts Used. The juice, the fruit
Habitat. West Indies, especially Montserrat. A native of Asia

¶ *Description.* The Lime is a small tree, crooked and prickly, only reaching as a rule a height of 8 feet. The leaves are ovate-oblong, and the stalk is not winged like that of the orange and lemon tree. The flowers are small and white and the fruit about half the size of a lemon, with a smoother, thinner rind, having a greenish tinge in its yellow. In Jamaica it is often planted for fences.

In London nurseries several varieties are found, the principal ones being the Chinese spreading, the West Indian, the Common, the broad-leaved and the weeping.

The juice is principally used in the manufacture of citric acid, and for medicinal purposes is often used indiscriminately with that of the lemon, although its flavour is not so popular.

Oil of Limes is used for flavouring purposes, especially in mineral waters and artificial lime-juice cordials, consisting of sweetened solutions of tartaric acid.

¶ *Constituents.* The National Formulary IV of America has defined and standardized Lime Juice as follows: the expressed juice of the ripe fruit of *Citrus medica acida*, containing in each *one hundred mils* not less than 5 gm. nor more than 10 gm. of total acids, calculated as crystallized citric acid ($H_3C_6H_5O_7$ plus H_2O : 210·08). It is clear or slightly turbid, pale yellow or greenish-yellow, with the characteristic odour and taste of limes. Specific gravity 1·025 to 1·040 at 25° C.

It must be free from sulphuric acid, and may contain 0·04 gm. of SO_2 in each 100 mils, but no other preservatives nor artificial colours.

The *rind* contains a volatile oil including the terpene *limonene* and citral.

¶ *Medicinal Action and Uses.* Antiscorbutic. Used in dyspepsia with glycerine of pepsin.

¶ *Dosage.* Of 40 per cent. glycerite of pepsin and 60 per cent. Lime juice, 2 fluid drachms.

¶ *Other Species.*

C. Limetta, grown in Italy, yields an oil resembling oil of Bergamot, called Italian Limette oil. It contains 26 per cent *ling* acetate. After standing it forms the yellow deposit *limettin.* It differs from the distilled West Indian oil of Limes.

See LEMON.

LIME TREE

Tilia Europœa (LINN.)
N.O. Tiliaceæ

Synonyms. Tilia vulgaris. Tilia intermedia. Tilia cordata. Tilia platyphylla. Linden Flowers. Linn Flowers. Common Lime. Flores Tiliæ. Tilleul
Parts Used. The flowers, the charcoal
Habitat. Northern Temperate Zone, especially British Isles

¶ *Description.* This tree will grow to 130 feet in height and when in bloom perfumes its whole neighbourhood. The leaves are obliquely heart-shaped, dark green above, paler below, from 2¼ to 4 inches long and sharply toothed. The yellowish-white flowers hang from slender stalks in flattened clusters. They have five petals and five sepals. The original five stamens have each developed a cluster, and there is a spoon-shaped false petal opposite each true one.

Linden Tea is much used on the Continent, especially in France, where stocks of dried lime-flowers are kept in most households for making 'Tilleul.'

The honey from the flowers is regarded as the best flavoured and the most valuable in the world. It is used exclusively in medicine and in liqueurs.

The wood is useful for small articles not requiring strength or durability, and where ease in working is wanted: it is specially valuable for carving, being white, close-grained, smooth and tractable in working, and admits of the greatest sharpness in minute details. Grinley Gibbons did most of his flower and figure carvings for St. Paul's Cathedral, Windsor Castle, and Chatsworth in Lime wood.

It is the lightest wood produced by any of the broad-leaved European trees, and is suitable for many other purposes, as it never becomes worm-eaten. On the Continent it is much used for turnery, sounding boards for pianos, in organ manufacture, as the framework of veneers for furniture, for packing-cases, and also for artists' charcoal making and for the fabrication of wood-pulp.

The *inner bark* or *bast* when detached from the outer bark in strands or ribands makes excellent fibres and coarse matting, chiefly used by gardeners, being light, but strong and elastic. Fancy baskets are often made of it. In Sweden, the inner bark, separated by maceration so as to form a kind of flax, has been employed to make fishing-nets.

The *sap*, drawn off in the spring, affords a considerable quantity of sugar.

The *foliage* is eaten by cattle, either fresh or dry. The leaves and shoots are mucilaginous and may be employed in poultices and fomentations.

¶ *Constituents.* The flowers contain a fragrant, volatile oil, with no colour, tannin, sugar, gum and chlorophyll.

The *bark* contains a glucoside, *tilicin*, and a neutral body, *tiliadin*.

The *leaves* exude a saccharine matter having the same composition as the manna of Mount Sinai.

¶ *Medicinal Action and Uses.* Lime-flowers are only used in infusion or made into a

distilled water as household remedies in indigestion or hysteria, nervous vomiting or palpitation. Prolonged baths prepared with the infused flowers are also good in hysteria.

In the Pyrenees they are used to soothe the temporary excitement caused by the waters, and M. Rostan has used them with success against spasms. The flowers of several species of Lime are used.

Some doctors prefer the light charcoal of lime wood to that of the poplar in gastric or dyspeptic disturbances, and its powder for burns or sore places.

If the flowers used for making the tisane are too old they may produce symptoms of narcotic intoxication.

LINSEED. *See* FLAX

LIPPIA

Lippia dulcis (TREV.)
N.O. Verbenaceæ

Synonyms. Yerba dulce. Mexican Lippia
Part Used. Leaves

A dozen species of *Lippias* are utilized in medicine and in perfumery for their fragrant oils.

The drug *Lippia Mexicana* consists of the leaves and flowers of *L. dulcis*, an evergreen shrub, about 18 feet high, with rough bark, the branches and leaves in pairs, the flower-stalks in the axils of the leaves, bearing many pyramidal, scaly heads about the size of a small grey pea, in which are many small yellow flowers between the scales. The leaves are 1 to 1½ inch long, ovate, narrowed into the petiole, acute, finely-toothed above, veiny and glandular-hairy. They have a peculiar, sweet and very delightful, aromatic odour and taste.

¶ *Constituents.* In 1886, Podwisrotzki separated an essential oil from the leaves, resembling that of fennel, as well as a camphor-like substance which he named Lippiol. (According to Maish, however, the plant used was probably the *Cedronella Mexicana*.)

¶ *Medicinal Action and Uses.* The drug finds employment as a stimulating expectorant, the tincture, in doses of ½ to 1 fluid drachm, is given as a respiratory sedative in coughs. It acts as an alterative on the mucous membrane.

Lippiol, in doses of 4½ grains, causes warmth, flushing, diaphoresis and drowsiness.

¶ *Other Species.*

L. GRAVEOLENS (H. B.) is similarly employed in Mexico, where it is known as *Yerba dulce.*

L. ORIGANOIDES (Kunth) is used as a substitute for *origanum.*

The yellowish-green leaves of L. CYMOSA of Jamaica are scented like Pennyroyal.

L. NODIFLORA (Mx.) is employed in India under the names of Buccar, Vakhar, Ratolia; and in Chile it is called *Yerba de la Sainte Maria.*

In Brazil, L. PSEUDO-THEA (Schauer) is used as a substitute for tea and its fruit is eaten.

L. SCABERRIMA (Souder) is the South African shrub Benkess Boas, and its leaves yield about 0·25 per cent. of volatile oil, somewhat resembling lavender in its odour. It contains the crystalline alcohol, *Lippianol.*

The Lemon-scented Verbena of gardens (the *Verveine odorante* of the French), so much valued for the fragrance of its leaves, was once referred to the genus *Verbena*, under the name of *Verbena triphylla*. Lyons subsequently assigned it to the genus *Aloysia* (hence a gardener's popular name for it: Herb Louisa, a corruption of the Latin name, *Aloysia*), but it is now classed in the genus *Lippia* and named L. CITRIODORA (Kunth). It differs from *Verbena* in having two, not four, nutlets in the fruit.

See VERBENA, LEMON-SCENTED.

LIPPIA CITRIODORA. *See* VERBENA

LIQUORICE   Glycyrrhiza glabra (LINN.) and Other Species
                                              N.O. Leguminosæ

Synonyms. Liquiritia officinalis. Lycorys (thirteenth century).
  (*Welsh*) Lacris
  (*French*) Reglisse
  (*German*) Lacrisse
  (*Italian*) Regolizia
Part Used. Root
Habitat. The Liquorice plants are shrubs, natives of South-east Europe and South-west
  Asia, as far as Persia, the *G. glabra* ranging more especially to the westward, the *G.
  glandulifera* more to the eastward and being the source of the Eastern Liquorice root
  of commerce

The Liquorice of medicine and commerce is derived from the sweet root of various species of *Glycyrrhiza*, a genus which contains about fourteen species, natives of warmer temperate countries in both the New and Old Worlds, ten of them having roots more or less sweet, but most of them not sufficiently so to be of use.

Hundreds of tons of Liquorice for commercial and medicinal purposes are imported annually from Spain, Russia, Germany, France and the East, most of our supply coming from Spain and Italy.

There are several well-marked species: *G. glabra, glandulifera, echinata,* etc. The chief source of the drug is *G. glabra,* which is cultivated in England, but is imported chiefly from Spain and Italy. There are several other varieties in commerce – Russian and Persian Liquorice – but these are not recognized by the British Pharmacopœia as suitable for medicinal purposes.

The use of the Liquorice plant was first learnt by the Greeks from the Scythians. Theophrastus (third century B.C.), in commenting on the taste of different roots (*Hist. Plant. lib.* IX. c. 13), instances the sweet Scythian root which grows in the neighbourhood of the Lake Mæotis (Sea of Azov), and is good for asthma, dry cough and all pectoral diseases.

Dioscorides, who names the plant Glyrrhiza (Greek *glukos,* sweet, and *riza,* a root), from his description of the plant possibly had in view *G. echinata,* as well as *G. glabra.*

The plant is often found under the name *Liquiritia officinalis.* The Latin name Liquiritia, whence is derived the English name Liquorice (Lycorys in the thirteenth century), is a corruption of Glycyrrhiza, as shown in the transitional form Gliquiricia. The Italian Regolizia, the German Lacrisse or Lakriz, the Welsh Lacris and the French Reglisse have the same origin.

The Roman writers, Celsus and Scribonius Largus, mention Liquorice as *Radix dulcis.* Pliny who describes it as a native of Cilicia, and Pontus makes no allusion to its growing in Italy.

Liquorice Extract was known in the times of Dioscorides and appears to have been in common use in Germany during the Middle Ages. In 1264, Liquorice (apparently the extract, not the root) is charged in the Wardrobe Accounts of Henry IV. Saladinus, who wrote about the middle of the fifteenth century, names it among the wares kept by the Italian apothecaries and it is enumerated in a list of drugs of the City of Frankfurt, written about the year 1450.

A writer in the first half of the sixteenth century notices the Liquorice plant as abundant in many parts of Italy, and describes the manner of making the Succus or Extract by crushing and boiling the fresh root.

The plant is described as being cultivated in Italy by Piero de Cresenzi of Bologna, who lived in the thirteenth century. As a medicine, the drug was well known in Germany in the eleventh century, and an extensive cultivation of the plant was carried on in Bavaria in the sixteenth century, but it is not mentioned in mediæval lists of plants.

Cultivation on a small scale has existed in England for a very long time. It appears from Turner's *Herbal* that it was cultivated in England in 1562, and Stow says 'the planting and growing of licorish began about the first year of Queen Elizabeth (1558).' Gerard, in 1597, tells us that he has plenty in his garden. It was known to and described by Culpepper who says: 'It is planted in fields and gardens, in divers places of this land and thereof good profit is made.'

John Parkinson grew Liquorice in his Holborn garden and John Josselyn gives the recipe for a beer which he used to brew for the Indians when they had bad colds. It was strongly flavoured with elecampane, liquorice, aniseed, sassafras and fennel.

Culpepper says:

'The English liquorice root shoots up several woody stalks, whereon are set, at several distances, many narrow, long green leaves, set together on both sides of the stalks and an odd one at the end, nearly resembling a young ash tree sprung up from the seed.

. . . This, by many years of continuance in a place without removal, and not else, will bring forth numerous flowers, standing together spike fashion, one above another upon the stalks in the form of pea-blossoms, but of a very pale blue colour, which turn into long, somewhat flat and smooth pods, wherein is contained small, round, hard seed. The root runneth down exceeding far into the ground, with divers smaller roots . . . they shoot out suckers in every direction, by which means the product is greatly increased.'

Liquorice is official in all pharmacopœias, which differ as to the variety or varieties recognized, as to the botanical name employed and as to the drug being peeled or unpeeled, dried Liquorice root being supplied in commerce either with or without the thin brown coat. In the latter state it is known as peeled or decorticated. The British Pharmacopœia requires that it be peeled, but others require that it be unpeeled.

¶ *Description.* The plants are graceful, with light, spreading, pinnate foliage, presenting an almost feathery appearance from a distance. The leaflets (like those of the False Acacia) hang down during the night on each side of the midrib, though they do not meet beneath it. From the axils of the leaves spring racemes or spikes of papilionaceous small pale-blue, violet, yellowish-white or purplish flowers, followed by small pods somewhat resembling a partly-grown pea-pod in form. In the type species *glabra*, the pods are smooth, hence the specific name; in others they are hairy or spiny.

The underground system, as in so many Leguminosæ, is double, the one part consisting of a vertical or tap root, often with several branches penetrating to a depth of 3 or 4 feet, the other of horizontal rhizomes, or stolons, thrown off from the root below the surface of the ground, which attain a length of many feet. These runners are furnished with leaf-buds and throw up stems in their second year. The perennial downward-running roots as well as the long horizontal stolons are equally preserved for use.

Various indications point to the habit of this plant of fixing atmospheric nitrogen, as do many others of the family.

In the species *glandulifera* (W. and K.) the pods are covered with thick, glandular spines, and the whole plant is pubescent or roughly glandular. The underground portion is not so spreading and produces a carrot-shaped root larger than the Spanish root derived from *G. glabra*. This species is indigenous to South-east Europe, Syria and Western Asia, and is both wild and cultivated in Russia.

Both the Russian and Persian Liquorice of commerce is derived from *G. glandulifera*, the Russian reaching this country is peeled or unpeeled: its taste although sweet, is accompanied by a more or less perceptible bitterness. It consists chiefly of roots, not runners.

Persian Liquorice root, collected in the valley of the Tigris and Euphrates, from *G. glandulifera*, and exported in bales from Bussorah, is usually unpeeled, and is in rather large, coarse pieces, closely resembling the Russian root. Both the Russian and Persian varieties are largely consumed in the United States; the root of *G. glandulifera* is equally official in the United States Pharmacopœia with that of *G. glabra*.

G. echinata, a native of Hungary, south Russia and Asia Minor, is the official German species. It has short globular heads of flowers and a small, ovoid pod with long spines. Probably a portion of the root from Italy and Sicily is the product of *G. echinata*, which grows wild in Apulia. The root is also somewhat bitter and there are contradictory statements concerning its quality, due perhaps to its having been confused with *G. glandulifera*.

Asiatic Liquorice is obtained from *G. uralensis* (Fisch.), found in Turkestan, Mongolia and Siberia, and little inferior to the best Russian Liquorice.

G. lepidota (Pursh), American Liquorice, is a species of the north-western United States. The rhizome is said to resemble that of Spanish Liquorice, but is smaller.

It is only grown now to a very limited extent in this country, being cultivated on a small scale near Pontefract in Yorkshire, though formerly it was extensively grown at Mitcham in Surrey, also at Godalming, and at Worksop (Notts).

The English Extract of Liquorice, made from the fresh home-grown root, sold in the lozenge form and known as Pontefract or Pomfrey cakes, is said to have a more delicate flavour than that imported, and it is considered that the cultivation of English Liquorice might well be extended, Essex and Surrey being suitable districts for its growth.

In southern Italy, large quantities of Liquorice root are grown, but it is chiefly converted into Extract, though some of the root is exported.

Spain and the south of France furnish quantities of carefully dried Liquorice root. Up to the year 1890, the cultivation of Spanish Liquorice was small or moderate in comparison with the wild collection. Owing, however, to the depletion of the natural supplies of root of good quality, this cultivation has grown rapidly in South and South-central Europe, where the climate is favourable.

Liquorice grows best on sandy soil near streams, usually not being found in the wild condition more than 50 yards from water.

It will not flourish on clay and prefers the rich, fine soil of bottom lands in river valleys, where there is an abundance of moisture during the growing period, but where the ground bakes hard during the hot, late summer months, when the dry heat is very favourable for the formation of the sweet constituents.

The plant succeeds most in a warm climate; not only can it not endure severe freezing, but cool weather interferes with the formation of its useful juice and renders it woody. It has been found that a climate particularly favourable to the production of the orange is favourable to that of Liquorice.

Owing to the depth to which the root penetrates and its ready propagation from detached pieces, the plant is a most persistent weed in cultivated grounds where it is indigenous and exceedingly difficult of extirpation. It is very healthy and robust and very little subject to disease, at the same time successfully occupying the ground to the exclusion of other plants. For this reason, the continuation of the natural supply may be considered as assured, though it is liable to suffer severe reduction from over-collection.

The supply of natural root has suffered severe fluctuations owing to the exhaustion of supplies in the districts previously worked, alternating with over-production from newly-opened districts. This fact, coupled with the operations of speculators, has resulted in equally great fluctuations in quality, the new districts yielding full-grown root of good quality, the older ones that which has not been allowed to develop properly.

The cultivation of Liquorice is easy, sure and profitable and, if properly conducted, conducive to the betterment of the soil.

On account of the depth to which the root strikes when the plant has room to flourish, the soil should have a good staple of mould 2 or 3 feet in depth and be manured if necessary.

The planting season is either October, or February and March; the latter is preferred. The plants are procured from old plantations, being waste from the harvesting process, consisting of those side roots or runners which have eyes or buds, cut into sections about 6 inches long. They are dibbled in, in rows 3 or 4 feet apart, about 4 inches underneath the surface and about 18 inches apart in the rows. In the autumn, the ground is dressed with farmyard manure, about 40 tons to the acre.

During the first two years the growth is slight, the plants not rising above a foot the first season, and in Calabria the intervening space is generally utilized for the production of potatoes, cabbages and similar crops. The soil being heavily fertilized for the production of Liquorice, these crops are usually very luxuriant. After the second year, the growing Liquorice plants cover the entire soil to the exclusion of other growth.

¶ *Harvesting and Preparation for Market.* Not until the end of the third season will the roots be ready to take up for use, but harvesting generally occurs only in the autumn of the fourth year. The soil is carefully removed from the space between the rows to a depth of 2 or 3 feet as required, thus exposing the roots and rhizomes at the side, the whole being then removed bodily. The earth from the next space is then removed and thrown into the trench thus formed and these operations are repeated continuously.

Every portion of the subterranean part of the plant is carefully saved, the drug consisting of both runners and roots, the former constituting the major part. The roots proper are washed, trimmed and sorted, and either sold in their entire state or cut into shorter lengths and dried, in the latter case the cortical layer being sometimes removed by scraping. The older or 'hard' runners are sorted out and sold separately; the young, called 'soft,' are reserved for propagation.

The average yield per acre is from 4 to 5 tons. The same ground yields a crop every three or four years, the fourth-year growth being the best. That of the third year and earlier is deficient in sweet substances, but immediately after the fourth year the texture begins to take on a tough, coarse and woody character. It is desirable also to collect the roots of those plants which have never borne fruit since that process exhausts the sweet substance of the sap.

English-grown Liquorice is dug up in late autumn and sold mostly in the fresh state for making extract, only a small amount being dried.

Fresh Liquorice (English) when washed is externally of a bright yellowish brown. It is very flexible, easily cut with a knife, exhibiting a light-yellow, juicy internal substance, which consists of a thick bark surrounding a woody column. Both bark and wood are extremely tough, readily tearing into long, fibrous strings. The root has a peculiar earthy odour and a strong, characteristic, sweet taste.

Most of the dried Liquorice root imported into this country comes from Spain and Russia, supplies of the official drug being drawn chiefly from Spain, the better quality of which comes from Tortosa and Alicante. Both Spanish and Russian Liquorice are usually exported in large bales or bundles, or rarely, in the case of the Spanish variety derived from Alicante, loose, or in bags. Spanish Liquorice root is in long, straight, nearly cylindrical, unpeeled pieces, several feet in length, varying in thickness from ¼ inch to about 1 inch, longitudinally wrinkled, externally greyish brown to dark brown, warty; internally tawny yellow; pliable, tough; texture coarsely fibrous; bark rather thick; wood porous, but dense, in narrow wedges; taste sweet, very slightly acrid. The underground stem which is often present has a similar appearance, but contains a thin pith. That from Alicante is frequently untrimmed and dirty in appearance, but that from Tortosa is usually clean and bright looking. When peeled, the pieces of root (including runners) are shorter, a pale yellow, slightly fibrous externally, and exhibit no trace of the small dark buds seen on the unpeeled runners here and there. Otherwise it resembles the unpeeled.

Nearly all the Russian Liquorice reaching this country has been peeled. It attains a much larger size than the Spanish, and the taste, although sweet, is accompanied by a more or less perceptible but not strong bitterness or acridity. It consists chiefly of roots, not runners, in long, often crooked pieces, about 2 inches in thickness, pale yellow externally and internally of a lighter yellow than the Spanish and softer. The size of all cells (when examined microscopically) is seen to be much larger than in the Spanish.

¶ *Extract.* The manufacture of Liquorice Juice, or *Extract*, is conducted on a liberal scale in Spain, southern France, Sicily, Calabria, Austria, southern Russia, Greece and Asia Minor, but the Extract with which England is supplied is almost exclusively the produce of Calabria, Sicily and Spain; Calabrian Liquorice is generally preferred. By far the larger part of the Italian and Sicilian crop is now manufactured there and exported in the form of Extract.

Spain formerly yielded most of the supply, hence the Extract is still termed 'Spanish Juice,' but that of the first grade has long since depleted to the point of scarcity.

The roots and runners of both wild and cultivated plants are taken up in late autumn and stacked through the winter in the cellars and yards of the factories. When required, they are crushed under millstones to a pulp, then transferred to boilers and boiled in water over a naked fire, the decoctions are run off and then evaporated in copper vessels over direct heat, till a suitable consistency is obtained, being constantly stirred to prevent burning. While warm, the mass is taken out and rolled into sticks, stamped and stacked on boards to dry. Vacuum pans and steam power have in some factories replaced the more simple methods.

The sticks vary in size, but are commonly about 1 inch in diameter and 6 or 7 inches in length and when imported are usually wrapped in bay leaves. At one end they are stamped with the maker's name or mark.

Stick Liquorice is very commonly impure, either from carelessness in its preparation, or from the fraudulent addition of other substances, such as starch, sand, carbonaceous matter, etc. Small particles of copper are also sometimes found in it.

Several varieties of Stick Liquorice are met with in English commerce, the most famous is the Solazzi Juice, manufactured at Corigliano, a small town of Calabria in the Gulf of Toranto.

The juice is also imported in a black form, having while warm and soft been allowed to run into the wooden cases of about 2 cwts. each, in which it is exported. This juice, known as *Liquorice Paste*, is largely imported from Spain and Asia Minor, but on account of a certain bitterness is unsuited for its use as a sweetmeat or in medicine, and is principally employed in the preparation of tobacco for chewing and smoking.

Extract of Liquorice in rolls has a black colour, is somewhat glossy and has a sharp and shining fracture. Some small cavities are found in the interior. The product of the different manufacturers of Stick Liquorice differ from one another not only in size, but often in the odour and taste; while some specimens are almost purely sweet, others are persistently acrid, rendering them unsuitable for medicinal purposes, for which they must be almost devoid of acridity.

Hard Extract of Liquorice, as described, is essentially different in composition and properties to the Extract of Liquorice of the British Pharmacopœia, which is entirely soluble in cold water, whereas the so-called Spanish Juice, when treated with cold water, leaves a large residue undissolved, retaining the shape of the stick. The amount soluble in cold water varies considerably and reaches in the best brands about 70 or 75 per cent. The United States and nearly all other Pharmacopœias recognize the commercial Extract of the root of *G. glabra*, but the British Pharmacopœia does not, and gives a process for making an extract which somewhat resembles the purified Extract of Liquorice of the United States Pharmacopœia. For the Liquid Extract of Liquorice, the British Pharmacopœia directs the exhaustion of the Liquorice root with two successive portions of cold water, using each time 50 fluid ounces for 20 oz. of the drug and allowing the mixture to macerate for 24 hours before expressing. The mixed infusions are heated to boiling point, strained through flannel and evaporated until the liquid has acquired, when cold, a specific gravity of 1·2, one-fourth of its volume of alcohol is added, and the mixture is set aside for 12 hours, after which it is filtered. It has a yellowish-brown colour and a pure sweet taste, free from all acridity.

¶ *Constituents.* The chief constituent of Liquorice root, to which its sweet taste is due, is Glycyrrhizin (6 to 8 per cent.), obtainable in the form of a sweet, white crystalline powder, consisting of the calcium and potassium salts of glycyrrhizic acid. The drug also contains sugar, starch (29 per cent.), gum, protein, fat (0·8 per cent.), resin, asparagin (2 to 4 per cent.), a trace of tannin in the outer bark of the root, yellow colouring matter, and 0·03 of volatile oil.

The amount of Glycyrrhizin present in Extract of Liquorice varies from 5 to 24 per cent., and the amount of moisture from 8 to 17 per cent. Upon ignition, the extract yields from 5 to 9 per cent. of ash.

The roots of *G. glandulifera* and *echinata* also contain in addition, Glycyrmarin, a bitter principle occurring mostly in the bark.

Glycyrrhizin, or a similar substance, has been obtained from other plants, viz. from the rhizome of *Polypodium vulgare*, the leaves of *Myrrhis odorata*, and the bark of *Lucuma glycyphlœa.*

¶ *Medicinal Action and Uses.* The action of Liquorice is demulcent, moderately pectoral and emollient.

It is a popular and well-known remedy for coughs, consumption and chest complaints generally, notably bronchitis, and is an ingredient in almost all popular cough medicines on account of its valuable soothing properties.

The Extract enters into the composition of cough lozenges and pastilles, with sedatives and expectorants. It is largely used in conjunction with infusion of linseed in the treatment of irritable cough, sore throat and laryngitis, and an infusion made by boiling 1 oz. of the bruised root deprived of its bark, with 1 pint of water for a few minutes, may be employed in the treatment of sore throat and in catarrhal conditions of the urinary intestinal tracts.

Beach mentions the following recipe as being used by the late Dr. Malone, of London, and speaks most highly of its efficacy:

'Take a large teaspoonful of Linseed, 1 ounce of Liquorice root, and ¼ lb. of best raisins. Put them into 2 quarts of soft water and simmer down to 1 quart. Then add to it ¼ lb. of brown sugar candy and a tablespoonful of white wine vinegar or lemon juice. Drink ½ pint when going to bed and take a little whenever the cough is troublesome.'

(N.B. – It is best to add the vinegar to that quantity which is required for immediate use.)

Fluid Extract of Liquorice is employed almost exclusively as a vehicle for disguising the taste of nauseous medicines, having a remarkable power of converting the flavour of acrid or bitter drugs, such as Mezereon, Quinine or Cascara.

The powdered root is useful in pill-making on account of its absorbent qualities, being used to impart stiffness to pill masses and to prevent the adhesion of pills.

As a remedial agent, powdered Liquorice root has been almost entirely replaced by the extract, though it is used in the well-known Compound Liquorice Powder, the mild laxative in which Senna and Fennel are the other ingredients. It is added mainly on account of its sweetness and emollient qualities, the action of the powder being mainly due to the Senna contained.

Liquorice was prescribed by early physicians from the time of Hippocrates, in cases of dropsy, to prevent thirst, for which it is an excellent thing, though probably the only sweet substance that has this effect. It is thought, however, that the property does not actually belong to the saccharine juice, but that if a piece of the root be chewed till all the juice is extracted, there remains a bitter, which acts on the salivary glands, and this may contribute to remove thirst.

The sugar of Liquorice may safely be taken by diabetic patients.

On the whole, Liquorice as a domestic medicine is far more largely used on the Continent than in Great Britain. It is much used in China and largely produced (both *L. glabra* and *L. echinata*) in some of the northern provinces, a variety of medicinal preparations being employed, not only as possessing tonic, alterative and expectorant properties, but also for the rejuvenating and highly nutritive qualities attributed to it.

It was recommended by Gervase Markham, a noted authority on husbandry and farriery in the early part of the seventeenth century, for the treatment of certain horses' ailments.

¶ *Preparations and Dosages.* Powdered root, ½ to 1 drachm. Fluid extract, 1 to 4 drachms. Comp. powder, B.P., 1 to 2 drachms. Solid extract, 1 drachm. Comp. lozenges, U.S.P. Solid extract in stick form, known as Liquorice Juice.

Liquorice is also largely used by brewers, being added to porter and stout to give thickness and blackness.

Block Liquorice is employed in the manufacture of tobacco for smoking and chewing.

According to the United States press, a new use for Liquorice Root has lately been discovered, the waste root being now utilized for the manufacture of boards for making boxes. After extraction of the Liquorice, the crushed root was formerly considered a waste product and destroyed by burning, but under a recently discovered process this refuse can now be made into a chemical wood pulp and pressed into a board that is said to have satisfactory resisting qualities and strength.

LIQUORICE, INDIAN

Abrus precatorius (LINN.)
N.O. Leguminosæ

Synonyms. Jequirity. Wild Liquorice. Prayer Beads (*Indian*) Gunga. (*Indian*) Goonteh. (*Indian*) Rati
Parts Used. Root, seeds

The root of an Indian leguminous plant, *Abrus precatorius* (Linn.), under the native names of Gunga or Goonteh, has been used as a demulcent. It contains Glycyrrhizin, and has been termed Indian Liquorice and used as a substitute for true Liquorice. Acrid resins, however, render the root irritant and poisonous.

An infusion and a paste of the seeds are included in the British Pharmacopœia. It has a strongly irritating effect upon the eyes and has been used both to produce and to allay certain ophthalmic diseases.

The hard, red, glossy seeds, nearly globular, with a large, black spot at one end, are known as Prayer Beads, or Jequirity seeds. The seeds, weighing about 1 carat each, have been used in India from very ancient times for the purpose of weighing gold, under the name of Rati. They are largely employed also for the making of rosaries and for ornamental purposes.

The weight of the famous Koh-i-noor diamond was ascertained by means of these seeds.

There is also a variety with perfectly white seeds.

Their medical importance is not great, but they have a notorious history in India as an agent in criminal poisoning. This practice has been directed chiefly against cattle and other live stock, but the poisoning of human beings has been not infrequent. That the attractive seeds form dangerous playthings for children has been proved by the records of a number of cases of poisoning which have occurred in this way.

The name Wild Liquorice has also been given to *Aralia nudicaulis* (Linn.), indigenous to Canada and the United States, and to the root of *Cephalanthus occidentalis*, a member of the Madder family, a large shrub, with rich, glossy foliage, growing in swamps almost throughout the United States and extending into Southern Canada, the bark and stem of which is used commercially.

Rest-Harrow has also been called Wild Liquorice.

LIQUORICE, WILD. *See* REST-HARROW, SARSAPARILLA

LITMUS

Roccella tinctoria (D. C.)
N.O. Lichenes

Synonyms. Lacmus. Orchella Weed. Dyer's Weed. Lacca cærulea. Lacca musica. Orseille. Persio. Rock Moss. Lichen Roccella. Roccella phycopsis. Roccella Pygmæa. Turnsole. Touresol. Laquebleu
Part Used. The whole plant, for its pigment
Habitat. Seashore rocks on all warm coasts and some mountain rocks

¶ *Description.* Various origins are ascribed to the name *Roccella*. It may be derived from *rocca* (a rock), or from the red colour produced by the plants. It occurs in an Italian *Natural History* of 1599.

Roccella tinctoria is a small, dry, perennial lichen, in appearance a bunch of wavy, tapering branched, drab-coloured stems from 2 to 6 inches high, springing from a narrow base. These bear nearly black warts at intervals, the *apothecia* or means of fructification peculiar to lichens. It is found principally on the Mediterranean coasts, but other species from other localities are also sources of commercial Litmus.

Blue and *Red Orchil* or *Archil* are used for dyeing, colouring and staining. The red is prepared by steeping the lichen in earthen jars and heating them by steam. The blue is similarly treated in a covered wooden vessel.

They are used as a thickish liquid for testing purposes.

Cudbear, prepared in a similar way, is also used as a dye. It is dried and pulverized, and becomes a purplish-red in colour.

The preparation of Litmus is almost exclusively carried on in Holland, the details being kept a secret. About nineteen kinds seem to be there, varying very much in value.

The lichens are coarsely ground with pearlashes, and macerated for weeks in wooden vessels in a mixture of urine, lime and potash or soda, with occasional stirring. In fermentation the mass becomes red and then blue, and is then moulded into earthy, crumbling cakes of a purplish-blue colour. The scent is like violets and indigo and the taste is slightly saline and pungent. Indigo is mixed with inferior kinds to deepen the colour.

Blue Litmus Paper is prepared by steeping unsized white paper in an infusion or Test Solution of Litmus, or by brushing the infusion over the paper, which must be carefully dried in the open air.

Red Litmus Paper is similarly prepared with an infusion faintly reddened by the addition of a small percentage of sulphuric or hydrochloric acid.

Vegetable red, much used in colouring foods, is a sulphonated derivative of orchil.

¶ *Constituents.* The lichen contains a brown resin, wax, insoluble and lichen starches, yellow extractive, gummy and glutinous matters, tartrate and oxalate of lime and chloride of sodium. The colouring principles are acids or acid anhydrides, themselves colourless but yielding colour when acted upon by ammonia, air and moisture.

The chief of these are Azolitmin and Erythro-litmin, sometimes called leconoric, orsellic and erythric acids.

The dye is tested by adding a solution of calcium hypochlorite to the alcoholic tincture, when a deep blood-red colour, quickly fading, should appear, or the plants can be macerated in a weak solution of ammonia, which should produce a rich violet-red.

¶ *Medicinal Action and Uses.* Demulcent and emollient. A decoction is useful in coughs and catarrhs.

Litmus is used officially as a test for acids and alkalis. Acids impart a red colour to blue Litmus and alkaloids cause reddened Litmus to return to its original blue. It may be used in solid or liquid forms as well as on the papers.

¶ *Adulterations.* Orchil is often adulterated with extracts of coloured woods, especially logwood and sappan wood.

¶ *Other Species.*

Two of the chief sources of Litmus are now *R. Montagnei* of Mozambique and *Dendrographa leucophœa* of California.

Lecanora Tartare, or Tartarean Moss, was formerly much used in Northern Europe.

R. pygmæa is found in Algeria.

R. fuciformis is larger, with flatter, paler branches.

R. phycopsis is smaller and more branched.

Inferior kinds of Litmus are prepared from species of *Variolaria, Lecanora* and *Parmelia*.

LIVERWORT, AMERICAN

Anemone hepatica (LINN.)
N.O. Ranunculaceæ

Synonyms. Hepatica triloba. Hepatica triloba, var. americana or obtusa. Round-leaved Hepatica. Noble Liverwort. Liverleaf. Liverweed. Trefoil. Herb Trinity. Kidneywort. Edellebere
Parts Used. Leaves and flowers
Habitat. Cooler latitudes of the North Temperate Zone

¶ *Description.* The name of the genus may be derived from *epatikos* (affecting the liver) or from *epar* (the liver), from a likeness in its appearance to that organ. The Hepaticas are distinguished by having carpels without feathery tails and by the involucre of three simple leaves being so close to the flower as to resemble a calyx.

The leaves are broad kidney or heart shaped, about 2 inches long and broad, with three broad, angular lobes, leathery, smooth and dark green above, almost evergreen, placed on long, slender foot-stalks growing direct from the root. In the wild state the flowers are generally blue, more rarely rose or white, but in cultivation many other tints are to be found. There are numerous garden varieties, growing best in deep loam or clay, several having double flowers.

The leaves should be gathered during flowering time in March.

¶ *Constituents.* Liverwort contains tannin, sugar, mucilage, etc.; its value is due to its astringent principle. A full analysis has not been made.

¶ *Medicinal Action and Uses.* Demulcent, tonic, astringent, vulnerary. It has been described as 'an innocent herb which may be taken freely in infusion and in syrup.' It is a mild remedy in disorders of the liver, indigestion, etc., and possessing pectoral properties it is employed in coughs, bleeding of the lungs and diseases of the chest generally.

The infusion, made from 1 oz. of the dried herb to 1 pint of boiling water, is slightly astringent and mucilaginous. Frequent doses of ½ teacupful have been recommended in the early stages of consumption. In some countries the whole plant is regarded as a vulnerary and astringent. In cataplasms it is valued in hernia, affections of the urinary passages and skin diseases.

A distilled water is used for freckles and sunburn. Though in use from ancient days, its mild character has caused it to be little used.

¶ *Dosage.* 30 to 120 grains. Fluid extract, ½ to 2 drachms.

¶ *Other Species.*
Marchantia polymorpha is the true Liverwort.

The lichen *Pettigora canina* is known as English or Ground Liverwort. It was formerly regarded as a remedy for hydrophobia.

¶ *Cultivation.* Hepaticas are hardy, longlived plants of a deep-rooting nature, preferring a rich, porous soil and a sheltered situation. They flourish best in a deep loam, but will thrive in clay: one condition of success is good drainage. It is not advisable to transplant them frequently; when left undisturbed for a few years, they form fine clumps.

The double varieties are propagated by division of roots. The strongest clumps should be lifted immediately after flowering and carefully divided into separate crowns, each division to have as many roots as can be secured to it. These must be at once planted in fresh soil and carefully closed in, and then lightly covered with some very fine earth. They will become established in the course of the season if the soil is well drained, care being taken to water when necessary. Being by nature woodside plants, they should not be exposed to long-continued sunshine.

The single varieties are raised by seed, which must be sown as soon as ripe in pans or shallow boxes, which should be filled with light rich, sandy loam, kept moist, and sheltered in a frame throughout the winter. Germination is very slow and the young plants will not appear till the end of September. Keep the seedlings in their seed-boxes, freely ventilated to prevent damping off, and in April remove them to a sheltered shady border. As the young plants make their proper leaves, carefully lift them out with a thin slip of wood and plant them in a border prepared for the purpose, where the soil must be sweet and sandy, without manure and a little shaded.

LIVERWORT, ENGLISH

Peltigera Canina (HOFFM.)
N.O. Lichenes

Synonyms. Lichen Caninus. Lichen Cinereus Terrestis. Ash-coloured Ground Liverwort
Part Used. Lichen
Habitat. Britain where the drainage is good; on mudwalls and molehills

¶ *Description.* The marginal disks of this lichen are at first veiled and project from the thallus, retaining fragments of the veil of the margin. The fronds are foliaceous, coriaceous, ascending, soft, underside is veined and attached to the ground or to whatever substance it grows upon – where they make handsome plants, especially when in fruit or studded with the little red parasite to which they are subject. The plant was formerly considered of great value in hydrophobia.

¶ *Medicinal Action and Uses.* Deobstruent, slightly purgative and held in esteem as a remedy for liver complaints.

¶ *Preparations and Dosages.* Infusion, 1 oz. to 1 pint of boiling water; take 4 oz. daily. Fluid extract, ½ to 2 drachms.

LOBELIA

Lobelia inflata (LINN.)
N.O. Lobeliaceæ

Synonyms. Rapuntium inflatum. Indian Tobacco. Pukeweed. Asthma Weed. Gagroot. Vomitwort. Bladderpod. Eyebright
Parts Used. The dried flowering herb, and seeds
Habitat. Dry places in the northern United States, Canada and Kamchatka. Grown in English gardens

¶ *Description.* The herb is named after the botanist Matthias de Lobel, a native of Lille, who died in London in 1616. It is an erect annual or biennial herb, 1 to 2 feet high; lower leaves and also flower are stalked, the latter being pale violet-blue in colour, tinted pale yellow within. Commercially, it is usually prepared in compressed, oblong packages, by the Shakers of New Lebanon for importation into England. The colour is a yellowish green, the odour irritating, the taste, after chewing, very like that of tobacco, burning and acrid, causing a flow of saliva. The powder has a greenish colour, but that of the seeds is brown, and stains paper with grease.

Several species are cultivated in English gardens for the splendour of their flowers, in every shade of scarlet, purple, and blue. *Lobelia Dortmanna* and *L. Urens* are British. The fixed oil, with constituents rather like that of linseed oil, possesses the drying qualities common to the fixed oils together with all the medicinal properties of the seed.

The plant was known to the Penobscot Indians and was widely used in New England long before the time of Samuel Thomson, who is credited with its discovery. It was brought into general professional use by Cutler of Massachusetts.

¶ *Constituents.* The activity of Lobelia is dependent upon a liquid alkaloid first isolated by Proctor in 1838 and named Lobeline. Pereira found a peculiar acid which he named Lobelic acid. Also, gum, resin, chlorophyl, fixed oil, lignin, salts of lime and potassium, with ferric oxide. Lobelacrine, formerly considered to be the acrid principle, is probably lobelate of lobeline. The seeds contain a much higher percentage of lobeline than the rest of the plant.

¶ *Medicinal Action and Uses.* Expectorant, diaphoretic, anti-asthmatic. It should not be employed as an emetic.[1] Some authorities attach great value to it as an expectorant in bronchitis, others as a valuable counter-irritant when combined with other ingredients in ointment form. It is sometimes given in convulsive and inflammatory disorders such as epilepsy, tetanus, diphtheria and tonsilitis. There is also difference of opinion with regard to its narcotic properties. Where relaxation of the system is required, as, for instance, to subdue spasm, Lobelia is invaluable. Relaxation can be counteracted by the stimulating and tonic infusion of capsicum. It may be used as an enema.

Externally, an infusion has been found useful in ophthalmia, and the tincture can be used as a local application for sprains, bruises, or skin diseases, alone, or in powder combined with an equal part of slippery elm bark and weak lye-water in a poultice. The oil of Lobelia is valuable in tetanus. One drop of oil triturated with one scruple of sugar, and divided into from 6 to 12 doses, is useful as an expectorant, nauseant, sedative, and diaphoretic, when given every one or two hours.

¶ *Preparations and Dosages.* Powdered bark, 5 to 60 grains. Fluid extract, 10 to 20 drops. Acid tincture, 1 to 4 drachms. Tincture, U.S.P., 1 to 4 drachms. Etherial tincture, B.P., 5 to 15 drops. Syrup, 1 to 4 drachms. Solid extract, 2 to 4 grains. Oil of seed, 1 drop rubbed up with 20 grains of ginger and divided into 6 to 12 doses. Lobelin, ¼ to 3 grains.

Acetum Lobellæ (Vinegar of Lobelia). Lobelia seed powder, 4 oz. Diluted acetic acid, 2 pints. Macerate in a close glass vessel for seven days, then express the liquor, filter, and add to the filtered product alcohol, or concentrated acetic acid, 1 fluid ounce. The whole should measure 2 pints. This medicated vinegar may also be prepared by percolation. It is an emetic, nauseant, and expectorant, and a valuable relaxant in spasmodic affections. A good application in such skin diseases as salt-rheum, erysipelas, poisoning by rhus, etc. As an expectorant, 5 to 30 drops every half-hour in elm or flaxseed infusion. One part of Vinegar of Lobelia to 1 part of syrup forms a pleasant preparation for children.

¶ *Poisonous, if any, with Antidotes.* In excessive doses the effects are those of a powerful acro-narcotic poison, producing great depression, nausea, cold-sweats, and possibly death.[2] Poisonous symptoms may occur from absorption of it through the epidermis.

¶ *Other Species.*
L. Dortmanna. This is indigenous to Great Britain, and is rather similar in action to *L. inflata.* A tincture of the fresh plant cures headaches and noises in the ears.

L. Erinus. A tincture of the plant has been used in cancer and has produced absolute freedom from pain; is also used as a remedy in syphilis.

LOBELIA, BLUE (*L. Syphilitica*) and LOBELIA RED (*L. Cardinalia*). Both used in homœopathy. The first is diaphoretic, emetic and cathartic and has been used in dropsy, diarrhœa, syphilis and dysentery, the root being the part used. The Red Lobelia is said to be anthelmintic, nervine and antispasmodic.

L. Kalmit. Said to be used by the Indians in the cure of syphilis.

L. purpurascens. A tincture of the whole plant is used in paralysis of the lungs and tongue.

[1] Herbalists, who use lobelia far more than the ordinary practitioners, nearly always prescribe it in doses large enough to prove emetic, and regard it as of greater value thus used. – EDITOR.
[2] Herbalists also deny that it has poisonous properties and that it has ever caused death. – EDITOR.

LOGWOOD

Hæmatoxylon Campeachianum (LINN.)
N.O. Leguminosæ

Synonyms. Hæmatoxylon Lignum. Lignum Campechianum. Lignum Cœruleum. Peachwood. Bois de Campechey de Sang or d'Inde. Bloodwood

Part Used. The heart-wood, or duramen, unfermented

Habitat. Tropical America, especially the shores of the Gulf of Campeachy. Naturalized in West Indies and elsewhere

¶ *Description.* The name of the genus comes from the Greek and refers to the blood-red colour of the heart-wood. *Hæmatoxylon Campeachianum* is a crookedly-branched, small tree, the branches spiny and the bark rough and dark. The leaves have four pairs of small, smooth leaflets, each in the shape of a heart with the points towards the short stem. The flowers, small and yellow, with five petals, grow in axillary racemes.

The tree was introduced into Jamaica and other countries in 1715 and has been grown in England since 1730.

The average yearly import of logwood into the United Kingdom is about 50,000 tons, the four kinds recognized in the market, in order of value, being Campeachy, Honduras, St. Domingo and Jamaica.

The trees are felled in their eleventh year, the red heartwood, in 3-foot logs, being exported.

The principal value of logwood is in dyeing violet, blue, grey and black. For dyeing, the wood is chipped and fermented, thus rendering it unsuitable for medicinal use.

The many disputes and difficulties that arose over the rights of growing and cutting logwood are a matter of history. It is used also as a microscopical stain. The odour is faint and pleasant, the taste astringent and sweetish. It gives a reddish-violet tinge to water made alkaline with a solution of sodium hydroxide.

¶ *Constituents.* A volatile oil, an oily or resinous matter, two brown substances, quercitin, tannin, a nitrogenous substance, free acetic acid, salts, and the colouring principle Hæmatoxylin or Hæmatin (not the hæmatin of the blood). The crystals are colourless, requiring oxygen from the air and an alkaline base to produce red, blue, and purple.

Hæmatein, produced by extraction of two equivalents of hydrogen, is found in dark violet crystalline scales, showing the rich, green colour often to be seen outside chips of logwood for dyeing purposes.

¶ *Medicinal Action and Uses.* A mild astringent, especially useful in the weakness of the bowels following cholera infantum. It may be used in chronic diarrhœa and dysentery, in hæmorrhages from uterus, lungs, or bowels, is agreeable to take, and suitable whether or not there is fever. It imparts a blood-red colour to urine and stools. It is incompatible with chalk or lime-water. The patient should be warned of these two characteristics.

In large doses hæmatoxylin can produce fatal gastro-enteritis in lower animals.

The infusion, internally, combined with a spray or lotion, is said to have cured obstinate cases of fœtid polypus in the nose.

¶ *Preparations and Dosages.* Decoction, 2 to 4 fluid ounces. Decoction, B.P. 1895, ¼ to 2 oz. Solid extract, B.P. 1885, 10 to 30 grains. Solid extract, U.S.P., 2 to 5 grains.

¶ *Other Species.*

'BASTARD LOGWOOD' from *Acacia Berteriana* and other species, contains no hæmatoxylin. It does not form a violet colour with alkalies, but yields a pure, yellowish-grey dye.

BRAZIL WOOD, a product of *Cæsalpinia*, is distinguished by forming a red colour with alkalis. It is now used only as a dye.

WEST INDIAN LOGWOOD is *Ceanothus Chloroxylon.*

LOOSESTRIFE, PURPLE

Lythrum salicaria
N.O. Lythraceæ

Synonyms. Lythrum. Purple Willow Herb. Spiked Loosestrife. Salicaire. Braune or Rother Weiderich. Partyke. Lysimaque rouge. Flowering Sally. Blooming Sally

Parts Used. Herb, root

Habitat. Europe, including Britain. Russian and Central Asia. Australia. North America

¶ *Description.* This handsome perennial, 2 to 4 feet in height, has a creeping rhizome, four to six angled, erect, reddish-brown stems, lanceolate leaves from 3 to 6 inches long, entire, sometimes opposite, sometimes in whorls clasping the stem, with reddish-purple or pink flowers in whorls forming terminal spikes. It grows in wet or marshy

PURPLE LOOSETRIFE
Lythrum Salicaria

MARSH MALLOW
Althæa Officinalis

places, varying in different districts in the comparative lengths of stamens and styles, colour of flowers and pollen grains. It is odourless, with an astringent taste. It has been used in tanning leather.

The name Lythrum is from the Greek *luthron*, meaning 'gore,' from the colour of the flowers.

¶ *Constituents.* Mucilage and an astringent principle, but it has not been analysed.

¶ *Medicinal Action and Uses.* Although scarcely used at present, Loosestrife has been highly esteemed by many herbalists. It is well established in chronic diarrhœa and dysentery, and is used in leucorrhœa and blood-spitting. In Switzerland the decoction was used successfully in an epidemic of dysentery. It has also been employed in fevers, liver diseases, constipation and cholera infantum, and for outward application to wounds and sores.

It has been stated to be superior to Eyebright for preserving the sight and curing sore eyes, the distilled water being applied for hurts and blows on the eyes and even in blindness if the crystalline humour is not destroyed.

An ointment may be made with the water – 1 oz. to 2 drachms of May butter without salt, and the same quantity of sugar and wax boiled gently together. It cleanses and heals ulcers and sores, if washed with the water, or covered with the leaves, green or dry according to the season.

A warm gargle and drink cures quinsy or a scrofulous throat.

¶ *Dosages.* Of powder, a drachm two to three times a day. Of decoction of root, 2 fluid ounces.

¶ *Other Species.*
Lythrum hyssopifolia has similar properties.

L. verticillatum (Decodon or Swamp Willow-herb) has similar properties, and is said to cure abortion in mares and cows who browse on it.

A Mexican Salicaria, *Apanxaloa*, is regarded as an astringent and vulnerary.

Loosestrife is the common name of many members of the genus *Lysimachia*.

LOOSESTRIFE, YELLOW

Lysimachia vulgaris (LINN.)
N.O. Primulaceæ

Synonyms. Yellow Willow Herb. Herb Willow. Willow-wort. Wood Pimpernel
Part Used. Herb

The Yellow Loosestrife is a tall, handsome plant, from 2 to 3 or even 4 feet high, found as a rule on shady banks or crowning the herbage of the stream-side vegetation. It has a creeping root, which persists year after year, and every spring throws up afresh the tall, golden-topped stems, whose flowers are at their best in July and August.

¶ *Description.* Its stems are slightly branched and covered with a soft, fine down. Closely set upon them are a number of nearly stalkless leaves, sometimes in pairs, sometimes three or four springing from the same spot. They are rather large and broad, 3 to 6 inches long by about 1¼ inches broad, oblong or lance-shaped and sharply tapering at the top. Their edges are unbroken. The undersurfaces are downy with soft, spreading hairs, especially on the veins, and the upper surfaces are marked with black dots which are glands. Whatever arrangement we find in any given plant holds throughout: we do not find in the same plant some of the leaves in pairs and others in three. When the leaves are in pairs, the stem is quadrangular and the angles increase as the leaves increase in number.

At the top of the stem arise the flower-buds, in the axils of the leaves. Each becomes a short stalk carrying a terminal flower, below which other flowers on smaller stalks arise – the ends of the main stem thus becoming covered with a mass of golden blossoms. The flower stalks are somewhat viscid, or sticky, to the touch.

Each flower is about ¾ inch in diameter, forming a cup of five petals, quite distinct at their tips, but joined together near the base. When the flowers droop, the five-pointed calyx, whose edges are fringed with fine red hairs, are seen at the back of the petals. The five stamens look quite separate, but are joined together at the bottom by a fleshy band attached to the petals, so that they seem to stand on a little glandular tube. This tube has not, as one would expect, any honey, and, in fact, there is neither honey nor scent in any part of the flower. Nevertheless, the plant is visited by one particular kind of bee, *Macropsis labiata*, which will visit no other flower, hence where the Loosestrife does not grow the Macropsis does not seem to exist. Self-fertilization also takes place in smaller, less attractive-looking flowers, sometimes found among the others. As a result of fertilization, whether self or effected by insects, the ovary develops into a rounded capsule, which when dried opens at the top by five valves. The swaying of the stems by the wind jerks out the minute seeds.

The Yellow Loosestrife, which is in no way related to the Purple Loosestrife, has often been known as the Yellow Willow Herb, Herb Willow, or Willow Wort, as if it belonged to the true Willow Herbs (which are quite a different family – Onagraceæ). There is a superficial resemblance between them, especially with regard to the leaves. The Yellow Loosestrife belongs, however, to the same family as the Primrose and the Pimpernel.

The Purple Loosestrife, on the other hand, is more nearly allied to the Willow herbs.

¶ *Other Species*. Four species of Lysimachia are native in this country – the Yellow Loosestrife; the Moneywort – our familiar Creeping Jenny; the Yellow Pimpernel (or 'Wood Loosestrife'), which is remarkably like the Scarlet Pimpernel in general habit and in form, and the Tufted Lysimachia, a rare plant confined to the northern portions of this island.

Both the scientific and popular names of the Loosestrife have interesting origins. The name Lysimachia is supposed to have been given in memory of King Lysimachus of Sicily, who, as Pliny tells us, first discovered its medicinal properties and then introduced it to his people. A belief in these properties persisted for many centuries; it was 'a singular good wound herb for green wounds,' says one old herbalist, and it had a great reputation for stanching bleeding of any sort. It had the credit of being so excellent a vulnerary, that the young leaves bound about a fresh wound are said to immediately check the bleeding and perform a cure in a very short time.

Its common name of Loosestrife is a very old one, and refers to the belief that the plant would quieten savage beasts, and that in particular it had a special virtue 'in appeasing the strife and unruliness which falleth out among oxen at the plough, if it be put about their yokes.' The plant appears to be obnoxious to gnats and flies, and so, no doubt, placing it under the yoke, relieved the beasts of their tormentors, thus making them quiet and tractable. For the same reason, the dried herb used to be burnt in houses, so that the smoke might drive away gnats and flies. It was particularly valuable in marshy districts. Snakes and serpents were said to disappear immediately the fumes of the burning herb came near them.

Gerard speaks of the 'yellow pimpernel growing in abundance between Highgate and Hampstead.'

Coles's *Art of Simpling*, the only herbal which devotes a chapter to herbs useful for animals, refers to the belief that

'if loosestrife is thrown between two oxen when they are fighting they will part presently, and being tied about their necks it will keep them from fighting.'

Even in Pliny's days, it was suggested that the plant did not really derive its name from a more or less mythical king, but that it was compounded from the Greek words, signifying 'dissolving strife' – it being held that not only cattle at the plough, but also restive horses could be subdued by it.

The plants can be transferred to the garden if the soil be somewhat moist, and especially if a stream or a piece of water is available. They will grow and thrive, then, in their new quarters, creeping by their perennial roots, so that when once fairly established, they will flourish permanently.

¶ *Part Used*. The whole herb, collected from wild plants in July and dried.

The taste of the dried herb is astringent and slightly acid, but it has no odour.

¶ *Medicinal Action and Uses*. Astringent, expectorant. Loosestrife proves useful in checking bleeding of the mouth, nose and wounds, restraining profuse hæmorrhage of any kind.

It has demulcent and astringent virtues which render it useful in obstinate diarrhœa, and as a gargle it finds use in relaxed throat and quinsy.

For the cure of sore eyes, this herb has been considered equal, if not superior to Eyebright. Culpepper states:

'This herb has some peculiar virtue of its own, as the distilled water is a remedy for hurts and blows on the eyes, and for blindness, so as the crystalline humours be not perished or hurt. It cleareth the eyes of dust or any other particle and preserveth the sight.'

For wounds, an ointment was used in his days, made of the distilled water of the herb, boiled with butter and sugar. The distilled water was also recommended for cleansing ulcers and reducing their inflammation, and also, applied warm, for removing 'spots, marks and scabs in the skin.'

See MONEYWORT, YELLOW PIMPERNEL.

LOVAGE

Levisticum officinale (KOCH.)
N.O. Umbelliferæ

Synonyms. Ligusticum Levisticum (Linn.). Old English Lovage. Italian Lovage. Cornish Lovage

Parts Used. Root, leaves, seeds, young stems

Habitat. It is not considered to be indigenous to Great Britain, and when occasionally found growing apparently wild, it is probably a garden escape. It is a native of the Mediterranean region, growing wild in the mountainous districts of the south of France, in northern Greece and in the Balkans

The Garden Lovage is one of the old English herbs that was formerly very generally cultivated, and is still occasionally cultivated as a sweet herb, and for the use in herbal medicine of its root, and to a less degree, the leaves and seeds.

It is a true perennial and hence is very easy to keep in garden cultivation; it can be propagated by offsets like Rhubarb, and it is very hardy. Its old-time repute has suffered by the substitution of the medicinally more powerful Milfoil and Tansy, just as was the case when 'Elecampane' superseded Angelica in medical use. The public-house cordial named 'Lovage,' formerly much in vogue, however, owed such virtue as it may have possessed to Tansy. Freshly-gathered leaf-stalks of Lovage (for flavouring purposes) should be employed in long split lengths.

¶ *Description.* This stout, umbelliferous plant has been thought to resemble to some degree our Garden Angelica, and it does very closely resemble the Spanish *Angelica heterocarpa* in foliage and perennial habit of growth. It has a thick and fleshy root, 5 or 6 inches long, shaped like a carrot, of a greyish-brown colour on the outside and whitish within. It has a strong aromatic smell and taste. The thick, erect hollow and channelled stems grow 3 or 4 feet or even more in height. The large, dark green radical leaves, on erect stalks, are divided into narrow wedge-like segments, and are not unlike those of a coarse-growing celery; their surface is shining, and when bruised they give out an aromatic odour, somewhat reminiscent both of Angelica and Celery. The stems divide towards the top to form opposite whorled branches, which in June and July bear umbels of yellow flowers, similar to those of Fennel or Parsnip, followed by small, extremely aromatic fruits, yellowish-brown in colour, elliptical in shape and curved, with three prominent winged ribs. The odour of the whole plant is very strong. Its taste is warm and aromatic, and it abounds with a yellowish, gummy, resinous juice.

It is sometimes grown in gardens for its ornamental foliage, as well as for its pleasant odour, but it is not a striking enough plant to have claimed the attention of poets and painters, and no myths or legends are connected with it. The name of the genus, *Ligusticum*, is said to be derived from Liguria, where this species abounds.

¶ *Cultivation.* Lovage is of easy culture. Propagation is by division of roots or by seeds. Rich moist, but well-drained soil is required and a sunny situation. In late summer, when the seed ripens, it should be sown and the seedlings transplanted, either in the autumn or as early in spring as possible, to their permanent quarters, setting 12 inches apart each way. The seeds may also be sown in spring, but it is preferable to sow when just ripe. Root division is performed in early spring.

The plants should last for several years, if the ground be kept well cultivated, and where the seeds are permitted to scatter the plants will come up without care.

¶ *Parts Used.* The root, *leaves* and *seeds* for medicinal purposes.

The *young stems*, treated like Angelica, for flavouring and confectionery.

¶ *Constituents.* Lovage contains a volatile oil, angelic acid, a bitter extractive, resins, etc. The colouring principle has been isolated by M. Niklis, who gives it the name of Ligulin, and suggests an important application of it that may be made in testing drinking water. If a drop of its alcoholic or aqueous solution is allowed to fall into distilled water, it imparts to the liquid its own fine crimson-red colour, which undergoes no change; but if limestone water be substituted, the red colour disappears in a few seconds and is followed by a beautiful blue, due to the alkalinity of the latter.

¶ *Medicinal Action and Uses.* Formerly Lovage was used for a variety of culinary purposes, but now its use is restricted almost wholly to confectionery, the young stems being treated like those of Angelica, to which, however, it is inferior, as its stems are not so stout nor so succulent.

The leafstalks and stem bases were formerly blanched like celery, but as a vegetable it has fallen into disuse.

A herbal tea is made of the leaves, when previously dried, the decoction having a very agreeable odour.

Lovage was much used as a drug plant in the fourteenth century, its medicinal reputation probably being greatly founded on its pleasing aromatic odour. It was never an official remedy, nor were any extravagant claims made, as with Angelica, for its efficacy in numberless complaints.

The roots and fruit are aromatic and stimulant, and have diuretic and carminative action. In herbal medicine they are used in disorders of the stomach and feverish attacks, especially for cases of colic and flatulence in children, its qualities being similar to those of Angelica in expelling flatulence, exciting perspiration and opening obstructions. The leaves eaten as salad, or infused dry as a tea, used to be accounted a good emmenagogue.

An infusion of the root was recommended by old writers for gravel, jaundice and urinary troubles, and the cordial, sudorific nature of the roots and seeds caused their use to be extolled in 'pestilential disorders.' In the opinion of Culpepper, the working of the seeds was more powerful than that of the root; he tells us that an infusion 'being dropped into the eyes taketh away their redness or dimness. . . . It is highly recommended to drink the decoction of the herb for agues. . . . The distilled water is good for quinsy if the mouth and throat be gargled and washed therewith. . . . The decoction drunk three or four times a day is effectual in pleurisy. . . . The leaves bruised and fried with a little hog's lard and laid hot to any blotch or boil will quickly break it.'

Several species of this umbelliferous genus are employed as domestic medicines. The root of LIGUSTICUM SINENSE, under the name of KAO-PÂU, is largely used by the Chinese, and in the north-western United States the large, aromatic roots of LIGUSTICUM FILICINUM (OSHA COLORADO COUGH-ROOT) are used to a considerable extent as stimulating expectorants.

The old-fashioned cordial, 'Lovage,' now not much in vogue, though still occasionally to be found in public-houses, is brewed not only from the Garden Lovage, *Ligusticum levisticum*, but mainly from a species of Milfoil or Yarrow, *Achillea ligustica*, and from Tansy, *Tanacetum vulgare*, and probably owes its merit more to these herbs than to Lovage itself. From its use in this cordial, Milfoil has often been mistakenly called Lovage, though it is in no way related to the Umbellifer family.

Several other plants have been termed Lovage besides the true Lovage, and this has frequently caused confusion. Thus we have the SCOTCH LOVAGE, known also as Sea Lovage, or Scotch Parsley, and botanically as *Ligusticum scoticum*; the BLACK LOVAGE, or Alexanders, *Smyrnium Olusatrum*; BASTARD LOVAGE, a species of the allied genus, *Laserpitum*, and WATER LOVAGE, a species of the genus *Œnanthe*.

Laserpitum may be distinguished from its allies by the fruit having eight prominent, wing-like appendages. The species are perennial herbs, chiefly found in south-eastern Europe. Some of them are employed as domestic remedies, on account of their aroma.

The scent of the root of MEUM ATHAMANTICUM (Jacq.), SPIGNEL (also called *Spikenel* or *Spiknel*), MEU or BALD-MONEY, has much in common with that of both Lovage and Angelica, and the root has been eaten by the Scotch Highlanders as a vegetable. It is a perennial, smooth and very aromatic herb. The elongated root is crowned with fibres, the leaves, mostly springing from the root, are divided into leaflets which are further cut into numerous thread-like segments, which gives them a feathery appearance. The stem is about 6 or 8 inches high, and bears umbels of white or purplish flowers. The aromatic flavour of the leaves is somewhat like Melilot, and is communicated to milk and butter when cows feed on the herbage in the spring. The peculiar name of this plant, 'Baldmoney,' is said to be a corruption of *Balder*, the *Apollo* of the northern nations, to whom the plant was dedicated.

LOVAGE, BASTARD

Laserpitum latifolia (LINN.)
N.O. Umbelliferæ

Synonym. White Gentian

Bastard Lovage is not a native of Great Britain. The species respectively comprised in the genera *Laserpitum* and *Ligusticum*, have much in common regarding foliage, manner of growth and aromatic odour.

LOVAGE, BLACK

Smyrnium Olisatrum (LINN.)

Synonyms. Alexanders. Alisanders. Black Pot-herb
Part Used. Herb

Black Lovage is in leaf and flower not unlike an Angelica, and amateur collectors have sometimes mistaken it for Wild Angelica.

Alexanders, to use its more common name, is a large perennial herb, growing 3 or 4 feet in height, with very large leaves, doubly and triply divided into three (ternate), with broad leaflets; the sheaths of the footstalks are very broad and membraneous in texture. The yellowish-green flowers are produced in numerous close, rounded umbels without involucres (the little leaves that are placed often at the spot where the various rays of the umbel spring). The whole herb is of a yellowish-green tint. The fruit is formed of two, nearly globular halves, with prominent ridges. When ripe, it is almost black, whence the plant received from the old herbalists the name of 'Black Pot-herb,' the specific name signifying the same. (*Olus*, a pot-herb, and *atrum*, black.)

LOVAGE, SCOTCH

Ligusticum Scoticum (LINN.)
N.O. Umbelliferæ

Synonym. Sea Lovage
Part Used. Root

The Scotch Lovage grows on cliffs and rocky shores in Scotland and Northumberland. It has a stout, branched rootstock, which is aromatic and pungent; a sparingly branched, erect, grooved stem, 1 to 3 feet high, and much cut-into dark green, shiny leaves, with three-lobed leaflets. The umbels of flowers, in bloom in July, are white or pink.

The leaves have been used in the Hebrides as a green vegetable, either boiled as greens, or eaten raw as salad, under the name of *Shunis*. The taste is strong and not very pleasant.

An infusion of the leaves in whey is used in Scotland as a purgative for calves, much valued, Green states in the *Universal Herbal*, in the Isle of Skye.

The root possesses aromatic and carminative properties; it has been applied in hysterical and uterine disorders.

When treated like celery, Sea Lovage proves quite inferior, though Angelica and Lovage have been thus used with a certain measure of success, even to the more fastidious modern palate.

This is one of the many cultivated plants that, escaping from gardens, have become apparently wild. It is now found rather abundantly in some parts of the sea-coast, on waste places near the mouth of rivers, especially in Scotland, and inland is occasionally seen in the neighbourhood of towns, or about the ruins of monasteries and other places where it was grown in olden times as a pot-herb and salad. It was formerly cultivated in the same manner as celery, which has now supplanted it, and boiled, was eaten by sailors returning from long voyages and suffering from scurvy. The young shoots and leaf-stalks eaten raw, have a rather agreeable taste, not very unlike that of celery, but more pungent. They were likewise used to flavour soups and stews, and some years ago were still so employed by the country people in parts where the plant abounds.

The seeds are sweetly aromatic and were formerly used as a carminative and stimulant medicine, and are still valued by herbalists for pleasantly flavouring confections of Senna and disguising the taste of other medicinal preparations.

(POISON)
LOVAGE, WATER

Œnanthe fistulosa (LINN.)
N.O. Umbelliferæ

Water Lovage is closely allied to Hemlock Water Dropwort (*Œnanthe crocata*, Linn.), and is by no means to be regarded as an edible plant. All the species of Water Dropwort are regarded as poisonous, and the Hemlock Water Dropwort should not be allowed to grow in places where cattle are kept, as instances are numerous in which cows have been poisoned by eating the roots, and it is equally poisonous to horses.

The genus *Œnanthe* is scattered throughout the whole of the Northern Hemisphere, but are rare in America; some of them are to be met with in Britain, and certain of them are very poisonous. *Œ. crocata* has been used with beneficial effect in certain skin-diseases; also in the form of poultices to ulcers, etc., as well as for the purpose of poisoning rats and moles.

See DROPWORT

LOVE LIES BLEEDING. *See* AMARANTHS

LUCERNE

Medicago sativa
N.O. Papilionaceæ

Synonyms. Purple Medicle. Cultivated Lucern
Part Used. Whole herb in flower
Habitat. Originally Medea, then old Spain, Italy, France; and cultivated in Persia and Peru

¶ *Description*. A deep-rooting perennial plant with numerous small clover-like spikes of blue or violet flowers of upright growth. Its herbage is green, succulent, and being an early crop is in a sense of some value as an agricultural plant. It yields two rather abundant green crops in the year – of a quality greatly relished by horses and cattle – it fattens them quickly and was much esteemed for increasing the milk of cows. One of the objections to growing it as a crop is the three to four years required before it attains full growth. When this plant is found in Britain growing wild it is merely an escape from cultivation. It may possibly have been a native of Europe; it is of great antiquity, having been imported into Greece from the East, after Darius had discovered it in Medea, hence its name. It is referred to by Roman writers, and is cultivated in Persia and Peru, where it is mown all the year round. It first came into notice in 1757 in Britain. Its chief characteristics are: herb, 1½ to 2 feet high; peduncled racemed; legumes contorted, twisted spirally, hairy; stem upright, smooth; leaves trifoliate; flowers in thick spikes, corolla purple.

To increase weight, an infusion of 1 oz. to the pint is given in cupful doses.

The root of Lucerne has sometimes been found as an adulterant of Belladonna root.

LUNGWORT

Sticta pulmonaria (LINN.)
N.O. Lichenes

Synonyms. Jerusalem Cowslip. Oak Lungs. Lung Moss
Part Used. Herb

Lungwort, a member of the Borage tribe, is found in woods and thickets, but is not common, and is by some only regarded as an escape from gardens, where it is cultivated now mostly for the sake of its ornamental leaves, which are curiously spotted with white.

¶ *Description.* The stem grows about a foot high, bearing rough, alternate, egg-shaped leaves, the lower ones stalked, and the flowers in a terminal inflorescence, red before expanding and pale purple when fully open.

The leaves of this plant, which are the part that has been used in medicine, have no peculiar smell, but when fresh have a slight astringent and mucilaginous taste, hence they have been supposed to be demulcent and pectoral, and have been used in coughs and lung catarrhs in the form of an infusion.

Its popular and Latin names seem to have been derived from the speckled appearance of the leaves resembling that of the lungs, and their use in former days was partly founded on the doctrine of signatures.

The Lungwort sold by druggists to-day is not this species, but a Moss, known also as Oak Lungs and Lung Moss.

The Lungwort formerly held a place in almost every garden, under the name of 'Jerusalem Cowslip'; and it was held in great esteem for its reputed medicinal qualities in diseases of the lungs.

Sir J. E. Smith says that

'every part of the plant is mucilaginous, but its reputation for coughs arose not from this circumstance, but from the speckled appearance of the leaves, resembling the lungs!'

¶ *Medicinal Action and Uses.* An infusion of 1 teaspoonful of the dried herb to a cup of boiling water is taken several times a day for subduing inflammation, and for its healing effect in pulmonary complaints.

Fluid extract, ½ to 1 drachm.

LUPINS

N.O. Leguminosæ

Synonyms. (*French*) Lupin. (*German*) Wolfsbohne
Parts Used. Seeds, herb

The *Lupinus* are a large genus of handsome plants, represented in Europe, Asia and North and South America, the poisonous properties of which are apparently very irregularly and unequally distributed.

A number of the species are cultivated only as ornamental plants, but others are grown for fodder, and if not over-fed, are found highly nutritive and wholesome. If the seeds of certain species are eaten in a more or less mature condition, poisoning is liable to occur, great numbers of animals sometimes being affected. These poisoning accidents have occurred in Europe and in the United States.

The species best known – as fodder – is the WHITE LUPIN of cultivation, *Lupinus albus* (Linn.) (French, *Lupin*; German, *Wolfs-bohne*), native of Southern Europe and adjacent Asia, a plant of about 2 feet high, with leaves cut palmately into five or seven divisions, 1 to 2 inches long, smooth above, and white, hairy, beneath. The flowers are in terminal racemes, on short footstalks, white and rather large, the pod 3 to 4 inches long, flattish, containing three to six white, circular, flattened seeds, which have a bitter taste.

¶ *History.* It is probably of Egyptian or East Mediterranean origin, and has been cultivated since the days of the ancient Egyptians. It is now very extensively used in Italy and Sicily, for forage, for ploughing-in to enrich the land, and for its seeds.

John Parkinson attributed wonderful virtues to the plant.

Many women, he says 'doe use the meale of Lupines mingled with the gall of a goate and some juyce of Lemons to make into a forme of a soft ointment.' He says that the burning of Lupin seeds drives away gnats.

Culpepper says they are governed by Mars in Ares:

'The seeds, somewhat bitter in taste, opening and cleansing, good to destroy worms. Outwardly they are used against deformities of the skin, scabby ulcers, scald heads, and other cutaneous distempers.'

This Lupin was cultivated by the Romans as an article of food. Pliny says:

'No kind of fodder is more wholesome and light of digestion than the White Lupine, when eaten dry. If taken commonly at meals, it will contribute a fresh colour and a cheerful countenance.'

Virgil, however, Dr. Fernie tells us (*Herbal Simples*, 1897), designated it '*tristis Lupinus*,' the sad Lupine. Dr. Fernie further states:

'The seeds were used as pieces of money by Roman actors in their plays and comedies, whence came the saying "nummus lupinus" – a spurious bit of money.'

The YELLOW LUPIN, also a native of Southern Europe and Western Asia, is called *Lupin luteus* from its yellow flowers. The BLUE-FLOWERED SPECIES of the North-eastern United States is *Lupinus perennis* (Linn.), the WILD or BLUE BEAN. In the Western United and southward into the Andes, the species are very numerous.

¶ *Cultivation.* If grown from seed, Lupins do not often come true to type, but if propagated, they will remain true. They must be isolated, owing to insects which might cross the pollen.

Lupins cross readily, hence isolation for propagation is absolutely necessary.

To intensify their colouring, sulphate of ammonia and sulphate of iron may both be employed.

Climatic conditions also more or less affect their colouring.

In a recent note in *The Western Gazette* (May 18, 1923) Lupins were spoken of as probably the best crop for light land, such as the poor land on the Suffolk coast, where Lupin growing is extending, as also on similar land in the northern part of Nottinghamshire.

In Suffolk the Blue Lupin is the local variety, and anyone travelling through that country in July will see whole fields devoted to it.

The great value of the plant lies in its capacity for growing luxuriantly on land which is so light and sandy that hardly anything else will thrive. Being a leguminous crop, it assimilates the free nitrogen of the air, greatly enriching the soil; and on light land it is probably quite the best plant we have for green manuring.

¶ *Constituents.* The bitter principle Lupinin is a glucoside occurring in yellowish needles. On boiling with dilute acids, it is decomposed into Lupigenin and a fermentable glucose.

Willstatter described the following alkaloids as occurring in the different species: Lupinine, a crystalline powder and Lupinidine, a syrupy liquid in LUPINUS LUTEUS and L. NIGER. Lupanine in L. ALBUS, L. ANGUSTIFOLIUS and L. PERENNIS, a pale yellow, syrupy fluid of an intensely bitter taste. E. Schmidt affirmed that the alkaloid of the seeds of *L. albus* is not the same as that of the herbage. A carbohydrate analogous to dextrin has been discovered in *L. luteus*.

According to Schwartz (1906) the seeds of LUPINUS ARABICUS contain a crystalline substance to which he gave the name of Magolan, which is a useful remedy in diabetes mellitus.

¶ *Medicinal Action and Uses.* The bruised seeds of White Lupine, after soaking in water, are sometimes used as an external application to ulcers, etc., and internally are said to be anthelmintic, diuretic and emmenagogue.

In 1917 a 'Lupin' banquet was given in Hamburg at a botanical gathering, at which a German Professor, Dr. Thoms, described the multifarious uses to which the Lupin might be put. At a table covered with a tablecloth of Lupin fibre, Lupin soup was served; after the soup came Lupin beefsteak, roasted in Lupin oil and seasoned with Lupin extract, then bread containing 20 per cent. of Lupin, Lupin margarine and cheese of Lupin albumen, and finally Lupin liqueur and Lupin coffee. Lupin soap served for washing the hands, while Lupin-fibre paper and envelopes with Lupin adhesive were available for writing.

¶ *Other Species.*

L. arboreus (the Tree Lupin), from California and Oregon, will, when well trained, produce a branching stem several feet in height that will live through four or five years, forming a trunk of light soft wood of the thickness of a man's arm.

L. polyphyllus and a few allied species from the same country are tall, erect, herbaceous perennials with very handsome richly-coloured spikes of flowers, which have become permanent inmates of our gardens.

MACE
Myristica fragrans (HONK.)
N.O. Myristicaceæ

Synonyms. Arillus Myristicæ. Myristica officinalis. Myristica moschata. Macis. Muscadier

Part Used. The dried arillus of the fruit or nutmeg

Habitat. Moluccas and Bandy Islands, New Guinea, West Indies, etc.

¶ *History.* The name is derived from a mediæval word for 'nut,' meaning 'suitable for an ointment.' The tree is a small evergreen, not more than 40 feet in height, with smooth, greyish-brown bark, green on the younger branches. The alternate leaves are oblong-ovate, acute, entire, smooth, and dark-green. The flowers are very small and unisexual. The fruits, smooth and yellow, resemble a pear grooved by a longitudinal furrow and contain a single erect seed about 1¼ inch long, the nucleus being the wrinkled 'nutmeg,' and the fleshy, irregular covering, scarlet when fresh and drying yellow and brittle, the 'mace.'

The principal harvest at Bencoolen is usually in the autumn, the smaller one in early summer. The fruits, which split open when ripe, are gathered with a long-handled hook and the products are separated. The mace when dried is often sprinkled with salt water to preserve it. If packed too moist it breeds worms.

Most of the supply comes from the Banda Islands by way of Java and Sumatra.

The 'blades,' 'bands,' or flattened, lobed pieces are about 25 mm. long, smooth, irregular, translucent, brittle or flexible, and if scratched or pressed exude an orange-coloured oil.

An inferior Mace is obtained from the long nutmeg, dark and very brittle and lacking the fragrant odour and aromatic taste of the official variety.

The medicinal properties resemble those of nutmeg, but it is principally used as a condiment.

¶ *Constituents.* The principal constituent is 7 to 9 per cent. of a volatile oil, protein, gum, resins, sugar and fixed oil. The volatile oil contains much pinene, and a little myristicin, which must be distinguished from the glyceride of myristic acid.

Two odorous fixed oils have been separated, a yellow one insoluble in boiling alcohol but soluble in ether, and a red one soluble in either.

The powder is brown or buff, orange-tinted.

Oil of Mace is practically identical with distilled oil of nutmeg or Nutmeg Butter.

¶ *Medicinal Action and Uses.* A flavouring agent, stimulant and tonic.

Both Mace and Nutmeg help digestion in stomachic weakness, but if used to excess may cause over-excitement. They increase circulation and animal heat. They have been employed in pestilential and putrid fevers, and with other substances in intermittent fevers, and enter into the composition of many French medicaments.

¶ *Dosage.* 5 to 20 grains.

¶ *Other Species.*

Myristica malabarica, yielding Bombay Mace, which is deficient in odour and taste. Several chemical tests provide means of detecting the substitution. It yields a much higher percentage of ether-soluble matter.

M. argentea, yielding Macassar Mace, which is of a dull brown colour with an odour like sassafras. It is too acrid for medicinal use.

M. otoba, yielding a Mace which, incorporated with fat, is used in gout and rheumatism.

See NUTMEG

MADDER
Rubia tinctorum (LINN.)
N.O. Rubiaceæ

Synonyms. Krapp. Dyer's Madder. Robbia (French) Garance

Part Used. Root

Habitat. Southern Europe, including southern Britain, and Mediterranean countries

¶ *Description.* The stalks of the Madder are so weak that they often lie along the ground, preventing the plant from rising to its maximum height of 8 feet. The stalks are prickly, and the whorls of leaves at the joints have spines along the midrib on the underside, a feature that the French turn to advantage by using them for polishing metal-work.

The herb is used as fodder for animals.

The flower-shoots spring from the joints in pairs, the loose spikes of yellow, starry flowers blooming only in the second or third year, in June.

The thick, fleshy fibres that compose the perennial are about ½ inch thick, and from their joining, or head, side roots run under the surface of the ground for some distance, sending up shoots. The main and side-roots are dried separately, their products being regarded as different, that of a young, parent root being the best. They are covered with a blackish rind, beneath which they are reddish, with a pale yellow pith. In France, after drying, the outer layer is threshed off and powdered and packed separately as an inferior product called *mall*. The stripped roots are again heated – excepting in hot climates – then powdered, and milled three times. The final product is packed in casks, which in Holland are stamped by sworn assayers.

The best European Madder is Dutch, but that from Smyrna is said to be even finer. The Turkey-red and other shades are adjective dyes, different mordants bringing many shades of red, pink, lilac, purple, brown, orange and black.

As a dye it colours milk, urine and bones, so that experiments in the growth of bones can be conducted with its help.

Rubia tinctoria differs very slightly from the Wild Madder or *R. peregrina*, and may be merely a variety.

¶ *Constituents*. The root contains rubian, rubiadin, ruberythric acid, purpurin, tannin, sugar and especially *alizarin*. *Pseudopurpurin* yields the orange dye and *xanthopurpurin* the yellow. The astringent taste, slight odour and red colour, are imparted to water or alcohol.

The most interesting of the colouring substances is the alizarin, and this is now termed dihydroscyanthraquinone. This occurs as orange-red crystals, almost insoluble in water, but readily soluble in alcohol, ether, the fixed oils and alkaline solutions. The alcoholic and aqueous solutions are rose-coloured, the ethereal, golden-yellow; the alkaline, violet and blue when concentrated, but violet red when sufficiently diluted. A beautiful rose-coloured lake is produced by precipitating a mixture of the solutions of alizarin and alum.

Alizarin was recognized by Græbe and Liebermann, in 1868, as a derivative of anthracene – a hydrocarbon contained in coal-tar, and in the same year they elaborated a method for preparing it commercially from anthracene. Upon this arose rapidly a great chemical industry, and the cultivation of Madder has, of course, decreased correspondingly until it may be said that the coal-tar products have entirely displaced the natural ones.

¶ *Medicinal Action and Uses*. Although not as a general rule employed medicinally, Madder has been reputed as effectual in amenorrhœa, dropsy and jaundice.

When taken into the stomach it imparts a red colour to the milk and urine, and to the bones of animals without sensibly affecting any other tissue. The effect is observed most quickly in the bones of young animals and in those nearest to the heart. Under the impression that it might effect some change in the nervous system, it has been prescribed in rachitis (rickets), but without noticeable favourable results. Dosage, ⅛ drachm three or four times daily.

¶ *Other Species*.

R. sylvestris, a nearly allied species, has been used as a remedy in liver diseases, jaundice, gall and spleen complaints. The root, leaves and seeds are all reputed as medicinally active.

R. cordifolia, or Bengal Madder, of India, yields the inferior dye called Munjeet.

In France it is thought that the root of *Galium cruciatum*, or Crosswort, might replace that of Madder.

MAGNOLIA

Magnolia acuminata
Magnolia virginiana (LINN.)
N.O. Magnoliaceæ

Synonyms. Cucumber Tree. Magnoliæ cortex. Blue Magnolia. Swamp Sassafras. Magnolia Tripetata

Parts Used. Bark of stem and root

Habitat. North America

¶ *Description*. The genus is named in commemoration of Pierre Magnol, a famous professor of medicine and botany of Montpellier in the early eighteenth century. All its members are handsome, with luxuriant foliage and rich flowers. The leaves of *Magnolia acuminata* are oval, about 6 inches long by 3 broad, and slightly hairy below, with a diameter of 6 inches, and the fruit or cone, about 3 inches long, resembles a small cucumber.

It is a large tree, reaching a height of 80 or more feet and a diameter of 3 to 5 feet, but only grows to about 16 feet in England. The wood is finely grained, taking a brilliant polish, and in its colour resembles that of the tulip or poplar, but it is less durable. It is sometimes used for large canoes and house interiors.

The bark of the young wood is curved or quilled, fissured outside, with occasional warts, and orange-brown in colour, being whitish and smooth within and the fracture short except for inner fibres. The older bark without the corky layer is brownish or whitish and fibrous. Drying and age cause the loss of its volatile, aromatic property.

¶ *Constituents.* The bark has no astringency. The tonic properties are found in varying degree in several species.

¶ *Medicinal Action and Uses.* A mild diaphoretic, tonic, and aromatic stimulant. It is used in rheumatism and malaria and is contra-indicated in inflammatory symptoms. In the Alleghany districts the *cones* are steeped in spirits to make a tonic tincture.

A warm infusion is laxative and sudorific, a cold one being antiperiodic and mildly tonic.

¶ *Dosage.* Fluid Extract. Frequent doses of ½ to 1 drachm, or the infusion in wineglassful doses.

¶ *Other Species.*
Both *M. virginiana* and *M. tripetala* were recognized as official with *M. acuminata.*

M. virginiana, or *M. glauca*, White Laurel, Beaver Tree, Swamp Sassafras, White Bay, Sweet Bay, Small or Laurel Magnolia, or Sweet Magnolia, is much used by beavers, who favour it both as food and building material. The light wood has no commercial use.

The bark and seed cones are bitter and aromatic, used as tonics, and in similar ways to *M. acuminata.* The leaves yield a green, volatile oil with a more pleasant odour than fennel or anise. There is probably also a bitter glucosidal principle.

M. tripetala, Umbrella Tree or Umbrella Magnolia. The fruit yields a neutral crystalline principle, Magnolin.

The bark, if chewed as a substitute for tobacco, is said to cure the habit.

MAIDENHAIR. *See* FERNS

MALABAR NUT

Adhatoda vasica (NEES)
N.O. Acanthaceæ

Synonyms. Justicia adhatoda (Linn.). Arusa. Adulsa Bakas
Parts Used. Leaves, flowers, fruit, root
Habitat. India

¶ *Description.* A common plant in India, the fresh leaves are 4 to 6 inches long, 2 inches wide, lanceolate entire, shortly petiolate, when dried dull brownish green, they become lighter when powdered, taste bitter and smell like strong tea. Its wood is soft and makes excellent charcoal for gunpowder.

¶ *Constituents.* The leaves contain a bitter crystalline alkaloid Vasicine, and an organic adhatodic acid, another alkaloid and an odorous volatile principle.

¶ *Medicinal Action and Uses.* In India the flowers, leaves, root and specially the fruit are considered a valuable antispasmodic for asthma and intermittent fever; used with success also as an expectorant in cases of chronic bronchitis and phthisis; the leaves are dried and smoked as cigarettes to relieve asthma. Large doses irritate the alimentary canal and cause diarrhœa and vomiting.

Adhatodic acid is believed to exert a strong poisoning influence upon the lower forms of animals and vegetable life, though non-poisonous to the higher animals.

¶ *Dosages.* Liquid extract of Adhatoda, 20 to 60 minims. The freshly expressed juice, 1 to 4 fluid drachms. Tincture from ½ to 1 fluid drachm.

MALE FERN. *See* FERNS

MALLOWS

N.O. Malvaceæ

The large and important family of Mallows are most abundant in the tropical region, where they form a large proportion of the vegetation; towards the poles they gradually decrease in number. Lindley states that about a thousand species had been discovered, all of which not only contain much mucilage, but are totally devoid of unwholesome properties. Besides the medicinal virtues of so many species, some are employed as food; the bark of others affords a substitute for hemp; the cotton of commerce is obtained from the seed vessels of yet other species, and many ornamental garden flowers are also members of this group, the Hibiscus and our familiar Hollyhock among the number.

MALLOW, MARSH   Althæa officinalis (LINN.)

Synonyms. Mallards. Mauls. Schloss Tea. Cheeses. Mortification Root
(*French*) Guimauve
Parts Used. Leaves, root, flowers
Habitat. Marsh Mallow is a native of most countries of Europe, from Denmark southward. It grows in salt marshes, in damp meadows, by the sides of ditches, by the
sea and on the banks of tidal rivers
    In this country it is local, but occurs in most of the maritime counties in the south
of England, ranging as far north as Lincolnshire. In Scotland it has been introduced

¶ *Description.* The stems, which die down in the autumn, are erect, 3 to 4 feet high, simple, or putting out only a few lateral branches. The leaves, shortly petioled, are roundish, ovate-cordate, 2 to 3 inches long, and about 1¼ inch broad, entire or three to five lobed, irregularly toothed at the margin, and thick. They are soft and velvety on both sides, due to a dense covering of stellate hairs. The flowers are shaped like those of the common Mallow, but are smaller and of a pale colour, and are either axillary, or in panicles, more often the latter.

The stamens are united into a tube, the anthers, kidney-shaped and one-celled. The flowers are in bloom during August and September, and are followed, as in other species of this order, by the flat, round fruit called popularly 'cheeses.'

The common Mallow is frequently called by country people, 'Marsh Mallow,' but the true Marsh Mallow is distinguished from all the other Mallows growing in Britain, by the numerous divisions of the outer calyx (six to nine cleft), by the hoary down which thickly clothes the stems, and foliage, and by the numerous panicles of blush-coloured flowers, paler than the Common Mallow.

The roots are perennial, thick, long and tapering, very tough and pliant, whitish-yellow outside, white and fibrous within.

The whole plant, particularly the root, abounds with a mild mucilage, which is emollient to a much greater degree than the common Mallow. The generic name, *Althæa*, is derived from the Greek, *altho* (to cure), from its healing properties. The name of the order, Malvaceæ, is derived from the Greek, *malake* (soft), from the special qualities of the Mallows in softening and healing.

Most of the Mallows have been used as food, and are mentioned by early classic writers in this connexion. Mallow was an esculent vegetable among the Romans, a dish of Marsh Mallow was one of their delicacies.

The Chinese use some sort of Mallow in their food, and Prosper Alpinus stated (in 1592) that a plant of the Mallow kind was eaten by the Egyptians. Many of the poorer inhabitants of Syria, especially the Fellahs, Greeks and Armenians, subsist for weeks on herbs, of which Marsh Mallow is one of the most common. When boiled first and fried with onions and butter, the roots are said to form a palatable dish, and in times of scarcity consequent upon the failure of the crops, this plant, which fortunately grows there in great abundance, is much collected for food.

In Job xxx. 4 we read of Mallow being eaten in time of famine, but it is doubtful whether this was really a true mallow. Canon Tristram thinks it was some saline plant; perhaps the *Orache*, or Sea-Purslane.

Horace and Martial mention the laxative properties of the Marsh Mallow leaves and root, and Virgil tells us of the fondness of goats for the foliage of the Mallow.

Dioscorides extols it as a remedy, and in ancient days it was not only valued as a medicine, but was used, especially the Musk Mallow, to decorate the graves of friends.

Pliny said: 'Whosoever shall take a spoonful of the Mallows shall that day be free from all diseases that may come to him.' All Mallows contain abundant mucilage, and the Arab physicians in early times used the leaves as a poultice to suppress inflammation.

Preparations of Marsh Mallow, on account of their soothing qualities, are still much used by country people for inflammation, outwardly and inwardly, and are used for lozenge-making. French druggists and English sweetmeat-makers prepare a confectionary paste (*Pâté de Guimauve*) from the roots of Marsh Mallow, which is emollient and soothing to a sore chest, and valuable in coughs and hoarseness. The 'Marsh Mallows' usually sold by confectioners here are a mixture of flour, gum, egg-albumin, etc., and contain no mallow.

In France, the young tops and tender leaves of Marsh Mallow are eaten uncooked, in spring salads, for their property in stimulating the kidneys, a syrup being made from the roots for the same purpose.

¶ *Cultivation.* Marsh Mallow used always to be cultivated in gardens on account of its medicinal qualities. It is said to have been introduced by the Romans.

It can be raised from seed, sown in spring, but cuttings will do well, and offsets of the root, carefully divided in autumn, when the stalks decay, are satisfactory, and will grow of their own accord.

Plant about 2 feet apart. It will thrive in any soil or situation, but grows larger in moist than in dry land, and could well be cultivated on unused ground in damp localities near ditches or streams.

¶ *Parts Used*. Leaves, root and flowers. The leaves are picked in August, when the flowers are just coming into bloom. They should be stripped off singly and gathered only on a fine day, in the morning, after the dew has been dried off by the sun.

¶ *Constituents*. Marsh Mallow contains starch, mucilage, pectin, oil, sugar, asparagin, phosphate of lime, glutinous matter and cellulose.

¶ *Medicinal Action and Uses*. The great demulcent and emollient properties of Marsh Mallow make it useful in inflammation and irritation of the alimentary canal, and of the urinary and respiratory organs. The dry roots boiled in water give out half their weight of a gummy matter like starch. Decoctions of the plant, especially of the root, are very useful where the natural mucus has been abraded from the coats of the intestines, The decoction can be made by adding 5 pints of water to ¼ lb. of dried root, boiling down to 3 pints and straining: it should not be made too thick and viscid. It is excellent in painful complaints of the urinary organs, exerting a relaxing effect upon the passages, as well as acting curatively. This decoction is also effective in curing bruises, sprains or any ache in the muscles or sinews. In hæmorrhage from the urinary organs and in dysentery, it has been recommended to use the powdered root boiled in milk. The action of Marsh Mallow root upon the bowels is unaccompanied by any astringency.

Boiled in wine or milk, Marsh Mallow will relieve diseases of the chest, constituting a popular remedy for coughs, bronchitis, whooping-cough, etc., generally in combination with other remedies. It is frequently given in the form of a syrup, which is best adapted to infants and children.

RECIPES
Marsh Mallow Water

'Soak one ounce of marsh mallow roots in a little cold water for half an hour; peel off the bark, or skin; cut up the roots into small shavings, and put them into a jug to stand for a couple of hours; the decoction must be drunk tepid, and may be sweetened with honey or sugar-candy, and flavoured with orange-flower water, or with orange-juice. Marshmallow water may be used with good effect in all cases of inveterate coughs, catarrhs, etc.' (Francatelli's *Cook's Guide*.)

For Gravel, etc.

'Put the flower and plant (all but the root) of Marsh Mallows in a jug, pour boiling water, cover with a cloth, let it stand three hours – make it strong. If used for gravel or irritation of the kidney, take ½ pint as a Tea daily for four days, then stop a few days, then go on again. A teaspoonful of gin may be added *when there is no tendency to inflammation*.' (From a family recipe-book.)

The powdered or crushed fresh roots make a good poultice that will remove the most obstinate inflammation and prevent mortification. Its efficacy in this direction has earned for it the name of Mortification Root. Slippery Elm may be added with advantage, and the poultice should be applied to the part as hot as can be borne and renewed when dry. An infusion of 1 oz. of leaves to a pint of boiling water is also taken frequently in wineglassful doses. This infusion is good for bathing inflamed eyes.

An ointment made from Marsh Mallow has also a popular reputation, but it is stated that a poultice made of the fresh root, with the addition of a little white bread, proves more serviceable when applied externally than the ointment. The fresh leaves, steeped in hot water and applied to the affected parts as poultices, also reduce inflammation, and bruised and rubbed upon any place stung by wasps or bees take away the pain, inflammation and swelling. Pliny stated that the green leaves, beaten with nitre and applied, drew out thorns and prickles in the flesh.

The flowers, boiled in oil and water, with a little honey and alum, have proved good as a gargle for sore throats. In France, they form one of the ingredients of the *Tisane de quatre fleurs*, a pleasant remedy for colds.

¶ *Preparations and Dosage*. Fluid extract leaves, ½ to 2 drachms.

MALLOW, BLUE   Malva sylvestris (LINN.)

Synonym. Common Mallow
Parts Used. Flowers, leaves

The Common or Blue Mallow is a robust plant 3 or 4 feet high, growing freely in field, hedgerows and on waste ground. Its stem is round, thick and strong, the leaves stalked, roundish, five to seven lobed, downy, with stellate hairs and the veins prominent on the underside. The flowers are showy, bright mauve-purple, with dark veins. When they first expand in June, the plant is handsome, but as the summer advances, the leaves lose their deep green colour and the stems assume a ragged appearance.

Cattle do not appear to be fond of this plant, every part of which abounds with a mild mucilage.

¶ *Medicinal Action and Uses.* The use of this species of Mallow has been much superseded by Marsh Mallow, which possesses its valuable properties in a superior degree, but it is still a favourite remedy with country people where Marsh Mallow is not obtainable. The roots are not considered of much value compared with those of the Marsh Mallow, and as a rule the leaves and flowers are used only, mainly externally in fomentations and poultices. The infusion has been a popular remedy for coughs and colds, but the internal use of the leaves has fallen into disuse, giving place to Marsh Mallow root, though they are still employed as a decoction for injection, which, made strong, cures strangury and gravel.

The foliage when boiled, forms a wholesome vegetable. The seeds, or 'cheeses,' are also edible.

A tincture of the flowers, which turn blue in fading, forms a very delicate test for alkalis.

The flowers were used formerly on May Day by country people for strewing before their doors and weaving into garlands.

¶ *Preparation and Dosage.* Fluid extract, ¼ to 2 drachms.

MALLOW, MUSK

Malva meschata

Parts Used. Leaves, root, flowers

The Musk Mallow is not an uncommon plant in dry pastures and in hedgerows. It grows 2 feet high, with round, thick, erect stems, somewhat hairy, often purple-spotted. The foliage is light-green, the lower leaves kidney-shaped, five to seven lobed, those on the stem finely divided into numerous narrow segments. The handsome rose-coloured flowers are three times the size of the Common Mallow, crowded towards the summit of the stem. It emits from its leaves a faint, musky odour, especially in warm weather, or when drawn through the hand.

This Mallow is not common in Kent and other counties, but in Essex it is very abundant.

The root is white and is the part used. It has the same virtues as the Common Mallow, but is not quite as strong, and the leaves have similar properties.

MALLOW, DWARF

Malva rotundifolia

Part Used. Leaves

Habitat. The Dwarf Mallow is self-fertilizing, while the other kinds are insect-visited. It is common in most parts of Europe, including Britain, and in Western Asia. In Egypt, especially upon the banks of the Nile, it is extensively cultivated and used by the natives as a pot-herb

The Dwarf Mallow, a smaller variety than any of the other wild Mallows, is easily distinguishable by its prostrate stems and pale lilac flowers. Its leaves are heart-shaped and have also sometimes been used medicinally.

MALLOW, TREE SEA

Lavatera arborea

Part Used. Herb

The velvety leaves of the Sea Tree Mallow, a tall, handsome plant growing 5 or 6 feet high, on sea cliffs, on many parts of the coast, are used for sprains, steeped in hot water and laid on the injured spot.

See HOLLYHOCK.

MANACA

Brunfelsia hopeana (HOOK.)
N.O. Solanaceæ

Synonyms. Vegetable Mercury. Franciscea uniflora
Parts Used. Root, stem
Habitat. South America, West Indies, Brazil

¶ *Description.* Small trees, a name often given to the genus *Solanaceæ*, in honour of Brunfels, the German herbalist of the sixteenth century. The genus is known by a five-cleft calyx with rounded lobes, bilabiate in æstivation, four fertile and anthers confluent at the top, where it is divided into two stigmatic lobes, capsules fleshy or leathery, more rarely indehiscent and drupe-like, several large seeds embedded in pulp. Flowers large and some very fragrant, blue or white. In commerce the pieces of root vary from a few inches to 1 foot long, ¼ inch in diameter, very tough and woody, centre yellow, with a very thin outer bark; the stem has a small yellow pith.

¶ *Constituents*. Alkaloid Mannacine and a peculiar substance fluorescent and supposed to be identical with gelseminic acid.

¶ *Medicinal Action and Uses*. From experiments made on animals, Manaca acts on the spinal cord, stimulating, then abolishing the activities of the motor centres; stimulating specially the kidneys and all the other glands. In large doses it causes lassitude,

perspiration and loose greenish discharges. It is highly recommended in the treatment of syphilis and chronic rheumatism of an arthritic nature.

¶ *Dosage*. Fluid extract, 10 to 30 minims three times daily.

¶ *Other Species*. *Franciscea uniflora* is the Brazilian name for Manaca, largely used for syphilitic complaints; root and leaves of this are used. It is a bitter purgative emetic, and in large doses poisonous.

MANDIOCA

Manihot utilissima
N.O. Euphorbiaceæ

Synonyms. Manioc. Yuca. Cassava. Farinha de Mandioca

Another food plant of enormous importance to tropical America in the present as well as in the past is *Manihot utilissima*, otherwise known as Manioc, Mandioca, or Yuca, from the tuberous root of which Cassava is prepared. It was, in fact, the plant of chief economic importance to the tribes of tropical South America east of the Andes, and its cultivation spread to the valley of Colombia, the Isthmus of Panama, and the West Indian Islands. Mandioca is a shrubby plant, with brittle stems, 6 feet to 8 feet high, large palmate leaves and green flowers. In the ordinary variety the tubers weigh up to 30 lb., and the juice, owing to the presence of hydrocyanic acid, is poisonous. A smaller non-poisonous variety is also found.

The true native method of preparing it for food, followed with slight variation throughout the Southern Continent and islands, is as follows: The root is sliced, and grated on a board set with small stones, washed in water, and packed into a long cylindrical 'press' of basketwork with a loop at either end. This press is so made that when it is suspended by one loop and a weight applied to the other, it increases in length and decreases in diameter, and the juice is squeezed from the contents, and falls into a vessel placed below. The paste is then spread in thin layers on griddles of pottery or slate and cooked over a fire. The root is also eaten roasted, especially the sweet variety, though even in the case of the poisonous tuber, the unwholesome

element is volatized by cooking. For this reason the juice is preserved and boiled, when it becomes wholesome, and is used as liquor for soup. If further inspissated by boiling, and sweetened in the sun, it is known as casareep, and is employed as a flavouring, especially in British Guiana, where it appears in almost every dish, and in the West Indies, where it is the foundation of the celebrated pepper pot. Casareep is highly antiseptic, and by its aid meat can be kept fresh for quite a long time.

An intoxicating drink can also be prepared from the Mandioca; the early West Indians fermented the sliced and grated tuber in water, adding a little chewed root or grated batata to assist the process. In British Guiana and North Brazil a similar process is still used; the chewed root is fermented in large wooden troughs of water, and the liquor is stored in gourds. At the present time Cassava flour, or *farinha de Mandioca*, is an important article of food throughout South America, and could be used much more extensively in Europe. The true starch of the Mandioca is known to commerce as Brazilian arrowroot, and this, after heating on hot plates and stirring with an iron rod, becomes tapioca. The cultivation is not difficult, the plant is propagated by cuttings, and the produce is at least six times that of wheat.

Sweet Cassava is nourishing, light and agreeable as a food for invalids, and infants during weaning.

See TAPIOCA.

MANDRAKE

Atropa mandragora
N.O. Solanaceæ

Synonyms. Mandragora. Satan's Apple
Part Used. Herb
Habitat. The Mandrake, the object of so many strange superstitions, is a native of Southern Europe and the Levant, but will grow here in gardens if given a warm situation, though otherwise it may not survive severe winters. It was cultivated in England in 1562 by Turner, the author of the *Niewe Herball*

The name *Mandragora* is derived from two Greek words implying 'hurtful to cattle.' The Arabs call it 'Satan's apple.'

¶ *Description*. It has a large, brown root, somewhat like a parsnip, running 3 or 4 feet deep into the ground, sometimes single and sometimes divided into two or three branches. Immediately from the crown of the root arise several large, dark-green leaves, which at first stand erect, but when grown to full size – a foot or more in length and 4 or 5 inches in width – spread open and lie upon the ground. They are sharp pointed at the apex and of a foetid odour. From among these leaves spring the flowers, each on a separate foot-stalk, 3 or 4 inches high. They are somewhat of the shape and size of a primrose, the corolla bell-shaped, cut into five spreading segments, of a whitish colour, somewhat tinged with purple. They are succeeded by a smooth, round fruit, about as large as a small apple, of a deep yellow colour when ripe, full of pulp and with a strong, apple-like scent.

¶ *Medicinal Action and Uses.* The leaves are quite harmless and cooling, and have been used for ointments and other external application. Boiled in milk and used as a poultice, they were employed by Boerhaave as an application to indolent ulcers.

The fresh root operates very powerfully as an emetic and purgative. The dried bark of the root was used also as a rough emetic.

Mandrake was much used by the Ancients, who considered it an anodyne and soporific. In large doses it is said to excite delirium and madness. They used it for procuring rest and sleep in continued pain, also in melancholy, convulsions, rheumatic pains and scrofulous tumours. They mostly employed the bark of the root, either expressing the juice or infusing it in wine or water. The root finely scraped into a pulp and mixed with brandy was said to be efficacious in chronic rheumatism.

Mandrake was used in Pliny's days as an anæsthetic for operations, a piece of the root being given to the patient to chew before undergoing the operation. In small doses it was employed by the Ancients in maniacal cases.

A tincture is used in homœopathy to-day, made from the fresh plant.

Among the old Anglo-Saxon herbals both Mandrake and periwinkle are endowed with mysterious powers against demoniacal possession. At the end of a description of the Mandrake in the *Herbarium of Apuleius* there is this prescription:

'For witlessness, that is devil sickness or demoniacal possession, take from the body of this said wort mandrake by the weight of three pennies, administer to drink in warm water as he may find most convenient – soon he will be healed.'

Bartholomew gives the old Mandrake legend in full, though he adds: 'It is so feynd of churles others of wytches.' He also refers to its use as an anæsthetic:

'the rind thereof medled with wine . . . gene to them to drink that shall be cut in their body, for they should slepe and not fele the sore knitting.'

Bartholomew gives two other beliefs about the Mandrake which are not found in any other English Herbal – namely, that while uprooting it the digger must beware of contrary winds, and that he must go on digging for it until sunset.

In the *Grete Herball* (printed by Peter Treveris in 1526) we find the first avowal of disbelief in the supposed powers of the Mandrake. Gerard also pours scorn on the Mandrake legend.

'There have been,' he says, 'many ridiculous tales brought up of this plant, whether of old wives or runnegate surgeons, or phisick mongers, I know not, all which dreames and old wives tales you shall from henceforth cast out your bookes of memorie.'

Parkinson says that if ivory is boiled with Mandrake root for six hours, the ivory will become so soft 'that it will take what form or impression you will give it.'

Josephus says that the Mandrake – which he calls *Baaras* – has but one virtue, that of expelling demons from sick persons, as the demons cannot bear either its smell or its presence. He even relates that it was certain death to touch this plant, except under certain circumstances which he details. (*Wars of the Jews*, book vii, cap. vi.)

The roots of the Mandrake are very nearly allied to Belladonna, both in external appearance and in structure. The plant is by modern botanists assigned to the same genus, though formerly was known as *Mandragora officinalis*, with varieties *M. vernalis* and *M. autumnalis*. According to Southall (*Organic Materia Medica*, 8th edition, revised by Ernest Mann, 1915), the root

'contains a mydriatic alkaloid, Mandragorine $(C_{17}H_{27}O_3N)$, which in spite of the name and formula which have been assigned to it, is probably identical with atropine or hyoscyamine.'

The roots of Mandrake were supposed to bear a resemblance to the human form, on account of their habit of forking into two and shooting on each side. In the old Herbals we find them frequently figured as a male with a long beard, and a female with a very bushy head of hair. Many weird superstitions collected round the Mandrake root. As an amulet, it was once placed on mantelpieces to avert misfortune and to bring prosperity and happiness to the house. Bryony roots were often cut into fancy shapes and passed off as Mandrake, being even trained to grow in moulds till they assumed the desired forms. In Henry VIII's time quaint little images made from Bryony roots, cut into the figure of a man, with grains of millet inserted into the face as eyes, fetched high prices. They were known as *puppettes* or *mammettes*, and were accredited with magical powers. Italian ladies were known to pay as much as thirty golden ducats for similar artificial Mandrakes.

Turner alludes to these 'puppettes and mammettes,' and says, 'they are so trymmed of crafty theves to mocke the poore people withall and to rob them both of theyr wit and theyr money.' But he adds:

'Of the apples of mandrake, if a man smell of them thei will make hym slepe and also if they be eaten. But they that smell to muche of the apples become dum . . . thys herbe diverse wayes taken is very jepardus for a man and may kill hym if he eat it or drynk it out of measure and have no remedy from it. . . . If mandragora be taken out of measure, by and by slepe ensueth and a great lousing of the streyngthe with a forgetfulness.'

The plant was fabled to grow under the gallows of murderers, and it was believed to be death to dig up the root, which was said to utter a shriek and terrible groans on being dug up, which none might hear and live. It was held, therefore, that he who would take up a plant of Mandrake should tie a dog to it for that purpose, who drawing it out would certainly perish, as the man would have done, had he attempted to dig it up in the ordinary manner.

There are many allusions to the Mandrake in ancient writers. From the earliest times a notion prevailed in the East that the Mandrake will remove sterility, and there is a reference to this belief in Genesis xxx. 14.

¶ *Cultivation.* Mandrake can be propagated by seeds, sown upon a bed of light earth, soon after they are ripe, when they are more sure to come up than if the sowing is left to the spring.

When the plants come up in the spring, they must be kept well watered through the summer and kept free from weeds. At the end of August they should be taken up carefully and transplanted where they are to remain. The soil should be light and deep, as the roots run far down – if too wet, they will rot in winter, if too near chalk or gravel, they will make little progress. Where the soil is good and they are not disturbed, these plants will grow to a large size in a few years, and will produce great quantities of flowers and fruit.

Culpepper tells us the Mandrake is governed by Mercury. The fruit has been accounted poisonous, but without cause. . . . The root formerly was supposed to have the human form, but it really resembles a carrot or parsnip.

See BELLADONNA.

MANDRAKE, AMERICAN

Podophyllum peltatum (LINN.)
N.O. Berberidaceæ

Synonyms. May Apple. Wild Lemon. Racoonberry. Duck's Foot. Hog Apple
Parts Used. Root, resin
Habitat. The American Mandrake is a small herb with a long, perennial, creeping rhizome, a native of many parts of North America, common in the eastern United States and Canada, growing there profusely in wet meadows and in damp, open woods

¶ *Description.* The root is composed of many thick tubers, fastened together by fleshy fibres which spread greatly underground, sending out many smaller fibres at the joints, which strike downward. The stems are solitary, mostly unbranched, 1 to 2 feet high, crowned with two large, smooth leaves, stalked, peltate in the middle like an umbrella, of the size of a hand, composed of five to seven wedge-shaped divisions, somewhat lobed and toothed at the apex. Between their foot-stalks, grows a solitary, drooping white flower, about 2 inches across, appearing in May. The odour of the flower is nauseous. When it falls off, the fruit that develops swells to the size and shape of the common rosehip, being 1 to 2 inches long. It is yellow in colour and pulpy. In taste it is sweet, though slightly acid and is edible. The leaves and roots are poisonous. The foliage and stems have been used as a pot-herb, but in some cases with fatal results.

The drug was well known to the North American Indians as an emetic and vermifuge. It was included in the British Pharmacopœia in 1864.

The Latin name is derived from *pous, podos* (a foot) and *phyllon* (a leaf), alluding to a fanciful resemblance in the palmate leaf to the foot of some web-footed aquatic bird. Hence one of the popular names of the plant – Duck's Foot.

¶ *Cultivation.* It grows in warm, sheltered spots, such as partially shaded borders, woods, and marshes, liking a light, loamy soil. It requires no other culture than to be kept clear of weeds, and is so hardy as to be seldom injured by frost.

Propagate (1) by sowing seeds, in sandy soil, planting out in the following spring or autumn; (2) by division of roots. It propagates so fast by its creeping roots that this mode of propagation is preferred. Every part of the root will grow. Divide either in autumn, when the leaves decay, or in spring, just before the roots begin to shoot, preferably the latter.

¶ *Part Used.* The dried rhizome, from which a resin is also extracted.

It must be carefully distinguished from English Mandrake (*Bryonia dioica*), which is sometimes offered as Mandrake root.

¶ *Constituents.* A neutral crystalline substance, podo-phyllotoxin, and an amorphous resin, podophylloresin, both of which are purgative. It also contains picro-podo-phyllin, a yellow colouring matter, quercetin, sugar, starch, fat, etc.

It yields about 3 per cent. of ash on incineration.

Podophyllum rhizome is said to be most active when it is beginning to shoot. It is used almost entirely in the form of podophyllum resin.

The resin is prepared by making a tincture of the rhizome, removing from this the greater part of the spirit by distillation and pouring the remaining liquor into water acidified with hydrochloric acid. By this means the resin is precipitated, and may be collected and dried.

¶ *Medicinal Action and Uses.* Antibilious, cathartic, hydragogue, purgative.

Podophyllum is a medicine of most extensive service; its greatest power lies in its action upon the liver and bowels. It is a gastro-intestinal irritant, a powerful hepatic and intestinal stimulant. In congested states of the liver, it is employed with the greatest benefit, and for all hepatic complaints it is eminently suitable, and the beneficial results can hardly be exaggerated.

In large doses it produces nausea and vomiting, and even inflammation of the stomach and intestines, which has been known to prove fatal. In moderate doses, it is a drastic purgative with some cholagogue action. Like many other hepatic stimulants, it does not increase the secretion of bile so much when it acts as a purgative.

Podophyllum is a powerful medicine, exercising an influence on every part of the system, stimulating the glands to healthy action. It is highly valuable in dropsy, biliousness, dyspepsia, liver and other disorders. Its most beneficial action is obtained by the use of small doses frequently given. In such circumstances, it acts admirably upon all the secretions, removing obstructions, and producing a healthy condition of all the organs in the system. In still smaller doses, it is a valuable remedy in skin diseases.

It may either be given in infusion, decoction, tincture or substance, but it is not to be given warm.

It is often employed in combination with other purgatives, such as colocynth, aloes or rhubarb, and also administered in pills, with extract of henbane or belladonna, to prevent griping.

Externally applied, the resin, of podophyllum acts as an irritant. If incautiously handled, it often produces conjunctivitis, and in America it has on this account, when dissolved in alcohol, been used as a counter-irritant.

¶ *Preparations and Dosages.* Powdered root, 5 to 30 grains. Fluid extract, 5 to 30 drops. Tincture root, 5 to 30 drops. Tincture resin, B.P., 5 to 15 drops. Solid extract, 1 to 5 grains. Podophyllum resin, ¼ to 1 grain.

¶ *Substitutes. Podophyllum Emodi* (Indian Podophyllum), a native of Northern India. The roots are much stouter, more knotty, and about twice as strong as the American. It is not identical with, nor should it be substituted for, the American rhizome. It contains twice as much podophyllotoxin, and in other respects exhibits differences. Indian podophyllum is official in India and the Eastern Colonies, where it is used in place of ordinary podophyllum.

MANNA. *See* ASH

MANZANILLO

Hippomane mancinella (LINN.)
N.O. Euphorbiaceæ

Synonym. Manchineel
Parts Used. Juice of berries, leaves, bark
Habitat. South America, West Indian Islands, Venezuela, Panama

¶ *Description.* A tree growing to a height of 40 to 50 feet, mostly on sandy seashores, said to be so poisonous that men die under the shade of it; leaves shiny green, stalked, elliptical edges cut like saw teeth, a single gland on upper side where the stalk and leaf join, very small inconspicuous flowers (of separate sexes) on long slender spikes, the few females placed singly at base of the spike with a three-parted calyx, the males in little clusters on the upper part with a two-parted calyx and two or four stamens joined by their filaments, the females with a many-celled ovary crowned with from four to eight styles and reflexed stigmas. Fruit a rounded, fleshy, yellow-green berry.

¶ *Constituents*. A milky, very acrid juice both in the bark and the berries.

¶ *Medicinal Action and Uses*. A violent irritant and powerful cathartic, diuretic, vesicant. The least drop applied to the eye will cause blindness for some days; the smoke from the wood when burnt will also seriously affect the eyes. Much used in Cuba for tetanus. Indians use the juice to poison their arrows.

¶ *Dosage*. 2 minims as a cathartic.

See EUPHORBIAS.

MAPLES

N.O. Aceraceæ

Habitat. The Maples, belonging to the genus *Acer*, natural order Aceraceæ, are for the most part trees, inhabitants of the temperate regions of the Northern Hemisphere, particularly North America, Northern India and Japan

¶ *Description*. The leaves are long-stalked, placed opposite to one another, and palmately lobed; the flowers, in fascicles appearing before the leaves as in the Norway Maple, or in racemes appearing with, or later than, the leaves as in the Sycamore Some of the flowers are often imperfect.

The dry fruit, termed a 'samara,' is composed of two one-seeded cells, furnished with wings, which divide when ripe, the winged seeds being borne by the wind to a considerable distance.

The leaves of the Maples commonly exhibit varnish-like smears, of sticky consistence, known as *honey-dew*. This is the excretion of the aphides which live on the leaves; the insect bores holes into the tissues, sucks their juices and ejects a drop of honey-dew, on an average once in half an hour. In passing under a tree infested with aphides the drops can be felt like a fine rain. The fluid is rich in sugar. When the dew falls, the honey-dew takes it up and spreads over

the leaf; later in the day evaporation reduces it to the state of a varnish on the leaf surface, which aids in checking transpiration. Many other trees exhibit this phenomenon, e.g. lime, beech, oak, etc.

Most of the Maples yield a saccharine juice from the trunk, branches and leaves. The wood of almost all the species is useful for many purposes, especially to the cabinet-maker, the turner and the musical instrument-maker, and for the manufacture of alkali the Maples of North America are of great value.

Many species with finely-cut or variegated leaves have been introduced, especially from Japan, as ornamental shrubs, most of them remarkable for the coppery-purple tint that pervades the leaves and younger growths.

The Common Maple (*Acer campestre*, Linn.) is the only species indigenous to Great Britain. This and the Sycamore, or Great Maple, were described by Gerard in 1597, the latter as 'a stranger to England.'

MAPLE, COMMON

Acer campestre

Though a native tree, *Acer campestre* is not often seen growing freely for the sake of its timber, being chiefly looked upon as a valuable hedge-tree, and is therefore frequently found in hedgerows.

When growing alone it is a small tree, seldom attaining more than 20 feet, but the wood is compact, of a fine grain, sometimes beautifully veined and takes a high polish. For this reason, it is highly praised by the

cabinet-maker and has always been used much for tables, also for inlaying, and is frequently employed for violin cases. The wood makes excellent fuel and affords very good charcoal.

The wood of the roots is often knotted and is valuable for small objects of cabinet-work.

The young shoots, being flexible and tough, are employed in France as whips.

Sap drawn from the trees in spring yields a certain amount of sugar.

MAPLE, BIRD'S EYE

Acer saccharinum (LINN.)

Acer saccharinum (Linn.), the Sugar or Bird's Eye Maple, is an American species, introduced into Britain in 1735.

It bears a considerable resemblance to the Norway Maple, especially when young, but

is not so hardy here as our native Maple and requires a sheltered situation.

So far it has only been grown as an ornamental tree, the vivid colours of its foliage in winter ranging from bright orange to dark crimson. Sometimes it attains a height of 70, or even 100 feet, though more commonly it does not exceed 50 or 60 feet. It is remarkable for the whiteness of its bark.

Where the tree is plentiful in America, the timber is much used for fuel and is extensively employed for house-building and furniture, used instead of Oak when the latter is scarce, being also employed for axle-trees and spokes, as well as for Windsor chairs, shoe-lasts, etc. The wood is white, but acquires a rosy tinge after exposure to light. The grain is fine and close and when polished has a silky lustre.

The wood of old trees is valued for inlaying mahogany. The name 'Bird's Eye Maple' refers to the twisting of the silver grain, which produces numerous knots like the eyes of birds. Considerable quantities of this Maple are imported from Canada for cabinet-making.

The wood forms excellent *fuel* and *charcoal*, while the ashes are rich in alkaline principles, furnishing a large proportion of the potash exported from Boston and New York.

Large quantities of sugar are made from the sap of this species of Maple. The sap is boiled and the syrup when reduced to a proper consistence is run into moulds to form cakes. Trees growing in moist and low situations afford the most sap, though the least proportion of sugar.

The trees are tapped in early spring, just before the foliage develops, either by making a notch in the stem, about 3 feet from the ground, with an axe, or by boring a hole about 2 inches deep and introducing a spout of sumach or elder, through which the sap flows into a trough below. The sap is purified and concentrated in a simple manner, the whole work being carried on by farmers, who themselves use much of the product for domestic and culinary purposes.

A cold north-west wind with frosty nights and sunny days tends to incite the flow, which is more abundant during the day than during the night. The flow ceases during a south-west wind and at the approach of a storm, and so sensitive are the trees to aspect and climatic variations that the flow of sap on the south and east sides has been noticed to be earlier than on the north and west sides of the same tree.

The sap continues flowing for five or six weeks, according to the temperature. A tree of average size yields 15 to 30 gallons of sap in a season, 4 gallons of sap giving about 1 lb. of sugar. The tree is not at all injured by the tapping operation.

The quality of Maple Sugar is superior to that of West Indian cane sugar: it deposits less sediment when dissolved in water and has more the appearance of sugar candy.

The profits of the Sugar Maple do not arise from the sugar alone: it affords good molasses and excellent vinegar. The sap which is suitable for these purposes is obtained after that which supplies the sugar has ceased to flow.

MAPLE, GREAT
Acer pseudo-Platanus (LINN.)

Acer pseudo-Platanus (Linn.), the Sycamore or Great Maple (the Plane-tree of the Scotch), grows wild in Switzerland, Germany, Austria and Italy. It is remarkably hardy and will grow with an erect stem, exposed to the highest winds or to the sea-breezes, which it withstands better than most timber trees, being often planted near farmhouses and cottages in exposed localities for the sake of its dense foliage.

¶ *Description.* It is a handsome tree, of quick growth, attaining a height of 50 or 60 feet in 50 years. Though not a native, it has been cultivated here for four or five centuries, and has become so naturalized that self-sown examples are common.

The timber was formerly much used by the turner for cups, bowls and pattern blocks; and is still in repute by the saddle-makers and the millwright, being soft, light and tough.

In spring and autumn, if the trunk is pierced, it yields an abundance of juice, from which a good wine has been made in the Highlands of Scotland. Sugar is to a certain extent procured from it by evaporation, but 1 ounce to 1 quart of sap is the largest amount of sugar obtainable.

The leaves may be dried and given to sheep in winter.

The lobed shape of its leaf and its dense foliage caused it to be confounded with the True Sycamore (*Ficus sycamorus*) of Scripture.

MAPLE, NORWAY
Acer Platanoides

Acer Platanoides, the Norway Maple, grows on the mountains of the northern countries of Europe, descending in some parts of Norway to the seashore. It abounds in the north of Poland and Lithuania, and is common through Germany, Switzerland, and Savoy.

It was introduced into Great Britain in

1683. It is a quick grower and on a tolerable soil it attains a large size (from 40 to 70 feet).

¶ *Description.* The leaves are smooth and of a shining green, as large or larger than those of the Sycamore, and are seldom eaten or defaced, because the tree is full of a sharp,

milky juice disliked by insects. In the spring, when the flowers, which are of a fine yellow colour, are out, this tree has great beauty.

The wood is used for the same purposes as that of the Sycamore.

Sugar has been made from the sap in Norway and Sweden.

MAPLE, RED   Acer rubrum (LINN.)

Synonyms. Swamp Maple. Curled Maple

Acer rubrum (Linn.), the Red or Swamp Maple, is another American species, a middle-sized tree, introduced here in 1656, but so far only cultivated in England as an ornamental tree, for the sake of its striking bright scarlet flowers, which appear before the leaves in March and April, its red fruit and leaves rendering it very attractive also in autumn.

The wood is applicable to many purposes, such as the seats of Windsor chairs, turnery, etc. The grain of very old trees is sometimes undulated, which has suggested the name of 'Curled Maple': this gives beautiful effects of light and shade on polished surfaces.

The most constant use of Curled Maple is for the stocks of fowling pieces and rifles, as it affords toughness and strength, combined with lightness and elegance, but on the whole the wood is considered inferior to that of the Bird's Eye Maple, both in strength and as fuel.

Sugar has been made from the sap by the French Canadians, and also molasses, but the yield is only half as great as that from the Sugar Maple.

The inner bark is dusky red: on boiling, it yields a purple colour, which with sulphate

of lead affords a black dye. It makes a good black ink.

¶ *Medicinal Action and Uses.* The bark has astringent properties and has been used medicinally as an application for sore eyes, a use which the early settlers learnt from the Red Indians.

It occurs in long quilled pieces 6 to 12 inches or more in length, ¼ to ¾ inch wide, externally blackish brown, slightly polished, with innumerable fine transverse lines and scattered, brownish, warts. The inner bark is in very tough and fibrous layers, pale reddish brown or buff. The bark has an astringent and slightly bitter taste.

The CHINESE SUGAR MAPLE is *Sorghum saccharatum* (known also as *Andropogon arundinaceus*, var. *saccharatus*), a cane-like plant containing sugary sap, belonging to the Grass family Gramineæ.

It somewhat resembles Indian corn, or maize, from which it is distinguished by producing large heads of small grains.

It is cultivated in the United States to some extent as a forage crop, but is not used in the manufacture of sugar, owing to the difficulty of effecting its crystallization.

MARE'S TAIL   Hippuris vulgaris (LINN.)
N.O. Haloragaceæ

Synonyms. Female Horsetail. Marsh Barren Horsetail

The Mare's Tail (*Hippuris vulgaris*) must not be confused with the Horsetail (*Equisetum arvense*). The Mare's Tail is an aquatic flowering plant, the only British species of a group of plants found growing nearly all over Europe, Russia, Central Asia, and North America. It has a superficial resemblance to the Horsetails, having the same erect, many-jointed stems about as thick as a goosequill, unbranched, except at the base, and tapering to a point, crowded *in* the whole length by whorls of eight to twelve very narrow leaves ½ to 1¼ inch long, closely set with hard tips.

The inconspicuous flowers are sessile, i.e. stalkless, in the axils of the upper leaves and consist of a minute calyx, forming an indistinctly two-lobed rim to the ovary, a solitary stamen, with red anthers and a single seed.

Some of the flowers are often without stamens. They appear in June and July.

In stagnant water the plant grows erect, in running water it bends with the stream, swimming on the surface. The stems are as a rule about 2 feet long.

Culpepper, in common with the older herbalists, considered it of great value as a vulnerary:

'It is very powerful to stop bleeding, either inward or outward, the juice or the decoction being drunk, or the juice, decoction or distilled water applied outwardly. . . . It also heals inward ulcers. . . . It solders together the tops of green wounds and cures all ruptures in children. The decoction taken in wine helps stone and strangury; the distilled water drunk two or three times a day eases and strengthens the intestines and is effectual in a cough that comes by distillation from the head. The juice or distilled water used as a warm fomentation is of service in inflammations and breakings-out in the skin.'

The Mare's Tail is not uncommon in shallow ponds, the margins of lakes, etc. where there is a depth of mud and frost cannot reach the roots, which are stout and creeping. When the water is shallow, the upper part of the stem is stout and projects out of the water to a height of 8 inches to a foot or more. The submerged leaves, when the plant grows in deep streams, are often 2 to 3 inches long, paler and broader than those above water.

In some countries it is a troublesome weed in rivers and chokes up the ditches. It has been supposed to assist in purifying the putrid air of marshes by absorbing a great quantity of marsh gas. Goats are said to eat it, and in the north wild ducks to feed on it.

Gerard calls the plant Female Horsetail, and Parkinson Marsh Barren Horsetail. The name, *Hippuris*, is the Greek word for Mare's Tail.

See (WATER) MILFOIL.

MARIGOLD

Calendula officinalis (LINN.)
N.O. Compositæ

Synonyms. Caltha officinalis. Golds. Ruddes. Mary Gowles. Oculus Christi. Pot Marigold. Marygold. Fiore d'ogni mese. Solis Sponsa

Parts Used. Flowers, herb, leaves

The Common Marigold is familiar to everyone, with its pale-green leaves and golden orange flowers. It is said to be in bloom on the calends of every month, hence its Latin name, and one of the names by which it is known in Italy – *fiore d'ogni mese* – countenances this derivation. It was not named after the Virgin, its name being a corruption of the Anglo-Saxon *merso-meargealla*, the Marsh Marigold. Old English authors called it Golds or Ruddes. It was, however, later associated with the Virgin Mary, and in the seventeenth century with Queen Mary.

¶ *History.* It was well known to the old herbalists as a garden-flower and for use in cookery and medicine. Dodoens-Lyte (*A Niewe Herball*, 1578) says:

'It hath pleasant, bright and shining yellow flowers, the which do close at the setting downe of the sunne, and do spread and open againe at the sunne rising.'

Linnæus assigned a narrower limit to the expansion of its flowers, observing that they are open from nine in the morning till three in the afternoon. This regular expansion and closing of the flowers attracted early notice, and hence the plant acquired the names of *solsequia* and *solis sponsa*. There is an allusion to this peculiarity in the poems of Rowley:

'The Mary-budde that shooteth (shutteth) with the light.'

And in the *Winter's Tale*:

'The Marigold that goes to bed wi' th' sun, And with him rises weeping.'

It has been cultivated in the kitchen garden for the flowers, which are dried for broth, and said to comfort the heart and spirits.

Fuller writes: 'We all know the many and sovereign virtues in your leaves, the Herbe Generalle in all pottage.' (*Antheologie*, 1655.) Stevens, in *Maison Rustique, or the Countrie Farme* (1699), mentions the Marigold as a specific for headache, jaundice, red eyes, toothache and ague. The dried flowers are still used among the peasantry 'to strengthen and comfort the hart.' He says further:

'Conserve made of the flowers and sugar, taken in the morning fasting, cureth the trembling of the harte, and is also given in the time of plague or pestilence. The yellow leaves of the flowers are dried and kept throughout Dutchland against winter to put into broths, physicall potions and for divers other purposes, in such quantity that in some Grocers or Sicesellers are to be found barrels filled with them and retailed by the penny or less, insomuch that no broths are well made without dried Marigold.'

Formerly its flowers were used to give cheese a yellow colour.

In Macer's *Herbal* it is stated that only to look on Marigolds will draw evil humours out of the head and strengthen the eyesight.

'Golde [Marigold] is bitter in savour
Fayr and zelw [yellow] is his flowur
Ye golde flour is good to sene
It makyth ye syth bryth and clene
Wyscely to lokyn on his flowres
Drawyth owt of ye heed wikked hirores [humours].

. . . .

Loke wyscely on golde erly at morwe [morning]
Yat day fro feures it schall ye borwe:
Ye odour of ye golde is good to smelle.'

'It must be taken only when the moon is in the Sign of the Virgin and not when Jupiter is in the ascendant, for then the herb loses its virtue. And the gatherer, who must be out of deadly sin, must say three Pater Nosters and three Aves. It will give the wearer a vision of anyone who has robbed him.'

From Eleanour Sinclair Rohde's *Old English Herbals*:

'Of marygold we learn that Summe use to make theyr here yelow with the floure of this herbe, not beyng contēt with the naturall colour which God hath geven thē.'

Gerard speaks of:

'The fruitful or much-bearing marigold, . . . is likewise called Jackanapes-on-horse-backe: it hath leaves stalkes and roots like the common sort of marigold, differing in the shape of his floures; for this plant doth bring forth at the top of the stalke one floure like the other marigolds, from which start forth sundry other small floures, yellow· likewise and of the same fashion as the first; which if I be not deceived commeth to pass per accidens, or by chance, as Nature often times liketh to play with other flowers; or as children are borne with two thumbes on one hande or such like; which living to be men do get children like unto others: even so is the seed of this Marigold, which if it be sowen it brings forth not one floure in a thousand like the plant from whence it was taken.'

Culpepper says it is a

'herb of the Sun, and under Leo. They strengthen the heart exceedingly, and are very expulsive, and a little less effectual in the smallpox and measles than saffron. The juice of Marigold leaves mixed with vinegar, and any hot swelling bathed with it, instantly gives ease, and assuages it. The flowers, either green or dried, are much used in possets, broths, and drink, as a comforter of the heart and spirits, and to expel any malignant or pestilential quality which might annoy them. A plaister made with the dry flowers in powder, hog's-grease, turpentine, and rosin, applied to the breast, strengthens and succours the heart infinitely in fevers, whether pestilential or not.'

¶ *Cultivation*. The Marigold is a native of south Europe, but perfectly hardy in this country, and easy to grow. Seeds sown in April, in any soil, in sunny, or half-sunny places germinate freely. They require no other cultivation but to keep them clean from weeds and to thin out where too close, leaving them 9 to 10 inches apart, so that their branches may have room to spread. The plants will begin to flower in June, and continue flowering until the frost kills them. They will increase from year to year, if allowed to seed themselves. The seeds ripen in August and September, and if permitted to scatter will furnish a supply of young plants in the spring.

Only the common deep orange-flowered variety is of medinical value.

¶ *Parts Used*. The flowers and leaves. *Leaves*. – Gather only in fine weather, in the morning, after the dew has been dried by the sun. *Flowers*. – The ray florets are used and need quick drying in the shade, in a good current of warm air, spread out on sheets of paper, loosely, without touching each other, or they will become discoloured.

¶ *Medicinal Action and Uses*. Marigold is chiefly used as a local remedy. Its action is stimulant and diaphoretic. Given internally, it assists local action and prevents suppuration. The infusion of 1 ounce to a pint of boiling water is given internally, in doses of a tablespoonful, and externally as a local application. It is useful in chronic ulcer, varicose veins, etc. Was considered formerly to have much value as an aperient and detergent in visceral obstructions and jaundice.

It has been asserted that a Marigold flower, rubbed on the affected part, is an admirable remedy for the pain and swelling caused by the sting of a wasp or bee. A lotion made from the flowers is most useful for sprains and wounds, and a water distilled from them is good for inflamed and sore eyes.

An infusion of the freshly-gathered flowers is employed in fevers, as it gently promotes perspiration and throws out any eruption – a decoction of the flowers is much in use in country districts to bring out smallpox and measles, in the same manner as Saffron. Marigold flowers are in demand for children's ailments.

The leaves when chewed at first communicate a viscid sweetness, followed by a strong penetrating taste, of a saline nature. The expressed juice, which contains the greater part of this pungent matter, has been given in cases of costiveness and proved very efficacious. Snuffed up the nose it excites sneezing and a discharge of mucous from the head.

The leaves, eaten as a salad, have been considered useful in the scrofula of children, and the acrid qualities of the plant have caused it to be recommended as an extirpator of warts.

A yellow dye has also been extracted from the flower, by boiling.

¶ *Preparations and Dosage*. Fluid extract, ¼ to 1 drachm. Tincture of Calendula,

MARIGOLD, BUR. *See* (WATER) AGRIMONY

MARIGOLD, MARSH

Caltha palustris (LINN.)
N.O. Ranunculaceæ

Synonyms. Kingcups. Water Blobs. Horse Blobs. Bull's Eyes. Leopard's Foot. Meadow Routs. Verrucaria. Solsequia. Sponsa solis
Parts Used. Whole plant, buds, leaves

The Marsh Marigold, a showy dark-green plant resembling a gigantic buttercup, is abundant in marshes, wet meadows, and by the side of streams, where it forms large tufts or masses.

¶ *Description.* It is a herbaceous perennial. The stems are about a foot in height, hollow, nearly round, erect, but at times creeping and rooting at intervals in the lower portions, which are generally of a purple colour.

Most of the leaves spring directly from the ground, on long stalks, kidney-shaped, large and glossy. The stem-leaves have very short stalks and are more pointed at the top.

It flowers from mid-March till the middle of June, the flowers being at the end of the stems, which divide into two grooved flower-stalks, each bearing one blossom, from 1 to 2 inches in diameter. The Marsh Marigold is closely allied to various species of buttercups, but the flower has no real corolla, the brilliant yellow cup being composed of the five petaloid sepals.

The generic name is derived from the Greek *calathos* (a cup or goblet), from the shape of its flowers; the specific name from the Latin *palus* (a marsh), in reference to its place of growth.

The English name Marigold refers to its use in church festivals in the Middle Ages, as one of the flowers devoted to the Virgin Mary. It was also used on May Day festivals, being strewn before cottage doors and made into garlands.

Shakespeare refers several times to the flower, 'Winking Marybuds begin to ope their golden eyes.'

It has been called *Verrucaria* because it is efficacious in curing warts; also *Solsequia* and *Sponsa solis* because the flower opens at the rising of the sun and closes at its setting.

¶ *Medicinal Action and Uses.* Every part of the plant is strongly irritant, and cases are on record of serious effects produced by rashly experimenting with it. Dr. Withering says:

'It would appear that medicinal properties may be evolved in the gaseous exhalations of plants and flowers, for on a large quantity of the flowers of Meadow Routs being put into the bedroom of a girl who had been subject to fits, the fits ceased.'

An infusion of the flowers was afterwards successfully used in various kinds of fits, both of children and adults.

A tincture made from the whole plant when in flower may be given in cases of anæmia, in small, well-diluted doses.

The buds have occasionally been used as capers, but rather inadvisedly; the soaking in vinegar may, however, somewhat remove the acid and poisonous character of the buds in their fresh state.

The leaves can be cooked and eaten like spinach.

The juice of the petals, boiled with a little alum, stains paper yellow, but the colour so produced is said not to be permanent.

¶ *Cultivation.* The Marsh Marigold is propagated by parting the roots in autumn. It should be planted in a moist soil and a shady situation. A double variety is cultivated in gardens.

See BUTTERCUP.

MARJORAM, SWEET

Origanum marjorana (LINN.)
N.O. Labiatæ

Synonyms. Knotted Marjoram. Marjorana hortensis
Parts Used. Herb, leaves

Sweet or Knotted Marjoram is not an annual, but is usually treated as such, as the plants – native to Portugal – will not stand the winter elsewhere, so must be sown every year.

Seeds may be sown, for an early supply, in March, on a gentle hot-bed and again, in a warm position, in light soil, in the open ground during April. Plants do well if sown in April, though they are long in germinating. The seed is small and should be sown either

in drills, 9 inches apart, or broadcast, on the surface, trodden, raked evenly and watered in dry weather. On account of the slowness of germination, care should be taken that the seedlings are not choked with weeds, which being of much quicker growth are likely to do so if not destroyed. They should be removed by the hand, until the plants are large enough to use the small hoe with safety. Seed may also be sown early in May. In common with other aromatic herbs, such as Fennel, Basil, Dill, etc., it is not subject to the attacks of birds, as many other seeds are. When about an inch high, thin out to 6 or 8 inches apart each way. It begins to flower in July, when it is cut for use, and obtains its name of Knotted Marjoram from the flowers being collected into roundish close heads like knots.

Marjoram has been cultivated on a small scale at Sfax, Tunis, for a long time, and is called by the natives 'Khezama' (the Arab name for lavender).

Before the War, the herb was bought by agents and exported to Marseilles and other places. The plant is suitable to the sandy soil of the country.

The Marjoram plants are obtained either by division of clumps in winter, or from seeds planted in parallel lines 2 metres apart, between the almond and olive trees; and the soil, being of necessity worked for cultivation of the trees, this also serves to fertilize the Marjoram. One cutting of plant-clumps is best, a second one weakens it. The stems are cut about 10 cms. from the ground, dried in the sun on earth which has been previously beaten slightly. The leaves are separated from the stems by being beaten with staves; they are discoloured by the sun, broken and mixed with the débris of stems of which the odour is less strong.

Drying in the shade obtains more aromatic and less broken leaves, with less impurities.

¶ *Medicinal Action and Uses.* The medicinal qualities of the oil extracted from Sweet Marjoram – *Oleum majoranæ* – are similar to that of the Wild Marjoram. Fifteen ounces of the oil are yielded by 150 lb. of the fresh herb. On being kept, it assumes a solid form. It is used as an external application for sprains, bruises, etc., and also as an emmenagogue. In powdered form the herb forms part of certain Sneezing Powders.

¶ *Other Species.* In addition to the species just mentioned, others are cultivated in this country as ornamental plants, such as O. *Dictamnus*, the Dittany of Crete, which has roundish leaves thickly invested with white down, and flowers in drooping spikes; and O. *sipyleum*, which is similar, but taller and less woolly. These last are popularly called Hop Plants, and are often seen in cottage windows.

RECIPE
Aromatic Herbaceous Seasoning

Take of nutmegs and mace 1 oz. each, of cloves and peppercorns 2 oz. of each, 1 oz. of dried bay-leaves, 3 oz. of basil, the same of *Marjoram*, 2 oz. of winter savoury, and 3 oz. of thyme, ¼ oz. of cayenne pepper, the same of grated lemon-peel, and 2 cloves of garlic; all these ingredients must be well pulverized in a mortar, and sifted through a fine wire sieve, and put away in dry corked bottles for use.

The following is from Halliwell's *Popular Rhymes and Superstitions*:

'On St. Luke's Day, says Mother Bunch, take marigold flowers, a sprig of *marjoram*, thyme, and a little wormwood; dry them before a fire, rub them to powder, then sift it through a fine piece of lawn, and simmer it over a slow fire, adding a small quantity of virgin honey and vinegar. Anoint yourself with this when you go to bed, saying the following lines three times, and you will dream of your future partner "that is to be":

> St. Luke, St. Luke, be kind to me,
> In dreams let me my true love see.

If a girl desires to obtain this information, let her seek for a green peascod in which there are full 9 peas, and write on a piece of paper –

> Come in, my dear,
> And do not fear;

which paper she must enclose in the peascod, and lay it under the door. The first person who comes into the room will be her husband.'

Shakespeare may allude to this in *As You Like It* (ii. iv.) when he talks about the wooing of a peascod.

MARJORAM, WILD

Origanum vulgare (LINN.)
N.O. Labiatæ

Parts Used. Herb, oil

Habitat. Generally distributed over Asia, Europe and North Africa; grows freely in England, being particularly abundant in calcareous soils, as in the south-eastern counties

The name *Origanum* is derived from two Greek words, *oros* (mountain) and *ganos* (joy), in allusion to the gay appearance these plants give to the hillsides on which they grow.

¶ *Description.* It is a perennial herb, with creeping roots, sending up woody stems about a foot high, branched above, often purplish. The leaves are opposite, petiolate, about an inch long, nearly entire, hairy beneath. The flowers are in corymbs, with reddish bracts, a two-lipped pale purple corolla, and a five-toothed calyx, blooming from the end of June, through August. There is a variety with white flowers and light-green stalks, another with variegated leaves. It is propagated by division of roots in the autumn.

When cultivated, the leaves are more elliptical in shape than the Wild Marjoram, and the flower-spikes thinner and more compact. Marjoram has an extensive use for culinary purposes, as well as in medicine, but it is the cultivated species, *Origanum Onites* (Pot Marjoram), *O. Marjorana* (Sweet or Knotted Marjoram), and *O. Heracleoticum* (Winter Marjoram) that are employed in cookery as a seasoning. They are little used for medicinal purposes for which the Wild Marjoram is employed.

¶ *History*. Marjoram has a very ancient medical reputation. The Greeks used it extensively, both internally and externally for fomentations. It was a remedy for narcotic poisons, convulsions and dropsy. Among the Greeks, if Marjoram grew on a grave, it augured the happiness of the departed, and among both the Greeks and Romans, it was the custom to crown young couples with Marjoram.

Either *O. Onites* or *O. Majorana* is supposed to be the plant called 'Amaracus' by Greek writers.

The whole plant has a strong, peculiar, fragrant, balsamic odour and a warm, bitterish, aromatic taste, both of which properties are preserved when the herb is dry. It yields by distillation with water a small quantity of a volatile oil, which may be seen in vesicles, on holding up the leaves between the eye and the light, and which is the chief source of its properties as a medicinal agent. 1 lb. of the oil is produced from about 200 lb. of the herb, which should be gathered when just coming into flower, early in July. Large quantities of it are still gathered and hung up to dry in cottages in Kent and other counties for making Marjoram tea.

The 'swete margerome' was so much prized before the introduction of various foreign perfumes that, as Parkinson tells us, 'swete bags,' 'swete powders' and 'swete washing water' made from this plant were widely used. Our forefathers also scoured their furniture with its aromatic juices, and it is one of the herbs mentioned by Tusser (1577) as used for strewing chambers.

The flowering tops yield a dye, formerly used in the country to dye woollen cloth purple, and linen a reddish brown, but the tint is neither brilliant nor durable. The tops are also sometimes put into table beer, to give it an aromatic flavour and preserve it, and before the introduction of hops they were nearly as much in demand for ale-brewing as the ground ivy or wood sage. It is said that Marjoram and Wild Thyme, laid by milk in a dairy, will prevent it being turned by thunder.

Goat and sheep eat this herb, but horses are not fond of it, and cattle reject it.

¶ *Medicinal Action and Uses*. Marjoram yields about 2 per cent. of a volatile oil, which is separated by distillation. This must not be confused with oil of Origanum, which is extracted from Thyme. Its properties are stimulant, carminative, diaphoretic and mildly tonic; a useful emmenagogue. It is so acrid that it has been employed not only as a rubefacient, and often as a liniment, but has also been used as a caustic by farriers. A few drops, put on cotton-wool and placed in the hollow of an aching tooth frequently relieves the pain. In the commencement of measles, it is useful in producing a gentle perspiration and bringing out the eruption, being given in the form of a warm infusion, which is also valuable in spasms, colic, and to give relief from pain in dyspeptic complaints.

Externally, the dried leaves and tops may be applied in bags as a hot fomentation to painful swellings and rheumatism, as well as for colic. An infusion made from the fresh plant will relieve nervous headache, by virtue of the camphoraceous principle contained in the oil.

¶ *Cultivation*. The Marjorams are some of the most familiar of our kitchen herbs, and are cultivated for the use of their aromatic leaves, either in a green or dried state, for flavouring and other culinary purposes, being mainly put into stuffings. Sweet Marjoram leaves are also excellent in salads. They have whitish flowers, with a two-lipped calyx, and also contain a volatile oil, which has similar properties to the Wild Marjoram.

Winter Marjoram is really a native of Greece, but is hardy enough to thrive in the open air in England, in a dry soil, and is generally propagated by division of the roots in autumn.

Pot Marjoram, a native of Sicily, is also a hardy perennial, preferring a warm situation and dry, light soil. It is generally increased by cuttings, taken in early summer, inserted under a hand-glass, and later planted out a space of 1 foot between the rows and nearly as much from plant to plant, as it likes plenty of room. It may also be increased by division of roots in April, or by offsets, slipping pieces off the plants with roots to them and planting with trowel or dibber, taking care to water well. In May, they grow quickly after the operation. May also be propagated by seed, sown moderately thin, in dry, mild weather in March, in shallow drills, about ½ inch deep and 8 or 9 inches apart, covered in evenly with the soil. Transplant afterwards to about a foot apart each way. The seeds are very slow in germinating.

MARSHMALLOW. *See* MALLOW

MASTERWORT

Imperatoria ostruthium (LINN.)
N.O. Umbelliferæ

Part Used. Root

Masterwort, though rare in the wild state, was formerly cultivated in this country for use as a pot-herb and in medicine. It is sometimes found in moist meadows in the north of England and in Scotland, but is generally regarded as naturalized, having originally been a garden escape. Its native habitat is Central Europe.

¶ *Description.* It is a smooth, perennial plant, the stout, furrowed stem growing 2 to 3 feet high. The dark-green leaves, which somewhat resemble those of Angelica, are on very long foot-stalks and are divided into three leaflets, each of which is often again sub-divided into three. The umbels of flowers are large and many-rayed, the corollas white; the fruit has very broad wings.

¶ *Medicinal Action and Uses.* Stimulant, antispasmodic, carminative; of use in asthma, dyspepsia, menstrual complaints.

The root, to quote Culpepper,

'is the hottest and sharpest part of the plant, hotter than pepper, and (in his opinion) very available in cold griefs and diseases both of the stomach and body.'

He tells us that it was also used 'in a decoction with wine against all cold rheums, distillations upon the lungs or shortness of breath,' and also states that it was considered effectual in dropsy, cramp, falling sickness, kidney and uterine troubles and gout. Also, that 'it is of a rare quality against all sorts of cold poison, to be taken as there is a cause; it provoketh sweat.'

'But,' he advises, 'lest the taste hereof or of the seed, should be too offensive, the best way is to take the water distilled both from the herb and root.'

¶ *Preparation.* Fluid extract, 1 to 2 drachms.

MASTIC

Pistacia Lentiscus (LINN.)
N.O. Anacardiaceæ

Synonyms. Mastich. Lentisk
Part Used. Resin

¶ *Description and Habitat.* A shrub rarely growing higher than 12 feet, much branched, and found freely scattered over the Mediterranean region, in Spain, Portugal, France, Greece, Turkey, the Canary Islands, and Tropical Africa. It has been cultivated in England since 1664. It is principally exported from Scio, on which island it has been cultivated for several centuries. The trees there are said to be entire male.

The best Mastic occurs in roundish tears about the size of a small pea, or in flattened, irregular pear-shaped, or oblong pieces covered with a whitish powder. They are pale yellow in colour, which darkens with age. The odour is agreeable and the taste mild and resinous, and when chewed it becomes soft, so that it can easily be masticated. This char-

acteristic enables it to be distinguished from a resin called Sanderach, which it resembles, but which when bitten breaks to powder.

¶ *Constituents.* Mastic contains a small proportion of volatile oil, 9 per cent. of resin soluble in alcohol and ether, and 10 per cent. of a resin insoluble in alcohol.

¶ *Medicinal Action and Properties.* Stimulant, diuretic. It has many of the properties of the coniferous turpentines and was formerly greatly used in medicine. Of late years it has chiefly been used for filling carious teeth, either alone or in spirituous solution, and for varnishes, and in the East in the manufacture of sweets and cordials.

In the East it is still used medicinally in the diarrhœa of children and masticated to sweeten the breath.

MATICO

Piper angustifolium (R. and P.)
N.O. Piperaceæ

Synonyms. Artanthe elongata. Stephensia elongata. Piper granulosum. Piper elongatum. Yerba soldado. Soldier's Herb. Thoho-thoho. Moho-moho
Part Used. The dried leaves
Habitat. Peru

The classical name for the genus came originally from the Sanscrit *pippali*. 'Matico' is the name of the Spanish soldier who accidentally discovered the properties of the leaves when wounded in Peru.

The plant has spread over many moist districts of tropical America, and though grown as a stove-plant in English botanical gardens it does not flower there. It is a shrub of about 8 feet high, with many branches thickened at

WILD MARJORAM
Origanum Vulgare

MASTIC
Pistacia Lentiscus

DOG'S MERCURY
Mercurialis Perennis

MEZEREON
Daphne Mezereum

the joints, the younger ones thickly covered with hairs that fall off later. The alternate, bright green leaves are of distinctive shape, oblong-lanceolate with a broad, uneven base and a long, bluntly-tipped point. They are 5 to 7 inches long, entire and rather solid, with a fine network of sunken veins, hairy along the prominent veins of the underside.

The long, flexible spikes, 4 to 7 inches long, consist of tight rings of tiny yellow flowers packed round a fleshy axis. The seed fills the black fruit, which is about the size of a poppy-seed.

Two principal varieties in the shape of the leaves are recognized, the 'cordulatum' as described above, and the 'ossanum' with narrowed leaf-bases.

The drug is imported in bales, via Panama, the whole herb being pressed into a greenish-yellow mass. It is aromatic in taste and odour.

¶ *Constituents.* A volatile oil, slightly dextro-gyrate, containing in some specimens Matico camphor. Some of the later specimens of oil are said to contain not camphor but asarol.

A crystallizable acid called artanthic acid and a little tannin and resin are also found.

¶ *Medicinal Action and Uses.* In South America Matico is used like cubeb. Its styptic properties are due to the volatile oil, and it is used for arresting hæmorrhages, as a local application to ulcers, in genito-urinary complaints, atonic diarrhœa, dysentery, etc.

In Peru it is considered aphrodisiac.

It is effective as a topical application to slight wounds, bites of leeches, or after the extraction of teeth. The under surface of the leaf is preferred to the powder for this purpose.

¶ *Dosages.* 45 to 75 grains. Of fluid extract, as intestinal astringent and diuretic, 1 fluid drachm.

¶ *Other Species.*
Piper aduncum, of Central America, yields a 'false matico'; the leaves are less tessellated above and hairy below, but the chemical properties are similar.

The name of Matico is also given to *Eupatorium glutinosum* and *Waltheria glomerata*, and possibly also to a species of Phlomis, but these are not recognized officially.

MATTE TEA. *See* PARAGUAY

MAYWEED

Anthemis cotula
N.O. Compositæ

Synonyms. Maroute. Maruta cotula. Cotula Maruta fœtida. Manzanilla loca. Dog Chamomile. Wild Chamomile. Camomille puante. Fœtid or Stinking Chamomile or Mayweed. Dog's Fennel. Maithes. Maithen. Mathor

Parts Used. Flowers, leaves

Habitat. Europe

¶ *Description.* This annual herb, growing freely in waste places, resembles the true Chamomile, having large, solitary flowers on erect stems, with conical, solid receptacles, but the white florets have no membraneous scales at their base. It is distinguished from the allied genera by its very fœtid odour, which rubbing increases.

The whole plant, including the fennel-like leaves, has this odour and is full of an acrid juice that has caused it to be classed among the vegetable poisons; it is liable to blister.

Its action resembles that of the Chamomiles, but it is weaker, and its odour prevents its general adoption.

Bees dislike it, and it is said to drive away fleas.

The flowers must not be gathered when wet, or they will blacken during drying.

¶ *Constituents.* The flowers have been found to contain volatile oil, oxalic, valeric and tannic acids, salts of magnesium, iron, potassium and calcium, colouring matter, a bitter extractive and fatty matter.

¶ *Medicinal Action and Uses.* The flowers are preferred for internal use, being slightly less disagreeable than the leaves. In hysteria it is used in Europe as an antispasmodic and emmenagogue. Applied to the skin fresh and bruised it is a safe vesicant. A poultice helpful in piles can be made from the herb boiled until soft, or it can be used as a bath or fomentation.

It is administered to induce sleep in asthma. In sick headache or convalescence after fever the extract may be used.

A strong decoction can cause sweating and vomiting. It is said to be nearly as valuable as opium in dysentery. It has also been used in scrofula, dysmennorrhœa and flatulent gastritis.

¶ *Dosage.* Of infusion, 1 to 4 fluid ounces.

¶ *Other Species.*
Anthemis tinctoria has similar properties and yields a yellow dye.

A. arvensis is considered in France to be one of the best indigenous febrifuges.

MAYWEED, SCENTLESS

Matricaria inodora
N.O. Compositæ

Synonym. Corn Feverfew
Part Used. Whole herb

The Scentless Mayweed owes its generic name to its reputed medicinal properties, which in a lesser degree resemble those of *Anthemis nobilis*.

It is an annual, commonly met with in fields, by the wayside, and on waste patches of ground, and flowers throughout the summer. The name 'Mayweed' is misleading, as it will be found in flower right up to the autumn. It is spreading and bunching in its growth, generally about 1 foot in height, but varying a good deal. The leaves, as in all the members of this group, are feather-like in character, springing direct from the main stems without leaf-stalks. The flower-heads are borne singly at the ends of long terminal flower-stems, the centre florets deep yellow on very prominent convex disks and the outer florets having very conspicuous white rays, much larger in proportion to the disk than in most of the allied species. Though compared with several of its allies, it may almost be termed 'scentless,' the term is not strictly appropriate as it yields slightly sweet and pleasant, aromatic odour.

The Finlanders use an infusion of this plant in consumption cases.

See CHAMOMILE.

MEADOWSWEET

Spiræa Ulmaria (LINN.)
N.O. Rosaceæ

Synonyms. Meadsweet. Dolloff. Queen of the Meadow. Bridewort. Lady of the Meadow
Part Used. Herb

¶ *Description.* The fragrant Meadowsweet is one of the best known wild flowers, decking our meadows and moist banks with its fernlike foliage and tufts of delicate, graceful, creamy-white flowers, which are in blossom from June to almost September. The leaves are dark green on the upper side and whitish and downy underneath, much divided, being interruptedly pinnate, having a few large serrate leaflets and small intermediate ones; the terminal leaflets are large, 1 to 3 inches long and three to five lobed. The stems are 2 to 4 feet high, erect and furrowed, sometimes purple. The flowers are small, clustered close together in handsome irregularly-branched cymes, and have a very strong, sweet smell. The whole herb possesses a pleasant taste and flavour, the green parts partaking of the aromatic character of the flowers.

A peculiarity of this flower is that the scent of the leaves is quite different from that of the flowers. The latter possess an almond-like fragrance; it is one of the fragrant herbs used to strew the floors of chambers. In allusion to this use, Gerard writes:

'The leaves and floures of Meadowsweet farre excelle all other strowing herbs for to decke up houses, to strawe in chambers, halls and banqueting-houses in the summer-time, for the smell thereof makes the heart merrie and joyful and delighteth the senses.'

Meadowsweet, water-mint, and vervain, were three herbs held most sacred by the Druids.

It is one of the fifty ingredients in a drink called 'Save,' mentioned in Chaucer's *Knight's Tale*, in the fourteenth century being called Medwort, or Meadwort, i.e. the mead or honey-wine herb, and the flowers were often put into wine and beer. It is still incorporated in many herb beers.

The name *Ulmaria* is given in allusion to the resemblance of its leaves to those of the Elm (*Ulmus*), being much wrinkled on the upper side.

Gerard says:

'It is reported that the floures boiled in wine and drunke do take away the fits of a quartaine ague and make the heart merrie. The distilled water of the floures dropped into the eies taketh away the burning and itching thereof and cleareth the sight.'

Culpepper says much the same and also: 'The leaves, when they are full grown, being laid on the skin will, in a short time, raise blisters thereon, as Tragus saith.' He also states that for acquiring the 'merry heart' (which Gerard mentions) 'some use the flowers and some the leaves.' He tells us that 'a leave hereof put into a cup of claret wine gives also a fine relish to it.'

¶ *Medicinal Action and Uses.* Aromatic, astringent, diuretic, and sub-tonic. It is a valuable medicine in diarrhœa, imparting to the bowels some degree of nourishment, as well as of astringency. It is also considered of some service as a corrector of the stomach, and not without some power as an alterative, and is frequently used in affections of the blood. It is a good remedy in strangury, dropsy, etc., and almost a specific in children's diarrhœa.

An infusion of 1 oz. of the dried herb to a pint of water is the usual mode of administration, in wineglassful doses. Sweetened with honey, it forms a very pleasant diet-drink, or beverage both for invalids and ordinary use.

The herb is collected in July, when in flower.

An infusion of the fresh tops produces perspiration, and a decoction of the root, in white wine, was formerly considered a specific in fevers.

Meadowsweet is visited by bees for the pollen.

¶ *Dosage.* Fluid extract, ¼ to 1 drachm.

¶ *Other Species.*
Another member of the *Spiræa* is *Spiræa Filipendula* (Dropwort). A herb about a foot high, with short rhizome and nodulose rootlets; leaves interruptedly pinnate, leaflets cut into narrow serrated segments; flowers in crowded, erect, compound cymes, pink externally in bud; when open, white and scentless. Dry pastures on a limestone (or chalky) soil. Distinguished from *S. Ulmaria* by its elegantly cut foliage, pink buds, and whiter scentless blossoms. A double-flowered variety is common in gardens. Flowering time – June, July. Perennial.

Culpepper speaks of *Filipendula*, or Drop-wort, as being a good remedy for kidney affections, by 'taking the roots in powder or a decoction of them in white wine, with a little honey.' He adds that it

'is also very effectual for all the diseases of the lungs, as shortness of breath, wheezing, hoarseness of the throat; and to expectorate tough phlegm, or any other parts thereabout.'

WILLOW-LEAVED SPIRÆA (*S. salyciflora*), a shrub with simple ex-stipulate leaves and spike-like clusters of rose-coloured flowers, grows in moist woods in the north and in Wales; but it is not indigenous. It flowers in July and August. Perennial.

There are several foreign species of *Spiræa*, one from Japan being a beautiful shrub with pure white flowers, and leaves like those of the plum, hence its name, *S. prunifolia*.

There is another from Nepaul, *S. bella*, with rose-coloured flowers growing in lateral and terminal corymbs; another from Canada, *S. tomentosa*, with cottony leaves and pyramidal panicles of rose-coloured flowers; and *S. Fortunei* from China, with ovate, smooth, toothed leaves often tinged with purple, and rose-coloured flowers.

See HARDHACK, INDIAN PHYSIC.

MELILOT

Melilotus officinalis (LINN.)
Melilotus alba (DESV.)
Melilotus arvensis (LAMK.)
N.O. Leguminosæ

Synonyms. Yellow Melilot. White Melilot. Corn Melilot. King's Clover. Sweet Clover. Plaster Clover. Sweet Lucerne. Wild Laburnum. Hart's Tree
Part Used. Herb

The Melilots or Sweet Clovers – formerly known as Melilot Trefoils and assigned, with the common clovers, to the large genus *Trifolium*, but now grouped in the genus *Melilotus* – are not very common in Britain, being not truly native, though they have become naturalized, having been extensively cultivated for fodder formerly, especially the common yellow species, *Melilotus officinalis* (Linn.).

Although now seldom seen as a crop, having, like the Medick, given place to the Clovers, Sainfoin and Lucerne, Melilot seems, however, to have been a very common crop in the sixteenth century, seeding freely, spreading in a wild condition wherever grown, since Gerard tells us,

'for certainty no part of the world doth enjoy so great plenty thereof as England and especially Essex, for I have seen between Sudbury in Suffolke and Clare in Essex and from Clare to Hessingham very many acres of earable pasture overgrowne with the same; in so much that it doth not only spoil their land, but the corn also, as Cockle or Darnel and is a weed that generally spreadeth over that corner of the shire.'

¶ *Description.* The Melilots are perennial herbs, 2 to 4 feet high, found in dry fields and along roadsides, in waste places and chalky banks, especially along railway banks and near lime kilns. The smooth, erect stems are much branched, the leaves placed on alternate sides of the stems are smooth and trifoliate, the leaflets oval. The plants bear long racemes of small, sweet-scented, yellow or white, papilionaceous flowers in the yellow species, the keel of the flower much shorter than the other parts and containing much honey. They are succeeded by broad, black, one-seeded pods, transversely wrinkled.

All species of Melilot, when in flower, have a peculiar sweet odour, which by drying becomes stronger and more agreeable, somewhat like that of the Tonka bean, this similarity being accounted for by the fact that they both contain the same chemical principle, Coumarin, which is also present in new-mown hay and woodruff, which have the identical fragrance.

The name of this genus comes from the words *Mel* (honey) and *lotus* (meaning honey-lotus), the plants being great favourites of the bees. Popular and local English names are Sweet Clover, King's Clover, Hart's Tree or Plaster Clover, Sweet Lucerne and Wild Laburnum.

The tender foliage makes the plant acceptable to horses and other animals, and it is said that deer browse on it, hence its name 'Hart's Clover.' Galen used to prescribe Melilot plaster to his Imperial and aristocratic patients when they suffered from inflammatory tumours or swelled joints, and the plant is so used even in the present day in some parts of the Continent.

In one Continental Pharmacopœia of recent date an emollient application is directed to be made of Melilot, resin, wax, and olive oil.

Gerard says that

'Melilote boiled in sweet wine untile it be soft, if you adde thereto the yolke of a rosted egge, the meale of Linseed, the roots of Marsh Mallowes and hogs greeace stamped together, and used as a pultis or cataplasma, plaisterwise, doth asswge and soften all manner of swellings.'

It was also believed that the juice of the plant 'dropped into the eies cleereth the sight.'

Water distilled from the flowers was said to improve the flavour of other ingredients.

There are three varieties of Melilot found in England, the commonest being *Melilotus officinalis* (Linn.), the Yellow Melilot; *M. alba* (Desv.), the White Melilot, and *M. arvensis* (Lamk.), the Corn Melilot, which is found occasionally in waste places in the eastern counties, but is not considered indigenous.

The dried leaves and flowering tops of all three species form the drug used in herbal medicine, though the drug of the German Pharmacopœia is *M. officinalis*. Two yellow-flowered species are, however, often sold under this name, the common *M. officinalis*, which has hairy pods, and *M. arvensis*, which has small, smooth pods.

The White Melilot found in waste places in England, particularly on railway banks, is not uncommon, but apparently not permanently established in any of its localities. It differs from *M. officinalis* by its more slender root and stems, which, however, attain as great a height, by its more slender and lax racemes and smaller flowers, which are about ½ inch long and white. The standard is larger than the keel and wings, which alone would distinguish it from *M. officinalis*. The pods are smaller and free from the hairs clothing those of *M. officinalis*.

A new kind of Sweet Clover, an *annual* variety of *M. alba*, has been discovered in the United States. To distinguish it from the other Sweet Clovers, it is called Hubam, after Professor Hughes, its discoverer, and Alabama, its native state. Some five or six years ago, small samples were distributed by Professor Hughes among various experimental stations, with the result that the superiority of the plant has been generally recognized and its spread has been rapid, over 5,000 acres now being cultivated. The plant has specially valuable characteristics – great resistance to drought, adaptability to a wide variety of soils and climates, abundant seed production, richness in nectar and great fertilizing value to the soil, and has been grown successfully in the United States, Canada, Australia, Italy, and many other countries. The quantity of forage produced from a given acre is second to no other forage plant, and the quality, if properly handled, is excellent. It is of very quick growth and blooms in three to four months after sowing, producing an unusual wealth of honey-making blooms. The flowers remain in bloom for a longer period than almost any other honey-bearing plant, and in the matter of nectar production the quantity is surprising, equal to that of any other honey produced in the United States, and the quality compares favourably with the best honey produced either there or in Great Britain. It is considered that this annual Sweet Clover will one day stand at the head of the list of honey plants of the world, if the present rate of spreading continues.

¶ *Parts Used Medicinally.* The whole herb is used, dried, for medicinal purposes, the flowering shoots, gathered in May, separated from the main stem and dried in the same manner as Broom tops.

The dried herb has an intensely fragrant odour, but a somewhat pungent and bitterish taste.

¶ *Constituents.* Coumarin, the crystalline substance developed under the drying process, is the only important constituent, together with its related compounds, hydrocoumaric (melilotic) acid, orthocoumaric acid and melilotic anhydride, or lactone, a fragrant oil.

¶ *Medicinal Action and Uses.* The herb has aromatic, emollient and carminative properties. It was formerly much esteemed in medicine as an emollient and digestive and is recommended by Gerard for many complaints, the juice for clearing the eyesight, and, boiled with lard and other ingredients, as an application to wens and ulcers, and mixed with wine, 'it mitigateth the paine of the eares and taketh away the paine of the head.'

Culpepper tells us that the head is to be washed with the distilled herb for loss of senses and apoplexy, and that boiled in wine, it is good for inflammation of the eye or other parts of the body.

The following recipe is from the Fairfax Still-room book (published 1651):

'To make a bath for Melancholy. Take Mallowes, pellitory of the wall, of each three handfulls; Camomell Flowers, *Mellilot* flowers, of each one handfull, senerick seed one ounce, and boil them in nine gallons of Water untill they come to three, then put in a quart of new milke and go into it bloud warme or something warmer.'

Applied as a plaster, or in ointment, or as a fomentation, it is an old-fashioned country remedy for the relief of abdominal and rheumatic pains.

It relieves flatulence and in modern herbal practice is taken internally for this purpose.

The flowers, besides being very useful and attractive to bees, have supplied a perfume, and a water distilled from them has been used for flavouring.

The dried plant has been employed to scent snuff and smoking tobacco and may be laid among linen for the same purpose as lavender. When packed with furs, Melilot is said to act like camphor and preserve them from moths, besides imparting a pleasant fragrance.

'In Switzerland, Melilot abounds in the pastures and is an ingredient in the green Swiss cheese called *Schabzieger*. The Schabzieger cheese is made by the curd being pressed in boxes with holes to let the whey run out; and when a considerable quantity has been collected and putrefaction begins, it is worked into a paste with a large proportion of the dried herb Melilotus, reduced to a powder. The herb is called in the country dialect "Zieger kraut," *curd herb*. The paste thus produced is pressed into moulds of the shape of a common flowerpot and the putrefaction being stopped by the aromatic herb, it dries into a solid mass and keeps unchanged for any length of time. When used, it is rasped or grated and the powder mixed with fresh butter is spread upon bread.' (Syme and Sowerby, *English Botany*.)

MELONS

N.O. Cucurbitaceæ

The order Cucurbitaceæ (the sole representative of which in the British Islands is the familiar hedge-climbing, red-berried Bryony) contains many genera of economic importance: *Cucumis* affords cucumber and melon; *Cucurbita*, pumpkin and marrow; to the genus *Lagenaria* belong the gourds; the well-known bath-loofah is formed of the closely-netted vascular bundles in the fruit of *Luffa ægyptica*, another member of the order, the unripe fruit itself being used as a pickle by the Arabians; *Sechium edule*, a tropical American species, is largely cultivated for its edible fruit, *Choko*; *Citrullus vulgaris* is the Water Melon, which serves the Egyptians both as food, drink and physic; *Citrullus Colecynthis* furnishes the drug called Celocynth, and equally valuable medicinally is *Ecbalium Elaterium*, the Squirting Cucumber.

MELON, COMMON

Cucumis melo (LINN.)

Synonym. Musk Melon

Habitat. The Melon is a native of South Asia – from the foot of the Himalayas to Cape Comorin, where it grows wild – but is cultivated in the temperate and warm regions of the whole world

¶ *Description.* It is an annual, trailing herb, with large palmately-lobed leaves and bears tendrils, by which it is readily trained over trellises. Its flowers (which have bell-shaped corollas, deeply five-lobed) are either male or female, both kinds being borne on the one plant. The male flowers have three stamens, the ovary in the female flowers, three cells. The many varieties of Melon show great diversity in foliage and still more in the size and shape of the fruit, which in some kinds is as small as an olive, in others as large as the Gourd (*Cucurbita maxima*). Some are globular, others egg-shaped, spindle-shaped or serpent-like, the outer skin smooth or netted, ribbed or furrowed, and variously coloured; the flesh, white, green or orange when ripe, scented or scentless, sweet or insipid, some bitter and even nauseous.

¶ *History.* The cultivation of the Melon in Asia is of very ancient date. It was grown by the Egyptians, and the Romans and Greeks were familiar with it. Pliny describes Melons as *Pepones*, Columella as *Melones*. It began to be extensively cultivated in France in 1629. Gerarde in his *Herball* (1597) figured and described several kinds of Melons or Pompions, but included gourds under the same name. The Common Melon was commonly known as the Musk Melon.

To grow it to perfection, the Melon requires artificial heat, being grown on hot beds of fermenting manure, with an atmospheric temperature of 75°, rising with sun-heat to 80°.

MELON, CANTALOUP

Cucumis Cantalupensis (HABERL.)

The Cantaloups (*Cucumis Cantalupensis*, Haberl., so called from a place near Rome where it was long cultivated) is grown by the market gardeners round Paris and other parts of France, and has its origin in Persia and the neighbouring Caucasian region. It was first brought to Rome from Armenia in the sixteenth century. The netted species probably also originally came from Persia.

MELON, DUDAIM

Cucumis dudaim

Synonym. Queen Anne's Pocket Melon

The Dudaim Melon (*Cucunis dudaim*), Queen Anne's Pocket Melon, as it has been called, is also a native of Persia. It produces a fruit variegated with green and orange and oblong green spots of varying size. When fully ripe, it becomes yellow and then whitish. It has a very fragrant, vinous, musky smell, and a whitish, flaccid, insipid pulp. *Dudaim* is the Hebrew name of the fruit.

MELON, SERPENT

Cucumis flexuosum (LINN.)

Synonym. Snake Cucumber

Cucumis flexuosum (Linn.) is the Serpent Melon, or Snake Cucumber. It grows to a great length and may be used either raw or pickled.

The 'Cucumber' of the Scriptures (Isaiah i. 8) is considered to have been *Cucumis chate*, the Hairy Cucumber, a kind of wild Melon, which produces a fruit, the flesh of which is almost of the same substance as the Common Melon, its taste being somewhat sweet and as cool as the Water Melon. It is common both in Arabia and in Egypt, where a dish is prepared from the ripe fruit. Peter Forskäl, a contemporary of Linnæus, in his work on the plants of Egypt (*Flora ægyptiaco-arabica*, 1775), describes its preparation. The pulp is broken and stirred by means of a stick thrust through a hole cut at the umbilicus of the fruit: the hole is then closed with wax, and the fruit, without removing it from its stem, is buried in a little pit; after some days, the pulp is found to be converted into an agreeable liquor.

MELON, WATER

Citrullus vulgaris (LINN.)

Parts Used. Seeds, juice

Melons are a staple and refreshing fruit in Egypt and Palestine, especially the Water Melon (*Citrullus vulgaris*, Linn.), a native of tropical Africa and the East Indies, which grows to a great size, even attaining 30 lb. in weight. It refreshes the thirsty as well as the hungry. It has a smooth rind, and though generally oblong and about a foot and a half in length, varies much in form and colour, the flesh being either red or pale, the seeds, black or reddish. There is a succession of crops from May to November. For its cool and refreshing fruit, it has been cultivated since the earliest times in Egypt and the East and was known in Southern Europe and Asia before the Christian era. The banks of the Burlus Delta lake, east of the Rosetta channel of the Nile Delta, are noted for their Water Melons, which are yellow within, and come into season after those grown on the banks of the Nile. Of the plants found in the Kalahari Desert of South Africa, in Bechuanaland, the most remarkable is the Water Melon, present in abundance, which supplies both man and beast with water.

¶ *Medicinal Action and Uses.* The fruit should be eaten cautiously by Europeans, especially when taken in the heat of the day, but it is much used in the tropics and in Italy. In Egypt, it is practically the only medicine the common people use in fevers; when it is ripe, or almost putrid, they collect the juice and mix it with rosewater and a little sugar. The seeds have been employed to a considerable extent as a domestic remedy in strangury and other affections of the urinary passages, and are regarded as having diuretic properties. The Russian peasants use them for dropsy and hepatic congestion, also for intestinal catarrh.

The *Four Greater Cold Seeds* of the old materia medica were the seeds of the Pumpkin (*Cucurbita pepo*), the Gourd (*C. maxima*), the Melon and the Cucumber. These were bruised and rubbed up with water to form an emulsion, which was much used in catarrhal affections, disorders of the bowels and urinary passages, fever, etc.

The seeds of both the Water Melon and the Common or Musk Melon are good vermicides, having much the same constituents as those of the PUMPKIN (sometimes known as the Melon Pumpkin), which have long been a popular worm remedy and in recent years have also been used for tapeworm.

¶ *Constituents*. Pumpkin seeds contain 30 per cent. or more of a reddish, fixed oil, traces of a volatile oil, together with proteids, sugar, starch and an acrid resin, to which the anthelmintic properties appear to be due, though recent experiments have failed to isolate any substance of physiological activity, either from the kernels or shells of the seeds. The value of the drug is said to be due to its mechanical effect.

The seeds are employed when quite ripe and must not be used if more than a month old. A mixture is made by beating up 2 oz. of the seeds with as much sugar and milk or water added to make a pint, and this mixture is taken fasting, in three doses, one every two hours, castor oil being taken a few hours after the last dose. An infusion of the seeds, prepared by pouring a pint of boiling water on 1 oz. of seeds, has likewise been used in urinary complaints.

The Pumpkin or Pompion (its older name, of which Pumpkin is a corruption) is a native of the Levant. Many varieties are cultivated in gardens, both for ornament and also for culinary use. It is a useful plant to the American backwoods-farmer, yielding both in the ripe and unripe condition a valuable fodder for his cattle and pigs, being frequently planted at intervals among the maize that constitutes his chief crop. The larger kinds acquire a weight of 40–80 lb., but smaller varieties are in more esteem for garden culture.

In England, Pumpkins were formerly called English Melons, which was popularly corrupted to Millions. They are used cut up in soups and make excellent pies, either alone or mixed with other fruit, and their pulp is also utilized as a basis by jam manufacturers, as it takes the flavour of any fruit juice mixed with it, and adds bulk without imparting any flavour of its own.

The SQUASHES, which have such extensive culinary use in America, are a variety of the Pumpkin (*C. melopepo*), and another familiar member of the genus, *C. evifera*, a variety of *C. pepo*, is the Vegetable Marrow. While small and green the Pumpkin may be eaten like the Marrow.

¶ *Medicinal Action and Uses*. The *root* of the Common Melon is purgative, and in large doses (7 to 10 grains) is said to be a certain emetic, the active and bitter principle having been called Melon-emetin.

The MELON-TREE, so-called, is the PAPAW, or Papaya (*Carica Papaya*, Linn.), a native of tropical America, where it is everywhere cultivated for its edible fruit and digestive properties.

The dried juice is largely used in the treatment of indigestion, under various trade names, 'Papain,' a white powder, being administered in all digestive disorders where albuminoid substances pass away undigested.

¶ *Dosage*. Papain, 1 to 5 grains.

See PAPAW (APPLE, BITTER).

MERCURY, DOG'S

Mercurialis perennis (LINN.)
N.O. Euphorbiaceæ

¶ *Description*. Dog's Mercury, a perennial, herbaceous plant, sending up from its creeping root numerous, undivided stems, about a foot high, is common in woods and shady places throughout Europe and Russian Asia, except in the extreme north. It is abundant at Hythe in Sussex.

Each stem bears several pairs of rather large roughish leaves, and from the axils of the upper ones grow the small green flowers, the barren on long stalks, the fertile sessile, the first appearing before the leaves are quite out. The stamens and pistils are on different plants. The perianth is three-cleft to the base. The barren flowers have nine stamens or more, the fertile flowers two styles and two cells to the two-lobed ovary.

Male and female plants are rarely found intermixed, each usually growing in large patches. The female are less common than the male, and the plant increases more by the spreading of its creeping rootstocks and stems than by seed. It flowers from the end of March to the middle of May and seeds in the summer. The leaves of the male flowering plants are more pointed and less serrated than those on the female plants, which have longer stalks.

Dog's Mercury has a disagreeable odour and is extremely acrid, being poisonous to animals in the fresh state. It has been said, however, that heat destroys its harmfulness, and that it is innocuous in hay. Its chemical constituents have not been ascertained.

Dog's Mercury has proved fatal to sheep, and Annual Mercury to human beings who had made soup from it.

¶ *History.* We find it spoken of in the old herbals as possessing wonderful powers, but it has been abandoned as a dangerous remedy for internal use.

Culpepper speaks strongly of the 'rank poisonous' qualities of Dog's Mercury, and adds, with some contempt:

'The common herbals, as Gerarde's and Parkinson's, instead of cautioning their readers against the use of this plant, after some trifling, idle observations upon the qualities of Mercurys in general, dismiss the article without noticing its baneful effects. Other writers, more accurate, have done this; but they have written in Latin, a language not very likely to inform those who stand most in need of this caution.'

It derives its name from the legend that its medicinal virtues were revealed by the god Mercury. The Greeks called it Mercury's Grass. The French call it *La Mercuriale*, the Italians, *Mercorella*. The name Dog's Mercury or Dog's Cole, was probably given it because of its inferiority from an edible point of view, either to the Annual, or Garden Mercury, or to a plant known to the older herbalists as English Mercury, which was sometimes eaten in this country and some parts of the Continent as a substitute for that vegetable. The prefix 'Dog' was often given to wild-flowers that were lacking in scent or other properties of allied species – as, for instance, Dog Violet, Dog Rose, etc.

That Dog's Mercury has been eaten in mistake for Good King Henry, with unfortunate results, we know from the report of Ray, one of the earliest of English naturalists, who relates that when boiled and eaten with fried bacon in error for this English spinach, it produced sickness, drowsiness and twitching. In another instance, when it was collected and boiled in soup by some vagrants, all partaking of it exhibited the ordinary symptoms of narcotic and irritant poisoning, two children dying on the following day.

The fact that some old books recommend Dog's Mercury as a good potherb arose probably from confusing it with the less harmful annual species, called by Gerard the French or Garden Mercury.

¶ *Medicinal Action and Uses.* Hippocrates commended this herb for women's diseases, used externally, as did also Culpepper, who says it is good for sore and watering eyes and deafness and pains in the ears. He advises the use of it, also, as a decoction, 'made with water and a cock chicken,' for hot fits of ague. It has been employed for jaundice and as a purgative.

The juice of the whole plant, freshly collected when in flower, mixed with sugar or with vinegar, is recommended externally for warts, and for inflammatory and discharging sores, and also, applied as a poultice, to swellings and to cleanse old sores.

A lotion is made from the plant for antiseptic external dressings, to be used in the same manner as carbolic.

The juice has also been used as a nasal douche for catarrh.

When steeped in water, the leaves and stems of the plant give out a fine blue colour, resembling indigo. This colouring matter is turned red by acids and destroyed by alkalis, but is otherwise permanent, and might prove valuable as a dye, if any means of fixing the colour could be devised. The stems are of a bright metallic blue, like indigo, and those that run into the ground have the most colouring matter.

MERCURY, ANNUAL

Mercurialis annua (LINN.)
N.O. Euphorbiaceæ

Annual Mercury (*Mercurialis annua*), known also to older writers as Garden Mercury and French Mercury, is a common weed in gardens.

It is taller than the Dog Mercury, and branched, and the leaves are smaller, perfectly smooth and of a light green hue.

Barren and fertile flowers are sometimes found on the same plant, the male flowers in peduncled axillary spikes.

It grows plentifully in waste places and seldom at any distance from inhabited districts.

It is in flower from July to October and increases so freely by the scattering of its rough seeds as to become a very troublesome weed in gardens, extremely hard to eradicate.

¶ *Medicinal Action and Uses.* The plant is mucilaginous and was formerly much employed as an emollient. The French made a syrup of the freshly-gathered herb, which was given as a purge, and the dried herb was used to make a decoction for injections, but as a herbal remedy it is now disregarded in England.

The seeds taste like those of hemp.

As a pot-herb, this plant had some reputation, the leaves being boiled and eaten as spinach, and it is still eaten in this way in some parts of Germany, the acrid qualities being dissipated, it is believed, by boiling. Pigs have also been fed with it in France.

(POISON)
MESCAL BUTTONS

Anhalonium Lewinii (HENN.)
N.O. Cactceæ

Synonyms. Lopophora Lewinii. Pellote. Muscal Buttons. Anhalonium Williamsii. Echinocactus Lewinii. Echinocactus Williamsii

Part Used. The tops, consisting of blunt leaves round a tuft of short, pale yellow hairs

Habitat. Mexico

¶ *Description.* These South American Cacti, formerly regarded as belonging to the *Anhalonium* genus, by the name of which they are chiefly known, were later attributed to the genus *Echinocactus* of the *Mammalaria* species, being spineless and flexible.

The principal species of *Williamsii* and *Lewinii*, found in the Rio Grande valley, grow to a height of only ½ inch, and the tops, or Mescal Buttons, are from 1 to 1½ inch across and ¼ inch thick. When dry they are hard and brittle, but become soft when moistened. The taste and smell are peculiar, bitter and disagreeable. The surface of *E. Lewinii*, or *Anhalonium Lewinii*, is crossed by thirteen irregular furrows, and that of *E. Williamsii* and *A. Williamsii* by eight regular ones. Small pink flowers are borne, but these do not appear in the drug.

The Kiowa Indians have used Mescal Buttons from ancient times for producing exaltation in their religious ceremonies.

¶ *Constituents.* Four alkaloids have been separated: Anhalonine, Mescaline, Anhalonidine, and Lophophorine, and two other bases, pellotine and anhalamine.

Pellotine is said to be found only in the Williamsii variety, but this is always present in the commercial drug.

¶ *Medicinal Action and Uses.* Cardiac, tonic, narcotic, emetic. The value of the drug in practice is uncertain, but it is stated to be useful in neurasthenia, hysteria, and asthma, and has been recommended in gout, neuralgia and rheumatism.

Four to five buttons, or 215 to 230 grains of the drug will produce a strange cerebral excitement with visual disturbance, the visions being at first of varied beauty and later of gruesome shapes and monsters. The physical effects include dilatation of the pupil, muscular relaxation, loss of time sense, partial anæsthesia, wakefulness, and sometimes nausea and vomiting. The mental symptoms in some ways resemble those of Indian Hemp.

Pellotine, in doses of ½ to 1 grain, has been used in hypodermic injection in cases of insanity, producing sleep without undesirable reactions. Care is needed, as collapse is said to have been observed after a dose of $\frac{7}{10}$ of a grain. The uses of the various alkaloids are in the experimental stage.

¶ *Dosage.* Of the crude drug, 7 to 15 grains. Of fluid extract, 10 to 15 minims. Of 10 per cent. tincture, 1 to 2 teaspoonsful.

¶ *Other Species.*
There are also found in parcels of the tops specimens of *Mammalaria fissuratus*, *M. retusus*, and *A. jourdanianum*.

Mescal is a name given in Mexico to a liquor distilled from a number of species of Agave.

MEZEREON

Daphne mezereum (LINN.)
N.O. Thymelæaceæ

Synonyms. Mezerei Cortex. Mezerei officinarum. Dwarf Bay. Flowering Spurge. Spurge Olive. Spurge Laurel. Laureole gentille. Camolea. Kellerhals. Wolt schjeluke

Parts Used. The bark of root and stem, berries, roots

Habitat. Europe, including Britain, and Siberia. Naturalized in Canada and the United States

¶ *Description.* The mediæval name Mezereum is derived from the Persian *Mazariyun*, a name given to a species of Daphne. The barks of *Daphne laureola*, or Spurge Laurel, and *D. Gnidium* are also official in the British Pharmacopœia and United States.

Though a hardy shrub and indigenous to England, *D. mezereum* is not often found wild. The leaves appear at the ends of the branches after the flowers, and are alternate, lanceolate, entire, 2 to 3 inches long and dark green in colour. The small, purplish-pink, four-segmented flowers grow in little clusters, and the bright-red, fleshy, ovoid, bluntly-pointed fruits, about ⅓ inch long, appear close to the stem in July.

There are varieties with yellow fruit and white flowers.

Occasionally the bark is found in commerce in quills, but more often in tough, flexible, thin, long strips, rolled like tape, splitting easily lengthways but difficult to break horizontally. The inner surface is silky, and the thin, outer, corky layer, of a light greenish-brown colour, separates easily in papery fragments.

The unpleasant odour of the fresh bark diminishes with drying, but the taste is intensely burning and acrid, though sweetish at first. The root bark is most active, but inadequate supplies led to the recognition of the stem bark also.

¶ *Constituents.* The acridity of the bark is chiefly due to mezeen, a greenish-brown, sternutatory, amorphous resin. Mezereic acid, into which it can be changed, is found in the alcoholic and ethereal extracts, together with a fixed oil, a bitter, crystalline glucoside, daphnin, and a substance like euphorbone. Daphnin can be resolved into daphnetin and sugar by the action of dilute acids.

¶ *Medicinal Action and Uses.* Stimulant and vesicant. A moist application of the recent bark to the skin will cause redness and blisters in from twenty-four to forty-eight hours. It may be softened in hot vinegar and water and applied as a compress, renewed every twelve hours. It can be used for a mild, perpetual blister.

An ointment was formerly used to induce discharge in indolent ulcers.

The bark is used for snake and other venomous bites, and in Siberia, by veterinary surgeons, for horses' hoofs.

The official compound liniment of mustard includes an ethereal extract, and one of its rare internal uses in England is as an ingredient in compound decoction of sarsaparilla.

Authorities differ as to its value in chronic rheumatism, scrofula, syphilis and skin diseases. A light infusion is said to be good in dropsies, but if too strong may cause vomiting and bloody stools. Thirty berries are used as a purgative by Russian peasants, though French writers regard fifteen as a fatal dose.

In Germany a tincture of the berries is used locally in neuralgia.

Slices of the root may be chewed in toothache, and it is recorded that an obstinate case of difficulty in swallowing, persisting after confinement, was cured by chewing the root constantly and so causing irritation.

¶ *Dosages.* Ten grains. Of decoction, 1 to 3 fluid ounces. Of fluid extract, 2 to 10 drops.

¶ *Poisons and Antidotes.* In large doses it is an irritant poison, causing vomiting and hypercatharsis.

The berries have proved fatal to children.

¶ *Other Species.*

D. Gnidium, or *D. paniculata,* garou, sainbois, or Spurge Flax, deriving its name from its native Cnidos, is one of the official species. The leaves are numerous and very narrow, like those of flax.

D. Laureola, or Spurge Laurel, is less acrid. The leaves were formerly used as an emmenagogue, but may cause vomiting and purging. Both leaves and bark have been used to procure abortion.

D. Thymelœa, D. Tartonaira, D. pontica and *D. alpina* are used as substitutes.

AMERICAN MEZEREON is a name of *Dirca Palustris* or Leatherwood.

MILFOIL. *See* YARROW

MILFOIL, WATER

N.O. Haloragaceæ

To the same natural order as the Mare's Tail (Haloragaceæ) belongs the Water Milfoil, which has the following varieties: SPIKED WATER MILFOIL (*Myriophyllum spicatum*), an aquatic plant forming a tangled mass of slender, much branched stems; leaves, four in a whorl, finely divided into numerous hair-like segments, the whole plant being submerged, except the spikes of inconspicuous greenish flowers, which rise a few inches above the surface.

WHORLED WATER MILFOIL (*M. verticillatum*) differs from the preceding in having the flowers in whorls at the base of the leaves: alternate-flowered Water Milfoil (*M. alterniflorum*) has the barren flowers alternately arranged in a short leafless spike, with the fertile flowers about three together, in the axils of the leaves, at its base. Both species are rare.

See MARE'S TAIL.

MILKWEED. *See* ASCLEPIAS

MIMOSAS

N.O. Leguminosæ

Mimosa fragifolia is an acrid astringent.

M. linguis is a diuretic astringent.

M. humilis, Brazilian Mimosa or Sensitive Plant, so called because the leaves close at the least contact. Tincture of the leaves is used by homœopaths for swelling of ankles.

Cassia nictitans, or Wild Sensitive Plant, is used for certain forms of rheumatism.

MINTS

N.O. Labiatæ

There are three chief species of mint in cultivation and general use: Spearmint (*Mentha viridis*), Peppermint (*M. piperita*), and Pennyroyal (*M. pulegium*), the first being the one ordinarily used for cooking.

The various species of mint have much in

common and have all been held in high medical repute. Dr. Westmacott, the author of a work on plants published in 1694, mentioning the different kinds of mint, states that they are well known to

'the young Botanists and Herb Women belonging to Apothecarys' shops. . . . In the shops are 1. The dry Herbs. 2ndly. Mint Water. 3rdly. Spirit of Mints. 4th. Syrup of Mints. 5th. The Conserve of the Leaves.

6th. The Simple Oyl. 7th. The Chemical Oyl.' He says 'the Mints have a biting, aromatick bitterish Sapor with a strong fragrant Smell abounding with a pungent Volatile Salt and a Subtil Sulphur which destroyeth Acids, and herein doth lodge the Causation of such medicinal Virtues in this Herb and others of the like Nature.'

All the Mints yield fragrant oils by distillation.

SPEARMINT

Mentha viridis (LINN.)
N.O. Labiatæ

Synonyms. Garden Mint. Mentha Spicata. Mackerel Mint. Our Lady's Mint. Green Mint. Spire Mint. Sage of Bethlehem. Fish Mint. Menthe de Notre Dame. Erba Santa Maria. Frauen Munze. Lamb Mint

Part Used. Herb

This common garden mint is not a native of these islands, though growing freely in every garden, but is originally a native of the Mediterranean region, and was introduced into Britain by the Romans, being largely cultivated not only by them, but also by the other Mediterranean nations. It was in great request by the Romans, and Pliny according to Gerard says of it: 'The smell of Mint does stir up the minde and the taste to a greedy desire of meate.' Ovid represents the hospitable Baucis and Philemon scouring their board with green mint before laying upon it the food intended for their divine guests. The Ancients believed that mint would prevent the coagulation of milk and its acid fermentation. Gerard, again quoting Pliny, says:

'It will not suffer milk to cruddle in the stomach, and therefore it is put in milk that is drunke, lest those that drinke thereof should be strangled.'

Many other references to it in old writings – among them, that of the payment by the Pharisees of tithes of Mint, Anise and Cumin – prove that the herb has been highly esteemed for many centuries. Mint is mentioned in all early mediæval lists of plants; it was very early grown in English gardens, and was certainly cultivated in the Convent gardens of the ninth century. Chaucer refers to 'a little path of mintes full and fenill greene.'

Turner states in his *Herball* (1568) that the garden mint of his time was also called 'Spere Mynte.' Gerard, in further praise of the herb, tells us that

'the smelle rejoiceth the heart of man, for which cause they used to strew it in chambers and places of recreation, pleasure and repose, where feasts and banquets are made.'

It has, in fact, been so universally esteemed, that it is to be found wild in nearly all the countries to which civilization has extended, and in America for 200 years it has been known as an escape from gardens, growing in moist soils and proving sometimes troublesome as a weed.

Parkinson, in his *Garden of Pleasure*, mentions 'divers sorts of mintes both of the garden and wilde, of the woods, mountain and standing pools or waters' and says:

'Mintes are sometimes used in Baths with Balm and other herbs as a help to comfort and strengthen the nerves and sinews. It is much used either outwardly applied or inwardly drunk to strengthen and comfort weak stomackes.'

The Ancients used mint to scent their bath water and as a restorative, as we use smelling salts to-day. In Athens where every part of the body was perfumed with a different scent mint was specially designated to the arms.

Gerard says of its medicinal properties:

'It is good against watering eies and all manner of breakings out on the head and sores. It is applied with salt to the bitings of mad dogs. . . . They lay it on the stinging of wasps and bees with good success.'

Culpepper gives nearly forty distinct maladies for which mint is 'singularly good.'

'Being smelled into,' he says, 'it is comfortable for the head and memory, and a decoction when used as a gargle, cures the mouth and gums, when sore.' Again, 'Garden Mint is most useful to wash children's heads when the latter are inclined to sores, and Wild Mint, mixed with vinegar is an excellent wash to get rid of scurf. Rose leaves and mint, heated and applied outwardly cause rest and sleep.'

In the fourteenth century, mint was used for whitening the teeth, and its distilled oil is still used to flavour tooth-pastes, etc., and in America, especially, to flavour confectionery, chewing gums, and also to perfume soap.

Mint ottos have more power than any other aromatic to overcome the smell of tobacco.

The application of a strong decoction of Spearmint is said to cure chapped hands.

Mice are so averse to the smell of mint, either fresh or dried, that they will leave untouched any food where it is scattered. As mice love Henbane and often prove very destructive to a crop, it has been suggested that their depredations might be checked if some mint were planted between the rows of Henbane.

It is probable that Spearmint was introduced by the Pilgrim Fathers when they landed in America, as it is mentioned among many other plants brought out from England, in a list given by John Josselyn. When in this country apparently found growing wild, it occurs in watery places, but is rather rare.

Professor Henslow (*Origin and History of our Garden Vegetables*) does not consider it truly native to any country. He says:

'The Garden Mint (*Mentha viridis*, Linn.) is a cultivated form of *M. sylvestris* (Linn.), the Horse Mint, which is recorded as cultivated at Aleppo. Either *M. sylvestris*, or some form approaching *M. viridis*, which is not known as a truly wild plant, was probably the mint of Scripture.'

Bentham also considers it not improbably a variety of *M. sylvestris*, perpetuated through its ready propagation by suckers, and though these two plants are sufficiently distinct as found in England, yet continental forms occur which bridge over their differences.

Its generic name, *Mentha*, is derived from the mythological origin ascribed to it, and was originally applied to the mint by Theophrastus. Menthe was a nymph, who because of the love Pluto bore her, was metamorphosed by Proserpine, from motives of jealousy, into the plant we now call mint.

¶ *Description.* From creeping root-stocks, erect, square stems rise to a height of about 2 feet, bearing very short-stalked, acute-pointed, lance-shaped, wrinkled, bright green leaves, with finely toothed edges and smooth surfaces, the ribs very prominent beneath. The small flowers are densely arranged in whorls or rings in the axils of the upper leaves, forming cylindrical, slender, tapering spikes, pinkish or lilac in colour. The little labiate flowers are followed by very few, roundish, minute brown seeds. The taste and odour of the plant are very characteristic.

There are several forms of Garden Mint, the true variety being of bold, upright growth, with fairly large and broad leaves, pointed and sharply serrated (or toothed) at the edges and of a rich, bright, green colour. Another variety, sometimes sold as Spearmint (*M. cardiaca*), is much smaller and less erect in growth, with darker leaves, the whorls of flowers distant and leafy, but possessing the same odour and flavour, and another has comparatively large, broad or rounded leaves. Yet another has soft hairs, but this, though distinct from what is known as Horse Mint, is inferior to the true Spearmint.

A form with its leaves slightly crisped is common in gardens under the name of *M. crispa.*

¶ *Cultivation.* A moist situation is preferable, but mint will succeed in almost any soil when once started into growth, though in dry, sandy soils it is sometimes difficult to grow, and should be planted in the coolest and dampest situations. Leaf mould, road scrapings, burnt ash and similar materials should, on the other hand, be used freely for lightening heavy, tenacious soils. It does best in a partially shaded position: if in a sheltered spot, it will start earlier in the spring than if exposed. Where a long or regular supply is required, it is a good plan to have at least one bed in a sunny and sheltered, and another in a shady position, where gatherings may be made both early and late.

As the plant is a perennial, spreading by means of its underground, creeping stems, propagation may be easily effected by lifting the roots in February or March, dividing them – every piece showing a joint will grow – and planting again in shallow trenches, covering with 2 inches of soil. Six inches apart in the rows and 8 inches between the rows are the right distances to allow. Cuttings in summer or offsets in spring may also be utilized for increasing a stock. Cuttings may be taken at almost any time during the summer, always choosing the young shoots, these being struck on a shady border of light soil and kept moist, or a better plan, if possible, is to insert them in a frame, keeping them close and moist till rooted. Cuttings or young shoots will also strike freely in good-sized boxes in a heated greenhouse, in the early spring, and after the tops have been taken off two or three times for use, the plants may be hardened off and planted outside.

The beds are much benefited by an annual top-dressing of rich soil, applied towards the close of autumn, when all remaining stalks should be cut down to the ground. A liberal top-dressing of short, decayed manure, such as that from an old hot-bed or mushroom bed, annually, either in the spring, when it commences to grow, or better still, perhaps, after the first or second cutting, will ensure luxuriant growth. Frequent cuttings of shoots constitute a great drain on the plants, and if not properly nourished they will fail, more or less. To have really good mint, the plantation should be re-made about every three years, or failing that, it is essential that a good top-dressing of rich soil be added.

A good stock should be kept up, so that plenty may be available for *forcing*. Cultivators having a greenhouse can easily force mint into an earlier development of new growth than would be in the open garden. Forcing is very easy, the only preparation being the insertion of a quantity of good roots in a box of light soil, which should be placed in a temperature of about 60° and watered freely as soon as growth starts. Cuttings may be made in two or three weeks. Forcing will generally be necessary from November to May – a succession being kept up by the introduction, at intervals of about three weeks, of an additional supply of roots, as forced roots soon decay. Often mint is so grown both upon and under the benches in greenhouses, and the demand for the young, tender stems and leaves during the winter is sufficient to make the plants pay well.

¶ *Mint Disease.* Unfortunately, mint is susceptible to a disease which in some gardens has completely destroyed it. This disease, which from its characteristic symptoms is known as Rust, is incurable. The fungus (*Puccinia Mentha*) which causes it develops inside the plant, and therefore cannot be reached by any purgicide, and as it is perennial, it cannot be got rid of by cutting off the latter. All that can be done is to prevent the spread of the disease by digging up all plants that show any sign of rust. The same ground should not be used again for mint for several years. Healthy stock should be obtained and planted in uninfected soil, some distance away. On account of this liability of mint to rust, it is advisable not to have it all in one bed, but to have several beds of it, placed at some distance from each other.

¶ *Harvesting.* When the plants are breaking into bloom, the stalks should be cut a few inches above the root, on a dry day, after the dew has disappeared, and before the hot sun has taken any oil from the leaves, and dried for culinary use for the winter. All discoloured and insect-eaten leaves should be removed and the stems tied loosely into bunches and hung to dry on strings in the usual manner directed for 'bunched' herbs. The bunches should be nearly equal in length and uniform in size to facilitate packing, if intended for sale, and placed when dry in airtight boxes to prevent re-absorption of moisture.

The leaves may also be stripped from the stems as soon as thoroughly dry and rubbed through a fine sieve, so as to be freed from stalks as much as possible, or pounded in a mortar and thus powdered, stored in stoppered bottles or tins rendered airtight. If preparing for market and not for home use, the rubbed herbs will, of course, command a higher price than the bunched herbs, and should be put up in tins or bottles containing a quantity of uniform weight.

When mint is grown commercially on a large scale, it has been estimated to yield from 4 to 5 tons per acre, from which 15 to 20 cwt. of dry should be obtained. Average yields per acre are, however, taken when crops are at maturity, and an estimate of the first cutting crop is hard to form, and is likely to be less profitable than succeeding years, on account of initial expenses.

If Spearmint is being grown as a *medicinal* herb, for the sake of the volatile oil to be extracted from it, the shoots should be gathered in August, when just coming into flower, and taken to the distillery as soon as possible after picking, the British Pharmacopœia directing that oil of Spearmint be distilled from the fresh, flowering plant. It is estimated that 350 lb. of Spearmint yield 1 lb. of oil. If the distillery is not on the ground or only a short distance away, and the crop has to be dispatched by train, the cutting should take place late in the afternoon on a fine day, before the dew falls, so as to be sent off by a night train to arrive at their destination next morning, having travelled in the cool, otherwise the leaves are apt to heat and ferment, losing colour.

¶ *Constituents.* The chief constituent of Spearmint oil is Carvone. There are also present Phellandrine, Limonene and dihydrocarveol acetate. Esters of acetic, butyric and caproic or caprylic acids are also present. (An Ester is a combination of an alcohol with an acid, the combination being associated with the elimination of water. The esters are highly important and in many cases dominant constituents of numerous essential oils, which owe their perfume largely, or in some cases entirely, to the esters contained. Many of the esters are used as flavouring or perfumery agents, and many are among the most important constituents of volatile salts.)

There are several different essential oils

known under the name of Spearmint oil, the botanical origin of the plant used for distillation differing with the country in which the plant is grown. In the United States and in this country several varieties of *M. viridis* are distilled. In Russia the plant distilled is *M. verticellata*, and in Germany either *M. longifolia*, or more generally *M. aquatica* var. *crispa* – a plant cultivated in Northern Germany, the oil (called there *Krausemünzöl*) being imported into this country as German Spearmint oil. It appears to be identical with that from *M. viridis*. Oil of Spearmint is little distilled in England, either German oil or American oil distilled from *M. viridis* being imported.

¶ *Medicinal Action and Uses*. Spearmint is chiefly used for culinary purposes. The properties of Spearmint oil resemble those of Peppermint, being stimulant, carminative and antispasmodic, but its effects are less powerful, and it is less used than Peppermint, though it is better adapted for children's maladies. From 2 to 5 drops may be given on sugar, or from ½ to 1 teaspoonful of spirit of Spearmint, with 2 tablespoonful of water. Spearmint oil is added to many compounds on account of its carminative properties, and because its taste is pleasanter and less strong than Peppermint. A distilled water of Spearmint will relieve hiccough and flatulence as well as the giddiness of indigestion. For infantile trouble generally, the sweetened infusion is an excellent remedy, and is also a pleasant beverage in fevers, inflammatory diseases, etc. Make the infusion by pouring a pint of boiling water on an ounce of the dried herb; the strained-off liquid is taken in doses of a wineglassful or less. It is considered a specific in allaying nausea and vomiting and will relieve the pain of colic. A homœopathic tincture prepared from the fresh plant in flower has been found serviceable in strangury, gravel, and as a local application in painful hæmorrhoids. Its principal employment is for its febrifuge and diuretic virtues.

¶ *Preparations and Dosages*. Fluid extract, ¼ to 1 drachm. Water, B.P. and U.S.P., 4 drachms. Spirit, U.S.P., 30 drops.

When eaten with lamb, very finely chopped in sweetened vinegar, in the form of mint sauce, mint greatly aids the digestion, as it makes the crude, albuminous fibres of the immature meat more digestible. The volatile oil stimulates the digestive system and prevents septic changes within the intestines.

The fresh sprigs of mint are used to flavour green peas and also new potatoes, being boiled with them, and the powdered, dried leaves are used with pea soup and also in seasonings. On the Continent, especially in Germany, the powdered, dried mint is often used at table for dusting upon pea and bean purées, as well as on gravies.

A grating of mint is introduced sometimes into a potato salad, or into a fowl stuffing, and in Wales it is not unusual to boil mint with cabbage.

Mint Jelly can be used instead of mint sauce, in the same manner as red currant jelly. It may be made by steeping mint leaves in apple jelly, or in one of the various kinds of commercial gelatine. The jelly should be a delicate shade of green. A handful of leaves should colour and flavour about half a pint of jelly. Strain the liquid through a jelly bag to remove all particles of mint before allowing to set.

Mint Vinegar is made as follows: Fill a jar or bottle with young mint leaves picked from the stalks. Cover with cold vinegar and cork or cover the bottle. Infuse for 14 days, then strain off the vinegar.

This vinegar is sometimes employed in making Mint Jelly, as follows:

Take 1 pint of water, 1¼ oz. gelatine, the white and shell of an egg, ¼ gill of Mint Vinegar, 1 dessertspoonful of Tarragon Vinegar, a bunch of herbs, 1 onion, 1 carrot, a stick of celery, 10 peppercorns, salt, 1 lemon. Peel the lemon very thinly, slightly whip the white of egg, wash and crush the shell. Put all the ingredients into a pan, then the juice of the lemon and whisk over the fire until just on boiling point. Boil up, then draw the pan to the side of the fire and simmer very gently for 20 minutes. Strain through a jelly bag until clear. Put into a mould to set. If liked, finely chopped mint may be added to the jelly after straining it, or more mint can be used and no Tarragon Vinegar.

To make *Mint Punch*: Pick a quart of fresh mint leaves, then wash and dry them by shaking them in a clean kitchen towel. Put them into a large jug and mash them with a wooden spoon till soft, when cover with freshly boiled water and infuse for ten minutes. Strain, cool, then set on ice till required. Add two cups of chilled grape juice and strained lemon juice to taste. Sweeten with castor sugar, stir till sugar is dissolved and then add a quart of ginger ale. Fill each tumbler to one-third with cracked ice and fill up with the punch.

The Garden Mint is also the basis of Mint Julep and Mint-water, the cordial distilled from the plant.

Mint Cake is a cake made of flour and dripping or lard, flavoured with sugar and chopped fresh mint and rolled out thin.

PEPPERMINT   Mentha piperita (SM.)
                                                              N.O. Labiatæ

Synonym. Brandy Mint
Part Used. Herb
Habitat. The plant is found throughout Europe, in moist situations, along stream banks
         and in waste lands, and is not unfrequent in damp places in England, but is not a
         common native plant, and probably is often an escape from cultivation. In America
         it is probably even more common as an escape than Spearmint, having long been
         known and grown in gardens

Of the members of the mint family under cultivation the most important are the several varieties of the Peppermint (*Mentha piperita*), extensively cultivated for years as the source of the well-known volatile oil of Peppermint, used as a flavouring and therapeutic agent.

¶ *Description.* The leaves of this kind of mint are shortly but distinctly stalked, 2 inches or more in length, and ¾ to 1¼ inches broad, their margins finely toothed, their surfaces smooth, both above and beneath, or only very slightly, hardly visibly, hairy on the principal veins and mid-rib on the underside. The stems, 2 to 4 feet high, are quadrangular, often purplish. The whorled clusters of little reddish-violet flowers are in the axils of the upper leaves, forming loose, interrupted spikes, and rarely bear seeds. The entire plant has a very characteristic odour, due to the volatile oil present in all its parts, which when applied to the tongue has a hot, aromatic taste at first, and afterwards produces a sensation of cold in the mouth caused by the menthol it contains.

¶ *History.* Pliny tells us that the Greeks and Romans crowned themselves with Peppermint at their feasts and adorned their tables with its sprays, and that their cooks flavoured both their sauces and their wines with its essence. Two species of mint were used by the ancient Greek physicians, but some writers doubt whether either was the modern Peppermint, though there is evidence that *M. piperita* was cultivated by the Egyptians. It is mentioned in the Icelandic Pharmacopœias of the thirteenth century, but only came into general use in the medicine of Western Europe about the middle of the eighteenth century, and then was first used in England.

It was only recognized here as a distinct species late in the seventeenth century, when the great botanist, Ray, published it in the second edition of his *Synopsis stirpium britannicorum*, 1696. Its medicinal properties were speedily recognized, and it was admitted into the London Pharmacopœia in 1721, under *M. piperitis sapore*. The oldest existing Peppermint district is in the neighbourhood of Mitcham, in Surrey, where its cultivation from a commercial point of view dates from about 1750, at which period only a few acres of ground there were devoted to medicinal plants. At the end of the eighteenth century, above 100 acres were cropped with Peppermint, but so late as 1805 there were no stills at Mitcham, and the herb had to be carried to London for the extraction of the oil. By 1850 there were already about 500 acres under cultivation at Mitcham, and at the present day the English Peppermint plantations are still chiefly located in this district, though it is grown in several other parts of England – in Herts at Hitchin, and in Cambs at Wisbech, in Lincolnshire at Market Deeping and also at Holbeach (where the cultivation and distillation of English Peppermint oil, now carried on with the most up-to-date improvements was commenced over seventy years ago).

There is room for a further extension of its cultivation, owing to the great superiority of the English product in pungency and flavour.

Most of London's supplies are grown in a triangle with its base on a line Kingston to Croydon, and its apex at Chipstead in Surrey. This triangle includes Mitcham, still the centre of the Peppermint-growing and distilling industry, the district proving to be specially suited to the crop. There are large Peppermint farms at Banstead and Cheam.

On the Continent Peppermint was first grown in 1771 at Utrecht, but it is now grown in considerable amounts in several countries. In France it is cultivated in the Departments of the Yonne and du Nord, French Peppermint Oil being distilled at Grasse and Cannes, as well as in the Basses-Alpes, Haute-Garonne and other parts, though the French varieties of *M. piperita* are not identical with those cultivated in England. The variety cultivated in France is known as 'Red Mint' and can grow on certain soils where the true Peppermint does not grow. The 'Red Mint' can be cultivated for four or five years in the same field, but the true *M. piperita* can be cultivated in the same field for two years only. 'Red Mint' gives a higher yield of oil, but is of inferior quality. In the Siagne Valley, it is calculated that 300 kilos of fresh plant produce 1 kilo of essential oil, elsewhere a yield of 2 kilos to about 1,000 kilos of stems and green leaves is claimed. It has been proved by experience that all parts of the plant do not give the same proportion of oil, and it is more abundant when the plants have been grown in a hot region and have flowered to the best advantage.

The product of absolutely genuine English plants cultivated in French soil varies according to the district, for the soil has a very important influence upon the flavour of the oil and also the climate: badly-drained ground is known to give unfavourable results both as to the quantity and quality of the oil.

An oil very similar to Mitcham oil, and of an excellent quality, is distilled from English plants grown in Italy, mostly in Piedmont and also in Sicily. Next to the essential oils of lemon and orange, that obtained from Peppermint enjoys a high reputation among the numerous volatile oils produced by Italy. Vigone and Pancalieri are the centres of the cultivation and distillation of Peppermint in the province of Turin. This district, which has been designated the 'Mitcham of Italy,' yields annually about 11,000,000 kilograms of Peppermint, from which 25,000 to 27,000 kilograms of essential oil are obtained. A new variety of Peppermint, found at Lutra on the island of Tino, in the Grecian Archipelago, has been cultivated in the Royal Colonial Garden at Palermo.

A small amount of Peppermint oil of good quality is distilled from plantations in Germany, at Miltitz, in Saxony and near Leipzig, where the little town of Colleda, before the War, produced annually as much as 40,000 cwt. of the herb. Russia also produces some Peppermint, in the Ukraine and the Caucasus, but most of it is used in the country itself.

With regard to Hungarian oil of Peppermint, organized effort to secure improvement began in 1904 and has been greatly developed. Hungarian oil compares favourably with American oil of Peppermint as regards percentage of Menthol contained: Hungarian oil yielding 43 to 56 per cent. of free menthol, and 35 to 65 per cent. of total menthol; while American oil yields 40 to 45 per cent. free menthol and 60 per cent. total menthol.

Peppermint oil distilled in 1914 from Mitcham plants grown at Molo, in the highlands of British East Africa, possesses a most excellent aroma, quite free of bitterness, and a very high figure indeed for the menthol contained, and there is no question that this source of supply should be an important one in the future.

The United States, however, are now the most important producers of Peppermint oil, producing – mostly in Michigan, where its cultivation was introduced in 1855, Indiana, the western districts of New York State, and to a smaller extent in Ohio – rather under half of the world's total output of the oil. The whole of the Peppermint cultivation is confined to the north-east portion of the United States, and the extreme south of Canada, where some is grown in the province of Ontario. The first small distillery was erected in Wayne County, New York State, in the early part of last century, and at the present day the industry has increased to such an extent, that there are portions of Michigan where thousands of acres are planted with nothing else but Peppermint.

English oil is incomparably the best, but it fetches a very high price, and the French oil, though much inferior, is of finer quality than the American.

The problem is to obtain a strain of mint plants which would yield larger quantities of oil in our climate. It is possible that varieties yielding a more abundant supply of essential oils might be secured by persistent endeavour, without reducing our English standard of refinement. Also economy in harvesting and distilling should be studied. If our English oils could be reduced in price, they would replace the foreign to a greater or less extent depending upon the reduction in cost of production.

There are several varieties of Peppermint. The two chief, the so-called 'Black' and 'White' mints are the ones extensively cultivated. Botanically there is little difference between them, but the stems and leaves of the 'Black' mint are tinged purplish-brown, while the stems of the 'White' variety are green, and the leaves are more coarsely serrated in the White. The oil furnished by the Black is of inferior quality, but more abundant than that obtained from the White, the yield of oil from which is generally only about four-fifths of that from an equal area of the Black, but it has a more delicate odour and obtains a higher price. The plant is also more delicate, being easily destroyed by frost or drought; it is principally grown for drying in bundles – technically termed 'bunching,' and is the kind chiefly dried for herbalists, the Black variety being more generally grown for the oil on account of its greater productivity and hardiness. The variety grown at Mitcham is classified by some authorities as *M. piperita*, var. *rubra*.

¶ *Cultivation.* Both Peppermint and Spearmint thrive best in a fairly warm, preferably moist climate, and in deep soils rich in humus and retentive of moisture, but fairly open in texture and well drained, either naturally or artificially.

These conditions are frequently combined in effectively drained swamp lands, but the plants may also be commercially cultivated in well-prepared upland soils, such as would produce good corn, oil or potatoes. Though a moist situation is preferable, Peppermint will succeed in most soils, when once started into growth and carefully cultivated. It flourishes well in what are known in America as muck land, that is, those broad level areas, often several thousand acres in extent, of deep fertile soil, the beds of ancient lakes and swamps where the remains of ages of growths of aquatic vegetation have accumulated. In Michigan and Indiana, where there are large areas of such land, mint culture has become highly specialized, a considerable part of the acreage being controlled by a few well-equipped growers able to handle the product in an economical manner, who have of late years installed their own up-to-date distilling plants. The cultivation of Peppermint is a growing industry now also on the reclaimed lands of Louisiana.

The usual method of mint cultivation on these farms in America is to dig runners in the early spring and lay them in shallow trenches, 3 feet apart in well-prepared soil. The growing crop is kept well cultivated and absolutely free from weeds and in the summer when the plant is in full bloom, the mint is cut by hand and distilled in straw. A part of the exhausted herb is dried and used for cattle food, for which it possesses considerable value. The rest is cut and composted and eventually ploughed into the ground as fertilizer.

The area selected for Peppermint growing should be cropped for one or two years with some plant that requires a frequent tillage. The tillage is also continued as long as possible during the growth of the mint, for successful mint-growing implies clean culture at all stages of progress.

In one of our chief English plantations the following mode of cultivation is adopted. A rich and friable soil, retentive of moisture is selected, and the ground is well tilled 8 to 10 inches deep. The plants are propagated in the spring, usually in April and May. When the young shoots from the crop of the previous year have attained a height of about 4 inches, they are pulled up and transplanted into new soil, in shallow furrows about 2 feet apart, lightly covered with about 2 inches of soil. They grow vigorously the first year and throw out numerous stolons and runners on the surface of the ground. After the crop has been removed, these are allowed to harden or become woody, and then farm-yard manure is scattered over the field and ploughed in. In this way the stolons are divided into numerous pieces and covered with soil before the frost sets in, otherwise if the autumn is wet, they are liable to become sodden and rot, and the next crop fails. In the spring the fields are dressed with Peruvian Guano.

¶ *Manuring.* Liberal manuring is essential, and the quantity and nature of the manure has a great effect on the characteristics of the oil. Mineral salts are found to be of much value. *Nitrate of Soda*, applied at the rate of 50 to 150 lb. to the acre both stimulates the growth of foliage and improves the quality of the essence. Half the total quantity should be applied a month before planting and the remainder a month before the harvest. *Potash*, also, is particularly useful against a form of chlorosis or 'rust' (*Puccinia menthœ*) due, apparently, to too much water in the soil, as it often appears after moist, heavy weather in August, which causes the foliage to drop off and leave the stems almost bare, in which circumstances the rust is liable to attack the plants. Some authorities have calculated that an acre of Peppermint requires 84 lb. of Nitrogen, 37 lb. of Phosphoric Acid and 139 lb. of Potash. Ground Bone and Lime do not seem to be of marked benefit. The top dressing of the running roots with fine loam either by ploughing as above described, or otherwise, is very essential before winter sets in.

In the south of France, sewage (1,300 lb. per acre) is extensively used, together with Sesame seeds from which the oil has been expressed. The latter are especially suited for light and limey soils, and are either worked in before planting or placed directly in the furrows with the plants. Up to 5,000 or 6,000 lb. per acre are applied, giving a crop of from 2,100 to 2,600 lb. per acre. The residues from the distillation of the crop are invariably used as manure. It is found, however, that although these manures supply sufficient nitrogen, they are deficient in phosphoric acid and potash. This shortage must be made up by chemical manures, otherwise the soil will become exhausted. Chemical manures *alone* are equally unsatisfactory in soils poor in organic matter. In conjunction with organic manures they give excellent results.

On suitable soil and with proper cultivation, yields of from 2 to 3 tons of Peppermint herb per acre may be expected, but large yields can only be expected from fields that are in the best possible condition. A fair average for well-managed commercial plantings may be said to be 30 lb. of oil per acre, but the yield of oil is always variable, ranging from only a few pounds to, in extremely favourable cases, nearly 100 lb. per acre. About 325 lb. of Peppermint, nearly 3 cwt., are required to produce a pound of oil in commercial practice, i.e. about 7 lb. of oil are generally obtained from 1 ton of the herb. The price varies as widely as the yield, the value depending upon the chemical composition.

The presence of weeds among the Peppermint, especially other species of *Mentha*, is an important cause of deterioration to the oil. *M. arvensis*, the Corn Mint, if allowed to settle and increase among the crop to such an extent as not to be easily separated, has been known when distilled to absolutely ruin the flavour of the latter. In new ground the Peppermint requires handweeding two or three times, as the hoe cannot be used without injury to the plant.

In America great detriment is occasioned by the growth of *Erigeron canadensis*, and newly cleared ground planted with Peppermint, is liable to the intrusion of another plant of the order Compositæ, *Erechtites hieracifolia*, which is also highly injurious to the quality of the oil.

¶ *Irrigation.* Peppermint requires frequent irrigation. In the south of France the crop is irrigated on the 15th of May, and thereafter every eight or ten days. When the plants are fully developed they are watered at least three times a week. It is important to keep the soil constantly moist, although well drained. Absorption of water makes the shoots more tender, thus facilitating cutting, and causes a large quantity of green matter to be produced.

A plantation lasts about four years, the best output being the second year. The fourth-year crop is rarely good. A crop that yields a high percentage of essential oil exhausts the ground as a rule, and after cropping with Peppermint for four years, the land must be put to some other purpose for at least seven years. In some parts of France the plantations are renewed annually with the object of obtaining vigorous plants.

Few pests trouble Peppermint, though crickets, grasshoppers and caterpillars may always do some damage.

¶ *Harvesting.* The herb is cut just before flowering, from the end of July to the end of August in England and France, according to local conditions. Sometimes when well irrigated and matured, a second crop can be obtained in September. With new plantations the harvest is generally early in September.

Harvesting should be carried out on a dry, sunny day, in the late morning, when all traces of dew have disappeared. The first year's crop is always cut with the sickle to prevent injury to the stolons. The herb of the second and third years is cut with scythes and then raked into loose heaps ready for carting to the stills.

In many places, the custom is to let the herb lie on the ground for a time in these small bundles or cocks. In other countries the herb is distilled as soon as cut. Again, certain distillers prefer the plants to be previously dried or steamed. The subject is much debated, but the general opinion is that it is best to distil as soon as cut, and the British Pharmacopœia directs that the oil be distilled from the fresh flowering plant. Even under the best conditions of drying, there is a certain loss of essential oil. If the herbs lie in heaps for any time, fermentation is bound to occur, reducing the quality and quantity of the oil, as laboratory experiments have proved. Should it be impossible to treat all the crop as cut, it should be properly dried on the same system as that adopted for other medicinal plants. The loss is then small. Variation in the chemical composition of the essence should be brought about by manuring, rather than by the system of harvesting, though in America the loss caused by partial drying in the field is not regarded by growers as sufficient to offset the increased cost of handling and distilling the green herb. Exposure to frost must, however, be avoided, as frozen mint yields scarcely half the quantity of oil which could otherwise be secured.

At Market Deeping the harvest usually commences in the beginning or middle of August, or as soon as the plant begins to flower and lasts for six weeks, the stills being kept going night and day. The herb is carted direct from the fields to the stills, which are made of copper and contain about 5 cwt. of the herb. Before putting the Peppermint into the still, water is poured in to a depth of about 2 feet, at which height a false bottom is placed, and on this the herb is then trodden down by men. The lid is then let down, and under pressure the distillation is conducted by the application of direct heat at the lowest possible temperature, and is continued for about 4¼ hours. The lid is then removed, and the false bottom with the Peppermint resting on it is raised by a windlass, and the Peppermint carried away in the empty carts on their return journey to the fields, where it is placed in heaps and allowed to rot, being subsequently mixed with manure applied to the fields in the autumn.

The usual yield of oil, if the season be warm and dry, is 1 oz. from 5 lb. of the fresh flowering plant, but if wet and unfavourable, the product is barely half that quantity.

If the cut green tops have some distance to travel to the distillery, they should be cut late in the afternoon, so as to be sent off by a night train to arrive at their destination next morning, or they would be apt to heat and ferment and lose colour.

Since the oil is the chief marketable product, adequate distilling facilities and a market for the oil are essential to success in the industry, and the prospective Peppermint grower should assure himself on these points before investing capital in plantations.

There is also a market, chiefly for herbalists, for the dried herb, which is gathered at the same time of year. It should be cut shortly above the base, leaving some leaf-buds, and not including the lowest shrivelled or discoloured leaves and tied loosely into bundles by the stalk-ends, about twenty to the bundle on the average, and the bundles of equal length, about 6 inches, to facilitate packing, and dried over strings as described for Spearmint. Two or three days will be sufficient to dry.

Peppermint culture on suitable soils gives fair average returns when intelligently conducted from year to year. The product, however, is liable to fluctuation in prices, and the cost of establishing the crop and the annual expenses of cultivation are high.

¶ Constituents. Among essential oils, Peppermint ranks first in importance. It is a colourless, yellowish or greenish liquid, with a peculiar, highly penetrating odour and a burning, camphorescent taste. It thickens and becomes reddish with age, but improves in mellowness, even if kept as long as ten or fourteen years.

The chief constituent of Peppermint oil is Menthol, but it also contains menthyl acetate and isovalerate, together with menthone, cineol, inactive pinene, limonene and other less important bodies.

On cooling to a low temperature, separation of Menthol occurs, especially if a few crystals of that substance be added to start crystallization.

The value of the oil depends much upon the composition. The principal ester constituent, menthyl acetate, possesses a very fragrant minty odour, to which the agreeable aroma of the oil is largely due. The alcoholic constituent, Menthol, possesses the well-known penetrating minty odour and characteristic cooling taste. The flavouring properties of the oil are due largely to both the ester and alcoholic constituents, while the medicinal value is attributed to the latter only. The most important determination to be made in the examination of Peppermint oil, is that of the total amount of Menthol, but the Menthone value is also frequently required. The English oil contains 60 to 70 per cent. of Menthol, the Japanese oil containing 85 per cent., and the American less than ours, only about 50 per cent. The odour and taste afford a good indication of the quality of the oil, and by this means it is quite possible to distinguish between English, American and Japanese oils.

Menthol is obtained from various species of *Mentha* and is imported into England, chiefly from Japan. The oils from which it is chiefly obtained are those from *M. arvensis*, var. *piperascens*, in Japan, *M. arvensis*, var. *glabrata* in China, and *M. piperita* in America.

Japan, and to a certain extent China, produce large quantities of Peppermint oil distilled from the plants just mentioned. The oils produced from these plants are greatly inferior to those distilled from *M. piperita*, but have the advantage of containing a large proportion of Menthol, of which they are the commercial source.

The Japanese Menthol plant is now being grown in South Australia, having been introduced there by the Germans from Japan.

Chinese Peppermint oil is largely distilled at Canton, a considerable quantity being sent to Bombay, also a large quantity of Menthol. Peppermint is chiefly cultivated in the province of Kiang-si.

M. incana, cultivated near Bombay as a herb, also possesses the flavour of Peppermint.

M. arvensis, var. *javanesa*, growing in Ceylon, has not the flavour of Peppermint, but that of the garden mint, while the type form of *M. arvensis*, growing wild in Great Britain, has an odour so different from Peppermint that it has to be carefully removed from the field lest it should spoil the flavour of the Peppermint oil when the herb is distilled.

The Japanese have long recognized the value of Menthol, and over 200 years ago carried it about with them in little silver boxes hanging from their girdles. The distillation of oil of Peppermint forms a considerable industry in Japan. The chief centre of cultivation is the province of Uzen, in the north-east of the island of Hondo, the largest of the Japanese Islands, and much is grown in the northern island of Hokkaido, but the best oil is produced in the southern districts of Okayama and Hiroshimo, the second largest Peppermint area in Japan, the yield of mint being yearly on the increase. The mint crop is a favourite one for farmers, owing to the distilling work it furnishes during the long and otherwise unprofitable winter.

The roots are planted at the end of November and beginning of December. The plant, which needs a light, well-drained soil, attains its full growth during the summer months and is cut in the latter part of July, during August and in the early part of September, three cuttings being made during the season. The third cutting yields the greatest percentage of oil and menthol crystals. The preliminary steps in the manufacture of Menthol are carried out by the farmers themselves, with the aid of stills of a simple design. The Peppermint plants are first dried in sheds, or under cover from the sun for thirty days. Then they are placed in the stills where they undergo a process of steaming. The resulting vapours are led off through pipes into cooling chambers, are condensed and deposited as crude Peppermint oil. This crude Peppermint is shipped to Yokohama and Kobe to the Menthol factories, of which there are over seventy in various parts of Japan, specially equipped for obtaining the full amount of Menthol. The residue of dementholized oil is further refined to the standard of purity required in the trade, and is known as Japanese Peppermint oil. The oil (known in Japan under the name of *Hakka no abura*) is exported from Hiogo and Osaka, but is frequently adulterated. The cheapest variety of Peppermint oil available in commerce is this partially dementholized oil imported from Japan, containing only 50 per cent. of Menthol.

Adulteration of American Peppermint oil with dementholized Japanese oil, known as Menthene, which is usually cheaper than American oil, is frequently practised. The failure of the mint crop in America in 1925 and the consequent scarcity and high price of the American oil caused this adulteration to be very extensive.

The Japanese oil, termed by the Americans Corn-Mint oil and not recognized by the United States Pharmacopœia, is at best only a substitute in confectionery and other products, such as tooth-pastes, etc. There are other varieties of so-called Peppermint oil on the market which are residues from Menthol-manufacture and are inferior even to the oil imported from Japan. These are not suitable for use in pharmacy.

As Japanese Peppermint oil, after being freed from Menthol crystals, is inferior both in taste and odour to English and American oil, experiments have been made in Japan with the cultivation of English and American Peppermint, but so far without success.

¶ *Adulterants.* Camphor oil is occasionally used as an adulterant of Peppermint oil, also Cedarwood oil and oil of African Copaiba. The oil is also often adulterated with one-third part of rectified spirit, which may be detected by the milkiness produced when the oil is agitated by water. Oil of Rosemary and oil of Turpentine are sometimes used for the same purpose. If the oil contains turpentine it will explode with iodine. If quite pure, it dissolves in its own weight of rectified spirits of wine.

In the form in which Menthol is imported, it bears some resemblance to Epsom Salts, with which it is sometimes adulterated.

Before the War about half the Menthol crystals exported from Japan were sent to Germany. During the War the United States became the largest purchaser of these crystals, followed in order by Great Britain, France and British India.

¶ *Medicinal Action and Uses.* Peppermint oil is the most extensively used of all the volatile oils, both medicinally and commercially. The characteristic anti-spasmodic action of the volatile oil is more marked in this than in any other oil, and greatly adds to its power of relieving pains arising in the alimentary canal.

From its stimulating, stomachic and carminative properties, it is valuable in certain forms of dyspepsia, being mostly used for flatulence and colic. It may also be employed for other sudden pains and for cramp in the abdomen; wide use is made of Peppermint in cholera and diarrhœa.

It is generally combined with other medicines when its stomachic effects are required, being also employed with purgatives to prevent griping. Oil of Peppermint allays sickness and nausea, and is much used to disguise the taste of unpalatable drugs, as it imparts its aromatic characteristics to whatever prescription it enters into. It is used as an infants' cordial.

The oil itself is often given on sugar and added to pills, also a spirit made from the oil, but the preparation in most general use is Peppermint Water, which is the oil and water distilled together.

Peppermint Water and spirit of Peppermint are official preparations of the British Pharmacopœia.

In flatulent colic, spirit of Peppermint in hot water is a good household remedy, also the oil given in doses of one or two drops on sugar.

Peppermint is good to assist in raising internal heat and inducing perspiration, although its strength is soon exhausted. In slight colds or early indications of disease, a free use of Peppermint tea will, in most cases, effect a cure, an infusion of 1 ounce of the dried herb to a pint of boiling water being employed, taken in wineglassful doses; sugar and milk may be added if desired.

An infusion of equal quantities of Peppermint herb and Elder flowers (to which either Yarrow or Boneset may be added) will banish a cold or mild attack of influenza within thirty-six hours, and there is no danger of an overdose or any harmful action on the heart. Peppermint tea is used also for palpitation of the heart.

In cases of hysteria and nervous disorders, the usefulness of an infusion of Peppermint has been found to be well augmented by the addition of equal quantities of Wood Betony, its operation being hastened by the addition to the infusion of a few drops of tincture of Caraway.

¶ *Preparations.* Fluid extract, ¼ to 1 drachm. Oil, ½ to 3 drops. Spirit, B.P., 5 to 20 drops. Water, B.P. and U.S.P., 4 drachms.

The following simple preparation has been found useful in insomnia:

1 oz. Peppermint herb, cut fine, ½ oz. Rue herb, ¼ oz. Wood Betony. Well mix and place a large tablespoonful in a teacup, fill with boiling water, stir and cover for twenty minutes, strain and sweeten, and drink the warm infusion on going to bed.

A very useful and harmless preparation for children during teething is prepared as follows:

½ oz. Peppermint herb, ½ oz. Scullcap herb, ½ oz. Pennyroyal herb. Pour on 1 pint of boiling water, cover and let it stand in a warm place thirty minutes. Strain and sweeten to taste, and given frequently in teaspoonful doses, warm.

Boiled in milk and drunk hot, Peppermint herb is good for abdominal pains. 'Aqua Mirabilis' is a term applied on the Continent to an aromatic water which is taken for internal pains. It is a water distilled from herbs, sometimes used in the following form:

Cinnamon oil, Fennel oil, Lavender oil, Peppermint oil, Rosemary oil, Sage oil, of each 1 part; Spirit, 350 parts; Distilled water, 644 parts.

Menthol is used in medicine to relieve the pain of rheumatism, neuralgia, throat affections and toothache. It acts also as a local anæsthetic, vascular stimulant and disinfectant. For neuralgia, rheumatism and lumbago it is used in plasters and rubbed on the temples; it will frequently cure neuralgic headaches. It is inhaled for chest complaints, and nasal catarrh, laryngitis or bronchitis are often alleviated by it. It is also used internally as a stimulant or carminative. On account of its anæsthetic effect on the nerve-endings of the stomach, it is of use to prevent sea-sickness, the dose being ½ to 2 grains. The bruised fresh leaves of the plant will, if applied, relieve local pains and headache, and in rheumatic affections the skin may be painted beneficially with the oil.

Oil of Peppermint has been recommended in puerperal fevers. 30 to 40 minims, in divided doses, in the twenty-four hours, have been employed with satisfactory results, a stimulating aperient preceding its use.

The local anæsthetic action of Peppermint oil is exceptionally strong. It is also powerfully antiseptic, the two properties making it valuable in the relief of toothache and in the treatment of cavities in the teeth.

Sanitary engineers use Peppermint oil to test the tightness of pipe joints. It has the faculty of making its escape, and by its pungent odour betraying the presence of leaks.

A new use for Peppermint oil has been found in connexion with the gas-mask drill on the vessels of the United States Navy.

Paste may be kept almost any length of time by the use of the essential oil of Peppermint to prevent mould.

Rats dislike Peppermint, a fact that is made use of by ratcatchers, who, when clearing a building of rats, will block up most of their holes with rags soaked in oil of Peppermint and drive them by ferrets through the remaining holes into bags.

See PENNYROYAL.

MINT, WILD

Mentha sativa (LINN.)
N.O. Labiatæ

Synonyms. Water or Marsh Mint. Whorled Mint. Hairy Mint
Part Used. Herb
Habitat. Common in Britain and found all over temperate and Northern Europe and Russian Asia

¶ *Description.* A rather coarse perennial 1 to 1½ feet high; leaves conspicuously stalked, ovate or oval-ovate, or oval-rounded or wedge-shaped at the base, subacute or acute serrate or crenate serrate, more or less hairy on both sides; flowers in whorls, usually all separate, beginning about or below the middle of the stem; bracts large, similar to leaves, sometimes the upper ones minute, uppermost ones often without flowers; bracteoles strap-shaped, subulate, hairy, shorter than flowers; pedicels hairy, rarely glabrous; calyx hairy, campanulate-cylindrical; teeth triangular, acuminate, half the length of tube, bristly, hairy; corolla scarcely twice as long as the calyx, hairy without and within; nucules rough with small points.

MINT, CORN

Mentha arvensis
N.O. Labiatæ

Habitat. It is a perennial, the root-stock, as in all the Mints, creeping freely, so that when the plant has once taken hold of the ground it becomes very difficult to eradicate it, as its long creeping roots bind the soil together and ultimately overrun a considerable area. It is generally an indication that the drainage of the land has been neglected. It is abundantly distributed throughout Britain, though less common in the northern counties and flourishes in fields and moist ground, and Peppermint growers must be ever watchful for its appearance

The Corn Mint (*Mentha arvensis*) is the type species of the Japanese Menthol plant, but is not endowed with useful medicinal properties, great care indeed, as has been mentioned, having to be taken to eradicate it from Peppermint plantations, for if mingled with that valuable herb in distilling its strong odour affects the quality of the oil.

¶ *Description.* It is a branched, downy plant. From the low, spreading, quadrangular stems that lie near the ground, the flowering stems are each year thrown up, 6 to 12 inches high. The leaves, springing from the stems, in pairs, are stalked, their outlines freely toothed. The upper leaves are smaller than the lower, and the flowers are arranged in rings (whorls) in their axils. The flowers themselves are small individually, but the

¶ *Medicinal and Other Uses.* The herb is considered to have emetic, stimulant, and astringent qualities, and is used in diarrhœa and as an emmenagogue. The infusion of 1 oz. of the dried herb to 1 pint of boiling water is taken in wineglassful doses.

delicacy of their colour and the dense clusters in which they grow, give an importance collectively, as ring after ring of the blossoms form as a whole a conspicuous head. The flowering season lasts throughout August and September.

This mint varies considerably in appearance in different plants, like all the other native species of mint, some being much larger than others, with a more developed foliage and a much greater hairiness of all the parts. It has a strong odour that becomes more decided still when the leaves are bruised in any way.

It is said that the effect of this plant, when animals eat it, is to prevent coagulation of their milk, so that it can hardly be made to yield cheese.

MINT, WILD WATER

Mentha aquatica (LINN.)
N.O. Labiatæ

Mentha aquatica, the Wild Mint, Water Mint or Marsh Mint in its many variations (of which *M. sativa*, the Hairy Mint, is by most botanists considered to be one, and not a distinct species), is the commonest of the Mints, growing abundantly 1 to 2 feet high, in extensive masses in wet places, banks of rivers and marshes, and well distinguished by its downy foliage and whorls of lilac flowers, which towards the summit of the stem are crowded into globose heads. The scent of the plant is strong and unpleasant to mbdern idea, but Dononæus says:

'The savour of scent of Mynte rejoiceth man, wherefore they sow and strow the wild Mynthe in this countrie in places where feasts are kept, and in Churches. The juyce of Mynte mingled with honied water cureth the payne of the eares when dropped therein, and taketh away the asperitie and roughness of the tongue when it is rubbed or washed therewith.'

The dried herb yields about 4 per cent. of essential oil, having an odour of Pennyroyal, the characters of which are not well determined. Russian Spearmint oil is derived from a form of this species.

¶ *Medicinal Action and Uses.* Emetic, stimulant and astringent. Used in herbal medicine in diarrhœa and as an emmenagogue, the infusion of 1 oz. of the dried herb to 1 pint of boiling water being taken in wineglassful doses.

In severe cold and influenza, or in any complaint where it is necessary to set up perspiration and in all inflammatory complaints, internal or external, the tea made from this plant may be taken warm as freely as the patient pleases. It can be used in conjunction with stomach remedies and in difficult menstruation. A strong infusion is inclined to be emetic.

A decoction of Water Mint prepared with vinegar is recommended to stop blood vomiting.

Pliny, describing the cultivation of mint, observes that the original name was *Mintha*, 'from which the Latin *Mentha* was derived, but of late it has been called Hedyosmon,' i.e. the sweet-scented. He speaks of 'a wild kind of Mint known to us as *Menastrum*.' This name was used in the fourteenth century for the Water Mint (*M. aquatica*).

Culpepper says it is good for the gravel, and in flatulent colics.

MINT, CURLED

Mentha crispa, which has wavy, broad, sharply-toothed leaves, woolly beneath, is a variety of *M. aquatica*. It is sometimes found

Mentha acrispa

in Britain in gardens and has quite a different odour to that of the common Wild Water Mint.

MINT, BERGAMOT

Synonym. Mentha odorata

Mentha citrata (Ehr.), syn. *M. odorata*, the Bergamot Mint, by some botanists considered a separate species, is by others looked on as a variety of *M. aquatica*.

The whole plant is smooth, dotted with yellow glands and is of a dark green colour, generally tinged with purple, especially the margins of the leaves, which are finelly toothed. There are very conspicuous lines of yellow glands on the purple calyx.

Mentha citrata

This Mint has a very pleasant, aromatic, lemon-like odour, somewhat resembling that of the Bergamot Orange, or that of the Oswego Tea (*Monarda didyma*), also called Bergamot, and its leaves like those of the latter can be employed in pot-pourri.

It is found in wet places in Staffordshire and Wales, though very rarely, but is often cultivated in gardens.

MINT, ROUND-LEAVED

Mentha rotundifolia
N.O. Labiatæ

Synonym. Egyptian Mint

Mentha rotundifolia is a sturdy plant having the habit of *M. sylvestris*, but is more branched. The leaves are very broad, somewhat resembling those of Sage, dull green in colour and much wrinkled above, often densely woolly and whitish beneath. The flowers are pink or white, in tapering, terminal spikes.

This species has somewhat the flavour of Spearmint, but is stronger. It is frequently found on the ruins of monasteries, the monks having used it for the languor following epileptic fits, as it was considered refreshing to the brain. It is sometimes found cultivated in cottage gardens under the name of Egyptian Mint.

The American Horsemint (*Monarda punctata*, Linn.) is of considerable importance, as it may before long be available as a regular source of Thymol, which has hitherto been manufactured principally from Ajowan seeds. It yields from 1 to 3 per cent. of a volatile oil, which contains a large proportion of Thymol, up to 61 per cent. having been obtained; Carvacrol also appears to be a constituent. The oil has a specific gravity of 0·930 to 0·940 and on prolonged standing deposits crystals of Thymol.

In 1907, Horsemint was observed to occur in abundance as a common weed on the sandy lands of central Florida, and the preliminary examinations of the oil from the wild plants which were made at that time seemed to indicate that a promising commercial source of Thymol could be developed by bringing this plant under cultivation and selecting for propagation types of plants best suited for oil production.

The leaf area of the wild plants is rather small: the first problem, therefore, seemed to be to increase the leaf area and thus increase the yield of oil per acre.

During several years of experiment, selection was also made to increase the size of the plants in order that the tonnage of herb per acre might be increased. This was also successful and a considerably increased yield was noted year by year.

In 1912 a series of fertilizer experiments was carried out. It was found that although certain special methods of treatment had a marked effect on the percentage of yield of oil and of Thymol in the oil, the greatest yield was obtained by promoting the growth of the plant and thus securing the largest possible yield of herb per acre.

On the scarcity of Thymol becoming acute on the outbreak of the Great War, the United States Department of Agriculture took up the matter, entered thoroughly into the question of utilizing the native American plant for the source of the valued product, and carried out exhaustive experiments in 1914 and 1915 as to the cultivation of the plant, the extraction of Thymol, the yield per acre and the commercial prospects of the cultivation of the plant, the conclusions arrived at being that the use is now warranted of the improved form of the plant – its luxuriance increased by cultivation – being used for the commercial production of Thymol in the United States.

It has been shown that Horsemint can be grown on the lighter types of soil at comparatively little expense, and as the cost of transportation for the finished product, Thymol, is very low, it would seem that the production of this crop might be profitable when grown in connexion with other oil-yielding plants for which a distilling apparatus is required. Distillation of the Horsemint herb is carried on by the usual methods in practice for distilling such volatile oils as Peppermint and Spearmint.

HORSEMINT
Mentha sylvestris (LINN.)
N.O. Labiatæ

The English Horsemint (*Mentha sylvestris*) is a strong-scented plant, frequent in damp, waste ground, usually growing in masses, with downy, egg-shaped leaves tapering to a point, with finely toothed margins, their undersides very white with silky hairs. The flowers are in thick cylindrical spikes, which are often interrupted below; the corollas are lilac in colour and hairy.

The taste and odour of the plant resemble those of the Garden Mint.

The dry herb yields about 1 per cent. of essential oil, having carminative and stimulant properties.

Culpepper says:

'It is good for wind and colic in the stomach. . . . The juice, laid on warm, helps the King's evil or kernels in the throat. . . . The decoction or distilled water helps a stinking breath, proceeding from corruption of the teeth; and snuffed up the nose, purges the head. It helps the scurf or dandruff of the head used with vinegar.'

HORSEMINT, AMERICAN
Monarda punctata (LINN.)
N.O. Labiatæ

Synonyms. Monarda lutea. Spotted Monarda
Part Used. Whole herb

¶ *Description*. In 1569 a doctor of Seville, Nicolas Monardes, wrote a great book, in Spanish, making known the medicinal plants of the New World, and the genus *Monarda* was named in his honour.

Monarda punctata is a perennial herb, growing in dry, sandy places. It has a strong erect stem, reaching 2 feet or more in height, with lanceolate, opposite leaves, 2 to 4 inches long, dotted on the under-surface with glands. The flowers form dense whorls, one being terminal, and have a large yellow corolla, the upper lip being spotted with purple. A circle of large, leaf-like bracts, purplish-pink in colour, surrounds them.

The plant, which is hardy, was introduced into England in 1714. The odour is strong and aromatic, the taste pungent and slightly bitter.

Wild Basil (*Pycnanthemum incanum*) is said to be often substituted for it in the United States.

¶ *Constituents*. The active virtues depend on the abundant volatile oil, which has been found to contain a hydrocarbon, thymol, and higher oxygenated compounds. It yields its virtues to boiling water, but particularly to alcohol.

Oleum Monardæ or Oil of Horsemint is official in the United States.

¶ *Medicinal Action and Uses*. Rubefacient, stimulant, carminative. The infusion is used for flatulent colic, sickness, and as a diaphoretic and emmenagogue, or as a diuretic in urinary disorders.

The principal use is external, and in its pure state it may be a vesicant. It should be diluted with olive oil or soap liniment, two or four parts of either being added to one of oil of Monarda. It may be employed in chronic rheumatism, cholera infantum, or whenever rubefacients are required.

It may be taken like Hedeoma, or American Pennyroyal.

¶ *Dosage*. Two to 10 minims of oil.

¶ *Other Species*.
M. Didyma and *M. Squarrosa* may be used as substitutes.

M. Fistulosa (Wild Bergamot, or Oswego Tea) is an active diuretic.

M. citriodora, or Prairie Bergamot, contains a phenol and a citral.

SWEET HORSEMINT is a name of *Cunila origanoides*, the essential oil of which is a stimulant aromatic.

See BERGAMOT.

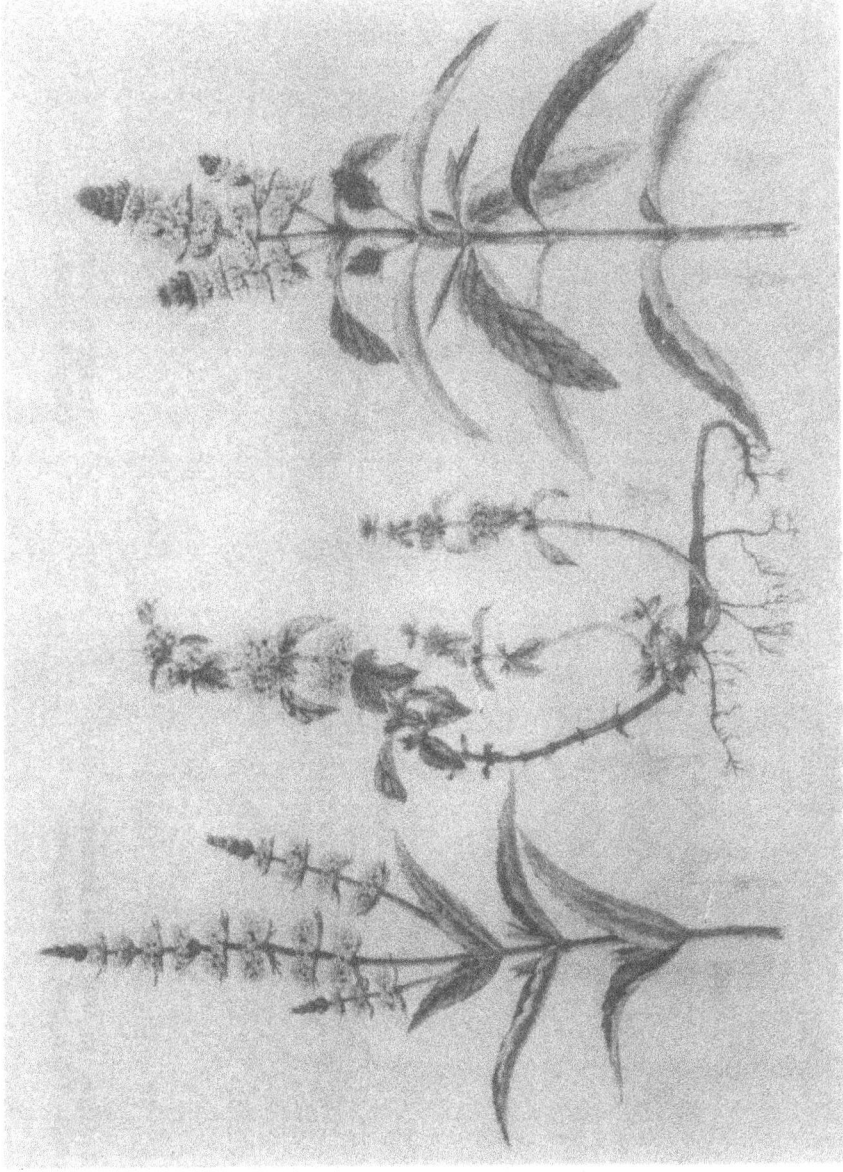

MINTS
Mentha Viridis, Mentha Pulegium, Mentha Piperita

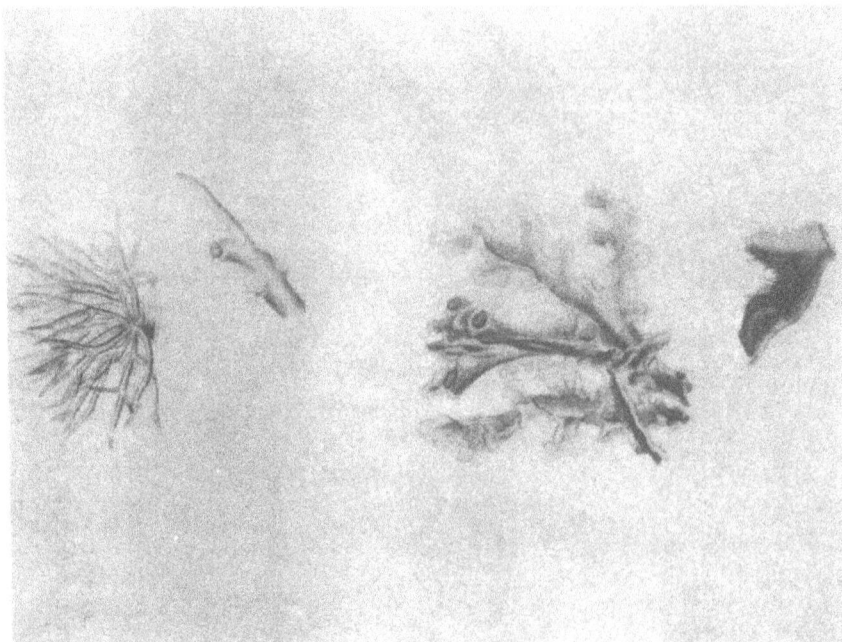

ICELAND MOSS
Cetraria Islandica

MUSTARDS, BLACK AND WHITE
Brassica Nigra and Brassica Alba

MISTLETOE

Viscum album (LINN.)
N.O. Loranthaceæ

Synonyms. Birdlime Mistletoe. Herbe de la Croix. Mystyldene. Lignum Crucis
Parts Used. Leaves and young twigs, berries

The well-known Mistletoe is an evergreen parasitic plant, growing on the branches of trees, where it forms pendent bushes, 2 to 5 feet in diameter. It will grow and has been found on almost any deciduous tree, preferring those with soft bark, and being, perhaps, commonest on old Apple trees, though it is frequently found on the Ash, Hawthorn, Lime and other trees. On the Oak, it grows very seldom. It has been found on the Cedar of Lebanon and on the Larch, but very rarely on the Pear tree.

When one of the familiar sticky berries of the Mistletoe comes into contact with the bark of a tree – generally through the agency of birds – after a few days it sends forth a thread-like root, flattened at the extremity like the proboscis of a fly. This finally pierces the bark and roots itself firmly in the growing wood, from which it has the power of selecting and appropriating to its own use, such juices as are fitted for its sustenance: the wood of Mistletoe has been found to contain twice as much potash, and five times as much phosphoric acid as the wood of the foster tree. Mistletoe is a true parasite, for at no period does it derive nourishment from the soil, or from decayed bark, like some of the fungi do -- all its nourishment is obtained from its *host*. The root becomes woody and thick.

¶ *Description.* The stem is yellowish and smooth, freely forked, separating when dead into bone-like joints. The leaves are tongue-shaped, broader towards the end, 1 to 3 inches long, very thick and leathery, of a dull yellow-green colour, arranged in pairs, with very short footstalks. The flowers, small and inconspicuous, are arranged in threes, in close short spikes or clusters in the forks of the branches, and are of two varieties, the male and female occurring on different plants. Neither male nor female flowers have a corolla, the parts of the fructification springing from the yellowish calyx. They open in May. The fruit is a globular, smooth, white berry, ripening in December.

Mistletoe is found throughout Europe, and in this country is particularly common in Herefordshire and Worcestershire. In Scotland it is almost unknown.

The genus *Viscum* has thirty or more species. In South Africa there are several, one with very minute leaves, a feature common to many herbs growing in that excessively dry climate; one in Australia is densely woolly, from a similar cause. Several members of the family are not parasitic at all, being shrubs and trees, showing that the parasitic habit is an acquired one, and now, of course, hereditary.

Mistletoe is always produced by seed and cannot be cultivated in the earth like other plants, hence the ancients considered it to be an excrescence of the tree. By rubbing the berries on the smooth bark of the underside of the branches of trees till they adhere, or inserting them in clefts made for the purpose, it is possible to grow Mistletoe quite successfully, if desired.

The thrush is the great disseminator of the Mistletoe, devouring the berries eagerly, from which the Missel Thrush is said by some to derive its name. The stems and foliage have been given to sheep in winter, when fodder was scarce, and they are said to eat it with relish.

In Brittany, where the Mistletoe grows so abundantly, the plant is called *Herbe de la Croix*, because, according to an old legend, the Cross was made from its wood, on account of which it was degraded to be a parasite.

The English name is said to be derived from the Anglo-Saxon *Misteltan*, *tan* signifying twig, and *mistel* from *mist*, which in old Dutch meant birdlime; thus, according to Professor Skeat, Mistletoe means 'birdlime twig,' a reference to the fact that the berries have been used for making birdlime. Dr. Prior, however, derives the word from *tan*, a twig, and *mistl*, meaning different, from its being unlike the tree it grows on. In the fourteenth century it was termed '*Mystyldene*' and also *Lignum crucis*, an allusion to the legend just mentioned. The Latin name of the genus, *Viscum*, signifying sticky, was assigned to it from the glutinous juice of its berries.

¶ *History.* Mistletoe was held in great reverence by the Druids. They went forth clad in white robes to search for the sacred plant, and when it was discovered, one of the Druids ascended the tree and gathered it with great ceremony, separating it from the Oak with a golden knife. The Mistletoe was always cut at a particular age of the moon, at the beginning of the year, and it was only sought for when the Druids declared they had visions directing them to seek it. When a great length of time elapsed without this happening, or if the Mistletoe chanced to fall to the ground, it was considered as an omen that some misfortune would befall the nation.

The Druids held that the Mistletoe protected its possessor from all evil, and that the oaks on which it was seen growing were to be respected because of the wonderful cures which the priests were able to effect with it. They sent round their attendant youth with branches of the Mistletoe to announce the entrance of the new year. It is probable that the custom of including it in the decoration of our homes at Christmas, giving it a special place of honour, is a survival of this old custom.

The curious basket of garland with which 'Jack-in-the-Green' is even now occasionally invested on May-day is said to be a relic of a similar garb assumed by the Druids for the ceremony of the Mistletoe. When they had found it they danced round the oak to the tune of 'Hey derry down, down, down derry!' which literally signified, '*In a circle move we round the oak.*' Some oakwoods in Herefordshire are still called '*the derry*'; and the following line from Ovid refers to the Druids' songs beneath the oak:

'*Ad viscum Druidæ cantare solebant.*'

Shakespeare calls it 'the baleful Mistletoe,' an allusion to the Scandinavian legend that Balder, the god of Peace, was slain with an arrow made of Mistletoe. He was restored to life at the request of the other gods and goddesses, and Mistletoe was afterwards given into the keeping of the goddess of Love, and it was ordained that everyone who passed under it should receive a kiss, to show that the branch had become an emblem of love, and not of hate.

¶ *Parts Used Medicinally.* The leaves and young twigs, collected just before the berries form, and dried in the same manner as described for Holly.

¶ *Constituents.* Mistletoe contains mucilage, sugar, a fixed oil, resin, an odorous principle, some tannin and various salts. The active part of the plant is the resin, Viscin, which by fermentation becomes a yellowish, sticky, resinous mass, which can be used with success as a birdlime.

The preparations ordinarily used are a fluid extract and the powdered leaves. A homœopathic tincture is prepared with spirit from equal quantities of the leaves and ripe berries, but is difficult of manufacture, owing to the viscidity of the sap.

¶ *Medicinal Action and Uses.* Nervine, antispasmodic, tonic and narcotic. Has a great reputation for curing the 'falling sickness' – epilepsy – and other convulsive nervous disorders. It has also been employed in checking internal hæmorrhage.

The physiological effect of the plant is to lessen and temporarily benumb such nervous action as is reflected to distant organs of the body from some central organ which is the actual seat of trouble. In this way the spasms of epilepsy and of other convulsive distempers are allayed. Large doses of the plant, or of its berries, would, on the contrary, aggravate these convulsive disorders. Young children have been attacked with convulsions after eating freely of the berries.

In a French work on domestic remedies, 1682, Mistletoe (*gui de chêne*) was considered of great curative power in epilepsy. Sir John Colbatch published in 1720 a pamphlet on *The Treatment of Epilepsy by Mistletoe*, regarding it as a specific for this disease. He procured the parasite from the Lime trees at Hampton Court, and recommended the powdered leaves, as much as would lie on a sixpence, to be given in Black Cherry water every morning. He was followed in this treatment by others who have testified to its efficacy as a tonic in nervous disorders, considering it the specific herb for St. Vitus's Dance. It has been employed in convulsions, delirium, hysteria, neuralgia, nervous debility, urinary disorders, heart disease, and many other complaints arising from a weakened and disordered state of the nervous system.

Ray also greatly extolled Mistletoe as a specific in epilepsy, and useful in apoplexy and giddiness. The older writers recommended it for sterility.

The tincture has been recommended as a heart tonic in typhoid fever in place of Foxglove. It lessens reflex irritability and strengthens the heart's beat, whilst raising the frequency of a slow pulse.

Besides the dried leaves being given powdered, or as an infusion, or made into a tincture with spirits of wine, a decoction may be made by boiling 2 oz. of the bruised green plant with ½ pint of water, giving 1 tablespoonful for a dose several times a day. Ten to 60 grains of the powder may be taken as a dose, and homœopathists give 5 to 10 drops of the tincture, with 1 or 2 tablespoonsful of cold water. Mistletoe is also given, combined with Valerian Root and Vervain, for all kinds of nervous complaints, cayenne pods being added in cases of debility of the digestive organs.

Fluid extract: dose, ½ to 1 drachm.

Country people use the berries to cure severe stitches in the side. The birdlime of the berries is also employed by them as an application to ulcers and sores.

It is stated that in Sweden, persons afflicted with epilepsy carry about with them a knife having a handle of Oak Mistletoe to ward off attacks.

MOMORDICA. *See* (BALSAM) APPLE

MONEYWORT

Lysimachia nummularia (LINN.)
N.O. Primulaceæ

Synonyms. Creeping Jenny. Creeping Joan. Wandering Jenny. Running Jenny. Wandering Tailor. Herb Twopence. Twopenny Grass. Meadow Runagates. Herbe 2 pence. Two Penigrasse. String of Sovereigns. Serpentaria

Part Used. Whole herb, dried or fresh

The Moneywort is far more often known by the familiar names of Creeping Jenny, Wandering Jenny, Running Jenny, Creeping Joan and Wandering Sailor – all names alluding to its rapid trailing over the ground. 'Meadow Runagates' has the same reference, and tells us also of its favourite home in damp pastures and by stream sides.

The earliest English Herbal, that of Turner, speaks of it as 'Herbe 2 pence' and 'Two penigrasse,' and it is still known in some localities as Herb Twopence and Twopenny Grass, the allusion here being to the leaves, which are set two and two on the stem, and rounded (though each has a short, sharp tip), and lying always faces turned to the sky, look like rows of pence. 'Moneywort' and 'Strings of Sovereigns,' though names based on the same idea, are probably suggested by the big golden flowers, rather than by the leaves. The leaves sometimes turn rose-pink in autumn. The specific name, *Nummularia*, is from the Latin *nummulus* (money).

¶ *Description*. The leaves and stems of the plant are all quite smooth, the stems being quadrangular. The flowers, which blossom through June and July, spring singly on slender stalks, just where each leaf joins the stem. Their five sepals are large, pale green and heart-shaped, somewhat 'frilly' round the base, perhaps as a protection against small creeping insects, which might otherwise make their way into the flowers, which are only just off the ground. The five petals are so deeply cut into that they appear separate, but are joined at the base to form a golden cup. The stamens, as in the Scarlet Pimpernel and others of this family, face their corresponding petals, instead of being alternate with them, and are also joined at their base to form a low ring. Their filaments, or little stalks, are covered with tiny golden hairs or knobs.

The ovary in the centre of the flower is so placed that the pollen from the stamens must fall on its stigma, but the flower is not only absolutely sterile to its own pollen, but also pollen from other Moneywort flowers seems to have little effect on its ovules, for as a rule no fruit follows the flowers. It has been thought, therefore, that the plant may not be a true native, and that there is something in our climate that does not suit it. It is probable, however, that it does not trouble to set seed, because it has adopted a simpler method of propagation. It frequently happens that plants which increase much in other ways seldom produce ripe seeds. This simple method of propagation lies in its trailing shoots – its 'stolons.' A stolon may be defined as a creeping stem which dies off every year, and is beset by leaves not very far apart. Close to the tip of each stolon, in the angle formed by little leaf-stalks, buds appear, which produce roots which pass into the ground. When winter comes, the stem and leaves die down between the old root and the new one, but when spring arrives, a new plant exists where the little roots entered the ground. In this way from a single plant which sends out stolons in various directions, many new plants appear by this so-called 'vegetative' method of reproduction.

In a damp situation, no plant thrives better in a garden, or requires less trouble to be taken with it.

¶ *Part Used*. The whole herb, used both dried and fresh. For drying, collect in June, and proceed as in Scarlet Pimpernel.

¶ *Medicinal Action and Uses*. The Moneywort in olden days was reputed to have many virtues. It was like the last species, one of the many 'best possible woundworts.' 'In a word, there is not a better wound-herb, no not tobacco itselfe, nor any other whatsoever,' said an old herbalist.

We are told by old writers that this herb was not only used by man, but that if serpents hurt or wounded themselves, they turned to this plant for healing, and so it was sometimes called 'Serpentaria.'

The bruised fresh leaves were in popular use as an application to wounds, both fresh and old, a decoction of the fresh herb being taken as a drink in wine or water, and also applied outwardly as a wash or cold compress to both wounds and inveterate sores. An ointment was made also for application to wounds.

The leaves are subastringent, slightly acid, and antiscorbutic. Boerhaave, the celebrated Dutch physician, recommended their use, dried and powdered, in doses of 10 grains in scurvy and hæmorrhages. Culpepper tells us:

'Moneywort is singularly good to stay all fluxes . . . bleeding inwardly or outwardly, and weak stomachs given to casting. It is very good for the ulcers or excoriations of the lungs.' Again, it was a specific for whooping-cough 'being boyled with wine or honey . . .

MONSONIA

Part Used. Plant, root
Habitat. Cape of Good Hope

¶ *Description*. Leaves oblong, subcordate, crenate, waved, flowers white axillary stalked, two on one peduncle, roots fleshy large, grown from seed.

¶ *Medicinal Action and Uses*. A valuable remedy for acute and chronic dysentery, specially of use in ulceration of the lower part of the intestines; the plant is not considered poisonous.

¶ *Dosage*. Saturated tincture, 1 to 2 fluid drachms, every three or four hours.

MORNING GLORY. *See* BINDWEED

MOSCHATEL, COMMON

Synonyms. Tuberous Moschatel. Musk Ranunculus

This plant, belonging to the natural order Caprifoliaceæ, is the only one of its species. The name *Adoxa* is from the Greek, signifying 'inglorious,' from its humble growth. It is an interesting little herbaceous plant, 4 to 6 inches high; stem four-angled; root-leaves long-stalked, ternate; leaflets triangular, lobed; cauline leaves or bracts two, smaller, with sheathing petioles; flowers arranged as if on five sides of a cube, small and pale green in colour; berry with one-seeded parchment-like chamber. Growing in hedgerows, local, but widely diffused, also in Asia and North America, even into the Arctic regions.

MOSQUITO PLANT. *See* THYME (WILD)

MOSS, AMERICAN CLUB

Synonym. American Ground Pine

The American Ground Pine is not a flowering plant, but one of the Club Mosses, which with the Ferns and Mosses belong to the great class of Cryptogams. The genus *Lycopodium* holds, as it were, an intermediate place between the Ferns and Mosses and includes only six British species, though there are about sixty-five distributed over the world.

Lycopodium complanatum, the American Club Moss, is a small mossy plant with aromatic, resinous smell and slightly turpentiny taste, the stalks hairy and the leaves close set, characteristics which have gained it the popular name of Ground Pine, as in

it prevaileth against that violent cough in children, commonly called the chinne-cough, but it should be chine-cough, for it doth make as it were the very chine-bone to shake.'

See PIMPERNEL (YELLOW), LOOSESTRIFE

Monsonia ovata (CAR.)
N.O. Geraniaceæ

The Pelargoniums belong to the same family, and all species have more or less astringent properties. Some have fragrant foliage, noticeably *Pelargonium roseum* and *P. capitatum*, from which a fragrant essential oil is extracted. In medicine they are used for dysentery and some for ulceration of the stomach and upper intestinal tracts. *P. Triste* has edible tubers.

See PELARGONIUMS

Adoxa Moschatellina
N.O. Caprifoliaceæ

The flowers, and indeed the whole plant, has a musk-like scent, which it emits towards evening when the dew falls – this scent, however, disappears if the plant is bruised. It flowers in April and May.

John Ray, in his early system of plant classification, placed the Moschatel amongst the berry-bearing plants. The early writers found considerable difficulty in classifying it botanically. One calls it the musk-ranunculus, whilst another classes it with the fumitories, probably because of its leaves.

Lycopodium complanatum (LINN.)
N.O. Lycopodiaceæ

the case of Yellow Bugle. The stem is long and creeping, only about ⅛ inch in diameter, yellowish-green, giving off at intervals erect, fan-shaped forked branches about 4 inches high, with minute scale-like leaves, leaving only the sharp tips free, the branches bearing fructification in the form of a stalked tuft of four to five cylindrical spikes, consisting of spore cases in the axils of minute bracts. The stem roots below at long intervals, the roots being pale, wiry and slightly branched.

¶ *Medicinal Action and Uses*. The whole plant is used, dried and powdered for infusion.

It has properties similar to the European Ground Pine, being a powerful diuretic, promoting urine and removing obstructions of the liver and spleen. It is, therefore, a valuable remedy in jaundice, rheumatism and most of the chronic diseases.

A decoction of this plant, combined with Dandelion and Agrimony, is a highly recommended herbal remedy for liver complaints and obstructions.

For EUROPEAN GROUND PINE, see (YELLOW) BUGLE.

MOSS, COMMON CLUB

Lycopodium clavatum (LINN.)
N.O. Lycopodiaceæ

Synonyms. Muscus Terrestris repens. Vegetable Sulphur. Wolf's Claw
Parts Used. The spores, the fresh plant

This species is found all over the world and occurs throughout Great Britain, being most plentiful on the moors of the northern counties.

Though this species of Club Moss occurs in Great Britain, the spores are collected chiefly in Russia, Germany and Switzerland, in July and August, the tops of the plants being cut as the spikes approach maturity and the powder shaken out and separated by a sieve. Probably the spores used commercially are derived also from other species in addition to *Lycopodium clavatum.*

¶ *Medicinal Action and Uses.* The part of the plant now employed is the minute spores which, as a yellow powder, are shaken out of the kidney-shaped capsules or sporangia growing on the inner side of the bracts covering the fruit spike. Under the names of *Muscus terrestris* or *M. clavatum* the whole plant was used, dried, by ancient physicians as a stomachic and diuretic, mainly in calculous and other kidney complaints; the spores do not appear to have been used alone until the seventeenth century, when they were employed as a diuretic in dropsy, a drastic in diarrhœa, dysentery and suppression of urine, a nervine in spasms and hydrophobia, an aperient in gout and scurvy and a corroborant in rheumatism, and also as an application to wounds. They were, however, more used on the Continent than in this country and never had a place in the London Pharmacopœia, though they have been prescribed for irritability of the bladder, in the form of a tincture, which is official in the United States Pharmacopœia.

The spores are still medicinally employed by herbalists in this country, both internally and externally, as a dusting powder in various skin diseases such as eczema and erysipelas and for excoriated surfaces, to prevent chafing in infants. Their chief pharmaceutical use is as a pill powder, for enveloping pills to prevent their adhesion to one another when placed in a box, and to disguise their taste. Dose, 10 to 60 grains. They have such a strong repulsive power that, if the hand is powdered with them, it can be dipped in water without becoming wet.

MOSS, CORSICAN

Fucus Helminthocorton (KÜTZ.)
N.O. Algæ

Synonym. Alsidium Helminthocorton
Part Used. Whole plant
Habitat. Mediterranean coast, specially Corsica

¶ *Description.* The drug is obtained from twenty to thirty species of Algæ, chiefly *Sphærococcus helminthocorton.* It is cartilaginous, filiform repeatedly forked, colour varies from white to brown, it has a nauseous taste, bitter and salt, odour rather pleasant.

¶ *Medicinal Action and Uses.* In Europe as an anthelmintic and febrifuge, it acts very successfully on lumbricoid intestinal worms. A decoction is made of it from 4 to 6 drachms to the pint. Dose, a wineglassful three times daily.
¶ *Dosage.* Ten to 60 grains in syrup or in infusion.

MOSS, CUP

Cladonia Pyxidata (FRIES.)
N.O. Lichenes

Part Used. Whole plant
Habitat. North-west America, but now a common weed in many counties in Britain

¶ *Description. Cladonia* is one of a numerous genus of lecidineous lichens. It grows abundantly in the woods and hedges and is a common species; it has no odour; taste sweetish and mucilagenous.

¶ *Medicinal Action and Uses.* Expectorant, a valuable medicine in whooping cough.
¶ *Dosage.* 2 oz. of the plant decocted and mixed with honey makes a good expectorant and a safe medicine for children's coughs.

¶ *Other Species.*
Cladonia rangiferina. The badge of the Clan McKenzie. Makes excellent food for reindeer.

C. sanguinea. In Brazil is rubbed down with sugar and water and applied in the thrush of infants.

MOSS, HAIR CAP

Polytrichium Juniperum (WILLD.)
N.O. Musci

Synonyms. Bear's Bed. Robin's Eye. Ground Moss. Golden Maidenhair. Female Fern Herb. Rockbrake Herb
Part Used. Whole herb
Habitat. High dry places, margins of woods, poor sandy soil

¶ *Description.* The genus have free veins, globose sort, and peltate indusia; only a few species are found in Britain. These are perennial, slender and reddish colour, from 4 to 7 inches high. Leaves lanceolate and spreading, fruit four-sided capsule, evergreen, darker in colour than other mosses.
¶ *Medicinal Action and Uses.* A very valuable remedy in dropsy as a powerful diuretic, and used with hydragogue cathartics of decided advantage. Very useful in urinary obstructions, gravel, etc., causing no nausea, can be given alone or combined with broom or wild carrot, and is excellent if it is necessary to give it indefinitely as an infusion, which is taken in 4-oz. doses.

MOSS, CELAND

Cetraria islandica (ACH.)
N.O. Lichenes

Synonyms. Cetraria. Iceland Lichen
Part Used. Lichen
Habitat. A common plant in northern countries and in the mountainous part of warmer countries

In spite of its name is not a Moss but a lichen. Found in Great Britain in barren stony ground, abundant in the Grampians, and in the Welsh hills, in Yorkshire, Norfolk, etc. It rarely fructifies but the thallus varies in size, amount of division and cusping as well as colour. It is sometimes much curled.

It contains about 70 per cent. of lichen starch and becomes blue on the addition of iodine. It also contains a little sugar, fumaric acid, oxalic acid, about 3 per cent. of cetrarin and 1 per cent. of licheno-stearic acid.
¶ *Medicinal Action and Properties.* Demulcent, tonic, and nutritive when deprived of its bitter principle. Excellent in chronic pulmonary troubles, catarrh, digestive disturbances, dysentery, advanced tuberculosis. Decoction, B.P. 1885, 1 to 4 oz. Ground, it can be mixed with chocolate or cocoa.

MOSS, IRISH

Chondrus crispus (STACKH.)
N.O. Algæ

Synonyms. Carrageen. Chondrus. Carrahan
Part Used. Plant, dried
Habitat. A perennial thallophyte common at low tide on all the shores of the North Atlantic, but remarkable for its extreme variability, the difference being mainly due to the great diversity in the width of the segments

¶ *Constituents.* It contains a large amount of mucilage with the presence of a big percentage of sulphur compounds.
¶ *Medicinal Action and Uses.* Demulcent, emollient, nutritive. A popular remedy made into a jelly for pulmonary complaints and kidney and bladder affections. Can be combined with cocoa. The decoction is made by steeping ½ oz. of the Moss in cold water for 15 minutes and then boiling it in 3 pints of milk or water for 10 or 15 minutes, after which it is strained and seasoned with liquorice, lemon or cinnamon and sweetened to taste. It can be taken freely.

MOSS, SPHAGNUM

Sphagnum Cymbifolium
N.O. Lichenes

Synonym. Bog Moss

Sphagnum Moss, commonly known as Bog Moss, is the only true Moss that has yet proved itself to be of appreciable economic value.

It is found in wet and boggy spots, preferably on peat soil, mostly near heather, on all our mountains and moors, in patches small or large, usually in water free from lime, growing so close together that it often forms large cushions or clumps. It is seldom found in woods; it grows best on heath moors, in water holes.

¶ *Description.* Sphagnum is easily distinguished from other mosses by its habit of growth, its soft thick fullness (each head resembling a full and elaborate bloom of *edelweiss*), and its vividly pale-green colour.

Its stem is densely beset with narrow, broken-up leaves, a branch being emitted at every fourth leaf; many of these are turned downwards and applied more or less closely to the stem.

Though the pale-green species is the most common, there are several others, large and small, varying in colour from the very light green (never dark green) to yellow, and all shades of pink to deep red and brown. The Moss often attracts attention by its display of beautiful shades of colour, such patches being avoided by wary persons, who do not wish to get their feet wet.

Every part of the moss is permeated with minute tubes and spaces, resulting in a system of delicate capillary tubes, having the effect of a very fine sponge. The cells readily absorb water and retain it. The water can be squeezed out, but the Moss does not collapse and is ready to take in fluid again.

The plant is not dependent on soil water, but also absorbs moisture from the atmosphere, and is laden throughout with water retained in its delicate cells.

The presence of these capillary cells makes Sphagnum economically useful. In horticulture, long before the war, this Moss had a marketable value, in combination with peat fibre, being widely used as a rooting medium for orchids, on account of the remarkable manner in which it retains moisture, a handful when wet being like a sponge, and when chopped and mixed with soil in pots preventing moisture passing too quickly through the soil.

In recent years, the light-brown layer of semi-decayed Sphagnum Moss deposits that lies above the actual peat on bogs and moors, has been largely employed as valuable stable litter in the place of straw, under the name of Moss Litter, entirely on account of its great absorptive powers.

On the outbreak of the late war a still wider economic use was found for this moss, as a dressing of wounds, and an interesting industry sprang up for war-workers living where this moss grows, mainly in Scotland, Ireland, Wales and Devon, much having also been collected from the Yorkshire moors, the Lake District and the Wye Valley.

Although this particular use of the moss is generally looked upon as an innovation, we owe the introduction of Sphagnum Moss as a modern surgical dressing to Germany, where its value for this purpose was quite accidentally discovered in the early eighties.

And though it is only in quite recent years that Sphagnum Moss has come to the fore in the dressing of wounds, bygone generations recognized its value for this purpose. A Gaelic Chronicle of 1014 relates that the wounded in the battle of Clontarf 'stuffed their wounds with moss,' and the Highlanders after Flodden stanched their bleeding wounds by filling them with bog moss and soft grass. Stricken deer are known to drag their wounded limbs to beds of Sphagnum Moss. The Kashmiri have used it from time immemorial and so have the Esquimaux. An old writer says:

'the Lapland matrons are well acquainted with this moss. They dry it and lay it in their children's cradles to supply the place of mattress, bolster and every covering, and being changed night and morning, it keeps the infant remarkable clean, dry and warm.'

The Lapps also use the moss for surgical purposes, and it has been used in Newfoundland as a dressing for wounds and sores from the earliest times.

For thirty years, Sphagnum Moss had been used as a surgical dressing in Germany.

The growing plant, with its underlying layers of withered stems and leaves, is collected, picked clean from other plants, pineneedles, etc., and dried. It is then lightly packed in bags of butter-muslin, which are sterilized before being placed on the wound.

Sphagnum Moss has important advantages (as an absorbent) over cotton-wool. Many materials, including other kinds of moss, are equally soft and light, but none can compare with it in power of absorption, due to its sponge-like structure. Prepared Sphagnum can absorb more than twice as much moisture as cotton, a 2-oz. dressing absorbing up to 2 lb. Even the best prepared cotton-wool lacks the power to retain discharges possessed by Sphagnum. A pad of Sphagnum Moss absorbs the discharge in lateral directions, as well as immediately above the wound, and holds it until fully saturated in all parts of the dressing before allowing any to escape. The even absorption of the moss is one of its chief virtues, for the patient is saved a good deal of disturbance, since the dressing does not require to be changed so frequently.

In civil hospitals, in times of peace, the deficiencies of cotton-wool are not so much noticed, the majority of wounds being those made by surgeons under ideal conditions, but for a variety of reasons the wounds of our men at the front were of such a suppurating character as to require specially absorbent dressings, and overworked doctors and nurses constantly expressed themselves thankful for a dressing that lasted longer than cotton-wool. Time and suffering are saved, as well as expense: the absorbent pads of moss are soft, elastic and very comfortable, easily packed and convenient to handle.

Fortunately the supply is practically an unlimited one; indeed, if the demand grew considerably, the artificial cultivation of Sphagnum for surgical purposes would be worth while. This Moss is easily propagated, as the stems and so-called leaves can be chopped up into fine particles and every morsel will grow and form a tassel-like head. Sphagnum only thrives in clean water and soil; it dislikes manure of any kind.

In gathering Sphagnum most people use their hands, though some employ a rake. The moss should be gathered as cleanly as possible, squeezed dry and carried home in sacks. The squeezing may be done with the hands, or with a towel or coarse sacking, further wringing being done at home, if necessary, with a laundry roller-wringer or mangle. Wringing or squeezing the moss does not harm it for surgical purposes, though it must not be allowed to dry in closely pressed pieces, because it tears when being opened up again. If squeezed with the hand, it must not be pressed into a hard ball.

While still damp, all clumps should be separated out, as the moss, whether picked or not, must be sent to the workrooms in a loose state.

Cleaning or picking the moss is best done while still damp, though it may also be done when dry. The moss is spread out on a table and all other substances, such as grasses, twigs, bits of heather and other plants, and above all, pine-needles, must be carefully removed by hand. The moss itself must not be torn or broken into short pieces.

Drying is best done in the open air; artificial heat is apt to overheat the moss and diminish its elasticity, making it brittle and easily rubbed into dust.

An empty hayshed may also be employed, open on all sides, or the floors of an empty room, with windows open, wire netting being used to keep the moss from blowing away.

Where a moor produces large patches of coherent Sphagnum – cushions – the following method has been employed. Large cushions of the moss are taken out and placed on a drier area near by – a couple of workers can put out about a hundred of these in an hour. On the next visit, these are turned and another set put out. In favourable weather a few days' sun and wind will dry these thoroughly, as the cushions are too bulky to be scattered by the wind. Several big sacks can be filled on a final visit, and the carriage of perfectly dry moss is an easy matter.

¶ *Preparation of the Dressings.* The moss after being dried and carefully picked over is now ready for the dressings. All used in home hospitals is put up loosely in small, flat muslin bags, of a fairly close but very thin muslin, the bags only being loosely filled (as a rule 2 oz. of the moss to each bag, 10 inches by 14 inches), as allowance has to be made for the way in which the moss swells on being brought into contact with moisture.

Sphagnum Moss pads are supplied both plain and sterilized (sublimated), some hospitals preferring to sterilize them themselves, but a considerable proportion being sterilized at the depots and sent out ready for use. The filled bags are passed through a solution of corrosive sublimate by a worker in rubber gloves, squeezed through a little mangle and dried again, that they may return to the specified weight, for after the bath they are 2 oz. too heavy. The object of sublimating the moss is not for any antiseptic effect on a wound (as of course it does not come into direct contact with the skin) but to neutralize the discharge which may come through the inner dressings.

For use in field-hospitals, etc., the moss is packed in compressed cakes cut to a certain size, which are more conveniently packed for sending abroad than the soft dressings, these small slabs being also placed, each in a muslin bag, very much too large for the size of the dry cake put in them, for obvious reasons. There was a munition factory in Scotland, where much of the moss was sublimated and part of it compressed by hydraulic power into these cakes. The very hydraulic press which one hour was moulding shell bases, was in the next devoting its energy to compressing the healing cakes of Sphagnum Moss.

Sphagnum Moss was also used during the War in conjunction with Garlic, one of the best antiseptics. The Government bought up tons of the bulbs, which were sent out to the front; the raw juice expressed, diluted with water, was put on swabs of sterilized Sphagnum Moss and applied to wounds. Where this treatment was adopted there were no specific complications, and thousands of lives were thus saved.

¶ *Peat Tar.* In connexion with the uses of Spaghnum Moss as a dressing for wounds, mention should be made of the Tar extracted from the Peat on which the Moss is usually found growing.

The Peat Tar contains similar antiseptic and preservative properties as the Moss itself – conclusively demonstrated by the fact that bodies of animals have lain buried in peat bogs for years, and when accidentally disinterred have been found in a state of perfect preservation.

¶ *Medicinal Action and Uses.* Preparations of calcined peat have long been regarded as effective and cheap germicides, and as a valuable aid to sanitation; peat water possesses astringent and antiseptic properties, and the air in proximity to tracts of peat moss is invariably salubrious, owing probably to the absorption of hydrogen and the exhalation of oxygen by the mosses. Sphagnol, a distillate of Peat Tar, is authori-

MOTHERWORT

Part Used. Herb

Motherwort, the only British representative of the genus *Leonurus*, is a native of many parts of Europe, on banks and under hedges, in a gravelly or calcareous soil. It is often found in country gardens, where it was formerly grown for medicinal purposes, but it is rare to find it truly wild in England, and by some authorities it is not considered indigenous, but merely a garden escape.

¶ *Description.* It is distinguished from all other British labiates by the leaves, which are deeply and palmately cut into five lobes, or three-pointed segments, and by the prickly calyx-teeth of its flowers. When not in flower, it resembles Mugwort in habit.

From the perennial root-stock rise the square, stout stems, 2 to 3 feet high, erect and branched, principally below, the angles prominent. The leaves are very closely set, the radical ones on slender, long petioles, ovate, lobed and toothed, those on the stem, 2 to 3 inches long, petioled, wedge-shaped; the lower roundish, palmately five-lobed, the lobes trifid at the apex, the upper three-fid, coarsely serrate, reticulately veined, the veinlets prominent beneath, with slender, curved hairs. The uppermost leaves and bracts are very narrow and entire, or only with a tooth on each side, and bear in their axils numerous whorls of pinkish, or nearly white, sessile flowers, six to fifteen in a whorl. The corollas, though whitish on the outside, are stained with paler or darker purple within. They have rather short tubes and nearly flat upper lips, very hairy above, with long, woolly hairs. The two front stamens are the longest and the anthers are sprinkled with hard, shining dots.

tatively recognized as an extremely useful application in eczema, psoriasis, pruritus, hæmorrhoids, chilblains, scabies, acne and other forms of skin diseases, while it is very beneficial for allaying irritation arising from insect bites. For the latter purpose it is a preventative no less than a cure.

The manufacture of spinning material out of peat-fibre has been attempted in Sweden, and experiments have advanced so far that cloth as well as clothing has been made out of peat fibre mixed with other textile materials. This does not, however, appear likely to lead to any important industry, but absorptive material has been produced from white Sphagnum Moss and Wood Pulp. It has also lately been reported from Sweden that successful attempts have been made to extract alcohol from Sphagnum.

Leonurus cardiaca (LINN.)
N.O. Labiatæ

The plant blossoms in August. It has rather a pungent odour and a very bitter taste. It is a dull green, the leaves paler below, pubescent, especially on the angles of the stem and the underside of the leaves, the hairs varying much in length and abundance.

The name of the genus, *Leonurus*, in Greek signifies a Lion's tail, from some fancied resemblance in the plant.

¶ *Cultivation.* When once planted in a garden, Motherwort will soon increase if the seeds are permitted to scatter. It is perfectly hardy and needs no special soil, and the roots will continue for many years.

Seedlings should be planted about a foot apart.

¶ *Part Used.* The whole herb, dried, cut in August. The drying may be carried out in any of the ways described for Scullcap.

¶ *Medicinal Action and Uses.* Diaphoretic, antispasmodic, tonic, nervine, emmenagogue. Motherwort is especially valuable in female weakness and disorders (hence the name), allaying nervous irritability and inducing quiet and passivity of the whole nervous system.

As a tonic, it acts without producing febrile excitement, and in fevers, attended with nervousness and delirium, it is extremely useful.

Old writers tell us that there is no better herb for strengthening and gladdening the heart, and that it is good against hysterical complaints, and especially for palpitations of the heart when they arise from hysteric causes, and that when made into a syrup, it will allay inward tremors, faintings, etc.

There is no doubt it has proved the truth of their claims in its use as a simple tonic, not only in heart disease, neuralgia and other affections of the heart, but also in spinal disease and in recovery from fevers where other tonics are inadmissable.

In Macer's *Herbal* we find 'Motherwort' mentioned as one of the herbs which were considered all-powerful against 'wykked sperytis.'

The best way of giving it is in the form of a conserve, made from the young tops, says one writer. It may be given in decoctions, or a strong infusion, but is very unpleasant to take that way. The infusion is made from 1 oz. of herb to a pint of boiling water, taken in wineglassful doses.

¶ *Preparations and Dosages.* Powdered herb, ½ to 1 drachm. Fluid extract, ½ to 1 drachm. Solid extract, 5 to 15 grains.

MOUNTAIN ASH. *See* ASH

MOUNTAIN FLAX. *See* FLAX

MOUNTAIN GRAPE. *See* GRAPE

MOUNTAIN LAUREL. *See* LAUREL

MOUSE-EAR. *See* HAWKWEED

MUGWORT

Culpepper wrote of Motherwort:

'Venus owns this herb and it is under Leo. There is no better herb to drive melancholy vapours from the heart, to strengthen it and make the mind cheerful, blithe and merry. May be kept in a syrup, or conserve, there-fore the Latins call it cardiaca. . . . It cleansethe the chest of cold phlegm, oppres-sing it and killeth worms in the belly. It is of good use to warm and dry up the cold humours, to digest and disperse them that are settled in the veins, joints and sinews of the body and to help cramps and convulsions.'

And Gerard says:

'Divers commend it against infirmities of the heart. Moreover the same is commended for green wounds; it is also a remedy against certain diseases in cattell, as the cough and murreine, and for that cause divers husband-men oftentimes much desire it.'

Artemisia vulgaris (LINN.)
N.O. Compositæ

Synonyms. Felon Herb. St. John's Plant. Cingulum Sancti Johannis
Parts Used. Leaves, root

Mugwort abounds on hedgebanks and waysides in most parts of England. It is a tall-growing plant, the stems, which are angular and often of a purplish hue, fre-quently rising 3 feet or more in height. The leaves are smooth and of a dark green tint on the upper surface, but covered with a dense cottony down beneath; they are once or twice pinnately lobed, the segments being lance-shaped and pointed. The flowers are in small oval heads with cottony involucres and are arranged in long, terminal panicles; they are either reddish or pale yellow. The Mugwort is closely allied to the Common Wormwood, but may be readily distinguished by the leaves being white on the under-surfaces only and by the leaf segments being pointed, not blunt. It lacks the essential oil of the Worm-wood.

The Mugwort is said to have derived its name from having been used to flavour drinks. It was, in common with other herbs, such as Ground Ivy, used to a great extent for flavouring beer before the introduction of hops. For this purpose, the plant was gathered when in flower and dried, the fresh herb being considered unsuitable for this object: malt liquor was then boiled with it so as to form a strong decoction, and the liquid thus prepared was added to the beer. Until recent years, it was still used in some parts of the country to flavour the table beer brewed by cottagers.

It has also been suggested that the name, Mugwort, may be derived not from 'mug,' the drinking vessel, but from *moughte* (a moth or maggot), because from the days of Dioscorides, the plant has been regarded, in common with Wormwood, as useful in keeping off the attacks of moths.

In the Middle Ages, the plant was known as *Cingulum Sancti Johannis*, it being be-lieved that John the Baptist wore a girdle of it in the wilderness. There were many super-stitions connected with it: it was believed to preserve the wayfarer from fatigue, sun-stroke, wild beasts and evil spirits generally: a crown made from its sprays was worn on St. John's Eve to gain security from evil possession, and in Holland and Germany one of its names is St. John's Plant, because of the belief, that if gathered on St. John's Eve it gave protection against diseases and misfortunes.

Dr. John Hill extols its virtues, and says:

'Providence has placed it everywhere about our doors; so that reason and authority, as well as the notice of our senses, point it out for use: but chemistry has banished natural medicines.'

Dioscorides praises this herb, and orders the flowering tops to be used just before they bloom.

The dried leaves were, sixty or seventy years ago, in use by the working classes in Cornwall as one of the substitutes for tea, at a time when tea cost 7s. per lb., and on the Continent Mugwort is occasionally employed as an aromatic culinary herb, being one of the green herbs with which geese are often stuffed during roasting.

The downy leaves have been used in the preparation of *Moxas*, which the Japanese use to cure rheumatism. The down is separated by heating the leaves and afterwards rubbing them between the hands until the cottony fibres alone remain, these are then made up into small cones or cylinders for use. *Artemisia Moxa* and *A. sinensis* are mainly used in Japan. This cottony substance has also been used as a substitute for tinder.

Sheep are said to enjoy the herbage of the Mugwort, and also the roots. The plant may, perhaps, be the Artemesia of Pontos, which was celebrated among the ancients for fattening these animals. It is said to be good for poultry and turkeys.

A variegated variety of Mugwort also occurs.

¶ *Parts Used Medicinally.* The leaves, collected in August and dried in the same manner as Wormwood, and the root, dug in autumn and dried. The roots are cleansed in cold water and then freed from rootlets. Drying may be done at first in the open air, spread thinly, as contact may turn the roots mouldy. Or they may be spread on clean floors, or on shelves, in a warm room for about ten days, and turned frequently. When somewhat shrunken, they must be finished more quickly by artificial heat in a drying room or shed, near a stove or gas fire, care being taken that the heated air can escape at the top of the room. Drying in an even temperature will probably take about a fortnight, or more. It is not complete until the roots are dry to the core and brittle, snapping when bent.

Mugwort root is generally about 8 inches long, woody, beset with numerous thin and tough rootlets, 2 to 4 inches long, and about $\frac{1}{12}$ inch thick. It is light brown externally; internally whitish, with an angular wood and thick bark, showing five or six resin cells. The taste is sweetish and acrid.

¶ *Constituents.* A volatile oil, an acrid resin and tannin.

¶ *Medicinal Action and Uses.* It has stimulant and slightly tonic properties, and is of value as a nervine and emmenagogue, having also diuretic and diaphoretic action.

Its chief employment is as an emmenagogue, often in combination with Pennyroyal and Southernwood. It is also useful as a diaphoretic in the commencement of cold.

It is given in infusion, which should be prepared in a covered vessel, 1 oz. of the herb to 1 pint of boiling water, and given in $\frac{1}{2}$ teaspoonful doses, while warm. The infusion may be taken cold as a tonic, in similar doses, three times daily: it has a bitterish and aromatic taste.

As a nervine, Mugwort is valued in palsy, fits, epileptic and similar affections, being an old-fashioned popular remedy for epilepsy (especially in persons of a feeble constitution). Gerard says: 'Mugwort cureth the shakings of the joynts inclining to the Palsie;' and Parkinson considered it good against hysteria. A drachm of the powdered leaves, given four times a day, is stated by Withering to have cured a patient who had been affected with hysterical fits for many years, when all other remedies had failed.

The juice and an infusion of the herb were given for intermittent fevers and agues. The leaves used to be steeped in baths, to communicate an invigorating property to the water.

¶ *Preparations.* Fluid extract, $\frac{1}{2}$ to 1 drachm.

Culpepper directs that the tops of the plant are to be used fresh gathered, and says:

'a very slight infusion is excellent for all disorders of the stomach, prevents sickness after meals and creates an appetite, but if made too strong, it disgusts the taste. The tops with the flowers on them, dried and powdered, are good against agues, and have the same virtues with wormseed in killing worms. The juice of the large leaves which grows from the root before the stalk appears is the best against the dropsy and jaundice, in water, ale, wine, or the juice only. The infusion drank morning and evening for some time helps hysterics, obstruction of the spleen and weakness of the stomach. Its oil, taken on sugar and drank after, kills worms, resists poison, and is good for the liver and jaundice.

The root has a slow bitterness which affects not the head and eyes like the leaves, hence the root should be accounted among the best stomachics. The oil of the seed cures quotidians and quartans. Boiled in lard and laid to swellings of the tonsils and quinsy is serviceable. It is admirable against surfeits. . . . Wormwood and vinegar are an antidote to the mischief of mushrooms and henbane and the biting of the seafish called Draco marinus, or quaviver; mixed with honey, it takes away blackness after falls, bruises, etc. . . . With Pellitory of the Wall used as poultice to ease all outward pains. Placed among woolen cloths it prevents and destroys the moths.'

Another old writer affirmed that Mugwort was good 'for quaking of the sinews.'
See WORMWOOD, SOUTHERNWOOD.

MULBERRY, COMMON

Morus nigra (LINN.)
N.O. Artocapaceæ

The Common or Black Mulberry is not one of our native trees, but with several other members of its genus – which contains a dozen or more species – can be grown without protection in the south of Britain. There they are small bushy-headed trees, with large alternate, deciduous, toothed and often variously lobed leaves. It is by no means unusual for a Mulberry tree to produce leaves of several different shapes, or differing considerably in outline. As a rule, abnormal-shaped leaves are produced from stem-shoots or sucker growths, and frequently by very vigorous young branches. The Chinese White Mulberry (*Morus alba*, Linn.), cultivated in other countries as food for the silkworm, is even more variable in leafage than the Common Mulberry, and quite a score of different forms of leaf have been gathered from a single tree and several from one shoot. Both species contain in every part a milky juice, which will coagulate into a sort of Indian rubber, and this has been thought to give tenacity to the filament spun by the silkworm.

¶ *Description*. The Common Mulberry is a handsome tree, 20 to 30 feet high, of rugged, picturesque appearance, forming a dense, spreading head of branches usually wider than the height of the tree, springing from a short, rough trunk.

It bears unisexual flowers, the sexes in separate spikes, or catkins, which are small, more or less cylindrical and in no way beautiful. The oblong, short-stalked 'fruit,' which when ripe is about an inch long and of an intense purple, is really a fruit-cluster, composed of little, closely-packed drupes, each containing one seed and enclosed by the four enlarged sepals, which have become succulent, thus forming the spurious berry. By detaching a single fruit from the cluster, the overlapping lobes of the former perianth may be still discerned.

Mulberries are extremely juicy and have a refreshing, subacid, saccharine taste, but they are devoid of the fine aroma that distinguishes many fruits of the order Rosaceæ.

¶ *Habitat*. The tree grows wild in northern Asia Minor, Armenia and the Southern Caucasus region as far as Persia and is now cultivated throughout Europe. It ripens its fruits in England and also as far north as Southern Sweden and Gothland. It flourishes more in the southern part of Great Britain than in the northern counties, but is always of slow growth. Gerard describes it as 'high and full of boughes' and growing in sundry gardens in England, and he grew in his own London garden both the Black and the White Mulberry. Lyte also, before Gerard, in 1578, describes it. It is definitely known to have been cultivated in England since the early part of the sixteenth century, and possibly long before, it being considered probable that it was introduced into Britain by the Romans, being imported from Italy for the soldiers' use.

The Black Mulberry was known in the whole of Southern Europe from the earliest times, and it is presumed that it was introduced from Persia. It is mentioned by most of the early Greek and Roman writers.

The Romans ate Mulberries at their feasts, as we know from the *Satires* of Horace, who (*Sat. ii*,) recommends that Mulberries be gathered before sunset. We also find mention of the Mulberry in Ovid, who in the *Metamorphoses* refers to the legend of Pyramus and Thisbe, who were slain beneath its shade, the fruit being fabled to have thereby changed from white to deep red through absorbing their blood. By Virgil, the tree is termed *sanguinea morus*. Pliny speaks of its employment in medicine and also describes its use in Egypt and Cyprus. He further relates:

'Of all the cultivated trees, the Mulberry is the last that buds, which it never does until the cold weather is past, and it is therefore called the wisest of trees. But when it begins to put forth buds, it dispatches the business in one night, and that with so much force, that their breaking forth may be evidently heard.'

It has been suggested that the generic name of the Mulberry, *Morus*, has been derived from the Latin word *mora* (delay), from this tardy expansion of the buds, and as the wisest of its fellows, the tree was dedicated by the Ancients to Minerva. In alluding to the Black Mulberry, Pliny observes that there is no other tree that has been so neglected by the wit of man, either in grafting or giving it names. It abounded in Italy at that time, as a reference in Virgil's *Georgics* (II, v. 121) clearly shows. The excavations at Pompeii also bear witness to this, for, in the peristyle of the 'House of the Bull,' a Black Mulberry is represented. Mulberry leaves are also to be found in a mosaic from the 'House of the Faun.' Schouw, who wrote about the plants of Pompeii in 1854, considered that *M. alba* was unknown to the Pompeians. At the time of Virgil (who died in 19 B.C.) silk was held to be a product of the Mulberry leaves, the work of the silkworms not being understood. Silkworm culture was first introduced by Justinian from Constantinople – he ruled from A.D. 527–65. In Italy the Black Mulberry was employed for feeding the silkworm until about 1434, when *M. alba* was introduced from the Levant and has ever since been commonly preferred.

References in various old Chronicles show that the Mulberry was far more esteemed in ancient times than at present. It was included among the large number of useful plants ordered by Charlemagne (A.D. 812) to be cultivated on the imperial farm. The cultivation of the Mulberry in Spain is implied by a reference to the preparation of Syrup of Mulberries in the Calendar of Cordova of the year 961.

There are many famous Mulberry trees in England. Those of Syon House, Brentford, are of special historical interest and include what is reported to be the oldest tree of its kind in England, said to be introduced from Persia in 1548. It is this particular and venerable tree which forms the subject of an illustration in London's *Aboretum and Fruticetum*. Although a wreck compared to its former self, it is regarded as one of the largest Mulberry trees in the country. Its height is given by Loudon as 22 feet, and additional interest is attached to this tree, as it is said to have been planted by the botanist Turner.

In 1608 James I, being anxious to further the silk industry by introducing the culture of the silkworm into Britain, issued an edict encouraging the cultivation of Mulberry trees, but the attempt to rear silkworms in England proved unsuccessful, apparently because the Black Mulberry was cultivated in error, whereas the White Mulberry is the species on which the silkworm flourishes. A letter was addressed by the King to the

'Lord Lieutenant of the several Shires of England urging them to persuade and require such as are of ability to buy and distribute in that County the number of ten thousand Mulberry plants which shall be delivered to them at our City of – , at the rate of 3 farthings the plant, or at 6s. the hundred containing five score plants.'

The following transaction is mentioned in the College accounts at Cambridge: 'Item for 300 mulberry plants, xviii. s.' This was in 1608–9, the date of Milton's birth, so that the old Mulberry tree growing in the grounds of Christ Church, Cambridge, still bearing excellent fruit, which is reputed to have been planted by Milton, is still older, probably the last of three hundred which cost the College 18s. in 1609.

There is another Mulberry tree still standing near the Vicarage at Stowmarket which, by tradition, is said to have been planted by Milton. A fine specimen of Mulberry tree is to be seen in front of the Head-master's house at Eton. It was measured in 1907, and found to be 30 feet high, with girth of 8 feet 3 inches, and there is a beautiful example in the Canons' old walled garden at Canterbury.

King James I not only issued his famous edict for introducing the culture of the silkworm into Britain, but he also planted largely himself, and directed payments to

'Master William Stallinge of the sum of £935 for the charge of 4 acres of land taken in for His Majesty's use, near to his Palace of Westminster, for the planting of Mulberry trees, together with the charge of walling, levelling and planting thereof with Mulberry trees.'

This plantation is the 'Mulberry Garden' often mentioned by the old dramatists and occupied the site of the present beautiful private grounds of Buckingham Palace, where one remaining Mulberry tree planted at that time is still to be seen. The tree still bears fruit, but is in no way remarkable either for size of its trunk or the spread of its branches.

'The Royal edict of James I,' writes Loudon, 'recommending the cultivation of silkworms and offering packets of Mulberry seeds to all who would sow them, no doubt rendered the tree fashionable, as there is scarcely an old garden or gentleman's seat throughout the country, which can be traced back to the seventeenth century, in which a Mulberry tree is not to be found. It is remarkable, however, that though these trees were expressly intended for the nourishment of silkworms, they nearly all belong to *M. nigra*, as very few instances exist of old trees of *M. alba* in England.' Shakespeare's famous Mulberry, of which there are descendants at Kew, is referable to this period. Shakespeare is said to have taken it from the Mulberry garden of James I, and planted it in his garden at New Place, Stratford-on-Avon, in 1609. This also was a Black Mulberry, 'cultivated for its fruit, which is very wholesome and palatable; and not for its leaves, which are but little esteemed for silkworms.'

'The tree,' Malone writes, 'was celebrated in many a poem, one especially by Dibdin, but about 1752, the then owner of New Place, the Rev. Mr. Gastrell, bought and pulled down the house and cut down Shakespeare's celebrated Mulberry tree, to save himself the trouble of showing it to those whose admiration of the poet led them to visit the ground on which it stood.'

The pieces were made into many snuff-boxes and other mementoes of the tree, some of them being inscribed with the punning motto, 'Memento Mori.' Ten years afterwards, when the freedom of the city was presented to Garrick, the document was enclosed in a casket made from the wood of this tree. A cup was also made from it, and at the Shakespeare Jubilee, Garrick, holding the cup, recited verses, composed by himself, in honour of the Mulberry tree planted by Shakespeare. A slip of it was grown by Garrick in his garden at Hampton Court, and a scion of the original tree is now growing in Shakespeare's garden.

¶ *Cultivation.* Mulberry trees like a warm, well-drained, loamy soil, and *M. nigra* is especially worth growing for its luxuriant leafage and picturesque form. It can be increased by cuttings with the greatest ease – in February, cut off some branches of a fairly large size (the old writers say that pieces 8 feet long or more will grow) and insert a foot deep, where neither sun nor wind can freely penetrate. Envelop the stem above the ground level with moss, all but the upper pair of buds, in order to check evaporation. Branches broken down, but not detached, will usually take root if they touch the ground. Layers made in the autumn will root in twelve months, and cuttings of the young wood taken off with a heel and planted deeply in a shady border late in the year will root slowly, but more quickly and surely if put into gentle heat under glass. *M. alba* will also root from autumn or winter cuttings.

The Mulberry can also be increased by seeds, which, if sown in gentle heat, or in the open early in the year, will produce young seedlings by the autumn.

In a paper by Mr. J. Williams of Pitmaston, published in the Horticultural Transactions for 1813, is the statement:

'The standard Mulberry receives great injury by being planted on grass plots with a view of preserving the fruit when it falls spontaneously. No tree, perhaps, receives more benefit from the spade and the dunghill than the Mulberry; it ought therefore to be frequently dug about the roots and occasionally assisted with manure.'

Mulberry trees do not begin to bear fruit early in life, and few fruits can be expected from a tree before it is fifteen years of age. It is commonly said that the fruit of the oldest Mulberry trees is the best.

There are few trees better able to withstand the debilitating effects of the close atmosphere of small town gardens, and numerous fine examples are met with about London, several within the City boundaries, familiar examples of which are those in Finsbury Circus and many smaller ones in St. Paul's Churchyard.

Mulberry trees are not easily killed, and old examples that have been reduced to a mere shell have been rejuvenated by careful pruning and cultivation.

The WHITE MULBERRY (*M. alba*), a deciduous tree, 30 to 45 feet high, native of China, to which we have referred as the tree upon which the silkworm is fed, succeeds quite well in the south of England but is not often grown in this country.

The RED MULBERRY (*M. rubra*), a native of the United States of America, is very difficult to grow here.

The FRENCH MULBERRY (*Callicarpa Americana*) is a shrub 3 to 6 feet high, with bluish flowers and violet fruit, but the species is too tender for any but the mildest parts of Great Britain.

¶ *Constituents* of the Black Mulberry Fruit: Glucose, protein, pectin, colouring matter, tartaric and malic acids, ash, etc. This composition varies much, as in all fleshy fruits, with the ripeness and other conditions.

In amount of grape sugar, the Mulberry is surpassed only by the Cherry and the Grape.

¶ *Uses.* Mulberries are refreshing and have laxative properties and are well adapted to febrile cases. In former days, they used to be made into various conserves and drinks.

RECIPES

Mulberry Wine

On each gallon of ripe Mulberries, pour 1 gallon of boiling water and let them stand for 2 days. Then squeeze all through a hair sieve or bag. Wash out the tub or jar and return the liquor to it, put in the sugar at the rate of 3 lb. to each gallon of the liquor; stir up until quite dissolved, then put the liquor into a cask. Let the cask be raised a little on one side until fermentation ceases, then bung down. If the liquor be clear, it may be bottled in 4 months' time. Into each bottle put 1 clove and a small lump of sugar and the bottles should be kept in a moderate temperature. The wine may be used in a year from time of bottling.

Mulberries are sometimes used in Devonshire for mixing with cider during fermentation, giving a pleasant taste and deep red colour. In Greece, also, the fruit is subjected to fermentation, thereby furnishing an inebriating beverage.

Scott relates in *Ivanhoe* that the Saxons made a favourite drink, Morat, from the juice of Mulberries with honey, but it is doubtful whether the *Morum* of the Anglo-Saxon 'Vocabularies' was not the Blackberry, so that the 'Morat' of the Saxons may have been Blackberry Wine.

Mulberry Jam

Unless very ripe Mulberries are used, the jam will have an acid taste. Put 1 lb. of Mulberries in a jar and stand it in a pan of water on the fire till the juice is extracted. Strain them and put the juice into a preserving pan with 3 lb. of sugar. Boil it and remove the scum and put in 3 lb. of very ripe Mulberries and let them stand in the syrup until thoroughly warm, then set the pan back on the fire and boil them very gently for a short time, stirring all the time and taking care not to break the fruit. Then take the pan off and let them stand in the syrup all night. Put the pan on the fire again in the morning and boil again gently till stiff.

¶ *Medicinal Action and Uses.* The sole use of Mulberries in modern medicine is for the preparation of a syrup, employed to flavour or colour any other medicine. Mulberry Juice is obtained from the ripe fruit of the Mulberry by expression and is an official drug of the British Pharmacopœia. It is a dark violet or purple liquid, with a faint odour and a refreshing, acid, saccharine taste. The British Pharmacopœia directs that *Syrupus Mori* should be prepared by heating 50 fluid drachms of the expressed juice to boiling point, then cooling and filtering. Ninety drachms of sugar is then dissolved in the juice, which is warmed up again. When once more cooled, 6·25 drachms of alcohol is added: the product should then measure

about 100 drachms (20 fluid ounces). The dose is 2 to 1 fluid drachm, but it is, as stated, chiefly used as an adjuvant rather than for its slightly laxative and expectorant qualities, though used as a gargle, it will relieve sore throat.

The juice of the American Red Mulberry may be substituted; it is less acid than the European, while that of the White Mulberry, native of China, is sweet, but rather insipid.

In the East, the Mulberry is most productive and useful. It is gathered when ripe, dried on the tops of the houses in the sun, and stored for winter use. In Cabul, it is pounded to a fine powder, and mixed with flour for bread.

The bark of *M. nigra* is reputed anthelmintic, and is used to expel tape worm.

The root-bark of *M. Indica* (Rumph) and other species is much used in the East under the name of San-pai-p'i, as a diuretic and expectorant.

The *Morinda tinctoria*, or Indian Mulberry, is used by the African aborigines as a remedial agent, but there is no reliable evidence of its therapeutic value.

A parasitic fungus growing on the old stems of Mulberry trees found in the island of Meshima, Japan, and called there *Meshimakobu*, brown outside and yellow inside, is used in Japan for medicine.

Gerard recommends the fruit of the Mulberry tree for use in all affections of the mouth and throat.

'The barke of the root,' he says, 'is bitter, hot and drie, and hath a scouring faculty: the decoction hereof doth open the stoppings of the liver and spleen, it purgeth the belly, and driveth forth wormes.'

With Parkinson, the fruit was evidently not in favour, for he tells us:

'Mulberries are not much desired to be eaten, although they be somewhat pleasant, both for that they stain their fingers and lips that eat them, and do quickly putrefie in the stomach, if they be not taken before meat.'

The Mulberry family, *Moraceæ*, formerly regarded, together with the *Ulmaceæ* (Elm family), as a division of the *Urticaceæ* (Nettle family), comprises upwards of 50 genera and about 900 species, of very diverse habit and appearance. Among them are the highly important food-plants *Ficus* (Fig) and *Artocarpus* (Bread fruit). *M. tinctoria* (Linn.), sometimes known as *Machura tinctoria* (D. Don), but generally now named *Chlorophora tinctoria* (Gaudich.), yields the dye-stuff Fustic, chiefly used for colouring wood of an orange-yellow colour. The tree is indigenous in Mexico and some of the West Indies, the wood being imported in logs of various sizes. This kind of fustic is known as old fustic, or Cuba fustic. Young fustic is a different product, obtained from *Rhus cotinus* (Linn.). It is known also as Venetian or Hungarian sumach, and is used in the Tyrol for tanning leather. The extract of fustic is imported as well as the wood. From *Maclura Brasiliensis* (Endl.) another important dye-wood is obtained. A yellow dye is also derived from the root of the Osage Orange (*Toxylon pomiferum*, Raf.), belonging to this order. The milky juice of *Brosimum Galactodendron* (Don) – the Cow or Milk-Tree of Tropical America – is said to be usable as cow's milk, and 'Bread-nuts' are the edible seeds of another member of this genus, *B. Alicastrum* (Swz.), of Jamaica. The famous deadly Upas Tree of the East Indies (*Antiaris toxicaria*, Lesc.) is a less useful member of this family.

The bast-fibres of many *Moraceæ* are tough and are used in the manufacture of cordage and paper. The Paper Mulberry (*Broussonetia papyrifera*, Vint.) is cultivated extensively in Japan. It is a native of China, introduced into Great Britain early in the eighteenth century and is a coarse-growing, vigorous shrub, or a tree up to 30 feet, forming a roundish, spreading head of branches. The young wood is thickly downy, soft and pithy, the leaves very variable in size and form, often shaped like fig-leaves, the upper surface dull, green and rough, the lower surface densely woolly. It is a diœcious plant, the male flowers in cylindrical, often curly, woolly catkins, the female flowers in ball-like heads, producing round fruits congregated of small, red, pulpy seeds. In Japan, the stems are cut down every winter, so that the shrub only attains a height of 6 or 7 feet, and the barks are stripped off as an important material for paper. *B. Kajinoki* (Sieb.) is a deciduous tree, wild in Japan, growing 29 to 30 feet high, similar to the Paper Mulberry and made use of in like manner, though inferior. The ripe fruits are beautifully red and sweet. Paper is also manufactured in Japan with the fibre of the bark of *B. kæmpferi* (Sieb.), a deciduous climber. A good paper may be manufactured from the bast of the *Morus alba*, var. *stylosa* (Bur.), Jap. 'Kuwa,' but as this plant is used especially for feeding silkworms, the paper made from the branches after the leaves are taken off for silkworms is of a very inferior quality.

MULLEIN, GREAT

Verbascum thapsus (LINN.)
N.O. Scrophulariaceæ

Synonyms. White Mullein. Torches. Mullein Dock. Our Lady's Flannel. Velvet Dock. Blanket Herb. Velvet Plant. Woollen. Rag Paper. Candlewick Plant. Wild Ice Leaf. Clown's Lungwort. Bullock's Lungwort. Aaron's Rod. Jupiter's Staff. Jacob's Staff. Peter's Staff. Shepherd's Staff. Shepherd's Clubs. Beggar's Stalk. Golden Rod. Adam's Flannel. Beggar's Blanket. Clot. Cuddy's Lungs. Duffle. Feltwort. Fluffweed. Hare's Beard. Old Man's Flannel. Hag's Taper

Parts Used. Leaves, flowers, root

Habitat. Verbascum thapsus (Linn.), the Great Mullein, is a widely distributed plant, being found all over Europe and in temperate Asia as far as the Himalayas, and in North America is exceedingly abundant as a naturalized weed in the eastern States. It is met with throughout Britain (except in the extreme north of Scotland) and also in Ireland and the Channel Islands, on hedge-banks, by roadsides and on waste ground, more especially on gravel, sand or chalk. It flowers during July and August

The natural order Scrophulariaceæ is an important family of plants comprising 200 genera and about 2,500 species, occurring mostly in temperate and sub-tropical regions, many of them producing flowers of great beauty, on which account they are frequently cultivated among favourite garden and greenhouse flowers. Of this group are the Calceolaria, Mimulus, Penstemon, Antirrhinum and Collinsia. Among its British representatives it embraces members so diverse as the Foxglove and Speedwell, the Mullein and Figworts, the Toadflax and the semi-parasites, Eyebright, Bartsia, Cowwheat, and the Red and Yellow Rattles.

Most of the flowers are capable of self-fertilization in default of insect visits.

Unlike the Labiatæ, to which they are rather closely related, plants belonging to this order seldom contain much volatile oil, though resinous substances are common. The most important constituents are glucosides, and many of them are poisonous or powerfully active.

A number of the Scrophulariaceæ are or have been valued for their curative properties and are widely employed both in domestic and in regular medicine.

The genus *Verbascum*, to which the Mullein belongs, contains 210 species, distributed in Europe, West and Central Asia and North Africa, six of which are natives of Great Britain. The Mulleins, like the Veronicas, are exceptions to the general character of the Scrophulariaceæ, having nearly regular, open corollas, the segments being connected only towards the base, instead of having the more fantastic flowers of the Snapdragon and others. They are all tall, stout biennials, with large leaves and flowers in long, terminal spikes.

¶ *Description.* In the first season of the plant's growth, there appears only a rosette of large leaves, 6 to 15 inches long, in form somewhat like those of the Foxglove, but thicker – whitish with a soft, dense mass of hairs on both sides, which make them very thick to the touch. In the following spring, a solitary, stout, pale stem, with tough, strong fibres enclosing a thin rod of white pith, arises from the midst of the felted leaves. Its rigid uprightness accounts for some of the plant's local names: 'Aaron's Rod,' 'Jupiter's' or 'Jacob's Staff,' etc.

The leaves near the base of the stem are large and numerous, 6 to 8 inches long and 2 to 2¼ inches broad, but become smaller as they ascend the stem, on which they are arranged not opposite to one another, but on alternate sides. They are broad and simple in form, the outline rather waved, stalkless, their bases being continued some distance down the stem, as in the Comfrey and a few other plants, the midrib from a quarter to half-way up the blade being actually joined to the stem. By these 'decurrent' leaves (as this hugging of the stem by the leaves is botanically termed) the Great Mullein is easily distinguished from other British species of Mullein – some with white and some with yellow flowers. The leaf system is so arranged that the smaller leaves above drop the rain upon the larger ones below, which direct the water to the roots. This is a necessary arrangement, since the Mullein grows mostly on dry soils. The stellately-branched hairs which cover the leaves so thickly act as a protective coat, checking too great a giving off of the plant's moisture, and also are a defensive weapon of the plant, for not only do they prevent the attacks of creeping insects, but they set up an intense irritation in the mucous membrane of any grazing animals that may attempt to browse upon them, so that the plants are usually left severely alone by them. The leaves are, however, subject to the attacks of a mould, *Peronospora sordida*.

The hairs are not confined to the leaves alone, but are also on every part of the stem, on the calyces and on the outside of the corollas, so that the whole plant appears whitish or grey. The homely but valuable Mullein Tea, a remedy of the greatest antiquity for coughs and colds, must indeed always be strained through fine muslin to remove any hairs that may be floating in the hot water that has been poured over the flowers, or leaves, for otherwise they cause intolerable itching in the mouth.

Towards the top of the stalk, which grows frequently 4 or even 5 feet high, and in gardens has been known to attain a height of 7 or 8 feet, the much-diminished woolly leaves merge into the thick, densely crowded flower-spike, usually a foot long, the flowers opening here and there on the spike, not in regular progression from the base, as in the Foxglove. The flowers are stalkless, the sulphur-yellow corolla, a somewhat irregular cup, nearly an inch across, formed of five rounded petals, united at the base to form a very short tube, being enclosed in a woolly calyx, deeply cut into five lobes. The five stamens stand on the corolla; three of them are shorter than the other two and have a large number of tiny white hairs on their filaments. These hairs are full of sap, and it has been suggested that they form additional bait to the insect visitors, supplementing the allurement of the nectar that lies round the base of the ovary. All kinds of insects are attracted by this plant, the Honey Bee, Humble Bee, some of the smaller wild bees and different species of flies, since the nectar and the staminal hairs are both so readily accessible, though the supply of nectar is not very great. The three short hairy stamens have only short, one-celled anthers – the two longer, smooth ones have larger anthers. The pollen sacs have an orange-red inner surface, disclosed as the anthers open.

In some species, *Verbascum nigrum*, the Dark Mullein, and *V. blattaria*, the Moth Mullein, the filament hairs are purple. The rounded ovary is hairy and also the lower part of the style. The stigma is mature before the anthers and the style projects at the moment the flower opens, so that any insect approaching it from another blossom where it has got brushed by pollen, must needs strike it on alighting and thus insure cross-fertilization, though, failing this, the flower is also able to fertilize itself. The ripened seed capsule is very hard and contains many seeds, which eventually escape through two valves and are scattered round the parent plant.

¶ *History*. The down on the leaves and stem makes excellent tinder when quite dry, readily igniting on the slightest spark, and was, before the introduction of cotton, used for lamp wicks, hence another of the old names: 'Candlewick Plant.' An old superstition existed that witches in their incantations used lamps and candles provided with wicks of this sort, and another of the plant's many names, 'Hag's Taper', refers to this, though the word 'hag' is said to be derived from the Anglo-Saxon word *Hæge* or *Hage* (a hedge) – the name 'Hedge Taper' also exists – and may imply that the sturdy spikes of this tall hedge plant, studded with pale yellow blossoms, suggested a tall candle growing in the hedge, another of its countryside names being, indeed, 'Our Lady's Candle.' Lyte (*The Niewe Herball*, 1578) tells us 'that the whole toppe, with its pleasant yellow floures sheweth like to a wax candle or taper cunningly wrought.'

'Torches' is another name for the plant, and Parkinson tells us:

'Verbascum is called of the Latines Candela regia, and Candelaria, because the elder age used the stalks dipped in suet to burne, whether at funeralls or otherwise.'

And Gerard (1597) also remarks that it is 'a plant whereof is made a manner of lynke (link) if it be talowed.' Dr. Prior, in *The Popular Names of British Plants*, states that the word Mullein was Moleyn in Anglo-Saxon, and Malen in Old French, derived from the Latin *malandrium*, i.e. the malanders or leprosy, and says:

'The term "malandre" became also applied to diseases of cattle, to lung diseases among the rest, and the plant being used as a remedy, acquired its name of "Mullein" and "Bullock's Lungwort." '

Coles, in 1657, in *Adam in Eden*, says that

'Husbandmen of Kent do give it their cattle against the cough of the lungs, and I, therefore, mention it because cattle are also in some sort to be provided for in their diseases.'

The name 'Clown's Lung Wort' refers to its use as a homely remedy. 'Ag-Leaf' and 'Ag-Paper' are other names for it. 'Wild Ice Leaf' perhaps refers to the white look of the leaves. Few English plants have so many local names.

The Latin name *Verbascum* is considered to be a corruption of *barbascum*, from the Latin *barba* (a beard), in allusion to the shaggy foliage, and was bestowed on the genus by Linnæus.

Both in Europe and Asia the power of driving away evil spirits was ascribed to the Mullein. In India it has the reputation among the natives that the St. John's Wort once had here, being considered a sure safeguard against evil spirits and magic, and from the ancient classics we learn that it was this plant which Ulysses took to protect himself against the wiles of Circe.

The Cowslip and the Primrose are classed together by our old herbalists as Petty Mulleins, and are usually credited with much the same properties. Gerard recommends both the flowers and leaves of the primrose, boiled in wine, as a remedy for all diseases of the lungs and the juice of the root itself, snuffed up the nose, for megrim.

All the various species of Mullein found in Britain possess similar medicinal properties, but *V. thapsus*, the species of most common occurrence, is the one most employed.

For medicinal purposes it is generally collected from *wild* specimens, but is worthy of cultivation, not merely from its beauty as an ornamental plant, but also for its medicinal value, which is undoubted. In most parts of Ireland, besides growing wild, it is carefully cultivated in gardens, because of a steady demand for the plant by sufferers from pulmonary consumption.

Its cultivation is easy: being a hardy biennial, it only requires sowing in very ordinary soil and to be kept free from weeds. When growing in gardens, Mulleins will often be found to be infested with slugs, which can be caught wholesale by placing in borders slates and boards smeared with margarine on the underside. Examine in the morning and deposit the catch in a pail of lime and water.

¶ *Parts Used*. The leaves and flowers are the parts used medicinally.

Fresh Mullein leaves are also used for the purpose of making a homœopathic tincture.

¶ *Constituents*. The leaves are nearly odourless and of a mucilaginous and bitterish taste. They contain gum as their principal constituent, together with 1 to 2 per cent. of resin, divisible into two parts, one soluble in ether, the other not; a readily soluble amaroid; a little tannin and a trace of volatile oil.

The flowers contain gum, resin, a yellow colouring principle, a green fatty matter (a sort of chlorophyll), a glucoside, an acrid, fatty matter; free acid and phosphoric acid; uncrystallizable sugar; some mineral salts, the bases of which are potassia and lime, and a small amount of yellowish volatile oil. They should yield not more than 6 per cent of ash. Their odour is peculiar and agreeable: their taste mucilaginous.

¶ *Medicinal Action and Uses.* The Mullein has very markedly demulcent, emollient and astringent properties, which render it useful in pectoral complaints and bleeding of the lungs and bowels. The whole plant seems to possess slightly sedative and narcotic properties.

It is considered of much value in phthisis and other wasting diseases, palliating the cough and staying expectoration, consumptives appearing to benefit greatly by its use, being given in the form of an infusion, 1 oz. of dried, or the corresponding quantity of fresh leaves being boiled for 10 minutes in a pint of milk, and when strained, given warm, thrice daily, with or without sugar. The taste of the decoction is bland, mucilaginous and cordial, and forms a pleasant emollient and nutritious medicine for allaying a cough, or removing the pain and irritation of hæmorrhoids. A plain infusion of 1 oz. to a pint of boiling water can also be employed, taken in wineglassful doses frequently.

The dried leaves are sometimes smoked in an ordinary tobacco pipe to relieve the irritation of the respiratory mucus membranes, and will completely control, it is said, the hacking cough of consumption. They can be employed with equal benefit when made into cigarettes, for asthma and spasmodic coughs in general.

Fomentations and poultices of the leaves have been found serviceable in hæmorrhoidal complaints.

Mullein is said to be of much value in diarrhœa, from its combination of demulcent with astringent properties, by this combination strengthening the bowels at the same time. In diarrhœa the ordinary infusion is generally given, but when any bleeding of the bowels is present, the decoction prepared with milk is recommended.

On the Continent, a sweetened infusion of the *flowers* strained in order to separate the rough hairs, is considerably used as a domestic remedy in mild catarrhs, colic, etc.

A conserve of the flowers has also been employed on the Continent against ringworm, and a distilled water of the flowers was long reputed a cure for burns and erysipelas.

An oil produced by macerating Mullein flowers in olive oil in a corked bottle, during prolonged exposure to the sun, or by keeping near the fire for several days, is used as a local application in country districts in Germany for piles and other mucus membrane inflammation, and also for frost bites and bruises. Mullein oil is recommended for earache and discharge from the ear, and for any eczema of the external ear and its canal. Dr. Fernie (*Herbal Simples*) states that some of the most brilliant results have been obtained in suppurative inflammation of the inner ear by a single application of Mullein oil, and that in acute or chronic cases, two or three drops of this oil should be made to fall in the ear twice or thrice in the day.

Mullein oil is a valuable destroyer of disease germs. The fresh flowers, steeped for 21 days in olive oil, are said to make an admirable bactericide. Gerarde tells us that 'Figs do not putrifie at all that are wrapped in the leaves of Mullein.'

An alcoholic tincture is prepared by homœopathic chemists, from the fresh herb with spirits of wine, which has proved beneficial for migraine or sick headache of long standing, with oppression of the ear. From 8 to 10 drops of the tincture are given as a dose, with cold water, repeated frequently.

¶ *Preparation and Dosage.* Fluid extract, ¼ to 1 drachm.

Formerly the flowers of several species of Mullein were officinal, but Mullein no longer has a place in the British Pharmacopœia, though Verbascum Flowers were introduced into the 4th Edition of the United States National Formulary, as one of the ingredients in pectoral remedies, and the leaves, in fluid extract of Mullein leaves, made with diluted alcohol were directed to be used as a demulcent, the dose being 1 fluid drachm.

In more ancient times, much higher virtues were attributed to this plant. Culpepper gives us a list of most extraordinary cures performed by its agency, and Gerard remarks that

'there be some who think that this herbe being but carryed about one, doth help the falling sickness, especially the leaves of the plant which have not yet borne flowers, and gathered when the sun is in Virgo and the moon in Aries, which thing notwithstanding is vaine and superstitious.'

A decoction of its roots was held to be an alleviation for toothache, and also good for cramps and convulsions, and an early morning draught of the distilled water of the flowers to be good for gout.

Mullein juice and powder made from the dried roots rubbed on rough warts was said to quickly remove them, though it was not recommended as equally efficacious for smooth warts. A poultice made of the seeds and leaves, boiled in hot wine, was also considered an excellent means to 'draw forth speedily thorns or splinters gotten into the flesh.' We also hear of the woolly leaves being worn in the stockings to promote circulation and keep the feet warm.

The flowers impart a yellow colour to boiling water and a rather permanent green colour with dilute sulphuric acid, the latter colour becoming brown upon the addition of alkalis. An infusion of the flowers was used by the Roman ladies to dye their hair a golden colour. Lyte tells us, 'the golden floures of Mulleyn stiped in lye, causeth the heare to war yellow, being washed therewithall,' and according to another old authority, Alexander Trallianus, the ashes of the plant made into a soap will restore hair which has become grey to its original colour.

The seeds are said to intoxicate fish when thrown into the water, and are used by poachers for that purpose, being slightly narcotic. According to Rosenthal (*Pharmaceutical Journal*, July, 1902), the seeds of *V. sinuatum* (Linn.), which are used in Greece as a fish poison, contain 6 to 13 per cent. of Saponin. Traces of the same substance were found in the seeds of *V. phlomoides* (Linn.) and *V. thapsiforme* (Schrad.), common in the south of Europe, which have been used for the same purpose. *V. pulverulentum* of Madeira (also used as a fish poisoner) and *V. phlomoides* are employed as tænicides (expellers of tapeworm).

MUSK SEED

Hibiscus Abelmoschus (LINN.)
N.O. Malvaceæ

Synonyms. Abelmoschus Moschatus. Semen Abelmoschi. Grana Moschata. Ambretta. Egyptian Alcée. Bisornkorner. Ambrakorner. Target-leaved Hibiscus. Ab-el-mosch. Bamia Moschata. Ketmie odorante. Galu gasturi. Capu kanassa
Part Used. Seeds
Habitat. Egypt, East and West Indies

¶ *Description.* This evergreen shrub is about 4 feet in height, having alternate, palmate leaves and large, sulphur yellow, solitary flowers with a purple base. The capsules are in the form of a five-cornered pyramid, filled with large seeds with a strong odour of musk. The capsules are used in soup and for pickles, and the greyish-brown, kidney-shaped seeds, the size of a lentil, with a strong aromatic flavour, are used by the Arabians to mix with coffee. They are used in perfumery for fats and oils, and for the adulteration of musk.

¶ *Constituents.* The seeds contain an abundance of fixed oil, and owe their scent to a coloured resin and a volatile, odorous body. They also contain albuminous matter.

¶ *Medicinal Action and Uses.* An emulsion made from the seeds is regarded as antispasmodic. In Egypt the seeds are chewed as a stomachic, nervine, and to sweeten the breath, and are also used as an aphrodisiac and insecticide. The seeds made into an emulsion with milk are used for itch.

¶ *Other Species.*

A variety is found in Martinique, of a lighter grey in colour and a more delicate odour.

Hibiscus esculentus or *A. esculentus*, okra, bendee, or gombo, is cultivated for its fruit, the abundant mucilage of which, called gombine, is used for thickening soup. The long roots have much odourless mucilage and when powdered are white, and are said to be better than marsh-mallow.

The bark is used for paper and cordage.

It is largely grown in Constantinople as a demulcent.

The leaves furnish an emollient poultice.

MUSTARDS

N.O. Cruciferæ

The Mustards, Black and White, are both wild herbs growing in waste places in this country, but are cultivated for their seeds, which are valuable medicinally and commercially. They were originally treated as members of a small genus of frequently cultivated European and Asiatic herbs named Sinapis, from the Greek *sinapi* (mustard), a name used by Theophrastus, but they are now generally included in the Cabbage genus, *Brassica*.

MUSTARD, WHITE

Brassica alba (BOISS.)

Synonym. Sinapis alba (LINN.)
Part Used. Seeds

The White Mustard, a native of Europe, common in our fields and by roadsides, and also largely cultivated, is an erect annual, about a foot or more in height, with pinnatifid leaves and large, yellow, cruciferous flowers. It closely resembles the Black Mustard, but is smaller. The fruit of the two plants differs considerably in shape, those of the White Mustard being more or less horizontal and hairy, while Black Mustard pods are erect and smooth. The pods of White Mustard are spreading, roundish pods, ribbed and swollen where the seeds are situated, and provided with a very large flattened, sword-shaped beak at the end. Each pod contains four to six globular seeds, about $\frac{1}{12}$ inch in diameter, yellow both on the surface and internally. The seed-coat, though appearing smooth, on examination with a lens, is seen to be covered with minute pits and to be finely reticulated. The inner seedcoats contain a quantity of mucilage, with which the seeds become coated when soaked in water, hence they are often employed to absorb the last traces of moisture in bottles which are not chemically dry. The cotyledons of the seeds contain oil and give a pungent but inodorous emulsion when rubbed with water.

The young seedling plants of White Mustard are commonly raised in gardens for salad, the seeds being usually sown with those of the garden cress and germinating with great rapidity. They may be grown all the year round, the seed readily vegetating under a hand-glass even in cold weather, if the ground is not absolutely frozen.

'When in the leaf,' wrote John Evelyn in 1699, in his *Acetaria*, 'Mustard, especially in young seedling plants, is of incomparable effect to quicken and revive the spirits, strengthening the memory, expelling heaviness, . . . besides being an approved antiscorbutic.'

In Gerard's time, a century earlier, White Mustard was not very common in England.

Both Mustards afford excellent fodder for sheep, and as they can be sown late in the summer are often used for this purpose after the failure of a turnip or rape crop, the White Mustard being more frequently employed, as it is less pungent, though equally nutritious. White Mustard makes a good catch crop, being ready for consumption on the land by sheep eight or nine weeks after being sown. It may be sown in southern counties after an early corn crop, about a peck of seed being sown broadcast to the acre. The plants are hoed sometimes to a distance of about 9 inches apart, if required for seed.

As *green manure*, both kinds of Mustard are employed, but the White Mustard is preferred for this purpose by English farmers, the seed being sown in August and September, and when the plants have attained a good size, about two months after sowing, they are ploughed in. Besides affording useful manure in itself, this green manure helps to prevent the waste of nitrates, which instead of being washed away in drainage water, which would probably happen if the soil were bare, are stored up in the growing plant.

The seeds of the Mustards retain their vitality for a great length of time when buried in the ground, so that after the plants have once been grown anywhere, it is difficult to get rid of them. It has been noticed in the Isle of Ely that whenever a trench was made, White Mustard sprang up from the newly-turned earth.

¶ *Part Used Medicinally.* The dried, ripe seeds are alone official. They possess rubefacient properties, and are mixed with Black Mustard seeds to produce mustard flour for preparing mustard poultices. The powder is not infrequently adulterated with farinaceous substances, coloured by turmeric.

¶ *Constituents.* The epidermal cells of the seed coat of White Mustard seeds contain mucilage, and the cotyledons contain from 23 to 26 per cent. of a fixed oil, which consists of the glycerides of oleic, stearic and erucic or brassic acids. The seeds also contain the crystalline glucoside Sinalbin and the enzyme Myrosin, which unite to form a volatile oil, called Sinalbin Mustard Oil, used for various purposes, though not so pungent as that of Black Mustard. This oil cannot be obtained by distillation, but is extracted by boiling alcohol after the seed has been deprived of its fixed oil. When cold, the volatile oil possesses only a faint, anise-like odour, but a pungent odour is given off on heating. The cake, after the oil is expressed, is pungent and therefore not well fitted for cattle food, but is used for manure.

¶ *Medicinal Action and Uses.* The seeds when ground form a pungent powder, but it is much inferior in strength to that prepared from the black-seeded species.

They have been employed medicinally from very early times. Hippocrates advised their use both internally and as a counter irritating poultice, made with vinegar. They have been administered frequently in disorders of the digestive organs. White Mustard seeds were at one time quite a fashionable remedy as a laxative, especially for old people, the dose being $\frac{1}{2}$ oz. in the entire state, but from the danger of their retention in the intestines, they are not very safe in large quantities, having in several cases caused inflammation of the stomach and intestinal canal.

An infusion of the seeds will relieve chronic bronchitis and confirmed rheumatism, and for a relaxed sore throat a gargle of Mustard Seed Tea will be found of service.

MUSTARD, BLACK

Brassica nigra (LINN.)
Sinapis nigra (LINN.)

Synonym. Brassica sinapioides (Roth.)
Part Used. Seeds
Habitat. The Black Mustard grows throughout Europe, except in the north-eastern
parts, also in South Siberia, Asia Minor and Northern Africa, and is naturalized in
North and South America. It is largely cultivated in England, Holland, Italy, Germany and elsewhere for the sake of the seed, used partly as a condiment, and partly
for its oil

¶ *Description.* It is an erect annual, 3 feet or
more in height, with smaller flowers than
the White Mustard. The spear-shaped,
upper leaves, linear, pointed, entire and
smooth, and the shortly-beaked pods, readily
distinguish it from the former species. The
smooth, erect flattened pods, each provided
with a short slender beak, contain about ten
to twelve dark reddish-brown or black seeds,
which are collected when ripe and dried.
They are about half the size of White
Mustard seeds, but possess similar properties.
The seedcoat is thin and brittle and covered
with minute pits. Like the White Mustard,
the seeds are inodorous, even when powdered,
though a pungent odour is noticeable when
moistened with water, owing to the formation of volatile oil of Mustard, which is
colourless or pale yellow, with an intensely
penetrating odour and a very acrid taste.

¶ *History.* The ancient Greek physicians
held this plant in such esteem for the
medicinal use of its seeds that they attributed
its discovery to Æsculapius.

When it was first employed as a condiment
is unknown, but it was most likely used in
England by the Saxons. Probably the
Romans, who were great eaters of mustard,
pounded and steeped in new wine, brought
the condiment with them to Britain.
Mustard gets its name from *mustum* (the
must), or newly-fermented grape juice, and
ardens (burning). It was originally eaten
whole, or slightly crushed. Gerard in 1623
says that

'the seede of Mustard pounded with vinegar
is an excellent sauce, good to be eaten with
any grosse meates, either fish or flesh, because it doth help digestion, warmeth the
stomache and provoketh appetite.'

Tusser mentions its garden cultivation and
domestic use in the sixteenth century, and
Shakespeare alludes more than once to it:
Tewkesbury mustard is referred to in *Henry
IV.* The herbalist Coles, writing in 1657,
says:

'In Glostershire about Teuxbury they
grind Mustard seed and make it up into balls
which are brought to London and other remote places as being the best that the world
affords.'

All mustard was formerly made up into
balls with honey or vinegar and a little
cinnamon, to keep till wanted, when they
were mixed with more vinegar. It was sold
in balls till Mrs. Clements, of Durham, at the
close of the eighteenth century, invented the
method of preparing mustard flour, which
long went under the name of Durham
Mustard. John Evelyn recommends for
mustard-making 'best Tewkesbury' or the
'soundest and weightiest Yorkshire seeds,'
and tells us that the Italians in making
mustard as a condiment mix orange and
lemon peel with the black seed. At Dijon,
where the best Continental mustard is made,
the condiment is seasoned with various spices
and savouries, such as Anchovies, Capers,
Tarragon and Catsup of Walnuts or Mushrooms.

The Black Mustard is said to have been
employed by the Romans as a green vegetable. The young leaves may be eaten as
salad in place of those of the White variety,
but are more pungent.

The Mustard Tree of Scripture is supposed by some authorities to be a species of
Sinapis, closely resembling the Black
Mustard, but as the latter never attains the
dimensions of a tree, it has been conjectured
that the plant in question is the *Khardal* of
the Arabs, a tree abounding near the Sea of
Galilee, which bears numerous branches and
has small seeds, having the flavour and properties of Mustard.

¶ *Cultivation.* Mustard is sown in spring,
either broadcast or in drills, a foot or more
apart, and ripens towards the end of summer, when, after it has stood in sheaves to
dry, the seed is threshed out and dried on
trays by gentle artificial heat. The crop is
very liable to injury from wet. It is grown for
market on rich, alluvial soil, chiefly in
Lincolnshire and Yorkshire. In Durham,
the cultivation of Mustard of an excellent
quality has been pursued on a considerable
scale for the last two hundred years. Before
grinding, the husk is usually removed, the
seeds are then passed between rollers and
afterwards reduced to powder in a mortar.
This is the system invented by Mrs.
Clements, of Durham. The so-called London Mustard is almost always adulterated and

many samples consist of little but flour, coloured with turmeric and flavoured with pepper.

The only seeds resembling those of Black Mustard are Colchicum seeds, which are larger, rougher, harder, bitter and not pungent.

¶ *Constituents*. The virtues of Black Mustard depend on an acrid, volatile oil contained in the seeds, combined with an active principle containing much sulphur. The acridity of the oil is modified in the seeds by being combined with another fixed oil of a bland nature, which can be separated.

The epidermal cells of the seed-coat contain much less mucilage than those of White Mustard seeds, but the cotyledons of Black Mustard seeds contain from 31 to 33 per cent. of a fixed oil, which consists of the glycerides of Oleic, Stearic and Erucic or Brassic and Behenic acids. The seeds also contain the crystalline glucoside Sinigrin and the enzyme Myrosin. These substances are stored in separate cells. When brought together in water, the volatile Oil of Mustard is formed. It is distilled from the seeds that have been deprived of most of the fixed oil and macerated in water for several hours, and contains from 90 to 99 per cent. of the active principle, Allyl isothiocyanate, which is used as a counter irritant. It is on account of the abundant sulphur contained by this active principle that mustard discolours silver spoons left in it, black sulphuret of silver being formed.

Neither White nor Black Mustard seeds contain starch when ripe.

It was formerly supposed that Black Mustard was deficient in the enzyme Myrosin, and White Mustard was added to correct this and to secure the maximum pungency. It has been proved, however, that Black Mustard contains sufficient of the enzyme, and that no increase in the yield of the volatile oil is effected by adding White Mustard. The main object in using both Black and White Mustard for preparing mustard flour, is probably the production of a commercial article with a better flavour than could be obtained otherwise.

¶ *Medicinal Action and Uses*. Irritant, stimulant, diuretic, emetic. Mustard is used in the form of poultices for external application near the seat of inward inflammation, chiefly in pneumonia, bronchitis and other diseases of the respiratory organs. It relieves congestion of various organs by drawing the blood to the surface, as in head affections, and is of service in the alleviation of neuralgia and other pains and spasms.

Mustard Leaves, used instead of poultices,

consist of the mustard seeds, deprived of fixed oil, but retaining the pungency-producing substances and made to adhere to paper.

Oil of Mustard is a powerful irritant and rubefacient, and when applied to the skin in its pure state, produces almost instant vesication, but when dissolved in rectified spirit, or spirit of camphor, or employed in the form of the Compound Liniment of Mustard of the British Pharmacopœia, is a very useful application for chilblains, chronic rheumatism, colic, etc.

Hot water poured on bruised Black Mustard seeds makes a stimulating footbath and helps to throw off a cold or dispel a headache. It also acts as an excellent fomentation.

Internally, Mustard is useful as a regular and mild aperient, being at the same time an alterative. If a tablespoonful of Mustard flour be added to a glass of *tepid* water, it operates briskly as a stimulating and sure emetic. In cases of hiccough, a teaspoonful of Mustard flour in a teacupful of *boiling* water is effective. The dose may be repeated in ten minutes if needed.

The bland oil expressed from the hulls of the seeds, after the flour has been sifted away, promotes the growth of the hair and may be used with benefit externally for rheumatism.

Whitehead's Essence of Mustard is made with spirits of turpentine and rosemary, with which camphor and the farina of Black Mustard seed are mixed. This oil is very little affected by frost or the atmosphere, and is therefore specially prized by clock-makers and makers of instruments of precision.

Parkinson says that Mustard 'is of good use, being fresh, for Epilepticke persons . . . if it be applyed hot inwardly and outwardly.'

Culpepper considered Mustard good for snake poison if taken in time, and tells us that mustard seed powder, mixed with honey in balls, taken every morning fasting, will clear the voice, and that

'the drowsy forgetful evil, to use it both inwardly and outwardly, to rub the nostrils, forehead and temples, to warm and quicken the spirits . . . the decoction of the seeds . . . resists the malignity of mushrooms. . . . Being chewed in the mouth it oftentimes helps the tooth-ache. It is also used to help the falling *off* the hair. The seed bruised, mixed with honey, and applied, or made up with wax, takes away the marks and black and blue spots of bruises or the like . . . it helps also the crick in the neck. . . .'

¶ *Preparations*. Linament, B.P.

Mustard flour is considered a capital antiseptic and sterilizing agent, as well as an excellent deodorizer.

MUSTARD, FIELD   Sinapis arvensis
> *Synonyms.* Charlock. Brassica Sinapistrum
> *Part Used.* Seeds

Charlock is a troublesome weed on arable land throughout England, growing so abundantly that it can at a distance be mistaken for a legitimate crop. It grows from 1 to 2 feet high, the stems upright, branched, grooved and often clothed with short rough hairs. The leaves are rough, unequally cut and serrated, and the flowers, which are yellow and large, are followed by nearly erect, angular, knotty pods, longer than their flattened conical beak.

It is an annual, flowering in May and June, and may easily be eradicated if pulled up before seeding. The seeds form a good substitute for Mustard, but are not equal to them in quality. They yield a good burning oil, which was much commended by Dodoens, as a preferable substitute for the 'Traine Oyle.'

Charlock varies in appearance in different plants and under varying conditions of growth, that growing in corn is taller and less branched than when growing by the roadside. It is capable of being used when boiled as a green vegetable, and is so employed in Sweden and Ireland. It is much liked by cattle and especially by sheep, and might be a useful fodder plant, though is usually regarded merely as a noxious intruder.

Spraying with 4 per cent. solution of copper sulphate or 15 per cent. solution of iron sulphate is employed for the destruction of Charlock in cornfields. It requires 40 gallons of solution for each acre. The weed should not exceed 3 inches in height at the time of spraying, or the remedy may be ineffectual.

RAPE   Brassica napus
> *Synonym.* Cole Seed
> *Habitat.* It is not indigenous to this country, though almost naturalized in parts

Rape is cultivated for the sake of the oil pressed from its seeds, the refuse being used to make oil-cake, or rape-cake, for feeding cattle.

It is frequently grown instead of White Mustard as a crop, being rather milder in flavour. When grown for feeding cattle, it should be sown about the middle of June, 6 or 8 lb. of seed to the acre. The plants are thinned by hoeing when young, and by the middle of November are ready for the cattle to feed on.

The seeds are also sown in gardens for winter and spring salads, as it is one of the small salad herbs, though little used.

It is also cultivated in cottage gardens for spring greens – the tops being cut first, and afterwards the side shoots.

MUSTARD, COMMON HEDGE   Sisymbrium officinale
> *Synonyms.* Singer's Plant. St. Barbara's Hedge Mustard. Erysimum officinale
> *Part Used.* Whole plant

The Common Hedge Mustard grows by our roadsides and on waste ground, where it is a common weed, with a peculiar aptitude for collecting and retaining dust. The blackish-green stalks, slender but tough, are branched and rough, the leaves hairy, deeply-lobed, with their points turned backwards, the terminal lobe larger. The yellow flowers are small and insignificant, placed at the top of the branches in long spikes, flowering by degrees throughout July. The pods are downy, close pressed to the stem and contain yellow, acrid seeds.

This plant is named by the French the 'Singer's Plant,' it having been considered up to the time of Louis XIV an infallible remedy for loss of voice. Racine, in writing to Boileau, recommends him to try the syrup of Erysimum in order to be cured of voicelessness. A strong infusion of the whole plant used to be taken in former days for all diseases of the throat.

FLIXWEED   Sisymbrium sophia (LINN.)

Another plant of the same genus, *Sisymbrium Sophia*, a more slender plant, bears the name of Flixweed, or Fluxweed, from having been given in cases of dysentery. It was called by the old herbalists *Sophia Chirugorum*, 'The Wisdom of Surgeons,' on account of its vulnerary properties.

The juice, mixed with an equal quantity of honey or vinegar, has been recommended for chronic coughs and hoarseness, and ulcerated sore throats. A strong infusion of the herb has proved excellent in asthma, and the seeds formed a special remedy for sciatica.

Chemically, the Hedge Mustard contains a soft resin and a sulphuretted volatile oil. Combined with Vervain it is supposed to have been Count Mattaei's famous remedy, *Febrifugo.*

MUSTARD, GARLIC   Sisymbrium alliaria

Synonyms. Jack-by-the-Hedge. Sauce Alone
Parts Used. Seeds, herbs

Garlic Mustard is an early flowering hedge plant, with delicate green leaves and snow-white flowers. The leaves are broadly heart-shaped, stalked, with numerous broad teeth. The whole plant emits when bruised a penetrating scent of Garlic, from which it derives its Latin and English names.

¶ *Medicinal Action and Uses.* The leaves used to be taken internally as a sudorific and deobstruent, and externally were applied antiseptically in gangrenes and ulcers. The juice of the leaves taken alone or boiled into a syrup with honey is found serviceable in dropsy.

Country people at one time used the plant in sauces, with bread and butter, salted meat and with lettuce in salads, hence it acquired also the name of Sauce Alone. The herb, when eaten as a salad, warms the stomach and strengthens the digestive faculties.

When cows eat it, it gives a disagreeable flavour to the milk.

The seeds, when snuffed up the nose, excite sneezing.

MUSTARD, TREACLE HEDGE   Erysimum Cheiranthoides

Synonyms. Wormseed. Treacle Wormseed
Part Used. Seeds

The Treacle Hedge Mustard has round stalks about a foot high, quite entire, or only slightly toothed, lanceolate leaves and small yellow flowers with whitish sepals, produced at the tops of the branches. The blackish-brown seeds are produced on each side of a pouch parted in the middle, about eighteen to each cell. The seeds are intensely bitter, and have been used by country people as a vermifuge, hence the second name of Wormseed or Treacle Wormseed. The seeds have also been given in obstructions of the intestines, and in rheumatism and jaundice with success. When taken in small doses they are purgative, but care must be taken not to administer in too large doses.

This plant flowers from May to August, and is a native of most parts of Europe, though it is not very common in England.

The Hedge Mustards and Garlic Mustard were all formerly allocated to the same genus to which this plant belongs, *Erysimum*.

Another species, *Erysimum Orientale* (Hare's Ear Treacle Mustard), with smooth, entire leaves and cream-coloured flowers, grows on some parts of the coast of Essex, Suffolk and Sussex.

MUSTARD, MITHRIDATE   Thlaspi arvense

Synonym. Pennycress
Part Used. Seeds

Mithridate Mustard, *Thlaspi arvense*, grows higher than Treacle Mustard; the leaves are small and narrower, smooth, toothed, arrow-shaped at the base. The flowers are small and white, growing on long branches, the seed-vessels form a round pouch, flat, with very broad wings, earning for the plant its other name of Pennycress.

It was formerly an ingredient in the Mithridate confection, an elaborate preparation used as an antidote to poison, but no longer used in medicine.

MYRRH   Commiphora myrrha (HOLMES)
                                                N.O. Burseraceæ

Synonyms. Balsamodendron Myrrha. Commiphora Myrrha, var. Molmol. Mirra. Morr.
        Didin. Didthin. Bowl
Part Used. The oleo-gum-resin from the stem
Habitat. Arabia, Somaliland

¶ *Description.* The bushes yielding the resin do not grow more than 9 feet in height, but they are of sturdy build, with knotted branches, and branchlets that stand out at right-angles, ending in a sharp spine. The trifoliate leaves are scanty, small and very unequal, oval and entire. It was first recognized about 1822 at Ghizan on the Red Sea coast, a district so bare and dry that it is called 'Tehama,' meaning 'hell.'

Botanically, there is still uncertainty about the origin and identity of the various species.

There are ducts in the bark, and the tissue between them breaks down, forming large cavities, which, with the remaining ducts, becomes filled with a granular secretion which is freely discharged when the bark is wounded, or from natural fissures. It flows as a pale yellow liquid, but hardens to a reddish-brown mass, being found in commerce in tears of many sizes, the average being that of a walnut. The surface is rough and powdered, and the pieces are brittle, with a granular fracture, semi-transparent, oily, and often show whitish marks. The odour and taste are aromatic, the latter also acrid and bitter. It is inflammable, but burns feebly.

Several species are recognized in commerce. It is usually imported in chests weighing 1 or 2 cwts., and wherever produced comes chiefly from the East Indies. Adulterations are not easily detected in the powder, so that it is better purchased in mass, when small stones, senegal gum, chestnuts, pieces of bdellium, or of a brownish resin called 'false myrrh,' may be sorted out with little difficulty.

It has been used from remote ages as an ingredient in incense, perfumes, etc., in the holy oil of the Jews and the *Kyphi* of the Egyptians for embalming and fumigations.

Little appears to be definitely known about the collection of myrrh. It seems probable that the best drug comes from Somaliland, is bought at the fairs of Berbera by the Banians of India, shipped to Bombay, and there sorted, the best coming to Europe and the worst being sent to China. The true myrrh is known in the markets as *karam*, formerly called *Turkey myrrh*, and the opaque bdellium as *meena harma*.

The gum makes a good mucilage and the insoluble residue from the tincture can be used in this way.

¶ *Constituents*. Volatile oil, resin (myrrhin), gum, ash, salts, sulphates, benzoates, malates, and acetates of potassa.

It is partially soluble in water, alcohol, and ether. It may be tested by a characteristic violet reaction if nitric acid diluted with an equal volume of water is brought into contact with the residue resulting from the boiling of 0·1 gramme of coarsely powdered myrrh with 2 c.c. of 90 per cent. alcohol, evaporated in a porcelain dish so as to leave a thin film.

The oil is thick, pale yellow, and contains myrrholic acid and heerabolene, a sesquiterpenene.

¶ *Medicinal Action and Uses*. Astringent, healing. Tonic and stimulant. A direct emmenagogue, a tonic in dyspepsia, an expectorant in the absence of feverish symptoms, a stimulant to the mucous tissues, a stomachic carminative, exciting appetite and the flow of gastric juice, and an astringent wash.

It is used in chronic catarrh, phthisis pulmonalis, chlorosis, and in amenorrhœa is often combined with aloes and iron. As a wash it is good for spongy gums, ulcerated throat and aphthous stomatitis, and the tincture is also applied to foul and indolent ulcers. It has been found helpful in bronchorrhœa and leucorrhœa. It has also been used as a vermifuge.

When long-continued rubefacient effect is needed, a plaster may be made with 1½ oz. each of camphor, myrrh, and balsam of Peru rubbed together and added to 32 oz. of melted lead plaster, the whole being stirred until cooling causes it to thicken.

Myrrh is a common ingredient of toothpowders, and is used with borax in tincture, with other ingredients, as a mouth-wash.

The Compound Tincture, or Horse Tincture, is used in veterinary practice for healing wounds.

Meetiga, the trade-name of Arabian Myrrh, is more brittle and gummy than that of Somaliland and has not its white markings.

The liquid Myrrh, or *Stacte*, spoken of by Pliny, and an ingredient of Jewish holy incense, was formerly obtainable and greatly valued, but cannot now be identified.

¶ *Dosages*. 10 to 30 grains. Of fluid extract, 5 to 30 minims. Tincture, B.P. and U.S.P., ¼ to 1 drachm. Of tincture of aloes and Myrrh, as purgative and emmenagogue, 30 minims. Of N.F. pills of aloes and Myrrh, 2 pills. Of Rufus's pills of aloes and Myrrh, as stimulant cathartic in debility and constipation, or in suppression of the menses, 4 to 8 grains of Br. mass.

¶ *Other Species*.

Bissa Bôl, or perfumed bdellium of the Arabs, has an odour like mushrooms. Though it is sent from Arabian ports to India and China, it was formerly known as East Indian Myrrh. It is of a dark colour, and may be a product of *Commiphora erythræa*, var. *glabrescens*, of *B. Kalaf*, *A. Kafal*, *B. Playfairii* or *Hemprichia erythræa*.

B. Kua of Abyssinia has been found to yield Myrrh.

Mecca balsam, a product of *B.* or *C. Opobalsamum*, is said to be the Myrrh of the Bible, the Hebrew word *mar* having been confused with the modern Arabic *morr* or Myrrh in translation.

Bdellium, recognized as an inferior Myrrh and often mixed with or substituted for it, is a product of several species of *Commiphora*, according to American writers, or *Balsamodendron* according to English ones. Four kinds are collected in Somaliland, making sub-divisions of African Bdellium:

Perfumed Bdellium or Habaghadi,
African Bdellium,
Opaque Bdellium,
Hotai Bdellium.

These African bdelliums, said by some writers to be products of *Balsamodendron*

(*Heudelotia*) *Africanum*, are in irregular, hard, roundish tears about an inch in diameter, pale yellow to red-brown, translucent, the fracture waxy, taste and odour slight.

The product of *Ceradia furcata* is also called African Bdellium.

The commercial *Gugul*, or Indian Bdellium, is said by some writers to be a product of *Commiphora roxburghiana*, by others of *B. Mukul*, and by others again of *B. roxbhurghii*

NARCISSUS

The bulbs of plants belonging to the natural order Amaryllideæ are in many cases poisonous, though they are widely cultivated for the sake of their flowers.

The chief of these is the DAFFODIL, or Lent Lily (*Narcissus pseudo-narcissus*, Linn.). The botanical name of the genus, *Narcissus*, is considered to be derived, not as is often said, from the name of the classical youth who met with his death through vainly trying to embrace his image reflected in a clear stream, but from the Greek word *narkao* (to benumb), on account of the narcotic properties which the plant possesses. Pliny describes it as *Narce narcissum dictum, non a fabuloso puero*, 'named Narcissus from *Narce*, not from the fabulous boy.'

Socrates called this plant the 'Chaplet of the infernal Gods,' because of its narcotic effects. An extract of the bulbs, when applied to open wounds, has produced staggering, numbness of the whole nervous system and paralysis of the heart.

The popular English names Daffodowndilly, Daffodily Affodily, are a corruption of Asphodel, with which blossoms of the ancient Greeks this was supposed to be identical. It is in France the *fleur d'asphodèle*, also 'pauvres filles de Sainte Claire.'

Herrick alludes in his *Hesperides* to the Daffodil as a portent of death, probably connecting the flower with the asphodel, and the habit of the ancient Greeks of planting that flower near tombs.

The bulbs of the Daffodil, as well as every other part of the plant are powerfully emetic, and the flowers are considered slightly poisonous, and have been known to have produced dangerous effects upon children who have swallowed portions of them.

The influence of Daffodil on the nervous system has led to giving its flowers and its bulb for hysterical affections and even epilepsy, with benefit.

A decoction of the dried flowers acts as an emetic, and has been considered useful for relieving the congestive bronchial catarrh of children, and also useful for epidemic dysentery.

or *Amyris Bdellium*. It is more moist than Myrrh; is found in irregular, dark reddish-brown masses, with a waxy fracture; softens with the heat of the hand; adheres to the teeth when chewed; and smells slightly of Myrrh.

It is used in the East Indies in leprosy, rheumatism and syphilis, and in Europe for plasters.

¶ *Dosage.* 10 to 40 grains.

N.O. Amaryllideæ

In France, Narcissus flowers have been used as an antispasmodic.

A spirit has been distilled from the bulb, used as an embrocation and also given as a medicine and a yellow volatile oil, of disagreeable odour and a brown colouring matter has been extracted from the flowers, the pigment being Quercetin, also present in the outer scales of the Onion.

The Arabians commended the oil to be applied for curing baldness and as an aphrodisiac.

An alkaloid was first isolated from the bulbs of *N. pseudo-narcissus* by Gerard in 1578, and obtained in a pure state as Narcissine by Guérin in 1910. The resting bulbs contain about 0·2 per cent. and the flowering bulbs about 0·1 per cent. With cats, Narcissine causes nausea and purgation.

N. princeps also contains a minute quantity of this alkaloid.

A case of poisoning by Daffodil bulbs, cooked by mistake in the place of leeks, was reported from Toulouse in 1923. The symptoms were acute abdominal pains and nausea, which yielded to an emetic.

The bulbs of *N. poeticus* (Linn.), the POET'S NARCISSUS, are more dangerous than those of the Daffodil, being powerfully emetic and irritant. The scent of the flowers is deleterious, if they are present in any quantity in a closed room, producing in some persons headache and even vomiting.

The bulb is used in homœopathy for the preparation of a tincture.

From the fragrant flowers of the JONQUIL (*N. jonquilla*) and the CAMPERNELLA (*N. odorus*), a sweet-smelling yellow oil is obtained in the south of France, used in perfumery.

The ease with which most species of Narcissus can be grown in this country is remarkable, since, being mostly natives of Southern Europe and Northern Africa, they have to adapt themselves to very different conditions of soil and climate.

No genus of flowering plants is more readily cultivated and less liable to disease, and the presence in its leaves and roots of innumerable bundles of needle-shaped crystals of calcium oxalate, termed raphides, protect it from injury of browsing and gnawing animals, rendering the plants indigestible and possibly poisonous to cattle and smaller animals.

The Crocus and Lily are not thus equipped for defence against browsing animals. Rabbits often fall prey to it.

The only insect enemy from which the Narcissus seems to suffer is the fly *Merodon equestris*, the grub of which lays an egg in or near the bulb, which then forms the food of the larva. This pest causes serious damage in Holland and the south of England.

See DAFFODIL.

NASTURTIUM. *See* WATERCRESS

NETTLES
N.O. Urticaceæ

The Nettle tribe, Urticaceæ, is widely spread over the world and contains about 500 species, mainly tropical, though several, like our common Stinging Nettle, occur widely in temperate climates. Many of the species have stinging hairs on their stems and leaves. Two genera are represented in the British Isles, *Urtica*, the Stinging Nettles, and *Parietaria*, the Pellitory. Formerly botanists included in the order Urticaceæ the Elm family, *Ulmaceæ*; the Mulberry, Fig and Bread Fruit family, *Moraceæ*; and that of the Hemp and Hop, *Cannabinaceæ*; but that these are now generally regarded as separate groups.

The British species of Stinging Nettle, belonging to the genus *Urtica* (the name derived from the Latin, *uro*, to burn), are well known for the burning properties of the fluid contained in the stinging hairs with which the leaves are so well armed. Painful as are the consequences of touching one of our common Nettles, they are far exceeded by the effects of handling some of the East Indian species: a burning heat follows the sensation of pricking, just as if hot irons had been applied, the pain extending and continuing for many hours or even days, attended by symptoms similar to those which accompany lockjaw. A Java species, *U. urentissima*, produces effects which last for a whole year, and are even said to cause death. *U. crenulato* and *U. heterophylla*, both of India, are also most virulent. Another Indian species, *U. tuberosa*, on the other hand, has edible tubers, which are eaten either raw, boiled or roasted, and considered nutritious.

NETTLE, GREATER
Urtica dioica (LINN.)

NETTLE, LESSER
Urtica urens (LINN.)
N.O. Urticaceæ

Synonyms. Common Nettle. Stinging Nettle
Parts Used. Herb, seeds

Our Common Nettle (*Urtica dioica*, Linn.) is distributed throughout the temperate regions of Europe and Asia: it is not only to be found in distant Japan, but also in South Africa and Australia and in the Andes.

A detailed description of this familiar plant is hardly necessary; its heart-shaped, finely-toothed leaves tapering to a point, and its green flowers in long, branched clusters springing from the axils of the leaves are known to everyone. The flowers are incomplete: the male or barren flowers have stamens only, and the female or fertile flowers have only pistil or seed-producing organs. Sometimes these different kinds of flowers are to be found on one plant; but usually a plant will bear either male or female flowers throughout, hence the specific name of the plant, *dioica*, which means 'two houses.'

The male flower consists of a perianth of four greenish segments enclosing an equal number of stamens, which bend inwards in the bud stage, but when the flower unfolds spring backwards and outwards, the anthers, with the sudden uncoiling, exploding and scattering the pollen. The flowers are thus adapted for wind-fertilization. The perianth of the female flower is similar, but only contains a single, one-seeded carpel, bearing one style with a brush-like stigma. The male flowers are in loose sprays or racemes, the female flowers more densely clustered together.

The Nettle flowers from June to September. As a rule the stem attains a height of 2 to 3 feet. Its perennial roots are creeping, so it multiplies quickly, making it somewhat difficult of extirpation.

The whole plant is downy, and also covered with stinging hairs. Each sting is a very sharp, polished spine, which is hollow and arises from a swollen base. In this base, which is composed of small cells, is contained the venom, an acrid fluid, the active principle of which is said to be bicarbonate of ammonia. When, in consequence of pressure, the sting pierces the skin, the venom is instantly expressed, causing the resultant irritation and inflammation. The burning property of the juice is dissipated by heat, enabling the young shoots of the Nettle, when boiled, to be eaten as a pot-herb.

It is a strange fact that the juice of the Nettle proves an antidote for its own sting, and being applied will afford instant relief: the juice of the Dock, which is usually found in close proximity to the Nettle, has the same beneficial action.

> 'Nettle in, dock out.
> Dock rub nettle out!'

is an old rhyme.

If a person is stung with a Nettle a certain cure will be effected by rubbing Dock leaves over the part, repeating the above charm slowly. Another version is current in Wiltshire:

> Out 'ettle, in dock,
> Dock zhall ha' a new smock;
> 'Ettle zhant ha' *narrun*! (none)

The sting of a Nettle may also be cured by rubbing the part with Rosemary, Mint or Sage leaves.

There are two other species of Nettle found in Britain, both annuals. The Lesser Nettle (*U. urens*) is widely distributed and resembles the Common Nettle in habit, but has smaller leaves and the flowers in short, mostly unbranched clusters, male and female in the same panicle. It is glabrous except for the stinging hairs, whereas *U. dioica* is softly hairy throughout. It rarely attains more than a foot in height and is a common garden weed.

The Roman Nettle (*U. pilulifera*), bearing its female flowers in little compact, globular heads, is not general and is considered a doubtful native. It is also smooth except for the stinging hairs, but these contain a far more virulent venom than either of the other species. It occurs in waste places near towns and villages in the east of England, chiefly near the sea, but is rare. It is supposed to have been introduced by the Romans. The antiquary Camden records in his work *Britannica* that this Nettle was common at Romney, saying that here or near it, Julius Cæsar landed and called it 'Romania,' from which Romney is a corruption. Camden adds:

'The soldiers brought some of the nettle seed with them, and sowed it there for their use to rub and chafe their limbs, when through extreme cold they should be stiff or benumbed, having been told that the climate of Britain was so cold that it was not to be endured.'

From their general presence in the neighbourhood of houses or spots where house refuse is deposited, it has been suggested that Nettles are not really natives, a supposition that to some extent receives countenance from the circumstance that the young shoots are very sensitive to frost. However that may be, they follow man in his migrations, and by their presence usually indicate a soil rich in nitrogen.

The common name of the Nettle, or rather its Anglo-Saxon and also Dutch equivalent, *Netel*, is said to have been derived from *Noedl* (a needle), possibly from the sharp sting, or, as Dr. Prior suggests, in reference to the fact that it was this plant that supplied the thread used in former times by the Germanic and Scandinavian nations before the general introduction of flax, *Net* being the passive participle of *ne*, a verb common to most of the Indo-European languages in the sense of 'spin' and 'sew' (Latin *nere*, German *na-hen*, Sanskrit *nah*, bind). Nettle would seem, he considers, to have meant primarily that with which one sews.

Its fibre is very similar to that of Hemp or Flax, and it was used for the same purposes, from making cloth of the finest texture down to the coarsest, such as sailcloth, sacking, cordage, etc. In Hans Andersen's fairy-tale of the Princess and the Eleven Swans, the coats she wove for them were made of Nettles.

Flax and Hemp bear southern names and were introduced into the North to replace it.

In the sixteenth and seventeenth century Nettle fibres were still used in Scotland for weaving the coarser household napery. The historian Westmacott says: 'Scotch cloth is only the housewifery of the nettle. In Friesland, also, it was used till a late period.' The poet, Campbell, complaining of the little attention paid to the Nettle in England, tells us:

'In Scotland, I have eaten nettles, I have slept in nettle sheets, and I have dined off a nettle tablecloth. The young and tender nettle is an excellent potherb. The stalks of the old nettle are as good as flax for making cloth. I have heard my mother say that she thought nettle cloth more durable than any other species of linen.'

After the Nettles had been cut, dried and steeped, the fibre was separated with instruments similar to those used in dressing flax or hemp, and then spun into yarn, used in manufacturing every sort of cloth, cordage, etc., usually made from flax or hemp. Green (*Universal Herbal*, 1832) says this yarn was particularly useful for making twine for fishing nets, the fibre of the Nettle being stronger than those of flax and not so harsh as those of hemps.

The fibre being, however, produced in less quantities than that of flax, and being somewhat difficult to extract, accounts, perhaps, for the fact that it is no longer used in Britain, though it was still employed in other countries in textile manufactures some sixty years ago. The greatest objection to its extensive employment is the necessity of growing it in rich, deep soil, for otherwise the fibre produced is short and coarse, and on land fitted for it flax can be grown at less cost compared to the value of the seed and fibre yielded. The most valuable sort of Nettle in regard to length and suppleness is most common in the bottom of ditches, among briars and in shaded valleys, where the soil is a strong loam. In such situations the plants will sometimes attain a great height, those growing in patches on a good soil, standing thick, averaging 5 to 6 feet in height, the stems thickly clothed with fine lint. Those growing in poorer soils and less favourable situations, with rough and woody stem and many lateral branches, run much to seed and are less useful, producing lint more coarse, harsh and thin.

When Germany and Austria ran short of cotton during the War, the value of the Nettle as a substitute was at once recognized, and the two ordinary species, *U. dioica* and *U. urens*, the great and the smaller Nettle, were specially selected for textiles.

Among the many fibrous plants experimented with, the Nettle alone fulfilled all the conditions of a satisfactory source of textile fibre, and it was believed that it would become an important factor in agriculture and in the development of the textile industry. Investigations and practical tests made in 1916 at Brünn and Reichenberg confirmed the hopes raised concerning the possibilities to be realized in Nettle fibre; the capabilities of the plant were thoroughly tested, and from the standpoint of the factory it was affirmed that goods woven from this fibre were for most purposes equal to cotton goods, so that it was believed that, for Central Europe at least, a large and increasing use of Nettle fibre seemed assured. Mixed with 10 per cent. cotton, it was definitely shown that underclothing, cloth, stockings, tarpaulins, etc., could be manufactured from the new fibre.

In 1915, 1·3 million kilograms of this material were collected in Germany, a quantity which increased to 2·7 million kilograms in 1916, and this without any attempt at systematic cultivation. The quantity of Nettles grown wild in Germany was estimated at 60,000 tons, but as time went on it was found that self-sown Nettles were insufficient in quantity for the need, and that their quality could be improved by cultivation, and great efforts were made to increase production, but the cultivation proved more difficult than was expected.

Cloth made from Nettle fibre was employed in many articles of army clothing. Forty kilograms were calculated to provide enough stuff for one shirt. In 1917 two captured German overalls, marked with the dates 1915 and 1916 respectively, were found to be woven of a mixed fibre consisting of 85 per cent. of the common Stinging Nettle and 15 per cent. of Ramie, the fibre of the Rhea, or Grass (*Boehmeria nivea*), a tropical member of the Nettle family, which is used in the manufacture of gas-mantles and is also valuable for making artificial silk and was largely employed in war-time in the making of gas-masks.

German army orders dated in March, April and May of 1918 give a good insight into the extent to which use was made of cloth woven from Nettle fibre. In these orders, Nettle is described as the only efficient cotton substitute.

In Austria, also, Nettles were cultivated on a large scale.

The length of the Nettle fibre varies from ¾ inch to 2½ inches: all above 1¾ inch is equal to the best Egyptian cotton. It can be dyed and bleached in the same way as cotton, and when mercerized is but slightly inferior to silk. It has been considered much superior to cotton for velvet and plush.

The Textile Department of the Bradford Technical College exhibited in March, 1918, samples of Nettle fibre. It had a pleasing appearance to the eye, but when examined under the microscope, magnification showed that it had a glass-like surface, devoid of the serrations which endow wool as a fibre for textile production, and experts considered that its employment in Germany seemed to point to very straitened circumstances as the motive, rather than any recognition of a true textile value in the fibre.

These properties of the Nettle were recognized before the War, and considerable sums of money were spent in the endeavour to utilize that plant, but trouble was experienced in the separation of the fibres. Recently, great progress has been made and some fifty processes have been patented for attaining this separation. In 1917 some 70,000 hectares of Nettles were cultivated, and it is thought possible to plant a million hectares of lowlands, giving a yield of Nettle fibres that would cover about 18 per cent. of Germany's cotton requirements.

The by-products of the Nettle were also stated to be of enormous production, the Nettle not only supplying a substitute for cotton, but for such indispensable articles as sugar, starch, protein and ethyl alcohol.

Another use of great importance is the application of the fibres of Nettle to the manufacture of paper of various qualities. They used to be collected in France in considerable quantities for that purpose, and though, owing to the different ages of the fibre, the attempts to use it for paper-making have not always met with complete success, the subject deserves further attention.

From a *culinary* point of view the Nettle has an old reputation. It is one of the few wild plants still gathered each spring by country-folk as a pot-herb. It makes a healthy vegetable, easy of digestion.

The young tops should be gathered when 6 to 8 inches high. Gloves should be worn to protect the hands when picking them. They should be washed in running water with a stick and then put into a saucepan, dripping, without any added water, and cooked with the lid on for about 20 minutes. Then chopped, rubbed through a hair-sieve and either served plain, or warmed up in the pan again, with a little salt, pepper and butter, or a little gravy, and served with or without poached eggs. They thus form a refreshing dish of spring greens, which is slightly laxative. In autumn, however, Nettles are hurtful, the leaves being gritty from the abundance of crystals (*cystoliths*) they contain.

In Scotland it was the practice to force Nettles for 'early spring kail.' Sir Walter Scott tells us in *Rob Roy* how Andrew Fairservice, the old gardener of Lochleven, raised early Nettles under hand-glasses. By earthing up, Nettles may be blanched in the same way as seakale and eaten in a similar manner. They also make a good vegetable soup, and in Scotland are used with leeks, broccoli and rice to make Nettle pudding, a very palatable dish.

RECIPES
Nettle Pudding

To 1 gallon of young Nettle tops, thoroughly washed, add 2 good-sized leeks or onions, 2 heads of broccoli or small cabbage, or Brussels sprouts, and ¼ lb. of rice. Clean the vegetables well; chop the broccoli and

leeks and mix with the Nettles. Place all together in a muslin bag, alternately with the rice, and tie tightly. Boil in salted water, long enough to cook the vegetables, the time varying according to the tenderness or otherwise of the greens. Serve with gravy or melted butter. These quantities are sufficient for six persons.

Pepys refers to Nettle pudding in his *Diary*, February, 1661: 'We did eat some Nettle porridge, which was very good.'

Nettle Beer

The Nettle Beer made by cottagers is often given to their old folk as a remedy for gouty and rheumatic pains, but apart from this purpose it forms a pleasant drink. It may be made as follows: Take 2 gallons of cold water and a good pailful of washed young Nettle tops, add 3 or 4 large handsful of Dandelion, the same of Clivers (Goosegrass) and 2 oz. of bruised, whole ginger. Boil gently for 40 minutes, then strain and stir in 2 teacupsful of brown sugar. When lukewarm place on the top a slice of toasted bread, spread with 1 oz. of compressed yeast, stirred till liquid with a teaspoonful of sugar. Keep it fairly warm for 6 or 7 hours, then remove the scum and stir in a tablespoonful of cream of tartar. Bottle and tie the corks securely. The result is a specially wholesome sort of ginger beer. The juice of 2 lemons may be substituted for the Dandelion and Clivers. Other herbs are often added to Nettles in the making of Herb Beer, such as Burdock, Meadowsweet, Avens Horehound, the combination making a refreshing summer drink.

As an arrester of bleeding, the Nettle has few equals and an infusion of the dried herb, or alcoholic tincture made from the fresh plant, or the fresh Nettle juice itself in doses of 1 to 2 tablespoonsful is of much power inwardly for bleeding from the nose, lungs or stomach. Old writers recommended a small piece of lint, moistened with the juice, to be placed in the nostril in bad cases of nose-bleeding. The diluted juice provides a useful astringent gargle. Burns may be cured rapidly by applying to them linen cloths well wetted with the tincture, the cloths being frequently re-wetted. An infusion of the fresh leaves is also soothing and healing as a lotion for burns.

Nettle is one of the best antiscorbutics. An infusion known as Nettle Tea is a common spring medicine in rural districts, and has long been used as a blood purifier. This tea made from young Nettles is in many parts of the country used as a cure for nettlerash. It is also beneficially employed in cases of gouty gravel, but must not be brewed too strong. A strong decoction of Nettle, drunk too freely, has produced severe burning over the whole body.

The homœopathic tincture, *Urtica*, is frequently administered successfully for rheumatic gout, also for nettlerash and chickenpox, and externally for bruises.

'Urtication,' or flogging with Nettles, was an old remedy for chronic rheumatism and loss of muscular power.

Young Nettles, mashed and pulped finely, mixed with equal bulk of thick cream, pepper and salt being added to taste, have been considered a valuable food for consumptives.

¶ *Medicinal Uses of the Nettle. Parts employed:* The whole herb, collected in May and June, just before coming into flower, and dried in the usual manner prescribed for 'bunched' herbs.

When the herb is collected for drying, it should be gathered only on a fine day, in the morning, when the sun has dried off the dew. Cut off just above the root, rejecting any stained or insect-eaten leaves, and tie in bunches, about six to ten in a bunch, spread out fanwise, so that the air can penetrate freely to all parts.

Hang the bunches over strings. If dried in the open, keep them in half-shade and bring indoors before there is any risk of damp from dew or rain. If dried indoors, hang up in a sunny room, and failing sun, in a well-ventilated room by artificial heat. Care must be taken that the window be left open by day so that there is a free current of air and the moisture-laden, warm air may escape. The bunches should be of uniform size and length, to facilitate packing when dry, and when quite dry and crisp must be packed away at once in airtight boxes or tins, otherwise moisture will be reabsorbed from the air.

The seeds and flowers are dried in the sun, or over a stove, on sheets of paper.

The Nettle is still in demand by wholesale herbalists, who stock the dried and powdered herb, also the seeds. Homœopathic chemists, in addition, employ the green herb for the preparation of a tincture.

¶ *Constituents.* The analysis of the fresh Nettle shows the presence of formic acid, mucilage, mineral salts, ammonia, carbonic acid and water.

It is the formic acid in the Nettle, with the phosphates and a trace of iron, which constitute it such a valuable food medicinally.

¶ *Action and Uses.* Although not prescribed by the British Pharmacopœia, the Nettle has still a reputation in herbal medicine, and is regarded in homœopathy as a useful remedy. Preparations of the herb have astringent properties and act also as a stimulating tonic.

Nettle is anti-asthmatic: the juice of the roots or leaves, mixed with honey or sugar, will relieve bronchial and asthmatic troubles and the dried leaves, burnt and inhaled, will have the same effect. The seeds have also been used in consumption, the infusion of herb or seeds being taken in wineglassful doses. The seeds and flowers used to be given in wine as a remedy for ague. The powdered seeds have been considered a cure for goitre and efficacious in reducing excessive corpulency.

In old Herbals the seeds, taken inwardly, were recommended for the stings or bites of venomous creatures and mad dogs, and as an antidote to poisoning by Hemlock, Henbane and Nightshade.

A quaint old superstition existed that a fever could be dispelled by plucking a Nettle up by the roots, reciting thereby the names of the sick man and also the names of his parents.

Preparations of Nettle are said to act well upon the kidneys, but it is a doubtful diuretic, though it has been claimed that incipient dropsy may be remedied by tea made from the roots.

A novel treatment for diabetes was reported by a sufferer from that disease in the daily press of April, 1926, it being affirmed that a diet of young Nettles (following a two days' fast) and drinking the brew of them had been the means of reducing his weight by 6 stone in three days and had vastly improved his condition.

An efficient Hair Tonic can be prepared from the Nettle: Simmer a handful of young Nettles in a quart of water for 2 hours, strain and bottle when cold. Well saturate the scalp with the lotion every other night. This prevents the hair falling and renders it soft and glossy. A good Nettle Hair Lotion is also prepared by boiling the entire plant in vinegar and water, straining and adding Eau de Cologne.

For stimulating hair growth, the old herbalists recommended combing the hair daily with expressed Nettle juice.

The homœopathic tincture of Nettle is made of 2 oz. of the herb to 1 pint of proof spirit.

The powder of the dried herb is administered in doses of 5 to 10 grains.

¶ *Preparations.* Fluid extract of herb, ½ to 1 drachm. Infusion, 1 oz. of the herb to a pint of boiling water.

¶ *Other Uses.* Nettles are of considerable value as fodder for live-stock, and might be used for this purpose where they occur largely. When Nettles are growing, no quadruped except the ass will touch them, on account of their stinging power, but if cut and allowed to become wilted, they lose their sting and are then readily cleared up by livestock. It is well known that when dried and made into hay, so as to destroy the poisonous matter of the stings, cows will relish them and give more milk than when fed on hay alone. In Sweden and Russia, the Nettle has sometimes been cultivated as a fodder plant, being mown several times a year, and given to milch cattle.

Nettles were much used as a substitute for fodder during the war, and instructions for their use were laid down by German military authorities. It was found that horses which had become thin and suffered from digestive troubles benefited from the use of Nettle leaves in their rations. When dried, the proportion of albuminoid matter in Nettles is as high as in linseed cake and the fat content is also considerable.

The Nettle is also of great use to the keeper of poultry. Dried and powdered finely and put into the food, it increases egg-production and is healthy and fattening. The seeds are also said to fatten fowls. Turkeys, as well as ordinary poultry, thrive on Nettles chopped small and mixed with their food, and pigs do well on boiled Nettles.

In Holland, and also in Egypt, it is said that horse-dealers mix the seeds of Nettles with oats or other food, in order to give the animals a sleek coat.

Although in Britain upwards of thirty insects feed solely on the Nettle plant, flies have a distaste for the plant, and a fresh bunch of Stinging Nettles will keep a larder free from them.

If planted in the neighbourhood of bee-hives, it is said the Nettle will drive away frogs.

The juice of the Nettle, or a decoction formed by boiling the green herb in a strong solution of salt, will curdle milk, providing the cheese-maker with a good substitute for rennet. The same juice, if rubbed liberally into small seams in leaky wooden tubs coagulates and will render them once more watertight.

A decoction of Nettle yields a beautiful and permanent green dye, which is used for woollen stuffs in Russia: the roots, boiled with alum, produce a yellow colour, which was formerly widely used in country districts to dye yarn, and is also employed by the Russian peasants to stain eggs yellow on Maundy Thursday.

The expressed seeds yield a burning oil, which has been extracted and used in Egypt.

The following passage from *Les Misérables* on the utilization of Nettles, shows how conversant Victor Hugo was with the virtues of this commonly despised 'weed':

'One day he (Monsieur Madeleine) saw some peasants busy plucking out Nettles; he looked at the heap of plants uprooted and already withered, and said – "They are dead. Yet it would be well if people knew how to make use of them. When the nettle is young, its leaf forms an excellent vegetable; when it matures, it has filaments and fibres like hemp and flax. Nettle fabric is as good as canvas. Chopped, the nettle is good for poultry; pounded it is good for cattle. The seed of the nettle mingled with fodder imparts a gloss to the coats of animals; its root mixed with salt produces a beautiful yellow colour. It is besides excellent hay and can be cut twice. And what does the nettle require? Little earth, no attention, no cultivation. Only the seed falls as it ripens, and is difficult to gather. That is all. With a little trouble, the nettle would be useful; it is neglected, and becomes harmful." '

Nettles are increasing all over the country, and for the benefit of those who desire their eradication, the Royal Horticultural Society, in their Diary for 1926, informed their members that if Nettles are cut down three times in three consecutive years, they will disappear.

NETTLE, WHITE DEAD-
Lamium album (LINN.)
N.O. Labiatæ

Synonyms. Archangel. White Dead Nettle. Blind Nettle. Dumb Nettle. Deaf Nettle. Bee Nettle

Part Used. Herb

The White Dead-Nettle owes its name of Nettle to the fact that the plant as a whole bears a strong general resemblance to the Stinging Nettle, for which it may easily be mistaken in the early spring, before it is in bloom; but the flowers are absolutely different in the two plants, which are quite unrelated. It can, moreover, be always readily distinguished from the Stinging Nettle, even when not in flower, by the squareness and hollowness of its stem.

The 'Dead' in its name refers to its inability to sting. Lord Avebury points out that this resemblance is a clever adaption of nature.

'It cannot be doubted that the true nettle is protected by its power of stinging, and that being so, it is scarcely less clear that the Dead Nettle must be protected by its likeness to the other,'

the two species being commonly found growing together. The resemblance serves probably not only as a protection against browsing quadrupeds, but also against leaf-eating insects.

Many other country names refer to this false suggestion of stinging power. In some localities it is called White Archangel, or Archangel alone, probably because it first comes into flower about the day dedicated to the Archangel Michael, May 8, old style – eleven days earlier than our May 8.

This plant is also known as the Bee Nettle, because bees visit it freely for the honey which it provides lavishly. The flower is specially built to encourage bee visitors – especially the humble bee. In the axils of the leaves are whorls, or rings, of the flowers, each ring composed of six to twelve blossoms of a delicate creamy white; out of the spiky, green, five-pointed calyx rises the white petal tube, which expands into an erection of very irregular shape, composed of five petals, one forming the lip, two the hood, and two form the little wings.

Four stamens lie in pairs along the back of the flower, with their heads well up under the hood and their faces downwards. The long column from the ovary also lies with them, but its top, the stigma, hangs a little out beyond the pollen-bearing anthers of the stamens. At the bottom of the corolla-tube is a rich store of honey.

When a bee visits the flower, he alights on the lower lip, thrusts his proboscis down the petal tube, which is nearly $\frac{1}{2}$ inch long, and reaches the honey, his back fitting meanwhile exactly into the conformation of the corolla, so that he first, as he settles on the lip, rubs the projecting stigmas with the pollen already on his back (thus affecting the fertilization of the flower), and then presses on to the stamens and gets dusted with their pollen in exchange, and this is then passed on to the next flower he visits. Unless the insect visitor is a big one, his back will not fill the cavity and neither stigma nor stamens are touched. The honey is placed in such a position that only the big humble bees with their long probosces can reach it. The flower also guards against smaller insects creeping down its tube by placing a barrier of hairs round it just above the honey. Some insects, whose tongues are too short to reach the honey, get at it by biting through the wall of the white tube right down at its base, and sucking away the honey without taking any share in the fertilization of the flower.

When the flower fades, the green calyx still remains to protect the tiny nutlets. It is somewhat stiffened, and when the nutlets are ripe and ready for dispersal, any pressure upon it forces it back and on the pressure being removed, the nuts are shot out with some force.

The plant is to be found in flower from May almost until December. The heart-shaped leaves, with their saw-like margins, are placed on the square, hollow stems in pairs, each pair exactly at right angles to the one above and below. Both stems and leaves are covered with small rough hairs, and contain certain essential oils which probably make them distasteful to cattle, even after their powerlessness to sting has been discovered. When bruised, the whole plant has a strong, rather disagreeable smell.

The corners of the hollow stems are strengthened by specially strong columns of fibres. In the country, boys often cut the stems and make whistles out of them.

The generic name of the Dead Nettles, *Lamium,* is derived from the Greek word *laimos* (the throat), in allusion to the form of the blossom.

NETTLE, PURPLE DEAD-

Lamium purpureum (LINN.)
N.O. Labiatæ

Synonym. Purple Archangel

The Purple Dead-Nettle is a common weed in cultivated ground and by waysides, found in the same spots as the other species, but less conspicuous.

It has heart- or kidney-shaped leaves, blunt, not pointed as in the preceding species, and is distinguished by the purple tinge of its foliage, crowded upper leaves and small, reddish flowers, which have much shorter petal tubes than the Yellow and White Dead-Nettles, so that bees with shorter tongues than the humble-bee, can reach its honey and fertilize it. It is, indeed, a favourite with bees, who find abundance of honey in its blossoms. The upper leaves are often densely clapped with silky hairs.

It flowers all the summer – from April to September and in mild seasons, both earlier and later. This species of Dead-Nettle is an annual, propagated by its seeds alone. It is one of the earliest weeds in gardens, but being an annual is easily eradicated.

The plant varies greatly in appearance, according to the situation in which it grows. On the open ground, it is somewhat spreading in habit, rarely more than 6 inches in height, whilst specimens growing in the midst of crowded vegetation are often drawn up to a considerable height, their leaves being of a dull green throughout, whereas those of the smaller specimens grown in the open are ordinarily more or less warm and rich in colour. At first glance the variation in the appearance of specimens grown under these different circumstances would leave the casual observer to suppose them to belong to different species.

¶ *Medicinal Action and Uses*. The herb and flowers, either fresh or dried, have been used to make a decoction for checking any kind of hæmorrhage.

The leaves are also useful to staunch wounds, when bruised and outwardly applied.

The dried herb, made into a tea and sweetened with honey, promotes perspiration and acts on the kidneys, being useful in cases of chill.

Linnæus reported that this species also has been boiled and eaten as a pot-herb by the peasantry in Sweden.

¶ *Other Species*.

The HENBIT DEAD-NETTLE (*Lamium amplexicaule*, Linn.), a small annual, fairly common on cultivated and waste ground, is not unlike the Purple Dead-Nettle, but somewhat lighter and more graceful. Its fine, deep rose-coloured flowers have a much slenderer tube, thrown out farther from the leaves.

The SPOTTED DEAD-NETTLE (*L. maculatum*), not considered a true wilding, but an escape from old-fashioned cottage gardens, is by some botanists regarded as a variety of the White Dead-Nettle, which it closely resembles, the flowers being, however, pale purple, instead of white and the foliage often marked by a broad, irregular streak of white down the centre of each leaf, with a few blotches on each side.

The HEMP NETTLE (*Galeopsis tetrahit*, Linn.) (named from *gale* (weasel) and *opsis* (a countenance), because of a fancied resemblance of its blossom to a weasel's face) is supposed to have been the source of one of Count Mattei's nostrums: *Pettorale*.

It is found on roadsides and borders of cornfields, tall-stemmed and erect, covered with long, dense bristles, the stem-joints thickened and the egg-shaped leaves hairy. The flowers, in dense whorls, are white, purple or yellow and are specially adapted for the visits of long-lipped bees, being much visited by the Humble Bee.

See DODDERS.

Gerard tells us:

'the White Archangel flowers compass the stalks round at certain distances, even as those of Horehound, whereof this is a kind and not of Nettle. The root is very threddy. The flowers are baked with sugar; as also the distilled water of them, which is said to make the heart merry, to make a good colour in the face, and to make the vital spirits more fresh and lively.'

Linnæus tells us that although refused by cattle, the leaves are eaten in Sweden as a pot-herb in the spring, in like manner as the True Nettle.

¶ *Part Used Medicinally*. The whole herb, collected in May and June, when just coming into flower and the leaves are in their best condition, and then dried in the manner directed for 'bunched' herbs.

The characteristic Dead-Nettle odour is lost in drying, but a slightly bitter taste remains.

The herb may be cultivated and propagated by means of seed sown in shallow drills, or by cuttings or division of roots – it spreads rapidly by means of its creeping, perennial roots, so that when once established, it is hard to get rid of it – but it would hardly pay for cultivation and is generally collected in the wild state.

¶ *Medicinal Action and Uses*. The whole plant is of an astringent nature, and in herbal medicine is considered of use for arresting hæmorrhages, as in spitting of blood and dysentery. Cotton-wool, dipped in a tincture of the fresh herb, is efficacious in staunching bleeding and a homœopathic tincture prepared from the flowers is used for internal bleeding, the dose being 5 to 10 drops in cold water.

As a blood purifier for rashes, eczema, etc., a decoction of Nettle flowers is excellent.

It has the reputation of being effectual in the healing of green wounds, bruises and burns.

This and the other species of Dead-Nettle have also been used in female complaints for their astringent properties.

Culpepper and the old herbalists tell us that the Archangel is an exhilarating herb, that it 'makes the heart merry, drives away melancholy, quickens the spirits, is good against the quartan agues, staunch-eth bleeding at the mouth and nose if it be stamped and applied to the nape of the neck.'

It was used with great success in removing the hardness of the spleen, which was supposed to be the seat of melancholy, a decoction being made with wine and the herb applied hot as a plaster to the region of the spleen, the decoction also being used as a fomentation.

Bruised and mixed with salt, vinegar and

lard, it has proved useful in the reduction of swellings and also to give ease in gout, sciatica and other pains in the joints and muscles.

NETTLE, YELLOW DEAD-

Lamium Galeobdolon (LINN.)
N.O. Labiatæ

Synonyms. Yellow Archangel. Weazel Snout. Dummy Nettle
Part Used. Herb

The closely-allied Yellow Archangel and the Purple Dead-Nettle (*Lamium purpureum*) have also been used medicinally for the same purposes as the White Dead-Nettle,' Culpepper telling us that the Yellow Archangel is most to be commended of the three for healing sores and ulcers.

All three species have hollow, square stalks, with the leaves opposite, in pairs.

The Yellow Archangel resembles in habit the White Dead-Nettle, but its stems are straighter and more upright, the pairs of leaves farther apart, the leaves themselves, narrower, longer and more pointed. The flowers, which also grow in whorls, are a little longer. They are large and handsome; pale yellow, blotched with red, visited by both Humble- and Honey-bee.

It has a much shorter flowering season than either of the other Dead-Nettles, being only in flower for two months – mid-April to mid-June, or May to July, according to district.

The plant is not infrequent in damp woods and shady hedgerows, but is much more local in its habitat than either the White or Purple Dead-Nettle, being common in some localities and altogether absent from others.

Its specific name, *Galeobdolon*, is made up from two Greek words, *gale* (a weasel) and *bdolos* (a disagreeable odour), an allusion to the somewhat strong odour of the plant when crushed.

The whole herb was used medicinally, dried and employed in the same manner as the White Archangel.

(*POISON*)
NIGHTSHADE, BLACK

Solanum nigrum (LINN.)
N.O. Solanaceæ

Synonyms. Garden Nightshade. Petty Morel
Parts Used. Whole plant, fresh leaves

The Black Nightshade is an annual plant, common and generally distributed in the South of England, less abundant in the North and somewhat infrequent in Scotland. It is one of the most cosmopolitan of wild plants, extending almost over the whole globe.

In this country, it is frequently to be seen by the wayside and is often found on rubbish heaps, but also among growing crops and in damp and shady places. It is sometimes called the Garden Nightshade, because it so often occurs in cultivated ground.

¶ *Description.* It rarely grows more than a foot or so in height and is much branched, generally making a bushy-looking mass. It varies much according to the conditions of its growth, both as to the amount of its dull green foliage and the size of its individual leaves, which are egg-shaped and stalked, the outlines bluntly notched or waved. The stem is green and hollow.

The flowers are arranged in clusters at the end of stalks springing from the main stems at the intervals between the leaves, not, as in the Bittersweet, opposite the leaves. They are small and white, resembling those of Bittersweet in form, and are succeeded by small round berries, green at first, but black

when ripe. The plant flowers and fruits freely, and in the autumn the masses of black berries are very noticeable; they have, when mature, a very polished surface.

On account of its berries, the Black Nightshade was called by older herbalists 'Petty Morel,' to distinguish it from the Deadly Nightshade, often known as Great Morel. Culpepper says: 'Do not mistake the deadly nightshade for this,' cautiously adding, 'if you know it not, you may then let them both alone.'

In the fourteenth century, we hear of the plant under the name of Petty Morel being used for canker and with Horehound and wine taken for dropsy.

¶ *Part Used.* The whole plant, gathered in early autumn, when in both flower and fruit and dried. Also the fresh leaves.

When the plant grows at all in a bunchy mass, strip off the stems singly and dry them under the same conditions as given above for Belladonna leaves, tying several stems together in a bunch, however, spread out fanwise for the air to penetrate to all parts, and hang the bunches over strings, rather than in trays. The bunches should be of uniform size.

¶ *Medicinal Action and Uses.* This species has the reputation of being very poisonous,

582

a fact, however, disputed by recent inquiries. In experimenting on dogs, very varying results have been obtained, which may be explained by the fact that the active principle, Solanine, on which the poisonous properties of this and the preceding species depend, and which exists in considerable quantity in the fresh herb, varies very much at different seasons.

The berries are injurious to children, but are often eaten by adults with impunity, especially when quite ripe, as the poisonous principle is chiefly associated with all green parts. Cattle will not eat the plant and sheep rarely touch it.

It is applied in medicine similarly to Bittersweet, but is more powerful and possesses greater narcotic properties.

According to Withering and other authorities, 1 or 2 grains of the dried leaves, infused in boiling water, act as a strong sudorific.

In Bohemia the leaves are placed in the cradles of infants to promote sleep. In the islands of Bourbon and Mauritius, the leaves are eaten in place of spinach: and the fruit is said to be eaten without inconvenience by soldiers stationed in British Kaffraria. (Lindley's *Treasury of Botany*.)

It has been found useful in cutaneous disorders, but its action is variable, and it is considered a somewhat dangerous remedy except in very small doses.

The bruised fresh leaves, used externally, are said to ease pain and abate inflammation, and the Arabs apply them to burns and ulcers. Their juice has been used for ringworm, gout and earache, and mixed with vinegar, is said to be good as a gargle and mouthwash.

Besides the above-mentioned species, others are used for medicinal, alimentary, and other purposes. Some are employed almost universally as narcotics to allay pain, etc.; others are sudorific and purgative. *Solanum toxicarium* is used as a poison by the natives of Cayenne. *S. pseudo-quina* is esteemed as a valuable febrifuge in Brazil. Among those used for food, are *S. Album* and *S. Æthiopicum*, the fruits of which are used in China and Japan. Those of *S. Anguivi* are eaten in Madagascar. *S. esculentum* and its varieties furnish the fruits known as Aubergines or Brinjals, which are highly esteemed in France, and may sometimes be met with in English markets; they are of the size and form of a goose's egg and usually of a rich purple colour. The Egg-plant, which has white berries, is only a variety of this. The Peruvians eat the fruits of *S. muricatum* and *S. quitoense*; those of *S. ramosum* are eaten as a vegetable in the West Indies. The Tasmanian Kangaroo Apple is the fruit of *S. laciniatum*; unless fully ripe this is said to be acrid. In Gippsland, Australia, the natives eat the fruits of *S. vescum*, which, like the preceding, is not agreeable till fully ripe, when it is said to resemble in form and flavour the fruits of *Physalis peruviana*. Of other species the leaves are eaten; as those of *S. oleraceum* in the West Indies and Fiji Islands, of *S. sessiflorum* in Brazil, etc.

Other species are used as dyes. *S. indigoferum*, in Brazil, cultivated for indigo. The juice of the fruit of *S. gnaphalioides* is said to be used to tint the cheeks of the Peruvian ladies, while their sisters of the Canary Isles employ similarly the fruits of *S. vespertilia*. The fruits of *S. saponaceum* are used in Peru to whiten linen in place of soap. *S. marginatum* is used in Abyssinia for tanning leather.

See POTATO, TOMATO, STRAMONIUM.

(POISON)
NIGHTSHADE, DEADLY

Atropa Belladonna (LINN.)
N.O. Solanaceæ

Synonyms. Belladonna. Devil's Cherries. Naughty Man's Cherries. Divale. Black Cherry. Devil's Herb. Great Morel. Dwayberry

Parts Used. Root, leaves, tops

Habitat. Widely distributed over Central and Southern Europe, South-west Asia and Algeria; cultivated in England, France and North America

Though widely distributed over Central and Southern Europe, the plant is not common in England, and has become rarer of late years. Although chiefly a native of the southern counties, being almost confined to calcareous soils, it has been sparingly found in twenty-eight British counties, mostly in waste places, quarries and near old ruins. In Scotland it is rare. Under the shade of trees, on wooded hills, on chalk or limestone, it will grow most luxuriantly, forming bushy plants several feet high, but specimens growing in places exposed to the sun are apt to be dwarfed, consequently it rarely attains such a large size when cultivated in the open, and is more subject to the attacks of insects than when growing wild under natural conditions.

¶ *Description.* The root is thick, fleshy and whitish, about 6 inches long, or more, and branching. It is perennial. The purplish-coloured stem is annual and herbaceous. It is stout, 2 to 4 feet high, undivided at the base, but dividing a little above the ground into three – more rarely two or four branches, each of which again branches freely.

The leaves are dull, darkish green in colour and of unequal size, 3 to 10 inches long, the lower leaves solitary, the upper ones in pairs alternately from opposite sides of the stem, one leaf of each pair much larger than the other, oval in shape, acute at the apex, entire and attenuated into short petioles.

First-year plants grow only about 1½ feet in height. Their leaves are often larger than in full-grown plants and grow on the stem immediately above the ground. Older plants attain a height of 3 to 5 feet, occasionally even 6 feet, the leaves growing about 1 to 2 feet from the ground.

The whole plant is glabrous, or nearly so, though soft, downy hairs may occur on the young stems and the leaves when quite young. The veins of the leaves are prominent on the under surface, especially the midrib, which is depressed on the upper surface of the leaf.

The fresh plant, when crushed, exhales a disagreeable odour, almost disappearing on drying, and the leaves have a bitter taste, when both fresh and dry.

The flowers, which appear in June and July, singly, in the axils of the leaves, and continue blooming until early September, are of a dark and dingy purplish colour, tinged with green, large (about an inch long), pendent, bell-shaped, furrowed, the corolla with five large teeth or lobes, slightly reflexed. The five-cleft calyx spreads round the base of the smooth berry, which ripens in September, when it acquires a shining black colour and is in size like a small cherry. It contains several seeds. The berries are full of a dark, inky juice, and are intensely sweet, and their attraction to children on that account, has from their poisonous properties, been attended with fatal results. Lyte urges growers 'to be carefull to see to it and to close it in, that no body enter into the place where it groweth, that wilbe enticed with the beautie of the fruite to eate thereof.' And Gerard, writing twenty years later, after recounting three cases of poisoning from eating the berries, exhorts us to 'banish therefore these pernicious plants out of your gardens and all places neare to your houses where children do resort.' In September, 1916, three children were admitted to a London hospital suffering from Belladonna poisoning, caused, it was ascertained, from having eaten berries from large fruiting plants of *Atropa Belladonna* growing in a neighbouring public garden, the gardener being unaware of their dangerous nature, and again in 1921 the Nor-

wich Coroner, commenting on the death of a child from the same cause, said that he had had four not dissimilar cases previously.

It is said that when taken by accident, the poisonous effects of Belladonna berries may be prevented by swallowing as soon as possible an emetic, such as a large glass of warm vinegar or mustard and water. In undoubted cases of this poisoning, emetics and the stomach-pump are resorted to at once, followed by a dose of magnesia, stimulants and strong coffee, the patient being kept very warm and artificial respiration being applied if necessary. A peculiar symptom in those poisoned by Belladonna is the complete loss of voice, together with frequent bending forward of the trunk and continual movements of the hands and fingers, the pupils of the eye becoming much dilated.

¶ *History.* The plant in Chaucer's days was known as Dwale, which Dr. J. A. H. Murray considers was probably derived from the Scandinavian *dool*, meaning delay or sleep. Other authorities have derived the word from the French *deuil* (grief), a reference to its fatal properties.

Its deadly character is due to the presence of an alkaloid, Atropine, $\frac{1}{10}$ grain of which swallowed by a man has occasioned symptoms of poisoning. As every part of the plant is extremely poisonous, neither leaves, berries, nor root should be handled if there are any cuts or abrasions on the hands. The root is the most poisonous, the leaves and flowers less so, and the berries, except to children, least of all. It is said that an adult may eat two or three berries without injury, but dangerous symptoms appear if more are taken, and it is wiser not to attempt the experiment. Though so powerful in its action on the human body, the plant seems to affect some of the lower animals but little. Eight pounds of the herb are said to have been eaten by a horse without causing any injury, and an ass swallowed 1 lb. of the ripe berries without any bad results following. Rabbits, sheep, goats and swine eat the leaves with impunity, and birds often eat the seeds without any apparent effect, but cats and dogs are very susceptible to the poison.

Belladonna is supposed to have been the plant that poisoned the troops of Marcus Antonius during the Parthian wars. Plutarch gives a graphic account of the strange effects that followed its use.

Buchanan relates in his *History of Scotland* (1582) a tradition that when Duncan I was King of Scotland, the soldiers of Macbeth poisoned a whole army of invading Danes by a liquor mixed with an infusion of Dwale

DEADLY NIGHTSHADE (BELLADONNA)
Atropa Belladonna

WOODY NIGHTSHADE (BITTERSWEET)
Solanum Dulcamara

NUTMEG
Myristica Fragrans

supplied to them during a truce. Suspecting nothing, the invaders drank deeply and were easily overpowered and murdered in their sleep by the Scots.

According to old legends, the plant belongs to the devil who goes about trimming and tending it in his leisure, and can only be diverted from its care on one night in the year, that is on Walpurgis, when he is preparing for the witches' sabbath. The apples of Sodom are held to be related to this plant, and the name Belladonna is said to record an old superstition that at certain times it takes the form of an enchantress of exceeding loveliness, whom it is dangerous to look upon, though a more generally accepted view is that the name was bestowed on it because its juice was used by the Italian ladies to give their eyes greater brilliancy, the smallest quantity having the effect of dilating the pupils of the eye.

Another derivation is founded on the old tradition that the priests used to drink an infusion before they worshipped and invoked the aid of Bellona, the Goddess of War.

The generic name of the plant, *Atropa*, is derived from the Greek *Atropos*, one of the Fates who held the shears to cut the thread of human life – a reference to its deadly, poisonous nature.

Thomas Lupton (1585) says: 'Dwale makes one to sleep while he is cut or burnt by cauterizing.' Gerard (1597) calls the plant the Sleeping Nightshade, and says the leaves moistened in wine vinegar and laid on the head induce sleep.

Mandrake, a foreign species of *Atropa* (*A. Mandragora*), was used in Pliny's day as an anæsthetic for operations. Its root contains an alkaloid, Mandragorine. The sleeping potion of Juliet was a preparation from this plant – perhaps also the Mandrake wine of the Ancients. It was called Circæon, being the wine of Circe.

Belladonna is often confused in the public mind with dulcamara (Bittersweet), possibly because it bears the popular name of woody nightshade. The cultivation of Belladonna in England dates at least from the sixteenth century, for Lyte says, in the *Niewe Herball*, 1578: 'This herbe is found in some places of this Countrie, in woods and hedges and in the gardens of some Herboristes.' Though not, however, much cultivated, it was evidently growing wild in many parts of the country when our great Herbals were written. Gerard mentions it as freely growing at Highgate, also at Wisbech and in Lincolnshire, and it gave a name to a Lancashire valley. Under the name of *Solanum lethale*, the plant was included in our early Pharma-

copœias, but it was dropped in 1788 and reintroduced in 1809 as *Belladonna folia*. Gerard was the first English writer to adopt the Italian name, of which he makes two words. The root was not used in medicine here until 1860, when Peter Squire recommended it as the basis of an anodyne liniment.

Before the War, the bulk of the world's supply of Belladonna was derived from plants growing wild on waste, stony places in Southern Europe. The industry was an important one in Croatia and Slavonia in South Hungary, the chief centre for foreign Belladonna, the annual crop in those provinces having been estimated at 60 to 100 tons of dry leaves and 150 to 200 tons of dry root. In 1908 the largest exporter in Slavonia is said to have sent out 29,880 lb. of dry Belladonna root.

The Balkan War of 1912–13 interrupted the continuity of Belladonna exports from South Hungary. Stocks of roots and leaves made shorter supplies last out until 1914, when prices rose, owing to increasing scarcity roots which realized 45s. per cwt. in January, 1914, selling for 65s. in June, 1914. With the outbreak of the Great War and the consequent entire stoppage of supplies, the price immediately rose to 100s. per cwt., and soon after, from 300s. to 480s. per cwt. or more. The dried leaves, from abroad, which in normal times sold at 45s. to 50s. per cwt., rose to 250s. to 350s. or more, per cwt. In August, 1916, the drug Atropine derived from the plant had risen from 10s. 6d. per oz. before the War to £7 per oz.

¶ *Cultivation.* Belladonna herb and root are sold by analysis, the value depending upon the percentage of alkaloid contained. A wide variation occurs in the amount of alkaloid present. It is important, therefore, to grow the crop under such conditions of soil and temperature as are likely to develop the highest percentage of the active principle.

In connexion with specimens of the wild plant, it is most difficult to trace the conditions which determine the variations, but it has been ascertained that a light, permeable and chalky soil is the most suitable for this crop. This, joined to a south-west aspect on the slope of a hill, gives specially good results as regards a high percentage of alkaloids. The limits of growth of Belladonna are between 50° and 55° N. Lat. and an altitude of 300 to 600 feet, though it may descend to sea-level where the soil is calcareous, especially where the drainage is good and the necessary amount of shade is found. The question of suitability of soil is especially important. Although the cultivated plant contains less alkaloid than that which grows wild, this in reality is only true of plants transported to a soil unsuited to them. It has been found, on the contrary, that artificial aids, such as the judicious selection of manure, the cleansing and preparation of the soil, destruction of weeds, etc., in accordance with the latest scientific practice, have improved the plants in every respect, not only in bulk, but even in percentage weight of alkaloidal contents.

Authorities differ on the question of manuring. Some English growers manure little if the plants are strong, but if the soil is really poor, or the plants are weak, the crop may be appreciably increased by the use of farmyard manure, or a mixture of nitrate of soda, basic slag and kainit. Excellent results have been obtained in experiments, by treating with basic slag, a soil already slightly manured and naturally suited to the plant, the percentage of total alkaloid in dry leaf and stem from third-year plants amounting to 0·84. In this case, the season was, however, an exceptionally favourable one, and, moreover, the soil being naturally suited to the plant, the percentage of alkaloid obtained without added fertilizer was already high. Speaking from the writer's own experience, Belladonna grows in her garden at Chalfont St. Peter. The soil is gravelly, even stony in some parts, with a chalk subsoil – the conditions similar to those that the plant enjoys in its wild state. This neighbourhood, in her opinion, is a suitable one for growing fields of Belladonna as crops for medicinal purposes.

Notes and statistics taken from season to season, extending over nine years, have shown that atmospheric conditions have a marked influence on the alkaloidal contents of Belladonna, the highest percentage of alkaloid being yielded in plants grown in sunny and dry seasons. The highest percentage of alkaloid, viz. 0·68 per cent., was obtained from the Belladonna crop of 1912, a year in which the months May and June were unusually dry and sunny; the lowest, just half, 0·34 was obtained on the same ground in 1907, when the period May and June was particularly lacking in sunshine. In 1905, August and September proving a very wet season, specimens analysed showed the low percentages of 0·38 and 0·35, whereas in July and October, 1906, the intervening period being very fine and dry, specimens analysed in those months showed a percentage of 0·54 and 0·64 respectively.

There appears to be no marked variation in alkaloidal contents due to different stages of growth from June to September, except when the plant begins to fade, when there is

rapid loss, hence the leaves may be gathered any time from June until the fading of the leaves and shoots set in.

In sowing Belladonna seed, 2 to 3 lb. should be reckoned to the acre. Autumn sown seeds do not always germinate, it is therefore more satisfactory to sow in boxes in a cool house, or frame, in early March, soaking the soil in the seed-boxes first, with boiling water, or baking it in an oven, to destroy the embryo of a small snail which is apt, as well as slugs and various insects, to attack the seedlings later. Pieces of chalk or lime can be placed among the drainage rubble at the bottom of the boxes. Belladonna seed is very slow in germinating, taking four to six weeks, or even longer, and as a rule not more than 70 per cent. can be relied on to germinate. On account of the seeds being so prone to attack by insect pests, if sown in the open, the seed-beds should first be prepared carefully. First of all, rubbish should be burnt on the ground, the soil earthed up and fired all over, all sorts of burnt vegetable rubbish being worked in. Then thoroughly stir up the ground and leave it rough for a few days so that air and sun permeate it well. Then level and rake the bed fine and finally give it a thorough drenching with boiling water. Let it stand till dry and friable, add sharp grit sand on the surface, rake fine again and then sow the seed very thinly.

Considerable moisture is needed during germination. The seedlings should be ready for planting out in May, when there is no longer any fear of frost. They will then be about 1½ inch high. Put them in after rain, or if the weather be dry, the ground should be well watered first, the seedlings puddled in and shaded from the sun with inverted flower-pots for several days. About 5,000 plants will be needed to the acre. If they are to remain where first planted, they may be planted 18 inches apart. A reserve of plants should be grown to fill in gaps.

The seedlings are liable to injury by late frosts and a light top dressing of farmyard manure or leaf-mould serves to preserve young shoots from injury during sudden and dangerous changes of temperature. They do best in shade. In America, difficulties in the cultivation of Belladonna have been overcome by interspersing plants with rows of scarlet runners, which, shading the herb, cause it to grow rapidly. Healthy young plants soon become re-established when transplanted, but require watering in dry weather. Great care must be taken to keep the crop clean from weeds and handpicking is to be recommended.

By September, the single stem will be 1½ to 2½ feet high. A gathering of leaves may then be made, if the plants are strong; 'leaves' include the broken-off tops of the plants, but the coarser stems are left on the plant and all discoloured portions rejected, and the plants should not be entirely denuded of leaves.

Before the approach of winter, plants must be thinned to 2½ to 3 feet apart, or overcrowding will result in the second year, in which the plant will bear one or two strong stems.

The writer finds that the green tips and cuttings from side branches root well and easily in early summer, and that buds with a piece of the root attached can be taken off the bigger roots in April, this being a very successful way of rapid propagation to get big, strong plants.

In the second year, in June, the crop is cut a few inches above the ground, while flowering, and delivered to the wholesale buyer the same day it is cut.

The average crop of fresh herb in the second and third years is 5 to 6 tons per acre, and 5 tons of fresh leaves and tops yield 1 ton of dried herb. A second crop is obtained in September in good seasons.

The yield per acre in the first year of growth should average about 6 cwt. of *dry* leaves.

The greatest loss of plants is in wet winters. Young seedling plants unless protected by dead leaves during the winter often perish. On the lighter soils there is less danger from winter loss, but the plants are more liable to damage from drought in summer.

One of the principal insect pests that attack Belladonna leaves is the so-called 'flea-beetle.' It perforates the leaves to such an extent as to make them unfit for sale in a dried state. It is when the plants are exposed to too much sunlight in open spots that the attacks of the beetle are worst, its natural habitat being well-drained slopes, partly under trees. If therefore the ground around the plants is covered with a thick mulch of leaves, they are not so likely to be attacked. The caterpillars from which the beetles come feed on the ground, and as they dislike moisture, the damp leaves keep them away. If napthalene is scattered on the soil, the vapour will probably help to keep the beetles off. The only way to catch them is to spread greased sheets of paper below the plants, and whenever the plants are disturbed a number of beetles will jump off like fleas and be caught on the papers. This at best only lessens the total quantity, however, and the other methods of precaution are the best.

The plant is dug or ploughed up during the autumn in the fourth year and the root collected, washed and dried, 3 to 4 tons of fresh root yielding a little over 1 ton of dry root. In time of great scarcity, it would probably pay to dig the root in the third year.

Old roots must be replaced by a planting of young ones or offsets, and if wireworm is observed, soot should be dug in with replacements.

Although Belladonna is not a plant that can be successfully grown in every small garden, yet in a chalky garden a few plants might be grown in a shady corner for the sake of the seed, for which there is a demand for propagation. Those, also, who know the haunts of the plant in its wild state might profitably collect the ripe berries, which should then be put into thin cotton bags and the juice squeezed out in running water. When the water is no longer stained, wring the bag well and turn out the seeds on to blotting paper and dry in the sun, or in a warm room near a stove. Sieve them finally, when dry, to remove all portions of the berry skin, etc.

Belladonna has been successfully cultivated in the neighbourhood of Leningrad since 1914, and already good crops have been obtained, the richness of the stems in alkaloids being noteworthy. It is stated that in consequence of the success that has attended the cultivation of Belladonna in Russia, it will no longer be needful to employ German drugs in the preparation of certain alkaloids. Much is also being collected wild in the Caucasus and in the Crimea.

It is hoped that if sufficient stocks can be raised in Britain, not only will it be unnecessary to import Belladonna, but that it may be possible to export it to those of our Dominions where the climate and local conditions prevent its successful culture, though at present it is still included among the medicinal plants of which the exportation is forbidden.

The following note on the growth and cultivation of Belladonna is from the *Chemist and Druggist*, of February 26, 1921:

'Belladonna is a perennial, but for horticultural purposes it is treated as a biennial, or triennial plant. The root in 3 years has attained very large dimensions around Edinburgh; in fact, often so large as to make the lifting a very heavy, and therefore costly, matter, and in consequence 2 years' growth is quite sufficient. One-year-old roots are just as active as the three-year-old stocks, and to the grower it is merely a matter of expediency which crop he chooses to dig up. The aerial growth is very heavy, two-year-old plants making 5 to 6 feet in the season if not cut for first crop, and if cut in July they make a second growth of 2 to 3 feet by September. To obtain a supply of seeds certain plantations must be left uncut, so as to get a crop of seeds for the next season. Moisture is, from a practical point of view, a very important matter. A sample, apparently dry to the touch, but not crisp, may have 15 per cent. to 20 per cent. of moisture present. Therefore if a pharmacist was to use a sample of such Belladonna leaves, although assayed to contain 0·03 per cent. of alkaloids, he would produce a weaker tincture than if he had used leaves with, say, only 5 per cent. of water present. The alkaloidal factor of this drug is the index to its value. Both the British and the United States Pharmacopœias adopt the same standard of alkaloidal value for the leaves, but the British Pharmacopœia does not require a standard for the root, which is one of those subtle conundrums which this quaint book frequently presents! Plants grown in a hard climate, such as Scotland, give a good alkaloidal figure, which compares favourably with any others. For roots, the British Pharmacopœia as just stated, requires no standard, but United States Pharmacopœia standard is 0·45 per cent., and Scottish roots yielded 0·78 per cent. and 0·72 per cent. There is not a great deal of alkaloidal value in the stalks. About 0·08 in the autumn.'

¶ *Constituents.* The medicinal properties of Belladonna depend on the presence of Hyoscyamine and Atropine. The root is the basis of the principal preparations of Belladonna.

The total alkaloid present in the *root* varies between 0·4 and 0·6 per cent., but as much as 1 per cent. has been found, consisting of Hyoscyamine and its isomer Atropine, 0·1 to 0·6 per cent.; Belladonnine and occasionally, Atropamine. Starch and Atrosin, a red colouring principle, are also present in the root. Scopolamine (hyoscine) is also found in traces, as is a fluorescent principle similar to that found in horse-chestnut bark and widely distributed through the natural order Solanaceæ. The greater portion of the alkaloidal matter consists of Hyoscyamine, and it is possible that any Atropine found is produced during extraction.

The amount of alkaloids present in the *leaves* varies somewhat in wild or cultivated plants, and according to the methods of drying and storing adopted, as well as on the conditions of growth, soil, weather, etc.

The proportion of the total alkaloid present in the dried leaves varies from 0·3 to 0·7 per cent. The greater proportion consists of Hyoscyamine, the Atropine being produced during extraction, as in the root. Belladonnine and Apoatropine may also be formed during extraction from the drug. The leaves contain also a trace of Scopolamine, Atrosin and starch.

The British Pharmacopœia directs that the leaves should not contain less than 0·3 per cent. of alkaloids and the root not less than 0·45 per cent.

A standardized liquid extract is prepared, from which the official plaster, alcoholic extract, liniment, suppository, tincture and ointment are made. The green extract is prepared from the fresh leaves.

¶ *Medicinal Action and Uses.* Narcotic, diuretic, sedative, antispasmodic, mydriatic. Belladonna is a most valuable plant in the treatment of eye diseases, Atropine, obtained during extraction, being its most important constituent on account of its power of dilating the pupil. Atropine will have this effect in whatever way used, whether internally, or injected under the skin, but when dropped into the eye, a much smaller quantity suffices, the tiny discs oculists using for this purpose, before testing their patient's sight for glasses, being made of gelatine with $\frac{1}{5000}$ grain of Atropine in each, the entire disk only weighing $\frac{1}{50}$ grain. Scarcely any operation on the eye can safely be performed without the aid of this valuable drug. It is a strong poison, the amount given internally being very minute, $\frac{1}{200}$ to $\frac{1}{100}$ grain. As an antidote to Opium, Atropine may be injected subcutaneously, and it has also been used in poisoning by Calabar bean and in Chloroform poisoning. It has no action on the voluntary muscles, but the nerve endings in involuntary muscles are paralysed by large doses, the paralysis finally affecting the central nervous system, causing excitement and delirium.

The various preparations of Belladonna have many uses. Locally applied, it lessens irritability and pain, and is used as a lotion, plaster or liniment in cases of neuralgia, gout, rheumatism and sciatica. As a drug, it specially affects the brain and the bladder. It is used to check excessive secretions and to allay inflammation and to check the sweating of phthisis and other exhausting diseases.

Small doses allay cardiac palpitation, and the plaster is applied to the cardiac region for the same purpose, removing pain and distress.

It is a powerful antispasmodic in intestinal colic and spasmodic asthma. Occasionally the leaves are employed as an ingredient of cigarettes for relieving the latter. It is well borne by children, and is given in large doses in whooping cough and false croup.

For its action on the circulation, it is given in the collapse of pneumonia, typhoid fever and other acute diseases. It increases the rate of the heart by some 20 to 40 beats per minute, without diminishing its force.

It is of value in acute sore throat, and relieves local inflammation and congestion.

Hahnemann proved that tincture of Belladonna given in very small doses will protect from the infection of scarlet fever, and at one time Belladonnna leaves were held to be curative of cancer, when applied externally as a poultice, either fresh or dried and powdered.

Belladonna plasters are often applied, after a fall, to the injured or sprained part. A mixture of Belladonna plaster, Salicylic acid and Lead plaster is recommended as an application for corns and bunions.

¶ *Preparations and Dosages.* Powdered leaves, 1 to 2 grains. Powdered root, 1 to 5 grains. Fluid extract leaves, 1 to 3 drops. Fluid extract root, B.P., ¼ to 1 drop. Tincture, B.P., 5 to 15 drops. Alkaloid Atropine, Alcoholic extract, B.P., ¼ to 1 grain. Green extract, B.P., ¼ to 1 grain. Juice, B.P., 5 to 15 drops. Liniment, B.P. Plaster, B.P. and U.S.P. Ointment, B.P.

NIGHTSHADE, WOODY

Solanum Dulcamara (LINN.)
N.O. Solanaceæ

Synonyms. Bittersweet. Dulcamara. Felonwood. Felonwort. Scarlet Berry. Violet Bloom
Part Used. Twigs

The large and important natural order of Solanaceæ contains, besides Henbane and the Nightshades, some of the most poisonous of our native plants, such useful economic plants as the Potato, Tomato, Aubergine, Capsicum and Tobacco, also the medicinally valuable Thornapple (*Datura Stramonium*), the Winter Cherry and the Mandrake, which in earlier days was supposed to possess miraculous properties.

The prevailing property of plants belonging to the Nightshade tribe is narcotic, rendering many of them in consequence highly poisonous.

The genus *Solanum* – to which the older herbalists formerly assigned *Atropa Belladonna*, and to which the Potato and Aubergine belong, is represented in this country by two species: *Solanum nigrum* (Black or Garden Nightshade) and *S. Dulcamara* (Bittersweet or Woody Nightshade). The leaves bear a certain resemblance to those of Belladonna, and the flowers of both Bittersweet and Belladonna are purple, though totally distinct in shape, and both have berries, red in the case of Bittersweet, not black as in the Belladonna. Bittersweet is common throughout Europe and America. It abounds in almost every hedgerow in England, where it is rendered conspicuous in the summer by its bright purple flowers, and in autumn by its brilliant red berries. Belladonna for which it is often mistaken is rare.

¶ *Description.* It is a perennial, shrubby plant, quite woody at the base, but throws out long, straggling, slender branches, which trail over the hedges and bushes among which it grows, reaching many feet in length, when supported by other plants. They are at first green and hairy, but become woody and smooth as they grow older, with an ashy-green bark.

The flowers, which are open all the summer, are in loose, drooping clusters, on short stalks opposite the leaves. They are of a bluish purple tint, with reflexed petals when expanded, so as almost to appear drooping. Their bright yellow stamens project in a conical form around the pistil, or seed-bearing portion of the flower.

The leaves are chiefly auriculate on the upper stems, i.e. with little ears, having at their base from one to two (rarely three) wing-like segments, but are heart-shaped below. They are placed alternately on either side of the stem and arranged so that they face the light. The flower-clusters always face a different direction to the leaves. 'One may gather a hundred pieces of the Woody Nightshade, and this strange perversity is rampant in all,' remarks an observer of this very curious habit.

The berries are green at first, afterwards becoming orange and finally bright red, and are produced in constant succession throughout the summer and early autumn, many remaining on the plant long after the leaves have fallen.

The plant was called the Woody Nightshade by the old herbalists to distinguish it from the Deadly Nightshade. Its generic name *Solanum* is derived from *Solor* (I ease), and testifies to the medicinal power of this group of plants. The second name, *Dulcamara*, used to be more correctly written in the Middle Ages, *Amaradulcis*, signifying literally 'bittersweet,' the common country name of the plant, given to it in reference to

589

the fact that the root and stem, if chewed, taste first bitter and then sweet. Another old name is Felonwood, probably a corruption of Felonwort, the plant for felons – felon being an old name for whitlow. We are told by an old writer that –

'the Berries of Bittersweet stamped with rusty Bacon, applied to the Joynts of the Finger that is troubled with a Felon hath been found by divers country people who are most subject thereto to be very successful for the curing of the same.'

In the days of belief in witchcraft, shepherds used to hang it as a charm round the necks of those of their beasts whom they suspected to be under the evil eye.

The older physicians valued Bittersweet highly and applied it to many purposes in medicine and surgery, for which it is no longer used. It was in great repute as far back as the time of Theophrastus, and we know of it being in use in this country in the thirteenth century.

Gerard says of it:

'The juice is good for those that have fallen from high places, and have been thereby bruised or beaten, for it is thought to dissolve blood congealed or cluttered anywhere in the intrals and to heale the hurt places.'

Boerhaave, the celebrated Dutch physician, considered the young shoots superior to Sarsaparilla as a restorative, and Linnæus, who at first had an aversion to the plant, later spoke of it in the highest terms as a remedy for rheumatism, fever and inflammatory diseases of all kinds. There are few complaints for which it has not been at some time recommended.

¶ *Part Used.* The limited demand for Bittersweet in modern pharmacy is supplied by the wild plant.

The dried young branches from indigenous plants, taken when they have shed their leaves, were the parts directed for use up to 1907, by the British Pharmacopœia, but it has been removed from the last two editions.

The shoots, preferably the extreme branches, are collected from two- to three-year-old branches, after the leaves have fallen in the autumn, cut into pieces about ½ inch long, with a chaff cutter, and then carefully dried by artificial heat. They require no other preparation. The peculiar unpleasant odour of the shoots is lost on drying.

An extract of the leaves or tops is frequently prepared also; 10 lb. of the dried shoots yield

about 2 lb. of the extract. A decoction of the dried herb is likewise used.

The drug occurs in commerce in short, cylindrical pieces of a light greenish, or brownish-yellow colour, about ¼ inch thick, bearing occasional alternate scars where the leaves have fallen off, and are quite free from hairs, and more or less longitudinally furrowed and wrinkled. A thin, shining bark surrounds the wood, which is lined internally by a whitish pith, which only partially fills it, leaving the centre hollow.

The active properties of Bittersweet are most developed when it grows in a dry and exposed situation. The bitterness is more pronounced in the spring than in the autumn, and in America the shoots are gathered while still pliant, when the plant is just budding, though the British Pharmacopœia directs that they shall be collected in the autumn.

¶ *Constituents.* Bittersweet contains the alkaloid Solanine and the amorphous glucoside Dulcamarine, to which the characteristic bittersweet taste is due. Sugar, gum, starch and resin are also present.

Solanine acts narcotically; in large doses it paralyses the central nervous system, without affecting the peripheral nerves or voluntary muscles. It slows the heart and respiration, lessens sensibility, lowers the temperature and causes vertigo and delirium, terminating in death with convulsions.

¶ *Medicinal Action and Uses.* The drug possesses feeble narcotic properties, with the power of increasing the secretions, particularly those of the skin and kidneys. It has no action on the pupil of the eye.

It is chiefly used as an alterative in skin diseases, being a popular remedy for obstinate skin eruptions, scrofula and ulcers.

It has also been recommended in chronic bronchial catarrh, asthma and whooping-cough.

For chronic rheumatism and for jaundice it has been much employed in the past, an infusion of 1 oz. of the dried herb to ½ pint water being taken in wineglassful doses, two or three times daily. From the fluid extract made from the twigs, a decoction is prepared of 10 drachms in 2 pints of boiling water, boiled down to 1 pint, and taken in doses of ½ to 2 oz. with an equal quantity of milk.

The berries have proved poisonous to a certain degree to children.

Fluid extract, ½ to 2 drachms.

¶ *Other Species.*

The four following species are all used in Homœopathic medicine:

SOLANUM ARRABENTA
Part Used. Leaves.
Habitat. Rio Janeiro.
Medicinal Use. Apoplexy.

SOLANUM MAMMOSUM
Synonym. Apple of Sodom.
Part Used. Fresh ripe fruit.
Medicinal Use. Irritability and restlessness.

SOLANUM OLERACEÆ
Synonym. Jagueribo.
Part Used. Flowers.
Habitat. Shores of Rio Janeiro.
Medicinal Use. Acts specifically on the mammary glands.

SOLANUM PSEUDO-CAPSICUM
Synonym. Jerusalem Cherry.
Part Used. Fruit.
Medicinal Use. Somnolence.

NUTMEG

Myristica fragrans (HOUTT.)
N.O. Myristicaceæ

Synonyms. Nux Moschata. Myristica officinalis (Linn.). Myristica aromata. Myristica
Part Used. Dried kernel of the seed
Habitat. Banda Islands, Malayan Archipelago, Molucca Islands, and cultivated in Sumatra, French Guiana

¶ *Description.* The tree is about 25 feet high, has a greyish-brown smooth bark, abounding in a yellow juice. The branches spread in whorls – alternate leaves, on petioles about 1 inch long, elliptical, glabrous, obtuse at base – acuminate, aromatic, dark green and glossy above, paler underside and 4 to 6 inches long. Flowers diœcious, small in axillary racemes. Peduncles and pedicles glabrous. Male flowers three to five more on a peduncle. Calyx urceolate, thick and fleshy, covered with an indistinct reddish pubescence dingy pale yellow, cut into three erect teeth. Female flowers differ little from the male, except pedicel is often solitary. Fruit is a pendulous, globose drupe, consisting of a succulent pericarp – the mace arillus covering the hard endocarp, and a wrinkled kernel with ruminated endosperm. When the arillus is fresh it is a brilliant scarlet, when dry more horny, brittle, and a yellowish-brown colour. The seed or nutmeg is firm, fleshy, whitish, transversed by red-brown veins, abounding in oil. The tree does not bloom till it is nine years old, when it fruits and continues to do so for seventy-five years without attention. In Banda Islands there are three harvests, the chief one in July or August, the next in November, and the last in March or April. The fruit is gathered by means of a barb attached to a long stick. The mace is separated from the nut and both are dried separately. The nutmeg or kernel of the fruit and the arillus or mace are the official parts.

After the mace is removed, the nutmegs are dried on gratings, three to six weeks over a slow charcoal fire – but are often sun-dried for six days previously. The curing protects them from insects.

When thoroughly dried, they rattle in the shell, which is cracked with a mallet. The nutmegs are graded, 1st Penang, 2nd Dutch (these are usually covered with lime to preserve them from insects), 3rd Singapore, and 4th long nutmegs.

Nutmegs have a strong, peculiar and delightful fragrance and a very strong bitter warm aromatic taste.

¶ *Constituents.* They contain lignin, stearin, volatile oil, starch, gum and 0·08 of an acid substance. By submitting nutmegs and water to distillation, a volatile oil is obtained. The small round heavy nutmeg is the best. Those that are larger, longer, lighter, less marbled, and not so oily, are inferior.

The powder of nutmegs, beaten to a pulp with water, then pressed between heated plates, gives from 10 to 30 per cent. of orange-coloured scented concrete oil erroneously called 'oil of mace' – an inferior oil is prepared in Holland from the spoiled or inferior nutmegs – and an artificial preparation is made by mixing together tallow, spermaceti, etc., colouring it with saffron and flavouring it with essential oil of nutmeg.

After the nutmegs have been collected, the outside fleshy pericarp is made into a preserve.

The mace of commerce should be somewhat flexible, cinnamon-yellow coloured, in single or double blades, with nutmeg-like smell and a warm, sharp, fatty, aromatic taste.

There is a large trade in wild nutmegs, which are known in commerce under the names of long, female, Macassar, Papua, Guinea, or Norse nutmegs. All these varieties have been traced to *Myristica argentea* of New Guinea, from whence they enter commerce as Macassar nutmegs.

There is much adulteration and fraud in the nutmeg trade. The essential oil has often been extracted before they are marketed – a fraud which can be detected by the light weight. This renders them more subject to attacks by insects.

Concrete oil of nutmeg, often erroneously termed 'oil of mace' or 'nutmeg butter,' is made by bruising the nuts and treating them with steam. The best nutmeg butter is imported from the East Indies in stone jars, or in blocks wrapped in palm leaves – it should be softly solid, unctuous to touch, orange yellow colour and mottled, with the taste and smell of nutmeg.

Holland prepares an inferior kind of oil sometimes offered for sale – it is said to be derived from nutmegs that have been deprived of their volatile oil by distillation. It is found in hard shining square cakes, light coloured and with less taste and smell than the East Indies oil. *Ucuhula* nut is the round or oval seed of *M. surinamensis*. It is distinguished by very large albuminous crystalloids, the seeds containing over 70 per cent. solid yellow fat. The Brazilian *M. officinalis* resembles the nutmeg in form and structure, it contains crystals like the preceding one, though less large; has a black shell covered with broad furrows and yields a fat or bicuhyba balsam very like the ordinary nutmeg, with a sharp sour taste, and a peculiar fatty acid, bicuhybastearic acid. From *M. otoba* otoba fat is procured. Almost colourless with a fresh smell of nutmeg, it contains myristin, olein, and otobite. The fruit of virola or *M. sebifera* also gives a fatty substance termed ocuba wax. The following are erroneously called nutmegs:

CALIFORNIAN NUTMEG. The seed of a coniferous tree, *Sorreya Californica* – its odour and taste terebinthinate.

JAMAICA or CALABACH NUTMEG. Obtained from *Monodora myristica*.

NEW HOLLAND or PLUME NUTMEG. Obtained from the *Atherosperma moschata*.

CLOVE NUTMEG. Obtained from *Agathophyllum aromaticum*.

Insects that attack nutmegs only extract the fat oil. They do not interfere in any way with the essential oil.

¶ *Medicinal Action and Uses.* The tonic principle is Myristicin. Oil of Nutmeg is used to conceal the taste of various drugs and as a local stimulant to the gastro-intestinal tract.

¶ *Uses of Nutmeg.* Powdered nutmeg is rarely given alone, though it enters into the composition of a number of medicines. The expressed oil is sometimes used externally as a gentle stimulant, and it was once an ingredient of the *Emplastrum picis*.

The properties of mace are identical to those of the nutmeg. Dose, 5 to 20 grains.

Both nutmeg and mace are used for flatulence and to correct the nausea arising from other drugs, also to allay nausea and vomiting.

Nutmeg is an agreeable addition to drinks for convalescents.

Grated nutmeg mixed with lard makes an excellent ointment for piles.

In some places roasted nutmeg is applied internally as a remedy for leucorrhœa. Dose of the powder, 5 to 20 grains. Fluid extract, 10 to 30 drops. Larger doses are narcotic and produce dangerous symptoms. Spirit, B.P., 5 to 20 drops.

See MACE.

(POISON)
NUX VOMICA

Strychnos Nux-vomica (LINN.)
N.O. Loganiaceæ

Synonyms. Poison Nut. Semen strychnos. Quaker Buttons
Part Used. Dried ripe seeds
Habitat. India, in the Malay Archipelago

¶ *Description.* A medium-sized tree with a short, crooked, thick trunk, the wood is white hard, close grained, durable and the root very bitter. Branches irregular, covered with a smooth ash-coloured bark; young shoots deep green, shiny; leaves opposite, short stalked, oval, shiny, smooth on both sides, about 4 inches long and 3 broad; flowers small, greeny-white, funnel shape, in small terminal cymes, blooming in the cold season and having a disagreeable smell. Fruit about the size of a large apple with a smooth hard rind or shell which when ripe is a lovely orange colour, filled with a soft white jelly-like pulp containing five seeds covered with a soft woolly-like substance, white and horny internally. The seeds are removed when ripe, cleansed, dried and sorted; they are exported from Cochin, Madras and other Indian ports. The seeds have the shape of flattened disks densely covered with closely appressed satiny hairs, radiating from the centre of the flattened sides and giving to the seeds a characteristic sheen; they are very hard, with a dark grey horny endosperm in which the small embryo is embedded; no odour but a very bitter taste.

¶ *Constituents.* Nux Vomica contains the alkaloids, Strychnine and Brucine, also traces of strychnicine, and a glucoside Loganin, about 3 per cent. fatty matter, caffeotannic acid and a trace of copper. The pulp of the fruit contains about 5 per cent. of loganin together with the alkaloid strychnicine.

¶ *Medicinal Action and Uses*. The properties of Nux Vomica are substantially those of the alkaloid Strychnine. The powdered seeds are employed in atonic dyspepsia. The tincture of Nux Vomica is often used in mixtures – for its stimulant action on the gastro-intestinal tract. In the mouth it acts as a bitter, increasing appetite; it stimulates peristalsis; in chronic constipation due to atony of the bowel it is often combined with cascara and other laxatives with good effects. Strychnine, the chief alkaloid constituent of the seeds, also acts as a bitter, increasing the flow of gastric juice; it is rapidly absorbed as it reaches the intestines, after which it exerts its characteristic effects upon the central nervous system, the movements of respiration are deepened and quickened and the heart slowed through excitation of the vagal centre. The senses of smell, touch, hearing and vision are rendered more acute, it improves the pulse and raises blood pressure and is of great value as a tonic to the circulatory system in cardiac failure. Strychnine is excreted very slowly and its action is cumulative in any but small doses; it is much used as a gastric tonic in dyspepsia. The most direct symptom caused by strychnine is violent convulsions due to a simultaneous stimulation of the motor or sensory ganglia of the spinal cord; during the convulsion there is great rise in blood pressure; in some types of chronic lead poisoning it is of great value. In cases of surgical shock and cardiac failure large doses are given up to $\frac{1}{10}$ grain by hypodermic injection; also used as an antidote in poisoning by chloral or chloroform. Brucine closely resembles strychnine in its action, but is slightly less poisonous; it paralyses the peripheral motor nerves. It is said that the convulsive action characteristic of strychnine is absent in brucine almost entirely. It is used in pruritis and as a local anodyne in inflammations of the external ear.

¶ *Preparations and Dosages*. Strychnine should not be administered in liquid form combined with bromides, iodides or chlorides, there being a risk of formation of the insoluble hydrobromide, etc.

Nux Vomica, 1 to 4 grains. Extract of Nux Vomica, B.P., $\frac{1}{4}$ to 1 grain. Extract of Nux Vomica, B.P. 1885, $\frac{1}{4}$ to 1 grain. Extract of Nux Vomica, U.S.P., $\frac{1}{4}$ grain. Liquid extract of Nux Vomica, B.P., 1 to 3 minims. Fluid extract of Nux Vomica, U.S.P., 1 minim. Tincture of Nux Vomica, B.P., 5 to 15 minims. Tincture of Nux Vomica, B.P. 1885, 10 to 20 minims. Tincture of Nux Vomica, U.S.P., 10 minims. Strychnine, B.P., $\frac{1}{8}$ to $\frac{1}{15}$ grain. Hypodermic injection of strychnine. Solution of Strychnine Hydrochloride, B.P., 2 to 8 minims. Acid Strychnine Mixture, B.P.C., $\frac{1}{2}$ to 1 fluid ounce.

¶ *Poisoning and Antidotes*. In cases of poisoning by strychnine an emetic or the stomach pump should be used at once and tannin or potassium permanganate given to render the strychnine inactive. Violent convulsions should be controlled by administration of chloroform or large doses of chloral or bromide. Urethane in large doses is considered an antidote. Amyl nitrite is also useful owing to its rapid action during the convulsion, and in absence of respiration 3 to 5 minims may be hypodermically injected.

¶ *Other Species*.

Strychnos tieute, a clumbing shrub growing in Java, gives a juice termed Upas tieute, said to be used by the natives as an arrow poison; it produces death by violent convulsions, the heart stopping before respiration.

S. toxifera yields the deadly poison Curare (Woorari or Urari) used by the natives of British Guiana.

S. ligustrina, the wood of which contains brucine, as does the bark.

S. pseudo is found in the mountains and forests of India. It supplies the seeds known as clearing nuts. The fruit is black, the size of a cherry, containing only one seed; fruit and seeds are used medicinally in India and also to clear muddy water, the seeds being rubbed for a minute inside the vessel and the water then allowed to settle; their efficiency depending on their albumen and casein contents acting as a fining agent similar to those employed to clarify wine and beer.

S. innocua. The fruit and pulp are harmless and are eaten by the natives of Egypt and Senegal.

S. Ignatii is found in the Philippines, the seeds containing strychnine and brucine, strychnine being present in greater quantity than in Nux Vomica. A tincture made from the beans is official in the British Pharmacopœia Codex.

OAK, COMMON

Quercus robur
N.O. Cupuliferæ

Synonym. Tanner's Bark

The Common, or British Oak, for many centuries the chief forest tree of England, is intimately bound up with the history of these islands from Druid times. A spray of oak was for long engraved on one side of our sixpences and shillings, but is now superseded by the British lion. The Oak, although widely distributed over Europe, is regarded as peculiarly English.

The genus *Quercus* comprises numerous species, distributed widely over the Northern Hemisphere, and found also in Java, and the Mountains of Mexico and South America. One species from Guatemala, *Quercus Skinneri*, is remarkable for its resemblance to the Walnut (*Juglans*) in its lobed and wrinkled seed-leaves or cotyledons.

The Oak is subject to a good deal of variation; many species have been defined and many oaks of foreign origin are grown in our parks, the longest established being the Evergreen or Holm Oak (*Q. ilex*). There are two principal varieties of *Q. robur*, often regarded as separate species: *Q. pedunculata*, the Common Oak, which is distinguished by having acorns in ones and twos attached to the twigs by long stems, the leaves having scarcely any stalk at all; and *Q. sessiliflora*, the Durmast Oak, often included with the former, but distinct, the leaves being borne on long stalks, while the acorns 'sit' on the bough. This variety of oak is more generally found in the lower parts of Britain and in North Wales. It is not so long-lived as the Common Oak, and the wood, which has a straighter fibre and a finer grain, is generally thought less tough and less resisting.

Q. pedunculata and *Q. sessiliflora* make good timber, the latter being darker, heavier and more elastic. The wood of these trees when stained green by the growth of a peculiar fungus known as *Peziza œriginosa* is much valued by cabinet-makers.

¶ *Description.* The shape of the oak leaves is too familiar to need description. The flowers are of two kinds; the male, or barren, in long drooping catkins, 1 to 3 inches long, appearing with the leaves, and the leaves and the fertile flowers in distant clusters, each with a cup-shaped, scaly involucre, producing, as fruit, an acorn 1 to 1 inch long.

The Oak is noted for the slowness of its growth, as well as for the large size to which it attains. In eighty years the trunk is said not to exceed 20 inches in diameter, but old trees reach a great girth. The famous Fairlop Oak in Hainault Forest measured 36 feet in girth, the spreading boughs extending above 300 feet in circumference. The Newland Oak in Gloucestershire measures 46 feet 4 inches at 1 foot from the ground, and is one of the largest and oldest in the kingdom, these measurements being exceeded, however, by those of the Courthorpe Oak in Yorkshire, which Hooker reports as attaining the extraordinary girth of 70 feet. King Arthur's Round Table was made from a single slice of oak, cut from an enormous bole, and is still shown at Winchester.

Humboldt refers to an oak in the Département de la Charente-Inférieure measuring nearly 90 feet in circumference near the base; near Breslau an oak fell in 1857 measuring 66 feet in circumference at the base. These large trees are for the most part decayed and hollow in the interior, and their age has been estimated at from one to two thousand years.

The famous Oak of Mamre, Abram's Oak, was illustrated formerly in the *Transactions of the Linnean Society*, by Dr. Hooker. It is a fine specimen of the species *Q. Coccifera*, the prickly evergreen or Kermes Oak, a native of the countries bordering on the Mediterranean; the insect (*coccus*) from which it derives its name yielding the dye known as 'Turkey red.' Abram's Oak is 22 feet in circumference; it is popularly supposed to represent the spot where the tree grew under which Abraham pitched his tent. There is a superstition that any person who cuts or maims this oak will lose his firstborn son.

The oak of Libbeiya in the Lebanon measures 37 feet in girth, and its branches cover an area whose circumference measured over 90 yards. The Arab name is *Sindian*.

The Greeks held the Oak sacred, the Romans dedicated it to Jupiter, and the Druids venerated it.

In England the name Gospel Oak is still retained in many counties, relating to the time when Psalms and Gospel truths were uttered beneath their shade. They were notable objects as resting-places in the 'beating of the parish bounds,' a practice supposed to have been derived from the feast to the god Terminus.

The following is a quotation from Withers:

'That every man might keep his own possessions,
Our fathers used, in reverent processions,
With zealous prayers, and with praiseful cheere,
To walk their parish limits once a year;
And well-known marks (which sacrilegious hands
Now cut or breake) so bordered out their lands,
That every one distinctly knew his owne,
And brawles now rife were then unknowne.'

The ceremony was performed by the clergyman and his parishioners going the boundaries of the parish and choosing the most remarkable sites (oak-trees being specially selected) to read passages from the Gospels, and ask blessings for the people.

NUX VOMICA
Strychnos Nux-Vomica

OAK GALLS
Quercus Infectoria

OLIVE
Olea Europœa

SWEET ORANGE
Citrus Aurantium

'Dearest, bury me
Under that holy oke, or Gospel Tree;
Where, though thou see'st not, thou may'st
think upon
Me, when you yearly go'st Procession.'
HERRICK

Many of these Gospel trees are still alive –
five in different parts of England.

An old proverb relating to the oak is still a
form of speculation on the weather in many
country districts.

'If the Oak's before the Ash,
Then you'll only get a splash;
If the Ash before the Oak,
Then you may expect a soak.'

The technical name of the Oak is said to be
derived from the Celtic *quer* (fine) and *cuez*
(tree).

A curious custom in connexion with wear-
ing an oak-leaf (or preferably an *oak-apple*)
on May 29, still exists in some villages in
South Wilts. Each one has the right to collect fallen branches in a certain large wood in
the district. To *claim* this privilege each
villager has to bring them home shouting
'*Grovely, Grovely, and all Grovely!*' (this
being the name of the large wood).

After the Oak has passed its century, it
increases by less than an inch a year, but the
wood matured in this leisurely fashion is
practically indestructible. Edward the Con-
fessor's shrine in Westminster Abbey is of
oak that has outlasted the changes of 800
years. Logs have been dug from peat bogs,
in good preservation and fit for rough building purposes, that were submerged a
thousand years ago. In the Severn, break-
waters are still used as casual landing-places,
where piles of oak are said to have been
driven by the Romans.

As timber, the particular and most valued
qualities of the Oak are hardness and toughness; Box and Ebony are harder, Yew and
Ash are tougher than Oak, but no timber is
possessed of both these requisites in so
great a degree as the British Oak. Its elasticity and strength made it particularly advantageous in shipbuilding, and the oaks of
the Forest of Dean provided much material
for the 'wooden walls of England.' We read
that Philip of Spain gave special orders to
the Armada to burn and destroy every oak in
that forest, and a century later, during a
period of twenty-five years, nearly 17,000
loads of oak timber, of the value of £30,000,
were despatched to naval dockyards from this
forest. Nelson drew up a special memorial to
the Crown on the desirability of replanting
this forest with oak trees, and at that time no
forester dared to cut down a *crooked* tree
before maturity, because its knees and
twisted elbows were so desirable in shipbuilding. A tree should be winter felled, if
perfection of grain is desired. Although not
employed as of old, for building ships of war,
it is in great request for peaceful land transit,
sharing with Ash in the making of railway
carriages and other rolling stock. The roots
were formerly used to make hafts for
daggers and knives.

Some of the American kinds also furnish
valuable timber. Such are *Q. alba*, the White
or Quebec Oak, the wood of which is used in
shipbuilding, and by wheelwrights and
coopers. *Q. virens*, the Live Oak, also yields
excellent timber for naval purposes. The
wood of *Q. ilex*, a Mediterranean species, is
said to be as good as that of the Common
Oak. *Q. cerris*, the Turkey Oak, supplies a
wood much in favour with wheelwrights,
cabinet-makers, turners, etc. There are also
several Japanese oaks, used for their excellent timber.

The False Sandalwood of Crete is the produce of *Q. abelicea*. This wood is of a reddish colour, and has an agreeable perfume.
The less valuable oaks furnish excellent
charcoal and firewood.

The bark is universally used to tan leather,
and for this purpose strips easily in April and
May. An infusion of it, with a small quantity
of copperas, yields a dye which was formerly
used in the country to dye woollen of a
purplish colour, which, though not very
bright, was said to be durable. The Scotch
Highlanders used it to dye their yarn. Oak
sawdust used also to be the principal indigenous vegetable used in dyeing fustian,
and may also be used for tanning, but is
much inferior to the bark for that purpose.
Oak apples have also been occasionally used
in dyeing as a substitute for the imported
Oriental galls, but the black obtained from
them is not durable.

In Brittany, tan compressed into cakes is
used as fuel. Oak-bark is employed for dyeing black, in conjunction with salts of iron.
With alum, oak-bark yields a brown dye;
with a salt of tin, a yellow colour; with a salt
of zinc, Isabella yellow. *Q. tinctoria*, a
North American species, yields *Quercitron
Bark*, employed for dyeing yellow; the
American Indians are said to dye their skins
red with the bark of *Q. prinus*. After the oak-
bark has been used for leather-tanning, it is
still serviceable to gardeners for the warmth
it generates and is largely used by them
under the name of Tan; it sometimes, however, favours the growth of certain fungi,
which are harmful to plants. Refuse tan is

also employed in the adulteration of chicory and coffee.

Acorns were of considerable importance formerly for feeding swine. About the end of the seventh century, special laws were made relating to the feeding of swine in woods, called pawnage, or pannage. In Saxon times of famine, the peasantry were thankful for a share of this nourishing, but somewhat indigestible food. The Board of Agriculture has lately issued a pamphlet, pointing out the use as fodder, which might be made both of the Acorn and of the Horse Chestnut. The analysis of the Acorn given by the *Lancet* is: water, 6·3 per cent.; protein, 5·2 per cent.; fat, 43 per cent.; carbohydrates, 45 per cent. The most important constituent of both the Acorn and the Horse Chestnut is the carbohydrate in the form of starch, while the Acorn should have further value on account of the substantial proportion of fat which it contains. The flavour of Acorns is improved if they are dried, and a flour with nourishing properties can be obtained by grinding the dried kernels.

In many country districts acorns are still collected in sacks and given to pigs; but these must be mixed with other vegetable food to counteract their binding properties.

Oak trees are more persistently attacked by insects than any other trees.

¶ *Medicinal Action and Uses.* The astringent effects of the Oak were well known to the Ancients, by whom different parts of the tree were used, but it is the *bark* which is now employed in medicine. Its action is slightly tonic, strongly astringent and antiseptic. It has a strong astringent bitter taste, and its qualities are extracted both by water and spirit. The odour is slightly aromatic.

Like other astringents, it has been recommended in agues and hæmorrhages, and is a good substitute for Quinine in intermittent fever, especially when given with Chamomile flowers.

It is useful in chronic diarrhœa and dysentery, either alone or in conjunction with aromatics. A decoction is made from 1 oz. of bark in a quart of water, boiled down to a pint and taken in wineglassful doses. Externally, this decoction has been advantageously employed as a gargle in chronic sore throat with relaxed uvula, and also as a fomentation. It is also serviceable as an injection for leucorrhœa, and applied locally to bleeding gums and piles.

¶ *Preparation and Dosage.* Fluid extract, ½ to 1 drachm.

Oak bark when finely powdered and inhaled freely, has proved very beneficial in consumption in its early stages. Working tanners are well known to be particularly exempt from this disease. A remedial snuff is made from the freshly collected oak bark, dried and reduced to a fine powder.

The bark is collected in the spring from young trees, and dried in the sun. It is greyish, more or less polished externally and brownish internally. The fracture is fibrous and the inner surface rough, with projecting medullary rays.

The older herbalists considered the thin skin that covers the acorn effectual in staying spitting of blood, and the powder of the acorn taken in wine was considered a good diuretic. A decoction of acorns and oak bark, made with milk, was considered an antidote to poisonous herbs and medicines.

The distilled water of the oak bud was also thought 'to be good used either inwardly or outwardly to assuage inflammation.'

Galen applied the bruised leaves to heal wounds.

OAK GALLS

Galls are excrescences produced in plants by the presence of the larvæ of different insects. The forms that they assume are many, and the changes produced in the tissues various. They occur in all parts of the plant and sometimes in great quantities.

The oak galls used in commerce and medicine are excrescences on the *Q. infectoria*, a small oak, indigenous to Asia Minor and Persia, and result from the puncture of the bark of the young twigs by the female Gall-wasp, *Cynips Gallæ-tinctoriæ*, who lays its eggs inside. This species of oak seldom attains the height of 6 feet, the stem being crooked, with the habit of a shrub rather than a tree.

The Common Oaks of this country are much affected by galls. They occur sometimes on the leaves, where they form the so-called 'Oak-apples,' sometimes on the shoots, where they do great mischief by checking and distorting the growth of the tree.

The young larva that hatches from the eggs feeds upon the tissues of the plant and secretes in its mouth a peculiar fluid, which stimulates the cells of the tissues to a rapid division and abnormal development, resulting in the formation of a gall.

The larva thus becomes completely enclosed in a nearly spherical mass, which projects from the twig, furnishing it with a supply of starch and other nutritive material.

The growth of the gall continues only so long as the egg or larva lives or reaches maturity and passes into a chrysalis, from which the fully-developed gall-wasp emerges and escapes into the air through a hole bored with its mandibles in the side of the gall.

The best Aleppo galls, collected in Asiatic Turkey, principally in the province of Aleppo, are collected before the insects escape.

Galls are also largely imported from Persia and to a lesser extent from Greece.

Aleppo Galls of good quality are hard and heavy, without perforations, dark bluish-green or olive green, nearly spherical in shape, 12 to 18 mm. in diameter (about ⅜ to ⅝ inch), and known in commerce as *blue* or *green* galls.

The Aleppo galls (from *Q. infectoria*) sometimes also called 'Mecca Galls,' are supposed to be the Dead Sea or Sodom Apples, 'the fruit that never comes to ripeness' – the fruit so pleasant to the eye, so bitter to the taste.

If collected after the insects have escaped, galls are of a pale, yellowish-brown hue, spongy and lighter in weight, perforated near the centre with a small hole. These are known in commerce as *white* galls.

On breaking a gall, it appears yellowish or brownish-white within, with a small cavity containing the remains of a larva of the Gall-wasp.

Galls have no marked odour, but an intensely astringent taste, and slightly sweet after-taste.

¶ *Constituents.* The chief constituents of *Aleppo* or Turkey Galls are 50 to 70 per cent. of gallotannic acid, 2 to 4 per cent. of gallic acid, mucilage, sugar, resin and an insoluble matter, chiefly lignin.

'White' galls contain less gallotannic acid than 'blue' or 'green.'

English Oak Galls, or Oak Apples, are smooth, globular, brown, usually perforated

OAK, POLYPODY OF. *See* FERNS

OATS

and much less astringent than Aleppo Galls, containing only 15 to 20 per cent. of gallo-tannic acid. They have no commercial value.

China Galls – produced by a species of Aphis on *Rhus semialata* – are used mainly for the manufacture of tannic and gallic acids, pyrogallol, ink, etc. They are not spherical, but of extremely diverse and irregular form, with a thick, grey, velvety down, making them a reddish-brown colour. They contain about 70 per cent of gallotannic acid.

Mecca Galls, from Bassorah, known as 'mala nisana,' are spherical in shape and surrounded about the centre by a circle of horned protuberances. They are not official.

¶ *Medicinal Action and Uses.* Galls are much used commercially in the preparation of gallic acid and tannic acid, and are extensively employed in tanning and dyeing, in the manufacture of ink, etc.

Medicinally, they are a powerful astringent, the most powerful of all vegetable astringents, used as a tincture internally, in cases of dysentery, diarrhoea, cholera, and as an injection in gonorrhœa, leucorrhœa, etc.

Preparations of gall are usually applied as a local astringent externally, mainly in Gall ointment (1 oz. powdered galls and 4 oz. benzoated lard), applied to painful hæmorrhoids, and also to arrest hæmorrhage from the nose and gums.

An infusion may be used also as a gargle in relaxed throat, inflamed tonsils, etc.

¶ *Preparations and Dosages.* Powdered gall, 5 to 20 grains. Fluid extract, 5 to 20 drops. Tincture, U.S.P., 1 drachm. Ointment, B.P. Compound ointment, B.P.

Avena sativa (LINN.)
N.O. Graminaceæ

Synonyms. Groats. Oatmeal
Part Used. Seeds
Habitat. It is unknown when Oats were first introduced into Britain

¶ *Description.* There are about twenty-five varieties cultivated. The nutritive quality of Oats is less in a given weight than that of any other cereal grain. In the best Oats it does not exceed 75 per cent. *Avena sativa*, the Common Oat, has a smooth stem, growing up to 4 feet high, with linear lanceolate, veined rough leaves; loose striate sheaves; stipules lacerate; panicle equal, loose; spikelets pedunculate, pendulous, two-flowered, both perfect. lower one mostly awned; paleæ cartilaginous, embracing the caryopsis; root fibrous, annual. The Naked or Pilcorn Oat differs slightly from the other: calyces three-flowered, receptacle exceeding the calyx; petals awned at the back; the third floscule awnless; and the chief difference lies

in the grains, which when ripe quit the husk and fall naked. The grains as found in commerce are enclosed in their pales and these grains divested of their paleæ are used for medicinal and dietary purposes; the grains when separated from their integuments are termed groats, and these when crushed are called Embden groats. Oatmeal is ground grain.

¶ *Constituents.* Starch, gluten, albumen and other protein compounds, sugar, gum oil, and salts.

¶ *Medicinal Action and Uses.* Nervine, stimulant, antispasmodic. Oats are made into gruel. This is prepared by boiling 1 oz. of oatmeal or groats in 3 pints of water till reduced to 1 quart, then straining it, sugar, lemons, wine, or raisins being added as flavouring. Gruel thus is a mild nutritious aliment, of easy digestion in inflammatory cases and fevers; it is very useful after parturition, and is sometimes employed in poisoning from acid substances. It is found useful also as a demulcent enema and boiled into a thick paste makes a good emollient poultice. Oatmeal is unsoluble in alcohol, ether, and the oils, but the two first move an oleoresinous matter from it. It is to be avoided in dyspepsia accompanied with acidity of the stomach. The pericarp of Oats con-

tains an amorphous alkaloid which acts as a stimulant of the motor ganglia, increasing the excitability of the muscles, and in horses causes excitement. A tincture is made by permeating 4 oz. of ground oatmeal to 1 pint diluted alcohol, keeping the first 5½ oz. (fluid), and evaporating the remainder down to ½ fluid ounce, and adding this to the first 5½ fluid ounces. The extract and tincture are useful as a nerve and uterine tonic.

¶ *Dosage.*[1] Fluid extract, 10 to 30 drops in hot water.

OLEANDER. *See* PERIWINKLE

OLIBANUM. *See* FRANKINCENSE

OLIVE

Olea Europæa (LINN.)
N.O. Oleaceæ

Synonyms. Olea Oleaster. Olea lancifolia. Olea gallica. Olivier
Parts Used. The oil of the fruit, leaves, bark
Habitat. Asia Minor and Syria. Cultivated in Mediterranean countries, Chile and Peru, and South Australia

¶ *History.* The high position held by the Olive tree in ancient as in modern days may be realized when it is remembered that Moses exempted from military service men who would work at its cultivation, and that in Scriptural and classical writings the oil is mentioned as a symbol of goodness and purity, and the tree as representing peace and happiness. The oil, in addition to its wide use in diet, was burnt in the sacred lamps of temples, while the victor in the Olympic games was crowned with its leaves.

¶ *Description.* Olea europæa is a small, evergreen tree, averaging 20 feet or more in height. It has many thin branches with opposite branchlets and shortly-stalked, opposite, lanceolate leaves about 2¼ inches long, acute, entire and smooth, pale green above and silvery below. The bark is pale grey and the flowers numerous, small and creamy-white in colour.

The dark purple fruit is a drupe about ¾ inch long, ovoid and often pointed, the fleshy part filled with oil. The thick, bony stone has a blunt keel down one side. It contains a single seed.

Being hardier than the lemon, the Olive may sometimes produce fruit in England. The largest of the varieties under cultivation is produced in Spain, but probably Italy prepares most oil, the annual average being 33 million gallons.

The beautifully-veined wood not only takes a fine polish, but is faintly fragrant, and is much valued for small cabinet-work. It was in olden days carved into statues of gods.

For use as a dessert fruit the unripe olives

are steeped in water to reduce their bitterness. Olives *à la Picholine* are steeped in a solution of lime and wood ashes. They are bottled in an aromatic solution of salt.

In warm countries the bark exudes a substance called *Gomme d'Olivier*, which was formerly used in medicine as a vulnerary.

The large 'Queen Olives' grown near Cadiz are chiefly exported to the United States; the smaller 'Manzanillo' is principally consumed in Spain and Spanish America.

The trees bear fruit in their second year; in their sixth will repay cultivation, and continue as a source of wealth even when old and hollow, though the crop varies greatly from year to year.

The groves are cut until the beauty of the trees is lost.

The ripe fruits are pressed to extract the oil, the methods varying in the different countries.

Virgin Oil, greenish in tint, is obtained by pressing crushed fruit in coarse bags and skimming the oil from the tubs of water through which it is conducted. The cake left in the bags is broken up, moistened, and repressed. Sometimes the fruit is allowed to reach fermenting point before pressure, the quantity of oil being increased and the quality lessened. The product is called *Huile fermentée.*

Huile ordinaire is made by expression and mixture with boiling water.

Provence oil is the most valued and the most refined.

Official Olive *soap* is made from olive oil and sodium hydroxide.

¶ *Constituents.* The exuding *gum-resin* contains benzoic acid and olivile. Mannite is

---

[1] The last dose at night should be taken in cold water instead of hot, or it may induce sleeplessness. – EDITOR.

found in the green leaves and unripe fruit. The oil, *Oleum Olivæ*, non-drying, fixed, solidifies on treatment with nitrous acid or mercuric nitrate, is slightly soluble in alcohol, miscible with ether, chloroform or carbon disulphide. The specific gravity is 0·910 to 0·915 at 25° C. or 77° F. It is pale yellow or greenish-yellow, with a faint odour and bland taste, becoming slightly acrid. At a lower temperature than 10° C. or 50° F. it may become a soft, granular mass. Tripalmitin crystallizes and the remaining fluid is chiefly triolein. There are also arachidic esters and a little free oleic acid.

¶ *Medicinal Action and Uses.* The *leaves* are astringent and antiseptic. Internally, a decoction of 2 handsful boiled in a quart of water until reduced to half a pint has been used in the Levant in obstinate fevers. Both leaves and bark have valuable febrifugal qualities.

The *oil* is a nourishing demulcent and laxative. Externally, it relieves pruritis, the effects of stings or burns, and is a good vehicle for liniments. With alcohol it is a good hair-tonic. As a lubricant it is valuable in skin, muscular, joint, kidney and chest complaints, or abdominal chill, typhoid and scarlet fevers, plague and dropsies. Delicate babies absorb its nourishing properties well through the skin. Its value in worms or gall-stones is uncertain.

Internally, it is a laxative and disperser of acids, and a mechanical antidote to irritant poisons. It is often used in enemas. It is the best fat for cooking, and a valuable article of diet for both sick and healthy of all ages. It can easily be taken with milk, orange or lemon juice, etc.

¶ *Dosage.* As a laxative, 1 to 2 fluid ounces.

¶ *Adulterants.* Cotton-seed, rape, sesame, arachis and poppy-seed oils are the many adulterants found, and several official chemical tests are practised for their detection.

¶ *Other Species.* The flowers of *Olea fragrans* or Lanhoa give its odour to the famous Chulan or Schoulang tea of China.

ONION

Allium cepa (LINN.)
N.O. Liliaceæ

Part Used. Bulb

¶ *Medicinal Action and Uses.* Antiseptic, diuretic. A roasted Onion is a useful application to tumours or earache.

The juice made into a syrup is good for colds and coughs. Hollands gin, in which Onions have been macerated, is given as a cure for gravel and dropsy.

ONION, POTATO

Allium cepa, var. aggregatum
N.O. Liliaceæ

Synonyms. The Underground Onion. Egyptian Onion
Part Used. Bulb

The Potato Onion, also known as the Underground Onion, from its habit of increasing its bulbs beneath the surface, is very prolific. It is a valuable vegetable because it furnishes sound, tender, full-sized bulbs at midsummer, three months before the ordinary Onion crop is harvested. The bulbs are rather large, of irregular shape, from 2 to over 3 inches in diameter and about 2 inches thick. The flesh of the bulb is agreeable to the taste and of good quality. The skin is thickish and of a coppery yellow colour.

In Lindley's *Treasury of Botany* this Potato Onion is called the 'Egyptian Onion,' and is stated to have been introduced from Egypt about the beginning of the nineteenth century. It is much cultivated in the West of England, being quite hardy, productive, and as mild in quality as the Spanish Onion.

This variety of Onion produces no seeds and is propagated by the lateral bulbs, which it throws out underground in considerable numbers. It requires a well-worked, moderately rich soil, and is largely grown in Devonshire, where in view of the mildness of the climate, the rule is to plant it in warm, sheltered situations in mid-winter, generally on the shortest day, with the hope of taking up the crop at mid-summer. In colder parts, however, the planting must be deferred until late winter, or early spring, yet the earlier it can be effected the better. The bulbs should be planted almost on the surface, in ground that has been previously well prepared and manured, and in rows 15 inches apart, with 6 to 10 inches space between the bulbs in the rows.

Each bulb will throw out a number of offsets all round it, which grow and develop into full-sized bulbs, which are taken up and dried when ready for pulling, and then stored for use and for future propagation. If the plants attain full maturity each bulb will produce seven or eight bulbs of various sizes. The strongest of these will in their turn produce a number of bulbs, while the weaker ones generally grow into a single, large bulb. The largest bulbs do not always keep so well as the medium-sized ones.

ONION,[1] TREE

Allium cepa, var. proliferum

Synonym. L'oignon d'Egypte
Part Used. Bulb

The Tree Onion is a peculiar kind of Onion that produces at the top of a strong stem about 2 feet high, instead of seeds, a cluster of small bulblets, green at first, but becoming of a brownish-red colour, and about the size of hazel nuts, the stems bearing so heavily that they often require some support.

This singular variety of Onion was introduced into this country from Canada in 1820. The French call it 'l'oignon d'Egypte,' but there is no proof that it is a native of that country. It is quite probable that it is the common Onion introduced from France into Canada by the early colonists and changed by the climate. Besides the stem Onions, a few effects are also produced underground.

The Tree Onion is propagated from the little stem bulbs alone, which are set in February, 2 inches deep and 4 inches apart, in rows 8 inches asunder. When planted in spring, these small bulbs form large ones by the end of the year, but do not produce any bulblets until the following year. When the bulbs are matured, they can be preserved in a cool place after they have been allowed to dry in the sun for a brief period. They are flat and of a coppery colour, their flesh being considered tolerably agreeable to the taste, but rather deficient in flavour. The bulblets are excellent for pickling and keep very well, though the large bulbs do not always keep very long.

¶ *Other Species.* A variety of the Tree Onion, called the Catawissa Onion, or Perennial Tree Onion, was introduced from America thirty or forty years ago. It is distinguished from the Ordinary Tree Onion by the great vigour of its growth and the rapidity with which the bulblets commence to grow without being detached from the top of the stem. They have hardly attained their full size when they emit stems, which also produce bulblets, and in favourable seasons this second tier of bulblets will emit green shoots, leaves and barren stems, bringing the height of the plant up to over 2½ feet. Only a small number of bulblets, generally two or three on each stem, are thus proliferous. The rest do not sprout in the first year and can be used for propagation. The plant is perennial, with long fibrous roots, and may be propagated by division of the tufts, in the same manner as Chives. No offsets are produced underground. A small bed of these is growing at the Whins:[2] they are very hardy, having lived outdoors in open ground all through the severe weather experienced in the early part of 1917. Moles greatly dislike the smell of Onions, and if one is planted in each mole run as it shows up, the mole will leave the ground altogether.

OPOPONAX

Opoponax chironium
N.O. Umbelliferæ

Synonym. Pastinaca Opoponax
Part Used. Concrete juice from the base of stem
Habitat. Levant, Persia, South France, Italy, Greece, Turkey

¶ *Description.* A perennial, with a thick, fleshy root, yellowish in colour. It has a branching stem growing about 1 to 3 feet high, thick and rough near the base. Leaves pinnate, with long petioles and large serrate leaflets, the terminal one cordate, the rest deficient at the base, hairy underneath. The flowers, yellowish, are in large, flat umbels at the top of the branches. The oleo resin is procured by cutting into the stem at the base. The juice that exudes, when sun-dried, forms the Opoponax of commerce. A warm climate is necessary to produce an oleo gum resin of the first quality; that from France is inferior, for this reason. In commerce it is sometimes found in tears, but usually in small, irregular pieces. Colour, reddish-yellow, with whitish specks on the outside, paler inside. Odour, peculiar, strongly unpleasant. Taste, acrid and bitter. It is inflammable, burning brightly.

¶ *Constituents.* Gum-resin, starch, wax, gum, lignin, volatile oil, malic acid, a slight trace of caoutchouc.

¶ *Medicinal Action and Uses.* Antispasmodic, deobstruent. It is now regarded as a medium of feeble powers, but was formerly considered of service as an emmenagogue, also in asthma, chronic visceral affections, hysteria and hypochondriasis. It is employed in perfumery.

---

[1] Onions are a valuable disinfectant. Country people hang up a string of Onions as a protection against an infectious disease, and it has constantly been observed that the Onions will take the disease while the inmates remain immune. For this reason it is important to examine Onions before they are cooked, and to discard any which are imperfect. – EDITOR.

[2] The author's house at Chalfont St Peter. – EDITOR.

¶ *Dose.* 10 to 30 grains.

¶ *Other Species.* From some species of *Mulinum*, and *Bolax Gillesii* and *B. clebaria* (belonging to same order), a gum-resin similar to Opopanax is obtained, which is employed by the native Chilian practitioners.

ORANGE, BITTER

Citrus vulgaris (RISSO.)
var. Bigaradia

ORANGE, SWEET

Citrus Aurantium (LINN.)
var. dulcis
N.O. Rutaceæ

Synonyms. Citrus vulgaris. Citrus Bigaradia. Citrus aurantium amara. Bigaradier. Bigarade Orange. Bitter Orange. Seville Orange. (Sweet) Portugal Orange. China Orange. Citrus dulcis

Parts Used. Fruit, flowers, peel

Habitat. India, China. Cultivated in Spain, Madeira, etc.

¶ *Description.* Both common and official names are derived from the Sanskrit *nagaranga* through the Arabic *naranj*.

It is a small tree with a smooth, greyish-brown bark and branches that spread into a fairly regular hemisphere. The oval, alternate, evergreen leaves, 3 to 4 inches long, have sometimes a spine in the axil. They are glossy, dark green on the upper side, paler beneath. The calyx is cup-shaped and the thick, fleshy petals, five in number, are intensely white, and curl back.

The fruit is earth-shaped, a little rougher and darker than the common, sweet orange: the flowers are more strongly scented and the glands in the rind are concave instead of convex.

The first mention of oranges appears in the writings of Arabs, the time and manner of their first cultivation in Europe being uncertain.

The small, immature fruits are sometimes used under the name of *Orange berries* for flavouring Curaçoa. They are the size of a cherry and dark greyish-brown in colour. Formerly an essence was extracted from them.

The peel is used both fresh and dried. Much is imported from Malta, cut more thinly than that prepared in England.

In Grasse the blossoms are candied in large quantities.

Oil of petit grain is made from the leaves and young shoots.

The volatile oil of the bitter Orange peel is known as Oil of Bigarade, and Sweet Orange oil as Oil of Portugal. For methods of extraction, *see* LEMON.

Orange oil is one of the most difficult to preserve, the most satisfactory method being to add 10 per cent. of its volume of olive oil.

The flowers yield by distillation an essential oil known as 'Neroli,' which forms one of the chief constituents of Eau-de-Cologne. A pomade and an oil are also obtained from them by maceration.

The oil from Sweet Orange blossoms is found in commerce under the name of 'Neroli petalæ.' Being far less fragrant it only fetches half the price of neroli oil and on that account is frequently used to adulterate the true neroli oil.

The largest Bigarade-tree plantations are to be found in the South of France, in Calabria and in Sicily. The centre of the industry of neroli oil is the South of France, where the bitter Orange is extensively cultivated for that purpose alone. The tree requires a dry soil with a southern aspect. It bears flowers three years after grafting, increasing every year until it reaches its maximum, when it is about twenty years old. The quantity depends on the age and situation, a full-grown tree yielding on an average 50 to 60 lb. of blossoms. One hundred Orange trees, at the age of ten years, will occupy nearly an acre of land, and will produce during the season about 2,200 lb. of Orange flowers. The flowering season is in May and the flowers are gathered two or three times a week, after sunrise. When the autumn is mild and atmospheric conditions are favourable, flowering takes place in October, and this supplementary harvest lasts until January, or till a frosty morning stops the flowering. These autumn flowers have much less perfume than those of the spring and the custom is to value them at only one-half the price of May flowers. The Bitter Orange and Edible Orange trees bear a great resemblance to each other, but their leaf-stalks show a marked difference, that of the Bitter Orange being broadened out in the shape of a heart. The yield of oil is greatly influenced by the temperature and atmospheric conditions prevailing at the time of gathering. In warm weather it may amount to as much as 1,400 grams per 100 kilogrammes of flowers, but under adverse conditions, such as damp, cool and changeable weather, considerable diminution is experienced. Generally the largest yields are obtained at the end of the flowering season, on account of the warmer temperature.

The method most followed for extraction of the oil is by distillation, which yields a higher percentage of oil from the flowers than maceration or absorption in fats and volatile solvents. The flowers are distilled immediately after gathering, the essential oil rising to the surface of the distillate is drawn off, while the aqueous portion is sold as 'Orange Flower Water.' Orange flower water is being increasingly used in France by biscuit-makers to give crispness to their products, and some of the English biscuit-makers have also adopted it for this purpose.

There is a marked difference in the scent of the oils obtained by the different processes. Neroli obtained by distillation has quite a different odour from the fresh Orange flower; the oils obtained by solvents and by maceration and enfleurage are truest to the scent of the natural flower. From 100 kilogrammes of flowers 1,000 grams of oil are obtained; by volatile solvents, 600 grams; by maceration, 400 grams; and by enfleurage, only about 100 grams of oil.

Orange Flower Oil as obtained from pomatum, slightly modified with other extracts, can be employed to make 'Sweet Pea' and 'Magnolia' perfumes, the natural odours of which it slightly resembles.

The use of Orange-blossom as a bridal decoration is neither long-established nor indigenous, as it was introduced into this country from France only about a hundred years ago.

¶ *Constituents.* The peel of var. *Bigaradia* contains volatile oil, three glucosides, hesperidin, isohesperidin, an amorphous bitter principle, Aurantiamarin, aurantiamaric acid, resin, etc.

The ethyl ether of -naphthol, under the name of *nerolin*, is an artificial oil of neroli, said to be ten times as strong.

Oil of Orange Flowers is

'soluble in an equal volume of alcohol, the solution having a violet fluorescence and a neutral reaction to litmus paper. The specific gravity is 0·868 to 0·880 at 25° C. (77° F.). When agitated with a concentrated solution of sodium bisulphate it assumes a permanent purple-red colour.'

It must not be coloured by sulphuretted hydrogen.

Oil of Sweet Orange Peel contains at least 90 per cent. δ-limonene, the remaining 10 per cent. being the odorous constituents, citral, citronellal, etc. It is a yellow liquid with the specific gravity 0·842 to 0·846 at 25° C. (77° F.).

Oil of Bitter Orange Peel, a pale yellow liquid, is soluble in four volumes of alcohol, the solution being neutral to litmus paper. The specific gravity is 0·842 to 0·848 at 25° C. (77° F.). The odour is more delicate than that of the Sweet Orange.

Fuming nitric acid gives a dark green colour to sweet peel and a brown to the bitter.

¶ *Medicinal Action and Uses.* The oil is used chiefly as a flavouring agent, but may be used in the same way as oil of turpentine in chronic bronchitis. It is non-irritant to the kidneys and pleasant to take.

On the Continent an infusion of dried flowers is used as a mild nervous stimulant.

The powdered Bitter Orange peel should be dried over freshly-burnt lime. For flavouring, the sweet peel is better, and as a tonic, that of the Seville or Bigaradia is preferred.

A syrup and an elixir are used for flavouring, and a wine as a vehicle for medicines.

The compound wine is too dangerous as an intoxicant, being mixed with absinthium, to be recommended as a tonic.

¶ *Preparations of Bitter Orange.* Syrup, B.P., ½ to 1 drachm. Tincture, B.P. and U.S.P., ½ to 1 drachm. Infusion of Orange, B.P., 4 to 8 drachms. Infusion of Orange Compound, B.P., 4 to 8 drachms. Compound spirit, U.S.P., 1 to 2 drachms. Syrup, B.P., ½ to 1 drachm. Wine, B.P., a wineglassful.

¶ *Preparations of Sweet Orange.* Syrup, B.P. and U.S.P., ½ to 1 drachm. Tincture, U.S.P., ½ to 1 drachm.

ORCHIDS

N.O. Orchidaceæ
Orchis maculata
Orchis latifolia
Orchis mascula
Orchis Morio
Orchis militaris
Orchis saccifera
Orchis pyrimidalis
Orchis coriphora
Orchis conopea

Synonyms. Salep. Saloop. Sahlep. Satyrion. Levant Salep
Part Used. Root

Most of the Orchids native to this country have tuberous roots full of a highly nutritious starch-like substance, called Bassorin, of a sweetish taste and with a faint, somewhat unpleasant smell, which replaces starch as a reserve material. In Turkey and Persia this has for many centuries been extracted from the tubers of various kinds of Orchis and exported under the name of *Sahlep* (an Arabian word, corrupted into English as Saloop or Salep), which has long been used, especially in the East, for making a wholesome and nutritious drink of the same name. Before coffee supplanted it, it used to be sold at stalls in the streets of London, and was held in great repute in herbal medicine, being largely employed as a strengthening and demulcent agent. The best English Salep came from Oxfordshire, but the tubers were chiefly imported from the East.

Charles Lamb refers to a 'Salopian shop' in Fleet Street, and says that to many tastes it has 'a delicacy beyond the China luxury,' and adds that a basin of it at three-halfpence, accompanied by a slice of bread-and-butter at a halfpenny, is an ideal breakfast for a chimney-sweep. Though Salep is no longer a popular London beverage, before the war it was regularly sold by street merchants in Constantinople as a hot drink during the winter.

Salep is collected in central and southern Europe and Asia. Most, if not all, of the species of *Orchis* and some allied plants found in Europe and Northern Asia, are provided with tubers which when duly prepared are capable of furnishing Salep. The varieties represent two forms, the one with branched, the other, and preferable one, with rounded and unbranched tubers. The tubers occur in pairs, one a little larger than the other.

Of those species actually used the following are the more important: *Orchis mascula* (Linn.), *O. Morio* (Linn.), *O. militaris* (Linn.), *O. ustulata* (Linn.), *O. pyramidalis* (Linn.), *O. coriophora* (Linn.), *O. longieruris* (Link.). These species, which have the tubers *entire*, are natives of the greater part of Central and Southern Europe, Turkey, the Caucasus and Asia Minor. The following species, with *palmate* or lobed tubers, are equally widely distributed: *O. maculata* (Linn.), *O. saccifera* (Brong.), *O. conopea* (Linn.), and *O. latifolia* (Linn.).

In the East, Salep is mostly obtained from *O. morio*, which is of frequent occurrence in this country in chalky soils, but it can be made here equally well from *O. mascula*, the Early Purple Orchis, *O. maculata* and *O. latifolia*, which are more common and very widely distributed throughout the country.

O. mascula (Linn.), the Early Purple Orchis, common in English woods, is in flower from mid-April to mid-June. A single flower-stem rises from the tuberous root, bearing flowers that as a rule are of a rich purple colour, mottled with lighter and darker shades, though often found of every tint from purple to pure white. Each flower has a long spur which turns upwards. The leaves are lance-shaped and do not rise far from the ground, giving a rosette-like effect, and are irregularly blotched with dark purple markings, which help to render the plant conspicuous. In woods and meadowland, the plant often attains a height of a foot or more, while on exposed and breezy downs it is seldom more than 6 inches high.

The blossoms are practically odourless in some specimens, whilst those of others are faintly fragrant, but in most cases the smell is not only strong, but offensive, especially in the evening. There is no honey in the flowers, but a sweet juice in the walls of the spur, which insects pierce with their probosces and suck out. The plant is provided with two fleshy, egg-shaped tubers, one serving to provide the necessities of the plant, shrinking as the plant reaches maturity, the other receiving the leaves' surplus supplies of foodstuffs to store for use in the following season.

Witches were supposed to use the tubers in their philtres, the fresh tuber being given to promote true love, and the withered one to check wrong passions. Culpepper speaks of them as 'under the dominion of Venus,' and tells us among other things, that 'being bruised and applied to the place' they heal the King's Evil.

This Early Purple Orchis in Northants is called 'Cuckoos,' because it comes into flower about the time when the cuckoo first calls. In Dorset it has the name of 'Granfer Griggles,' and the wild Hyacinth, which often flowers by its side, bears the name of 'Granny Griggles.'

O. Morio (Linn.), the Green-winged Meadow Orchis, is in flower about the same time as the Early Purple Orchis and resembles it in habit. It grows in meadows and is often very abundant. It is, however, a shorter plant, bearing fewer flowers in the spike, and is best distinguished by its two lateral sepals, which are bent upwards to form a kind of hood, being strongly marked with parallel green veins.

O. maculata (Linn.), the Spotted Orchis, receives its name from the blotches of reddish-brown, which mark the upper surfaces of the leaves similarly to those of *O. mascula*. The flowers, massed in spikes, about 3 inches long, on a stem about a foot high, with the leaves springing from it at distant intervals, vary in hue from pale lilac to rich purple, are curiously marked with dark lines and spots, and are very similar in structure to those of the Early Purple Orchis. It grows abundantly on heaths and commons, flowering in June and July.

In this species, the tubers are divided into two or three finger-like lobes, hence the plant has been known as 'Dead Men's Fingers' (*Hamlet*, IV, vii), Hand Orchis, or Palma Christi. Gerard calls it the 'Female Satyrion,' orchids being known in his time as Satyrions, from a legend that they were specially connected with the Satyrs. The plants were believed to be the food of the Satyrs, and to have incited them to excesses. Orchis, in the old mythology, was the son of a Satyr and a nymph, who, when killed by the Bacchanalians for his insult to a priestess of Bacchus, was turned, on the prayer of his father, into the flower that bears his name.

O. latifolia (Linn.), the March Orchis, is a taller plant than the last, but has also palmate roots. The broad leaves are very erect, the flowers rose-coloured or purple, the finely-tapering bracts being longer than the flowers. This species, in common with the three preceding ones, sometimes bears white flowers. It is very frequent in marshes and damp pastures, and will be found in bloom in June and July.

The Salep of commerce is prepared chiefly in the Levant, being largely collected in Asia Minor, but to some extent also in Germany and other parts of Europe. The European Salep is always smaller than the Oriental Salep. The drug found in English trade is mostly imported from Smyrna. That sold in Germany is partly obtained from plants growing wild in the Taunus Mountains, the Odenwald and other districts. Salep is also collected in Greece and used in that country and in Turkey in the form of a decoction, which is sweetened with honey and taken as an early morning drink. The Salep of India is mostly produced on the hills of Afghanistan, Beluchistan, Kabul and Bokhara, and also from the Nilgiri Hills and Ceylon.

The drug was known to Dioscorides and the Arabians, as well as to the herbalists and physicians of the Middle Ages, by whom it was mostly prescribed in the fresh state. Gerard (1636 edition) gives excellent figures of the various orchids, whose tubers, he says, 'our age useth.' Geoffrey (1740), having recognized the salep imported from the Levant to be the tubers of an Orchis, pointed out how it might be prepared from the species indigenous to France.

Levant Salep, as occurring in commerce, consists of tubers ½ inch to 1 inch in length, oblong in form, often pointed at the lower end and rounded at the upper, where is a depressed scar left by the stem; palmate tubers are infrequent. They are generally shrunken and contorted, covered with a roughly granular skin, pale brown, translucent, very hard and horny, practically inodorous and with an insipid, mucilaginous taste. After maceration in water for several hours the tubers regain their original form and size.

The branched or palmate Salep tubers (*Radix palmæ Christi*) are somewhat flattened and palmately two to five branched. The elongated mucilage cells are not so large as in the other form.

German Salep is more translucent and gummy-looking than that of the Levant, and more carefully prepared.

The Oriental Royal Salep, said to be much used as a food in Afghanistan, has been identified as the product of a bulbous plant related to the onion, *Allium Macleanii* (*Pharm. Journal*, Sept., 1889).

The Salep of the Indian bazaars, known as *Salib misri*, for fine qualities of which great prices are paid, is derived from certain species of *Eulophia*.

¶ *Collection and Preparation.* Tubers required for making Salep are taken up at the close of the summer, when the seed-vessels are fully formed, as the next year's tubers then contain the largest amount of starchy matter and are full and fleshy.

The shrivelled ones having been thrown aside, those which are plump are washed and then immersed for a short time in boiling water, this scalding process destroying their vitality and removing the bitterness of their fresh state and making them dry more readily. The outer skins are then rubbed off and the tubers are dried, either by exposure to the sun, or to a gentle artificial heat in an oven for ten minutes and heated to about bread-making temperature. On removing from the oven, their milky appearance will have changed to an almost transparent and horny state, though the bulk will not be reduced. They are then placed in the fresh air to dry and harden for a few days, when they are ready for use, or to be stored for as long as desired, as damp does not affect them. The dried tubers are generally ground to powder before using; it has a yellowish colour.

¶ *Constituents and Uses.* The constituents of Salep are subject to great variation, according to the season of collection. Raspail found the old tuber, collected in autumn, to be free from starch, while the young one was richly supplied with it.

The most important constituent is mucilage, amounting to 48 per cent. It also contains sugar (1 per cent.), starch (2·7 per cent.), nitrogenous substance (5 per cent.), and when fresh a trace of volatile oil. It yields

2 per cent. of ash, consisting chiefly of phosphates and chlorides of potassium and calcium.

Salep is very nutritive and demulcent, for which properties it has been used from time immemorial. It forms a diet of especial value to convalescents and children, being boiled' with milk or water, flavoured and prepared in the same way as arrowroot. A decoction flavoured with sugar and spice, or wine, is an agreeable drink for invalids. Sassafras chips were sometimes added, or cloves, cinnamon and ginger.

From the large quantity of farinaceous matter contained in a small bulk, it was considered so important an article of diet as to constitute a part of the stores of every ship's company in the days of sailing ships and long voyages, an ounce, dissolved in 2 quarts of boiling water, being considered sufficient subsistence for each man per day, should provisions run short. In this form it is employed in some parts of Europe and Asia as an article of diet. It is to the mucilage contained in the tuber that Salep owes its power of forming jelly, only 1 part of Salep to 50 parts of boiling water being needed for the purpose.

To allay irritation of the gastro-intestinal canal, it is used in mucilage made by shaking 1 part of powdered Salep with 10 parts of cold water, until it is uniformly diffused, when 90 parts of boiling water are added and the whole well agitated. It has thus been recommended as an article of diet for infants and invalids suffering from chronic diarrhœa and bilious fevers. In the German Pharmacopœia, a mucilage of Salep appears as an official preparation.

OSIER, RED AMERICAN

Cornus sericea (LINN.)
N.O. Cornaceæ

Synonyms. Swamp's Dogwood. Red Willow. Silky Cornel. Female Dogwood. Blueberry. Kinnikinnik. Rose Willow.
(*French*) Cornouille
Parts Used. Root-bark and bark
Habitat. North America, Florida to Mississippi

¶ *Description.* A water-loving shrub, growing from 6 to 12 feet high. Branches spreading, dark purplish; branchlets silky downy; leaves narrowly ovate or elliptical, pointed, smooth above, silky downy below and often hairy upon ribs on petioles from half an inch to an inch long. Flowers yellowish white, small, disposed in large terminal, depressed and woolly cymes or corymbs. Berries globose, bright blue, stone compressed. It is found in moist woods and on the margins of rivers, flowering in June and July.

¶ *Constituents.* The active properties are similar to those found in Peruvian Bark, except that there is more gum mucilage and extractive matter and less resin quinine and tannin.

¶ *Medicinal Action and Uses.* It is tonic astringent and slightly stimulant, used in periodical and typhoid fever. Taken internally it increases the strength and frequency of the pulse, elevating the temperature of the body. It should be used in the dried state, the fresh bark being likely to upset the stomach.

The powdered bark has been used as toothpowder, to preserve the gums and make the teeth white; the flowers have been used in place of chamomile.

OSIER, GREEN

Cornus circinata
N.O. Cornaceæ

Part Used. Fresh bark

A homœopathic tincture of the fresh bark is administered in ulcerated conditions of the mucous membranes and in liver complaints and jaundice.

OX-EYE DAISY. *See* DAISY

OX-TONGUE

Helminthia echioides

Part Used. Herb

Closely allied to the Sow Thistles and somewhat resembling them in general appearance is the Bristly Ox Tongue (*Helminthia echioides*), frequently met with in England on hedgebanks and on waste ground, especially on clay soil, but less common in Ireland and rare in Scotland.

¶ *Description.* It is somewhat stout and coarse, the sturdy stems attaining a height of from 2 to 3 feet, branching freely and covered with short, stiff hairs, each of which springs from a raised spot and is hooked at the end.

The lower leaves are much longer than the

upper, of lanceolate or spear-head form, with their margins coarsely and irregularly toothed and waved. The upper leaves are small and stalkless, heart-shaped and clasping the stem with their bases. All the leaves are of a greyish-green hue and very tough to the touch.

The flower-heads are ordinarily somewhat clustered together on short stalks and form an irregular, terminal mass at the ends of the main stems. The involucre, or ring of bracts from which the florets spring, is doubled – outside the ring of eight to ten narrow and nearly erect scales, simple in form and thin in texture, is an outer ring composed of a smaller number of spiny bracts of a broad heart-shape, in their roughness of surface and general character resembling the leaves of the plant. The combination of the inner and outer bracts may be roughly compared to a cup and saucer, and gives the plant a singular appearance.

The Ox Tongue is in blossom during June and July; all the florets of the flower-heads, as in the Dandelion, are of a rich golden yellow.

The generic name, *Helminthia*, is Greek in origin and signifies a small kind of worm. It is suggested that the name was bestowed from the form of the fruit, but it seems more likely that the name may have been applied to the plant from some former belief in its power as a vermifuge. It has by some botanists been assigned to the genus *Picris*. The specific name, *echioides*, refers to the rough, prickly character of the stems and leaves.

In spite of its spiny character, the Ox Tongue was used as a pot-herb in the same manner as the Sow Thistles, but can only be eaten when young, when it is said to have a pleasant taste. The juice is milky, bitter, but not extremely acrid.

¶ *Other Species.*

The HAWKWEED OX-TONGUE (*Picris hieracioides*), a closely allied plant, has been similarly employed as a pot-herb. It is a rather slender plant, 2 to 3 feet high, the stems rough with hooked bristles, the stalkless leaves narrow, rough and toothed; flowers numerous and yellow. It is abundant on the edges of fields, especially in a gravelly or calcareous soil, and flowers from July to September. The name of the genus is derived from the Greek *picros* (bitter), from the bitter taste of the plant.

See (SOW) THISTLE.

PÆONY

Pæonia officinalis (LINN.)
N.O. Ranunculaceæ

Synonym. Pæonia Corallina
Part Used. Root

The Pæony is not indigenous to Great Britain, and only grows wild on an island called the Steep Holmes, in the Severn, where it was probably introduced some centuries ago.

The varieties Female and Male Pæony have no reference to the sexes of the flowers. The roots of the Female or Common Pæony are composed of several roundish, thick knobs or tubers, which hang below each other, connected by strings. The stems are green (red when quite young) and about 2½ feet high. The leaves are composed of several unequal lobes, which are cut into many segments; they are of a paler green colour than those of the so-called Male Pæony, and the flowers are of a deeper purple colour. From this variety are derived the double garden Pæonies.

Many of the species have very fragrant flowers.

The roots of the Male Pæony – the kind found wild on the island in the Severn – are composed of several oblong knobs, hanging by strings fastened to the main head. The stems are the same height as in the preceding, and bear large single flowers, composed of five or six large roundish red (or sometimes white) petals. The flowers of both sorts open in May, the seeds ripening in the autumn.

The last-named variety is the kind formerly much cultivated for the roots, which were celebrated for their medicinal value in disorders of the head and nerves. It has been known also as *Pæonia Corallina*.

The genus is supposed to have been named after the physician Pæos, who cured Pluto and other gods of wounds received during the Trojan War with the aid of this plant.

The superstitions connected with the Pæony are numerous. In ancient times, it was thought to be of divine origin, an emanation from the moon, and to shine during the night, protecting shepherds and their flocks, and also the harvest from injury, driving away evil spirits and averting tempests. Josephus speaks of the Pæony as a wonderful and curious plant. He says – according to Gerard – that 'to pluck it up by the roots will cause danger to he that touches it, therefore a string must be fastened to it in the night and a hungry dog tied thereto, who being allured by the smell of roasted flesh set towards him may pluck it up by the roots.' Pliny and Theophrastus assert

'that of necessity it must be gathered in the

night, for if any man shall pluck of the fruit in the daytime, being seen of the woodpecker, he is in danger to lose his eyes.'

Gerard adds:

'But all these things be most vaine and frivolous, for the root of Peionne may be removed at any time of the yeare, day, or houre whatsoever.'

The seeds used to be strung as a necklace and worn as a charm against evil spirits.

Gerard says:

'The black graines (that is the seed) to the number of fifteene taken in wine or mead is a speciall remedie for those that are troubled in the night with the disease called the Nightmare, which is as though a heavy burthen were laid upon them and they oppressed therewith, as if they were overcome with their enemies, or overprest with some great weight or burthen; and they are also good against melancholie dreames.'

A drink called 'Pæony-water' made from the plant was once much used, and the kernels or seeds were used in cookery as a spice.

'Stick the cream with Pæony kernels,' *Mrs. Glasse's Cookery* (1796).

¶ *Cultivation.* Pæonies are extremely hardy and will grow in almost any soil or situation, in sun or shade. The best soil, however, is a deep, rich loam, which should be well trenched and manured, previous to planting.

Propagation is by division of roots, which increase very quickly. The best season for transplanting is towards the end of August, or the beginning of September. In dividing the roots, care must be taken to preserve a bud upon the crown of each offset.

Single varieties are generally propagated from seeds, sown in autumn, soon after they are ripe, upon a bed of light soil, covering them with ¼ inch of soil. Water well in dry weather and keep clear from weeds. Leave the young plants in this bed two years, transplanting in September.

¶ *Part Used.* The root, dried and powdered. It is dug in the autumn, from plants at least two years old. The roots should be cleansed carefully in cold water with a brush and only be allowed to remain in the water as short a time as possible. Then spread out on trays in the sun, or on the floor, or on shelves in a kitchen, or other warm room for ten days or more. When somewhat shrunken, roots may be finished off more quickly in greater heat over a stove or gas fire, or in an open oven, when the fire has just gone out. Dried roots must always be dry to the core and brittle.

Pæony root occurs in commerce in pieces averaging 3 inches long and ⅛ to ¼ inch in diameter, spindle-shaped, strongly furrowed and shrunken longitudinally, of a pinkish grey or dirty white colour, generally having been scraped. The transverse section is starchy and radiate, the rays more or less tinged with purple. The root has no odour, but its taste is sweet at first, and then bitter.

¶ *Medicinal Action and Uses.* Antispasmodic, tonic. Pæony root has been successfully employed in convulsions and spasmodic nervous affections, such as epilepsy, etc.

It was formerly considered very efficacious for lunacy. An old writer tells us: 'If a man layeth this wort over the lunatic as he lies, soon he upheaveth himself whole.'

The infusion of 1 oz. of powdered root in a pint of boiling water is taken in wineglassful doses, three or four times daily.

An infusion of the powdered root has been recommended for obstructions of the liver, and for complaints arising from such obstructions.

¶ *Other Species.*
Pæonia Albiflora, distinguished by its smooth recurved follicles, is a native of Siberia, and the whole of Northern Asia; the roots of this are sometimes boiled by the natives, and eaten in broth; they also grind the seeds and put them into their tea.

PAPAW

Carica Papaya (LINN.)
N.O. Cucurbitaceæ

Synonyms. Melon Tree. Mamæire. Papaya Vulgaris (D.C.)
Parts Used. Fruit juice, seeds, leaves – pawpain
Habitat. South America, West Indies, and cultivated in most tropical countries

¶ *Description.* A small tree seldom above 20 feet high, 1 foot in diameter, tapering to about 4 or 5 inches at its summit. It has a spongy soft wood, hollow in centre; leaves are as large as 2 feet in diameter, deeply cut into seven lobes, ending in sharp points and margins irregularly waived; foot-stalks 2 feet long, diverge horizontally from the stem;

fruit oblong, dingy green yellow colour, about 10 inches long, 3 or 4 broad with projecting angles, a rind like a gourd, thick and fleshy; the central cavity contains a quantity of black wrinkled seeds.

¶ *Constituents.* The seeds of the Papaw tree contain a glucoside, Caricin, which resembles Sinigrin, also the ferment Myrosin, and by reaction of the two a volatile, pungent body suggestive of mustard oil. From the leaves an alkaloid called carpaine has been obtained; physiologically this alkaloid has the same effect on the heart as digitalis. Papain is often adulterated with starch; in cases of acidity it is said to be much superior to pancreatin because its action is not affected to any extent by its contact with the acid. This plant must not be confounded with the custard apple, which is often called Papaw and botanically known as *Uvaria triloba*.

¶ *Medicinal Action and Uses*. The juice of the tree or an infusion of the leaves and fruit makes the toughest meat tender when rubbed with it or cooked in the leaves; if chickens and pigs are fed on the leaves it will make their flesh tender. The ripe fruit is refreshing and palatable; it is sometimes used as a sauce; the seeds cannot be detected from capers; it is sometimes preserved in sugar or boiled like turnips. The juice is used to remove freckles; it is also a strong vermifuge. The leaves are used as a substitute for soap; when the unripe fruit is pierced with a bone knife a milky juice exudes which is collected in a basin and allowed to coagulate; this is dried in the sun and contains a propeolytic enzyme which acts as a neutral or alkaline solution, and is given for impaired digestion. Pawpain is the dried white powdered unripe juice of Papaw, a ferment, and strongly suggests pepsin in odour, taste and appearance. It is said to dissolve the fibrinous membrane in croup and diphtheria, a solution over the pharynx painted every five minutes; when injected into the circulation in large doses it paralyses the heart; it is recommended to destroy warts and epithelioma, tubercules, etc.; is not caustic or astringent, but has the virtue of dissolving muscular and connective tissue.

The fresh leaves have been used as a dressing for foul wounds; internally the juice is useful in dyspepsia and catarrh of the stomach; the juice has a tendency to deteriorate by undergoing butyric fermentation, but this can be overcome by the addition of glycerine, which preserves it without impairing its digestive power.

See PAPAW SEEDS.

PAPAW SEEDS

Asimina triloba
N.O. Anonaceæ

Synonyms. Custard Apple. Uvaria triloba
Parts Used. Seeds, bark, and leaves
Habitat. Middle, Southern and Western States, also India, Africa, Asia

¶ *Description*. A small beautiful tree, growing up to 20 feet. The young shoots and leaves are at first clothed in a rusty down which soon becomes glabrous. The leaves are thin, smooth, entire, ovate, oblong, acuminate, 8 to 12 inches long by 3 broad, and tapering to very short petioles. Flowers dull purple, axillary, solitary; petals veiny, round, ovate, outer one orbicular, three or four times as large as the calyx. Flowers appear same time as leaves, March to June, and are about 1½ inches wide. Fruit, yellowish, ovoid oblong, pulpy pod about 3 inches long and 1 inch diameter, fragrant, sweet, ripe in autumn and contains about eight seeds; before fruit is ripe it has an unpleasant smell and when ripe after frost it is luscious and similar to custard; it is considered healthy to eat, being sedative and laxative; the seeds are the part used; these have a fœtid smell like straminium; they are covered with an exterior coat which is tough and hard, light brown colour and smooth externally, wrinkled and lighter inside. It encloses a white kernel, deeply fissured on both sides and compressed, almost scentless, slightly bitter and sweet and dry and powdery when chewed; it leaves a faint, persistent, unpleasant sensation of sickness; seeds vary in shape, being flat ovoid, sometimes circular and somewhat reniform, with a depression along the centre of each flat surface, and frequently a ridge in place of the furrow.

¶ *Constituents*. Fixed oil, a resin, a resin insoluble in ether, glucose and extractive.

¶ *Medicinal Action and Uses*. Emetic, for which a saturated tincture of the bruised seeds is employed; dose, 10 to 60 drops. The bark is a bitter tonic and is said to contain a powerful acid, the leaves are used as an application to boils and ulcers.

¶ *Other Species*.

Uvaria Natrum. Root aromatic and fragrant, used in India in intermittent fevers and liver complaints. Bruised in salt water is used as an application to certain skin diseases. A fragrant greenish oil is distilled from it.

U. tripelaloidea. When incised, gives a fragrant gum.

U. febrifuga, so called by the Indians of Orinoco, who use its flowers for fevers.

U. longifolia. A perfume oil is extracted from the flowers in Bourbon and several other species are also fragrant.

U. Zeylandica and *U. cordata* have edible fruits.

PARADISE GRAINS. *See* PEPPER, HUNGARIAN

PARAGUAY TEA

Ilex Paraguayensis (A. ST. HIL).
N.O. Aquifoliaceæ

Synonyms. Paraguay Herb. Paraguay. Maté. Ilex Maté. Yerba Maté. Houx Maté. Jesuit's Tea. Brazil Tea. Gôn gouha
Part Used. Leaves
Habitat. Brazil, Argentina, Paraguay

¶ *Description.* This large, white-flowered shrub grows wild near streams, but is largely cultivated in South America for the drink obtained by infusing the leaves. The leaves are alternate, large, oval or lanceolate and broadly toothed. The fruit is a red drupe the size of pepper grains. Its name of Yerba signifies the herb *par excellence*, and the consumption in South America is vast, as it is drunk at every meal and hour. 'Maté' is derived from the name of the vessel in which it is infused in the manner of tea, burnt sugar or lemon-juice being added. It is sucked through a tube, usually of silver, with a bulb strainer at the end, and the cup is passed round.

If the powder is dropped into water and stirred the mixture is called *cha maté*.

Large sums are paid to the Government for permission to gather the leaves, which are dried by heat and powdered. The season is from December to August. Paraguay exports 5 to 6 million pounds annually.

The tea is very sustaining, and sometimes it is the only refreshment carried for a journey of several days.

The odour is not very agreeable, but is soon unnoticed. The taste is rather bitter.

¶ *Constituents.* Fresh leaves dried at Cambridge were found to contain caffeine, tannin, ash and insoluble matter.

¶ *Medicinal Action and Uses.* Tonic, diuretic, diaphoretic, and powerfully stimulant. In large doses it causes purging and even vomiting. Fluid extract, ½ to 1 drachm.

¶ *Other Species.*
In South America the infusion of leaves of different species are used, such as *Cassina paragua*, *Psoralea glandulosa* and a *Luxemburgia*.

Ilex vomitoria and *I. Dahoon*, Apalachin or Cassena and Dahoon holly, have emetic properties. A decoction is used by the North Carolina Indians as Yaupon, or ceremonial black drink, as well as in medicine.

PAREIRA

Chondrodendron tomentosum (RUIZ and P.)
N.O. Menispermaceæ

Synonyms. Pereira Brava. Cissampelos Pareira. Velvet Leaf. Ice Vine
Parts Used. Dried root, bark, bruised leaves
Habitat. West Indies, Spanish Main Brazil, Peru

¶ *Description.* A woody vine, climbing a considerable height over trees; very large leaves, often 1 foot long with a silky pubescence, on the inner side grey colour; flowers diœcious in racemes; in the female plant the racemes are longer than the leaves, bearing the flowers in spike fascicles; the berries, first scarlet, then black, are oval, size of large grapes in commerce. The root is cylindrical in varying lengths from ⅓ inch to 5 inches in diameter and from 2 or 3 inches to several feet long; externally blackish brown, longitudinally furrowed, transversed knotty ridges; it is hard, heavy, tough, and when freshly cut has a waxy lustre; interior woody, reddy yellow; transversed section shows several successive eccentric and distinctly radiate concentric zones of projecting secondary bundles fibro-vascular. Stem deeply furrowed; colour grey and covered with patches of lichen; odour, slight, aromatic, sweetish flavour, succeeded by an intense nauseating bitterness, yielding its bitterness and active properties to water or alcohol.

¶ *Constituents.* A soft resin, yellow bitter principle, brown colouring, a nitrogenous substance, fecula, acid calcium malate, various salts and potassium nitrate.

¶ *Medicinal Action and Uses.* Tonic, diuretic, aperient; acts as an antiseptic to the bladder, chiefly employed for the relief of chronic inflammation of the urinary passages, also recommended for calculus affections, leucorrhœa, rheumatism, jaundice, dropsy, and gonorrhœa. In Brazil it is used for poisonous snake bites; a vinous infusion of the root is taken internally, while the bruised leaves of the plant are applied externally.

¶ *Dosages.* Infusion, 1 to 4 fluid ounces. Solid extract, 10 to 20 grains. Fluid extract, ¼ to 2 drachms.

¶ *Other Species.*
Cissampelos Glaberrima, growing in Brazil, appears to possess similar properties, Beberine chondrodine, some stearic acid, tannin and starch.

C. convolulaceum, called by the Peruvians the Wild Grape with reference to the form of the fruit and their acid and not unpleasant flavour; the bark is used as a febrifuge.

Arbuta rufescens, or White Pareira Brava, has a thick woody root which exhibits concentric layers, transversed by very distinct dark medullary rays, interradial spaces being white and rich in starch.

The COMMON FALSE PAREIRA, botanical origin unknown. The arrangement of the woody zones is eccentric and the wavy appearance of true Pareira is absent. It contains no starch, and the root is much lighter and less waxy than the genuine variety.

PARILLA, YELLOW

Menispermum Canadense (LINN.)
N.O. Menispermaceæ

Synonyms. Canadian Moonseed. Texas Sarsaparilla. Moonseed Sarsaparilla. Vine Maple

Parts Used. The rhizome and roots

Habitat. Canada and United States of America. Cultivated in Britain as a hardy, deciduous, ornamental shrub. A closely allied species is indigenous to the temperate parts of Eastern Asia

¶ *Description.* A climbing, woody plant, with a very long root of a fine yellow colour, and a round, striate stem, bright yellow-green when young; leaves, roundish, cordate, peltate, three to seven angled, lobed. Flowers small, yellow, borne in profusion in axillary clusters. Drupes, round, black, with a bloom on them, one-seeded. Seed, crescent-shaped, compressed, the name Moonseed being derived from this lunate shape of the seed. The rhizome is wrinkled longitudinally and has a number of thin, brittle roots; fracture, tough, woody; internally reddish; a thick bark encloses a circle of porous, short, nearly square wood wedges and a large central pith. The root is the official part; it has a persistent bitter, acrid taste and is almost inodorous.

¶ *Constituents.* Berberine and a white amorphous alkaloid termed Menispermum, which has been used as a substitute for Sarsaparilla, some starch and resin.

¶ *Medicinal Action and Uses.* In small doses it is a tonic, diuretic, laxative and alterative. In larger doses it increases the appetite and action of the bowels; in *full* doses, it purges and causes vomiting. It is a superior

laxative bitter; considered very useful in scrofula, cutaneous, rheumatic, syphilitic, mercurial and arthritic diseases; also for dyspepsia, chronic inflammation of the viscera and in general debility. Externally, the decoction has been applied as an embrocation in cutaneous and gouty affections.

¶ *Preparations and Dosages.* Powdered root, ¼ to 1 drachm. Fluid extract, ½ to 1 drachm. Saturated tincture, ½ to 1 drachm. Menispermum, 1 to 4 grains. Decoction, 1 to 4 fluid ounces, three times daily. Menisperine in powder is recommended as a nervine and is considered superior to Sarsaparilla, taken in doses of 1 to 3 grains, three times daily.

¶ *Other Species.*

Some of the species closely allied to *Menispermum* have narcotic properties and are very poisonous: *Anamirta paniculata* yields *Cocculus Indicus,* illegally used to impart bitterness to malt liquor; *Jateorhiza palmata* supplies bitter Columba root, used as a tonic; and *Cissampelos Pareira* is the tonic Pareira Brava.

See COLUMBA, COCCULUS, PAREIRA.

(POISON)
PARIS, HERB

Paris quadrifolia (LINN.)
N.O. Trilliaceæ

Synonyms. Herba Paris. Solanum quadrifolium. Aconitum pardalianches. True Love. One Berry

(French) Parisette

(German) Einbeere

Part Used. The entire plant, just coming into bloom

Habitat. Europe, Russian Asia, and fairly abundant in Britain, but confined to certain places

¶ *Description.* This singular plant gets its generic name of *Paris* from *par* (paris), equal on account of the regularity of its leaves. In olden times it was much esteemed and used in medicine, but to-day its use is almost confined to homœopathy. It is a

herbaceous perennial plant found in moist places and damp shady woods. It has a creeping fleshy rootstock, a simple smooth upright stem about 1 foot high, crowned near its top with four pointed leaves, from the centre of which rises a solitary greeny-white

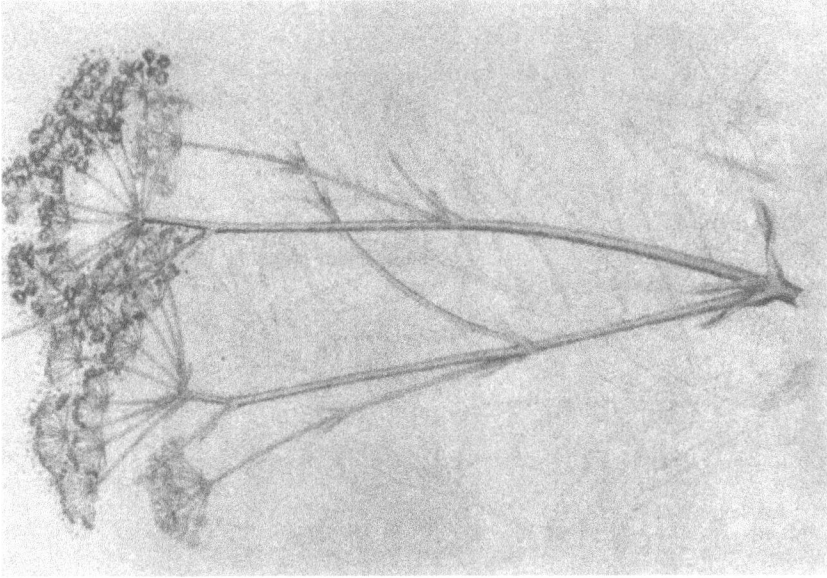

OPOPONAX
Opoponax Chironium

FOOLS' PARSLEY
Æthusa Cynapium

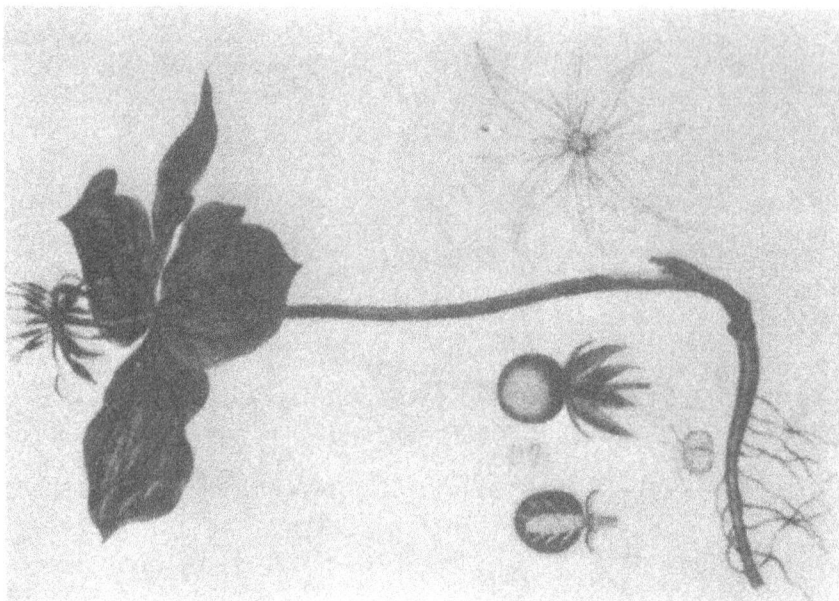

HERB PARIS
Paris Quadrifolia

BLACK PEPPER
Piper Nigrum

flower, blooming May and June with a foetid odour; the petals and sepals remain till the purply-blackberry (fruit) is ripe, which eventually splits to discharge its seeds.

¶ *Constituents.* A glucoside called Paradin.

¶ *Medicinal Action and Uses.* Narcotic, in large doses producing nausea, vomiting, vertigo, delirium convulsions, profuse sweating and dry throat. The drug should be used with great caution; overdoses have proved fatal to children and poultry. In *small doses* it has been found of benefit in bronchitis; spasmodic coughs, rheumatism; relieves cramp, colic, and palpitation of the heart; the juice of the berries cures inflammation of the eyes. A cooling ointment is made from the seeds and the juice of the leaves for green wounds and for outward application for tumours and inflammations. The powdered root boiled in wine is given for colic. One or 2 scruples acts as an emetic in place of Ipecacuanha.

It has been used as an aphrodisiac – the seeds and berries have something of the nature of opium. The leaves in Russia are prescribed for madness. The leaves and berries are more actively poisonous than the root.

Herb Paris is useful as an *antidote* against mercurial sublimate and arsenic. A tincture is prepared from the fresh plant.

¶ *Other Species. Paris polyphylla,* which grows in Nepaul.

PARSLEY

Carum petroselinum (BENTH.)
N.O. Umbelliferæ

Synonyms. Apium petroselinum (Linn.). Petroselinum lativum (Hoffm.). Petersylinge. Persely. Persele

Parts Used. Root, seeds

Habitat. The Garden Parsley is not indigenous to Britain: Linnæus stated its wild habitat to be Sardinia, whence it was brought to England and apparently first cultivated here in 1548. Bentham considered it a native of the Eastern Mediterranean regions; De Candolle of Turkey, Algeria and the Lebanon. Since its introduction into these islands in the sixteenth century it has been completely naturalized in various parts of England and Scotland, on old walls and rocks

Petroselinum, the specific name of the Parsley, from which our English name is derived, is of classic origin, and is said to have been assigned to it by Dioscorides. The Ancients distinguished between two plants *Selinon,* one being the Celery (*Apium graveolens*) and called *heleioselinon* – i.e. 'Marsh *selinon,*' and the other – our parsley -- *Oreoselinon,* 'Mountain selinon'; or *petroselinum,* signifying 'Rock selinon.' This last name in the Middle Ages became corrupted into *Petrocilium* – this was anglicized into Petersylinge, Persele, Persely and finally Parsley.

There is an old superstition against transplanting parsley plants. The herb is said to have been dedicated to Persephone and to funeral rites by the Greeks. It was afterwards consecrated to St. Peter in his character of successor to Charon.

In the sixteenth century, Parsley was known as *A. hortense,* but herbalists retained the official name *petroselinum.* Linnæus in 1764 named it *A. petroselinum,* but it is now assigned to the genus *Carum.*

The Greeks held Parsley in high esteem, crowning the victors with chaplets of Parsley at the Isthmian games, and making with it wreaths for adorning the tombs of their dead. The herb was never brought to table of old, being held sacred to oblivion and to the dead.

It was reputed to have sprung from the blood of a Greek hero, Archemorus, the forerunner of death, and Homer relates that chariot horses were fed by warriors with the leaves. Greek gardens were often bordered with Parsley and Rue.

Several cultivated varieties exist, the principal being the common plain-leaved, the curled-leaved, the Hamburg or broad-leaved and the celery-leaved. Of the variety *crispum,* or curled-leaved, there are no less than thirty-seven variations; the most valuable are those of a compact habit with close, perfectly curled leaves. The common sort bears close leaves, but is of a somewhat hardier nature than those of which the leaves are curled; the latter are, however, superior in every way. The variety *crispum* was grown in very early days, being even mentioned by Pliny.

Turner says, 'if parsley is thrown into fishponds it will heal the sick fishes therein.'

The Hamburg, or turnip-rooted Parsley, is grown only for the sake of its enlarged fleshy tap-root. No mention appears to have been made by the Ancients, or in the Middle Ages, of this variety, which Miller in his *Gardeners' Dictionary* (1771) calls 'the large-rooted Parsley,' and which under cultivation develops both a parsnip-like as well as a turnip-shaped form. Miller says:

'This is now pretty commonly sold in the London markets, the roots being six times as large as the common Parsley. This sort was many years cultivated in Holland before the English gardeners could be prevailed upon to sow it. I brought the seeds of it from thence in 1727; but they refused to accept it, so that I cultivated it several years before it was known in the markets.'

At the present day, the 'long white' and the 'round sugar' forms are sold by seed-growers and are in esteem for flavouring soups, stews, etc., the long variety being also cooked and eaten like parsnips.

Neapolitan, or celery-leaved, parsley is grown for the use of its leafstalks, which are blanched and eaten like those of celery.

The plain-leaved parsley was the first known in this country, but it is not now much cultivated, the leaves being less attractive than those of the curled, of a less brilliant green, and coarser in flavour. It also has too close a resemblance to Fool's Parsley (*Anthriscus cynapium*), a noxious weed of a poisonous nature infesting gardens and fields. The leaves of the latter, though similar, are, however, of a rather darker green and when bruised, emit an unpleasant odour, very different to that of Parsley. They are, also, more finely divided. When the two plants are in flower, they are easily distinguished, *Anthriscus* having three tiny, narrow, sharp-pointed leaflets hanging down under each little umbellule of the white umbel of flowers, whereas in the Garden Parsley there is usually only one leaflet under the main umbel, the leaflets or bracts at the base of the small umbellules only being short and as fine as hairs. *Anthriscus* leaves, also, are glossy beneath. Gerard called *Anthriscus* 'Dog's Parsley,' and says 'the whole plant is of a naughty smell.' It contains a peculiar alkaloid called Cynapium.

Stone Parsley (*Sison*), or Breakstone, is an allied plant, growing in chalky districts.

S. Amomum is a species well known in some parts of Britain, with cream-coloured flowers and aromatic seeds. The name is said to be derived from the Celtic *sium* (running stream), some of the species formerly included growing in moist localities.

Of our Garden Parsley (which he calls Parsele) Gerard says, 'It is delightful to the taste and agreeable to the stomache,' also 'the roots or seeds boiled in ale and drank, cast foorth strong venome or poyson; but the seed is the strongest part of the herbe.'

Though the medicinal virtues of Parsley are still fully recognized, in former times it was considered a remedy for more disorders than it is now used for. Its imagined quality of destroying poison, to which Gerard refers, was probably attributed to the plant from its remarkable power of overcoming strong scents, even the odour of garlic being rendered almost imperceptible when mingled with that of Parsley.

The plant is said to be fatal to small birds and a deadly poison to parrots, also very injurious to fowls, but hares and rabbits will come from a great distance to seek for it, so that it is scarcely possible to preserve it in gardens to which they have access. Sheep are also fond of it, and it is said to be a sovereign remedy to preserve them from footrot, provided it be given them in sufficient quantities.

¶ *Cultivation.* Parsley requires an ordinary, good well-worked soil, but a moist one and a partially-shaded position is best. A little soot may be added to the soil.

The seed may be sown in drills, or broadcast, or, if only to be used for culinary purposes, as edging, or between dwarf or short-lived crops.

For a continuous supply, three sowings should be made: as early in February as the weather permits, in April or early in May, and in July and early August – the last being for the winter supply, in a sheltered position, with a southern exposure. Sow in February for the summer crop and for drying purposes. Seed sown then, however, takes several weeks to germinate, often as much as a full month. The principal sowing is generally done in April; it then germinates more quickly and provides useful material for cutting throughout the summer. A mid-August sowing will furnish good plants for placing in the cold frames for winter use.

An even broadcast sowing is preferable, if the ground is in the condition to be trodden, which appears to fix the seed in its place, and after raking leaves a firm even surface.

The seed should be but slightly covered, not more than ⅓ inch deep and thinly distributed; if in drills, these should be 1 foot apart.

It is not necessary, however (though usual), to sow the seed where the plants are to be grown, as when large enough, the seedlings can be pricked out into rows.

When the seedlings are well out of the ground – about an inch high – adequate thinning is imperative, as the plants dislike being cramped, and about 8 inches from plant to plant must be allowed: a well-grown plant will cover nearly a square foot of ground.

The rows should be liberally watered in dry weather; a sheltered position is preferred, as the plants are liable to become burnt up in very hot and dry summers. The rows should be kept clean of weeds, and frequent dressings may be applied with advantage.

If the growth becomes coarse in the summer, cut off all the leaves and water well. This will induce a new growth of fine leaves, and may always be done when the plants have grown to a good size, as it encourages a stocky growth.

Soon after the old or last year's plants begin to grow again in the spring, they run to flower, but if the flower stems are promptly removed, and the plants top dressed and watered, they will remain productive for some time longer. Renew the beds every two years, as the plant dies down at the end of the second season.

When sowing Parsley to stand the winter, a plain-leaved variety will often be found superior to the curled or mossy sorts, which are, perhaps, handsomer, but the leaves retain both snow and rain, and when frost follows, the plants soon succumb. A plain-leaved Parsley is far hardier, and will survive even a severe winter and is equally good for cooking, though not so attractive for garnishing. Double the trouble is experienced in obtaining a supply of Parsley during the winter, when only the curled-leaved varieties are given.

Where curled Parsley is desired and is difficult to obtain, because there is no sufficiently sheltered spot in the garden for it, it may often be saved by placing a frame-light over the bed during severe weather to protect the plants, or they may be placed altogether in cold frames. Care must be taken with all Parsley plants grown thus in frames, to pick off all decaying leaves directly noticed, and the soil should be stirred occasionally with a pointed stick between the plants, to prevent its becoming sour. Abundance of air should be given on all favourable occasions, removing the light altogether on fine days.

¶ *Medicinal Action and Uses.* The uses of Parsley are many and are by no means restricted to the culinary sphere. The most familiar employment of the leaves in their fresh state is, of course, finely-chopped, as a flavouring to sauces, soups, stuffings, rissoles, minces, etc., and also sprinkled over vegetables or salads. The leaves are extensively cultivated, not only for sending to market fresh, but also for the purpose of being dried and powdered as a culinary flavouring in winter, when only a limited supply of fresh Parsley is obtainable.

In addition to the leaves, the *stems* are also dried and powdered, both as a culinary colouring and for dyeing purposes. There is

a market for the seeds to supply nurserymen, etc., and the roots of the turnip-rooted variety are used as a vegetable and flavouring.

Medicinally, the two-year-old *roots* are employed, also the *leaves*, dried, for making Parsley Tea, and the *seeds*, for the extraction of an oil called Apiol, which is of considerable curative value. The best kind of seed for medicinal purposes is that obtained from the Triple Moss curled variety. The wholesale drug trade generally obtains its seeds from farmers on the East coast, each sample being tested separately before purchases are made. It has been the practice to buy second-year seeds which are practically useless for growing purposes: it would probably hardly pay farmers to grow for Apiol producing purposes only, as the demand is not sufficiently great.

¶ *Constituents.* Parsley Root is faintly aromatic and has a sweetish taste. It contains starch, mucilage, sugar, volatile oil and Apiin. The latter is white, inodorous, tasteless and soluble in boiling water.

Parsley fruit or 'seeds' contain the volatile oil in larger proportion than the root (2·6 per cent.); it consists of terpenes and Apiol, to which the activity of the fruit is due. There are also present fixed oil, resin, Apiin, mucilage and ash. Apiol is an oily, non-nitrogenous allyl compound, insoluble in water, soluble in alcohol and crystallizable when pure into white needles. The British Pharmacopœia directs that Apiol be prepared by extracting the bruised fresh fruits with ether and distilling the solvent. The residue is the commercial liquid Apiol. It exercises all the virtues of the entire plant. Crystallized Apiol, or Parsley Camphor, is obtained by distilling the volatile oil to a low temperature. The value of the volatile oil depends on the amount of Apiol it contains. Oil obtained from German fruit contains this body in considerable quantity and becomes semi-solid at ordinary temperature, that from French fruit is much poorer in Apiol. In France, only the crystalline Apiol is official, but three different varieties, distinguished as green, yellow and white, are in use.

Apiol was first obtained in 1849 by Drs. Joret and Homolle, of Brittany, and proved an excellent remedy there for a prevailing ague. It is greatly used now in malarial disorders. The name Apiol has also been applied to an oleoresin prepared from the plant, which contains three closely-allied principles: apiol, apiolin and myristicin, the latter identical with the active principle of oil of Nutmeg. The term 'liquid Apiol' is frequently applied to the complete oleoresin.

This occurs as a yellowish liquid with a characteristic odour and an acrid pungent taste. The physiological action of the oleoresin of Parsley has not been sufficiently investigated, it exercises a singular influence on the great nerve centres of the head and spine, and in large doses produces giddiness and deafness, fall of blood-pressure and some slowing of the pulse and paralysis. It is stated that the paralysis is followed by fatty degeneration of the liver and kidney, similar to that caused by myristicin.

Parsley has carminative, tonic and aperient action, but is chiefly used for its diuretic properties, a strong decoction of the root being of great service in gravel, stone, congestion of the kidneys, dropsy and jaundice. The dried leaves are also used for the same purpose. Parsley Tea proved useful in the trenches, where our men often got kidney complications, when suffering from dysentery.

A fluid extract is prepared from both root and seeds. The extract made from the root acts more readily on the kidneys than that from other parts of the herb. The oil extracted from the seeds, the Apiol, is considered a safe and efficient emmenagogue, the dose being 5 to 15 drops in capsules. A decoction of bruised Parsley seeds was at one time employed against plague and intermittent fever.

In France, a popular remedy for scrofulous swellings is green Parsley and snails, pounded in a mortar to an ointment, spread on linen and applied daily. The bruised leaves, applied externally, have been used in the same manner as Violet leaves (also Celandine, Clover and Comfrey), to dispel tumours suspected to be of a cancerous nature. A poultice of the leaves is said to be an efficacious remedy for the bites and stings of poisonous insects.

Culpepper tells us:

'It is very comfortable to the stomach . . . good for wind and to remove obstructions both of the liver and spleen . . . Galen commendeth it for the falling sickness . . . the seed is effectual to break the stone and ease the pains and torments thereof. . . . The leaves of parsley laid to the eyes that are inflamed with heat or swollen, relieves them if it be used with bread or meat. . . . The juice dropped into the ears with a little wine easeth the pains.'

Formerly the distilled water of Parsley was often given to children troubled with wind, as Dill water still is.

¶ *Preparations and Dosages.* Fluid extract root, ¼ to 1 drachm. Fluid extract seeds, ¼ to 1 drachm. Apiol (oil), 5 to 15 drops in capsule.

¶ *Preparation for Market.* The roots are collected for medicinal purposes in the second year, in autumn or late summer, when the plant has flowered.

To dry Parsley towards the close of the summer for culinary use, it may be put into the oven on muslin trays, when cooking is finished, this being repeated several times till thoroughly dry and crisp, when the leaves should be rubbed in the hands or through a coarse wire sieve and the powder then stored in tins, so that neither air nor light can reach it, or the good colour will not be preserved. In the trade, there is a special method of drying which preserves the colour.

The oil is extracted from the 'seeds' or rather fruits, when *fresh*, in which condition they are supplied to manufacturing druggists.

PARSLEY, FOOL'S

Æthusa cynapium (LINN.)
N.O. Umbelliferæ

Synonyms. Lesser Hemlock. Smaller Hemlock. Dog Parsley. Dog Poison
Part Used. Herb

¶ *Description.* This annual plant is not unlike both Parsley and Hemlock. Its leaves, which are very similar to those of Parsley, are more acute, of a darker green and when bruised emit a disagreeable odour. When in flower it is easily distinguished because it has no general involucre and the partial involucre is composed of three to five long pendulous bracts which are drawn to one side, also the flowers, instead of being yellow, are white. It differs from Hemlock in being smaller, having its stem unspotted and the ridges of its fruit not wavy, also in the odour of the leaves, which is less unpleasant than that of Hemlock.

¶ *Constituents.* The active principle is an alkaloid, Cynopine.

¶ *Medicinal Action and Uses.* Though poisonous, the plant is less so than Hemlock. Poisoning from Fool's Parsley showed symptoms of heat in the mouth and throat and a post-mortem examination showed redness of the lining membrane of the gullet and windpipe and slight congestion of the duodenum and stomach.

It is used medicinally as a stomachic and sedative for gastro-intestinal troubles in children, for summer diarrhœa and cholera infantum.

PARSLEY PIERT

Alchemilla arvensis (SCOP.)
N.O. Rosaceæ

Synonyms. Parsley Breakstone. Parsley Piercestone. Field Lady's Mantle
Part Used. Herb

Parsley Piert is common in Great Britain everywhere, especially in dry soil, being abundant in fields and waste places, on the tops of walls and in gravel-pits.

It is widely distributed throughout Europe and North Africa and has been introduced into North America. Unlike the Common Lady's Mantle, it is not found in this country above an altitude of 1,600 feet.

¶ *Description.* Parsley Piert is a smaller and even more inconspicuous plant than the Common Lady's Mantle. The stem is sometimes prostrate, but generally erect, and much branched from the base. It is rarely more than 4 inches high.

The leaves are of a dusky green colour, wedge-shaped, three-cleft, the lobes deeply cut, the whole leaf less than ⅛ inch wide, narrowed into a short foot-stalk with leafy, palmately-cut stipules, sheathing and cleaving to the footstalk. The whole plant is downy with slender, scattered hairs.

The greenish, minute and stalkless flowers are crowded together in tufts almost hidden by the leaves and their large stipules. There is no corolla, the stamens, which have jointed filaments, being inserted at the mouth of the calyx, which is usually four-cleft, as in the preceding species. The plant is in bloom from May to August. It is an annual.

This species is still in high repute with herbalists, and has been used for many centuries for its action on stone in the bladder, on account of which it was given the name of 'Parsley Breakstone' and 'Parsley Piercestone,' which has been corrupted into Parsley Piert, the 'parsley' referring to the form of its cut-into leaves, not to any relationship to the true Parsley.

¶ *Part Used.* The whole herb, either fresh or dried. It has an astringent taste, but no odour.

¶ *Medicinal Action and Uses.* Diuretic, demulcent and refrigerant. Its chief employment is in gravel, stone, dropsy and generally for complaints of the bladder and kidneys. Acting directly on the parts affected, it is found very valuable, even in apparently incurable cases. It operates violently, but safely, by urine and also removes obstructions of the liver, being therefore useful in jaundice.

Fluid extract: dose, 1 drachm.

It is prescribed in the form of an infusion – a handful of the herb to a pint of boiling water – taken daily in half-teacupful doses, three or four times daily. When used alone, it forms a useful remedy in all these complaints; its best action is seen, however, when compounded with other diuretics, such as Broom, Buchu leaves, Wild Carrot, Juniper Berries, Parsley Root and Pellitory-of-the-Wall. To soothe and help the passage of the irritating substance, it is also often combined with a demulcent such as Comfrey, Marshmallow or Sweet Flagroot, Hollyhock or Mullein flowers, Gum Arabic, or Slippery Elm Bark.

Some of the older herbalists considered it best when fresh gathered. Culpepper, after telling us of its powers in expelling stone, tells us that

'it is a very good salad herb and it were well that the gentry would pickle it up as they pickle up Samphire for their use all the winter because it is a very wholesome herb, and may be kept either dried or in a syrup. You may take a drachm of the powder of it in sherry wine: it will bring away gravel from the kidneys insensibly and without pain. It cures strangury.'

See LADY'S MANTLE.

PARSNIP

Pastinaca sativa
N.O. Umbelliferæ

Synonyms. (*French*) Le Panais. (*German*) Die Pastinake
Part Used. Root
Habitat. The Wild Parsnip is a native of most parts of Europe, growing chiefly in calcareous soils, by the wayside and on the borders of fields

The food value of Parsnips exceeds that of any other vegetable except potatoes. It is easy of production and should be more extensively grown.

The Parsnip, together with the carrot, was cultivated by the Ancients, but the Roman horticulturists evidently knew nothing of the advantage of selecting seeds, by means of

which the best existing variety has been developed. Pliny tells us it was grown either from the root transplanted or else from seed, but that it was impossible to get rid of the pungent flavour. The finest strain raised by Professor Buckman, between 1848 and 1850, as a result of his experiments in selection, was named by him the 'Student,' and having been further improved, still takes the first rank. It differs in several respects from the wild plant.

According to Pliny, Parsnips were held in such repute by the Emperor Tiberius that he had them annually brought to Rome from the banks of the Rhine, where they were then successfully cultivated. They are dressed in various ways and are much eaten with salt-fish during Lent.

In Holland, Parsnips are used in soups, whilst in Ireland cottagers make a beer by boiling the roots with water and hops, and afterwards fermenting the liquor. A kind of marmalade preserve has also been made from them, and even wine which in quality has been said to approach the famed Malmsey of Madeira.

It has a tough, wiry root, tapering somewhat from the crown, from which arises the erect stem, 1 to 2 feet high, tough and furrowed. The leaf-stalks are about 9 inches long, the leaves divided into several pairs of leaflets, each 1 to 2 inches long, the larger, terminal leaflet, ¾ inch broad. All the leaflets are finely toothed at their margins and softly hairy, especially on the underside. The sheath at the base of the leaf-stalk is about 1½ inch long, the first pair of leaflets being 4 inches above it.

The modern cultivated Parsnip has developed a leaf-stalk 2 feet long, the first pair of leaflets being several inches above the sheath. The leaflets are oblong, about 2 inches across at the basal part and 4½ inches in length (more than double the size of those of the wild plant), and are entirely smooth and somewhat paler in colour. The flowers in each case are yellow and in umbels at the ends of the stems, like the carrot, though the umbels do not contract in seeding, like those of the carrot. The flowers of the cultivated Parsnip are of a deeper yellow colour than those of the wild plant. The Parsnip is a biennial, flowering in its second year, throughout June and August. The fruit is flattened and of elliptical form, strongly furrowed. Parsnip 'seeds' as the fruit is commonly called, are pleasantly aromatic, and were formerly collected for their medicinal value and sold by herbalists. They contain an essential oil that has the reputation of curing intermittent fever. A strong decoction of the root is a good diuretic and assists in removing obstructions of the viscera. It has been employed as a remedy for jaundice and gravel.

¶ *Medicinal Action and Uses.* Culpepper wrote:

'The wild Parsnip differeth little from the garden, but groweth not so fair and large,

nor hath so many leaves, and the root is shorter, more woody and not so fit to be eaten and, therefore, more medicinal. The Garden Parsnip nourisheth much and is good and wholesome, but a little windy, but it fatteneth the body if much used. It is good for the stomach and reins and provoketh urine. The wild Parsnip hath a cutting, attenuating, cleansing and opening quality therein. It easeth the pains and stitches in the sides and expels the wind from the stomach and bowels, or colic. The root is often used, but the seed much more, the wild being better than the tame.'

Gerard, speaking of its uses as a vegetable, observes:

'The Parsneps nourish more than do the Turneps or the Carrots, and the nourishment is somewhat thicker, but not faultie nor bad. . . . There is a good and pleasant foode or bread made of the rootes of Parsneps, as my friend Master Plat hath set foorth in his booke of experiments.'

Tournefort, in *The Compleat Herbal* (1730), wrote of Parsnips, that

'they are commonly boiled and eaten with butter in the time of Lent; for that they are the sweetest, by reason the juice has been concocted during the winter, and are desired at that season especially, both for their agreeable Taste and their Wholesomeness. For they are not so good in any respect, till they have been first nipt with Cold. It is likewise pretty common of late to eat them with salt-fish mixed with hard-boiled eggs and butter . . . and much the wholesomer if you eat it with mustard.'

John Wesley, in his *Primitive Physic*, says: '*Wild parsnips* both leaves and stalks, bruised, seem to have been a favorite application; and a very popular internal remedy for cancer, asthma, consumption and similar diseases.'

The roots are sweeter than carrots. They contain both sugar and starch, and for this reason beer and spirits are sometimes prepared from them. In the north of Ireland, they have been often brewed with malt instead of hops and fermented with yeast, the result being a pleasant drink, and Parsnip wine, when properly made, is esteemed by many people.

Parsnips are not only a valuable item of human food, but equal, if not superior to carrots for fattening pigs, making the flesh white, and being preferred by pigs to carrots. Washed and sliced and given with bran, horses eat them readily and thrive on them. In Brittany and the Channel Islands, they are largely given to cattle and pigs, and milch cows fed on them in winter are said to give as much and as good milk, and yield butter as well-flavoured as when feeding on grass in May and June.

¶ *Cultivation.* Parsnips require a long period of growth, and should be started, if possible, the latter part of February. In choosing the seed, the older varieties should be avoided, as there is no comparison between them and the newer and better kinds. The 'Student,' already mentioned, is suited in every way for the average small garden.

No specially good soil is required, though a strong soil is preferable to a sandy one; poorish or partially exhausted soil is no drawback, as there should be no recent manure in the top spit, for in common with carrots, its presence tends to form forked roots. The ground, however, should be deeply trenched and a slight dressing of manure may be buried deeply. Roots will be poor if grown in soil which has hardly been turned over, but if the land is deeply dug, plenty of lime, old mortar rubbish or wood ashes being mixed in, fine roots will be produced.

One ounce of Parsnip seed will sow a row 300 feet long. The seed is best sown in drills about 1 inch deep, as soon as the land is anything like dry enough to work. Drop three seeds together, 8 inches apart, and let the rows stand 15 inches asunder. After the plants appear, there is very little to do except to thin them and hoe, at intervals; no stimulants are needed. Thinning may be done as soon as they are well in their second leaf.

As the Parsnip is hardy, there is no need to lift the roots in autumn. The crop will be ready for use in September, but it may be left in the ground and be dug throughout the winter as required, and the remainder not finally raised till the middle or end of February, when the site the roots occupy has to be prepared for the crop of the ensuing summer.

PARSNIP, WATER

Synonym. Water Hemlock

Sium latifolium, the Broad-leaved Water Parsnip, is another of the umbelliferous plants sometimes called Water Hemlock. It occurs in watery places all over the British Isles. The long creeping root-stock of this and the somewhat smaller, closely allied species *S. angustifolium* is poisonous, but

RECIPES

To prepare *Parsnip Soup*, scrape and cut up 2 large Parsnips or 4 small ones, and wash them carefully. Peel 6 large potatoes and boil them with the Parsnips in a quart of water. When soft, mash and pass through a sieve. Boil up again in the water and pour on to slices of bread in the tureen, adding 2 oz. of butter. The addition of a little cream, in more favourable times, of course makes the soup more savoury.

Stewed Parsnips

Wash, peel and cut 3 Parsnips into slices, then boil them till they are nearly done, drain them and let them cool. Melt 2 or 3 oz. bacon fat in a stewpan; when hot, fry the Parsnips to a light brown colour. Next add a tablespoonful of flour and moisten with sufficient brown stock just to cover the Parsnips. Season with salt and pepper, and 1 or 2 tablespoonsful of tomato sauce. Bring to the boil and let the Parsnips simmer slowly for another 20 minutes. Dish up and serve with the prepared sauce.

Parsnip Cakes

Parsnips mashed with a little butter and pepper and salt, and then dipped into flour and formed into small, round cakes, are nice if fried in lard, dripping or bacon fat.

Parsnip Salad

Plainly-boiled Parsnips, when cold, make an excellent salad. Slice the Parsnips, not too thinly, and season with salt and pepper, and mix with a simple French oil and vinegar salad dressing.

Parsnip Wine

Take 15 lb. of sliced Parsnips, and boil until quite soft in 5 gallons of water; squeeze the liquor well out of them, run it through a sieve and add 3 lb. of coarse lump sugar to every gallon of liquor. Boil the whole for ¾ hour. When it is nearly cold, add a little yeast on toast. Let it remain in a tub for 10 days, stirring it from the bottom every day; then put it into a cask for a year. As it works over, fill it up every day.

Sium latifolium
N.O. Umbelliferæ

pigs and oxen eat the stem and leaves without harm. However, cows in milk should not be allowed to eat it, as it communicates a disagreeable taste to the milk.

Both species are easily recognized by their pinnate leaves, the leaf-stalks carrying about six to eight pairs of ovate, toothed leaflets.

The umbels of white flowers are flat and have a general involucre composed of broadish or lance-shaped bracts, and there is also an in-volucel. The fruit bears slender ribs. The erect, furrowed stems are from 3 to 6 feet high.

PASSION FLOWER

Passiflora incarnata (LINN.)
N.O. Passifloraceæ

Synonyms. Passion Vine. Granadilla. Maracoc. Maypops
Part Used. The dried herb, collected after some of the berries have matured
Habitat. Virginia

¶ *Description.* The Passion Flowers are so named from the supposed resemblance of the finely-cut corona in the centre of the blossoms to the Crown of Thorns and of the other parts of the flower to the instruments of the Passion of Our Lord. *Passiflora incarnata* has a perennial root, and the herbaceous shoots bear three-lobed, finely-serrated leaves and flesh-coloured or yellowish, sweet-scented flowers, tinged with purple. The ripe, orange-coloured, ovoid, many-seeded berry is about the size of a small apple; when dried, it is shrivelled and greenish-yellow. The yellow pulp is sweet and edible.

¶ *Constituents.* There appears to be no detailed analysis of this species, but its active principle, which has been called Passiflorine, would appear to be somewhat similar to morphine.

¶ *Medicinal Action and Uses.* The drug is known to be a depressant to the motor side of the spinal cord, slightly reducing arterial pressure, though affecting circulation but little, while increasing the rate of respiration. It is official in homœopathic medicine and used with bromides, it is said to be of great service in epilepsy. Its narcotic properties cause it to be used in diarrhœa and dysentery, neuralgia, sleeplessness and dysmenorrhœa.

¶ *Dosages.* 3 to 10 grains. Of Fluid extract, 10 to 20 minims.

¶ *Other Species.*
Many species yield edible fruits or are cultivated for their beauty and fragrance.

P. cærulea, the familiar Blue Passion Flower, hardy in southern districts of this country as a wall-climber, was introduced into England from Brazil in 1699.

P. quadrangularis, the Common Granadilla, a native of Jamaica and South America grown for its large edible fruit, the purple, succulent pulp of which is eaten with wine and sugar, has a root said to be very poisonous and a powerful narcotic; in small doses it is anthelmintic. It is used in Mauritius as a diuretic and emetic.

The fruit of *P. edulis* in colour and flavour resembles that of the orange, with a mixture of acid.

P. macrocarpa bears a gourd-like, oblong fruit, much larger than any of the other species, attaining a weight of 7 to 8 lb.

P. maliformis, the Apple-fruited Granadilla, the Sweet Calabash of the West Indies, has a fruit 2 inches in diameter, full of a pleasant gelatinous pulp. The juice of the leaves, and also of those of *P. pallida*, is used by the Brazilians against intermittent fevers.

P. laurifolia, the Water Lemon of the West Indies, is much cultivated throughout South America for its fruit, the aromatic juice of which quenches thirst, allays heat and induces appetite. Its bitter and astringent leaves are employed as an anthelmintic.

The roots of *P. contrayerva* and *P. normalis* are reputed to have counter-poison properties.

P. fœtida is used in hysteria, female complaints and as an expectorant, and the leaves as a poultice in skin inflammations.

The flowers of *P. rubra* yield a narcotic tincture.

P. capsularia is said to possess emmenagogue properties.

PATCHOULI

Pogostemon patchouli (PILL.)
N.O. Labiatæ

Synonym. Pucha-pat
Part Used. The herb, yielding a volatile oil by distillation
Habitat. East and West Indies and Paraguay

¶ *Description.* This fragrant herb, with soft, opposite, egg-shaped leaves and square stems, grows from 2 to 3 feet in height, giving out the peculiar, characteristic odour of patchouli when rubbed. Its whitish flowers, tinged with purple, grow in both axillary and terminal spikes. The crop is cut two or three times a year, the leaves being dried and packed in bales and exported for distillation of the oil. The best oil is freshly distilled near the plantations. That obtained from leaves imported into Europe, often damaged and adulterated even up to 80 per cent., is inferior. It is used in coarser perfumes and in 'White Rose' and 'Oriental' toilet soaps. Although the odour is objectionable to some, it is widely-used both in Asia and India. Sachets are made of the coarsely-powdered leaves, and before its common use in Europe, genuine Indian shawls and Indian ink were distinguished by the odour, which has the unusual quality of improving with age. Hence the older oil is preferred by perfumers and used to confer more lasting properties upon other scents.

¶ *Constituents.* Oil of Patchouli is thick, the colour being brownish-yellow tinted green. It contains cœrulein, the vivid blue compound found in matricaria, wormwood and other oils. It deposits a solid, or stearoptene, patchouli alcohol, leaving cadinene.

It is lævorotatory, with the specific gravity of 0·970 to 0·990 at 15° C. (59° F.).

¶ *Medicinal Action and Uses.* Its use is said to cause sometimes loss of appetite and sleep and nervous attacks. The Chinese, Japanese and Arabs believe it to possess prophylactic properties.

¶ *Other Species and Adulterations.*

Java patchouli, often grown in Indian gardens for home use, is a product of *Pogostemon Heyneanus.*

The inferior oil of Assam is from *Microtœna cymosa.*

Cubeb and cedar oils are said to be usual adulterants.

PAPYRUS. *See* SEDGES

PEACH

Prunus Persica (STOKES)
N.O. Rosaceæ

Synonyms. Amygdalis Persica (Linn.). Persica vulgaris Null
(*Chinese and Japanese*) 'Too'
Parts Used. Bark, leaves

The Peach is included by Hooker and other botanists in the genus *Prunus*, its resemblance to the plum being obvious. Others have classed it with the Almond as a distinct genus, *Amygdalus*, and others again have considered it sufficiently distinct to constitute it a separate genus, *Persica*.

As we now know it, the Peach has been nowhere recognized in the wild state. De Candolle attributes all cultivated varieties to a distinct species, probably of Chinese origin. Other naturalists, among them Darwin, look on the Peach as a modification of the Almond.

It has been cultivated from time immemorial in most parts of Asia, and appears to have been introduced into Europe from Persia, as its name implies. At what period it was introduced into Greece is uncertain. The Romans seem to have brought it direct from Persia during the reign of the Emperor Claudius.

When first introduced it was called *Malus persica*, or Persian Apple. The expedition of Alexander probably made it known to Theophrastus, 392 B.C., who speaks of it as a Persian fruit. It has no name in Sanskrit; nevertheless, the people speaking that language came into India from the Northwest, the country generally assigned to the species.

In support of the supposed *Chinese* origin, it may be added that the Peach-tree was introduced from China into Cochin-China, and that the Japanese call it by the Chinese name, *Too.*

The Peach is mentioned in the books of Confucius, fifth century before the Christian era, and the antiquity of the knowledge of the fruit in China is further proved by representations of it in sculpture and on porcelain.

It is said to have been first cultivated in England in the first half of the sixteenth century. Gerard describes several varieties as growing in his garden, and speaks of a 'double-flowered peach,' as a rarity, in his garden.

It is always cultivated here trained against walls or under glass. When growing naturally, it is a medium-sized tree, with spreading branches, of quick growth and not longlived. The leaves are lance-shaped, about 4 inches long and 1½ inch broad, tapering to a sharp point, borne on long, slender, relatively unbranched shoots, and with the flowers arranged singly, or in groups of two or more at intervals along the shoots of the previous year's growth. The blossoms come out before the leaves are fully expanded, and are of a delicate, pink colour. They have a hollow tube at the base, bearing at its free edge five sepals, and an equal number of petals, usually concave, and a great number of stamens. They have very little odour.

The fruit is a drupe, like the plum, having a delicate, thin outer downy skin enclosing the flesh of the Peach, the inner layers becoming woody to form the large, furrowed, rugged stone, while the ovule ripens into the kernel or seed. This is exactly the structure of the plum and apricot, and differs from that of the almond, which is identical in the first instance, only in that the fleshy part of the latter eventually becomes dry and leathery, and cracks along a line called the suture, which is merely represented in the Peach by a furrow on one side.

In the South of France, and in other Continental countries possessing a similar climate, Peach-trees ripen their fruit very well as standards in the open air. In America, the

Peach grows almost without any care – extensive orchards, containing from 10,000 to 20,000 trees, being raised from the stones. At first, the trees there make rapid and healthy growth, and in a few years bear in great abundance; but they soon decay, their leaves becoming tinged with yellow even in summer, when they should be green. This is owing to their being grown on their own roots, for when that is the case in Britain the trees present a similar appearance. They require, therefore, to be budded on the plum or on the almond.

In America, the Peach is chiefly used for feeding pigs, and for making Peach Brandy.

¶ *Cultivation.* The soil best suited for the Peach is three parts mellow, unexhausted loam, mixed with vegetable mould or manure. Peaches require a lighter soil than pears or plums.

To perpetuate and multiply the choicer varieties, both the Peach and the newly-allied nectarine are budded upon plums or almond stocks. For dry soil, the almond stocks are preferable; for damp or clayey loam, it is better to use certain kinds of plums.

The fruit is produced on the ripened shoots of the preceding year, and the formation of young shoots in sufficient abundance, and of requisite strength, is the great object of peach training and pruning.

In cold soils and bleak situations, it is considered best to cover the walls upon which the trees are trained with a casing of glass, so that the trees may be under shelter during uncongenial spring weather.

Various kinds of *Aphis* and the *Acarus,* or Red Spider, infest the leaves of the Peach.

¶ *Medicinal Action and Uses.* The fruit is wholesome and seldom disagrees if eaten ripe, though the skin is indigestible. The quantity of sugar is only small.

All Peaches have in the kernel a flavour resembling that of noyau, which depends on the presence of prussic or hydrocyanic acid. Not only the kernels, but also the young branches and flowers, after maceration in water, yield a volatile oil, which is chemically identical with that of bitter almonds, and is the cause of this flavour. Infused in white brandy, sweetened with barley sugar, Peach leaves have been said to make a fine cordial, similar to noyau, and the flowers when distilled furnish a white liquor, which communicates a flavour resembling the kernels of the fruit.

The leaves, bark, flowers and kernels have medicinal virtue. Both the *leaves* and *bark* are still employed for their curative powers. They have demulcent, sedative, diuretic and expectorant action. An infusion of ½ oz. of the bark or 1 oz. of the dried leaves to a pint of boiling water has been found almost a specific for irritation and congestion of the gastric surfaces. It is also used in whooping cough, ordinary coughs and chronic bronchitis, the dose being from a teaspoonful to a wineglassful as required.

The fresh leaves were stated by the older herbalists to possess the power of expelling worms, if applied outwardly to the body as a poultice. An infusion of the dried leaves was also recommended for the same purpose.

Culpepper informs us that a powder of the leaves 'strewed on fresh bleeding wounds stayeth their bleeding and closeth them.'

In Italy, at the present day, there is a popular belief that if fresh Peach leaves are applied to warts and then buried, the warts will fall off by the time the buried leaves have decayed.

A syrup and infusion of Peach *flowers* was formerly a preparation recognized by apothecaries, and praised by Gerard as a mildly acting efficient purgative. The syrup was considered good for children and those in weak health, and to be good against jaundice.

A tincture made from the flowers has been said to allay the pain of colic caused by gravel.

Culpepper recommends the milk or cream of the kernels applied to the forehead and temples as a means of procuring 'rest and sleep to sick persons,' and says 'the oil drawn from the kernels and the temples annointed therewith doth the like.' He tells us that 'the liquor that drops from the tree, being wounded,' added to coltsfoot, sweet wine and saffron, is 'good for coughs, hoarseness and loss of voice,' and that it 'clears and strengthens the lungs and relieves those who vomit and spit blood.' He concludes:

'If the kernels be bruised and boiled in vinegar until they become thick and applied to the head, it marvellously causes the hair to grow again upon any bald place or where it is too thin.'

'Peach cold' is an affection which prevails in some parts where Peach trees are largely cultivated, just as rose fever and rose catarrh are caused by roses in parts of America.

¶ *Collection.* The *bark* for medicinal purposes is stripped from the tree in the spring and taken from young trees. It is best dried in a moderate sun-heat, being taken indoors at night. The pieces of bark if thin are often threaded on strings and hung up in a warm current of air. They must not touch each other. Peach bark occurs in commerce in small, thin, pale-brown fragments, rarely exceeding 1½ inch in length, and ⅛ inch in thickness, having a smooth, dark brown skin and an inner surface with a faint network of fibres. It has a bitter, very astringent taste and slight odour.

Peach *leaves* should be collected for drying purposes in June and July, when at their best.

PEACH WOOD, known also as Nicaragua Wood, is in no way related to the fruit-tree, but is a much-used dyewood that dyes a delicate peach and cherry colour. It is obtained from the tree CÆSALPINIA ECHINATA, belonging to the Pea and Bean tribe, Leguminosae, and is imported into this country in blocks about 4 feet in length and 8 inches in diameter. We receive annually about 8,000 tons in normal times. That which comes from Peru yields the finest shades of colour, mainly tints of red and orange.

PELARGONIUMS

Pelargonium antidysentericum
And other Species
N.O. Geraniaceæ

Synonym. T'Namie
Part Used. Root
Habitat. Cape of Good Hope

¶ *Description.* This is a very extensive genus, and the greater number are natives of the Cape of Good Hope, most species possess astringent properties, and have been found valuable in dysentery (particularly *Pelargonium antidysentericum*), also for ulcerations of the stomach and upper part of the intestines.

¶ *Other Species.*
P. triste, native also of the Cape. This has yellow flowers with a purple spot, always open, but only fragrant after the sun has left them. The tuberous roots are eaten by the natives.

Others are cultivated for the distillation of a volatile oil (from the leaves) which is not unlike that from rose petals; *P. roseum* has very fragrant foliage; *P. capitatum* gives a good essential oil and yields Pelargonic fatty acid, this specie is often called rose geranium.

The oil of *P. odoratissimum* is much used as an adulterant to oil of Roses.

See MONSONIA.

PELLITORY

Anacyclus pyrethrum (D.C.)
N.O. Compositæ

Synonyms. Anthemis Pyrethrum. Pyrethrum officinarum. Pyrethrum. Pyrethri Radix. Roman Pellitory. Pellitory of Spain. Spanish Chamomile. Pyrethre. Matricaria Pyrethrum
Part Used. Root
Habitat. Algeria. Cultivated in Mediterranean countries

¶ *Description.* This perennial plant, in habit and appearance like the chamomile, has stems that lie on the ground for part of their length, before rising erect. Each bears one large flower, the disk being yellow and the rays white, tinged with purple beneath. The leaves are smooth, alternate, and pinnate, with deeply-cut segments.

The root is almost cylindrical, very slightly twisted and tapering and often crowned with a tuft of grey hairs. Externally it is brown and wrinkled, with bright black spots. The fracture is short, and the transverse section, magnified, presents a beautiful radiate structure and many oleoresin glands. The taste is pungent and odour slight.

¶ *Cultivation.* Planting may be done in autumn, but the best time is about the end of April. Any ordinary good soil is suitable, but better results are obtained when it is well-drained, and of a stiff loamy character, enriched with good manure. Propagation is done in three ways, by seed, by division of roots and by cuttings. If grown by *seed*, sow in February or March, thin out to 2 to 3 inches between the plants, and plant out early in June to permanent quarters, allowing a foot or more between the plants and 2 feet between the rows, selecting, if possible, a showery day for the operation. The seedlings will quickly establish themselves. Weeding should be done by hand, the plants when first put out being small, might be injured by hoeing. To propagate by *division*, lift the plants in March, or whenever the roots are in an active condition, and with a sharp spade, divide them into three or five fairly large pieces. *Cuttings* should be made from the young shoots that start from the base of the plant, and should be taken with a heel of the old plant attached, which will greatly assist their rooting. They may be inserted at any time from October to May. The foliage should be shortened to about 3 inches, when the cuttings will be ready for insertion in a bed of light, sandy soil. Plant very firmly, surface the bed with sand, and water in well. Shade is necessary while the cuttings are rooting.

¶ *Constituents*. Analysis has shown a brown, resinous, acrid substance, insoluble in potassium hydroxide and probably containing *pelletonin*, two oils soluble in potassium hydroxide – one dark brown and acrid, the other yellow – tannin, gum, potassium sulphate and carbonate, potassium chloride, calcium phosphate and carbonate, silica, alumina, lignin, etc.

An alkaloid, Pyrethrine, yielding pyrethric acid, is stated to be the active principle.

¶ *Medicinal Action and Uses*. Pellitory root is widely used because of its pungent efficacy in relieving toothache and in promoting a free flow of saliva. The British Pharmacopœia directs that it be used as a masticatory, and in the form of lozenges for its reflex action on the salivary glands in dryness of the mouth and throat. The tincture made from the dried root may be applied to relieve the aching of a decayed tooth, applied on cotton wool, or rubbed on the gums, and for this purpose may with advantage be mixed with camphorated chloroform. It forms an addition to many dentifrices.

A gargle of Pellitory infusion is prescribed for relaxed uvula and for partial paralysis of the tongue and lips. To make a gargle, two or three teaspoonsful of Pellitory should be mixed with a pint of cold water and sweetened with honey if desired. Patients seeking relief from rheumatic or neuralgic affections of the head and face, or for palsy of the tongue, have been advised to chew the root daily for several months.

Being a rubefacient and local irritant, when sliced and applied to the skin, it induces heat, tingling and redness.

The powdered root forms a good snuff to cure chronic catarrh of the head and nostrils

and to clear the brain, by exciting a free flow of nasal mucous and tears.

Culpepper tells us that Pellitory 'is one of the best purges of the brain that grows' and is not only 'good for ague and the falling sickness' (epilepsy) but is 'an excellent approved remedy in lethargy.' After stating that 'the powder of the herb or root snuffed up the nostrils procureth sneezing and easeth the headache,' he goes on to say that 'being made into an ointment with hog's lard it taketh away black and blue spots occasioned by blows or falls, and helpeth both the gout and sciatica,' uses which are now obsolete.

In the thirteenth century we read in old records that Pellitory of Spain was 'a proved remedy for the toothache' with the Welsh physicians. It was familiar to the Arabian writers on medicine and is still a favourite remedy in the East, having long been an article of export from Algeria and Spain by way of Egypt to India.

In the East Indies the infusion is used as a cordial.

¶ *Dosages*. 20 grains. Tincture, B.P. and U.S.P., 20 to 30 drops.

¶ *Other Species*.

Anacyclus officinarum is indigenous to Africa, cultivated in Germany, and formerly official in the German Pharmacopœia. The roots are smaller and very pungent. It is also known as *A. pyrethrum*, *Pyrethrum germanicum* and German Pellitory.

P. umbelliferum is said to be used also, the Pyrethrum of Dioscorides being an Umbellifer.

Though dandelion and other roots, especially *Corrigiola littoralis* (Illecebraceæ), are named as adulterants, it is stated by French authorities that the roots of *A. pyrethrum* are often old when found in commerce, but are never mixed with others.

PELLITORY, DALMATIAN

Chrysanthemum cinerariæfolium (VIS.)

PELLITORY, PERSIAN

Chrysanthemum roseum (ADAM)
Pyrethrum roseum (BIEB.)
Chrysanthemum carneum
N.O. Compositæ

Synonyms. Insect Flowers. Insect Plants
Part Used. Closed flowers

The Insect Powder of commerce, used to stupefy and kill various small insects, especially the larvæ of Cochylis, which attacks the vine, was first known as Persian Insect Powder, or Persian Pellitory, being prepared from the closed flowers of *Pyrethrum roseum* and *P. carneum*, plants native to the north of Persia, where they flourish on the mountain slopes up to a height of 6,500 feet, and also in the Caucasus. These two species are

familiar in this country as garden flowers, of which there are many varieties in cultivation, blossoming freely in May, the tufts of foliage of a dark green, much cut into, and the flowers of all shades of rose and crimson.

Some years ago, a Dalmatian species, *Chrysanthemum cinerariæfolium*, was found to be more active, and the Persian or Caucasian Insect Powder Plants are now seldom imported, being superseded by the Dalmatian species, which has white flowers, smaller than our Ox-Eye Daisy. It is cultivated both in Dalmatia and in California.

The cultivation of the Insect Powder plants has not yet been taken up on a commercial scale, either in Great Britain or the colonies, but it could be grown successfully in certain districts in this country.

There is a great demand for the flowers in commerce, and the flowers received from their usual source are so frequently adulterated by the addition of other composite flowers which are lacking in stupefying power, that the cultivation of the plant would be most desirable, either here or in our colonies. It can be profitably grown on dry, stony soil.

The conditions suiting the Dalmatian variety are sunny, pebbly, calcareous hillsides, dry, without irrigation, and in a fairly dry atmosphere. In ordinary garden soil, it does not flourish in shade and often dies off after flowering. All three species grown experimentally at Berne often succumbed during moist summers.

On the warmer southern and western coasts of Great Britain, the plant could easily be cultivated. It might be grown with success on the hilly slopes of oolite and limestone and chalk and on sandhills on the shore in Cornwall, Devon and Lancashire, or on the pebbly beach of Lydd, in Kent. In Jersey, on the pebbly and sandy shores, it would grow luxuriantly.

Attempts have already been made to cultivate the plant in Australia and South Africa.

Insect Powder is harmless to human beings. Besides being used as an insecticide in the form of a powder, it is also used as a lotion, a tincture of the flowers being prepared and used, diluted with 10 parts of water, to dab on the exposed skin to keep away insects. It is also employed as a fumigator. The smoke of the burnt flowers is as effective as the powder in keeping down insects, and might be valuable in Africa as a means against the tsetse-flies, and in sleeping sickness districts, if grown on the shores where they breed, and burnt when the flies emerge from the chrysalis.

In Dalmatia, the plant grows on the seashore, but it also grows well in the inland, mountainous districts of Herzegovina and Montenegro, the wild Montenegrin flowers being very highly esteemed. In the Adriatic islands, its cultivation is very remunerative.

¶ *Cultivation.* Sow seeds at the end of March on rich, light soil, in sunny situation and cover with $\frac{1}{4}$ to $\frac{1}{3}$ inch of fine soil and then with dry leaves. If the autumn be mild, the seeds may also be sometimes sown in

August, or early September, as soon as the seed is ripe, but then they need shading with canvas, placed about 6 inches above the soil, or more. Prick out the seedlings in the following March, or later, if sown in September. On the average only about half of the seedlings are fit for pricking out.

It is difficult to obtain seed that will germinate, the Dalmatian growers apparently dry the seeds by heat before disposing of them, to prevent germination.

Arrange the plants in deep furrows, prepared the previous autumn, about 15 to 20 inches apart, the seedlings 15 inches apart in the furrows. Of every 100 plants pricked out, fifteen to thirty generally die off and have to be replaced.

Weed several times during growth.

The plants begin to flower about the third week in May. The flower-buds are collected in the middle of May, or if it should then be damp, not till June. They must always be collected in dry weather.

A second gathering is made in August and September. The unopened flower-buds are kept separately, as they obtain the best price. The flower-heads are collected at different stages of development, the commercial varieties being known as 'closed,' 'half-closed' and 'open' flowers respectively. They are most active if collected when fully developed, but before they have expanded. They are cut off just below the involucre of bracts.

The flowers retain their insecticidal properties for an indefinite period, if kept under suitable condition, even if in the state of dry powder. It is the flowers alone that are active; the leaves have no insecticidal properties whatever.

The powder prepared from the Dalmatian flowers is distinguished from that of Persian flowers by numerous hairs. The better the quality of the powder, the larger will be the proportion of pollen and the smaller the proportion of stem issue.

One of the best tests of the quality of the powder is to keep a few house-flies under a tumbler with a little of the powder; they should be stupefied within a minute. Adulterated or less active powder will take about twenty minutes to effect this.

Each plant yields 80 to 100 flowers, and in one day 1,500 to 2,500 flowers can be gathered by one person. One hundred flowers weigh about 50 grammes ($1\frac{3}{5}$ oz.). One hundred kilos (220 lb.) of fresh flowers yield 25 to 33 kilos (55 to 72 lb.) of dried flowers.

In Dalmatia the flowers are dried in the shade on frames of cloth, in layers 1 to $1\frac{1}{2}$ inch deep, turned over two or three times daily. The Persian flowers are dried first in the sun and then in the shade.

After harvesting, the land is tilled in the autumn and again in the spring, the soil being forked between the rows to keep it porous. Being a mountain plant, it requires a dry surface, well drained below. Sunlight and heat are necessary for luxuriant growth.

The plants live on the average for six years, but sometimes will remain healthy and strong for as much as twenty years.

PELLITORY-OF-THE-WALL

Parietaria officinalis (LINN.)
N.O. Urticaceæ

Synonym. Lichwort
Part Used. Herb

Pellitory-of-the-Wall is a humble, inconspicuous plant belonging to the same group as the Stinging Nettle and the Hop. It is the only representative of its genus in Britain. The name of this genus, *Parietaria*, is derived from the Latin word *paries* (a wall), for it is very commonly found growing from crannies in dry walls, as its popular English name also tells us, and will frequently luxuriate in the midst of stony rubbish.

¶ *Description.* It is a much-branched, bushy, herbaceous, perennial plant, 1 to 2 feet high, with reddish, brittle stems and narrow, stalked leaves 1 to 2 inches long. The stems and veins of the under surface of the leaves are furnished with short, soft hairs, the upper surface of the leaves is nearly smooth, with sunken veins. The small, green stalkless flowers grow in clusters in the axils of the leaves and are in bloom all the summer. The filaments of their stamens are curiously jointed and so elastic that if touched before the expansion of the flower, they suddenly spring from their incurved position and scatter their pollen broadcast.

¶ *Constituents.* All parts of the plant contain nitre abundantly.

¶ *Medicinal Action and Uses.* Diuretic, laxative, refrigerant and slightly demulcent.

Pellitory-of-the-Wall is a most efficacious remedy for stone in the bladder, gravel, dropsy, stricture and other urinary complaints. Its action upon the urinary calculus is perhaps more marked than any other simple agent at present employed.

It is given in infusion or decoction, the infusion – the most usual form – 1 oz. to 1 pint of boiling water being taken in wineglassful doses. Frequently it is combined with Wild Carrot and Parsley Piert.

Fluid extract: dose, 1 drachm.

The decoction, says Gerard, 'helpeth such as are troubled with an old cough,' and 'the decoction with a little honey is good to gargle a sore throat.' He gives us many other uses:

'The juice held awhile in the mouth easeth pains in the teeth; the distilled water of the herb drank with sugar worketh the same effect and cleanseth the skin from spots, freckles, pimples, wheals, sunburn, etc. . . . 'The juice dropped into the ears easeth the noise in them and taketh away the pricking and shooting pains therein.'

In the form of an ointment he tells us it is capital for piles and a remedy for gout and fistula.

The leaves may be usefully applied as poultices.

The juice of the fresh herb, made into a thin syrup will stimulate the kidneys in the same way as the infusion of the dried herb.

Ben Jonson says:

'A good old woman . . . did cure me
With sodden ale and pellitorie o' the wall.'

PENNYROYAL

Mentha Pulegium (LINN.)
N.O. Labiatæ

Synonyms. Pulegium. Run-by-the-Ground. Lurk-in-the-Ditch. Pudding Grass. Piliole-rial
Part Used. Herb

This species of Mint, a native of most parts of Europe and parts of Asia, is the Pulegium of the Romans, so named by Pliny from its reputed power of driving away fleas – *pulex* being the Latin for flea, hence the Italian *pulce* and the French *puce*. This name given the plant in ancient times has been retained as its modern specific name. It is sometimes known to the country-people as 'Run by the Ground' and 'Lurk in the Ditch,' from its manner of growth.

It was formerly much used in medicine, the name Pennyroyal being a corruption of the old herbalists' name 'Pulioll-royall' (*Pulegium regium*), which we meet also in the Middle Ages as 'Piliole-rial.' It has been known to botanists since the time of Linnæus as *Mentha Pulegium*.

One of its popular names is 'Pudding Grass,' from being formerly used in stuffings for hog's puddings ('grass' being, like 'wort,' a word simply meaning 'herb'). It is still used abroad in various culinary preparations, but in this country it is now in disuse, as its taste and odour is too pronounced.

A famous stuffing was once made of Pennyroyal, pepper and honey.

¶ *Description*. Pennyroyal is the smallest of the Mints and very different in habit from any of the others. Two forms of the plant are met with in Great Britain: the commonest, the variety *decumbens*, has weak, prostrate stems, bluntly quadrangular, 3 inches to a foot long, which readily take root at the lower joints or nodes. The leaves are opposite, shortly stalked, more or less hairy on both sides, roundish oval, greyish green, about 1 to 1¼ inch long and ¼ inch broad. The flowers are in whorled clusters of ten or a dozen, rising in tiers one above the other at the nodes, where the leaves spring in pairs, beginning about the middle of the stem, their colour reddish purple to lilac blue, and in bloom during July and August. The seed is light brown, oval and very small. The other variety, *erecta*, has much stouter stems, not rooting at the nodes and not decumbent, but erect or sub-erect, 8 to 12 inches high. It is rarer, but the best for cultivation, as it can be reaped and tied up in bundles easily, whereas the stems of *decumbens* form a dense green turf, the flowering stems, sparingly produced, lying on the leafy cushions of the plant. There are other varieties on the Continent. The plant has been introduced into North and South America. It is mentioned in the Herbals of the New World as one of the plants the Pilgrim Fathers introduced.

It is found wild and naturalized throughout the civilized world in strong, moist soil on the borders of ponds and streams, and near pools on heaths and commons. Gerard speaks of it as found abundantly

'on a common at Mile End, near London, about the holes and ponds thereof, in sundrie places, from whence poore women bring plenty to sell in London markets.'

Turner says:

'It crepeth much upon the ground and hath many little round leves not unlyke the leves of mesierum gentil, but that they are a little longer and sharper and also little indented rounde about, and grener than the leves of mariurum ar. The leves grow in little branches even from the roote of certayn ioyntes by equall spaces one devyded from an other. Whereas the leves grow in little tuftes upon the over partes of the braunches. . . . Pennyroyal groweth much, without any setting, besyd hundsley (Hounslow) upon the heth beside a watery place.'

Like most of its near relatives, Pennyroyal is highly aromatic, perhaps even more so than any other Mint, containing an essential oil resembling in properties that of other mints, though less powerful. The flavour is more pungent and acrid and less agreeable than that of Spearmint or Peppermint.

Pennyroyal was in high repute among the Ancients. Both Pliny and Dioscorides described its numerous virtues. In Northern Europe it was also much esteemed, as may be inferred from the frequent references to it in the Anglo-Saxon and Welsh works on medicine.

'The boke of Secretes of Albertus Magnus of the vertues of Herbes, Stones and certaine Beastes' states that, by putting drowning flies and bees in warm ashes of Pennyroyal, 'they shall recover their lyfe after a little tyme as by ye space of one houre' and be revived.

Pennyroyal is often found in cottage gardens, as an infusion of the leaves, known as Pennyroyal Tea, is an old-fashioned remedy for colds and menstrual derangements.

¶ *Cultivation*. Locally, Pennyroyal grows abundantly, but being required by the hundredweight it has been cultivated to a certain extent in this country, on account of the difficulty of obtaining sufficient quantities from the widely separated localities in which it is found.

As a crop, it presents uncertainty, being diminished by drought, its natural habitat being on moist heaths and commons by the sides of pools. It is easily grown from seed and succeeds best in loamy soil, in a moist situation, but propagation is commonly by division of old roots in autumn or spring, March or April, like Spearmint, or more rarely by cuttings. The roots may be divided up in September where the winters are mild, in April where the winters are frosty.

In planting, allow a space of 12 inches between the rows and 6 inches between the plants in the row. Water shortly afterwards should the weather be at all dry. When a good stock of healthy roots has been obtained, Pennyroyal may be forced with advantage. The creeping underground roots grow in horizontal masses, as with the other mints, and if some of these are taken up at any time during the winter and laid out on a bed of good soil, covering them with 2 or 3 inches of the same, they will soon push up fresh shoots in quantity. They can be put in boxes in a moderately warm house or pit. If all the tops are not wanted they may be made into cuttings, each with four or five joints, and, inserted in boxes of light, sandy soil, will soon form roots in the same temperature, and after being duly hardened off, may be planted out in the open, in due course, and a healthy, vigorous stock thus be maintained. Towards the close of autumn all the stalks that remain should be cut down to the ground and the bed covered with fresh soil to the depth of 1 inch.

Plantations generally last for four or five years when well managed and on favourable soil, but frosts may cause the crop to die off in patches, so it is a safe plan to make new plantings yearly.

¶ *Harvesting*. Pennyroyal is mostly sold in the dry state for making tea, the stems being cut when the plant is just about to flower and dried in the usual manner.

¶ *Constituents*. The fresh herb yields about 1 per cent. of a volatile oil, oil of Pulegium, a yellow or greenish-yellow liquid, obtained by distillation, and having a strong aromatic odour and taste. The chief constituent is ketone pulegone.

A yield of 12 lb. of oil to the acre of crop is considered good.

¶ *Medicinal Action and Uses*. Pliny gives a long list of disorders for which Pennyroyal was a supposed remedy, and especially recommends it for hanging in sleeping rooms, it being considered by physicians as more conducive to health even than roses.

It was likewise thought to communicate its purifying qualities to water, and Gerard tells us: 'If you have Pennyroyale in great quantity dry and cast it into corrupt water, it helpeth it much, neither will it hurt them that drink thereof.' As a purifier of the blood, it was highly spoken of: 'Penny-royale taken with honey cleanseth the lungs and cleareth the breast from all gross and thick humours.'

It was deemed by our ancestors valuable in headaches and giddiness. We are told: 'A garland of Penny-royale made and worn about the head is of great force against the swimming in the head and the pains and giddiness thereof.'

Pennyroyal Water was distilled from the leaves and given as an antidote to spasmodic, nervous and hysterical affections. It was also used against cold and 'affections of the joints.'

Culpepper says of Pennyroyal:

'Drank with wine, it is good for venomous bites, and applied to the nostrils with vinegar revives those who faint and swoon. Dried and burnt, it strengthens the gums, helps the gout, if applied of itself to the place until it is red, and applied in a plaster, it takes away spots or marks on the face; applied with salt, it profits those that are splenetic, or liver-grown. . . . The green herb bruised and put into vinegar, cleanses foul ulcers and takes away the marks of bruises and blows about the eyes, and burns in the face, and the leprosy, if drank and applied outwardly. . . . One spoonful of the juice sweetened with sugar-candy is a cure for hooping-cough.'

Its action is carminative, diaphoretic, stimulant and emmenagogic, and is principally employed for the last-named property in disorders caused by sudden chill or cold.

It is also beneficial in cases of spasms, hysteria, flatulence and sickness, being very warming and grateful to the stomach.

The infusion of 1 oz. of herb to a pint of boiling water is taken warm in teacupful doses, frequently repeated, and the oil is also given on sugar, as well as being made up into pills and other preparations.

In France and Germany oil of Pennyroyal is also used commercially.

¶ *Preparations and Dosages*. Fluid extract, ¼ to 1 drachm. Essence, 5 to 20 drops. Oil, ¼ to 3 drops.

The following is reprinted by special permission from *Punch*:

PENNYROYAL. – A CAROL

'Far away in Sicily!'
    A home-come sailor sang this rhyme,
Deep in an ingle, mug on knee,
    At Christmas time.

In Sicily, as I was told,
    The children take them Pennyroyal,
The same as lurks on hill and wold
    In Cotsall soil.

The Pennyroyal of grace divine
    In little cradles they do weave –
Little cradles therewith they line
    On Christmas Eve.

And there, as midnight bells awake
    The Day of Birth, as they do tell,
All into bud the small buds break
    With sweetest smell.

All into bud that very hour;
    And pure and clean, as they do say,
The Pennyroyal's full in flower
    On Christmas Day.

Far away in Sicily!
    Hark, the Christmas bells do chime!
So blossom love in thee and me
    This Christmas time!

W. B.

December 19, 1917.

See MINTS.

PEPPER

PEPPER
Piper nigrum (LINN.)
N.O. Piperaceæ

Synonyms. Black Pepper. Piper (United States Pharmacopœia)

Part Used. Dried unripe fruit

Habitat. In South India wild, and in Cochin-China; also cultivated in East and West Indies, Malay Peninsula, Malay Archipelago, Siam, Malabar, etc.

¶ *Description.* The best Pepper of commerce comes from Malabar. Pepper is mentioned by Roman writers in the fifth century. It is said that Attila demanded among other items 3,000 lb. of Pepper in ransom for the city of Rome. Untrained, the plant will climb 20 or more feet, but for commercial purposes it is restricted to 12 feet. It is a perennial with a round, smooth, woody stem, with articulations, swelling near the joints and branched; the leaves are entire, broadly ovate, acuminate, coriaceous, smooth, with seven nerves; colour dark green and attached by strong sheath-like foot-stalks to joints of branches. Flowers small, white, sessile, covering a tubular spadix; fruits globular, red berries when ripe, and surface coarsely wrinkled. The plant is propagated by cuttings and grown at the base of trees with a rough, prickly bark to support them. Between three or four years after planting they commence fruiting and their productiveness ends about the fifteenth year. The berries are collected as soon as they turn red and before they are quite ripe; they are then dried in the sun. In England, for grinding they mix Peppers of different origin. Malabar for weight, Sumatra for colour, and Penang for strength. Pepper has an aromatic odour, pungent and bitterish taste.

¶ *Constituents.* Piperine, which is identical in composition to morphia, volatile oil, a resin called Chavicin. Its medicinal activities depends mainly on its pungent resin and volatile oil, which is colourless, turning yellow with age, with a strong odour, and not so acrid a taste as the peppercorn; it also contains starch, cellulose and colouring.

The concrete oil is a deep green colour and very acrid.

¶ *Medicinal Action and Uses.* Aromatic, stimulant, carminative; is said to possess febrifuge properties. Its action as a stimulant is specially evident on the mucous membrane of the rectum, and so is good for constipation, also on the urinary organs; externally it is a rubefacient, useful in relaxed conditions of the rectum when prolapsed; sometimes used in place of cubebs for gonorrhœa; given in combination with aperients to facilitate their action, and to prevent griping. As a gargle it is valued for relaxed uvula, paralysis of the tongue. On account of its stimulant action it aids digestion and is specially useful in atonic dyspepsia and torbid condition of the stomach. It will correct flatulence and nausea. It has also been used in vertigo, paralytic and arthritic disorders. It is sometimes added to quinine when the stomach will not respond to quinine alone. It has also been advised in diarrhœa, cholera, scarlatina, and in solution for a wash for *tinea capititis.* Piperine should not be combined with astringents, as it renders them inert.

¶ *Dosages.* Black Pepper, 5 to 15 grains in powder. Piperine, 1 to 8 grains.

The root of the Pepper plant in India has been used by the natives as a cordial tonic and stimulant.

B.P. dose of Pepper, 1 to 2 drachms.

Oleoresin, U.S.P.: dose, ¼ grain.

Heliotropin is recommended medicinally as an antiseptic and antipyretic. It is obtained by the oxidation of piperic acid and is used in perfumery. From the time of Hippocrates Pepper has been used as a medicine and condiment.

¶ *Adulteration of Pepper.* Linseed mustard seed, wheat and pea-flour, sago, ground rice. At one time when the duty levied on Pepper was very high, fictitious peppercorns were made of oil-cake, clay, with a little cayenne added.

¶ *Other Species Used.*

Piper trioicum, nearly allied to *P. nigrum,* is also used in commerce.

The female plant does not ripen properly, and is deficient in pungency, but the Peppers on plants with hermaphrodite flowers on same spike are very pungent, and equal to the best Malabar Pepper.

WHITE PEPPER (*Piper album*).

From the same plant as *P. nigrum,* White Pepper is ripe fruit, partially deprived of its pericarp by maceration in water, then rubbed and dried in the sun. It contains albuminous seed, having small starch grains, taste and smell like Pepper, more aromatic than black and not so pungent. Same as the black, but containing more starch and less ash. Sold as whole White Pepper or broken White Pepper. The removed hulls are sold separately as Pepper hulls, and form a brownish powder, very pungent in smell and flavour and containing a large quantity of oleoresin of Pepper, but no piperine.

Sometimes the hulls are mixed with the broken White Pepper; this mixture has more oleoresin in it and less piperine.

¶ *Medicinal Action and Uses.* Teaspoonful doses taken several times a day are recommended to overcome the obstinate constipation of dyspeptics.

LONG PEPPER (*Piper longum*).

Part Used. The dried, unripe spikes of *Pipers officinum* and *longum*.

Habitat. Java, India, Philippines, the best coming from Batavia, and Singapore.

P. officinarum is principally used and is considered the best; both are gathered when green, when they are hotter than when quite ripe. In *P. officinarum* the fruit is a dark grey colour with a weak aromatic odour and a very fiery pungent taste. In *P. longum* the fruits are shorter and thicker and the constituents almost identical with *P. nigrum*. It contains piperine, a soft green resin, a burning acridity, a volatile oil which possibly gives it its odour; it is inferior to *P. nigrum* and most used as its adulterant.

PIPER BETEL.

Habitat. East Indies.

The leaves are used to wrap round areca nut; rubbed with shell lime they are chewed by the Indians to sweeten their breath and strengthen the stomach. The trade in it forms considerable commerce. The Asiatic use of it amongst men destroys the teeth from the lime used with it. The women of the Malabar Coast, on the other hand, stain their teeth black with antimony, which preserves theirs to old age.

PIPER AMALAGO, or rough-leaved Pepper, a shrub growing up to 10 feet. It is called the small-grained Black Pepper, and grows on the hilly parts of Jamaica. The berries differ only in size from the East Indian Black Pepper, being only the size of mustard seed, good for seasoning, taste and flavour being the same as Black Pepper. It is picked when full-grown before it ripens, otherwise it loses its pungency and grows soft and succulent.

It is dried in the sun and often left on its stalks, which have the same flavour and pungency as the Peppers and are as easily ground in the mills.

¶ *Medicinal Action and Uses.* Leaves and tender shoots are used in discutient baths and fomentations and pounded for application to ulcers; root is warm and very useful as a resolutive and sudorific or diaphoretic, but best for infusions and decoctions; a good deobstruent for dropsy.

PIPER PELLUCIDUM, or pellucoid-leaved Pepper.

Habitat. South America and West Indian Islands.

¶ *Description.* An annual found growing on moist, gravelly banks, etc.

Has very small berries each containing a small seed like dust. In Martinico the leaves are eaten with lettuce, vinegar and oil as a salad and called 'Cresson,' but they are too strong and hot for most Europeans.

PIPER ROTUNDIFOLIUM.

Habitat. Jamaica and Martinique.

A herbaceous plant living in close, moist woods covering the trunks of old trees and stones.

¶ *Description.* Leaves greasy, bright green, fragrant, reviving odour; good aromatics and cephalics, retaining perfume several years; water distilled from them smells deliciously of the plants.

PIPER UMBELLATUM.

Synonyms. Unbelled Pepper. Santa Maria Leaf.

Habitat. Jamaica.

This plant is a very common annual and found growing up to 4 feet high. Has large round leaves; the root is a warm, active remedy against poisons, and in many parts of the sugar colonies is made up into a syrup much used by the inhabitants for colds and catarrhs.

PEPPER, HUNGARIAN

Synonyms. Paprika. Sweet Pepper. Grains of Paradise

Paprika, or Hungarian Pepper, a tasteless cayenne, is recognized by the German Pharmacopœia, and in the United States is imported in three grades. The first grade is savoury and of a fine red colour; it is made of the selected pericarp, the stems and placenta removed, the seeds first washed, then ground. The second grade is made by grinding the entire pod with the stems. Third grade is all the waste and spoiled pods being ground together, the residue of other grades. This is a yellowish colour and much more pungent than the other. Paprika is generally made

from *Croton annum*, and sometimes called Sweet Pepper. It is mostly used to dilute the strength of other powdered chillies, and it is used by bird fanciers to improve the colour of canaries.[1]

Grains of Paradise, Guinea Grains, Melegueta or Mallaguetta Pepper, from *Ampelopsis Grana Paradisi*, or *Habzeli* of Ethiopia (Kanang of Ethiopia). Two kinds of these grains are known in the English markets, one plumper than the other. One may be that imported into America from West Africa, and into England from plants introduced into Deme-

---

[1] This is the paprika which flavours so many Hungarian dishes. – EDITOR.

GRAINS OF PARADISE (HUNGARIAN PEPPER)
Amomum Melegueta

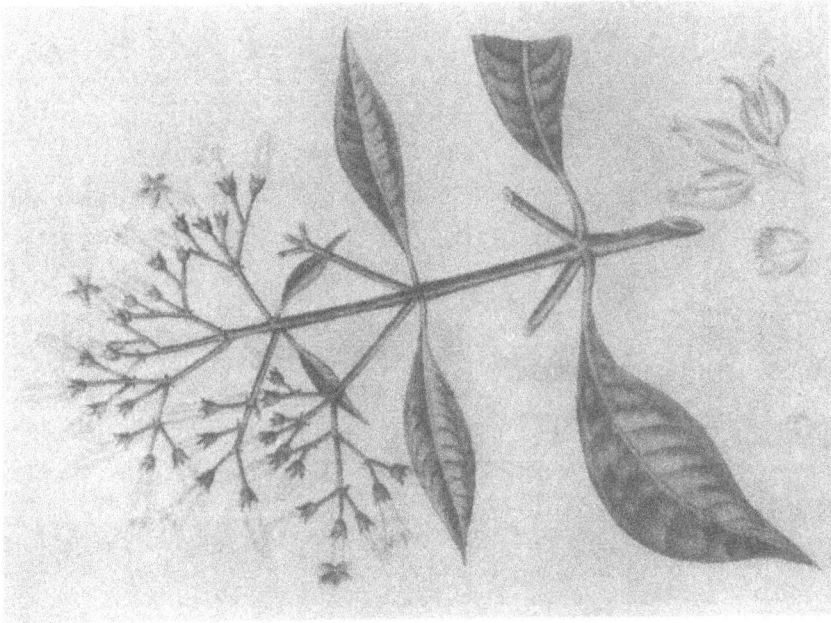

PERUVIAN BARK
Cinchona Succirubra

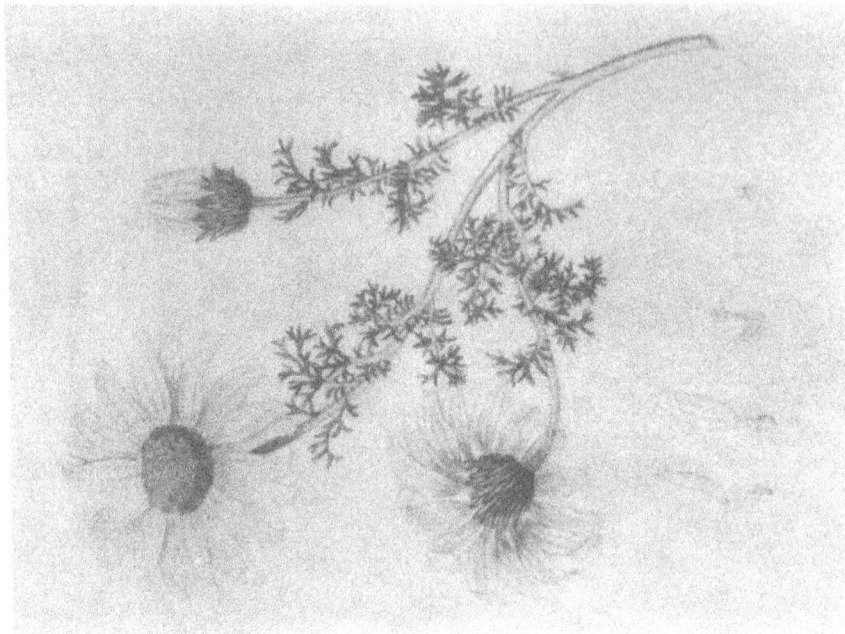

PELLITORY
Anacyclus Pyrethrum

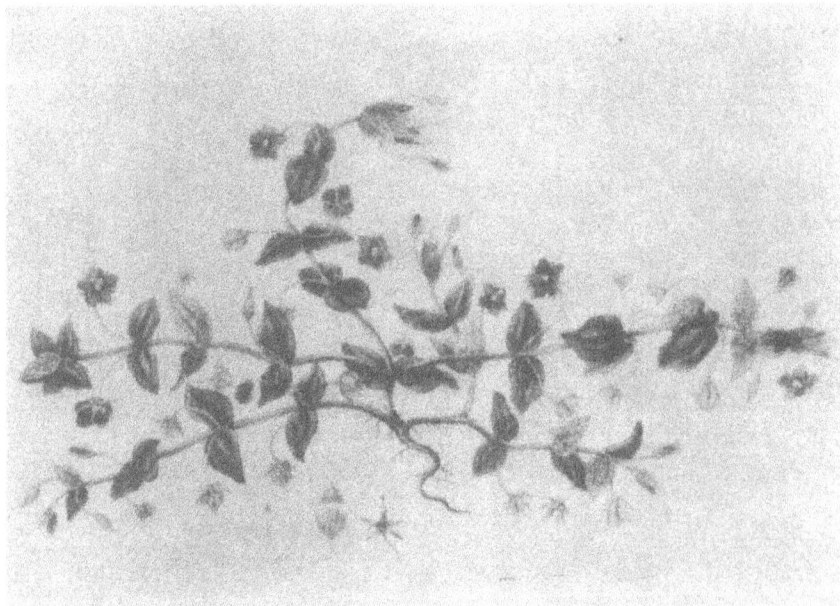

SCARLET PIMPERNEL
Anagallis Arvensis

rara, where they are thought to be a product of *A. Melegueta*. They resemble Pepper in their effects, but are seldom used except in

PEPPERMINT. *See* MINTS

PERIWINKLES

GREATER PERIWINKLE (*Vinca major*, Linn.)

This is the species more generally used in herbal medicine, as an astringent and tonic, in menorrhagia and in hæmorrhages, also as a laxative, and gargle. Made into an ointment, useful for piles and inflammatory conditions of the skin.

LESSER PERIWINKLE (*Vinca minor*, Linn.)

Employed in homœopathy for preparation of a tincture used for hæmorrhages.

MADAGASCAR PERIWINKLE (*Vinca rosea*, Linn.)

A reputed cure for diabetes. (Synonym *Lochnera rosea*, Reichb.)

The well-known Periwinkles – both Greater and Lesser – familiar plants of our woods and gardens, are members of the genus *Vinca*, so named by Linnæus, which includes *five* in Europe, and the Orient, and three species native to the East Indies, Madagascar and America, assigned by a later botanist, Reichberg, to a separate genus, *Lochnera*, as they differ from Vinca in the stamens and head of the style not being hairy, though the main characteristics are the same.

Vinca is a genus of the natural order Apocynaceæ, which includes many tropical trees and shrubs with showy flowers, a large number of which are very poisonous, among these being the beautiful Oleander, so frequently grown in our greenhouses.

The Periwinkles are the only representatives of their order in our flora, and there is, in fact, considerable doubt among botanists whether the Periwinkle should be considered a true native of Great Britain. It was a familiar flower in the days of Chaucer, who refers to it as the 'fresh Pervinke rich of hew,' and it is now commonly found in woods and hedgerows, and, where it occurs, is generally in great profusion.

The plant is perennial and retains its glossy leaves throughout the winter. Occasionally, in the smaller kind, when cultivated in gardens, leaves occur with streaks of lighter green upon the dark rich colour that is characteristic of the rest of the foliage. The leaves are always placed in pairs on the stem, the flowers springing from their axils. In the Greater Periwinkle, the leaves are large and egg-shaped, with the margins minutely fringed. Those of the Lesser are much smaller, myrtle-like in form, their margins not fringed.

The plant seldom, if ever, ripens its seed, a

veterinary practice and to give strength to spirits, wine, beer, and vinegar. The seeds have a rich reddish-brown colour.

N.O. Apocynaceæ

fact that has been considered confirmatory of the theory that the Periwinkle is not truly indigenous, as in more southern countries it does so. It propagates itself by long, trailing and rooting stems, and by their means not only extends itself in every direction, but succeeds in obtaining an almost exclusive possession of the soil, since little or nothing else can maintain its ground against the dense mass of stems, which deprive other and weaker plants of light and air.

The flowers of the Periwinkle vary somewhat in intensity of colour, but the average colour is a deep purplish-blue. A white variety of the Lesser Periwinkle occurs in Devonshire and in gardens; it is often met with bearing purple, blue and white flowers, sometimes double.

The calyx is deeply cleft into five very narrow divisions. The corolla consists of a distinctly tubular portion terminating in a broad flat disk, composed of five broad lobes, twisted when in bud, curiously irregular in form, having the sides of the margin unequally curved, so that although the effect of the whole corolla is symmetrical, when each separate lobe is examined, it will be seen that an imaginary line from apex to the centre of the flower would divide it into two very unequal portions – very unusual in the petals of a flower. The whole effect is as if the lobes of the corolla were rotating round the mouth of its tube, and the movement had suddenly been arrested.

The mouth of the tube is angular and the tube closed with hairs, and the curiously curved anthers of the stamens, which are five in number, are inserted in the tube. The pistil of this flower, as well as of the smaller species, is a singularly beautiful object, resembling the shaft of a pillar with a double capital. The anthers stand above the stigmatic disk, but the stigma itself is on the under surface of the disk, so that self-fertilization is not caused as the insect's tongue enters the flowers.

The Lesser Periwinkle is not only smaller in all the parts, but has a more trailing habit of growth, matting itself together. The stems are very slender, only those bearing flowers being erect, growing to a height of 6 to 8 inches, the others trailing and rooting freely at intervals, so that a large space of ground is quickly monopolized by it.

Both the English and botanical names of the Periwinkle are derived from the Latin *vincio* (to bind), in allusion to these long, trailing stems that spread over and keep down the other plants where it grows. This is described by Wordsworth:

'Through primrose tufts in that sweet bower
The fair periwinkle trailed its wreaths.'

It is assumed that the *Vincapervinca* of Pliny is this plant.

¶ *History*. The old English form of the name, as it appears in early Anglo-Saxon Herbals, as well as in Chaucer, was 'Parwynke,' and we also find it called 'Joy of the Ground.' In Macer's *Herbal* (early sixteenth century) it is described:

'Parwynke is an erbe grene of colour
In Tyme of May he beryth blo flour,
His stalkys ain (are) so feynt and feye
Yet never more growyth he hey (high).'

And we are also told that 'men calle it ye Juy of Grownde.'

In more modern days it has locally been called 'Ground Ivy,' though that name is now generally assigned to quite another little, blue-flowered plant of the hedgerow, *Glechoma hederacea*. In Gloucestershire, we find the name 'Cockles' given locally to it; in Hampshire, its name is corrupted to 'Pennywinkle.' In some parts of Devonshire, the flowers from their use are known as 'Cut Finger,' and the more fanciful name of 'Blue Buttons' is also there given to it. In France, it has been known as *Pucellage*, or Virginflower, no doubt also from the madonnablue of its blossoms.

An old name, given both in reference to its colour and its use in magic, was 'Sorcerer's Violet' (corresponding to its old French name *'Violette des sorciers'*). It was a favourite flower with 'wise folk' for making charms and love-philtres. It was one of the plants believed to have power to exorcize evil spirits. In Macer's *Herbal* we read of its potency against 'wykked spirytis.'

Apuleius, in his *Herbarium* (printed 1480), gives elaborate directions for its gathering:

'This wort is of good advantage for many purposes, that is to say, first against devil sickness and demoniacal possessions and against snakes and wild beasts and against poisons and for various wishes and for envy and for terror and that thou mayst have grace, and if thou hast the wort with thee thou shalt be prosperous and ever acceptable. This wort thou shalt pluck thus, saying, "I pray thee, vinca pervinca, thee that art to be had for thy many useful qualities, that thou come to me glad blossoming with thy mainfulness, that thou outfit me so that I be shielded and ever prosperous and undamaged by poisons and by water"; when thou shalt pluck this wort, thou shalt be clean of every uncleanness, and thou shalt pick it when the moon is nine nights old and eleven nights and thirteen nights and thirty nights and when it is one night old.'

These superstitions about the Periwinkle are of great age and are repeated by all the old writers. In *The Boke of Secretes of Albartus Magnus of the Vertues of Herbs, Stones and certaine Beastes*, we find:

'Perwynke when it is beate unto pouder with worms of ye earth wrapped about it and with an herbe called houslyke, it induceth love between man and wyfe if it bee used in their meales . . . if the sayde confection be put in the fyre it shall be turned anone unto blue coloure.'

In olden days it was used in garlands. An old chronicle tells us that when, in 1306, Simon Fraser, after he had been taken prisoner fighting for William Wallace, rode heavily ironed through London to the place of execution, a garland of Periwinkle was placed in mockery on his head.

The flower is called by the Italians *Centocchio*, or 'Hundred Eyes,' but it is also called 'The Flower of Death,' from the ancient custom of making it into garlands to place on the biers of dead children. To the Germans, it is the 'Flower of Immortality.' In France, the Periwinkle is considered an emblem of friendship, probably in allusion to Rousseau's recollection of his friend Madame de Warens, after a lapse of thirty years, by the sight of the Periwinkle in flower.

¶ *Uses*. Both species of Periwinkle are used in medicine for their acrid, astringent and tonic properties.

'The Periwinkle is a great binder,' said an old herbalist, and both Dioscorides and Galen commended it against fluxes. Culpepper says that it

'stays bleeding at the mouth and nose, if it be chewed . . . and may be used with advantage in hysteric and other fits. . . . It is good in nervous disorders, the young tops made into a conserve is good for the night-mare. The small periwinkle possesses all the virtues of the other kind and may very properly supply its place.'

It was considered a good remedy for cramp, Lord Bacon himself testifying that a limb suffering from cramp would be cured if bands of green Periwinkle were tied round it;

and William Coles, in his *Adam in Eden* (1657), gives a definite case of a friend who was

'vehemently tormented with the cramp for a long while which could be by no means eased till he had wrapped some of the branches hereof about his limbs.'

An ointment prepared from the bruised leaves with lard has been largely used in domestic medicine and is reputed to be both soothing and healing in all inflammatory ailments of the skin and an excellent remedy for bleeding piles.

Vinca major is used in herbal practice for its astringent and tonic properties in menorrhagia and in hæmorrhages generally. For obstructions of mucus in the intestines and lungs, diarrhœa, congestions, hæmorrhages, etc., Periwinkle Tea is a good remedy. In cases of scurvy and for relaxed sore throat and inflamed tonsils, it may also be used as a gargle. For bleeding piles, it may be applied externally, as well as taken internally.

A homœopathic tincture is prepared from the fresh leaves of *Vinca minor* and

'is given medicinally for the milk-crust of infants as well as for internal hæmorrhages, the dose being from 2 to 10 drops, three or four times in the day, with a spoonful of water.'

PERUVIAN BALSAM. *See* BALSAM

PERUVIAN BARK

The flowers of the Greater (and probably also of the Lesser) Periwinkle are gently purgative, but lose their effect on drying. If gathered in the spring and made into a syrup, they will impart thereto all their virtues, and this, it is stated, is excellent as a gentle laxative for children and also for overcoming chronic constipation in grown persons.

The bruised leaves put into the nostrils will, it is asserted, allay bleeding from the nose.

A still more important use has been found for another species, *V. rosea*, Linn. (synonym *Lochnera rosea*, Reichb.), sometimes known as the Madagascar Periwinkle, a small undershrub up to 3 feet high in its native habitat, the general appearance much resembling our English species, *V. major*, but with the stems more upright. It is widely spread in Tropical Africa and naturalized in the Tropics in general. It is not sufficiently hardy to stand our climate without protection, though it is often grown in conservatories in this country. The blossoms are a rich crimson.

In 1923, considerable interest was aroused in the medical world by the statement that this species of *Vinca* had the power to cure diabetes, and would probably prove an efficient substitute for Insulin, but *V. major* has long been used by herbalists for this purpose.

¶ *Preparation.* Fluid extract.

Cinchona succirubra (PAVON.)
N.O. Rubiaceæ

Synonyms. Red Bark. Jesuits' Powder. Cinchona Bark
Part Used. Bark dried from stem and branches
Habitat. South America, but cultivated in India, Java, Ceylon, etc.

¶ *Description.* The species most cultivated in India and elsewhere are *Cinchona succirubra*, or Peruvian Bark, and *C. officinalis.* These evergreen trees grow in the hottest part of the world and are said to constitute a twenty-ninth part of the whole flowering plants of the tropics. Peruvian bark was introduced to Europe in 1640, but the plant producing it was not known to botanists till 1737; a few years later it was renamed Cinchona after the Countess of Chinchon, who first made the bark known in Europe for its medicinal qualities. The history of Cinchona and its many vicissitudes affords a striking illustration of the importance of Government aid in establishing such an industry. It was known and used by the Jesuits very early in its history, but was first advertized for sale in England by James Thompson in 1658, and was made official in the London Pharmacopœia of 1677. The

bark is spongy, very slight odour, taste astringent and strongly bitter.

¶ *Constituents.* Alkaloids, quinine, cinchonidine, cinchonine, quinidine, hydrocinchonidine, quinamine, homocinchonidine, hydroquinine, quinic and cincholannic acids, bitter amorphous glucoside, starch and calcium oxalate. The history of the formation of the alkaloids, in different parts and age of the tree, is interesting. The process of 'mossing' introduced by Mr. M'Ivor, viz. the protection of the bark from light and air by layers of damp moss, increases the quantity of the alkaloids, allows of the periodical renewal of the bark, and increases the quantity of the alkaloid in the new bark.

¶ *Medicinal Action and Uses.* Febrifuge, tonic and astringent; valuable for influenza, neuralgia and debility. Large and too constant doses must be avoided, as they produce headache, giddiness and deafness. The liquid extract is useful as a cure for drunkenness. The powdered bark is often used in tooth-powders, owing to its astringency, but not much used internally (except as a bitter wine); it creates a sensation of warmth, but sometimes causes gastric intestinal irritation. Cinchona in decoction is a useful gargle and a good throat astringent.

¶ *Dosage.* 3 to 10 grains.

See CALISAYA.

PHEASANT'S EYE. *See* (FALSE) HELLEBORE

PICHI

Fabiana imbricata (RUTZ. and PARON.)
N.O. Solanaceæ

Synonym. Fabiana
Parts Used. Dried leaf and twig
Habitat. Chile, Peru, Bolivia, and Argentine Republic

¶ *Description.* A neat half-hardy shrub, very like a heath in general appearance. Fastigiate habit, has small branches covered with scale-like imbricated leaves, colour bluish green, leaves are smooth, entire, flowers solitary, terminal, corolla tubular, usually white, sometimes purple. A dwarf decorative plant; will grow in warmer parts of England; it needs a bright sheltered sunny spot, and would do well on a rockery. The fruit is a capsule containing a few sub-globular seeds. The odour of the drug is aromatic, the taste bitter, and terebinthinate.

¶ *Constituents.* Volatile oil, fat, resin, bitter fluorescent glucoside, and an alkaloid fabianine and tannin.

¶ *Medicinal Action and Uses.* Tonic, cholagogue, a valuable terebinthic diuretic, largely used in acute vesical catarrh, giving very favourable results where urinary irritation is caused by gravel. Is said to ease the irritability and assist in the expulsion of renal, urethal or cystic calculi, very useful in the treatment of jaundice and dyspepsia due to lack of biliary secretion. Is contraindicated in organic disease of the kidneys, though cases of renal hæmorrhages from Bright's disease have been greatly benefited by its use; it has been used also for gonorrhœa and gonorrhœal prostatitis.

¶ *Dosage.* Solid extract, 2 to 10 grains. Fluid extract, 1 to 40 minims.

A strong tincture is made from the resinoid precipitate and is considered the best preparation of the drug.

PILEWORT. *See* CELANDINE

PIMPERNEL, SCARLET

Anagallis arvensis (LINN.)
N.O. Primulaceæ

Synonyms. Shepherd's Barometer. Poor Man's Weatherglass. Adder's Eyes
　(*Old English*) Bipinella
Parts Used. Leaves, herb
Habitat. The Scarlet Pimpernel grows on the roadside in waste places and on the dry sandy edges of corn and other fields; it is widely distributed, not only over Britain, but throughout the world, being found in all the temperate regions in both hemispheres

¶ *Description.* Its creeping, square stems, a foot in length at most, have their egg-shaped, stalkless leaves arranged in pairs. The edges of the leaves are entire (i.e. quite free from indentations of any sort), and in whatever direction the stem may run, either along the ground, or at an angle to it, the leaves always keep their faces turned to the light.

The Pimpernel flowers from May until late into August. The flowers appear singly, each on longish, thin stalks, springing from the junction of each leaf with the stem. The little flower-stalks are erect during flowering, but curved backward when the seed is ripening. The corolla is made up of five petals, joined together at their base into a ring. A purple spot often appears in the centre of the flower. The petals are very sensitive, the flowers closing at once if the sky becomes overcast and threatens rain. Even in bright weather, the flowers are only open for a comparatively short time – never opening until between eight and nine in the morning and shutting up before three o'clock in the afternoon. As the petals are only brilliantly coloured on their upper faces, the flowers when closed disappear from view among the greenness of the leaves.

Inside the petals are five stamens, each standing exactly opposite to a petal. Upon the stamens are a number of delicate, violet hairs, which seem to serve as a bait to insects, taking the place, perhaps, of honey, of which the Pimpernel has none.

As the autumn comes on, the fruit in the centre of each flower swells and ripens. It is in the form of a little urn or capsule, full of tiny seeds. When the latter are quite ripe, the urn splits round its circumference into two halves – the upper half lifts up like a lid and the seeds are shaken out with every movement of the wind.

Propagation is entirely by seeds, as the plant is an annual, completely dying at the end of each season, both above and below ground.

A blue variety of an intense deep colour is occasionally found in Great Britain, and more commonly in central and southern Europe. A number of scientific experiments have been made on these blue and red Pimpernels by Darwin, Henslow and others. Henslow found that of the offspring of the blue, some had red and some blue petals, while Darwin discovered that by crossing the red and blue, some of the offspring were red, some blue, and some an intermediate colour. Gerard thought that the scarlet variety was the male plant, and that the blue was the female.

This blue variety (*Anagallis cerulea*) is described as growing in beautiful little tufts about the hills of Madeira.

The common variety (*A. arvensis*) is mentioned in lists of plants growing in Persia, Nepaul, China, New Holland, Mauritius, Cape of Good Hope, Japan, Egypt, Abyssinia, U.S.A., Mexico, and Chile. It is to be found in all the temperate regions in both hemispheres, but shuns the Arctic cold and hardly bears more than the sub-tropical heat.

Occasionally flesh-coloured and pure white blossoms have been found as varieties of this plant.

The plant appears in the Herbals and Vocabularies of the sixteenth century as 'Bipinella,' a name originally applied to the Great and Salad Burnet. It was much used as a cosmetic herb. Howard, in *The Old Commodore*, 1837, says: 'If she'd only used my pimpernel water, for she has one monstrous freckle in her forehead.' The plant was also said to be a remedy for the bites of mad dogs and to dispel sadness.

This plant once had a great reputation in medicine, and was used as a universal panacea.

'No heart can think, no tongue can tell
  The virtues of the Pimpernel.'

Pliny speaks of its value in liver complaints, and its generic name *Anagallis* (given it by Dioscorides) is derived from the Greek *Anagelao*, signifying 'to laugh,' because it removes the depression that follows liver troubles.

The Greeks used it for diseases of the eye, and Gerard and Culpepper affirm that 'it helpeth them that are dim-sighted,' the juice being mixed with honey and dropped into the eyes.

It is 'a gallant, Solar herb, of a cleansing attractive quality, whereby it draweth forth thorns and splinters gotten into the flesh.'

'Used inwardly and applied outwardly,' Culpepper tells us, 'it helpeth also all stinging and biting of venomous beasts or mad dogs.'

And again, 'the distilled water or juice is much celebrated by French dames to cleanse the skin from any roughness, deformity or discolourings thereof.'

Another old writer says 'the Herb Pimpernel is good to prevent witchcraft, as Mother Bumby doth affirm.'

¶ *Part Used*. The whole herb, gathered in the wild condition, when the leaves are at their best, in June, and used both fresh and dried.

Pimpernel has no odour, but a bitter taste, which is rather astringent.

¶ *Constituents*. The plant possesses very active properties, although its virtues are not fully understood. It is known to contain Saponin, such as the Soapwort also specially furnishes.

The leaves are sufficiently inert to be eaten in salads, of which they often form a component part in France and Germany, but Professor Henslow tells us that caged birds have died from eating them instead of Chickweed, which it somewhat resembles.

Experiments have shown that it contains some injurious properties which neither drying nor boiling destroys. Though too small to be eaten in quantities by browsing animals, an extract made from it has been found to have a strong narcotic effect on them and to be of such a poisonous nature as to cause the deaths of some dogs to whom it was experimentally given in considerable doses.

¶ *Medicinal Action and Uses*. Diuretic, diaphoretic and expectorant. The ancient reputation of Scarlet Pimpernel has survived to the present day, especially in dealing with diseases of the brain. Doctors have considered the herb remedial in melancholy and in the allied forms of mental disease, the decoction or a tincture being employed.

John Hill (*British Herbal*, 1756) tells us that the whole plant, dried and powdered, is good against epilepsy, and there are well authenticated accounts of this disease being absolutely cured by it. The flowers alone have also been found useful in epilepsy, 20 grains dried being given four times a day.

It is of a cordial sudorific nature, and a strong infusion of it has been considered an excellent medicine in feverish complaints, which it relieves by promoting a gentle perspiration. It was recommended by Culpepper on this account as a preservative in pestilential and contagious diseases. The same simple preparation has also been much used among country people in the first stages of pulmonary consumption, it being stated to have often checked the disorder and prevented its fatal consequences.

The dried leaves may be given in powder, or an infusion made of the whole plant dried, but according to Green (*Universal Herbal*, 1832) nothing equals the infusion of the fresh plant.

The expressed juice has been found serviceable in the beginnings of dropsies and in obstructions of the liver and spleen. A tincture has also been used for irritability of the urinary passages, having been found effective in cases of stone and gravel.

In Gerard's days, a preparation of this herb, called 'Diacorallion,' was used for gout, and in California a fluid extract is given for

rheumatism, in doses of 1 teaspoonful with water, three times a day.

Modern authorities consider that caution should be exercised in the use of this herb for dropsy, rheumatic affections, hepatic and renal complaints.

The tincture is made from the fresh leaves, in the proportion of 10 oz. to a pint of diluted alcohol; the dose is from 1 to 5 drops. A homœopathic tincture is also prepared from the flowers.

The powder of the dried leaves is given in 15 to 60 grain doses.

The seeds of the plant, which are very numerous, and enclosed in small capsules, are much eaten by birds.

¶ *Other Species.*

The BOG PIMPERNEL (*A. tenella*) is another of this species. Its blossoms are larger than those of the Scarlet Pimpernel, and of a pale rose colour, and the leaves which are numerous, are very small in proportion to the blossoms. It is found on marshy grounds, but is rare: it is a perennial; whereas the scarlet variety is an annual.

Gerard speaks of the '*pimpernel rose* in a pasture as you goe from a village hard by London called Knightsbridge unto Fulham, a village thereby.'

PINE

Various Species
N.O. Pinaceæ

Pines are among the most important commercial trees. Most of them have straight, unbranched, cylindrical trunks, which furnish large amounts of excellent saw timber. On account of the straight grain, strength, and other qualities of pine timber, it is used for nearly every sort of constructional work and the trade in it is enormous.

All the Pines yield *resin* in greater or smaller quantities, which is obtained by tapping the trees. The crude resin is almost entirely used for the distillation of *Oil of Turpentine* and *Rosin*, only small quantities being employed medicinally – for ointments, plasters, etc. When the Oil of Turpentine is entirely distilled off, the residuum is *Rosin* or *Colophony*, but when only part of the oil is extracted, the viscous mass remaining is known commercially as common *Crude Turpentine*.

Oil of Turpentine is a good solvent for many resins, wax, fats, caoutchouc, sulphur, and phosphorus, and is largely employed in making varnish, in oil-painting, etc. Medicinally, it is much employed in both general and veterinary practice as a rubefacient and vesicant, and is valuable as an antiseptic. It is used for horses and cattle internally as a vermifuge, and externally as a stimulant for

rheumatic swellings, and for sprains and bruises, and to kill parasites.

Rosin is used not only by violinists, for rubbing their bows, but also in making sealing wax, varnish, and resinous soaps for sizing paper and *papier maché* and dressing hemp cordage, but one of its special uses is for making *brewer's pitch* for coating the insides of beer casks and for distilling resinous oils, when the *pitch* used by shoemakers is left as residuum. Pitch is also used in veterinary practice.

Tar is an impure turpentine, viscid and brown-black in colour, procured by destructive distillation from the roots of various coniferous trees, particularly from *Pinus sylvestris*. Tar is used medicinally, especially in veterinary practice, for its antiseptic, stimulant, diuretic and diaphoretic action. Tar-water is given to horses with chronic cough and used internally and externally as a cutaneous stimulant and antiseptic in eczema. Oil of Tar is used instead of Oil of Turpentine in the case of mange, etc.

A considerable industry has grown up in the United States in the distillation of Pine *wood* by means of steam under pressure. One of the products thus obtained, which has considerable commercial importance, is known as

Pine Oil. It has a pleasant odour, resembling that of caraway or Juniper Oil, and has been largely used for making paints which dry without gloss and as a 'flatting' material. It flows well under the brush and is a powerful solvent, and is useful for emulsion paints such as are now employed for inside work.

Pine resins are largely employed by the soap-maker for the manufacture of brown soaps.

The trade in resins was for many years almost exclusively a French industry, and only in France were the Pine forests turned to account for the production of resin on a commercial scale. Now, however, Switzerland, Sweden, Russia and North America furnish quantities, though, from the point of view of quality, the Pines which flourish near Bordeaux furnish a resin still much in request, and the turpentine extracted therefrom is abundant and one of the best qualities produced.

¶ *Medicinal Action and Properties.* Rubefacient, diuretic, irritant. A valuable remedy in bladder, kidney, and rheumatic affections and diseases of the mucous membrane and respiratory complaints; *externally* in the form of liniment plasters and inhalants.

¶ *Preparations and Dosages.* Oil of Turpentine. Spirits of Turpentine, B.P., 2 to 10 drops. As a vermifuge, 2 to 4 drachms. Tar, B.P., Pin. Sylv. Tar, U.S.P., Pin. Palust. Ointment Tar, B.P. Syrup Tar, U.S.P., 1 drachm.

See TAMARAC.

SPECIES OF PINES HAVING MEDICINAL PRODUCTS

Pinus balsamea. Abies canadensis. A. balsamea. Balsam Fir. Balm of Gilead Fir. Perusse. Hemlock Spruce.
  Canada Turpentine. Pills for mucous discharge.

P. Canadensis. A. canadensis. Hemlock Spruce.
  Pitch and Oil.

P. Cedrus of Mount Lebanon.
  A false manna used in phthisis in Syria.

P. Cembra (Siberian Cedar or Tannenbaum). Europe and Asia.
  Edible seeds eaten by Russians as nuts. Coniferin from the cambium.

P. Cubensis. Cuban Pine.
  Turpentine.

P. Damaris. Agathis Damara.
  Damara Turpentine that hardens into a hard rosin.

P. Densiflora. Japan.
  An exudation called akamatsu. Timber.

P. Echinata. Short-leaved Pine.
  Turpentine. Timber.

P. Gerardiana. Neosa Pine. N.W. India.
  Edible seeds called neosa or chilgoza seeds.

P. Halepensis. Mediterranean countries.
  Spirits of Turpentine.

P. Heterophylla. Eastern America.
  Spirits of Turpentine. Timber.

P. Khasya. Burma.
  Turpentine resembling French Oil.

P. Larix. Larix Europæa. A. larix. L. decidua. Larch.
  Briançon manna, containing no mannite. Venice Turpentine.

P. Maritima. P. pinaster. Cluster Pine. Mediterranean countries.
  Bordeaux Turpentine. Pitch. French Oil of Turpentine, 25 per cent.

P. Merkusii. Burma.
  Turpentine resembling French Oil.

P. Microcarpa. P. pendula. L. Americana. Black or American Larch. Hackmatack. Tamarac.
  A decoction of the bark used.

P. Mughus. Hungarian terebinth.

P. Nigra. Pieca Mariana. Black or Bog Spruce.
  Decoction of young branches gives Essence of Spruce used for Spruce Beer.

P. Palustris. P. Australia. Long-leaved Pine. Yellow, Southern, Hard, Virginia.
  Spirits of Turpentine, 17 per cent. oil. Carpets woven from leaves.

P. Picea. A. pectinata. Picea vulgaris. P. abies. A. vulgaris. A. alba. Spruce Fir. Norway Spruce.
  Strassbourg Turpentine. Térébinthine au citron.

P. Pinea. Mediterranean countries.
  Edible seeds. 'Pignons' or 'Pinocchi.'

P. Ponderosa. Heavy Pine. California.
  Exudation is almost pure heptane; a chief constituent of American petroleum. Timber.

P. Pumilio. P. montana.
  Volatile Oil from the leaves. Oil of Dwarf Pine Needles. Oil of Pine.

P. Rigida. Pitch Pine.
  Tar.

P. Roxburghii. Himalayas.
  Spirits of Turpentine.

P. Sabiniana. Nut or Digger Pine.
  Turpentine, the oil being called abietene. Edible seeds.

P. Scropica.
  Occasionally its Turpentine is used for American Rosin.

P. Strobus. P. alba. White Pine.
  Coniferin from the Cambium Bark. Compound Syrup with Morphine. Timber.

P. Succinifera. Extinct.
Fossil resin or amber.

P. Sylvestris. Scotch Pine or Fir. Norway Pine.
Spirits of Turpentine, 32 per cent. of oil. Russian Turpentine. Finnan Turpentine is the oleoresin. Timber.

P. Toeda. Loblolly Pine. Old Field Pine. United States.
Occasionally its turpentine used for American rosin.

P. Teocoty. Mexican or Brea Turpentine.

P. Thunbergii. Japan.
Exudation called Kuromatsu. Timber.

PINE (LARCH)

Pinus larix (D.C.)
N.O. Coniferæ

Synonyms. Larix Europæa. Abies larix. Larix decidua. Laricis Cortex. Meleze. European Larch. Venice Turpentine
Part Used. The bark, deprived of its outer layer
Habitat. Central Europe

¶ *Description*. 'Larix' was the name given to Pine resin in the time of Dioscorides, and the term has been kept for these lofty trees. The leaves, bright green in spring, grow in small, spreading tufts like brushes. The male catkins, ½ inch long, are sessile and ovoid, with a cup of persistent bracts and inner, resinous, fringed, brown scales. The female cones, ¾ inch long, grow on short stalks, with hard, greyish-brown scales.

Larch is only indigenous to the hilly regions throughout Central Europe, where it forms large forests in the Alps, but it has for long been largely cultivated throughout Europe. It was first introduced into England in 1639.

It is one of the most valuable trees ever introduced into the country, both with respect to the rapidity of its growth (it grows six times quicker than Oak) and the value of its durable timber. Its wood is far tougher, stronger and more durable than that of any other conifer, excepting perhaps the Yew. Its durability makes it specially adapted for mining operations and there is also considerable demand for it for railway sleepers, because it lasts longer than any other kind of home-grown wood when under the wear and tear of traffic and the decomposing influence of damp, warmth, and fungi. It is also employed both in ship- and house-building, and in cabinet-work is capable of taking a very high polish. Gilding has a better effect on it than over almost any other, and it is a favourite for placing behind pictures, as it resists worm attacks. It is the one wood for which a ready sale can always be found in any part of the United Kingdom.

None of our forest trees is hardier than the Larch. The young trees establish themselves readily and soon grow rapidly. They are therefore, like the birch, used as 'nurses' for slow-growing and less hardy kinds of trees. The ground beneath a larch wood speedily improves in quantity and quality.

Large quantities of turpentine are collected from full-grown trees from May to October, holes being bored in the trunk and wooden tubes inserted. The exudation that flows is perfectly clear and needs no further preparation than straining through a coarse hair-cloth to free it from impurities. It was used in medicine and for making several kinds of varnish. In commerce it is known as 'Venice Turpentine,' being formerly exclusively exported from Venice. It is produced now mainly in the Tyrol, Switzerland, and Piedmont.

The frequently-found substitutes may be detected by their strong odour, and by drying into a hard varnish when painted on paper. The bark, which is not official in India or the United States, should be removed and stripped of its roughest outer portion in spring, and dried rapidly. In commerce it is found in flat pieces or quills of various sizes. The outer surface is rosy in colour, and the inner either yellowish or pinkish, easily separating into layers. It breaks with a close fracture, excepting the whitish fibres. The odour is a little like balsam and terebinth, and the taste astringent. The bark is sometimes used for tanning, but is inferior to oak, so that in Britain it is not always worth the cost of peeling and carriage.

¶ *Constituents*. The bark contains tannic acid, larixinic acid and turpentine. The larixin, a crystalline principle, resembles pyrogallol.

Briançon Manna is exuded from the leaves in summer. It is white and sweet, occurring in oblong tears and almost odourless. Its peculiar sugar is termed *Melezitose*. Its use is obsolete.

If the trees are burnt, a gum exudes from the trunk called *Gummi Orenbergense*, soluble in water like Gum Arabic.

¶ *Medicinal Action and Uses*. Stimulant, diuretic, astringent, balsamic and expectorant. As an external application it has been found useful in chronic eczema and psoriasis. Its chief official use is as a stimulant expec-

636

LARCH PINE
Pinus Larix

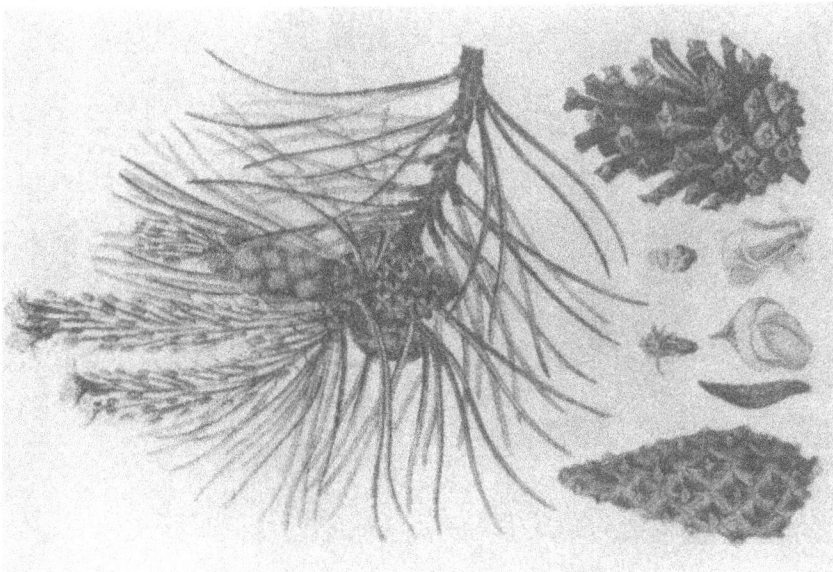

WILD PINE
Pinus Sylvestris

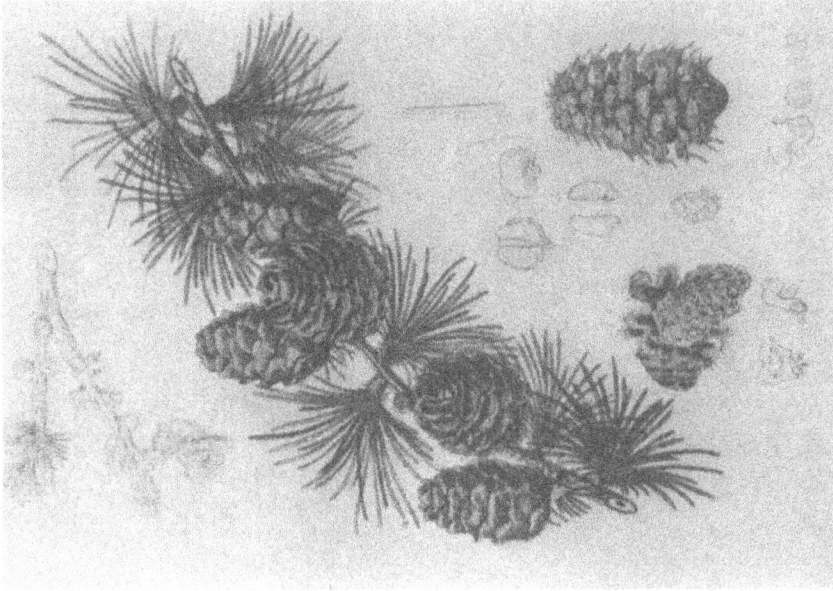

PINK ROOT
Spigelia Marilandica

POMEGRANATE
Punica Granatum

torant in chronic bronchitis, with much secretion. Its action is that of oil of turpentine.

It has also been given internally in hæmorrhage and cystitis.

The turpentine is used in veterinary practice. It has been suggested for combating poisoning by cyanide or opium, and as a disinfectant in hospital gangrene.

¶ *Dosage.* Of B.P. Tincture Laricis, 20 to 30 minims. Venice Turpentine.

See TAMARAC.

PINE, WHITE

Pinus strobus (LINN.)
N.O. Pinaceæ

Synonyms. Weymouth Pine. Pin du Lord. Pinus Alba
Part Used. Dried inner bark
Habitat. Eastern North America. Cultivated in Europe

¶ *Description.* The name of Weymouth Pine, common in Europe, refers to a Lord Weymouth who planted numbers of the trees shortly after their introduction in 1705. The French name is a similarly derived contraction.

In the United States it grows up to 200 feet in height, but rarely reaches half that stature in England. The wood is peculiarly adapted for the masts of ships, and in Queen Anne's reign legal measures were taken for the encouragement of its cultivation. The bark is very smooth, and the leaves grow in small bundles of five, the cylindrical cones being a little longer than these.

The bark is found in small, flattened pieces, the outer surface light, with a pinkish or yellowish tinge, sometimes patched with greyish-brown fragments, and the inner surface lighter or darker and finely striate. The tough, fibrous fracture shows yellowish and whitish layers. The odour is like terebinth, and the taste both bitter and sweet, astringent and mucilaginous.

¶ *Constituents.* The powder shows starch and resin. The bark yields a maximum of 3 per cent. of ash. It is a source of the terebinth of America. Coniferin is found in the cambium.

¶ *Medicinal Action and Uses.* Expectorant, demulcent, diuretic, a useful remedy in coughs and colds, having a beneficial effect on the bladder and kidneys.

The compound syrup contains sufficient morphine to assist in developing the morphine habit and should be used with caution.

¶ *Dosage.* Of Compound Syrup, 1 fluid drachm. Of Compound Syrup, with Morphine, 30 minims. Fluid Extract, ½ to 1 drachm.

(GROUND) PINE. *See* (YELLOW) BUGLE

PINE, AMERICAN GROUND. *See* (AMERICAN CLUB) MOSS

PINK ROOT

Spigelia Marylandica (LINN.)
N.O. Loganiaceæ

Synonyms. Indian Pink. Maryland Pink. Wormgrass. American Wormgrass. Carolina-, Maryland-, American-Wormroot. Starbloom
Parts Used. Dried rhizome and rootlets, or entire plant
Habitat. Southern United States of America

¶ *Description.* This herbaceous perennial plant has been known in commerce for many years and used to be collected by the Creek and Cherokee Indians for sale to the white traders. It is official in the United States Pharmacopœia. It has several smooth simple stems, arising from the same rhizome; these stems are rounded below and square above. Leaves, few, opposite, sessile, ovate-lanceolate, at apex acuminate, tapering at the base. The flowers are borne in a brilliant red-pink spike at top of the stem, the long corollas (terminating in spreading, star-like petals), externally red, yellow within, surrounding a double, many-seeded capsule. It grows in rich, dry soils on the edges of woods and flowers from May to July. The entire plant is collected in autumn and dried, but only the rhizome and rootlets are official in the United States Pharmacopœia, though in several other pharmacopœias on the Continent, in which Spigelia is official, a closely allied species is named and the flowering plant is specified. The rhizome is tortuous, knotty and dark-brown externally, with many thin, wiry motlets attached to it and the short branches on the upper side are marked with scars of the stems of former years; internally, the rhizome is whitish, with a dark-brown pith; the rootlets are lighter coloured than the rhizome, thin, brittle and long. Odour, aromatic; taste, bitter, sweetish, pungent and somewhat nauseous. It is usually powdered and then is of a greyish colour. Age impairs its strength. When imported from the Western United States, where it is very abundant, it is received in bales and casks.

Constituents. A poisonous alkaloid, named Spigeline; also a bitter acrid principle, soluble in water or alcohol, but insoluble in ether; a small amount of volatile oil, a tasteless resin, tannin, wax, fat, mucilage, albumen, myricin, a viscid, saccharine substance, lignin, salts of sodium, potassium and calcium. The reactions of the poisonous alkaloid resemble those of nicotine, lobeline and coniine.

Medicinal Action and Uses. Its chief use is as a very active and certain vermifuge, most potent for tapeworm and specially so for the round worm; its use was known among the Indians for worms long before America was discovered. It is a safe and efficient drug to give to children, if administered in proper doses and always followed by a saline aperient, such as magnesium sulphate, otherwise unpleasant and serious symptoms may occur, such as disturbed vision, dizziness, muscular spasms, twitching eyelids, increased action of the heart. In large doses, these are increased, both circulation and respiration being depressed and loss of muscular power caused, and cases have been known resulting, in children, in death from convulsions. It is also useful for children's fevers not caused by the irritation of vermin, such as those occurring from hydrocephalus.

Dosage. The official U.S.P. preparation is the Fluid Extract: average dose, 1 fluid drachm.

It is also given in infusion and in powder.

It is often combined with a cathartic – Senna, Fennel and Manna – the narcotic ill-effects being thereby avoided.

Dose of powdered root for an adult: 1 to 2 drachms, morning and evening, for several successive days, followed by an active purgative. For children, 10 to 20 grains.

The infusion is made of ¼ oz. troy of the bruised root to 1 pint boiling water. Dose for children, 1 tablespoonful, night and morning; for adults, a teacupful.

There is a preparation much in use called Worm Tea, composed of Spigelia, Savin, Senna and Manna, in the proportion of amounts to suit the individual need.

Adulterations. Spigelia is frequently adulterated, so that an absolutely genuine and pure article is said to be the exception. The rhizomes are often extensively adulterated with those of *Ruellia ciliosa* (Acanthaceæ); they are, however, longer, straighter and thicker and the rootlets less wiry.

The rhizomes of species of Alpine Phlox, *Phlox ovata*, *P. Carolina* and *P. glaberrima*, are used in some localities and sometimes offered entirely as Spigelia. Those of *P. glaberrima* are somewhat darker and less ridged than *Ruellia* and more closely resemble Spigelia. Those of *P. Carolina* are rather coarse and straight, brownish-yellow, with a straw-coloured wood underneath and a readily removable bark.

The rhizomes of Golden Seal and *Caulophyllum* have often been found intermixed with the genuine Spigelia.

Other Varieties.

The genus *Spigelia* comprises some thirty species, all American, mostly tropical, and several of them are employed like the official. Chief of these is *S. Anthelmia* (Linn.), native of the West Indies and northern South America, where it is abundant and is largely used as an anthelmintic. It is an annual, growing up to 2 feet high, of a similar habit to Pink Root, but the leaves, lanceolate below, and very broad, almost ovate, above, are mostly in whorls of four, the light reddish flowers only ¼ inch long, the rhizome short, blackish externally, whitish internally and bearing numerous long, thin roots. The drug has a stronger narcotic and bitter taste than the official. It has been introduced into Europe and the Belgian Pharmacopœia specifically states that it is more active than the United States Pharmacopœia official species and directs that the flowering plant shall be employed. In large doses this is said to be a very powerful poison, causing death to animals and humans.

In cases of poisoning, the stomach should be emptied and stimulants administered, the patient being kept warm in bed. Artificial respiration with oxygen must be immediately resorted to if there are signs of respiratory failure. As an antidote, give strong tea or 15 to 20 grains of tannic acid in aqueous solution.

PINUS BARK. HEMLOCK SPRUCE

Tsuga Canadensis (CARR.)
N.O. Pinaceæ

Synonyms. Hemlock Pitch. Canada Pitch. Pix Canadensis. Hemlock Bark. Pinus Canadensis. Abies Canadensis. Hemlock Gum. Hemlock Spruce

Part Used. The bark encrusted with hardened juice

Habitat. North America

Description. The flow of juice from incisions in the bark is much less than in most of the species, but at the time of late maturity a spontaneous exudation partly evaporates, hardening on the bark, which is stripped, broken in pieces, and boiled in water. The melted pitch is skimmed off and boiled for a second time. The product is of a dark reddish-brown colour, brittle, hard, opaque, almost tasteless, and with a very slight odour. It melts and softens at a low temperature.

An extract of the bark is used in tanning.

¶ *Constituents*. Besides resin, there is found a volatile oil, *oil of spruce* or *oil of hemlock*, and tannin.

¶ *Medicinal Action and Uses*. Canada Pitch is softer than Burgundy Pitch, so that even the temperature of the body makes it inconvenient to handle. It is a mild rubefacient, The liquid extract has been used as an astringent. It resembles rhatany in its action.

The volatile oil is used in veterinary liniments, and to procure abortion, but it is very dangerous for this purpose.

Hemlock or Canada Pitch Plaster can be made by melting together 90 parts of Canada Pitch to 10 parts of Yellow Wax, straining and stirring until it cools and thickens.

Fluid extract, ¼ to 1 drachm.

¶ *Other Species*.

Pseudotsuga tascifolia, the branches of which give out an emanation which, after being inhaled for some hours, is reported to have caused stupor, involuntary evacuation of urine, and collapse followed by psychic disturbance.

See PINES.

PIPSISSEWA

Chimaphila umbellata (LINN.)
N.O. Ericaceæ

Synonyms. Pyrola umbellata. Winter Green. Butter Winter. Prince's Pine. King's Cure. Ground Holly. Love in Winter. Rheumatism Weed

Parts Used. Dried leaves only are official, though the whole plant, including root, is used

Habitat. Europe, Asia, Siberia, America, and found in all parts of the United States

¶ *Description*. The name Chimaphila is derived from two Greek words meaning 'winter' and 'to love.' There are two varieties of this plant, *Chimaphila umbellata* and *C. maculata*. The former alone is the official plant, a small evergreen perennial with a creeping yellow rhizome, which has several creeping, erect or semi-procumbent stems, angular, marked with the scars of former leaves, and woody at the base. These are 4 to 8 inches high, with the leaves on upper surface, shiny, coriaceous, dark green and underside paler. Flowers corymbose, light purple colour, corolla five cream-coloured petals, fragrantly perfumed, purplish at base. Capsule erect, depressed five-celled, five-valved, numerous seeds, linear, chaffy. It flowers May till August; leaves when dried have only a slight odour, but when fresh and rubbed are sweet-smelling; taste astringently sweetish and not disagreeably bitter.

¶ *Constituents*. Leaves contain various crystalline constituents, Chimaphilin, etc., also arbutin gum, resin, starch, pectic acid, extractive fatty matter, chlorophyll tannic acid, sugar, potassa, lime, iron, magnesia, chloride of sodium, sulphuric phosphoric and silicic acids.

¶ *Medicinal Action and Uses*. Diuretic, astringent, tonic, alterative. The fresh leaves, when bruised and applied to the skin, act as vesicants and rubefacients, of great use in cardiac and kidney diseases, chronic rheumatism and scrofula. The decoction is advantageous for chronic gonorrhœa, strangury, catarrh of the bladder, and a good cure for ascites. It is said to diminish lithic acid in the urine; for dropsy it is useful combined with other medicines; it is a substitute for uva-ursi and less obnoxious; said to be of value in diabetes, but this has not yet been confirmed; and it is very efficacious for skin diseases.

¶ *Dosage*. Decoction, 1 to 4 fluid ounces three times daily. Fluid extract, B.P.C., 15 to 45 grains. Fluid extract, B.P.C., 3 parts syrup to 1 part fluid extract. Fluid extract, 1 to 45 grains.

Syrup. – Macerate 4 oz. finely bruised leaves in 8 fluid ounces of water; let it stand 36 hours, strain till 1 pint of the fluid is obtained, evaporate to ¼ pint, add ¾ lb. sugar; dose, 1 to 2 tablespoonful.

Dose of Chimaphilin, 1 to 5 grains. This is very valuable for scrofulous complaints, hence its name, 'King's Cure'; also used externally in the form of a decoction to unhealthy scrofulous sores.

C. maculata, or Spotted Wintergreen, is very similar, but the leaves are a deep olive-green colour with greenish-white veins. When fresh and bruised they have a peculiar odour, which is lost on drying; taste pleasantly bitter, astringent and sweetish. A solution of perchloride of iron makes the infusion green colour. The leaves only are official, but all parts of the plant have active properties, and stem and leaves are often used together. The stem and root have a pungent taste and combine bitterness and astringency. Medicinal properties, diuretic with an antiseptic influence on the urine, occasionally prescribed for cystitis. The best preparation is the fluid extract.

See PYROLA, WINTERGREEN.

PITCHER PLANT

Sarracenia purpurea (LINN.)
N.O. Sarraceniaceæ

Synonyms. Sarazina Gibbosa. Sarracenie. Eve's Cups. Fly-catcher. Fly-trap. Huntsman's Cup. Purple Side-saddle Flower. Side-saddle Plant. Water-cup. Nepenthes distillatoria

Parts Used. Root, leaves

Habitat. North America

¶ *Description.* A strange, perennial plant, the leaves of which form cups, often richly coloured, which become filled with water and small insects, and are covered by a lid in hot weather, due to the contraction of the fibres of the modified leaf-stalk. Water is sometimes present before opening. The insects gradually form a decaying mass, which emits a strong odour and probably serves as a fertilizer.

There appears to be little, if any, difference botanically between the American *Sarracenia* and the *Nepenthes distillatoria* of Ceylon, the East Indies and China. For lack of other definite information it may be concluded from the name that the latter is also used medicinally. (*Nepenthe*, from the Greek 'not' and 'grief.') In antiquity a magic potion, Nepenthe, is mentioned by Greek and Roman poets. It was said to cause forgetfulness of sorrows and misfortunes.

¶ *Cultivation.* The plant requires a moist, well-drained situation, and being a creeping plant needs trellis-work for support. The flowers are insignificant, with five petals shaped like a violin.

¶ *Constituents.* An alkaloid, Sarracenine resin, a yellow colouring principle (probably sarracenic acid) and extractive. 'Sarracenine is white, soluble in alcohol and ether, combines with acids to form salts, and with sulphuric acid forms handsome needles which are bitter, and communicate this taste to its members.'

¶ *Medicinal Action and Uses.* Tonic, laxative, stomachic, diuretic. Used in the southern United States in dyspepsia. The drug was unknown in Europe until a few years ago, when Mr. Herbert Miles introduced it as a specific for smallpox, as used by the North American Indians with great success, saving life and even the unsightly pitting. Some homœopaths confirm the value of the remedy, but allopaths do not appear to have been successful in its use, either in America, England or France.

Its principal value appears to be in torpid liver, stomach, kidney and uterus complaints.

¶ *Dosages.* Of tincture, 1 fluid drachm. Of fluid extract, 10 to 20 minims. Of powder, 10 to 30 grains.

PLANTAIN, COMMON

Plantago major (LINN.)
N.O. Plantaginaceæ

Synonyms. Broad-leaved Plantain. Ripple Grass. Waybread. Slan-lus. Waybroad. Snakeweed. Cuckoo's Bread. Englishman's Foot. White Man's Foot
(*Anglo-Saxon*) Weybroed

Parts Used. Root, leaves, flower-spikes

The Common Broad-leaved Plantain is a very familiar perennial 'weed,' and may be found anywhere by roadsides and in meadow-land.

¶ *Description.* It grows from a very short rhizome, which bears below a great number of long, straight, yellowish roots, and above, a large, radial rosette of leaves and a few long, slender, densely-flowered spikes. The leaves are ovate, blunt, abruptly contracted at the base into a long, broad, channelled footstalk (petiole). The blade is 4 to 10 inches long and about two-thirds as broad, usually smooth, thickish, five to eleven ribbed, the ribs having a strongly fibrous structure, the margin entire, or coarsely and unevenly toothed. The flower-spikes, erect, on long stalks, are as long as the leaves, ⅛ to ⅓ inch thick and usually blunt. The flowers are somewhat purplish-green, the calyx four-parted, the small corolla bell-shaped and four-lobed, the stamens four, with purple anthers. The fruit is a two-celled capsule, not enclosed in the perianth, and containing four to sixteen seeds.

The Plantain belongs to the natural order Plantaginaceæ, which contains more than 200 species, twenty-five or thirty of which have been reported as in domestic use.

The drug is without odour: the leaves are saline, bitterish and acrid to the taste; the root is saline and sweetish.

The glucoside Aucubin, first isolated in *Aucuba japonica*, has been reported as occurring in many species.

¶ *Medicinal Action and Properties.* Refrigerant, diuretic, deobstruent and somewhat astringent. Has been used in inflammation of the skin, malignant ulcers, intermittent fever, etc., and as a vulnerary, and externally as a stimulant application to sores. Applied to a bleeding surface, the leaves are of some value in arresting hæmorrhage, but they are useless in internal hæmorrhage, although they were formerly used for bleeding of the lungs and stomach, consumption and dysentery. The fresh leaves are applied whole or bruised in the form of a poultice. Rubbed on parts of the body stung by insects, nettles, etc., or as an application to burns and scalds, the leaves will afford relief and will stay the bleeding of minor wounds.

Fluid extract: dose, ½ to 1 drachm.

In the Highlands the Plantain is still called 'Slan-lus,' or plant of healing, from a firm belief in its healing virtues. Pliny goes so far as to state, 'on high authority,' that if 'it be put into a pot where many pieces of flesh are boiling, it will sodden them together.' He also says that it will cure the madness of dogs. Erasmus, in his *Colloquia*, tells a story of a toad, who, being bitten by a spider, was straightway freed from any poisonous effects he may have dreaded by the prompt eating of a Plantain leaf.

Another old Herbal says: 'If a wood hound (mad dog) rend a man, take this wort, rub it fine and lay it on; then will the spot soon be whole.' And in the United States the plant is called 'Snake Weed,' from a belief in its efficacy in cases of bites from venomous creatures; it is related that a dog was one day stung by a rattlesnake and a preparation of the juice of the Plantain and salt was applied as promptly as possible to the wound. The animal was in great agony, but quickly recovered and shook off all trace of its misadventure. Dr. Robinson (*New Family Herbal*) tells us that an Indian received a great reward from the Assembly of South Carolina for his discovery that the Plantain was 'the chief remedy for the cure of the rattlesnake.'

The Broad-leaved Plantain seems to have followed the migrations of our colonists to every part of the world, and in both America and New Zealand it has been called by the aborigines the 'Englishman's Foot' (or the White Man's Foot), for wherever the English have taken possession of the soil the Plantain springs up. Longfellow refers to this in 'Hiawatha.'

Our Saxon ancestors esteemed it highly, and in the old *Lacnunga* the Weybroed is mentioned as one of nine sacred herbs. In this most ancient source of Anglo-Saxon medicine, we find this 'salve for flying venom':

'Take a handful of hammer wort and a handful of maythe (chamomile) and a handful of *waybroad* and roots of water dock, seek those which will float, and one eggshell full of clean honey, then take clean butter, let him who will help to work up the salve, melt it thrice: let one sing a mass over the worts, before they are put together and the salve is wrought up.'

Some of the recipes for ointments in which Plantain is an ingredient have lingered to the present day. Lady Northcote, in *The Book of Herbs* (1903), mentions an ointment made by an old woman in Exeter that up to her death about twenty years ago was in much request. It was made from Southernwood, Plantain leaves, Black Currant leaves, Elder buds, Angelica and Parsley, chopped, pounded and simmered with clarified butter and was considered most useful for burns or raw surfaces. A most excellent ointment can also be made from Pilewort (Celandine), Elder buds, Houseleek and the Broad Plantain leaf.

Decoctions of Plantain entered into almost every old remedy, and it was boiled with Docks, Comfrey and a variety of flowers.

A decoction of Plantain was considered good in disorders of the kidneys, and the root, powdered, in complaints of the bowels. The expressed juice was recommended for spitting of blood and piles. Boyle recommends an electuary made of fresh Comfrey roots, juice of Plantain and sugar as very efficacious in spitting of blood. Plantain juice mixed with lemon juice was judged an excellent diuretic. The powdered dried leaves, taken in drink, were thought to destroy worms.

To prepare a plain infusion, still recommended in herbal medicine for diarrhœa and piles, pour 1 pint of boiling water on 1 oz. of the herb, stand in a warm place for 20 minutes, afterwards strain and let cool. Take a wineglassful to half a teacupful three or four times a day.

The small mucilaginous seeds have been employed as a substitute for linseed. For 'thrush' they are recommended as most useful, 1 oz. of seeds to be boiled in 1½ pint of water down to a pint, the liquid then made into a syrup with sugar and honey and given to the child in tablespoonful doses, three or four times daily.

The seeds are relished by most small birds and quantities of the ripe spikes are gathered near London for the supply of cage birds.

Abercrombie, writing in 1822 (*Every Man his own Gardener*), giving a list of forty-four Salad herbs, includes Plantain.

Dr. Withering (*Arrangement of Plants*) states that sheep, goats and swine eat it, but that cows and horses refuse it.

It is a great disfigurement to lawns, rapidly multiplying if allowed to spread, each plant quite destroying the grass that originally occupied the spot usurped by its dense rosette of leaves.

Salmon's *Herbal* (1710) gives the following manifold uses for *Plantage major*:

'The liquid juice clarified and drunk for several days helps distillation of rheum upon the throat, glands, lungs, etc. Doses, 3 to 8 spoonsful. An especial remedy against ulceration of the lungs and a vehement cough arising from same. It is said to be good against epilepsy, dropsy, jaundice and opens obstructions of the liver, spleen and reins. It cools inflammations of the eyes and takes away the pin and web (so called) in them. Dropt into the ears, it eases their pains and restores hearing much decayed. Doses, 3 to 6 spoonsful more or less, either alone or with some fit vehicle morning and night. The powdered root mixed with equal parts of powder of Pellitory of Spain and put into a hollow tooth is said to ease the pain thereof. Powdered seeds stop vomiting, epilepsy, lethargy, convulsions, dropsy, jaundice, strangury, obstruction of the liver, etc. The liniment made with the juice and oil of Roses eases headache caused by heat, and is good for lunatics. It gives great ease (being applyed) in all hot gouts, whether in hands or feet, especially in the beginning, to cool the heat and repress the humors. The distilled water with a little alum and honey dissolved in it is of good use for washing, cleansing and healing a sore ulcerated mouth or throat.'

'Salmon also tells us that a good cosmetic is made with essence of Plantain, houseleeks and lemon juice.

Culpepper tells us that the Plantain is 'in the command of Venus and cures the head by antipathy to Mars, neither is there hardly a martial disease but it cures.' He also states that 'the water is used for all manner of spreading scabs, tetters, ringworm, shingles, etc.'

From the days of Chaucer onwards we find reference in literature to the healing powers of Plantain. Gower (1390) says: 'And of Plantaine he hath his herb sovereine,' and Chaucer mentions it in the *Prologue of the Chanounes Yeman*. Shakespeare, both in *Love's Labour's Lost, iii*, i, and in *Romeo and Juliet*, I, ii, speaks of the 'plain Plantain' and 'Plantain leaf' as excellent for a broken shin, and again in *Two Noble Kinsmen*, I, ii: 'These poore slight sores neede not a Plantin.' His reference to it in *Troilus and Cressida*, III. ii: 'As true as steel, as Plantage to the moon,' is an allusion that is now no longer clear to us. Again, Shenstone in the *Schoolmistress*: 'And plantain rubb'd that heals the reaper's wound.'

PLANTAIN, BUCK'S HORN

Plantago Coronopus (LINN.)
N.O. Plantaginaceæ

Synonyms. Cornu Cervinum. Herba Stella. Herb Ivy. Buckshorne. Hartshorne
Parts Used. Whole plant, leaves
Habitat. It is an annual, found on sandy commons, waste places and chalky banks, especially near the sea, being fairly common and generally distributed in England.

The Buck's Horn Plantain is the only British species which has divided leaves more or less downy and usually prostrate. It is very variable in the size and in the lobing of the leaves, which are from 1 to 12 inches in length, one-ribbed, either deeply divided nearly to the base, or merely toothed and almost entire. The flower-spikes are slender, many-flowered, short or long, the bracts to the flowers have a long point and the sepals are strongly winged. The pale brown seeds are mucilaginous and adhere to the soil when they fall.

In Salmon's *Herbal* we find 'Our Common Buck's Horn Plantain' described thus:

'Root single, long and small, with several fibres. If sown or planted from seed, it rises up at first with small, long, narrow, hairy, dark-green leaves, almost like grass, without any division, but those that come after have deep divisions and are pointed at the end, resembling the snaggs of a Buck's Horn, from whence it took its name. When it is well grown, the leaves lie round about the root on the ground, resembling the form of a star and thereby called *Herba Stella*. There is also a prickly Buck's Horn Plantain, which is rougher, coarser and more prickly than the other. In Italy, they grow the first in their garden as a Sallet herb. The second grows on mountains and rocks. They both flower in May, June and July, their seeds ripening in the mean season and their leaves abide fresh and green in a manner all the winter. The qualities, specifications, preparation and virtues are the very same as those of Plantage major. The decoction in wine, if it is long drank, cureth the strangury and is profitable for such as are troubled with sand, gravel, stones, etc. The cataspasm of leaves and roots with bay salt applied to both wrists and bound on pretty hard (yet not too hard) cures agues admirably.'

¶ *Medicinal Action and Uses.* As a remedy for ague, the whole plant, roots included, was even hung round the neck as an amulet.

Gerard says: 'The leaves boyled in drinke and given morning and evening for certain days together helpeth most wonderfully those that have sore eyes, watery or blasted, and most of the griefs that happen unto the eyes.

PLANTAIN, HOARY

Plantago media (LINN.)
N.O. Plantaginaceæ

Part Used. Seeds

The Hoary Plantain is a common meadow species. The broadly-elliptical leaves, on short flat stalks, spread horizontally from the crown of the root and lie so close to the ground as to destroy all vegetation beneath and to leave the impression of their ribs on the ground. The flowers are in a close, cylindrical spike, shorter than in *Plantago major*, but growing on a longer stalk, which is downy. They are very fragrant, and are conspicuous by their light purple anthers, the filaments being long and pink or purplish.

¶ *Medicinal Action and Uses.* This species is a reputed cure for blight on fruit-trees. A few green leaves from the plant, if rubbed on the part of the tree affected, it has been recently discovered, will effect an instantaneous cure, and the wounds on the stem afterwards heal with smooth, healthy coverings. The plant is often found growing underneath the trees in orchards.

The medicinal virtues of this species were considered to be much the same as the preceding ones, the seeds, boiled in milk, being laxative and demulcent.

PLANTAIN, ISPAGHUL

Plantago ovata (FORSK.)
N.O. Plantaginaceæ

Synonyms. Ispaghula. Spogel Seed. Plantago Ispaghula. Plantago decumbens
Part Used. Dried seeds
Habitat. India, Persia, Spain, Canary Islands

¶ *Description.* The corolla gives attachment to four protruded stamina, ovary free with one or two cells, containing one or more ovules.

The style capillar, terminated by a single subulate stigma. The fruit is a small pyxidium covered by the persistent corolla; seeds composed of a proper integument which covers a fleshy endosperm at the centre of which is a cylindrical axile and a homotype embryo, boat-shaped, acute at one end $\frac{1}{12}$ to $\frac{1}{4}$ inch long and $\frac{1}{24}$ inch wide, pale-green brown with a darker elongated spot on the convex side; on concave side hilium is covered with the remains of a thin white membrane. It has no odour or taste, but the herbage is demulcent and bitter and somewhat astringent.

¶ *Constituents.* Mucilage contained in seed coat (sometimes used to stiffen linen), fixed oil, proteins.

¶ *Medicinal Action and Uses.* Useful in place of linseed or barley, also for diarrhœa and dysentery; the decoction is a good demulcent drink, or seeds mixed with sugar and taken dry invaluable in this form for reducing inflamed mucous membranes of the intestinal canal – a mild laxative. When roasted the seeds become astringent and are used for

children's diarrhœa. In European medicine they are used chiefly for chronic diarrhœa and for catarrhal conditions of the genito-urinary tract. Dose, 2 to 2½ drachms of the seeds, mixed with sugar and taken dry. Decoction, ½ to 2 fluid ounces.

¶ *Other Species.* The seeds of the Indian species, *Plantago Amplexicaulis*, are sold in the bazaars as Ispaghula. They are of a darker colour than the official seeds, and are used in India as a demulcent in dysentery and other intestinal complaints.

P. decumbens (Forsk.), of South Africa, is regarded by some as the wild plant of which the preceding is a cultivated variety.

The seeds of *P. arenaria* (Waldst.), the SAND PLANTAIN, somewhat smaller, black and less glossy, and those of *P. Cynops* (Linn.), somewhat larger and lighter brown, are used similarly.

P. arenaria is an annual, with an erect, leafy, branched stem, bearing opposite, linear leaves and flowers in a spike, on long stalks, greenish-white. It flowers from June to September and grows in sandy, waste places, but in Britain has only been found on sandhills in one spot in Somerset and is not regarded as an indigenous species.

PLANTAIN, PSYLLIUM

Plantago Psyllium (LINN.)
N.O. Plantaginaceæ

Synonyms. Psyllium Seeds. Fleaseed. Psyllion. Psyllios
(*Barguthi*) Barguthi
Parts Used. Seeds, leaves

In Southern Europe, as well as in Northern Africa and Southern Asia, *Plantago Psyllium* (Linn.), Fleaseed is used similarly to *P.*

major. The seeds are also used for their large yield of mucilage. *Semen psyllii* is the name given to the seeds of several species of European Plantago, but the best are those of *P. Psyllium*. They are dark brown on the convex side, shiny, inodorous and nearly tasteless, but mucilaginous when chewed. They are demulcent and emollient and may be used internally and externally in the same manner as flaxseed, which they closely resemble in medicinal properties.

P. Psyllium has once been found on ballast hills in Jersey, but has not permanently established itself.

PLANTAIN, RIBWORT

Plantago lanceolata
N.O. Plantaginaceæ

Synonyms. Snake Plantain. Black Plantain. Long Plantain. Ribble Grass. Ribwort. Black Jack. Jackstraw. Lamb's Tongue. Hen Plant. Wendles. Kemps. Cocks. Quinquenervia. Costa Canina
Parts Used. Leaves, seeds

Several of the wild Plantains have been used indiscriminately for *Plantago major*. Of these, the most important is *Plantago lanceolatus* (Linn.), the Ribwort Plantain.

¶ *Description.* This is a very dark green, slender perennial, growing much taller than *P. major*. Its leaf-blades rarely reach an inch in breadth, are three to five ribbed, gradually narrowed into the petioles, which are often more than a foot long. The flower-stalks are often more than 2 feet long, terminating in cylindrical blunt, dense spikes, $\frac{1}{2}$ to 3 or 4 inches long and $\frac{1}{8}$ to $\frac{1}{2}$ inch thick. It has the same chemical constituents as *P. major*.

When this Plantain grows amongst the tall grasses of the meadow its leaves are longer, more erect and less harsh, than when we find it by the roadside, or on dry soil. The leaves are often slightly hairy and have at times a silvery appearance from this cause, especially in the roadside specimens. The flower-stalks are longer than the leaves, furrowed and angular and thrown boldly up. The flower-head varies a good deal in size and form, sometimes being much smaller and more globular than others. The sepals are brown and paper-like in texture and give the head its peculiar rusty look. The corolla is very small and inconspicuous, tubed and having four spreading lobes. The stamens, four in number, are the most noticeable feature, their slender white filaments and pale yellow anthers forming a conspicuous ring around the flower-head.

In some old books we find this species called *Costa canina*, in allusion to the prominent veinings on the leaves that earned it the name of Ribwort, and it is this feature that caused it to receive also the mediæval name of *Quinquenervia*. Another old popular name was 'Kemps,' a word that at first sight seems without meaning, but when fully understood has a peculiar interest. The stalks of this plant are particularly tough and wiry, and it is an old game with country children to strike the heads one against the other until the stalk breaks. The Anglo-Saxon word for a soldier was *cempa*, and we can thus see the allusion to 'kemps.'

This species of Plantain abounds in every meadow and was brought into notice at one time as a possible fodder plant. Curtis, in his *Flora Londonensis*, says:

'The farmers in general consider this species of plantain as a favourite food of sheep and hence it is frequently recommended in the laying down of meadow and pasture land, and the seed is for that purpose kept in the shops.'

But its cultivation was never seriously taken up, for though its mucilaginous leaves are relished by sheep and to a certain extent by cows and horses, it does not answer as a crop, except on very poor land, where nothing else will grow. Moreover, it is very bitter, and in pastures destroys the more delicate herbage around it by its coarse leaves.

The seeds are covered with a coat of mucilage, which separates readily when macerated in hot water. The gelatinous substance thus formed has been used at one time in France for stiffening some kinds of muslin and other woven fabrics.

The leaves contain a good fibre, which, it has been suggested, might be adapted to some manufacturing purpose.

PLANTAIN, SEA

Plantago maritimo
N.O. Plantaginaceæ

Synonyms. Sheep's Herb
Part Used. Herb

The Sea Plantain has linear leaves grooved, fleshy and woolly at the base. It is common on the seashore and tops of mountains and is easily distinguished from the rest of the genus by its fleshy leaves.

It is so relished by sheep as food and considered so good for them, that in North Wales, where it has been cultivated, it is called Sheep's Herb, and the Welsh have two names for it, signifying 'the sheep's favourite morsel' and 'the suet producer.'

The RATTLESNAKE or NET-LEAVED PLANTAINS of the United States, *Peramium ripens* (Salisb.) (syn. *Goodyera ripens*, R. Br.), the White Plantain or Squirrel-ear, and *P. pubescens* (Willd.), peculiar little woodland herbs, their ovate leaves beautifully reticulated with white lines, are not allies of our common Plantains, but belong to the Orchid family.

The name WHITE PLANTAIN is also applied in the United States to *Antennaria plantaginifolia* (Linn.), the Ladies or Indian Tobacco, Spring Cudweed, or Life-Everlasting, to give several of its names, exceedingly common throughout Eastern North America, and one of the earliest blooming of spring plants in dry meadows, where it grows in patches.

It is used as a soothing expectorant with more or less marked stomachic properties.

PLANTAIN, WATER

Alisma Plantago
N.O. Alismaceæ

Synonym. Mad-Dog Weed
Part Used. Leaves

The Water Plantain, though its name suggests a similarity, is in fact widely different to the Plantago species, and belongs to another natural order, Alismaceæ. It is a water-plant, widely distributed in Europe, Northern Asia and North America and abundant in many parts of England, though only naturalized in Scotland. It grows freely around the margins of lakes or streams and in watery ditches, in company with the forget-me-not, brooklime, and other well-known waterside plants.

The name *Alisma* is said to be from the Celtic word for water, *alis*, in allusion to the aquatic habitat of the plant. The name *Plantago* was given by the early botanists because they were impressed with the similarity of form between the leaves of this plant and those of the plantain, and ignoring its dissimilarity in flower and fruit, etc., called it the 'Water Plantain.'

The roots of the Water Plantain are fibrous, but the base of the stem is swollen and fleshy, or tuberous and furnished with a tuft of numerous whitish hairs. The flower-stalk, which rises directly from it, is obtusely three-cornered, a form specially suitable to enable it to stem the current; it is from 1 to 3 feet in height. The flower-bearing branches that spring laterally from this at its upper extremity are thrown off in rings or whorls, and these branches are themselves branched in like fashion, the whole forming a loose pyramidal panicle. The large leaves, broad below, but tapering to a point, all spring directly from the root also and are borne on long, triangular stalks, growing in a nearly erect position. They are smooth in texture, their margins often more or less waved and are very strongly veined, the mid-rib and about three on each side being very conspicuous. The leaf-stems are deeply channelled, broadening out and sheathing at their bases. The flowers are attractive in form and colour. The calyx is composed of three ovate, concave, spreading sepals, while the corolla has three showy petals of a delicate, pale pink colour, somewhat round in form, slightly jagged at their edges. The stamens are six in number, their anthers being of a greenish tint. The fruit is composed of some twenty or more three-cornered, clustering carpels, each containing one seed.

¶ *Medicinal Action and Uses.* The Water Plantain has been considerably used medicinally, and is a drug of commerce. It contains a pungent, volatile oil and an acrid resin, to which all its virtues must be ascribed

The drug has diuretic and diaphoretic properties, and has been recommended by herbalists in renal calculus, gravel, cystitis, dysentery and epilepsy.

The powdered rhizome and leaves are employed by herbalists, also an infusion and a tincture prepared from the swollen rhizome, in its fresh state, is a homœopathic drug.

The powdered seeds were recommended by older herbalists as an astringent in cases of bleeding.

The bruised leaves are rubefacient and will inflame and sometimes even blister the skin, being injurious to cattle. They have been applied locally to bruises and swellings.

The roots formerly enjoyed some repute as a cure for hydrophobia (hence one of its names, formerly, Mad-Dog Weed), and have been regarded in Russia as a specific, but repeated experiments made with them in this country and a searching inquiry, have not confirmed their use as a remedy for this disease. Their acridity is lost in drying.

In America it has earned a reputation against the bite of the rattlesnake. The roots are also used medicinally in Japan, under the name of *Saji Omodaka*.

This group of plants, the Alismaceæ, in

general contains acrid juices, on account of which a number of species, besides the Water Plantain, have been used as diuretics and antiscorbutic.

PLANTAIN FRUIT

Musa paradisiaca
Musa sapientum
N.O. Musæ

Synonym. Bananas
Parts Used. Fruit, unripe and ripe, juice

The tropical fruit known as Plantain belongs to the genus *Musa*, which contains about forty species, widely distributed throughout the tropics of the Old World and in some cases introduced into the New World.

The great use of the family resides in the use of the unripe fruits as food and to a much less extent in that of the ripe fruit – Bananas. In many parts of the tropics they are as important to the inhabitants as are the grain plants to those living in cooler regions. The northern limit of their cultivation is reached in Florida, the Canary Islands, Egypt and Southern Japan, and the southern limit in Natal and South Brazil. There has been considerable discussion as to whether they were growing in America before the discovery of the New World.

The unripe fruit is rich in starch, which on ripening turns into sugar.

The most generally used fruits are derived from *Musa paradisiaca*, of which an enormous number of varieties and forms exist in cultivation. The sub-species, *sapientum*, formerly regarded as a distinct species (*M. sapientum*), is the source of the fruits generally known in England as Bananas and eaten raw, while the name Plantain is given to forms of the species itself which require cooking. The species is probably a native of India and Southern Asia.

Other species are *M. acuminata* in the Malay Archipelago, *M. Fehi*, in Tahiti, and *M. Cavendishii*, the so-called Chinese Banana, which has a thinner rind and is found in cooler countries.

Plantains often reach a considerable size. The hardly-ripe fruit is eaten (whole or cut into slices) roasted, baked, boiled, fried, as an ingredient of soups and stews, and in general as potatoes are used, possessing, like the potato, only a slight or negative flavour and no sweetness. They are also dried and ground into flour as meal, Banana meal forming an important food-stuff, to which the following constituents have been assigned: Water 10·62, albuminoids 3·55, fat 1·15, carbohydrates 81·67 (more than ¾ starch), fibre 1·15, phosphates 0·26, other salts, 1·60. The sugar is chiefly cane-sugar.

Several species of *Sagittaria*, natives of Brazil, are astringent, and their expressed juice has been used in making ink.
See ARROWHEAD.

In East Africa and elsewhere an intoxicating drink is prepared from the fruit. The rootstock which bears the leaves is, just before the flowering period, soft and full of starch, and is sometimes used as food in Abyssinia, and the young shoots of several species are cooked and eaten.

The leaves cut into strips are plaited to form mats and bags; they are also largely used for packing and the finer ones for cigarette papers. The mature leaves of several species yield a valuable fibre, the best of which is 'Manila hemp.'

¶ *Medicinal Action and Uses.* The Banana family is of more interest for its nutrient than for its medicinal properties. Banana root has some employment as an anthelmintic and has been reported useful in reducing bronchocele.

The use of Plantain juice as an antidote for snake-bite in the East has been reported in recent years by the *Lancet*, an alleged cure at Colombo (reported in the *Lancet*, April 1, 1916), and again, in the same year, at Serampore:

'A servant of the Principal of the Government Weaving College was bitten by a venomous snake in the foot. The Principal applied a ligature eight inches above the bitten part and then cut it with a lancet and applied permanganate of potash, making the wound bleed freely. He then extracted some juice from a plantain tree and gave the patient about a cupful to drink. After drinking the plantain juice the man seemed to recover a little, and the wound was washed. He was made to walk up and down, and in the morning, when the ligature was removed, the man was declared cured.' – *Lancet*, June 10, 1916.

The BASTARD PLANTAIN (*Heliconia Bihai*) belongs to a genus containing thirty species, natives of tropical America. Although it belongs to the same order as the Banana, and has very large leaves, 6 to 8 feet long and 18 inches wide, it has quite different fruit, namely, small succulent berries, each containing three hard, rugged seeds, and is not employed economically.

PLEURISY ROOT

Asclepias tuberose (LINN.)
N.O. Asclepiadaceæ

Synonyms. Butterfly-weed. Swallow-wort. Tuber Root. Wind Root. Colic Root. Orange Milkweed

Part Used. Root

The genus *Asclepias* contains about eighty species, mostly natives of North America, a few being indigenous to South America and Africa.

Asclepias tuberosa, common from Canada southwards, growing from Ontario to Minnesota, most abundantly southward and southwestward, is known popularly as Pleurisy Root, from its medicinal use. Its stem forms an exception to Asclepias in general, by being almost or entirely devoid of the acrid milky juice containing caoutchouc, that distinguishes the rest of the genus and has gained them the name of Milkweeds.

¶ *Description.* It is a handsome, fleshy-rooted, perennial plant, growing 1 to 1½ foot high and bearing corymbs of deep yellow and orange flowers in September. When cultivated, it does not like being disturbed, and prefers good peat soil.

The rootstock, the part used medicinally, is spindle-shaped and has a knotty crown, slightly but distinctly annulate, the remainder longitudinally wrinkled.

The dried root as found in commerce is usually in cut or broken pieces of variable size, 1 to 6 inches long and about ¾ inch in thickness, externally pale orange-brown, becoming greyish-brown when kept long, internally whitish. It is tough and has an uneven fracture; the broken surface is granular; that of the bark is short and brittle. The wood is yellowish, with large white medullary rays. The drug is almost inodorous, but has a bitterish and disagreeable, somewhat acrid taste.

The powdered drug is yellowish brown and when examined under the microscope shows numerous simple or 2 to 4 compound starch grains, also calcium oxalate crystals.

The Western Indians boil the tubers for food, prepare a crude sugar from the flowers and eat the young seed-pods, after boiling them, with buffalo meat. Some of the Canadian tribes use the young shoots as a pot-herb, after the manner of asparagus.

¶ *Constituents.* The root contains a glucosidal principle, Asclepiadin, which occurs as an amorphous body, is soluble in ether, alcohol and hot water. It also contains several resins, and odorous fatty matter, and a trace of volatile oil. It yields not more than 9 per cent. of ash.

¶ *Medicinal Action and Uses.* Antispasmodic, diaphoretic, expectorant, tonic, carminative and mildly cathartic.

From early days this Asclepias has been regarded as a valuable medicinal plant. It is one of the most important of the indigenous American remedies, and until lately was official in the United States Pharmacopœia.

It possesses a specific action on the lungs, assisting expectoration, subduing inflammation and exerting a general mild tonic effect on the system, making it valuable in all chest complaints. It is of great use in pleurisy, mitigating the pain and relieving the difficulty of breathing, and is also recommended in pulmonary catarrh. It is extensively used in the Southern States in these cases, also in consumption, in doses of from 20 grains to a drachm in a powder, or in the form of a decoction.

It has also been used with great advantage in diarrhœa, dysentery and acute and chronic rheumatism, in low typhoid states and in eczema. It is claimed that the drug may be employed with benefit in flatulent colic and indigestion, but in these conditions it is rarely used.

In large doses it acts as an emetic and purgative.

A teacupful of the warm infusion (1 in 30) taken every hour will powerfully promote free perspiration and suppressed expectoration. The infusion may be prepared by taking 1 teaspoonful of the powder in a cupful of boiling water.

The decoction is taken in doses of 2 to 3 fluid ounces.

The dose of the fluid extract is ½ to 1 drachm; of Asclepin, 1 to 4 grains.

A much-recommended herbal recipe is: Essence of composition powder, 1 oz.; fluid extract of Pleurisy Root, 1 oz. Mix and take a teaspoonful three or four times daily in warm sweetened water.

It is often combined with Angelica and Sassafras for producing perspiration in fever and pleurisy and for equalizing the circulation of the blood.

More than a dozen other species have similar properties.

See ASCLEPIAN, CALOTROPIS and SWAMP MILKWEED.

PLOUGHMAN'S SPIKENARD. *See* SPIKENARD

PLUMBAGO

Plumbago Europæa (LINN.)
N.O. Plumbaginaceæ

Synonyms. Leadwort. Dentallaria
(*French*) Dentelaire
Parts Used. Root, herb
Habitat. China, Southern Europe, and cultivated in England in hot-houses

¶ *Description.* A half-hardy herbaceous climbing, half-shrubby plant, with large trusses of pale-blue flowers, which are in bloom continuously through the summer. This variety is also known under the name of *Plumbago Capensis*, and is greatly used in German gardening.

¶ *Constituents.* Plumbagin, a crystallizable acrid principle obtained from the root.

¶ *Medicinal Action and Uses.* It is acrid, and when chewed creates a free flow of saliva, particularly if root is used; said to be of benefit to relieve toothache, and has long been used in France for that purpose, hence its name, dentalaire; also useful for itch – a decoction of the root in olive oil is much used.

¶ *Other Species.* P. *Zeylanica* is said to be a strong diaphoretic.

POISON IVY ⎫
}*See* IVY
POISON OAK ⎭

POKE ROOT

Phytolacca decandra (LINN.)
N.O. Phytolaccaceæ

Synonyms. Phytolacca Root. Phytolaccæ Radix. Phytolacca Berry. Phytolaccæ Bacca. Phytolacca Vulgaris. Phytolacca Americana. Blitum Americanum. Branching Phytolacca. Phytolaque. Garget. Pigeon Berry. Méchoacan du Canada. Bear's Grape. Poke Weed. Raisin d'Amérique. Red-ink Plant. American Spinach. Skoke. Crowberry. Jalap. Cancer-root. American Nightshade. Pocan or Cokan. Coakum. Chongras. Morelle à Grappes. Herbe de la Laque. Amerikanische scharlachbeere. Kermesbeere. Virginian Poke. Poke Berry
Parts Used. Dried root, berries
Habitat. Indigenous to North America. Common in Mediterranean countries

¶ *Description.* This is regarded as one of the most important of indigenous American plants, and one of the most striking in appearance. The perennial root is large and fleshy, the stem hollow, the leaves alternate and ovate-lanceolate, and the flowers have a white calyx with no corolla. The fruit is a deep purple berry, covering the stem in clusters and resembling blackberries.

The young shoots make a good substitute for asparagus, and poultry eat the berries, though large quantities give the flesh an unpleasant flavour, also causing it to become purgative, when eaten.

In Portugal the use of the juice of the berries to colour port wines was discontinued because it spoilt the taste. The stain of the juice is a beautiful purple, and would make a useful dye if a way of fixing it were found.

A decoction of the roots has been used for drenching cattle.

As found in commerce the roots are usually sliced either longitudinally or transversely, are grey in colour, hard and wrinkled. The fracture is fibrous. It is inodorous, and the taste is acrid and slightly sweet.

It is often used to adulterate belladonna, but may be recognized by the concentric rings of wood bundles in the transverse section. The leaves are used for the same purpose, requiring microscopical identification.

¶ *Constituents.* Phytolaccic acid has been obtained from the berries, and tannin. In the root a non-reducing sugar, formic acid, and a small percentage of bitter resin have been found. The alkaloid Phytolaccin may be present in small quantities, but it has not been proved. A resinoid substance is called phytolaccin. The virtues are extracted by alcohol, diluted alcohol, and water. The powder is said to be sternutatory.

¶ *Medicinal Action and Uses.* A slow emetic and purgative with narcotic properties. As an alterative it is used in chronic rheumatism and granular conjunctivitis. As an ointment, in the proportion of a drachm to the ounce, it is used in psora, tinea capitis, favus and sycosis, and other skin diseases, causing at first smarting and heat.

The slowness of action and the narcotic effects that accompany it render its use as an emetic inadvisable. It is used as a cathartic in paralysis of the bowels. Headaches of many sources are benefited by it, and both lotion and tincture are used in leucorrhœa.

As a poultice it causes rapid suppuration in

felons. The extract is said to have been used in chronic rheumatism and hæmorrhoids.

Authorities differ as to its value in cancer. Great relief towards the close of a difficult case of cancer of the uterus was obtained by an external application of 3 oz. of Poke Root and 1 oz. of Tincture used in the strength of 1 tablespoonful to 3 pints of tepid water for bathing the part. It is also stated to be of undoubted value as an internal remedy in cancer of the breast.

The following prescription has been recommended: Fluid extracts of Phytolacca (2 oz.), Gentian (1 oz.) and Dandelion (1 oz.), with Simple Syrup to make a pint. One teaspoonful may be taken after each meal.

Infused in spirits, the fruit is used in chronic rheumatism, being regarded as equal to Guaicum.

It is doubtful if the root will cure syphilis without the help of mercury.

¶ *Dosages.* As emetic, 10 to 30 grains. As alterative, 1 to 5 grains. Of fluid extract of berries, ½ to 1 drachm. Of fluid extract of root, ¼ to ½ drachm; as an emetic, 15 drops; as an alterative, 2 drops. Phytolaccin, 1 to 3 grains.

¶ *Poisons and Antidotes.* In the lower animals convulsions and death from paralysis of respiration may be caused. Overdoses may produce considerable vomiting and purging, prostration, convulsions and death.

¶ *Other Species. Phytolacca drastica* of Chile is a violent purgative.

POLYPODY ROOT. *See* FERNS

POLYPORUS OF LARCH. *See* FUNGI

POMEGRANATE

Punica granatum (LINN.)
N.O. Lythraceæ

Synonyms. Grenadier. Cortex granati. Ecorce de Granade. Granatwurzelrinde. Melogranato. Malicorio. Scorzo del Melogranati. Cortezade Granada

Parts Used. The root, bark, the fruits, the rind of the fruit, the flowers

Habitat. Western Asia. Now grows widely in Mediterranean countries, China and Japan

¶ *History.* The Latin name of the tree was *Malus punica*, or *Punicum Malum*, the Lybian or Carthaginian apple; while the name of *granatum* was bestowed on account of its many seeds. Having no close relations, the tree has been placed by various authorities in different orders, some giving it an order of its own, Granateæ.

¶ *Description.* It is a small tree, not more than 15 feet high, with pale, brownish bark. The buds and young shoots are red, the leaves opposite, lanceolate, entire, thick, glossy and almost evergreen. The flowers are large and solitary, the crimson petals alternating with the lobes of the calyx. The fruit is the size of an orange, having a thick, reddish-yellow rind, an acid pulp, and large quantities of seeds.

The dried root bark is found in quills 3 to 4 inches long. It is yellowish-grey and wrinkled outside, the inner bark being smooth and yellow. It has a short fracture, little odour and a slightly astringent taste.

The rind of the fruit is in curved, brittle fragments, rough and yellowish-brown outside, paler and pitted within. It is called Malicorium.

The fruit is used for dessert, and in the East the juice is included in cooling drinks.

The flowers yield a red dye, and with leaves and seeds were used by the Ancients as astringent medicines and to remove worms. The Pomegranate is mentioned in the Papyrus Ebers.

It is still used by the Jews in some ceremonials, and as a design has been used in architecture and needlework from the earliest times. It formed part of the decoration of the pillars of King Solomon's Temple, and was embroidered on the hem of the High-Priest's ephod.

There are three kinds of Pomegranates: one very sour, the juice of which is used instead of verjuice, or unripe grape juice; the other two moderately sweet or very sweet. These are (in Syria) eaten as dessert after being cut open, seeded, strewn with sugar and sprinkled with rosewater. A wine is extracted from the fruits, and the seeds are used in syrups and conserves.

The bark is used in tanning and dyeing, giving the yellow hue to Morocco leather.

The barks of three wild Pomegranates are said to be used in Java: the red-flowered *merah*, the white-flowered *poetih*, and the black-flowered *hitam*.

¶ *Constituents.* The chief constituent of the *bark* (about 22 per cent.) is called punicotannic acid. It also contains gallic acid, mannite, and four alkaloids, Pelletierine, Methyl-Pelletierine, Pseudo-Pelletierine, and Iso-Pelletierine.

The liquid pelletierine boils at 125° C., and is soluble in water, alcohol, ether and chloroform.

The drug probably deteriorates with age.

The *rind* contains tannic acid, sugar and gum.

Pelletierine Tannate is a mixture of the

tannates of the alkaloids obtained from the bark of the root and stem, and represents the tænicidal properties.

¶ *Medicinal Action and Uses*. The *seeds* are demulcent. The *fruit* is a mild astringent and refrigerant in some fevers, and especially in biliousness, and the bark is used to remove tapeworm.

In India the *rind* is used in diarrhœa and chronic dysentery, often combined with opium.

It is used as an injection in leucorrhœa, as a gargle in sore throat in its early stages, and in powder for intermittent fevers. The flowers have similar properties.

As a tænicide a decoction of the *bark* may be made by boiling down to a pint 2 oz. of bark that has been macerated in spirits of water for twenty-four hours, and given in wineglassful doses. It often causes nausea and vomiting, and possibly purging. It should be preceded by strict dieting and fol-

lowed by an enema or castor oil if required. It may be necessary to repeat the dose for several days.

A hypodermic injection of the alkaloids may produce vertigo, muscular weakness and sometimes double vision.

The root-bark was recommended as a vermifuge by Celsus, Dioscorides and Pliny. It may be used fresh or dried.

¶ *Dosages*. Of rind and flowers in powder, 20 to 30 grains. Of pelletierine tannate, 3 to 5 grains. Of rind, 1 to 2 drachms. Fluid extract, root-bark, ¼ to 2 drachms. Decoction, B.P., ½ to 2 oz. Of decoction of 4 oz. of bark to 20 of water, ½ a fluid ounce.

¶ *Adulterations*. The bitter but non-astringent barks of Barberry and Box (*Boxux sempervirens*). Their infusion does not produce the deep blue precipitate with a persalt of iron.

Pinana is a dwarf variety naturalized in the West Indies.

POPLAR

Populus tremuloides (MICHX.)
N.O. Salicaceæ

Synonyms. American Aspen. White Poplar. Quaking Aspen
Part Used. Bark
Habitat. North America

¶ *Description*. This tree does not grow well in Britain, but in America it grows up to 100 feet in height. It has a pale yellowish bark on the young trunk and main branches; broadly ovate finely-toothed leaves averaging 1¾ inch long and wide, and having fine hairs on the margin.

The bark should be collected in spring. It has a bitterish taste and no odour.

¶ *Constituents*. The bark probably has similar properties to that of *Populus tremula* of Europe, i.e. salicin and populin.

¶ *Medicinal Action and Uses*. Febrifuge and tonic, chiefly used in intermittent

fevers. It has been employed as a diuretic in urinary affections, gonorrhœa and gleet. The infusion has been found helpful in debility, chronic diarrhœa, etc. Is a valuable and safe substitute for Peruvian bark.

¶ *Dosages*. Fluid extract, 1 drachm. Of salicin, in intermittents, 10 to 30 grains. Of populin, 1 to 4 grains.

¶ *Other Species*.
P. grandidentata, the large Aspen, is said to have more activity and bitterness.

P. candicans is also used.

POPPY, PLUME

Bocconia cordata
N.O. Papaveraceæ

Synonym. Macleaya
Part Used. Juice of stems of leaves
Habitat. China, but grows freely in author's garden

¶ *Description*. This plant was named in honour of a Sicilian botanist. A handsome and vigorous perennial, growing in erect tufts up to 8 feet. Flowers in very large panicles; the inflorescence is a soft creamy to brown plume, not showy, but has a fine effect; the blue-green downy leaves are very effective and elegant; the plant is propagated by seeds and division of the root.

¶ *Constituents*. Protopine, homo-chilidonine chelerythrine and sanguinarine have been isolated from the plant.

¶ *Medicinal Action and Uses*. The liquid from the root and the juice of the stems of the leaves are a deep orange and stains the hands; the juice from the *stems of the leaves* is used for insect-bites.

It is considered probable that the various species of this genus may have active medicinal qualities.

¶ *Other Species*.
The Mexican (*Bocconia arborea*, Watson) has been found to contain two alkaloids, one of which is probably Sanguinarine, and the

leaves of other species are used in South America as purgatives and abortifacients.

B. frutescens and *B. integrifolia* are natives of the West Indies and Mexico, and are more tender than *B. cordata*, and are best protected or taken into greenhouse during the winter. It is easier to raise these by seeds than by cuttings.

POPPY, RED

Papaver Rhœas (LINN.)
N.O. Papaveraceæ

Synonyms. Corn Rose. Corn Poppy. Flores Rhœados. Headache
Parts Used. Flowers, petals

The Common Red Poppy, growing in fields and waste places, has petals of a rich scarlet colour when fresh, and is often nearly black at the base. They have the peculiar heavy odour of opium when fresh, but becomes scentless on drying.

There are several varieties, differing in the size of the lobes of the leaves and in the character of the fruit, which may be nearly cylindrical or globular, smooth or furnished with stiff hairs. The intensity of the scarlet colouring of the petals also varies. The fresh petals are used for preparing a syrup. The Red Poppy with petals having a dark spot at the base makes the deepest-coloured syrup; that with the oblong capsule should not be used, as it contains an alkaloid resembling Thebaine in action.

¶ *Collection.* The petals find a steady, though limited market, but must be collected in large quantities, by an organized band of collectors, to be of any use. Farmers might arrange to deliver the fresh petals to manufacturers. They can be collected by children in small muslin bags suspended from the neck, so that both hands are left free for gathering. The petals should not be taken out of the bags, but packed in them, among straw, and sent off the same day as collected, before they fade or lose their bright colour. All the collecting should be done in dry weather, and all handling possible should be avoided.

Although in this country the Field Poppy is only regarded as a weed, and only a limited amount of the petals are used, it is cultivated in Flanders and several parts of Germany for the sake of its seeds, which are not only used in cakes, but from which an excellent oil is made, used as a substitute for olive oil.

The foliage is said to have been used as a vegetable, and the syrup prepared from the petals has been employed as an ingredient in soups and gruels.

Attempts have also been made to utilize the brilliant red of the petals as a dye, but the colour has proved too fugitive to be of use. The syrup has, however, been used as a colouring matter for old ink.

¶ *Constituents. Papaver Rhœas* is very slightly narcotic. The chief constituent of the fresh petals is the red colouring matter, which consists of Rhœadic and Papaveric acids. This colour is much darkened by alkalis.

All parts of the plant contain the crystalline non-poisonous alkaloid Rhœadine. The amount of active ingredients is very small and rather uncertain in quantity. There is great controversy as to the presence of Morphine. Also it has not been determined whether Meconic Acid, which is present in opium, is a constituent.

(POISON)
POPPY, WHITE

Papaver somniferum (LINN.)
N.O. Papaveraceæ

Synonyms. Opium Poppy. Mawseed
Parts Used. Capsules, flowers
Habitat. The Opium Poppy (*Papaver somniferum*, var. *album*) is indigenous to Asia Minor, and is cultivated largely in European and Asiatic Turkey, Persia, India and China for the production of Opium
It has been observed growing on the cliffs between Folkestone and Dover.

The word opium is derived from the Greek *opos* (juice).

¶ *Description.* The plant is an erect, herbaceous annual, varying much in the colour of its flowers, as well as in the shape of the fruit and colour of the seeds. All parts of the plant, but particularly the walls of the capsules, or seed-vessels, contain a system of laticiferous vessels, filled with a white latex.

The flowers vary in colour from pure white to reddish purple. In the wild plant, they are pale lilac with a purple spot at the base of each petal. In England, mostly in Lincolnshire, a variety with pale flowers and whitish seeds is cultivated medicinally for the sake of the capsules. Belgium has usually supplied a proportion of the Poppy Heads used in this country, though those used for fomentations are mostly of home growth.

The capsules vary much in shape and size. They are usually hemispherical, but depressed at the top, where the many-rayed stigma occupies the centre; they have a swollen ring below where the capsule joins the stalk. Some varieties are ovoid, others again depressed both at summit and base. The small kidney-shaped seeds, minute and very numerous, are attached to lateral projections from the inner walls of the capsule and vary in colour from whitish to slate. The heads are of a pale glaucous green when young. As they mature and ripen they change to a yellowish brown, and are then cut from the stem if the *dried* poppy heads are required.

Opium is extracted from the poppy heads before they have ripened, and from Poppies grown in the East, those grown in Europe yielding but little of the drug. When the petals have fallen from the flowers, incisions are made in the wall of the unripe capsules, care being taken not to penetrate to the interior. The exuded juice, partially dried, is collected by scraping – the scrapings being formed eventually into cakes, which are wrapped in poppy leaves or paper and further dried in the sun, the white milky juice darkening during the drying.

The first poppies cultivated in this country for the purpose of extracting opium were grown by Mr. John Ball, of Williton, in 1794, but the production of opium has not become a home industry, as was expected at the time. The cultivation of the Opium Poppy has also been experimentally carried out in France and Germany, but the expense of the necessary labour and land has been too great to render it profitable. The British Pharmacopœia directs that opium, when used officially, must be obtained from Asia Minor. A certain amount is cultivated in Macedonia and exported from Salonica, and much of that cultivated in Persia is also sent to European markets. Chinese Opium is entirely consumed in the country and is not exported.

¶ *Constituents*. The most important constituents of opium are the alkaloids, which constitute in good opium about one-fifth of the weight of the drug. No fewer than twenty-one have been reported.

The principal alkaloid, both as regards its medicinal importance, and the quantity in which it exists, is Morphine. Next to this, Narcotine and Codeine are of secondary importance. Among the numerous remaining alkaloids, amounting in all to about 1 per cent. of the drug, are Thebaine, Narceine, Papaverine, Codamine and Rhœadine.

Meconic acid exists to the extent of about 5 per cent. combined with morphine. This acid is easily identified, and is important in toxicological investigation, as corroborative of the presence of opium.

Meconin and meconiasin exist in small quantity only. Mucilage, sugar, wax, caoutchouc and salts of calcium, and magnesium are also contained in opium, and sulphuric acid is found in the ash. The presence of starch, tannin, oxalic acid and fat, common constituents of most plants, indicates adulteration, as these substances do not occur normally in the drug. Powdered poppy capsules stones, small shot, pieces of lead, gum, grape must, sugary fruits, and other mechanical impurities, have also been used as adulterants of opium. The drug should not contain more than 12½ per cent. of moisture.

¶ *Medicinal Action and Uses*. Hypnotic, sedative, astringent, expectorant, diaphoretic, antispasmodic.

The drug was known in very remote times and the Greeks and Romans collected it. It is probable that the physicians of the Arabian school introduced the drug into India, as well as into Europe. It was originally used only as a medicine, the practice of opium eating having first arisen, probably in Persia.

Opium is one of the most valuable of drugs, Morphine and Codeine, the two principal alkaloids, being largely used in medicine.

It is unexcelled as a hypnotic and sedative, and is frequently administered to relieve pain and calm excitement. For its astringent properties, it is employed in diarrhœa and dysentery, and on account of its expectorant, diaphoretic, sedative and antispasmodic properties, in certain forms of cough, etc.

Small doses of opium and morphine are nerve stimulants. The Cutch horsemen share their opium with their jaded steeds, and increased capability of endurance is observed alike in man and beast.

Opium and morphine do not produce in animals the general calmative and hypnotic effects which characterize their use in man, but applied locally, they effectually allay pain and spasm. Owing to the greater excitant action in veterinary patients, the administration of opium does not blunt the perception of pain as effectually as it does in human patients.

The British Pharmacopœia Tincture of Opium, popularly known as Laudanum, is made with 3 oz. of Opium and equal parts of distilled water and alcohol, and for immediate effects is usually preferable to solid Opium. Equal parts of Laudanum and Soap Liniment make an excellent anodyne, much used externally.

¶ *Preparations*. Syrup of Poppy, B.P., 1885. Syrup Papav. alba. Capsules, 1 to 2 drachms.

¶ *Antidotes*. Opium is not very quickly absorbed. When a poisonous dose has been swallowed, the stomach should be

WHITE POPPY
Papaver Somniferum

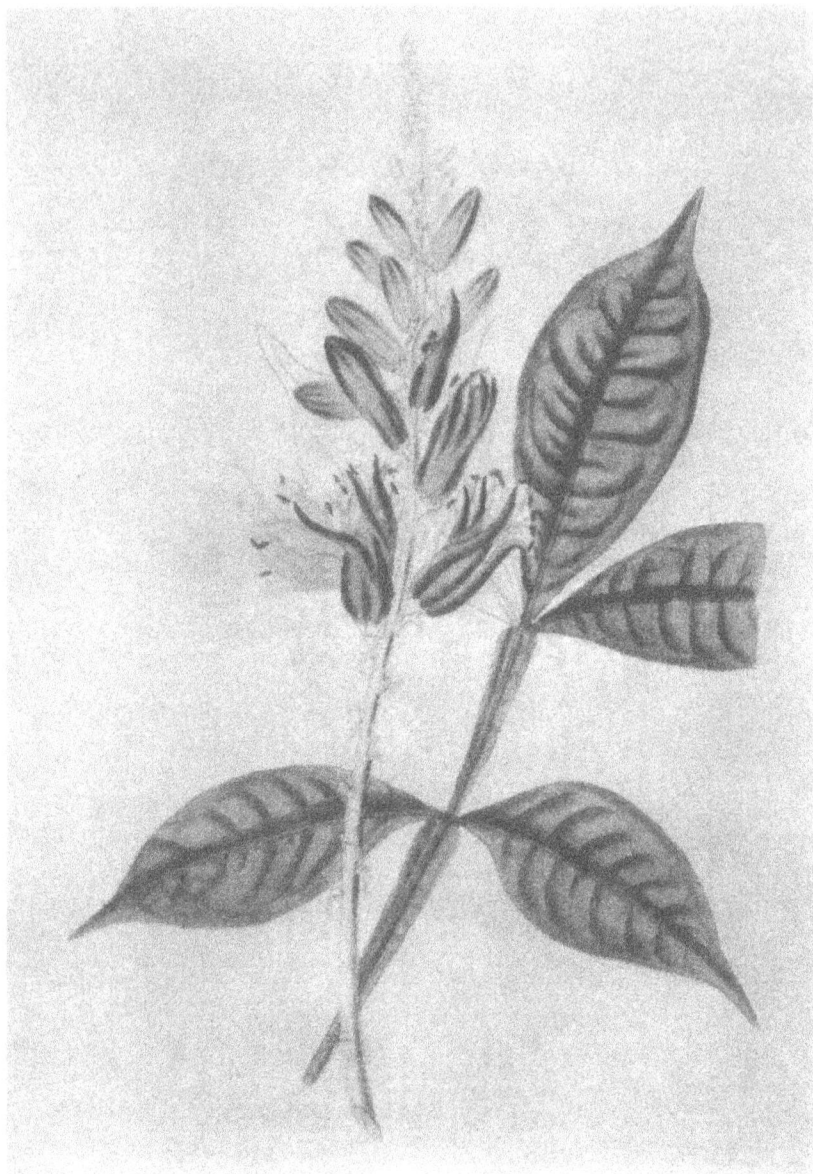

QUASSIA
Picræna Excelsa

emptied as soon as possible by the stomach pump and washed with a solution of potassium permanganate. Administration of nitrites and of small doses of atropine hypodermically maintain cardiac action, but the atropine must be used cautiously, as full doses are apt to intensify paralysis both of the heart and spinal cord. The lethal tendency is further combated by strychnine used hypodermically and by artificial respiration. Coma is prevented by giving strong coffee and stimulant enemata and keeping the patient moving. Tincture of gall and other chemical antidotes are of little avail.

The leaves of *Combretum Sundaicum*, a plant native to the Malay Peninsula and Sumatra, have been used in the form of a decoction of the roasted leaves, as a cure for the opium habit among the Chinese.

¶ *Cultivation.* The plants prefer rich, moist soil and much sun, and are often grown in succession to wheat and barley.

The land is manured and ploughed in autumn, to ensure a fine tilth in spring. Sowing is done at the end of March or in April – according to weather – allowing 1 lb. of seed per acre, and drilling in rows a foot apart. The whitest seeds are preferred.

Plants which are too forward are liable to be cut down by late frosts, while if the seed is sown too late, the seedlings may become dwarfed if dry weather sets in before they are well established. A light roller is sufficient to ensure the seeds being covered.

When the plants are 3 or 4 inches high, cut them with the hoe into clumps about 6 to 9 inches apart, and afterwards 'single' them, leaving a solitary strong plant from each group. Weeding is necessary, and a dressing of soot may be given if support appears to be needed.

Poppy heads of pale colour are most desired, but a week's rain, or even a few nights' heavy dew, may spoil the colour of the ripening fruit. High winds and heavy rains may cause much destruction, as the plants become top-heavy. The yield is very variable.

The capsules are left on the stems after the petals have fallen, until they cease to enlarge. The stems should then be bent in the middle and the capsules left on the plant until they are firm, which will be about September.

In India, when the flowers are in bloom, the first step is the removal of the petals, which are used in packing the prepared drug. After a few days, the imperfectly ripened capsules are scarified from above downwards by two or three knives tied together and called 'mushturs.' These make a superficial incision, or series of incisions, into the capsule, whereupon a milky juice exudes, which is allowed to harden and is then removed and collected in earthen pots. The time of day chosen for slicing the capsules is about two o'clock in the afternoon, when the heat of the sun causes the speedy formation of a film over the exuded juice; great attention is also paid to the weather, as all these causes modify the quantity, quality, or speediness of exudation of the opium.

The capsules are submitted to two or three slicing processes at intervals of a few days, and the drug is ultimately conveyed to the government factory where it is kneaded into a homogeneous mass by native workmen.

The capsules contain the principal constituents of opium, the most important of which is the alkaloid Morphine, which exists in combination with meconic and sulphuric acids. The seeds are free from morphine; their principle constituent is the pale yellow fixed oil, used as a drying oil by artists, as well as for culinary and various technical purposes.

The action of poppy capsules is the same as that of opium, anodyne and narcotic, but much weaker.

The crushed capsules are used as a poultice, together with chamomile.

A syrup is prepared from the capsules, prescribed as an ingredient in cough medicine. Syrup of Poppy is often employed to allay cough and likewise as an opiate for children; in the latter case it should be used with great caution.

Decoction of Poppy, made from the bruised capsules and distilled water, is not given internally, but is employed as an external application to allay pain and soothe.

The broken capsules are sold at a cheaper rate, for making fomentations.

The grey seeds are sold for birds' food, under the name of 'maw' seed, and are derived from the dark-red flowered form of *Papaver Somniferum*; the var. *album* having white seeds.

On the Continent the seeds are much used in special poppy cakes and are sprinkled on rolls, as also in India, where they are used in the native pancakes or 'chupaties.'

Anodyne, expectorant. The fresh petals are directed by the British Pharmacopœia for preparing a syrup, which may be given in 1 drachm doses, occasionally, as a mild astringent, but is principally employed as a colouring agent for mixtures and gargles.

Culpepper tells us that a syrup made of the leaves and flowers is effectual in pleurisy and erysipelas, or the green leaves can be applied outwardly, made into an ointment, but Gerard says these claims are without foundation and that 'it is only chance when persons are relieved by it.'

Culpepper also tells us :

'it is more cooling than any of the other Poppies, and therefore cannot but be as effectual in hot agues, frenzies, and other inflammations either inward or outward. Galen saith, The seed is dangerous to be used inwardly.'

There are other varieties of the Field Poppy – *P. Dubium*, frequently met with in some parts of the country, is a smaller, more slender plant than *P. Rhœas*, and may be at once distinguished by the capsule, which is twice as long as broad, and by the bristles, which are flattened up against the stem. *P. hybridum* is less branched than the Field Poppy, which it greatly resembles, but differs in the filaments of the stamens, which are dilated from below upwards; and in the capsule, which, though globular, is covered with stiff bristles. This species is rare in this country.

P. Argemone is the smallest of the British Poppies; its capsule is in shape like that of *P. Dubium*, but it has a few stiff hairs or bristles which are directed upwards.

POTATO

Solanum tuberosum (LINN.)
N.O. Solanaceæ

Part Used. Edible tubers

The Potato is nearly related to the Night-shades, belonging to the same genus, *Solanum*. Its flowers are very similar in form, but larger and paler in colour than those of *Solanum Dulcamara*.

The stalks, leaves and green berries possess the narcotic and poisonous properties of the Nightshades, but the tubers we eat (which are not the root, but mere enlargements of underground stems, shortened and thickened, in which starch is stored up for the future use of the plant), not being acted on by light, do not develop the poisonous properties contained by that part of the plant above ground. The influence of light on the tubers can be observed if in spring-time young green potatoes are exposed to daylight, when it will be found that they become poisonous and have a disagreeable taste.

The Potato was introduced into Europe early in the sixteenth century, being brought to Spain from Peru, and was first brought into England in 1586 from North America, the colonists sent out by Sir Walter Raleigh bringing it back with them from Virginia.

Gerard, in his *Herbal* published in 1597, gives a figure of the Potato, under the name of 'Potato of Virginia' – to distinguish it from the Sweet Potato. The Herbal contains a portrait of himself on the frontispiece holding in his hand a spray of the Potato plant with flowers and berries.

Though Sir Walter Raleigh was the first to plant the Potato, on his estate at Youghall, near Cork, it is said that he knew so little about it that he tried to eat the berries, and on discovering their noxious character, ordered the plants to be rooted out. It is said that the gardener in doing so, first learnt the value of their wholesome tubers.

From Ireland, the Potato was soon after carried into Lancashire, but for some time Potatoes were only grown as a delicacy for the epicure, not as food for the people. Both Gerard and Parkinson refer to them in this manner. The Puritans opposed their cultivation, because no mention of them could be found in the Bible, and it was not until the middle of the eighteenth century that potatoes became common in this country as a vegetable. As late as 1716, Bradley, in his *Historia Plantarum Succulentarum*, speaks of them as 'inferior to skirrets and radishes.'

The Potato is indigenous in various parts of South America, plants in a wild state having been found on the Peruvian coast, as well as on the sterile mountains of Central Chile and Buenos Aires. The Spaniards are believed to have first brought it to Europe, from Quito, in the early part of the sixteenth century. It afterwards found its way into Italy, and from thence it was carried to Mons, in Belgium, by one of the attendants of the Pope's legate. In 1598 it was sent from Mons to the celebrated botanist Clusius at Vienna, who states that in a short time it spread rapidly throughout Germany.

In the time of James I, potatoes cost 2s. a pound, and are mentioned in 1619 among the articles provided for the royal household. In 1633, when their valuable properties had become more generally known, they were noticed by the Royal Society, and measures were taken to encourage their cultivation in case of famine; but it was not till nearly a century after this that they were grown to any extent in England. In 1725 they were introduced into Scotland and cultivated with much success, first in gardens, and afterwards (about 1760), when they had become plentiful, in the open fields.

On the Continent, the adoption of the Potato as a vegetable met with considerable prejudice, and it did not become a general article of food for some time after it was in general use here. Gerard says: 'Bauhine saith that he heard that the use of these roots was forbidden in Burgundy for that they were persuaded the too frequent use of them caused the leprosie' – a belief without any foundation, for the disease is now confined to countries where the Potato is not grown, and its antiscorbutic properties have been proved.

Linnæus for some time objected to the use of the Potato on account of its connexion with the Deadly Nightshade and Bittersweet. Solanine, the poisonous active principle contained in the stalks, leaves and unripe fruit, is very powerful, and has not yet been fully investigated. It is also present in the peel of the tuber, but is dissipated and rendered inert when the whole potato is boiled and steamed, and is decomposed by baking.

¶ *Constituents*. The tuber is composed mainly of starch, which affords animal heat and promotes fatness, but the proportion of muscle-forming food is very small – it is said that 10½ lb. of the tubers are only equal in value to 1 lb. of meat. The raw juice of the Potato contains no alkaloid, the chief ingredient being potash salts, which are present in large quantity. The tuber also contains a certain amount of citric acid – which, like Potash, is antiscorbutic – and phosphoric acid, yielding phosphorus in a quantity less only than that afforded by the apple and by wheat.

It is of paramount importance that the valuable potash salts should be retained by the Potato during cooking. If peeled and then boiled, the tubers lose as much as 33 per cent. of potash and 23 per cent. of phosphoric acid, and should, therefore, invariably be boiled or steamed with their coats on. Too much stress cannot be laid on this point. Peeled potatoes have lost half their food-value in the water in which they have been boiled.

The Potato is not only important as a valuable article of diet, but has many other uses, both medicinal and economic.

To carry a raw potato in the pocket was an old-fashioned remedy against rheumatism that modern research has proved to have a scientific basis. Ladies in former times had special bags or pockets made in their dresses in which to carry one or more small raw potatoes for the purpose of avoiding rheumatism if predisposed thereto. Successful experiments in the treatment of rheumatism and gout have in the last few years been made with preparations of raw potato juice. In cases of gout, rheumatism and lumbago the acute pain is much relieved by fomentations of the prepared juice followed by an application of liniment and ointment. Sprains and bruises have also been successfully treated by the Potato-juice preparations, and in cases of synovitis rapid absorption of the fluid has resulted. Although it is not claimed that the treatment in acute gout will cure the constitutional symptoms, local treatment by its means relieves the pain more quickly than other treatment.

Potato starch is much used for determining the diastatic value of malt extract.

Hot potato water has in years past been a popular remedy for some forms of rheumatism, fomentations to swollen and painful parts, as hot as can be borne, being applied from water in which 1 lb. of unpeeled potatoes, divided into quarters, has been boiled in 2 pints slowly boiled down to 1 pint. Another potato remedy for rheumatism was made by cutting up the tubers, infusing them together with the fresh stalks and unripe berries for some hours in cold water, and applying in the form of a cold compress. The potatoes should not be peeled.

Uncooked potatoes, peeled and pounded in a mortar, and applied cold, have been found to make a very soothing plaster to parts that have been scalded or burnt.

The mealy flour of baked potato, mixed with sweet oil, is a very healing application for frost-bites. In Derbyshire, hot boiled potatoes are used for corns.

Boiled with weak sulphuric acid, potato starch is changed into glucose, or grape sugar, which by fermentation yields alcohol – this spirit being often sold under the name of British Brandy.

A volatile oil – chemically termed Amylic alcohol, in Germany known as *Fuselöl* – is distilled by fermentation from potato spirit.

Although young potatoes contain no citric acid, the mature tubers yield enough even for commercial purposes, and ripe potato juice is an excellent cleaner of silks, cottons and woollens.

A fine flour is prepared from the Potato, and more used on the Continent than in this country for cake-making.

POTATO, PRAIRIE

Psoralea
N.O. Leguminosæ

Synonyms. Prairie Turnip. Tipsinah. Taahgu
Parts Used. Root, leaf, seeds
Habitat. United States. Other species of the genus in India and Europe

¶ *Description*. The tubers of *Psoralea esculenta* are eaten by the Indians and settlers of the North-western United States. The other species have various medicinal qualities. *P. pedunculata* or *P. melilotoides*, the Virginian variety, is also known as Congo

Root, Bob's Root, and Samson's Snakeroot.

Leaflets of *P. obliqua*, bitter, and of a distinct odour, have been found to be mixed with Buchu.

¶ *Constituents.* Of the tuber, 70 per cent. starch and 5 per cent. of a new sugar not yet fully investigated. The root of the Virginian variety contains a volatile oil of pungent taste, and a bitter principle, not tannin. The Indian *P. corylifolia* yields a useful oleoresin.

¶ *Medicinal Action and Uses. P. glandulosa,* or yolochiahitl, has a leaf included in the Mexican Pharmacopœia as a tonic or anthelmintic, and an emetic root. *P. bituminosa* of Europe and *P. physodes* of California are tonic and emmenagogic. The root of the Virginian variety is a valuable, aromatic tonic, useful in chronic diarrhœa, while the Indian species is useful for leucoderma and other skin diseases.

POTATO, WILD

Convolvulus panduratus
N.O. Convolvulaceæ

Synonyms. Mechameck. Wild Jalap. Man-in-the-earth. Man-in-the-ground. Manroot. Now Ipomœa fastigiata, Sweet

Part Used. Root

Habitat. United States and a small amount in South America

¶ *Description.* The perennial, tapering root is very large, being from 2 to 8 feet in length, and 2 to 5 inches in diameter. It is brownish-yellow outside, whitish and lactescent within, having an acrid taste and disagreeable odour. It loses 75 per cent. of weight in drying. Usually it arrives in transverse, circular sections, not readily reducible to greyish powder. It is stated that the Red Indians can handle rattlesnakes with ease and safety after wetting their hands with the milky juice of the root. The leaves are 2 to 3 inches long, the flowers large and white, and the fruit an oblong, two-celled capsule.

¶ *Constituents.* Unknown.

¶ *Medicinal Action and Uses.* Mildly cathartic and diuretic. It was formerly used in strangury and calculous diseases, and also slightly influences lungs, liver, and kidneys without excessive diuresis or catharsis. Probably the active principle would prove stronger than the crude root.

¶ *Dosage.* 40 grains of the dried root.

See BINDWEED, JALAP, POTATO (SWEET).

PRICKLY ASH. *See* ASH

PRIMROSE

Primula vulgaris (HUDS.)
N.O. Primulaceæ

Parts Used. Root, herb

Habitat. The plant is abundant in woods, hedgerows, pastures and on railway embankments throughout Great Britain, and is in full flower during April and May. In sheltered spots in mild winters it is often found in blossom during the opening days of the year

The Primrose possesses somewhat similar medicinal properties to those of the Cowslip. It has a root-stock, knotty with the successive bases of fallen leaves and bearing cylindrical, branched rootlets on all sides. The leaves are egg-shaped and oblong, about 5 inches long when fully developed, tapering into a winged stalk, about 1¼ inch broad in the middle, smooth above, the veins and veinlets prominent beneath and hairy, the margins irregularly toothed. The young leaf appears as a stout mid-rib, with the blade rolled on itself on either side into two crinkled coils laid tightly along it, in similar manner to the Cowslip.

The flowers are each on separate stalks.

There are two kinds of flowers, externally apparently identical, but inwardly of different construction. Only one kind is found on each plant, never both, one kind being known as 'pin-eyed' and the other as 'thrum-eyed.' In both, the green-tubed calyx and the pale yellow corolla of five petals, joined into a tube below and spreading into a disk above are identical, but in the centre of the pin-eyed flowers there is only the green knob of the stigma, looking like a pin's head, whereas in the centre of the thrum-eyed flowers there are five anthers, in a ring round the tube, but no central knob. Farther down the tube, there are in the pin-eyed flowers five anthers hanging on to the wall of the corolla tube, while in the thrum-eyed, at this same spot, is the stigma knob. At the bottom of the tube in both alike is the seed-case and round it the honey.

It was Darwin who first pointed out the reason for this arrangement. Only a long-tongued insect can reach the honey at the base of the tube and when he starts collecting the honey on a pin-eyed flower, pollen is rubbed on the middle part of his proboscis from the anthers midway down the tube. As he goes from flower to flower on the same plant, there is the same result, but when he visits another plant with thrum-eyed flowers, then the pollen on his proboscis is just in the right place to rub on the stigma which only reaches half-way up the tube, his head meanwhile getting pollen from the long stamens at the throat of the tube, which in turn is transferred to the tall stigmas of the next pin-eyed flower he may visit. Thus both kinds of flowers are cross-fertilized in an ingenious manner. It is also remarkable that the pollen of the two flowers differs, the grains of that in the thrum-eyed flower being markedly larger, to allow it to fall on the long stigmas of the pin-eyed flowers and to put out long tubes to reach to the ovary-sac far below, whereas the smaller pollen destined for the shorter stigmas has only to send out a comparatively short tube to reach the seeds waiting to be fertilized. This diversity of structure ensures cross-fertilization only by such long-tongued insects as bees and moths.

¶ *Parts Used Medicinally and Preparation for Market.* The whole herb, used fresh, and in bloom, and the root-stock (the so-called root) dried.

The roots of two- or three-year-old plants are used, dug in autumn. The roots must be thoroughly cleansed in cold water, with a brush, allowing them to remain in water as short a time as possible. All smaller fibres are trimmed off. Large roots may be split lengthwise to facilitate drying, but as a rule this will not be necessary with Primrose roots.

¶ *Constituents.* Both the root and flowers of the Primrose contain a fragrant oil and Primulin, which is identical with Mannite, whilst the somewhat acrid active principle is Saponin.

¶ *Medicinal Action and Uses.* Antispasmodic, vermifuge, emetic, astringent.

In the early days of medicine, the Primrose was considered an important remedy in muscular rheumatism, paralysis and gout.

Pliny speaks of it as almost a panacea for these complaints.

The whole plant is sedative and in modern days a tincture of the fresh plant in bloom, in a strength of 10 oz. to 1 pint of alcohol, in doses of 1 to 10 drops has been used with success in America in extreme sensitiveness, restlessness and insomnia. The whole plant has somewhat expectorant qualities.

An infusion of the flowers was formerly considered excellent against nervous hysterical disorders. 'Primrose Tea,' says Gerard, 'drunk in the month of May is famous for curing the phrensie.' The infusion may be made of 5 to 10 parts of the petals to 100 of water.

In modern herbal medicine the infusion of the root is generally taken in tablespoonful doses as a good remedy against nervous headaches. A teaspoonful of the powdered dry root serves as an emetic.

'Of the leaves of Primrose,' Culpepper tells us, 'is made as fine a salve to heal wound as any I know.'

The leaves are said to be eagerly eaten by the common silkworm.

In ancient cookery the flowers were the chief ingredient in a pottage called 'Primrose Pottage.' Another old dish had rice, almonds, honey, saffron, and ground Primrose flowers. (From *A Plain Plantain.*)

The Primrose family is remarkable for the number of hybrids it produces. The garden 'Polyanthus of unnumbered dyes,' as the poet Thomson calls it in 'The Seasons,' is only another form (probably of the Cowslip or Oxlip) produced by cultivation. The Oxlip is distinguished from the Primrose by its flowers being stalked umbels and of a deeper shade of yellow and by its leaves becoming suddenly broader above the middle. It varies from the Cowslip by its tubular, not bell-shaped calyx and flat, not concave corolla.

The following note is from the *Chemist and Druggist* (March 5, 1921):

'The Oxlip is of more interest to the botanist than to the pharmacist, though at one time it shared with its cousins the cowslip and primrose the name *Herba paralysis*, and had, like them, a considerable reputation as a remedy in several diseases. Our official books distinguished between *Herba paralysis* and *Primula veris*, and attributed different virtues to them.'

See COWSLIP, CYCLAMEN.

PRIMROSE, EVENING

Œnothera biennis (LINN.)
N.O. Onagraceæ

Synonym. Tree Primrose
Parts Used. Bark, leaves
Habitat. The Evening or Tree Primrose, though originally a native of North America, was imported first into Italy and has been carried all over Europe, being often naturalized on river-banks and other sandy places in Western Europe. It is often cultivated in English gardens, and is apparently fully naturalized in Lancashire and some other counties of England, having been first a garden escape

¶ *Description.* The root is biennial, fusiform and fibrous, yellowish on the outside and white within. The first year, many obtuse leaves are produced, which spread flat on the ground. From among these in the second year, the more or less hairy stems arise and grow to a height of 3 or 4 feet. The later leaves are 3 to 5 inches long, 1 inch or more wide, pointed, with nearly entire margins and covered with short hairs. The flowers are produced all along the stalks, on axillary branches and in a terminating spike, often leafy at the base. The uppermost flowers come out first in June. The stalks keep continually advancing in height, and there is a constant succession of flowers till late in the autumn, making this one of the showiest of our hardy garden plants, if placed in large masses. The flowers are of a fine, yellow colour, large and delicately fragrant, and usually open between six and seven o'clock in the evening, hence the name of Evening Primrose. From a horticultural point of view, the variety *grandiflora* or *Lamarkiana* should always be preferred to the ordinary kind, as the flowers are larger and of a finer colour, having a fine effect in large masses, and being well suited for the wild garden.

The generic name is derived from *oinos* (wine) and *thera* (a hunt), and is an old Greek name given by Theophrastus to some plant, probably an Epilobium, the roots of which were eaten to provoke a relish for wine, as olives are now; others say it dispelled the effects of wine.

The large, bright yellow, fragrant flowers are mostly fertilized by twilight-flying insects, especially in the early season. Later the plants keep 'open house' practically all day. In America it is considered a troublesome pest; in England it is not formidable.

The roots of the Evening Primrose are eaten in some countries in the spring, and the French often use it for garnishing salads.

¶ *Cultivation.* The Evening Primrose will thrive in almost any soil or situation, being perfectly hardy. It flourishes best in fairly good sandy soil and in a warm sunny position.

Sow the seeds an inch deep in a shady position out-doors in April, transplanting the seedlings when 1 inch high, 3 inches apart each way in sunny borders. Keep them free from weeds, and in September or the following March, transplant them again into the flowering positions. As the roots strike deep into the ground, care should be taken not to break them in removing.

Seeds may also be sown in cold frames in autumn for blooming the following year.

If the plants are once introduced and the seeds permitted to scatter, there will be a supply of plants without any special care.

¶ *Parts Used.* Bark and leaves. The bark is peeled from the flower-stems and dried in the same manner as the leaves, which are collected in the second year, when the flower-stalk has made its appearance.

¶ *Medicinal Action and Uses.* Astringent and sedative. The drug extracted from this plant, though not in very general use, has been tested in various directions, and has been employed with success in the treatment of gastro-intestinal disorders of a functional origin, asthma and whooping cough.

It has proved of service in dyspepsia, torpor of the liver, and in certain female complaints, such as pelvic fullness.

The dose ranges from 5 to 30 grains.

Henslow mentions another species, *Œnothera odorata*, which he states is found wild in the south of England, but only as a garden escape. It grows to 2 feet in height, with purplish stems and yellow flowers, 3 to 4 inches across. They are sweet-smelling, hence its specific name.

In *The Treasury of Botany* a large white-flowered species is also mentioned, said to have run wild over some parts of the Nilghiri Hills in India.

PRIMULAS

N.O. Primulaceæ

The leaves of some species produce irritation to face and hands resulting sometimes in a form of eczema. This is caused by a secretion in the glandular hairs and is termed primula dermatitis. The roots of *Primula grandiflora* give a crystalline polyatomic alcohol, 'primulite,' said to be identical with hepatomic alcohol 'volemite.' Two glucosides, Primverin and Primulaverin, and an enzyme, primverase, have also been isolated in it.

The Primrose family is remarkable for the number of hybrids it produces. The garden 'Polyanthus of unnumbered dyes,' as the poet Thomson calls it in 'The Seasons,' is only another form (probably of the Cowslip or Oxlip) produced by cultivation, and is one of the most favourite plants in cottage gardens, of endless variety and easy cultivation. The Oxlip is distinguished from the Primrose by its flowers being stalked umbels and of a deeper shade of yellow and by its leaves becoming suddenly broader above the middle. It varies from the Cowslip by its tubular, not bell-shaped calyx and flat, not concave corolla.

All the hardy varieties of Primula, whether Primrose, Cowslip, Polyanthus or Auricula, may be easily propagated by dividing the roots of old plants in autumn. New varieties are raised from seed, which should be sown as soon as ripe, in leaf-mould, and pricked out into beds when large enough.

Among the many splendid flowers that are grown in our greenhouses none shows more improvement under the fostering hand of the British florist than the Chinese Primula, which originally had small, inconspicuous flowers, but now bears trusses of magnificent blooms ranging from the purest white to the richest scarlet and crimson. The Star Primulas which have attained an even greater popularity in late years are considered perhaps even more elegant, being looser in growth and carrying their plentiful blossoms in more graceful, if not more beautiful trusses. Both varieties are among the most beautiful of our winter-flowering plants, the toothed and lobed, somewhat heart-shaped leaves being extremely handsome with their crimson tints.

Seeds of these greenhouse Primulas should be sown in the spring in gentle heat, the soil used being very fine and pleasantly moist. The seedlings must be pricked off and potted on as necessary, with a view to ensuring sturdy, healthy growth.

P. obconica is a slightly varying type of these greenhouse Primulas, the leaves approaching more the shape of those of the common Primrose; the plants are exceedingly floriferous and graceful, the full trusses of delicate lilac flowers are borne on tall slender stems and care must be used in the handling of it, as the leaves sometimes cause an eruption like eczema. Homœopaths make a tincture from this species.

The broad, thick leaves of the Auricula (*P. auricula*), a frequent garden plant in this country, though not native to Great Britain, are used in the Alps as a remedy for coughs.

See PRIMROSE, COWSLIP.

PRUNES

Prunus domestica (LINN.)
N.O. Rosaceæ

Synonym. Plum Tree
Part Used. Fruit, dried
Habitat. Asia and parts of Europe; best from Bordeaux

¶ *Description.* A small tree, 15 to 20 feet high, with numerous spreading branches without spines, young branches smooth, leaves small, alternate on longish petioles, provided with linear, fimbriated, pubescent stipules which are quickly deciduous, blade about 2 inches long, oval, acute at both ends, crenate-dentate, smooth above, more or less pubescent underneath, convolute in the bud, flowers appear before leaves. The cultivated plum has been developed from the wild plum, the thorns being lost in the process. Plums were known to the Romans in Cato's time.

¶ *Constituents.* Prunes have a faint peculiar odour and a sweetish slightly acidulous and viscid taste. The ripe fruit contains sugar, gum, albumen, malic acid, pectin, vegetable fibre, etc.

¶ *Medicinal Action and Uses.* Dried prunes are mildly laxative and are frequently employed in decoction. They form a pleasant and nourishing diet for invalids when stewed; they enter into the composition of Confection of Senna. A medicinal tincture is prepared from the fresh flower-buds of the Blackthorn. Some 20 per cent. of oil is obtainable by crushing the Plum kernel – this is clear, yellow in colour and has an agreeable almond flavour and smell. It is used for alimentary purposes. The residue after pressing is used in the manufacture of a brandy, which is largely consumed in Hungary.

PSYLLIUM SEEDS. *See* PLANTAIN

PULSATILLA. *See* ANEMONE

PUMPKIN. *See* MELON

PURSLANE, GREEN

Portulaca oleracea

PURSLANE, GOLDEN

Portulaca sativa
N.O. Caryophylleæ

Synonyms. Garden Purslane. Pigweed
Parts Used. Herb, juice, seeds
Habitat. The Purslanes are distributed all over the world. *Portulaca oleracea*, the Garden, or Green Purslane, is a herbaceous annual, native of many parts of Europe, found in the East and West Indies, China, Japan and Ascension Island, and though found also in the British Isles is not indigenous there

¶ *Description.* It has a round, smooth, procumbent, succulent stem, growing about 6 inches high, with small, oblong, wedge-shaped, dark-green leaves, thick and stalked, clustered together, destitute of the bristle in their axils which others of the genus have. The flowers are small, yellow, solitary or clustered, stalkless, placed above the last leaves on the branches, blooming in June and July, and opening only for a short time towards noon.

The growth of the plant somewhat resembles Samphire, and the rich red colour of the stems is very striking and most decorative in herb borders. The Golden Purslane (*Portulaca sativa*) is a variety of Purslane with yellow leaves, less hardy than the Green Purslane, but possessing the same qualities. The seeds of an individual plant have been known to produce both green and golden-leaved plants.

Purslane is a pleasant salad herb, and excellent for scorbutic troubles. The succulent leaves and young shoots are cooling in spring salads, the older shoots are used as a pot-herb, and the thick stems of plants that have run to seed are pickled in salt and vinegar to form winter salads. Purslane is largely cultivated in Holland and other countries for these purposes. It is used in equal proportion with Sorrel to make the well-known French soup *bonne femme.* Gerard said of this herb: 'Raw Purslane is much used in sallads, with oil, salt and vinegar. It cools the blood and causes appetite;' and Evelyn tells us that, 'familiarly eaten alone with Oyl and Vinegar,' moderation should be used, adding that it is eminently moist and cooling, 'especially the golden,' and is 'generally entertained in all our sallets. Some eate of it cold, after it has been boiled, which Dr. Muffit would have in wine for nourishment.'

Most of the plants in this order are mucilaginous. The root of one species, *Lewisia rediviva*, the Tobacco root, a native of North America, so called from its odour when cooked, possesses great nutritive properties. It is boiled and eaten by the Indians, and Hogg tells us that it proves most sustaining on long journeys, and that 2 or 3 oz. a day are quite sufficient for a man, even while undergoing great fatigue. *Claytonia tuberosa,* another plant belonging to the same order as the Purslanes, likewise a native of North America, has also an edible root.

Purslane in ancient times was looked upon as one of the anti-magic herbs, and strewn round a bed was said to afford protection against evil spirits. We are told that it was a sure cure for 'blastings by lightening or planets and burning of gunpowder.'

¶ *Medicinal Action and Uses.* It was highly recommended for many complaints. The expressed juice, taken while fresh, was said to be good for strangury, and taken with sugar and honey to afford relief for dry coughs, shortness of breath and immoderate thirst, as well as for external application in inflammation and sores.

It was supposed to cool 'heat in the liver' and to be excellent for 'hot agues,' and all pains in the head 'proceeding from the heat, want of sleep or the frenzy,' and also to stop hæmorrhages.

The herb, bruised and applied to the forehead and temple, was said to allay excessive heat, and applied to the eyes to remove inflammation. Culpepper says: 'The herb if placed under the tongue assuayeth thirst. Applied to the gout, it easeth pains thereof, and helps the hardness of the sinews, if it come not of the cramp, or a cold cause.'

The juice, with oil of Roses, was recommended for sore mouths and swollen gums and also to fasten loose teeth. Another authority declared that the distilled water took away pains in the teeth, both Gerard and Turner telling us too, that the leaves eaten raw are good for teeth that are 'set on edge with eating of sharpe and soure things.'

The seeds, bruised and boiled in wine, were given to children as a vermifuge.

¶ *Cultivation.* Sow the seeds in drills, on a bed of rich light earth, during any of the summer months, from May onwards. To have it early in the season, it should be sown upon a hot bed, at the end of March and planted out in a warm border in May. The Green Purslane is quite hardy, the Golden Purslane less so.

Keep the plants clear from weeds, and in dry weather water them two or three times a week. The Purslanes need rather more watering than most herbs.

In warm weather, they will be fit for use in six weeks. When the leaves are gathered, the plants must be cut low and then a fresh crop will appear.

To continue a succession, sow three or four times, at an interval of a fortnight or three weeks.

If the seeds are to be saved, leave some of the earliest plants for that purpose.

¶ *Other Species*.

Professor Hulme, in *Familiar Wild Flowers*, speaks of a variety which he calls the SEA PURSLANE (*Atriplex portulacoides*), common enough on the sea-shores of England and Ireland, though much less so in Scotland. It grows in saline marshes and muddy fore-shores. It is a shrubby and much-branching plant, attaining to no great height, usually a foot to 18 inches – though occasionally to 2 feet. The lower portion of the stem is often somewhat creeping and rooting, which gives it a greater grip of the ground in view of fierce gales. The stems are often of a delicate purple colour, more or less covered with a grey bloom. The foliage is of pointed, lance-head form, thick and fleshy, and entirely silvery white in colour. The minute flowers are in little clusters that succeed one another at intervals on the short branches near the top of the plant and form a terminal head. The flowers are of two kinds: one is stamen-bearing, these stamens being five in number and within a five-cleft perianth; the other is pistil-bearing and consists of two flattened segments, closing somewhat like the leaves of a book, and contained within the ovary. After the flowering is over, this flattened perianth considerably enlarges. This construction of the seed-bearing flower is of some specific importance, for in the present species and the *A. pedunculata* the two segments are united nearly to the top, while in another species, the *A. rosea*, these segments are not joined above their centres; and in a third, the *A. hortensis*, they are not joined at all.

An entirely different plant, one of the great Pink family, the *Houckenya peploides*, is sometimes called the 'ovate-leaved Sea Purslane.' It is a common plant on sea-beaches, with large white five-petalled blossoms. Another name for it is 'ovate Sand-wort.'

The generic title of the Sea Purslane, *Atriplex*, is one of Pliny's plant names. It is derived from two Greek words signifying 'not to flourish,' the meaning of the word applied to the plant is obscure. The specific name, *Potrulacoides*, signifies 'resembling the purslane plant,' the *portulaca*. Another name for the Sea Purslane is 'Shrubby Orache.'

The origin of the name 'Purslane' is unknown. Turner calls the plant 'purcellaine,' and in the *Grete Herball*, 1516, it is 'procelayne.'

In the North American prairies Purslane is called 'Pussly.'

PYROLAS

N.O. Pyrolaceæ

The species are known by the common name of Wintergreen.

The name Pyrola is a diminutive of *Pyrus* (a pear tree), from the resemblance of its leaves to those of the pear.

WINTERGREEN

Pyrola secunda is known as Yevering Bells, from the resemblance of its flowers to little bells hung one above the other.

¶ *Description*. Low herbs, with a slender shortly creeping stock; orbicular or ovate, nearly radical leaves; and white or greenish, drooping flowers, either solitary or several in a short raceme, on leaflets, erect peduncles. Sepals five, small. Petals five, distinct or slightly joined at the base, forming at first a spreading corolla, which persists round the young capsule, assuming a globular shape. Stamens ten. Capsule five-celled, opening by slits in the middle of the cells.

Pyrola uniflora (one-flowered Winter-green), found in woods, in Northern and Arctic Europe, Asia and America, and along the high mountain ranges of Central Europe. In pine woods from Perth and Aberdeen northwards. Flowers in the summer.

P. media (Intermediate Wintergreen), not found in England south of Warwick and Worcester, whence it extends to Shetland; it also is found in the north and west of Ireland.

P. minor (Common Wintergreen). In woods and moist shady places in Europe, Northern Asia and the extreme north of America, becoming a mountain plant in Southern Europe and the Caucasus. Frequent in Scotland, northern England, more local in southern England. Rare in Ireland. Flowers in the summer.

P. secunda. Very local in Britain, found in Monmouthshire and from Yorkshire northward to Ross-shire. It is very rare in the north-east of Ireland only. Flowers in the summer.

LARGE WINTERGREEN   Pyrola rotundifolia

Synonym. Round-leaved Wintergreen

¶ *Description.* A larger plant than *Pyrola minor*, with larger and whiter flowers and the petals more spreading, but chiefly distinguished from it by the long, protruding, much-curved style, usually at least twice as long as the capsule with a much smaller stigma, with short erect lobes.

¶ *Medicinal Action and Uses.* Astringent, diuretic, tonic, antispasmodic. The decoction much used in skin diseases and to eradicate a scropulous condition from the system. The decoction also valuable as a gargle and wash for ophthalmic eyes.

Used internally for epilepsy and other nervous affections.

Dose of decoction, 1 fluid ounce three times daily. Solid extract, 2 to 4 grains. The Germans use this plant in their wound drinks and in many ointments and plasters. A decoction of the leaves with the addition of a little cinnamon and red wine cures bloody stools, ulcers of the bladder and restrains the menses.

Salmon says:

'The liquid juice. It consolidates green wounds, uniting their lips speedily together; and taken inwardly 2 or 3 spoonfuls at a time in wine and water, it stops inward fluxes of the blood and cures inward wounds. It stops the overflowing of the Terms in women, cures spitting and vomiting of Blood, the Hepatick Flux, Bloody Flux and all other Fluxes of the Bowels. It is said to cure ulcers and wounds in the Reins and Bladder, Womb and other secret parts, as also ulcers and Fistulas in any other part of the Body, being inwardly taken and outwardly applied. The decoction in wine and water . . . has all the former virtues, but not altogether so powerful and may be given morning and night from 3 ounces to 6, sweetened with syrup of the juice of the same. . . . The Balsam or Ointment is made with Hog's Lard, or with oil olive, Bees Wax and a little Turpentine . . . heals cankers of the mouth and gums.'

See PIPSISSEWA, WINTERGREEN.

QUASSIA

Picræna excelsa (LINDL.)
N.O. Simarubeæ

Synonyms. Bitter Wood. Jamaica Quassia. Bitter Ash. Quassia Amara (Linn.). Quassia Lignum, B.P.

Part Used. Wood of trunks and branches

Habitat. Jamaica

¶ *Description.* A tree growing 50 to 100 feet, erect stem over 3 feet in diameter. Bark smooth and greyish. Leaves alternate, unequally pinnate, leaflets opposite, oblong, acuminate, and unequal at the base. Flowers small pale yellowish green, blooming October and November. Fruit three drupes size of a pea (maturing its fruit December and January), black, shining, solitary, globose, with a thin shell. The wood of this tree furnishes the Quassia of commerce. It is imported in large logs varying from a foot or more in diameter and 1 to 8 feet in length, occasionally much bigger, then it is split into quarters, retaining a friable and feebly attached cortex which has the same medicinal qualities as the wood, which is very tough, close grained and white, but changes to yellow on contact with the air. It is odourless and very bitter, the bark is thin and dark brown or thick greyish brown transversed by reticulating lines.

Quassia Amara, or Surinan Quassia, as found in commerce, is in much smaller billets than the Jamaica Quassia, and is used in its place on the Continent, and is easily recognized from the Jamaica one, which it closely resembles, by its medullary rays, which are only one cell wide, and contain no calcium oxalate.

¶ *Constituents of Jamaica Quassia.* Volatile oil, quassin, gummy extractive pectin, woody fibre, tartrate and sulphate of lime, chlorides of calcium, and sodium, various salts such as oxalate and ammoniacal salt, nitrate of potassa and sulphate of soda. Quassia, U.S.P., may be either Jamaica or Surinan Quassia.

¶ *Medicinal Action and Uses.* Quassia, found in the shops in the form of chips or raspings, has no smell but an intense bitter taste, which will always distinguish the pure drug from adulterations; the infusion of these by persalt of iron gives a bluish-black colour, but as the blue Quassia chips contain no tannic acid, no result is produced in the infusion. Quassia wood is a pure bitter tonic and stomachic; it is also a vermicide and slight narcotic; it acts on flies and some of the higher animals as a narcotic poison. It is a valuable remedy in convalescence, after acute disease and in debility and atonic dyspepsia; an antispasmodic in fever. Having no tannic acid, it is frequently given with chalybeates and therefore can be prescribed with salts of iron; as an aromatic bitter stomachic it acts in the same way as calumba. In small doses Quassia increases the appetite; large doses act as an irritant and cause vomiting; its action probably lessens putrefaction in the stomach, and prevents the formation of acid substances during digestion. A decoction used as an injection will move ascarides; for an enema for this purpose, 3 parts Quassia to 1 part mandrake root are used, and to each ounce of the mixture, 1 fluid drachm of asafœtida or diluted carbolic acid is added; for a child up to three years, 2 fluid ounces are injected into the rectum twice daily. Cups made of the wood and filled with liquid will in a few hours become thoroughly impregnated and this drink makes a powerful tonic. The infusion is made by macerating in cold water for twelve hours 3 drachms of the rasped Quassia to 1 pint of cold water, 2 oz. of the infusion alone, or with ginger tea, taken three times a day, proves very useful for feeble emaciated people with impaired digestive organs. The extract can be made by evaporating the decoction to a pilular consistence, and taken in 1 grain doses, three or four times daily, this will be found less obnoxious to the stomach than the infusion or decoction. Quassia with sulphuric acid acts as a cure for drunkenness, by destroying the appetite for alcoholics.

¶ *Preparations and Dosages.* Fluid extract, 15 to 30 drops. Tincture, B.P. and U.S.P., ½ to 1 drachm. Conc. Solut., B.P., ½ drachm. Powdered Quassia, 30 grains. The infusion for killing flies should be sweetened with sugar.

See SIMARUBA.

QUEBRACHO

Aspidosperma quebracho-blanco
N.O. Apocynaceæ

Synonyms. Quebracho Bark. Quebracho-blanco
Part Used. Bark
Habitat. Chile and Argentina, Bolivia, Southern Brazil

¶ *History.* Quebracho is an evergreen tree which sometimes rises to 100 feet, with an erect stem and wide-spreading crown. The wood of all the species of this genus is valuable, and the name is due to its hardness, being derived from two Spanish words, *quebrar* and *hacha*, meaning 'the axe breaks.' It is used for tanning.

The bark was not introduced into Europe until 1878, though was for long used in South America as a febrifuge. Commercially, it is met with in large, thick pieces, covered on the outside with a very thick and rough, corky layer of a greyish-brown colour, and deeply divided by furrows and excavations. The inner bark is greyish or yellowish, smooth or somewhat fibrous, and often with small, black spots. The taste is very bitter, but there is scarcely any odour.

Two other plants are known as Quebracho: *Schinopsis Lorenzii*, the wood of which is sold in commerce as 'quebracho wood,' and *Iodina rhombifolia*, 'quebracho flojo,' the wood and bark of which are sometimes substituted for the 'quebracho colorado.'

¶ *Constituents.* Contains six alkaloids: Aspidospermine, Aspidospermatine, Aspidosamine, Quebrachine, Hypoquebrachine and Quebrachamine. All agree that quebrachine is the most active.

Two new sugars, quebrachite and lævogyrate inosite, tannin and starch have also been extracted.

¶ *Medicinal Action and Uses.* Tonic, febrifuge and anti-asthmatic.

When a preparation of Quebracho or Aspidosperma is injected into the circulation, the rate and depth of the respiration increases largely, apparently due to direct action on the respiratory centre, and the blood-pressure falls.

Aspidosperma is used in medicine for the relief of various types of dyspnœa, especially in emphysema and in asthma. It is not generally useful to interrupt the paroxysm, but, as a rule, if used continuously, it will reduce the frequency and severity of attacks.

Under the name of amorphous aspidospermine, a mixture of the various alkaloids has become known in commerce.

Quebracho Colorado, or *S. Lorenzii*, has been used as a substitute, but is essentially different, being probably a simple and gastro-intestinal stimulant, though it has been said to be a much weaker form of quebracho-blanco.

¶ *Dosages.* Of amorphous aspidospermine, ¼ to 1 grain. Of crystalline aspidospermine, $\frac{1}{10}$ to $\frac{1}{20}$ grain. Of aspidospermine, 15 grains, but it is not used in the crude state. Fluid extract, ¼ to ½ drachm.

QUEEN'S DELIGHT

Stillingia sylvatica (LINN.)
N.O. Euphorbiaceæ

Synonyms. Queen's Root. Silver Leaf. Also Sapium Sylvaticum Yaw Root
Part Used. Root
Habitat. In the southern United States of America from Virginia to Florida and westward to Texas

¶ *Description.* A perennial herb, with an angled glabrous stem, growing to 4 feet high, with a milky sap. The leaves are sessile, leathery and tapering at the base. Flowers yellow on terminal spike. Fruit a three-grained capsule. The plant was named after Dr. B. Stillingfleet. It flowers from April to July; a milky juice exudes from the plant or root when cut or broken. This should be used when fresh as it deteriorates if kept. As found in commerce, the root is 1 to 4 inches long and 1 inch or more thick, covered with a bark wrinkled longitudinally, greyish brown externally, and reddish-brown or rose-coloured internally, odour peculiar, oleaginous, taste bitter and unpleasant, followed by a persistent pungent acridity in mouth and throat. Fracture fibrous, short, irregular, and shows a pithy soft, yellowish-pink interior porous woody portion. The inner bark and medullary rays with brown resin cells, its best solvent is alcohol.

¶ *Constituents.* Its resinous acrid constituent is Sylvacrol, an acrid fixed oil, volatile oil, tannin, starch, calcium oxalate. Woody fibre, colouring matter extractive.

¶ *Medicinal Action and Uses.* In large doses it is emetic and purgative causing a disagreeable, peculiar, burning sensation in the stomach or alimentary canal with considerable prostration of the system; in smaller doses it is an excellent alterative, and influences the secretory functions; it has almost a specific action in the different forms of primary and secondary syphilis, also in skin diseases, scrofula and hepatic affections, acting with most successful results. The fluid extract combined with oils of anise or caraway, proves very beneficial in chronic bronchitis and laryngitis. Some pieces of fresh root chewed daily have permanently and effectually cured these troubles, it is also useful for leucorrhœa. The oil is too acrid for internal use uncombined with saccharine or mucilaginous substance, for internal use the fluid extract or syrup is sufficiently efficacious. As an external stimulating application in most cases the oil will be found very valuable. For croup 1 drop on the tongue three or four times daily, has been found successful for severe attacks. The dried root is said to be inferior in strength to the fresh one, but some chemists consider it more powerful. It may be given either alone or combined with sarsaparilla and other alteratives. It acts reflexly as a sialagogue and expectorant. It is often given for syphilitic complaints in place of mercury.

¶ *Dosages.* Tincture, ½ to 2 drachms. Decoction, 1 to 2 fluid ounces. Powdered root, 6 to 10 grains. Solid extract, 2 to 5 grains. Stillingin, 1 to 3 grains. Fluid extract, 10 to 30 drops.

QUINCE

Pyrus Cydonia (LINN.)
N.O. Rosaceæ

Synonym. Cydonia vulgaris (PERS.)
Parts Used. Seeds, fruit

The Quince has been under cultivation since very remote times. It is a native of Persia and Anatolia and perhaps also of Greece and the Crimea, though it is doubtful if in the latter localities the plant is not a relic of former cultivation. It is certain that the ancient Greeks knew a common variety, upon which they grafted scions of a better variety, which they obtained from Cydon in Crete, from which place the fruit derived its name of *Cydonia*, of which the English name Quince is a corruption.

Botanically, the plant used to be called *Pyrus Cydonia*, but modern botanists now place it in the genus *Pyrus* and assign it to a separate genus, to which the former specific name *Cydonia* has been given.

In old English literature we find the fruit called a Coyne, as in the *Romaunt of the Rose* and the old English Vocabularies of the fourteenth and fifteenth centuries, this name being adapted from the French *coin*, whence Middle English *Coin, Quin*, the plural *quins*, becoming corrupted to the singular *Quince*.

The Quinces differ from the *Pyrus* genus in the twisted manner in which the petals are arranged in the bud and in the many-celled ovary, in which the numerous ovules are disposed horizontally, not vertically as in the Pears. They are much-branched shrubs, or small trees, with entire leaves and large, solitary, white or pink flowers, like those of a pear or apple, but with leafy calyx lobes.

The Quince as we know it in this country

is a different fruit to that of Western Asia and tropical countries, where the fruit becomes softer and more juicy. In colder climates, the fruit is of a fine, handsome shape, of a rich golden colour when ripe and has a strong fragrance, by some judged to be rather heavy and overpowering. The rind is rough and woolly and the flesh harsh and unpalatable, with an astringent, acidulous taste. In hotter countries, the woolly rind disappears and the fruit can be eaten raw. This is the case not only in Eastern countries, where it is much prized, but also in those parts of tropical America to which the tree has been introduced from Europe. This explains the fact that it figured so prominently in classical legends. It was very widely cultivated in the East and especially in Palestine, and many commentators consider that the *Tappuach* of Scripture, always translated Apple, was the Quince. It is also supposed to be the fruit alluded to in the *Canticles*, 'I sat down under his shadow with great delight and his fruit was sweet to my taste'; and in *Proverbs*, 'A word fitly spoken is like Apples of gold in pictures of silver.'

Pliny, who speaks at length of the medicinal virtues of the Quince, says that the fruit warded off the influence of the evil eye, and other legends connect it with ancient Greek mythology, as exemplified by statues on which the fruit is represented, as well as by representations in the wall-paintings and mosaics of Pompeii, where Quinces are almost always to be seen in the paws of a bear.

By the Greeks and Romans, the Quince was held sacred to Venus, who is often depicted with a Quince in her right hand, the gift she received from Paris. The 'golden Apples' of Virgil are said to be Quinces, as they were the only 'golden' fruit known in his time, oranges having only been introduced into Italy at the time of the Crusades.

The fruit, being dedicated to Venus, was regarded as the symbol of Love and Happiness, and Plutarch mentions the bridal custom of a Quince being shared by a married pair. Quinces sent as presents, or shared, were tokens of love. The custom was handed down, and throughout the Middle Ages Quinces were used at every wedding feast, as we may read in a curious book, *The Praise of Musicke*:

'I come to marriages, wherein as our ancestors did fondly and with a kind of doating, maintain many rites and ceremonies, some whereof were either shadowes or abodements of a pleasant life to come, as the eating of a Quince Peare to be a preparative

of sweet and delightful dayes between the married persons.'

Quinces are mentioned among the curious recipes in Manuscripts relating to domestic life in England. Wynkyn de Worde, in the *Boke of Kervynge*, speaks of 'char de Quynce,' and John Russell, in the *Boke of Nurture*, speaks of 'chare de Quynces' – the old name for Quince Marmalade. This preserve is now practically the only use made of the Quince as an article of food, though it is sometimes added to apple-tarts, to improve their flavour, but in Shakespeare's time, Browne spoke of the fruit as 'the stomach's comforter, the pleasing Quince,' and a little later, Parkinson says:

'There is no fruit growing in the land that is of so many excellent uses as this [the Quince], serving as well to make many dishes of meat for the table, as for banquets, and much more for their physical virtues.'

¶ *Cultivation*. The Quince is little cultivated in Great Britain, though it will thrive almost anywhere, but is best adapted to a damp spot, in a rich, high and somewhat moist soil. In Scotland, it seldom approaches maturity unless protected by a wall.

Propagation is generally by cuttings or layers, the former making the best plants, but taking longer to grow. The Quince forms a thick bush and is generally not pruned, unless required to form standard fruit-bearing trees, when it should be trained up to a single stem till a height of 5 or 6 feet is attained.

There are three principal varieties of the Quince: the Portugal, Apple-shaped and Pear-shaped. The Portugal is a taller and more vigorous grower than the others and has larger and finer fruit; the Apple-shaped, which is sometimes considered to have a finer flavour, has roundish fruit, is more productive and ripens under less favourable conditions than either of the others and earlier than the Pear-shaped variety and is therefore preferred to it.

The Quince is much used as a dwarfing stock for certain kinds of pears and for this purpose the young plants when bedded out in the quarters should be shortened back to about 18 to 20 inches. The effect is to restrain the growth of the tree, increase and hasten its fruitfulness and enable it to withstand the effects of cold.

¶ *Medicinal Action and Uses*. A syrup prepared from the fruit may be used as a grateful addition to drinks in sickness, especially in looseness of the bowels, which it is said to restrain by its astringency.

The seeds may be used medicinally for the sake of the mucilage they yield. When soaked in water they swell up and form a mucilaginous mass. This mucilage is analogous to, and has the same properties as, that which is formed from the seeds of the flax – linseed.

The seeds somewhat resemble apple-pips in size and appearance. They are of a dark brown colour, flattened on two sides, owing to mutual pressure and frequently adhere to one another by a white mucilage, which is derived from the epidermal cells of the seed-coats. The seed contains two firm, yellowish-white cotyledons, which have a faintly bitter taste resembling that of bitter almonds.

¶ *Chemical Constituents.* The cotyledons contain about 15 per cent. fixed oil and protein, together with small proportions of amygdalin and emulsion or some allied ferment. The chief constituent of the seed is about 10 per cent. mucilage, contained in the seed-coat. The pulp of the fruit contains 3 to 3·5 per cent. of malic acid.

Pereira considers the mucilage peculiar to this fruit; the chemists Tollens and Kirchner regard it as a compound of gum and cellulose. It differs from Arabin in not yielding a precipitate with potassium silicate and in being soluble both in hot and cold water. It is almost free from adhesive properties.

The seeds, on account of their mucilage, have soothing and demulcent properties and are used internally in the form of *Decoctum Cydoniæ*, an official preparation of the British Pharmacopœia. It is prepared by boiling 2 drachms of Quince seed in a pint of water in a tightly-covered vessel for 10 minutes and straining off. Large quantities of the decoction may be drunk in dysentery, diarrhœa and gonorrhœa and it is used in thrush and irritable conditions of the mucous membrane. The decoction also forms a usefu adjunct to boric-acid eye-lotions. On account of its mucilaginous character, it is not so readily washed away by the tears.

It is also used as an adjunct to skin lotions and creams.

It has been proposed to evaporate the decoction to dryness and powder the residue: 3 grains of this powder form a sufficiently consistent mucilage with an ounce of water. According to Grant (*Journal de Pharmacie et de Chénie*, Paris), 1 part communicates to a thousand parts of water a semi-syrupy consistence.

Mucilago Cydoniæ (Mucilage of Quince Seeds, B.P.) is stronger than the decoction and has similar properties. It forms a useful suspending agent for such liquids as tincture of Benzoin, when added to toilet preparations. When used for this purpose, it is sometimes prepared with rose-water.

RECIPES
Quince Marmalade

Pare and core the Quinces and cut them up, putting them into water as they are cored, to prevent them from blackening. Put them into a preserving pan with 1 lb. sugar and 1 pint water for every lb. of fruit. Boil over a gentle fire until soft. Then put through a sieve, or mash with a spoon, boil up again and tie down in the same way as any other preserve.

In France, before putting the marmalade into pots, a little rosewater and a few grains of musk, mixed together, are added. This is most delicious and among the French, by whom it is called *Cotiniat*, has a reputation for its digestive powers.

Quince and Apple Marmalade

Take equal quantities of Apple and Quinces. Put into an earthenware jar, 2 quarts of water and, as quickly as they can be pared and sliced, 4 lb. of Quinces. Stew them gently till soft and then strain them. They must not be boiled too long, or they will become red. Boil together, for ¾ hour, 4 lb. of sliced Apples, with the same weight of Quince juice. When it boils, take it off the fire and add 1½ lb. sugar. When dissolved, put it back on the fire and boil, together with the Quinces, for another 20 minutes, stirring all the time and removing the scum. Then pot.

Quince Jelly

Pare and core some ripe Quinces, cut them up, weigh them and put them at once into part of the water in which they will be cooked. Put the Quinces on the fire, with 1 pint water to each pound of fruit and let it simmer, but not long enough to change the colour to red – it should be quite pale. Strain through a jelly-bag. Weigh the juice the next day and put it in a preserving pan and boil it quickly for 15 minutes. Then take it from the fire and stir into it 12 oz. sugar for each lb. of juice. Boil for another 15 or 20 minutes, till cooked, stirring all the time, and remove the scum.

Quinces and Apples can be mixed, making a good combination.

QUINCE, JAPANESE

Cydonia Japonica
Pyrus Japonica

The Japanese Quince, familiar in our gardens, and formerly known as *Pyrus Japonica*, now usually described as *Cydonia Japonica*, is grown for the sake of its blossoms, which vary in colour from creamy white to rich red and are produced during the winter and early spring months. It is a handsome shrub, generally planted in a sheltered spot, often against a dwarf wall or a trellis, the brilliant flowers of the ordinary red variety being produced soon after the New Year. For the last hundred years it has been the chief spring ornament of English gardens and being quite hardy and easily grown is often seen covering the walls of cottages. A deep, moist loam suits it exactly. The flowers appear before the leaves, and later on in the year, old trees on warm walls will in a dry, hot summer produce a few fruits (Quinces), though it cannot be described as a fruitful tree in this country. They are nearly round and about the size of a tangerine orange, ripening off a dull green colour, very fragrant and as hard as flints. When cut up, they are found to be packed with large dark pips, around which is a broad rim of flesh of a most uninviting character and quite uneatable, the flavour being rough and styptic.

There are many varieties, differing chiefly in the colour of the flowers: there is often abundance of fruit on the white variety. *C. Maulei*, a more recently introduced shrub from Japan, bears a profusion of beautiful orange-red flowers, followed by fruit of a yellow colour and agreeable fragrance, so that when cooked with sugar, it forms a pleasant conserve.

QUINOA. *See* CHENOPODIUM

QUINSY-WORT

Asperula cynanchica (LINN.)

Synonym. Squinancy-wort

Quinsy-Wort was formerly esteemed a remedy for the disorder the name of which it bears. The specific name, *cynanchica*, is derived from the Greek *Kunanchi* (dog strangle), from its choking nature.

Its roots, like those of the *Galiums* and *Rubia*, yield a red dye, which has been occasionally used in Sweden.

It is no longer applied in medicine.

This is not a common British plant, except locally in dry pastures on a chalky or limehouse soil.

It is a small, smooth plant, 6 to 10 inches high, with very narrow, close-set leaves, four in a whorl, two of each whorl much smaller than the others.

The flowers are in loose terminal bunches, the corollas only $\frac{1}{8}$ inch in diameter, pink externally and white inside, and are in bloom during June and July.

RADISH

Raphanus sativus
N.O. Cruciferæ

Parts Used. Root, seed-pods

Habitat. Europe, especially Britain, and temperate Asia. A native of China, Cochin-China and Japan

¶ *Description.* The name of this familiar garden plant is suggested by its colour, being derived from the Saxon, *rude, rudo,* or *reod* (ruddy), or from the Sanskrit *rudhira,* meaning blood. The genus is distinguished by its elongated pod, which has no longitudinal partition when ripe, but contains several seeds separated by a pithy substance filling the pod. The actual plant is unknown in a wild state, but is supposed to have come from Southern Asia, and may be descended from the wild *Raphanus Raphanistrum* of the Mediterranean shores, the long roots developing seeds sown in a loose soil, and the turnip-rooted kinds in a stiff soil. In the days of the Pharaohs, the Radish was extensively cultivated in Egypt, but apparently it did not reach Britain until A.D. 1548. Gerard mentions four varieties as being recognized in 1597. The leaves are rough and partly divided into segments, the outer one being larger and broader than the rest. The flower stem grows to about 3 feet in height, bearing medium-sized flowers that vary in colour from white to pale violet, with strongly-marked, dark veins. Structurally, it resembles the turnip, as the swollen, fleshy portion is really a stem which gradually passes downwards into the real root. Many kinds are named, the best known being (1) turnip-rooted, both red and white, including the white and black Spanish kinds; (2) olive-shaped, including the white, scarlet, and French breakfast forms; (3) the long, tapering varieties, like Long Red and Lady's Finger. The flesh is white, crisp, and tender, not specially nourishing, but valued as an antiscorbutic because of its quantity of nitrous juice. When too large for eating raw, they can be steamed for half an hour and served like asparagus. They should be well washed, but never peeled except when preparing the juice for medicinal purposes; in dry weather the bed should be watered the day before they are pulled. The young, green, seed-pods may be used for pickling, alone or with other vegetables, and are considered a fair substitute for capers.

¶ *Constituents*. Phenyl-ethyl isothiocyanite, a pungent, volatile oil, and an amylclytic enzyme.

¶ *Medicinal Action and Uses*. Radishes are an excellent food remedy for stone, gravel and scorbutic conditions. The juice has been used in the treatment of cholelithiasis as an aid in preventing the formation of biliary calculi. The expressed juice of white or black Spanish radishes is given in increasing doses of from ¼ to 2 cupfuls daily. The 2 cupfuls are continued for two or three weeks. then the dose is decreased until ½ cupful is taken three times a week for three or four more weeks. The treatment may be repeated by taking 1 cupful at the beginning, then ½ daily, and later, ½ every second day.

The colouring matter is recommended as a sensitive indicator in alkalimetry.

¶ *Other Species*.
R. Raphanistrum (Wild Radish, or Jointed-podded Charlock). It was stated by Linnæus that in wet seasons this abounds as a weed among barley, in Sweden, and being ground with the corn, it is eaten in barley bread, causing violent convulsive complaints, or an epidemic, spasmodic disease. Other authorities say that it is harmless, liked by domestic animals and bees. It is bristly, and has rather large, straw-coloured flowers.

R. Sibiricus, or Siberian Radish, has cylindrical pods.

R. caudatus, the Java, or Rat's Tail Radish, a native of Final, furnishes long, edible pods, purple or violet in colour. They should be used half-grown. The root of this species is not used.

R. maritimus is an indigenous, seaside variety.

R. Erucoides, of Italy, has pods with a beak of their own length, and a simple, biennial root, scarcely thicker than the stem.

R. Tenellus, another native of Siberia, flowers in Britain in June and July, having awl-shaped, jointed, two-celled, smooth pods.

RAGWORT

Senecio Jacobæa (LINN.)
N.O. Compositæ

Synonyms. St. James-wort. Ragweed. Stinking Nanny. Staggerwort. Dog Standard. Cankerwort. Stammerwort
Part Used. Herb

¶ *Description*. Ragwort grows about 2 to 3 feet high, with a much branched, furrowed stem, without hairs, and deep, glossy, green leaves, irregularly divided and toothed. The root-leaves are broader, jagged at the base, those on the stalk deeply divided down to the rib. The flowers are arranged in rather large, flat-topped bunches (corymbs), into which the branches divide at the summit and are a beautiful bright yellow, ¾ to 1 inch across, with narrow rays, toothed at the outer edge. The plant is a perennial and abundant in most parts of the country, on dry roadsides and waste ground and pastures, often growing in large patches and flowering in July and August. It is distributed over Europe, Siberia and North-West India. In the Highlands it is found at a height of 1,200 feet above sea-level.

Ragwort was formerly much employed medicinally for various purposes. The leaves are used in the country for emollient poultices and yield a good green dye, not, however, permanent. The flowers boiled in water give a fair yellow dye to wool previously impregnated with alum. The whole plant is bitter and aromatic, of an acrid sharpness, but the juice is cooling and astringent, and

of use as a wash in burns, inflammations of the eye, and also in sores and cancerous ulcers – hence one of its old names, Cankerwort. It is used with success in relieving rheumatism, sciatica and gout, a poultice of the green leaves being applied to painful joints and reducing the inflammation and swelling. It makes a good gargle for ulcerated throat and mouth, and is said to take away the pain caused by the sting of bees. A decoction of the root has been reputed good for inward bruises and wounds. In some parts of the country Ragwort is accredited with the power of preventing infection.

In olden days it was supposed to be 'a certaine remedie to help the Staggers in Horses,' whence one of its popular names, Staggerwort. One of its other names, Stammerwort, probably indicates a belief in its efficacy as a remedy for impediment of speech.

Fluid extract, ½ to 1 drachm.

Ragwort is collected in August.

Culpepper says it is 'under the command of Dame Venus, and cleanses, digests, and discusses. In Sussex we call it Ragweed.'

Senecio aquaticus (MARSH RAGWORT) is a form of *S. Jacobæa*, common on the sides of rivers and ditches throughout the country, growing freely at an elevation of 1,500 feet above sea-level, in the Lake district and resembling the common Ragwort, but usually of laxer growth and readily distinguished by its less divided, longer-stalked leaves and larger heads of flowers, which are 1 to 1¼ inch in diameter.

All forms of this genus are not of beneficial use, and one at least has lately been found to be distinctly harmful, for Molteno disease, a cattle and horse disease prevalent in certain parts of South Africa, has been definitely traced to the presence of a poisonous alkaloid in *S. latifolius*, a near relative of the Common Groundsel.

Some botanists refer the genus *Cineraria* to the same order as the *Senecio*; these differ from *Senecio* in the achenes of the ray-florets being winged. The beautiful spring-flowering plants cultivated in greenhouses as *Cinerarias* belong, however, to *Senecio*, and have been obtained by horticulturists by intercrossing with each other a number of the Canary Island species, such as *S. populifolius*, *S. Tussilaginis*, etc. The deep blue colour of some of the garden varieties of these plants is singular in the genus, and not at all common in the family.

From the report of the Board of Agriculture's Chief Veterinary Officer (1917):

'It is not generally recognized that the common British Ragwort is *poisonous to cattle*. This probably arises from the fact that poisoning under natural conditions is a slow process, that is to say, an animal does not receive, and could not eat enough of the weed at one meal to cause acute poisoning. On the other hand, the poison is cumulative in its action; with continuous doses the amount of poison which becomes available is sufficient in time to cause very serious symptoms which often end in death. Much more attention has been given to the subject of poisoning by certain species of Ragwort in South Africa, Canada, and New Zealand, and in certain districts where it is commonly met with it was believed to be a disease of cattle until its actual cause was discovered. Thus, we find such names applied to it as Pictou, Winton, and Molteno disease. The following represent broadly the circumstances of the cases which have recently come to the notice of the Board. Pastures containing a considerable proportion of the weed were cropped in the hope that the comparatively early cropping might help to get rid of it. The crop was made into hay, and owing to the prolonged spell of cold weather and the scarcity of other feeding stuffs, this was fed later and in considerable amount to animals at pasture.

'The actively poisonous agent in the plant seems to be one or two more alkaloids which have been extracted in more or less pure form from various species of Ragwort. . . . Some of the animals fed on the Ragwort died in a few days after the first appearance of definite symptoms. In others the symptoms continued for a month or more and deaths occurred at later dates. It would appear also that although animals which had received a toxic amount of Ragwort over a certain period may seem healthy at the time when feeding on the material is discontinued, they nevertheless develop active symptoms of poisoning and die at a later period. Thus in the cases investigated some of the animals did not show definite symptoms until twelve days or more after the feeding with Ragwort had been discontinued. In the early stages the animals have the appearance of being hide-bound. Later, they walk with a staggering gait, some appearing to be partially blind or heedless of where they go. Later, they may become very excitable, and will charge at anyone who approaches them. In some there may be diarrhœa, but usually constipation is so marked that it causes violent straining. The pulse is weak and rapid, but the temperature remains normal. . . . There is no cure, and prevention resolves itself into removing the Ragwort from the forage, or eradicating it from the pastures.'

McGovern makes the following recommendations for eradicating the weed:

'Ragwort may be exterminated by preventing the plant from seeding. This may be done in the following ways:

'(a) By grazing infested land with sheep in the winter and early spring.

'(b) By cutting the plants in the flowering stage either –

'(i) Twice, the first cut being made early in July, and the second about six weeks later, there being no necessity to gather up the cut portions; or

'(ii) Once only, cutting being done late in July or early in August. The cut portions of the plants must be gathered up at once and burnt.

'(c) By pulling the plants, if circumstances permit, preferably early in July, when there is no need to collect and burn the pulled plants. If pulled later the plants must be collected and burned to prevent seeding . . .

'It is not certain that sheep are absolutely immune to poisoning by Ragwort. Prob-ably the flowering season – June, July, and early August – is when Ragwort is most actively poisonous.'

See GROUNDSEL, LIFE ROOT, CINERARIA MARITIME.

RAMPION

Campanula rapunculus (LINN.)
N.O. Campanulaceæ

Synonym. Ramps
Part Used. Herb
Habitat. The plant is found wild in England, on gravelly roadsides and hedgebanks and in open pastures, from Stafford southwards, but it is uncertain whether it should be held as a true native in the localities in southern England, where it is now established

The Rampion formerly regularly culti-vated in English kitchen gardens, and much valued as a wholesome esculent vegetable, is seldom grown for use now, though its grace-ful flowers are sometimes seen to advantage in the borders as an ornamental plant.

The name Rampion is derived from its Latin specific name, *Rapunculus*, a diminu-tive of *rapa* (a turnip). It is still much culti-vated in France, Germany and Italy, and occasionally here, for the roots which are boiled tender like parsnips and eaten hot with a sauce. They are sweetish, with a slight pungency, but though wholesome, are con-sidered inferior to other roots now more widely grown for culinary use. The larger roots are reserved for boiling, sometimes the young roots are eaten raw with vinegar and pepper, and occasionally the leaves, as well as the roots, are eaten as a winter salad. The leaves can be used in the summer and autumn as a substitute for spinach. The young shoots may be blanched like asparagus and pre-pared in the same manner.

¶ *Description*. The roots are fleshy and biennial (but can be made perennial), the stems are 2 to 3 feet high, erect, stiff, though rather slender, generally simple, more or less covered with stiff, white hairs, which almost disappear when cultivated. The leaves are variable, 1 to 3 inches long, the radical leaves oblong or ovate, on long stalks and slightly crenate, the stem-leaves narrow and mostly entire, or obscurely toothed. The flowers, which bloom in July and August, are about ¾ inch long, reddish purple, blue or white, on short peduncles, forming long, simple or slightly branched panicles. The corolla is divided to about the middle into five lanceolate segments. The capsule is short and erect, opening in small lateral clefts, close under the narrow linear seg-ments of the calyx.

Drayton names it among the vegetables and pot-herbs of the kitchen garden, in his poem *Polyolbion*, and there is a reference to it in the slang of Falstaff, showing how gener-ally it was in cultivation in this country in Shakespeare's time.

There is an Italian tradition that the possession of a rampion excites quarrels among children. The plant figures in one of Grimm's tales, the heroine, Rapunzel, being named after it, and the whole plot is woven around the theft of rampions from a magician's garden. In an old Calabrian tale, a maiden, uprooting a rampion in a field, discovers a staircase that leads to a palace far down in the depths of the earth.

¶ *Cultivation*. Rampion is easily cultivated and will flourish in ordinary good soil, though a moist, sandy soil suits it best.

Seeds should be sown in shallow drills, a foot apart, in May, and thinned out to 5 or 6 inches in the rows. The young plants should be moderately watered at first.

If grown for culinary use, it must not be allowed to flower, and the roots should be earthed up several inches on each side in order to blanch them. They are fit for use in November, and should be lifted then and stored in a frost-proof place.

¶ *Medicinal Action and Uses*. Gerard tells us: 'Some affirme that the decoction of the roots are good for all inflammation of the mouth and almonds of the throte and other diseases happening in the mouth and throte, as the other Throte warts.'

An old writer states that the distilled water of the whole plant is excellent for the com-plexion and 'maketh the face very splendent.'

¶ *Other Species*.
Two other native species have been em-ployed dietetically, *Campanula rapunculoides* and *C. persicifolia*, but they have fallen into disuse as culinary vegetables, though the latter is a favourite in the flower border.

All the plants of the genus have a milky juice, which is more or less acrid, though not sufficiently so to act poisonously.

RAPE SEED. *See* MUSTARD

RASPBERRY

Rubus Idæus (LINN.)
N.O. Rosaceæ

Synonyms. Raspbis. Hindberry. Bramble of Mount Ida
(*Danish*) Hindebar
(*Dutch*) Braamboss
(*German*) Hindbur
(*Saxon*) Hindbeer
Parts Used. Leaves, fruit

The well-known Raspberry, grown so largely for its fruit, grows wild in some parts of Great Britain. It is a native of many parts of Europe. The stems are erect and shrubby, biennial, with creeping perennial roots. It flowers in May and June.

¶ *Cultivation.* The plant is generally propagated by suckers, though those raised from layers should be preferred, because they will be better rooted and not so liable to send out suckers. In preparing these plants their fibres should be shortened, but the buds which are placed at a small distance from the stem of the plant must not be cut off, as they produce the new shoots the following summer. Place the plants about 2 feet apart in the rows, allowing 4 or 5 feet between the rows. If planted too closely, without plenty of air between the rows, the fruit will not be so fine.

The most suitable soil is a good, strong loam. They do not thrive so well in a light soil.

In October, cut down all the old wood that has produced fruit in the summer and shorten the young shoots to about 2 feet in length. Dig the spaces between the rows well and dress with a little manure. Beyond weeding during the summer, no further care is needed. It is wise to form new plantations every three or four years, as the fruit on old plants is apt to deteriorate.

¶ *Constituents.* The Raspberry contains a crystallizable fruit-sugar, a fragrant volatile oil, pectin, citric and malic acids, mineral salts, colouring matter and water. The ripe fruit is fragrant, subacid and cooling: it allays heat and thirst, and is not liable to acetous fermentation in the stomach.

Raspberry vinegar is an acid syrup made with the fruit-juice, sugar and white-wine vinegar, and when added to water forms an excellent cooling drink in summer, suitable also in feverish cases, where the acid is not an objection. It makes a useful gargle for relaxed, sore throat.

A home-made wine, brewed from the fermented juice of ripe Raspberries, is antiscrofulous, and Raspberry syrup dissolves the tartar of the teeth.

The fruit is also utilized for dyeing purposes.

¶ *Medicinal Action and Uses.* Astringent and stimulant. Raspberry Leaf Tea, made by the infusion of 1 oz. of the dried leaves in a pint of boiling water, is employed as a gargle for sore mouths, canker of the throat, and as a wash for wounds and ulcers. The leaves, combined with the powdered bark of Slippery Elm, make a good poultice for cleansing wounds, burns and scalds, removing proud flesh and promoting healing.

An infusion of Raspberry leaves, taken cold, is a reliable remedy for extreme laxity of the bowels. The infusion alone, or as a component part of injections, never fails to give immediate relief. It is useful in stomach complaints of children.

Raspberry Leaf Tea is valuable during parturition. It should be taken freely – warm.

¶ *Preparation.* Fluid extract, 1 to 2 drachms.

The Raspberry grows wild as far north as lat. 70°, and southward it appears to have been abundant on Mount Ida, in Asia Minor, lat. 39° 40′. It was known to the Ancients, and Linnæus retained the classic name of Ida, with which it was associated by Dioscorides. It was called in Greek *Batos Idaia,* and in Latin *Rubus Idæa,* the Bramble of Mount Ida. Gerard calls it Raspis or Hindberry, and Hindberry is a derivation of the Saxon name *Hindbeer.*

'Twas only to hear the yorling sing,
And pu' the crawflower round the spring,
The scarlet hep and the *hindberrie,*
And the nut that hang frae the hazel tree.'

The Wild Raspberry differs from the cultivated variety mainly in its size.

RECIPES

Raspberry Wine

To every 3 pints of fruit, carefully cleared from mouldy or bad, put 1 quart of water; bruise the former. In 24 hours strain the liquor and put to every quart 1 lb. of sugar, of good middling quality, of Lisbon. If for white currants, use lump sugar. It is best to put the fruit, etc., into a large pan, and when, in three or four days, the scum rises, take that off before the liquor be put into the barrel. Those who make from their own gardens may not have a sufficiency to fill the barrel at once; the wine will not hurt if made in the pan in the above proportions, and added as the fruit ripens, and can be gathered in dry weather.

Keep an account of what is put in each time.

Raspberry Vinegar

Raspberry Vinegar is made either with malt vinegar or white vinegar (i.e. either white-wine vinegar or dilute acetic acid). Malt vinegar adds to the colour, which with white vinegar generally needs the addition of a little caramel to deepen it. When made from the fruit 2 lb. of raspberries is required to a pint of vinegar. Another method is to acidulate Raspberry-juice with acetic acid and sweeten with plain syrup.

Another Recipe for the Same

Put 1 lb. of fine fruit into a china-bowl, and pour upon it 1 quart of the best white-wine vinegar; next day strain the liquor on 1 lb. of fresh raspberries; and the following day do the same, but do not squeeze the fruit, only drain the liquor as dry as you can from it.

The last time pass it through a canvas, previously wet with vinegar, to prevent waste. Put it into a stone jar, with 1 lb. of sugar to every pint of juice, broken into large lumps; stir it when melted, then put the jar into a saucepan of water or on a hot hearth, let it simmer and skim it. When cold, bottle it.

This is one of the most useful preparations that can be kept in a house, not only as affording the most refreshing beverage, but being of singular efficacy in complaints of the chest. A large spoonful or two in a tumbler of water. Be careful to use no glazed nor metal vessels for it.

(Old Cookery-Book.)

Raspberry Brandy

Pick fine dry fruit, put it into a stone jar, and the jar into a kettle of water, or on a hot hearth, till the juice will run; strain, and to every pint add ¼ lb. of sugar, give one boil and skim it; when cold, put equal quantities of juice and brandy, shake well and bottle. Some people prefer it stronger of the brandy.

(Old Cookery-Book.)

RATTLE, DWARF RED

Pedicularis sylvatica
N.O. Labiatæ

Synonyms. Red Rattle Grass. Lousewort. Lesser Red Rattle
Part Used. Herb

The Dwarf Red Rattle (*Pedicularis sylvatica*) and the Yellow Rattle or Cock's Comb (*Rhinanthus Crista-galli*) are very closely allied to the Eyebright. As remedies they have now fallen into disuse.

There are two Red Rattles, but the commoner and medicinal one is the Dwarf or Lesser Red Rattle, frequent in moist pastures and on swampy heaths. It is quite a small plant, generally nestling rather closely to the ground, the short root-stock sending up many prostrate and spreading, leafy stems, 3 to 10 inches long, branching a good deal at the base and rarely more than 3 or 4 inches high when in flower. The leaves are very deeply cut into numerous segments. The flowers are in terminal, loose spikes, the calyx smooth on the outside, but woolly inside at the mouth, broadly inflated and marked over with a fine network of veins, and at the top, cut into five unequal, leaf-like lobes. The lower portion of the corolla forms a tube hidden within the calyx, but then emerging projects boldly beyond it; it is labiate in form, like the Eyebright, the upper lip tall and dome-like, but compressed at the sides, the lower lip flatly expanded and cut into three

very distinct lobes. Both are of a bright rose colour and the whole flower is very striking and quaint. As the seeds ripen, they may be heard rattling in their capsule within the inflated calyx, hence the popular name Red Rattle. Another name for the plant is 'Lousewort,' from a belief that sheep eating it became diseased and covered with parasites, but when sheep do suffer in this manner after eating this plant, it is really because the presence of it in a pasture indicates a very bad and unsuitable pasture, since marshy land, the best suited to its growth, is the worst from the health point of view for the sheep. The generic name, *Pedicularis* (from the Latin *pediculus* = a louse), refers also to the suppositious vermin-producing qualities of the plant.

The old herbalists considered the Red Rattle a wound herb and styptic. Culpepper tells us that —

'The Red Rattle is accounted profitable to heal fistulas and hollow ulcers and to stay the flux of humours in them as also the abundance of the courses or any other flux of blood, being boiled in port wine and drunk.'

RATTLE, YELLOW

Rhinanthus Crista-galli
N.O. Labiatæ

Synonyms. Cock's Comb. Yellow Rattle Grass. Pennygrass
(*Welsh*) Crivell Melyn
(*French*) Crête-de-coq
(*Gœlic*) Boden chloigin

The Yellow Rattle, a near relative of the Red Rattle, also obtains its name from the fact that the seeds rattle in the husky capsules when ripe. This is an erect, somewhat rigid plant, common in cultivated land, composed of a single stem, about a foot high, smooth and more or less spotted with purple, bearing pairs of stalkless, wedge-shaped leaves, with deeply notched margins and conspicuous veins, and terminated by a loose spike of yellow, labiate flowers, in which the calyx is large and very inflated (flattened so that its side view is much larger than its end view), of an uncommon pale green in colour and contracting at the mouth, where it is divided into four equal teeth. The upper lip of the corolla is very convex and ordinarily has a purple spot upon it; the lower lip is divided into three segments, the middle one being the largest. The stamens, which rest closely under the upper lip, have curious anthers, covered with little, bristly hairs.

Culpepper and other old writers call this plant Rattle Grass, like the preceding species, but Gerard gives also the name of 'Pennygrass,' an allusion to the flattened, fairly circular outline of the capsules. The generic name, *Rhinanthus*, is derived from the two Greek words signifying *nose* and *flower*, from the projecting beak of the upper portion of the corolla. The specific name, *Crista-galli*, means the crest or comb of a cock, because, according to Pliny, it has numerous leaves resembling a cock's comb. Parkinson, writing in 1640, also explains the name by saying the deeply-dented edges of the leaves 'resemble therein the crest or combe of a cocke,' but others have thought the name 'Coxcomb' refers rather to the notched calyx. In France it is called the 'Crête-de-coq.'

Both the Red Rattle and the Yellow Rattle are semi-parasites like the Eyebright, in similar manner extracting nourishment from the roots of the grasses among which they grow, the Yellow Rattle, however, to a more considerable degree than the others, impoverishing thereby the pastures in which it flourishes, and on the Continent it is often harmful to Rye crops, if not eradicated in time.

The Yellow Rattle was considered to have certain properties in common with Eyebright. Culpepper tells us that it 'is held to be good for those that are troubled with a cough or dimness of sight, if the herb being boiled with beans and some honey; put thereto be drunk or dropped into the eyes. The whole seed being put into the eyes draweth forth any skin, dimness or film from the sight without trouble or pain.'

RED CLOVER. *See* CLOVER

RED ROOT

Ceanothus Americanus (LINN.)
N.O. Rhamnaceæ

Synonyms. New Jersey Tea. Wild Snowball
Parts Used. Root or bark of the root
Habitat. North America

¶ *History*. This is a half-hardy shrub growing to 4 or 5 feet high. It has downy leaves and stems and small ornamental white flowers in great numbers, coming into bloom June or July, followed by bluntly triangular seedvessels. It is usually called 'New Jersey Tea' in America because its leaves were used as a substitute for tea during the War of Independence. In Canada it is used to dye wool a cinnamon colour. It takes its name from its large red roots. Its wood is tough, pale brown red, with fine rays – taste bitter and astringent with no odour. Fracture hard, tough, splintering. Its bark is brittle, dark-coloured and thin.

¶ *Constituents*. The leaves are said to contain tannin, a soft resin and bitter extract, a green colouring matter similar to green tea in colour and taste, gum a volatile substance, lignin, and a principle called Ceanothine.

¶ *Medicinal Action and Uses*. Astringent, antispasmodic, anti-syphilitic expectorant and sedative, used in asthma, chronic bronchitis, whooping-cough, consumption, and dysentery; also as a mouth-wash and gargle, and as an injection in gonorrhœa, gleet and leucorrhœa.

¶ *Dosages*. Of the decoction, $\frac{1}{2}$ oz. Fluid extract, 1 to 30 drops.

¶ *Other Species*. Mexican *Ceanothus azurea* (Desf.), a powerful febrifuge.

RED SAGE. *See* SAGE

REST-HARROW

Ononis arvensis
N.O. Leguminosæ

Synonyms. Wild Liquorice. Cammock. Stinking Tommy. Ground Furze. Land Whin
Part Used. Whole herb

¶ *Description.* A troublesome weed, with a root that affords a sweet, viscid juice. Common in arable land. Its long, thickly-matted root will arrest the progress of the harrow, hence its name.

It is a favourite food of the donkey, from which the generic name is derived, *onos* being the Greek word for an ass.

A tradition exists that this was the plant from which the crown of thorns was plaited for the Crucifixion.

The plant is obnoxious to snakes.

¶ *Medicinal Action and Uses.* The young shoots were much used at one time as a vegetable, being boiled, eaten in salad or pickled.

In medicine it was used for stone in the bladder and to subdue delirium.

RHATANY

Krameria triandra (R. and P.)
N.O. Polygalaceæ

Synonyms. Rhatanhia. Ratanhiawurzel. Krameria Root. Peruvian Rhatany. Mapato. Pumacuchu. Raiz para los dientes. Red Rhatany
Part Used. Dried root
Habitat. Peru

¶ *Description.* A low shrub with large red flowers, growing on dry, sandy places on mountain-slopes, 3,000 to 8,000 feet above sea-level in several provinces of Peru, especially near the city of Huanuco. The root, as found in commerce, consists of long, cylindrical pieces, varying in thickness from ¼ to ½ inch or more (long Rhatany), or a short, thick portion, knotted, and as large as a man's fist (short, or stumpy Rhatany). The difference is caused by the diggers, the former being removed by them with care, and the latter torn up with force. The bark of the root is thin, readily separable, rough and scaly; of a dark, reddish-brown colour outside, and bright brownish-red within. It breaks with a somewhat fibrous fracture, is tough and difficult to powder, and has a strong, purely astringent taste, tingeing the saliva red when chewed. The central woody portion is very hard and almost tasteless. Neither bark nor wood has any marked odour. As the virtues of Rhatany reside in the bark, the smaller pieces are preferable.

A strong tincture of these roots in brandy is used in Portugal to impart roughness to port wines.

The genus *Krameria* was named after Kramer, a Hungarian physician and botanist. The name Rhatany is said to describe the creeping character of the plant, in the language used by the Peruvian Indians, while its Spanish name is derived from its dental properties.

The dried roots of two species besides the Peruvian are official: *Krameria Ixené*, or Savanilla Rhatany, and *Krameria Argentea*, known in commerce as Para or Brazilian Rhatany.

Krameria was dropped from the United States Pharmacopœia but retained in the British Pharmacopœia and National Formulary.

¶ *Constituents.* The essential constituent is a peculiar tannic acid, known as Rhatania-tannic acid or Krameria tannic acid, closely allied to catechu-tannic acid. By the action of dilute acid it is decomposed into a crystallizable sugar, and Rhatania-red. No gallic acid is present. Rhatanin is a homologue of tyrosine, and is identical with angelin, geoffrayin, and andirin. It appears to contain also lignin, and small quantities of gum, starch, saccharine matter, and a peculiar acid, krameric acid. The mineral acids and most of the metallic salts throw down precipitates with the infusion, decoction and tincture of Rhatany, and are incompatible in prescription.

Cold water extracts all the astringency of Rhatany.

Very inferior extracts of Rhatany are often sold. Its virtues may be considered as in proportion to its solubility.

¶ *Medicinal Action and Uses.* An active astringent, and slightly tonic. It has been found useful for internal administration in chronic diarrhœa, dysentery, menorrhagia, incontinence of urine, hæmaturia, and passive hæmorrhage from the bowels. In the form of an infusion it has been used locally in fissure of the anus, prolapsus ani, and leucorrhœa; as a gargle in relaxed, sore throat; and as an astringent wash for the mucous membrane of the eyes, nose, gums, etc.

The powder is also used as a dentifrice when mixed with equal parts of orris rhizome and charcoal, or with prepared chalk and myrrh.

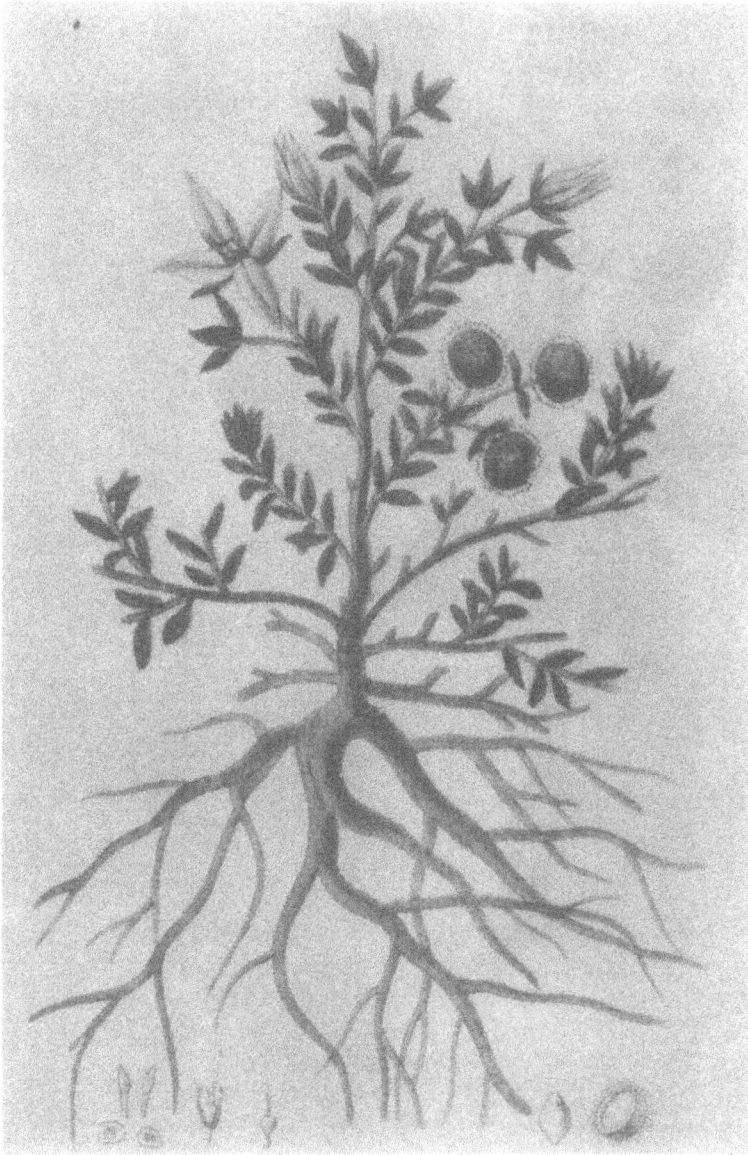

PERUVIAN RHATANY
Krameria Triandra

YELLOW RHODODENDRON
Rhododendron Chrysanthum

¶ *Preparations and Dosages.* Tincture of 20 per cent. krameria and diluted alcohol, 1 fluid drachm. Syrup of 45 per cent. fluid extract of krameria and syrup – as an intestinal astringent – 1 fluid drachm. Of the powder (rarely used), 20 to 30 grains. Lozenges are also prepared, with cocaine. Powdered root, 10 to 30 grains. Fluid extract, 10 to 60 drops. Tincture, B.P., and U.S.P., ½ to 1 drachm. Infusion, B.P., ½ to 1 oz. Solid extract, U.S.P., 5 to 8 grains. Solid extract, B.P., 5 to 15 grains. Concentrated solution, B.P., ½ to 1 drachm.

Other Species.

A Rhatany from Guayaquil appeared on the London market, yielding a larger quantity of tannin than the Peruvian drug, but less than the other two species. A spurious Rhatany from Peru, of unknown botanical origin, has also been put on the market. The Krameria lanceolate (*Texan Rhatany*) of North America, is richer in tannin than the official drug. It takes a deep purple colour when treated with iron, while Para gives a dirty brown and Savanilla violet.

The powder is of a reddish-brown colour.

RHODODENDRON, YELLOW

Rhododendron Chrysanthum
N.O. Ericaceæ

Synonyms. Rosebay. Snow Rose. Rosage Alpenrose
Part Used. Leaves
Habitat. Mountains of Siberia

¶ *Description.* A small bush, stem 1 to 1½ foot high, spreading, much branched, often concealed by moss, tips of shoots only being visible. Leaves alternate like laurel, ovate, somewhat acute, tapering to stalk, reticulated, rough above, paler and smoother underneath. Flowers large, showy, nodding, on clustered terminal, loose peduncles emerging from large downy scales. Corolla campanulate, five cleft, rounded segments, three upper largest and streaked with livid dots next the tube, lower unspotted. Stamens ten, unequal deflexed; anthers oblong, incumbent, without appendages, opening by two terminal pores, capsule ovate, rather angular, five-celled, five-valved, septicidal; seeds numerous, minute. The leaves should be gathered directly the capsules have ripened. They have a faint odour when first gathered, and a bitter, acrid, astringent taste.

¶ *Constituents.* The leaves contain a stimulant narcotic principle, which they yield to water or alcohol.

¶ *Medicinal Action and Other Uses.*[1] Much used in Siberia as a remedy for rheumatism. Also useful in gout and syphilis.

¶ *Dosage.* 2 teaspoonsful of the infusion.

RHUBARBS

N.O. Polygonaceæ

Rhubarb is the root of different species of *Rheum*, growing in the mountains of the Western and North-western provinces of China and in the adjoining Thibetan terrtory.

Rhubarb occurs in commerce under various names: Russian, Turkey, East Indian and Chinese; but the geographical source of all species is the same, the commercial names of the drug indicating only the route by which it formerly reached the European market. Previous to 1842, Canton being the only port of the Chinese Empire holding direct communication with Europe, Rhubarb mostly came by overland routes: the Russian Rhubarb used to be brought by the Chinese to the Russian frontier town of Kiachta; the Turkey Rhubarb received its name because it came to us by way of Asiatic Turkey, through the Levant; East Indian came by way of Singapore and other East Indian ports, and Chinese Rhubarb was shipped from Canton. At the present day practically all is conveyed to Europe via Shanghai.

According to Lindley's *Treasury of Botany*, the technical name of the genus is said to be derived from *Rha*, the ancient name of the Volga, on whose banks the plants grow; other authorities derive the name from the Greek *rheo* ('to flow'), in allusion to the purgative properties of the root.

RHUBARB, TURKEY

Rheum palmatum
Rheum Rhaponticum

Synonyms. East Indian Rhubarb. China Rhubarb
Part Used. Root

¶ *Description.* The leaves of the Turkey Rhubarb are palmate and somewhat rough. The root is thick, of an oval shape, sending off long, tapering branches; externally it is brown, internally a deep yellow colour.

The stem is erect, round, hollow, jointed,

[1] In homœopathic medicine a tincture of the fresh leaves is said to be curative of diarrhœa, amenorrhœa, chorea, affections of the eyes and ears, and neuralgia. – EDITOR.

branched towards the top, from 6 to 10 feet high.

This species is distinguished from our familiar garden Rhubarb by its much larger size, the shape of its leaves, with their oblong, sharpish segments, and the graceful looseness of its little panicles of greenish-white flowers. The first buds which appear in spring are yellow, not red.

It was not until the year 1732 that botanists knew any species of Rheum from which the true Rhubarb seemed likely to be obtained. Then Boerhaave, the celebrated Dutch physician, procured from a Tartarian Rhubarb merchant the seeds of the plant which produced the roots he annually sold, and which were admitted at St. Petersburg to be the real Rhubarb. These seeds on being sown produced two distinct species: *Rheum Rhaponticum*, our Garden Rhubarb, and *Rheum* and *R. palmatum*, Turkey Rhubarb.

The Turkey Rhubarb grows remarkably quickly – a six-year-old plant was found to grow between April, when the stalk first emerged from the ground, to the middle of July, when it was at its greatest height, to 11 feet 4 inches. In one day it was observed to grow 3 inches and over 4 inches in one night. Many of its leaves were 5 feet long. The root, taken up in October, weighed 36 lb. when cleaned, washed and deprived of its small fibres.

'J. D. B. (31/10). – The rhubarb rhizome official in the British Pharmacopœia, 1914, must be collected in China and Thibet. English-grown rhubarb is inferior to the official rhubarb in medicinal qualities.'

We still depend upon Northern China and Thibet for Rhubarb; that grown in the English climate, near Banbury, does not command a high price in the market, although its medicinal properties are the same as those of the Chinese roots. If English growers would endeavour to produce a more marketable root by experimenting with different soils and methods of cultivation, the results might meet with success. It is possible that English roots are harvested when too young, and that not so much attention is paid to trimming the roots for market as is done by the Chinese. It is never collected from plants that are less than six years old.

It is said that the odour of the best samples is so delicate that the assistants in the wholesale drug-houses are not permitted to touch it without gloves.

¶ *Part Used*. The root, scraped or rasped, halved longitudinally when very large, and then cut into transverse pieces and strung on cords to dry in the sun, the drying afterwards being completed by stove heat. It is dug in October.

Chinese or Turkey Rhubarb occurs in commerce in brownish-yellow pieces of various size, usually perforated, the holes often containing a portion of the cord used to hang the sections of the root on during drying. The outer surface is generally powdery (the bark having been removed) and shows a network of white lines.

The taste is astringent and nauseous, and there is a characteristic odour.

The preparations used in medicine are: the powdered root, a fluid extract, a tincture, syrup, infusion and solution. It is also employed as a principal ingredient in compound powder (Gregory's Powder) and in compound pills.

¶ *Constituents*. The chemical constituents of Rhubarb root are not yet completely known. Recent investigations indicate that the most important constituents are a number of substances which may be divided into two groups, viz. tannoid constituents and purgative constituents, several of which have been isolated in a free state: the former are astringent and the latter laxative.

Three crystalline tannoids have been extracted. The purgative constituents apparently exist in the form of an unstable crystalline substance: Rheopurgarin. This splits up into four glucosides: two of these yield Chrysophanic acid (so named from its forming yellow crystals) and Rheochrysidin respectively. The other two glucosides have not yet been isolated, but they appear to yield Emodin and Rhein.

There are also several resinous matters, one of which, Phaoretin, is purgative, and mineral compounds are also present, especially Oxalate of Calcium. The astringency of Rhubarb is due to a peculiar tannic acid (Rheo-tannic), which is soluble in water and alcohol.

¶ *Medicinal Action and Uses*. Astringent, tonic, stomachic, aperient. In large doses, Rhubarb powder acts as a simple and safe purgative, being regarded as one of the most valuable remedies we possess, effecting a brisk, healthy purge, without clogging the bowels and producing constipation, too often consequent upon the use of the more active purgatives.

It is especially useful in cases of diarrhœa, caused by an irritating body in the intestines: the cause of irritation is removed and the after-astringent action checks the diarrhœa.

The following note from *The Chemist and Druggist* of March 31, 1923, supports this:

'*Rhubarb in Bacillary Dysentery*. – An investigation was undertaken to determine the way in which rhubarb acts in this disease and which constituent was responsible for its action, one writer having stated in regard to the treatment of bacillary dysentery that no remedy in medicine has such a magical effect. (*Lancet*, I, 1923, 382.) A solution containing all the purgative constituents of rhubarb soluble in water (1 gr. of B.P. rhubarb extract) was allowed to act on *B. dysenterial Shiga and Flexner* of the bacillus No. 1 of Morgan without affecting growth in the broth tubes. Fresh undiluted ox bile has not distinct action on the bacilli, thus indicating that the therapeutic effect of rhubarb is not due to its cholagogue action. Neither does the serum of a rabbit treated with rhubarb have any germicidal action. The nature of the therapeutic effect of rhubarb in bacillary dysentery therefore still remains obscure.'

And again, September 3, 1921, in the *Lancet*, by Dr. R. W. Burkitt:

'In the former journal, Dr. R. W. Burkitt, of Nairobi, British East Africa, states that acute bacillary dysentery has been treated in that colony almost exclusively with powdered rhubarb for the past three years. The dose given has been 30 grains every two or three hours until the rhubarb appears in the stools. After a few doses the stools become less frequent, hæmorrhage ceases, and straining and the other symptoms of acute general poisoning, which characterize the disease, rapidly disappear. In children 5 grains is given every two hours for three doses only, as, if the administration is continued longer, the drug will cure the dysentery, but produce an obstinate simple diarrhœa. In both adults and children the thirst is combated by small, frequent doses of bicarbonate of soda and citrate of potash. Dr. Burkitt concludes: "I know of no remedy in medicine which has such a magical effect. No one who has ever used rhubarb would dream of using anything else. I hope others will try it in this dreadful tropical scourge." '

Rhubarb in small doses exhibits stomachic and tonic properties, and is employed in atonic dyspepsia, assisting digestion and creating a healthy action of the digestive organs, when in a condition of torpor and debility.

The tincture is chiefly used, but the powder is equally effective and reliable.

Rhubarb when chewed increases the flow of saliva.

¶ *Preparations and Dosages.* Powdered root, 3 to 30 grains. Comp. powder, B.P. (Gregory's), 20 to 60 grains. Comp. pill, B.P., 4 to 8 grains. Solid extract, U.S.P., 4 grains. Solid extract, B.P., 2 to 8 grains. Tincture comp., B.P., ½ to 4 drachms. Tincture, U.S.P., 1 drachm. Tincture aromat., U.S.P., ½ drachm. Fluid extract, 10 to 30 drops. Syrup, B.P., ½ to 2 drachms. Infusion, B.P., ½ to 1 oz. Syrup, B.P. and U.S.P., ½ to 2 drachms. Arom. syrup, U.S.P., 2 drachms. Rheum, 1 to 4 grains.

RHUBARB, ENGLISH   Rheum Rhaponticum (WILLD.)

Synonyms. Garden Rhubarb. Bastard Rhubarb. Sweet Round-leaved Dock
Parts Used. Root, stems

English Rhubarb is similar in action to Turkey or Chinese Rhubarb, though milder. It is derived from *Rheum Rhaponticum*, the ordinary Garden Rhubarb, and from *R. officinale*.

It has blunt, smooth leaves; large, thick roots, running deep into the ground, reddish-brown outside and yellow within, and stems 2 to 3 feet high, jointed and purplish. The flowers are white.

About 1777, Hayward, an apothecary, of Banbury, in Oxfordshire, commenced the cultivation of Rhubarb with plants of *R. Rhaponticum*, raised from seeds sent from Russia in 1762, and produced a drug of excellent quality, which used to be sold as the genuine Rhubarb, by men dressed up as Turks. The Society for the encouragement of Arts, Manufactures and Commerce exerted itself for many years in promoting the cultivation of Rhubarb, granting medals not only to this original pioneer, but also, some years later, to growers of Rhubarb in Somersetshire, Yorkshire and Middlesex, some of whom, it appears, attempted also to cultivate *R. palmatum*. When Hayward died, he left his Rhubarb plantations to the ancestor of the present cultivators of the Rhubarb fields at Banbury, where *R. officinale* is also now cultivated, from specimens first introduced into this country in 1873. Both *R. Rhaponticum* and *R. officinale* are at the present time grown, not only in Oxfordshire but also in Bedfordshire. Although specimens of *R. palmatum* were raised from seed as early as 1764, in the Botanical Gardens in Edinburgh, it is not grown now in this country for medicinal purposes, experiments having shown that it is the least easily cultivated of the rhubarbs, the main root in this climate being liable to rot. *R. officinale* and *R. Emodi* have to some extent been grown also as an ornamental plant, being also quite hardy and readily propagated.

¶ *Cultivation*. Rhubarb may be raised from seed, but it is better and more usual to obtain established roots. Seeds may be sown, however, in drills a foot or more apart, in the open, from March to April, and the young plants thinned out to 10 inches, transplanting them in the autumn, allowing about 4 feet every way to each plant.

Rhubarb roots may be planted at any time of the year, although mild weather in autumn or early spring is best; it should be planted on a clear, open spot, on good soil, which should be well trenched 3 feet deep, and before planting, a good substance of rotten manure should be worked into the soil.

When the plants are to be increased, it is merely necessary to take up large roots and divide them with a spade: every piece that has a crown to it will grow. Fresh plantations are generally made in February or March, but Rhubarb may still be divided early in May.

To ensure fine rhubarb for table use, a large dressing of well-rotted manure should be dug in about the roots as soon as the last of the leaves have been pulled. It is not right to wait until the winter, before the plants are dressed.

Old roots ought to be divided and re-planted every fourth or fifth year, when the plants are grown for the use of the stems.

If Rhubarb be forced on the ground where it grows, nothing more is required than to cover with large pots, half casks, or boxes, round and over which should be placed plenty of stable manure. Roots forced in green-house or in frames do not need to have the light excluded from them. Such roots, however, require dividing and replanting in the spring out of doors.

¶ *Part Used Medicinally and Preparation*. The roots of English Rhubarb are generally taken from plants from four years old and upwards. They are dug up in October, washed thoroughly and the fibres taken away. The bark of English Rhubarb is not usually removed.

The roots of both *R. Officinale* and *R. Rhaponticum* are much smaller than those of the Chinese Rhubarb and are easily distinguished by their distinctly radiate structure. They are also more shrunken, more or less distinctly pink in colour, and have a diffuse circle of isolated star-spots on the transverse section. The roots of *R. officinale* cultivated in England resemble Chinese Rhubarb, but are more spongy, and shrink and wrinkle as they dry, and are softer to cut. They have a less rich colour than the Chinese, and have no network of white lines on the outer surface, the dark red and white lines usually running parallel to each other and the star-spots being less developed, fewer and more scattered.

The English Rhubarb from *R. Rhaponticum* shows red veins, that of *R. officinale* is usually in larger pieces and has blackish veins.

The root is used as a drug in powdered form.

¶ *Constituents. Root*. The constituents of *R. officinale* are similar to those of Chinese Rhubarb.

Rhapontic or Garden Rhubarb contains no emodine, rhein or rhabarberine, but has in it a crystalline body, rhaponticin.

Stem and Leaves of R. Rhaponticum. Potassium oxalate is present in quantity in Rhubarb *leaf-stems*, and certain persons who are constitutionally susceptible to salts of oxalic acid, show symptoms of irritant poisoning after eating rhubarb stewed in the ordinary manner. Many people of a gouty tendency do well to avoid it, and those subject to urinary irritation should take it very sparingly or not at all.

Rhubarb stems did not come into general use as a substitute for fruit till about 100 years ago. We hear of a pioneer grower, Joseph Myatt, of Deptford, sending, in 1810, five bunches of Rhubarb to the Borough Market and only being able to dispose of three. But he persevered in his efforts to make a market for Rhubarb, raised improved varieties, and a few years after, Rhubarb had become established in public favour as a culinary plant.

It was, however, soon realized that the use of Rhubarb as food was sometimes attended with some risk to health. Lindley, in his *Vegetable Kingdom*, 1846, remarks that oxalic acid exists in both Docks and Rhubarb, and that the latter contains also an abundance of nitric and malic acid, and goes on to say that whilst these give an agreeable taste to the Rhubarb when cooked, he considers them ill-suited to the digestion of some persons. The *Penny Cyclopædia*, 1841, warned persons subject to calculous complaints against eating Rhubarb stalks, owing to the presence of oxalic acid, stating that 'the formation of oxalate of lime, or mulberry calculus, may be the consequence of indulgence.'

The chemical constituents of Rhubarb *leaves* were till recently not fully ascertained, but the analysis has lately been undertaken under orders from the Home Office, in consequence of fatal and injurious effects having resulted from eating the leaves cooked as

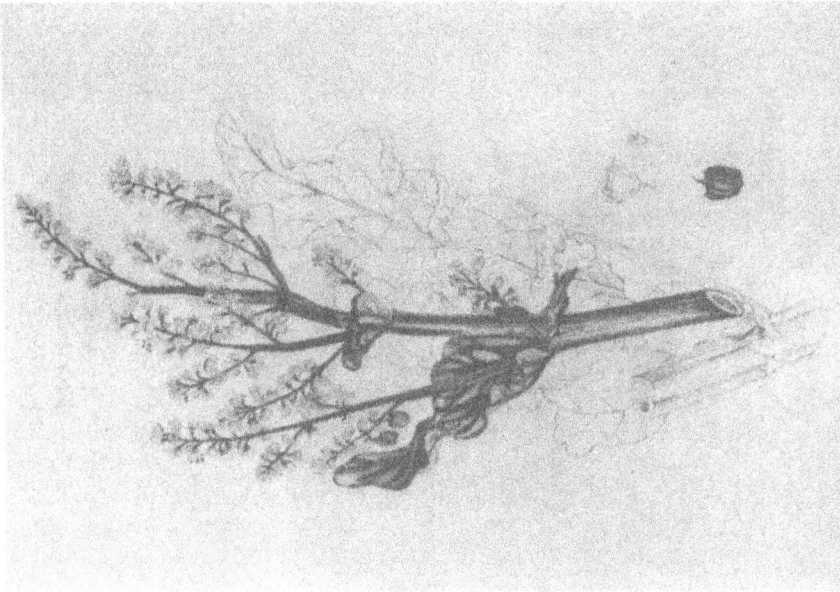

FRENCH RHUBARB
Rheum Undulatum

EAST INDIAN RHUBARB
Rheum Palmatum

ROSEMARY
Rosmarinus Officinalis

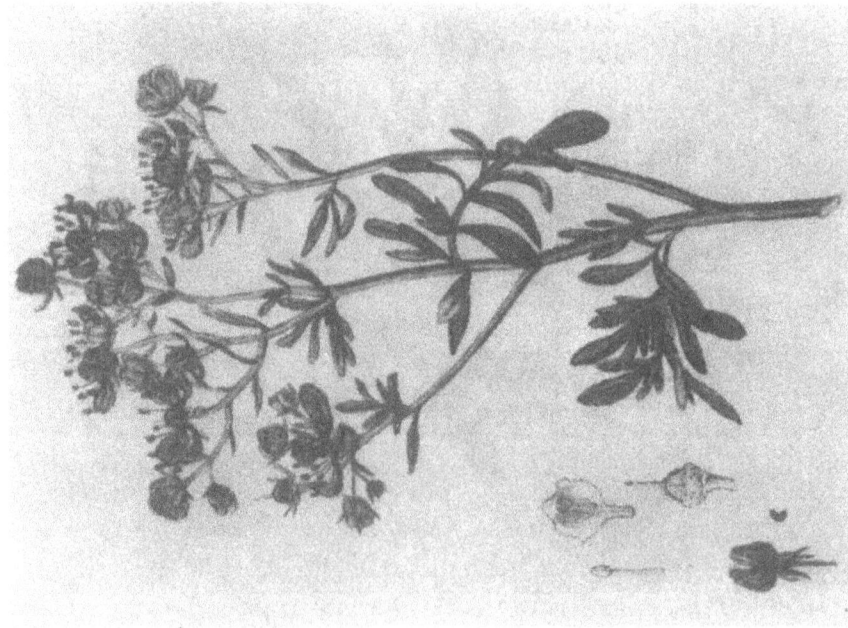

RUE
Ruta Graveolens

spinach. The report of the official analyist states that the leaves contain some 0·3 per cent. oxalates of potassium and calcium oxalates. It is possible that the recent cases of poisoning occurred in subjects specially susceptible to oxalic poisoning, as there are also many cases reported of no harm ensuing from a use of Rhubarb leaves as a vegetable.

In Maunders' *Treasury of Botany* Rhubarb leaves are mentioned as a pot-herb. Green (*Universal Herbal*, 1832) says: 'The leaves are also used by the French in their soups, to which they impart an agreeable acidity, like that of Sorrel.' Reference has recently been made in the press to a letter which appeared in the *Gardeners' Chronicle* for 1846, in which the gardener of the Earl of Shrewsbury at Alton Towers, Staffordshire, told how rhubarb leaves had been used there for many years as a vegetable. He also mentioned that the flower of the plant (before the leaves expanded) could be used like broccoli. A subsequent note by him makes it clear, however, that the leaf-stems were meant, for he then says:

'I have no experience in the eating of the leaves and think them nauseous to the taste and unpleasant to the smell. . . . I tasted them boiled and they did not appear to me to have one redeeming feature. . . .'

The flower of the plant, when in bud form, has been eaten as a pleasant substitute for broccoli; when cooked *au gratin*, with white sauce over it, the cheese quite obviates any bitterness of taste.

Further reference to the *Gardeners' Chronicle*, of 1847, shows records of the varying results of eating the young inflorescence, producing no ill-effects in some cases and serious illness in others, and a case is recorded of severe sickness attacking a whole family after partaking of the leaves boiled as a vegetable. In 1853 we find the question again raised. In 1872 we hear of deaths from eating the leaves in America, and in 1899 we find a revival of interest in Rhubarb leaves as a vegetable, quite opposite opinions being expressed in a correspondence in the gardening papers. In 1901 we hear of a man dying after eating stewed Rhubarb leaves, the verdict at the inquest being: 'Accidental death, caused by eating rhubarb-leaves.' It was stated then that the leaves were used as a vegetable in parts of Hampshire. The *British Medical Journal* in December, 1910, mentions several cases of rhubarb poisoning.

The leaves are sometimes made use of in the fabrication of fictitious cigars and tobacco. The shape of the hairs, however, as seen under a microscope, can enable the observer to detect the presence or absence of tobacco, but it is not so easy to determine the source of the fraudulent admixtures.

It is possible that the chemical composition of Rhubarb varies to some extent according to the variety and the soil on which it is grown. It has been stated that the amount of water present is less when the plants are grown on poor soil, while the acid principle is more abundant.

As regards the method of cooking, the *British Medical Journal* points out that hard water would precipitate the oxalate, while a soft water might leave it in the form of soluble oxalate, more readily assimilated into the systems of those susceptible to this kind of poisoning. In a recent case that terminated fatally, the leaves were well washed, drained, cut up and put into boiling water, in an iron saucepan, for 20 minutes. A little salt and kitchen soda were added, but nothing else. Being acid, the leaves should, of course, not be cooked in a copper vessel.

¶ *Medicinal Action and Uses.* Though the English Rhubarb root is milder as a purgative, it is more astringent, and has been considered a better stomachic than the foreign.

It is specially useful in infantile stomach troubles and looseness of the bowels.

In fairly large doses it acts as a laxative.

Dose of powdered root, 5 to 60 grains. The dose is entirely individual, 12 grains acting on some persons, as much as 20 on others of the same age. It has been held that 20 grains of the seed are equal to 30 of the root, as regards purgative power. The properties of the seeds are similar to those of the root.

A decoction of the seeds is supposed not only to ease pains in the stomach, but to strengthen it by increasing the appetite.

A strong decoction of the root has been employed as a good wash for scrofulous sores.

If a portion of the root be infused in water, and when strained a few grains of salt of tartar be added, a very beautiful red tincture results, which might prove valuable for the purposes of a dye.

Culpepper says of Rhubarb:

'If your body be anything strong, you may take 2 drams of it at a time being sliced thin and steeped all night in white wine, in the morning strain it out and drink the white wine; it purges but gently, it leaves a binding quality behind it, therefore dried a little by the fire and beaten into powder, it is usually given in Fluxes.'

RHUBARB, MONK'S   Rumex alpinus (LINN.)

Synonym. Garden Patience

Monk's Rhubarb is, as Culpepper tells us, 'a Dock bearing the name of Rhubarb for some purging quality within.'

The root was formerly used medicinally, and the leaves as a pot-herb.

It is found on roadsides near cottages in the North of England and in Scotland, but is rare and naturalized.

The root-stock is very stout, of a yellow colour; the stem 2 to 4 feet high, bearing pale green leaves, broad and very long, the edges waved, but not cut into. The tops of the stems are divided into many small branches, bearing reddish or purple flowers, succeeded by angular seeds, as in other docks.

The medicinal virtues of the root, when dried, are similar to the Garden or Bastard Rhubarb, but are not so strong.

Culpepper says:

'A dram of the dried root of Monk's Rhubarb with a scruple of Ginger made into powder, and taken fasting in a draught or mess of warm broth, purges choler and phlegm downwards very gently and safely without danger. . . . The distilled water thereof is very profitably used to heal scabs; also foul ulcerous sores, and to allay the inflammation of them. . . .'

See DOCKS.

RICE   Oryza sativa (LINN.)
                                                     N.O. Graminaceæ

Synonyms. Nivara. Dhan. O. montana. O. setegera. O. latifolia. Bras. Paddy
Part Used. The seeds
Habitat. East Indies. Most sub-tropical countries

¶ *Description.* Rice is an annual plant with several jointed culms or stems from 2 to 10 feet long, the lower part floating in water or prostrate, with roots at the nodes, the rest erect. The panicle is terminal and diffuse, bowing when the seed is weighty. It is probably indigenous to China, and certainly to India, where the wild form grows by tanks, ditches and rivers. It was early introduced into East Africa and Syria, and later into America, where it already appears as a native plant. In Europe, rice was brought into the Mediterranean basin from Syria by the Arabs in the Middle Ages, but is now grown largely only in the plain of Lombardy, and a little in Spain. In England it has been cultivated merely as a curiosity, and may be seen in the hothouses of most botanic gardens, treated as a water plant. The Cingalese distinguish 160 kinds, while 50 or 60 are cultivated in India, not including the wild form, from which the grain is collected, though it is never cultivated. Most kinds require irrigation, but some need little water, or can be grown on ordinary, dry ground.

Oryza (the classical name of the grain), or the husked seeds, is called Bras by the Malays, and Paddy when it is enclosed in the husk. Carolina and Patna rice are the most esteemed in England and the United States. The grain of the first is round and flat, and boils soft for puddings; the latter has a long and narrow grain that keeps its shape well for curries, etc.

The *flour* procured from the seeds is called Oryzæ Farina, or rice flour, commonly known as *ground rice*.

The granules of *rice starch* are the smallest of all known starch granules.

A kind of spirit called Arrack is sometimes distilled from the fermented infusion, but the name Arrack is usually applied to Palm wine or Toddy.

¶ *Medicinal Action and Uses.* The chief consumption of rice is as a food substance, but it should never be forgotten that the large and continued consumption of the white, polished rices of commerce is likely to be injurious to the health. The nations of which rice is the staple diet eat it unhusked as a rule, when it is brownish and less attractive to the eye, but much more nutritious as well as cheaper. Having no laxative qualities, rice forms a light and digestible food for those in whom there is any tendency to diarrhœa or dysentery, but it contains less potash and vegetable acids than potatoes.

A decoction of rice, commonly called *rice-water* is recommended in the Pharmacopœia of India as an excellent demulcent, refrigerant drink in febrile and inflammatory diseases, and in dysuria and similar affections. It may be acidulated with lime-juice and sweetened with sugar. This may also be used as an enema in affections of the bowels.

A poultice of rice may be used as a substitute for one of linseed meal, and finely-powdered rice flour may be used, like that of wheat flour, for erysipelas, burns, scalds, etc.

Rice starch may be used medicinally and in other ways in place of wheat starch.

A few years ago the injurious habit of chewing the raw white grains was practised by fashionable women and girls to produce a white velvety complexion.

ROCKET, GARDEN

Hesperis matronalis
N.O. Cruciferæ

Synonyms. Eruca sativa. Dame's Rocket. White Rocket. Purple Rocket. Rucchette. Roquette. Dame's Violet. Vesper-Flower

Part Used. Whole plant

Habitat. Central Europe

¶ *Description.* These biennial plants are natives of Italy, but are found throughout most of Central and Mediterranean Europe, and in Britain and Russian Asia as escapes from gardens. The stems are very erect, and grow from 2 to 3 feet in height, with spear-shaped, pointed leaves. The flowers, white purple, or variegated, are produced in a simple thyrse at the top of the stalk. Johnson wrote of a double-white variety in 1633. The Siberian Rocket is almost identical. The seeds are like those of mustard, but larger.

The leaves are very acrid in taste, and in many countries, especially in Germany, they are eaten like cress in salads.

In the language of flowers, the Rocket has been taken to represent deceit, since it gives out a lovely perfume in the evening, but in the daytime has none. Hence its name of Hesperis, or Vesper-Flower, given it by the Ancients.

For eating purposes, the plant should be gathered before flowering, but for medicinal use, when in flower.

¶ *Constituents.* The properties of the cultivated Rocket resemble those of the Cochlearea, but its taste is less acrid and piquant.

¶ *Medicinal Action and Uses.* In former days doctors combined with poets in attributing marvellous virtues to this plant. It is regarded principally as antiscorbutic.

A strong dose will cause vomiting, and may be taken in the place of ipecacuanha. Powdered, the effect is less strong than that of mustard.

¶ *Other Species.* The *Sea-Rocket* or *Cakile maritima, Eruca marina,* often found on sandhills, is very acrid, and can be used as an antiscorbutic, being prescribed in scrofulous affections, lymphatic disturbances, and the malaise that follows malaria. It is important not to confuse it with the real Rocket.

ROSEMARY

Rosmarinus officinalis (LINN.)
N.O. Labiatæ

Synonyms. Polar Plant. Compass-weed. Compass Plant. Rosmarinus coronarium (*Old French*) Incensier

Parts Used. Herb, root

¶ *Description.* The evergreen leaves of this shrubby herb are about 1 inch long, linear, revolute, dark green above and paler and glandular beneath, with an odour pungently aromatic and somewhat camphoraceous. The flowers are small and pale blue. Much of the active volatile principle resides in their calyces. There are silver and gold-striped varieties, but the green-leaved variety is the kind used medicinally.

¶ *Cultivation.* Rosemary is propagated by seeds, cuttings and layers, and division of roots. (1) Seeds may be sown upon a warm, sunny border. (2) Cuttings, taken in August, 6 inches long, and dibbled into a shady border, two-thirds of their length in the ground, under a hand-glass, will root and be ready for transplanting into permanent quarters the following autumn. (3) Layering may be readily accomplished in summer by pegging some of the lower branches under a little sandy soil.

Rosemary succeeds best in a light, rather dry soil, and in a sheltered situation, such as the base of a low wall with a south aspect. On a chalk soil it grows smaller, but is more

fragrant. The silver- and gold-striped kinds are not quite so hardy.

The finest plants are said to be raised from seed.

¶ *History.* The Ancients were well acquainted with the shrub, which had a reputation for strengthening the memory. On this account it became the emblem of fidelity for lovers. It holds a special position among herbs from the symbolism attached to it. Not only was it used at weddings, but also at funerals, for decking churches and banqueting halls at festivals, as incense in religious ceremonies, and in magical spells.

At weddings, it was entwined in the wreath worn by the bride, being first dipped into scented water. Anne of Cleves, we are told, wore such a wreath at her wedding. A Rosemary branch, richly gilded and tied with silken ribands of all colours, was also presented to wedding guests, as a symbol of love and loyalty. Together with an orange stuck with cloves it was given as a New Year's gift – allusions to this custom are to be found in Ben Jonson's plays.

Miss Anne Pratt (*Flowers and their Associations*) says:

'But it was not among the herbalists and apothecaries merely that Rosemary had its reputation for peculiar virtues. The celebrated Doctor of Divinity, Roger Hacket, did not disdain to expatiate on its excellencies in the pulpit. In a sermon which he entitles "A Marriage Present," which was published in 1607, he says: "Speaking of the powers of rosemary, it overtoppeth all the flowers in the garden, boasting man's rule. It helpeth the brain, strengtheneth the memorie, and is very medicinable for the head. Another property of the rosemary is, it affects the heart. Let this rosmarinus, this flower of men, ensigne of your wisdom, love and loyaltie, be carried not only in your hands, but in your hearts and heads." '

Sir Thomas More writes:

'As for Rosmarine, I lett it runne all over my garden walls, not onlie because my bees love it, but because it is the herb sacred to remembrance, and, therefore, to friendship; whence a sprig of it hath a dumb language that maketh it the chosen emblem of our funeral wakes and in our buriall grounds.'

In early times, Rosemary was freely cultivated in kitchen gardens and came to represent the dominant influence of the house mistress. 'Where Rosemary flourished, the woman ruled.'

The *Treasury of Botany* says:

'There is a vulgar belief in Gloucestershire and other counties, that Rosemary will not grow well unless where the mistress is "master"; and so touchy are some of the lords of creation upon this point, that we have more than once had reason to suspect them of privately injuring a growing rosemary in order to destroy this evidence of their want of authority.'

Rosemary was one of the cordial herbs used to flavour ale and wine. It was also used in Christmas decoration.

'Down with the rosemary and so,
Down with the baies and mistletoe,
Down with the holly, ivie all
Wherewith ye deck the Christmas Hall.'
HERRICK.

In place of more costly incense, the ancients used Rosemary in their religious ceremonies. An old French name for it was *Incensier*. The Spaniards revere it as one of the bushes that gave shelter to the Virgin Mary in the flight into Egypt and call it *Romero*, the Pilgrim's Flower. Both in Spain and Italy, it has been considered a safeguard from witches and evil influences generally. The Sicilians believe that young fairies, taking the form of snakes, lie amongst the branches.

It was an old custom to burn Rosemary in sick chambers, and in French hospitals it is customary to burn Rosemary with Juniper berries to purify the air and prevent infection. Like Rue, it was placed in the dock of courts of justice, as a preventative from the contagion of gaol-fever. A sprig of Rosemary was carried in the hand at funerals, being distributed to the mourners before they left the house, to be cast on to the coffin when it had been lowered into the grave. In many parts of Wales it is still a custom.

One old legend compares the growth of the plant with the height of the Saviour and declares that after thirty-three years it increases in breadth, but never in height.

There is a tradition that Queen Philippa's mother (Countess of Hainault) sent the first plants of Rosemary to England, and in a copy of an old manuscript in the library of Trinity College, Cambridge, the translator, 'danyel bain,' says that Rosemary was unknown in England until this Countess sent some to her daughter.

Miss Rohde gives the following quotation from *Banckes' Herbal*:

'Take the flowers thereof and make powder thereof and binde it to thy right arme in a linnen cloath and it shale make *theee* light and merrie.

'Take the flowers and put them in thy chest among thy clothes or among thy Bookes and Mothes shall not destroy them.

'Boyle the leaves in white wine and washe thy face therewith and thy browes, and thou shalt have a faire face.

'Also put the leaves under thy bedde and thou shalt be delivered of all evill dreames.

'Take the leaves and put them into wine and it shall keep the wine from all sourness and evill savours, and if thou wilt sell thy wine thou shalt have goode speede.

'Also if thou be feeble boyle the leaves in cleane water and washe thyself and thou shalt wax shiny.

'Also if thou have lost appetite of eating boyle well these leaves in cleane water and when the water is colde put thereunto as much of white wine and then make sops, eat them thereof wel and thou shalt restore thy appetite againe.

'If thy legges be blowen with gowte, boyle the leaves in water and binde them in a linnen cloath and winde it about thy legges and it shall do thee much good.

'If thou have a cough drink the water of the leaves boyld in white wine and ye shall be whole.

'Take the Timber thereof and burn it to coales and make powder thereof and rubbe thy teeth thereof and it shall keep thy teeth from all evils. Smell it oft and it shall keep thee youngly.

'Also if a man have lost his smellyng of the ayre that he may not draw his breath, make a fire of the wood, and bake his bread therewith, eate it and it shall keepe him well.

'Make thee a box of the wood of rosemary and smell to it and it shall preserve thy youth.'

From the *Grete Herbal*:

'ROSEMARY. – For weyknesse of ye brayne. Against weyknesse of the brayne and coldenesse thereof, sethe rosemaria in wyne and lete the pacyent receye the smoke at his nose and keep his heed warme.'

¶ *Parts Used.* The oil of Rosemary, distilled from the flowering tops, as directed in the British Pharmacopœia, is a superior oil to that obtained from the stem and leaves, but nearly all the commercial oil is distilled from the stem and leaves of the wild plant before it is in flower.[1]

The upper portions of the shoots are taken, with the leaves on and the leaves are stripped off the portions of the shoots that are very wooden.

¶ *Constituents.* The plant contains some tannic acid, together with a resin and a bitter principle and a volatile oil. The chief constituents of the oil are Borneol, bornyl acetate and other esters, a special camphor similar to that possessed by the myrtle, cineol, pinene and camphene. It is colourless, with the odour of Rosemary and a warm camphoraceous taste. The chief adulterants of oil of Rosemary are oil of turpentine and petroleum. Rosemary yields its virtues partly to water and entirely to rectified spirits of wine.

From 100 lb. of the flowering tops, 8 oz. of the oil are usually obtained.

¶ *Medicinal Action and Uses.* Tonic, astringent, diaphoretic, stimulant. Oil of Rosemary has the carminative properties of other volatile oils and is an excellent stomachic and nervine, curing many cases of headache.

It is employed principally, externally, as *spiritus Rosmarini*, in hair-lotions, for its odour and effect in stimulating the hair-bulbs to renewed activity and preventing premature baldness. An infusion of the dried plant (both leaves and flowers) combined with borax and used when cold, makes one of the best hairwashes known. It forms an effectual remedy for the prevention of scurf and dandruff.

The oil is also used externally as a rubefacient and is added to liniments as a fragrant stimulant. Hungary water, for outward application to renovate the vitality of paralysed limbs, was first invented for a Queen of Hungary, who was said to have been completely cured by its continued use. It was prepared by putting 1½ lb. of fresh Rosemary tops in full flower into 1 gallon of spirits of wine, this was allowed to stand for four days and then distilled. Hungary water was also considered very efficacious against gout in the hands and feet, being rubbed into them vigorously.

A formula dated 1235, said to be in the handwriting of Elizabeth, Queen of Hungary, is said to be preserved in Vienna.

Rosemary Wine when taken in small quantities acts as a quieting cordial to a weak heart subject to palpitation, and relieves accompanying dropsy by stimulating the kidneys. It is made by chopping up sprigs of green Rosemary and pouring on them white wine, which is strained off after a few days and is then ready for use. By stimulating the brain and nervous system, it is a good remedy for headaches caused by feeble circulation.

The young tops, leaves and flowers can be made into an infusion, called Rosemary Tea, which, taken warm, is a good remedy for removing headache, colic, colds and nervous diseases, care being taken to prevent the escape of steam during its preparation. It will relieve nervous depression. A conserve, made by beating up the freshly gathered tops with three times their weight of sugar, is said to have the same effect.

A spirit of Rosemary may be used, in doses of 30 drops in water or on sugar, as an antispasmodic.

Rosemary and Coltsfoot leaves are considered good when rubbed together and smoked for asthma and other affections of the throat and lungs.

Rosemary is also one of the ingredients used in the preparation of Eau-de-Cologne.

¶ *Preparations.* Oil, ½ to 3 drops. Spirit, B.P., 5 to 20 drops.

ROSES

N.O. Rosaceæ

Roses are a group of herbaceous shrubs found in temperate regions throughout both hemispheres. All the Roses of the Antipodes, South Africa and the temperate parts of South America have been carried there by cultivation.

[1] Rosemary is one of the plants like lavender which grows better in England than anywhere else, and English oil of Rosemary, though it is infinitely superior to that of other countries, is hardly found in commerce to-day. The bulk of the commercial oil comes from France, Dalmatia, Spain and Japan. – EDITOR.

The birthplace of the cultivated Rose was probably Northern Persia, on the Caspian, or Faristan on the Gulf of Persia. Thence it spread across Mesopotamia to Palestine and across Asia Minor to Greece. And thus it was that Greek colonists brought it to Southern Italy. It is beyond doubt that the Roses used in ancient days were cultivated varieties. Horace, who writes at length on horticulture, gives us an interesting account of the growing of Roses in beds. Pliny advises the deep digging of the soil for their better cultivation. In order to force their growth, it was the practice to dig a ditch round the plants and to pour warm water into the ditch just as the rose-buds had formed. The varieties were then very limited in number, but it would appear that the Romans, at all events, knew and cultivated the red Provins Rose (*Rosa gallica*), often mistakenly called the Provence Rose. The word *rosa* comes from the Greek word *rodon* (red), and the rose of the Ancients was of a deep crimson colour, which probably suggested the fable of its springing from the blood of Adonis.

The voluptuous Romans of the later Empire made lavish use of the blossoms of the Rose. Horace enjoins their unsparing use at banquets, when they were used not only as a means of decoration, but also to strew the floors, and even in winter the luxurious Romans expected to have petals of roses floating in their Falernian wine. Roman brides and bridegrooms were crowned with roses, so too were the images of Cupid and Venus and Bacchus. Roses were scattered at feasts of Flora and Hymen, in the paths of victors, or beneath their chariot-wheels, or adorned the prows of their war-vessels. Nor did the self-indulgent Romans disdain to wear rose garlands at their feasts, as a preventive against drunkenness. To them, the Rose was a sign of pleasure, the companion of mirth and wine, but it was also used at their funerals.

As soon as the Rose had become known to nations with a wide literature of their own, it was not only the theme of poets, but gave rise to many legends. Homer's allusions to it in the *Iliad* and *Odyssey* are the earliest records, and Sappho, the Greek poetess, writing about 600 B.C., selects the Rose as the Queen of Flowers. (The 'Rose of Sharon' of the Old Testament is considered to be a kind of Narcissus, and the 'Rose of Jericho' is a small woody annual, also not allied to the Rose.)

It was once the custom to suspend a Rose over the dinner-table as a sign that all confidences were to be held sacred. Even now the plaster ornament in the centre of a ceiling is known as 'the rose.' It has been suggested that because the Pretender could only be helped secretly, *sub rosa*, that the Jacobites took the white rose as his symbol. Although we have no British 'Order of the Rose,' our national flower figures largely in the insignia of other orders, such as the Garter, the order of the Bath, etc.

¶ *Constituents*. The essential oil to which the perfume of the Rose is due is found in both flowers and leaves, sometimes in one, sometimes in both, and sometimes in neither, for there are also scentless roses. In the flower, the petals are the chief secreting part of the blossom, though a certain amount of essential oil resides in the epidermal layers of cells, both surfaces of the petals being equally odorous and secretive. An examination of the stamens, which are transformed into petals in the cultivated roses, shows that the epidermal cells also contain essential oil.

More than 10,000 roses are known in cultivation and three types of odours are recognized, viz. those of the Cabbage Rose (*R. centifolia*), the Damask Rose (*R. damascena*) and the Tea Rose (*R. indica*), but there are many roses of intermediate character as regards perfume, notably the 'perpetual hybrid' and 'hybrid tea' classes, which exhibit every gradation between the three types and no precise classification of roses by their odour is possible.

The flowers adapted for the preparation of essence of roses are produced by several species of rose trees. The varieties cultivated on a large scale for perfumery purposes are *R. damascena* and *R. centifolia*. *R. damascena* is cultivated chiefly in Bulgaria, Persia and India: it is a native of the Orient and was introduced into Europe at the period of the Crusades. *R. centifolia* is cultivated in Provence, Turkey and Tunis; it has been found wild in the forests of the Caucasus, where double-flowered specimens are often met with.

Although the Rose was highly esteemed in the dawn of history, it does not appear that it was then submitted to the still, the method of preserving the aroma being to steep the petals in oil, or possibly to extract it in the form of a pomade. The *Oleum Rosarum*, *Ol. rosatum* or *Ol. rosacetum* of the Ancients was not a volatile oil, but a fatty oil perfumed with rose petals. The first preparation of rosewater by Avicenna was in the tenth century. It was between 1582 and 1612 that the oil or OTTO OF ROSES was discovered, as recorded in two separate histories of the Grand Moguls. At the wedding feast of the princess Nour-Djihan with the Emperor Djihanguyr, son of Akbar, a canal circling the whole gardens was dug and filled with rose-water. The heat of the sun separating the water from the essential oil of the Rose, was observed by the bridal pair when rowing on the fragrant water. It was skimmed off and found to be an exquisite perfume. The discovery was immediately turned to account and the manufacture of Otto of Roses was commenced in Persia about 1612 and long before the end of the seventeenth century the distilleries of Shiraz were working on a large scale. The first mention of Persian Otto or Attar of Roses is by Kampfer (1683), who alludes to the export to India. Persia no longer exports Attar of Roses to any extent, and the production in Kashmir and elsewhere in India – probably as ancient as that of Persia – practically serves for local consumption only.

Through the Turks, the manufacture was introduced into Europe, by way of Asia Minor, where it has long been produced. It is probable that the first otto was distilled in Bulgaria, then part of the Turkish Empire, about 1690 – its sale in Europe, at a high cost, is first alluded to in 1694 – but the importance of the Turkish otto industry is of comparatively late growth, and Turkish otto is not mentioned as an article of English commerce until the beginning of the last century.

A small amount of Otto of Roses has been produced in the South of France for at least 150 years, having been an established industry there before the French Revolution, but these earlier French ottos, almost entirely derived from *R. centifolia*, as a by-product in rose-water distillation, were consumed in the country itself. French roses were almost exclusively used for the manufacture of rose-pomade and of rose-water, the French rose-water having the reputation of being superior in odour to any that can be produced in England. In spite of their unrivalled delicacy of fragrance, which always commanded a high place in the estimation of connoisseurs, until recent years the high price and lack of body of French ottos did not enable them to compete for general purposes with the Balkan concrete oil. When, however, Bulgaria joined the Central Empires, the French seized their opportunity, and methods of distillation were modernized, improved stills were erected and many other blooms than those of *R. centifolia* were experimented with, until now French otto has made itself a place in perfumery. Large plantations of roses have been laid down, and the output of otto is increasing steadily, 10,000 to 20,000 oz. being at present the annual production. French chemists, botanists and horticulturists have studied the scientific aspect of the Rose, and in the new roses introduced, the chief object has been to improve the odour rather than the appearance of the flower. The variety of rose mostly cultivated is the *Rose de Mai*, a hybrid of *R. gallica* and *R. centifolia*, bearing recurved prickles on the flowering branches. Two types are grown in the Grasse district, one more spiny than the other. They are mingled in the plantations, but the more spiny is preferred for less irrigated ground and the one with fewer thorns for well-watered land. The bushes are planted half a metre apart, in rows one metre asunder. The first fortnight in May sees the rose harvest. The buds open gradually and are numerous, as each stalk bears a dense cluster and all the annual stems are well-covered. In the second half of May, after flowering, they are cut back and the complete pruning takes place in the following November. A rose plantation lasts from eight to ten years. Five thousand rose-trees will occupy about ¼ acre of land and will produce about 2,200 lb. of flowers during the season. It is necessary to distil about 10,000 lb. of roses to obtain 1 lb. of oil. By the volatile solvents process a similar quantity will give anything up to 10 lb. of concrete. The rose-trees cultivated at Grasse in the last few years have been much attacked by disease, and in the opinion of some authorities the variety most grown hitherto would appear to be degenerating. The plantations are all more or less attacked by the rose rust parasite (*Pragmidium subcorticium*).

Quite recently a new and very promising rose has been introduced, known as the *Rose de Hai*, produced by crossing *R. damascena* with 'General Jacqueminot,' which in its turn is derived from *R. rugosa*, or the Japanese and Kamschatkan Rose. It has the advantage of not being so sensitive to heat and cold as the *Rose de Mai* and can be cultivated in the north of France, or as far south as Algeria. Its flowering period is much longer than that of the *Rose de Mai* and it gives more blooms and the oil is of almost equal quality. A certain amount of French otto is also distilled from garden roses. 'Ulrich Brunner,' distilled with other garden blooms, give a fair quality oil or concrete, known as 'Roses de France.' Other varieties which frequently enter into the composition of 'Roses de France' concretes are 'Grussan Teplitz,' 'Frau Karl Druschky,' Narbonnand, Van Houtte, Safrano, Paul Neyron, Madame Gabriel Luizet, Madame Caroline Testout, Baronne de Rothschild, Mrs. John Laing, Madame Maurice de Luze, François Juranville, Gerbe Rose and Gloire d'un Enfant d'Hiram.

Oil of Rose is light yellow in colour, sometimes possessing a green tint. It has a strong odour of fresh roses. When cooled, it congeals to a translucent soft mass, which is again liquefied by the warmth of the hand. The congealing point lies between 15° and 22° C., mostly between 17° and 21° C.

The composition of Rose oil is not quite uniform, the variation being due to a number of influences, the chief being the kind of flower and the locality in which it has been grown. The Rose oil from plants grown in colder climates contains a very high percentage of the waxy substance stearoptene, odourless and valueless as a perfume. This was the first constituent of Rose oil to be studied and was recognized as paraffin hydrocarbon by Fluckiger: it consists of a mixture of hydrocarbons. Sometimes this stearoptene is removed by large distillers and the resulting oil sold at a higher price as stearoptene-free Otto of Roses. Geraniol and Citronellol are the chief ingredients of Rose oil as regards percentage, though not the most characteristic as regards odour. Citronellol, a fragrant, oily liquid, forms about 35 per cent. of the oil. Geraniol, which may be present to the amount of 75 per cent., is a colourless liquid, with a sweet, rose-like odour. It is also found in Palmarosa or Turkish Geranium oil and in oils of Citronella, Lavender, Neroli, Petit Grain, Ylang Ylang, Lemongrass and some Eucalyptus oils. It is largely obtained industrially from the oils of Palmarosa and Citronella and is much used to adulterate Otto of Roses. The temptation to adulterate so expensive an oil is great and it is widely practised. Bulgaria usually exports from 30 to 60 per cent. more otto than is distilled in the country. This is due to the enormous amount of adulteration that takes place. This is so well done that a chemical analysis is imperative to ascertain the purity of the oil. The principal adulterant is Geraniol. The addition of this, or of Palmarosa oil, which contains it, either to the rose leaves before distillation, or to the product, reduces the congealing point, but this can be brought up to the normal standard by the addition of spermaceti. Hence in addition to the congealing point, the determination of the absence of spermaceti may become necessary. Another recent adulterant of importance, employed in Bulgaria, is the Guaiac Wood Oil, from *Bulnesia sarmienti*, which has an agreeable tea-rose-like odour. It can be recognized by the microscopic examination of the form of the crystals of guaicol, which separate from the oil on cooling. Guaicol forms needle-shaped crystals which are characterized by a channel-like middle-line. The crystals of the Rose oil paraffin are smaller and thinner and possess less sharply-outlined forms. The addition of Guaiac Wood oil to Rose oil raises the congealing point of the oil and increases the specific gravity and its presence may thus be detected.

A satisfactory artificial Otto of Rose cannot be obtained by the exclusive combination of aromatic chemicals, some of the natural oil must always enter into the composition of any artificial rose oil, or a purely synthetic oil may be distilled over a certain quantity of rose petals. A striking difference between synthetic and natural rose oils is that the former is almost entirely deodorized by iodine, while the latter is unaffected in this respect.

Apart from French Otto of Roses, the world's supply is mainly drawn from Bulgaria, the greater part being distilled by small peasant growers. The Bulgarian rose industry is confined to one special mountain district, having for its centre the town of Kazanlik. The rose district is about 80 miles long and about 30 miles wide and its average elevation about 1,300 feet above the sea-level. Attempts to extend the rose culture to other neighbouring districts in Bulgaria have proved a failure. The rose bush seems to thrive best in sandy soil, well exposed to the sun, protected from the cold winter winds and having perfect drainage. It is chiefly the mountain formation, the climatic peculiarities and the special sandy soil of the rose district which adapt it for this industry, in which, in addition to their other farm culture, about 180 villages are engaged. There are about 20,000 small proprietors of rose gardens, each one owning about 1 acre of rose plantation, which, when well tended, is calculated to yield at the average 100 lb. of flowers every day for three weeks.

Only two varieties of roses are cultivated in Bulgaria, the Damask Rose (*R. damascena*), light red in colour and very fragrant, with 36 petals, and the Musk Rose (*R. muscatta*), a snow-white rose, far less fragrant, yielding an oil of poorer quality, very rich in stearoptene, but containing very little otto. It is of more vigorous growth and is grown chiefly for hedges between the plantations to indicate the divisions of the rose fields. The rose bushes only yield one crop a year, the harvest beginning in the latter half of May and lasting from two to five weeks, according to the weather. The weather during the rose harvest has a great influence on the quality and quantity of the crop – should it be exceptionally dry and hot, the crop may only last two weeks and be poor, but if it be cool, with some rainfall, there is a rich yield, lasting over four or even six weeks. The weather during the budding season has also to be reckoned with, dry and hot weather causing the bushes to throw out only very small clusters of buds, while in favourable weather 13, 21 and even 18 buds will be found in the clusters. The flowers are gathered in the early morning, just before the sun rises and the picking should cease by ten or eleven o'clock, unless the day be cloudy, when it continues all day. The flowers are distilled on the same day. It takes 30 roses to make 1 drop of otto and 60,000 roses (about 180 lb. of flowers) to make 1 oz. of otto.

The small stills used by the farmers are very simple and primitive and are only capable of distilling at a time 24 lb. of flowers, but they are gradually being replaced by modern, improved, large steam stills, which obtain results immeasurably greater. In 1918, some far-sighted and influential rose-essence producers in Bulgaria combined to unite all parties interested in this industry into an association for mutual advantage. Of the membership of 5,000 nearly half were collective members, i.e. co-operative societies, so that the membership represents a very large number of growers. The objects of the association are: (1) to procure cheap credit for its members; (2) to prevent adulteration; (3) to organize joint distillation; (4) to provide the societies with the requisite apparatus for producing the otto.

The Bulgarian rose industry has developed steadily since 1885, though the Great War seriously handicapped it.

Bulgarian rose distillers do not obtain all their otto direct from the petals, but draw the greater part by treating the water. They charge the alembic with ten kills of flowers (about 25 lb.) and about 50 litres of water. They draw from this charge, 10 litres of distilled water, from which they gather a very small quantity of green concrete essence. When they have made four distillations, they carefully collect the 40 litres of water and re-distil, and obtain 10 or 15 litres of liquid. It is reckoned that 4,000 kilos of flowers yield 1 kilo of otto, of which only one-third – the green essence – comes from the first distillation and the other two-thirds – yellow – are the result of re-distilling the waters. This is the reason why in France, some 10,000 kilos of flowers are required for 1 kilo of oil, as French distillers do not re-distil the waters; these are sold separately. The product of the first operation is of markedly superior quality.

In 1919 the entire Bulgarian crop of Otto of Roses was taken over by the Government of that country in consequence of an agreement between the Bulgarian Government and the United States Food Administration, by which payment for food supplied to Bulgaria from America was to be made out of the proceeds of the Bulgarian otto crop.

¶ *Cyprus Otto of Roses.* In Cyprus, rose cultivation for Otto has of late years been keenly developed. It had been prepared since 1897 in a very small way with native stills at the village of Milikouri, where the Damask Rose is abundant, but no attempt had been made to extract the Rose oil by means of a modern still. The closing of the market for Bulgarian Otto of Roses, owing to the War, gave an impetus to the industry, and in the spring of 1917 the Department of Agriculture of Cyprus sent qualified officers to superintend the work at Milikouri and to carry out an experimental distillation. The samples of 1917 oil sent to the Imperial Institute were found to be similar to the Bulgarian article, though rather weaker.

¶ *Roses in Germany, Algiers and Morocco.* Otto of Roses is also prepared in Algiers to a limited extent and in Germany, from large rose plantations near Leipzig.

The cultivation of roses is already extensively practised in Morocco for the distillation of rose-water, which enters so largely into native perfumery, but there is no production of Otto of Roses on a commercial scale.

¶ *Indian Rose Otto.* The two main centres of the Rose industry in India are Ghazipore and Hathras, in Upper India. Rose plantations exist in the neighbourhood of both these places, but the industry is confined to the manufacture of rose-water and small quantities of Aytar – a mixture of Sandalwood oil and Otto of Roses.

¶ *Medicinal Action and Uses.* The petals of the dark red Rose, *R. gallica*, known as the Provins Rose, are employed medicinally for the preparation of an infusion and a confection. In this country it is specially grown for medicinal purposes in Oxfordshire and Derbyshire.

The petals of this rose are of a deep, purplish-red, velvety in texture, paler towards the base. They have the delicate fragrance of the Damask Rose and a slightly astringent taste.

The British Pharmacopœia directs that Red Rose petals are to be obtained only from *R. gallica*, of which, however, there are many variations, in fact there are practically no pure *R. gallica* now to be had, only hybrids, so that the exact requirements of the British Pharmacopœia are difficult to follow. Those used in medicine and generally appearing in commerce are actually any scented roses of a deep red colour, or when dried of a deep rose tint. The main point is that the petals suitable for medicinal purposes must yield a deep rose-coloured and somewhat astringent and fragrant infusion when boiling water is poured upon them. The most suitable are the so-called Hybrid Perpetuals, flowering from June to October, among which may be specially recommended the varieties:

Eugène Furst, deep dark red, sweet-scented.

General Jacqueminot, a fine, rich crimson, scented rose.

Hugh Dickson, rather a large petalled one, but of a fine, deep red colour and sweet-scented.

Ulrich Brunner, bright-red.

Richmond, deep crimson-red.

Liberty, scarlet-red.

¶ *Collection and Preparation*. When employed for the preparation of the drug, only flower-buds just about to open are collected, no fully-expanded flowers. They must only be gathered in dry weather and no petals of any roses that have suffered from effects of damp weather must be taken. The whole of the unexpanded petals are plucked from the calyx so that they remain united in small conical masses, leaving the stamens behind. Any stamens that may have come away with the petals should be shaken out. The lighter-coloured, lower portion is then cut off from the deep purplish-red upper part. The little masses, kept as entire as possible, are used in the fresh state for preparation of the 'confection,' but for making the infusion, they are dried carefully and quickly on trays in a good current of warm air. They are dried until crisp and while crisp packed in tins that the colour and crispness may be retained. If exposed to the air, they will re-absorb moisture and lose colour.

¶ *Constituents*. The important constituent of Red Rose petals is the red colouring matter of an acid nature. There have also been isolated two yellow crystalline substances, the glucoside *Quercitrin*, which has been found in many other plants and *Quercetin*, yielded when Quercitrin is boiled with a dilute mineral acid. The astringency is due to a little gallic acid, but it has not yet been definitely proved whether quercitannic acid, the tannin of oak bark, is also a constituent. The odour is due to a very small amount of volatile oil, not identical with the official *Ol. Rosæ*. A considerable amount of sugar, gum, fat, etc., are also present.

¶ *Preparations*. Red Rose petals are official in nearly all Pharmacopœias. Though formerly employed for their mild astringency and tonic value, they are to-day used almost solely to impart their pleasant odour to pharmaceutical preparations. The British Pharmacopœia preparations are a Confection, Acid Infusion and a Fluid Extract. The *Confection* is directed to be made by beating 1 lb. of fresh Red Rose petals in a stone mortar with 3 lb. of sugar. It is mostly used in pill making. Formerly this was prescribed for hæmorrhage of the lungs and for coughs. The United States official confection is made by rubbing Red Rose petals, powdered, with heated rose-water, adding gradually fine, white sugar and heating the whole together till thoroughly mixed. The *Fluid Extract* is made from powdered Red Rose petals with glycerine and dilute alcohol. It is of a deep red colour, an agreeable odour of rose and of a pleasant, mildly astringent taste. The *Acid Infusion* is made from dried, broken-up, Red Rose petals, diluted with sulphuric acid, sugar and boiling water, infused in a covered vessel for 15 minutes and strained. It has a fine red colour and agreeable flavour and has been employed for its astringent effects in the treatment of stomatitis and pharyngitis. Its virtue is principally due to the aromatic sulphuric acid which it contains and the latter ingredient renders it a useful preparation, in the treatment of night-sweats resulting from depression. A *Simple* (non-acid) *Infusion* is mainly used as a flavouring for other medicines. It is also used as a lotion for ophthalmia, etc.

Syrup of Red Rose, official in the United States Pharmacopœia, is used to impart an agreeable flavour and odour to other syrups and mixtures. The syrup is of a fine red colour and has an agreeable, acidulous, somewhat astringent taste. *Honey of Roses*, also official in the United States Pharmacopœia, is prepared from clarified honey and fluid extract of roses. It is considered more agreeable than ordinary honey and somewhat astringent. In olden days, Honey of Roses was popular for sore throats and ulcerated mouth and was made by pounding fresh petals in a small quantity of boiling water, filtering the mass and boiling the liquid with honey. *Rose Vinegar*, a specific on the Continent for headache caused by hot sun, is prepared by steeping dried rose petals in best distilled vinegar, which should not be boiled. Cloths or linen rags are soaked in the liquid and are then applied to the head.

Two liqueurs made by the French also have rose petals as one of the chief ingredients. A small quantity of spirits of wine is distilled with the petals to produce 'Spirit of Roses.' The fragrant spirit, when mixed with sugar, undergoes certain preparatory processes and makes the liqueur called 'L'Huile de Rose.' It is likewise the base of another liqueur, called 'Parfait Amour.'

ROSA CENTIFOLIA.

The pale petals of the Hundred-leaved Rose or Cabbage Rose are also used in commerce. On account of its fragrance, the petals of this variety of rose are much used in France for distillation of rose-water. Though possessing aperient properties, they are seldom now used internally and preparations of them are not official in the British Pharmacopœia.

The roses grouped as varieties of *R. centifolia* have all less scent than *R. gallica*.

The best of them is the old Cabbage Rose. It is a large rose, sweet-scented, of a pink or pale rose-purple colour, the petals whitish towards the base. Its branches are covered with numerous nearly straight spines: the petioles and peduncles are nearly unarmed, but more or less clothed with glandular bristles and the leaves have five or sometimes seven ovate, glandular leaflets, softly hairy beneath. This species and its varieties have given rise to innumerable handsome garden roses.

The flowers are collected and deprived of the calyx and ovaries, the petals alone being employed. In drying, they become brownish and lose some of their delicious rose odour.

The *Constituents* of the Pink Rose are closely similar to those of the Red. The very little colouring matter is apparently identical with that of the Red Rose. A little tannin is present.

Rose-water. The British Pharmacopœia directs that it shall be prepared by mixing the distilled rose-water of commerce, obtained mostly from *R. damascena*, but also from *R. centifolia* and other species, with twice its volume of distilled water immediately before use. It is used as a vehicle for other medicines and as an eye lotion. *Triple rose-water* is water saturated with volatile oil of Rose petals, obtained as a by-product in the distillation of oil of Roses. The finest rose-water is obtained by distillation of the fresh petals. It should be clear and colourless, not mucilaginous, and to be of value medicinally must be free from all metallic impurities, which may be detected by hydrogen sulphide and ammonium sulphide, neither of which should produce turbidity in the water.

Ointment of rose-water, commonly known as *Cold Cream*, enjoys deserved popularity as a soothing, cooling application for chapping of the hands, face, abrasions and other superficial lesions of the skin. For its preparation, the British Pharmacopœia directs that 1½ oz. each of spermaceti and white wax be melted with 9 oz. of Almond oil, the mixture poured into a warmed mortar and 7 fluid ounces of rose-water and 8 minims of oil of Rose then incorporated with it.

¶ *Medicinal Action and Uses.* The old herbalists considered the Red Rose to be more binding and more astringent than any of the other species:

'it strengtheneth the heart, the stomach, the liver and the retentive faculty; is good against all kinds of fluxes, prevents vomiting, stops tickling coughs and is of service in consumption.'

Culpepper gives many uses for the Rose, both white and red and damask.

'Of the Red Roses are usually made many compositions, all serving to sundry good uses, viz. electuary of roses, conserve both moist and dry, which is usually called sugar of roses, syrup of dry roses and honey of roses; the cordial powder called aromatic rosarum, the distilled water of roses, vinegar of roses, ointment and oil of roses and the rose leaves dried are of very great use and effect.'

'The electuary,' he tells us, 'is purging and is good in hot fevers, jaundice and joint-aches. The moist conserve is of much use both binding and cordial, the old conserve mixed with aromaticum rosarum is a very good preservative in the time of infection. The dry conserve called the sugar of roses is a very good cordial against faintings, swoonings, weakness and trembling of the heart, strengthens a weak stomach, promotes digestion and is a very good preservative in the time of infection. The dry conserve called the sugar of roses is a very good cordial to strengthen the heart and spirit. The syrup of roses cooleth an over-heated liver and the blood in agues, comforteth the heart and resisteth putrefaction and infection. Honey of roses is used in gargles and lotions to wash sores, either in the mouth, throat or other parts, both to cleanse and heal them. Red rose-water is well known, it is cooling, cordial, refreshing, quickening the weak and faint spirits, used either in meats or broths to smell at the nose, or to smell the sweet vapours out of a perfume pot, or cast into a hot fire-shovel. It is of much use against the redness and inflammation of the eyes to bathe therewith and the temples of the head. The ointment of roses is much used against heat and inflammation of the head, to anoint the forehead and temples and to cool and heal red pimples. Oil of roses is used to cool hot inflammation or swellings and to bind and stay fluxes of humours to sores and is also put into ointments and plasters that are cooling and binding. The dried leaves of the red roses are used both outwardly and inwardly; they cool, bind and are cordial. Rose-leaves and mint, heated and applied outwardly to the stomach, stay castings, strengthen a weak stomach and applied as a fomentation to the region of the liver and heart, greatly cool and temper them, quiet the over-heated spirits and cause rest and sleep. The decoction of red roses made with white wine and used is very good for head-ache and pains in the eyes, ears, throat and gums.'

¶ *Preparations*. Rose-water, B.P., 1 to 2 oz. Fluid extract, ½ to 1 drachm. Confec., B.P. and U.S.P., 2 to 4 drachms. Infusion acid, B.P., ½ to 1 oz. Syrup, U.S.P. Oil, B.P.

In modern herbal medicine the flowers of the common Red Rose dried are given in infusions and sometimes in powder for hæmorrhage. A tincture is made from them by pouring 1 pint of boiling water on 1 oz. of the dried petals, adding 15 drops of oil of Vitriol and 3 or 4 drachms of white sugar. The tincture when strained is of a beautiful red colour. Three or four spoonsful of the tincture taken two or three times a day are considered good for strengthening the stomach and a pleasant remedy in all hæmorrhages.

Culpepper mentions a syrup made of the *pale* red petals of the Damask Rose by infusing them 24 hours in boiling water, then straining off the liquor and adding twice the weight of refined sugar to it, stating that this syrup is an excellent purge for children and adults of a costive habit, a small quantity to be taken every night. A conserve of the buds has the same properties as the syrup.

WILD ROSES.

The actual number of the roses indigenous to Great Britain is a subject open to dispute among botanists, as the roses found wild show many variations. Most authorities agree that there are only five distinct types or species: *R. canina*, the Dog Rose; *R. arvensis*, the Field Rose; *R. rubiginosa*, Sweet Briar; *R. spinosissima*, the Burnet Rose; and *R. villosa*, the Downy Rose.

The DOG ROSE (*R. canina*) is a flower of the early summer, its blossoms expanding in the first days of June and being no more to be found after the middle of July. The general growth of the Dog Rose is subject to so much variation that the original species defined by Linnæus has been divided by later botanists into four or five subspecies. The flowers vary very considerably in colour, from almost white to a very deep pink, and have a delicate but refreshing fragrance. The scarlet fruit, or hip (a name that has come down from the Anglo-Saxon *hiope*), is generally described as 'flask-shaped.' It is what botanists term a false fruit, because it is really the stalk-end that forms it and grows up round the central carpels, enclosing them as a case; the *real*

fruits, each containing one seed, are the little hairy objects within it. Immediately the flower has been fertilized, the receptacle round the immature fruits grows gradually luscious and red and forms the familiar 'hip,' which acts as a bait for birds, by whose agency the seeds are distributed. At first the hips are tough and crowned with the five-cleft calyx leaves, later in autumn they fall and the hips are softer and more fleshy. The pulp of the hips has a grateful acidity. In former times when garden fruit was scarce, hips were esteemed for dessert. Gerard assures us that 'the fruit when it is ripe maketh the most pleasante meats and banketting dishes as tartes and such-like,' the making whereof he commends 'to the cunning cooke and teethe to eate them in the riche man's mouth.' Another old writer says:

'Children with great delight eat the berries thereof when they are ripe and make chains and other pretty geegaws of the fruit; cookes and gentlewomen make tarts and suchlike dishes for pleasure.'

The Germans still use them to make an ordinary preserve and in Russia and Sweden a kind of wine is made by fermenting the fruit.

Rose hips were long official in the British Pharmacopœia for refrigerant and astringent properties, but are now discarded and only used in medicine to prepare the confection of hips used in conjunction with other drugs, the pulp being separated from the skin and hairy seeds and beaten up with sugar. It is astringent and considered strengthening to the stomach and useful in diarrhœa and dysentery, allaying thirst, and for its pectoral qualities good for coughs and spitting of blood. Culpepper states that the hips are 'grateful to the taste and a considerable restorative, fitly given to consumptive persons, the conserve being proper in all distempers of the breast and in coughs and tickling rheums' and that it has 'a binding effect and helps digestion.' He also states that 'the pulp of the hips dried and powdered is used in drink to break the stone and to ease and help the colic.' The constituents of rose hips are malic and citric acids, sugar and small quantities of tannin, resin, wax, malates, citrates and other salts.

The *leaves* of the Dog Rose when dried and infused in boiling water have often been used as a substitute for tea and have a grateful smell and sub-astringent taste. The *flowers*, gathered in the bud and dried, are said to be more astringent than the Red Roses. They contain no honey and are visited by insects only for their pollen. Their scent is not strong enough to be of any practical use for distillation purposes.

Two explanations have been put forward for the popular name of this wild rose. The first is founded on an ancient tradition that the root would cure a bite from a mad dog (Pliny affirming that men derived their knowledge of its powers from a dream); and the other and more probable theory that it was the Dag Rose – 'dag' being a dagger – because of its great thorns, and like the 'Dogwood' (originally Dagwood) became changed into 'Dog' by people who did not understand the allusion.

The FIELD ROSE (*R. arvensis*) is generally a much more trailing rose than the Dog Rose, a characteristic which distinguishes it from all our other wild roses. It is widely distributed throughout England, but is much less common in Scotland and Ireland.

The leaves in general form are similar to those of the Dog Rose, but are often rather smaller and their surfaces more shining. The prickles, too, are somewhat smaller in size, but are more hooked. The flowers are white, much less fragrant than those of the Dog Rose and sometimes even scentless. Though occasionally occurring singly on the stem, they are generally in small bunches of three or four at the ends of the twigs, though only one of these at a time will as a rule be found expanded. This species generally comes into blossom rather later than the Dog Rose and continues in bloom a good deal longer. It is one of the chief ornaments of our hedge-rows, in the summer, from the profusion of its blossoms and long trailing stems; and in the autumn, by its scarlet hips, which are more globular in form than those of the Dog Rose. It has its styles united into a central column and not free or separate, as in the Dog Rose.

SWEET BRIAR (*R. rubiginosa*). The flowers of the Sweet Briar are a little smaller than those of the Dog Rose and generally of a deeper hue, though of a richer tint in some plants than in others. They are in bloom during June and July. The fruit is eggshaped, its broadest part being uppermost or farthest from the stem.

The specific name *rubiginosa* signifies, in Latin, 'rusty,' the plant having been thus named as both stems and leaves are often of a brownish-red tint. It delights in open copses, though is sometimes found also in old hedgerows and is more specially met with in chalk districts in the south of England.

Its fragrance of foliage is peculiarly its own and has led to it holding a cherished place in many old gardens. Under its older name of Eglantine its praises have been sung by poets.

It takes a shower to bring out the full sweetness of Sweet Briar, when its strong and refreshing fragrance will fill the air and be borne a long distance by the breeze. Though the leaves are so highly odorous, the flowers are almost entirely without scent.

Sweet Briar only obtains a place among perfumes in name, for like many other sweet-scented plants, it does not repay the labour of collecting its odour, the fragrant part of the plant being destroyed more or less under treatment. An Essence under this name is, however, prepared, compounded of various floral essences so blended as to resemble the spicy fragrance of the growing plant. In olden days the Sweet Briar was used medicinally.

Briarwood pipes are not made from the wood of either the Sweet Briar or of any wild rose, but from that of the Tree Heath (*Erica arborea*).

The BURNET ROSE (*R. spinosissima*), known also as the Pimpernel Rose, or Scotch Rose, is generally found on waste land near the sea, more rarely on dry, heath-clad hills inland. The whole plant rarely attains to more than a foot or so in height. Its stems are armed with numerous, straight thorns – hence its specific name, signifying in Latin 'exceedingly prickly.' The English name is given it from the fact that the general form of its small leaves, with seven or nine leaflets to each leaf, is very similar to those of the Burnet (*Poterium sanguisorba*) and the Burnet Saxifrage (*Pimpinella*).

The white or sulphur-tinted flowers are usually placed singly and are rather small. The roundish fruit is so deep a purple as to appear almost black. The juice of the ripe fruit has been used in the preparation of dye: diluted with water, it dyes silk and muslin of a peach colour and mixed with alum gives a beautiful violet, but is considered too fugitive to be of any real economic value.

This rose is frequently cultivated in gardens and a great many varieties have been raised from it. The first double variety was found in a wild state in the neighbourhood of Perth and from this one were produced about 50 others. The French have over 100 distinct varieties.

The DOWNY ROSE (*R. villosa*) is found only in England in the north and west, but is common in Scotland, Ireland and Wales. It receives its specific name from the downy texture of both sides of the leaves, the Latin word *villosa* meaning softly hairy.

This species is subject to many variations, five or six of which have been by some botanists considered separate species. The flowers are white or pale pink. The fruit, which is globular, is covered with fine prickles.

The stems of the various kinds of wild rose are often found tufted with little fluffy balls of what look like crimson moss. These are really galls and result from the puncture of a small insect, a kind of wasp – the *Rose Gall* – in a similar manner as Oak Galls are formed. The wasp punctures a leaf while it is yet undeveloped in the bud and there lays its eggs. Immediately the normal growth of the leaf alters and numerous larvæ are formed, which hatch out and creep further into the leaf tissues until the whole swells into the moss-like gall we know. In the Middle Ages these Rose Galls, under the name of Bedeguar, were held in high repute in medicine for their astringency and supposed power of inducing sleep if placed under the pillow at night.

POT-POURRI OF ROSES.

All varieties of both *R. gallica* and *R. centifolia* are used in the making of pot-pourri, the dried petals of all scented roses being valuable for the purpose as they retain their scent for a considerable time. Nearly every fragrant flower and scented leaf can be used as an ingredient of pot-pourri, blending with suitable spices to give charm to this favourite, old-fashioned sweet mixture, which in winter recalls so delightfully the vanished summer days. It must be understood that rose-petals should preponderate, and that the other component parts ought to be added in such proportions that the scent of one cannot kill the perfume of another.

There are two principal methods of making pot-pourri, the *dry* and the *moist*.

For the *dry* kind, the bulk of the rose-petals is fully dried and everything else – Sweet Geranium and Sweet Verbena leaves, Bay leaves and Lavender is also dried. The best way of drying is to spread out on sheets of paper in an airy room. Anything of lasting scent, such as cedar or sandalwood sawdust, or shavings, can be added. When all is ready, the spices and sweet gums, all in powder, are put together and the whole is thoroughly mixed. For two-thirds of a bushel of dried petals and leaves, the *spice mixture* is 2 oz. each of Cloves, Mace and Cinnamon, ½ oz. each of Coriander, Allspice, Gum Storax and Gum Benzoin, and 4 oz. Violet Powder.

The *moist* method of preparation takes more time and needs greater care. The rose leaves are not fully, but only partly dried, so that they lose a good half of their bulk and acquire a kind of tough, leathery consistency. To preserve them and to maintain them in this state, a certain proportion of salt is added. The salt is a mixture of half Bay salt and half common salt. Bay Salt is sold in lumps; these are roughly pounded, so that some of it is quite small and the larger pieces are about the size of a small hazel nut, and then mixed with the common salt. The roses must be absolutely dry when picked. The petals are stripped off and carefully separated and laid out to partially dry. The length of time depends on the temperature and atmospheric conditions, but they are usually ready the second day after picking. Large jars of glazed earthenware should be employed for storing the rose leaves, the most convenient being cylindrical, with lids of the same glazed ware and with flat leaded disks (supplied with handles), for pressing down the contents. Put two good handsful of the rose leaves in at a time and press them down with the handled rammer. Then sprinkle a small handful of the salt mixture, then more rose leaves and so on. Then weight down till the next batch is put in. Besides rose leaves, the other chief ingredient is leaves of the Sweet Geranium, torn into shreds, dried like the Roses and put into the jars in the same way, rammed, salted and pressed. Bay leaves, Sweet Verbena and Lavender are all of a drier nature and can be put into the jars and salted just as they are. When all is ready, the contents of the preparation jars are taken out and broken up small; the mass, especially of the rose-petals, will come out in thick flakes, closely compacted. It is then mixed with the spices and sweet powders. If the freshly made mixture be rammed rather tightly into a jar or wooden barrel and left for six months, or better still for a year, the quality is much improved by being thus matured.

Mr. Donald McDonald, in *Sweet-scented Flowers and Fragrant Leaves*, gives the following pot-pourri recipes.

1. Gather early in the day and when perfectly dry, a peck of Roses, pick off the petals and strew over them ¾ lb. common salt. Let them remain two or three days and if fresh flowers are added, some more salt must be sprinkled over them. Mix with the roses ½ lb. of finely powdered Bay salt, the same quantity of allspice, cloves and brown sugar, ¼ lb. gum benzoin, and 2 oz. Orris root. Add 1 gill of brandy and any sort of fragrant flowers, such as Orange and Lemon flowers, Lavender and lemon-scented Verbena leaves and any other sweet-scented flowers. They should be perfectly dry when added. The mixture must be occasionally stirred and kept in close-covered jars, the covers to be raised only when the perfume is desired in the room. If after a time the mixture seems

to dry, moisten with brandy only, as essences too soon lose their quality and injure the perfume.

This mixture is said to retain its fragrance for fifty years.

II. Prepare 2 pecks of dry Rose leaves and buds, 1 handful each of Orange flowers, Violets and Jessamine, 1 oz. sliced Orris root and Cinnamon, ¼ oz. Musk, ¼ lb. sliced Angelica root, ¼ lb. of red part of Cloves (carnations), 2 handsful of Lavender flowers, Heliotrope and Mignonette, 1 handful each of Rosemary flowers, Bay and Laurel leaves, 3 sweet Oranges stuck full of cloves and dried in the oven and then powdered in a mortar, ¼ handful of Marjoram, 2 handfuls of Balm of Gilead dried, 1 handful each of Bergamot, Balm, Pineapple and Peppermint leaves. Mix well together and put in a large china jar; sprinkle salt between the layers, add a small bottle of extract of New-Mown Hay and moisten with brandy. If the mixture becomes too dry, stir it, adding liquid or additional leaves when wanted for use. If the jar is tightly corked, the preparation will keep and be fragrant for many years.

III. Take the rind of 2 Lemons, cut thin, 1 lb. Bay salt, 1 oz. of powdered Orris root, 1 oz. Gum Benzoin, 1 oz. Cinnamon, ½ oz. Cloves, 1 oz. Nutmegs, 1 grain Musk, 12 Bay leaves, a few Sage leaves, Rosemary and Lavender, cut small, 1 oz. Lavender Water, 1 oz. Eau-de-Cologne, 1 oz. Bergamot oil. Mix all together in a pan and add sweet flowers in their natural state as they come into blossom, stir up frequently – at least once a day. It must be put into a covered stone pot, with a wooden spoon to stir it with. At the end of two or three months, this will be a sweet-scented mass ready to fill any number of Japanese rose jars. From time to time throw in fresh Rose petals.

Lady Rosalind Northcote in *The Book of Herbs* gives:

I. *A Devonshire Recipe*

'Gather flowers in the morning when dry and lay them in the sun till the evening:
Roses, Orange flowers, Jasmine, Lavender, Thyme, Sage, Marjoram, Bay, } in smaller quantities.

'Put them into an earthen wide jar or hand basin in layers. Add the following ingredients:

6 lb. Bay Salt
4 oz. Yellow Sandal Wood
4 oz. Acorus Calamus Root
4 oz. Cassia Buds
2 oz. Cinnamon
2 oz. Cloves

4 oz. Gum Benzoin
1 oz. Storax Calamite
1 oz. Otto of Rose
1 drachm Musk
¼ oz. Powdered Cardamine Seeds.

'Place the rose leaves, etc., in layers in the jar. Sprinkle the Bay salt and other ingredients on each layer, press it tightly down and keep for two or three months before taking it out.'

II. *Sweet-Jar*

'¼ lb. Bay salt, ¼ lb. saltpetre and common salt, all to be bruised and put on six baskets of rose-leaves, 24 bay leaves torn to bits, a handful of sweet myrtle leaves, 6 handfuls of lavender blossom, a handful of orange or syringa blossoms, the same of sweet violets and the same of the red of clove carnations. After having well stirred every day for a week add ½ oz. cloves, 4 oz. orris root, ½ oz. cinnamon and 2 nutmegs, all pounded; put on the roses, kept well covered up in a china jar and stirred sometimes.

'Put alternate layers of rose leaves and Bay salt in an earthern pot. Press down with a plate and pour off the liquor that will be produced, every day for six weeks, taking care to press as dry as possible. Break up the mass and add the following ingredients well pounded and mixed together: Nutmeg, ¼ oz.; cloves, mace, cinnamon, gum benzoin, orris-root (sliced) 1 oz. each. Mix well with a wooden spoon. The rose leaves should be gathered on a dry, sunny afternoon, and the Bay salt roughly crushed before using. Orris root may be replaced with advantage by good violet powder.'

Besides the ingredients mentioned in these various recipes, the following may also be added: *leaves* of Basil, Bergamot, Mint, Lad's Love or Southernwood, Santolina, Costmary, Bog Myrtle, Anise and Sweet Woodruff and Cowslip and Agrimony *flowers*. The dried petals of Cornflower, Borage, Broom, Hollyhock and Marigold and any other bright petals that, though scentless, keep their colour when dried, are also often added to give a brighter and more attractive appearance to the mixture.

Sweet oils and essences played an important part in the recipes of a hundred years ago, as, for example, the following formula:

Four grains of Musk, 1 oz. of Pimento, crushed Cloves and powdered gum Benzoin, 80 drops of oil of Cassia, 6 drops of Otto of Roses, 150 drops of essence of Bergamot and the same quantity of oil of Lavender, the whole being thoroughly worked in and mixed with whatever petals are handy.

Another recipe (which was used by an old-fashioned Scottish chemist for some fifty years) was purely a liquid one, the essences consisting of Musk, Vanilla, Sandalwood, Patchouli, Verbena, Neroli and Otto of Roses. The mixture was bottled and sold under the all-bracing and appropriate title, 'A' the floers o' th' gairden in a wee bit bottle.'

RECIPE FOR CRYSTALLIZED ROSES

Choose a dry day for gathering the roses and wait until the dew evaporates, so that the petals are dry. Before gathering the roses, dissolve 2 oz. of gum-arabic in ¼ pint of water. Separate the petals and spread them on dishes. Sprinkle them with the gum-arabic solution, using as many petals as the solution will cover. Spread them on sheets of white paper and sprinkle with castor sugar, then let them dry for 24 hours. Put 1 lb. of sugar (loaf) and ¼ pint of cold water into a pan, stir until the sugar has melted, then boil fast to 250° F., or to the thread degree. This is ascertained by dipping a stick into cold water, then into the syrup and back into the water. Pinch the syrup adhering to the stick between the thumb and finger and draw them apart, when a thread should be formed. Keep the syrup well skimmed. Put the rose-petals into shallow dishes and pour the syrup over. Leave them to soak for 24 hours, then spread them on wire trays and dry in a cool oven with the door ajar. The syrup should be coloured with cochineal or carmine, in order to give more colour to the rose-petals.

Rose-petals have also been employed to flavour butter, for which the following recipe may be of interest:

Rose-Petal Sandwiches

Put a layer of Red Rose-petals in the bottom of a jar or covered dish, put in 4 oz. of fresh butter wrapped in waxed paper. Cover with a thick layer of rose-petals. Cover closely and leave in a cool place overnight. The more fragrant the roses, the finer the flavour imparted. Cut bread in thin strips or circles, spread each with the perfumed butter and place several petals from fresh Red Roses between the slices, allowing edges to show. Violets or Clover blossoms may be used in place of Roses.

ROSIN-WEED

Silphium Paciniatum (LINN.)
N.O. Compositæ

Synonyms. Compass Plant. Compass-weed. Polar Plant
Part Used. Root
Habitat. Western United States, especially Ohio

¶ *Description.* The plant is so closely allied to *Silphium laciniatum* (Compass Plant, Compass-weed, or Polar Plant) that some authorities identify them. Both are closely connected with *S. perfoliatum* (Indian Cup-Plant or Ragged Cup). They yield by exudation and incision a fragrant and bitter gumlike frankincense, white or amber colour, which is chewed by the American Indians to sweeten the breath. The taste of Compass-Plant roots is bitter and then acrid. They are odourless.

¶ *Constituents.* Rosin-weed yields an abundance of a resinous secretion, resembling mastic so closely that it might very well be used as an inexpensive substitute.

¶ *Medicinal Action and Uses.* Tonic, diaphoretic, alterative.

The resin has diuretic properties and imparts a strong, aromatic odour to the urine. The root has been used as an expectorant in cough and other pulmonary troubles. It is cut into slices, arranged in a dish in layers, each layer being strewn with sugar and the whole covered with brandy. It is then expressed and strained, and after standing for a few days is bottled.

Both Rosin-weed and Compass-weed are said to be emetic in decoction, and to have effected cures in intermittent fevers, and to have cured the heaves in horses. They are beneficial in dry, obstinate coughs, asthmatic affections, and pulmonary catarrhal diseases. A strong infusion or extract is said to be one of the best remedies for the removal of ague cake, or enlarged spleen, and for internal bruises, liver affections, and ulcers.

¶ *Dosage.* Of Silphium perfoliatum, 20 grains. Of fluid extract of Silphium laciniatum, ¼ to 1 drachm.

See CUP PLANT.

RUE

Ruta graveolens (LINN.)
N.O. Rutaceæ

Synonyms. Herb-of-Grace. Herbygrass. Garden Rue
Part Used. Herb
Habitat. Southern Europe

Rue, a hardy, evergreen, somewhat shrubby plant, is a native of Southern Europe. The stem is woody in the lower part, the leaves are alternate, bluish-green, bi- or tri-pinnate, emit a powerful, disagreeable odour and have an exceedingly bitter, acrid and nauseous taste. The greenish-yellow flowers are in terminal panicles, blossoming from June to September. In England Rue is one of our oldest garden plants, cultivated for its use medicinally, having, together with other herbs, been introduced by the Romans, but it is not found in a wild state except rarely on the hills of Lancashire and Yorkshire. This wild form is even more vehement in smell than the garden Rue. The whole plant has a disagreeable and powerful odour. The first flower that opens has usually ten stamens, the others eight only.

¶ *Cultivation.* The plant grows almost anywhere, but thrives best in a partially sheltered and dry situation. Propagation may be effected: (1) by seeds, sown outside, broadcast, in spring, raked in and the beds kept free from weeds, the seedlings, when about 2 inches high, being transplanted into fresh beds, allowing about 18 inches each way, as the plants become busy; (2) by cuttings, taken in spring and inserted for a time, until well rooted, in a shady border; (3) by rooted slips, also taken in spring. Every slip or cutting of the young wood will readily grow, and this is the most expeditious way of raising a stock.

Rue will live much longer and is less liable to be injured by frost in winter when grown in a poor, dry, rubbishy soil than in good ground.

Rue is first mentioned by Turner, 1562, in his *Herbal*, and has since become one of the best known and most widely grown simples for medicinal and homely uses.

The name *Ruta* is from the Greek *reuo* (to set free), because this herb is so efficacious in various diseases. It was much used by the Ancients; Hippocrates specially commended it, and it constituted a chief ingredient of the famous antidote to poison used by Mithridates. The Greeks regarded it as an antimagical herb, because it served to remedy the nervous indigestion they suffered when eating before strangers, which they attributed to witchcraft. In the Middle Ages and later, it was considered – in many parts of Europe – a powerful defence against witches, and was used in many spells. It was also thought to bestow second sight.

Piperno, a Neapolitan physician, in 1625, commended Rue as a specific against epilepsy and vertigo, and for the former malady, at one time, some of this herb used to be suspended round the neck of the sufferer.

Pliny, John Evelyn tells us, reported Rue to be of such effect for the preservation of sight that the painters of his time used to devour a great quantity of it, and the herb is still eaten by the Italians in their salads. It

was supposed to make the sight both sharp and clear, especially when the vision had become dim through over-exertion of the eyes. It was with 'Euphrasy and Rue' that Adam's sight was purged by Milton's Angel.

At one time the holy water was sprinkled from brushes made of Rue at the ceremony usually preceding the Sunday celebration of High Mass, for which reason it is supposed it was named the Herb of Repentance and the Herb of Grace. 'There's rue for you and here's some for me; we may call it herb of grace o' Sundays.'

Gerard tells us: 'the garden Rue, which is better than the wild Rue for physic's use, grows most profitably, as Dioscorides said, under a fig tree.' But this is, probably, only a reference, originally, to the fact that it prefers a sheltered position.

Country-people boil its leaves with treacle, thus making a conserve of them. These leaves are curative of croup in poultry. It has also been employed in the diseases of cattle.

Shakespeare refers again to Rue in *Richard III*:

'Here in this place
I'll set a bank of *rue*, sour herb of grace;
Rue, even for ruth, shall shortly here be seen,
In the remembrance of a weeping queen.'

The following is a quotation from Drayton:

'Then sprinkles she the juice of *rue*,
With nine drops of the midnight dew
From lunarie distilling.'

The latter was the Moonwort (*Lunaria*), often called 'honesty' – a common garden flower, with cross-shaped purple blossoms, and round, clear silvery-looking seed-vessels.

Chaucer also calls it Lunarie.

Gerard says:

'If a man be anointed with the juice of rue, the poison of wolf's bane, mushrooms, or todestooles, the biting of serpents, stinging of scorpions, spiders, bees, hornets and wasps will not hurt him.'

Rue-water sprinkled in the house 'kills all the fleas,' says an old book.

The juice was used against earache.

Rue has been regarded from the earliest times as successful in warding off contagion and preventing the attacks of fleas and other noxious insects. It was the custom for judges sitting at assizes to have sprigs of Rue placed on the bench of the dock against the pestilential infection brought into court from gaol by the prisoner, and the bouquet still presented in some districts to judges at the assizes was originally a bunch of aromatic herbs, given to him for the purpose of warding off gaol-fever.

It is one of the ingredients in the 'Vinegar of the Four Thieves.'

Culpepper recommends it for sciatica and pains in the joints, if the latter be 'anointed' with it, as also for 'the shaking fits of agues, to take a draught before the fit comes.' He also tells us that

'the juice thereof warmed in a pomegranate shell or rind, and dropped into the ears, helps the pains of them. The juice of it and fennel, with a little honey, and the gall of a cock put thereunto, helps the dimness of the eyesight.'

In Saxony Rue has given its name to an Order. A chaplet of Rue, borne bendwise on bars of the Coat Armour of the Dukedom of Saxony, was granted by Frederick Barbarossa to the first Duke of Saxony, in 1181. In 1902 the King of Saxony conferred the Order of the Rautenkrone (Crown of Rue) on our present King, then Prince of Wales. Since the latter half of the seventeenth century, sprigs of Rue have been interlaced in the Collar of our Order of the Thistle.

¶*Parts Used and Constituents.* The whole herb is used, the drug consisting of both the fresh and the dried herb. The tops of the young shoots contain the greatest virtues of any part of the plant. The shoots are gathered before the plant flowers.

The volatile oil is contained in glands distributed over the whole plant and contains caprinic, plagonic, caprylic and œnanthylic acids – also a yellow crystalline body, called rutin. Oil of Rue is distilled from the fresh herb. Water serves to extract the virtues of the plant better than spirits of wine. Decoctions and infusions are usually made from the fresh plant, or the oil may be given in a dose of from 1 to 5 drops. The dried herb – which is a greyish green – has similar taste and odour, but is less powerful. It is used, powdered, for making tea.

¶ *Medicinal Action and Uses.* Strongly stimulating and antispasmodic – often employed, in form of a warm infusion, as an emmenagogue. In excessive doses, it is an acro-narcotic poison, and on account of its emetic tendencies should not be administered immediately after eating.

It forms a useful medicine in hysterical affections, in coughs, croupy affections, colic and flatulence, being a mild stomachic. The oil may be given on sugar, or in hot water.

Externally, Rue is an active irritant, being employed as a rubefacient. If bruised and applied, the leaves will ease the severe pain of sciatica. The expressed juice, in small quantities, was a noted remedy for nervous nightmare, and the fresh leaves applied to the temples are said to relieve headache. Compresses saturated with a strong decoction of the plant, when applied to the chest, have been used beneficially for chronic bronchitis.

If a leaf or two be chewed, a refreshing aromatic flavour will pervade the mouth and any nervous headache, giddiness, hysterical spasm, or palpitation will be quickly relieved.

¶ *Preparations and Dosages.* Powdered herb, 15 to 30 grains. Fluid extract, ¼ to 1 drachm.

RUE, GOAT'S

Galega officinalis (LINN.)
N.O. Leguminosæ

Synonyms. Herba ruta caprariæ. Italian Fitch
(*German*) Pestilenzkraut
Parts Used. Leaves, flowering tops

Goat's Rue, known in the old Herbals as *Herba rutæ caprariæ,* is a leguminous plant that in former times was much employed on account of its diaphoretic properties in malignant fevers and the plague, hence one of its German popular names of *Pestilenzkraut.*

'The leaves, gathered just as the plant is going into flower and dried, with the addition of boiling water, make an infusion which being drunk plentifully, excites sweating and is good in fevers.' (Hill's *Universal Herbal,* 1832.)

It was also used as a remedy for worms and recommended as a cure for the bites of serpents. Parkinson says it is 'good for fattening hens.'

This profuse-flowering, hardy perennial herb is a native of Southern Europe and the Mediterranean – Gerard calls it Italian Fitch – and it is widely cultivated in gardens in England.

¶ *Description.* From the several-headed root, rise erect stems, about 3 feet high, smooth and branched, bearing pinnate leaves with from six to eight pairs of lance-shaped leaflets, ¾ to 2 inches long, and an odd terminal one. The leaflets are bright green, smooth (or very slightly hairy), on short foot-stalks.

The small lilac, purplish or white flowers are in axillary racemes and produce narrow, almost cylindrical pods.

The plant is without scent, unless bruised, when it emits a disagreeable odour, whence perhaps its name of Goat's Rue.

It has a mucilaginous and somewhat bitter

and astringent taste. It colours the saliva yellowish-green, if chewed.

¶ *Cultivation.* Being pea-like in character, its chief requirements are deep soil and moisture. Given these it will grow strongly each season, producing great masses of flowers, and will grow undisturbed for many years. Autumn planting is best.

¶ *Constituents.* The constituents of Goat's Rue have not been investigated fully. It contains a bitter principle and tannin and yields not more than 12 per cent. of ash.

¶ *Medicinal Action and Uses.* Diaphoretic, galactagogue. The herb is official in the National Formulary IV attached to the United States Pharmacopœia; the dried flowering tops are made into a fluid extract with diluted alcohol.

In 1873 Gillet-Damitte, in a communication to the French Academy, stated that this plant when given to cows would increase the secretion of milk from 35 to 50 per cent., since which time, Cerisoli, Millbank and several French physicians have affirmed that Goat's Rue is a powerful galactagogue. The best preparation is stated to be an aqueous extract prepared from the fresh plant. This almost black extract has a pronounced odour and is recommended to be given in doses of from 8 to 15 grains, from three to five times a day.

Culpepper says:

'A bath made of it is very refreshing to wash the feet of persons tired with over-walking. In the northern countries they use this herb for making their cheeses instead of Rennet, whence it is called also "Cheese-Rennet"; the flowers contain an acidity, which may be got by distillation. This plant is seldom used in the shops.'

The root of an American species of Goat's Rue (*Galega virginiana*, Linn.) is said to be diaphoretic and powerfully anthelmintic. It is given in decoction.

See BROOM, GORSE, MELILOT.

RUSHES. *See* SEDGES, GRASSES

RUPTUREWORT

Herniaria glabra (LINN.)
N.O. Caryophyllaceæ

Part Used. Herb
Habitat. Temperate and Southern Europe and Russian Asia, extending into Scandinavia, but not to high latitudes. A native of Britain, especially southern and central England

¶ *Description.* The *Herniaria* were formerly included in the *Illecebraceæ*. They are small annuals or undershrubs, with small green flowers crowding along the stems intermixed with leaves.

There are very few species of the genus.

H. hirsuta is a common Continental and west Asiatic species, and has been found near Christchurch, in Hampshire.

The taste is insipid and the plant is odourless.

¶ *Constituents.* A crystalline principle has been obtained, called Herniarine, which proved to be methylumbelliferone.

An alkaloid, Paronychine, has also been found.

¶ *Medicinal Action and Uses.* Very active diuretic properties have been attributed to Herniarine, which has been found successful in the treatment of dropsy, whether of cardiac or nephritic origin.

It is recommended for catarrh of the bladder.

SABADILLA

Veratrum sabadilla
N.O. Liliaceæ

Synonyms. Cevadilla. Schœnocaulon officinale. Melanthium sabadilla. Veratrum officinale. Helonias officinalis. Sabadilla officinarum. Asagræa officinalis. Sabadillermer
Parts Used. Seeds, dried fruit
Habitat. Southern North America, Guatemala and Venezuela

¶ *Description.* The name Schœnocaulon indicates the habit of the scape, meaning 'a rush' and 'a stem.' The name *Asagræa* commemorates Professor Asa Gray of Harvard University, the most distinguished of living American botanists. It is not quite certain whether the seeds are obtained from the *Veratrum Sabadilla*, a plant 3 or 4 feet high, or from the *V. officinale*, differing slightly in appearance and construction. The seeds are black, shining, flat, shrivelled and winged, odourless, with a bitter, acrid, persistent and disagreeable taste, the pale grey, amorphous powder being errhine and violently sternutatory. The seeds were known in Europe as early as 1752, but officially only as the source of veratrine.

¶ *Constituents.* Sabadilla contains several alkaloids, the most important being Cevadine, yielding cevine on hydrolysis; Veratrine, obtained from the syrupy liquor from which the cevadine has crystallized; and Cevadilline or Sabadillie, obtained after the extraction of the veratrine with ether.

Two other alkaloids have been isolated: Sabadine, which is less sternutatory than veratrine, and Sabadinine, which is not sternutatory. Sabadilla yields about 0·3 per cent. of veratrine. The seeds also contain veratric acid, cevadic acid, fat and resin.

¶ *Medicinal Action and Uses.* Sabadilla, or cevadilla, is an acrid, drastic emeto-cathartic, in overdoses capable of producing fatal results. Cevine was found to be less poisonous than cevadine, though producing similar symptoms. The powdered seeds have been used as a vermifuge, and to destroy vermin in the hair, being the principal ingredient of the *pulvis capucinorum* used in Europe. Cevadilla was formerly used internally as an anthelmintic, and in rheumatic and neuralgic affections. The highly poisonous *veratria*, which is derived from it, has been given in minute doses internally in acute rheumatism

and gout, and in some inflammatory diseases, but it must be used with caution. Veratria is useful as an ointment in rheumatism and neuralgia, but is regarded as being less valuable than aconite. The ointment is also employed for the destruction of pedicule. Applied to unbroken skin it produces tingling and numbness, followed by coldness and anæsthesia. Given subcutaneously, it causes violent pain and irritation, in addition to the symptoms following an internal dose. The principal reason against its internal use is its powerful action on the heart, the contractions of the organ becoming fewer and longer until the heart stops in systole.

¶ *Dosage.* From 5 to 20 grains as a tænicide. Ointment veratrine, B.P.

¶ *Poisonous, if any, with Antidotes.* Large doses paralyse heart action and respiration, and its use is so dangerous that it is scarcely ever taken internally.

SAFFLOWER

Carthamus tinctorius
N.O. Compositæ

Synonyms. Dyer's Saffron. American Saffron. Fake Saffron. Flores Carthami. Bastard Saffron

Part Used. Flowers

This plant is not in any way related to Saffron, though the flowers are used similarly.[1]

The Safflower plant, known in India as Koosumbha and in China as Hoang-tchi, is extensively cultivated in India, China and other parts of Asia, also in Egypt and Southern Europe; but its native country is unknown. It grows about 2 to 3 feet high, with a stiff, upright whitish stem, branching near the top; and has oval, spiny, sharp-pointed leaves, their bases half-clasping the stem. Its fruits are about the size of barleycorns, somewhat four-sided, white and shining, like little shells.

Safflower contains two colouring matters, yellow and red, the latter being most valued.

It is chiefly used for dyeing silk, affording various shades of rose and scarlet. Mixed with finely-powdered talc it forms the well-known substance called 'rouge.' Another common use of Safflower is in adulterating Saffron. The seeds yield an oil much used in India for burning and for culinary purposes.

¶ *Medicinal Action and Uses.* The flowers are the part used, their action is laxative and diaphoretic. In domestic practice these flowers are used in children's and infants' complaints – measles, fevers, and eruptive skin complaints. An infusion is made of ¼ oz. of the flowers to a pint of boiling water taken warm to produce diaphorasis.

SAFFRON

Crocus sativus
N.O. Iridaceæ

Synonyms. Crocus. Karcom. Krokos (*Arabian*) Zaffer

Part Used. Flower pistils

The true Saffron is a low ornamental plant with grass-like leaves and large lily-shaped flowers, inhabiting the European continent, and frequently cultivated for the sake of the yellow stigmas, which are the part used in medicine, in domestic economy and in the arts.

Saffron is the *Karcom* of the Hebrews (Song of Solomon iv. 14). The plant was also known to the ancient Greeks and Romans.

In the course of an inquest held in 1921 at

Poplar (London, E.), a medical witness testified to the prevalence of a domestic custom of giving Saffron 'tea' flavoured with brandy in cases of measles.

The *Emplastrum Oxycroceum* of the Edinburgh Pharmacopœia contained, in olden days, a large proportion of Saffron (from which – and vinegar – it derived its name), with the addition of colophony, gum ammoniacum, mastic and vinegar.

Saffron was imported to England from the

[1] It largely replaces the use of Saffron owing to the large price of the latter. – EDITOR.

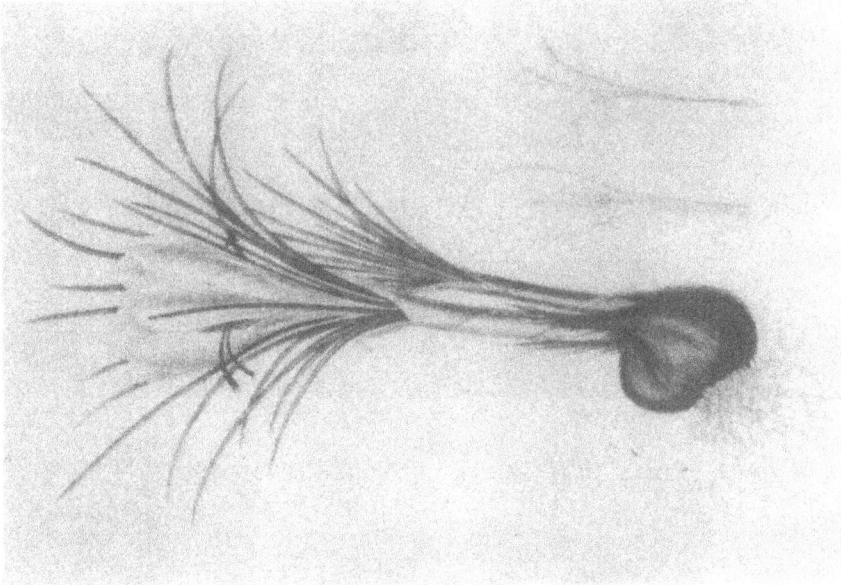

LXXX

SAFFRON
Crocus Sativus

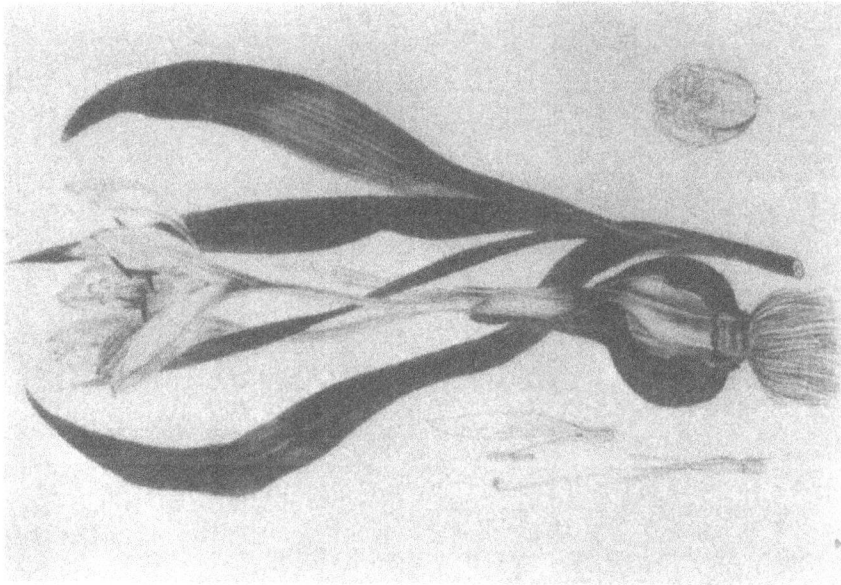

MEADOW SAFFRON
Colchicum Autumnale

East many centuries ago, and was once grown extensively round Saffron Walden, in Essex. One smoke-pervaded spot in the heart of London still bears the name of 'Saffron Hill.' It is a somewhat expensive product, the economic value residing in the *stigmas* of the flower, of which it is said 60,000 are needed to make 1 lb. of Saffron.

According to Dr. Pereira, a grain of good commercial Saffron contains the stigmas and styles of nine flowers, and consequently 4,320 flowers are required to yield 1 oz. of Saffron! English-grown Saffron is now very seldom met with in commerce; the best comes from Spain, while that imported from France is usually considered of second-rate quality. The quantity imported has been computed at between 5,000 and 20,000 lb. weight per annum. Saffron has a bitter taste and a penetrating aromatic odour.

Lately, Persian Saffron has made its appearance in the English market – although of rare occurrence – owing to the high and increasing price of the European article. It has long been known as a wild product of Persia, and was formerly sent from that country and Kashmir to Bombay, but was driven out of the market by the superior Saffrons of Europe.

Saffron was cultivated at Derbena and Ispahan in Persia in the tenth century. It differs a little in appearance from European Saffron in being rather more slender and in the unbranched part of the *style* being paler, but the characteristic odour is remarkably strong. On immersion in water it does not seem to give out so much colour as European Saffron, and could only compete with it if the price enabled it to be used in sufficient quantity to give a colour equal to that used in Europe. The wild Persian crocus is the variety *Hausknechtii*, which occurs on the Delechani and Sangur mountains between Kermanshah and Hamada in West Persia, and at Karput in Kurdistan, which is the most easterly point where any form of *Crocus sativus* occurs in the wild state.

It may be mentioned that five forms of *C. sativus* are known in the wild state. (1) Var. *Orsinii*, which may be regarded as the Italian form and is found at Ascoli, the most westerly point from which any wild form of the plant is recorded. It nearly resembles the cultivated type in purplish colour and habit, but the stigmas are erect and do not hang out between the segments of the perianth, as in the cultivated plant. (2) Var. *Cartwrightianus*, a Greek form common in the Piræus, in which the flowers are smaller and paler, but the stigma is erect and longer than the stamens, as in the cultivated plant. (3) Var. *Pallasii*,

a still smaller form with pale flowers and smaller corms, the stigmas being nearly always shorter than the stamens. It is the commonest of the wild forms, extending through Bulgaria to the Crimea, and reaching Italy on the west. (4) Var. *Elwesii*. This is similar to the last, but has short stigmas and larger flowers, and occurs in Asia Minor. (5) Var. *Hausknechtii*. This, like Nos. 1 and 2, has long stigmas, but the perianth is usually white; it may be regarded as the Persian form, extending from West Persia to Kurdistan. But records of the collection of Saffron from the wild plants are wanting. Only Nos. 1, 2 and 5 are fitted for collection in having long stigmas, but the cultivated purple-flowered form with its stigmas hanging outside the flower would naturally be the easiest to collect, and it would only be the wild varieties from Italy, Greece and Persia that could be utilized. There is no doubt that the cultivated form is also grown from France to Kashmir, whence it was introduced from Persia, and also that it is largely cultivated in Burma (near the Youngaline River at Kuzeih, about ten miles from Pahun) and in China. But it is not always a paying crop, as it does not produce seeds unless cross-fertilized, and the corms are subject to disease if grown in the same ground too long.

In these circumstances it is quite likely that the Persian Saffron at present offered in commerce may have been derived from the wild Persian form, var. *Hausknechtii*; at all events, the pale, almost white, lower part of the styles gives it a characteristic appearance.

These details concerning the different forms are largely taken from the *Chemist and Druggist* of March 29, 1924.

¶ *Cultivation.* The corms are planted in rows, 6 inches apart from corm to corm, in a well-pulverized soil, neither poor nor a very stiff clay, and in the month of July. The flowers are collected in September and the yellow stigmas and part of the style are picked out and dried on a kiln between layers of paper and under the pressure of a thick board, to form the mass into cakes. Two pounds of dried cake is the average crop of an acre after the first planting, and 24 lb. for the next two years. After the third crop the roots are taken up, divided and transplanted.

The Arabs, who introduced the cultivation of the Saffron Crocus into Spain as an article of commerce, bequeathed to us its modern title of *Zaffer*, or 'Saffron,' but the Greeks and Romans called it *Krokos* and *Karkom* respectively.

To the nations of Eastern Asia, its yellow dye was the perfection of beauty, and its odour a perfect ambrosia. 'Saffron yellow shoes formed part of the dress of the Persian Kings,' says Professor Hehn. Greek myths and poetry exhibit an extravagant admiration of the colour and perfume. Homer sings 'the Saffron morn'; gods and goddesses, heroes and nymphs and vestals, are clothed in robes of Saffron hue. The Saffron of Lydia, Cilicia and Cyrene was much prized. The scent was valued as much as the dye; saffron water was sprinkled on the benches of the theatre, the floors of banqueting-halls were strewn with crocus leaves, and cushions were stuffed with it.

¶ *Medicinal Action and Uses.* Carminative, diaphoretic, emmenagogue. Used as a diaphoretic for children and for chronic hæmorrhage of the uterus in adults.

¶ *Preparations.* Powdered Saffron: Tincture, B.P., 5 to 15 drops.

(POISON)
SAFFRON, MEADOW

Colchicum autumnale (LINN.)
N.O. Liliaceæ

Synonym. Naked Ladies
Parts Used. Root, seeds
Habitat. Grows wild in meadows, especially on limestone

¶ *Description.* It has lanceolate leaves, dark green, glabrous, often a foot long. Flowers light purple or white, like crocus but for their six stamens; the ovaries remain underground until the spring after flowering, when they are borne up by the elongating peduncles and ripen. It flowers in September and October. The leaves and fruit are poisonous to cattle.

The root is called a *corm*, from which in autumn the light-purplish mottled flowers arise.

¶ *Cultivation.* Requires light, sandy loam, enriched with decayed manure or leafmould. Plant the bulbs 3 inches deep and 3 inches apart in July or August, in moist beds or rockeries, shrubbery, borders or lawns near shade of trees. The foliage dies down in June and July, and does not reappear until after the plant has flowered. It may also be propagated by seeds sown ½ inch deep in a bed of fine soil outdoors in August or September, or in pans or boxes of similar soil in cold frame at the same time, transplanting seedlings 3 inches apart when two years old; or by division of bulbs in August. Seedling bulbs do not flower till four or five years old.

¶ *Medicinal Action and Uses.* The Colchicum is valued for its medicinal properties. The parts used are the root and seeds, these being anti-rheumatic, cathartic, and emetic.

Its reputation rests largely upon its value in acute gouty and rheumatic complaints. It is mostly used in connexion with some alkaline diuretic; also in pill form. Overdoses cause violent purging, etc.

The active principle is said to be an alkaline substance of a very poisonous nature called Colchinine. It is acrid, sedative, and acts upon all the secreting organs, particularly the bowels and kidneys. It is apt to cause undue depression, and in large doses acts as an irritant poison. Dr. Lindley relates the case of a woman who was poisoned by the sprouts of Colchicum, which had been thrown away in Covent Garden Market and which she mistook for onions.

The Hermodactyls of the Arabians, formerly celebrated for soothing pains in the joints, are said to be this plant.

The corm or root is usually sold in transverse slices, notched on one side and somewhat reniform in outline, white and starchy internally, about ⅛ inch thick, and varying from ¾ to 1 inch in diameter. Taste sweetish, then bitter and acrid. Odour radish-like in fresh root, but lost in drying.

¶ *Preparations.* Powdered root, 2 to 5 grains. Extract, B.P., ½ to 1 grain. Fluid extract (root), 1 to 10 drops. Fluid extract (seed), U.S.P., 1 to 10 drops. Tincture, B.P., 5 to 15 drops. Wine, B.P., 10 to 30 drops. Acetic solid extract, ½ to 1 grain.

SAGES

Salvias
N.O. Labiatæ

SAGE, COMMON

Salvia officinalis (LINN.)
N.O. Labiatæ

Synonyms. (*Old English*) Sawge. Garden Sage. Red Sage. Broad-leaved White Sage. Narrow-leaved White Sage. Salvia salvatrix
Parts Used. Leaves, whole herb

The Common Sage, the familiar plant of the kitchen garden, is an evergreen undershrub, not a native of these islands, its natural habitat being the northern shores of the Mediterranean. It has been cultivated for culinary and medicinal purposes for many centuries in England, France and Germany, being sufficiently hardy to stand any ordinary winter outside. Gerard mentions it as being in 1597 a well-known herb in English gardens, several varieties growing in his own garden at Holborn.

¶ *Description.* Sage generally grows about a foot or more high, with wiry stems. The leaves are set in pairs on the stem and are 1½ to 2 inches long, stalked, oblong, rounded at the ends, finely wrinkled by a strongly-marked network of veins on both sides, greyish-green in colour, softly hairy and beneath glandular. The flowers are in whorls, purplish and the corollas lipped. They blossom in August. All parts of the plant have a strong, scented odour and a warm, bitter, somewhat astringent taste, due to the volatile oil contained in the tissues.

¶ *Habitat.* Sage is found in its natural wild condition from Spain along the Mediterranean coast up to and including the east side of the Adriatic; it grows in profusion on the mountains and hills in Croatia and Dalmatia, and on the islands of Veglia and Cherso in Quarnero Gulf, being found mostly where there is a limestone formation with very little soil. When wild it is much like the common garden Sage, though more shrubby in appearance and has a more penetrating odour, being more spicy and astringent than the cultivated plant. The best kind, it is stated, grows on the islands of Veglia and Cherso, near Fiume, where the surrounding district is known as the Sage region. The collection of Sage forms an important cottage industry in Dalmatia. During its blooming season, moreover, the bees gather the nectar and genuine Sage honey commands there the highest price, owing to its flavour.

In cultivation, Sage is a very variable species, and in gardens varieties may be found with narrower leaves, crisped, red, or variegated leaves and smaller or white flowers. The form of the calyx teeth also varies, and the tube of the corolla is sometimes much longer. The two usually absent upper stamens are sometimes present in very small-sterile hooks. The Red Sage and the Broad-leaved variety of the White (or Green) Sage – both of which are used and have been proved to be the best for medical purposes – and the narrow-leaved White Sage, which is best for *culinary* purposes as a seasoning, are classed merely as varieties of *Salvia officinalis*, not as separate species. There is a variety called Spanish, or Lavender-leaved Sage and another called Wormwood Sage, which is very frequent.

A Spanish variety, called *S. Candelabrum*, is a hardy perennial, the upper lip of its flower greenish yellow, the lower a rich violet, thus presenting a fine contrast.

S. Lyrala and *S. urticifolia* are well known in North America.

S. hians, a native of Simla, is hardy, and also desirable on account of its showy violet-and-white flowers.

The name of the genus, *Salvia*, is derived from the Latin *salvere*, to be saved, in reference to the curative properties of the plant, which was in olden times celebrated as a medicinal herb. This name was corrupted popularly to *Sauja* and *Sauge* (the French form), in Old English, 'Sawge,' which has become our present-day name of Sage.

In the United States Pharmacopœia, the leaves are still officially prescribed, as they were formerly in the London Pharmacopœia, but in Europe generally, Sage is now neglected by the regular medical practitioner, though is still used in domestic medicine. Among the Ancients and throughout the Middle Ages it was in high repute: *Cur moriatur homo cui Salvia crescit in horto?* ('Why should a man die whilst sage grows in his garden?') has a corresponding English proverb:

'He that would live for aye,
    Must eat Sage in May.'

The herb is sometimes spoken of as *S. salvatrix* ('Sage the Saviour'). An old tradition recommends that Rue shall be planted among the Sage, so as to keep away noxious toads from the valued and cherished plants. It was held that this plant would thrive or wither, just as the owner's business prospered or failed, and in Bucks, another tradition maintained that the wife rules when Sage grows vigorously in the garden.

In the Jura district of France, in Franche-Comte, the herb is supposed to mitigate grief, mental and bodily, and Pepys in his Diary says : 'Between Gosport and Southampton we observed a little churchyard where it was customary to sow all the graves with Sage.'

The following is a translation of an old French saying:

'Sage helps the nerves and by its powerful might
Palsy is cured and fever put to flight,'

and Gerard says:

'Sage is singularly good for the head and brain, it quickeneth the senses and memory, strengtheneth the sinews, restoreth health to those that have the palsy, and taketh away shakey trembling of the members.'

He shared the popular belief that it was efficacious against the bitings of serpents, and says:

'No man need to doubt of the wholesomeness of *Sage Ale*, being brewed as it should be with Sage, Betony, Scabious, Spikenard, Squinnette (Squinancywort) and Fennell Seed.'

Many kinds of Sage have been used as substitutes for tea, the Chinese having been said to prefer Sage Tea to their own native product, at one time bartering for it with the Dutch and giving thrice the quantity of their choicest tea in exchange. It is recorded that George Whitfield, when at Oxford in 1733, lived wholesomely, if sparingly, on a diet of Sage Tea, sugar and coarse bread. Balsamic Sage, *S. grandiflora*, a broad-leaved Sage with many-flowered whorls of blossoms, used to be preferred to all others for making tea. An infusion of Speedwell (*Veronica officinalis*), Sage and Wood Betony is said to make an excellent beverage for breakfast, as a substitute for tea, Speedwell having somewhat the flavour of Chinese green tea. In Holland the leaves of *S. glutinosa*, the yellow-flowered Hardy Sage, both flowers and foliage of which exhale a pleasant odour, are used to give flavour to country wines, and a good wine is made by boiling with sugar, the leaves and flowers of another Sage, *S. sclarea*, the Garden Clary. The latter is known in France as 'Toute bonne' – for its medicinal virtues.

It was formerly thought that Sage used in the making of Cheese improved its flavour, and Gay refers to this in a poem:

'Marbled with Sage, the hardening cheese she pressed.'

Italian peasants eat Sage as a preservative of health, and many other country people eat the leaves with bread and butter, than which, it has been said, there is no better and more wholesome way of taking it.

A species of Sage, *S. pomifera*, the APPLE-BEARING SAGE, of a very peculiar growth, is common on some of the Greek islands. It has firm, fleshy protuberances of about ¾ inch thickness, swelling out from the branches of the plant and supposed to be produced in the same manner as oak apples, by the puncture of an insect of the *Cynips* genus. These excrescences are semi-transparent like jelly. They are called Sage Apples, and under that name are to be met with in the markets. They are candied with sugar and made into a kind of sweetmeat and conserve which is regarded by the Greeks as a great delicacy, and is said to possess healing and salutary qualities. It has an agreeable and astringent flavour. This plant is considerably larger than the common Sage of our gardens and its flavour and smell are much more powerful,

being more like a mixture of Lavender and Sage. It grows very abundantly in Candia, Syros and Crete, where it attains to the size of a small shrub. The leaves are collected annually, dried and used medicinally as an infusion, the Greeks being particular as to the time and manner in which they are collected, the date being May 1, before sunrise. The infusion produces profuse perspiration, languor, and even faintness if used to excess. There is a smaller Salvia in Greece, the *S. Candica*, without excrescences.

Another south European species, an annual, *S. Horminum*, the RED-TOPPED SAGE, has its whorls of flowers terminated by clusters of small purple or red leaves, being for this peculiarity often grown in gardens as an ornamental plant. The leaves and seed of this species, put into the vat, while fermenting, greatly increase the inebriating quality of the liquor. An infusion of the leaves has been considered a good gargle for sore gums, and powdered makes a good snuff.

Certain varieties of Sage seeds are mucilaginous and nutritive, and are used in Mexico by the Indians as food, under the name of *Chia*.

¶ *Cultivation.* The Garden Sage succeeds best in a warm and rather dry border, but will grow well almost anywhere in ordinary garden soil; it thrives in a situation somewhat shaded from sunshine, but not strictly under trees.

¶ *Description.* It is a hardy plant, but though a perennial, does not last above three or four years without degenerating, so that the plantation should be renewed at least every four years. It is propagated occasionally by seed, but more frequently by cuttings. New plantations are readily made by pulling off the young shoots from three-year-old plants in spring, generally in the latter end of April, as soon as they attain a sufficiency of hardness to enable them to maintain themselves on the moisture of the ground and atmosphere, while the lower extremities are preparing roots. If advantage be taken of any showery weather that may occur, there is little trouble in obtaining any number of plants, which may either be struck in the bed where they are to grow, inserting a foot apart each way, or in some other shady spot whence they may be removed to permanent quarters when rooted. The latter plan is the best when the weather is too bright and sunny to expect Sage to strike well in its ordinary quarters. See the young plants do not suffer from want of water during their first summer, and hoe the rows regularly to induce a bushy growth, nipping off the growing tips if shooting up too tall. Treat the ground with soot and mulch in winter with old manure. Cuttings may also be taken in the autumn, as soon as the plants have ceased flowering.

Sage is also often propagated by layers, in the spring and autumn, the branches of old plants being pegged down on the ground and covered with ¼ inch of earth. The plant, being like other of the woody-stemmed garden herbs, a 'stem rooter,' each of the stems thus covered will produce quantities of rootlets by just lying in contact with the ground, and can after a time be cut away from the old plant and transplanted to other quarters as a separate plant.

Red Sage is always propagated by layering or by cuttings, as the seed does not produce a red-leaved plant, but reverts back to the original green-leaved type, though efforts are being made to insure the production of a Red Sage that shall set seed and remain true and develop into the red-leaved plant.

Sages backed by late-flowering Orange Lilies go very well together, and being in flower at the same time make an effective grouping. The calyces of Sage flowers remain on the plants well into late summer and give a lovely haze of reddish spikes; the smell of these seeding spikes is very distinct from the smell of the leaves, and much more like that of the Lemon-scented Verbena, pungent, aromatic and most refreshing.

At the present day, by far the largest demand for Sage is for culinary use, and it should pay to grow it in quantity for this purpose as it is little trouble. For this, the White variety, with somewhat pale green leaves should be taken.

In Dalmatia, where the collection of Sage in its wild condition forms an important cottage industry, it is gathered before blooming, the leaves being harvested from May to September, those plucked in midsummer being considered the best. The general opinion is that it should be gathered before the bloom opens, but the Austrian Pharmacopœia states that it is best when gathered *during* bloom.

¶ *Chemical Constituents.* The chief constituent of Sage and its active principle is a yellow or greenish-yellow volatile oil (sp. gr. 0·910 to 0·930) with a penetrating odour. Tannin and resin are also present in the leaves; 0·5 to 1·0 per cent. of the oil is yielded from the leaves and twigs when fresh, and about three times this quantity when dry.

The Sage oil of commerce is obtained from the herb *S. officinalis*, and distilled to a considerable extent in Dalmatia and recently in Spain, but from a different species of *Salvia*. A certain amount of oil is also distilled in Germany. The oil distilled in Dalmatia and in Germany is of typically Sage

odour, and is used for flavouring purposes. The botanical origin of Spanish Sage oil is now identified as *S. triloba*, closely allied to *S. officinalis*, though probably other species may also be employed. The odour of the Spanish oil more closely resembles that of Spike Lavender than the Sage oil distilled in Germany for flavouring purposes, and is as a rule derived from the wild Dalmatian herb, *S. officinalis*. The resemblance of the Spanish oil to Spike Lavender oil suggests the possibility of its use for adulterative purposes, and it is an open secret that admixture of the Spanish Sage oil with Spanish Spike Lavender oil does take place to a considerable extent, though this can be detected by chemical analysis. It is closer in character to the oil of *S. sclarea*, Clary oil, which has a decided lavender odour, although in the oil of *S. triloba*, the ester percentage does not appear to be as high as in the oil of the *S. sclarea* variety.

Pure Dalmatian or German Sage oil is soluble in two volumes of 80 per cent. alcohol, Spanish Sage oil is soluble in six volumes of 70 per cent. alcohol.

Sage oil contains a hydrocarbon called Salvene; pinene and cineol are probably present in small amount, together with borneol, a small quantity of esters, and the ketone thujone, the active principle which confers the power of resisting putrefaction in animal substances. Dextro-camphor is also present in traces. A body has been isolated by certain chemists called Salviol, which is now known to be identical with Thujone.

English distilled Sage oil has been said to contain Cedrene.

S. cypria, a native of the island of Cyprus, yields an essential oil, having a camphoraceous odour and containing about 75 per cent of Eucalyptol.

S. mellifer (syn. *Ramona stachyoides*) is a labiate plant found in South California, known as BLACK SAGE, with similar constituents, and also traces of formic acid.

¶ *Medicinal Action and Uses.* Stimulant, astringent, tonic and carminative. Has been used in dyspepsia, but is now mostly employed as a condiment. In the United States, where it is still an official medicine, it is in some repute, especially in the form of an infusion, the principal and most valued application of which is as a wash for the cure of affections of the mouth and as a gargle in inflamed sore throat, being excellent for relaxed throat and tonsils, and also for ulcerated throat. The gargle is useful for bleeding gums and to prevent an excessive flow of saliva.

When a more stimulating effect to the

throat is desirable, the gargle may be made of equal quantities of vinegar and water, ½ pint of hot malt vinegar being poured on 1 oz. of leaves, adding ½ pint of cold water.

The infusion when made for *internal* use is termed Sage Tea, and can be made simply by pouring 1 pint of boiling water on to 1 oz. of the dried herb, the dose being from a wine-glassful to half a teacupful, as often as required, but the old-fashioned way of making it is more elaborate and the result is a pleasant drink, cooling in fevers, and also a cleanser and purifier of the blood. Half an ounce of fresh Sage leaves, 1 oz. of sugar, the juice of 1 lemon, or ¼ oz. of grated rind, are infused in a quart of boiling water and strained off after half an hour. (In Jamaica, the negroes sweeten Sage Tea with lime-juice instead of lemon.)

Sage Tea or infusion of Sage is a valuable agent in the delirium of fevers and in the nervous excitement frequently accompanying brain and nervous diseases and has considerable reputation as a remedy, given in small and oft-repeated doses. It is highly serviceable as a stimulant tonic in debility of the stomach and nervous system and weakness of digestion generally. It was for this reason that the Chinese valued it, giving it the preference to their own tea. It is considered a useful medicine in typhoid fever and beneficial in biliousness and liver complaints, kidney troubles, hæmorrhage from the lungs or stomach, for colds in the head as well as sore throat and quinsy and measles, for pains in the joints, lethargy and palsy. It will check excessive perspiration in phthisis cases, and is useful as an emmenagogue. A cup of the strong infusion will be found good to relieve nervous headache.

The infusion made strong, without the lemons and sugar, is an excellent lotion for ulcers and to heal raw abrasions of the skin. It has also been popularly used as an application to the scalp, to darken the hair.

The fresh leaves, rubbed on the teeth, will cleanse them and strengthen the gums. Sage is a common ingredient in tooth-powders.

The volatile oil is said to be a violent epileptiform convulsant, resembling the essential oils of absinthe and nutmeg. When smelt for some time it is said to cause a sort of intoxication and giddiness. It is sometimes prescribed in doses of 1 to 3 drops, and used for removing heavy collections of mucus from the respiratory organs. It is a useful ingredient in embrocations for rheumatism.

In cases where heat is required, Sage has been considered valuable when applied externally in bags, as a poultice and fomentation.

In Sussex, at one time, to munch Sage leaves on nine consecutive mornings, whilst fasting, was a country cure for ague, and the dried leaves have been smoked in pipes as a remedy for asthma.

In the region where Sage grows wild, its leaves are boiled in vinegar and used as a tonic.

Among many uses of the herb, Culpepper says that it is

'Good for diseases of the liver and to make blood. A decoction of the leaves and branches of Sage made and drunk, saith Dioscorides, provokes urine and causeth the hair to become black. It stayeth the bleeding of wounds and cleaneth ulcers and sores. Three spoonsful of the juice of Sage taken fasting with a little honey arrests spitting or vomiting of blood in consumption. It is profitable for all pains in the head coming of cold rheumatic humours, as also for all pains in the joints, whether inwardly or outwardly. The juice of Sage in warm water cureth hoarseness and cough. Pliny saith it cureth stinging and biting serpents. Sage is of excellent use to help the memory, warming and quickening the senses. The juice of Sage drunk with vinegar hath been of use in the time of the plague at all times. Gargles are made with Sage, Rosemary, Honeysuckles and Plantains, boiled in wine or water with some honey or alum put thereto, to wash sore mouths and throats, as need requireth. It is very good for stitch or pains in the sides coming of wind, if the place be fomented warm with the decoction in wine and the herb also, after boiling, be laid warm thereto.'

CULINARY RECIPES

Sage and Onion stuffing for ducks, geese and pork enables the stomach to digest the rich food.

From Warner's *Ancient Cookery*, 1791, for 'Sawgeat,' Sawge.

'Sawgeat

'Take Pork and seeth (boil) it wel and grinde it smale and medle (mingle) it with ayren (eggs) and ygrated (grated) brede (bread). Do thereto salt sprinkled and saffron. Take a close litull ball of it in foiles (leaves) of Sawge. Wet it with a bator (batter) of ayren, fry and serve forth.'

From *The Cook's Oracle*, 1821:

'Sage and Onion Sauce

'Chop very fine an ounce of onion and ½ oz. of green Sage leaves, put them in a stamper with 4 spoonsful of water, simmer gently for 10 minutes, then put in a teaspoonful of pepper and salt and 1 oz. of fine bread-crumbs. Mix well together, then pour to it ¼ pint of Broth, Gravy or Melted Butter, stir well together and simmer a few minutes longer. This is a relishing sauce for Roast Pork, Geese or Duck, or with Green Peas on Maigre Days.'

The same book gives:

'A Relish for Roast Pork or Goose

'2 oz. of leaves of Green Sage, an ounce of fresh lemon peel, pared thin, same of salt, minced shallot and ¼ drachm of Cayenne pepper, ditto of citric acid, steeped for a fortnight in a pint of claret. Shake it well every day; let it stand a day to settle and decant the clear liquid. Bottle it and cork it close. Use a tablespoonful or more in ¼ pint of gravy or melted butter.'

Another modern Sage Sauce, excellent with Roast Pork is

Sagina Sauce

Take 6 large Sage leaves, 2 onions, 1 teaspoonful of flour, 1 teaspoonful of vinegar, butter the size of a walnut, salt, pepper, and ½ pint of good, brown gravy. Scald the Sage leaves and chop them with the onions to a mincemeat. Put them in a stewpan with the butter, sprinkle in the flour, cover close and steam 10 minutes. Then add the vinegar, gravy and seasoning and simmer half an hour.

From Walsh's *Manual of Domestic Economy*, 1857:

'Sage Cheese

'Bruise the tops of young red Sage in a mortar with some leaves of spinach and squeeze the juice; mix it with the rennet in the milk, more or less, according to the preferred colour and taste. When the curd is come, break it gently and put it in with the skimmer till it is pressed two inches above the vat. Press it 8 or 10 hours. Salt it and turn every day.'

MEDICINAL RECIPES

A Gargle for a Sore Throat

A small glass of port wine, a tablespoonful of Chile vinegar, 6 Sage leaves, and a dessert-spoonful of honey; simmer together on the fire for 5 minutes.

A Cure for Sprains

Bruise a handful of Sage leaves and boil them in a gill of vinegar for 5 minutes; apply this in a folded napkin as hot as it can be borne to the part affected.

SAGE, CLARY
                                      Salvia sclarea
                                      N.O. Labiatæ

Synonyms. Clary. Horminum. Gallitricum. Clear Eye. See Bright
   (*German*) Muskateller Salbei
Parts Used. Herb, leaves, seeds
Habitat. The Common Clary, like the Garden Sage, is not a native of Great Britain, having first been introduced into English cultivation in the year 1562. It is a native of Syria, Italy, southern France and Switzerland, but will thrive well upon almost any soil that is not too wet, though it will frequently rot upon moist ground in the winter

Gerard describes and figures several varieties of Clary, under the names of *Horminum* and *Gallitricum*. He describes it as growing 'in divers barren places almost in every country, especially in the fields of Holborne neare unto Grayes Inne . . . and at the end of Chelsea.'

Salmon, in 1710, in *The English Herbal*, gives a number of varieties of the Garden Clary, which he calls *Horminum Hortense*, in distinction to *H. Sylvestre*, the Wild Clary, subdividing it into the Common Clary (*H. commune*), the True Garden Clary of Dioscorides (*H. sativum verum Dioscorides*), the Yellow Clary (*Calus Jovis*), and the Small or German Clary (*H. humile Germanicum* or *Gallitricum alterum Gerardi*). This last variety being termed *Gerardi*, indicates that Gerard classified this species when it was first brought over from the Continent, evidently taking great pains to trace its history, giving in his *Herbal* its Greek name and its various Latin ones. That the Clary was known in ancient times is shown by the second variety, the True Garden Clary, being termed *Dioscoridis*.

Another variety of *Horminum* is given in *The Treasury of Botany*, called *H. pyrenaicum*, and described as 'a tufted perennial herb, with numerous root-leaves, simple almost leafless stems and purplish-blue flowers which grow in whorls of six, all turned the same way. It is a native of the temperate parts of Europe, on the mountains.'

¶ *Description.* The Common Garden Clary is a biennial plant, its square, brownish stems growing 2 to 3 feet high, hairy and with few branches. The leaves are arranged in pairs, almost stalkless and are almost as large as the hand, oblong and heart-shaped, wrinkled, irregularly toothed at the margins and covered with velvety hairs. The flowers are in a long, loose, terminal spike, on which they are set in whorls. The lipped corollas, similar to the Garden Sage, but smaller, are of a pale blue or white. The flowers are interspersed with large coloured, membraneous bracts, longer than the spiny calyx. Both corollas and bracts are generally variegated with pale purple and yellowish-white. The seeds are blackish brown, 'contained in long, toothed husks,' as an old writer describes the calyx. The whole plant possesses a very strong, aromatic scent, somewhat resembling that of Tolu, while the taste is also aromatic, warm and slightly bitter.

According to Ettmueller, this herb was first brought into use by the wine merchants of Germany, who employed it as an adulterant, infusing it with Elder flowers, and then adding the liquid to the Rhenish wine, which converted it into the likeness of Muscatel. It is still called in Germany *Muskateller Salbei* (Muscatel Sage).

Waller (1822) states it was also employed in this country as a substitute for Hops, for sophisticating beer, communicating considerable bitterness and intoxicating property, which produced an effect of insane exhilaration of spirits, succeeded by severe headache. Lobel says:

'Some brewers of Ale and Beere doe put it into their drinke to make it more heady, fit to please drunkards, who thereby, according to their several dispositions, become either dead drunke, or foolish drunke, or madde drunke.'

In some parts of the country a wine has been made from the herb in flower, boiled with sugar, which has a flavour not unlike Frontiniac.

The English name Clary originates in the Latin name *sclarea*, a word derived from *clarus* (clear). Clary was gradually modified into 'Clear Eye,' one of its popular names, and from the fact that the seeds have been used for clearing the sight.

Sometimes we find the plant not only called 'Clear Eye,' but also 'See Bright' and even 'Eyebright,' though this name belongs to another plant – *Euphrasia officinalis*.

¶ *Cultivation.* Clary is propagated by seed, which should be sown in spring. When fit to move, the seedlings should be transplanted to an open spot of ground, a foot apart each way, if required in large quantities. After the plants have taken root, they will require no further care but to keep them free of weeds. The winter and spring following, the leaves will be in perfection. As the plant is a biennial only, dying off the second summer,

after it has ripened seeds, there should be young plants annually raised for use.

¶ *Parts Used.* The herb and leaves, used both fresh and dry, dried in the same manner as the Garden Sage. Formerly the root was used, dry, in domestic medicine, and also the seeds.

¶ *Constituents. Salvia sclarea* yields an oil with a highly aromatic odour, resembling that of ambergris. It is known commercially as Clary oil, or Muscatel Sage, and is largely used as a fixer of perfumes. Pinene, cineol and linalol have been isolated from this oil.

French oil of Clary has a specific gravity of 0·895 to 0·930, and is soluble in two volumes of 80 per cent. alcohol. German oil of Clary has a specific gravity of 0·910 to 0·960, and is soluble in two volumes of 90 per cent. alcohol.

¶ *Medicinal Action and Uses.* Antispasmodic, balsamic, carminative, tonic, aromatic, aperitive, astringent, and pectoral.

The plant has been used, both fresh and dry, either alone or with other herbs, as an infusion or a tincture.

It has mostly been employed in disordered states of the digestion, as a stomachic, and has also proved useful in kidney diseases.

For violent cases of hysteria or wind colic, a spirituous tincture has been found of use, made by macerating in warm water for 14 days, 2 oz. of dried Clary leaves and flowers, 1 oz. of Chamomile flowers, ½ ox. bruised Avens root, 2 drachms of bruised Caraway and Coriander seeds, and 3 drachms of bruised Burdock seeds, adding 2 pints of proof spirit, then filtering and diluting with double quantity of water – a wineglassful being the dose.

Culpepper says:

'For tumours, swellings, etc., make a mucilage of the seeds and apply to the spot. This will also draw splinters and thorns out of the flesh. . . . For hot inflammation and boils before they rupture, use a salve made of the leaves boiled with hot vinegar, honey being added later till the required consistency is obtained.' He recommends a powder of the dry roots taken as snuff to relieve headache, and 'the fresh leaves, fried in butter, first dipped in a batter of flour, egges, and a little milke, serve as a dish to the table that is not unpleasant to any and exceedingly profitable.'

The juice of the herb drunk in ale and beer, as well as the ordinary infusion, has been recommended as very helpful in all women's diseases and ailments.

In Jamaica, where the plant is found, it was much in use among the negroes, who considered it cooling and cleansing for ulcers, and also used it for inflammations of the eyes.

A decoction of the leaves boiled in coco-nut oil was used by them to cure the stings of scorpions. Clary and a Jamaican species of Vervain form two of the ingredients of an aromatic warm bath sometimes prescribed there with benefit.

SAGE, VERVAIN

Salvia Verbenaca
N.O. Labiatæ

Synonyms. Wild English Clary. Christ's Eye. Oculus Christi
Parts Used. Leaves, seeds.

The Wild English Clary, or Vervain Sage, is a native of all parts of Europe and not uncommon in England in dry pastures and on roadsides, banks and waste ground, especially near the sea, or on chalky soil. It is a smaller plant than the Garden Clary, but its medicinal virtues are rather more powerful.

¶ *Description.* The perennial root is woody, thicky and long, the stem 1 to 2 feet high, erect with the leaves in distinct pairs, the lower shortly stalked, and the upper ones stalkless. The radical leaves lie in a rosette and have foot-stalks 1½ to 4 inches long, their blades about the same length, oblong in shape, blunt at their ends and heart-shaped at the base, wavy at the margins, which are generally indented by five or six shallow, blunt lobes on each side, their surfaces much wrinkled. The whole plant is aromatic, especially when rubbed, and is rendered conspicuous by its long spike of purplish-blue flowers, first dense, afterwards becoming rather lax. The whorls of the spike are six-flowered, and at the base of each flower are two heart-shaped, fringed, pointed bracts. The calyx is much larger than the corolla. The plant is in bloom from June to August. The seeds are smooth, and like the Garden Clary, produce a great quantity of soft, taste-less mucilage, when moistened. If put under the eyelids for a few moments the tears dissolve this mucilage, which envelops any dust and brings it out safely. Old writers called this plant 'Oculus Christi,' or 'Christ's Eye.'

¶ *Medicinal Action and Uses.* 'A decoction of the leaves,' says Culpepper, 'being drank, warms the stomach, also it helps digestion and scatters congealed blood in any part of the body.'

This Clary was thought to be more efficacious to the eye than the Garden variety.

'The distilled water strengthening the eyesight, especially of old people,' says Culpepper, 'cleaneth the eyes of redness water-ishness and heat: it is a gallant remedy for dimness of sight, to take one of the seeds of it and put it into the eyes, and there let it remain till it drops out of itself, the pain will be nothing to speak on: it will cleanse the eyes of all filthy and putrid matter; and repeating it will take off a film which covereth the sight.'

¶ *Other Species.*
Salvia pratensis, the MEADOW SAGE – our other native Sage – is a very rare plant, found only in a few localities in Cornwall, Kent and Oxfordshire, and by some authorities is considered hardly a true native.

It is common in some parts of Italy and the Ionian Islands.

It has the habit of *S. Verbenaca*, but is larger. The flowers are very showy, large and bright blue, arranged on a long spike, four flowers in each whorl, the corolla (about four times as long as the calyx) having the prominent upper lip much arched and compressed and often glutinous. The stem bears very few leaves.

Several plants, though not true Sages, have been popularly called 'Sage': *Phlomis fruticosa*, a hardy garden shrub, 2 to 4 feet high, with flowers either yellow or dusky yellow, was known as Jerusalem Sage; Turner (1548) terms it so and he is followed in this by Green (1832), whereas Lyte (1578) gives this name to *Pulmonaria officinalis*, the Common Lungwort, and Gerard (1597), describing *Phlomis fruticosa*, gives it another name, saying, 'The leaves are in shape like the leaves of Sage, whereupon the vulgar people call it French Sage.' Gerard gives the name of 'Sage of Bethlem' to *Pulmonaria officinalis*; in localities of North Lincolnshire, the name has been given to the Garden Mint, *Mentha viridis*. 'Garlick Sage' is one of the names quoted by Gerard for *Teucrium scorodonia*, which we find variously termed by old writers, Mountain Sage, Wild Sage and Wood Sage.

See GERMANDER.

ST. JOHN'S WORT

Hypericum perforatum (LINN.)
N.O. Hypericaceæ

Parts Used. Herb tops, flowers
Habitat. Britain and throughout Europe and Asia

¶ *Description.* A herbaceous perennial growing freely wild to a height of 1 to 3 feet in uncultivated ground, woods, hedges, roadsides, and meadows; short, decumbent, barren shoots and erect stems branching in upper part, glabrous; leaves pale green, sessile, oblong, with pellucid dots or oil glands which may be seen on holding leaf to light. Flowers bright cheery yellow in terminal corymb. Calyx and corolla marked with black dots and lines; sepals and petals five in number; ovary pear-shaped with three long styles. Stamens in three bundles joined by their bases only. Blooms June to August, followed by numerous small round blackish seeds which have a resinous smell and are contained in a three-celled capsule; odour peculiar, terebenthic; taste bitter, astringent and balsamic.

There are many ancient superstitions regarding this herb. Its name *Hypericum* is derived from the Greek and means 'over an apparition,' a reference to the belief that the herb was so obnoxious to evil spirits that a whiff of it would cause them to fly.

SALEP. *See* ORCHIDS and SAFFRON

SALSAFY

Tragopogon porrifolius (LINN.)
N.O. Compositæ

Synonyms. Purple Goat's Beard. Vegetable Oyster
(*French*) Salsifis des prés
Part Used. Root

The Salsafy, familiar as a kitchen-garden plant, is very similar to Goat's Beard, the main difference being the colour of the flowers – yellow in our native species, purple in the Salsafy.

Salsafy is often called the Purple Goat's Beard, from its likeness in general character to the Yellow Goat's Beard of the countryside. Some writers, again, invert this distinction and call the Yellow Goat's Beard, 'Meadow Salsafy.' The French call it '*Salsifis des prés.*'

Salsafy is a corruption of the old Latin name *solsequium*. This was derived from the Latin words *sol* (sun) and *sequens* (following), meaning the flower that followed the course of the sun.

It is a taller plant than the Goat's Beard, the stem being nearly 3 feet high. The leaves and flowers are similar in form, the flowers having the same peculiarity of closing at noon. The florets are of a delicate pale purple colour.

Though not a British species, it is occasionally found in moist meadows, having been originally a garden escape. It was formerly much cultivated for the sake of its fleshy, tapering roots.

¶ *Cultivation*. Salsafy is a very easy crop to grow and matures in a year.

A friable, open soil is preferable, though it will also grow on heavy soil. On a stony soil, or one made up of clay with flints scattered in it, it will not be a success, as the roots get coarse and forked. No manure should be added to the soil, as forking will also then result, but wood-ash, lime, soot, superphosphates, etc., may be used freely.

The seeds should be sown 1 inch or more deep, 4 inches apart, in drills 9 inches asunder, as early in March as possible, to give a long season for its growth.

The roots may be lifted in October and stored in the same way as Beet, Carrot, etc., or they may remain in the ground until the spring.

Salsafy seed frequently fails, unless kept wet from sowing time till the seedlings are well up.

¶ *Medicinal Action and Uses*. Culpepper says of Purple Goat's Beard:

'The virtues of this are the same as the other, only less pleasant, therefore more bitter, astringent, detersive and medicinal. This, however, may be eaten in great quantities, and so will be useful in chronic complaints. The roots are particularly specific in obstructions of the gall and the jaundice; the best way to use them is stewed like chardoons.'

It ranks as one of the most salubrious of culinary vegetables, being antibilious, cooling, deobstruent, and slightly aperient; but although it is deservedly esteemed as an esculent, it is nevertheless decidedly inferior to *Scorzonera* in properties, nor does it keep so well when taken out of the ground, as it

¶ *Medicinal Action and Uses*. Aromatic, astringent, resolvent, expectorant and nervine. Used in all pulmonary complaints, bladder troubles, in suppression of urine, dysentery, worms, diarrhœa, hysteria and nervous depression, hæmoptysis and other hæmorrhages and jaundice. For children troubled with incontinence of urine at night an infusion or tea given before retiring will be found effectual; it is also useful in pulmonary consumption, chronic catarrh of the lungs, bowels or urinary passages. Externally for fomentations to dispel hard tumours, caked breasts, ecchymosis, etc.

¶ *Preparations and Dosages*. 1 oz. of the herb should be infused in a pint of water and 1 to 2 tablespoonsful taken as a dose. Fluid extract, ⅓ to 1 drachm.

The oil of St. John's Wort is made from the flowers infused in olive oil.

soon becomes hardened, insipid, and difficult to cook properly.

See GOAT'S BEARD (YELLOW).

RECIPES

Baked Salsafy

Scrape 1 bundle of Salsafy, wash and cut into short pieces, and put into a basin of cold water containing lemon juice or vinegar. Drain and cook in stock or seasoned water till tender. Make a white sauce, put in the Salsafy previously drained and blend both carefully. Place on a buttered dish, pour over the sauce, sprinkle breadcrumbs over, add a few small pieces of butter and bake for 10 minutes in a sharp oven.

Salsafy with Cheese

Cook and drain and place a layer of Salsafy in a shallow dish. Sprinkle with grated cheese, then a layer of Bechamel sauce, again a layer of Salsafy, then more cheese and sauce, and sprinkle breadcrumbs over the top. Place in a quick oven to get well hot through and brown.

To serve plain boiled, the roots must be scraped lightly first, cut up into two or three portions, and placed in water, with a few drops of lemon juice or vinegar, to prevent them discolouring. Then boiled for an hour, quickly, in salt water till tender, drained and served with a white sauce.

SALVIAS. *See* SAGES

SAMPHIRE

Crithmum maritimum (LINN.)
N.O. Umbelliferæ

Stewed Salsafy

Scrape about 20 heads of Salsafy, cut into pieces about 2 inches long, sprinkle them with salt and steep in water and milk. Cut a small onion, half a carrot, half a turnip and half a head of celery into small pieces. Put these on in a stewpan with ¼ lb. of lean bacon cut into pieces. Cook for 20 minutes. Mix 1 oz. flour with a little milk and stir in, fill up with a quart of stock or water, stir and bring to the boil. Put in the Salsafy and let it simmer till tender. Add a tablespoonful of cream, one of chopped parsley, and a little lemon juice. Season with pepper, grated nutmeg and castor sugar. Reheat and arrange the Salsafy neatly on a dish, garnish with button mushrooms, pour over the sauce and serve.

Salsafy Cream Soup

Scrape and wash a bundle of Salsafy. Cut it up small and place in a stewpan, with 3 oz. of butter and a finely-minced onion, and stir for a few minutes. Then moisten with about a quart of white stock, add also 1 oz. rice. When cooked, drain and pound with the rice and pass all through a fine sieve. Then put the purée with a stock, stir over the fire, boil up the soup, season with salt, pepper and nutmeg. At the last add half a gill of cream, 2 beaten-up yolks of eggs, but do not let the soup boil again.

Synonyms. Sea Fennel. Crest Marine. Sampier
    (*German*) Meerfenchel
    (*Italian*) Herba di San Pietra. Sanpetra
Part Used. Herb

Occasionally we find the name SEA FENNEL given to a plant which is far more familiar under the name of SAMPHIRE, and which also belongs to the great order of umbelliferous plants, though not to the same genus as the fennel. In German, this plant is also given a name equivalent to sea-fennel: *Meerfenchel*.

Prior tells us that the name of this plant is more properly zas; it was formerly spelt Sampere, or Sampier, from Saint Pierre, and Herba di San Pietra (contracted to Sanpetra) is its Italian name. It is dedicated to the fisherman saint, because it likes to grow on sea-cliffs.

The Samphire is a succulent, smooth, much-branched herb, woody at the base, growing freely on rocks on the sea-shore moistened by the salt spray.

¶ *Description.* It is well distinguished by its long, fleshy, bright-green, shining leaflets (full of aromatic juice) and umbels of tiny, yellowish-green blossoms. The whole plant is aromatic and has a powerful scent.

The young leaves, if gathered in May, sprinkled with salt (after freeing them from stalks and flowers), boiled and covered with vinegar and spice, make one of the best pickles, on account of their aromatic taste.

On those parts of the coast where Samphire does not abound, other plants which resemble it in having fleshy leaves are sometimes sold under the same name, but are very inferior.

Samphire gathering is referred to in *King Lear* :

        'Half-way down
Hangs one that gathers samphire; dreadful trade!'

At the present time it grows but sparingly

709

on the white cliffs of Dover, where Shakespeare described it, but in his days it was probably more abundant there. From his description of the perilous nature of the collection of Samphire, it might be assumed that it grows where none but the adventurous can reach it, but it is to be found growing freely in the clefts of the rocks, and is in many places easily accessible from the beach, and is even sometimes to be found in the salt marshes that in some districts fringe the coast.

Samphire is abundantly met with where circumstances are favourable to its growth, around the coasts of western or southern England, but is rarer in the north and seldom met with in Scotland.

The use of Samphire as a condiment and pickle, or as an ingredient in a salad is of ancient date. It used at one time to be cried in London streets as 'Crest Marine.'

SAMPHIRE, GOLDEN

Part Used. Herb

Inula crithmoides, popularly named Golden Samphire, is a species growing in salt marshes and on sea-cliffs, but rare, and in England only plentiful in the Isle of Sheppey.

¶ *Description.* It has narrow, fleshy leaves and large yellow flowers, growing singly at the extremity of the branches. Formerly, when Samphire (*Crithmum Maritimum*) was

¶ *Medicinal Action and Uses.* In Gerard's time it was in great reputation as a condiment. He wrote in 1597:

'The leaves kept in pickle and eaten in sallads with oile and vinegar is a pleasant sauce for meat, wholesome for the stoppings of the liver, milt and kidnies. It is the pleasantest sauce, most familiar and best agreeing with man's body.'

Culpepper, writing some fifty years later, deplores that it had in his days much gone out of fashion, for it is well known almost to everybody that ill digestions and obstructions are the cause of most of the diseases which the frail nature of man is subject to; both of which might be remedied by a more frequent use of this herb. It is a safe herb, very pleasant to taste and stomach.

In some seaside districts where Samphire is found, it is still eaten pickled by country people.

Inula crithmoides (LINN.)

N.O. Compositæ

sold in the London markets for a pickle, the young branches of this species were sometimes mixed with it, causing Green in his *Universal Herbal* (1832) to indignantly remark: 'but it is a villainous imposition because this plant has none of the warm aromatic taste of the true Samphire.'

See ELECAMPANE.

SANDALWOOD

Synonym. Sanders-wood
Parts Used. Wood, oil
Habitat. India

Santalum album (LINN.)
N.O. Santalaceæ

¶ *Description.* A small tree 20 to 30 feet high, with many opposite slender drooping branches, bark smooth grey-brown. Young twigs glabrous; leaves opposite, without stipules, petiole slender, about ⅓ inch long, blade 1½ to 2½ inches long, oval, ovate-oval or lanceolate, acute or obtuse at apex, tapering at base into petiole entire, smooth on both sides, glaucous beneath. Flowers small, numerous, shortly stalked in small pyramidal erect terminal and axillary, trichotomus paniculate, cymes panicle, branches smooth, bracts small passing into leaves below.

Perianth campanulate, smooth, about ⅕ inch long, divided into four (rarely five) triangular, acute, spreading segments, valvate, in bud rather fleshy, at first straw coloured, changing to deep reddish purple provided at the mouth with four erect, fleshy, rounded lobes. Stamens four, opposite, perianth segments, filaments short, in-

serted in mouth of perianth alternating with erect lobes. Anthers short, two-celled, introrse, ovary half, inferior, tapering, one-celled, an erect central placenta, rising from base and not reaching to the top, to the summit of which are attached three or four pendulous ovules without the usual coverings, style filiform, stigma small, three or four lobed on a level with anthers.

Fruit concealed about size of a pea, spherical, crowned by rim-like remains of perianth tube, smooth, rather fleshy, nearly black, seed solitary.

The trees are felled or dug up by roots; the branches are worthless, so are cut off. It is usual to leave the trunk on the ground for several months for the white ants to eat away the sap wood, which is also of no value; it is then trimmed and sawn into billets 2 to 2½ feet long and taken to mills in the forests, where it is again trimmed and sorted into grades. It is heavy, hard, but splits easily; colour light yellow, transverse sections yellow to light reddish brown, with alternating light and dark concentric zones nearly equal in diameter, numerous pores, and traversed by many very narrow medullary rays. Odour characteristic, aromatic, persistent; taste peculiar, strongly aromatic. Indian Sandalwood is a Government monopoly.

¶ *Medicinal Action and Uses.* Used internally in chronic bronchitis, a few drops on sugar giving relief; also in gonorrhœa and gleet; in chronic cystitis, with benzoic and boric acids. Much used as a perfume for different purposes. The wood is used for making fancy articles and is much carved.

Fluid extract, 1 to 2 drachms. Oil, 5 to 20 drops.

¶ *Adulterants.* Castor oil is often added, and on the Continent oil of cedar, made by distilling the chips remaining from the manufacture of lead pencils.

¶ *Other Species.* Pterocarpus santalinus or *Santalum rubrum* (*Red Sandalwood*), solely used for colouring and dyeing. Other varieties come from the Sandwich Islands, Western Australia and New Caledonia.

SANDSPURRY, COMMON

Arenaria rubra (LINN.)
N.O. Caryophyllaceæ

Synonyms. Spergularia rubra. Sabline rouge. Tissa rubra. Birda rubra
Part Used. Herb
Habitat. Europe, Russia, Asia, North America, Australia

Common in Britain in sandy, gravelly heaths and waste places near the sea. Flowers all the summer. There are two marked varieties: the one growing inland has small flowers, thin leaves, short capsules, seeds rarely bordered. The other, often called *Spergularia Marina*, is larger in every respect and has fleshy leaves. For medicinal purposes the one most used is found in Malta, Sicily and Algiers, growing in dry sandy soil from Quebec to Virginia.

¶ *Description.* An annual or biennial plant, glabrous or with a short viscid down in the upper parts; numerous stems branching from the base forming prostrate tufts 3 to 6 inches long; leaves narrow, linear; very short conspicuous scarious stipules at the base. Flowers usually pink, sometimes white, but variable size; short pedicels in forked cymes, usually leafy at base. Petals shorter, rarely longer than the sepals. Seeds more or less flattened.

¶ *Medicinal Action and Uses.* Long used in bladder diseases. It contains a resinous, aromatic substance which presumably is its active principle. Very valuable for calculus diseases and acute and chronic cystitis.

¶ *Dosages.* Aqueous extract up to 30 grains, or of the fluid extract, 1 fluid drachm three or four times a day. Infusion, 1 oz. to 1 pint. Its taste is saline and slightly aromatic.

SANICLE, WOOD

Sanicula Europæa (LINN.)
N.O. Umbelliferæ

Synonyms. Poolroot. Self-Heal
Part Used. Herb
Habitat. Wood Sanicle is an umbelliferous perennial plant, common in woods and thickets and damp moist places, and generally distributed over the British Isles. It is most abundant in the middle and north of Europe and is found on the mountains of tropical Africa. It is the only representative in this country of the genus Sanicula, to which very few species are assigned

¶ *Description.* The root-stock (the short underground stem from which each year's new stalks grow upward) is shortly creeping and fibrous, with a few thick, brownish scales at the top, the remains of decayed leafstalks. The stem, erect, 8 inches to 2 feet high, is simple, often leafless or with a single leaf. The radical leaves are on stalks 2 to 8 inches long, the leaves themselves palmately three to five partite and divided nearly to the base of the leaf, the lobes, or divisions, often three-cleft again. The leaves are heart-shaped at the base near the stalk and toothed like a saw.

The flowers are in umbels. Each little group, or umbellule, forms a hemispherical head. The little stalks, each bearing a head of flowers, join together at one spot again to form what is termed a compound or general umbel, as in most plants of this order. In the case of the Sanicle, the umbel is said to be irregular, as the converging stalks forming these rays are often divided into two or three prongs. The flowers are pinkish-white, $\frac{1}{16}$ inch across, the outer flowers of the umbellules being without stamens; the inner, without pistils. They blossom in May and June and are succeeded in August by roundish seeds, which are covered with prickles, causing them to adhere to everything they touch.

The plant is glabrous and bright green, the leaves paler beneath and the stems often reddish.

The origin of the name of this genus is the Latin word *sano* (I heal or cure), in reference to the medicinal virtues.

In the Middle Ages the power of Sanicle was proverbial:

> Celuy qui sanicle a
> De mire affaire il n'a.

and

> Qui a la Bugle et la Sanicle fait aux chirugiens la niche.

It was as a vulnerary that this plant gained its medical reputation. Lyte and other herbalists say that it will 'make whole and sound all wounds and hurts, both inward and outward.'

Wood Sanicle has locally often been known as Self-Heal, a name which belongs rightly to another quite distinct herb, *Prunella vulgaris*, belonging to the Labiate order.

¶ *Cultivation*. Sanicle is generally collected from wild specimens.

In a moist soil and a shady situation, Sanicle will thrive excellently, especially in rich soil.

Propagation may be effected by division of roots, any time from September to March, the best time for the operation being in the autumn. Plant from 8 to 9 inches apart each way.

¶ *Part Used*. The whole herb, collected in June and dried. Gather the herb only on a fine day, in the morning, when the sun has dried off the dew.

¶ *Constituents*. As yet no analysis has been made of this plant, but evidence of tannin in its several parts is afforded by the effects produced by the plant.

In taste it is at first very bitter and astringent, afterwards acrid, and probably partakes of the poisonous acridity which is so frequent in the Umbelliferæ. In the fresh leaves, the taste is very slight, but considerable in the dry leaves, and in the extract made from them.

¶ *Medicinal Action and Uses*. Astringent, alterative. Sanicle is usually given in combination with other herbs in the treatment of blood disorders, for which it is in high esteem.

As an internal remedy, it is of great benefit in all chest and lung complaints, chronic coughs and catarrhal affections, inflammation of the bronchii, spitting of blood, and all affections of the pulmonary organs.

As an alterative, it has a good reputation, and it is useful in leucorrhœa, dysentery, diarrhœa, etc.

It effectually cleanses the system of morbid secretions and leaves the blood healthier and in better condition. The infusion of 1 oz. to a pint of boiling water is taken in wineglassful doses.

Sanicle is used as a gargle in sore throat, quinsy, and whenever an astringent gargle is required. Culpepper mentions the use of Sanicle for disease of the lungs and throat, and recommends the gargle being made from a decoction of the leaves and root in water, a little honey being added.

In scald-head of children and all cases of rashes, the decoction or infusion forms an admirable external remedy.

Sanicle is popularly employed in France and Germany as a remedy for profuse bleeding from the lungs, bowels, and other internal organs and for checking dysentery, the fresh juice being given in tablespoonful doses.

¶ *Preparations*. Fluid extract, ¼ to 1 drachm. A strong decoction of the leaves used to be a popular remedy for bleeding piles.

The root of an American species, *Sanicula marilandica*, contains resin and volatile oil, and has been used with alleged success in intermittent fever and in chorea, in doses of 10 to 60 grains.

American Bastard Sanicle belongs, not to this genus, but to the genus *Mitella*, and the Bear's Ear Sanicle (*Cortusa Matthiola*) is likewise not a true Sanicle, being related to the Primroses and Auriculas.

Yorkshire Sanicle is one of the names given sometimes to Butterwort, or Marsh Violet (*Pinguicula vulgaris*), a plant with violet-coloured flowers and thick plaintain-shaped leaves, which grow in a tuft or rosette on the ground, and to the touch are greasy, causing them to be used for application to sores and chapped hands.

SARSAPARILLA, AMERICAN

Aralia nudicaulis (LINN.)
N.O. Araliaceæ

Synonyms. False Sarsaparilla. Wild Sarsaparilla. Shot Bush. Small Spikenard. Wild Liquorice. Rabbit Root
Part Used. Root
Habitat. Canada to the Carolinas

¶ *Description*. A herbaceous perennial, with large, tortuous, fleshy, horizontal, creeping, long roots, externally yellow brown, from which grows a large solitary compound leaf. Leaflets oval, obovate, acute, finely serrate. Flower-stem also comes from root, naked, about 1 foot high, terminating in three small many-flowered greenish umbels, no involucres. Fruit a small, black berry the size of elderberry. The root has a sweet spicy taste, and a pleasant aromatic smell.

¶ *Medicinal Action and Uses.* Alterative, pectoral, diaphoretic, sudorific. Used as a substitute for Smilax Sarsaparilla is useful in pulmonary diseases and externally as a wash for indolent ulcers and shingles. It is said to be used by the Crees under the name of Rabbit Root for syphilis and as an application to recent wounds. It contains resin, oil, tannin, albumen, an acid, mucilage and cellulose.

Fluid extract, ½ to 1 drachm.

SARSAPARILLA, CARACAO

Habitat. La Guayra

¶ *Description.* The radicals are often very amylaceous internally and in this respect is very like *Sarsaparilla papyracea*, but the plant has now almost been destroyed and is difficult to obtain. The roots contain large quantities of starch.

S. papyracea, native of Trinidad, French Guiana and North Brazil, is a near ally of *S. officinalis*, and like it, is only known by is leaf specimens; it is recognized by the old stems and lower branches, which instead of being cylindrical, as in most other species, always remain intensely quadrangular, their angles having very flat closely crowded prickles and leaves more membranaceous. The *Rio Negro Smilax* is an allied species *Smilax Spruceana*. This plant is known as affording *Guatemala Sarsaparilla* and is considered to be identical with *Sarsaparilla papyracea*. *Smilax syphilitica* is a native of New Grenada, has a smooth round stem, bearing at the knots two to four short, thick, straight prickles. Leaves 1 foot long, oblong, lanceolate, acuminate, shining, coriaceous, three nerved, ending in a long point.

Guayaquil Sarsaparilla grows in the valleys of the Western slopes of Equatorial Andes. It appears in commerce carelessly packed in bales. The rhizome and parts of the stem often mixed with the root, the stem is round and prickly, root dark, large and coarse, with much fibre. The bark furrowed thick and not mealy in the thinner portions of the root, which is near the foot-stalks. As the root gets thicker, the bark becomes thicker, smoother and amylaceous, showing when cut a pale yellow interior.

SARSAPARILLA, JAMAICA

Smilax ornata
N.O. Liliaceæ

Synonyms. Smilax Medica. Red-bearded Sarsaparilla
Part Used. Root
Habitat. Central America, principally Costa Rica

¶ *Description.* This plant derived its name from being exported to Europe through Jamaica. The word Sarsaparilla comes from the Spanish *Sarza*, meaning a bramble, and *parilla*, a vine, in allusion to the thorny stems of the plant. This is a non-mealy Sarsaparilla. It is a large perennial climber, rhizome underground, large, short, knotted, with thickened nodes and roots spreading up to 6 or 8 feet long. Stems erect, semi-woody, with very sharp prickles ½ inch long. Leaves large, alternate stalked, almost evergreen with prominent veins, seven nerved, mid-rib very strongly marked. Flowers and fruit not known. Cortex thick and brownish, with an orange red tint; when chewed it tinges the saliva, and gives a slightly bitter and mucilaginous taste, followed by a very acrid one; it contains a small proportion of starch, also a glucoside, sarsaponin, sarsapic acid, and fatty acids, palmitic, stearic, behenic, oleic and linolic.

Jamaica Sarsaparilla was introduced in the middle of the sixteenth century as a remedy for syphilis, and later came to be used for other chronic diseases, specially rheumatism. It is a mild gastric irritant due to its saponin content. The smoke of Sarsaparilla was recommended for asthma. It is also very useful as a tonic, alterative, diaphoretic and diuretic. Its active principle is a crystalline body, Parillin or Smilacin.

¶ *Preparations and Dosages.* Powdered root, ½ to 1 drachm. Fluid extract, U.S.P., ½ to 1 drachm. Fluid extract, B.P., 2 to 4 drachms. Solid extract, 10 to 20 grains. Compound solution, 2 to 8 drachms. Compound syrup, U.S.P., 4 drachms.

Smilax officinalis has a twining stem, angular and prickly; young shoots unarmed; leaves ovate, oblong, acute, cordate, smooth, 1 foot long; petioles 1 inch long, having tendrils above the base. This plant grows in New Granada, on the banks of Magdaline near Bajorgne. Commercially it consists of very long roots, with a thick bark, grey or brown colour. Almost odourless. Taste mucilaginous. The deep orange-tinted roots are the best.

¶ *Constituents.* Salseparin, starch, colouring matter, essential oil chloride of potassium, bassorin, albumen, pectic and ascitic acids, and salts of lime, oxide of iron, potassa and magnesia. It is said to be the source of *Honduras* Sarsaparilla and is considered the best of all Sarsaparillas. It is exported from the bay of Honduras in over 2 feet long roots folded into a sort of hank, with a few rootlets attached, grey or reddy brown, with mealy cortex. It has the same properties as the other varieties, but if alcohol is added to the infusions of the root it will greatly increase their medicinal qualities.

¶ *Medicinal Action and Uses.* Alterative, tonic. Used in chronic skin diseases, rheumatism, passive dropsy.

¶ *Dosages.* Powder, 20 grains. Infusion or syrup, 4 fluid ounces.

SARSAPARILLA, INDIAN

Hemidesmus Indica
N.O. Asclepiadeæ

Synonyms. Hemidesmus. Periploca Indica. Nunnari Asclepias. Pseudosarsa
Part Used. Dried root
Habitat. All parts of India, the Moluccas, and Ceylon

¶ *Description.* A climbing slender plant with twining woody stems, and a rust-coloured bark, leaves opposite, petiolate, entire, smooth, shiny and firm, varying in shape and size according to their age. Flowers small green outside, deep purple inside, in axillary, sessile racemes, imbricated with flowers, followed with scale-like bracts. Fruit two long slender spreading follicles.

This plant has long been used in India as an antisyphilitic in place of Sarsaparilla, but was not introduced into England till 1831. The root is long, tortuous, rigid, cylindrical, little branched, consisting of aligneous centre, a brownish corky bark, furrowed and with annular cracks, odour aromatic, probably due to Coumarin and not unlike Sassafras or new-mown hay, with a bitter, sweetish, feeble aromatic taste. One side of the root is sometimes separated from the cork and raised above the cortex and transversely fissured, showing numerous laticiferous cells in the cortex.

¶ *Constituents.* Unknown. No satisfactory investigation has yet been made of the chemical properties. But a volatile oil has been found in it and a peculiar crystallizable principle, called by some Hemidesmine; others suggest that the substance is only a stearoptene. It also contains some starch, saponin, and in the suberous layer tannic acid.

¶ *Medicinal Action and Uses.* Alterative, tonic and diuretic. Useful for rheumatism, scrofula, skin diseases and thrush; it is used as an infusion, but not as a decoction as boiling dissipates its active volatile principle. Two oz. of the root are infused in 1 pint of boiling water and left standing for 1 hour then strained off and drunk in 24 hours.

It has been successfully used in the cure of venereal disease, proving efficacious where American Sarsaparilla has failed. Native doctors utilize it in nephritic complaints and for sore mouths of children.

Syrup, B.P., ½ to 1 drachm.

Particularly indicated for inveterate syphilis, pseudo-syphilis, mescurio-syphilis and struma in all its forms. Also valuable in gonorrhœal neuralgia and other depraved conditions of the system as well as for other diseases treated by other varieties.

Powder, 30 grains three times daily. Infusion or syrup, 4 fluid ounces.

An Alterative Mixture

1 lb. Rio Negro Sarsaparilla root, or in place of it Stillingia Sylvatica; 6 oz. rasped guaiac wood; aniseed and liquorice root bruised 2 oz. of each; 1 lb. molasses; 1 oz. Mezereon root-bark and 6 Cloves. Put all these into 2 gallons of boiling water and shake vessel well. When fermentation starts, take 4 fluid ounces three times daily.

SARSAPARILLA, WILD

Aralia nudicaulis (LINN.)
N.O. Araliaceæ

Synonyms. Bamboo Brier. Smilax Sarsaparilla
Part Used. Root
Habitat. A native of the southern United States and grows in swampy woods and thickets

¶ *Description.* It has a stout, flexuous and square stem, with a few hooked prickles above. Leaves unarmed, elliptical-ovate, cuspidate, abruptly contracted at each end; three strong veins, two lateral smaller secondary ones; underside glaucous, 3 inches diameter, on short margined petioles, with two long tendrils at their bases. Flowers

LXXXI

JAMAICA SARSAPARILLA
Smilax Ornata

SASSAFRAS
Sassafras Officinale

yellowish-white, appearing May to August, in small thin umbels of three or four red or black berries, three-seeded.

¶ *Medicinal Action and Uses.* Alterative, tonic, antisyphilitic. Said to be inferior to all other Sarsaparillas. Much used by the American Indians. Used freely in decoction.

¶ *Other Species.*

Smilax Medica has an angular stem armed with straight prickles at joints, and a few hooked ones at intervals; paper-like leaves, bright green both sides, smooth, cordate, auriculate, shortly acuminate, five-nerved prominent veins underneath and otherwise variable in form. Mid-rib and petioles, when old, have straight, subulate prickles,

peduncles three lines to 1 inch; umbels twelve flowers; pedicle three lines long. Found growing in Papantla, Inspan, etc. Said to be similar to the Mexican or Vera Cruz Sarsapa of commerce, which may be derived from this species.

SARSAPARILLA MEXICAN (*Synonym.* Vera Cruz Sarsaparilla), as found in commerce, has a caudex with a number of long radicles which are smaller and have a thinner bark than the Honduras variety, contain little starch and have square endodermal cells with thickened walls, and more or less oval lumen. The taste is acrid and the plant contains the medical properties of other Sarsaparillas.

See SMILAX.

SASSAFRAS

Sassafras officinale (LEES and EBERM.)
N.O. Lauraceæ

Synonyms. Sassafras varifolium. Laurus Sassafras. Sassafrax. Sassafras radix
Parts Used. Bark-root and the root, pith
Habitat. Eastern United States, from Canada to Florida, and Mexico

¶ *Description.* The name 'Sassafras,' applied by the Spanish botanist Monardes in the sixteenth century, is said to be a corruption of the Spanish word for saxifrage. The tree stands from 20 to 40 feet high, with many slender branches, and smooth, orange-brown bark. The leaves are broadly oval, alternate, and 3 to 7 inches long. The flowers are small, and of an inconspicuous, greenish-yellow colour. The roots are large and woody, their bark being soft and spongy, rough, and reddish or greyish-brown in colour. The living bark is nearly white, but exposure causes its immediate discoloration. The roots are imported in large, branched pieces, which may or may not be covered with bark, and often have attached to them a portion of the lower part of the trunk. The central market for all parts is Baltimore. The entire root is official in the British Pharmacopœia, but only the more active bark in the United States, where wood and bark form separate articles of commerce. The bark without its corky layer is brittle, and the presence of small crystals cause its inner surface to glisten. Both bark and wood have a fragrant odour, and an aromatic, somewhat astringent taste.

The tree, which has berries like those of cinnamon, appears to have been cultivated in England some centuries ago, for in 1633 Johnston wrote: 'I have given the figure of a branch taken from a little sassafras tree which grew in the garden of Mr. Wilmot at Bon.' Probably it was discovered by the Spaniards in Florida, for seventy years earlier there is mention of the reputation of its roots in Spain as a cure for syphilis, rheu-

matism, etc., though its efficacy has since then been much disputed.

The fragrant oil distilled from the root-bark is extensively used in the manufacture of the coarser kinds of perfume, and for scenting the cheapest grades of soap. The oil used in perfumes is also extracted from the fruits. The wood and bark of the tree furnish a yellow dye. In Louisiana, the leaves are used as a condiment in sauces, and also for thickening soups; while the young shoots are used in Virginia for making a kind of beer. Mixed with milk and sugar, Sassafras Tea, under the name of 'Saloop,' could, until a few years ago, be bought at London street-corners in the early mornings.

SASSAFRAS PITH (*Sassafras medulla*) is only official in the United States. It is usually found in thin, cylindrical pieces, which are light and spongy, white and insipid. Its principal constituent is mucilage, which may be prepared by adding 60 grains of the pith to a pint of boiling water. This remains limpid when alcohol is added. It is used as a demulcent, especially for inflammation of the eyes, and as a soothing drink in catarrhal affection.

¶ *Constituents.* The root-bark contains a heavy and a light volatile oil, camphorous matter, resin, wax, a decomposition product of tannic acid called Sassafrid, tannic acid, gum, albumen, starch, lignin and salts. Sassafrid bears some analogy to cinchonic red. The bark yields from 6 to 9 per cent. of oil, of which the chief constituent is Safrol (80 per cent.). It is one of the heaviest of the volatile oils, and when cold deposits four- or six-sided prisms of Sassafras camphor, which retain the odour. It should be preserved in well-stoppered, amber-coloured bottles, away from the light. Three bushels of the root yield about 1 lb.

Safrol has been found to be one of those bodies which can exist either in a solid or a liquid condition long after freezing or melting-point. Chemically, it has been found to be the methylene ether of allyl-dioxibenene. It is found in many other species, is now commercially extracted from oil of Camphor, and could possibly be obtained from some members of the Cinnamomum family. Physiologically and therapeutically it is equivalent to oil of Sassafras.

Oil of Sassafras is *chiefly* used for flavouring purposes, particularly to conceal the flavour of opium when given to children. In the United States of America it is employed for flavouring effervescing drinks.

¶ *Medicinal Action and Uses.* Aromatic, stimulant, diaphoretic, alterative. It is rarely given alone, but is often combined with guaiacum or sarsaparilla in chronic rheumatism, syphilis, and skin diseases.

The oil is said to relieve the pain caused by menstrual obstructions, and pain following parturition, in doses of 5 to 10 drops on sugar, the same dose having been found useful in gleet and gonorrhœa.

Safrol is found to be slowly absorbed from the alimentary canal, escaping through the lungs unaltered, and through the kidneys oxidized into piperonalic acid.

A teaspoonful of the oil produced vomiting, dilated pupils, stupor and collapse in a young man.

It is used as a local application for wens and for rheumatic pains, and it has been praised as a dental disinfectant.

Its use has caused abortion in several cases.

Dr. Shelby of Huntsville stated that it would both prevent and remove the injurious effects of tobacco.

A lotion of rose-water or distilled water, with Sassafras Pith, filtered after standing for four hours, is recommended for the eyes.

¶ *Dosage.* Of fluid extract, ½ to 1 drachm. Of Sassafras bark, 1 to 2 drachms. Of oil of Sassafras, 1 to 5 drops. Mucilage, U.S.P., 4 drachms.

¶ *Poison and Antidotes.* The oil can produce marked narcotic poisoning, and death by causing widespread fatty degeneration of the heart, liver, and kidneys, or, in a larger dose, by great depression of the circulation, followed by a centric paralysis of respiration.

¶ *Other Species.* The name is also applied to the following:

BLACK SASSAFRAS, or *Oliveri Cortex* (Oliver's Bark), a substitute for cinnamon in Australia.

SWAMP SASSAFRAS, or *Magnolia glauca*, an aromatic, diaphoretic, tonic bitter.

AUSTRALIAN SASSAFRAS, or *Atherosperma moschatum*, a powerful poison, useful in rheumatism, syphilis and bronchitis.

SASSAFRAS GOESIANUM, or *Massoja aromatica*, yielding Massoi Bark.

CALIFORNIA SASSAFRAS, or *Umbellularia californica*, the leaves of which are employed in headache, colic and diarrhœa.

SASSY BARK

Erythrophlœum guineense (G. DON)
N.O. Leguminosæ

Synonyms. Nkasa. Mancona Bark. Doom Bark. Ordeal Bark. Casca Bark. Saucy Bark. Red Water Bark. Cortex erythrophlei
Part Used. Bark of the tree and branches
Habitat. Upper Guinea and Senegambia

¶ *Description.* The tree is large and spreading, and the bark very hard, breaking with a short, granular fracture. It varies in size and thickness according to the age of the stem or branch. It may be flat or curved, dull grey, red-brown, or almost black, with reddish warts or circular spots merging into bands running longitudinally. It is inodorous, with an astringent, acrid taste.

In West Africa the drug is used as an ordeal poison in trials for witchcraft and sorcery.

Possibly other species yield the Sassy Bark of commerce, differences being noticed in its properties at different periods.

¶ *Constituents.* Sassy Bark yields its properties to water. The poisonous principle Erythrophleine was obtained and confirmed

in several experiments, possessing an action similar to that of digitalis. From this an acid called erythrophleic acid and a volatile alkaloid called Manzçonine were obtained by the action of hydrochloric acid. In contact with sulphuric acid and black manganese oxide, a violet colour is obtained, rather paler than that produced with strychnine. The bark also contains tannin and resin.

¶ *Medicinal Action and Uses.* Astringent, analgesic. The hydrochloride has been used in dental surgery. Erythrophleine causes a slow, strong pulse, with a rise in the arterial pressure. Purging is probably due to local action on peristalsis, and vomiting, the result of influence on the nerve centres, as it occurs when the alkaloid is given hypodermically. There has been much controversy concerning its anæsthetic powers. It has not yet been obtained in crystalline form, and needs fuller investigation.

Observations in West Africa about 1859 showed that Sassy Bark produced constriction in the fauces, with prickling, and later, numbness. It is asserted that it gives great relief in dyspnœa, but is uncertain as a heart tonic. The powder is strongly sternutatory.

It has been useful in mitral disease and dropsy, but disturbs the digestion even more than digitalis.

¶ *Dosages.* Of the alkaloid, $\frac{1}{20}$ to $\frac{1}{30}$ grain. Of the extract, $\frac{1}{4}$ to $\frac{1}{3}$ grain.

A solution of $\frac{1}{10}$ of 1 per cent. is used as an application to the cornea.

¶ *Poison with Antidotes.* An overdose causes stricture across the brow, severe pain in the head, coma, and death.

SAUNDERS, RED

Pterocarpus santalinus
N.O. Leguminosæ

Synonyms. Pterocarpi Lignum. Santalum rubrum. Lignum rubrum. Red Sandalwood. Rubywood. Rasura Santalum Ligni. Red Santal Wood. Sappan

Part Used. Wood

Habitat. Madras Presidency and Ceylon

¶ *Description.* A tree of 20 to 25 feet high, covered with rough bark resembling that of the Common Alder, and bearing spikes of yellow flowers. Plantations have been formed for its cultivation in Southern India, where it is very rare.

The name *Santalinus* refers to its name of red Sandalwood, which all its Indian titles signify, though it bears no relationship to *Santalum*. It is imported, usually from Ceylon, in the form of irregular logs or billets, without bark and sapwood, and about 3 to 5 feet in length. They are heavy, dense, reddish or blackish brown outside, and, if cut transversely, a deep blood-red inside, variegated with zones of a lighter red colour. In pharmacy the wood is in the form of chips, raspings, or coarse red powder. When rubbed, the wood has a faint peculiar odour, but is otherwise odourless, with a slight, astringent taste.

Gum Kino is obtained from other species of *Pterocarpus*. The chief use of Red Saunders wood is as a dye-stuff. In India it is employed mixed with sapan wood, for dyeing silk, cotton and wool, the shade of red varying according to the mordant used.

¶ *Constituents.* The colouring principle, called Santalin, is readily soluble in alcohol (90 per cent.), but almost insoluble in water. Ether, alkalis, and three other crystalline principles have also been described as being present: Santal, Pterocarpin, and Homopterocarpin. A small quantity of tannin, probably kino-tannic acid, has also been found in the wood. The colouring principle is partially soluble in some of the essential oils, such as lavender, rosemary, cloves, and oil of bitter almonds, and as a colouring agent it forms part of the official Comp. Tincture of Lavender.

The colouring principles of the West African Barwood (*Pterocarpus angolensis*) and Camwood (*Baphia nitida*) are closely allied with that of Red Saunders, if not identical.

¶ *Medicinal Action and Uses.* Astringent, tonic. Chiefly used medicinally in India, and employed in pharmacy for colouring tinctures.

SAVINE

Sabina cacumina
N.O. Coniferæ

Synonyms. Savine Tops

Part Used. Fresh dried tops of Juniperas Sabina collected in spring from plants grown in Britain

Habitat. Britain. Indigenous to Northern States of America, Middle and Southern Europe

¶ *Description.* A shrub growing to a height of a few feet in Britain, but found as a tree in some Greek Islands, evergreen and compact in growth, spreads horizontally, branches round, tough, and slender; bark, when young, pale green, becoming rough with age on trunk; leaves small, ovate, dark green, in four rows, opposite, scale-like, ovate-lanceolate, having on back a shallow groove containing an oblong or roundish gland. The fruit is a blackish purple berry, ovoid in shape, containing three seeds. Flowers unisexual; odour peculiar, terebinthinate; taste disagreeable, resinous and bitter.

¶ *Constituents.* Volatile oil, resin, gallic acid, chlorophyl extractive, lignin, calcareous salts, a fixed oil, gum and salts of potassia.

¶ *Medicinal Action and Uses.* Savine is an irritant when administered internally or locally; it is a powerful emmenagogue in large doses; it is an energetic poison leading to gastro enteritis collapse and death. It should never be used in pregnancy, as it produces abortion. It is rarely given internally, but is useful as an ointment and as a dressing to blisters in order to promote discharge; also applied externally to syphilitic warts, and other skin trouble. The powdered leaves mixed with an equal part of verdigris are used to destroy warts.

¶ *Adulterant.* Red Cedar (*Juniperus Virginiana*, Linn.) is often commonly referred to as Savin and is substituted commercially, the tops of *J. Phœnicæ* (Linn.), which contain volatile oil, are also admixed in Europe.

See CEDARS.

SAVORY, SUMMER

Satureia hortensis (LINN.)
N.O. Labiatæ

Part Used. Herb

The genus *Satureia* (the old Latin name used by Pliny) comprises about fourteen species of highly aromatic, hardy herbs or under-shrubs, all, except one species, being natives of the Mediterranean region.

Several species have been introduced into England, but only two, the annual Summer or Garden Savory and the perennial, Winter Savory are generally grown. The annual is more usually grown, but the leaves of both are employed in cookery, like other sweet herbs, the leaves and tender tops being used, with marjoram and thyme, to season dressings for turkey, veal or fish.

Both species were noticed by Virgil as being among the most fragrant of herbs, and on this account recommended to be grown near bee-hives. There is reason to suppose that they were cultivated in remote ages, before the East Indian spices were known and in common use. Vinegar, flavoured with Savory and other aromatic herbs, was used by the Romans in the same manner as mint sauce is by us.

In Shakespeare's time, Savory was a familiar herb, for we find it mentioned, together with the mints, marjoram and lavender, in *The Winter's Tale*.

In ancient days, the Savorys were supposed to belong to the Satyrs, hence the name Satureia. Culpepper says:

'Mercury claims dominion over this herb. Keep it dry by you all the year, if you love yourself and your ease, and it is a hundred pounds to a penny if you do not.'

He considered Summer Savory better than Winter Savory for drying to make conserves and syrups.

John Josselyn, one of the early settlers in America, gives a list of plants introduced there by the English colonists to remind them of the gardens they had left behind. Winter and Summer Savory are two of those mentioned.

¶ *Description.* Summer Savory is a hardy, pubescent annual, with slender erect stems about a foot high. It flowers in July, having small, pale lilac labiate flowers, axillary, on short pedicels, the common peduncle sometimes three-flowered. The leaves, about ⅓ inch long, are entire, oblong-linear, acute, shortly narrowed at the base into petioles, often fascicled. The hairs on the stem are short and decurved.

¶ *Cultivation.* Summer Savory is raised from seeds, sown early in April, in shallow drills, 9 inches or a foot apart. Select a sunny situation and thin out the seedlings, when large enough, to 6 inches apart in the rows. It likes a rich, light soil.

The seeds may also be sown broadcast, when they must be thinned out, the thinned out seedlings being planted in another bed at 6 inches distance from each other and well watered. The seeds are very slow in germinating.

The early spring seedlings may be first topped for fresh use in June. When the plants are in flower, they may be pulled up and dried for winter use.

¶ *Uses.* As a *pot-herb*, Savory, which has a distinctive taste, though it somewhat recalls that of marjoram, is not only added to stuffings, pork pies and sausages as a wholesome seasoning, but sprigs of it, fresh, may be boiled with broad beans and green peas, in the same manner as mint. It is also boiled with dried peas in making pea-soup. For garnishing it has been used as a substitute for parsley and chervil.

¶ *Medicinal Action and Uses.* Savory has aromatic and carminative properties, and though chiefly used as a culinary herb, it may be added to medicines for its aromatic and warming qualities. It was formerly deemed a sovereign remedy for the colic and a cure for flatulence, on this account, and was also considered a good expectorant.

Culpepper tells us that

'The juice dropped into the eyes removes dimness of sight if it proceed from thin humours distilled from the brain. The juice heated with oil of Roses and dropped in the ears removes noise and singing and deafness: outwardly applied with wheat flour, it gives ease to them.'

He says:

'Keep it dry, make conserves and syrups of it for your use; for which purpose the Summer kind is best. This kind is both hotter and drier than the Winter kind. . . . It expels tough phlegm from the chest and lungs, quickens the dull spirits in the lethargy, if the juice be snuffed up the nose; dropped into the eyes it clears them of thin cold humours proceeding from the brain . . . outwardly applied with wheat flour as a poultice, it eases sciatica and palsied members.'

Both the old authorities and modern gardeners agree that a sprig of either of the Savorys rubbed on wasp and bee stings gives instant relief.

SAVORY, WINTER

Satureia montana (LINN.)
N.O. Labiatæ

Part Used. Herb

Winter Savory is a dwarf, hardy, perennial, glabrous or slightly pubescent under shrub, also a native of Southern Europe, and it has been known in Great Britain since 1562.

The stems are woody at the base, diffuse, much branched. The leaves are oblong, linear and acute, or the lower ones spatulate or wedge-shaped and obtuse. The flowers, in bloom in June, are very pale-purple, the cymes shortly pedunculate, approximating to a spike or raceme.

¶ *Cultivation.* It is propagated either from seeds, sown at a similar period and in the same manner as Summer Savory, or from cuttings and divisions of root. It is woodier and more bushy than Summer Savory.

Cuttings formed of young side shoots, with a heel attached, may be taken in April or June, and will readily root under a hand-glass, or in a shady border outside.

Divisions of the roots should be made in March or April, and plants obtained in this way, or from cuttings, should be permanently inserted during a showery period in the latter part of summer, in rows, at the distance of 1 foot apart.

The plant grows better in a poor, stony soil than a rich one. In a rich soil, plants take in too much moisture to stand the severity of our winter. In soil that suits it, Winter Savory makes a good-sized shrub. It will continue for several years, but when the plants are old the shoots are short and not so well furnished with leaves. It is, therefore, well to raise a supply of young plants every other year.

Parkinson tells us that Winter Savory used to be dried and powdered and mixed with grated bread-crumbs, 'to breade their meate, be it fish or flesh, to give it a quicker relish.' It is recommended by old writers, together with other herbs, in the dressing of trout.

When dried, it is used as seasoning in the same manner as Summer Savory, but is not employed medicinally.

Culpepper says that it is a good remedy for the colic.

¶ *Other Species.*
Satureia thymbra, which is used in Spain as a spice and is closely allied to the Savories grown in English kitchen gardens, yields an oil containing about 19 per cent. of thymal. Other species of *Satureia* contain carvacrol. The oil from wild plants of Winter Savory contains 30 or 40 per cent. of carvacrol, and that from cultivated plants still more.

SAW PALMETTO

Sarenoa serrulata (HOOK. F.)
N.O. Palmaceæ

Synonyms. Sabal. Sabal serrulata
Part Used. Partially-dried ripe fruit
Habitat. The Atlantic Coast from South Carolina to Florida, and southern California

¶ *Description.* The plant grows from 6 to 10 feet high, forming what is called the 'palmetto scrub.' It has a crown of large leaves, and the fruit is irregularly-spherical to oblong-ovoid, deep red-brown, slightly wrinkled, being from ½ to 1 inch long and about ⅓ inch in diameter. It contains a hard brown seed. The taste is sweetish and not agreeable, and the panicle containing it may weigh as much as 9 lb. It has no odour.

¶ *Constituents.* Volatile oil, fixed oil, glucose, about 63 per cent. of free acids, and 37 per cent. of ethyl esters of these acids. The oil obtained exclusively from the nut is a glyceride of fatty acids, thick and of a greenish colour, without fruity odour. From the whole fruit can be obtained by pressure about 1⅓ per cent. of a brownish-yellow to dark red oil, soluble in alcohol, ether, chloroform and benzene, and partly soluble in dilute solution of potassium hydroxide. The fixed oil is soluble in alcohol, ether, and petroleum benzin. The presence of an alkaloid is uncertain.

The following formula will give elixir of sabal with terpinhydrate. Dissolve 1·75 gram of terpinhydrate in 40 mm. of fluid extract of sabal and 10 mm. of alcohol. Add 1 mm. of tincture of sweet orange peel, 0·2 mm. of solution of saccharin, 40 mm. of glycerin, and 100 mm. of syrup. This preparation will contain 8 grains of terpinhydrate and 184 grains of sabal in each fluid ounce.

¶ *Medicinal Action and Uses.* Diuretic, sedative, tonic. It is milder and less stimulant than cubeb or copaiba, or even oil of sandalwood. Like these, it has the power of affecting the respiratory mucous membrane, and is used for many complaints which are accompanied by chronic catarrh. It has been claimed that sabal is capable of increasing the nutrition of the testicles and mammæ in functional atony of these organs. It probably acts by reducing catarrhal irritation and a relaxed condition of bladder and urethra. It is a tissue builder.

¶ *Dosages.* Of fluid extract, ½ to 1 drachm. Of solid extract, 5 to 15 grains.

SAXIFRAGE, BURNET

Pimpinella Saxifraga (LINN.)
N.O. Umbelliferæ

Synonyms. Lesser Burnet. Saxifrage
Parts Used. Root, herb
Habitat. It grows abundantly in dry, chalky pastures, and is very generally distributed over the country

The Burnet Saxifrage, sometimes cultivated for kitchen use, is neither a Burnet nor a Saxifrage, but has obtained the latter name because supposed to break up stone in the bladder, and the former from the similarity of its leaves to the Greater and Lesser Burnets, though its umbels of white flowers mark the difference at the first glance.

¶ *Description.* The root-stock is slender, the stem also slender, round, striate, 9 inches to 3 feet high. The root-leaves are numerous, shortly stalked, pinnate, the leaflets oval or roundish, four to eight pairs, sometimes so deeply cut as to be bipinnate, sometimes merely serrated. The stem-leaves are few, with the petiole dilated, particularly in the uppermost ones, the leaflets narrower than in the radical leaves, and pinnatifid. The upper leaves are reduced to dilated sheaths, the leaflets represented by one or more linear lobes. The umbels are regular, flat-topped, the umbelules many-flowered, the individual flowers ¹⁄₁₀ inch across, white, with notched petals. The whole plant is dark green, generally glabrous.

¶ *Parts Used.* The leaves and roots. The whole herb is cut in July and dried in the same way as the Burnets.

¶ *Medicinal Action and Uses.* Resolvent, diaphoretic, stomachic, diuretic. The root is very hot and acrid, burning the mouth like pepper. On drying, or on being kept long, its pungency is considerably diminished. It contains a bitter resin and a blue essential oil, which communicates that colour to water or spirit on distillation, and is said to be used in Germany for colouring brandy.

The oil and resin contained are useful to relieve flatulent indigestion.

The fresh root chewed is good for toothache and paralysis of the tongue. A decoction has the reputation of removing freckles. It is said to dissolve mucus, and on this account is used as a gargle in hoarseness and some cases of throat affection.

It is also prescribed in asthma and dropsy.

Small bunches of the leaves and shoots, tied together and suspended in a cask of beer impart to it an agreeable aromatic flavour, and are thought to correct tart or spoiled wines.

Cows which feed on this plant have their flow of milk increased.

Culpepper says:

'The whole plant is binding . . . it is a cordial. In the composition of the *Syrupus Altheæ* it is generally used instead of the Great Burnet Saxifrage.'

SAXIFRAGE, GREATER BURNET

Pimpinella magna
N.O. Umbelliferæ

Parts Used. Herb, seeds

The Greater Burnet Saxifrage is very like large specimens of *Pimpinella Saxifraga*, but larger in all its parts and of a paler green in colour, the root-stock much thicker and the stems generally 2 to 4 feet high, stouter and more angular. The leaflets are larger and broader, generally less deeply cut. The umbels and flowers are similar, though the styles are longer and more slender.

¶ *Medicinal Action and Uses.* This plant has much the same medicinal properties as the former species, and has been employed in a similar manner.

The root is very acrid, and is powerfully diuretic, having been prescribed with success, in strong infusion, in disorders arising from obstructions of the viscera. The seeds are carminative, and have been used in colic and for dispersing wind in the stomach, administered in powdered form.

The Aniseed of medicine and commerce is a foreign species of this same genus.

Culpepper says this plant

'has the properties of the parsleys but eases

SCABIOUS, FIELD

Synonyms. Scabiosa arvensis
Part Used. Herb

¶ *Description*. There are several species of Scabious indigenous to these islands, of which the Field Scabious (*Knautia arvensis*) is the largest. It is abundant throughout Britain, flowering best, however, on chalk, and very frequent in meadows, hedgerows or amidst standing corn, where its large blossoms, of a delicate mauve, render it very conspicuous and attractive. The root is perennial, dark in colour and somewhat woody, and takes such a firm hold on the ground that it is only eradicated with difficulty. The stems are round and only slightly branched, 2 to 3 feet high, somewhat coarse with short, whitish hairs and rather bare of leaves, except at the base. The leaves vary in character in different plants and in different parts of the same plant; they grow in pairs on the stem and are hairy. The lowest leaves are stalked and very simple in character, about 5 inches long and 1 inch broad, lance-shaped, their margins cut into by large teeth. The upper ones are stalkless, their blades meeting across the main stem and cut into almost to the mid-rib, to form four or five pairs of narrow lobes, with a terminal big lobe. The flowers are all terminal and borne on long stalks. The heads are large and convex in outline, the inner florets are regularly cleft into four lobes or segments, the outer ones are larger and generally, though not always, with rays cut into very unequal segments. The florets when in bud are packed tightly, but with beautiful regularity. The fruit is rather large, somewhat four-cornered and crowned by several short, bristly hairs that radiate from its summit.

The generic name, *Knautia*, is derived

SCABIOUS, LESSER

Part Used. Herb

The Lesser Scabious is not uncommon on a chalky soil, and is distinguished from the former by its smaller size. The foliage is of a light hue and the leaves very finely cut into. The flowers are lilac, but in nearly globular heads, not so convex, the corollas being five-cleft, not four-cleft, and the outer

pains and provokes urine more effectually. . . . The distilled water, boiled with castoreum, is good for cramps and convulsions, and the seed used in comfits (like carraway seeds) will answer the same purpose. The juice of the herb dropped into bad wounds in the head, dries up their moisture and heals them.'

Knautia arvensis
N.O. Compositæ

from a Saxon botanist of the seventeenth century, Dr. Knaut. The name Scabious is supposed to be connected with the word 'scab' (a scaly sore), a word derived from the Latin *scabies* (a form of leprosy), for which and for other diseases of a similar character, some of these species were used as remedies.

¶ *Medicinal Action and Uses*. Gerard tells us: 'The plant gendereth scabs, if the decoction thereof be drunke certain daies and the juice used in ointments.' We are told that this juice 'being drunke, procureth sweat, especially with Treacle, and atenuateth and maketh thin, freeing the heart from any infection or pestilence.' Culpepper informs us also that it is 'very effectual for coughs, shortness of breath and other diseases of the lungs,' and that the 'decoction of the herb, dry or green, made into wine and drunk for some time together,' is good for pleurisy. The green herb, bruised and applied to any carbuncle was stated by him to dissolve the same 'in three hours' space,' and the same decoction removed pains and stitches in the side. The decoction of the root was considered a cure for all sores and eruptions, the juice being made into an ointment for the same purpose. Also, 'the decoction of the herb and roots outwardly applied in any part of the body, is effectual for shrunk sinews or veins and healeth green wounds, old sores and ulcers.' The juice of Scabious, with powder of Borax and Samphire, was recommended for removing freckles, pimples and leprosy, the head being washed with the same decoction, used warm, for dandruff and scurf, etc.

Scabiosa Columbaria
N.O. Compositæ

florets larger than the inner, though not quite so large as in the Field Scabious. Its properties are similar to the larger species just described.

Scabious herb should be collected in July and August and dried. The root is no longer used.

SCABIOUS, DEVIL'S BIT

Scabiosa succisa (LINN.)
N.O. Compositæ

Synonyms. Ofbit. Premorse Scabious
Part Used. Herb

The Devil's Bit Scabious is almost as common a plant as the preceding species, but is more often to be found in open meadows and on heaths than in the hedgerow and the cornfield.

¶ *Description.* It is a slender, little-branched plant, with a hairy stem, few leaves, which are oblong and not cut into, and almost globular heads of deep purplish-blue flowers. It is to be found in bloom from July to October. The florets composing the head are all very much the same size, the outer ones being scarcely larger than the inner. The stamens of each floret, as in the other species of Scabious are a very conspicuous feature, the anthers being large and borne upon filaments or threads that are almost as long again as the corolla. The root is, when fully grown, nearly the thickness of a finger, and ends in so abrupt a way as almost to suggest that it had been bitten off, a peculiarity that has given it a place in legends. In the first year of the plant's existence the root is like a diminutive carrot or radish in shape; it then becomes woody and dies away, the upper part excepted; as it decays and falls away, the gnawed or broken look results. The portion left throws out numerous lateral roots, which compensate for the portion that has perished. The plant derives its common name from this peculiarity in the form of the root. Gerard tells us:

'The greater part of the root seemeth to be bitten away; old fantastick charmers report that the divel did bite it for envie, because it is an herbe that hath so many good vertues and it is so beneficial to man-kinde.'

The legend referred to by Gerard tells how the devil found it in Paradise, but envying the good it might do to the human race, bit away a part of the root to destroy the plant, in spite of which it still flourishes, but with a stumped root. The legend seems to have been very widely spread, for the plant bears this name, not only in England but also on the Continent.

SCAMMONY. *See* BINDWEED, CONVOLVULUS

¶ *Medicinal Action and Uses.* This plant is still used for its diaphoretic, demulcent and febrifuge properties, the whole herb being collected in September and dried.

It makes a useful tea for coughs, fevers and internal inflammation. The remedy is generally given in combination with others, the infusion being given in wineglassful doses at frequent intervals. It purifies the blood, taken inwardly, and used as a wash externally is a good remedy for cutaneous eruptions. The juice made into an ointment is effectual for the same purpose. The warm decoction has also been used as a wash to free the head from scurf, sores and dandruff.

Culpepper assigned it many uses, saying that the root boiled in wine and drunk was very powerful against the plague and all pestilential diseases, and fevers and poison and bites of venomous creatures, and that 'it helpeth also all that are inwardly bruised or outwardly by falls or blows, dissolving the clotted blood,' the herb or root bruised and outwardly applied, taking away black and blue marks on the skin. He considered 'the decoction of the herb very effectual as a gargle for swollen throat and tonsils, and that the root powdered and taken in drink expels worms.' The juice or distilled water of the herb was deemed a good remedy for green wounds or old sores, cleansing the body inwardly and freeing the skin from sores, scurf, pimples, freckles, etc. The dried root used also to be given in powder, its power of promoting sweat making it beneficial in fevers.

The SHEEP'S (or SHEEP'S-BIT) SCABIOUS (*Jasione montana*) is not a true Scabious, though at first sight its appearance is similar. It may be distinguished from a Scabious by its united anthers, and it differs from a Compound Flower (Compositæ, to which the Scabious belongs) in having a two-celled capsule. It is a member of the Campanulaceæ, and is the only British species. The whole plant, when bruised, has a strong and disagreeable smell.

See CORNFLOWER, KNAPWEED, TEAZLE THISTLE.

SCOPOLIA

Scopola carniolica (JACQ.)
N.O. Solanaceæ

Synonyms. Scopolia atropoides. Scopola. Belladonna Scopola. Japanese Belladonna
Part Used. Dried rhizome
Habitat. Bavaria, Austro-Hungary, South-western Russia

¶ *Description.* The genus *Scopola* is a connecting link between *Atropa* and *Hyoscya-* mus, its leaf, flower and rhizome resembling the former, and the fruit the latter. The

Japanese *Scopola japonica* is so closely allied that it is doubtful if it can be regarded as a distinct species.

S. Carniolica grows in damp, stony places in hilly districts and resembles belladonna both in appearance and characteristics. It only grows to the height of 1 foot, and has thin leaves, its fruit being a transversely dehiscent capsule.

The rhizome is horizontal, curved, almost cylindrical, and somewhat flattened vertically. It is usually found in pieces from 2½ to 7½ cm. long and 0·8 to 1·6 cm. broad, often split before drying. The upper surface is marked with closely-set, large, cup-shaped stem-scars, and the colour varies from yellowish-brown to dark, brownish-grey; the fracture is short and sharp, showing a yellowish-white bark, its corky layer dark brown, or pale brown, the central pith being rather horny. It has scarcely any odour, and the taste is sweetish at first, but afterwards bitter and strongly acrid. The Japanese rhizome is larger, with circular scars, not whitish when broken, and having a slightly mousy, narcotic odour, and practically no bitterness in taste.

The bark of *S. Carniolica* is less thick than in belladonna and the starch grains smaller.

Scopolia is but little used in Britain, but has been used in America for many years in the manufacture of belladonna plasters.

¶ *Constituents.* The alkaloidal constituents are similar to those of Belladonna Root, hyoscine (scopolamine), however, predominating. Inactive scopolamine, also known as atroscine, is present, melting at 82° C. (179·6° F.) and yielding by hydrolysis tropic acid and scopoline. The result of an assay of many tons of the root of *Atropa Belladonna* and of the rhizome of Scopolia, each of the best qualities to be found in the American market, showed that while belladonna yielded on an average 0·50 per cent. of alkaloid, Scopolia yielded 0·58 per cent.

The root of *S. Carniolica* is official in the United States Pharmacopœia for the production of an extract and fluid extract. It should contain not less than 0·5 per cent. of alkaloids.

Scopolamine hydrobromide is recognized in the United States Pharmacopœia.

Scopolamine or hyoscine must be preserved in well-closed containers, protected from light. When pure, it forms a syrupy liquid. Great care must be used in tasting it, and then only in dilute solutions. When dried at 100° C. (212° F.) it loses about 12 per cent. of its weight. It is the same substance as Hyoscinæ Hydrobromicum. *Atro-*scine is an optically inert isomer of scopolamin and *Euscopol* is an optically inactive scopolaminum hydrobromicum.

¶ *Medicinal Action and Uses.* Narcotic and mydriatic. The medicinal properties are very like those of belladonna, but the crude drug has been scarcely used at all in internal medicine. Much of the hyoscine of commerce has been obtained from it during the last decade.

Many of the older investigations into the effects of scopolamine are contradictory because of the failure to realize the quantitative difference between *racemic* and *lævo-scopolamine*. The former, sometimes called *atrocine*, is very much less powerful in its effects upon the autonomic nerves, though its action upon the central nervous system is about equal.

Its most important use is as a cerebral sedative, especially in manias, hysteria, and drug habits, while in insomnias and epilepsy it increases the effects of other drugs, such as morphine and bromides. It is also useful to allay sexual excitement. In 1900 the use of a combination of morphine and scopolamine was introduced as a means of producing anæsthesia, under the name of 'Twilight Sleep,' either alone or as a preliminary to chloroform or ether, as its peculiar effect in large doses is to cause loss of memory, including that of pain. However, the anæsthesia has often been found to be unsatisfactory, while the mortality has been high.

¶ *Dosages.* Powdered extract, U.S.P., 1 to 5 grains. Of the drug, 1 to 2 grains. Of the fluid extract, U.S.P., 1 to 5 minims. Extract of Scopolia, ⅛ to ¼ grain. (Prepared by evaporating the fluid extract and assaying it so that it contains 2 per cent. of mydriatic alkaloids.) Of Scopolamine, ₁⁄₁₀₀ to ₁⁄₈₀ grain.

¶ *Poisonous, if Any, with Antidotes.* Many persons being very susceptible to the influence of the drug, the above doses of scopolamine may produce toxic symptoms, which are alarming, though the poisoning rarely ends fatally.

Sometimes there is disorientation, sometimes active delirium as in atropine poisoning. There may or may not be somnolence. The pupils may be dilated, the pulse rate accelerated and there is dryness of the mouth with a peculiar husky character of voice that appears to be due to laryngeal paralysis. If there should be serious difficulty in breathing, strychnine may be used. It is better not to give drugs for the relief of the delirium, but if very active, small doses of paraldehyde and bromides may be employed.

SCULLCAPS

Scutellarias
N.O. Labiatæ

Habitat. The Scullcaps, belonging to the genus *Scutellaria*, are herbaceous, slender, rarely shrubby, labiate plants, scattered over different parts of the world, in temperate regions and tropical mountains, being specially abundant in America. There are about ninety known species belonging to this genus, only two members of which are natives of Great Britain – *Scutellaria galericulata* and *S. minor*. Both are found on the banks of rivers and lakes, and in watery places generally, and are decumbent or spreading, seldom quite erect

N.O. Labiatæ

The generic name is from the Latin *scutella* (a little dish), from the lid of the calyx. The form of the latter is a peculiarity by which they can be recognized; it is bell-shaped, lipped, as Hooker describes it: 'the tube being dilated opposite to the posterior lip, with a broad, flattened hollow pouch, the lip and pouch being deciduous in fruit and the mouth closed after flowering.' Hooker adds: 'The only insect known to visit the first species is a butterfly.'

SCULLCAP, COMMON

Scutellaria galericulata (LINN.)

Synonyms. Greater Scullcap. Helmet Flower. Hoodwort.
(*French*) Toque
Part Used. Herb

The Common or Greater Scullcap is fairly common in England, though rare in Scotland and local in Ireland.

¶ *Description.* The root-stock is perennial and creeping. The square stems, 6 to 18 inches high, are somewhat slender, either paniculately branched, or, in small specimens, nearly simple, with opposite downy leaves, oblong and tapering, heart-shaped at the base, ¼ to 2½ inches long, notched and shortly petioled.

The flowers are in pairs, each growing from the axils of the upper, leaf-like bracts, which are quite indistinguishable from the true leaves, and are all turned one way, the pedicels being very short. The corollas are bright blue, variegated with white inside, the tube long and curved, three or four times as long as the calyx, the lips short, the lower lip having three shallow lobes.

Soon after the corolla has fallen off, the upper lip of the calyx, which bulges outward about the middle, closes on the lower as if on a hinge, and gives it the appearance of a capsule with a lid. When the seed is ripe, the cup being dry, divides into two distinct parts, and the seeds, already detached from the receptacle, fall to the ground.

The plant is in flower from July to September. It is subglabrous, with the angles of the stem, the leaves and flowering calyx finely pubescent.

SCULLCAP, LESSER

Scutellaria minor (LINN.)

Part Used. Herb

The Lesser Scullcap, which grows chiefly in bogs, is not common, except in the western counties and in Ireland.

It has the habit of the preceding species, but is more slender and often much branched, and rarely attains 6 inches in height. The whole plant is more glabrous than *Scutellaria galericulata*.

The leaves are egg-shaped, the upper, quite entire, the lower ones often slightly toothed at the base. The flowers are small, dull pink-purple, the calyx having the same peculiarity as the larger species.

It flowers from July to October.

SCULLCAP, VIRGINIAN

Scutellaria lateriflora (LINN.)
N.O. Labiatæ

Synonyms. Mad-dog Scullcap. Madweed
Part Used. Herb

The American species, Virginian Scullcap, flowering in July, with inconspicuous blue flowers in one-sided racemes, is one of the finest nervines ever discovered.

Popularly this plant is known in America as Mad-dog Scullcap or Madweed, having the reputation of being a certain cure for hydrophobia.

The English species, *Scutellaria galericulata* and *S. minor*, possess similar nervine properties to the American, and with *S. integrifolia* and other American species with the flowers in one-sided terminal racemes, are often used as substitutes.

Among the cultivated species are *S. micrantha*, from Siberia and the north of China, a handsome species with spiked racemes of blue flowers; and *S. Coccinea*, from Mexico, with scarlet flowers.

The French name for this plant is *Toque*.

¶ *Cultivation.* The various species of *Scutellaria* will grow in any ordinary garden soil, preferring sunny, open borders, where they will live much longer and grow more strongly than on a rich soil, though they seldom continue more than two or three years.

Plant in March or April, 6 inches apart.

Propagation is mostly effected by seeds, sown in gentle heat in February or March or out of doors, in half-shady positions, in light soil in April. Transplant into permanent quarters in the autumn. No further care is necessary than weeding.

Propagation may also be effected by division of roots in March or April, but the roots are generally lifted, divided and replanted only when overgrown.

¶ *Part Used.* The whole herb, collected in June, dried and powdered.

¶ *Constituents.* A volatile oil, Scutellarin, and a bitter glucoside, yielding Scutellarein on hydrolysis. Also tannin, fat, some bitter principle, sugar and cellulose.

¶ *Medicinal Action and Uses.* Scullcap has strong tonic, nervine and antispasmodic action, and is slightly astringent.

In hysteria, convulsions, hydrophobia, St. Vitus's dance and rickets, its action is invaluable. In nervous headaches, neuralgia and in headache arising from incessant coughing

and pain, it offers one of the most suitable and reliable remedies. The dried extract, given in doses of from 1 to 3 grains as a pill, will relieve severe hiccough.

Many cases of hydrophobia have been cured by this remedy alone.

It is considered a specific for the convulsive twitchings of St. Vitus's dance, soothing the nervous excitement and inducing sleep when necessary, without any unpleasant symptoms following.

Fluid extract, ½ to 1 drachm.

It may be prescribed in all disorders of the nervous system, and has been suggested as a remedy for epilepsy. Writing on this point in the *British Medical Journal*, 1915, Dr. William Bramwell says: 'Its efficacy appears to be partly due to its stimulating the kidneys to increased activity. . . .'

Overdoses of the tincture cause giddiness, stupor, confusion of mind, twitchings of the limbs, intermission of the pulse and other symptoms indicative of epilepsy, for which in diluted strength and small doses it has been successfully given.

The usual dose is an infusion of 1 oz. of the powdered herb to a pint of boiling water, given in half-teacupful doses, every few hours. Both fluid and solid extracts are prepared and Scutellarin is also administered in doses of 1 to 2 grains.

Fluid extract, ½ to 1 drachm.

The European species, *S. galericulata*, was at one time given for the tertian ague, and was said to have proved beneficial where the fits were more obstinate than violent, 1 to 2 oz. of the expressed juice, or an infusion of a handful or two of the herb, being given. In England, however, the remedy was not in use.

SCURVY GRASS

Cochlearia officinalis (LINN.)
N.O. Cruciferæ

Synonym. Spoonwort
Part Used. Herb
Habitat. Abundant on the shores in Scotland, growing inland along some of its rivers and Highland mountains and not uncommon in stony, muddy and sandy soils in England and Ireland, also in the Arctic Circle, sea-coasts of Northern and Western Europe and to high elevations in the great European mountain chains

¶ *Description.* It is a small, low-growing plant, annual or biennial, with thick, fleshy, glabrous, egg-shaped, cordate leaves (hence its name of spoonwort). The upper leaves are sessile – lower ones stalked, deltoid orbicular or reniform entire or toothed angularly. Flowers all summer in white short racemes – pods nearly globular – prominent valves of the mid-rib when dry. It has an unpleasant smell and a bitter, warm, acrid taste, very pungent when fresh.

¶ *Constituents.* Leaves abound in a pungent oil containing sulphur, of the butylic series.

¶ *Medicinal Action and Uses.* Formerly the fresh herb was greatly used on sea-voyages as a preventative of scurvey. It is stimulating, aperient, diuretic, antiscorbutic. The essential oil is of benefit in paralytic and rheumatic cases; scurvy-grass ale was a popular tonic drink.

The infusion of 2 oz. to a pint of boiling water is taken in frequent wineglassful doses.

SEA FENNEL. *See* FENNEL

SEA LAVENDER. *See* LAVENDER

SEAWEED. *See* BLADDERWRACK, (CORSICAN) MOSS, (IRISH) MOSS

SEDGE, SWEET

Acorus Calamus (LINN.)
N.O. Araceæ

Synonyms. Calamus. Sweet Flag. Sweet Root. Sweet Rush. Sweet Cane. Gladdon. Sweet Myrtle. Myrtle Grass. Myrtle Sedge. Cinnamon Sedge
Part Used. Root
Habitat. Found in all European countries except Spain. Southern Russia, northern Asia Minor, southern Siberia, China, Japan, northern United States of America, Hungary, Burma, Ceylon and India

The Sweet Sedge is a vigorous, reed-like, aquatic plant, flourishing in ditches, by the margins of lakes and streams and in marshy places generally, associated with reeds, bull-rushes and bur-reed.

Its erect, sword-shaped leaves bear considerable resemblance to those of the Yellow Flag, hence its equally common popular name of 'Sweet Flag,' though it is not related botanically to the Iris, being a member of the Arum order, Araceæ. All parts of the plant have a peculiar, agreeable fragrance.

Formerly, on account of its pleasant odour, it was freely strewn on the floors of churches at festivals and often in private houses, instead of rushes. The specific name, *calamus*, is derived from the Greek *calamos* (a reed).

The floors of Norwich Cathedral until quite recently were always strewn with calamus at great festivals.

As the Sweet Sedge did not grow near London, but had to be fetched at considerable expense from Norfolk and Suffolk, one of the charges of extravagance brought against Cardinal Wolsey was his habit of strewing his floors with fresh rushes.

Most species of this order give out a considerable amount of heat within the spathe at the time of flowering, so that the temperature rises noticeably above that of the external air. Many of the varieties also have lurid colouring and a fetid odour.

The generic name, *Acorus*, is from *Acoron*, the Greek name of the plant used by Dioscorides and said to be derived from *Coreon* (the pupil of the eye), diseases of which the Ancients used this plant to cure.

The rhizomes are an important commercial commodity and of considerable medicinal value.

Though now common throughout Europe, there is little doubt that the Sweet Flag is a native of eastern countries, being indigenous to the marshes of the mountains of India.

It is said to have been introduced into Poland by the Tartars, but not till 1588 is it recorded as abundant in Germany. Clusius, the famous botanist, first cultivated it at Vienna in 1574, from a root obtained from Asia Minor and distributed it to other botanists in Belgium, Germany and France. It is readily propagated and rapidly becomes established. In England, it was probably introduced about 1596, being first grown by Gerard, who says that 'Anthony Coline the apothecarie sent him pieces from Lyons,' telling him that he had used it in his composition of Treacle. ('Treacle' was a term used by the old herbalists for a medicine composed of many herbal ingredients.) Gerard looked upon it as an Eastern plant, which he says is grown in many English gardens and might hence be fitly called the 'Sweet Garden Flag.'

Calamus was largely grown from time immemorial for its rhizomes in the East and the Indian rhizomes were imported extensively long after it was common in Europe. The Indian rhizome is said to have a stronger and more agreeable flavour than that obtained in Europe or the United States.

If the Calamus of the Bible is this plant, Exodus xxx. 23, Canticles iv. 14, and Ezekiel xxvii. 19, are the earliest records of its use.

The *Calamus aromaticus* of the Ancients is thought by some to be a plant belonging to the Gentian family, though the description of the plant '*Acoron*,' a native of Colchis, Galatia, Pontus and Crete, given by Dioscorides and Pliny, seems to refer to the Sweet Flag.

It is now found wild on the margins of ponds and rivers in most of the English counties, and is in some parts abundant, especially in the Fen districts. In Scotland it is scarce. It is found in all European countries except Spain, and becomes more abundant eastward and in southern Russia, northern Asia Minor and southern Siberia, China and Japan. It is also found in the northern United States of America, where it appears to be indigenous.

It is cultivated to a small extent in Hungary, Burma and Ceylon, and is common in gardens in India. In northern China another species is cultivated as an ornamental greenhouse plant, but the wild plant is that generally collected for use, especially in Russia, on

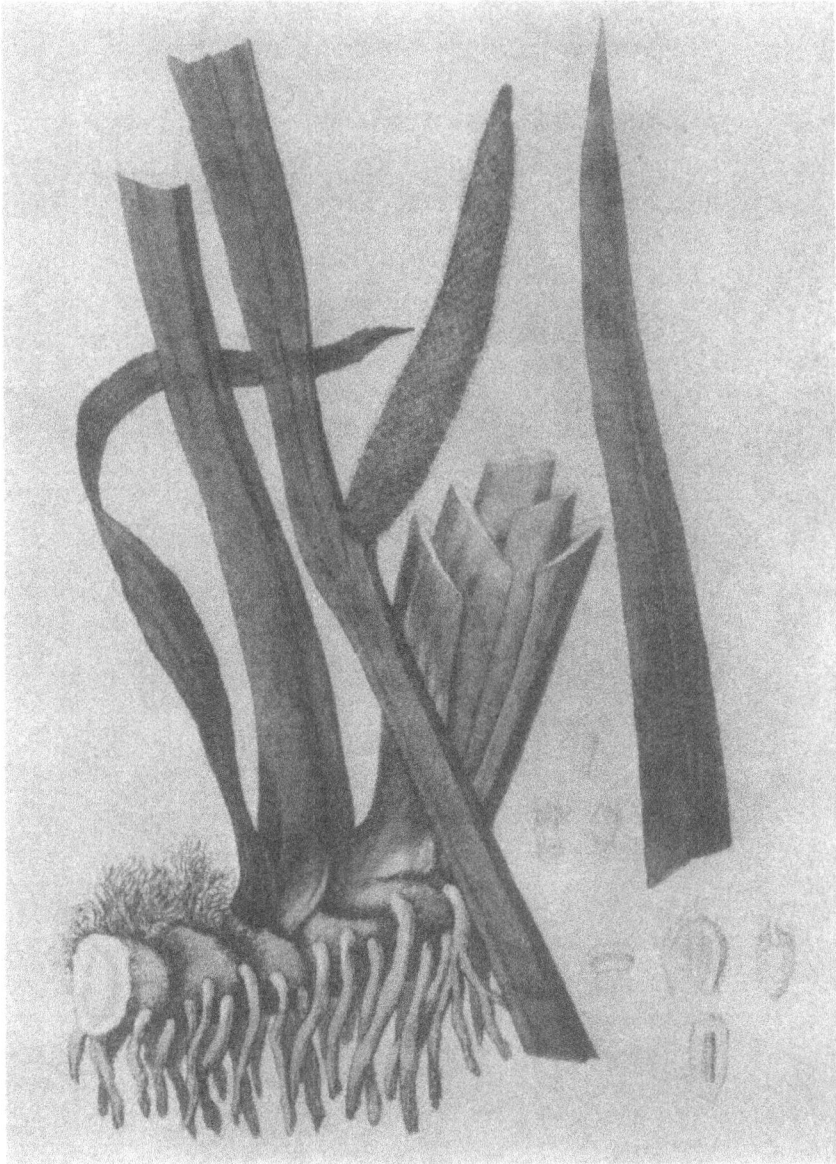

SWEET SEDGE
Acorus Calamus

SENNA
Cassia Acutifolia

the shores of the Black Sea. In 1724, Berlu (*Treasury of Drugs*) states that it was 'brought in quantities from Germany,' hence it may be inferred it was not collected in England until a later period, when the London market was supplied from the rivers and marshes of Norfolk, where it was cultivated in the Fen districts, and from the banks of the Thames, as much as £40 having been obtained for the year's crop of a single acre of the riverside land on which it naturally grows. But for many years now the native source has been neglected and the rhizomes for medicinal and commercial use are imported. In dry summers, large quantities are collected in the ditches in Germany, but the greater proportion of the imported drug is derived from southern Russia, via Germany.

In the districts in Norfolk where the plant flourishes the villagers call it 'Gladdon,' so the name would appear to apply to more than one species of the family. A few years since, the 'Gladdon harvest' was an important episode in the country of the 'Broads,' and many small boats might be seen laden with this plant, being brought to shore for marketing purposes. Some of the Norfolk churches in country districts are thatched with this 'reed.'

¶ *Description.* The Sweet Sedge is a perennial herb, in habit somewhat resembling the Iris, with a long, indefinite, branched, cylindrical rhizome immersed in the mud, usually smaller than that of the Iris, about the thickness of a finger and emitting numerous roots. The erect leaves are yellowish-green, 2 to 3 feet in length, few, all radical, sheathing at their bases (which are pink), sword-shaped, narrow and flat, tapering into a long, acute point, the edges entire, but wavy or crimped. The leaves are much like those of Iris, but may readily be distinguished from these and from all others by the peculiar crimped edges and their aromatic odour when bruised.

The scape or flower-stem arises from the axils of the outer leaves, which it much resembles, but is longer and solid and triangular. From one side, near the middle of its length, projecting upwards at an angle, from the stem, it sends out a solid, cylindrical, blunt spike or spadix, tapering at each end, from 2 to 4 inches in length, often somewhat curved and densely crowded with very small greenish-yellow flowers. Each tiny flower contains six stamens enclosed in a perianth with six divisions and surrounding a three-celled, oblong ovary with a sessile stigma. The flowers are sweet-scented and so formed that cross-pollination is ensured, but the plant is not usually fertile in the British Isles, as it is in Asia, the proper insects being ab-

sent here. The fruit, which does not ripen in Europe, is a berry, being full of mucus, which falls when ripe into the water or to the ground, and is thus dispersed, but it fruits sparingly everywhere and propagates itself mainly by the rapid growth of its spreading rhizome.

It is easily distinguished from all other British plants by its peculiar spadix, which appears in June and July, and by the fragrance of its roots, stems and leaves.

In most localities the flowers are not very abundantly produced: it never flowers unless actually growing in water.

¶ *Cultivation.* The plants can be propagated very readily by the division of the clumps or of the rhizomes in early spring, or at the commencement of autumn, portions of the rhizome being planted in damp, muddy spots, in marshes or on the margins of water, set 1 foot apart and well covered. It will succeed very well in a garden if the ground is moist, but a rich, moist soil is essential, or it has to be frequently watered.

¶ *Collection.* It is the root-stock or rhizome that is used for medicinal purposes, a digestive medicine being made from it which is official in the United States Pharmacopœia and in several others.

Calamus root has also value as a commercial commodity in various industries.

Experiments have lately been made with a distillation of the leaves, and if the fragrant volatile oil contained in them can be obtained successfully on economic conditions, this will create a trade.

The rhizomes are gathered when large enough, generally after two or three years, and before they lose their firmness and become hollow. Late autumn or early spring is the time chosen for collection.

If actually growing in water, the raft-like masses of interwoven roots and mud, which in a river or lake float about a foot below the surface of the water, are cut out in square sections, raked to the lake edge, the leaves stripped off and separated. Whether growing thus actually in water, or in moist ground, the rhizomes are next thoroughly washed in a trough, and then, deprived of the far less aromatic and brittle rootlets, which are 4 to 6 inches long, unbranched, but near the tip beset with soft, thin fibres.

The fresh root-stock is brownish-red, or greenish-white and reddish within and of a spongy texture, tolerably uniform in transverse section. It has an aromatic sweet odour and a bitterish, pungent taste.

The dried rhizome appears in commerce in tortuous, sub-cylindrical or flattened pieces, a few inches long and from $\frac{1}{4}$ to 1 inch in diameter; externally, yellowish-brown, with blackish patches; sharply longitudinally wrinkled, the upper surface obliquely marked with broad, dark, often fibrous leaf-scales, which are often broadly V-shaped and have sharply projecting margins, the lower surface is thickly pitted with a zigzag line of circular root-scars, which exhibit a low whitish rim and a dark depressed centre. The fracture is short, sharp, corky, whitish and starchy. The texture is spongy, exhibiting numerous oil-cells and scattered wood-bundles.

On drying, Calamus loses from 70 to 75 per cent. in weight, but improves in odour and taste. It deteriorates, however, after long keeping.

Since the oil-cells containing the aromatic essential oil are situated in the outer part, peeling the rhizomes before shipping or distilling, as is often done on the Continent, should not be resorted to. Most of the commercial article has the outer portion of the cortex removed, but the handsome, white peeled (German) Calamus of the market cannot be used in accordance with the official requirements of other pharmacopœias. The peeled rhizome is usually angular and often split. Though white when fresh, it turns pinkish on drying and is less aromatic and bitter than the unpeeled.

¶ *Constituents.* The properties of Calamus are almost entirely due to its volatile oil, obtained by steam distillation. The oil is contained in all parts of the plant, though in greatest quantity in the rhizome, the leaves yielding to distillation 0·2 per cent., the fresh root 1·5 to 3·5 per cent., the dried German root 0·8 per cent., and the Japan root as much as 5 per cent.

The oil is strong and fragrant, its taste warm, bitterish, pungent and aromatic. Its active principles are taken up by boiling water. It is a thick, pale yellow liquid. Little is known of its chemistry, though it possibly contains pinene and the chief aromatic constituent is asaryl aldehyde.

The rhizome also contains alkaloidal matter, mainly Choline (formerly thought to be a specific alkaloid, Calamine); soft resin, gum, starch and the bitter glucoside, Acorin, which is amorphous, semi-fluid, resinous, of neutral reaction, aromatic odour and bitter aromatic taste.

Calamus Oil is used in perfumery – an alcoholate is made with 3 kilos to 3·5 kilos of rhizome to 20 litres of 85 per cent. alcohol.

¶ *Medicinal Action and Uses.* Calamus was formerly much esteemed as an aromatic stimulant and mild tonic. A fluid extract is an official preparation in the United States and some other Pharmacopœias, but it is not now official in the British Pharmacopœia, though it is much used in herbal medicine as an aromatic bitter.

On account of the volatile oil which is present, it also acts as a carminative, removing the discomfort caused by flatulence and checking the growth of the bacteria which give rise to it.

It is used to increase the appetite and benefit digestion, given as fluid extract, infusion or tincture. Tincture of Calamus, obtained by macerating the finely-cut rhizome in alcohol for seven days and filtering, is used as a stomachic and flavouring agent. It has a brownish-yellow colour and a pungent, spicy taste.

The essential oil is used as an addition to inhalations.

The dried root may be chewed *ad libitum* to relieve dyspepsia or an infusion of 1 oz. to 1 pint of boiling water may be taken freely in doses of a teacupful. The dried root is also chewed to clear the voice.

Fluid extract, U.S.P., 15 to 60 drops.

Calamus has been found useful in ague and low fever, and was once greatly used by country people in Norfolk, either in infusion, or powdered, as a remedy against the fever prevalent in the Fens. Its use has been attended with great success where Peruvian bark has failed. It is also beneficial as a mild stimulant in typhoid cases.

The tonic medicine called Stockton Bitters, formerly in much esteem in some parts of England, is made from the root of this plant and that of *Gentiana campestris.*

Waller's *British Herbal* says:

'It is of great service in all nervous complaints, vertigoes, headaches and hypochondriacal affections. Also commended in dysentry and chronic catarrhs. The powdered root may be given, 12 grs. to ½ drachm. In an infusion of 2 drachms to a pint of water or of white wine, it is an agreeable stomachic, even to persons in health, to take a glass about an hour before dinner. When the root is candied with sugar, it is convenient to dyspeptic patients, who may carry it in a small box, in the pocket, and take it as they find occasion.'

On the Continent the candied rhizome is widely employed. The Turks use the candied rhizome as a preventive against contagion.

The rhizome is largely used in native Oriental medicines for dyspepsia and bronchitis and chewed as a cough lozenge, and from the earliest times has been one of the most popular remedies of the native practitioners of India. The candied root is sold as a favourite medicine in every Indian bazaar.

The powdered root is also esteemed in Ceylon and India as a vermifuge and an insecticide, especially in relation to fleas. Sprinkled round a tree attacked by white ants in Malay (Perak) it was found to destroy those that were near the surface and prevented others from attacking the tree.

In powder, Calamus root on account of its spicy flavour serves as a substitute for cinnamon, nutmeg and ginger.

It is said also to be used by snuff manufacturers and to scent hair-powders and in tooth-powders, in the same way as orris.

The highly aromatic volatile oil is largely used in perfumery.

The oil is used by rectifiers to improve the flavour of gin and to give a peculiar taste and fragrance to certain varieties of beer.

In the United States, Calamus was also formerly used by country people as an ingredient in making wine bitters.

In Lithuania, the root is preserved with sugar-like angelica.

The young and tender inflorescence is often eaten by children for its sweetness. In Holland, children use the rhizomes as chewing-gum and also make pop-gun projectiles of them.

The aroma that makes the leaves attractive to us, renders them distasteful to cattle, who do not touch the plant.

There is a seventeenth-century reference to broth 'flavoured with Angelica seed and Calamus.'

An extract from Salmon's *Herbal* (1710), giving no less than sixteen different preparations of Calamus, will show in how much greater esteem it was held in former days:

'It is a good stimulant and carminative. The preparations: The root only is of use, and you may have therefrom 1, A liquid Juice. 2, An Essence. 3, An Infusion of Wine. 4, A Decoction in Wine. 5, A Powder. 6, A Cataplasm. 7, A spirituous Tincture. 8, An acid Tincture. 9, An oily Tincture. 10, A Spirit. 11, A chemical Oil. 12, Potestates or Powers. 13, An Elixir. 14, A Collegium. 15, A Preserve. 16, A Syrup. The Liquid Juice, No. 1, was said "to prevail against the bitings of mad dogs and other venomous creatures." It is a peculiar thing against poison, the Plague and all contagious diseases.'

Culpepper says:

'The spicy bitterness of the root of this plant (which he calls the Bastard Flag) bespeaks it as a strengthener of the stomach and head and therefore may fitly be put into any composition of that intention. The root preserved with good success may be used by itself. The leaves, having a very grateful flavour, are by some nice cooks put into sauce for fish.'

¶ *Adulterations.* The rhizome of the Common Yellow Flag (*Iris pseudacorus*) is sometimes mixed with those of the Sweet Flag, when collected in this country, but is readily detected by its darker colour, different structure and want of aromatic odour and taste.

Calamus Draco (Willd.) (*Dæmonorops Draco*, Martius) is a slender palm of the East Indies, yielding the resin 'Dragon's Blood,' obtained from the fruit, used in former times as a mild astringent in diarrhœa, but now never given internally. It was formerly an ingredient of many plasters.

At present, it is mainly used as a colouring agent in pharmacy and the arts, to colour tooth-powders, tinctures and plasters and to impart a mahogany colour to varnishes and wood stains.

The term 'Dragon's Blood' has also been applied to the resin of *Dracæna draca* (Socotra), *Pterocarpus Draco* (West Indies) and *Croton Draco*.

See DRAGON'S BLOOD.

OTHER SEDGES

N.O. Araceæ

The Sedge family is of comparatively slight economic importance. The plants are distinguished from the true Grasses, which they closely resemble, by their solid stems, leaf-sheaths which are not connate, and the presence of but a single scale to each flower.

They are mostly coarse, harsh and indigestible, and not adapted for food purposes, though the rhizomes of several have been utilized as starchy foods.

Quite a number possess volatile oils and aromatic principles, while others are rich in astringents – chiefly the species indigenous to India and China.

Among the more important aromatics and carminatives are *Cyperus sanguinea-fuscus* (Nees), the Cure-pire of Paraguay, *C. elegans* (Rottb.) of Mexico; *C. pertenuis* (Roxb.), the Indian Nagar-motha or Koriak, whose roots, when dried and powdered, are used by the Indian ladies for perfuming their hair; and *C. tegetum* (Roxb.); *Adrue* or *Guinea Rush* is the rhizome of *C. articulatus* (Linn.), which, besides being used as a carminative, has a high repute in the East Indies for anti-emetic properties. The blackish tubers have a somewhat bitter, aromatic taste, resembling that of Lavender. A fluid extract is prepared from them used in herbal medicine. The aromatic properties of the drug cause a feeling of warmth to be diffused throughout the system and act as a sedative in dyspeptic disorders. It is common also in Jamaica and on the banks of the Nile.

Two Indian species of Sedge, *C. rotundus* and *C. scarious*, also possess fragrant roots, largely employed in Eastern perfumes, but they are little used in Europe.

The tubers of *C. hexastachys* are said to be successfully used by Hindu practitioners in cases of cholera. They call the plant 'Mootha.'

The tubers of *C. bulbosus* are said to taste like potatoes when roasted, and would be valuable for food if they were bigger.

The root of *C. odoratus* has a warm, aromatic taste, and is given in India in infusions as a stomachic.

The roots of the Sweet Cyperus or English Galingale (*C. longus*, Linn.) were once esteemed as an aromatic tonic, considered good as a stomachic and serviceable in the first stages of dropsy, but they have now fallen into disuse. This species is a native of France, Germany, Italy and Sicily, but very rare in this country, being only found in a few places in Dorsetshire and Wales. The plants throw up erect triangular stems, about 2 feet high, bearing three long, channelled, drooping leaves and a lax, compound umbel of flat flower-spikes, which renders it very ornamental when in flower.

C. esculentus is a native of Italy and Sicily and the Levant. Its roots are fibrous, with small round tubers hanging from them, of the size of peas, which taste like sweet filberts and are eaten in Italy, and sold in the markets.

The French call the tubers *Souchet comestible* or *Amande de terre*.

C. Papyrus is the Egyptian Papyrus, the fibrous stems of which provided the earliest form of paper known.

This plant had various economic uses, as Pliny and other writers have shown, though as the Egyptians cultivated other Sedges, it is probable that these became more exclusively used for food and fuel, sails and cordage, baskets and sieves, not to speak of punts or canoes to which the prophet Isaiah refers (Isaiah xviii. 2), where the Ethiopians are spoken of as sending ambassadors by the sea even in *vessels of bulrushes* upon the waters (the Hebrew word is *gome*). The papyrus was, in ancient times, carefully cultivated, especially in certain districts of Lower, and probably of Upper Egypt also, for the great and important purpose with which its name must ever be associated.

For this manufacture the rind was removed, the pith cut in strips and laid lengthwise on a flat board, their edges united by some glue or cement (Pliny says 'Nile water'), and the whole subjected to pressure, compacting the several strips into one uniform fabric. This material was well known to the Ancients, and continued to be used in Europe until the time of Charlemagne, when it was superseded by parchment. It is remarkable that although we have no trace in Scripture of the use of papyrus or other vegetable substance by the Jews for writing purposes, the plant has been found to exist in vast quantities in the Lake Merom at the northern end of the Lake of Tiberias, and in some of the streams which flow into the Mediterranean.

On the other hand, it has disappeared from Egypt, where it once grew in quantity. It is also grown in Sicily and Sardinia, but on a limited scale.

Of the Papyrus, or some allied species of Sedge, Heliodorus relates that the Ethiopians made swift-sailing wherries, capable of carrying two or three men; and the traveller Bruce refers to a similar use of this ancient plant among the modern Abyssinians.

Other writers give similar testimony, and it is highly probable that such light vessels were coated with bitumen, like the rude basket made by Jochabed for the infant Moses (Exod. ii. 3).

The stems of the Papyrus were likewise used for ornamenting Egyptian temples, and crowning the statues of their gods.

This plant, if grown in Britain, requires the aid of a stove to grow it properly, and then it must have a good supply of water.

Scirpus lacustris, the Great Club-Rush or Common Bulrush, is used for making chair seats, mats and hassocks, being imported dried, in large bundles from Holland. The roots are astringent and diuretic and were formerly employed in medicine, but are now no longer used.

S. capillaris is used in Spanish America under the name of Espartillo, as a pectoral.

Other British species are the chocolate-headed Club-Rush (*S. pauciflorus*), Deer's-hair (*S. cæspitosus*), Dwarf Club-Rush (*S. nanus*), Floating Mud-Rush (*S. fluitans*), Savi's Mud-Rush (*S. cernuus*), Bristle-like Mud-Rush (*S. sætaceus*), Round-headed Mud-Rush (*S. Holoschœuus*), and eight others of the genus *Scirpus*.

Kyllingia monocephala is used in Paraguay as a substitute for Calamus.

Carex arenaria (Linn.), the Sand Sedge, is a familiar seaside species of Sedge, which is very widely distributed and common on sandy coasts, growing on sand-dunes and elsewhere at high-water mark, amongst grasses and herbage, helping to bind it together.

The plant is perennial, propagating itself rapidly in loose sand, on which account it is planted on dykes in Holland for the purpose of binding the sand by means of its long and interlacing underground stems, which penetrate horizontally about 4 inches below the surface, thus helping to prevent the incursions of the sea. It has been used for this purpose also on the British East Coast.

The rhizomes have been used medicinally in Germany as a substitute for Sarsaparilla, in the same way that Couch Grass is here employed, having diuretic and sudorific properties.

C. vulpinoides, an allied species to C. vulpina (Great or Fox Sedge), is a North American plant, but has been found on the banks of the Thames near Kew.

There are sixty-nine species of Carex given by Johns (Flowers of the Field), besides those mentioned above; some only grow in Scotland, and none have medicinal or practical uses.

Eriophorum angustifolium (Cotton Grass),

with its long white tufts of hair, is very decorative on our bogs and mosses in the middle of summer. The down is used in moorland districts for stuffing pillows, and attempts have been made to employ it as a substitute for cotton, under the name of 'Arctic Wool,' thread having been spun from it, but the fibres are more brittle than those of cotton and do not bear twisting as well. Candles and lamp wicks have been made from the down by country people.

In former days the leaves and roots had some reputation in northern countries as a medicine in diarrhœa, as like most members of the Sedge family, they possess considerable astringency.

The name Eriophorum is from the Greek erion (wool) and phero (I bear).

Culpepper approved of the use of 'Bulrushes' and 'some of the smoother sorts,' but considered they should be 'given with caution,' as they were apt to 'cause head-ache, and provoke sleep. The root, boiled in water, to the consumption of one-third, helps the cough.'

See GRASSES.

SELF-HEAL

Prunella vulgaris (LINN.)
N.O. Labiatæ

Synonyms. Prunella. All-Heal. Hook-Heal. Slough-Heal. Brunella. Heart of the Earth. Blue Curls

Part Used. Herb

Habitat. Common throughout the British Isles and Europe

The Self-Heal holds an equal place with Bugle in the esteem of herbalists.

¶ Description. It may at once be distinguished from other members of the great Labiate order because on the top of its flowering stalks, the flowers – to quote Culpepper – are 'thicke set together like an eare or spiky knap.' No other plant is at all like it. Immediately below this ear are a pair of stalkless leaves standing out on either side like a collar. The flowers and bracts of this spike or 'ear' are arranged in most regular tiers or whorls, each tier composed of a ring of six stalkless flowers, supported by a couple of spreading, sharp-pointed bracts. The number of whorls varies from half a dozen to a dozen. The flower-spike is at first very short, compact and cylindrical, but then opens out somewhat, maintaining much the same size throughout its length, not tapering as in the flower spikes of most other flowers. The flowers do not come out simultaneously in any one ring, so that a somewhat ragged-looking head of flowers is produced.

Each flower consists of a two-lipped calyx, the upper lip very wide and flat, edged with three blunt teeth, the lower lip much narrower and with two long, pointed teeth. Both lips have red margins and carry hairs. The two-lipped corolla is of a deep purple hue, the upper lip strongly arched, on the top of the arch many hairs standing on end, and the lower lip of much the same length, spreading out into three holes. Under the roofing upper lip are two pairs of stamens, one pair longer than the other, their filaments ending in two little branches, one of which carries an anther, the other remaining a little spike. Through the centre of the two pairs of stamens the long style runs, curving so as to fit under the lip, its lower end set between four nutlets. Honey lies at the bottom of the corolla tube, protected from tiny insects by a thick hedge of hairs placed just above it. The flower is adapted by this formation, like the rest of the Labiate group, for fertilization by bees, who alight on the lower lip and in thrusting their probosces down the tube for the honey, dust their heads with the pollen from the anthers and then on visiting the next flower, smear this pollen on the end of the curving style that runs up the arch of the upper lip and thus effect fertilization. After fertilization is effected, the corolla falls out of the sheath-like calyx, which, however, remains in place, as do also the two bracts supporting each whorl. When all the purple corollas have fallen and only the rings of the persistent calyces remain, the resemblance to an ear of corn, which Culpepper points out, is very marked.

The plant does not rely wholly for its propagation on the four little nutlets that ripen within the continually reddening calyx, even though the flowering season is particularly long, lasting through all the summer months, for its creeping stems can throw out roots at every point, new plants thus being formed, as in the case of the Bugle. It is from the creeping stems that the flowering spikes arise, standing upright among the herbage, 3 inches to a foot in height.

The leaves, oblong in form and blunt, about an inch long and ¼ inch broad, grow on short stalks in pairs down the square stem, from which they stand out boldly, and are often roughish on the top, with scattered, close hairs, their mid-rib at the back also carrying hairs and their margins fringed with tiny hairs. Their outline is either one continuous line, or they are slightly indented along their margins.

¶ *Habitat.* Self-Heal is a very common plant throughout Britain and all over Europe, abundant in pastures and on waste ground. In open and exposed situations, the plant is diminutive, while in more sheltered spots it is larger in all its parts. It branches freely, lateral stems being thrown out in pairs at almost every node, from which the leaves spring. The main stem is often deeply grooved and rough to the touch, the lower parts tinted with reddish purple.

Self-Heal is one of those common wildflowers that have found their way to North America, tending even to oust the native flowers. It is known there as 'Heart of the Earth' and 'Blue Curls.'

Cole, in *Adam in Eden* (1657), says:

'It is called by modern writers (for neither the ancient Greek nor Latin writers knew it) Brunella, from Brunellen, which is a name given unto it by the Germans, because it cureth that inflammation of the mouth which they call "die Breuen," yet the general name of it in Latin nowadays is Prunella, as being a word of a more gentile pronunciation.'

Cole further explains that the disease in question 'is common to soldiers when they lye in camp, but especially in garrisons, coming with an extraordinary inflammation or swelling, as well in the mouth as throat, the very signature of the Throat which the form of the Floures so represent signifying as

much' – an instance of the doctrine of signatures of which William Cole was such a ready exponent.

'There is not a better Wound herbe,' says Gerard, 'in the world than that of Self-Heale is, the very name importing it to be very admirable upon this account and indeed the Virtues doe make it good, for this very herbe without the mixture of any other ingredient, being onely bruised and wrought with the point of a knife upon a trencher or the like, will be brought into the form of a salve, which will heal any green wounde even in the first intention, after a very wonderful manner. The decoction of Prunell made with wine and water doth join together and make whole and sound all wounds, both inward and outward, even as Bugle doth. To be short, it serveth for the same that the Bugle serveth and in the world there are not two better wound herbs as hath been often proved.'

¶ *Constituents.* The chemical principles of Bugle and Self-Heal resemble those of the other Labiate herbs, comprising a volatile oil; some bitter principle, not yet analysed; tannin, to which its chief medicinal use is due; sugar and cellulose.

¶ *Part Used.* The whole herb, collected when in best condition in mid-summer.

¶ *Medicinal Action and Uses.* Astringent, styptic and tonic.

Self-Heal is still in use in modern herbal treatment as a useful astringent for inward or outward use.

An infusion of the herb, made from 1 oz. to a pint of boiling water, and taken in doses of a wineglassful, is considered a general strengthener. Sweetened with honey, it is good for a sore and relaxed throat or ulcerated mouth, for both of which purposes it also makes a good gargle. For internal bleeding and for piles, the infusion is also used as an injection.

Culpepper, explaining the name 'Self-Heal whereby when you are hurt, you may heal yourself,' tells us that

'it is an especial herb for inward or outward wounds. Take it inwardly in syrups for inward wounds, outwardly in unguents and plasters for outward. As Self-Heal is like Bugle in form, so also in the qualities and virtues, serving for all purposes, whereunto Bugle is applied with good success either inwardly or outwardly; for inward wounds or ulcers in the body, for bruises or falls and hurts. If it be combined with Bugle, Sanicle and other like wound herbs, it will be more effectual to wash and inject into ulcers in the parts outwardly. . . . It is an especial remedy for all green wounds to close the lips of them and to keep the place from further inconveniences. The juice used with oil of roses to annoint the temples and forehead is very effectual to remove the headache, and the same mixed with honey of roses cleaneth and healeth ulcers in the mouth and throat.'

SENEGA

Polygala Senega (LINN.)
N.O. Polygaleæ

Synonyms. Snake Root. Senegæ Radix. Seneca. Seneka. Polygala Virginiana. Plantula Marilandica. Senega officinalis. Milkwort. Mountain Flax. Rattlesnake Root
Part Used. Dried Root
Habitat. North America

¶ *Description.* This perennial herb, about a foot high, grows throughout central and western North America, in woods, and on dry, rocky soil. The leaves are small alternate, and narrowly lanceolate, and the numerous, small pinky-white flowers are crowded on to a narrow, terminal spike from 1 to 2 inches long.

The name of the genus, *Polygala*, means 'much milk,' alluding to its own profuse secretions and their effects. 'Senega' is derived from the Seneca tribe of North American Indians, among whom the plant was used as a remedy for snake-bites.

The root, varying in colour from light yellowish grey to brownish grey, and in size from the thickness of a straw to that of the little finger, has as its distinguishing mark a projecting line, along its concave side. It is usually twisted, sometimes almost spiral, and has at its upper end a thick, irregular, knotty crown, showing traces of numerous, wiry stems. It breaks with a short fracture, the wood often showing an abnormal appearance, since one or two wedge-shaped portions may be replaced by parenchymatous tissue, as if a segment of wood had been cut out. The keels are due to the development of the bast, and not to any abnormality in the wood. The odour and taste resemble that of Wintergreen.

About 1735, Dr. John Tennent, a Scottish physician living in Pennsylvania, was introduced to the use of the root by the Seneca Indians for curing rattlesnake-bite. As the symptoms were similar to those of pleurisy and the latter stages of pleuropneumonia, he experimented with it in those diseases with success, and as a result the drug was accepted in Europe and cultivated in England in 1739. The roots should be gathered when the leaves are dead, and before the first frost. From carelessness in collection other roots are often found mixed with it, but not for intentional adulteration. The root of commerce is obtained from *Polygala latifolia* also, this species being several inches taller and having larger leaves than *P. Senega*. The dried roots, usually in broken pieces, are brought into market in bales weighing from 50 to 400 lb. They vary a little in appearance according to their locality. The official Senega is the small Southern Senega, 400 to 500 of the dried roots of which are required to make a pound. Manitoba Senega is larger and darker, often with purple markings near the crown. The Northern, White, False, or Large Senega, comes from Wisconsin, Minnesota, and farther west. About 80 to 100 of its roots will make a pound. It is stated that it is not possible to distinguish the two when powdered.

¶ *Constituents.* The root contains polygalic acid, virgineic acid, pectic and tannic acids, yellow, bitter, colouring matter, cerin fixed oil, gum, albumen, woody fibre, salts, alumina, silica, magnesia and iron. The powder is yellowish-grey to light yellowish-brown.

The active principle, contained in the bark, is Senegin (which some authorities regard as another name for polygalic acid, while others differentiate between the two). It is a white powder easily soluble in hot water and alcohol, forming a soapy emulsion when mixed with boiling water. It is almost identical with the saponin of *Saponaria officinalis* and *Quillaria Saponaria*. Thus its influence counteracts, or can be counteracted, by digitalis.

Another analysis, in 1889, gives fixed oil and resin, traces of volatile oil (a mixture of valeric ether and methyl salicylate), 7 per cent. sugar, from 2 to 5 per cent. senegin, yellow colouring-matter, and malates.

It is advisable to use an alkali in small proportion in making galenical preparations of senega.

Oil of Senega is bitter, rancid, and disagreeable, with the consistency of syrup and an acid reaction. It is not Seneca oil.

¶ *Medicinal Action and Uses.* A stimulating expectorant, diuretic and diaphoretic. The Ancients regarded its action as identical with that of ipecacuanha, but in doses of three times the strength. It should be used when the power to expectorate is small – very useful in the second stage of acute bronchial catarrh or pneumonia. It is of little value when the expectoration is tough and scanty, but very helpful in chronic pneumonia or bronchitis or dropsy dependent on renal disease. Spirit of chloroform will lessen its disagreeable taste. It has been used also in croup, whooping-cough, and rheumatism.

As it stimulates most of the secretions, it is also useful as a sialagogue and emmenagogue. In active inflammation its use is contra-indicated.

In large doses it is emetic and cathartic.

¶ *Dosages.* Powdered root, 5 to 20 grains. Fluid extract, 10 to 20 drops. Of infusion, B.P., 4 to 8 drachms. Of syrup, U.S.P., 1 drachm. Of tincture, B.P., ½ to 1 drachm. Conct. Solut., B.P., ½ to 1 drachm.

¶ *Poisons and Antidotes.* In overdose it can act as an irritant or general protoplasmic poison, with violent vomiting and purging. A dose of from 10 minims of the tincture to a scruple of the powdered root will cause heaviness and vertigo, dazzling vision, sneez-

ing, inflammation of the œsophagus, with constriction, thirst, nausea, mucous vomiting, colic, scalding, frothy urine, irritation of the larynx, and general debility. Like saponin, it causes a paresis of the muscles of the respiratory tract and the vaso-motor system in general, resulting in capillary congestions followed by rapid exosmosis.

¶ *Adulterations and Other Species.*

Panax quinquefolium, or American Ginseng Root, is the most common admixture. It is larger and has no ridge.

Various species of *Gillenia*, *Asclepias Vincetoxicum*, or Swallow-wort, *Triosteum perfoliatum*, and the rhizome of *Cypripedium pubescens* have also been found in parcels. They have a different taste and odour, and show no ridge.

P. Boykinii or *P. Alba* resemble *P. Senega*, but have no ridge and are much less acrid.

Arnica, Valerian, Serpentary and Green Hellebore roots resemble it, but have no keel.

SENNA

Cassia Acutifolia (DELL.)
N.O. Leguminosæ

Synonyms. Alexandrian Senna. Nubian Senna. Cassia Senna. Cassia lenitiva. Cassia Lanceolata. Cassia officinalis. Cassia æthiopica. Senna acutifolia. Egyptian Senna. Sĕnĕ de la palthe. Tinnevelly Senna. Cassia angustifolia. Eâst Indian Senna

Parts Used. Dried leaflets, pods

Habitat. Egypt, Nubia, Arabia, Sennar

¶ *Description.* Several species of *Cassia* contribute to the drug of commerce, and were comprised in a single species by Linnæus under the name of *Cassia Senna*. Since his day, the subject has been more fully investigated, and it is known that several countries utilize the leaves of their own indigenous varieties in the same way. The two most widely exported and officially recognized are *C. acutifolia* and *C. angustifolia* (India or Tinnevelly Senna).

C. acutifolia, yielding the finest and most valuable variety of the drug is a small shrub about 2 feet high. The stem is erect, smooth, and pale green, with long, spreading branches, bearing leaflets in four or five pairs, averaging an inch long, lanceolate or obovate, unequally oblique at the base, veins distinct on the under surface, brittle, greyish-green, of a faint, peculiar odour, and mucilaginous, sweetish taste. The form of the base, and freedom from bitterness, distinguish the Senna from the Argel leaves, which are also thicker and stiffer. The flowers are small and yellow. The pods are broadly oblong, about 2 inches long by ⅜ inch broad, and contain about six seeds.

Senna is an Arabian name, and the drug was first brought into use by the Arabian physicians Serapion and Mesue, and Achi-

arius was the first of the Greeks to notice it. He recommends not the leaves but the fruit, and Mesue also prefers the pods to the leaves, thinking them more powerful, though they are actually less so, but they do not cause griping.

The leaves of *C. acutifolia* are collected principally in Nubia. Ignatius Pallme, who travelled much in Africa, wrote:

'Senna is found in abundance in many parts of Kardofan, but the leaves are not collected on account of the existing monopoly. The Government draws its supplies from Dongola in Nubia.'

Two crops are collected annually in Nubia, the more abundant in September, after the rains, the other in April, in dry seasons a very bad one. The plants are cut down, exposed on the rocks in hot sunshine until thoroughly dry, then stripped, and packed in palm-leaf bags, being sent thus on camels to Essouan and Darao, and by the Nile to Cairo, or via Massowah and Suakin on the Red Sea. It is made up at Boulak, near Cairo, under the superintendence of the Egyptian Government, though much adulteration takes place there. The leaves are loosely packed, and as they curl when drying, often present this appearance, while Indian

Senna is packed tightly, and the leaves come out flat.

Senna appears to have been cultivated in England about 1640. By keeping the plants in a hot-bed all the summer, they frequently flowered; but rarely perfected their seeds.

Commercial Senna is prepared for use by *garbling*, or picking out the leaflets and rejecting the lead-stalks, impurities, and leaves of other plants. The amount annually exported is about 8,000 bales of each of the varieties, and the price is high, owing to the failure of the crops at certain seasons. Good Senna may be known by the bright, fresh, yellowish-green colour of the leaves, with a faint and peculiar odour rather like green tea, and a nauseous, mucilaginous, sweetish, slightly bitter taste. It should be powdered only as wanted, because the powder absorbs moisture, becomes mouldy, and loses its value. Boiling destroys its virtues, unless it be in *vacuo*, or in a covered vessel.

¶ *Constituents*. Water and diluted alcohol extract the active principles of Senna. Pure alcohol only extracts them imperfectly. The leaves yield about one-third of their weight to boiling water.

The purgative constituents are closely allied to those of Aloes and Rhubarb, the activities of the drug being largely due to anthraquinone derivatives and their glucosides. It contains rhein, aloe-emedin, kæmpferol, isormamnetin, both free and as glucosides together with myricyl alcohol, etc. The ash amounts to about 8 per cent., consisting chiefly of earthy and ashy carbonates.

The active purgative principle was discovered in 1866. It is a glucoside of weak acid character, and was named Cathartic Acid. By boiling its alcoholic solution with acids it yields Cathartogenic Acid and sugar. There were also found Chrysophanic Acid, Sennacrol and Sennapicrin, and a peculiar non-fermentable saccharine principle which was named Cathartomannite or Sennit.

The conclusions reached after experimenting with Senna leaves washed with alcohol were as follows:

(1) Strong spirit does not remove any of the active principle from Senna leaves.

(2) The therapeutic action of cathartic acid is assisted by one or more of the constituents yielded by Senna to strong alcohol, though these constituents produce no purgative effect when taken alone.

(3) Senna exhausted by alcohol is a reliable and pleasant purgative, but somewhat weaker in its action than the unexhausted leaves.

Many substances produce precipitates with the infusion of Senna, but they may remove only inert ingredients, and not be really incompatible medicinally. Cathartic acid is precipitated by infusion of galls and solution of lead subacetate. Lead acetate and tartar emetic, which disturb the infusion, have no effect upon a solution of this substance.

Cathartin is the name of a mixture of the salts of cathartic acid which may be used in doses of from 3 to 6 grains.

Sennax is the name applied to the water-soluble glucoside of Senna, marketed in tablets containing 0·075 gram each.

¶ *Medicinal Action and Uses*. Purgative. Its action being chiefly on the lower bowel, it is especially suitable in habitual costiveness. It increases the peristaltic movements of the colon by its local action upon the intestinal wall. Its active principle must pass out of the system in the secretions unaltered, for when Senna is taken by nurses, the suckling infant becomes purged. It acts neither as a sedative nor as a refrigerant, but has a slight, stimulating influence. In addition to the nauseating taste, it is apt to cause sickness, and griping pains, so that few can take it alone; but these characteristics can be overcome or removed, when it is well adapted for children, elderly persons, and delicate women. The colouring matter is absorbable, and twenty or thirty minutes after the ingestion of the drug it appears in the urine, and may be recognized by a red colour on the addition of ammonia.

The addition of cloves, ginger, cinnamon, or other aromatics are excellent correctives of the nauseous effects. A teaspoonful of cream of tartar to a teacupful of the decoction of infusion of Senna, is a mild and pleasant cathartic, well suited for women if required soon after delivery. Some practitioners add neutral laxative salts, or saccharine and aromatic substances. The purgative effect is increased by the addition of pure bitters; the decoction of guaiacum is said to answer a similar purpose. Senna is contraindicated in an inflammatory condition of the alimentary canal, hæmorrhoids, prolapsus, ani, etc. The well-known 'black draught' is a combination of Senna and Gentian, with any aromatic, as cardamom or coriander seeds, or the rind of the Seville orange. The term 'black draught,' it is stated, should never be used, as mistakes have been made in reading the prescriptions, and 'black drop' or vinegar of opium has been given instead, several deaths having been caused in this way.

SENNA PODS, or the dried, ripe fruits, are official in the British Pharmacopœia, though the quantity is restricted, as an adulterant, in the United States Pharmacopœia.

They are milder in their effects than the leaflets, as the griping is largely due to the resin, and the pods contain none, but have about 25 per cent. more cathartic acid and emodin than the leaves, without volatile oil. From 6 to 12 pods for the adult, or from 3 to 6 for the young or very aged, infused in a claret-glass of cold water, act mildly but thoroughly upon the whole intestine.

The fluid extract was formerly treated with alcohol for the removal of the griping principles, but the process was deleted from the United States Pharmacopœia. The fluid extract is a dark, blackish, thick and somewhat turbid liquid, with a strong flavour of Senna. It is well adapted for exhibition with saline cathartics, such as Epsom salt or cream of tartar. In this case not more than half the full dose should be given at once. The British Pharmacopœia 1898 'Liquor Sennæ Concentratus' was more like a concentrated infusion than a fluid extract, but had the same strength as the latter, the menstrum being distilled water; tincture of ginger and alcohol being added.

The infusion of Senna, or Senna Tea, consists of 100 grams of Senna leaves, 5 grams of sliced Ginger, 1,000 millilitres of distilled water, boiling. Infuse in a covered vessel for fifteen minutes, and strain, while hot. The United States Pharmacopœia prefers coriander to ginger. The infusion deposits, on exposure to air, a yellowish precipitate, so it is advisable to make it in very small quantities, as the deposit aggravates its griping tendency. It is usual to prescribe manna and one of the saline cathartics with it. The cold infusion is said to be less unpleasant in taste, and equal in strength to the hot.

SYRUP OF SENNA is prepared by mixing 8 fluid ounces, 218 minims of fluid extract of Senna, with 81 minims of oil of Coriander and sufficient syrup to make 33 fluid ounces (6½ fluid drachms).

The Aromatic Syrup includes also jalap, rhubarb, cinnamon, clove, nutmeg, oil of lemon, sugar, and diluted alcohol.

The Compound Syrup includes rhubarb, frangula, methyl salicylate, alcohol, and syrup.

¶ *Dosages.* Powdered leaves, 1 drachm. Conct. solution, B.P., ½ to 1 drachm. Of compound or aromatic syrup, 2 fluid drachms. Of U.S.P. syrup, for an adult, 1 to 4 fluid drachms. Of B.P. syrup, 1 to 2 fluid drachms. Of Senna, ½ to 2 drachms. Of compound mixture, B.P., 4 to 16 drachms. Of infusion, B.P., ½ to 2 fluid ounces. Of fluid extract, for an adult, ½ to 2 fluid drachms. Of confection, B.P., 1 to 2 drachms.

¶ *Adulterations and Other Species Used.* Owing to the high price, what is known as 'broken Senna' is found on the market and sold for the genuine article with government sanction in the United States of America. Also, 'Senna siftings,' containing sand and other foreign matter have been offered for sale, causing trouble to government inspectors.

Formerly there was an intentional mixture of 5 parts of *C. acutifolia*, 3 of *C. obovata*, and 2 of *Cynanchum*, but now Alexandrian Senna is more uniform. It is often called in the French Pharmacopœia *séné de la palthe*, because of the duty formerly laid upon it by the Ottoman Porte. A parcel of Alexandrian Senna in the market formerly consisted of (1) leaflets of *C. acutifolia*, (2) leaflets of *C. obovata*, (3) the pods, broken leaf-stalks, flowers, and fine fragments of either, (4) leaves of *Cynanchum oleofolium*. The last are larger, thicker, regular at the base, and have no lateral nerves visible on their undersurface. They must be regarded as an adulteration.

C. angustifolia or *Tinnevelly Senna, Senna Indica, C. elongata,* is an annual growing in the Yemen and Hadramaut provinces of Arabia Felix, in Somaliland, Mozambique, Scind, and the Punjab. In Southern India it is cultivated and grows to a larger size. In the German and Swiss Pharmacopœias, the official drug is restricted to Tinnevelly Senna, and also in the British Pharmacopœia and the Pharmacopœia of India. *Senna Indica* also includes the variety known as Arabian, Mocha, Bombay, or East Indian Senna. Both varieties, as well as Alexandrian Senna, are official in the United States Pharmacopœia.

There is a certain difference in the qualities and also in the names of the species imported into Britain and America. The fine Tinnevelly Senna goes from Madras or Tuticorin to Britain. The leaflets are unbroken, from 1 to 2 or more inches long, thin, flexible, and green.

It has been stated that it contains only two-thirds as much of the active principle as the Alexandrian.

The other, or Arabian variety, comes via Mocha and Bombay, and is less pure and less carefully prepared. The leaflets are long and narrow, pike-like, so are called in France *séné de la pique*. Leaflets resembling these were brought by Livingstone from Southeast Africa. *Mecca Senna*, also known in America as Arabian or Bombay Senna, is obtained from both the wild and the cultivated kinds of *C. angustifolia*. The best comes from British India. The variety has sometimes a yellowish or tawny colour, more like the Indica than the Alexandrian, and may be the product of *C. lanceolata* of Forskhal. *C. obovata*, *C. obtusa* or *Senna obtusa* is usually a perennial, found wild in Egypt, Nubia, Abyssinia, Tripoli, Senegal and Benguella, Arabia and India. It was the first kind of Senna known, and being brought by the Moors into Europe, was formerly cultivated in Northern Italy, Spain, and Southern France, and called *S. italica*. It is official in the British Pharmacopœia and the Pharmacopœia of India as one of the botanical sources of Alexandrian Senna, but now few of its leaflets are included. It is called by the Arabs *S. baladi*, i.e. indigenous or wild Senna, to distinguish it from *C. acutifolia*, *S. jebeli*, or Mountain Senna. It is common in Jamaica, where its cultivation has been suggested, and where it is called Port Royal Senna or Jamaica Senna.

C. Marilandica or *American Senna, Wild Senna, Poinciana pulcherima*, formerly *Maryland Senna*, is a common perennial from New England to Northern Carolina. Its leaves are compressed into oblong cakes like other herbal preparations of the Shakers. It acts like Senna, but is weaker, and should be combined with aromatics. The dose in powder is from ½ to 2½ drachms. For the infusion, add 1 ounce of the leaves and 1 drachm of coriander seeds to 1 pint of boiling water. Macerate for an hour in a covered vessel, and strain. Dose: 4 to 5 fluid ounces. These leaves are also found mixed with or substituted for Alexandrian Senna.

C. Chamœcrista, Prairie Senna, Partridge Pea, Dwarf Cassia, or *Sensitive Pea*, found on the Western Prairies, is an excellent substitute for the above.

C. fistula, or *Purging Cassia, C. Stick, Pudding Pipe-Tree*, or *Alexandrian Purging Cassia*, is a tree rising to 40 feet in height, the pulp of the pods being used in the electuary of Senna. It is found in Egypt, the Indies, China, etc.

Colutea arborescens, or *Bladder-Senna* (*see* SENNA, BLADDER), *Baguenaudier, Séné Indigène*, the *Sutherlandia frutescens* of the Cape, formerly often met with as a substitute, is now usually replaced by *Globularia Turbith* or *Alypum*, the leaves of which are milder, so that a double dose may be taken. It is the Wild Senna of Europe.

Coriaria Myrtifolia is a Mediterranean shrub and highly poisonous, so that it should be recognized when present. The leaves are green, very thin, and soft, three veined, ovate-lanceolate, and equal at the base. It grows wild in Southern Europe, and its leaves are used as a black dye. It is also used to adulterate sweet marjoram. Deaths are recorded from eating the small, black berries. A Mexican drug, Tlolocopetale, containing coriarin and coriamurtin, is said to be a product. Other names are *Curriers Sumach* and *Redoul*.

Argel leaves (*Solenostemma* or *Cynanchum Argel*), from Nubia, are paler in colour, have less conspicuous veins, and an equal base.

Tephrosia leaflets and legumes (*Tephrosia Apollinea*), from the banks of the Nile, are silky or silvery, equal at the base and usually folded longitudinally on their mid-rib.

Jaborandi Leaflets (*Bilocarpus Microphyllus*) have been imported under the name of Senna.

Aden Senna is believed to be obtained from *C. holosericeæ*.

C. montana yields a false Senna from Madras, partly resembling the Tinnevelly Senna, though the colour of the upper surface of the leaves is browner.

It must be remembered that the Senna leaf contains no tannic acid and does not alter a ferric solution, while most of those encountered as adulterations precipitate ferric-chloride.

Other varieties used in their native countries, of which little appears to be known, are also:

C. cathartica, C. rugosa, C. splendida, C. lævigata, C. multijuja, Coronilla Emerus or *Scorpion Senna, C. obovata* or *Senegal Senna*.

SENNA, BLADDER

Colutea arborescens
N.O. Leguminosæ

Part Used. Leaves

Habitat. Indigenous to Southern Europe, Mediterranean region, said to be the sole vegetation found growing on the crater of Vesuvius

¶ *Description.* Cultivated in Britain as a decorative shrub, flowers yellow, papilionaceous, specially characterized by membraneous, bladder-like pods, which when pressed go off with a loud bang, hence its name of Bladder Senna. The plant grows well in the author's garden.

¶ *Medicinal Action and Uses.* The leaflets are purgative and on the Continent are often substituted for Senna leaves, but they are much milder in action than the true Senna. Taken in the form of an infusion, 1 or 2 drachms of the seeds will excite vomiting.

SENSITIVE PLANT. *See* MIMOSAS

SHALLOT. *See* GARLIC, ONION

SHEEP'S SORREL. *See* SORREL

SHEPHERD'S PURSE
Capsella bursa-pastoris (MEDIC.)
N.O. Cruciferæ

Synonyms. Shepherd's Bag. Shepherd's Scrip. Shepherd's Sprout. Lady's Purse. Witches' Pouches. Rattle Pouches. Case-weed. Pick-Pocket. Pick-Purse. Blind-weed. Pepper-and-Salt. Poor Man's Parmacettie. Sanguinary. Mother's Heart. Clappedepouch (*Irish*)
(*French*) Bourse de pasteur
(*German*) Hirtentasche

Part Used. Whole plant

Habitat. All over the world, outside the tropics. It is probably of European or West Asiatic origin, and is abundant in Britain, flowering all the year round

Shepherd's Purse is so called from the resemblance of the flat seed-pouches of the plant to an old-fashioned common leather purse. It is similarly called in France *Bourse de pasteur*, and in Germany *Hirtentasche*.

The Irish name of 'Clappedepouch' was given in allusion to the begging of lepers, who stood at cross-roads with a bell or clapper, receiving their alms in a cup at the end of a long pole.

It is a common weed of the Cruciferous order, said to be found all over the world and flourishing nearly the whole year round.

A native of Europe, the plant has accompanied Europeans in all their migrations and established itself wherever they have settled to till the soil. In John Josselyn's *Herbal* it is one of the plants named as unknown to the New World before the Pilgrim Fathers settled there.

It will flourish and set seed in the poorest soil, though it may only attain the height of a few inches. In rich soil it luxuriates and grows to 2 feet in height.

¶ *Description.* The plant is green, but somewhat rough with hairs. The main leaves, 2 to 6 inches long, are very variable in form, either irregularly pinnatifid or entire and toothed. When not in flower, it may be distinguished by its radiating leaves, of which the outer lie close to the earth.

The slender stem, which rises from the crown of the root, from the centre of the rosette of radical leaves, is usually sparingly branched. It is smooth, except at the lower part, and bears a few, small, oblong leaves, arrow-shaped at the base, and above them, numerous small, white, inconspicuous flowers, which are self-fertilized and followed by wedge-shaped fruit pods, divided by narrow partitions into two cells, which contain numerous oblong yellow seeds.

When ripe, the pod separates into its two boat-shaped valves.

The odour of the plant is peculiar and rather unpleasant, though more cress-like than pungent.

It has an aromatic and biting taste, but is less acrid than most of the Cruciferæ, and was formerly used as a pot-herb, the young radical leaves being sold in Philadelphia as greens in the spring. It causes taint of milk when freely eaten by dairy cattle.

¶ *Part Used.* In modern herbal medicine the whole plant is employed, dried and administered in infusion, and in fluid extract.

A homœopathic tincture is prepared from the fresh plant.

¶ *Constituents.* During the summer, the plant has a sharp, acrid taste, due to the stimulating principle.

Several partial analyses have been made of it, but no characteristic principle has been definitely separated. The active constituent is said to be an organic acid, which Bombelon, a French chemist, termed bursinic acid. He also found a tannate and an alkaloid, Bursine, which resembles sulphocyansinapine.

A peculiar sulphuretted volatile oil, closely similar to, if not identical with oil of mustard, as well as a fixed oil, have been determined and 6 per cent. of a soft resin.

¶ *Medicinal Action and Uses.* Shepherd's Purse is one of the most important drug-plants of the family Cruciferæ.

When dried and infused, it yields a tea which is still considered by herbalists one of the best specifics for stopping hæmorrhages of all kinds – of the stomach, the lungs, or the uterus, and more especially bleeding from the kidneys.

Its hæmostyptic properties have long been known and are said to equal those of ergot and hydrastis. During the Great War, when these were no longer obtainable in German commerce, a liquid extract of *Capsella bursa-*

pastoris was used as a substitute, the liquid extract being made by exhausting the drug with boiling water. Bomelon found the herb of prompt use to arrest bleedings and flooding, when given in the form of a fluid extract, in doses of 1 to 2 spoonfuls.

Culpepper says it helps bleeding from wounds – inward or outward – and

'if bound to the wrists, or the soles of the feet, it helps the jaundice. The herb made into poultices, helps inflammation and St. Anthony's fire. The juice dropped into ears, heals the pains, noise and matterings thereof. A good ointment may be made of it for all wounds, especially wounds in the head.'

It has been used in English domestic practice from early times as an astringent in diarrhœa; it was much used in decoction with milk to check active purgings in calves.

It has been employed in fresh decoction in hæmaturia, hæmorrhoids, chronic diarrhœa and dysentery, and locally as a vulnerary in nose-bleeding, which is checked by inserting the juice on cotton-wool. It is also used as an application in rheumatic affections, and has been found curative in various uterine hæmorrhages, especially those with which uterine cramp and colic are associated, and also in various passive hæmorrhages from mucous surfaces.

It is a remedy of the first importance in catarrhal conditions of the bladder and ureters, also in ulcerated conditions and abscess of the bladder. It increases the flow of urine. Its use is specially indicated when there is white mucous matter voided with the urine; relief in these cases following at once.

Its antiscorbutic, stimulant and diuretic action causes it to be much used in kidney complaints and dropsy; other similar stimulating diuretics such as Couch Grass may be combined with it.

Dr. Ellingwood, in his valuable work on Therapeutics, says of Shepherd's Purse:

'This agent has been noted for its influence in hæmaturia . . . soothing irritation of the renal or vesical organs. In cases of uncomplicated chronic menorrhagia (excessive menstruation) it has accomplished permanent cures, especially if the discharge be persistent. The agent is also useful where uric acid or insoluble phosphates or carbonates produce irritation of the urinary tract. Externally, the bruised herb has been applied to bruised and strained parts, to rheumatic joints, and where there was ecchymosis, or extravasations within or beneath the skin.

'The herb is rather unpleasant to take, but it is valuable mixed with Pellitory of the Wall, and a little Spirits of Juniper much disguises the flavour. A small quantity of Nitrate of Potash will further disguise it, and not detract from its medicinal value. The infusion may be taken in wineglassful doses, four times a day.'

The medicinal infusion should be made with an ounce of the plant to 12 oz. of water, reduced by boiling to ½ pint, strained and taken cold.

The fluid extract is given in doses of ½ to 1 drachm. In the United States, the fluid extract is given for dropsy in doses of ½ to 1 teaspoonful in water.

Shepherd's Purse was said to be the principal herb in the blue 'Electric Fluid' used by Count Matthei to control hæmorrhage.

Small birds are fond of the seeds of Shepherd's Purse: chaffinches and other wild birds may often be observed feeding on them, and they form valuable food for all caged birds.

When poultry have fed freely on the green plant in the early spring, it has been noticed that the egg yolks become dark in colour, a greenish brown or olive colour, and stronger in flavour.

SIEGESBECKIA

Siegesbeckia orientalis (LINN.)
N.O. Compositæ

Synonym. The Holy Herb
Parts Used. Juice, leaves, and whole plant
Habitat. Isle of Bourbon

¶ *Description.* A small composite plant or small shrub growing in hot climates. The heads are small with an involucre of five bracts covered with very sticky glandular hairs. The secretion continues till after the fruit is ripe and aids in its distribution, the whole head breaking off and attaching itself to some passing animal. In China it is a common weed. The drug contains a white crystalline body resembling salicylic acid.

¶ *Medicinal Action and Uses.* Used by Creoles as a protective covering for wounds, burns, etc. The juice when applied to the skin leaves a coating similar to that of collodion. Creoles call it 'Colle Colle' – Stick Stick.

In China it is used as a remedy for ague,

rheumatism, and renal colic; used in Britain chiefly as a cure for ringworm in conjunction with glycerine. Used in Mauritius Islands for syphilis, leprosy, and various skin diseases.

¶ *Dose*: 10 minims of the fluid extract.

SILVERWEED

Potentilla anserina (LINN.)
N.O. Rosaceæ

Synonyms. Prince's Feathers. Trailing Tansy. Wild Tansy. Goosewort. Silvery Cinquefoil. Goose Tansy. Goose Grey. Moor Grass. Wild Agrimony

Part Used. Herb

The Silverweed, one of the commonest of the *Potentillas*, is very abundant in Great Britain and throughout the temperate regions, extending from Lapland to the Azores, and is equally at home in regions as remote as Armenia, China, New Zealand and Chile.

All soils are congenial to its growth. It spreads rapidly by means of long, creeping runners and thrives in moist situations, especially in clay, where the water is apt to stagnate, and is common by waysides, though on dusty ground it becomes much dwarfed.

It has a slender, branched root-stock, dark brown outside, which has been eaten in the Hebrides in times of scarcity.

The leaves are covered on both sides with a silky, white down of soft hairs, mostly marked on the underside, hence its English name of Silverweed. They are 2 to 5 inches long, much cut or divided, interruptedly pinnate, i.e. divided into twelve to fifteen pairs of oval, toothed leaflets along the midrib, each pair being separated by a shorter pair all the way up.

The buttercup-like flowers, in bloom from early summer till later autumn, are borne singly on long footstalks from the axils of the leaves on the slender runners. They are large, with five petals of a brilliant yellow colour and the calyx is cleft into ten divisions.

The Silverweed is a favourite food of cattle, horses, goats, pigs and geese. Only sheep decline it.

Older writers call it *Argentina* (Latin, *argent*, silver) from its appearance of frosted silver. The name Anserina (Latin, *anser*, a goose) was probably given it because geese were fond of it.

The generic name, *Potentilla*, is derived from the Latin adjective, *potens*, powerful, in allusion to the medicinal properties of some of the species.

¶ *Parts Used*. All parts of the plant contain tannin.

In modern herbal medicine the whole herb is used, dried, for its mildly astringent and tonic action. It has an astringent taste, but no odour.

The roots, which are even more astringent, have been used, also the seeds.

The herb is gathered in June, all shrivelled, discoloured or insect-eaten leaves being rejected. Collect only in dry weather, in the morning, after the dew has been dried by the sun. Failing the convenience of a specially-fitted drying-shed, where drying is carried on by artificial heat, drying may be done in warm, sunny weather out of doors, but in half-shade, as leaves dried in the shade retain their colour better than those dried in the sun. They may be placed on wire sieves, or wooden frames covered with wire or garden netting, at a height of about 3 or 4 feet from the ground, to ensure a current of air. The herbs must be brought indoors to a dry room or shed at night, before there is any chance of them becoming damp by dew.

For drying indoors, a warm, sunny attic may be employed, the window being left open by day, so that there is a current of air for the moist, hot air to escape; the door may also be left open. The leaves and herbs can be placed on coarse butter-cloth, stented, i.e. if hooks are placed beneath the window and on the opposite wall, the butter cloth can be attached by rings sewn on each side of it and hooked on so that it is stretched quite taut. The temperature should be from 70° to 100° F. Failing sun, any ordinary shed, fitted with racks and shelves can be used, provided that it is ventilated near the roof, and has a warm current of air, caused by an ordinary coke stove or anthracite stove. The important point is rapidity and the avoidance of steaming; the quicker the process of drying, the more even the colour obtained, making the product more saleable.

All dried leaves should be packed away at once in wooden or tin boxes, in a dry place, as otherwise they re-absorb about 12 per cent. of moisture from the air, and are liable to become mouldy and to deteriorate in quality.

¶ *Medicinal Action and Uses*. A strong infusion of Silverweed, if used as a lotion, will check the bleeding of piles, the ordinary infusion (1 oz. to a pint of boiling water) being meanwhile taken as a medicine.

The same infusion, sweetened with honey, constitutes an excellent gargle for sore throat. A tablespoonful of the powdered herb may also be taken every three hours.

It is also an excellent remedy for cramps in the stomach, heart and abdomen. In addition to the infusion taken internally, it is advisable to apply it to the affected parts on compresses.

On the Continent, a tablespoonful of the herb, boiled in a cup of milk, has been recommended as an effective remedy in tetanus, or lockjaw. The tea should be drunk as hot as possible. If the patient dislikes milk, boiling water may be used.

The dried and powdered leaves have been successfully administered in ague: the more astringent roots have been given in powder in doses of a scruple and upwards.

As a diuretic, Silverweed has been considered useful in gravel. Ettmueller extolled it as a specific in jaundice. Of the fresh plant, 3 oz. or more may be taken three or four times daily.

The decoction has been used for ulcers in the mouth, relaxation of the uvula, spongy gums and for fixing loose teeth, also for toothache and preserving the gums from scurvy.

A distilled water of the herb was in earlier days much in vogue as a cosmetic for removing freckles, spots and pimples, and for restoring the complexion when sunburnt.

In Leicestershire, Silverweed fomentations were formerly used to prevent pitting by smallpox.

Salmon (1710) says:

'It is very cold and dry in the second degree, astringent, anodyne, vulnerary and arthritic. It stops all fluxes of the bowels, even the bloody flux, also spitting, vomiting of blood, or any inward bleeding. It helps the whites in women and is profitable against ruptures in children and is good to dissipate contusions, fastens loose teeth and heals wounds or ulcers in the mouth, throat or in any part of the body, drying up old, moist, corrupt and running sores. It resists the fits of agues, is said to break the stone, and is good to cool inflammation in the eyes, as eke to take away all discolourings of the skin and to cleanse it from any kind of depredation.'

See FIVE-LEAF GRASS, TORMENTIL.

SIMARUBA

Simaruba Amara (D. C.)
Simaruba officinalis
N.O. Simarubaceæ

Synonyms. Dysentery Bark. Mountain Damson. Bitter Damson. Slave Wood. Stave Wood. Sumaruppa. Maruba. Quassia Simaruba

Part Used. Dried root-bark

Habitat. French Guiana, the Islands of Dominica, Martinique, St. Lucia, St. Vincent and Barbados

¶ *Description.* The name given by the founder of the genus was Carib *Simarouba*, but later writers adopted the present spelling.

The tree is 60 feet or more in height, with many long, crooked branches covered with smooth, greyish bark, leaves 9 to 12 inches long, and flowers growing in small clusters, with rather thick, dull-white petals. The bark is usually found in pieces several feet long, the roots being long, horizontal, and creeping. Very often the outer bark has been removed, when it shows a pale yellowish or pinkish-brown surface. It is odourless, difficult to powder, and intensely bitter. It is usually imported from Jamaica, in bales.

¶ *Constituents.* Simaruba root-bark contains a bitter principle identical with quassin, a resinous matter, a volatile oil having the odour of benzoin, malic acid, gallic acid in very small proportion, an ammoniacal salt, calcium malate and oxalate, some mineral salts, ferric oxide, silica, ulmin, and lignin.

It readily imparts its virtues at ordinary temperatures to water and alcohol. The infusion is as bitter as the decoction, which becomes turbid as it cools.

¶ *Medicinal Action and Uses.* A bitter tonic. It was first sent from Guiana to France in 1713 as a remedy for dysentery. In the years 1718 and 1725 an epidemic flux prevailed in France, which resisted all the usual medicines. Simaruba was tried with great success, and established its medical character in Europe. It restores the lost tone of the intestines, promotes the secretions, and disposes the patient to sleep. It is only successful in the latter stage of dysentery, when the stomach is not affected. In large doses it produces sickness and vomiting. On account of its difficult pulverization, it is seldom given in substance, the infusion being preferred, but like many bitter tonics, it is now seldom used. From its use, it has been called 'dysentery bark.'

¶ *Dosage.* From 20 grains to a drachm. A ¼ oz. of simaruba may be infused for 12 hours in 12 oz. of cold or boiling water, and a wineglassful of the infusion taken every three or four hours.

Fluid extract, ½ to 1 drachm.

¶ *Other Species.*

Simaruba glauca of Jamaica, San Domingo, Bahama Islands, Panama and Guatemala has identical properties, and by some writers is regarded as the same tree, others distinguishing it by a slight difference in the flowers. It is also known as Winged-leaved Quassia, and *S. medicinalis.*

S. versicolor of Brazil, has similar properties, the fruit and bark being also used as anthelmintics, and an infusion of the latter being employed in cases of snake-bite. The plant is so bitter that insects will not attack it, on which account the powdered bark has been employed to kill vermin.

S. glauca of Cuba furnishes a glutinous juice, which is employed in certain skin diseases.

S. excelsa or Quassia Excelsa yields quassin from boiled slices of the wood, furnishing the Quassia of commerce, substituted for the true *Surinam Quassia.*

Samadera Indica contains a similar bitter principle in its bark.

See QUASSIA.

SKIRRET

Sium Sisarum
N.O. Umbelliferæ

Part Used. Root

Sium Sisarum, or Skirret, is a plant of Chinese origin, cultivated in Europe. It has a sweetish, somewhat aromatic root, which is used as a vegetable in much the same manner as the Oyster plant or Salsify (*Tragopogon porrifolius*) and the Parsnip. It is supposed to be a useful diet in chest complaints.

The name (*Sium*) is from the Celtic *siu* (water), in allusion to their habitat.

S. Sisarum has been cultivated in this country since A.D. 1548. When boiled and served with butter, the roots form a dish, declared by Worlidge, in 1682, to be 'the sweetest, whitest, and most pleasant of roots.'

Culpepper says:

'*Sisari, secacul.* Of Scirrets. – They are hot and moist, of good nourishment, something windy, as all roots; by reason of which they . . . stir up appetite . . .'

SKUNK-CABBAGE

Symplocarpus fœtidus
N.O. Araceæ

Synonyms. Dracontium. Dracontium fœtidum (Linn.). Skunkweed. Polecatweed. Meadow Cabbage. Spathyema fœtida. Ictodes fœtidus
Parts Used. Seeds, root
Habitat. United States

¶ *Description.* The plant grows in abundance in moist places of the northern and middle United States. All parts of it have a strong, fœtid odour, dependent upon a volatile principle, which is quickly dissipated by heat. The rhizome should be collected in the autumn or early spring, and should not be kept more than one season, as it deteriorates with age and drying. In commerce it is found in cylindrical pieces, 2 inches or more in length and about 1 in. in diameter, or, more commonly, in transverse slices, much compressed and corrugated. It is dark brown outside, white or yellowish within. The seeds are regarded as more energetic than the root, and preserve their virtues longer. They have an acrid taste, and emit the fœtid odour only when bruised. The acridity of the root is absent in the decoction.

¶ *Constituents.* A fixed oil, wax, starch, volatile oil, fat, salts of lime, silica, iron and maganese.

¶ *Medicinal Action and Uses.* Antispasmodic, diaphoretic, expectorant, narcotic. Large doses cause nausea, vomiting, headache, vertigo and dimness of vision. It has been used with alleged success in asthma, chronic catarrh, chronic rheumatism, chorea, hysteria and dropsy. It is said to be helpful in epilepsy, and convulsions during pregnancy and labour. It is an ingredient in well-known herbal ointments and powders. Externally, as an ointment, it stimulates granulations, eases pain, etc.

The powdered root may be used, alone, or mixed with honey ($\frac{1}{2}$ oz. to 4 oz. of honey), but the best method of use is probably a saturated tincture of the fresh root.

¶ *Dosage.* Of powder, 10 to 20 grains. Of tincture, 1 to 2 fluid drachms. Of fluid extract, $\frac{1}{2}$ to 1 drachm.

SLIPPERY ELM. *See* ELM

SENEGA
Polygala Senega

SIMARUBA
Simaruba Amara

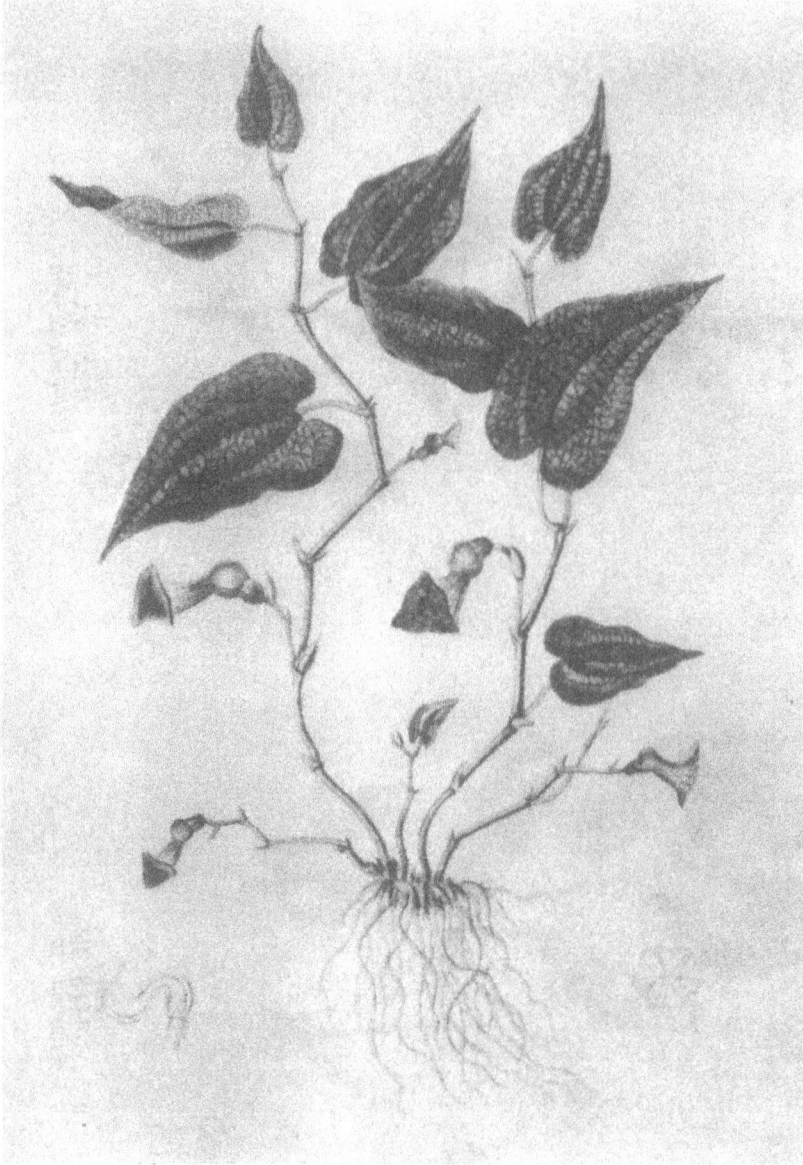

SNAKEROOT
Aristolochia Serpentaria

SMARTWEED

Polygonum Hydropiper (LINN.)
N.O. Polygonaceæ

Synonyms. Water Pepper. Biting Persicaria. Bity Tongue. Arcmart. Pepper Plant. Smartass. Ciderage. Red Knees. Culrage. Bloodwort. Arsesmart

Parts Used. Whole herb and leaves

Habitat. Great Britain and Ireland, rarer in Scotland; is a native of most parts of Europe, in Russian Asia to the Arctic regions. Found abundantly in places that are under water during the winter

¶*Description.* Annual. The branched stem, 2 to 3 feet in length, creeps at first, then becomes semi-erect. The leaves are lance-shaped, shortly stalked, wavy, more or less acute, glandular below, fringed with hairs. The stipules form a short inflated ochrea. The greenish-pink flowers are in long, slender, loose racemes, that mostly droop at their tips. There are six to eight stamens, two of which are functionless; two to three styles to the pistil. The fruit is black and dotted, as long as the perianth, three-sided and nut-like. The leaves have a pungent, acrid, bitter taste (something like peppermint), which resides in the glandulat dots on its surface, no odour.

¶*Constituents.* The plant's irritant medicinal properties are due to an active principle not fully understood, called Polygonic Acid (when discovered by Dr. C. J. Rademaker in 1871), which forms in green deliquescent crystals, having a bitter and acrid taste and strong acid reaction. It is destroyed by heating or drying. Other authorities later considered this body to be simply a mixture of impure tannic and gallic acids, together with chlorophyll, and failed to isolate a stable active principle. The plant contains 3 or 4 per cent. of tannin. It imparts its properties to alcohol or water. The tincture must be made from the fresh plant; heat and age destroy its qualities.

It is said that this herb, together with Arbor Vitæ, constituted the anti-venereo remedy of Count Mattei.

Linnæus observes that the Water Pepperwort will dye woollen cloths of a yellow colour, if the material be first dipped in a solution of alum, and that all domestic quadrupeds reject it.

¶*Medicinal Action and Uses.* Stimulant, diuretic, diaphoretic, emmenagogue, efficacious in amenorrhœa. A cold water infusion is useful in gravel, colds and coughs.

In combination with tonics and gum myrrh, it is said to have cured epilepsy – probably dependent on some uterine derangement. The infusion in cold water, which may be readily prepared from the fluid extract, has been found serviceable in gravel, dysentery, gout, sore mouths, colds and coughs, and mixed with wheat bran, in bowel complaints. Antiseptic and desiccant virtues are also claimed for it. The fresh leaves, bruised with those of the Mayweed (*Anthemis Cotula*), and moistened with a few drops of oil of turpentine, make a speedy vesicant.

Simmered in water and vinegar, it has proved useful in gangrenous, or mortified conditions. The extract, in the form of infusion or fomentation, has been beneficially applied in chronic ulcers and hæmorrhoidal tumours, also as a wash in chronic erysipetalous inflammations, and as a fomentation in flatulent colic.

A hot decoction made from the whole plant has been used in America as a remedy for cholera, a sheet being soaked in it and wrapped round the patient immediately the symptoms start.

In Mexico, the infusion is used not only as a diuretic, but also put into the bath of sufferers from rheumatism.

A fomentation of the leaves is beneficial for chronic ulcers and hæmorrhoids – in tympanitis and flatulent colic, and as a wash in chronic inflammatory erysipelas.

It was once held that a few drops of the juice put into the ear would destroy the worms that it was believed caused earache.

There is a tradition, quoted in old Herbals, that if a handful of the plant be placed under the saddle, a horse is enabled to travel for some time without becoming hungry or thirsty, the Scythians having used this herb (under the name of Hippice) for that purpose.

It was an old country remedy for curing proud flesh in the sores of animals. Culpepper tells us also that 'if the Arsemart be strewed in a chamber, it will soon kill all the fleas.'

The root was chewed for toothache – probably as a counter-irritant – and the bruised leaves used as a poultice to whitlows.

A water distilled from the plant, taken in the quantity of a pint or more in a day, has been found serviceable in gravel and stone.

The expressed juice of the freshly gathered plant has been found very useful in jaundice and the beginning of dropsies, the dose being from 1 to 3 tablespoonfuls.

In Salmon's *Herbal*, it is stated:

'It is known by manifold and large experience to be a peculiar plant against gravel and stone. The Essence causes a good digestion, it is admirable against all cold and moist diseases of the brain and nerves, etc., such as falling sickness, vertigo, lethargy, apoplexy, palsy, megrim, etc., and made into a syrup with honey it is a good pectoral. The oil dissolves and discusses all cold swellings, scrofulous and scirrhous tumours, quinsies, congealed blood, pleurisies, etc.'

Waller recommends it also for 'hypochondriacal diseases.'

SMILAX, CHINA

Smilax, China (LINN.)
N.O. Liliaceæ

Synonym. China
Part Used. Root
Habitat. Eastern Asia

It has a hard, large, knotty, uneven rhizome, blackish externally, pale coloured or whitish internally. Stem without support, about 3 feet high, but growing much taller if it has a bush to cling to. Leaves thin, membraneous, round, five-nerved acute or obtuse at each end, mucronate at points. Stipules distinct obtuse; umbels greenish yellow, small ten-flowered; fruit red, size of bird cherry. This is the commercial China root, used as a substitute for Sarsaparilla. It is in large ligneous pieces 2 to 6 inches long and about 2 inches in diameter. Odourless, taste at first slightly bitter and acrid like Sarsaparilla. The root-stocks yield a yellow dye with alum and a brown one with sulphate of iron.

Brazilian or Rio Negro or Lisbon Sarsaparilla is furnished by *Smilax Papyracea.*

S. Aspera (habitat, South of France, Italy, etc.) yields the Italian Sarsaparilla which has the same properties as the American ones.

S. ovalifolia is used medicinally in India.

S. lanceæfolia is used in India and has very large tuberous root-stocks.

S. glyciphylla is the Australian medicinal Sarsaparilla.

S. macabucha is used in the Philippines for dysentery and other complaints.

S. anceps is the medicinal Sarsaparilla of Mauritius.

¶ *Preparations and Dosage.* Infusion, 1 oz. to 1 pint – 1 tablespoonful three times daily. Fluid extract, 1 to 2 drachms. Tincture, 2 to 4 drachms.

¶ *Other Species.* From the AMERICAN SMART-WEED (*Polygonum*, Linn.), which possesses properties similar to those of the English species; a homœopathic tincture is prepared from the fresh plant, which has been used with great advantage in diarrhœa and dysentery, in doses of 20 to 60 minims.

In Persia the young shoots of some of the species are eaten as asparagus.

S. pseudo-China and other species are used in basket-making.

S. rotundifolia – Mexican – is said to be a diaphoretic and depurative.

All the Sarsaparillas have medicinal properties and can be used in the same way. Sarsaparilla is efficacious in proportion to its acrid taste. The properties reside chiefly in the cortex, though the bark is generally used.

The name Smilax was used by the Greeks to denote a poisonous tree – others derive the name from *Smile*, i.e. a cutting or scratching implement, in allusion to the rough prickles on the stem.

In commerce the varieties of Sarsaparillas are grouped as mealy and non-mealy, according to the starch they contain. The farinaceous matter is found under the rind.

The mealy group include Smilax officinalis, Honduras, Caracas, Brazilian, Syphilitica and Papyraceæ.

The non-mealy species are Jamaica Sarsaparilla, Mexican, Media and Lima.

The most esteemed varieties are Jamaica and Lima on account of their acrid taste.

See (AMERICAN) SPIKENARD.

See SARSAPARILLA

SNAKEROOT

Aristolochia serpentaria (LINN.)
N.O. Aristolochiaceæ

Synonyms. Aristolochia reticulata. Serpentatiæ Rhizoma. Serpentary Rhizome. Serpentary Radix. Virginian Snakeroot. Aristolochia officinalis. Aristolochia sagittata. Endodeca Bartonii. Endodeca Serpentaria. Snakeweed. Red River or Texas Snakeroot. Pelican Flower. Virginia serpentaria. Snagrel. Sangrel. Sangree. Radix Colubrina. Radix Viperina
Parts Used. Dried rhizome and roots
Habitat. The Central and Southern United States

¶ *Description.* Many species of *Aristolochia* have been employed in medicine, the classical name being first applied to *A. Clem*-atitis and *A. rotunda*, from their supposed emmenagogue properties. *A. serpentaria* and *A. reticulata*, or Texas Snakeroot, differ slightly in leaves and flowers, the latter having a slightly coarser root. Both are recognized as official in the United States of America.

The plant is a perennial herb, growing in rich, shady woods, the roots being collected in Western Pennsylvania, West Virginia, Ohio, Indiana and Kentucky, where it is packed in bales containing about 100 lb., often mixed with leaves, stems and dirt.

It has a short, horizontal rhizome, giving off numerous long, slender roots below. The flowers are peculiar, growing from the joints near the root and drooping until they are nearly buried in the earth or in their dried leaves. They are small, and brownish-purple in colour. Attempts at cultivation are being made, as the rather large use of *serpentaria* has caused the drug to become scarcer. A specimen was grown in an English garden as far back as 1632. There is one in cultivation at Kew, but it has not flowered there. The genus *Endodeca* was defined from this species, but it has no characters to distinguish it. Serpentaria has a yellowish or brownish colour, and both smell and taste are aromatic and resemble a mixture of valerian and camphor. Several kinds are cultivated in hothouses for the singularity and, in some cases, the handsome appearance of their flowers, though their colours are usually dingy. The bent shape causes some blossoms to act as a fly-trap. *A. sipho*, a native of the Alleghany Mountains, is cultivated as an outdoor climbing plant, for the sake of its large leaves, the shape of its flowers inspiring the name of Pipe-Vine or Dutchman's Pipe.

¶ *Constituents.* A volatile oil in the proportion of about ¼ per cent., and a bitter principle – Aristolochin – an amorphous substance of yellow colour and bitter and slightly acrid taste, soluble in both water and alcohol. The medicinal properties are due to these two substances, but the root also contains tannic acid, resin, gum, sugar, etc.

A more recent analysis gives volatile oil, resin, a yellow, bitter principle considered analagous to the bitter principle of quassia, gum, starch, albumen, lignin, malate and phosphate of lime, oxide of iron and silica.

About ¼ oz. of the oil is furnished by 100 lb. of the root, the coarser, *A. reticulata*, yielding rather more. The resinous aristinic acid has been obtained from a number of species, including *A. serpentaria*. The alkaloid Aristolochine, found in several varieties, requires fuller investigation.

¶ *Medicinal Action and Uses.* Stimulant, tonic and diaphoretic, properties resembling those of valerian and cascarilla. Too large doses occasion nausea, griping pains in the bowels, sometimes vomiting and dysen-teric tenesmus. In small doses, it promotes the appetite, toning up the digestive organs. It has been recommended in intermittent fevers, when it may be useful as an adjunct to quinine. In full doses it produces increased arterial action, diaphoresis, and frequently diuresis. In eruptive fevers where the eruption is tardy, or in the typhoid stage where strong stimulants cannot be borne, it may be very valuable. An infusion is an effective gargle in putrid sore-throat. It benefits sufferers from dyspepsia and amenorrhœa.

Long boiling impairs its virtues. A cold infusion is useful in convalescence from acute diseases.

It is probable that as it does not disturb the bowels, it may often be used where *Guaiacum* is not easily tolerated, for stimulating capillary circulation and promoting recovery in chronic forms of gouty inflammation.

Many powers are claimed for the drug as an antidote to the bites of snakes and mad dogs, but though there is much direct testimony, the claim is not considered to be authoritatively proved.

¶ *Dosage.* Powdered root, 10 to 30 grains. Fluid extract, ½ to 1 drachm. Tincture, B.P. and U.S.P., ½ to 1 drachm. Infusion, B.P., ½ to 1 oz. Conc. solution, B.P., ½ to 2 drachms.

¶ *Poisonous, if any, with Antidotes.* According to Pohl, aristolochine in sufficient dose produces in the higher animals violent irritation of the gastro-intestinal tract and of the kidneys, with death in coma from respiratory paralysis.

The celebrated Portland powder for the cure of gout contained aristolochia, with gentian, centaury and other bitters in the dose of a drachm every morning for three months, afterwards diminishing for a year or more, but its prolonged use injured the stomach and nervous system, bringing on premature decay and death.

¶ *Other Species.*

Analyses have been made of *A. Clematitis*, *A. rotunda*, *A. longa*, *A. argentea*, *A. indica* and *A. bracteata*, yielding aristolochine, aristolin, or aristinic acid. A closely allied if not identical resinous acid has been obtained from the plant *Bragantia Wallichii*, besides an alkaloid, which, under the name of *Alpam*, has long been used in Western India as an antidote to snake-venom. The allied species, *Bragantia tomentosa*, is said to be employed in Java as an emmenagogue.

Several species are found in the herbalists' stores of India which do not enter commerce.

A. bracteata is employed as an emmenagogue. *Aristolochia* of the Br. Add. was the dried stem and root of *A. indica*, the stems with attached roots being used for the cure of snake-bite.

Of *A. rotunda*, the Br. Add. recognized the concentrated liquor, i.e. 1 in 2 of 20 per cent. alcohol (dose, ¼ to 2 fluid drachms), and the tincture, i.e. 1 in 5 of 70 per cent. alcohol (dose, ¼ to 1 fluid drachm).

A. Clematitis, *A. longa* and *A. rotunda* are still retained in official catalogues in Europe, where they are indigenous. *A. Pistolochia*, of Southern Europe, appears to have been the aristolochia of Pliny, and is still used under the name of Pistolochia.

A. Clematitis, or Birthwort, is found in England, usually near old ruins, as if it had been cultivated for its medical use, as an aid to parturition.

It is stated that Egyptian jugglers use some of these plants to stupefy snakes before they handle them, while it is related that the juice of the root of *A. anguicida*, if introduced into the mouth of a serpent, will stupefy it, and if it be compelled to swallow a few drops it will die in convulsions.

It is conjectured that the Guaco of South America, a root of which is carried by all Indians and Negroes who traverse the country, is some species of Aristolochia, probably *A. cymbifera*, known in Brazil as milhommen, jarra, and jarrinha.

In the Argentine Republic the root of *A. argentina* is used as a diuretic and diaphoretic, especially in rheumatism.

In Arabia, Forskhal states that the leaves of *A. sempervirens* are used as a counter-poison.

A. fœtida, of Mexico, or Yerba del Indio, is used as a local stimulant to foul ulcers.

For snake-bite, in addition to *A. serpentaria* in North America, *A. maxima* or *Contra Capitano* is employed in South America, *A. anguicida* in the Antilles, *A. brasiliensis*, *A. cymbifera*, *A. macroura*, *A. trilobata*, etc.

See BIRTHWORT

SNAKEROOT, BUTTON

Liatris spicata (WILLD.)
N.O. Compositæ

Synonyms. Gay Feather. Devil's Bite. Colic Root
Part Used. Root
Habitat. Southern Ontario southwards

¶ *Description.* An indigenous perennial composite plant, growing in moist fields and grounds, found from Southern Ontario and Minnesota southwards. Root tuberous; has a herbaceous erect stem, which in August gives a beautiful spike of crimson-purple compound flowers. The odour of the root is terebinic, taste bitterish; the plant grows well in the author's garden at Chalfont St. Peter.

¶ *Constituent.* Coumarin.

¶ *Medicinal Action and Uses.* Useful for its diuretic properties and as a local application for sore throat and gonorrhœa, for which it is exceedingly efficacious. Being an active diuretic it is valuable in the treatment of Bright's disease. Its agreeable odour is due to Coumarin, which may be detected on the surface of its spatulate leaves.

¶ *Dosage.* A decoction is taken three or four times daily in 2-oz. doses.

¶ *Other Species.* Several varieties of *Liatris* are largely used in Southern United States to flavour tobacco, and are said to keep moths away from clothing. All varieties are active diuretics, and *L. squarrosa* (syn. 'Rattlesnake Master') has been utilized to cure rattlesnake-bite.

SNAPDRAGON

Antirrhinum magus (LINN.)
N.O. Scrophularaceæ

Part Used. Leaves

Snapdragon is closely allied to the Toad-flaxes. It is really not truly a native herb, but has become naturalized in many places, on old walls and chalk cliffs, being an escape from gardens, where it has been long cultivated.

The botanical name, *Antirrhinum*, refers to the snout-like form of the flower.

¶ *Medicinal Action and Uses.* The plant has bitter and stimulant properties, and the leaves of this and several allied species have been employed on the Continent in cataplasms to tumours and ulcers.

It was valued in olden times like the Toad-flax as a preservative against witchcraft.

The numerous seeds yield a fixed oil by expression, said to be little inferior to olive oil, for the sake of which it has been cultivated in Russia.

¶ *Other Species.*
Antirrhinum Orontium (Linn.), the Calf's Snout or Small Snapdragon, an annual found occasionally in cornfields, in lime or chalk soil, with narrow, hairy leaves and small, reddish flowers, resembling those of the Snapdragon in form, is said to be poisonous, but the fact is not well established.

Its properties seem similar to those of the other species.

The name, *Orontium*, given it by Dodonæus, is an old mediæval generic name for the Snapdragon.

See TOADFLEX.

SNOWDROP

Galanthus nivalis (LINN.)
N.O. Amaryllidaceæ

Synonyms. Fair Maid of February. Bulbous Violet

Snowdrop, usually spoken of as the first flower of our year, though the Winter Aconite has perhaps a better title to be so considered, has never been of much account in physic, and has never been recognized. Gerard says 'nothing is set down hereof by the ancient Writers, nor anything observed by the moderne.' He calls it the Bulbous Violet, but adds that some call it the Snowdrop, the earliest mention of it by this name, and it was known to all the old botanists as a bulbous violet.

The generic name, *Galanthus*, is Greek in its origin and signifies Milkflower. *Nivalis* is a Latin adjective, meaning relating to or resembling snow.

Gerard speaks of it as not a native of England, though somewhat common in gardens, having been introduced from Italy. It is a native of Switzerland, Austria and of Southern Europe generally, but where naturalized here spreads into considerable masses, and is plentiful wherever it occurs, generally growing in shady pastures, woods and orchards. There is probably no bulbous plant, however, which for all its extreme hardiness in resisting cold, shows such a marked preference or distaste for certain localities, even though there may be little variation in soil or altitude. In some districts snowdrops will grow and spread in woods as readily as the wild hyacinth; in others, with apparently identical conditions, it is difficult to get them to grow and they will refuse to spread.

The bulbs grow in compact masses. Each sends up a one-flowered stem. The points of the leaves protecting the flower-head are thickened and toughened at the tips, enabling them to push through the soil. This simple device shows on the mature leaf like a delicate nail on a green finger.

The flowers remain open a long time; the bud is erect, but the open flowers pendulous and adapted to bees. The perianth is in two whorls, on the inner surface of the inner perianth leaves are green grooves secreting honey – the stamens dehisce, or open, by apical slots and lie close against the style, forming a cone. The stigma projects beyond the anther cone and is first touched by an insect, which in probing for nectar, shakes the stamens and receives a shower of pollen.

Gerard appears to be wrong in saying that the plant has no medicinal use.

An old glossary of 1465, referring to it as *Leucis i viola alba*, classes it as an emmenagogue, and elsewhere, placed under the narcissi, its healing properties are stated to be 'digestive, resolutive and consolidante.'

SOAP TREE

Quillaja saponaria (MOLINA.)
N.O. Rosaceæ

Synonyms. Soap Bark. Panama Bark. Cullay
Part Used. Dried inner bark
Habitat. Peru and Chile, and cultivated in Northern Hindustan

¶ *Description.* A tree 50 to 60 feet high. Leaves smooth, shiny, short-stalked, oval, and usually terminal white flowers, solitary, or three to five on a stalk. Bark thick, dark coloured, and very tough. In commerce it is found in large flat pieces $\frac{1}{5}$ inch thick, outer surface brownish-white, with small patches of brownish cork attached, otherwise smooth; inner surface whitish and smooth, fracture splintery, chequered with pale-brown vast fibres, embedded with white tissue; it is inodorous, very acrid and astringent.

¶ *Constituents.* Its chief constituent is saponin, which is a mixture of two glucosides, guillaic acid and guillaia-sapotoxin. The latter is very poisonous and possesses marked foam-producing properties. Calcium oxalate is also present in the bark. The drug also contains cane-sugar and a non-toxic modification of guillaic acid. As the active principles of Soap Bark are the same as those of Senega, Quillaia has been suggested as a cheap substitute for Sarsaparilla.

¶ *Medicinal Action and Uses.* It can be used as a stimulating expectorant. As a decoction (5 parts to 200), adult-dose 1 tablespoonful. Syrup of guillaia can be utilized as a substitute for syrup of Senega, by adding 4 parts of the fluid extract to 21 parts of syrup, using diluted alcohol as the menstruum.

¶ *Doses of Quillaia Bark.* Fluid extract, 2 to 8 drops. Solid extract, $\frac{1}{2}$ to 2 grains. Tincture, B.P. and U.S.P., $\frac{1}{2}$ to 1 drachm.

Might be useful in cases of aortic disease with hypertrophy, its efficacy depending on the diminished action of the cardiac ganglia and muscle which its active principle, Saponine, produces. Saponin appears to be identical with Cyclamin, from Cyclamen European, and with primulin from *Primula officinalis*. Digitonin from Digitalis appears to be a kind of Saponin differing somewhat from the others. Saponin, when applied locally, is a powerful irritant, local anæsthetic and muscular poison. On account of its local irritation, when injected hypodermically it causes intense pain; sneezing when applied to the nose; vomiting, diarrhœa and gastro-enteritis if taken in large doses internally. Locally applied, it paralyses motor and sensory nerves, and voluntary and involuntary muscular fibre; in the voluntary muscles it produces a condition of *rigor mortis*, and the muscular substance becomes brittle and structureless. Saponin acts as an emeto-cathartic and a diuretic if it is absorbed; in its excretion it irritates the bronchial mucous membrane, and is a protoplasmic poison. In poisoning produced from it, digitalis is indi-cated, as it is antagonistic to Saponin. Saponin is contained in agrostemma seeds, and has caused death; the symptoms were headache, vertigo, vomiting, hot skin, rapid feeble pulse, progressive muscular weakness, and finally coma.

Quillaia bark is used in its native country for washing clothes, and in this country is used by manufacturers and cleaners for washing or cleaning delicate materials. For washing hair: Powdered Soap Tree bark, 100 parts; alcohol, 400 parts; essence of Berga-mot, 20 drops; mix. It is said to promote the growth of the hair. Was once used in the production of foam on non-alcoholic beverages, but its use in this way is now generally prohibited by law.

¶ *Other Species.*

The Brazilian species, *Quillaia Selloniana*, or *Fontenellea braziliensis*, has similar properties to *Quillaia Saponaria*.

SOAPWORT

Saponaria officinalis (LINN.)
N.O. Caryophylleæ

Synonyms. Soaproot. Bouncing Bet. Latherwort. Fuller's Herb. Bruisewort. Crow Soap. Sweet Betty. Wild Sweet William
Parts Used. Dried root and leaves
Habitat. Central and Southern Europe. Grows well in English gardens

¶ *Description.* A stout herbaceous perennial with a stem growing in the writer's garden to 4 or 5 feet high. Leaves lanceolate, slightly elliptical, acute, smooth, 2 or 3 inches long and ½ inch wide. Large pink flowers, often double in paniculate fascicles; calyx cylindrical, slightly downy; five petals, unguiculate; top of petals linear, ten stamens, two styles; capsule oblong, one-celled, flowering from July till September. No odour, with a bitter and slightly sweet taste, followed by a persistent pungency and a numbing sensation in the mouth.

¶ *Constituents.* Constituents of the root, Saponin, also extractive, resin, gum, woody fibre, mucilage, etc.

Soapwort root dried in commerce is found in pieces 10 and 12 inches long, $\frac{1}{12}$ inch thick, cylindrical, longitudinally wrinkled, outside light brown, inside whitish with a thick bark. Contains number of small white crystals and a pale yellow wood.

¶ *Medicinal Action and Uses.* A decoction cures the itch. Has proved very useful in jaundice and other visceral obstructions. For old venereal complaints it is a good cure, specially where mercury has failed. It is a tonic, diaphoretic and alterative, a valuable remedy for rheumatism or cutaneous troubles resulting from any form of syphilis. It is also sternutatory. Should be very cautiously used owing to its saponin content.

Dose. – Decoction, 2 to 4 fluid ounces three or four times daily. Extract or the inspissated juice will be found equally efficacious: dose, 10 to 20 grains. As a sternutatory 2 to 6 grains. Fluid extract, ¼ to 1 drachm.

SOAPWORT ROOT, EGYPTIAN

Gypsophila struthium (LINN.)
N.O. Caryophylleæ

Habitat. Europe and United States of America

¶ *Description.* The root is generally in lengths of 4 to 6 inches, ½ to 1½ inches in diameter; colour a yellowish white, furrowed down its length externally with lighter places where the cortex has been rubbed. The section is of a radiate and concentric structure. Taste bitter, then acrid; odour slight; powder irritating to the nostrils. This variety is rarely used medicinally, the Soapwort (*Saponaria officinalis*) being used as a sub-stitute. This is a perennial herbaceous plant with a stem 1 to 2 feet in height, growing in Europe and United States of America.

¶ *Medicinal Action and Uses.* Tonic, dia-phoretic, alterative. A valuable remedy in the treatment of syphilitic, scrofulous and cutaneous diseases, also in jaundice, liver affections, rheumatism and gonorrhœa, the decoction is generally used. Saponin is produced from this plant.

748

SOLOMON'S SEAL   Polygonatum multiflorum (ALLEM.)
                N.O. Liliaceæ

Synonyms. Lady's Seals. St. Mary's Seal. Sigillum Sanctæ Mariæ
 (*French*) Scean de Solomon
 (*German*) Weusswurz
 Part Used. Root

A close relative to the Lily-of-the-Valley, and was formerly assigned to the same genus, *Convallaria*. It is a popular plant in gardens and plantations; a native of Northern Europe and Siberia, extending to Switzerland and Carniola. In England it is found, though rarely, growing wild in woods in York, Kent and Devon, but where found in Scotland and Ireland is regarded as naturalized. The Dwarf Solomon's Seal is found in the woods of Wiltshire.

¶ *Description.* The creeping root-stock, or underground stem, is thick and white, twisted and full of knots, with circular scars at intervals, left by the leaf stems of previous years. It throws up stems that attain a height of from 18 inches to 2 feet, or even more, which are for some considerable portion of their length erect, but finally bend gracefully over. They are round, pale-green in colour, and bare half-way up; from thence to the top, large and broadly-oval leaves grow alternately on the stem, practically clasping it by the bases. All the leaves have the character of turning one way, being bent slightly upward, as well as to one side, and have very marked longitudinal ribbing on their surfaces.

The flowers are in little drooping clusters of from two to seven, springing from the axils of the leaves, but hanging in an opposite direction to the foliage. They are tubular in shape, of a creamy or waxy white, topped with a yellowish-green, and sweet-scented, and are succeeded by small berries about the size of a pea, of a blackish-blue colour, varying to purple and red, and containing about three or four seeds.

The generic name *Polygonatum* signifies many-angled, and is supposed to be derived either from the numerous knots or swellings of the root or from the numerous nodes or joints of the stem, but the characteristics are not very marked ones. The specific name, *multiflorum*, serves to distinguish this many-flowered species from another in which the blossoms are solitary, or only in pairs from each axil.

The origin of the common English name of the plant is variously given. Dr. Prior tells us it comes from 'the flat, round scars on the rootstocks, resembling the impressions of a seal and called Solomon's, because his seal occurs in Oriental tales.'

Another explanation is that these round depressions, or the characters which appear when the root is cut transversely, and which somewhat resemble Hebrew characters, gave rise to the notion that Solomon 'who knew the diversities of plants and the virtues of roots,' has set his seal upon them in testimony of its value to man as a medicinal root.

Gerard maintained that the name Sigillum Solomons was given to the root partly because it bears marks something like the stamp of a seal, but still more because of the virtue the root hath in sealing and healing up green wounds, broken bones and such like, being stamp't and laid thereon.'

The name Lady's Seal was also conferred on the plant by old writers, as also St. Mary's Seal (*Sigillum Sanctæ Mariæ*).

¶ *Cultivation.* Solomon's Seal is a very hardy plant. It prefers a light soil and a shady situation, being a native of woods. If in a suitable soil and situation and not crowded by shrubs, it will thrive and multiply very rapidly by the creeping rootstocks. It will be better for occasional liberal dressings of leaf-mould, or an annual top dressing of decayed manure in March.

Seeds, sown as soon as gathered in the autumn, germinate in early spring, or the roots may be divided to any extent. The best time to transplant or part the roots is in autumn, after the stalks decay, but it may safely be done at any time, if taken up with plenty of soil, until they begin to shoot in the spring, when the ground should be dug about them and kept clean from weeds. They should also have room to spread and must not be removed oftener than every third or fourth year.

To give Solomon's Seal a good start when planting, the soil should be well broken up with a fork and have a little mild manure worked in.

¶ *Part Used.* The root dug in autumn and dried.

¶ *Constituents.* The rhizome and herb contain Convallarin, one of the active constituents of Lily-of-the-Valley, also Asparagin, gum, sugar, starch and pectin.

¶ *Medicinal Action and Uses.* Astringent, demulcent and tonic. Combined with other remedies, Solomon's Seal is given in pulmonary consumption and bleeding of the lungs. It is useful also in female complaints. The infusion of 1 oz. to a pint of boiling water is taken in wineglassful doses and is also used as an injection. It is a mucilaginous tonic, very healing and restorative, and is good in inflammations of the stomach and bowels, piles, and chronic dysentery.

A strong decoction given every two or three hours has been found to cure erysipelas, if at the same time applied externally to the affected parts.

The powdered roots make an excellent poultice for bruises, piles, inflammations and tumours. The bruised roots were much used as a popular cure for black eyes, mixed with cream. The bruised leaves made into a stiff ointment with lard served the same purpose. Gerard says:

'The roots of Solomon's Seal, stamped while it is fresh and greene and applied, taketh away in one night or two at the most, any bruise, blacke or blew spots gotten by fals or women's wilfulness in stumbling upin their hastie husband's fists, or such like.'

A decoction of the root in wine was considered a suitable beverage for persons with broken bones, 'as it disposes the bones to knit.' On this point, Gerard adds:

'As touching the knitting of bones and that truly which might be written, there is not another herb to be found comparable to it for the purposes aforesaid; and therefore in briefe, if it be for bruises inward, the roots must be stamped, some ale or wine put thereto and strained and given to drinke . . . as well unto themselves as to their cattle,'

it being applied 'outwardly in the manner of a pultis' for external bruises.

Parkinson says, 'The Italian dames, however, doe much use the distilled water of the whole plant of Solomon's Seal' – for their complexions, etc.

In Galen's time, the distilled water was used as a cosmetic, and Culpepper says:

'the diluted water of the whole plant used to the face or other parts of the skin, cleanses it from freckles, spots or any marks whatever, leaving the place fresh, fair and lovely, for which purpose it is much used by the Italian ladies and is the principal ingredient of most of the cosmetics and beauty washes advertised by perfumers at high price.'

The roots macerated for some time in water yield a substance capable of being used as food and consisting principally of starch. The young shoots form an excellent vegetable when boiled and eaten like Asparagus, and are largely consumed in Turkey. The roots of another species have been made into bread in times of scarcity, but they require boiling or baking before use.

The flowers and roots used as snuff are celebrated for their power of inducing sneezing and thereby relieving head affections. They also had a wide vogue as aphrodisiacs, for love philtres and potions.

The berries are stated to excite vomiting, and even the leaves, nausea, if chewed.

The properties of these roots have not been very fully investigated. It is stated that a decoction will afford not only relief but ultimate cure in skin troubles caused by the poison vine, or poisonous exalations of other plants.

Dosage of the decoction: 1 to 4 oz. three times daily.

As a remedy for piles the following has been found useful: 4 oz. Solomon's Seal, 2 pints water, 1 pint molasses. Simmer down to 1 pint, strain, evaporate to the consistence of a thick fluid extract, and mix with it from ⅓ to 1 oz. of powdered resin. Dosage: 1 teaspoonful several times daily.

¶ *Other Species.*

Polygonatum biflorum, an American Solomon's Seal, has characters and constitution similar to the European.

P. uniflorum, now *P. officinale,* is said to be no longer used. The plant bears a single fragrant flower.

P. verticillatum, bearing its leaves in whorls, is only found in Scotland, and then rarely.

Smilacina Racemosa is known as False Solomon's Seal.

SORREL, COMMON	Rumex acetosa
SORREL, FRENCH	Rumex scutatus
SORREL, MOUNTAIN	Oxyria reniformis
	N.O. Germaniaceæ
SORREL, SHEEP'S	Rumex acetosella
SORREL, WOOD	Oxalis acetosella

Synonyms. Wood Sour. Sour Trefoil. Stickwort. Fairy Bells. Hallelujah. Cuckowes Meat. Three-leaved Grass. Surelle. Stubwort

(*Scotch*) Gowke-Meat (*French*) Pain de Coucou

(*Irish*) Seamsog (*Italian*) Iuliole

Parts Used. Leaves and herb

The Sour Docks or Sorrels, cultivated for pot-herbs, *Rumex acetosa* (Common Sorrel) and *R. scutatus* (French Sorrel), as well as the smaller *R. acetosella* (Sheep's Sorrel) and

Oxyria reniformis (Mountain Sorrel), owe the grateful acidity of their herbage to the presence of a special salt, binoxalate of potash, which is also present in Rhubarb. This, however, is absent in the common Docks. We find it to a marked degree in the WOOD SORREL (*Oxalis acetosella*), which indeed receives its name on this account, and not for any similarity in the structure of the plant, which is in no way related to the Sorrels and Docks.

¶ *Description.* It is a little plant of a far more delicate, even dainty character, growing abundantly in woods and shady places. From its slender, irregular creeping rootstock covered with red scales, it sends up thin delicate leaves, each composed of three heart-shaped leaflets, a beautiful bright green above, but of a purplish hue on their under surface. The long slender leaf-stalks are often reddish towards the base. The leaflets are usually folded somewhat along their middle, and are of a peculiarly sensitive nature. Only in shade are they fully extended: if the direct rays of the sun fall on them they sink at once upon the stem, forming a kind of three-sided pyramid, their under surfaces thus shielding one another and preventing too much evaporation from their pores. At night and in bad weather, the leaflets fold in half along the midrib, and the three are placed nearly side by side to 'sleep,' a security against storm and excessive dews.

The flowers, each set on long stalks, are fragile, in form somewhat like the Crane's-bills, to which they are closely allied, being bell-shaped, the corolla composed of five delicate white petals, veined with purple, enclosed in a five-scalloped cup of sepals and containing ten stamens, and in the centre, five green, thread-like columns, arising from a single five-celled ovary. At the base of the petals, a little honey is stored, but the flower seems to find favour with few insects.

As the flower fades, its stalk bends towards the ground and conceals the seed capsule under the leaves, till ripe, when it straightens again. The case of the capsule is elastic and curls back when the fruit is quite ripe, jerking the seeds out several yards, right over the leaves.

A second kind of flower is also produced. These are hidden among the leaves and are inconspicuous, their undeveloped petals never opening out. The ripening and seed scattering processes of these self-fertilized cleistogamous (or hidden) flowers are the same as with the familiar white-petalled ones. Wood Sorrel droops its blossoms in stormy weather, and also folds its leaves.

Neither the flowers nor any part of the plant has any odour, but the leaves have a pleasantly acid taste, due to the presence of considerable quantities of binoxalate of potash. This, combined with their delicacy, has caused them to be eaten as a spring salad from time immemorial, their sharpness taking the place of vinegar. They were also the basis of a green sauce, that was formerly taken largely with fish. 'Greene Sauce,' says Gerard, 'is good for them that have sicke and feeble stomaches . . . and of all Sauces, Sorrel is the best, not only in virtue, but also in pleasantness of his taste.'

Both botanical names *Oxalis* and *acetosella* refer to this acidity, *Oxalis* being derived from the Greek *oxys*, meaning sour or acid, and *acetosella*, meaning vinegar salts. Salts of Lemon, as well as Oxalic acid, can be obtained from the plant: 20 lb. of fresh herb yield about 6 lb. of juice, from which, by crystallization, between 2 and 3 oz. of Salts of Lemon can be obtained.

An old writer tells us:

'The apothecaries and herbalists call it Alleluya and Paniscuculi, or Cuckowes meat, because either the Cuckoo feedeth thereon, or by reason when it springeth forth and flowereth the Cuckoo singeth most, at which time also Alleluya was wont to be sung in Churches.'

It flowers between Easter and Whitsuntide.

By many, the ternate leaf has been considered to be that with which St. Patrick demonstrated the Trinity to the ancient Irish, though a tiny kind of clover is now generally accepted as the 'true Shamrock.'

The early Italian painters often depicted the blossom. Ruskin writes: 'Fra Angelico's use of the Oxalis acetosella is as faithful in representation as touching in feeling.'

¶ *Cultivation.* If roots are planted in a moist, shady border, they will multiply freely, and if kept clean from weeds will thrive and need no other care.

¶ *Part Used Medicinally.* The leaves, fresh or dried.

¶ *Medicinal Action and Uses.* It has diuretic, antiscorbutic and refrigerant action, and a decoction made from its pleasant acid leaves is given in high fever, both to quench thirst and to allay the fever. The Russians make a cooling drink from an infusion of the leaves, which may be infused with water or boiled in milk. Though it may be administered freely, not only in fevers and catarrhs, but also in hæmorrhages and urinary disorders, excess should be guarded against, as the oxalic salts are not suitable to all constitutions, especially those of a gouty and rheumatic tendency.

The old herbalists tell us that Wood Sorrel is more effectual than the true Sorrels as a blood cleanser, and will strengthen a weak stomach, produce an appetite, check vomiting, and remove obstructions of the viscera.

The juice of the leaves turns red when clarified and makes a fine, clear syrup, which was considered as effectual as the infusion. The juice used as a gargle is a remedy for ulcers in the mouth, and is good to heal wounds and to stanch bleeding. Sponges and linen cloths saturated with the juice and applied, were held to be effective in the reduction of swellings and inflammation.

An excellent conserve, *Conserva Ligulæ*, used to be made by beating the fresh leaves up with three times their weight of sugar and orange peel, and this was the basis of the cooling and acid drink that was long a favourite remedy in malignant fevers and scurvy.

In Henry VIII's time this plant was held in great repute as a pot-herb, but after the introduction of French Sorrel, with its large succulent leaves, it gradually lost its position as a salad and pot-herb.

From *Le Dictionnaire des Ménages* (Paris, 1820):

'*Limonade sans Citrous, Limonade Sèche*

'Take three drachms of *Salt of Sorrel* and one pound of white sugar; reduce them to powder separately, and then mix them. Keep the powder, which is known as dry lemonade, in a well-corked bottle. Substitute tartaric acid for Salt of Sorrel, divide the powder into suitable portions, and you have "lemonade powders without lemons." '

From *A Plain Plantain*:

'*A Sirrup for a Feaver*

'Take Sirrup of Violets two ounces; Sirrup of Woodsorrell two ounces; Sirrup of Lemmon two ounces, mixed altogether, and drink it.'

¶ *Other Species.*
R. Conglomeratus (Clustered Dock). *R. obtusifolin. R. pulcher*, the Fiddle Dock, so called from the resemblance in the form of its leaves to a violin.

SORRELS

SORREL, FRENCH
Rumex scutatus (LINN.)

Synonym. Buckler-shaped Sorrel
Part Used. Herb
Habitat. It is a common plant in mountainous districts, being a native of the South of France, Italy, Switzerland, Germany and Barbary

This has a more grateful acid than Common Sorrel, and is therefore preferred for kitchen use in soups, especially by the French. Their Sorrel soup is made from this species.

It is distinguished from the Common Sorrel by the form of the leaves, which are cordate-hastate, very succulent, fleshy and brittle. The whole plant is intensely glaucous. The flowers are hermaphrodite, the stamens and pistils not on separate plants as in the Common Sorrel.

It is sometimes met with in Scotland, or in the North of England, but is a doubtful native.

It is said to have been introduced into this country in 1596.

SORREL, GARDEN
Rumex acetosa (LINN.)
N.O. Polygonaceæ

Synonyms. Green Sauce. Sour Sabs. Sour Grabs. Sour Suds. Sour Sauce. Cuckoo Sorrow. Cuckoo's Meate. Gowke-Meat
Part Used. Leaves

Of the two kinds of Sorrel cultivated for use as vegetables or salads, *Rumex acetosa*, the Garden Sorrel, is an indigenous English plant, common, too, in the greater part of Europe, in almost all soils and situations. It grows abundantly in meadows, a slender plant about 2 feet high, with juicy stems and leaves, and whorled spikes of reddish-green flowers, which give colour, during the months of June and July, to the grassy spots in which it grows.

It is generally found in pastures where the soil contains iron.

The leaves are oblong, the lower ones 3 to 6 inches in length, slightly arrow-shaped at the base, with very long petioles. The upper ones are sessile. They frequently become a beautiful crimson.

As the flowers increase in size, they become a purplish colour. The stamens and pistils are on different plants. The seeds, when ripe, are brown and shining. The perennial roots run deeply into the ground.

Sorrel is well known for the grateful acidity of its herbage, which is most marked when the plant is in full season, though in early spring it is almost tasteless.

The plant is also called 'Cuckoo's-meate'

from an old belief that the bird cleared its voice by its agency. In Scotland it is 'gowke-meat.'

Domestic animals are fond of this and other species of Sorrel. The leaves contain a considerable quantity of binoxalate of potash, which gives them their acid flavour and medicinal and dietetic properties. They have been employed from the most distant time as a salad. In France, Sorrel is put into ragouts, fricassées and soups, forming the chief constituent of the favourite *Soupe aux herbes*.

In the time of Henry VIII, this plant was held in great repute in England, for table use, but after the introduction of French Sorrel, with large succulent leaves, it gradually lost its position as a salad and a potherb, and for many years it has ceased to be cultivated.

John Evelyn thought that Sorrel imparted 'so grateful a quickness to the salad that it should never be left out.' He wrote in 1720:

'Sorrel sharpens the appetite, assuages heat, cools the liver and strengthens the heart; is an antiscorbutic, resisting putrefaction and in the making of sallets imparts a grateful quickness to the rest as supplying the want of oranges and lemons. Together with salt, it gives both the name and the relish to sallets from the sapidity, which renders not plants and herbs only, but men themselves pleasant and agreeable.'

Culpepper tells us

'Sorrel is prevalent in all hot diseases, to cool any inflammation and heat of blood in agues pestilential or choleric, or sickness or fainting, arising from heat, and to refresh the overspent spirits with the violence of furious or fiery fits of agues: to quench thirst, and procure an appetite in fainting or decaying stomachs: For it resists the putrefaction of the blood, kills worms, and is a cordial to the heart, which the seed doth more effectually, being more drying and binding. . . . Both roots and seeds, as well as the herb, are held powerful to resist the poison of the scorpion. . . . The leaves, wrapt in a colewort leaf and roasted in the embers, and applied to a large imposthume, botch, boil, or plague-sore, doth both ripen and break it. The distilled water of the herb is of much good use for all the purposes aforesaid.'

In this country, the leaves are now rarely eaten, unless by children and rustics, to allay thirst, though in Ireland they are still largely consumed by the peasantry with fish and milk. Our country people used to beat the herb to a mash and take it mixed with vinegar and sugar, as a green sauce with cold meat, hence one of its popular names: Green-sauce.

Because of their acidity, the leaves, treated as spinach, make a capital dressing with stewed lamb, veal or sweetbread. A few of the leaves may also with advantage be added to turnips and spinach. When boiled by itself, without water, it serves as an excellent accompaniment to roast goose or pork, instead of apple sauce.

'To Stew Sorrel for Fricandean and Roast Meat.

'Wash the Sorrel, and put it into a silver vessel, or stone jar, with no more water than hangs to the leaves. Simmer it as slow as you can, and when done enough, put a bit of butter and beat it well.'

Unless cooked carefully, Sorrel is likely to disagree with gouty persons, from the acid oxalate of potash it contains, but this may be got rid of if it is plunged for two or three minutes in boiling water, before cooking, this first water being then thrown away.

In Scandinavia, Sorrel has sometimes been used in time of scarcity to put into bread. The leaves contain a little starch and mucilage, and the root is rather farinaceous.

The juice of the leaves will curdle milk as well as rennet, and the Laplanders use it as a substitute for the latter.

The dried root affords a beautiful red colour when boiled and used for making barley water look like red wine, when in France they wish to avoid giving anything of a vinous nature to the sick.

The salt of Sorrel, binoxalate of potash, is much used for bleaching straw and removing ink stains from linen, and is often sold in the shops under the name of 'essential salt of lemons.'

¶ *Cultivation.* Sorrel of two kinds is cultivated, *R. acetosa*, or Garden Sorrel, and *R. scrutatus*, or French Sorrel. Garden Sorrel likes a damp situation, French Sorrel a dry soil and an open situation.

The finest plants are propagated from seed, sown in March, though it may be sown in any of the spring months. Sow moderately thin, in drills 6 inches apart, and thin out when the plants are 1 or 2 inches high. When the stalks run up in July, they should be cut back. The roots will then put out new leaves, which will be tender and better for kitchen use than the older leaves, so that by cutting down the shoots of some plants at different times, there will always be a supply of young leaves.

Both varieties are generally increased by dividing the roots, which may be done either in spring or autumn, the roots being planted about a foot apart each way, and watered.

¶ *Parts Used Medicinally*. The leaves both dried and fresh.

¶ *Constituents*. The sour taste of Sorrel is due to the acid oxalate of potash it contains; tartaric and tannic acids are also present.

¶ *Medicinal Action and Uses*. The medicinal action of Sorrel is refrigerant and diuretic, and it is employed as a cooling drink in all febrile disorders.

It is corrective of scrofulous deposits: for cutaneous tumours, a preparation compounded of burnt alum, citric acid, and juice of Sorrel, applied as a paint, has been employed with success.

Sorrel is especially beneficial in scurvy.

Both the root and the seed were formerly esteemed for their astringent properties, and were employed to stem hæmorrhage.

A syrup made with the juice of Fumitory and Sorrel had the reputation of curing the itch, and the juice, with a little vinegar, was considered a cure for ringworm, and recommended as a gargle for sore throat.

A decoction of the flowers, made with wine, was said to cure jaundice and ulcerated bowels, the root in decoction or powder being also employed for jaundice, and gravel and stone in the kidneys.

Gerard enumerated eight different kinds of Sorrel – the Garden, bunched or knobbed, Sheep, Romane, Curled, Barren and Great Broad-leaved Sorrel, and said of them:

'The Sorrells are moderately cold and dry. Sorrell doth undoubtedly cool and mightily dry, but because it is sour, it likewise cutteth tough humours. The juice thereof in summer time is a profitable sauce in many meats and pleasant to the taste. It cooleth a hot stomach. The leaves are with good success added to decoctions, and are used in agues. The leaves are taken in good quantity, stamped and stained into some ale and cooleth the body. The leaves are eaten in a tart spinach. The seed of Sorrell drunk in wine stoppeth the bloody flow.'

SORREL, MOUNTAIN

Oxyria reniformis (HOOK)

Part Used. Herb

The Mountain Sorrel is found distributed in the Arctic regions and the Alps of the north temperate zone, and grows by streams in Wales, Yorks and northwards.

It has the characters of the allied genus *Rumex*, approaching the Common Sorrel in habit, but is shorter and stouter. The leaves are all from the root, fleshy and kidney-shaped. The flowers are green, growing in clustered spikes. The generic name, *Oxyria*, is derived from the Greek *oxys* (sharp), from the acid flavouring of the stem and leaves, which make it, like the other Sorrels, an excellent pot-herb and antiscorbutic.

SORREL, SHEEP'S

Rumex acetosella

Synonym. Field Sorrel
Part Used. Herb

Sheep's Sorrel is much smaller than either French or Garden Sorrel, and is often tinged, especially towards the end of the summer, a deep red hue. It is a slender plant, the stems from 3 to 4 inches to nearly a foot high, often many and tufted, decumbent at the base. The leaves, ⅓ to 2 inches in length, have long petioles and are variable in breadth, mostly narrow-lanceolate, the lower ones hastate and the lobes of the base usually spreading and often divided.

It grows in pastures and dry gravelly places in most parts of the globe, except the tropics, penetrating into Arctic and Alpine regions, and is abundant in Britain, where it is sometimes called Field Sorrel.

Like the other Sorrels, it is highly acid, though is less active in its properties than the French or Garden species.

¶ *Medicinal Action and Uses*. The whole herb is employed medicinally, in the fresh state. The action is diuretic, refrigerant and diaphoretic, and the juice extracted from the fresh plant is of use in urinary and kidney diseases.

SOUTHERNWOOD

Artemisia abrotanum (LINN.)
N.O. Compositæ

Synonyms. Old Man. Lad's Love. Boy's Love. Appleringie
(*French*) Garde Robe
Part Used. Herb

The Southernwood is the southern Wormwood, i.e. the foreign, as distinguished from the native plant, being a native of the South of Europe, found indigenous in Spain and Italy. It is a familiar and favourite plant in our gardens, although it rarely if ever flowers in this country. It has finely-divided, greyish-green leaves. It was introduced into this country in 1548. An ointment made with its ashes is used by country lads to promote the growth of a beard. St. Francis de Sales says: 'To love in the midst of sweets, little children could do that, but to love in the bitterness of Wormwood is a sure sign of our affectionate fidelity.' This refers to the habit of including a spray of the plant in country bouquets presented by lovers to their lasses.

The volatile essential oil contained in the plant consists chiefly of Absinthol and is common in other Wormwoods. The scent is said to be disagreeable to bees and other insects, for which reason the French call the plant *Garderobe*, as moths will not attack clothes among which it is laid.

It used to be the custom for women to carry to church large bunches of this plant and Balm, that the keen, aromatic scent might prevent all feeling of drowsiness. Southernwood in common with Wormwood was thought to ward off infection. Even in the early part of last century, a bunch of Southernwood and Rue was placed at the side of the prisoner in the dock as a preventive from the contagion of jail fever.

It Italy, Southernwood, like Mugwort, is employed as a culinary herb.

¶ *Part Used*. The whole herb, collected in August and dried in the same manner as Wormwood.

¶ *Medicinal Action and Uses*. Tonic, emmenagogue, anthelmintic, antiseptic and deobstruent.

The chief use of Southernwood is as an emmenagogue. It is a good stimulant tonic and possesses some nervine principle. It is given in infusion of 1 oz. of the herb to 1 pint of boiling water, prepared in a covered vessel, the escape of steam impairing its value. This infusion or tea is agreeable, but a decoction is distasteful, having lost much of the aroma.

Fluid extract, ½ to 1 drachm.

Considerable success has also attended its use as an anthelmintic, being chiefly used against the worms of children, teaspoonful doses of the powdered herb being given in treacle morning and evening.

The branches are said to dye wool a deep yellow.

Culpepper says:

'Dioscorides saith that the seed bruised, heated in warm water and drunk helpeth those that are troubled in the cramps or convulsions of the sinews or the sciatica. The same taken in wine is an antidote and driveth away serpents and other venomous creatures, as also the smell of the herb being burnt doth the same. The oil thereof annointed on the backbone before the fits of agues come, preventeth them: it taketh away inflammation of the eyes, if it be put with some part of a wasted quince or boiled in a few crumbs of bread, and applied. Boiled in barley meal it taketh away pimples . . . that rise in the face or other parts of the body. The seed as well as the dried herb is often given to kill worms in children. The herb bruised helpeth to draw forth splinters and thorns out of the flesh. The ashes thereof dry up and heal old ulcers that are without inflammation, although by the sharpness thereof, it makes them smart. The ashes mingled with old salad oil helps those that have their hair fallen and are bald, causing the hair to grow again, either on the head or beard. A strong decoction of the leaves is a good worm medicine, but is disagreeable and nauseous. The leaves are a good ingredient in fomentation for easing pain, dispersing swellings or stopping the progress of gangrenes. The distilled water of the herb is said to helpe . . . diseases of the spleen. The Germans commend it for a singular wound herb. . . . Wormwood has thrown it into disrepute.'

SOUTHERNWOOD, FIELD

Artemisia campestris

Part Used. Herb

The Field Southernwood is common in most parts of Europe, but rare in Britain, occurring only on sandy heaths in Norfolk and Suffolk. It is perennial, like the other species of Artemisia, with a rather thick, tapering root, but unlike them, its foliage is not aromatic. The slender, grooved stems, until flowering, are prostrate; the leaves are silky when young, but nearly smooth when mature, the segments few in number, but very slender, ¼ to ½ inch long, terminating in a point with their margins recurved. The flower-heads are small and numerous, in

long, slender, drooping racemes, the florets yellow and are in bloom in August and September.

¶ *Medicinal Action and Uses*. Dr. John Hill says of Field Southernwood that it is of a

'warm, fine, pleasant, aromatic taste, with a little bitterness, not enough to be disagreeable. It wants but to be more common and more known to be very highly valued . . . and one thing it is in particular, it is a composer; and always disposes the person to sleep. Opiates weaken the stomach and must not be given often where we wish for their assistance; this possesses the soothing quality without the mischief.'

This species of Artemisia has the same qualities, in a lesser degree, as the garden Southernwood, and Linnæus recommended an infusion of it as of use in pleurisy.

¶ *Cultivation of Species of Artemisia.* The Common Wormwood, Mugwort and Southernwood are regularly cultivated on some of the old established drug farms. They are grown in rows about 2 feet apart each way, and need no further care than to be kept free from weeds, growing in almost any soil. Mugwort and Common Wormwood may also be collected in the wild state.

Artemisia Dracunculus is the well-known culinary herb 'Tarragon,' a native of Siberia. It differs from the majority of its fellows in that its leaves are narrow and lance-shaped, of a bright green colour, and possess a peculiar aromatic taste, without the characteristic bitterness of the genus.

The Wormwood so frequently mentioned in Scripture is most probably *A. judaica,* growing in the Southern Desert.

See MUGWORT, TARRAGON, WORMWOOD.

SOW-THISTLES
SOW-THISTLE, COMMON

N.O. Compositæ
Sonchus oleraceus (LINN.)

> *Synonyms.* Hare's Thistle. Hare's Lettuce
> *Parts Used.* Leaves, stems, milky juice

The Sow-Thistle is a well-known weed in every field and garden. It is a perennial, growing from 1 to 3 feet high, with hollow, thick, branched stems full of milky juice, and thin, oblong leaves, more or less cut into (pinnatifid) with irregular, prickly teeth on the margins. The upper leaves are much simpler in form than the lower ones, clasping the stem at their bases.

The flowers are a pale yellow, and when withered, the involucres close over them in a conical form. The seed vessels are crowned with a tuft of hairs, or pappus, like most of this large family of Compositæ.

This plant is subject to great variations which are merely owing to soil and situation, some being more prickly than others.

The name of the genus, *Sonchus,* is derived from the Greek word for *hollow,* and bears allusion to the hollow nature of the succulent stems.

The Sow Thistles are sometimes erroneously called Milk Thistles from the milky juice they contain; the true Milk Thistle is, however, a very different plant (*see* THISTLES).

The Latin name of the species, *oleraceus,* refers to the use to which this weed has been put as an esculent vegetable. Its use as an article of food is of very early date, for it is recorded by Pliny that before the encounter of Theseus with the bull of Marathon, he was regaled by Hecale upon a dish of Sow-Thistles. The ancients considered them very wholesome and strengthening, and administered the juice medicinally for many disorders, considering them to have nearly the same properties as Dandelion and Succory.

The young leaves are still in some parts of the Continent employed as an ingredient in salads. It used in former times to be mingled with other pot herbs, and was occasionally employed in soups; the smoothest variety is said to be excellent boiled like spinach.

Its chief use nowadays is as food for rabbits. There is no green food they devour more eagerly, and all keepers of rabbits in hutches should provide them with a plentiful supply. Pigs are also particularly fond of the succulent leaves and stems of the Sow-Thistle.

One of the popular names of the Sow-Thistle: 'Hare's Thistle' or 'Hare's Lettuce,' refers to the fondness of hares and rabbits for this plant. An old writer tells us: 'when fainting with the heat she (the hare) recruits her strength with this herb: or if a hare eat of this herb in the summer when he is mad, he shall become whole.' Sheep and goats also eat it greedily, but horses will not touch it.

There are three or four other kinds of Sow Thistle, and as an old herbal tells us: 'They have all the same virtue, but this has them in perfection.'

SOW-THISTLE, CORN

Sonchus arvensis (LINN.),

> *Parts Used.* Leaves, milky juice

The Corn Sow-Thistle is a perennial, with a large fleshy, creeping root. It is found in similar situations as the common species, though mainly in cornfields, where its large, bright golden flowers, externally tinged with red, showing above the corn, make it a conspicuous plant. It is readily distinguished from the Common Sow-Thistle by its stem, which is 3 to 4 feet high – being unbranched and by the much larger size of its flowers, the involucres and stalks of which are covered by numerous glandular hairs. The leaves, like those of the Common Sow-Thistle, applied outwardly by way of cataplasm, have been found serviceable in inflammatory swellings.

SOW-THISTLE, MARSH

Part Used. Milky juice

The Marsh Sow-Thistle is a much taller species than either of the preceding, attaining a height of 6 to 8 feet, being one of the tallest of our English herbaceous plants. The root is perennial, fleshy and branched, but not creeping; the leaves, arrow-shaped at the base, large, shiny on the under surfaces; the flowers, large and pale yellow, with hairy involucres, are in bloom in September and October, much later than the last species,

Sonchus palustris (LINN.)

which it somewhat resembles, though the edges of the leaves are minutely toothed, not waved. It grows in marshy places but is rare in this country, being now extinct in most of the places in Norfolk, Suffolk, Kent and Essex where it was formerly found, and only occurring on the Thames below Woolwich. This thistle was placed by mediæval botanists under the planetary influences of Mars: 'Mars rules it, it is such a prickly business.'

SOW-THISTLE, MOUNTAIN

Synonym. Blue Sow-Thistle
Parts Used. Milky juice, leaves

The Blue or Mountain Sow-Thistle, a tall, handsome plant with very large blue flowers, but also very rare in these islands (it grows on the Clova Mountains), has been used as a salad in Lapland, the young shoots being stripped of their skin and eaten raw, but Linnæus informs us that it is somewhat bitter and unpalatable.

Of the Siberian Sow-Thistle (*Sonchus Tartaricus*), Anne Pratt, in *Flowers and Their Associations* (1840) says:

'This plant during that clear weather which is generally favourable to flowers, never uncloses; but let a thick mist over-spread the atmosphere or a cloud arise large enough to drive home the Honey Bee, and it will soon unfold its light blue blossoms.'

¶ *Medicinal Action and Uses.* Culpepper considers that the Sow-Thistles possess great medicinal virtues, which lie chiefly in the milky juice. He tells us:

'They are cooling and somewhat binding, and are very fit to cool a hot stomach and ease the pain thereof. . . . The milk that is taken from the stalks when they are broken, given in drink, is very beneficial to those that are short-winded and have a wheezing.'

He goes on to inform us, on the authority of Pliny, that they are efficacious against gravel, and that a decoction of the leaves and stalks is good for nursing mothers; that the juice or distilled water is good 'for all inflammation,

Sonchus alpinus (LINN.)

wheals and eruptions, also for hæmorrhoids.' Also that

'the juice is useful in deafness, either from accidental stoppage, gout or old age. Four spoonsful of the juice of the leaves, two of salad oil, and one teaspoonful of salt, shake the whole well together and put some on cotton dipped in this composition into the ears and you may reasonably expect a good degree of recovery.'

Again, that

'the juice boiled or thoroughly heated in a little oil of bitter almonds in the peel of a pomegranite and dropped into the ears is a sure remedy for deafness.'

Finally, he informs us that the juice 'is wonderfully efficacious for women to wash their faces with to clear the skin and give it lustre.'

Another old herbalist also says:

'The leaves are to be used fresh gathered; a strong infusion of them works by urine and opens obstructions. Some eat them in salads, but the infusion has more power.'

The whole plant has stiff spines on the leaf margin, and the seeds and roots are used in homœopathic medicine.

The milky juice of all the Sow-Thistles is an excellent cosmetic. The leaves are said to cure hares of madness.

See HAWKWEED, OX-TONGUE.

SPAGHNUM. *See* MOSS

SPEARMINT. *See* MINTS

SPEARWORT, LESSER

Part Used. Whole plant

The Lesser Spearwort has been used in the Isle of Skye and in many parts of the Highlands of Scotland to raise blisters, the leaves

Ranunculus flammula (LINN.)
N.O. Ranunculaceæ

being well bruised in a mortar and applied in one or more limpet shells to the part where the blister is to be raised.

It was used in the fourteenth century under the name of 'flame' for 'cankers,' a term probably used for ulcers. Its distilled water has been employed as a harmless emetic.

This plant is very common throughout Britain, growing in wet and boggy parts of heaths and commons, where it flowers from June to September.

The stems often root at the lower joints, being more or less horizontal to start with, but afterwards rising to a foot or more in height, being terminated by a few loose flower-bearing branches. It has undivided, lanceolate (lance-shaped) leaves, the uppermost being the narrowest and smallest. The flowers are numerous, on long stalks, a light golden-yellow, ½ to ¾ inch across.

¶ *Medicinal Action and Uses.* A tincture is used to cure ulcers.

See BUTTERCUP, CELANDINE.

SPEEDWELL, COMMON

Part Used. Herb

Veronica officinalis (LINN.)

N.O. Scrophulariaceæ

The Common Speedwell is a native of the Old World, but is abundantly naturalized in the eastern United States, where it grows in open, grassy places.

In this country, it is generally found on heaths, moors, dry hedgebanks and in coppices, where it is very common and generally distributed.

¶ *Description.* The plant is a perennial, of a prostrate habit, with ascending branches, bearing erect, spike-like clusters of blue flowers, the stems 3 to 18 inches long, varying very much in length according to soil. The leaves are opposite, shortly stalked, generally about an inch long, oval and attenuated into their foot-stalks, their margins finely toothed. The flowers are in dense, axillary, many-flowered racemes, 1½ to 6 inches long, the individual flowers nearly stalkless on the main flower-stalk, their corollas only ⅛ inch across, pale blue with dark blue stripes and bearing two stamens with a very long style. The capsule is inversely heart-shaped and notched, longer than the oblong, narrow sepals. The plant is of a dull green and is generally slightly hairy, having short hairs, sometimes smooth.

The fresh herb is faintly aromatic. After drying, it is inodorous. It has a bitterish, warm, and somewhat astringent taste.

¶ *Constituents.* Enz found a bitter principle, soluble in water and alcohol, but scarcely so in ether, and precipitated by the salts of lead, but not by tannic acid; an acrid principle; red colouring matter; a variety of tannic acid, producing a green colour with ferric salts; a crystallizable, fatty acid, with malic, tartaric, citric, acetic and lactic acids; mannite; a soft, dark green bitter resin.

Mayer, of New York (in 1863), found evidences of an alkaloid and of a saponaceous principle. Vintilesco (1910) found a gluco-side both in this species and in *Veronica chamædrys.*

¶ *Medicinal Action and Uses.* This species of Veronica retained a place among our recognized remedies until a comparatively late period, and is still employed in herbal medicine.

Its leaves possess astringency and bitterness.

Among the Welsh peasantry, great virtues are attributed to the Speedwell. The plant has diaphoretic, alterative, diuretic, expectorant and tonic properties, and was formerly employed in pectoral and nephritic complaints, hæmorrhages, diseases of the skin and in the treatment of wounds. Modern herbalists still consider that an infusion of the dried plant is useful in coughs, catarrh, etc., and is a simple and effective remedy in skin diseases.

¶ *Other Species.*

In *Familiar Wild Flowers* (and also in Lindley's *Treasury of Botany*) mention is made of another Speedwell called 'Buxbaum's Speedwell' (*V. Buxbaumii*) which the author states is sometimes mistaken for *V. Agrestis,* but is a distinct species. It branches freely and attains to a height of a foot or so; its stem and leaves are thickly clothed with soft and silky hairs. The leaves are placed singly at irregular intervals along the stem, but are more numerous towards the summit; they are broadly heart-shaped, with margins deeply-cut into teeth, each leaf has a short leaf-stalk; all leaves are of the same character. The flower-bearing stems that spring from the axils of the leaves are very long, and give a decided character to the plant, while the flowers themselves have the curious Veronica character – three large and fairly equal segments and then a lower and narrower one. The blossoms are a clear blue in colour, and for a Veronica are decidedly large. The fruit or capsule that succeeds the flower is twice as broad as it is long, and this flattened-out character is a specific feature. It derived its name from a distinguished botanist of the eighteenth century.

Buxbaum's Speedwell is a plant of cultivation, springing up in gardens and fields, and never far from human society and influence. It is a southerner, and though found throughout England and even Southern Scotland, it is more at home in less northern latitudes, and was probably introduced with some kind of foreign seed.

V. Serpyllifolia (Thyme-leaved Speedwell); the Marsh Speedwell (*V. scutellata*); the Ivy-leaved Speedwell (*V. hederifolia*); the Procumbent Speedwell (*V. agrestis*); and the Wall Speedwell (*V. arvensis*).

The Spiked Speedwell (*V. spicata*) is decidedly rare, but a handsome species; the Rock Veronica (*V. saxatilis*), a fine species with few flowers, is chiefly found in the highlands of Scotland.

Three other extremely rare species are *V. verna* (Vernal Speedwell), *V. alpina* (Alpine Speedwell) and *V. triphyllos* (The Finger Speedwell).

See VERONICAS.

SPEEDWELL, GERMANDER

Veronica chamædrys (LINN.)
N.O. Scrophulariaceæ

Synonyms. Fluellin the Male. Veronique petit Chêne. Paul's Betony. Eye of Christ. Angels' Eyes. Cat's Eye. Bird's Eye. Farewell

Part Used. Herb

Speedwell, Germander, is the commonest British species of Speedwell, found everywhere, on banks, pastures, in copses, etc., flowering in spring and early summer.

The name Germander is a corruption of the Latin *chamædrys*. Gerard commenting on the name says: 'The Germander from the form of the leaves like unto small oak leaves, has the name chamædrys given it, which signifieth a dwarf oak' – though the likeness is not very pronounced.

¶ *Description.* This little plant has a creeping, branched root-stock, passing insensibly into the stem, which is weak and decumbent to the point where the leaves commence, and then raises itself about a foot, to carry up the flowers. The leaves are in pairs, nearly stalkless, ½ to 1¼ inches long, egg-shaped to heart-shaped, deeply furrowed by the veins, the margins coarsely toothed. On the whole length of the stem are two lines of long hairs running down between each pair of leaves, shifting from side to side wherever they arrive at a fresh pair of leaves. These hairy lines act as barriers to check the advance of unwelcome crawling insects. The leaves themselves bear jointed hairs, and the flower-stalks, calyx and capsule also have long, gland-tipped hairs. The leaves are sometimes attacked by a gall mite, *Cecidomyia Veronica*, and white galls like white buttons are the result on the ends of the shoots.

The numerous flowers are in loose racemes, 2 to 6 inches long in the axils of the leaves, the flowers are rather close together on first expanding, but become distant after the fall of the corolla, which is ½ inch across, bright blue with darker lines, and a white eye in the centre, where the four petals join into the short tube. The corolla is so lightly attached that the least jarring causes it to drop, so that the plant at the slightest handling loses its bright blossom – hence, perhaps, its name Speedwell and similar local names, 'Farewell' and 'Good-bye.' The under lip of the corolla covers the upper in bud. The flower closes at night and also in rainy weather, when the brightness of the blossoms quite disappears, only the pale and pearly underside of its petals being visible.

The cross fertilization of the flower is performed chiefly by drone flies. On either side of the big, double, top petal, a little stamen stretches outward like a horn. When an insect approaches, it grasps the stamens with its front legs and they are thus drawn forwards and onwards, so that they dust the under-side of the insect with their pollen. He steadies himself for a moment, probing the flower for the nectar round the ovary and then flies away. As the stamens in any flower do not discharge their pollen until after the stigma, which projects over the lower petal, has been ready for some time to receive it, and since the stigmas also rub on the insect's abdomen, it is evident that it will probably be fertilized from some neighbouring flower before its own pollen is ready for use. When before and during rain the flower is closed, in the absence of insect visitors, it then, however, successfully carries on self-fertilization. Kerner, in *Flowers and their Unbidden Guests*, notes this fact in referring to the Speedwells, saying: 'In the mountainous districts of the temperate zones, it often happens that rainy weather sets in just at the time when the flowers are about to open, and that it lasts for weeks. Humble and hive-bees, butterflies and flies retire to their hiding-places, and for a considerable time cease to pay any visits to flowers. The growth of the plants is not, however, arrested during this period, and even in the flowers themselves, development quietly progresses if the temperature be not too low. The stigmatic tissue becomes receptive, the anthers attain to maturity, dehisce, and liberate their pollen, notwithstanding that no ray of sunshine penetrates the clouds, and that rain falls continuously. In such circumstances the mouth of the flower is not opened, self-fertilization takes place in the closed flower, and all the adjustments evolved with the object of securing cross-fertilization are ineffectual.'

The two-celled ovary matures into a flattened capsule, deeply notched at the top, which opens round the edges by two valves. The *Seeds* are said to be specially good as food for birds.

¶ *Medicinal Action and Uses*. Old writers of all countries speak highly of the virtues of the Speedwell as a vulnerary, a purifier of the blood, and a remedy in various skin diseases, its outward application being considered

efficacious for the itch. It was also believed to cure smallpox and measles, and to be a panacea for many ills. Gerard recommends it for cancer, 'given in good broth of a hen,' and advocates the use of the root as a specific against pestilential fevers.

It is not to be confused with Germander (*Teucrium chamædrys*), the celebrated specific for gout, used by the Emperor Charles V.

The Germander Speedwell has a certain amount of astringency, and an infusion of its leaves was at one time famous for coughs, the juice of the fresh plant also, boiled into a syrup with honey, was used for asthma and catarrh, and a decoction of the whole plant was employed to stimulate the kidneys.

SPIKENARD, AMERICAN

Aralia racemosa (LINN.)
N.O. Araliaceæ

Synonyms. Spignet. Life of Man. Pettymorell. Old Man's Root. Indian Spikenard. Indian Root
Part Used. Root
Habitat. North America, New Zealand, Japan

¶ *Description*. The much-branched stem grows from 3 to 6 feet high. Very large leaves, consisting of thin oval heart-shaped, double saw-toothed leaflets. Small greenish flowers in many clusters – blooming later than *Aralia medicaulis* (for which it is often substituted), July to August. Has roundish red-brown berries going dark purple. Root-stock thick and large, spicy and aromatic. Fracture of cortex short, of the wood also short and fibrous. Odour aromatic, taste mucilaginous, pungent and slightly acrid. Transverse section of root shows thick bark, several zones containing

oil. The plant grows freely in the author's garden.

¶ *Constituents*. Volatile oil, resin, tannin, etc.

¶ *Medicinal Action and Uses*. Stimulant, diaphoretic, alterative for syphilitic, cutaneous and rheumatic cases, and used in same manner and dosage as genuine Sarsaparilla. Much used also for pulmonary affections, and enters into the compound syrup of Spikenard. Fluid extract, ¼ to 1 drachm. Infusion of ½ oz. to a pint of water in wineglassful doses.

See ARALIAS, SARSAPARILLAS.

SPIKENARD, CALIFORNIAN

Aralia Californica or Californian Spikenard may be used for same purposes as the other species. It is very like *A. racemosa*, but bigger in herbage and root.

See ANGELICA TREE, DWARF ELDER (AMERICAN), SARSAPARILLAS.

SPIKENARD, PLOUGHMAN'S

Inula Conyza
N.O. Compositæ

Synonyms. Conyza Squarrosa (Linn.). Cloron's Hard. Horse Heal. Cinnamon Root. Great Fleabane
Part Used. Herb
Habitat. It is found on dry banks and in copses, principally on limestone or chalky soil.

Ploughman's Spikenard is another member of this genus that – as its name implies – has had a popular reputation for its curative powers.

¶ *Description*. Its upright stems, rising from a biennial root, generally only a foot or two in height, often purplish in colour and downy, are branched and terminated by numerous small flower-heads of a dingy yellow or dusky purple, only about two-thirds of an inch across, the ray florets inconspicuous and the

leaf-like scales of the involucre rolled back. The leaves of the plant are narrow, of a dull green, egg-shaped and downy. Their margins are either entire, or toothed, the teeth ending in horny points.

The plant has a slight, but not unpleasant, aromatic odour, hence, perhaps, one of its local names: Cinnamon Root.

¶ *Medicinal Action and Uses*. The older herbalists considered Ploughman's Spikenard a good wound herb, and it was frequently taken in decoction for bruises, ruptures, inward wounds, pains in the side and difficulty of breathing. It also had a reputation as an emmenagogue, and the juice of the while plant was applied externally to cure the itch.

The very smell of the plant was said to destroy fleas, and the leaves have been used, burnt, as an insecticide. Great Fleabane is one of its popular names.

Its specific name, *Conyza*, is derived from the Greek word for dust or powder, and refers to its power of killing noxious insects.

The leaves are sometimes substituted for Digitalis, but may be readily distinguished by their entire margins to the leaves or, when toothed, by the horny points terminating the teeth.

Inula of several species (especially *Inule Britannica*, Linn.) has been used to adulterate Arnica flowers. *En masse*, this spurious drug is pale and dull-looking, and its rays are small and narrow and of a pale yellow, whereas Arnica flower rays are broad and bright yellow. Also Inula has the involucral scales in several series, the receptacle is not hairy, and the anther-bases are long-tailed.

See ELECAMPANE, FLEABANE.

SPINACH

Spinacia oleracea (LINN.)
N.O. Chenopodiaceæ

Part Used. Leaves

Habitat. The Spinach is an annual plant, long cultivated for the sake of its succulent leaves, a native of Asia, probably of Persian origin, being introduced into Europe about the fifteenth century

¶ *Constituents.* Spinach is relatively rich in nitrogenous substances, in hydrocarbons, and in iron sesqui-oxide, which last amounts to 3·3 per cent. of the total ash. It is thus more nourishing than other green vegetables. It is a valuable part of the diet in anæmia, not only on account of its iron, but also for its chlorophyll. Chlorophyll is known to have a chemical formula remarkably similar to that of hæmoglobin, and it is stated that the ingestion of chlorophyll will raise the hæmoglobin of the blood without increasing the formed elements. The plant contains from 10 to 20 parts per 1,000 by weight of chlorophyll. During the war, wine fortified with Spinach juice (1 in 50) was given to French soldiers weakened by hæmorrhage.

According to Chick and Roscoe (*Biochem. Journal*, 1926, XX, 137), fresh leaves of Spinach are a rich source of vitamin A, a small daily ration (0·1 gram and upward) encouraging growth and lessening or preventing xerophthalmia in young rats on diets devoid of fat-soluble vitamins. Spinach grown in the open in winter, spring or autumn possesses no antirachitic properties that can be demonstrated by the methods employed. Spinach leaves when irradiated with ultraviolet rays from a Hg vapour quartz lamp become powerfully antirachitic.

Boas (*Biochem. Journal*, 1926, XX, 153) found that the fresh leaves of winter-grown Spinach added to an experimental diet caused an even greater improvement in the well-being of rats and in the rate of growth than was caused by the addition of cod-liver oil. The weight of the skeleton was not, however, proportionally increased. The conclusion was drawn by Boas that winter Spinach contains an amount of vitamin D which is negligible compared with its content of vitamin A.

The leaves contain a large proportion of saltpetre. The water drained from Spinach, after cooking, is capable of making as good match-paper as that made by a solution of nitre.

¶ *Cultivation.* Spinach should be grown on good ground, well worked and well manured, and for the summer crops abundant water will be necessary.

To afford a succession of Summer Spinach, the seeds should be sown about the middle of February and again in March. After this period, small quantities should be sown once a fortnight, as Summer Spinach lasts a very short time. The seeds are generally sown in shallow drills, between the lines of peas. If occupying the whole of a plot, the rows should be 1 foot apart.

The Round-seeded is the best kind for summer use.

The Prickly-seeded and the Flanders kinds are the best for winter and should be thinned out early in the autumn to about 2 inches apart, and later on to 6 inches. The Lettuce-leaved is a good succulent winter variety but not quite so hardy.

The first sowing of Winter Spinach should be made early in August and again towards the end of that month, in some sheltered but not shaded situation, in rows 18 inches apart, the plants as they advance being thinned and the ground hoed. By the beginning of winter, the outer leaves will have become fit for use, and if the weather is mild successive gatherings may be obtained up to the beginning of May.

SPINACH, NEW ZEALAND

Tetragonia expansar
N.O. Picoideæ

New Zealand Spinach is a half-hardy annual, a native of New Zealand, sometimes used as a substitute for Spinach during the summer months, but decidedly inferior to it. It is unrelated to the Spinach, belonging to the *Picoideæ*.

When cultivated in this country, seeds are sown in March on a gentle hot-bed. They must be previously steeped in water for several hours. The seedlings should be potted and placed in a frame till the end of May and then planted out in light, rich soil.

Only the young leaves are gathered for use, a succession being produced during summer and autumn.

See ARRACHS, CHENOPODIUMS, GOOSEFOOTS.

SPINDLE TREE

Euonymus atropurpureus
Euonymus Europœus (JACQ.)
N.O. Celastraceæ

Synonyms. Fusanum. Fusoria. Skewerwood. Prickwood. Gatter. Gatten. Gadrose. Pigwood. Dogwood. Indian Arrowroot. Burning Bush. Wahoo

(*French*) Fusain. Bonnet-de-prêtre
(*German*) Spindelbaume
Parts Used. Root, bark, berries

¶ *Description*. The Spindle Tree found in our hedges and copses is a smooth-leaved shrub. The leaves have very short stalks, are opposite in pairs and have minute teeth on the margin. It bears small greenish-white flowers, in loose clusters, during May and June, followed by an abundance of fruits. The fruit is three or more lobed, and becomes a beautiful rose-red colour; it bursts when ripe, disclosing ruddy-orange-coloured seeds, which are wrapped in a scarlet arillus. This yields a good yellow dye when boiled in water, and a green one with the addition of alum, but these dyes are fugitive. The berries attract children, but are harmful, for they are strongly emetic and purgative: they have proved fatal to sheep. The bark, leaves and fruit are all injurious, and no animal but the goat will browse upon them.

The Latin name for Spindle is *Fusus*, and by some of the old writers this plant is called Fusanum and the Fusoria. By the Italians it is still called Fusano. The fruit is given three or four as a dose, as a purgative in rural districts; and the decoction, adding some vinegar, is used as a lotion for mange in horses and cattle. In allusion to the actively irritating properties of the shrub, its name *Euonymus* is associated with that of Euonyme, the mother of the Furies. In old herbals it is called Skewerwood or prickwood (the latter from its employment as toothpicks), and *gatter*, *gatten*, or *gadrose*. Chaucer, in one of his poems, calls it *gaitre*.

Prior says:

Gatter is from the Anglo-Saxon words, *gad* (a goad) and *treow* (a tree); *gatten* is made up of *gad* again and *tan* (a twig); and *gadrise* is from *gad* and *hris* (a rod).'

The same hardness that fitted it for skewers, spindles, etc., made it useful for the ox-goad.

Turner apparently christened the tree Spindle Tree. He says:

'I coulde never learne an Englishe name for it. The Duche men call it in Netherlande, *spilboome*, that is, spindel-tree, because they use to make spindels of it in that country, and me thynke it may be as well named in English seying we have no other name. . . . I know no goode propertie that this tree hath, saving only it is good to make spindels and brid of cages (bird-cages).'

The wood, which is of a light yellow hue, strong, compact and easily worked, fulfils many uses. On the Continent it is used for making pipe-stems, and an excellent charcoal is made from the young shoots, which artists approve for its smoothness, and the ease with which it can be erased. It is also employed in the making of gunpowder.

¶ *Cultivation*. It is found in woods and hedgerows. The green and variegated Spindle Trees are familiar in British gardens. They all grow freely in any kind of soil, and are easily increased by inserting the ripened tips of the branches, about 3 inches long, into a fine, sandy loam in autumn, keeping them damp and fresh with a frequent spraying overhead. A species from South Europe and another from Japan are cultivated.

¶ *Parts Used*. The variety of Spindle Tree (*Euonymus atropurpureus*), common in the eastern United States, is known there as Wahoo, Burning Bush, or Indian Arrowwood. This is the kind generally used in medicine.

It is a shrub about 6 feet high, with a smooth ash-coloured bark, and has small dark purple flowers and leaves purple-tinged at the serrated edges.

Wahoo bark, as it is called commercially, is the dried root-bark of this species.

The root-bark is alone official, but the stem-bark is also collected and used as a substitute.

The root-bark, when dried, is in quilled or curved pieces, $\frac{1}{12}$ to $\frac{1}{4}$ inch thick, ash-grey, with blackish ridges or patches, outer surface whitish, or slightly tawny and quite smooth. Fracture friable, smooth, whitish, the inner layer appearing tangentially striated. The taste is sweetish, bitter and acrid. It has a very faint, characteristic odour, resembling liquorice.

The stem-bark is in longer quills, with a smooth outer surface, with lichens usually present on it, and a greenish layer under the epidermis.

¶ *Constituents*. Little is definitely known of the chemical constituents of Euonymus Bark. Its chief constituent is a nearly colourless intensely bitter principle, a resin called Euonymin. There are also present euonic acid, a crystalline glucoside, asparagin, resins, fat, dulcitol, and 14 per cent. of ash.

Commercial Euonymin is a powdered extract.

¶ *Medicinal Action and Uses*. Tonic, alterative, cholagogue, laxative and hepatic stimulant.

SPERGULARIA. *See* SANDSPURRY

SPURGES

Genera more than 200, species more than 3,000, representing almost all habits of growth and exhibiting a high degree of adaptability to varying environments. The valuable rubbers produced by the family are of great importance, notably that from the prepared milk juice of several species of *Hevea*, known in commerce as Para rubber.

The medicinal properties of the family depend chiefly upon two classes of constituents; first, fixed oils, or the fatty acids freed by their decomposition, typical properties of which are castor oil, from *Recinus communis*, and Croton oil, from *Croton tigilum*; also valuable drying oils, the artists' oil or lambang from the seeds of *Aleurites moluccana*, tung oil, said to be the most perfect drying oil known, from seeds of *A. cordata*. From *A. laccifera* gum-lac, of a very superior quality, is obtained; another excellent drying oil is obtained from *Sapium sebiferum*, known as Chinese tallow. Besides the cathartic properties resident in the fixed oils of these seeds,

In small doses, Euonymin stimulates the appetite and the flow of the gastric juice. In larger doses, it is irritant to the intestine and is cathartic. It has slight diuretic and expectorant effects, but its only use is as a purgative in cases of constipation in which the liver is disordered, and for which it is particularly efficacious. It is specially valuable in liver disorders which follow or accompany fever. It is mildly aperient and causes no nausea, at the same time stimulating the liver somewhat freely, and promoting a free flow of bile.

To make the decoction, add an ounce to a pint of water and boil together slowly. A small wineglassful to be given, when cold, for a dose, two or three times a day.

Of the tincture made with spirit from the bark, 5 to 10 drops may be taken in water or on sugar.

Euonymin is generally given in pill form and in combination with other tonics, laxatives, etc.

¶ *Preparations*. Fluid extract, $\frac{1}{2}$ to 1 drachm. Powdered extract, B.P. and U.S.P., 2 grains. Euonymin, 1 to 4 grains.

¶ *Other Species*. The green leaves of one species of *Euonymus* are said to be eaten by the Arabs to produce watchfulness, and a sprig of it is believed to be – to the person who carries it – a protection from plague. Another species is said to inflict painful wounds.

Euphorbias
N.O. Euphorbiaceæ

somewhat similar properties, almost always accompanied by more or less emesis, exists in the plant-parts generally, the active constituents being usually carried in the milk juices, so that the family has yielded a large number of drugs used somewhat like Ipecacuanha.

The genus *Euphorbia* comprises nearly a thousand species, and a large number of these species yield a milky juice. Some are herbaceous or shrubby, with or without leaves, the leafless varieties flourishing on African deserts like the cactus, having spiny stems. The milky juice of the stem coagulates on exposure to the air, forming a resinous mass which is generally marketed in the form of tears.

For external use it is of service in chronic rheumatism and paralysis as a counter-irritant, alone, or combined with cantharides, merezeon bark, etc., or as a plaster when mixed with Burgundy pitch or resin.

It is a violent irritant and caustic poison. At the Cape, the capsules are used for destroying animals. It may produce delirium.

(*POISON*)

SPURGE, OFFICINAL

Euphorbia resinifera
N.O. Euphorbiaceæ

Synonyms. Euphorbia officinarum. Poisonous Gum-Thistle. Dergmuse. Darkmous. Euphorbium Bush. Gum Euphorbium

Part Used. Concrete resinous juice

Habitat. The slopes of the Great Atlas range in Morocco

¶ *Description.* Resembling a cactus in appearance, this leafless perennial plant has a stem about 4 feet in height, and many branches. The flowers are small, simple, and bright yellow, and the fruit a small capsule with one seed in each cell. Specimens sent to Kew in 1870 have never flowered, but others have done so in Paris. Both Pliny and Dioscorides knew the drug, and its name is classical.

The milky juice is collected from incisions made in the fleshy branches, and is so acrid that it burns the fingers. It flows down the stems and encrusts them as it hardens in the sun. Poor Arabs bring in the resinous masses for sale in Morocco, whence it is chiefly exported from Mogador. The dust is so intensely irritant to the mucous membrane, that the mouth and nose of those handling it must be covered by a cloth.

In commerce the drug is found in yellowish-brown 'tears' that have a waxy appearance. They are almost transparent, slightly aromatic only when heated, and often pierced with holes made by the prickles of the plant while drying. The taste is slight, but becomes very acrid.

It is said to be employed as an ingredient of paint used for preserving ships' bottoms.

At Mogador, the branches are used for tanning leather.

¶ *Constituents.* The chief constituent is resin, and it also contains wax, calcium malate, potassium malate, lignin, bassorin, volatile oil, and water, with no soluble gum. Another analysis gives euphorbone, euphorbo-resene, euphorbic acid, calcium malate, a very acrid substance not yet isolated, and vegetable debris.

The acrid resin is soluble in alcohol, and will burn brilliantly, becoming very aromatic.

The powder is yellowish, and violently sternatatory.

¶ *Medicinal Action and Uses.* The internal use of the drug has been abandoned, owing to the severity of its action. It is an irritant emetic and cathartic. Its chief use is as a vesicant, and principally in veterinary practice. It has been used in dropsy; mixed with cantharides as a 'gout plaister'; and as an errhine in chronic brain, ear, or eye complaints, sometimes mitigated with the powder of *Convallaria maialis*, but accidents have led to its use being discontinued.

SPURGES, VARIOUS

Euphorbia cerifera is one of the sources of Candelilla wax which occurs as a coating on all parts of the plant.

'PILLBEARING SPURGE' (*E. pilulifera*) is commonly known as Queensland asthma weed, cat's hair, in allusion to its globular, axillary inflorescences. Is very common in all tropical countries. Its principal constituents are resins described as glucosidal, wax, and volatile matter; it is collected whilst flowering and fruiting, and has been utilized by some practitioners with a certain success in the treatment of subacute and chronic inflammation of the respiratory duct. Toxic doses have killed small animals through failure of respiration. The decoction is taken in asthmatic conditions, chronic bronchitis, and emphysema, the tincture being used in coryza and hay fever.

¶ *Dosage.* Compound Elixir of Euphorbia, C.F., from *E. pilulifera*. Tincture of Euphorbia, B.P.C., from *E. pilulifera*, 10 to 30 minims. Fluid extract of *E. pilulifera*, ½ to 1 drachm. Decoction of *E. pilulifera*, 1 in 40, 1 tablespoonful.

E. corollata: dose of dried root as an emetic, 10 to 20 grains; as a cathartic, 3 to 10 grains.

E. hypericifolia: an infusion of the dried leaves, ¼ oz. infused in a pint of boiling water for ½ hour and a tablespoonful taken for a dose.

¶ *Other Species.*

E. tetragona, *E. antiguorum* of the African coast, and *E. canariensis* of the Canary Islands also supply the drug.

WHITE IPECACUANHA (*E. ipecacuanha*), the root of which is used, contains a fixed oil, starch, glucose, and various salts, also resin. Its medicinal properties are similar to *E. corollata*.

WHITE PURSLANE (*E. corollata*). Syn. White Parsley, Purging or Emetic Root, Apple Root, Wild Hippo. The whole plant is used, including the root. Its habitat is east and central North America. It abounds in lactiferous ducts, which contain starch; the resin is or carries the actual principle, the presence of glucoside is conjecture. Formerly it was used as an emetic in 10 to 20 grains, and as a cathartic in 3 to 10 grains, but because of its irritating and uncertain properties its use has been practically abandoned; the recent root bruised and applied to the skin produces vesication.

CAPER SPURGE (*E. lathyris*). (Syn. Mole Plant.) Has a milky juice of an acrid nature. Its seeds yield an abundance of fine clear oil called oil of Euphorbia; this is obtained by expression or by the action of alcohol or ether, and is colourless, inodorous, and almost insipid; it rapidly becomes rancid, and acquires a dangerous acrimony. The oil is a very violent poison, producing violent purgation and having an irritating effect upon the mucous membrane of the intestinal canal, and especially on the larger intestines; the oil resembles croton oil. In doses of 5 drops it is said to be less acrid and irritating than croton oil; it must be recently extracted. The seeds to the number of twelve or fifteen are used by country people in France as a purgative. The root of the plant is equally purgative and emetic; the leaves are vesicant and are used by beggars to produce ulcers by which to excite pity; the juice is depilatory; the seeds contain æsculetin in the free state.

E. hypericifolia is regarded in tropical America as a powerful astringent and has a reputation in the cure of diarrhœa and dysentery; it has also narcotic properties. The juice is said to cause temporary blindness when applied to the eyes; it contains caoutchouc, gallic acid, resin and tannin.

SPOTTED SPURGE (*E. maculata*) represents a group used by eclectics and homœopaths with claims for properties more or less special. It has been used in cholera, diarrhœa and dysentery in the form of an infusion of the leaves, and has been found to contain caoutchouc resin, tannin, and apparently euphorbon. Is said to be a valuable astringent; an infusion may be employed as an injection in the treatment of leucorrhœa. To this medicinal group belongs:

E. esula (Linn.) (Leafy Spurge) of Europe.
E. peplus (Linn.) of Europe.
E. helioscopia (Linn.) of Europe (Sun or Wart Spurge, Churnstaff, Seven Sisters).
E. humistrata (Engl.) of central North America.
E. hypericifolia (Linn.) of North America.
E. portulacoides of Chile.
E. iata (Eng.) of U.S.A.
E. marginata (Pursh.) (Mountain Snow) of western U.S.A.
E. Drummondii, the juice, has caused many fatalities to sheep and cattle in Australia.
E. cremocarpus is used in Australia for the poisoning of fish in calm pools and streams.

E. heterodoxa, a Brazilian species, said to have been used with extraordinary success against cancerous and syphilitic ulcers. It is a powerful irritant, mildly caustic; the milky juice preserved with salicylic acid is used.

E. prostata grows in the south-western portions of the U.S.A., and has the reputation of being a specific against the bite of the rattlesnake, spiders, etc.; the juice is used.

E. parviflora and *E. hirta*. Both used in India as antisyphilitics, and *E. canescens* similarly in Spain.

The juice of *E. linearis* is employed in Brazil for syphilitic ulcers of the cornua. *E. hiberna* was formerly much used in syphilis before the introduction of mercury. The plant is extensively employed by the peasantry of Kerry for stupefying fish, and so powerful are its qualities that a small basket filled with the bruised leaves will poison the fish for several miles down the river. The same properties are possessed by *E. platyphylla*, and in Brazil *E. cotinifolia* is used for the same purpose, and the acrid juice which drops from it is used by the natives to poison their arrows.

The seeds and leaves of *E. thymifolia* of India are given by the Tamuls as an anthelmintic and in bowel affections of children.

E. balsamifera, when cooked, is eaten in the Canaries.

The juice of *E. Mauritanica*, when dried, is employed as a condiment, and forms one of the adulterations of Scammony.

In countries bordering on the Mediterranean, *E. Peplis, E. spinosa, E. Dendroides, E. Aleppica, E. Apois*, are used as purgatives in domestic practice.

E. peplus, E. peploides, E. pilosa, E. palustris have the reputation of being remedies in hydrophobia.

E. Helisscopia juice is commonly applied to warts, and sometimes, though improperly, used to cure sore eyelids, causing in many instances intolerable pain and inflammation.

The bark of the roots of *E. Gerardiane, E. amydaloides* and *E. Cyparissias* have febrifuge reputations; but the latter is known to possess dangerous properties. It is destructive to sheep, and La Motte has seen a woman perish from having taken a lavement prepared with the plant. In France it is used as a popular purgative, under the name of *Rhubarbe des pauvres*. Orfila regards it as a poison.

The milky juice of *E. amydaloides* is very acrid, and though not highly poisonous, corrodes and ulcerates the flesh wherever it is applied.

Warts and corns anointed with it are said soon to disappear, but great caution is needed in using it, or injury is likely to result to the surrounding skin. Though said to be a remedy for toothache, it is not to be recommended on account of its very acrid nature.

The juice of *E. tribuloides*, a small cactus-shaped species growing in the Canaries, is there used as a diaphoretic.

It is reported by Scopoli, in his *Flora Carnoilica*, that he has seen death occasioned by the administration of 30 grains of the seed of *E. esula*, and gangrene caused on the belly by the application of the plant on that part; he also adds that people have lost their eyesight by rubbing their eyes with its juice.

E. buxifolia in the West Indies, *E. papillosa*

in Brazil, *E. laurifolia* in Peru, and *E. portulacoides* in Chile are used as purgatives.

E. tirucalli is employed in India as a vesicant, and in Java as a powerful emetic and purgative. It is said that exhalations from the tree cause the loss of eyesight; the juice is considered sudorific and, according to Sonnerat, is administered in India, in doses of a drachm, mixed with flour, daily as an antisyphilitic.

E. ligularia, another native of India, is held sacred to Munsa, the goddess of serpents; the root of the tree, mixed with black pepper, is employed for the cure of snake-bites, both internally and externally.

SQUAW VINE

Mitchella repens (LINN.)
N.O. Rubiaceæ

Synonyms. Partridgeberry. Checkerberry. Winter Clover. Deerberry. One-berry
Part Used. Herb
Habitat. United States

¶ *Description.* The plant grows in dry woods, among hemlock timber, and in swampy places; in flower in June and July. The leaves resemble those of clover and remain green throughout the winter. The fruit or berry also remains bright scarlet, is edible, and nearly tasteless, dry, and full of stony seeds. The use of the drug is peculiarly American.

¶ *Constituents.* It has been found to contain resin, wax, mucilage, dextrin, and what appears to be saponin.

¶ *Medicinal Action and Uses.* Parturient, diuretic, tonic, astringent. Beneficial in all uterine complaints. It resembles in its action pipsissewa (Chimaphila), for which it is often substituted. It is taken by Indian women for

weeks before confinement, in order to render parturition safe and easy. A herbal physician should be consulted for a safe and effectual preparation.

It is used in dropsy, suppression of urine, and diarrhœa. The following preparation is a cure for sore nipples: 2 oz. of the herb (fresh, if possible), 1 pint of water. Make a strong decoction, strain, and add an equal quantity of good cream. Boil the whole down to the consistency of a soft salve, and when cool, anoint the nipple every time the child is removed from the breast.

¶ *Dosages.* Of a strong decoction, 2 to 4 fluid ounces, two or three times a day. Fluid extract, $\frac{1}{2}$ to 1 drachm.

SQUILL

Urginea scilla (STEINHEIL)
N.O. Liliaceæ

Synonyms. Maritime Squill. Scilla maritima (Linn.). Urginea maritima. Urginea Indica. White Squill. Red Squill
Part Used. Bulb, cut into slices, dried and powdered
Habitat. The Squill is found in dry, sandy places, especially the seacoast in most of the Mediterranean districts, being abundant in southern Spain, where it is by no means confined to the coast, and is found in Portugal, Morocco, Algeria, Corsica, southern France, Italy, Malta, Dalmatia, Greece, Syria and Asia Minor. In Sicily, where it grows most abundantly, it ascends to an elevation of 3,000 feet. Its range also includes the Canary Islands and the Cape of Good Hope. It is often grown under fig-trees in the Italian Riviera, and is grown in many botanical gardens, having first been recorded as cultivated in England in 1648, in the Oxford Botanic Gardens

¶ *Description.* It is a perennial plant with fibrous roots proceeding from the base of a large, tunicated, nearly globular bulb, 4 to 6 inches long, the outer scales of which are thin and papery, red or orange-brown in colour. The bulb, which is usually only half immersed in the sand, sends forth several long, lanceolate, pointed, somewhat undulated, shining, dark-green leaves, when fully grown

2 feet long. From the middle of the leaves, a round, smooth, succulent flower-stem rises, from 1 to 3 feet high, terminating in a long, close spike of whitish flowers, which stand on purplish peduncles, at the base of each of which is a narrow, twisted, deciduous floral leaf or bract. The flowers are in bloom in April and May and are followed by oblong capsules.

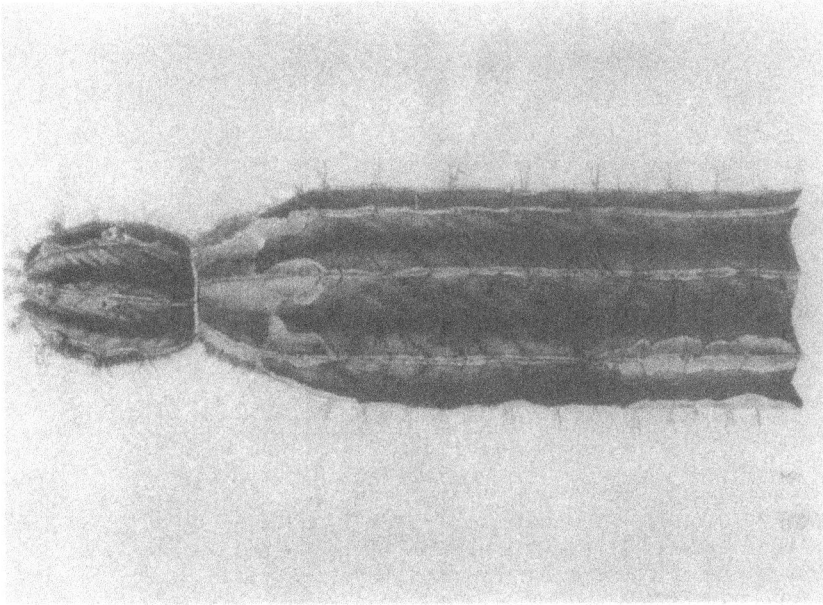

SPURGE (EUPHORBIUM)
Euphorbia Resinifera

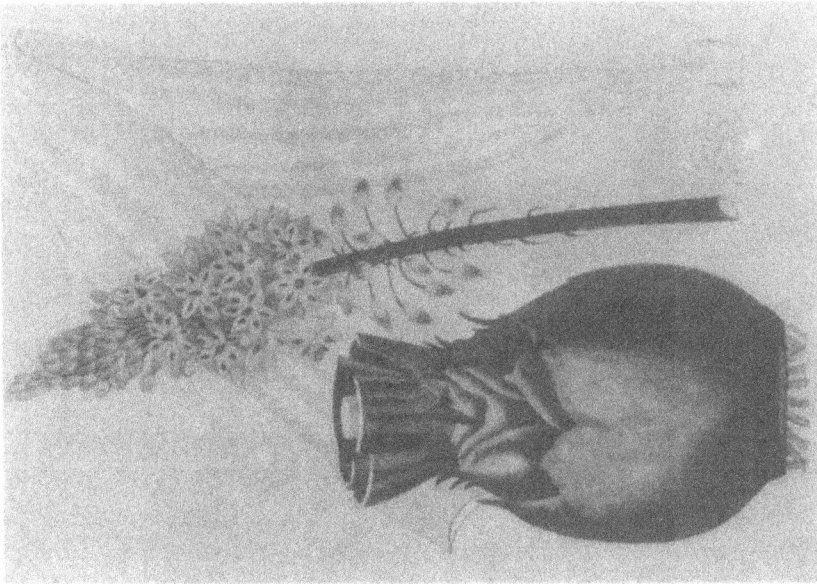

SQUILL
Urginea Scilla

STAVESACRE
Delphinium Staphisagria

STORAX
Liquidambar Orientalis

It is a very variable plant, the bulb differing greatly in size and colour, and the leaves of the flower presenting similar varieties, which has led to the formation of several species, about twenty-five species having been described. Two varieties of Squill, termed respectively *white* and *red*, are distinguished by druggists. In the first named, the bulb scales are whitish or yellowish in colour, whereas the red species has deep, reddish-brown outer scales and yellowish white inner scales, covered with a pinkish epidermis, intermediate forms also occurring. No essential difference exists in the medicinal properties of the two kinds.

The White Squill, collected in Malta and Sicily, is preferred in England, while the Red Squill, collected in Algeria, is used in France. Both varieties are mentioned by Pliny and other ancient writers: the white is more mentioned in mediæval literature, though the medical school of Salerno preferred the red variety of the drug.

The United States Pharmacopœia defines the drug Scilla as the inner scales of the bulb of the white variety of *Urginea maritima* (Linn.).

Scilla, the classical name of the plant, is derived from a Greek word meaning to excite or disturb, as an emetic does the stomach. *Scilla maritima* was the name given by Linnæus, but this was changed to *Urginea*, in allusion to the Algerian tribe Ben Urgin, near Boma, where Steinheil in 1834 examined this plant, removing it from the genus *Scilla*. The main difference between the genera is that the genus *Urginea* has flat, discoid seeds, while in *Scilla* proper they are triquetrous (three-angled, with three concave faces). Baker named it *Urginea maritima*, but it now retains *Scilla* as its specific name.

As seen in commerce, the undried bulb is somewhat pear-shaped, and generally about the size of a man's fist, but often larger, weighing from ¼ lb. to more than 4 lb.

It has the usual structure of a bulb, being formed of smooth juicy scales, closely wrapped over one another. It has little odour, but its inner scales have a mucilaginous, bitter, acrid taste, owing to the presence of bitter glucosides.

In its home, it is frequently used fresh, but in other countries it is directed by the pharmacopœias to be deprived of its dry membraneous outer scales (which are destitute of activity), cut into thin, transverse slices and carefully dried, either in the sun, or by artificial heat, the inmost part being rejected, as this central portion, being the youngest growth, is deficient in activity.

Owing to the mucilaginous nature of the tissue, drying is tedious and difficult. When fresh, the bulb abounds in a viscid, very acrid juice, which is capable of causing inflammation of the skin. On drying, the bulb loses four-fifths of its weight, and its acridity is largely diminished, with slight loss of medicinal activity.

Squill is generally imported in ready-dried slices, packed in casks, from Malta, where the largest collections are made.

The dried slices are narrow, flattish, curved, yellowish-white, or with a roseate hue, according to the variety of Squill from which they are obtained, from 1 to 2 inches long, more or less translucent.

When quite dry, the strips are brittle and can easily be powdered, but they are tough and flexible when moist and dried. Squill should be kept in well-stoppered bottles, on account of its readiness to absorb moisture, when the slices become tough and cannot be reduced to powder. When kept in a dry place, Squill retains its virtues for a long time. When powdered, unless carefully preserved in a dried state by absorption of moisture, it forms a hard mass, and it is therefore officially recommended that powdered Squill should be kept quite dry over quicklime.

Occasionally, entire bulbs are imported, but are difficult to keep in the fresh state as they preserve their vitality for a long time, and if allowed to remain in a warm place, rapidly develop an aerial shoot. Professor Henslow reports (*Poisonous Plants in Field and Garden*) that a bulb was found attempting to grow after being stowed away for more than twenty years in the museum of St. Bartholomew's Hospital Medical School.

¶ *Constituents.* The chemical constituents of Squill are imperfectly known. Merck, in 1879, separated the three bitter glucosidal substances Scillitoxin, Scillipicrin and Scillin. The first two are amorphous and act upon the heart, the former being the more active; Scillin is crystalline and causes numbness and vomiting. Other constituents are mucilaginous and saccharine matter, including a peculiar mucilaginous carbohydrate named Sinistrin, an Inulin-like substance, which yields Lævulose on being boiled with dilute acid. The name Sinistrin (in 1834, first proposed by Macquart for Inulin) has also been applied to a mucilaginous matter extracted from barley, but it remains to be proved that the latter is identical with the Sinistrin of Squill. Calcium oxalate is also present, in bundles of long, acicular crystals, which easily penetrate the skin when the bulbs are handled, and causes intense irritation, sometimes eruption, if a piece of fresh Squill is rubbed on the skin.

The toxicity of Squills has more recently been ascribed to a single, bitter, non-nitrogenous glucoside, to which the name Scillitin is given, and which is the active diuretic and expectorant principle.

The bulbs also yield when distilled in a current of steam, a slightly coloured liquid oil of unpleasant odour.

The chemistry of Squills cannot yet be regarded as fully worked out, since most of the glucosides described have only been prepared in an amorphous condition of uncertain chemical identity.

¶ *Medicinal Action and Uses.* The Medicinal Squill was valued as a medicine in early classic times and has ever since been employed by physicians, being official in all pharmacopœias. Oxymel of Squill, used for coughs, was invented by Pythagoras, who lived in the sixth century before Christ.

It is mentioned by Theophrastus in the third century before Christ, and was known to all the ancient Greek physicians. Epimenides, a Greek, is said to have made much use of it, from which circumstance we find it called *Epimenidea.*

It is considered to be the Sea Onion referred to by Homer. Pliny was acquainted with it, and Dioscorides, who lived about the same time, describes the different varieties of the bulb and the method of making vinegar of Squills. A similar preparation, as well as compounds of Squill with honey, was administered by the Arabian physicians of the Middle Ages, who introduced the drug into European medicine, these preparations still remaining in use.

The mediæval reputation of Squill was originally as a diuretic, the older authorities attributing its diuretic action to a direct stimulant effect upon the kidney.

As a diuretic, it is frequently employed in dropsy, whether due to chronic disease of the kidneys or to the renal congestion consequent to chronic cardiac disease. Squill is not employed, however, when the kidneys are acutely inflamed. In the treatment of cardiac dropsy, Squill is frequently combined with digitalis.

Squill stimulates the bronchial mucous membrane and is given in bronchitis after subsidence of the acute inflammation. It is generally used in combination with other stimulating expectorants, its effects being thereby increased, and is considered most useful in chronic bronchitis, catarrhal affections and asthma. The tincture is administered combined with other expectorants, especially ipecacuanha and ammonium carbonate. Vinegar, Oxymel and Syrup of Squill are also common constituents of expectorant cough mixtures.

It is largely sued for its stimulating, expectorant and diuretic properties, and is also a cardiac tonic, acting in a similar manner to digitalis, slowing and strengthening the pulse, though more irritating to the gastro-intestinal mucous membrane. On account of its irritant qualities it is not administered in diseases of an acute inflammatory nature. It has also been given as an emetic in whooping-cough and croup, usually combined with ipecacuanha, but as an emetic is considered very uncertain in its action.

To prevent its too great action on the stomach, it is frequently combined with a portion of opium. With calomel, it forms a powerful stimulant of the urinary organs. (A pill containing 1 grain each of Squill, digitalis and calomel is popularly known as Niemeyer's pill.)

In poisonous doses, Squill produces violent inflammation of the gastro-intestinal and genito-urinary tracts, manifested by nausea, vomiting, abdominal pains and purging, and, in addition, dullness, stupour, convulsions, a marked fall in temperature, enfeebled circulation and sometimes death.

The powdered drug and extracts made from it have been largely used as rat poisons and are said to be very efficacious, the red variety being preferred for this purpose, although there would not seem to be sufficient evidence of its superiority

¶ *Dosage.* When given in substance, Squill is most conveniently administered in the form of pill. Dose: 1 to 3 grains.

Vinegar of Squill, B.P. Dose: 5 to 15 minims.

Vinegar of Squill, U.S.P. Average dose: 15 minims.

Liquid Extract of Squill, B.P. Codex. Dose: 1 to 3 minims.

Fluid Extract of Squill, U.S.P. Average dose: 1½ minim.

Opiate Linctus, B.P.C. Dose: ½ to 1 fluid drachm.

Linctus of Squill, B.P.B. Dose: ½ to 1 fluid drachm. (Used as cough linctus for children.)

Syrup of Squill, B.P. Used as an expectorant in acid cough mixtures. Dose: ½ to 1 fluid drachm.

Syrup of Squill, U.S.P. (The preparation commonly administered in bronchitis.) Average dose: 30 minims.

Compound Syrup of Squill, U.S.P. Average dose: 30 minims.

Compound Squill Tablets, B.P.C. Dose: 1 to 2 tablets.

Tincture of Squill, B.P. (Used with other expectorants to relieve cough and in chronic bronchitis.) Dose: 5 to 15 minims.

Tincture of Squill, U.S.P. Average dose: 15 minims.

Compound Linctus of Squill, B.P.C. (Gee's Linctus.) Dose: ⅓ to 1 fluid drachm.

Squill Mixture, B.P.C. (Fothergill's Cough Mixture.) Given for coughs. Dose: 2 to 4 fluid drachms.

Compound Squill Mixture, B.P.C. (Used as diaphoretic and expectorant.) Dose: ½ to 1 fluid ounce.

Squill and Ipecacuanha Mixture, B.P.C. Dose: ⅓ to 1 fluid ounce.

Squill and Opium Mixture (Abercrombie's Cough Mixture), B.P.C. Dose: 2 to 4 fluid drachms.

Oxymel of Squill, B.P. (Vinegar of Squill 20, purified honey 50.) Employed in coughs and colds to assist expectoration. Dose: ½ to 1 fluid drachm.

Compound Squill Pill, B.P. Dose: 4 to 8 grains.

Compound Syrup of Squill, B.P.C. (For coughs.) Dose: ½ to 1 fluid drachm.

¶ *Substitutes.* There are several bulbs used in place of the official Squill which, owing to the abundance and low price of the latter, do not appear in the European market.

Indian Squill consists of the younger bulbs of *Urginea indica* (Knuth), or of *Scilla indica* (Baker), which is also known as *Ledebouria hyacinthina* (Roth.).

U. indica, Knuth (*S. indica*, Roxb.) is a widely diffused plant occurring in northern India, Abyssinia, Nubia and Senegambia. It is known by the same Arabic and Persian names as *U. scilla* and its bulbs are used for similar purposes, but are considered to have no action when old and large. The bulbs consist of whitish, fleshy coats or scales, which enclose each other completely. They resemble common onions in shape.

S. indica, Baker (*L. hyacinthina*, Roth.), a native of India and Abyssinia, has a bulb often confused in the Indian bazaars with the preceding, but easily distinguished when entire by being *scaly*, not *tunicated*, its cream-coloured scales overlapping one another. The bulbs are about the size and shape of a small pear, somewhat smaller than those of *U. indica.* It is considered a better representative of the European Squill.

The bulbs of both species have a nauseous odour and a bitter acrid taste. They are collected soon after the plants have flowered, divested of their dry, outer, membraneous coats, cut into slices and dried.

The chief constituents in each case are bitter principles, similar to the glucosidal substances found in ordinary Squill, and needle-shaped crystals of calcium oxalate are also present.

The drug possesses stimulant, expectorant and diuretic principles, and is official in the India and Colonial Addendum for use in India and the Eastern Colonies as an equivalent of ordinary Squill.

U. altissima, Baker (*Ornithogalum altissimum*, Linn.), a South African species very closely related to the common Squill, has apparently the same properties.

The bulb of *S. Peruviana* (Linn.) has also been used and exported as a substitute for Squill.

Drimia ciliaris (Jacq.), native of the Cape of Good Hope, much resembles the official Squill, but has a juice so irritating if it comes into contact with the skin, that it was called by the Dutch colonists *Jeukbol*, i.e. Itch-bulb. It is used medicinally as an emetic, expectorant and diuretic.

Crinum asiaticum, var. *toxicarium* (Hubert), is a large plant with handsome white flowers and showy leaves, cultivated in Indian gardens and growing wild in low, humid spots in various parts of India and on the coast of Ceylon. The bulb was admitted in 1868 to the Pharmacopœia of India as a valuable emetic, but is not widely used.

The European Squills belonging to the genus *Scilla* possess in a milder form the same active principle, and some of the species are deleterious, if not absolutely dangerous.

The bulbs of *S. lilio-hyacinthus* are used as a purgative by the inhabitants of the Pyrenees.

SQUIRTING CUCUMBER. *See* CUCUMBER

STAR ANISE. *See* ANISEED

STAR OF BETHLEHEM [1]

Ornithogalum umbellatum (LINN.)
N.O. Liliaceæ

Synonyms. Bath Asparagus. Dove's Dung. Star of Hungary. White Filde Onyon
Part Used. Bulb

The Star of Bethlehem is a bulbous plant nearly allied to the Onion and Garlic.

The leaves are long and narrow and dark-green; the flowers, in bloom during April and May, are a brilliant white internally, but with the petals striped with green outside. They expand only in the sunshine.

The bulbs, in common with those of many Liliaceous plants, are edible and nutritious. They were in ancient times eaten, both raw

The homœopaths make a tincture from the bulbs which is useful in some cases of cancer. – EDITOR.

and cooked, as Dioscorides related, and form a palatable and wholesome food when boiled. They are still often eaten in the East, being roasted like chestnuts, and Linnæus and others considered that they were probably the 'Dove's Dung' mentioned in the Second Book of Kings, vi. 25, as being sold at a high price during the siege of Samaria by the King of Syria, when 'the fourth part of a cab of dove's dung was sold for five pieces of silver.' The Greek name, *Ornithogalum*, signifies the 'birds' milk flower.' The plains of Syria and Palestine are sheeted in spring with the white flowers of a species of Star of Bethlehem, the bulbs of which are used as food, and are still called by the Arabs, 'Dove's Dung,' a name in common use among them for vegetable substances. Bochart tells us that the Arabs give this name to a moss that grows on trees and stony ground, and also to a pulse or pea, which appears to have been common in India. Large quantities of the bulb, it is stated, were parched and dried and stored at Cairo and Damascus, being much used during journeys, and especially by the great pilgrim caravans to Mecca.

In Lyte's *Dodoens* (1578) it is described as 'the white filde onyon,' growing in plenty near Malines. In Turner's *Herbal* (1548) it is not mentioned, but in Gerard's six species are enumerated. He says: 'There be sundry sorts of wild field Onions, called "Starres of Bethlehem," differing in stature, taste and smell, as shall be declared,' and calls them 'the Star of Hungary,' 'the Lesser Spanish Star,' 'the Star of Bethlehem,' 'the great Arabische star floure,' etc.

Though there are numerous species in this genus, only one is truly native to Great Britain, the spiked Ornithogalum, *O. pyrenaicum* (Linn.), and is not common, being a local plant, found only in a few counties. It is abundant, however, in woods near Bath, and the unexpanded inflorescence used to be collected and sold in that town under the name of 'Bath Asparagus,' and was cooked and served as a vegetable.

A leafless stalk, about 2 feet high, rises from the bulb, bearing greenish-white flowers in a long, erect spike.

¶ *Other Species.*

O. divaricatum (Lindl.) is the CALIFORNIAN

SOAPROOT, Soap Bulb, Soap Apple or Amole. Its large bulb, resembling that of Squill, is universally used by the Indians of the regions where it grows as a detergent and as a fish poison. It has other uses dependent upon the action of its Saponin, and it is an emetico-cathartic poison.

O. thyroides (Jacq.), of South Africa, is a fatal stock poison.

O. Capense (Linn.), also of South Africa, yields a tuber used as an emmenagogue: the action is due to saponin.

Over the deserts of the south-western United States and Mexico, the tuberous rhizomes of large species of *Yucca* (also belonging to the order Liliaceæ) are called Soap Root, and have the same uses as those of the Californian variety of *Ornithogalum*. There is said to be no better tonic or stimulant for the hair than a free application of a solution of this juice in alcohol, water, or glycerine. Besides the Saponin, it contains a large number of raphides, which probably add mechanically to the stimulation.

Yucca filamentosa (Linn.), of the south-eastern United States, commonly known as 'Adam's Needle,' has a large rhizome which contains nearly 2 per cent. of Saponin, and which is used as a stimulant owing to the action of this constituent.

Gagea lutea (Ker Gawl.), the YELLOW STAR OF BETHLEHEM, has a small, egg-shaped or nearly round bulb, about the size of a large pea.

It flowers from March to May, and is a plant 6 to 10 inches high, with narrow leaves and yellow flowers (arranged in an umbel), which only open in the middle of the day. It occurs in woods and pastures in this country, but is not common.

It is recorded that the Swedes have eaten this bulb in times of scarcity. Round the main small bulb there are usually a number of bulbules about the size of sago grains, but only the parent bulb is enclosed in a yellowish outer skin.

Some species of Gagea have been used as diuretics, much like Squill, and probably contain related, if not identical, substances.

The tuberous root-stock of *Melanthium Virginicum* (Linn.), the Bunch Flower of the eastern and central United States, is poisonous and is used as a parasticide.

(POISON)
STAVESACRE

Synonym. Lousewort
Part Used. Seeds
Habitat. Asia Minor and Europe

Delphinium Staphisagria (LINN.)
N.O. Ranunculaceæ

Stavesacre is a species of Larkspur, a stout, erect herb attaining 4 feet in height, indigenous to Asia Minor and southern Europe. It

is cultivated in France and Italy, our supplies having before the War been drawn chiefly from Trieste and from the south of Italy.

Stavesacre was well known to both the Greeks and Romans. Dioscorides mentions it, and Pliny describes its use as a parasiticide. It continued to be extensively employed throughout the Middle Ages.

This Delphinium is an annual, with a hairy stem and hairy palmate leaves, composed of five to seven oblong lobes, which have frequently one or two acute indentures on their sides. The flowers form a loose spike at the upper part of the stalk, each on a short peduncle, and are of a pale-blue or purple colour.

¶ *Cultivation*. The seeds of this species should be sown in April, where the plants are intended to remain and require no special treatment, growing in almost any soil or situation, but the plants are most luxuriant when given a deep, yellow loam, well enriched with rotted manure and fairly moist. They should be thinned to a distance of 2 feet apart.

¶ *Part Used*. The dried, ripe seeds. Shake the seeds out of the pods on trays and spread them out to dry in the sun. Then pack away in airtight boxes or tins. The dried, ripe seeds are brown when fresh, changing to a dull, earthy colour on keeping. In shape they are irregularly quadrangular, one side being curved and larger than the others, and the surface of the seed is wrinkled and pitted. They average about 6 mm. (nearly $\frac{1}{4}$ inch) long and rather less in width, ten weighing about 6 grains. The seed coat is nearly tasteless, but the endosperm is oily and has a bitter and acrid taste. The seeds have no marked collour.

¶ *Constituents*. The chief constituents of Stavesacre seeds are from 20 to 25 per cent. of alkaloidal matter, which consists chiefly of the bitter, acrid, crystalline, alkaloid Delphinine, an irritant poison, and a second crystalline alkaloid named Delphisine, and the amorphous alkaloid Delphinoidine. Less important are staphisagroine, of which traces only are present, and staphisagrine, which appears to be a mixture of the first three elements.

¶ *Medicinal Action and Uses*. Vermifuge and vermin-destroying. Stavesacre seeds are extremely poisonous and are only used as a parasiticide to kill pediculi, chiefly in the form of the official ointment, the expressed oil, the powdered seeds, or an acid aqueous extract containing the alkaloids.

These seeds are so violently emetic and cathartic that they are rarely given internally, though the powdered seeds have been given as a purge for dropsy, in very small quantities at first and increased till the effect is produced. The dose at first should not exceed 2 or 3 grains, given in powder or decoction, but the administration of the drug must always be accompanied by great caution, as staphisagrine paralyses the motor nerves like curare.

The seeds are used as an external application to some cutaneous eruptions, the decoction, applied with a linen rag, being effectual in curing the itch. It is made by boiling the seeds in water.

Delphinine has also been employed similarly to aconite, both internally and externally, for neuralgia. It resembles aconite in causing slowness of pulse and respiration, paralysis of the spinal cord and death from asphyxia. By depressing the action of the spinal cord it arrests the convulsions caused by strychnine.

See ACONITE, LARKSPUR (FIELD).

STONECROPS

Sedums
N.O. Crassulaceæ

STONECROP, WHITE

Sedum album
N.O. Crassulaceæ

Synonym. Small Houseleek (Culpepper)
Parts Used. Leaves, stalks

Culpepper's Small Houseleek is now generally called the White Stonecrop. It is not very common, and is found wild on rocks and walls. As a rule, however, when growing on garden walls and the roofs of cottages and outhouses, it owes its presence indirectly to human agency, and is to be considered a garden escape. The root is perennial and fibrous, the flowerless stems prostrate, of a bluish-green colour, round and leafy. The leaves are bright green and very succulent, oblong, cylindrical, blunt and spreading, $\frac{1}{3}$ to $\frac{1}{4}$ inch long. The flowering stems are 6 to 10 inches high, with a few leaves growing alternately on them and terminated by much-branched, flat tufts (cymes) of numerous, small, star-like flowers, about $\frac{1}{6}$ inch in diameter, the white petals twice as large as the green sepals.

This Stonecrop, which flowers in July and August, is not to be confounded with another white-flowered Stonecrop (*Sedum Anglicum*), which flowers earlier – June and July – and is an annual. It is a plant of smaller and compacter growth, the leaves shorter and less cylindrical, with less numerous flowers, the white petals of which are spotted with red.

The White Stonecrop is said to be indigenous in the Malvern Hills and Somerset, but a garden escape elsewhere, being grown as rock-plants.

S. Anglicum is abundant on the bank of a hedge close to Poole Harbour.

The older herbalists considered the White Stonecrop to possess all the virtues of the Houseleek. The leaves and stalks were recommended and used for all kinds of inflammation, being especially applied as a cooling plaster to painful hæmorrhoids. Culpepper tells us: 'it is so harmless an herb you can scarce use it amiss.' It was the custom, too, to prepare and eat it as a pickle, in the same way as the juicy Samphire.

STONECROP, COMMON

Sedum acre
N.O. Crassulaceæ

Synonyms. Biting Stonecrop. Wallpepper. Golden Moss. Wall Ginger. Bird Bread. Prick Madam. Gold Chain. Creeping Tom. Mousetail. Jack-of-the-Buttery (*French*) Pain d'oiseau
Part Used. Herb

The Common or Biting Stonecrop is the commonest of the Stonecrops, growing freely upon walls and cottage roofs, on rocks and in sandy places, especially near the sea, forming tufts or cushions, 3 to 10 inches across, which in June and July are a mass of golden blossom, but its flowering season is very soon over.

The root is perennial and very fibrous, its minute threads penetrating into the smallest crevices. The stalks are numerous, many of them trailing and flowerless, others erect – generally 3 to 5 inches high – bearing the clusters of flowers. When growing among other foliage, or on rockwork, the flower-stalks are often drawn up to some height, at other times much dwarfed. They branch and are clothed with numerous leaves. The little upright and very succulent leaves that closely overlap on the flowerless stems are a distinguishing characteristic from the other yellow-flowering species of *Sedum*; they are so fleshy as to be almost round. The starlike flowers are of a brilliant yellow colour, the five sepals small and inconspicuous, but the five petals, spreading and acutely pointed, are a striking feature. There are ten stamens, with anthers the same tint as the petals.

The pungency of the leaves has obtained for the plant its specific name of *acre*, and the popular English name of Wallpepper and Wall Ginger. Gerard tells us it was known in his day as Mousetail, or Jack of the Butterie. As regards the latter name, Dr. Fernie says: 'this and the Sedums *album* and *reflexum* were ingredients in a famous worm-expelling medicine or "theriac" (treacle), and "Jack of the Buttery" is a corruption of *Bot. theriaque*.'

De Lobel called it *vermicularis*, partly – we are told – from the grub-like shape of the leaves, and partly from its medical efficacy as a vermifuge.

Some old writers considered this species to possess considerable virtues, but others, from the durability of its acrimony and the violence of its operation, have thought it unsafe to be administered. Culpepper tells us:

'Its qualities are directly opposite to the other Sedums, and more apt to raise inflammations than to cure them; it ought not to be put into any ointment, nor any other medicine.'

He considered it, however, good for scurvy, both inwardly in decoction and outwardly, bathed as a fomentation, and he also commended it for King's Evil. Other writers have likewise considered it to be a beneficial remedy in some scorbutic diseases, when properly and carefully used, recommending it in the form of a gargle for scurvy of the gums, and as a lotion for scrofulous ulcers. It has been considered useful in intermittent fever and in dropsy. In large doses it is emetic and cathartic, and applied externally will sometimes produce blisters.

Pliny recommends it as a means of procuring sleep, for which purpose he says it must be wrapped in a black cloth and placed under the pillow of the patient, without his knowing it, otherwise it will not be effectual.

STONECROP, CROOKED YELLOW

Sedum reflexum
N.O. Crassulaceæ

Synonym. Stonecrop Houseleek
Parts Used. Leaves, young shoots

The Stonecrop Houseleek of the old herbalists goes now by the name of Crooked Yellow Stonecrop.

¶ *Description.* It is not considered truly indigenous, though often found on rocks, old walls, house-tops, and sometimes on dry banks, in many parts of the British Isles. The slender but tough stems, tinged with pink, are elongated, lying on the ground, sending up numerous ascending, short, leafy, barren shoots and erect, and somewhat flexuous flowering stems, 9 inches to 1 foot high, clothed with spreading and reflexed leaves, which are cylindrical and pointed, ⅛ to ¾ inch long, spurred at their bases. The leaves are distant towards the lower ends of the barren shoots, but crowded towards the apex, forming a kind of tuft: they are only curved back, or reflexed, on the flowering stems. This Stonecrop also blossoms in July and August:

STONECROP, ORPINE

Synonyms. Live Long. Life Everlasting
(*French*) Herbe aux charpentiers
Parts Used. Whole plant, leaves

The Orpine, the largest British species of this genus, is readily distinguished from most of the other plants allied to it by its large, broad, flattened leaves and terminal heads of pinkish flowers, being the only British species with flat leaves.

It has a wide distribution: in warmer countries it is a mountain plant. Lindley gives its true habitat as mountainous woods, and Cesalpinus, an early Italian botanist, calls it *Crassula montana*, but in this country it grows freely in lower situations. It is probable that it was originally an introduced plant, though it is now not uncommonly found in hedgebanks on shady sides of fields and in woods, though probably escaped from cultivation in many of its localities. In its wild state, the plant is from 1 to 2 feet high, though in gardens it may attain as much as 3 feet.

The root-stock is perennial, large and fleshy, producing small parsnip-shaped tubers, with a whitish-grey rind, containing a considerable store of nourishment. The stalks are numerous, erect, unbranched, round and solid, generally of a reddish tint, spotted and streaked with a deeper red above. The flat, fleshy leaves, bluish-green in colour, are numerous, placed alternately on the stem at very short intervals, and coarsely toothed. The upper leaves are rounded at their bases and without foot-stalks, the lower ones taper at the base to a short stalk, being almost wedge-shaped; they are largest and closest together about the middle of the stem, where they are 1½ to 3 inches long.

The flowers are in compact heads at the top of the stems, forming a brilliant mass of crimson, in most cases, though sometimes whitish, suffused with dull purplish rose. They are spreading and acutely pointed, three times as long as the calyx. In their

the flowers are in terminal cymes as in the previous species, but are bright yellow.

In Holland, the leaves and young shoots of this species are used for salad.

Culpepper considered that as 'it is more frequent than the white stonecrop, flowering at the same time, it may very well supply its place.' He goes on to tell us that the House-leek, 'though not given inwardly, yet is recommended by some to quench thirst in fever.' Mixed with posset drink, 3 oz. of the juice of this and *Persicaria maculata*, boiled to the consistence of a julep, are recommended to allay the heat of inflammation.

Sedum Telephium
N.O. Crassulaceæ

centre are ten conspicuous stamens, with reddish anthers, and the ovaries they surround are also reddish.

The whole plant is smooth and somewhat shiny. It flowers in July and seeds in August.

The specific name is derived from Telephus, the son of Hercules, who is said to have discovered its virtues. Its most familiar English name, Orpine, is derived from *Auripigmentum*, the gold-coloured pigment, called Orpiment, or Orpin, a yellow sulphuret of the metal arsenic. This name, which might have been appropriate enough for the brilliant yellow flowers of the last two species described, is quite out of place applied to the crimson blossoms of this *Sedum*.

Its tenacity of life has earned it the name of 'Live Long' and 'Life Everlasting,' the length of time it will continue fresh after being gathered being remarkable. It will live a long time if uprooted and hung up in a room without earth or water, subsisting on the store of nourishment in its fleshy leaves and swollen roots.

¶ *Constituents.* The whole plant is mucilaginous and slightly astringent. It contains lime, sulphur, ammonia and probably mercury.

The leaves have sometimes been used as a salad, like the other *Sedums*, but though sheep and goats eat it, horses will refuse it.

¶ *Medicinal Action and Uses.* It has been used as a popular remedy for diarrhœa. The leaves are boiled in milk, and a large teacupful of the decoction taken three or four times a day is said also to stimulate the action of the kidneys, and to be serviceable for piles and hæmorrhages. Orpine has also an anticancerous reputation.

Culpepper stated that it was seldom used internally in his days, but that the celebrated

German herbalist, Tragus, considered its distilled water –

'profitable for gnawings or excoriation in the stomach or bowels, for ulcers in the lungs, liver or other inward parts and cures those diseases, being drunk for days together,'

and that the root has the same action, even stronger. He says that it is

'used outwardly to cool inflammations upon

any hurt or wound, and easeth the pain of them; as also to heal scaldings and burnings, the juice thereof being beaten with some green salad oil and anointed. The leaf bruised and laid to any green wound in the head or legs doth heal them quickly, and being bound to the throat cureth the quinsy; and it reduceth ruptures. If you make the juice into a syrup with honey or sugar, you may safely take a spoonful or two at a time for sore throat and quinsy.'

STONECROP, VIRGINIAN

Penthorum sedoides (LINN.)
N.O. Crassulaceæ

Synonyms. Ditch Stonecrop. Penthorum
Part Used. Herb

The Virginian Stonecrop is a native of America.

¶ *Description.* It is a biennial, with stems about a foot high, on which the leaves are placed on alternate sides, on short stalks. They are oblong, 2 to 3 inches long and about a third as broad, smooth and thin, the apex pointed and the margins finely toothed. The flowers are small and greenish, on short flower-stalks, in rows along the upper sides of the branches of the terminal cyme: there are five very small petals and five sepals, and the ovary is five-cleft and five-celled, surrounded by ten stamens with filaments twice as long as the calyx. The genus *Penthorum* differs from the genus *Sedum*, in having no nectaries in its flowers.

This plant has of late attracted much notice, especially in America, as a remedy for catarrh, catarrhal inflammation of the larynx, chronic bronchitis, with increased secretion of mucus and catarrhal affections of the stomach and bowels. It has also been employed with success in the treatment of diarrhœa, hæmorrhoids and infantile cholera.

It is demulcent, laxative and somewhat astringent in its action. A fluid extract is prepared from the whole herb and administered in doses of from 10 to 20 drops. It has a slightly astringent taste.

¶ *Other Species.*

Among other species of *Sedum* are the HAIRY STONECROP (*Sedum villosum*), frequent in Scotland and the North of England, a small species with viscid stems and leaves and pinkish-white flowers. The THICK-LEAVED STONECROP (*S. dasyphyllum*), also a small species, but very rare, distinguished from the preceding by its fleshy, almost globular leaves, viscid flower-stalks and blunt petals. Other British species belonging to this group are: TASTELESS YELLOW STONECROP (*S. sexangulare*), distinguished from *S. acre* by its leaves, which are six in a whorl, growing in Greenwich Park, the Isle of Sheppey and a few other places. ST. VINCENT'S ROCK STONECROP (*S. rupestre*), a species allied to *S. reflexum*, with slightly flattened leaves, which grow five in a whorl, found on St. Vincent's Rocks and other limestone cliffs, rare; and WELSH STONECROP (*S. Fosterianum*), another species allied to *S. reflexum*, with leaves flattened at the base and compact cymes of flowers – which grows on the rocks in Wales and Shropshire.

See HOUSELEEK, KIDNEYWORT.

STONE ROOT

Collinsonia Canadensis (LINN.)
N.O. Labiatæ

Synonyms. Horseweed. Richweed. Richleaf. Knob-Root. Knobweed. Horsebalm. Hardback. Heal-all. Oxbalm. Knot-Root. Baume de Cheval. Guérit-tout
Parts Used. Whole plant, fresh root
Habitat. North America, from Canada to the Carolinas

¶ *Description.* The plant has a four-sided stem, from 1 to 4 feet in height, and bears large, greenish-yellow flowers. It grows in moist woods and flowers from July to September. The rhizome is brown-grey, about 4 inches long, knobby, and very hard. The whole plant has a strong, disagreeable odour and a pungent and spicy taste. The chief virtue of the plant is in the root, which should always be used fresh. The name is derived from its discoverer, Peter Collinson.

¶ *Constituents.* In the root there is resin, starch, mucilage and wax. In the leaves, resin, tannin, wax and volatile oil. The alkaloid discovered in the root appears to be a magnesium salt.

¶ *Medicinal Action and Uses.* Sedative, antispasmodic, astringent, tonic, diaphoretic, diuretic.

A decoction of the fresh root has been given in catarrh of the bladder, leucorrhœa, gravel and dropsy. It is largely used by American veterinary surgeons as a diuretic. It is valuable in all complaints of urinary organs and rectum, and is best combined with other drugs.

It can be used externally, especially the leaves, for poultices and fomentations, bruises, wounds, sores, cuts, etc., and also as a gargle, in the strength of 1 part of fluid extract to 3 of water.

¶ *Preparations and Dosages.* Of fluid extract, 15 to 60 drops. Of Collinsonin, 2 to 4 grains.

STORAX

Liquidambar orientalis (MILL.)
N.O. Hamamelaceæ

Synonyms. Liquidambar imberbe. Styrax Præparatus. Prepared Storax. Styrax liquidus. Flussiger Amber. Liquid Storax. Balsam Styracis

Part Used. Balsam obtained from the wood and inner bark

Habitat. Asia Minor

¶ *Description.* A tree of 40 feet or more in height, with many branches, and a thick, purplish-grey bark; leaves palmately cut into five, three-lobed sections, and white flowers arranged in little, round solitary heads. The name *Liquidambar* was given by Monardes in the sixteenth century as the name of the resin obtained in Mexico from the American species, now *L. styraciflua*. *L. orientalis* was not known botanically until the middle of the last century, when it was grown in Chelsea, Kew, and other botanical gardens from seed brought from the Levant via Paris. It forms forests near Budrum, Melasso, Moughla, Marmorizza and a few places near, but does not appear to be found wild in any other district. The genus *Liquidambar* is very similar to that of *Platanus*, and this species to *L. styraciflua*.

Styrax officinale has been proved to be the source of the solid Storax of the Ancients, which was always scarce and valuable, and is now never found in commerce, though it is probable that the cultivated *S. officinale* of Europe is capable of yielding Storax. Storax appears to be a pathological rather than a physiological product; when the young wood is injured, oil-ducts are formed in which the Storax is produced. Its extraction is chiefly carried on by a tribe of wandering Turcomans called Yuruks. The outer bark of the tree is removed, the inner bark is stripped off and thrown into pits until a sufficient quantity has been collected. It is then packed in strong, horse-hair bags and pressed in a wooden press. After removal, hot water is thrown on the bags, which are pressed a second time, when the greater part of the balsam will be extracted. Another account says that the bark is first boiled in water in a large copper over a brick fire, by which process the balsam is separated, and can then be skimmed off. The boiled bark is then put into bags over which hot water is thrown, and submitted to pressure as described above, by which an additional quantity of balsam

(Yagh, or oil) is obtained. In either mode of procedure the product is the semi-liquid, opaque substance called Liquid Storax. This is chiefly forwarded in barrels to Constantinople, Smyrna, Syria and Alexandria; some to Smyrna, in goat-skins, with a certain proportion of water; thence it is forwarded to Trieste in barrels. Much goes to Bombay for India and China, but little comes to the United States or Britain. Liquid Storax is known in the East as Rosemalloes or Rosemalles. The residual bark left after the extraction of the balsam constitutes the fragrant, leaf-like cakes known as *Cortex Thymiamatis*, *Cortex Thuris* and *Storax Bark*.

The quality of Storax now on the market appears to be much inferior to that of a few years ago, and is usually much adulterated. As imported, Liquid Storax is a soft, viscid, opaque substance, about the consistence of honey, of a greyish-brown colour, and containing a variable quantity of water, which, after it has been allowed to stand for a time, floats on the surface. It has an agreeable, balsamic odour, though, when fresh, this is a little contaminated by naphthalin or bitumen. Its taste is burning, pungent, and aromatic.

The Prepared Storax is obtained from Liquid Storax by means of rectified spirit and straining. It is then described officially as 'a semi-transparent, brownish-yellow, semi-fluid balsam, of the consistence of thick honey, agreeable fragrance, and aromatic, bland taste.' The odour is slightly less agreeable than that of the balsam of Peru. It is imported in jars holding 14 lb. each.

¶ *Constituents.* The most abundant constituent of Storax is Storesin, in two forms, called alpha and beta, both free and in the form of a cinnamic ester. It is an amorphous substance, melting at 168° C. (334·4° F.), and readily soluble in petroleum benzin. Cinnamic esters of phenylprophyl, of ethyl, of benzyl, and especially cinnamate of cinnamyl, the so-called Styrasin, have also been observed. The yield of cinnamic acid varies from 6 to 12 per cent., or even as much as 23 per cent. of crystallized cinnamic acid can be obtained.

Another analysis gives free cinnamic acid, vanillin, styrol, styracin, cinnamic acid-ethyl ester, cinnamic acid-phenylprophyl ester, and storesinol partly free and partly as cinnamic acid ester.

Crude Storax contains from 1 to 9 per cent. of matter insoluble in alcohol, and up to 30 per cent. of water. When purified, it is brownish-yellow, viscous, and transparent in thin layers; entirely soluble in alcohol (90 per cent.) and in ether. Boiled with solution of potassium chromate and sulphuric acid, it evolves an odour of benzaldehyde. It loses not more than 5 per cent. of its weight when heated in a thin layer on a water-bath for one hour.

Owing to the demand for the cinnamic esters of Storax for perfumery purposes, much of the commercial drug has been deprived of these before it is put on the market.

¶ *Medicinal Action and Uses.* A stimulating expectorant and feeble antiseptic, at present very seldom used except as a constituent of the compound tincture of benzoin. Externally, mixed with 2 or 3 parts of olive oil, it has been found a useful local remedy in scabies. It has the same action as balsams of Tolu and Peru and benzoin. It has been recommended as a remedy in diphtheria, in pulmonic catarrhs, and as a substitute for South American copaiba in gonorrhoea and leucorrhoea. Combined with tallow or lard, it is valuable for many forms of skin disease, such as ringworm, especially in children. The taste and smell of opium is well concealed by the addition of Storax in pills, its fragrance being used frequently also in ointments.

¶ *Dosage.* 10 to 20 grains.

¶ *Adulterations, Substitutes, Allied Balsams.* L. styraciflua, or Sweet Gum, the American variety, is sometimes confused because its product, obtained by spontaneous exudation, is often called Liquidambar, as well as Liquid Storax or copalm balsam. It contains cinnamyl cinnamate, with ethyl, benzyl, and other esters of cinnamic acid. Another of its products, obtained by boiling the young branches, has also been confounded with Liquid Storax, which it resembles. It is used in Texas for coughs. A syrup of the bark is used for diarrhoea and dysentery in the Western States.

L. storesin is said to be known also in Eastern markets.

Aromatic resins are also obtained in China from *L. Formosana*, and in Java and Burma from *L. Altingea* (*Altingia excelsa*), where the Storax-like substance varies in colour from white to red.

Styrea reticulata and other species in Brazil have a fragrant secretion similar to benzoin, which is used in churches as frankincense.

The commonest adulterations are sawdust and turpentine.

STRAMONIUM. *See* THORNAPPLE

STRAWBERRY

Fragaria vesca (LINN.)
N.O. Rosaceæ

Part Used. Leaves

Habitat. The whole of the Northern Hemisphere, exclusive of the tropics

¶ *Description.* The Wild Strawberry, a delicate, thin-leaved plant, with small, scarlet berries, cone-shaped and studded with tiny, brown 'seeds,' has a fragrance and flavour more delicate even than the cultivated Strawberry. It chooses a slightly sheltered position, and, being very small, considerable labour goes to the collection of its fruit, which is much more used and appreciated in France than in Great Britain.

1629 is the date assigned to the introduction of the Scarlet Strawberry from Virginia, and the earliest mention of the Strawberry in English writings is in a Saxon plant list of the tenth century, and in 1265 the 'Straberie' is mentioned in the household roll of the Countess of Leicester. 'Strabery ripe,' together with 'Gode Peascode' and 'Cherrys in the ryse,' were some of the London cries mentioned by Lydgate in the fifteenth century. Ben Jonson, in a play written in 1603, speaks of

'A pot of Strawberries gathered in the wood
To mingle with your cream.'

The common idea that the word Strawberry is derived from the habit of placing straw under the cultivated plants when the berries are ripening is quite erroneous. The name is older than this custom, and preserves the obsolete preterit 'straw' of the verb 'to strew,' referring to the tangle of vines with which the Strawberry covers the ground.

¶ *Constituents.* Cissotanic, malic, and citric acids, sugar, mucilage and a peculiar volatile aromatic body uninvestigated.

Bacon found in the odour of the dying

leaves 'a most excellent cordial smell,' next in sweetness to the muskrose and violet.

¶ *Medicinal Action and Uses.* Laxative, diuretic, astringent. Both the leaves and the fruit were in early pharmacopœias, though the leaves were mostly used. The fruit contains malic and citric acids, a volatile matter, sugar, mucilage, pectin, woody fibre and water. It is easily digested and is not subject to acetous fermentation in the stomach. In feverish conditions the fruit is invaluable, and is also recommended for stone. Strawberry vitamins are of value in sprue. Culpepper declares the plant to be 'singularly good for the healing of many ills,' but Linnæus was the first to discover and prove the efficacy of the berries as a cure for rheumatic gout.

The root is astringent and used in diarrhœa. The leaves have the same property, and a tea made from them checks dysentery. The stalks only entered into the composition of the once-famous Antioch drink and vulnerary. Some recipes order that the drink should be prepared between the feasts of St. Philip and St. James and the Nativity of St. John the Baptist.

The Strawberry is a useful dentifrice and cosmetic. The fresh fruit removes discoloration of the teeth if the juice is allowed to remain on for about five minutes and the teeth are then cleansed with warm water, to which a pinch of bicarbonate of soda has been added. A cut Strawberry rubbed over the face immediately after washing will whiten the skin and remove slight sunburn. For a badly sunburnt face it is recommended to rub the juice well into the skin, to leave it on for half an hour, and then wash off with warm water to which a few drops of simple tincture of benzoin have been added; no soap should be used.

¶ *Dosage.* Infusion, 1 to 2 tablespoonsful.

AN OLD RECIPE

'Gather strawberry leaves on Lamas Eve, press them in the distillery until the aromatick perfume thereof becomes sensible. Take a fat turkey and pluck him, and baste him, then enfold him carefully in the strawberry leaves. Then boil him in water from the well, and add rosemary, velvet flower, lavender, thistles, stinging nettles, and other sweet-smelling herbs. Add also a pinte of canary wine, and half a pound of butter and one of ginger passed through the sieve. Sieve with plums and stewed raisins and a little salt. Cover him with a silver dish cover.'

(POISON)
STROPHANTHUS

Strophanthus Kombé (OLIV.)
N.O. Apocynaceæ

Synonyms. Strophanthus hispidus. Kombé Seeds. Strophanti Semina
Part Used. Dried, ripe seeds, deprived of their awns
Habitat. Tropical East Africa

¶ *Description.* The name *Strophanthus* is derived from the Greek *strophos* (a twisted cord or rope) and *anthos* (a flower), thus expressing the chief peculiarity of its appearance, the limb of the corolla being divided into five, long, tail-like segments. The official description of the seeds is 'lance-ovoid, flattened and obtusely-edged; from 7 to 20 mm. in length, about 4 mm. in breadth, and about 2 mm. in thickness; externally of a light fawn colour with a distinct greenish tinge, silky lustrous form, a dense coating of flat-lying hairs (*S. Kombé*) or light to dark brown, nearly smooth, and sparingly hairy (*S. hispidus*), bearing on one side a ridge running from about the centre to the summit; fracture short and somewhat soft, the fractured surface whitish and oily; odour heavy when the seeds are crushed and moistened; taste very bitter.'

In Germany the seeds of *S. hispidus* are preferred because of their guaranteed purity. This plant when growing alone is in the form of a bush, but is usually found as a woody climber inhabiting the forests between the coasts and the centre of the African continent. It then reaches to the tops of the highest trees, coiling on the ground and hanging in festoons from tree to tree. The stem is several inches in diameter. The flowers are cream-coloured, yellow at the base, purple-spotted above.

The British, French and Swiss officially favour *S. Kombé*, while the United States Pharmacopœia recognizes both. There is a voluminous literature on the subject.

The seeds of all species of the genus possess hairs that have a characteristic, thickened base, somewhat like those of nux vomica seeds; those of several species are used for the preparation of arrow poison in Africa, at Kombé in the Manganja country, in the Gaboon district, and in Guinea and Senegambia. In Gaboon the poison is called inée, onayé, or onage. Some of the poisons closely resemble those of the genus *Acocanthera*, which are used for a similar purpose. The plant yielding the arrow poison of Kombé was first brought to Europe by Sir John Kirke, and described as a new species by

Oliver, of Kew, under the name of *S. Kombé*. In preparing the arrow poison, the seeds, deprived of their hairs, are pounded to a pulp, the adhesive sap of another plant is added, and the mixture smeared for 6 inches along the point of the arrow. Game wounded by such an arrow is said to be rarely able to move 100 yards, while the flesh can be eaten without bad effect.

Strophanthus is found in commerce either in pods or as clean seeds. It must be preserved in tightly-closed containers, adding a few drops of chloroform or carbon tetrachloride from time to time, to prevent attacks by insects.

The usual course for the qualitative examination has been found insufficient, and a supplementary microscopical test is recommended. The question of its relative variability of strength as compared with digitalis is not definitely settled.

The seeds are reduced to powder with great difficulty. They are sometimes bruised in an iron mortar with broken glass, after drying.

As the active principle of Strophanthus is most abundant in the seeds, but is also found in the husks and hairs, pharmaceutical preparations of the drug should be made from the separated seeds, while other parts may be employed for the manufacture of Strophanthin.

¶ *Constituents*. A glucoside, Strophanthin, an alkaloid, Inœine, and fixed oil.

Sulphuric acid, diluted with one-fifth of its volume of water, colours the endosperm, and sometimes the cotyledons, dark green (presence of Strophanthin).

Herr Lampart and Müller received the Hagen Bucholz prize of the German Apothecaries Society for the proposed assay method following, based upon the preliminary extraction of the drug with absolute alcohol, the removal of oil from the precolate with petroleum ether, the conversion of the glucosides into strophanthidin by boiling with hydrochloric acid, and the subsequent extraction with chloroform, weighing, and calculating to strophanthin by multiplying by the factor 2·187.

The strophanthins from different species were found to vary somewhat in chemical composition, and Thoms proposes to name them as follows: *k*-strophanthin when obtained from *S. Kombé*, *g*-strophanthin when obtained from *S. gratus*, *e*-strophanthin when obtained from *S. Emini*, *h*-strophanthin when obtained from *S. hispidus*.

g-strophanthin is the one appearing to be identical with the glucoside Ouabain of Acocanthera.

Strophanthinum, a mixture of glucosides prepared from *S. Kombé*, is a whitish, crystalline powder freely soluble in water and giving a green coloration with sulphuric acid. Warmed with dilute acids it is readily hydrolized into Strophanthidin and a sugar.

Great care must be used in tasting it, and then only in very dilute solutions.

¶ *Medicinal Action and Uses*. The sole official use of Strophanthus in medicine is for its influence on the circulation, especially in cases of chronic heart weakness. As its action is the same as that of digitalis, although more likely to cause digestive disturbances,[1] it is often useful as an alternative or adjuvant to the drug. Believed to have greater diuretic power, it is esteemed of greater value in cases complicated with dropsies.

In urgent cases, the effects upon the circulation can be obtained almost immediately by means of the intravenous injection of its active principle. The hypodermic injection of Strophanthin is not recommended, owing to the intense local irritation it causes, and because of its strength it should be used with great care and under medical direction.

¶ *Dosages*. Of Extractum Strophanthi of the B.P., from ¼ to 1 grain. This extract takes the place of a solid preparation and can be administered in pills and capsules, 1 grain being equal to 5 minims of the United States tincture.

Of tincture of Strophanthus, B.P. and U.S.P., 5 to 15 drops.

Of Strophanthin, $\frac{1}{300}$ of a grain.

The maximum *daily* dose should not exceed: For *g*-strophanthin, intravenously, $\frac{1}{64}$ grain; by mouth, ⅛ grain. For *k*-strophanthin, intravenously, $\frac{1}{40}$ grain; by mouth, $\frac{1}{10}$ grain.

¶ *Poisonous, if any, with Antidotes*. The greatest caution should always attend the use of strophanthin, though, unlike digitalis, its effects are not cumulative.

¶ *Varieties and Substitutions*. There are twenty-eight recognized species of the genus in Africa and Asia, extending to China, the East Indies and the Philippines. The commercial drug is often largely compounded of other than the recognized species, and may contain the seeds of related varieties, especially those of *Kickxia (Funtumia) africana*, which are beardless and spindle-shaped. They turn brown, then red, instead of green, when treated with concentrated sulphuric acid.

S. Kombé grows solely in East Africa, but the seeds from different regions are often mixed before they are shipped.

S. hispidus, S. glabra, S. Emini, S. courmontii (both var. *Kerkii* and var. *Fallax*), *S.*

Many practitioners are of opinion that Strophanthus does not cause digestive disturbances. – EDITOR.

gratus of Sierra Leone, and *S. Nicholsoni*, all contribute seeds.

The two most mixed with the official drug before exportation are those of *S. gratus* from the Senegal and Congo, where *S. hispidus* is found, and which are recommended by some authorities because easily recognized and yielding strophanthin readily in crystalline form, and *S. Thallone*.

At present Strophanthus seeds are less mixed than formerly. In 1892 the commercial seeds were classified as follows:

1. The official products of *S. Kombé* and *S. hispidus*, which contain strophanthin and no crystals of calcium oxalate.

2. Those resembling the official seeds, but coming from Mozambique and Sierra Leone.

3. Those containing calcium oxalate crystals but no strophanthin (from Senegal, Lagos, Niger, German East Africa, Togoland, and Baol of Senegal).

4. A very hairy seed from the Upper Niger, varying from a silky white to brown; the embryo contains calcium oxalate crystals, but the seeds do not contain strophanthin.

5. Seeds said to be glabrous, but having hairs in the region of the raphe, come from Lagos and Zambesi and contain neither calcium oxalate crystals nor strophanthin.

SUMACHS

N.O. Anacardiaceæ

The American Poison Ivy (*Rhus Toxicodendron*, Linn.) is one of the species of Sumachs, an attractive group of plants widely distributed in Europe, Asia and North America, varying much in habit from low bushes to moderately-sized trees, many of them familiar denizens of our gardens, for the sake of their ornamental foliage, which assumes beautiful tints in autumn, some of the varieties also bearing showy fruits.

Several species are of considerable importance, their value being chiefly in their leaves and sap, and in the large galls that are found on their leaves after they have been punctured by a tiny insect. The so-called Chinese Galls, of an irregular shape and astringent taste, which are imported into this country from China for tanning purposes, are formed by the puncture of the leaves of *Rhus semialata*, a species of aphis, and are of considerable economic value, containing 70 to 80 per cent. of gallotannic acid.

SUMACH, SMOOTH

Rhus glabra (LINN.)
N.O. Anacardiaceæ

Synonyms. Upland Sumach. Pennsylvania Sumach. Rhus copallinum (Mountain Sumach). Rhus typhinum (Staghorn or Velvet Sumach).
Parts Used. Bark of branches and root, dried, ripe berries, and exudation
Habitat. Almost all parts of the United States and Canada

¶ *Description.* There are several varieties of the plant, such as *Rhus typhinum* (Staghorn or Velvet Sumach), the berries of which now often replace those of *R. glabra* and *R. copallinum* (Mountain or Dwarf Sumach), and they should be carefully distinguished from the poisonous species. The non-poisonous have their fruit clothed with acid, crimson hairs, and their panicles are compound, dense, and terminal; the poisonous varieties have axillary panicles, and smooth fruit.

The flowers of *R. glabra* are greenish-red, and the fruit grows in clusters of small berries. It is a shrub from 6 to 15 feet high, with straggling branches and a pale-grey bark, sometimes slightly red. It grows in thickets and waste places. The berries should be gathered before the rain has removed their downy covering, for they are no longer acid when this has been washed off. They have a sour, astringent, not unpleasant taste, and are eaten freely by the country people. Their powder is a brownish-red.

When broken on the plant, a milky fluid is exuded from both bark and leaves, which forms later a solid gum-like body.

Excrescences are produced under the leaves containing quantities of tannic and gallic acid. They have been used as a substitute for imported Chinese galls, and found preferable.

The leaves, and, to a less extent, the bark, are largely used in tanning leather and dyeing. This Sumach, for the manufacture of extract for tanner's use, is largely cultivated in Virginia, where the annual crop amounts to from 7,000 to 8,000 tons. The percentage of tannin in Virginian Sumach varies from 16 to 25 per cent. That in the European or Sicilian Sumach (*R. coriaria*) falls from 6 to 8 per cent. below the percentage of the Virginian Sumach, yet the European is preferred by tanners and dyers, since by its use it is possible to make the finer, white leathers for gloves and fancy shoes.

The American product gives the leather a yellow colour, apparently due to the presence of quercitrin and quercitin.

Large quantities of a dark-red, semi-fluid, bitter, astringent extract are prepared in Virginia from Sumach, and is said to contain 25 to 30 per cent. of tannin. It is used both in

Europe and America. An infusion of the berries affords an excellent black dye for wool. A medicinal wine can also be prepared from them.

Oil of Rhus may be extracted from the seeds of this and other species of the genus. It will attain a tallow-like consistency on standing, and can be made into candles, which burn brilliantly, though they emit a pungent smoke.

¶ *Constituents*. The berries contain free malic acid and acid calcium malate co-exist, with tannic and gallic acids, fixed oil, extractive, red colouring matter, and a little volatile oil. The active properties of both bark and berries yield to water.

¶ *Medicinal Action and Uses*. The bark is tonic, astringent, and antiseptic; the berries refrigerant and diuretic.

A strong decoction, or diluted fluid extract, affords an agreeable gargle in angina, especially when combined with potassium chlorate. Where tannin drugs are useful, as in diarrhœa, the fluid extract is an excellent astringent.

The bark, in decoction or syrup, has been found useful in gonorrhœa, leucorrhœa, diarrhœa, dysentery, hectic fever, scrofula and profuse perspiration from debility. Combined with the barks of slippery elm and white pine and taken freely, the decoction is said to have been greatly beneficial in syphilis. As an injection for prolapsus uteri and ani, and for leucorrhœa, and as a wash in

many skin complaints, the decoction is valuable. For scald-head it can be simmered in lard, or the powdered root-bark can be applied as a poultice to old ulcers, forming a good antiseptic.

A decoction of the inner bark of the root is helpful for the sore-mouth resulting from mercurial salivation, and also for internal use in mercurial diseases. A free use of the bark will produce catharsis.

The berries may be used in infusion in diabetes, strangury bowel complaints, and febrile diseases; also as a gargle in quinsy and ulcerations of the mouth and throat, and as a wash for ringworm, tetters, offensive ulcers, etc.

The astringent excrescences, when powdered and mixed with lard or linseed oil, are useful in hæmorrhoids.

The mucilagic exudation, if the bark be punctured in hot weather, has been used advantageously in gleet and several urinary difficulties.

¶ *Dosages*. Of the fluid extract of bark, 1 to 2 drachms. Of the fluid extract of berries, 1 to 2 drachms. Of the decoction of bark, or infusion of berries, 1 to 4 fluid ounces. Rhusin, 1 to 2 grains.

The following has been recommended for gonorrhœa: Take 1 scruple each of the exudation and Canada balsam. Form into a pill mass with a sufficient quantity of powdered pokeroot, and divide into 10 pills, of which 1 or 2 may be taken three or four times daily.

SUMACH, SWEET

Rhus aromatica (AIT.)
N.O. Anacardiaceæ

Synonyms. Fragrant Sumach
Part Used. Bark

This species of Sumach, usually growing about 4 feet high, was introduced into England as an ornamental shrub in 1759.

The bark is used in tanning.

¶ *Medicinal Action and Uses*. The root-bark is astringent and diuretic. Used in diabetes and excessive discharge from kidneys and bladder. The wood exudes a peculiar odour and is used by the Indians in Arizona, California and New Mexico for making baskets.

¶ *Other Species*.

Rhus Diversilobe (CALIFORNIAN POISON OAK).

¶ *Medicinal Action and Uses*. A tincture of the fresh leaves is used for eczema and skin diseases.

The American species, *R. venenata* and *R. toxicodendron*, produce effects imputed to the Upas-tree of Java. The hands and arms, and sometimes even the whole body, becomes greatly swollen from simply touching or carrying a branch of one of these plants, and

the swelling is accompanied with intolerable pain and inflammation, ending in ulceration. Some people, however, are able to handle the plants with impunity. *R. venenata*, called the POISON SUMACH or POISON ELDER, is a tall shrub with pinnate leaves composed of eleven or thirteen smoothish leaflets.

From the sap of *R. vernicifera*, the VARNISH SUMACH or Lacquer-tree of China and Japan, the varnish used in the manufacture of the famous Japanese lacquer-ware is prepared. The leaves and galls are also rich in tannin, and are used extensively for tanning various kinds of leather, and the expressed oil of the seed serves for candles. Japan Wax is obtained in Japan by expression and heat, or by the action of solvents from the fruit of another Sumach, *R. succedanea*. It consists almost entirely of palmitin and free palmitic acid, and is not a true wax; it is used in candle-making, for adulterating white beeswax and in making pomades.

R. copallina, a North American tree, provides copal resin, a transparent substance with a slight tinge of brown, which when dissolved in any volatile liquid, generally in oil of turpentine, forms one of the most perfect and beautiful of all the varnishes (known by the name of Copal Varnish).

The VENETIAN SUMACH, *R. cotinus*, though a native of Southern Europe, is so hardy a shrub as not to be injured by the frost of our winters, and is a familiar plant in our gardens, being cultivated for the very singular and ornamental appearance of its elongated, feathery fruit-stalks, which, combined with its blue-green leaves, have led to its common name of SMOKE PLANT. Both root and stem have been used for dyeing a yellow, approaching to orange, the colour obtained being, however, somewhat fugitive. The leaves are largely used for tanning.

Sumac Yellow is obtained from the dried and powdered branches of *R. coriana*, the ELM-LEAVED SUMACH, a shrub indigenous to the Mediterranean region, where it is cultivated for dyeing yellow and for tanning leather, the SICILIAN SUMACH being considered the best quality. The shoots are cut down every year close to the root, and after being dried are reduced to powder by means of a mill. An infusion of this yields a fawn colour, bordering on green, which may be improved by the judicious application of mordants. The principal use, however, of Sumach in dyeing is the production of black, by means of the large quantity of gallic acid which it affords. The bark is used instead of the oak for tanning leather, and it is said that all Turkey leather is tanned with this plant. The leaves and seeds are used in medicine and are considered astringent and styptic: the Tripoli merchants sell the seeds at Aleppo, where they are used to provoke an appetite before meals. The shrub is frequent in our gardens, retaining its dense clusters of deep red, rough berries till winter, after the leaves have fallen. It is quite hardy, and like most of the Sumachs is easily propagated by seed.

See (POISON) IVY.

SUMBUL

Ferula Sumbul (HOOK, F.)
N.O. Umbelliferæ

Synonyms. Euryangium Musk Root. Jatamansi. Ouchi. Ofnokgi. Sumbul Radix. Racine de Sumbul. Sumbulwurzel. Moschuswurzel

Parts Used. Root and rhizome

Habitat. Turkestan, Russia, Northern India

¶ *Description*. The plant reaches a height of 8 feet, and has a solid, cylindrical, slender stem which gives rise to about twelve branches. The root-leaves are 2½ feet long, triangular in outline, while the stem-leaves rapidly decrease in size until they are mere sheathing bracts. The pieces of root, as met with in commerce, are from 1 to 3 inches in diameter and ¾ to 1 inch in thickness. They are covered on the outside with a dusky-brown, papery, transversely-wrinkled cork, sometimes fibrous; within they are spongy, coarsely fibrous, dry, and dirty yellowish-brown, with white patches and spots of resin. The odour is strong and musk-like, the taste bitter and aromatic.

Sumbul – a Persian and Arabic word applied to various roots – was discovered in 1869 by the Russian Fedschenko, in the mountains south-east of Samarkand near the small town of Pentschakend on the River Zarafshan, at an elevation of 3,000 to 4,000 feet. A root was sent to the Moscow Botanical Gardens, and in 1872 two were sent from there to Kew, one arriving alive. In 1875 the plant died after flowering. The genus *Euryangium* (i.e. 'broad reservoir') was based by Kauffmann on the large, solitary dorsal vittæ, or oil tubes, which are filled with a quantity of latex – the moisture surounding the stigma – which pours out freely when a section is made, smelling strongly of musk, especially if treated with water, but they almost disappear in ripening, making the plant difficult to classify.

The root has long been used in Persia and India medicinally and as incense in religious ceremonies.

The physicians of Moscow and Petrograd were the first to employ it on the Continent of Europe, and Granville first introduced it to Great Britain and the United States.

The root of *Ferula suaveolens*, having only a faint, musky odour, is one of the species exported from Persia to Bombay by the Persian Gulf. It is the Sambul Root of commerce which differs from the original drug, being apparently derived from a different species of Ferula than that officially given.

The recognized source in the United States Pharmacopœia is *F. Sumbul* (Hooker Fil.). False Sumbul is the root of *Dorema Ammoniacum*; it is of closer texture, denser, and more firm, of a red or yellow tinge and feeble odour.

¶ *Constituents*. Volatile oil, two balsamic resins, one soluble in alcohol and one in ether; wax, gum, starch, a bitter substance soluble in water and alcohol, a little angelic and valeric acid. The odour seems to be connected with the balsamic resins. The volatile oil has a bitter taste like peppermint, and on dry distillation yields a bluish oil containing umbelliferone. A 1916 analysis shows moisture, starch, pentrosans, crude fibre, protein, dextrin, ash, sucrose, reducing sugar, volatile oil and resins. Alkaloids were not detected. The volatile oil did not show the presence of sulphur. Both betaine and umbelliferon were detected. In the resin, vanillic acid was identified and a phytosterol was present. Among the volatile acids were acetic, butyric, angelic and tiglic acid, and among the non-volatile oleic, linoleic, tiglic, cerotic, palmitic and stearic.

¶ *Medicinal Action and Uses.* Stimulant and antispasmodic, resembling valerian in its action, and used in various hysterical conditions. It is believed to have a specific action on the pelvic organs, and is widely employed in dysmenorrhœa and allied female disorders.

It is also a stimulant to mucous membranes, not only in chronic dysenteries and diarrhœas, but in chronic bronchitis, especially with asthmatic tendency, and even in pneumonia.

Half an ounce of a tincture produced narcotic symptoms, confusing the head, causing a tendency to snore even when awake, and giving feelings of tingling, etc., with a strong odour of the drug from breath and skin which only passed off after a day or two.

The tincture of 10 per cent. Sumbul, with 2 volumes of alcohol and 1 of water, is used as an antispasmodic and nervine. The fluid extract, being superior, superseded the tincture. (Sumbul, in No. 30 powder, 1,000 grams, with a mixture of 4 volumes of alcohol and 1 of water as the menstruum.)

¶ *Dosages.* B.P., ½ to 1 drachm. Of fluid extract, ½ to 1 fluid drachm. Of extract of Sumbul or Muskroot, 2 to 5 grains. Solid extract, U.S.P., 4 grains.

SUNDEW

Drosera rotundifolia (LINN.)
N.O. Droseraceæ

Synonyms. Dew Plant. Round-leaved Sundew. Red Rot. Herba rosellæ. Sonnenthau rosollis. Rosée du Soleil
Part Used. The flowering plant dried in the air, *not* artificially
Habitat. Britain, and in many parts of Europe, India, China, Cape of Good Hope, New Holland, North and South America, Russian Asia

¶ *Description.* This little insectivorous plant is found growing in muddy edges of ponds, bogs and rivers, where the soil is peaty. It is a small herbaceous, perennial, aquatic plant, with short and slender fibrous root, from which grow the leaves. These are remarkable for their covering of red glandular hairs, by which they are readily recognized, apart from their flowers which only open in the sunshine. Their leaves are orbicular on long stalks, depressed, lying flat on ground and have on upper surface long red viscid hairs, each having a small gland at top, containing a fluid, which looks like a dewdrop, hence its name. This secretion is most abundant when the sun is at its height. Flower-stems erect, slender, 2 to 6 inches high, at first coiled inward bearing a simple raceme, which straightens out as flowers expand; these are very small and white, appearing in summer and early autumn. Seeds numerous, spindle-shaped in a loose chaffy covering contained in a capsule. These hairs are very sensitive, they curve inward slowly and catch any insects which alight on them; the fluid on the

points also retains them. After an insect has been caught, the glandular heads secrete a digestive fluid which dissolves all that can be absorbed from the insect. It has been noted that secretion does not take place when inorganic substances are imprisoned.

¶ *Constituents.* The juice is bitter, acrid, caustic, odourless, yielding not more than 30 per cent. ash, and contains citric and malic acids.

¶ *Medicinal Action and Uses.* Used with advantage in whooping-cough, exerting a peculiar action on the respiratory organs; useful in incipient phthisis, chronic bronchitis, asthma, etc., the juice is said to take away corns and warts, and may be used to curdle milk. In America it has been advocated as a cure for old age; a vegetable extract is used together with colloidal silicates in cases of arterio sclerosis.

¶ *Dosages.* 2 fluid drachms of the saturated tincture added to 4 fluid drachms of water or wine and a teaspoonful taken for a dose. Fluid extract, 10 to 20 drops. Solid extract, 2 to 5 grams.

SUNFLOWER

Helianthus annuus
N.O. Compositæ

Synonyms. Marigold of Peru. Corona Solis. Sola Indianus. Chrysanthemum Peruvianum
The common Sunflower is a native of Mexico and Peru, introduced into this country in the sixteenth century and

now one of our most familiar garden plants.

It is an annual herb, with a rough, hairy

stem, 3 to 12 feet high, broad, coarsely-toothed, rough leaves, 3 to 12 inches long, and circular heads of flowers, 3 to 6 inches wide in wild specimens and often a foot or more in cultivation. The flower-heads are composed of many small tubular flowers arranged compactly on a flattish disk: those in the outer row have long strap-shaped corollas, forming the rays of the composite flower.

The genus *Helianthus*, to which the Sunflower belongs, contains about fifty species, chiefly natives of North America; many are indigenous to the Rocky Mountains, others to tropical America, and a few species are found in Peru and Chile.

They are tall, hardy, annual or perennial herbs, several of which are grown in gardens, being of easy cultivation in moderately good soil, and that useful plant of the kitchen garden, the Jerusalem Artichoke (*Helianthus tuberosus*), is also a member of the genus.

The name *Helianthus*, being derived from *helios* (the sun) and *anthos* (a flower), has the same meaning as the English name Sunflower, which it is popularly supposed to have been given these flowers from a supposition that they follow the sun by day, always turning towards its direct rays. But since the word 'Sunflower' existed in English literature before the introduction of *H. annuus*, or at any rate before its general diffusion in English gardens, it is obvious that some other flower must have been intended. The Marigold (*Calendula officinalis*) is considered by Dr. Prior to have been the plant described by Ovid as turning to the sun, likewise the *solsæce* of the Anglo-Saxon, a word equivalent to *solsequium* (sun-following). The better explanation for the application of the name to a flower is its resemblance to 'the radiant beams of the sun.'

In Peru, this flower was much reverenced by the Aztecs, and in their temples of the Sun, the priestesses were crowned with Sunflowers and carried them in their hands. The early Spanish conquerors found in these temples numerous representations of the Sunflower wrought in pure gold.

In some of the old Herbals we find the Rock-rose (*Helianthemum vulgare*) also termed Sunflower, its flowers opening only in the sunshine. The so-called 'Pigmy sunflower' is *Actinella grandiflora*, a pretty perennial 6 to 9 inches high, from the Colorado mountains.

The Sunflower is valuable from an *economic*, as well as from an ornamental point of view. Every part of the plant may be utilized for some economic purpose. The *leaves* form a cattle-food and the *stems* contain a fibre which may be used successfully in making paper. The *seed* is rich in oil, which is said to approach more nearly to olive oil than any other vegetable oil known and to be largely used as a substitute. In pre-war days, Sunflower seed was sometimes grown in this country, especially on sewage farms, as an economical crop for pheasants, as well as poultry. The *flowers* contain a yellow dye.

One of the many effects of the War in its relation to agriculture was the increase in the use of the Sunflower.

It forms one of the well-known crops in Russia, Spain, France, Germany, Italy, Egypt, India, Manchuria and Japan. The average acre will produce about 50 bushels of merchantable seeds, and each bushel yields approximately 1 gallon of oil, for which there is a whole series of important uses.

The oil is produced mainly in Russia, but to an increasing extent also in Roumania, Hungary, Bulgaria and Poland. In 1913 some 180,000 tons of oil were produced, practically all of which was consumed locally.

The oil pressed from the seeds is of a citron yellow colour and a sweet taste and is considered equal to olive oil or almond oil for table use. The resulting oil-cake when warm pressed, yields a less valuable oil which is used largely for technical purposes, such as soap-making, candle-making and in the art of wool-dressing. As a drying oil for mixing paint, it is equal to linseed oil and is unrivalled as a lubricant.

The residue after the oil is expressed forms an important cattle-food. This oil-cake is relished by sheep, pigs, pigeons, rabbits and poultry.

The seed makes excellent chicken-food and feeding fowls on bruised Sunflower seeds is well known to increase their laying power.

The seeds of the large-seeded varieties are also much liked by Russians and are sold in the street as are chestnuts in this country. Big bowls of Sunflower seeds are to be seen in the restaurants of railway stations, for people to eat. Indian natives are also fond of the seeds.

Roasted in the same manner as coffee, they make an agreeable drink, and the seeds have been used in Portugal and Russia to make a wholesome and nutritious bread.

The pith of the sunflower stalk is the lightest substance known; its specific gravity is 0·028, while that of the Elder is 0·09 and of Cork 0·24. The discovery of the extreme lightness of the pith of the stalk has essentially increased the commercial value of the plant. This light cellular substance is now carefully removed from the stalks and applied to a good many important uses, chiefly in the making of life-saving appliances. The pith has been recommended for moxa, owing to the nitre its contains.

¶ *Chemical Constituents.* The black-seeded variety yield between 50 and 60 per cent. of the best grade of oil.

The oil has a specific gravity of from 0·924 to 0·926, solidifies at 5° F., is slightly yellowish, limpid, of a sweetish taste and odourless. It dries slowly and forms one of the best burning oils known, burning longer than any other vegetable oil.

Ludwig and Kromayer obtained a tannin which they called Helianthitanic acid, and gave it the formula $C_{14}H_9O_8$. On boiling with moderately diluted hydrochloric acid, they obtained a fermentable sugar and a violet colouring matter. E. Diek found only small quantities of Inulin, large quantities of Levulin and a dextro-rotatory sugar.

All parts of the plant contain much carbonate of potash.

¶ *Extraction.* For the extraction of the oil, the seeds are bruised, crushed and ground to meal in a five-roller mill, under chilled iron or steel cylinders. The meal, after being packed in bags, is placed in hydraulic presses, under a pressure of 300 atmospheres or more, and allowed to remain under pressure for about seven minutes. All edible oils are thus obtained and are known in commerce as 'cold-drawn oils' or 'cold pressed oils.' As a preliminary operation, the seeds are freed from dust, sand and other impurities by sifting in an inclined revolving cylinder or sieving machine, covered with woven wire, having meshes varying according to the size and nature of the seeds operated upon. This preliminary purification is of the greatest importance. The seeds are then passed through a hopper over the rollers, which are finely grooved, so that the seed is cut up whilst passing in succession between the first and second rollers in the series, then between the second and the third, and so on to the last, when the grains are sufficiently bruised, crushed and ground. The distance between the rollers can be easily regulated, so that the seed leaving the bottom roller has the desired fineness. The resulting more or less coarse meal is either expressed in this state, or subjected to a preliminary heating, according to the quality of the product to be manufactured. The oil exuding in the cold dissolves the smallest amount of colouring matter, etc., and hence has suffered least in its quality.

By pressing in the cold, only part of the oil or fat is recovered. A further quantity is obtained by pressing the seed meal at a somewhat elevated temperature, reached by warming the crushed seeds either immediately after they leave the five-roller mill, or after the 'cold-drawn oil' has been taken off. The cold pressed cakes are first disintegrated, generally under an edge-runner. This oil is of a second-grade quality.

Vertical hydraulic presses are at present almost exclusively in use, the Anglo-American type of press being most employed. It represents an open press, fitted with a number (usually sixteen) of iron press plates, between which the cakes are inserted by hand. A hydraulic ram then forces the table carrying the cakes against a press-head and the exuding oil flows down the sides into a tank below.

According to the care exercised by the manufacturer in the range of temperature to which the seed is heated, various grades of oils are obtained.

¶ *Cultivation.* In growing crops of the Sunflower, various methods of planting and spacing are recommended in different countries. It is best, says a scientific American authority, to plant in rows running noith and south, the seeds to be placed 9 inches apart, in rows 30 inches apart.

But in this country, instead of sowing in the open, the most successful growers sow in boxes, or singly in pots under glass, afterwards planting the seedlings out in ground that has been well prepared and enriched with manure. Not that rich soil is essential, practically any kind of soil is suitable so long as it is open to sun and light and splendid returns of seed have been obtained from waste land without any preparation beyond digging the soil.

A well-tilled soil is, however, desirable for successful Sunflower cultivation, preferably with not too much clay in its composition. It should be well ploughed in the autumn and harrowed in the spring. A certain depth is necessary, as the roots will spread from 12 inches to 15 inches in each direction.

In the latter years of the War, the Ministry of Food and the Food Production Department supplied full information as to cultivation and harvesting and undertook to purchase the ripened seed in quantities of ¼ cwt. and upwards: they were used in the manufacture of margarine and other essential fats used in the making of munitions.

The seed should be sown thinly in boxes in March and when the plants have made three or four leaves, they should be potted off into small pots and grown on if possible in gentle heat. Where no heat is available, a cold frame is the next best thing. Provided that frost can be excluded, a cool, unheated glasshouse may be used.

When established, they should be gradually hardened off for planting out in May, after all danger of late spring frosts is past.

Suitable compost for seeds and potting off is: 1 part leaf mould, 1 part sand, 2 parts loam. If this is not available, any good garden soil will do and it need not be very finely sifted. The seeds germinate readily and grow very rapidly.

Ordinary farmyard manure should be dug into the soil at the rate of 3 cwt. per rod, as they are gross feeders. The Sunflower plants should be planted 3 feet apart between the rows and 2 feet from plant to plant in good soils, and slightly closer on poor soils.

An application of superphosphate before or at the time of planting, at the rate of 1½ oz. per square yard will encourage early maturing of the seed.

It is of interest to note that the plant assimilates a large quantity of potash and therefore it must not be planted in the same soil the second year.

Seeds should not be sown *in the open* until late in April, only a sunny border being chosen.

The Food Production Department advised cultivators who intended growing largely for munitions to sow seed early in May, in drills 1 to 1½ inch deep and stated the amount of seed required to be at the rate of 1 oz. to 8 rods, or 1¼ lb. per acre.

In exposed positions, the plants will require support and this is best done by placing a good strong stake each end and one in centre of row, and running a length of wire or thick string from stake to stake and tying the plants to this loosely.

¶ *Harvesting*. No more attention will be needed until the heads commence to ripen, when they should be looked to daily, as the seed soon falls if left too long and also, as the seed ripens, garden pests of the larger sort, birds and squirrels in particular, are always troublesome.

Some growers prevent the loss caused by the attacks of birds to whom the seeds are particularly attractive and by the shaking out of the ripe seeds, by surrounding the heads with bags of rough muslin, but this can only be done when growing on a small scale. With a large plantation, scare away birds by any of the usual methods.

It is, of course, impossible to say exactly when the harvesting should commence. Everything depends upon climatic conditions. If the weather is warm and dry, the best plan is to leave the plants alone, so that the ripening process can be carried out naturally, the heads being cut when about to shed their seeds. In a fine autumn, Sunflower seed will ripen well in the open and the best results are got when the seed can thus be allowed to mature.

When the head shrivels and the seeds are ripe, cut the plants at the ground level, standing them with their heads uppermost, like shocks or sheaves of corn. When the heads are thoroughly dry, cut them off and thresh out the remaining seeds by standing each head on its side and hammering it with a mallet. Store the seeds in bags, in a dry place.

If the weather is dull or wet, unfavourable for ripening of the seed out-of-doors, hasten the ripening by cutting the plants at ground level as soon as the seeds are plump.

Stand them shock-wise, if possible under cover, in a damp-proof outside house, barn or room, and wind being as good a drying agent as the sun, see that the store is well ventilated and leave windows and doors wide open when the weather is propitious. When the heads shrivel, cut them off and complete drying in a very slow oven. Place the heads in single layers on the shelves of the oven in the evening, leaving the door slightly open. Remove them when the fire is made up in the morning and replace them in the evening.

If a kiln or hop oast is available, it may be used for finishing off the drying, but if the seeds are exposed to a high temperature, they will be useless for next year's sowing.

The important things to remember are that the seeds are not ready if they cannot be removed from the heads without difficulty, and they will not keep very long if not dry when stored.

In Russia, where Sunflowers are extensively grown for human food the method adopted by the peasants for removing the seed from the heads is interesting. A wooden disk is made, through which nails are hammered in rows radiating from the centre. The disk is attached to a handle and the seed-head is held in contact with the nails when the disk is turned, with the result that the seed, which is collected in sacks, is raked out very quickly. The disk is so arranged that one man can hold the seed-head in position and at the same time turn the handle to extract the seeds.

The Mammoth or Giant Sunflower, which comes from Russia and is called the Russian Sunflower, is the best kind to grow, these being nearly double the size of the ordinary variety. During the War, the only seed available was the American Giant, which was said, however, to be equal to the Russian.

The tall Mammoth Sunflower, bearing heads of an average width of 15 inches, containing 2,000 seeds, yields about 50 bushels an acre, producing 50 gallons of oil and about 150 lb. of oil-cake, the stems giving 10 per cent. of potash.

It has been estimated in Denmark, that the crops of one season in that country would produce 2,000 tons of seed, yielding 350 tons of oil, and about 1,550 tons of oil-cake and oil waste to be used as fodder.

With the exception of Cambridgeshire, the Sunflower grows best in England in the Southern and South-Western counties.

They have been proved to do best on deep, stony soil, and it is an advantage to grow them where bees are kept, as they are much visited by the honey-bee, fertilization of the flowers ensuing.

¶ *Sunflower-seeds as Poultry and Cattle Food.* Sunflower seeds have a high feeding value – the analysis in round figures is 16 per cent. albumen and 21 per cent. fat.

Being so rich in oil, they are too stimulating to use alone and should only be used in combination with other feeding stuffs. Fed with oats in equal quantities, they make a perfectly balanced ration. Since both of these articles contain a big proportion of indigestible matter, particularly in the husks, grit must on no account be withheld, if the birds are to derive full benefit.

As food for laying poultry, it ought in the opinion of some authorities, not to be used in excess of one-third of the total mixture of corn, owing to its fat-producing properties.

The seeds are palatable to poultry and greedily devoured by them. A very common way to supply the birds with the seeds is to hang up the ripe heads just high enough to compel the chicks to pick them out, for when the heads are thrown into the yard, they are trodden on and wasted.

Sunflower-seed oil-cake is a valuable article for bringing up the feeding value of some of the poultry foods and was specially in demand for this purpose in war-time, when the supply of good cereals ran short. It is more fattening to cattle than Linseed cake, being richer in nitrogenous substances, containing 34 per cent. albumen. As well as being an excellent food for poultry, and also for rabbits, it keeps both horses and cattle in good condition. It is said that cows, fed on Sunflower-seed oil-cake, mixed with bran, will have an increased flow of good, rich milk.

It is largely exported by Russia to Denmark, Sweden and elsewhere for stock feeding.

¶ *Sunflower Plants as Green Food.* With Sunflowers there need be little waste. The green leaves, when gathered young, make a good succulent green food for poultry stock of all ages. They can be finely minced up and added – raw – to the mash for young or adult stock, or they can be boiled and put in the soft food. The leaves are much appreciated by rabbits, horses, cows and other stock.

The dried leaves can be rubbed up or reduced to a meal form and be well scalded prior to inclusion in the mash, and the ripe seeds can also be ground into a meal if desired.

¶ *Litter.* Even the stems and seedless heads need not be wasted where fowls are kept. Many may prefer to use them as fire-kindlers, but they will, when thoroughly dry, come in useful as litter for the laying-houses. When dry, they can be passed through a chaff-cutting machine and be added to the other litter – peat-moss or dried leaves. They need to be made into a scratchable material for hens, but for ducks, the material can be placed deeply in the house as a bedding. Ducks need litter to 'squat' on rather than to scratch in.

¶ *Silage.* The value of the Giant Sunflower as a silage crop is discussed in the March, 1918, number of *The Journal of Heredity*, by F. B. Linfield, the Director of the Montana Agricultural Station. Trials were made of this plant in the higher valleys, where Beans and Maize were not well adapted, owing to the uncertainty of their yield. In three successive years, the yield of the Sunflower varied from 22 to 30 tons of green fodder per acre, being about two and a half times that of Maize, and more than twice as great as that of Lucerne, for the season. It had, moreover, the advantage of so shading the ground as to keep all weeds under. Feeding experiments were made with it, both as a green crop and as silage. Cows were found to eat it as readily as Maize fodder, and control experiments showed that the milk flow was maintained as readily as with the latter crop; nor was there evidence of any taint in the milk. A portion of the Sunflower fodder was put into the silo and fed in the winter, both to cows and fattening steers, with satisfactory results. It matures in the English climate better than Maize, and, consequently, would not be so liable to become sour in the silo and its relatively high oil content would probably render it valuable.

¶ *As Fuel. As Source of Potash for Manure.* Sunflowers, when the stalks are dry, are as hard as wood and make an excellent fire.

Those who undertake to grow Sunflowers should, however, bear in mind that the ash obtained from the plants after the seed has been harvested is, owing to its richness in potash, a manure of considerable value, so that it is really wasteful to use up the dry stems merely on the domestic fire; it is of more advantage to make them up in heaps on the ground, burn them there and save the ash.

At the time of cutting, strip off the leaves and feed them to rabbits or poultry. When the stems are dry and after the seed crop has been gathered, choose a fine day to burn both stems and empty seed-heads.

Of the ash obtained from burning the Sunflower stems and heads (apart from seeds) 62 per cent. consists of potash, and as an acre of Sunflowers produces from 2,500 to 4,000 lb. of top, the total yield of potash is considerable. Allowing 3,000 lb. of top, there would be produced 160 lb. of ashes per acre of crop, which should contain upwards of 50 lb. of potash.

The ash should either be spread at once or stored under cover; if left exposed to rain, the potash will be washed away and the ash rendered of little manurial value. It can be used with advantage for the potato or other root crop in the following year, being spread a little while before the crop is planted, at the rate of from ⅓ to 1 oz. to the square yard.

¶ *As Soil Improver*. The growing herb is extremely useful for drying damp soils, because of its remarkable ability to absorb quantities of water. Swampy districts in Holland have been made habitable by an extensive culture of the Sunflower, the malarial miasma being absorbed and nullified, whilst abundant oxygen is emitted.

¶ *Textile Use*. The Chinese grow this plant extensively, and it is believed that a large portion of its fibre is mixed with their silks.

¶ *A Bee Plant*. The Sunflower is a good bee plant, as it furnishes hive bees with large quantities of wax and nectar.

¶ *As Vegetable*. The unexpanded buds boiled and served like Artichokes form a pleasant dish.

¶ *Medicinal Action and Uses*. The seeds have diuretic and expectorant properties and have been employed with success in the treatment of bronchial, laryngeal and pulmonary affections, coughs and colds, also in whooping cough.

The following preparation is recommended: Boil 2 oz. of the seeds in 1 quart of water, down to 12 oz. and then strain. Add 6 oz. of good Holland gin and 6 oz. of sugar. Give in doses of 1 to 2 teaspoonsful, three or four times a day.

The oil possesses similar properties and may be given in doses of 10 to 15 drops or more, two or three times a day.

A tincture of the flowers and leaves has been recommended in combination with balsamics in the treatment of bronchiectasis.

The seeds, if browned in the oven and then made into an infusion are admirable for the relief of whooping cough.

Tincture of Helianthus has been used in Russia. Kazatchkoft says that in the Caucasus the inhabitants employ the Sunflower in malarial fever. The leaves are spread upon a bed covered with a cloth, moistened with warm milk and then the patient is wrapped up in it. Perspiration is produced and this process is repeated every day until the fever has ceased.

A tincture prepared from the seed with rectified spirit of wine is useful for intermittent fevers and ague, instead of quinine. It has been employed thus in Turkey and Persia, where quinine and arsenic have failed, being free from any of the inconveniences which often arise from giving large quantities of the other drugs.

The leaves are utilized in herb tobaccos.

SWAMP MILKWEED

Asclepias incarnata (LINN.)
N.O. Asclepiadaceæ

Synonyms. Flesh-coloured Asclepias. Swamp Silkweed. Rose-coloured Silkweed
Part Used. Root

¶ *Description*. A herb growing in wet places, flowering in the United States in July and August. Stem erect, smooth, with two downy lines above, about 2½ feet high, branched above, very leafy; leaves opposite, petiolate, oblong, lanceolate, hairy, acute, cordate at base, 4 to 7 inches long, 1 to 2 inches wide; flowers rose-purple, fragrant, disposed in terminal-crowded umbels two to six on a peduncle 2 inches long, consisting of ten to twenty small flowers; pods smooth; rhizome oblong, 1 inch in diameter, knotty, surrounded with rootlets, 4 to 6 inches long, yellow-brown externally, white internally; bark thin, wood with fine medullary rays.

The roots exudes a milky juice with a heavy odour, which is lost in drying.

Solvents: Alcohol, water.

¶ *Constituents*. Asclepiadin (the emetic principle), an alkaloid, two acrid resins, volatile oil, fixed oil, albumen, starch, pectin and glucose.

¶ *Medicinal Action and Uses*. Emetic, diuretic, anthelmintic, stomachic. Swamp Milkweed strengthens the heart in the same way as digitalis and is a quick and certain diuretic. It is given in dropsy as a diuretic in place of digitalis, also in coughs, colds, rheumatism from cold, threatened inflammation of the lungs. Also in diarrhœa, gastric catarrh, certain skin eruptions of an erysipelatous nature and in asthma and dyspnœa. It may also be used with advantage in the early stages of dysentery.

It acts as a vermifuge in doses of 10 to 20 grains.

TAG ALDER. *See* ALDER

TALLOW TREE

Sapium Salicifolium
N.O. Euphorbiaceæ

Synonym. Sapium
Parts Used. Leaves, fruit
Habitat. Tropics of both Hemispheres and cultivated in China and Paraguay

¶ *Description.* It yields a milky juice, which is acrid and even poisonous, the leaves are willow-like, and at their point of union with the stalk have two round glands; the flowers are small and greenish, and grow in terminal spikes, the lower portion bearing the fertile, and the upper ones the sterile flowers. The bark of *Sapium Salicifolium* yields a substance for tanning which is used instead of oak; most modern writers unite this genus with *Stillingia*, from which there are no reliable characters to distinguish it. In America, *S. Biglandulosum* is a source for rubber. Sapium or *S. Indicum* is known in Borneo under the name of Booroo; the leaves are used for dye-

¶ *Preparations and Dosages.* Specific Swamp Milkweed, 1 to 20 minims. The infusion is made of ½ oz. of the powdered root to a pint of boiling water. Dose of the powder, 15 to 60 grains.

ing and staining rotang a dark colour; the acrid milky juice burns the mouth as Capsicum does; the young fruit is acid and eaten as a condiment; the fruit is also used to poison alligators; the ripe fruit are woolly, trilobed capsules, about 1 inch across, three-celled and containing only one seed in each.

S. sebiyerum, the Chinese Tallow Tree, gives a fixed oil which envelops the seeds. The tallow occurs in hard brittle opaque white masses, which consists of palmatin and stearin. The oil is used for lighting and the waste from the nuts for fuel and manure.

See QUEEN'S DELIGHT.

TAMARAC

Larix Americana (MICHX.)
N.O. Coniferæ

Synonyms. American Larch. Black Larch. Hackmatack. Pinus Pendula (Salisb.)
Part Used. Bark
Habitat. Eastern North America

¶ *Description.* The tree has a straight slender trunk with thin horizontal branches growing to 80 to 100 feet high; leaves short, 1 or 2 inches long, very fine, almost thread-form, soft deciduous, without sheaths in fascicles of from twenty to forty, being developed early in the spring from lateral scaly and globular buds which produce growing shoots on which the leaves are scattered. Cones oblong of a few rounded scales widening upward from ½ to 1 inch in length, deep purple colour, scales thin, inflexed on the margin. Bracts elliptical, often hollowed

at the sides, abruptly acuminate, with a slender point and, together with the scales, persistent.

¶ *Medicinal Action and Uses.* The bark used as a decoction is laxative, tonic, diuretic and alterative, useful in obstructions of the liver, rheumatism, jaundice and some cutaneous diseases. A decoction of the leaves has been used for piles, hæmoptysis, menorrhagia, diarrhœa and dysentery.

¶ *Dosage.* 2 tablespoonsful of the bark decoction.

See PINES.

TAMARINDS

Tamarindus Indica (LINN.)
N.O. Leguminosæ

Synonyms. Imlee. Tamarindus officinalis (Hook)
Part Used. The fruits freed from brittle outer part of pericarp
Habitat. India; tropical Africa; cultivated in West Indies

¶ *Description.* A large handsome tree with spreading branches and a thick straight trunk, ash-grey bark, height up to 40 feet. Leaves alternate, abruptly pinnated; leaflets light green and a little hairy, in twelve to fifteen pairs. In cold damp weather and after sunset the leaflets close. Flowers fragrant,

yellow-veined, red and purple filaments, in terminal and lateral racemes. Legume oblong, pendulous, nearly linear, curved, somewhat compressed, filled with a firm acid pulp. Bark hard and scabrous, never separates into valves; inside the bark are three fibres, one down, on the upper concave margin, the

TAMARIND
Tamarindus Indica

TANSY
Tanacetum Vulgare

other two at equal distances from the convex edge. Seeds six to twelve, covered with a shiny smooth brown shell, and inserted into the convex side of the pericarp. There are three varieties of Tamarinds. The East Indian, with long pods containing six to twelve seeds, the West Indian, with shorter pods containing about four seeds, and a third, with the pulp of the pod a lovely rose colour. West Indian Tamarinds are usually imported in syrup, the outer shell having been removed; East Indian Tamarinds are exported in a firm black mass of shelled legumes; the third kind are usually preserved in syrup.

¶ *Constituents.* Citric, tartaric and malic acids, potassium, bitartrate, gum, pectin, some grape sugar, and parenchymatous fibre.

¶ *Medicinal Action and Uses.* Cathartic, astringent, febrifuge, antiseptic, refrigerant. There are no known constituents in Tamarinds to account for their laxative properties; they are refrigerant from the acids they contain, an infusion of the Tamarind pulp making a useful drink in febrile conditions, and the pulp a good diet in convalescence to maintain a slightly laxative action of the bowels; also used in India as an astringent in bowel complaints. The pulp is said to weaken the action of resinous cathartics in general, but is frequently prescribed with them as a vehicle for jalap, etc. Tamarind is useful in correcting bilious disorders; 3 drachms up to 2 oz. of the pulp to render it moderately cathartic are required according to the case. The leaves are some-times used in subacid infusions, and a decoction is said to destroy worms in children, and is also useful for jaundice, and externally as a wash for sore eyes and ulcers. A punch is made from the fruit in the West Indies, mixed with a decoction of borage to allay the scalding of urine. Tamarind Whey, made by boiling 1 oz. of the pulp in 1 pint of milk and then strained, makes a cooling laxative drink. In some forms of sore throat the fruit has been found of service. In Mauritius the Creoles mix salt with the pulp and use it as a liniment for rheumatism and make a decoction of the bark for asthma. The Bengalese employ Tamarind pulp in dysentery, and in times of scarcity use it as a food, boiling the pods or macerating them and removing the dark outer skin. The natives of India consider that the neighbourhood in which Tamarind trees grow becomes unwholesome, and that it is unsafe to sleep under the tree owing to the acid they exhale during the moisture of the night. It is said that no plant will live under the shade of it, but in the Author's experience some plants and bulbs bloomed luxuriantly under the Tamarind trees in her garden in Bengal. The wood is very hard and durable, valuable for building purposes and furnishes excellent charcoal for gunpowder; the leaves in infusion give a yellow dye. Tamarinds in Indian cookery is an important ingredient in curries and chutneys, and makes a delicious sauce for duck, geese and water fowl, and in Western India is used for pickling fish, Tamarind fish being considered a great delicacy.

TANSY

Tanacetum vulgare (LINN.)
N.O. Compositæ

Synonym. Buttons
Part Used. Herb
Habitat. Tansy, a composite plant very familiar in our hedgerows and waste places, is a hardy perennial, widely spread over Europe

¶ *Description.* The stem is erect and leafy, about 2 to 3 feet high, grooved and angular. The leaves are alternate, much cut into, 2 to 6 inches long and about 4 inches wide. The plant is conspicuous in August and September by its heads of round, flat, dull yellow flowers, growing in clusters, which earn it the name of 'Buttons.' It has a very curious, and not altogether disagreeable odour, somewhat like camphor.

It is often naturalized in our gardens for ornamental cultivation. The feathery leaves of the Wild Tansy are beautiful, especially when growing in abundance on marshy ground, and it has a more refreshing scent than the Garden Tansy.

¶ *Cultivation.* Tansy will thrive in almost any soil and may be increased, either in spring or autumn, by slips or by dividing the creeping roots, which if permitted to remain undisturbed, will, in a short time, overspread the ground. When transplanting the slips or portions of root, place therefore at least a foot apart.

The name Tansy is probably derived from the Greek *Athanaton* (immortal), either, says Dodoens, because it lasts so long in flower, or, as Ambrosius thought, because it is capital for preserving dead bodies from corruption. It was said to have been given to Ganymede to make him immortal.

Tansy was one of the Strewing Herbs, mentioned by Tusser in 1577, and was one of the native plants dedicated to the Virgin Mary.

Perhaps it found additional favour as a 'Strewing Herb' because it was said to be effectual in keeping flies away, particularly if mixed with elder leaves.

Parkinson grew Tansy amongst other aromatic and culinary herbs in his garden.

It is connected with some interesting old customs observed at Easter time, when even archbishops and bishops played handball with men of their congregation, and a Tansy cake was the reward of the victors. These Tansy cakes were made from the young leaves of the plant, mixed with eggs, and were thought to purify the humours of the body after the limited fare of Lent. In time, this custom obtained a kind of symbolism, and Tansies, as these cakes were called, came to be eaten on Easter Day as a remembrance of the bitter herbs eaten by the Jews at the Passover. Coles (1656) says the origin of eating it in the spring is because Tansy is very wholesome after the salt fish consumed during Lent, and counteracts the ill-effects which the 'moist and cold constitution of winter has made on people . . . though many understand it not, and some simple people take it for a matter of superstition to do so.'

'This balsamic plant,' says Boerhaave (the Danish physician), 'will supply the place of nutmegs and cinnamon,' and the young leaves, shredded, serve as a flavouring for puddings and omelets. Gerard tells us that Tansy Teas were highly esteemed in Lent as well as Tansy puddings.

From an old cookery book:

'A Tansy.

'Beat seven eggs, yolks and whites separately; add a pint of cream, near the same of spinach-juice, and a little tansy-juice gained by pounding in a stone mortar; a quarter of a pound of Naples biscuit, sugar to taste, a glass of white wine, and some nutmeg. Set all in a sauce-pan, just to thicken, over the fire; then put it into a dish, lined with paste, to turn out, and bake it.'

Culpepper says: 'Of Tansie. The root eaten, is a singular remedy for the gout: the rich may bestow the cost to preserve it.'

Cows and sheep eat Tansy, but horses, goats and hogs refuse to touch it, and if meat be rubbed with this plant, flies will not attack it. In Sussex, at one time, Tansy leaves had the reputation of curing ague, if placed in the shoes.

The Finlanders employ it in dyeing green.

¶ *Parts Used.* The leaves and tops. The plant is cut off close above the root, when first coming into flower in August.

¶ *Constituents.* Tanacetin, tannic acid, a volatile oil, mainly thujone, waxy, resinous and protein bodies, some sugar and a colouring matter.

¶ *Medicinal Action and Uses.* Anthelmintic, tonic, stimulant, emmenagogue.

Tansy is largely used for expelling worms in children, the infusion of 1 oz. to a pint of boiling water being taken in teacupful doses, night and morning, fasting.

It is also valuable in hysteria and in kidney weaknesses, the same infusion being taken in wineglassful doses, repeated frequently. It forms an excellent and safe emmenagogue, and is of good service in low forms of fever, in ague and hysterical and nervous affections. As a diaphoretic nervine it is also useful.

In moderate doses, the plant and its essential oil are stomachic and cordial, being anti-flatulent and serving to allay spasms.

In large doses, it becomes a violent irritant, and induces venous congestion of the abdominal organs.

In Scotland, an infusion of the dried flowers and seeds ($\frac{1}{2}$ to 1 teaspoonful, two or three times a day) is given for gout. The roots when preserved with honey or sugar, have also been reputed to be of special service against gout, if eaten fasting every day for a certain time.

From 1 to 4 drops of the essential oil may be safely given in cases of epilepsy, but excessive doses have produced seizures.

Tansy has been used externally with benefit for some eruptive diseases of the skin, and the green leaves, pounded and applied, will relieve sprains and allay the swelling.

A hot infusion, as a fomentation to sprained and rheumatic parts, will in like manner give relief.

¶ *Preparations and Dosages.* Fluid extract, $\frac{1}{2}$ to 2 drachms. Solid extract, 5 to 10 grains.

In the fourteenth century we hear of Tansy being used as a remedy for wounds, and as a bitter tonic, and Tansy Tea has an old reputation in country districts for fever and other illnesses.

Gerard also tells us that cakes were made of the young leaves in the spring, mixed with eggs,

'which be pleasant in taste and good for the stomache; for if bad humours cleave thereunder, it doth perfectly concoct them and carry them off. The roote, preserved in honie, or sugar, is an especiall thing against the gout, if everie day for a certaine space, a reasonable quantitie thereof be eaten fasting.'

See COSTMARY.

TAPIOCA

Manihot utilissima (POHL.)
Jatropha Manihot (LINN.)
N.O. Euphorbiaceæ

Synonyms. Cassara. Manioc. Manihot. Brazilian Arrowroot. Cassara Starch. Janipha Manihot (Kunth.)

Part Used. The starch grains obtained from the Bitter and Sweet Cassara Root

Habitat. Brazil and tropical America

¶ *Description.* Irregular hard white rough grains possessing little taste, partially soluble in cold water and affording a fine blue colour when iodine solution is added to its filtered solution. Many of the starch grains are swollen by the heat of drying. The root of the Sweet Cassara may be eaten with impunity; that of the Bitter, which is the more extensively cultivated, contains an acrid milky juice, which renders it highly poisonous if eaten in the recent state; this poison is entirely eliminated in the process of washing and drying for the production of Tapioca.

The name 'Tapioca' is that used by the Brazilian Indians.

¶ *Medicinal Action and Uses.* A nutritious diet for invalids; is baked into bread by the natives of Central America; it is used to adulterate arrowroot.

¶ *Other Species.*

Arum arrowroot derived from *Arum Dracunculus* (see ARUM).

East India arrowroot, or Aircuma arrowroot, is derived from the tubers of *Aircuma angustifolia* and *C. Leucophiza*, belonging, like the true arrowroot, to the order Marantaceæ, according to some botanists, and by others assigned to the same order as the ginger, viz. Zingiberaceæ.

See MANDIOCA.

TARRAGON

Artemisia Dracunculus (LINN.)
N.O. Compositæ

Synonyms. Little Dragon, Mugwort (*French*) Herbe au Dragon

Parts Used. Leaves, herb

Tarragon, a member of the Composite tribe, closely allied to Wormwood, is a perennial herb cultivated for the use of its aromatic leaves in seasoning, salads, etc., and in the preparation of Tarragon vinegar.

It grows to a height of about 2 feet and has long, narrow leaves, which, unlike other members of its genus, are undivided. It blossoms in August, the small flowers, in round heads, being yellow mingled with black, and rarely fully open. The roots are long and fibrous, spreading by runners.

Tarragon is more common in Continental than in English cookery, and has long been cultivated in France for culinary purposes.

The name Tarragon is a corruption of the French *Esdragon*, derived from the Latin *Dracunculus* (a little dragon), which also serves as its specific name. It was sometimes called little Dragon Mugwort and in French has also the name *Herbe au Dragon*. To this, as to other Dragon herbs, was ascribed the faculty of curing the bites and stings of venomous beasts and of mad dogs. The name is practically the same in most countries.

One of the legends told about the origin of Tarragon, which Gerard relates, though without supporting it, is that the seed of flax put into a radish root, or a sea onion, and set in the ground, will bring forth this herb.

¶ *Cultivation.* Two kinds of Tarragon are cultivated in kitchen gardens. The French

Tarragon, with very smooth, dark green leaves and the true Tarragon flavour, which is a native of the South of Europe, and Russian Tarragon, a native of Siberia, with less smooth leaves of a fresher green shade and somewhat lacking the peculiar tartness of the French variety.

As Tarragon rarely produces fertile flowers, either in England or France, it is not often raised by seed, but it may be readily propagated by division of roots in March or April, or by cuttings struck when growth is commencing in spring or later in the summer, under a hand-glass, placed outside. A few young plants should be raised annually to keep up a supply.

It loves warmth and sunshine and succeeds best in warm, rather dry situations, and a little protection should also be afforded the roots through the winter, as during severe frost they are liable to be injured. Both varieties need a dry, rather poor soil, for if set in a wet soil, they are likely to be killed by our winter.

The green leaves should be picked between Midsummer and Michaelmas. The foliage may also be cut and dried in early autumn for use in a dry state afterwards. The beds should then be entirely cut down and top-dressed, to protect from frost. If green leaves are required during winter, a few roots should be lifted in the autumn and placed in heat: it will only need a small quantity to maintain a succession.

If the herb is required dried, for winter use, gather in August, choosing a fine day, in the morning after the sun has dried off the dew. Cut off close above the root and reject any stained or insect-eaten leaves. Tie in bunches – about six stalks in a bunch – spread out fanwise, so that the air may penetrate freely to all parts and hang over strings, either on a hot, sunny day, in the open, but in half-shade, or indoors, in a sunny room, or failing sun, in a well-ventilated room by artificial heat, care being taken that the window be left open by day, so that there is a free current of air and the moisture-laden air may escape. If dried in the open, bring in before there is any risk of damp from dew or showers. A disused green-house may be used as drying-shed, provided that the glass is shaded and that there is no tank in the house to cause steaming. Heating may be either by pipes or by any ordinary coke or anthracite stove, should sun fail, but ventilation is in all cases essential. The drying temperature for aromatic herbs should never exceed 80°.

The bunches of herbs should be of uniform size and length, to facilitate packing, and when quite dry and crisp, must be packed away at once, in airtight boxes or tins, otherwise moisture will be re-absorbed from the air.

¶ *Medicinal Action and Uses.* John Evelyn says of Tarragon: ' 'Tis highly cordial and friend to the head, heart and liver.'

In Continental cookery its use is advised to temper the coolness of other herbs in salads. The leaves, which have a fragrant smell in addition to their aromatic taste, make an excellent pickle.

Fresh Tarragon possesses an essential volatile oil, chemically identical with that of Anise, which becomes lost in the dried herb.

To make Tarragon vinegar, fill a wide-mouthed bottle with the freshly-gathered leaves, picked just before the herb flowers, on a dry day. Pick the leaves off the stalks and dry a little before the fire. Then place in a jar, cover with vinegar, allow to stand some hours, then strain through a flannel jelly bag and cork down in the bottles. The best white vinegar should be used.

Tarragon vinegar is the only correct flavouring for Sauce Tantare, but must never be put into soups, as the taste is too strong and pungent. French cooks usually mix their mustard with Tarragon vinegar.

Russian Tarragon is eaten in Persia to induce appetite.

The root of Tarragon was formerly used to cure toothache.

See MUGWORT, WORMSEED.

TEA

Camellia Thea (LINK.)
N.O. Camelliaceæ

Synonyms. Thea sinensis (Sims). Thea Veridis. Thea bohea. Thea stricta Jassamica. Camellia theifera (Griff.)

Part Used. Dried leaf

Habitat. Assam; cultivated in Ceylon, Japan, Java, and elsewhere where climate allows

¶ *Description.* A small evergreen shrub cultivated to a height of 7 to 8 feet, but growing wild up to 30 feet high, much branched. Bark rough, grey. Leaves dark green, lanceolate or elliptical, on short stalks, blunt at apex, base tapering, margins shortly serrate, young leaves hairy, older leaves glabrous. Flowers solitary or two or three together on short branchlets in the leaf axils, somewhat drooping, on short stalks with a few small bracts, 1 to 1½ inches wide; sepals five, imbricate, slightly united below, ovate or rounded, blunt smooth, persistent; petals usually five or up to nine, unequal, strongly rounded, concave, spreading, white, caducous; stamens indefinite, adherent to petals at base in two rows, filaments flexuose, half the length of petals; anthers large, versatile; ovary small, free, conical, downy, three-celled with three or four pendulous ovules in each cell; styles three distinct or combined at base, slender simple stigmas. Fruit a smooth, flattened, rounded, trigonous three-celled capsule; seed solitary in each cell; size of a small nut.

It was formerly supposed that black and green tea were the produce of distinct plants, but they are both prepared from the same plant. Green tea is prepared by exposing the gathered leaves to the air until superfluous moisture is eliminated, when they are roasted over a brisk wood fire and continually stirred until they become moist and flaccid; after this they pass to the rolling table, and are rolled into balls and subjected to pressure, which twists them and gets rid of the moisture; they are then shaken out on flat trays, again roasted over a slow and steady charcoal fire, and kept in rapid motion for an hour to an hour and a half, till they assume a dullish green colour. After this they are winnowed, screened, and graded into different varieties. With black tea, the gathered leaves are exposed to the air for a longer period, then gathered up and tossed until soft and flaccid, and after further exposure, roasted in an iron pan for about five minutes. After rolling and pressing, they are shaken out, exposed to the outer air for some hours, re-roasted for three or four minutes, re-rolled, spread out in baskets and exposed to the heat of a charcoal fire for five or six minutes and then rolled for the third time and again heated, and finally dried in baskets over charcoal fires, from which process they become black in colour. China is the great tea-producing country, over four million acres of ground being devoted to its cultivation. In India also it is a very important product.

TEAZLES

The Fuller's Thistle was an old name for the Teazle, of which there are three varieties in this country, *Dipsacus Fullonum*, the FULLER'S TEAZLE, the COMMON TEAZLE (*D. sylvestris*), and the SMALL TEAZLE (*D. pilosus*), a distinct species sometimes found in moist hedgerows, but not generally distributed, being in height, shape of its flower-heads and form of the foliage, quite distinct from the two first named species and having

¶ *Constituents*. Caffeine (theine), tannin (10 to 20 per cent. gallotannic acid), boheic acid, volatile oil, aqueous extract, protein wax, resin, ash and theophylline.

¶ *Medicinal Action and Uses*. Stimulant, astringent. It exerts a decided influence over the nervous system, generally evinced by a feeling of comfort and exhilaration; it also causes unnatural wakefulness when taken in quantity. Taken moderately by healthy individuals it is harmless, but in excessive quantities it will produce unpleasant nervous and dyspeptic symptoms, the green variety being decidedly the more injurious. Tea is rarely used as a medicine, but, the infusion is useful to relieve neuralgic headaches.

N.O. Dipsaceæ

more the habit of a Scabious than of a Teazle.

Many botanists consider the Fuller's Teazle only a variety of the Common Wild Teazle, in which the spines of the flower-heads are strongly developed into a hooked form, a feature preserved by cultivation and apt to disappear by neglect, or on poor soil, causing it to relapse into the ordinary wild variety.

TEAZLE, COMMON

Dipsacus sylvestris
N.O. Dipsaceæ

Synonyms. Venus' Basin. Card Thistle. Barber's Brush. Brushes and Combs. Church Broom

Parts Used. Root, heads

Habitat. The Common Teazle is to be found on waste land, in hedgerows and dykesides, mainly in the south of England, being rarer in the north

¶ *Description*. It is a biennial, with a tall, rigid, prickly, furrowed stem, generally attaining the height of 4 or 5 feet, bearing cylindrical flower-heads, globular when young, but lengthening out to a cone-like shape when in full flower. The whole plant is very harsh and prickly to the touch.

For some distance below the head, the stems are bare except for prickles, then small pairs of leaves appear, joined directly by their bases to the main stem, with a shining, white midrib, on the back of which are many prickles. In the lower and larger pairs of leaves the bases are joined round the stem and form deep cups, which are capable of holding dew and rain. This conspicuous feature has earned the plant its older name of Venus' Basin, and it was held that the water which collects there acquired curative properties. It was regarded as a remedy for warts, and was also used as a cosmetic and an eye-wash. The generic name of the plant, *Dipsacus*, also refers to this peculiarity in

structure, being derived from the Greek verb, *to be thirsty*.

The English name, Teazle, is from the Anglo-Saxon *tæsan*, signifying to tease cloth, and refers to the use of the flower-heads by cloth-workers. These heads are a mass of semi-stiff spines, the spines longest at the top of the head, each head being enclosed by curving, narrow, green bracts, set with small prickles, arising in a ring at the base of the head and following the line of the head, though a little outside it, curved inward at the tip. When the head commences to flower, the purple petals of the floret show in a ring about one-third of the way down and then spread upward and downwards simultaneously.

¶ *Medicinal Action and Uses*. Culpepper tells us that the medicinal uses of both the Wild and Fuller's Teazle are the same, and that 'the roots, which are the only parts used, are said to have a cleansing faculty.' He refers to the use of the water in the leaf-basins as a cosmetic and eye-wash, and tells us, on the authority of Dioscorides, that an ointment made from the bruised roots is good, not only for warts and wens, but also against cankers and fistulas.

Other old writers have recommended an infusion of the root for strengthening the stomach and creating an appetite. Also for removing obstructions of the liver, and as a remedy for jaundice.

Lyte, in his translation of Dodoens, 1586, says that the small worms found often within the heads 'do cure and heale the quartaine ague, to be worne or carried about the necke or arme,' a theory which Gerard contemptuously discards, from his own personal experience.

But the principal use of the Teazle, dating from long before Gerard's time, still remains unchallenged, and that is for wool 'fleecing,' or raising the nap on woollen cloth. The cultivated variety, *D. Fullonum*, Gerard's 'tame Teasell' is used, because, as already mentioned, its spines are crooked, not straight. These heads are fixed on the rim of a wheel, or on a cylinder, which is made to revolve against the surface of the cloth to be 'fleeced,' thus raising the nap. No machine has yet been invented which can compete with the Teazle in its combined rigidity and elasticity. Its great utility is that while raising the nap, it will yet break at any serious obstruction, whereas all metallic substances in such a case would cause the cloth to yield first and tear the material.

This particular Teazle is grown largely in the west of England, and also imported from France, Germany, Italy, Africa and America, to meet the needs of our manufacturers. One large firm uses 20,000 Teazle heads in a year.

The heads are cut as soon as the flowers wither, about 8 inches of stem remaining attached to them, and they are then dried and sorted into qualities.

The arms of the Clothworkers' Company are three Teazle-heads.

Closely allied to the Teazle, though very different in appearance, is the Scabious, also belonging to the natural order Dipsaceæ, a family of plants having affinities with the large order Compositæ, to which the Thistles belong.

See KNAPWEED, CENTAURY, STAR THISTLE, SCABIOUS.

THAPSIA

Thapsia Garganica
N.O. Umbelliferæ

Synonym. Drias
Habitat. Southern Europe, from Spain to Greece, also Algeria

¶ *Description.* The plant was well known to the Ancients who gave it its peculiar name, believing it to be obtained originally from the Isle of Thapsus. It is considered by the Algerians to be a specific against pain, every part of the plant being efficacious, though deadly poisonous to Camels. The root is a strong purgative. Thapsia Silphion is thought to be identical with *Thapsia Garganica*, is found on the mountains near the site of Ancient Cyrene, and is said to have yielded the gum resin to the Ancients as *Laser Cyrenaicum* or *Asa Dulces*, the Greek name being *Silphion*. Representations of it occur on Cyrene coins.

¶ *Medicinal Action and Uses.* Theophrastus speaks of the purgative and emetic properties of the root, and modern French doctors recognize its value and include it in their Codex as *Resin Thapsiæ*. An extract is made from the bark of the root with alcohol, the moisture is evaporated and made into a plaster with 7 per cent. of the resin combined with yellow wax, turps and colophony. Great caution has to be exercised in unpacking the commercial bales of the roots because the dust or powder arising in the process causes itching and swelling of the face and hands. The French Thapsia plaster is a very drastic counter-irritant, creating much inflammation with an eczematous eruption (and intolerable itching) which leaves scars. Another variety, *T. Villosa*, also contains in its root a vesicant resin which acts more gently than *T. Garganica*.

THISTLES

N.O. Compositæ

Thistle is the old English name – essentially the same in all kindred languages – for a large family of plants occurring chiefly in Europe and Asia, of which we have fourteen species in Great Britain, arranged under the botanical groups Carduus, Carlina, Onopordon and Carbenia, or Cnicus.

In agriculture the Thistle is the recognized sign of untidiness and neglect, being found not so much in barren ground, as in good ground not properly cared for. It has always been a plant of ill repute among us; Shakespeare classes 'rough Thistles' with 'hateful Docks,' and further back in the history of our race we read of the Thistle representing part of the primeval curse on the earth in general, and on man in particular, for – 'Thorns also and Thistles shall it bring forth to thee.'

Thistles will soon monopolize a large extent of country to the extinction of other plants, as they have done in parts of the American prairies, in Canada and British Columbia, and as they did in Australia, till a stringent Act of Parliament was passed, about twenty years ago, imposing heavy penalties upon all who neglected to destroy Thistles on their land, every man being now compelled to root out, within fourteen days, any Thistle that may lift up its head, Government inspectors being specially appointed to carry out the enforcement of the law.

The growth of weeds in Great Britain, having, in the opinion of many, also reached disturbing proportions, it is now proposed to enact a similar law in this country, and the Smallholders' Union is bringing forward a 'Bill to prevent the spread of noxious weeds in England and Wales,' the provisions being similar to the Australian law – weed-infested roadsides, as well as badly-cleared cultivated land, to come within the scope of the enactment.

Among the thirteen noxious weeds enumerated in the proposed Bill, the name of Thistle is naturally to be found. And yet in medicine Thistles are far from useless.

When beaten up or crushed in a mill to destroy the prickles, the leaves of all Thistles have proved excellent food for cattle and horses. This kind of fodder was formerly used to a great extent in Scotland before the introduction of special green crops for the purpose. The young stems of many of the Thistles are also edible, and the seeds of all the species yield a good oil by expression.

Two or three of our native species are handsome enough to be worthy of a place in gardens. Some species which flourish in hotter and drier climates than our own, such as the handsome Yellow Thistles of the south of Europe, *Scolymus*, are cultivated for that purpose, and have a classical interest, being mentioned by Hesiod as *the* flower of summer. This striking plant, crowned with its golden flowers, is abundant throughout Sicily. The Fish-bone Thistle (*Chamæpeuce diacantha*), from Syria, is also a very handsome plant. A grand Scarlet Thistle from Mexico (*Erythrolena conspicua*) was grown in England some fifty years ago, but is now never seen.

THISTLE, HOLY   Carbenia benedicta (BERUL.)

> *Synonyms.* Blessed Thistle. Cnicus benedictus (Gætn.). Carduus benedictus (Steud.)
> *Part Used.* Herb

A Thistle, however, that has been cultivated for several centuries in this country for its medicinal use is known as the Blessed or Holy Thistle. It is a handsome annual, a native of Southern Europe, occurring there in waste, stony, uncultivated places, but it grows more readily in England in cultivation.

It is said to have obtained its name from its high reputation as a heal-all, being supposed even to cure the plague. It is mentioned in all the treatises on the Plague, and especially by Thomas Brasbridge, who in 1578 published his *Poore Man's Jewell, that is to say, a Treatise of the Pestilence, unto which is annexed a declaration of the vertues of the Hearbes Carduus Benedictus and Angelica.* Shakespeare in *Much Ado about Nothing*, says: 'Get you some of this distilled Carduus Benedictus and lay it to your heart; it is the only thing for a qualm. . . . I mean plain Holy Thistle.' The 'distilled' leaves, it says 'helpeth the hart,' 'expelleth all poyson taken in at the mouth and other corruption that doth hurt and annoye the hart,' and 'the juice of it is outwardly applied to the bodie' ('lay it to your heart,' *Sh.*), 'therefore I counsell all that have Gardens to nourish it, that they may have it always to their own use, and the use of their neighbours that lacke it.'

It has sometimes been stated that the herb was first cultivated by Gerard in 1597, but as this book was published twenty years previously it would appear to have been in cultivation much earlier, and in fact it is described and its virtues enumerated in the *Herbal* of Turner in 1568.

¶ *Description.* The stem of the Blessed Thistle grows about 2 feet high, is reddish, slender, very much branched and scarcely able to keep upright under the weight of its leaves and flowerheads. The leaves are long, narrow, clasping the dull green stem, with prominent pale veins, the irregular teeth of the wavy margin ending in spines. The flowers are pale yellow, in green prickly heads, each scale of the involucre, or covering of the head, ending also in a long, brown bristle. The whole plant, leaves, stalks and also the flowerheads, are covered with a thin down. It grows more compactly in some soils than in others.

¶ *Cultivation.* Being an annual, Blessed Thistle is propagated by seed. It thrives in any ordinary soil. Allow 2 feet each way when thinning out the seedlings. Though occurring sometimes in waste places in England as an escape from cultivation, it cannot be considered indigenous to this country. The seeds are usually sown in spring, but if the newly-ripened seeds are sown in September or October in sheltered situations, it is possible to have supplies of the herb green, both summer and winter.

¶ *Part Used*. The whole herb. The leaves and flowering tops are collected in July, just as the plant breaks into flower, and cut on a dry day, the best time being about noon, when there is no longer any trace of dew on them.

About 3½ tons of fresh herb produce 1 ton when dried, and about 35 cwt. of dry herb can be raised per acre.

¶ *Chemical Constituents*. Blessed Thistle contains a volatile oil, and a bitter, crystalline neutral body called Cnicin (soluble in alcohol and slightly also in water) which is said to be analogous to salicin in its properties.

¶ *Medicinal Action and Uses*. Tonic, stimulant, diaphoretic, emetic and emmenagogue. In large doses, Blessed Thistle acts as a strong emetic, producing vomiting with little pain and inconvenience. Cold infusions in smaller draughts are valuable in weak and debilitated conditions of the stomach, and as a tonic, creating appetite and preventing sickness. The warm infusion – 1 oz. of the dried herb to a pint of boiling water – in doses of a wineglassful, forms in intermittent fevers one of the most useful diaphoretics to which employment can be given. The plant was at one time supposed to possess very great virtues against fevers of all kinds.

Fluid extract, ¼ to 1 drachm.

It is said to have great power in the purification and circulation of the blood, and on this account strengthens the brain and the memory.

The leaves, dried and powdered, are good for worms.

It is chiefly used now for nursing mothers, the warm infusion scarcely ever failing to procure a proper supply of milk. It is considered one of the best medicines which can be used for the purpose.

Turner (1568) says:

'It is very good for the headache and the megram, for the use of the juice or powder of the leaves, preserveth and keepeth a man from the headache, and healeth it being present. It is good for any ache in the body and strengtheneth the members of the whole body, and fasteneth loose sinews and weak. It is also good for the dropsy. It helpeth the memory and amendeth thick hearing. The leaves provoke sweat. There is nothing better for the canker and old rotten and festering sores than the leaves, juice, broth, powder and water of Carduus benedictus.'

Culpepper (1652) writes of it:

'It is a herb of Mars, and under the Sign Aries. It helps swimmings and giddiness in the head, or the disease called vertigo, because Aries is the House of Mars. It is an excellent remedy against yellow jaundice and other infirmities of the gall, because Mars governs choller. It strengthens the attractive faculty in man, and clarifies the blood, because the one is ruled by Mars. The continual drinking the decoction of it helps red faces, tetters and ringworm, because Mars causeth them. It helps plague-sores, boils and itch, the bitings of mad dogs and venomous beasts, all which infirmities are under Mars. Thus you see what it doth by sympathy.

'By Antypathy to other Planets: it cures the French Pox by Antypathy to Venus who governs it. It strengthens the memory and cures deafness by Antypathy to Saturn, who hath his fall in Aries which Rules the Head. It cures Quarten Agues and other diseases of Melancholy, and a dust Choller by Sympathy to Saturn, Mars being exalted in Capricorn. Also it provokes Urine, the stopping of which is usually caused by Mars or the Moon.'

Mattheolus and Fuschius wrote also of *Carduus benedictus*:

'It is a plant of great virtue; it helpeth inwardly and outwardly; it strengthens all the principal members of the body, as the brain, the heart, the stomach, the liver, the lungs and the kidney; it is also a preservative against all disease, for it causes perspiration, by which the body is purged of much corruption, such as breedeth diseases; it expelleth the venom of infection; it consumes and wastes away all bad humours; therefore, give God thanks for his goodness, Who hath given this herb and all others for the benefit of our health.'

Four different ways of using Blessed Thistle have been recommended: It may be eaten in the green leaf, with bread and butter for breakfast, like Watercress; the dried leaves may be made into a powder and a drachm taken in wine or otherwise every day; a wineglassful of the juice may be taken every day, or, which is the usual and the best method, an infusion may be made of the dried herb, taken any time as a preventive, or when intended to remove disease, at bed time, as it causes copious perspiration.

Many of the other Thistles may be used as

HOLY THISTLE
Carbenia Benedicta

THORNAPPLE
Datura Stramonium

TOBACCO
Nicotiana Tabacum

substitutes for the Blessed Thistle. The seeds of the Milk Thistle (*Carduus Marianus*), known also as *Silybum Marianum*, have similar properties and uses, and the Cotton Thistle, Melancholy Thistle, etc., have also been employed for like purposes.

THISTLE, MILK

Silybum Marianum

Synonym. Marian Thistle
Parts Used. Whole herb, root, leaves, seeds and hull

The Marian, or Milk Thistle, is perhaps the most important medicinally among the members of this genus, to which all botanists do not, however, assign it, naming it *Silybum Marianum.*

¶ *Description.* It is a fine, tall plant, about the size of the Cotton Thistle, with cut-into root-leaves, waved and spiny at the margin, of a deep, glossy green, with milk-white veins, and is found not uncommonly in hedgebanks and on waste ground, especially by buildings, which causes some authorities to consider that it may not be a true native. In Scotland it is rare.

This handsome plant is not unworthy of a place in our gardens and shrubberies and was formerly frequently cultivated. The stalks, like those of most of our larger Thistles, may be eaten, and are palatable and nutritious. The leaves also may be eaten as a salad when young. Bryant, in his *Flora Dietetica*, writes of it: 'The young shoots in the spring, cut close to the root with part of the stalk on, is one of the best boiling salads that is eaten, and surpasses the finest cabbage. They were sometimes baked in pies. The roots may be eaten like those of Salsify.' In some districts the leaves are called 'Pig Leaves,' probably because pigs like them, and the seeds are a favourite food of goldfinches.

The common statement that this bird lines its nest with thistledown is scarcely accurate, the substance being in most cases the down of Colt's-foot (*Tussilago*), or the cotton down from the willow, both of which are procurable at the building season, whereas thistledown is at that time immature.

Westmacott, writing in 1694, says of this Thistle: 'It is a Friend to the Liver and Blood: the prickles cut off, they were formerly used to be boiled in the Spring and eaten with other herbs; but as the World decays, so doth the Use of good old things and others more delicate and less virtuous brought in.'

The heads of this Thistle formerly were eaten, boiled, treated like those of the Artichoke.

There is a tradition that the milk-white veins of the leaves originated in the milk of the Virgin which once fell upon a plant of Thistle, hence it was called Our Lady's Thistle, and the Latin name of the species has the same derivation.

¶ *Medicinal Action and Uses.* The seeds of this plant are used nowadays for the same purpose as Blessed Thistle, and on this point John Evelyn wrote: 'Disarmed of its prickles and boiled, it is worthy of esteem, and thought to be a great breeder of milk and proper diet for women who are nurses.'

It is in popular use in Germany for curing jaundice and kindred biliary derangements. It also acts as a demulcent in catarrh and pleurisy. The decoction when applied externally is said to have proved beneficial in cases of cancer.

Gerard wrote of the Milk Thistle that

'the root if borne about one doth expel melancholy and remove all diseases connected therewith. . . . My opinion is that this is the best remedy that grows against all melancholy diseases,'

which was another way of saying that it had good action on the liver. He also tells us:

'Dioscorides affirmed that the seeds being drunke are a remedy for infants that have their sinews drawn together, and for those that be bitten of serpents:'

and we find in a record of old Saxon remedies that 'this wort if hung upon a man's neck it setteth snakes to flight.' The seeds were also formerly thought to cure hydrophobia.

Culpepper considered the Milk Thistle to be as efficient as *Carduus benedictus* for agues, and preventing and curing the infection of the plague, and also for removal of obstructions of the liver and spleen. He recommends the infusion of the fresh root and seeds, not only as good against jaundice, also for breaking and expelling stone and being good for dropsy when taken internally, but in addition, to be applied externally, with cloths, to the liver. With other writers, he recommends the young, tender plant (after removing the prickles) to be boiled and eaten in the spring as a blood cleanser.

A tincture is prepared by homœopathists for medicinal use from equal parts of the root and the seeds with the hull attached.

It is said that the empirical nostrum, *antiglaireux*, of Count Mattaei, is prepared from this species of Thistle.

Thistles in general, according to Culpepper, are under the dominion of Jupiter.

THISTLE, SCOTCH   Onopordon Acanthium

Synonyms. Cotton Thistle. Woolly Thistle
Parts Used. Leaves, root

The Scotch Thistle, or Cotton Thistle (*Onopordon Acanthium*) is one of the most beautiful of British plants, not uncommon in England, by roadsides and in waste places, particularly in chalky and sandy soils in the southern counties.

¶ *Description.* It is a biennial, flowering in late summer and autumn. The erect stem, 18 inches to 5 feet high, is very stout and much branched, furnished with wing-like appendages (the decurrent bases of the leaves) which are broader than its own diameter. The leaves are very large, waved and with sharp prickles on the margin. The flowers are light purple and surrounded with a nearly globular involucre, with scales terminating in strong, yellow spines.

The whole plant is hoary with a white, cottony down, that comes off readily when rubbed, and causes the young leaves to be quite white. From the presence of this covering, the Thistle has obtained its popular name of Cotton or Woolly Thistle.

This species is one of the stiffest and most thorny of its race, and its sharp spines well agree with Gerard's description of the plant as 'set full of most horrible sharp prickles, so that it is impossible for man or beast to touch the same without great hurt and danger.'

Which is the true Scotch Thistle even the Scottish antiquarians cannot decide, but it is generally considered to be this species of Thistle that was originally the badge of the House of Stuart, and came to be regarded as the national emblem of Scotland. The first heraldic use of the plant would appear to be in the inventory of the property of James III of Scotland, made at his death in 1458, where a hanging embroidered with 'thrissils' is mentioned. It was, undoubtedly, a national badge in 1503, in which year Dunbar wrote his poetic allegory, 'The Thrissill and the Rose,' on the union of James IV and Princess Margaret of England. The Order of the Thistle, which claims, with the exception of the Garter, to be the most ancient of our Orders, was instituted in 1540 by James V, and revived by James VII of Scotland and Second of England, who created eight Knights in 1687. The expressive motto of the Order, *Nemo me impune lacessit* (which

would seem to apply most aptly to the species just described), appears surrounding the Thistle that occupies the centre of the coinage of James VI. From that date until now, the Thistle has had a place on our coins.

Pliny states, and mediæval writers repeat, that a decoction of Thistles applied to a bald head would restore a healthy growth of hair.

¶ *Medicinal Action and Uses.* The Ancients supposed this Thistle to be a specific in cancerous complaints, and in more modern times the juice is said to have been applied with good effect to cancers and ulcers.

A decoction of the root is astringent and diminishes discharges from mucous membranes.

Gerard tells us, on the authority of Dioscorides and Pliny, that 'the leaves and root hereof are a remedy for those that have their bodies drawn backwards,' and Culpepper explains that not only is the juice therefore good for a crick in the neck, but also as a remedy for rickets in children. It was considered also to be good in nervous complaints.

The name of the genus is derived from the Greek words *onos* (an ass) and *perdon* (I disperse wind), the species being said to produce this effect in asses.

The juicy receptacle or disk on which the florets are placed was used in earlier times as the Artichoke – which is also a member of the Thistle tribe. The young stalks, when stripped of their rind, may be eaten like those of the Burdock.

The cotton is occasionally collected from the stem and used to stuff pillows, and the oil obtained from the seeds has been used on the Continent for burning, both in lamps and for ordinary culinary purposes. Twelve pounds of the seeds are said to produce, when heat is used in expression, about 3 lb. of oil.

The greater number of the Thistles are assigned to the genus *Carduus*. The derivation of the name of this genus is difficult to determine; by some orders it is said to come from the Greek *cheuro*, a technical word denoting the operation of carding wool, to which process the heads of some of the species are applicable.

THISTLE, DWARF   Carduus acaulis

Synonyms. Ground Thistle. Dwarf May Thistle (Culpepper)
Part Used. Root

Carduus acaulis, the Dwarf Thistle, is found in pastures, especially chalk downs, and is rather common in the southern half of

England, particularly on the east side. It is a perennial, with a long, woody root-stock. The stem in the ordinary form is so short that the flowers appear to be sessile, or sitting, in the centre of the rosette of prickly leaves, but very occasionally it attains the length of a foot or 18 inches, and then is usually slightly branched. The leaves are spiny and rigid, with only a few hairs on the upper side, and on the veins beneath, and are of a dark, shining green. The flowers are large and dark crimson in colour, and are in bloom from July to September.

THISTLE, CREEPING PLUME

Synonym. Way Thistle
Parts Used. Root, leaves

Carduus arvensis, the Creeping Plume Thistle, or Way Thistle, has many varieties. It is found in cultivated fields and waste places, and is very common and widely distributed. The root-stock is perennial, creeping extensively and sending up leafy barren shoots and flowering stems about 3 feet high.

THISTLE, WELTED

Synonym. Field Thistle
Parts Used. Root, leaves

Carduus crispus, the Welted Thistle, or Field Thistle, is one of the taller species. The stem, 3 to 4 feet high, is erect, branched, continuously spinous-winged throughout. The leaves are green on both sides, downy on the veins beneath, narrow, cut into numerous lobes and very prickly. The flowers are purplish-crimson, not very large, sometimes clustered three or four together on short stalks. The plant varies much in the degree

THISTLE, WOOLLY-HEADED

Parts Used. Root, leaves

Carduus eriophorus, the Woolly-headed Thistle, is a biennial. The stem is elongated, branched, not winged, short and furrowed, woolly, 3 to 5 feet high. The lowest leaves are very large, often 2 feet long, the stem leaves much smaller, all deeply cut into, with strap-shaped lobes joined together in pairs in the lower ones. The flowers are light reddish-purple, the large woolly heads covered with reddish curled hairs. The

THISTLE, MELANCHOLY

Parts Used. Root, leaves

Carduus heterophyllus, the Melancholy Thistle, is said by some to have been the original badge of the House of Stuart, instead of the Cotton Thistle; it is the *Cluas an fleidh* of the Highlanders, and is more common in Scotland than in England, where it only occurs in the midland and northern counties, growing no farther south than the

The Thistle is very injurious in pastures; it kills all plants that grow beneath it, and ought not to be tolerated, even on the borders of fields and waste places. At one time the root used to be chewed as a remedy for toothache.

Johns (*Flowers of the Field*) calls this the Ground Thistle, and Culpepper calls it the Dwarf May Thistle, and says that 'in some places it is called the Dwarf Carline Thistle.'

Carduus arvensis

The leaves are attenuated, embracing the stems at their base, with strong spines at their margins. The flowers are in numerous small heads, and are pale purple in colour. The plant is bright green, the leaves often white beneath, but varying much in this respect.

Carduus crispus

of soft hairiness, and consequently in the green or whitish colour of the leaves. It is common and generally distributed in England, growing in hedgebanks, borders of fields and by roadsides, occurring less frequently in Scotland. This is one of the least troublesome of the Thistles, being an annual and less abundant than some others. Like the last species, it has many variations of form.

Carduus eriophorus

whole plant is a deep dull green. It flowers in August.

This Thistle is eaten when young as a salad. The young stalks, peeled and soaked in water to take off the bitterness, are excellent, and may be eaten either boiled or baked in pies after the manner of Rhubarb, though Gerard says: 'concerning the temperature and virtues of these Thistles we can allege nothing at all.'

Carduus heterophyllus

northern counties of Wales. It is a perennial, with a long and creeping root. The stems are tall and stout, often deeply furrowed, and more or less covered with a white or cotton-like down. The leaves clasp the stem at their bases and white dark green above, have their under-surfaces thickly covered with white and down-like hairs

Unlike most of the Thistles, the leaves are not continued down the stem at all, and are much simpler in form than the ordinary type of Thistle foliage. Their edges have small bristle-like teeth. The flowerheads are borne singly on long stalks, the bracts that form the involucre being quite destitute of prickles.

Culpepper considered that a decoction of this Thistle in wine 'being drank expels superfluous melancholy out of the body and makes a man as merry as a cricket.'

And he further adds:

'Dioscorides saith, the root borne about one doth the like, and removes all diseases of melancholy: Modern writers laugh at him: *Let them laugh that win*: my opinion is, that it is the best remedy against all melancholy diseases that grows; they that please may use it.'

THISTLE, SPEAR
Carduus lanceolatus

Parts Used. Root, leaves

Carduus lanceolatus, the Spear Thistle, is one of our most striking and common Thistles. It grows in waste places, by roadsides, in pastures and cultivated ground, and is generally distributed over the whole kingdom. The plant is a biennial, the stem 1 to 5 feet high, stout and strong, more or less woolly with narrow, spinous wings. The leaves have the segments elongated or lance-shaped, palmately cleft sometimes in large plants, but short and scarcely cleft at all in weaker specimens, each lobe terminating in a long and acute prickle. They are dark, dull green above, paler beneath, where they are sometimes nearly white from the abundance of hair present. The flowerheads stand singly and are large and conspicuous. The flowers are a beautiful purple and, like those of the Artichoke, have the property of curdling milk.

THISTLE, MUSK
Carduus nutans

Synonym. Nodding Thistle
Parts Used. Root, seeds

Carduus nutans, the Musk Thistle, or Nodding Thistle, occurs in waste places, and is particularly partial to chalky and limestone soils. It is not uncommon in England, but is rare in Scotland, where it is confined to sandy seashores in the southern counties. The stem is erect, 2 to 3 feet high, branched only in larger plants, furrowed, interruptedly winged. The leaves are long, undulated, with scattered hairs on both surfaces, somewhat shiny, green and very deeply cut. This is a common Thistle on a dry soil, and may be known by its large drooping, crimson-purple flowers, the largest of all our Thistle blooms, handsome both in form and colour, and by its faint, musky scent.

The down of this, as of some other species, may be advantageously used as a material in making paper.

THISTLE, MARSH PLUME
Carduus palustris

Synonym. Cirsium palustre
Parts Used. Root, leaves

Carduus palustris, or *Cirsium Palustre*, the Marsh Plume Thistle, is very common in meadows, marshes and bogs, by the sides of ditches, etc., and is generally distributed over the country. It is a biennial, the stem stout, erect, furrowed, 1 to 5 feet high, scarcely branched at all, the branches, when occurring, being much shorter than the main stem, which is narrowly winged, the wings having numerous, long slender spines. The spines on the edges of the narrow, long leaves are similar to those on the wings of the stem. The flowers are dark, dull, crimson purple, small in themselves, but grouped together in large clusters, which distinguish it from most of our thistles, though one or two others exhibit their characteristic in a lesser degree. The plant is a deep dull green, the leaves sometimes slightly hoary beneath.

The stalks of this species are said to be as good as those of the Milk Thistle, and in Evelyn's time were similarly employed.

Culpepper tells us that, in his day, it was 'frequent in the Isle of Ely.'

THISTLE, CARLINE
Carlina vulgaris

Parts Used. Root, leaves

Carlina vulgaris, the Carline Thistle, closely related to the last-named Thistles, but assigned to a special genus, of which it is the sole representative in this country, is found on dry banks and pastures, being rather scarce except on chalk, where it is plentiful. It is rare in Scotland. It is a biennial, the root, a taproot, producing in the first year a tuft of strap-shaped, nearly flat leaves, hoary, especially beneath, very spinuous, but with the spines short and weak. The flower stem, appearing in the second year, is from 3 inches to 2 feet high, purple, not winged, the leaves on it decreasing in length and increasing in width from bottom to top, strongly veined, spinous and waved at the edges. The whole plant is pale green, the leaves rigid and scarcely altering after the plant is dead, except in colour. The flowers are straw yellow, the inner florets purplish, the heads distinguished by the straw-coloured, glossy, radiating long inner scales of the involucre, or outer floral cup. The outer bracts are very prickly. The flowers expand in dry and close in moist weather. They retain this property for a long time and form rustic hygrometers, being often seen on the Continent nailed over cottage doors for this purpose. The presence of the Carline Thistle indicates a very poor soil; it particularly infests dry, sandy pastures.

Culpepper describes the 'Wild Carline Thistle (*C. vulgaris*)' as having flowers 'of a fine purple,' so he must have confused it with another species, or given it a wrong name.

The original name of this plant was Carolina, so called after Charlemagne, of whom the legend relates that

'a horrible pestilence broke out in his army and carried off many thousand men, which greatly troubled the pious emperor. Wherefore he prayed earnestly to God, and in his sleep there appeared to him an angel who shot an arrow from a crossbow, telling him to mark the plant upon which it fell, for with that plant he might cure his army of the pestilence.'

The herb so miraculously indicated was this Thistle. Its medicinal qualities appear to be very like those of Elecampane, it has diaphoretic action, and in large doses is purgative. The herb contains some resin and a volatile essential oil of a camphoraceous nature, like that of Elecampane, which has made it of use for similar purposes as a cordial and antiseptic.

In Anglo-Saxon, the plant was called from the bristly appearance of its flowerheads, *ever throat*, i.e. boar's throat. It was formerly used in magical incantations.

The texture of Carline Thistles is like that of Everlasting Flowers; they scarcely alter their appearance when dead; and the whole plant is remarkably durable.

Other Thistles are the SLENDER-FLOWERED THISTLE (*C. pycnocephalous*) which has stems 2 to 4 feet high, slightly branched, hoary, with broad continuous, deeply-lobed, spinous wings; leaves cottony underneath; heads many, clustered, cylindrical, small; florets pink. It grows in sandy, waste places, especially near the sea: frequent. Biennial.

The TUBEROUS PLUME THISTLE (*C. tuberosus*). The root is spindle-shaped with tuberous fibres; stem 2 feet high, single, erect, round, hairy, leafless above; leaves not decurrent, deeply pinnatifid, fringed with minute prickles; heads generally solitary, large, egg-shaped; florets crimson. Grows only in Wiltshire. Perennial.

The MEADOW PLUME THISTLE (*C. pratensis*). A small plant, 12 to 18 inches high, with fibrous roots; a cottony stem, giving off runners; few leaves, mostly radical, soft, wavy, fringed with minute spines, not decurrent; and generally solitary heads, with adpressed, slightly cottony bracts and crimson florets. Found in wet meadows; not general. Flowers in August. Perennial.

The SOW THISTLE is in no sense a Thistle, but is more nearly allied to the Dandelion.

The Star Thistles belong to the genus *Centaurea*.

See KNAPWEEDS, TEAZLE, SCABIOUS, CORNFLOWER, SOW THISTLE

THISTLE, COMMON STAR

Centaurea Colcitrapa
N.O. Compositæ

Parts Used. Herb, seeds, root
Habitat. South-east England

Centaurea Calcitrapa, the Common Star Thistle, occurs in waste places and by roadsides, but is somewhat rare and chiefly found in south-east England.

¶ *Description.* The stem is branched, not winged, like most of the true Thistles; the lower leaves are much cut into, almost to the midrib, but the uppermost are merely toothed or with entire margins. On the flowerheads are long sharp spines, ½ inch to 1 inch long. The flowers themselves are pale, purplish rose, the ray florets no longer than the central ones. The plant is a dull green, somewhat hairy, and flowers in July.

The specific name of this species is due to the resemblance of the flower-head to the *Caltrops*, or iron ball covered with spikes, formerly used for throwing under horses' feet to lame them on a field of battle.

It is a troublesome weed to agriculturists in certain districts, and is only eradicated by breaking up the ground.

THISTLE, YELLOW STAR

Synonym. St. Barnaby's Thistle
Parts Used. Herb, seeds, root

Centaurea solstitialis, the Yellow Star Thistle, St. Barnaby's Thistle, is rare and hardly to be considered a native, though found in dry pastures in south-east Kent.

¶ *Description.* The plant forms a scrubby bush, 18 inches to 2 feet high, with the lower part of the stems very stiff, almost woody, the branches when young very soft, with broad wings, decurrent from the short, strap-shaped leaves. The lower leaves are deeply cut into, the upper ones narrow and with entire margins. The spines of the flower-heads are very long, ½ inch to 1 inch in length, pale yellow. The whole plant is hoary.

This plant obtains its name from being

Centaurea solstitalis
N.O. Compositæ

¶ *Medicinal Action and Uses.* The seeds used to be made into powder and drunk in wine as a remedy for stone, and the powdered root was considered a cure for fistula and gravel.

supposed to flower about St. Barnabas' Day, June 11 (old style). It is an annual.

¶ *Medicinal Action and Uses.* It has been used for the same purposes as the Common Star Thistle.

Many species of *Centaurea* grow wild in Palestine, some of formidable size. Canon Tristram mentions some in Galilee through which it was impossible to make way till the plants had been beaten down. 'Thistle' mentioned several times in the Bible refers to some member of this family (*Centaurea*), probably *C. Calcitrapa*, which is a Palestinian weed.

See CENTAURY, KNAPWEEDS.

(*POISON*) [1]
THORNAPPLE

Datura Stramonium (LINN.)
N.O. Solanaceæ

Synonyms. Stramonium. Datura. Devil's Apple. Jamestown-weed. Jimson-weed. Stinkweed. Devil's Trumpet. Apple of Peru
Parts Used. Leaves, seeds
Habitat. Throughout the world, except the colder or Arctic regions

The Thornapple is, like the Henbane, a member of the order Solaneæ. It belongs to the genus *Datura*, which consists of fifteen species, distributed throughout the warmer portion of the whole world, the greatest number being found in Central America. Nearly all of them are used locally in medicine, and are characterized by similar properties to those of the official species, *Datura Stramonium*. The plants vary from herbs to shrubs, and even trees.

The question of the native country and early distribution of *D. Stramonium* has been much discussed by botanical writers. It is doubtful to what country this plant originally belonged. Many European botanists refer it to North America, while there it is looked on as a denizen of the Old World. Nuttall considers it originated in South America or Asia, and it is probable that its native country is to be found in the East. Alphonse de Candolle, *Géographie Botanique* (1855), gives it as his opinion that *D. Stramonium* is indigenous to the Old World, probably to the borders of the Caspian Sea or adjacent regions, but certainly not India; it grows wild abundantly in southern Russia from the

borders of the Black Sea eastward to Siberia. Its seeds are very retentive of life, and being often in the earth put on shipboard for ballast, from one country to another, the plant is thus propagated in all regions, and it is now spread throughout the world, except in the colder or Arctic regions. Gypsies are also said to have had a share in spreading the plant by means of its seeds from western Asia into Europe. In the United States, it is now a familiar weed, found everywhere in the vicinity of cultivation, especially about barnyards, timber-yards, docks and waste places, frequenting dung-heaps, the roadsides and commons, and other places where a rank soil is created by the deposited refuse of towns and villages. Where the plant grows abundantly, its vicinity may be detected by the rank odour which it diffuses. Notwithstanding the abundance of the plant in North America, it is cultivated there in order to obtain a drug of uniform quality. The Bureau of Plant Industry, United States Department of Agriculture, has conducted experiments on a large scale: several hundred pounds of leaf were grown and cured by artificial heat in a tobacco barn, proving of excellent quality,

The dried leaves are not regarded as poisonous. – EDITOR.

being marketed at a price in advance of the highest quoted figures.

In Great Britain, it is only occasionally found and can scarcely be considered naturalized here, though it is sometimes met with in the south of England, generally in rich, waste ground, chiefly near gardens or dwellings. It is sometimes grown in private gardens in England as an ornamental plant. It was cultivated in London towards the close of the sixteenth century.

The name Stramonium is of uncertain origin: some authorities claim that it is derived from the Greek name of the madapple. *Stramonia* was the name of *D. metel* at Venice, in the middle of the sixteenth century, and the plant is figured under that title in the great Herbals of Tragus and Fuchsius. *D. Stramonium* seems to have been a later introduction into Europe than *D. metel*, not becoming general till after the middle of the sixteenth century, but as it rapidly spread and became a common plant, the name of the latter was transferred to it.

The generic name, *Datura*, is from the Hindoo *Dhatura*, derived from the Sanskrit, *D'hustúra*, applied to the Indian species *fastuosa*, well known to the mediæval Arabian physicians under the name of *Tatorea*.

¶ *Description*. The Thornapple is a large and coarse herb, though an annual, branching somewhat freely, giving a bushy look to the plant. It attains a height of about 3 feet, its spreading branches covering an area almost as broad. On rich soil it may attain a height of even 6 feet.

The root is very long – thick and whitish, giving off many fibres. The stem is stout, erect and leafy, smooth, a pale yellowish-green in colour, branching repeatedly in a forked manner, and producing in the forks of the branches a leaf and a single, erect flower. The leaves are large and angular, 4 to 6 inches long, uneven at the base, with a wavy and coarsely-toothed margin, and have the strong, branching veins very plainly developed. The upper surface is dark and greyish-green, generally smooth, the under surface paler, and when dry, minutely wrinkled.

The plant flowers nearly all the summer. The flowers are large and handsome, about 3 inches in length, growing singly on short stems springing from the axils of the leaves or at the forking of the branches. The calyx is long, tubular and somewhat swollen below, and very sharply five-angled, surmounted by five sharp teeth. The corolla, folded and only half-opened, is funnel-shaped, of a pure white, with six prominent ribs, which are extended into the same number of sharp-pointed segments. The flowers open in the evening for the attraction of night-flying moths, and emit a powerful fragrance.

The flowers are succeeded by large, egg-shaped seed capsules of a green colour, about the size of a large walnut and covered with numerous sharp spines, hence the name of the plant. When ripe, this seed-vessel opens at the top, throwing back four valve-like forms, leaving a long, central structure upon which are numerous rough, dark-brown seeds. The appearance of the plant when in flower and fruit is so peculiar that it cannot be mistaken for any other native herb.

The plant is smooth, except for a slight downiness on the younger parts, which are covered with short, curved hairs, which fall off as growth proceeds. It exhales a rank, very heavy and somewhat nauseating narcotic odour. This fœtid odour arises from the leaves, especially when they are bruised, but the flowers are sweet-scented, though producing stupor if their exhalations are breathed for any length of time.

The plant is strongly narcotic, but has a peculiar action on the human frame which renders it very valuable as a medicine. The whole plant is poisonous, but the seeds are the most active; neither drying nor boiling destroys the poisonous properties. The usual consequences of the poison when taken in sufficient quantity are dimness of sight, dilation of the pupil, giddiness and delirium, sometimes amounting to mania, but its action varies greatly on different persons. Many fatal instances of its dangerous effects are recorded: it is thought to act ·more powerfully on the brain than Belladonna and to produce greater delirium. The remedies to be administered in case of poisoning by Stramonium are the same as those described for Henbane poisoning, and also Belladonna poisoning. It is classed in Table II of the poison schedule. The pupils have become widely dilated even by accidentally rubbing the eyes with the fingers after pulling the fresh leaves of Stramonium from the plant.

The seeds have in several instances caused death, and accidents have sometimes occurred from swallowing an infusion of the herb in mistake for other preparations, such as senna tea.

Browsing animals as a rule refuse to eat Thornapple, being repelled by its disagreeable odour and nauseous taste, so that its presence is not really dangerous to any of our domestic cattle. Among human beings the greater number of accidents have occurred among children, who have eaten the half-ripe seeds which have a sweetish taste.

The poisonous properties of the seeds are well known in India, where the Datura is abundant, the thieves and assassins not unfrequently administering them to their victims to produce insensibility.

In America it is called the 'Devil's Apple,' from its dangerous qualities and the remarkable effects that follow its administration. When the first settlers arrived in Virginia, some ate the leaves of this plant and experienced such strange and unpleasant effects that the colonists (so we are told) gave it this name by which it is still known in the United States. It is also known very commonly there by the name of 'Jamestown (or Jimson) Weed,' derived probably from its having been first observed in the neighbourhood of that old settlement in Virginia.

There are two varieties of this species of Datura, one with a green stem and white flowers, the other with a dark-reddish stem, minutely dotted with green and purplish flowers, striped with deep purple on the inside. The latter is now considered as a distinct species, being the *D. Tatula* of Linnæus. The leaves are mostly of a deeper green, and have purplish foot-stalks and mid-ribs.

De Candolle considered *D. Tatula* to be a native of Central America, whence it was imported into Europe in the sixteenth century, and naturalized first in Italy and then in South-west Europe, where it is very common. It occurs in England more rarely than *D. Stramonium*, under similar conditions and seems a more tender plant. It is sometimes cultivated here. The properties of both species are the same.

In early times, the Thornapple was considered an aid to the incantation of witches, and during the time of the witch and wizard mania in England, it was unlucky for anyone to grow it in his garden.

¶ *Cultivation.* Thornapple is easily cultivated, growing well in an open, sunny situation. It will flourish in most moderately good soils, but will do best in a rich calcareous soil, or in a good sandy loam, with leaf mould added.

Seeds are sown in the open in May, in drills 3 feet apart, barely covered. Sow thinly, as the plants attain a good size and grow freely from seed. Thin out the young plants to a distance of 12 to 15 inches between each plant in the drill. From 10 to 15 lb. of seed to the acre should be allowed.

The soil should be kept free from weeds in the early stages, but the plants are so umbrageous and strong that they need little care later. If the summer is hot and dry, give a mulching of rotted cow-manure.

The plants may also be raised from seeds, sown in a hot-bed in February or March, or in April in boxes in a cool greenhouse, the seedlings, when large enough, being transferred to small pots, in which they are grown with as much light and air as possible till June, when they are planted in the open. Thornapple transplants readily.

If grown for leaf crop, the capsules should be picked off as soon as formed, as in a wind the spines tear the leaves. Some seed, for propagation purposes, should always be collected from plants kept specially for the purpose.

Though cultivated in this country, on some of the herb farms, such as Long Melford and Brentford, Thornapple was not much grown on a commercial scale before the War, considerable quantities of the dried leaves having always been imported from Germany and Hungary.

¶ *Parts Used, Harvesting and Preparation for Market.* All parts of the Thornapple have medicinal value, but only the leaves and seeds are official. The United States Pharmacopœia formerly recognized leaves, root and seeds, but since 1900 the leaves alone are recognized as official. They are used in the dried state and are referred to as *Stramonium*.

Stramonium leaves are official in all Pharmacopœias. Many require that they be renewed annually. The Belgian excludes discoloured leaves. The Portuguese directs the use of the entire plant except the root, and allows the substitution of *D. Tatula*. To how great an extent it is true that the quality deteriorates on being kept is conjectural.

The commercial drug as imported into Great Britain consists of the leaves and young shoots, collected while the plant is in flower, and subsequently dried, and containing the shrivelled, bristly young fruits, tubular calyx, and yellowish corolla, but the official description, for medicinal purposes, permits of the use of the leaves only.

The leaves should be gathered when the plant is in full bloom and carefully dried. The United States Pharmacopœia considers that they may be gathered at any time from the appearance of the flowers till the autumnal frosts. In this country they are generally harvested in late summer, about August, the crop being cut by the sickle on a fine day in the morning, after the sun has dried off the dew, and the leaves stripped from the stem and dried carefully as quickly as possible, as for Henbane.

The dried leaves are usually much shrivelled and wrinkled, and appear in commerce either loose, or more or less matted together, of a dark-greyish green colour, especially on the upper surface, stalked and often unequal at the base, and are characterized by the very coarse pointed teeth. About 34 parts of dried leaves are produced from 100 parts of fresh leaves.

The fresh leaves, when bruised, emit a fœtid, narcotic odour, which they lose on drying. Their taste is bitter and nauseous. These properties, together with their medicinal virtues, are imparted to water and alcohol and the fixed oils. The leaves if carefully dried retain their bitter taste.

The inspissated juice of the *fresh* leaves was formerly commonly prescribed, but the alcoholic extract is now almost exclusively used.

Stramonium *seeds* are official in a number of Pharmacopœias. The thorny capsules are gathered from the plants when they are quite ripe, but still green. They should then be dried in the sun for a few days, when they will split open and the seeds can be readily shaken out. The seeds can then be dried, either in the sun or by artificial heat.

The dried, ripe seeds are dark brown or dull black in colour, flattened, kidney-shaped in outline, wrinkled and marked with small depressions, and average about ⅛ inch in length. Though ill-smelling when fresh, when dry they have a scarcely perceptible odour till crushed, but a bitter, oily taste. They should not be stored in a damp place, or will mildew. *Kiln-dried* seeds, it should be noted, are no use for cultivation.

The demand for the seed is very limited, but the dry leaves find a ready market. The south of Europe furnishes a quantity, but owing to careless collection and neglect of botanical characters, the South European product is often mixed with other leaves of no value, which are sometimes entirely substituted for it, especially species of *Xanthium*, which has spiny though smaller fruits. Spanish Stramonium which contains no Stramonium at all has been offered in London and Liverpool. The imported commercial Stramonium leaves are also frequently found freely adulterated with those of *Carthamus helenoides*.

¶ *Constituents.* Stramonium *leaves* contain the same alkaloids as Belladonna, but in somewhat smaller proportion, the average of commercial samples being about 0·22 per cent.: the percentage may, however, rise to as much as 0·4 per cent. The mid-rib and footstalk of the leaf contain a far larger proportion than the blade. It is generally considered that the main stems and the root contain little alkaloid, and should, therefore, not be present in the drug. The *American Journal of Pharmacy* (January, 1919) directs attention to the fact that if the stems could be utilized, the cost of labour in harvesting a crop of Stramonium would be only one-fourth or one-fifth of what it is where the leaves alone are gathered, since machinery for the purpose could be employed. Dr. G. B. Koch, of the Biological Laboratories of the H.K. Mulford Co., Philadelphia, has been making careful experiments on the relative value of the stem and root of this plant, and has arrived at the following conclusions:

1. The whole plant, either with or without the root, can be harvested and used for the commercial preparations without fear of the total alkaloid content falling below 0·25 per cent., which is the desired standard of the United States Pharmacopœia.

2. The total mydriatic (pupil-dilating) alkaloids of the leaf and secondary stems when analysed individually, or the leaves with 10 per cent. of the secondary stems, run much higher than the United States Pharmacopœia requirement.

3. Of the whole plant, including stem, root and leaf, the leaf represents about 41 per cent.

4. Excluding the root, the ratio of the leaf to the stem is about 47·5 to 52·3 per cent.

In general it has been found that fresh parts yielded more alkaloid than the dried parts. The alkaloid consists chiefly of hyoscyamine, associated with atropine and hyoscine (scopolamine), malic acid also being present. The Daturin formerly described as a constituent is now known to be a mixture of hyoscyamine and atropine. The leaves also yield 17 to 20 per cent. of ash, and are rich in potassium nitrate, to which, doubtless, part of the antispasmodic effects are due, and they contain also a trace of volatile oil, gum, resin, starch, and other unimportant substances.

Seeds. Except that they contain about 25 per cent. of fixed oil, the constituents of the seeds are practically the same as those of the leaves, though considered to contain a much greater proportion of alkaloid, which renders them more powerful than the leaves. But the presence of the large amount of fixed oil makes it difficult to extract the alkaloids or to make stable preparations and the leaves have, therefore, greatly taken the place of the seeds.

¶ *Medicinal Action and Uses.* Antispasmodic, anodyne and narcotic. Its properties are virtually those of hyoscyamine. It acts similarly to belladonna, though without constipating, and is used for purposes similar to those for which belladonna is employed, dilating the pupil of the eyes in like manner. It is considered slightly more sedative to the central nervous system than is belladonna.

Stramonium is, in fact, so similar to belladonna in the symptoms produced by it in small or large doses, in its toxicity and its general physiological and therapeutic action, that the two drugs are practically identical, and since they are about the same strength in activity, the preparations may be used in similar doses.

Stramonium has been employed in all the conditions for which belladonna is more commonly used, but acts much more strongly on the respiratory organs, and has acquired special repute as one of the chief remedies for spasmodic asthma, being used far more as the principal ingredient in asthma powders and cigarettes than internally. The practice of smoking *D. ferox* for asthma was introduced into Great Britain from the East Indies by a certain General, and afterwards the English species was substituted for that employed in Hindustan. Formerly the roots were much used: in Ceylon, the leaves, stem and fruit are all cut up together to make burning powders for asthma, but in this country the dried *leaves* are almost exclusively employed for this purpose. The beneficial effect is considered due to the presence of atropine, which paralyses the endings of the pulmonary branches, thus relieving the bronchial spasm. It has been proved that the smoke from a Stramonium cigarette, containing 0.25 grams of Stramonium, leaves contains as much as 0.5 milligrams of atropine. The leaves may be made up into cigarettes or smoked in a pipe, either alone, or with a mixture of tobacco, or with cubebs, sage, belladonna and other drugs. More commonly, however, the coarsely-ground leaves are mixed into cones with some aromatic and with equal parts of potassium nitrate, in order to increase combustion and are burned in a saucer, the smoke being inhaled into the lungs. Great relief is afforded, the effect being more immediate when the powdered leaves are burnt and the smoke inhaled than when smoked by the patient in the form of cigars or cigarettes, but like most drugs, after constant use, the relief is not so great and the treatment is only palliative, the causation of the attack not being affected. Accidents have also occasionally happened from the injudicious use of the plant in this manner.

Dryness of the throat and mouth are to be regarded as indications that too large a quantity is being taken.

The *seeds*, besides being employed to relieve asthma in the same manner as the leaves, being smoked with tobacco, are employed as a narcotic and anodyne, generally used in the form of an extract, prepared by boiling the seeds in water, or macerating them in alcohol. A tincture is sometimes preferred. The extract is given in pills to allay cough in spasmodic bronchial asthma, in whooping-cough and spasm of the bladder, and is considered a better cough-remedy than opium, but should only be used with extreme care, as in over-doses it is a strong narcotic poison.

Applied locally, in ointment, plasters or fomentation, Stramonium will palliate the pain of muscular rheumatism, neuralgia, and also pain due to hæmorrhoids, fistula, abscesses and similar inflammation.

¶ *Preparations and Dosages.* Powdered leaves, $\frac{1}{10}$ to 5 grains. Fluid extract leaves, 1 to 3 drops. Fluid extract seeds, 1 to 2 drops. Tincture leaves, B.P. and U.S.P., 5 to 15 drops. Powdered extract, U.S.P., $\frac{1}{8}$ grain. Solid extract, B.P., $\frac{1}{4}$ to 1 grain. Ointment, U.S.P.

Gerard declared that

'the juice of Thornapple, boiled with hog's grease, cureth all inflammations whatsoever, all manner of burnings and scaldings, as well of fire, water, boiling lead, gunpowder, as that which comes by lightning and that in very short time, as myself have found in daily practice, to my great credit and profit.'

It has been conjectured that the leaves of *D. Stramonium* were used by the priests of Apollo at Delphi to assist them in their prophecies, and in the Temple of the Sun, in the city of Sagomozo the seeds of the Floripondio (*D. Sanguinea*) are used for a similar purpose. The Peruvians also prepare an intoxicating beverage from the seeds, which induces stupefaction and delirium if partaken of in large quantities. The Arabs of Central Africa are said to dry the leaves, the flowers, and the rind of the rootlet, which is considered the strongest preparation, and to smoke them in a common bowl, or in a waterpipe. It is esteemed by them a sovereign remedy for asthma and influenza, and although they do not use it like the Indian Datura poisoners, accidents nevertheless occur from its narcotic properties.

Stramonium was at one time esteemed as a sedative in epilepsy, and in acute mania and other forms of active insanity, but its action is very uncertain.

The introduction of Stramonium into medicine is due chiefly to the exertions of Baron Storch, in the latter half of the eighteenth century, who was also instrumental in re-introducing Henbane into modern medicine.

In a recent issue of an American medical journal, the opinion was expressed that Stramonium was a remedy for hydrophobia, the writer saying 'there is no drug so far proven that deserves as thorough and careful a trial in this dread disease as Stramonium.'

The poorer Turks are said to use Stramonium instead of opium, for smoking.

¶ *Other Species.*

In India and the Eastern and West Indian Colonies, the leaves and seeds of *D. fastuosa* var. *alba* are also official, under the name of Datura. They possess similar properties, and are regarded as of equal strength.

D. fastuosa is a small shrub indigenous to tropical India. There are said to be several varieties of this species, and it is generally conceded to be the most toxic of the Indian Daturas. The leaves are ovate and more or less angular, the flowers being mostly purplish, sometimes white.

Of the varieties of *D. fastuosa*, the British Pharmacopœia recognizes that known as *alba*. From it the Thugs prepared the poison *Dhât*, with which they used to stupefy their victims. It is used in India as a criminal poison, the professional poisoners being called *Dhatureeas*.

The drug has a slight, unpleasant odour and a bitter taste. It contains the alkaloid Hyoscine, a resin and a fixed oil, hyoscyamine being also present and a small proportion of atropine.

It is used by the native doctors (India) for the relief of rheumatic and other painful affections.

While this drug produces effects more or less similar to those of belladonna, its precise action has not been clearly determined.

This species of Datura grows in abundance in almost all the islands of the Philippine group, in some localities reaching a height of 6 feet, and might afford a favourable source of atropine and hyoscyamine, though it has not so far been made use of commercially, there being no attempt at cultivation or even systematic collection of the

drug, though attention was drawn to its latent possibilities during the War.

Under the names of *Man t'o lo fa, Wan t'o hua* and *Nau Yeung fa* the Chinese use as a medicine the flowers of the *D. alba*.

D. metel is also an Indian plant and resembles *D. fastuosa*; it differs in that the leaves are heart-shaped, almost entire and downy, and the flowers always white. The leaves contain 0·55 per cent. alkaloid, the seeds 0·5 per cent., all hyoscine.

D. alba or *D. metel* also produce similar effects. The Rajpoot mothers are said to smear their breasts with the juice of the leaves, to poison their newly-born female infants.

D. arborea, a South American species (the Tree Datura), growing freely in Chile, contains about 0·44 per cent. alkaloid, nearly all hyoscine. A tincture of the flowers is used to induce clairvoyance.

D. quercifolia, of Mexico, contains 0·4 per cent. in the leaves and 0·28 per cent. of alkaloids in the seeds, about half hyoscyamine and half hyoscine.

El Bethene, a Datura of the Sahara Desert, is capable of causing delirium, coma and death.

D. Tatula, Purple Stramonium has already been mentioned. It owes its activity to the same alkaloids as *D. Stramonium*, and its leaves are also much used in the form of cigarettes as a remedy for spasmodic asthma.

D. ferox, Chinese Datura, is used in homœopathy.

A tincture is made from the unripe fruit and a trituration of the seeds.

An Old Recipe 'for A Burne'

'Take of the plant called *Thorneaple*, and Elder leaves, 2 good handfuls; pound both leaves and apples very small in A stone mortar; then take a pound of Barow hogs lard watered and putt them altogether in an earthen pan, working them well together; lett itt stand till it begins to hoare [grow musty], and then sett itt over A soft fire, not letting it boyle; then straine it, and putt in fresh herbs; order itt as before; this doe three times; and then keep itt for your use; it will keep seven years.'—(*A Plain Plantain.*)

THUJA. *See* CEDAR

THYME, BASIL

Calamintha acinos
N.O. Labiatæ

Synonyms. Common Calamint. Calamintha officinalis. Calamintha menthifolia. Thymos acinos. Acinos vulgaris. Mountain Mint

Part Used. Herb

Habitat. Rather scarce in England, though fairly generally distributed over the country; it is rare in Scotland and very rare in Ireland

¶ *Description.* This species is found on dry banks and in fields, in chalky, gravelly and sandy soils: a small, bushy herb, its stems 6 to

8 inches high, branching at the base, slender and leafy.

The shortly stalked leaves, ¼ to ½ inch long,

with the veins prominent beneath, are egg-shaped and hairy. The flowers, in bloom in July and August, are ¼ inch long and grow in whorls from the axils of the leaves, like in the preceding species, as well as at the summit of the stem. The corollas are bluish-purple, variegated with white on the lower lip, in the middle of which there is a purple spot. The calyx is distinctly two-lipped, the lower lip bulged at the base and has prominent ribs, fringed with bristly hairs.

The plant varies much in degree of hairiness. It has a pleasant, aromatic smell, somewhat similar, though weaker, than that of Thyme, to which, however, in general appearance, it bears little resemblance.

Basil Thyme was a great favourite with the old herbalists. Gerard enumerates twelve uses to which it can be applied without fear of failure. Among them he states that

'it cureth them that are bitten of serpents; being burned or strewed, it drives serpents away; it taketh away black and blew spots that come by blows or by beatings, making

the skinne faire and white; but for such things, saith Galen, it is better to be laid to greene than dry.'

Externally, its use has been recommended as an addition to warm baths, especially for children, as a strengthener and nerve soother.

The oil, which is very heating, is of service as a rubefacient, applied to the skin in sciatica and neuralgia.

One drop of the oil, on cotton wool, put into a decayed tooth, will alleviate the pain.

The flowering tops are used to flavour jugged hare, etc., they have a milder and rather more grateful flavour than the common Thyme.

Although it has been stated that animals will seldom eat this plant and that rabbits do not touch it, it has been alleged that sheep love to crop its fragrant leaves and that, as a consequence, a fine flavour is imparted to their flesh.

It is said that Wild Thyme and Marjoram laid by milk in the dairy will prevent it being turned by thunder.

THYME, CAT

Teucrium Marum (LINN.)
N.O. Labiatæ

Synonym. Marum
Parts Used. Leaves, root-bark, whole herb

The Cat Thyme, or Marum, is not a British plant, but a native of Spain, though with care it can be grown here and will live through the winter in the open, on a dry soil and in a good situation, when the frosts are not severe, though it is frequently killed in hard winters, if unprotected by mats or other covering.

In the southern countries of Europe, this species of *Teucrium* forms a shrub 3 or 4 feet high, but in England it rarely attains even half that height. It has oval leaves, broader at the base, downy beneath, with uncut margins. The flowers are in one-sided spikes, the corollas crimson in colour.

The leaves and younger branches when fresh, on being rubbed emit a volatile, aromatic smell, which excites sneezing, but in taste they are somewhat bitter, accompanied with a sensation of heat.

¶ *Medicinal Action and Uses.* The plant is supposed to possess very active powers,

having been recommended in many diseases requiring medicine of a stimulant, aromatic and deobstruent quality. It has been considered good in most nervous complaints, the leaves being powdered and given in wine. The powdered leaves, either alone, or mixed with other ingredients of a like nature, when taken as snuff, have been recommended as excellent for 'disorders of the head,' under the name of compound powder of Assarabacca, but lavender flowers are now generally substituted for Cat Thyme.

Cat Thyme is more nearly related to the Germanders and to Wood Sage than to the Thymes.

The bark of the root is considerably astringent and has been used for checking hæmorrhages.

A homœopathic tincture is made from the whole herb, said to be effectual against small thread-worms in children.

THYME, GARDEN

Thymus vulgaris (LINN.)
N.O. Labiatæ

Synonym. Common Thyme
Part Used. Herb

The Garden Thyme is an 'improved' cultivated form of the Wild Thyme of the mountains of Spain and other European countries bordering on the Mediterranean, flourishing also in Asia Minor, Algeria and Tunis, and

is a near relation to our own Wild Thyme (*Thymus serpyllum*), which has broader leaves (the margins not reflexed as in the Garden Thyme) and a weaker odour.

It is cultivated now in most countries with

temperate climates, though we do not know at what period it was first introduced into northern countries. It was certainly commonly cultivated in England before the middle of the sixteenth century, and is figured and described by Gerard.

¶ *Description.* T. *vulgaris* is a perennial with a woody, fibrous root. The stems are numerous, round, hard, branched, and usually from 4 to 8 inches high, when of the largest growth scarcely attaining a foot in height. The leaves are small, only about $\frac{1}{4}$ inch long and $\frac{1}{16}$ inch broad, narrow and elliptical, greenish-grey in colour, reflexed at the margins, and set in pairs upon very small foot-stalks. The flowers terminate the branches in whorls. The calyx is tubular, striated, closed at the mouth with small hairs and divided into two lips, the uppermost cut into three teeth and the lower into two. The corolla consists of a tube about the length of the calyx, spreading at the top into two lips of a pale purple colour, the upper lip erect or turned back and notched at the end, the under lip longer and divided into three segments. The seeds are roundish and very small, about 170,000 to the ounce, and 24 oz. to the quart: they retain their germinating power for three years. The plant has an agreeable aromatic smell and a warm pungent taste. The fragrance of its leaves is due to an essential oil, which gives it its flavouring value for culinary purposes, and is also the source of its medicinal properties. It is in flower from May to August.

There are three varieties usually grown for use, the broad-leaved, narrow-leaved and variegated: the narrow-leaved, with small, greyish-green leaves, is more aromatic than the broad-leaved, and is also known as Winter or German Thyme. The fragrant Lemon Thyme, likewise grown in gardens, has a lemon flavour, and rather broader leaves than the ordinary Garden Thyme, is not recurved at the margins, and ranks as a variety of T. *serpyllum*, the Wild Thyme. It is of a more trailing habit and of still smaller growth than the common Garden Thyme, and keeps its foliage better in the winter, though is generally considered to be not as hardy as the common Thyme. Another variety, the Silver Thyme, is the hardiest of all and has perhaps the best flavour. There is a variety, also, called the Orange Thyme, which Dr. Kitchener, in *The Cook's Oracle*, describes as a delicious herb that deserves to be better known. This and other varieties of Thyme, including the Caraway Thyme, which was used to rub the baron of beef, before it was roasted, and so came to be called 'Herbe Baronne,' are all worth cultivating.

The name Thyme, in its Greek form, was first given to the plant by the Greeks as a derivative of a word which meant 'to fumigate,' either because they used it as incense, for its balsamic odour, or because it was taken as a type of all sweet-smelling herbs. Others derive the name from the Greek word *thumus*, signifying courage, the plant being held in ancient and mediæval days to be a great source of invigoration, its cordial qualities inspiring courage. The antiseptic properties of Thyme were fully recognized in classic times, there being a reference in Virgil's *Georgics* to its use as a fumigator, and Pliny tells us that, when burnt, it puts to flight all venomous creatures. Lady Northcote (in *The Herb Garden*) says that among the Greeks, Thyme denoted graceful elegance; 'to smell of Thyme' was an expression of praise, applied to those whose style was admirable. It was an emblem of activity, bravery and energy, and in the days of chivalry it was the custom for ladies to embroider a bee hovering over a sprig of Thyme on the scarves they presented to their knights. In the south of France, Wild Thyme is a symbol of extreme Republicanism, tufts of it being sent with the summons to a Republican meeting.

This little plant, so familiar also in its wild form, has never been known in England by any familiar name, though occasionally 'Thyme' is qualified in some way, such as 'Running Thyme,' or 'Mother-of-Thyme.' 'Mother Thyme' was probably derived from the use of the plant in uterine disorders, in the same way that 'Motherwort' (*Leonurus Cardiaca*) has received its popular name for use in domestic medicine.

The affection of bees for Thyme is well known and the fine flavour of the honey of Mount Hymettus near Athens was said to be due to the Wild Thyme with which it was covered (probably T. *vulgaris*), the honey from this spot being of such especial flavour and sweetness that in the minds and writings of the Ancients, sweetness and Thyme were indissolubly united. 'Thyme, for the time it lasteth, yieldeth most and best honie and therefor in old time was accounted chief,' says an old English writer. Large clumps of either Garden or Wild Thyme may with advantage be grown in the garden about 10 feet away from the hives.

Though apparently not in general use as a culinary herb among the ancients, it was employed by the Romans to give an aromatic flavour to cheese (and also to liqueurs).

¶ *Cultivation.* Sow about the middle of March or early April, in dry, mild weather, moderately thin, in shallow drills about $\frac{1}{2}$ inch deep, and 8 or 9 inches apart, in good, light soil, in a warm position. Cover in evenly with the soil. Some of the plants may remain where planted, after a thinning for early use, others plant out in the summer. Thyme thrives best with lots of room to spread in. It is well to make new beds annually. Self-sown plants will answer for this where found.

Stocks may also be increased by dividing old roots, or making cuttings, by slipping pieces off the plants with roots to them and planting out with trowel or dibber, taking care to water well. This may be done as soon as the weather is warm enough, from May to September. The old clumps may be divided to the utmost extent and provided each portion has a reasonable bit of root attached, success is assured. The perfume of Lemon Thyme is sweeter if raised from cuttings or division of roots, rather than from seed.

Although Thyme grows easily, especially in calcareous light, dry, stony soils, it can be cultivated in heavy soils, but it becomes less aromatic. It dislikes excess of moisture. To form Thyme beds, choose uncultivated ground, with soil too poor to nourish cereals. If Thyme grows upon walls or on dry, stony land, it will survive the severest cold of this country. If the soil does not suit it very well and is close and heavy, some material for lightening it, such as a little road-sand or sweepings, ensuring reasonable porosity, will be welcomed, and should be thoroughly incorporated – in a gritty soil it will root quickly, but it does not like a close, cold soil about its roots.

According to Gattefosse, the Thyme is 'a faithful companion of the Lavender. It lives with it in perfect sympathy and partakes alike of its good and its bad fortune.' Generally speaking, the conditions most suitable to the growth of Thyme are identical with those favoured by Lavender.

The plant is often overrun by Dodder (*Cuscuta epithymum*). If this happens, cut off the affected plants and burn them, or use a solution of sulphate of iron.

At the close of the summer, as soon as the herbs have been cut sufficiently, the beds should be attended to, all weeds cleared away and the soil well forked on the surface.

In winter, protect the plants from frost by banking up with earth.

Thyme roots soon extract the goodness from the soil, hence whatever is sown or planted afterwards will seldom thrive unless the ground is first trenched deeper than the Thyme was rooted, and is well manured.

The whole herb is used, fresh and dried. Though cultivated in gardens for culinary use, Common Thyme is not grown in England on a large scale, most of the dried

Thyme on the market having been imported from the Continent, mainly from Germany.

Its essential oil is distilled in the south of France, the flowering herb being used for the production of oil of Thyme. In the neighbourhood of Nîmes, the entire plant is used and the distillation is carried on at two periods of the year, in May and June, and again in the autumn. In England, only a comparatively small amount of the essential oil is distilled, but it is considered to be of a high quality. For distilling, the fresh herb should be collected on a dry day, when just coming into flower; the lower portions of the stem, together with any yellow or brown leaves, should be rejected and the herbs conveyed to the distillery as soon as possible.

¶ *Constituents.* Oil of Thyme is the important commercial product obtained by distillation of the fresh leaves and flowering tops of *T. vulgaris*. Its chief constituents are from 20 to 25 per cent. of the phenols Thymol and Carvacrol, rising in rare cases to 42 per cent. The phenols are the principal constituents of Thyme oil, Thymol being the most valuable for medicinal purposes, but Carvacrol, an isomeric phenol, preponderate in some oils. Cymene and Pinene are present in the oil, as well as a little Menthone. Borneol and Linalol have been detected in the high boiling fractions of the oil and a crystalline body, probably identical with a similar body found in Juniper-berry oil.

Two commercial varieties of Thyme oil are recognized, the 'red,' the crude distillate, and the 'white' or colourless, which is the 'red' rectified by re-distilling. The yield of oil is very variable, from 2 per cent. to 1 per cent. in the fresh herb (100 lb. of the fresh flowering tops yielding from ½ to 1 lb. of essential oil) and 2·5 per cent. in the dried herb, the yield of oil from the dried German herb being on the average 1·7 per cent. and from the dried French herb 2·5 to 2·6 per cent. The phenols present in French and German oils consist mainly of Thymol, but under certain conditions the latter may be replaced by Carvacrol. The value of Thyme oil depends so much upon the phenols it contains, that it is important that these should be estimated, as the abstraction of Thymol is by no means uncommon.

Red oil of Thyme is frequently imported and sold under the name of oil of Origanum: it is often adulterated with oils of turpentine, spike lavender and rosemary, and coloured with alkanet root, and is not infrequently more or less destitute of Thymol. *True* oil of Origanum is extracted from Wild Marjoram, *Origanum vulgare*, and other species of *Origanum*.

French oil of Thyme is the most esteemed variety of the oil known. A considerable quantity of Thyme oil is also distilled in Spain, but probably from mixed species of Thyme oil, the origin of Spanish Thyme oil not having been definitely proved; a certain amount is also distilled in Algeria from *T. Algeriensis*. French oil (specific gravity 0·905 to 0·935) contains 20 to 36 per cent. of phenols, chiefly Thymol, on which the value of the oil chiefly depends. Spanish oil contains a much higher percentage of phenols, 50 to 70 per cent., mostly Carvacrol, but sometimes a fairly large proportion of Thymol is present. The production of Thymol or Carvacrol seems to depend on some variation in the soil or climatic conditions which favours the formation of one or the other. The specific gravity of Spanish oil is 0·928 to 0·958.

T. capitans also yields an oil of a specific gravity about 0·900, closely resembling that obtained from *T. vulgaris*. A similar oil is obtained from *T. camphoratus*. A somewhat different oil is obtained from the Lemon Thyme, *T. serpyllum*, var *citriodorus*. This oil has an odour resembling Thyme, Lemon and Geranium. It contains only a very small amount of phenols. Admixture with the oil of *T. serpyllum* does not alter the specific gravity of Thyme oil. *T. mastichina*, the so-called Spanish Wood Marjoram, also yields an oil of Thyme, of a bright yellow colour, turning darker with age and with a camphoraceous odour like Thyme.

¶ *Medicinal Action and Uses.* Antiseptic, antispasmodic, tonic and carminative.

The pounded herb, if given fresh, from 1 to 6 oz. daily, mixed with syrup, has been employed with success as a safe cure for whooping cough. An infusion made from 1 oz. of the dried herb to 1 pint of boiling water, sweetened with sugar or honey, is also used for the same purpose, as well as in cases of catarrh and sore throat, given in doses of 1 or more tablespoonsful, several times daily. The wild plant may be equally well used for this.

Thyme tea will arrest gastric fermentation. It is useful in cases of wind spasms and colic, and will assist in promoting perspiration at the commencement of a cold, and in fever and febrile complaints generally.

In herbal medicine, Thyme is generally used in combination with other remedies.

Fluid extract, ¼ to 1 drachm. Oil, 1 to 10 drops.

According to Culpepper, Thyme is

'a noble strengthener of the lungs, as notable a one as grows, nor is there a better remedy growing for hooping cough. It purgeth the body of phlegm and is an excellent remedy for shortness of breath. It is so harmless you need not fear the use of it. An ointment made of it takes away hot swellings and warts, helps the sciatica and dullness of sight and takes away any pains and hardness of the spleen: it is excellent for those that are troubled with the gout and the herb taken anyway inwardly is of great comfort to the stomach.'

Gerard says it will 'cure sciatica and pains in the head,' and is healing in leprosy and the falling sickness.

Oil of Thyme is employed as a rubefacient and counter-irritant in rheumatism, etc.

Thyme enters into the formula for Herb Tobacco, and employed in this form is good for digestion, headache and drowsiness.

In Perfumery, Essence of Thyme is used for cosmetics and rice powder. It is also used for embalming corpses.

The dried flowers have been often used in the same way as lavender, to preserve linen from insects.

In this country, Thyme is principally in request for culinary requirements, for its use in flavouring stuffings, sauces, pickles, stews, soups, jugged hare, etc. The Spaniards infuse it in the pickle with which they preserve their olives.

All the different species of Thyme and Marjoram yield fragrant oils extensively used by manufacturing perfumers for scenting soaps. When dried and ground, they enter into the composition of sachet powders.

THYMOL, a most valuable crystalline phenol, is the basis of the fragrant volatile Essence of Sweet Thyme, and is obtainable from *Carum copticum, Monarda punctata* and various other plants, as well as from *T. vulgaris*, being present to the extent of from 20 to 60 per cent. in the oils which yield it. Ajowan oil, its principal commercial source (from the seeds of *C. copticum*), contains from 40 to 55 per cent. of Thymol; the oil of *T. vulgaris* contains from 20 to 30 per cent. as a rule of Thymol and Carvacrol in varying proportions, while the oil of *M. punctata* contains 61 per cent. of Thymol.

The extraction of Thymol is effected by treating the oil with a warm solution of sodium hydroxide: this alkali dissolves the Thymol, and on dilution with hot water the undissolved oil (terpenes, etc.) rises to the surface. The alkaline thymol compound is decomposed by treatment with hydrochloric acid and subsequent crystallization of the oily layer into large, oblique, prismatic crystals. Thymol (*methyl-propyl-phenol*) has been prepared synthetically.

When treated with caustic potash and

iodine, it yields iodo-thymol, commonly known as 'Aristol.'

Camphor of Thyme was noticed first by Neumann, apothecary to the Court at Berlin in 1725. It was called Thymol and carefully examined in 1853 by Lallemand and recommended instead of Phenol (carbolic acid) in 1868 by Bouilhon, apothecary, and Paquet, M.D., of Lille.

Thymol is a powerful antiseptic for both internal and external use; it is also employed as a deodorant and local anæsthetic. It is extensively used to medicate gauze and wool for surgical dressings. It resembles carbolic acid in its action, but is less irritant to wounds, while its germicidal action is greater. It is therefore preferable as a dressing and during recent years has been one of the most extensively used antiseptics.

Thymol is also a preservative of meat.

In respect of its physiological action, Thymol appears to stand between carbolic acid and oil of turpentine. Its action as a disinfectant is more permanent and at the same time more powerful than that of carbolic acid. It is less irritating to the skin, does not act as a caustic like carbolic acid, and is a less powerful poison to mammals. In the higher animals it acts as a local irritant and anæsthetic to the skin and mucous membrane. It is used as an antiseptic lotion and mouth wash; as a paint in ringworm, in eczema, psoriasis, broken chilblains, parasitic skin affections and burns; as an ointment, half-strength, perfumed with lavender, to keep off gnats and mosquitoes. Thymol in oily solution is applied to the respiratory passages by means of a spray in nasal catarrh, and a spirituous solution may be inhaled for laryngitis, bronchial affections and whooping cough. It is most useful against septic sore throat, especially during scarlet-fever. Internally, it is given in large doses, to robust adults, in capsules, as a vermifuge, to expel parasites, especially the miner's worm, and it has also been used in diabetes and vesical catarrh.

Thymol finds no place in perfumery, but the residual oil after extracting the crystalline Thymol from Ajowan oil, which amounts to about 50 per cent. of the original oil, is generally sold as a cheap perfume for soap-making and similar purposes, under the name of 'Thymene.'

Till the outbreak of war, Thymol was manufactured almost exclusively in Germany. One of the chief commercial sources of Thymol, Ajowan seed (C. copticum), is an annual umbelliferous plant, a kind of caraway, which is abundant in India, where it is widely cultivated for the medicinal properties of its seeds. Almost the whole of the exports of Ajowan seed from India, Egypt, Persia and Afghanistan went to Germany for the distillation of the oil and extraction of Thymol, the annual export of the seed from India being about 1,200 tons, from which the amount of Thymol obtainable was estimated at 20 tons. On the outbreak of war the export of Ajowan seed dropped to 2 tons per month, and there was a universal shortage of Thymol, just when it was urgently needed for the wounded.

As a result of investigations by the Imperial Institute, Thymol is now being made by several firms in this country, and the product is equal in quality and appearance to that previously imported from Germany. In India, also, good samples were obtained as a result of experiments conducted in Government laboratories in the early months of the War, and by the close of 1915 companies were already established at Dehra and Calcutta for its manufacture on a large scale. In the two years ending June, 1919, as much as 10,500 lb. of Thymol were exported from Calcutta.

Several other plants can be utilized as sources of Thymol, although none yield such high percentages as Ajowan seed. The following new sources of Thymol were suggested when the scarcity of the valuable antiseptic made itself so severely felt on curtailment of Continental supplies: Garden Thyme and Wild Thyme (T. vulgaris and serpyllum), American Horse Mint (M. punctata), Cunila mariana, Mosla japonica, Origanum hirtum, Ocimim viride and Satureja thymbra.

The oil of Thyme obtained by distilling the fresh-flowering herb of T. vulgaris is already an article of commerce, and contains varying amounts of Thymol, but the actual amount present is not very high, varying, as already stated, from 20 to 25 per cent., only in very rare cases amounting to more; and the methods of separation in order to obtain a pure compound are necessarily more complicated than in the manufacture from Ajowan oil.

The American Horsemint (M. punctata), native to the United States and Canada, seems likely to prove a more valuable source of Thymol than T. vulgaris. It yields from 1 to 3 per cent. of a volatile oil, which contains a large proportion of Thymol, up to 61 per cent. having been obtained; Carvacrol also appears to be a constituent. The oil has a specific gravity of 0·930 to 0·940, and on prolonged standing deposits crystals of Thymol.

Another species also found in America (M. didyma) (called also 'Oswego tea' from the use sometimes made of its leaves in America) is said to yield an oil of similar composition, though not to the same degree, and so far *M. punctata* is considered the only plant indigenous to North America which can be looked upon as a fruitful source of Thymol, though from *C. mariana*, also found in North America, an oil is derived – Oil of Dittany – which is stated to contain about 40 per cent. of phenols, probably Thymol.

Thymol is also contained in the oil distilled from the dry herb of *Mosla japonica*, indigenous to Japan. It is stated to yield about 2·13 per cent. of oil, containing about 44 per cent. of Thymol.

Satureja thymbra, which is used in Spain as a spice and is closely allied to the Savouries grown in the English kitchen garden, yields an oil containing about 19 per cent. of Thymol. Other species of *Satureja* contain Carvacrol.

A new source of Thymol is also *Ocimum viride*, the 'Mosquito Plant' of West Africa and the West Indies, which yield 0·35 to 1·2 of oil from which 32 to 65 per cent. of Thymol can be extracted. This plant occurs wild on all soils in every part of Sierra Leone, and is also grown in the Seychelles. In Sierra Leone it bears the name of 'Fever-plant' on account of its febrifugal qualities; a decoction is made from the leaves.

The Origanum oils shipped from Trieste and Smyrna generally contain only Carvacrol, the only species yielding Thymol exclusively and to a considerable degree being *Origanum hirtum*, which may be regarded as a promising source of Thymol.

Recently a Spanish species of Thyme has been used as a source of Thymol (*T. zygis*, Linn.), known to Theophrastus as *Serpyllum zygis*. It is common throughout Spain and Portugal, occurring in oak and other woods, in desert and dry gravelly places among the sierras of the central, eastern and southern provinces. In consequence of its wide distribution, the common names for the plant vary greatly; in Portugal it is known as Wood Marjoram, *ouregao do mato*; but the most frequently recurring name in Spain is *Tomillo salsero* or Sauce Thyme, from its use as a condiment. The species is very similar to *T. vulgaris*, but is easily distinguished by the comparatively large white hairs at the base of the leaves. The flowers are either purple or white, the white form being the only one occurring in the Balearic Islands, where it is called *Senorida de flor blanca*. There are two well-known varieties, var. *floribunda* and var. *gracillis*, a simpler, less-branched form, and it is the latter (not such a decided alpine as *floribunda*) which is now being used by a British manufacturer as a source of Thymol. See *Chemist and Druggist*, June 12th and July 17th, 1920. Var. *gracilis* is more easily collected on account of its lower station, and further unguarded exploitation of the wild plant might result in the substitution of var. *floribunda*, which it seems probable yields an oil with quite different characters and content from those of the oil obtained from var. *gracilis*.

Carvacrol has not hitherto been employed in medicine, but the antiseptic properties of Origanum oil, consisting principally of Carvacrol, as well as of the phenol itself, have been investigated and Iodocrol – iodide of Carvacrol – a reddish-brown powder, has been used lately as an antiseptic in place of iodoform in treatment of eczema and other skin diseases.

If required, a British Possession can provide Carvacrol as a substitute for Thymol. It can be obtained from oils derived from a variety of plants, but most profitably from the Origanum of Cyprus (*Origanum dubium*), which contains 82·5 per cent. of Carvacrol. At the instance of the Imperial Institute, this Cyprus Origanum oil has been produced in commercial quantities from wild plants in Cyprus, and already in 1913 was exported thence to the United Kingdom to the value of £980. It is believed that the plant can be cultivated profitably and on a large scale in Cyprus, and experiments in this direction were begun shortly after the outbreak of war. The oil from *O. onites*, var. *Symrnæum* – Smyrna Origanum oil – contains 68 per cent. phenols, almost wholly Carvacrol. Other sources of Carvacrol are *Monarda fistulosa* (Wild Bergamot), which yields 52 to 58 per cent. of Carvacrol; *Satureja montana* (Winter Savoury or White Thyme), oil from wild plants of this species containing 35 to 40 per cent. of Carvacrol; while that from cultivated plants has been found to contain as much as 65 per cent. A sample of Dalmatian *Satureja*, a form of *S. montana*, yielded at the Imperial Institute 68·75 of phenolic constituents, consisting mostly of Carvacrol.

THYME, WILD

Thymus serpyllum (LINN.)
N.O. Labiatæ

Synonyms. Mother of Thyme. Serpyllum
Part Used. Herb

The Wild Thyme is indigenous to the greater part of the dry land of Europe, though is a great deal less abundant than the Common Thyme so widely cultivated. It is found up to a certain height on the Alps, on high plateaux, and in valleys, along ditches and roads, on rocks, in barren and dry soil, and also in damp clay soil destitute of chalk. It is seen in old stony, abandoned fields, dried-up lawns and on clearings. In England it is found chiefly on heaths and in mountainous situations, and is also often cultivated as a border in gardens or on rockeries and sunny banks. It was a great favourite of Francis Bacon, who in giving us his plan for the perfect garden, directs that alleys should be planted with fragrant flowers: 'burnet, wild thyme and watermints, which perfume the air most delightfully being trodden upon and crushed,' so that you may 'have pleasure when you walk or tread.'

The herb wherever it grows wild denotes a pure atmosphere, and was thought to enliven the spirits by the fragrance which it diffuses into the air around. The Romans gave Thyme as a sovereign remedy to melancholy persons.

Wild Thyme is a perennial, more thickset than the Garden Thyme, though subject to many varieties, according to the surroundings in which it grows. In its most natural state, when found on dry exposed downs, it is small and procumbent, often forming dense cushions; when growing among furze or other plants which afford it shelter, it runs up a slender stalk to a foot or more in height, which gives it a totally different appearance. The specific name, *serpyllum*, is derived from a Greek word meaning to creep, and has been given it from its usually procumbent and trailing habit.

¶ *Description*. The root is woody and fibrous, the stems numerous, hard, branched, procumbent, rising from 4 inches to 1 foot high, ordinarily reddish-brown in colour. The bright green oval leaves ⅛ inch broad, tapering below into very short foot-stalks, are smooth and beset with numerous small glands. They are fringed with hairs towards the base and have the veins prominent on the under surfaces. Their margins are entire and not recurved as in Garden Thyme. As with all other members of the important order Labiatæ, to which the Thymes belong, the leaves are set in pairs on the stem. The plant flowers from the end of May or early June to the beginning of autumn, the flowers, which are very similar to those of the Garden Thyme, being purplish and in whorls at the top of the stems.

Bees are especially fond of the Thyme blossoms, from which they extract much honey. Spenser speaks of the 'bees-alluring time,' and everyone is familiar with Shakespeare's the 'bank whereon the wild thyme blows,' the abode of the queen of the Fairies. It was looked upon as one of the fairies'

flowers, tufts of Thyme forming one of their favourite playgrounds.

In some parts it was a custom for girls to wear sprigs of Thyme, with mint and lavender, to bring them sweethearts!

Thyme has also been associated with death. It is one of the fragrant flowers planted on graves (in Wales, particularly), and the Order of Oddfellows still carry sprigs of Thyme at funerals and throw them into the grave of a dead brother. An old tradition says that Thyme was one of the herbs that formed the fragrant bed of the Virgin Mary.

Wild Thyme is the badge of the Drummond clan.

¶ *Cultivation*. Wild Thyme will grow on any soil, but prefers light, sandy or gravel ground exposed to the sun.

Propagate by seeds, cuttings, or division of roots. Care must be taken to weed. Manure with farmyard manure in autumn or winter and nitrates in spring.

Cut when in full flower, in July and August, and dry in the same manner as Common Thyme.

It is much picked in France, chiefly in the fields of the Aisne, for the extraction of its essential oil.

¶ *Constituents*. When distilled, 100 kilos (about 225 lb.) of dried material yield 150 grams of essence (about 5 or 6 oz.). It is a yellow liquid, with a weaker scent than that of oil of Thyme extracted from *T. vulgaris*, and is called oil of Serpolet. It contains 30 to 70 per cent. of phenols: Thymol, Carvacrol, etc. It is made into an artificial oil, together with the oil of Common Thyme. In perfumery, oil of Serpolet is chiefly used for soap.

The flowering tops, macerated for 24 hours or so in salt and water, are made into a perfumed water.

¶ *Medicinal Action and Uses*. In medicine, Wild Thyme or Serpolet has the same properties as Common Thyme, but to an inferior degree. It is aromatic, antiseptic, stimulant, antispasmodic, diuretic and emmenagogue.

The infusion is used for chest maladies and for weak digestion, being a good remedy for flatulence, and favourable results have been obtained in convulsive coughs, especially in whooping cough, catarrh and sore throat. The infusion, prepared with 1 oz. of the dried herb to a pint of boiling water, is usually sweetened with sugar or honey and made demulcent by linseed or acacia. It is given in doses of 1 or more tablespoonfuls several times daily.

The infusion is also useful in cases of drunkenness, and Culpepper recommends it as a certain remedy taken on going to bed for 'that troublesome complaint the nightmare,' and says: 'if you make a vinegar of the herb as vinegar of roses is made and annoint the head with it, it presently stops the pains thereof. It is very good to be given either in phrenzy or lethargy.'

Wild Thyme Tea, either drunk by itself or mixed with other plants such as rosemary, etc., is an excellent remedy for headache and other nervous affections.

Formerly several preparations of this plant were kept in shops, and a distilled spirit and water, which were both very fragrant.

TIGER LILY. *See* LILY

TOADFLAX

Linaria vulgaris (MILL.)
N.O. Scrophulariaceæ

Synonyms. Fluellin. Pattens and Clogs. Flaxweed. Ramsted. Snapdragon. Churnstaff. Dragon-bushes. Brideweed. Toad. Yellow Rod. Larkspur Lion's Mouth. Devils' Ribbon. Eggs and Collops. Devil's Head. Pedlar's Basket. Gallwort. Rabbits. Doggies. Calves' Snout. Eggs and Bacon. Buttered Haycocks. Monkey Flower

Part Used. Herb

Habitat. The genus *Linaria*, to which it belongs, contains 125 species, native to the Northern Hemisphere and South America, seven of which are found in England

The Toadflax grows wild in most parts of Europe, on dry banks, by the wayside, in meadows by hedge sides, and upon the borders of fields. It is common throughout England and Wales, though less frequent in Ireland. In Scotland, it is found, as a rule, only in the southern counties. Having been introduced into North America, probably originally with grain, it has become there a troublesome weed. It is especially abundant in sandy and gravelly soil and in chalk and limestone districts.

¶ *Description.* From a perennial and creeping root, the Toadflax sends up several slender stems, erect and not much branched, generally between 1 and 2 feet long, bearing numerous leaves, which are very long and narrow in form. Both stems and leaves are glaucous, i.e. of a pale bluish tint of green, and are quite destitute of hairs.

The stems terminate in rather dense spikes of showy yellow flowers, the corolla in general shape like that of the Snapdragon, but with a long spur, and with the lower lip orange. The Toadflax flowers throughout the summer, from late June to October.

The mouth of the flower is completely closed and never opens until a bee forces its entrance. The only visitors are the large bees – the humble-bee, honey-bee, and several wild bees – which are able to open the flower, and whose tongues are long enough to reach the nectar, which is so placed in the spur that only long-lipped insects can reach it. The closing of the swollen lower lip excludes beetles from the spur. When the bee alights on the orange palate, the colour of which is specially designed to attract the desired visitor, acting as a honey-guide, it falls a little, disclosing the interior of the flower, which forms a little cave, on the floor of

which are two ridges of orange hairs, a track between them leading straight to the mouth of the long, hollow spur. Above this is the egg-shaped seed-vessel with the stamens. Between the bases of the two longer stamen filaments, nectar trickles down along a groove to the spur, from the base of the ovary where it is secreted. The bee pushes into the flower, its head fitting well into the cavity below the seed-vessel and thrusting its proboscis down the spur, sucks the nectar, its back being meanwhile well coated by the pollen from the stamens, which run along the roof, the stigma being between the short and long stamens. It is reckoned that a humble-bee can easily take the nectar from ten flowers in a minute, each time transferring pollen from a previous flower to the stigma of the one visited, and thus effecting cross-fertilization.

The Toadflax is very prolific. Its fruit is a little rounded, dry capsule, which when ripe, opens at its top by several valves, the many minute seeds being thrown out by the swaying of the stems. The seeds are flattened and lie in the centre of a circular wing, which, tiny as it is, helps to convey the seed some distance from the parent plant.

Sometimes a curiously-shaped Toadflax blossom will be found: instead of only one spur being produced, each of the five petals whose union builds up the toad-like corolla forms one, and the flower becomes of regular, though almost unrecognizable shape. This phenomenon is termed by botanists, 'peloria,' i.e. a monster. As a rule it is the terminal flower that is thus symmetrical in structure, but sometimes flowers of this type occur all down the spike.

The name Toadflax originated in the resemblance of the flower to little toads, there being also a resemblance between the mouth of the flower and the wide mouth of a toad. Coles says that the plant was called Toadflax, 'because Toads will sometimes shelter themselves amongst the branches of it.'

The general resemblance of the plant in early summer to a Flax plant, accounts for the latter part of its name, and also for another of its country names, 'Flaxweed.' The Latin name, *Linaria*, from *linum* (flax), was given it by Linnæus, from this likeness to a flax plant before flowering. The mixture of light yellow and orange in the flowers has gained for it the provincial names of 'Butter and Eggs,' 'Eggs and Bacon,' etc.

Gerard says:

'Linaria being a kind of Antyrrhinum, hath small, slender, blackish stalks, from which do grow many long, narrow leaves like flax. The floures be yellow with a spurre hanging at the same like unto a Larkesspurre, having a mouth like unto a frog's mouth, even such as is to be seene in the common Snapdragon; the whole plant so much resembleth Esula minor, that the one is hardly knowne from the other but by this olde verse: "Esula lactescit, sine lacte Linaria crescit."

' "Esula with milke doth flow,
Toadflax without milke doth grow." '

This *Esula* is one of the smaller spurge, *Euphorbia esula*, which before flowering so closely resembles Toadflax that care must be taken not to collect it in error; the milky juice contained in its stems (as in all the Spurges) will, however, at once reveal its identity.

The leaves of the Toadflax also contain an acrid, rather disagreeable, but not *milky* juice, which renders them distasteful to cattle, who leave them untouched. Among the many old local names given to this plant we find it called 'Gallwort,' on account of its bitterness, one old writer affirming that it received the name because an infusion of the leaves was used 'against the flowing of the gall in cattell.' The larvæ of several moths feed on the plant, and several beetles are also found on it.

¶ *Part Used Medicinally. Cultivation.* For medicinal purposes, Toadflax is generally gathered in the wild condition, but it can be cultivated with ease, though it prefers a dry soil. No manure is needed. Seeds may be sown in spring. All the culture needed is to thin out the seedlings and keep them free of weeds. Propagation may also be carried out by division of roots in the autumn.

The whole herb is gathered just when coming into flower and employed either fresh or dried.

When fresh, Toadflax has a peculiar, heavy, disagreeable odour, which is in great measure dissipated by drying. It has a weakly saline, bitter and slightly acrid taste.

¶ *Constituents.* Toadflax abounds in an acrid oil, reputed to be poisonous, but no harm from it has ever been recorded. Little or nothing is known of its toxic principle, but its use in medicine was well known to the ancients.

Its constituents are stated to be two glucosides, Linarin and Pectolinarian, with linarosin, linaracin, antirrhinic, tannic and citric acids, a yellow colouring matter, mucilage and sugar.

¶ *Medicinal Action and Uses.* Astringent, hepatic and detergent. It has some powerful qualities as a purgative and diuretic, causing it to be recommended in jaundice, liver, skin diseases and scrofula; an infusion of 1 oz. to the pint has been found serviceable as an alterative in these cases and in incipient dropsy. The infusion has a bitter and unpleasant taste, occasioned by the presence of the acrid essential oil. It was at one time in great reputation among herb doctors for dropsy. The herb distilled answers the same purpose, as a decoction of both leaves and flowers in removing obstructions of the liver. It is very effectual if a little Peruvian bark or solution of quinine and a little cinnamon be combined with it. Gerard informs us that 'the decoction openeth the stopping of the liver and spleen, and is singular good against the jaundice which is of long continuance, and further states that 'a decoction of Toadflax taketh away the yellownesse and deformitie of the skinne, being washed and bathed therewith.'

The fresh plant is sometimes applied as a poultice or fomentation to hæmorrhoids, and an ointment of the flowers has been employed for the same purpose, and also locally in diseases of the skin. A cooling ointment is made from the fresh plant – the whole herb is chopped and boiled in lard till crisp, then strained. The result is a fine green ointment, a good application for piles, sores, ulcers and skin eruptions.

The juice of the herb, or the distilled water, has been considered a good remedy for inflammation of the eyes, and for cleansing ulcerous sores.

Boiled in milk, the plant is said to yield an excellent fly poison, and it is an old country custom in parts of Sweden to infuse Toadflax flowers in milk, and stand the infusion about where flies are troublesome.

The flowers have been employed in Germany as a yellow dye.

TOADFLAX, IVY-LEAVED

Linaria Cymbalaria
N.O. Scrophulariaceæ

Synonyms. Ivywort. Aaron's Beard. Climbing Sailor. Creeping Jenny. Mother of Millions. Mother of Thousands. Thousand Flower. Oxford-weed. Pedlar's Basket. Pennywort. Rabbits. Roving Jenny. Wandering Jew

Part Used. Herb

Ivy-leaved Toadflax (Mill.) (*Linaria Cymbalaria*). This little trailing plant, with ivy-like leaves and small lilac flowers, was not originally a British plant, but a native of the Mediterranean region, but it has become naturalized over almost the whole of Europe, from Holland southwards, except in Turkey, and is now thoroughly at home in England, having first been introduced into the Chelsea Botanic Gardens from Italy.

It is mostly found near houses, on old garden walls, where it hangs down from the interstices between the stones, the roots being thin and fibrous, and finding their way into crevices. The stems are purple in colour and very numerous, slender and stringy, rooting at intervals and very long, growing to a length of 2 or 3 feet.

¶ *Description.* The ivy-like leaves, somewhat thick in texture, and smooth, are cut up into five prominent, rounded lobes or divisions, and are on long stalks. The backs of the leaves are of a reddish-purple. The flower-stalks, about equal in length to the leaf-stalks, arise singly from the axils of the leaves and bear small flowers similar in form to those of the common Toadflax, of a delicate lilac colour, the palate being bright yellow and each blossom ending in a spur, which in this case is only as long as the calyx. Before fertilization each flower pushes itself out into the light and sun, standing erect, but when the seeds are mature, it bends downward, buries the capsule in the dark crannies between the stones on which it grows, the seeds being thus dispersed by direct action of the plant itself.

This little Toadflax is in flower from May right up to November, and is visited only by bees. It has become a favourite garden flower for planting on rockeries.

Gerard illustrates the plant in his *Herbal*, springing from brickwork, but the block of his illustration was incorrectly placed upside down, so that the plant instead of being represented as growing downwards, stands erect. Parkinson, in 1640, also figures this plant in the same way, and names it *Cymbalaria hederacea.*

In Italy it is the 'plant of the Madonna.'

¶ *Medicinal Action and Uses.* The Ivy-leaved Toadflax has anti-scorbutic properties, and has been eaten as a salad in southern Europe, being acrid and pungent like Cress.

It is reported to have been successfully administered in India for diabetes.

The flowers yield a clear but not permanent yellow dye.

TOBACCO

Nicotiana Tabacum (LINN.)
N.O. Solanaceæ

Synonyms. Tabacca. Tabaci Folia (B.P.C.)
Part Used. Leaves, cured and dried
Habitat. Virginia, America; and cultivated with other species in China, Turkey, Greece, Holland, France, Germany and most sub-tropical countries

¶ *Description.* The genus derives its name from Joan Nicot, a Portuguese who introduced the Tobacco plant into France. The specific name being derived from the Haitian word for the pipe in which the herb is smoked. Tobacco is an annual, with a long fibrous root, stem erect, round, hairy, and viscid; it branches near the top and is from 3 to 6 feet high. Leaves large, numerous, alternate, sessile, somewhat decurrent, ovate, lanceolate, pointed, entire, slightly viscid and hairy, pale-green colour, brittle, narcotic odour, with a nauseous, bitter acrid taste. Nicotine is a volatile oil, inflammable, powerfully alkaline, with an acrid smell and a burning taste. By distillation with water it yields a concrete volatile oil termed nicotianin or Tobacco camphor, which is tasteless, crystalline, and smells of Tobacco; other constituents are albumen, resin, gum, and inorganic matters.

¶ *Constituents.* The most important constituent is the alkaloid Nicotine, nicotianin, nicotinine, nicoteine, nicoteline. After leaves are smoked the nicotine decomposes into pyridine, furfurol, collidine, hydrocyanic acid, carbon-monoxide, etc. The poisonous effects of Tobacco smoke are due to these substances of decomposed nicotine.

¶ *Medicinal Action and Uses.* A local irritant; if used as snuff it causes violent sneezing, also a copious secretion of mucous; chewed, it increases the flow of saliva by irritating the mucous membrane of the mouth; injected into the rectum it acts as a cathartic. In large doses it produces nausea, vomiting, sweats and great muscular weakness.

The alkaloid nicotine is a virulent poison, producing great disturbance in the digestive and circulatory organs. It innervates the heart, causing palpitation and cardiac irregularities and vascular contraction, and is considered one of the causes of arterial degeneration.

Nicotine is very like coniine and lobeline in its pharmacological action, and the pyridines in the smoke modify very slightly its action.

Tobacco was once used as a relaxant, but is no longer employed except occasionally in chronic asthma. Its active principle is readily absorbed by the skin, and serious, even fatal, poisoning, from a too free application of it to the surface of the skin has resulted.

The smoke acts on the brain, causing nausea, vomiting and drowsiness.

Medicinally it is used as a sedative, diuretic, expectorant, discutient, and sialagogue, and internally only as an emetic, when all other emetics fail. The smoke injected into the rectum or the leaf rolled into a suppository has been beneficial in strangulated hernia, also for obstinate constipation, due to spasm of the bowels, also for retention of urine, spasmodic urethral stricture, hysterical convulsions, worms, and in spasms caused by lead, for croup, and inflammation of the peritoneum, to produce evacuation of the bowels, moderating reaction and dispelling tympanitis, and also in tetanus. To inject the smoke it should be blown into milk and injected; for croup and spasms of the rima glottides it is made into a plaster with Scotch snuff and lard and applied to throat and breast, and has proved very effectual. A cataplasm of the leaves may be used as an ointment for cutaneous diseases. The leaves in combination with the leaves of belladonna or stramonium make an excellent application for obstinate ulcers, painful tremors and spasmodic affections. A wet Tobacco leaf applied to piles is a certain cure. The inspissated juice cures facial neuralgia if rubbed along the tracks of the affected nerve. The quantity of the injection must never exceed a scruple to begin with; half a drachm has been known to produce amaurosis and other eye affections, deafness, etc.

The Tobacco plant was introduced into England by Sir Walter Raleigh and his friends in 1586, and at first met with violent opposition.

Kings prohibited it, Popes pronounced against it in Bulls, and in the East Sultans condemned Tobacco smokers to cruel deaths. Three hundred years later, in 1885, the leaves were official in the British Pharmacopœia.

Externally nicotine is an antiseptic. It is eliminated partly by the lungs, but chiefly in the urine, the secretion of which it increases. Formerly Tobacco in the form of an enema of the leaves was used to relax muscular spasms, to facilitate the reduction of dislocations.

A pipe smoked after breakfast assists the action of the bowels.

The pituri plant contains an alkaloid, Pitarine, similar to nicotine, and the leaves are used in Australia instead of Tobacco. An infusion of Tobacco is generally used in horticulture as an insecticide.

In cases of nicotine poisoning, the stomach should be quickly emptied, and repeated doses of tannic acid given, the person kept very warm in bed, and stimulants such as caffeine, strychnine, or atropine given, or if there are signs of respiratory failure, oxygen must be given at once.

¶ *Other Species.*

Tobacco (*Nicotiana rustica*). Turkish Tobacco is grown in all parts of the globe.

N. quadrivalis, affording Tobacco to the Indians of the Missouri and Columbia Rivers, has, as the name implies, four-valved capsules.

N. fruticosa – habitat, China – is a very handsome plant and differs from the other varieties in its sharp-pointed capsules.

N. persica. Cultivated in Persia; is the source of Persian Tobacco.

N. repandu. Cultivated in Central and southern North America. Havannah is used in the manufacture of the best cigars.

Latakria Tobacco (syn. *N. Tabacum*) is the only species cultivated in Cuba.

N. latissima yields the Tobacco known as Orinoco.

N. multivulvis has several valved capsules.

TOLU BALSAM. *See* BALSAM

TONKA BEANS. *See* TONQUIN

TONQUIN BEAN

Dipteryx odorata (WILLD.)
N.O. Leguminosæ

Synonyms. Tonka Bean. Coumarouna odorata
Part Used. Seeds
Habitat. A forest tree native to Brazil and British Guiana and called there 'Rumara'

¶ *Description*. The odour of coumarin, which distinguishes the Tonka Bean, is found in many plants, especially in Melilotus, sweet vernal grass, and related grasses.

One pound of the beans has yielded 108 grains of coumarin, which is the anhydride of coumaric acid. In addition to its use in perfumery as a fixative, coumarin is used to flavour castor-oil and to disguise the odour of iodoform.

The fatty substance of the beans is sold in Holland as *Tonquin butter*.

¶ *Medicinal Action and Uses*. Aromatic, cardiac, tonic, narcotic. The fluid extract has been used with advantage in whooping cough, but it paralyses the heart if used in large doses.

¶ *Dosage*. For children of five years' old, 5 to 8 grains.

TORMENTIL

Potentilla Tormentilla (NECK.)
N.O. Rosaceæ

Synonyms. Septfoil. Thormantle. Biscuits. Bloodroot. Earthbank. Ewe Daisy. Five Fingers. Flesh and Blood. Shepherd's Knapperty. Shepherd's Knot. English Sarsaparilla
Parts Used. Root, herb

In *Potentilla Tormentilla* the flowers are yellow as in *P. reptans*, but smaller, and have four petals instead of five, and eight sepals, not ten, so separated as to form a Maltese cross when regarded from above.

From the root-stock come leaves on long stalks, divided into three or five oval leaflets (occasionally, but rarely, seven, hence the names Septfoil and Seven Leaves), toothed towards their tips. The stem-leaves, in this species, are stalkless with three leaflets.

A small-flowered form is very frequent on heaths and in dry pastures, a larger-flowered, in which the slender stems do not rise, but trail on the ground, is more general in woods, and on hedge-banks. From the ascending form, 6 to 12 inches high, this species has been called *P. erecta*, but even in this case the long stems are more often creeping and ascending rather than actually erect.

The name Tormentil is said to be derived from the Latin *tormentum*, which signifies such gripings of the intestines as the herb will serve to relieve, likewise the twinges of toothache.

The plant is very astringent, and has been used in some places for tanning.

It has been official in various Pharmacopœias and was formerly in the Secondary List of the United States Pharmacopœia.

It is considered one of the safest and most powerful of our native aromatic astringents, and for its tonic properties has been termed 'English Sarsaparilla.'

All parts of the plant are astringent, especially the red, woody rhizome.

The rhizome is 1 to 2 inches long, as thick as the finger, or smaller, tapering to one end, usually with one to three short branches near the larger end, ridged, with several strong, longitudinal wrinkles between them, bearing numerous blunt indentations. It is brown or blackish externally; internally, light brownish red; the fracture short and somewhat resinous, showing a thin bark, one or two circles of small, yellowish wood-wedges, broad medullary rays and a large pith. It has a peculiar faint, slightly aromatic odour and a strongly astringent taste.

¶ *Chemical Constituents*. It contains 18 to 30 per cent. of tannin, 18 per cent. of a red colouring principle – Tormentil Red, a product of the tannin and yielding with potassium hydroxide, protocatechuic acid and phloroglucin. It is soluble in alcohol, but insoluble in water. Also some resin and ellagic and kinovic acids have been reported.

¶ *Medicinal Action and Uses*. There is a great demand for the rhizome, which in modern herbal medicine is used extensively as an astringent in diarrhœa and other discharges, operating without producing any stimulant effects. It also imparts nourishment and support to the bowels.

It is employed as a gargle in sore, relaxed and ulcerated throat and also as an injection in leucorrhœa.

It may be given in substance, decoction or extract. The dose of the powdered root or fluid extract is ½ to 1 drachm.

The fluid extract acts as a styptic to cuts, wounds, etc.

A strongly-made decoction is recommended as a good wash for piles and inflamed eyes. The decoction is made by boiling 2 oz. of the bruised root in 50 oz. of water till it is reduced one-third. It is then strained and taken in doses of 1½ oz. It may be used as an astringent gargle.

If a piece of lint be soaked in the decoction and kept applied to warts, they will disappear.

The decoction for internal use should be made with 4 drachms to ½ pint of water, boiled for 10 minutes, adding ¼ drachm of cinnamon stick at the end of boiling. Dose, 1 or 2 tablespoonsful.

Compound Powder of Tormentil. (A very reliable medicine in diarrhœa and dysentery.) Powdered Tormentil, 1 oz; Powdered Galangal, 1 oz.; Powdered Marshmallow root, 1 oz.; Powdered Ginger, 4 drachms.

An infusion is made of the powdered ingredients by pouring 1 pint of boiling water upon them, allowing to cool and then straining the liquid. Dose, 1 or 2 fluid drachms, every 15 minutes, till the pain is relieved – then take three or four times a day.

A *simple infusion* is made by scalding 1 oz. of the powdered Tormentil with 1 pint of water and taking as required in wineglassful doses for chronic diarrhœa, fluxes, etc.

A continental recipe for an astringent decoction is equal parts of Tormentilla, Bistort and Pomegranate.

Dr. Thornton declared that in fluxes of blood, 1 drachm of Tormentil given four times a day in an infusion of Hops did wonders.

Thornton tells of a poor old man who made wonderful cures of ague, smallpox, whooping cough, etc., from an infusion of this herb and became so celebrated locally that Lord William Russell gave him a piece of ground in which to cultivate it, which he did, keeping it a secret for long.

It was much given for cholera, and also sometimes in intermittent fevers, and used in a lotion for ulcers and long-standing sores. The juice of the fresh root, or the powder of

the dried, was used in compounding ointments and plasters for application to wounds and sores.

The fresh root, bruised, and applied to the throat and jaws was held to heal the King's Evil.

Culpepper says:

'Tormentil is most excellent to stay all fluxes of blood or humours, whether at nose, mouth or belly. The juice of the herb and root, or the decoction thereof, taken with some Venice treacle and the person laid to sweat, expels any venom or poison, or the plague, fever or other contagious disease, as the pox, measles, etc., for it is an ingredient in all antidotes or counterpoisons.' . . . 'It resisteth putrefaction.' . . . 'The root taken inwardly is most effectual to help any flux of the belly, stomach, spleen or blood and the juice wonderfully opens obstructions of the spleen and lungs and cureth yellow jaundice. Tormentil is no less effectual and powerful a remedy against outward wounds, sores and hurts than for inward and is therefore a special ingredient to be used in wound drinks, lotions and injections. . . . It is also effectual for the piles. . . . The juice or powder of the root, put into ointments, plasters and such things that are applied to wounds or sores is very effectual.'

In the Western Isles of Scotland and in the Orkneys the roots were used for tanning leather and considered superior even to oak bark, being first boiled in water and the leather steeped in the cold liquor. The Laplanders employed the thickened red juice of the root for staining leather red.

The Americans use the name Tormentil for *Geranium maculatum*, the Spotted Cranesbill, which has similar properties.

Many other of the 150 species of Potentilla have been similarly used in medicine.

See FIVE-LEAF GRASS, SILVERWEED, CINQUE-FOILS.

TRAGACANTH

Astragalus gummifer (LABILL.)
N.O. Leguminosæ

Synonyms. Gum Tragacanth. Syrian Tragacanth. Gum Dragon (known in commerce as Syrian Tragacanth)
Part Used. Gummy exudation
Habitat. Asia Minor, Persia and Kurdistan

¶ *Description.* The plant is a small branching thorny shrub, the stem of which exudes a gum, vertical slits giving flat ribbon-shaped pieces and punctures giving tears; these have a horny appearance, are nearly colourless or faintly yellow, marked with numerous concentric ridges; the flakes break with a short fracture, are odourless and nearly tasteless;

soaked in cold water, they swell and form a gelatinous mass 8 or 10 per cent. only dissolving.

¶ *Constituents.* The portion soluble in water contains chiefly polyarabinan-trigalætangeddic acid; the insoluble part is called bassorin. Tragacanth also contains water, traces of starch, cellulose, and nitrogen-

WOOD SORREL
Oxalis Acetosella

TORMENTIL
Potentilla Tormentilla

TRAGACANTH
Astragalus Gummifer

BEARBERRY (UVA-URSI)
Arbutus Uva-Ursi

ous substances, yielding about 3 per cent. ash.

¶ *Medicinal Action and Uses.* Demulcent, but owing to its incomplete solubility is not often used internally. It is much used for the suspension of heavy, insoluble powders to impart consistence to lozenges, being superior to gum arabic, also in making emulsions, mucilago, etc. Mucil-age of Tragacanth has been used as an application to burns; it is also employed by manufacturers for stiffening calico, crape, etc.

Mucilage, B.P. and U.S.P. Comp. Powder, B.P., 20 to 60 grains.

¶ *Adulterants.* The Indian gum, the product of *Coplospermum gossypium,* also acacia, dextrin wheat and corn starch.

TRAVELLERS' JOY. *See* CLEMATIS

TREE OF HEAVEN

Ailanthus glandulosa (DESF.)
N.O. Simarubeæ

Synonyms. Chinese Sumach. Vernis de Japon. Ailanto. (Trans. as Tree of the Gods. – Götterbaum.)

Parts Used. Inner bark of tree, root

Habitat. China and India. Cultivated throughout Europe and the United States

¶ *Description.* A large, handsome tree of rapid growth, bearing leaves from 1 to 2 feet long, and greenish flowers of a disagreeable odour. Was introduced into England in 1751 and is frequently found in gardens as a shade tree.

The *Ailanthus imberiflora* occurs in Australia, and in India the *A. excelsa* has a bark used as a bitter tonic.

In France it is cultivated for its leaves, on which the caterpillar of the silk-spinning Ailanthus Moth (*Bombyx Cynthia*) is fed, yielding a silk more durable and cheaper than Mulberry silk, though inferior to it in fineness and gloss. Its name of Japan Varnish shows that it was mistaken for the true Japanese Varnish Tree, a species of Sumach. At one time it was classed as a Rhus.

The wood is satiny, yellowish-white, and well suited for cabinet-making when climates permit of adequate growth.

The bark has a nauseating, bitter taste, and, when fresh, a sickening odour.

The leaves have been found in commerce adulterated with those of senna.

¶ *Constituents.* Lignin, chlorophyll, a yellow colouring matter, a gelatinous substance (pectin), quassin, an odorous resin, traces of a volatile oil, a nitrogenous, fatty matter, and several salts. A later analysis found starch, tannin, albumen, gum, sugar, oleoresin, and a trace of volatile oil, potash, phosphoric acid, sulphuric acid, iron, lime, and magnesia.

All the characteristic properties of either the fresh or carefully dried bark can be exhausted by alcohol, to which a deep, green colour will be imparted, changing to yellowish-brown with age and more quickly if exposed to air.

¶ *Medicinal Action and Uses.* Antispasmodic, cardiac depressant, astringent. The effect produced by Hetet when experimenting on dogs, was copious stools and the discharge of worms. The resin purges, but rarely acts as an anthelmintic. In China the bark is popular for dysentery and other bowel complaints. A smaller dose of the oleoresin produces similar results, and keeps better than the bark.

The vapours of the evaporating extract have a prostrating effect, as have the emanations from the blossoms, while the action upon patients of powder or extract is disagreeable and nauseating, though they have been successfully used in dysentery and diarrhœa, gonorrhœa, leucorrhœa, prolapsus ani, etc., and also as a tænifuge.

The infusion may be given in sweetened orange-flower or other aromatic water, to lessen the bitterness and resultant sickness. Though it produces vomiting and great relaxation, it is stated not to be poisonous.

A tincture of the root-bark has been used successfully in cardiac palpitation, asthma and epilepsy.

The action of the trees in malarial districts is considered to resemble that of the Eucalyptus.

The statement that the resin is purgative has been disputed, some asserting that it is inert.

¶ *Dosages.* From 7 to 20 grains. Of the tincture, 5 to 60 drops from two to four times a day. Of the infusion, a teaspoonful, night and morning, cold. (50 grams of the root-bark infused for a short time in 75 grams of hot water, then strained.)

TURKEY CORN

Dicentra Canadensis (D.C.)
N.O. Fumariaceæ

Synonyms. Turkey Pea. Squirrel Corn. Staggerweed. Bleeding Heart. Shone Corydalis. Corydalis. Corydalis Canadensis (Goldie). Bicuculla Canadensis (Millsp.)
Part Used. Dried tubers
Habitat. Westward and south of New York to North Carolina

¶ *Description.* This plant is essentially indigenous to America, a perennial 6 to 10 inches high, with a tuberous root, flowering in early spring (often in March) having from six to nineteen nodding, greenish-white, purple-tinged flowers, the root or tuber small and round. It should be collected only when the plant is in flower. It grows in rich soil on hills and mountains. The tubers are tawny yellow-coloured, the colour being a distinctive character. The plant must not be confounded with *Corydalis (Dicentra) Cuccularia* (Dutchman's Breeches), which flowers at the same time and very much resembles it (though smaller), except in the root, the rind of which is black with a white inside, and when dried, turns brownish-yellow, and under the microscope is full of pores. It has also a peculiar faint odour, the taste at first slightly bitter, then followed by a penetrating taste, which influences the bowels and increases the saliva; the differences in the colour after drying may be caused by the age of the root. Under the miscroscope, it is porous, spongy, resinous, with a glistening fracture. Another *Corydalis* also somewhat like Turkey Corn is *C. Formosa*, the fresh root of which is darkish yellow throughout and has a fracture much resembling honeycomb. The true Turkey Corn is much used by American eclectic practitioners. It is slightly bitter in taste and almost odourless. Tannic acid and all vegetable astringents are incompatible with preparations containing Turkey Corn, or with its alkaloid, Corydalin.

¶ *Constituents.* The amount of alkaloids in the dried tubers is about 5 per cent.; they have been found to contain corydalin, fumaric acid, yellow bitter extractive, an acrid resin and starch. The constituents of the drug have not been exactly determined, but several species of the closely allied genus *Corydalis* have been carefully studied and *C. tuberosa, cava* and *bulbosa* have been found to yield the following alkaloids: Corycavine, Bulbocapnine and Corydine; Corydaline is a tertiary base, Corycavine is a difficult soluble base; Bulbocapnine is present in largest amount and was originally called Corydaline. Corydine is a strong base found in the mother liquor of Bulbocapnine and several amorphous unnamed bases have been found in it. All these alkaloids have narcotic action. Protopine, first isolated from opium, has been found in several species of *Dicentra* and in *C. vernyi, ambigua* and *tuberosa*.

¶ *Medicinal Action and Uses.* Tonic, diuretic and alterative; useful in chronic cutaneous affections, syphilis and scrofula and in some menstrual complaints. The corydalin sold by druggists is often impure.

Turkey Corn is often combined with other remedies, such as Stillingia, Burdock or Prickly Ash.

¶ *Dosages.* An infusion is prepared of 5 grams of the powdered Corydalin in 100 c.c. of hot distilled water stirred for 10 minutes and then filtered. This gives a light amber fluid and a precipitate with mercuric-potassium iodide T.S. and a dark blue colour with Iodine T.S.

Infusion, ½ oz. in 1 pint of boiling water, in wineglassful doses three or four times daily. Fluid extract, ½ to 1 drachm. Corydalin, in ¼ grains, three or four times daily. Saturated tincture, ½ drachm to 2 fluid drachms.

¶ *Other Species.*
Dicentra pusilla (Sieb et Zuce), of Japan, is there popularly used for dysentery.

C. ambigua, used by the Chinese in medicine. A number of the same alkaloids are found in it and others closely allied.

As commonly understood in medicine, the name Corydalis applies to the tubers of Turkey Corn, but several others of the genus *Dicentra* and *Corydalis* are used.

TURMERIC

Curcuma longa (LINN.)
N.O. Zingiberaceæ

Synonyms. Curcuma. Curcuma rotunda (LINN.). Amomum curcuma (Jacq.)
Part Used. Dried rhizome
Habitat. Southern Asia. Cultivated in China, Bengal and Java

¶ *Description.* A perennial plant with roots or tubers oblong, palmate, and deep orange inside; root-leaves about 2 feet long, lanceolate, long, petioled, tapering at each end, smooth, of a uniform green; petioles sheathing spike, erect, central, oblong, green; flowers dull yellow, three or five together surrounded by bracteolæ. It is propagated by cuttings from the root, which when dry is in curved cylindrical or oblong tubers 2 or 3 inches in length, and an inch in diameter, pointed or tapering at one end, yellowish externally, with transverse, parallel rings internally deep orange or reddish brown, marked with shining points, dense, solid, short, granular fracture, forming a lemon yellow powder. It has a peculiar fragrant odour and a bitterish, slightly acrid taste, like ginger, exciting warmth in the mouth and colouring the saliva yellow. It yields its properties to water or alcohol.

¶ *Constituents*. An acrid, volatile oil, brown colouring matter, gum, starch, chloride of calcium, woody fibre and a yellowish colouring matter named curcumin; this is obtained by digesting tumeric in boiling alcohol,

filtering and evaporating the solution to dryness, the residue being digested in ether, filtered and evaporated.

¶ *Medicinal Action and Uses*. Tumeric is a mild aromatic stimulant seldom used in medicine except as a colouring. It was once a cure for jaundice. Its chief use is in the manufacture of curry powders. It is also used as an adulterant of mustard and a substitute for it and forms one of the ingredients of many cattle condiments. Tincture of Turmeric is used as a colouring agent, but the odour is fugitive. It dyes a rich yellow. Turmeric paper is prepared by soaking unglazed white paper in the tincture and then drying. Used as a test for alkaloids and boric acid.

TURPETH

Ipomœa Turpethum
N.O. Convolvulaceæ

Synonyms. Turpeth Root. Indian Jalap. Trivrit. Nisoth. Operculina Turpethum
Parts Used. Dried root, stem
Habitat. India. Ceylon, Pacific Islands, China, Australia

¶ *Description*. There are two varieties of this convolvulaceous plant, the Sveta, or White Turpeth, preferred as a mild cathartic, and the black or Kirshna, a powerful drastic. The pieces of root are cylindrical, somewhat twisted, and dull grey outside. The drug has a faint odour, and the taste becomes nauseous after it has been in the mouth for some time, though less so than the true jalap. The genus *Ipomœa* are closely related to the *Batatas*.

¶ *Constituents*. Resin, a fatty substance, volatile oil, albumen, starch, a yellow colouring matter, lignin, salts, and ferric oxide. The root contains 10 per cent. of resin, which is a glucoside, Turpethin, insoluble in ether, but soluble in alcohol, to which it gives a brown colour not removable by animal charcoal. To obtain pure, the alcoholic solution is concentrated; the resin is precipitated by, and afterwards boiled with,

water, then dried, reduced to powder, digested with ether, and finally redissolved by absolute alcohol and deposited by ether. After being treated several times in this way, it is obtained in the state of a brownish resin, yielding on pulverization a grey powder, which irritates the mucous membrane of the nostrils and mouth. It is inflammable, burning with a smoky flame and emitting irritant vapours. With strong bases it acts like jalapin, takes up water, and is transferred into a soluble acid, while with dilute acids it is decomposed into turpetholic acid, and glucose.

¶ *Medicinal Action and Uses*. Cathartic and purgative. It is rather slow in its action, less powerful and less unpleasant than jalap.

¶ *Dosage*. 5 to 20 grains.

See BINDWEED, CONVOLVULUS.

UNICORN ROOT, FALSE

Chamælirium luteum (A. GRAY)
N.O. Liliaceæ

Synonyms. Starwort. Helonias. Helonias dioica (Pursh.). Helonias lutea (Ker-Gawl). Chamælirium Carolinianum (Willd.). Veratrum luteum (Linn.)
Part Used. Root

¶ *Description*. A herbaceous perennial found in low moist ground east of the Mississipi and flowering in May and June. Stem 1 to 3 feet high, simple, smooth, angular; leaves alternate, spatulate below, lanceolate above, radical leaves, 8 inches long, ¼ inch wide, narrow at base and formed into a whorl; flowers numerous, small, greenish white, bractless, diœcious, in a dense, terminal raceme, nodding like a plume, 6 inches long,

petals of such flowers narrow, stamens longer than the petals, filaments tapering; anthers terminal, two lobed; petals of female flowers linear; stamens short; ovary ovate, triangular, furrowed; stigmas three-capsule, oblong, three-furrowed, opening at summit; fruit many, compressed, acute; rhizome bulbous, terminating abruptly, 1 inch long; odour faint; taste bitter. Solvents: alcohol, water.

¶ *Constituents*. Chamælirin, fatty acid.

¶ *Medicinal Action and Uses*. Emetic, tonic, diuretic, vermifuge. In large doses a cardiac poison. Of the greatest value in female disorders of the reproductive organs. The indication for its use is a dragging sensation in the extreme lower abdomen. It is useful in impotence, as a tonic in genito-urinary weakness or irritability, for liver and kidney diseases. Especially in diseases due to poor action of the liver and not to weakness of the heart or circulation. It is a good remedy in albuminaria.

¶ *Preparations*. Fluid extract, 5 to 30 drops. Helonin, 2 to 4 grains. Specific helonias, 1 to 20 drops.

UNICORN ROOT, TRUE

Aletris farinosa (LINN.)
N.O. Hæmodoraceæ

Synonyms. Colic-root. Stargrass. Starwort. Star-root. Blazing Star. Ague-root. Aloe-root. Ague Grass. Black-root. Bitter Grass. Crow Corn. Bettie Grass. Devil's Bit
(*French*) Aletris Farinseu
(*German*) Mehlige Aletria
Parts Used. Root, dried rhizome
Habitat. North America. Found at edges of swampy or wet sandy woods, from Florida northward, specially on seashore

¶ *Description*. A low-growing, spreading perennial herb, with tuberous cylindrical, somewhat horizontal root, having many fibres from its lower surface. No stem, leaves lanceolate, acute, ribbed, sessile, or slightly sheathing at base, smooth and flat, pale coloured, thin and coriaceous. Flower-stem simple with remote scales, 1 to 3 feet high, topped with a spiked raceme of short-stalked, white, bell-shaped oblong flowers blooming May to August; the outer surface of these has a mealy frosted appearance. Fruit is an ovate, tapering, coriaceous capsule, enclosed in a persistent envelope. Seeds numerous, ovate, ribbed, albuminous, fleshy, and oily.

In commerce the rhizome is found dried in pieces about 2 inches long and ⅜ inch thick, light brown colour, flattish on upper surface and densely tufted with the remains of the leaves, fracture yellow and slightly fibrous; the roots from the rhizome are wiry about 3 inches long and of a glossy black colour, but when first dried brownish. Taste intensely bitter, peculiar; it loses a great part of its nauseous bitterness with age. Odour very faint.

¶ *Constituents*. The bitter principle in the root has not yet been determined. Its best solvent is alcohol. It contains a large percentage of bitter extractive, colouring matter and resin, and a quantity of starch.

¶ *Medicinal Action and Uses*. The fresh root in large doses is somewhat narcotic, emetic and cathartic; when dried, these properties are lost. In smaller doses it gives colic in hypogastrium, and a sense of stupefaction and vertigo. When dried it becomes a valuable bitter tonic and its tincture or decoction has been used in flatulence, colic, hysteria, and to tone up the stomach; of value in dyspepsia and where there is an absence of urinary phosphates. Its most valuable property is its tonic influence on the female generative organs, proving of great use in cases of habitual miscarriage and as a general tonic. *Extraction Aletridis alcoholicum* is the official preparation.

¶ *Dosages*. The dried powdered root, 5 to 10 grains. Saturated tincture, 5 to 15 drops in water. Fluid extract, ½ to 1 drachm.

UVA URSI. *See* BEARBERRY

VALERIAN

Valeriana officinalis (LINN.)
N.O. Valerianaceæ

Synonyms. Phu (Galen). All-Heal. Great Wild Valerian. Amantilla. Setwall. Setewale Capon's Tail
Part Used. Root
Habitat. Europe and Northern Asia

Two species of Valerian, *Valeriana officinalis* and *V. dioica*, are indigenous in Britain, while a third, *V. pyrenaica*, is naturalized in some parts. The genus comprises about 150 species, which are widely distributed in the temperate parts of the world.

In medicine, the root of *V. officinalis* is intended when Valerian is mentioned. It is supposed to be the *Phu* (an expression of aversion from its offensive odour) of Dioscorides and Galen, by whom it is extolled as an aromatic and diuretic.

It was afterwards found to be useful in

certain kinds of epilepsy. The plant was in such esteem in mediæval times as a remedy, that it received the name of All Heal, which is still given it in some parts of the country.

The plant is found throughout Europe and Northern Asia, and is common in England in marshy thickets and on the borders of ditches and rivers, where its tall stems may generally be seen in the summer towering above the usual herbage, the erect, sturdy growth of the plant, the rich, dark green of the leaves, their beautiful form, and the crowning masses of light-coloured flowers, making the plant conspicuous.

¶ *Description.* The roots tend to merge into a short, conical root-stock or erect rhizome, the development of which often proceeds for several years before a flowering stem is sent up, but slender horizontal branches which terminate in buds are given off earlier, and from these buds proceed aerial shoots or stolons, which produce fresh plants where they take root. Only one stem arises from the root, which attains a height of 3 or 4 feet. It is round, but grooved and hollow, more or less hairy, especially near the base. It terminates in two or more pairs of flowering stems, each pair being placed at right angles to those above and below it. The lower flowering stems lengthen so as to place their flowers nearly or often quite on a level with the flowers borne by the upper branches, forming a broad and flattened cluster at the summit, called a *cyme.* The leaves are arranged in pairs and are united at their bases. Each leaf is made up of a series of lance-shaped segments, more or less opposite to one another on each side of the leaf (pinnate). The leaflets vary very much in number, from six to ten pairs as a rule, and vary also in breadth, being broad when few in number and narrower when more numerous; they are usually 2 to 3 inches long. The margins are indented by a few coarsely-cut teeth. The upper surface is strongly veined, the under surface is paler and frequently more or less covered with short, soft hairs. The leaves on the stem are attached by short, broad sheaths, the radical leaves are larger and long-stemmed and the margins more toothed.

The flowers are in bloom from June to September. They are small, tinged with pink and flesh colour, with a somewhat peculiar, but not exactly unpleasant smell. The corolla is tubular, and from the midst of its lobes rise the stamens, only three in number, though there are five lobes to the corolla. The limb of the calyx is remarkable for being at first inrolled and afterwards expanding in the form of a feathery pappus, which aids the dissemination of the fruit. The fruit is a capsule containing one oblong compressed seed. Apart from the flowers, the whole plant has a fœtid smell, much accentuated when bruised.

Although more often growing in damp situations, Valerian is also met with on dry, elevated ground. It is found throughout Britain, but in the northern counties is more often found on higher and dryer ground – dry heaths and hilly pastures – than in the south, and then is usually smaller, not more than 2 feet high, with narrow leaves and hairy, and is often named *sylvestris.* The medicinal qualities of this form are considered to be especially strong.

Though none of the varieties differ greatly from the typical form, Valerian is more subject than many plants to deviations, which has caused several more or less permanent varieties to be named by various botanists. One of the chief is *V. sambucifolia* (Mikan), the name signifying 'Elder-leaved,' from the form of its foliage, the segments being fewer (only four to six pairs) and broader than in the type form, and having somewhat of the character of the elder.

V. celtica is supposed to be the *Saliunca* of ancient writers. It is used by Eastern nations to aromatize their baths. The roots are collected by the Styrian peasants, and are exported by way of Trieste to Turkey and Egypt, whence they are conveyed to India and Ethiopia. *V. sitchensis*, a native of north-western America, is considered by the Russians the most powerful of all species.

Valerian is cultivated for the sake of the drug in England (in Derbyshire), but to a much greater extent in Prussia, Saxony (in the neighbourhood of Colleda, north of Weimar), in Holland and in the United States (Vermont, New Hampshire and New York). English roots have always commanded about four times the price of the imported. In Derbyshire, the cultivation of Valerian takes place in many villages near Chesterfield, the wild plants occurring in the neighbourhood not being sufficient to supply the demand. Derbyshire Valerian plants are of two varieties: *V. Milkanii* (Syme), on limestone, and *V. sambucifolia* (Mikan) on the coal measures. The former yields most of the cultivated Derbyshire rhizome.

The derivation of the name of this genus of plants is differently given. It is said by some authors to have been named after Valerius, who first used it in medicine; while others derive the name from the Latin word *valere* (to be in health), on account of its medicinal qualities. The word *Valeriana* is not found in the classical authors; we first meet with it in the ninth or tenth century, at which period and for long afterwards it was used as synonymous with *Phu* or *Fu*; *Fu, id est valeriana*, we find it described in ancient medical works of that period. The word *Valerian* occurs in the recipes of the Anglo-Saxon leeches (eleventh century). Valeriana, Amantilla and Fu are used as synonymous in the *Alphita*, a mediæval vocabulary of the important medical school of Salernum. Saladinus of Ascoli (about 1450) directs the collection in the month of August of *radices fu, id est Valerianæ*. Referring to the name *Amantilla*, by which it was known in the fourteenth century, Professor Henslow quotes a curious recipe of that period, a translation of which runs as follows: 'Men who begin to fight and when you wish to stop them, give to them the juice of Amantilla *id est Valeriana* and peace will be made immediately.' *Theriacaria, Marinella, Genicularis* and *Terdina* are other old names by which Valerian has been known in former days. Another old name met with in Chaucer and other old writers is 'Setwall' or 'Setewale,' the derivation of which is uncertain. Mediæval herbalists also called the plant 'Capon's Tail,' which has rather fantastically been explained as a reference to its spreading head of whitish flowers.

Drayton (*Polyolbion*) mentions the use of Valerian for cramp; and a tea was made from its roots.

¶ *Cultivation*. Valerian does well in all ordinary soils, but prefers rich, heavy loam, well supplied with moisture.

In Derbyshire, cultivation is from wild plants collected in local woods and transplanted to the prepared land. Preference is given in collecting to root offsets – daughter plants and young flowering plants, which develop towards the close of summer, at the end of slender runners given off by the perennial rhizomes of old plants. These should be set 1 foot apart in rows, 2 or 3 feet apart. The soil should first be treated with farmyard manure, and after planting it is well to give liquid manure from time to time, as well as plenty of water. The soil must be well manured to secure a good crop. Weeding requires considerable attention.

Propagation may also be by seed, either sown when ripe in cold frames, or in March in gentle heat, or in the open in April. In the first two cases, transplant in May to permanent quarters. But to ensure the best alkaloidal percentage, it is best to transplant and cultivate the daughter plants of the wild Valerian.

¶ *Harvesting and Preparation for Market*. The flowering tops must be cut off as they appear, thus enabling the better develop-ment of the rhizome. Many of the young plants do not flower in the first year, but produce a luxuriant crop of leaves, and yield rhizome of good quality in the autumn.

In September or early October, all the tops are cut off with a scythe and the rhizomes are harvested, the clinging character of the Derbyshire soil not allowing them to be left in the ground longer.

The drug as found in commerce consists usually of the entire or sliced erect rhizome, which is dark yellowish-brown externally, about 1 inch long and $\frac{1}{4}$ inch thick, and gives off numerous slender brittle roots from $2\frac{1}{2}$ to 4 inches long, whilst short, slender, lateral branches (stolons) are also occasionally present. The root-stock, which is sometimes crowned with the remains of flowering stems and leaf-scales is usually firm, horny and whitish or yellowish internally, but old specimens may be hollow. A transverse section is irregular in outline and exhibits a comparatively narrow bark, separated by a dark line from an irregular circle of wood bundles of varying size.

The drug may also consist of small, undeveloped rhizomes about $\frac{1}{4}$ inch long, crowned with the remains of leaves and bearing short slender roots, the young rhizome having been formed where the stolons given off from mature root-stocks have taken root and produced independent plants.

The roots of Valerian are of similar colour to the erect rhizome, about $\frac{1}{16}$ inch thick, striated longitudinally and usually not shrivelled to any great extent; a transverse section shows a thick bark and small wood.

The drug has a camphoraceous, slightly bitter taste and a characteristic, powerful, disagreeable odour, which gradually develops during the process of drying, owing to a change which occurs in the composition of the volatile oil contained in the sub-epidermal layer of cells: the odour of the fresh root, though not very agreeable, is devoid of the unpleasant valerianaceous odour.

The colour and odour of Valerian rhizome distinguish it readily from other drugs. The rhizome somewhat resembles Serpentary rhizome (*Aristolochia Serpentaria*, Virginian Snakeroot), but may be distinguished therefrom by its odour, erect method of growth, and by the roots being thicker, shorter and less brittle.

¶ *Substitutes*. Valerian root is often fraudulently adulterated with those of other species, notably with those of *V. dioica* (Linn.) (Marsh Valerian), which are smaller and of much feebler odour, and not possessed of such active properties. This Valerian is also a native of Great Britain, found in wet meadows and bogs, but rather scarce. It is a smaller plant than the official Valerian, its stem only growing 6 to 18 inches high. The leaves are very variable, the lower ones generally entire, oval but broader at the base, the upper ones cut into pairs of leaflets, and the flowers *diœcious*, i.e. stamens and pistil, or seed-producing organs in different flowers, the male flowers being arranged rather loosely, and the female flowers, which are smaller and darker, being in more compact heads.

The roots of *V. Phu* (Linn.) are also frequently found mingled with those of the official plant in the imported drug. This species is a native of Southern Europe and Western Asia, often grown in gardens for its decorative golden foliage, being easy of culture. Its rhizome is sometimes known as *V. Radix Majoris*. It is from 4 to 6 inches long, ½ inch in thickness, brown and with a feeble, valerian-like odour and taste. Its thicker rhizome lies obliquely in the earth instead of being erect like that of *V. officinalis*, and is rooted at the bottom only, the roots being numerous and yellowish.

It is stated also that in Germany various Ranunculaceous (or Buttercup) roots are a dangerous adulterant of Valerian; they may be readily detected by their want of the peculiar odour of the official root. The Valerian in the markets of Paris is often largely adulterated with the roots of Scabious (*Scabiosus succisa*, Linn.) and *S. arvensis* (Linn.). They are shorter than the genuine root, less rough, very brittle, not striated, or channelled, and with a white fracture. Though inodorous in themselves, they are very apt to acquire odour from contact with the Valerian. The roots of *Geum urbanum*, or Avens, which in themselves are pleasingly aromatic, but may also on contact acquire some of the odour, have also occasionally been found in parcels of imported Valerian root.

¶ *Chemical Constituents.* The chief constituent of Valerian is a yellowish-green to brownish-yellow oil, which is present in the dried root to the extent of 0·5 to 2 per cent. though an average yield rarely exceeds 0·8 per cent. This variation in quantity is partly explained by the influence of locality, a dry, stony soil, yielding a root richer in oil than one that is moist and fertile.

Lindley's *Treasury of Botany* states: 'What is known to chemists as volatile oil of Valerian seems not to exist naturally in the plant, but to be developed by the agency of water.'

The oil is contained in the sub-epidermal ayer of cells in the root, not in isolated cells or glands. It is of complex composition, containing valerianic, formic and acetic acids, the alcohol known as borneol, and pinene. The valerianic acid present in the oil is not the normal acid, but isovalerianic acid, an oily liquid to which the characteristically unpleasant odour of Valerian is due. It is gradually liberated during the process of drying, being yielded by the decomposition of the chief constituent, bornyl-isovalerianate, by the ferment present. It is strongly acid, burning to the palate and with the odour of the plant. The oil is soluble in 30 parts of water and readily in alcohol and ether. It is found in nature in the oil of several plants, also in small proportion in train oil and the oil of *Cetacea* (whales, porpoises, etc.), which owe their smell to it. It is also one of the products of oxidation of animal matters and of fat oils, and is secreted in certain portions of animal bodies. Its salts are soluble and have a sweetish taste and fatty aspect.

The root also contains two alkaloids – Chatarine and Valerianine – which are still under investigation and concerning which little is known, except that they form crystalline salts. There are also a glucoside, alkaloid and resin all physiologically active, discovered in the fresh rhizome by Chevalier as recently as 1907. He claims that the fresh root is of greater medicinal value than the dry on this account.

On incineration, the drug, if free from adherent earthy matter, yields about 8 or 9 per cent. of ash.

The chief preparation of the British Pharmacopœia is the *Tinctura Valerianæ Ammoniata*, containing Valerian, oil of Nutmeg, oil of Lemon and Ammonia: it is an extremely nauseous and offensive preparation. An etherial tincture and the volatile oil are official in some of the Continental Pharmacopœias, and a distilled water and syrup in the French Codex.

Valerianate of oxide of ethyl, or valerianic ether is a fragrant compound occurring in some vegetable products. The valerianic acid in use is not prepared from the root, but synthetically from amyl alcohol. Valerianic acid combines with various bases (the oxides of metals) to form salts called Valerianates. Valerianate of zinc, prepared by double decomposition, is used as an antispasmodic and is official in the British Pharmacopœia.

¶ *Medicinal Action and Uses.* Valerian is a powerful nervine, stimulant, carminative and antispasmodic.

It has a remarkable influence on the cerebro-spinal system, and is used as a sedative to the higher nerve centres in conditions of nervous unrest, St. Vitus's dance, hypochrondriasis, neuralgic pains and the like.

The drug allays pain and promotes sleep. It is of especial use and benefit to those suffering from nervous overstrain, as it possesses none of the after-effects produced by narcotics.

During the recent War, when air-raids were a serious strain on the overwrought nerves of civilian men and women, Valerian, prescribed with other simple ingredients, taken in a single dose, or repeated according to the need, proved wonderfully efficacious, preventing or minimizing serious results.

Though in ordinary doses, it exerts an influence quieting and soothing in its nature upon the brain and nervous system, large doses, too often repeated, have a tendency to produce pain in the head, heaviness and stupor.

It is commonly administered as *Tinctura Valerianæ Ammoniata*, and often in association with the alkali bromides, and is sometimes given in combination with quinine, the tonic powers of which it appreciably increases.

Oil of Valerian is employed to a considerable extent on the Continent as a popular remedy for cholera, in the form of cholera drops, and also to a certain extent in soap perfumery.

Ettmuller writes of its virtues in strengthening the eyesight, especially when this is weakened by want of energy in the optic nerve.

The juice of the fresh root, under the name of Energetene of Valerian, has of late been recommended as more certain in its effects, and of value as a narcotic in insomnia, and as an anti-convulsant in epilepsy. Having also some slight influence upon the circulation, slowing the heart and increasing its force, it has been used in the treatment of cardiac palpitations.

Valerian was first brought to notice as a specific for epilepsy by Fabius Calumna in 1592, he having cured himself of the disease with it.

¶ *Preparations and Dosages.* Fluid extract, ½ to 1 drachm. Solid extract, 5 to 10 grains. Tincture, B.P. and U.S.P., 1885, 1 to 2 drachms. Ammoniated tincture, B.P. and U.S.P. 1898, ½ to 1 drachm.

Culpepper (1649) joins with many old writers to recommend the use both of herb and root, and praises the herb for its longevity and many comforting virtues, reminding us that it is 'under the influence of Mercury, and therefore hath a warming faculty.' Among other uses, he adds:

'The root boiled with liquorice, raisons and aniseed is good for those troubled with cough. Also, it is of special value against the plague, the decoction thereof being drunk and the root smelled. The green herb being bruised and applied to the head taketh away pain and pricking thereof.'

Gerard tells us that herbalists of his time thought it 'excellent for those burdened and for such as be troubled with croup and other like convulsions, and also for those that are bruised with falls.' He relates that the dried root was held in such esteem as a medicine among the poorer classes in the northern counties and the south of Scotland, that 'no broth or pottage or physicall meats be worth anything if Setewale (the old name for Valerian) be not there.'

Sutherland describes many varieties of Valerian, and himself grew the Indian Valerian which is still sent to Mincing Lane, and offered on the British market. Hanbury states that, according to its habitat, it has many variations which some botanists take as separate species. In the south of England, when once it obtains a hold of the ground, nothing will eradicate it. It was well known to the Anglo-Saxons, who used it as a salad.

Valerian has an effect on the nervous system of many animals, especially cats, which seem to be thrown into a kind of intoxication by its scent. It is scarcely possible to keep a plant of Valerian in a garden after the leaves or root have been bruised or disturbed in any way, for cats are at once attracted and roll on the unfortunate plant. It is equally attractive to rats and is often used by rat-catchers to bait their traps. It has been suggested that the famous Pied Piper of Hamelin owed his irresistible power over rats to the fact that he secreted Valerian roots about his person.

In the Middle Ages, the root was used not only as a medicine but also as a spice, and even as a perfume. It was the custom to lay the roots among clothes as a perfume (*vide* Turner, *Herbal*, 1568, Pt. III, p. 56), just as some of the Himalayan Valerians are still used in the East, especialiy *V. Jatamansi*, the Nard of the Ancients, believed to be the Spikenard referred to in the Scriptures. It is still much used in ointments. Its odour is not so unpleasant as that of our native Valerians, and this and other species of Valerian are used by Asiatic nations in the manufacture of precious scents. Several aromatic roots were known to the Ancients under the name of *Nardus*, distinguished according to their origin or place of growth by the names of

Nardus indica, N. celtica, N. montana, etc., and supposed to have been derived from different valerianaceous plants. Thus the *N. indica* is referred to *V. Jatamansi* (Roxb.), of Bengal, the *N. celtica* to *V. celtica* (Linn.), inhabiting the Alps and the *N. montana* to *V. tuberosa,* which grows in the mountains of the south of Europe.

¶ *Other Species.*

JAPANESE VALERIAN, or Kesso Root, was formerly believed to be the product of *Patrinia scabiosæfolia* (Link.), but is now known to be obtained from a Japanese variety of *V. officinalis.* It yields a volatile oil. By the absence of a well-marked, upright rhizome, it widely differs from true Valerian, though at first sight agrees to some extent with it. In colour and taste it is almost identical.

The roots of *V. Mexicana* (D.C.), MEXICAN VALERIAN, which occurs in Mexican commerce in slices, or fleshy disks, contain a large percentage of valerianic acid, which they yield readily and economically. As much as 3·3 per cent. of oil has been extracted from the roots of this species.

V. pyrenaica (Linn.), the HEART-LEAVED VALERIAN, a native of the Pyrenees, is occasionally found in Great Britain naturalized in plantations. It is a large, coarse herb, the stem 2 to 4 feet high, the radical leaves sometimes very large, often a foot in diameter, heart-shaped, the upper ones smaller, with a few basal leaflets, the flowers much as in *V. officinalis.* It is not employed medicinally.

V. montana and *V. angustifolia* are Alpine varieties, but can be grown in this country with a little care. They are almost entirely grown for decorative purposes, flowering from May to August, and possessing none of the unpleasant smell of Valerian.

Culpepper describes a plant which he calls 'Water Valerian' (*V. Aquatica*), with 'much larger' flowers than the garden Valerian, which, however, they resemble, and of a 'pale purple colour.' He states it grows 'promiscuously in marshy grounds and moist meadows' and flowers in May.

VALERIAN, AMERICAN

Cypripedium pubescens (WILLD.)
Cyprepedium parviflorum
N.O. Orchidaceæ

Synonyms. Lady's Slipper. Cypripedium hirsutum. American Valerian. Noah's Ark. Yellow Lady's Slipper. Nerve-root

Part Used. Root

American Valerian is one of the names given to the Yellow Lady's Slipper (*Cypripedium*). The roots of several varieties, the principal being *Cypripedium pubescens* and *Cyprepedium parviflorum,* are employed in hysteria, being a gentle, nervous stimulant and antispasmodic, less powerful than Valerian.

American Valerian is official in the United States Pharmacopœia for the production of a fluid extract. *Cypridenin* is a complex, resinoid substance, obtained by precipitating with water a concentrated tincture of the rhizome.

¶ *Preparations and Dosages.* Powdered root, 1 drachm. Fluid extract, ½ to 1 drachm. Cypripedin, 1 to 3 grains. Solid extract alc., 5 to 10 grains.

VALERIAN, INDIAN

Valeriana Wallichii (DE CANDOLLE)
N.O. Valerianaceæ

Synonym. Tagar.

Indian Valerian is a perennial, herbaceous plant, indigenous to India, being found in the temperate Himalayan region. The dried rhizome and rootlets are used for medicinal purposes, and the drug is known in India as 'tagar.' It possesses stimulant and antispasmodic properties, and is official in the Indian and Colonial Addendum for use in the Eastern Colonies. The chief preparation of the drug is *Tinctura Valerianæ Indicæ Ammoniata.* Indian Valerian is practically identical in its composition with the European drug, but contains a slightly larger amount of volatile oil. It may be employed in the same way as Valerian, but is more used as a perfume than in medicine. It is largely employed in preparations for the hair, and the dried rhizome is used as incense.

It occurs in commerce in crooked pieces of a dull brown colour, about 2 inches long, and from ¼ to ½ inch in diameter, with a number of bracts at the crown and blunt at the lower extremity. The rhizome is marked with transverse ridges and studded thickly with prominent circular tubercles to a few of which thick rootlets may be attached. The crown usually bears the remains of the leaf-stalks. In transverse section it is dark, with a large pith and diffuse ring of small wood-bundles. The drug is very hard and tough, and shows a greenish-brown surface when fractured. This and its crooked form distinguish it from Common Valerian. Its colour, due to the presence of volatile oil resembles that of ordinary Valerian rhizome, but is much stronger. The chief constituent of the drug is this oil, but it also contains valerianic and other organic acids, together with resin, tannin, etc. As in the case of ordinary Valerian, the valerianic acid is probably formed by the gradual decomposition of other constituents present in the volatile oil.

¶ *Preparations.* Tincture Valerianæ Indicæ Ammoniata.

The INDIAN NARD, or Spikenard, sometimes called Syrian Nard, is still occasionally to be found in commerce. It is a small, delicate root, from 1 to 3 inches long, beset with a tuft of soft, light brown, slender fibres, of an agreeable odour and a bitter aromatic taste. It was formerly very much esteemed as a medicine, but is now almost out of use. Its properties are analogous to those of Valerian, but it must not be confused with Indian Valerian.

VALERIAN, RED-SPUR

Centranthus rubra (D. C.)
N.O. Valerianaceæ

Synonyms. Pretty Betsy. Bouncing Bess. Delicate Bess. Drunken Sailor. Bovisand Soldier
Habitat. England, Scotland and the Mediterranean countries

The Red-Spur Valerian, a plant with lance-shaped, untoothed leaves and red flowers with a spur at the base, grouped in dense clusters, must not be confounded with the true medicinal Valerian, though the mistake is often made. It is destitute of the properties of the official Valerian, and is not usefully applied in England, though in some parts of Continental Europe the leaves are eaten. They are exceedingly good in salad, or cooked as a vegetable, and in France there is a sale for the roots for soups.

This plant is not truly British, but is perfectly naturalized in the south of England, being found quite often growing on rocks or walls, in old chalk-pits, railway cuttings and waste places in Kent and Devonshire, though less frequently in the northern counties and only in a few places in Scotland. It is naturally a native of the Mediterranean countries, and was probably originally introduced as a decorative plant. It is mentioned by many of the older writers as a garden flower. Gerard, writing in 1597, saying: 'It groweth plentifully in my garden, being a great ornament to the same.' Parkinson (1640) says that it grows 'in our gardens chiefly, for we know not the natural place.'

¶ *Description.* The root-stock is perennial and very freely branching, enabling it to take a firm hold in the crevices in which it

has once gained possession. The stems are stout, somewhat shrubby at the base, between 1 and 2 feet long, hollow and very smooth in texture. The leaves 2 to 4 inches long and pointed, opposite one another in pairs, are somewhat fleshy, their outlines generally quite entire. The very numerous flowers are in masses, either of a rich crimson colour, a delicate pink, or much more rarely, white, and are in bloom from June to September. The spur to the long, tubular corolla is a marked feature. Each flower only contains one stamen. The fruit is small and dry, the border of the surrounding calyx forming a feathery rosette or pappus.

Linnæus included this species with the Valerians, as *Valeriana rubra*, but De Candolle assigned it to a separate genus, *Centranthus*, in which all later botanists have followed him. The name of the genus comes from the Greek *kentron* (a spur) and *anthos* (a flower), in reference to the corolla being furnished with a spur at the base, which absolutely distinguishes it from the true Valerian, apart from other differences.

'Pretty Betsy' and 'Bouncing Bess' are popular names for the Red Valerian. Near Plymouth, we find the names 'Drunken Sailor' and 'Bovisand Soldier,' and in West Devon, the smaller, paler kind is known as 'Delicate Bess.'

VERBENA, LEMON

Lippia citriodora
N.O. Verbenaceæ

Synonyms. Aloysia citriodora. Verveine citronelle or odorante. Herb Louisa. Lemon-scented Verbena. Verbena triphylla. Lippia triphylla
Parts Used. Leaves, flowering tops
Habitat. Chile and Peru. Cultivated in European gardens

¶ *Description.* This deciduous shrub was introduced into England in 1784, reaching a height of 15 feet in the Isle of Wight and in sheltered localities. The leaves are very fragrant, lanceolate, arranged in threes, 3 to

4 inches long, with smooth margins, pale green in colour, having parallel veins at right-angles to the mid-rib and flat bristles along the edges. The many small flowers are pale purple, blooming during August in slim,

terminal panicles. The leaves, which have been suggested to replace tea, will retain their odour for years and are used in perfumery. They should be gathered at flowering time.

All the species of Lippia abound in volatile oil.

¶ *Constituents.* The odour is due to an essential oil obtainable by distillation. It has not been analysed in detail.

¶ *Medicinal Action and Uses.* Febrifuge, sedative. The uses of Lemon Verbena are similar to those of mint, orange flowers, or melissa, as a stomachic and antispasmodic in dyspepsia, indigestion and flatulence, stimulating skin and stomach.

SWEET VERNAL GRASS. *See* GRASSES

VERONICAS

The genus *Veronica* includes some of our most beautiful native flowers, the Speedwells, which differ from the other British *Scrophularicæ* in having only two stamens, which project horizontally from the rotate, or wheel-shaped corolla, which has only four unequal spreading lobes, the lower segment being the smallest, the two posterior petals, according to the theory of botanists, being united into one large one. The numerous species found in England have generally blue petals with dark diverging lines at the base, though in a few cases, pinkish flowers are found.

All the species of Veronica possess a slight degree of astringency, and many of them were formerly used in medicine, some

¶ *Dosage.* The decoction may be taken in several daily doses of three tablespoonsful.

¶ *Other Species.*

Lippia Scaberrima, or Beukessboss of South Africa, yields an essential oil with an odour like lavender, named Lippianol. It has a peculiar crystalline appearance, with the qualities of a monohydric alcohol.

From *L. mexicana* or possibly *Cedronella mexicana*, an essential oil resembling that of fennel was separated, and also a substance like camphor, called Lippioil.

The essence of Lemon-Grass, or *Andropogon Schœnanthus*, should not be confused with that of Lemon-Scented Verbena.

N.O. Scrophulariaceæ

20 of them have been employed as drugs, those with the chief reputaticn being *Veronica Chamædrys*, *V. officinalis*, and *V. Beccabunga*, all natives of Great Britain; the American species *V. leptandra*, now known as *Leptandra veronica* and another species, native to Asia Minor, called *V. peduncularis* (Bieb.) or *V. nigricans* (Koch.), the root of which is used there under the name Batitjoe.

The name of this genus of plants is said to have been derived from the Saint; others say it is from the Greek words *phero* (I bring) and *nike* (victory), alluding to its supposed efficacy in subduing diseases.

See BROOKLIME, SPEEDWELL, GERMANDER SPEEDWELL.

VERVAIN

Verbena officinalis (LINN.)
Verbena hastata
N.O. Verbenaceæ

Synonyms. Herb of Grace. Herbe Sacrée. Herba veneris
Parts Used. Leaves, flowering heads
Habitat. Europe, Barbary, China, Cochin-China, Japan

¶ *Description.* In England the Common Vervain is found growing by roadsides and in sunny pastures. It is a perennial bearing many small, pale-lilac flowers. The leaves are opposite, and cut into toothed lobes. The plant has no perfume, and is slightly bitter and astringent in taste. The name *Vervain* is derived from the Celtic *ferfaen*, from *fer* (to drive away) and *faen* (a stone), as the plant was much used for affections of the bladder, especially calculus. Another derivation is given by some authors from *Herba veneris*, because of the aphrodisiac qualities attributed to it by the Ancients. Priests used it for sacrifices, and hence the name *Herba Sacra*. The name *Verbena* was the classical Roman name for 'altar-plants' in general, and

for this species in particular. The druids included it in their lustral water, and magicians and sorcerers employed it largely. It was used in various rites and incantations, and by ambassadors in making leagues. Bruised, it was worn round the neck as a charm against headaches, and also against snake and other venomous bites as well as for general good luck. It was thought to be good for the sight. Its virtues in all these directions may be due to the legend of its discovery on the Mount of Calvary, where it staunched the wounds of the crucified Saviour. Hence, it is crossed and blessed with a commemorative verse when it is gathered. It must be picked before flowering, and dried promptly.

¶ *Constituents.* The plant appears to contain a peculiar tannin, but it has not yet been properly analysed.

¶ *Medicinal Action and Uses.* It is recommended in upwards of thirty complaints, being astringent, diaphoretic, antispasmodic, etc. It is said to be useful in intermittent fevers, ulcers, ophthalmia, pleurisy, etc., and to be a good galactogogue. It is still used as a febrifuge in autumn fevers.

As a poultice it is good in headache, earneuralgia, rheumatism, etc. In this form it colours the skin a fine red, giving rise to the idea that it had the power of drawing the blood outside. A decoction of 2 oz. to a quart, taken in the course of one day, is said to be a good medicine in purgings, easing pain in the bowels. It is often applied externally for piles. It is used in homœopathy.

Fluid extract, ½ to 1 drachm.

¶ *Other Species.*

Verbena Jamaicensis (JAMAICA VERVAIN) grows in Jamaica, Barbados, and other West Indian islands, bearing violet flowers.

The juice is used in dropsy and for children as an anthelmintic and cooling cathartic. The negroes use it as an emmenagogue, and for sore and inflamed eyes. As a poultice, with wheat-flour, the bruised leaves are used for swelling of the spleen, and for hard tumours at their commencement.

V. Lappulaceæ (BURRY VERVAIN), another West Indian herb, with pale blue flowers, is a vulnerary sub-astringent, being used even for very severe bleeding wounds in men and cattle, especially in Jamaica.

V. hastata (BLUE VERVAIN, Wild Hyssop, Simpler's Joy) is indigenous to the United States, and is used unofficially as a tonic, emetic, expectorant, etc., for scrofula, gravel, and worms. A fluid extract is prepared from the dried, over-ground portion.

V. Urticifolia. The root, boiled in milk and water with the inner bark of *Quercus Alba*, is said to be an antidote to poisoning by *Rhus Toxicodendron*.

V. Sinuata. An infusion of the root, taken as freely as possible, is said to be a valuable antisyphilitic.

VINE

Vitis vinifera (LINN.)
N.O. Vitaceæ

Synonym. Grape Vine
Parts Used. Fruit, leaves, juice
Habitat. Asia, Central and Southern Europe, Greece, California, Australia, and Africa

¶ *Description.* The name vine is derived from *viere* (to twist), and has reference to the twining habits of the plant which is a very ancient one; in the Scriptures the vine is frequently mentioned from the time of Noah onward. Wine is recorded as an almost universal drink throughout the world from very early times. The vine is a very longlived plant. Pliny speaks of one 600 years old, and some existent in Burgundy are said to be 400 and over.

The stem of old vines attains a considerable size in warm climates, planks 15 inches across may be cut therefrom, forming a very durable timber.

Artificial heat for forcing the grapes was not used till the early part of last century and the first accounts of vineries enclosed by glass date from the middle of that period.

The vine is propagated by seeds, layers, cuttings and grafting and succeeds in almost any gravelly soil; that of a volcanic nature produces the finest wines. It is a climbing shrub with simple, lobed, cut or toothed leaves (seldom compound) with thyrsoid racemes of greenish flowers, the fruit consisting of watery or fleshy pulp, stones and skin, two-celled, four-seeded.

¶ *Constituents.* The leaves gathered in June contain a mixture of cane sugar and glucose, tartaric acid, potassium bi-tartrate, quercetine, quercitrin, tannin, amidon, malic acid, gum, inosite, an uncrystallizable fermentable sugar and oxalate of calcium; gathered in the autumn they contain much more quercetine and less trace of quercitrin.

The ripe fruit juice termed 'must' contains sugar, gum, malic acid, potassium bitartrate and inorganic salts; when fermented this forms the wine of commerce.

The dried ripe fruit commonly called raisins, contain dextrose and potassium acid tartrate.

The seeds contain tannin and a fixed oil.

The juice of the unripe fruit, 'Verjuice,' contains malic, citric, tartaric, racemic and tannic acids, potassium bi-tartrate, sulphate of potash and lime.

¶ *Medicinal Action and Uses.* Grape sugar differs from other sugars chemically. It enters the circulation without any action of the saliva. The warming and fattening action of grape sugar is thus more rapid in increasing strength and repairing waste in fevers but is unsuitable for inflammatory or gouty conditions.

The seeds and leaves are astringent, the leaves being formerly used to stop hæmorrhages and bleeding. They are used dried and powdered as a cure for dysentery in cattle.

The sap, termed a tear or lachryma, forms an excellent lotion for weak eyes and specks on the cornea.

Ripe grapes in quantity influence the kidneys producing a free flow of urine and are apt to cause palpitation in excitable and full-blooded people. Dyspeptic subjects should avoid them.

In cases of anæmia and a state of exhaustion the restorative power of grapes is striking, especially when taken in conjunction with a light nourishing diet.

In cases of small-pox grapes have proved useful owing to their bi-tartrate of potash content; they are also said to be of benefit in cases of neuralgia, sleeplessness, etc.

Three to 6 lb. of grapes a day are taken by people undergoing the 'grape cure,' sufferers from torpid liver and sluggish biliary functions should take them not quite fully ripe, whilst those who require animal heat to support waste of tissue should eat fully ripe and sweet grapes.

Dried grapes; the raisins of commerce, are largely used in the manufacture of galencials, the seeds being separated and rejected as they give a very bitter taste. Raisins are demulcent, nutritive and slightly laxative.

¶ *Other Species.*

Vitis labrusca, indigenous to North America, is the Wild Vine or Foxgrape.

V. cordifolia, the Heart-leaved Vine or Chickengrape.

V. riparia, the Riverside or Sweet-scented Vine.

VIOLET, DOG

Viola canina (LINN.)
N.O. Violaceæ

Parts Used. Leaves and flowers

¶ *Description.* The Dog Violet differs principally from the Sweet Violet in its long straggling stems and paler blue flowers. It possesses the same properties, being powerfully cathartic and emetic. At one time a medicine made from it had some reputation in curing skin diseases. It may be found on dry hedge-banks and in the woods, flowering from April to August, a longer flowering period than the Sweet Violet. It is a very variable plant in size of leaf and blossom, form of leaf and other parts, but there seem to be no permanent and reliable differences to justify the division into distinct sub-species. The root-stock of the Dog Violet is short and from it rises a tuft of leaves. The flowering stems are at first short, but as time goes on they elongate considerably until sometimes they may be found nearly a foot long. The leaves are heart-shaped and with serrated edges, but vary much in their proportions. They are ordinarily, like the stems, quite smooth, while in the Sweet Violet we often get them more or less covered with soft hairs. The flowers are scentless, generally larger than those of the Sweet Violet, not only paler in colour, but like most purple flowers, occasionally varying to white.

The popular name of this plant is a reproach for its want of perfume.

VIOLET, HAIRY

Viola hirta
N.O. Violaceæ

Part Used. Whole plant

The Hairy Violet (*Viola hirta*), the Dog Violet (*V. canina*), the Marsh Violet (*V. palustris*) (which has pale lilac flowers) and the Heartsease or Pansy (*V. tricolor*) are other well-defined species of indigenous Violets, most of them, however, being subject to variations, which have been described by botanists as sub-species.

Henslow says *V. palustris* is not uncommon in the north, but rarer in southern counties. It has very smooth leaves, as is usually the case with semi-aquatic plants; the flowers are scentless. The same authority mentions another variety, *V. calcarea*, a dwarfed, starved form of *V. hirta*.

¶ *Description.* The Hairy Violet bears a very considerable resemblance to *V. odorata*, the Sweet Violet. The main points of difference are as follows: in the Hairy Violet the flowers are almost or quite scentless; it but rarely throws out the trailing shoots that are so characteristic a feature in the Sweet Violet; the hairs on the stem are in the Sweet Violet deflexed, while in the Hairy Violet they are spreading and are thus more conspicuous, sufficiently so to give the popular name to the plant. The little scales on the flower-stems, called bracts, are in Sweet Violet ordinarily above the middle of the stalk, while in the Hairy Violet they are ordinarily (in neither case invariably) below this point. This species is more frequently found in the east of England than the west, and is common in chalk and limestone districts or near the sea.

VIOLET, SWEET

Viola odorata (LINN.)
N.O. Violaceæ

Synonyms. Sweet-Scented Violet
Parts Used. Flowers and leaves dried, and whole plant fresh
Habitat. The Violet family comprises over 200 species, widely distributed in the temperate and tropical regions of the world, those natives of Europe, Northern Asia and North America being wholly herbaceous, whilst others, native of tropical America and South America, where they are abundant, are trees and shrubs. The genus *Viola* contains about 100 species, of which five are natives of Great Britain

¶ *Description.* The sweet-scented Violet appears at the end of February and has finished blooming by the end of April.

The familiar leaves are heart-shaped, slightly downy, especially beneath, on stalks rising alternately from a creeping rhizome or underground stem, the blades of the young leaves rolled up from each side into the middle on the face of the leaf into two tight coils. The flower-stalks arise from the axils of the leaves and bear single flowers, with a pair of scaly bracts placed a little above the middle of the stalk.

The flowers are generally deep purple, giving their name to the colour that is called after them, but lilac, pale rose-coloured or white variations are also frequent, and all these tints may sometimes be discovered in different plants growing on the same bank.

They bear five sepals extended at their bases, and five unequal petals, the lower one lengthened into a hollow spur beneath and the lateral petals with a hairy centre line. The anthers are united into a tube round the three-celled capsule, the two lower ones furnished with spurs which are enclosed within the spur of the corolla.

The flowers are full of honey and are constructed for bee visitors, but bloom before it is really bee time, so that it is rare that a Violet flower is found setting seed. There is indeed a remarkable botanical curiosity in the structure of the Violet: it produces flowers both in the spring and in autumn, but the flowers are different. In spring they are fully formed, as described, and sweet-scented, but they are mostly barren and produce no seed, while in autumn, they are very small and insignificant, hidden away amongst the leaves, with no petals and no scent, and produce abundance of seed. This peculiarity is not confined to the Violet. It is found in some species of *Oxalis, Impatiens, Campanula, Eranthemum,* etc. Such plants are called *cleistogamous* and are all self-fertilizing. The cleistogamous flowers of the Violet are like flowers which have aborted instead of developing, but within each one are a couple of stamens and some unripe seeds. In warmer climates, like Italy, these 'cleistogamous' buds develop into perfect flowers. Only

occasionally do they do so in England. In the woodland species (*Viola sylvatica*) all the flowers on the plant may be cleistogamous.

The Violet propagates itself, also, in another way by throwing out scions, or runners, from the main plant each summer after flowering, and these in turn send out roots and become new plants, a process that renders it independent of seed.

The Violet is very abundant in the neighbourhood of Stratford-on-Avon, where it is nowadays much cultivated for commercial purposes.

Violet is the diminutive form of the Latin *Viola,* the Latin form of the Greek name *Ione.* There is a legend that when Jupiter changed his beloved Io into a white heifer for fear of Juno's jealousy, he caused these modest flowers to spring forth from the earth to be fitting food for her, and he gave them her name. Another derivation of the word Violet is said to be from *Vias* (wayside).

Other flowers besides the Violet formerly bore that name, e.g. the Snowdrop was called the 'bulbous or narcissus Violet'; the plant now called 'Honesty' (or Moonwort) had the apellation of 'Strange Violet'; and two species of Gentian were called 'Autumn Bell-flower' or 'Calathian Violet,' and another 'Marion's Violet.' The periwinkle, now generally known in France by the name of *Pervenche,* in other times was known as '*du lisseron*' or '*Violette des sorciers*'; and our own Violet was called, in distinction from the others, 'March Violet,' and in French *Violette de Mars.*

At Pæstum, which has been and still is famous for its Violets as well as for its roses, several kinds of Violets are found, and one species that grows in the woods has exceedingly large leaves and seed-vessels; but the flower is so small that it can hardly be seen; this has given rise to the idea that it blooms underground. The flowers are of a pale yellow.

The Violet of India bears its blossom in an erect position, while our own native plant hangs down its head. It has been suggested by Professor Rennie that the drooping position of the purple petals shaded still more by the large green flower-cup, serves as an umbrella to protect the seed while unripe, from the rains and dews, which would injure it. As soon as the seed is matured and the little canopy no longer wanted, the flower rises and stands upright on its stem.

Some butterflies feed entirely on Violet, and the stem of the plant is often swelled and spongy in appearance, due to insects, whose eggs were deposited on the stalk during the preceding summer. The little animal, on hatching out, finds its food ready for it, and penetrating the plant, disturbs its juices and causes this excrescence.

Violets were mentioned frequently by Homer and Virgil. They were used by the Athenians 'to moderate anger,' to procure sleep and 'to comfort and strengthen the heart.' Pliny prescribes a liniment of Violet root and vinegar for gout and disorder of the spleen, and states that a garland or chaplet of Violets worn about the head will dispel the fumes of wine and prevent headache and dizziness. The ancient Britons used the flowers as a cosmetic, and in a Celtic poem they are recommended to be employed steeped in goats' milk to increase female beauty, and in the Anglo-Saxon translation of the Herbarium of Apuleius (tenth century), the herb *V. purpureum* is recommended 'for new wounds and eke for old' and for 'hardness of the maw.'

In Macer's *Herbal* (tenth century) the Violet is among the many herbs which were considered powerful against 'wykked sperytis.'

Askham's *Herbal* has this recipe for insomnia under Violet:

'For thē that may not slepe for sickness seeth this herb in water and at even let him soke well hys feete in the water to the ancles, whā he goeth to bed, bind of this herbe to his temples.'

Violets, like Primroses, have been associated with death, especially with the death of the young. This feeling has been constantly expressed from early times. It is referred to by Shakespeare in *Hamlet* and *Pericles* and by Milton in *Lycidas*.

In parts of Gloucestershire the country people have an aversion to bringing Violets into their cottages because they carry fleas. This idea may have arisen from these insects in the stem.

When Napoleon went to Elba his last message to his adherents was that he should return with Violets. Hence he was alluded to and toasted by them in secret as Caporal Violette, and the Violet was adopted as the emblem of the Imperial Napoleonic party.

Violets were also and still are used in cookery, especially by the French. '*Vyolette: Take flowrys of Vyolet, boyle hem, presse hem, bray (pound) hem smal,*' and the recipe continues that they are to be mixed with milk and floure of rys and sugar or honey, and finally to be coloured with Violets. A recipe called *Mon Amy* directs the cook to 'plant it with flowers of Violets and serve forth.'

A wine made from the flowers of the Sweet Violet was much used by the Romans.

Violets impart their odour to liquids, and vinegar derives not only a brilliant tint, but a sweet odour from having Violet flowers steeped in it.

The chief use of the Violet in these days is as a colouring agent and perfume, and as the source of the medicinally employed Syrup of Violets, for which purposes the plant is largely cultivated, especially in Warwickshire. The Syrup can be made as follows: To 1 lb. of Sweet Violet flowers freshly picked, add 2½ pints of boiling water, infuse these for twenty-four hours in a glazed china vessel, then pour off the liquid and strain it gently through muslin; afterwards add double its weight of the finest loaf sugar and make it into a syrup, but without letting it boil. This is an old-fashioned recipe.

Another recipe, from a seventeenth century recipe book:

'Sirrup of Violets

'Take a quantity of Blew Violets, clip off the whites and pound them well in a stone morter; then take as much fair running water as will sufficiently moysten them and mix with the Violets; strain them all; and to every halfe pint of the liquor put one pound of the best loafe sugar; set it on the fire, putting the sugar in as it melts, still stirring it; let it boyle but once or twice att the most; then take it from the fire, and keep it to your use. This is a daynty sirrup of Violets.'

Syrup of Violet with Lemon Syrup and acetic acid makes an excellent dish in summer. The Syrup forms a principal ingredient in Oriental sherbet.

¶ *Cultivation.* The Wild Violet has been developed by cultivation till its blossoms in some varieties are many times the original size.

One of the essential points for the successful cultivation of Violets, either for the sake of marketing the cut blooms, or for medicinal purposes, is clear atmosphere. They seldom do well near a town, because the undersides of the leaves are covered with hairs, which catch the grit, thus blocking the breathing pores.

Neglect of a few simple rules is invariably the cause of failure. One frequently finds a bed of Violets which produces nothing but leaves. The plants may have been healthy enough to begin with and they were probably well and truly planted, but after the first season of bloom they were allowed to spread and become overcrowded. The Violet must be renewed and replanted every year. Failure to perform this operation spells failure.

If the amateur contemplates growing Violets in order to obtain bloom during autumn and winter, April is a favourable time to set about the task of making a Violet bed. The Violet in summer time delights in partial shade, therefore the bed should be made if possible under the north-east side of a fence or hedge. The bed should be, however, placed fairly well in the open, and if grown in private gardens not in the dense shadow cast by house walls, nor under trees, though shade to a certain amount is absolutely essential in summer, as when exposed to sun the plants become overrun with red spider, an insect pest to which the Violet is specially liable. At the same time, it is as essential that the plants be exposed to the full sun in the autumn. If grown on a large scale, a suitable situation for summer quarters is between rows of sweet peas.

Ordinary garden soil will suffice for successful Violet culture, but the soil must be carefully prepared and deep digging is essential. This should be done some time before planting-out time; if possible in autumn, so that the ground may be left open to the effects of winter. Avoid, if possible, stiff clay, as in very wet soil Violets are apt to become diseased. Violets flourish best on a good medium soil, neither too heavy, nor too light. The ideal soil is a deep, sandy soil. Where the soil is heavy, it can be improved by an admixture of well-decayed manure, road grit, leaf-mould and burnt vegetable refuse. Rank stable manure must be avoided or the roots will produce any quantity of foliage and very few flowers. A dressing of leaf-mould is advantageous, as it will prevent the surface from becoming cracked in hot weather and will at the same time supply the roots with the medium in which they are most at home naturally.

The young plants should be rooted runners; plant not less than a foot apart each way. Choose a moist, dull day for planting, or if dry, puddle in the roots. If an inverted flower-pot be placed over each young Violet during the day in hot sunshine and lifted off during rain and at night, the plants will become established at much greater ease than if the ground were allowed to become baked by the sun. Water must be given copiously in dry weather, and the plants will also benefit at such times from a mulching or top dressing of leaf-mould or decayed manure, old mushroom-bed manure being useful for this purpose.

If the foliage assumes a yellow tint, it is almost an indication of the presence of red spider. The plants should then be sprinkled at frequent intervals with a mixture of sulphur and well-seasoned soot and a thorough syringing such as will reach the under-part of the foliage should also be given, using a solution of Gishurst compound, repeating the operation at intervals of a day or two, until the pest is eradicated.

The soil between the rows should be hoed frequently and the runners of most varieties must be removed in the summer. The single varieties, on account of their stronger growth, require more room than the double forms. Single varieties of the more modern kinds, such as the Princess of Wales, flower freely on the runners which issue from the parent plant, and for this reason such runners may be left. The double varieties, on the contrary, must have the runners removed so as to strengthen the crowns which give the finest blooms. Good single varieties besides the Princess of Wales are Wellsiana, La France, Admiral Avellan and California, and among the doubles Mrs. J. J. The double garden variety, especially the pale blue Neapolitan Violet which forms a stem 6 inches in height, is often called the Tree Violet.

From plants thus established in the open, a plentiful supply of blooms will be forthcoming in the following spring. It is, however, only in sheltered places that Violets will thrive in the open during winter. It is generally found necessary to transfer the plants to cold frames for flowering, and to grow the flowers for the sake of marketing the cut blooms for profit; this is absolutely essential, as without glass, Violets can only be obtained in March and April, when they are plentiful, cheap and unprofitable. Frames in which melon or cucumbers have been grown during the summer will be found eminently suitable for the purpose. A foundation of stable litter and leaves, a foot deep or more, turned frequently to allow the volatile gases to escape from the litter, and then well trodden, and covered with a layer of about 6 inches of rich loamy soil, makes a very suitable bed. A great point to bear in mind is the desirability of keeping the crowns of plants as near to the glass as possible. If therefore it is necessary to raise the bed this should be done before the plants are put in the winter quarters.

Water the Violets from the outdoor bed a day before lifting; by taking this precaution, it will be possible to lift the roots so that they bring away with them a good-sized ball of earth. All straggling runners should be cut away, leaving only two or three, already rooted probably, and showing flowers close up to the old plants. These reserved runners, if not already rooted, should be pegged down, and, in addition to flowering freely, will be just what are wanted for planting out next spring. There must be no crowding of the plants as, unless they are kept perfectly clear of each other, damping off is likely to take place, especially if the ventilation is faulty. They should be planted a foot apart, firmly and deeply, or sufficiently to bury the stems, keeping the crowns well out of the soil. Level all and give a good watering immediately to settle the roots, and keep the frame closed for a few days until the plants begin to make roots, but no longer. Plenty of air must be supplied day and night, as long as the weather remains mild. In frost keep the lights down, and when severe cover with mats, but do not keep the frames too close or dark from excessive covering. For Violets in frames, light and air cannot be overstudied, and whilst not allowing the frost to exercise a too severe influence upon them, it is advisable to expose them to all the fresh air and light obtainable, to keep the plants in healthy condition. The leaves when the plants are kept close and in darkness will turn yellow and lose their vitality, and under such conditions the plants soon become weakened and rendered incapable of producing flowers. It is a good plan to sprinkle the soil around the plants with a little finely-powdered charcoal, as the latter will absorb the moisture that unavoidably arises through the frames being kept closed and darkened during severe weather. Application of water to the roots of Violets in midwinter is not necessary, but later, when the sun exercises a greater evaporative influence and air in abundance can be admitted to the plants, it will be necessary to occasionally apply water as well as manure in liquid form. Care must be taken to keep the glass clean and free from any smoky deposit which obscures the light; in cleaning the glasses both sides regularly, avoid any drip on to the plants. Remove all decaying foliage and constantly watch for slugs. Fog is bad for Violets in frames: it causes the leaves to damp off and sometimes kills the plants outright.

Plants removed to frames in the latter half of September, if properly attended to, will begin to bloom early in October and continue to flower till April. In this month, after suitable cuttings and runners have been taken from them for next season's use, they may be thrown or given away, for each season young plants alone should be cultivated. If a little fresh soil is given early in March as a top-dressing to the plants in the frames, the runners become stronger and better rooted for planting out-of-doors. Besides being kept moist at the roots by occasional watering, their growth is much benefited by an overhead sprinkling in the evening during the summer, when the surrounding soil is hot and dry. While this promotes a healthy growth, it tends also to keep down red spider.

Some growers raise their young plants from cuttings taken early in October, when lifting the plants to put them into frames or cool greenhouses. At this time, it is easy to secure a few hundreds of the healthiest cuttings, heeling them in till time permits of their being dealt with. Inserted in boxes of soil or preferably under spare lights, model plants for putting out in March or early April will result, which in turn give the finest flowering clumps.

¶ *Parts Used Medicinally.* The flowers *dried* and the leaves and whole plant *fresh*.

The odour of the flowers is in a great measure destroyed by desiccation and the degree to which they retain their colour depends on the method of collecting and drying them.

The Violet flowers used for Syrup of Violets are not always the ordinary wild *V. odorata*, the colour of which soon fades, except under special treatment. Other species with deeper-coloured and larger blue flowers, and also deep-coloured garden Violas and Pansies are often substituted for the Sweet Violet, for upon the colour their value depends.

¶ *Constituents.* The chief chemical constituents of the flowers are the odorous principle and the blue colouring matter, which may be extracted from the petals by infusion with water and turns green and afterwards yellow with alkalis and red with acids. The flowers yield their odour and slightly bitter taste to boiling water and their properties may be preserved for some time by means of sugar in the form of Syrup of Violets.

A glucoside, Viola-quercitin, is also a constituent, found throughout the plant and especially in the rhizome. It may be isolated by exhausting the fresh plant with warm alcohol, removing the alcohol by distillation and treating the residue with warm distilled water, from which it crystallizes in fine yellow needles, which are soluble in water, less so in alcohol and insoluble in ether. On boiling with mineral acids, the glucoside is split up into quercitin and a fermentable sugar. The activity of the plant, according to the British

Pharmacopœia, is probably due to this glucoside and its products of decomposition, or a ferment associated with it.

Salicylic acid has also been obtained from the plant.

The scientist Boullay discovered in the root, leaves, flowers and seeds of this plant an alkaloid resembling the Emetin of Ipecacuanha (which also belongs to the same group of plants), which he termed Violine. The same alkaloid was found by the French physician Orfila (1787–1853) to be an energetic poison, which may be identical with Emetin.

It has been found that the Toulouse Violet, which is *without scent* when cultivated in the land from which it takes its name, develops a very agreeable and pronounced perfume when raised at Grasse.

The growth of Violet flowers for the extraction of their perfume is not carried out to such an extent as formerly, as the natural perfume is suffering severely from the competition of the artificial product which forms the greater part of the Violet perfume of commerce. The natural perfume is very expensive to extract, an enormous quantity of flowers being required to scent a pomade. The largest Violet plantations are at Nice. The species used are the double Parma Violet and the Victoria Violet. A certain amount of perfume of a distinctive character is also now made from the green leaves of Violet plants, taken just before flowering.

¶ *Medicinal Action and Uses.* The Violet is still found in the Pharmacopœias.

Violet flowers possess slightly laxative properties. The best form of administration is the Syrup of Violets. *Syrop Violæ* of the British Pharmacopœia directs that it may be given as a laxative to infants in doses of ½ to 1 teaspoonful, or more, with an equal volume of oil of Almonds.

Syrup of Violets is also employed as a laxative, and as a colouring agent and flavouring in other neutral or acid medicines.

The older writers had great faith in Syrup of Violets: ague, epilepsy, inflammation of the eyes, sleeplessness, pleurisy, jaundice and quinsy are only a few of the ailments for which it was held potent. Gerard says: 'It has power to ease inflammation, roughness of the throat and comforteth the heart, assuageth the pains of the head and causeth sleep.'

The flowers are crystallized as an attractive sweetmeat, and in the days of Charles II, a favourite conserve, Violet Sugar, named then 'Violet Plate,' prepared from the flowers, was considered of excellent use in consumption, and was sold by all apothecaries. The flowers have undoubted expectorant qualities.

The fresh flowers have also been used as an addition to salads; they have a laxative effect.

An infusion of the flowers is employed, especially on the Continent, as a substitute for litmus, as a test of acids and alkalis.

Of the *leaves*, Gerard tells us that they

'are used in cooling plasters, oyles and comfortable cataplasms or poultices, and are of greater efficacies amongst other herbs as Mercury, Mallowes and such like in clisters for the purposes aforesaid.'

They are an old popular remedy for bruises.

Culpepper says:

'It is a fine pleasing plant of Venus, of a mild nature and no way hurtful. All the Violets are cold and moist, while they are fresh and green, and are used to cool any heat or distemperature of the body, either inwardly or outwardly, as the inflammation in the eyes, to drink the decoction of the leaves and flowers made with water or wine, or to apply them poulticewise to the grieved places; it likewise easeth pains in the head caused through want of sleep, or any pains arising of heat if applied in the same manner or with oil of Roses. A drachm weight of the dried leaves or flowers of Violets, but the leaves more strongly, doth purge the body of choleric humours and assuageth the heat if taken in a draught of wine or other drink; the powder of the purple leaves of the flowers only picked and dried and drank in water helps the quinsy and the falling sickness in children, especially at the beginning of the disease. It is also good for jaundice. The flowers of the Violets ripen and dissolve swellings. The herbs or flowers while they are fresh or the flowers that are dry are effectual in the pleurisy and all diseases of the lungs. The green leaves are used with other herbs to make plasters and poultices for inflammation and swellings and to ease all pains whatsoever arising of heat and for piles, being fried with yoke of egg and applied thereto.'

The underground stems or rhizomes (the so-called roots) are strongly emetic and purgative. They have occasionally been used as adulterants to more costly drugs, notably to ipecacuanha. A dose of from 40 to 50 grains of the powdered root is said to act violently, inciting nausea and great vomiting and nervous affection, due to the pronounced emetic qualities of the alkaloid contained.

The seeds are purgative and diuretic and have been given in urinary complaints, and are considered a good corrective of gravel.

A modern homœopathic medicinal tincture is made from the whole fresh plant, with proof spirit, and is considered useful for a spasmodic cough with hard breathing, and also for rheumatism of the wrists.

The glucosidal principles contained in the leaves have not yet been fully investigated, but would appear to have distinct antiseptic properties.

Of late years, preparations of fresh Violet leaves have been used both internally and externally in the treatment of cancer, and though the British Pharmacopœia does not uphold the treatment, it specifies how they are employed. From other sources it is stated that Violet leaves have been used with benefit to allay the pain in cancerous growths, especially in the throat, which no other treatment relieved, and several reputed cures have been recorded.

An infusion of the leaves in boiling water (1 in 5) has been administered in doses of 1 to 2 fluid ounces. A syrup of the petals and a liquid extract of the fresh leaves are also used, the latter taken in teaspoonful doses, or rubbed in locally. The fresh leaves are also prepared as a compress for local application.

The *infusion* is generally drunk cold and is made as follows: Take 2½ oz. of Violet leaves, freshly picked. Wash them clean in cold water and place them in a stone jar and pour over them 1 pint of boiling water. Tie the jar down and let it stand for twelve hours, till the water is green. Then strain off the liquid into a well-stoppered bottle and the tea is ready for drinking cold at intervals of every two hours during the day, taking a wineglassful at a time till the whole has been consumed each day. It is essential that the tea should be made fresh every day and kept in a cool place to prevent it turning sour. If any should be left over it should be thrown away.

As a cure for cancer of the tongue, it is recommended to drink half this quantity daily at intervals and apply the rest in hot fomentations.

Injection. – About a couple of wineglassfuls made tepid can be used, if required, as an injection, night and morning, but this infusion should be made separate from the tea and should not be of greater strength than 1 oz. of leaves to ½ pint of water.

As a hot *Compress*, for external use, dip a piece of lint into the infusion, made the same strength as the tea, of which a sufficient quantity must be made warm for the purpose. Lay the lint round or over the affected part and cover with oilskin or thin mackintosh. Change the lint when dry or cold. Use flannel, not oilskin, for open wounds, and in cold weather it should be made fresh about every alternate day. Should this wet compress cause undue irritation of the skin, remove at once and substitute the following compress or *poultice*: Chop some fresh-gathered young Violet leaves, without stems, and cover with boiling water. Stand in a warm place for a quarter of an hour and add a little crushed linseed.

A *concentrated preparation* is also recommended, made as follows: Put as many Violet leaves in a saucepan as can boil in the water. Boil for ½ hour, then strain, squeezing tightly. Evaporate this decoction to one-fourth its bulk and add alcohol (spirits of wine 1 in 15); 1½ oz. or 3 tablespoonsful of spirits of wine will keep 24 oz. for a month. This syrupy product is stated to be extremely efficacious, applied two or three times a day, or more, on cotton-wool about the throat. This will not cause irritation unless applied to the skin with waterproof over for a considerable time, as under such circumstances moisture will cause irritation.

For *lubricating* the throat, dry and powder Violet leaves and let them stand in olive oil for six hours in a water bath. Make strong. It will keep any time.

A continuous daily supply of fresh leaves is necessary and a considerable quantity is required. It is recorded that during the nine weeks that a nurseryman supplied a patient suffering from cancer in the colon – which was cured at the end of this period – a Violet bed covering six rods of ground was almost entirely stripped of its foliage.

Violet Ointment. – Place 2 oz. of the best lard in a jar in the oven till it becomes quite clear. Then add about thirty-six fresh Violet leaves. Stew them in the lard for an hour till the leaves are the consistency of cooked cabbage. Strain and when cold put into a covered pot for use. This is a good old-fashioned Herbal remedy which has been allowed to fall into disuse. It is good as an application for superficial tubercles in the glands of the neck, Violet Leaves Tea being drunk at the same time.

VIOLET, WATER

Hottonia palustris
N.O. Violaceæ

Synonyms. Water Milfoil. Water Yarrow. Feather Foil

The Water Violet, an aquatic plant, is in no wise related to the familiar Violets and Pansies, but is a member of the Primrose tribe – named after Hotton, an early Leyden professor of Botany.

Description. It is common in ponds and

ditches. From the abundance of its finely-divided leaves, which are all submersed, it was also called Millefolium by older writers and Water Milfoil, Water Yarrow and Feather Foil popularly. It flowers in May and June, the flowers being large and handsome, pink or pale purple, with a yellow eye, arranged in whorls one above the other around a leafless stalk, which rises several inches out of the water and forms a handsome spike.

VIRGINIA CREEPER

Vitis Hederacea (WILLD.)
N.O. Vitaceæ

Synonyms. American Ivy. Five-leaved Ivy. Ampolopsis quinquefolia (Mich.). Cissus Hederacea (Ross.). Cissus quinquefolia (Desf.). Vitis quinquefolia (LINN.). Wood Vine

Parts Used. Bark, twigs, fresh leaves, berries, resin

This common creeper is familiar to all on account of its rapid growth and the magnificence of its autumn colouring. It is specially useful in town gardens, where it is not affected by the smoky atmosphere.

The stem is extensively climbing, reaching out in all directions and fastening itself by the disk-like appendages of the tendrils, and also by rootlets. It will shoot about 20 feet in one year, and in time it becomes very woody.

The flowering branches become converted into tendrils, as in the case of the Vine. An inspection of any vine in summer will generally show some tendrils with buds upon them, revealing their origin. Occasionally, what *ought* to have been a tendril becomes a flowering branch and bears a full bunch of grapes. The two together are called a 'double cluster.'

¶ *Description.* The leaves have long petioles, or foot-stalks, and are divided into five leaflets. The flowers are in small clusters—yellowish-green in colour and open in July, a few at a time. They are much liked by bees, and are succeeded by dark purplish-blue berries, which are ripe in October, being then about the size of a pea.

Under the name of *Hedera quinquefolia,* this creeper was first brought to Europe from Canada, and was cultivated here as early as 1629. Parkinson, in whose days it was introduced, described it –

'The leaves are crumpled or rather folded together at the first coming forth and very red, which after growing forth are very fair, large and green, divided into four, five, six or seven leaves standing together upon a small foot-stalk – set without order on the branches, at the ends whereof, as also at other places sometimes, come forth short tufts of buds for flowers, but we could never see them open themselves to show what manner of flower it would be or what fruit would follow in our country.'

¶ *Part Used.* Bark and twigs. A tincture is made of the fresh young shoots and bark, which are chopped and pounded to a pulp, mixed with 2 parts by weight of alcohol, and left for 8 days in the dark before being strained and filtered off. The tincture is not official in either the United States or the British Pharmacopœia.

The generic name *Hedera* is supposed to be derived either from the Celtic *hædra* (a cord), or from the Greek *hedra* (a seat). The specific name *Helix* was given by Linnæus, on account of its being a great harbourer of snails, Helix being the scientific name of the Snail family. The English name of Ivy is said to be from *iw* (green), from its evergreen character. Yew is derived from the same word.

¶ *Constituents.* The properties depend on the special balsamic resin contained in its leaves and stems, as well as in its particular aromatic gum. The berries contain a very bitter principle somewhat like quinine. The alkaloid contained in it is termed Hederin.

¶ *Medicinal Action and Uses.* Stimulating, diaphoretic and cathartic. Many virtues were attributed by our forefathers to this plant. Its berries have been found of use in febrile disorders, and were regarded as a specific against the plague and similar disorders, for which they were infused in vinegar. During the Great Plague of London, Ivy berries were given with some success for their antiseptic virtues and to induce perspiration.

In India the leaves are used as an aperient, and a resinous matter that in warm climates exudes from the bark of the main stems (and may be procured by wounding them) is considered a useful stimulant, antispasmodic and emmenagogue. This gum possesses mildly aperient properties, and was at one time included as a medicine in the Edinburgh Pharmacopœia, but has now fallen out of use. Dissolved in vinegar it had the reputation of being a good filling for a hollow tooth causing neuralgic toothache.

The leaves have a very unpleasant taste. Taken inwardly in infusion, they act as an aperient and emetic, but are sudorific. They have been given on the Continent to children suffering from atrophy. The juice is said to cure headache, when applied to the nostrils. An infusion of the leaves and berries will also mitigate a severe headache.

The fresh leaves of Ivy, boiled in vinegar and applied warm to the sides of those who are troubled with the spleen, or stitch in the sides, will give much ease. The same applied with Rose-water, and oil of Roses to the temples and forehead eases headaches. Cups made from Ivywood have been employed, from which to sip hot or cold water for diseases of the spleen.

A decoction of the leaves applied externally will destroy head lice in children, and fresh Ivy leaves bruised and applied will afford great relief to bunions and shooting corns, a remedy to the excellence of which John Wesley has testified.

The leaves have also been employed as poultices and fomentations in glandular enlargements, indolent ulcers, etc.

A decoction of the leaves has been used as a black dye.

The berries possess much the same properties as the leaves, being strongly purgative and emetic. An infusion of the berries has been frequently found serviceable in rheumatic complaints and is reported to have cured the dropsy.

The dried bark is also used in a decoction. When stripped from the branches (after the berries have ripened) and dried in the sun, it occurs in quilled pieces 2 to 3 inches long and from $\frac{1}{4}$ to $\frac{1}{2}$ inch in diameter, externally brown with enlarged transverse scars, the fracture showing a white bark with coarse flattened fibres in the inner portion. One ounce of the bark to a pint of boiling water is taken in wineglassful doses.

A fluid extract is also prepared from the bark and twigs, of which the dose is $\frac{1}{2}$ to 1 drachm; another preparation, Ampelopsin, is taken in doses of 2 to 4 grains.

¶ *Constituents.* Pyrocatachin (Oxyphenic acid) in the green leaves. Cisso-tannic acid has been determined as the pigment of the red coloration in the autumnal coloured leaves, and has an astringent, bitter taste. The leaves when green contain also free tartaric acid and its salts, with sodium and potassium. Glycollic acid and calcium glycollate exist in the ripe berries.

In scrofulous affections the drug is principally employed in the form of a syrup.

WAFER ASH. *See* ASH

WAHOO. *See* SPINDLE

(POISON)
WAKE ROBIN, AMERICAN

Arum triphyllum (LINN.)
N.O. Araceæ

Synonyms. Dragon Root. Wild Turnip. Devil's Ear. Pepper Turnip. Indian Turnip. Jack-in-the-Pulpit. Memory Root. Arisamæ triphyllum (Schott.)
(*French*) Gouet à trois feuilles
(*German*) Dreiblattiger Aron
Part Used. The root (fresh corm)
Habitat. Eastern North America in damp places. Indigenous almost all over United States and Canada

¶ *Description.* The plant has a round flattened perennial rhizome, the upper part tunicated as in the onion, the lower and larger portion tuberous and fleshy, with numerous long white radicles in a circle from its upper edge, the under-side covered with a dark, loose, wrinkled epidermis. Spathe ovate, acuminate, convoluted into a tube at the bottom, flattened and bent at top like a hood, varying in colour internally, supported by an erect scape inverted at base by petioles and their acute sheaths. Spadix club-shaped, shorter than spathe, rounded at end, contracted at base, surrounded by stamens or ovaries; the upper portions of the spadix withers together with the spathe, whilst the ovaries grow into a large compact bunch of shining scarlet berries. Leaves, one or two standing on long sheathing foot-stalks, ternate. Leaflets oval, mostly entire, acuminate, smooth, paler on under-side, becoming glaucous with growth, the two lateral ones rhomboidal.

¶ *Constituents.* In the recent state it has a peculiar odour and is violently acrid. It has been found to contain besides the acrid principle, 10 to 17 per cent. of starch, albumen, gum, sugar, extractive, lignin and salts of potassium and calcium.

¶ *Medicinal Action and Uses.* Acrid, expectorant, and diaphoretic. Used in flatulence, croup, whooping-cough, stomatitis, asthma, chronic laryngitis, bronchitis and pains in chest.

In the fresh state it is a violent irritant to the mucous membrane, when chewed burning the mouth and throat; if taken internally this plant causes violent gastro-enteritis which may end in death.

¶ *Dosage.* Powdered root, 10 grains two or three times daily.

The perfectly fresh root should not be used and the fully dried root is inactive.

¶ *Antidote.* Strong tea and stimulants.
  See CUCKOO PINT.

WALLFLOWER [1]

Cherranthus cheiri (LINN.)
N.O. Cruciferæ

Synonyms. Gillyflower. Wallstock-gillofer. Giroflier. Gillyflower. Handflower. Keiri. Beeflower. Baton d'or
Parts Used. Flowers, stems
Habitat. All Southern Europe, on old walls, quarries and seacliffs

¶ *Description.* This homely perennial plant of the cabbage family was introduced into this country over 300 years ago, and its delightful fragrance soon made it a general favourite. It has single flowers, yellowy orange in its wild state, and quickly spreads abundantly from seed, commencing to bloom in early spring, and continuing most of the summer. In olden times this flower was carried in the hand at classic festivals, hence it was called Cherisaunce by virtue of its cordial qualities.

¶ *Constituents.* Oil, a powerful glucoside, of the digitalis group, and cherinine, a crystalline alkaloid.

¶ *Medicinal Action and Uses.* The oil has a pleasing perfume if diluted, but in full strength a disagreeable odour. The alkaloid is useful acting on nerve centres and on the muscles.

WALL RUE. *See* FERNS

WALNUT

Juglans nigra (LINN.)
N.O. Juglandaceæ

Synonyms. Carya. Jupiter's Nuts
  (*Dutch*) Walnoot
  (*Greek*) Carya persica. Carya basilike
  (*Roman*) Nux persica. Nux regia
Parts Used. Leaves, bark
Habitat. According to Dr. Royle *Juglans regia* extends from Greece and Asia Minor, over Lebanon and Persia, probably all along the Hindu-Kush to the Himalayas. It is abundant in Kashmir, and is found in Sirmore, Kumdon and Nepal. The walnuts imported into the plains of India are chiefly from Kashmir. Dr. Hooker states that in the Sikkim Himalaya, the Walnut inhabits the mountain slopes at an elevation of 4,000 to 7,000 feet.
  According to Pliny, it was introduced into Italy from Persia, and it is mentioned by Varro, who was born B.C. 116, as growing in Italy during his lifetime.
  There is no certain account of the time it was brought into this country. Some say 1562; but Gerard, writing about thirty years later, mentions the Walnut as being very common in the fields near common highways, and in orchards.

The Common Walnut, a large and handsome tree, with strong, spreading boughs, is not a native of Britain. Its native place is probably Persia. Other varieties of Walnut, the Black Walnut, the various kinds of Hickory, etc., are mostly natives of North America.

The Romans called the tree *nux*, on account of its fruit. The English name Walnut is partly of Teutonic origin, the Germans naming the nut *Wallnuss*, or *Welsche Nuss* – *Welsche* signifying foreign.

It was said that in the 'golden age,' when men lived upon acorns the gods lived upon Walnuts, and hence the name of *Juglans*, *Jovis glans*, or Jupiter's nuts.

¶ *Description.* The tree grows to a height of 40 or 60 feet, with a large spreading top, and thick, massive stem. One accurately measured by Professor du Breuil, in Normandy, was upwards of 23 feet in circumference; and in some parts of France there are Walnut trees 300 years old, with stems of much greater thickness. In the southern parts of England the trees grow vigorously and bear abundantly, when not injured by late frosts in spring.

The flowers of separate sexes are borne upon the same tree and appear in early spring before the leaves. The male flowers have a calyx of five or six scales, surrounding from eighteen to thirty-six stamens; whilst the

---

[1] In homœopathic medicine a tincture of the whole plant has been found useful in the effects of cutting the wisdom tooth. – EDITOR.

calyx of the female flowers closely envelops the ovary, which bears two or three fleshy stigmas. The deciduous leaves are pinnate.

For drying indoors, a warm, sunny attic, or loft may be employed, the window being left open by day, so that there is a current of air and the moist, hot air may escape: the door may also be left open. The leaves can be placed on coarse butter-cloth, stented – if hooks are placed beneath the window and on the opposite wall the butter-cloth can be attached by rings sewn on each side of it and hooked on so that it is stretched taut. The temperature should be from 70° to 100°.

Failing sun, any ordinary shed, fitted with racks and shelves, can be used, provided it is ventilated near the roof and has a warm current of air, caused by an ordinary coke or anthracite stove. Empty glasshouses can readily be adapted into drying-sheds (especially if heated by pipes) if the glass is shaded. Ventilation is essential, and there must be no open tank in the house to cause steaming.

The leaves should be spread in a single layer, preferably not touching, and may be turned during drying.

All dried leaves should be packed away at once, in airtight, wooden or tin boxes in a dry place, otherwise they re-absorb moisture from the air.

Walnut leaves are parchment-like when dry, and the leaf-stalks brown, but the leaves themselves keep their good colour when dried. They have a bitter and astringent taste. By long keeping, the leaves become brown and lose their characteristic, aromatic odour.

The bark is dried in the same manner as the leaves. When dry, it occurs in quilled or curbed pieces, 3 to 6 inches long or more, and ¾ inch broad, dull blackish-brown, with traces of a thin, whitish epidermal layer, tough and fibrous and somewhat mealy. The inner fibres are tough and flattened, the outer ones, white and silky. The taste is bitter and astringent, but it has no odour.

¶ *Constituents*. The active principle of the whole Walnut tree, as well as of the nuts, is Nucin or Juglon. The kernels contain oil, mucilage, albumin, mineral matter, cellulose and water.

¶ *Medicinal Action and Uses*. The bark and leaves have alterative, laxative, astringent and detergent properties, and are used in the treatment of skin troubles. They are of the highest value for curing scrofulous diseases, herpes, eczema, etc., and for healing indolent ulcers; an infusion of 1 oz. of dried bark or leaves (slightly more of the fresh leaves) to the pint of boiling water, allowed to stand

for six hours, and strained off is taken in wineglassful doses, three times a day, the same infusion being also employed at the same time for outward application. Obstinate ulcers may also be cured with sugar, well saturated with a strong decoction of Walnut leaves.

The bark, dried and powdered, and made into a strong infusion, is a useful purgative.

The husk, shell and peel are sudorific, especially if used when the Walnuts are green. Whilst unripe, the nut has worm-destroying virtues.

The fruit, when young and unripe, makes a wholesome, anti-scorbutic pickle, the vinegar in which the green fruit has been pickled proving a capital gargle for sore and slightly ulcerated throats. Walnut catsup embodies the medicinal virtues of the unripe nuts.

It is much cultivated in some parts of Italy, France, Germany and Switzerland, and formerly also in England, particularly on the chalk-hills of Surrey, for the sake of its timber, as well as for its fruit.

On the Continent, the wood is still in great request for furniture, but when mahogany became a favourite wood in this country, in the early part of last century, the old walnut trees that were cut down were not always replaced by young ones, so that plantations of this tree diminished.

At one time as much as £600 was given for a single Walnut tree.

The leaves have a very strong, characteristic smell, aromatic and not unpleasant, but said to be injurious to sensitive people. They have three, sometimes four pairs of leaflets and a terminal one, the leaflets varying in size on the same leaf, being 2½ to 4 inches in length and 1 to 1½ inch wide, entire, smooth, shining, and paler below.

The flowers begin to open about the middle of April and are in full bloom by the middle of May, before which time the tree is in full leaf.

Even in the south of France, this tree is frequently injured by spring frosts.

The wood has been much used, not only for furniture and wainscoting, but for the wheels and bodies of coaches, for making gun-stocks, and by the cabinet-maker for inlaying. It is unfit for use as beams because of its brittleness.

The oil yielded by the kernel of the fruit (the part eaten) is used to polish the wood. Not congealing by cold, it is found on this account most useful for painters for mixing gold-size and varnish with white and delicate colours. The oil has been used in some parts of France for frying, eaten as butter and employed as lamp oil. One bushel of nuts, producing about 15 lb. of peeled kernels, will yield about 7 lb. of the oil.

The green husks of the fruit, boiled, make a good yellow dye.

No insects will touch the leaves of the Walnut, which yield a brown dye, which gypsies use to stain their skin. It is said to contain iodine.

The husks and leaves, macerated in warm water impart to it an intense bitterness, which will destroy all worms (if the liquid be poured on to lawns and grass walks) without injuring the grass itself.

¶ *Parts Used Medicinally.* The leaves and bark. The leaves are stripped off the tree singly, in June and July and dried.

Gather the leaves only in fine weather, in the morning, after the dew has been dried by the sun. The prevalence of an east wind is favourable, as the dry air facilitates the process of drying. Reject all stained leaves.

Drying may be done in warm, sunny weather, out-of-doors, but in half-shade as leaves dried in the shade retain their colour better than those dried in the sun and do not become so tindery. They may be placed on wire sieves, or frames covered with wire or garden netting – at a height of about 3 or 4 feet from the ground, to ensure a current of air – and must be taken indoors to a dry room or shed, before there is any chance of them becoming damp from dew or showers.

The juice of the green husks, boiled with honey, is also a good gargle for a sore mouth and inflamed throat, and the distilled water of the green husks is good for quinsy and as an application for wounds and internally is a cooling drink in agues.

The thin, yellow skin which clothes the inner nut is a notable remedy for colic, being first dried, and then rubbed into powder. It is administered in doses of 30 grains, with a tablespoonful of peppermint water.

The oil extracted from the ripe kernels, taken inwardly in ½ oz. doses, has also proved good for colic and is efficacious, applied externally, for skin diseases of the leprous type and wounds and gangrenes.

¶ *Preparations.* Fluid extract leaves, 1 to 2 drachms. Walnut oil.

The Walnut has been termed 'vegetable arsenic,' on account of its curative effect in eczema and other skin diseases.

William Cole, an exponent of the doctrine of signatures, says in *Adam in Eden,* 1657:

'Wall-nuts have the perfect Signature of the Head: The outer husk or green Covering, represent the *Pericranium,* or outward skin of the skull, whereon the hair groweth, and therefore salt made of those husks or barks, are exceeding good for wounds in the head. The inner wooddy shell hath the Signature of the Skull, and the little yellow skin, or Peel, that covereth the Kernell, of the hard *Meninga* and *Pia-mater,* which are the thin scarfes that envelope the brain. The Kernel hath the very figure of the Brain, and therefore it is very profitable for the Brain, and resists poysons; For if the Kernel be bruised, and moystned with the quintessence of Wine, and laid upon the Crown of the Head, it comforts the brain and head mightily.'

Culpepper says of Walnuts :

'if they' [the leaves] 'be taken with onions, salt, and honey, they help the biting of a mad dog, or the venom or infectious poison of any beast, etc. Caius Pompeius found in the treasury of Mithridates, King of Pontus, when he was overthrown, a scroll of his own handwriting, containing a medicine against any poison or infection; which is this: Take two dry walnuts, and as many good figs, and twenty leaves of rue, bruised and beaten together with two or three corns of salt and twenty juniper berries, which take every morning fasting, preserves from danger of poison, and infection that day it is taken. . . . The kernels, when they grow old, are more oily, and therefore not fit to be eaten, but are then used to heal the wounds of the sinews, gangrenes, and carbuncles. . . . The said kernels being burned, are very astringent . . . being taken in red wine, and stay the falling of the hair, and make it fair, being anointed with oil and wine. The green husks will do the like, being used in the same manner. . . . A piece of the green husks put into a hollow tooth, eases the pain.'

RECIPES

'To preserve green Walnuts in Syrup

'Take as many green Walnuts as you please, about the middle of July, try them all with a pin, if it goes easily through them they are fit for your purpose; lay them in Water for nine days, washing and shifting them Morning and Night; then boil them in water until they be a little Soft, lay them to drain; then pierce them through with a Wooden Sciver, and in the hole put a Clove, and in some a bit of Cinnamon, and in some the rind of a Citron Candi'd: then take the weight of your Nuts in Sugar, or a little more; make it into a syrup, in which boil your Nuts (scimming them) till they be tender; then put them up in Gally potts, and cover them close. When you lay them to drain, wipe them with a Course cloth to take off a thin green Skin. They are Cordial and Stomachal.' – (From *The Family*

Physician, 'by Geo. Hartman, Phylo Chymist, who liv'd and Travell'd with the Honourable Sir Kenelm Digby, in several parts of Europe, the space of Seven Years till he died.')

The next is from a seventeenth-century household MS. Receipt Book inscribed *Madam Susanna Avery, Her Book, May ye 12th, Anno Domini* 1688.

'To Pickel Wallnutts Green

'Let your nutts be green as not to have any shell; then run a kniting pin two ways through them; then put them into as much ordinary vinegar as will cover them, and let them stand thirty days, shifting them every too days in ffrech vinegar; then ginger and black peper of each ounce, rochambole two ounces slised, a handfull of bay leaves; put all togeather cold; then wrap up every wall nutt singly in a vine leaf, and put them in putt them into [*sic*] the ffolloing pickel: for 200 of walnutts take two gallans of the best whit vineager, a pint of the best mustard seed, fore ounces of horse radish, with six lemons sliced with the rin(d)s on, cloves and mace half an ounce, a stone jar, and put the pickel on them, and cork them close up; and they will be ffitt for use in three months, and keep too years.'

WALNUT, WHITE

Juglans cinerea (LINN.)
N.O. Juglandaceæ

Synonyms. Oil Nut
See BUTTERNUT

WATER BETONY. *See* BETONY

WATERCRESS

Nasturtium officinale
N.O. Cruciferæ

Parts Used. Leaves, flowers, seeds
Habitat. Europe and Russian Asia

¶ *Description.* A hardy perennial found in abundance near springs and open running watercourses, of a creeping habit with smooth, shining, brownish-green, pinnatifid leaves and ovate, heart-shaped leaflets, the terminal one being larger than the rest. Flowers small and white, produced towards the extremity of the branches in a sort of terminal panicle.

The true nasturtium or Indian Cress cultivated in gardens as a creeper has brilliant orange-red flowers and produces the seeds which serve as a substitute for capers in pickles.

The poisonous Marshwort or 'Fool's Cress' is often mistaken for Watercress, with which it is sometimes found growing. It may readily be distinguished by its hemlock-like white flowers, and when out of flower, by its finely toothed and somewhat pointed leaves, much longer than those of the watercress and of a paler green. The Latin name 'Nasturtium' is derived from the words *nasus tortus* (a convulsed nose) on account of its pungency.

¶ *Constituents.* A sulpho-nitrogenous oil, iodine iron, phosphates, potash, with other mineral salts, bitter extract and water. Its volatile oil rich in nitrogen combined with some sulphur in the sulpho-cyanide of allyl.

¶ *Medicinal Action and Uses.* Watercress is particularly valuable for its antiscorbutic qualities and has been used as such from the earliest times. As a salad it promotes appetite. Culpepper says that the leaves bruised or the juice will free the face from blotches, spots and blemishes, when applied as a lotion.

¶ *Dosage.* Expressed juice, 1 to 2 fluid ounces.

Watercress has also been used as a specific in tuberculosis. Its active principles are said to be at their best when the plant is in flower.

WATER DOCK. *See* DOCK

WATER DROPWORT. *See* DROPWORT, HEMLOCK WATER

WATER FENNEL. *See* FENNEL

WATER SOLDIER

Stratiotes aloides
N.O. Hydrocharidaceæ

Synonyms. Water Houseleek. Water Aloe. Water Sengren. Sea Green. Crab's Claws. Knight's Pondweed. Freshwater Soldier. Water Parsnip
(*French*) Aloides
(*German*) Wasserfeder
Part Used. Herb

Culpepper describes under the name of Water Houseleek, Water Sengren or Sea-green, a plant that has nothing to do with any of these other succulent plants, and that

845

nowadays generally goes by one of its other popular names, Water Soldier, and is botanically known as *Stratiotes aloides*.

It is an aquatic plant, the only British representative of its genus, and is found growing in ditches in the Eastern counties of England, mostly in the Fen district. The roots extend some distance into the mud and throw up numerous deep-green, spreading, narrow, rigid and brittle leaves, from 6 to 18 inches long, very sharply pointed, with sharp prickles on each margin. They are strikingly similar to the foliage of an aloe, hence its specific name, *aloides*, and another of its popular English names, Water Aloe. The name of the genus is derived from the Greek word for a soldier, in reference to its crowded, sword-like leaves.

¶ *Description.* The flower-stalk is stout and short, about 6 inches high, bearing at its summit a two-leaved sheath, which is likened by old writers to the claws of a crab, from which another of its names, Crab's Claws, is derived. Stamens and pistils are on different plants. In the case of the staminate flowers, the sheath contains several delicate white flowers, with three petals and numerous stamens, twelve of which are perfect, as well as many other imperfect ones. The flowers containing the ovary – which is six-celled and six-angled, and develops into a pulpy, flask-shaped berry – are solitary on the stem.

After flowering in the month of July, the plant sinks to the bottom and ripens its fruit while submerged. It is a perennial and propagates itself freely by stolons as well as by seed. Although each root only flowers once, the parent plant rooted in the mud at the bottom of the ditch, after flowering, sends out buds of leaves at the end of long runners, which rise to the surface in the spring, and become separate plants, forming roots, flower, and then sink to the bottom, where they fix themselves in the mud, ripen their seeds and become, in their turn, parents of another race of young offsets, which in turn rise in the spring and float on the surface, sometimes eight or ten in a circle, so thick as to entirely fill up the surface of the ditches, and prevent all other plants from growing.

¶ *Medicinal Action and Uses.* Culpepper tells us that the herb 'is good against St. Anthony's Fire, and assuages swelling and inflammations in wounds; an ointment made of it is good to heal them.' He also informs us it is good for 'bruised kidneys.' It had in olden times the reputation of being an unfailing cure for all wounds made by iron weapons.

WHITE POND LILY. *See* LILY

WILD CARROT. *See* CARROT

WILD CHERRY. *See* CHERRY

WILD GINGER. *See* GINGER

WILD INDIGO. *See* INDIGO

WILD YAM. *See* YAMS

WILD MINT. *See* MINTS

WILLOW, BLACK AMERICAN

Salyx nigra (MARCH)
N.O. Salicaceæ

Synonym. Pussy Willow
Parts Used. Bark, berries
Habitat. America (New York and Pennsylvania)

¶ *Description.* A tree growing on banks of rivers up to 15 to 25 feet high, with a rough blackish bark. Leaves narrowly lanceolate, pointed, tapering at each end, serrulate, smooth, and green on both sides, petioles and midveins tomentose. Stipules small, decuduous, dentate; aments erect, cylindric, villous. Scales oblong, very villous. Sterile aments 3 inches long, glands of sterile flowers two large and deeply two or three cleft. Stamens four to six, often but three in the upper scales, filaments bearded at base. Ovary pedicillate, smooth, ovoid. Style very short, stigmas bifid.

¶ *Constituents.* The bark contains tannin and about 1 per cent. of Salinigrin, a white crystalline glucoside soluble in water and alcohol.

¶ *Medicinal Action and Uses.* An aphrodisiac, sedative, tonic. The bark has been prescribed in gonorrhœa and to relieve ovarian pain; a liquid extract is prepared and used in mixture with other sedatives. Largely used in the treatment of nocturnal emissions.

Fluid extract, ½ to 1 drachm.

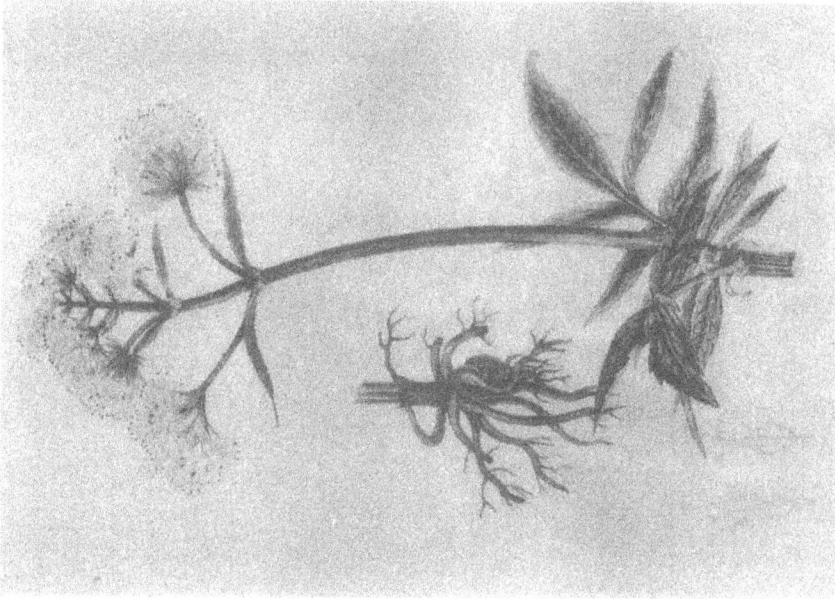

COMMON VALERIAN
Valeriana Officinalis

WILLOW
Salix Russeliana

WINTER'S BARK
Drimys Winteri

WINTERGREEN
Chimophila Umbellata

WILLOW, WHITE

Salix alba (LINN.)
N.O. Salicaceæ

Synonym. European Willow
Part Used. Bark
Habitat. Central and Southern Europe

¶ *Description.* A large tree with a rough greyish bark, the twigs being brittle at the base; the leaves are pubescent on both surfaces and finely serrulate; it hybridizes with other species of *Salix*, it flowers in April and May and the bark is easily separable throughout the summer; flowers and leaves appear coincidently from March to June.

¶ *Constituents.* The bark contains up to 13 per cent. of tannin as its chief constituent, also a small quantity of salicin.

¶ *Medicinal Action and Uses.* Tonic, antiperiodic and astringent. It has been used in dyspepsia connected with debility of the digestive organs. In convalescence from acute diseases, in worms, in chronic diarrhœa and dysentery, its tonic and astringent combination renders it very useful.

¶ *Dosages.* 1 drachm of the powdered root. 1 or 2 fluid ounces of the decoction.

WILLOW-HERBS

N.O. Onagrariaceæ

The Willow-herbs (*Epilobium*), nine species of which are natives of Great Britain, belong to the order Onagraceæ, to which belong also the familiar garden flowers the Fuchsia, Clarkia and Godetia, and the Evening Primrose (*Œnothera biennis*) (a native of North America, which, as a garden escape, is sometimes found apparently wild). The insignificant wild plant *Circæa lutetiana*, the Enchanter's Nightshade, also belongs to the same family. Many of the members of the order, being rich in tannin, find considerable domestic use as astringents.

The name of the genus *Epilobium* is from two Greek words *epi* (upon) and *lobos* (a pod), from the fact that the flowers stand upon the top of long, thin, pod-like seed-vessels, having somewhat the appearance of rather thick flower-stems. The name Willow-herb refers to the willow-like form of the leaves.

WILLOW-HERB, ROSE BAY

Epilobium angustifolium (LINN.)
N.O. Onagrariaceæ

Synonyms. Flowering Willow. French Willow. Persian Willow. Rose Bay Willow. Blood Vine. Blooming Sally. Purple Rocket. Wickup. Wicopy. Tame Withy
Part Used. Herb

Epilobium angustifolium (Linn.), the Rose Bay Willow-herb, is one of our handsomest wild flowers, and like the Foxglove, is for its beauty often cultivated as a garden plant.

Its tall, erect stems, 4 to 8 feet high, densely clothed with long, narrow, minutely-toothed leaves, terminate in long, showy spikes of flowers of a light rose-purple, hence the name Rose Bay, the leaves having likewise been compared to those of the Bay Laurel. The plant has also been named Blood Vine, because it has a red appearance. In Ireland, we find it called 'Blooming Sally,' Sally being a corruption of the Latin *Salix*, the Willow, really a reference to the willow-like leaves.

Gerard calls it:

'A goodly and stately plant having leaves like the greatest willow or osier, garnished with brave flowers of great beautie, consisting of four leaves apiece of an orient purple colour.'

It is a native of most countries of Europe. In this country, it has apparently become more common than it was in Gerard's day.

He tells us he had received some plants of this species from a place in Yorkshire, apparently as a rarity, 'which doe grow in my garden very goodly to behold, for the decking up of houses and gardens.'

It is to be found by moist riversides and in copses, but will sometimes spring up in a town, self-sown, on waste ground recently cleared of buildings: the site of Kingsway and Aldwych in London, adjoining the Strand, where many buildings, centuries old, had been pulled down, was the following summer covered by the Rose Bay Willow-herb, as by a crimson mantle, though no one could explain where the seeds had come from. The same phenomenon was repeated, in Westminster, when other old buildings were demolished for improvements and the ground remained waste for a considerable time. In America, it springs up on ground recently cleared by firing, being one of the plants called 'Fireweed' in the United States where it is known as the Great or Spiked Willow-herb, Bay Willow, Flowering Willow, Purple Rocket, Wickup and Wicopy.

The plant is in bloom for about a month. The individual flowers are about an inch in diameter, calyx and corolla each four-parted; the stamens, eight in number, standing up, form an arch or dome over the ovary, on the green, fleshy, upper surface of which nectar is secreted. Sprengel, in 1790, showed that the flowers, which open soon after sunrise, are protenandrous, i.e. the anthers ripen first, and self-pollination would occur if insects did not visit them. Bees, who much visit the flowers in search of nectar, get smeared by the pollen, which is sticky. It is not left by them on the stigma of the same flower, however, which at this stage is a mere knob, immature and unable to receive the pollen grains. On reaching another flower, further advanced, the stigma, ripe for reception of pollen, has opened out to become a white, four-rayed cross of great distinctness and perforce receives any pollen the insect visitor may have collected as he pushes by to get to the nectar below, and the ovules thus become fertilized.

The dead flowers, when fertilization has been effected, fall off cleanly from the long, projecting, quadrangular pods, which later split into four long strands, which stretch wide apart, disclosing a mass of silky white hairs, in which are embedded the very tiny seeds, a few hairs being attached to the top of each seed. The slightest wind scatters them broadcast over the neighbourhood. All the Willow-herbs distribute their seeds in the same manner, and as the plant spreads extensively by creeping stems it is very difficult to keep it within bounds.

¶ Uses. The leaves of the Rose Bay Willow-herb have been used as a substitute and adulterant of Tea. Though no longer so employed in England, the leaves of both this species and of the Great Hairy Willow-herb (E. hirsutum, Linn.) are largely used in Russia, under the name of Kaporie Tea.

Green (Universal Herbal, 1832) reports:

'The young shoots are said to be eatable, although an infusion of the plant produces a stupifying effect.

'The pith when dried is boiled, and becoming sweet, is by a proper process made into ale, and this into vinegar, by the Kamtschatdales; it is also added to the Cow Parsnip, to enrich the spirit that is prepared from that plant.

'As fodder, goats are said to be extremely fond of it and cows and sheep to eat it.

'The down of the seeds, mixed with cotton or fur, has been manufactured into stockings, etc.'

The young shoots are boiled and eaten like asparagus.

The ale made from the plant in Kamchatka is rendered still more intoxicating with a toadstool, the Fly Agaric, Agaricus muscarius.

¶ Medicinal Action and Uses. The roots and leaves have demulcent, tonic and astringent properties and are used in domestic medicine in decoction, infusion and cataplasm, as astringents.

Used much in America as an intestinal astringent.

The plant contains mucilage and tannin.

The dose of the herb is 30 to 60 grains. It has been recommended for its antispasmodic properties in the treatment of whooping-cough, hiccough and asthma.

In ointment, it has been used locally as a remedy for infantile cutaneous affections.

By some modern botanists, this species is now assigned to a separate genus and designated: Chamænerion angustifolium (Scop.).

WILLOW-HERB, GREAT HAIRY   Epilobium hirsutum (LINN.)
                                           N.O. Onagrariaceæ

Synonyms. Son-before-the-Father. Codlings and Cream. Apple Pie. Cherry Pie. Gooseberry Pie. Sod Apple and Plum Pudding
Part Used. Herb

The Great Hairy Willowherb, though it has not so conspicuous a flower as the Rose Bay, is yet a striking plant, growing in great masses by pond sides, along the margins of lakes and rivers and in marshes and pools.

It is tall and erect, branched, with underground creeping shoots, like the Rose Bay. The leaves are placed opposite one another on the stem, are 3 to 5 inches long, their bases clasping the stem and like it, very woolly, hence the specific Latin name hirsutum, and the common English name.

The flowers are numerous and large, rose-purple, though not so brilliant as those of the Rose Bay, bell-shaped and partly drooping, the petals broad and notched.

In this species, stigmas and anthers ripen together and the plant is capable of self-pollination, but cross-pollination is ensured by insect visitors by the more prominent position of the stigmas. Insect visitors are, however, not very numerous, and in their absence the stigmas curl back and touch the anthers. (In another smaller species, Epilobium parviflorum (Schreb.) rarely visited by insects, four stamens are shorter, four longer than the style; the former are only useful for cross-pollination, the latter self-pollinate the flower. Stamens and stigma ripen simultaneously.)

The seeds, contained in similar long pods, are provided as in the Rose Bay, with a tuft of hairs which aid in wind dispersal.

The leaves, and particularly the top-shoots, when slightly bruised, have a delicate, cool fragrance, resembling scalded codlings, whence its popular name of Codlings and Cream, but this fragrance is very soon lost after the plant is gathered. It is also called, in allusion to this delicate scent, Apple Pie, Cherry Pie, Gooseberry Pie, Sod Apple and Plum Pudding. It is said to be the 'St. Anthony's Herb' of antiquity.

The old English country name of 'Son-before-the-Father' arises because, as Lyte says: 'the long huskes in which the seede is contained doe come forth and waxe great before that the flouere openeth.'

The name 'Hooded Willow-herb' does not refer to one of these species, but is another name for the Scullcap (*Scutellaria*), and the 'Purple Willow-herb' is also not this species, but another name for *Lythrum Salicaria*, the Purple Loosestrife, a plant that is often present in the same riverside situations.

Although the leaves of *E. hirsutum* have also been used as astringents there are reports of violent poisoning with epileptic-like convulsions having been caused by its employment.

WINTERGREEN

Gaultheria procumbens (LINN.)
N.O. Ericaceæ

Synonyms. Teaberry. Boxberry. Mountain Tea. Checkerberry. Thé du Canada. Aromatic Wintergreen. Partridge Berry. Deerberry

Part Used. Leaves

Habitat. Northern United States from Georgia to Newfoundland; Canada

¶ *Description.* A small indigenous shrubby, creeping, evergreen plant, growing about 5 to 6 inches high under trees and shrubs, particularly under evergreens such as Kalmias and Rhododendrons. It is found in large patches on sandy and barren plains, also on mountainous tracts. The stiff branches bear at their summit tufts of leaves which are petiolate, oval, shiny, coriaceous, the upper side bright green, paler underneath. The drooping white flowers are produced singly from the base of the leaves in June and July, followed by fleshy, bright red berries (with a sweetish taste and peculiar flavour), formed by the enlargement of the calyx. The *leaves* were formerly official in the United States Pharmacopœia, but now only the oil obtained from them is official, though in some parts the whole plant is used. The odour is peculiar and aromatic, and the taste of the whole plant astringent, the leaves being particularly so.

¶ *Constituents.* The volatile oil obtained by distillation and to which all the medicinal qualities are due, contains 99 per cent. Methyl Salicylate: other properties are 0·3 of a hydrocarbon, Gaultherilene, and an aldehyde or ketone, a secondary alcohol and an ester. To the alcohol and ester are due the characteristic odour of the oil. The oil does not occur crudely in the plant, but as a non-odorous glucoside, and before distillation, the leaves have to be steeped for twelve to twenty-four hours for the oil to develop by fermentation – a reaction between water and a neutral principle: Gaultherin.

¶ *Medicinal Action and Uses.* Tonic, stimulant, astringent, aromatic. Useful as a diuretic and emmenagogue and for chronic mucous discharges. Is said to be a good galactogogue. The oil of Gaultheria is its most important product. It has all the properties of the salicylates and therefore is most beneficial in acute rheumatism, but must be given internally in capsules, owing to its pungency, death from inflammation of the stomach having been known to result from frequent and large doses of it. It is readily absorbed by the skin, but is liable to give rise to an eruption, so it is advisable to use for external application the synthetic oil of Wintergreen, Methyl Salicylate, or oil from the bark of *Betula lenta*, which is almost identical with oil of Gaultheria. In this form, it is a very valuable external application for rheumatic affections in all chronic forms of joint and muscular troubles, lumbago, sciatica, etc. The leaves have found use as a substitute for tea and as a flavouring for genuine tea. The berries form a winter food for animals, partridges, deer, etc. They have been used, steeped in brandy, to produce a bitter tonic taken in small quantities. The oil is a flavouring agent for tooth powders, liquid dentifrices, pastes, etc., especially if combined with menthol and eucalyptus.

¶ *Dosage.* Capsules of oil of Gaultheris, 10 minims in each, 1, three times daily.

¶ *Other Species.*

Gaultheria hispidula, or Cancer Wintergreen, supposed to remove the cancerous taint from the system. Is also used for scrofula and prolapsus of the womb.

G. Shallon is the Sallol of North-west America, whose edible fruit deserves to be more widely known and cultivated.

Pyrola rotundifolia, known as False Wintergreen or British Wintergreen, was formerly considered a vulnerary.

With *Chimophila umbellata,* the Bitter Wintergreen, Rheumatism Weed or Pipsissewa, *C. maculata,* the Spotted Wintergreen was used internally by North American Indians for rheumatism and scrofula. For its diuretic action it is occasionally prescribed, in fluid extract, for cystitis and considered useful in disordered digestion.

Trientalis Europæa, the Chickweed Wintergreen, a British plant, was formerly esteemed in ointment as a wound salve, and an infusion taken internally for blood poisoning or eczema. The root is emetic.

See PYROLA.

WINTER'S BARK

Drimys winteri (FORST.)
N.O. Magnoliaceæ

Synonyms. True Winter's Bark. Winter's Cinnamon. Wintera aromatica. Wintera
Part Used. Bark
Habitat. Antarctic America, southern parts of South America, along the Straits of Magellan and north to Chile, Brazil

¶ *Description.* This very large evergreen tree took its name from Captain Winter, who discovered its medicinal properties while attending Drake in his voyage round the world. It will grow to 50 feet high. The bark is green and wrinkled, that of the branches smooth and green, erect and scarred, leaves alternate, oblong, obtuse, with a midrib veinless, glabrous and finely dotted underside. Flowers small on terminal peduncles, approximately one-flowered, simple. Fruits up to six obovate, baccate, and many seeded. The bark is the official part and is found in small carved pieces ⅓ inch thick, dull yellow grey externally. Both Canella and Cinnamodendron are found in its transverse section, exhibiting radiating white lines at the end of the last rays, diverging towards the circumference; odour aromatic with a warm pungent taste.

¶ *Constituents.* An inodorous acrid resin, pale yellow volatile oil, tannic acid, oxide of iron, colouring matter and various salts.

¶ *Medicinal Action and Uses.* Stimulant, aromatic tonic, antiscorbutic, may be substituted in all cases for canella and cinnamon barks. Dose, 30 grains powdered bark; this bark is becoming very scarce and is seldom imported into Britain.

¶ *Other Species.*
Under the name of *Winter's Bark* Malambo Bark was imported into the United States (or Croton Malambo) or Matias bark, is the product of a small shrubby tree, found on the coast of Venezuela and Columbia. It has an aromatic smell and a pungent bitter taste with a calamus flavour. Active contents, a volatile oil, and bitter extractive, found most useful for dyspepsia, hemicrania, intermittent fever, and as a general aromatic tonic, also a useful adjuvant to diuretics and a good substitute for Peruvian bark.

Drimys Chilensis, growing in Chile, has analogous properties to Winter's Bark.

Cinnamodendron axillaris. The bark is used in fevers and called Casca Paratuds.

D. aromatica. An Australian species.

See (WHITE) CINNAMON.

WINTER'S BARK, FALSE

Cinnamodendron corticosum
N.O. Canallaceæ

Synonyms. Red Canella. Mountain Cinnamon
Part Used. Dried bark
Habitat. Jamaica

¶ *Description.* This is pungent like Winter's Bark, but a much paler brown colour, resembling canella bark, but without its chalky white inner surface. It has a ferruginous grey-brown colour, darker externally, with scars of the nearly circular subereous warts smooth and finely striated on the inner surface. Like canella bark in odour and pungent taste but is not bitter.

¶ *Constituents.* Volatile oil and tannic acid, it may be distinguished from canella bark by its decoction becoming blackened by a persalt of iron, can be used for the same diseases as Winter's Bark. In South America it is much used for diarrhœa, etc.

WITCH HAZEL
Hamamelis virginiana (LINN.)
N.O. Hamamelidaceæ

Synonyms. Spotted Alder. Winterbloom. Snapping Hazelnut
Parts Used. Bark, dried; leaves, fresh and dried
Habitat. The Eastern United States and Canada

¶ *Description.* The name *Hamamelis* was adopted from a Greek word to indicate its resemblance to an apple-tree.

This shrub, long known in cultivation, consists of several crooked branching trunks from one root, 4 to 6 inches in diameter, 10 to 12 feet in height, with a smooth grey bark, leaves 3 to 5 inches long and about 3 inches wide, on short petioles, alternate, oval or obovate, acuminate, obliquely sub-cordate at the base, the margin crenate, dentate, scabrous, with raised spots underneath, pinnately veined and having stellate hairs. The leaves drop off in autumn, then the yellow flowers appear, very late in September and in October, in clusters from the joints, followed by black nuts, containing white seeds which are oily and edible. In Britain, the nut does not bear seeds, but in America, they are produced abundantly, but often do not ripen till the following summer. The seeds are ejected violently when ripe, hence the name Snapping Hazelnut. The leaves are inodorous, with an astringent and bitterish aromatic taste. The twigs are flexible and rough, colour externally, yellowish-brown to purple, wood greeny white, pith small. The bark as found in commerce is usually in quilled pieces $\frac{1}{16}$ inch thick, 2 to 8 inches long, with silvery grey, scaly cork; longitudinally striated; fracture fibrous and laminated; taste and odour slight.

¶ *Constituents.* Of the *leaves* (official in the United States Pharmacopœia), tannic and gallic acids, an unknown bitter principle and some volatile oil.

The *bark* contains tannin, partly amorphous and partly crystal, gallic acid, a physterol, resin, fat and other bitter and odorous bodies.

¶ *Medicinal Action and Uses.* The properties of the leaves and bark are similar, astringent, tonic, sedative, valuable in checking internal and external hæmorrhage, most efficacious in the treatment of piles, a good pain-killer for the same, useful for bruises and inflammatory swellings, also for diarrhœa, dysentery and mucous discharges.

It has long been used by the North American Indians as poultices for painful swellings and tumours.

The decoction has been utilized for incipient phthisis, gleet, ophthalmia, menorrhagia and the debilitated state resulting from abortion.

A tea made of the leaves or bark may be taken freely with advantage, being good for bleeding of the stomach and in complaints of the bowels, and an injection of this tea is excellent for inwardly bleeding piles, the relief being marvellous and the cure speedy. An ointment made of 1 part fluid extract of bark to 9 parts simple ointment is also used as a local application, the concentration Hamamelin being also employed, mainly in the form of suppositories.

Witch Hazel has been supposed to owe its utility to an action on the muscular fibre of veins. The distilled extract from the fresh leaves and young twigs forms an excellent remedy for internal or external uses, being beneficial for bleeding from the lungs and nose, as well as from other internal organs. In the treatment of varicose veins, it should be applied on a lint bandage, which must be constantly kept moist: a pad of Witch Hazel applied to a burst varicose vein will stop the bleeding and often save life by its instant application.

Pond's Extract of Witch Hazel was much used in our grandmother's days as a general household remedy for burns, scalds, and inflammatory conditions of the skin generally and it is still in general use.

In cases of bites of insects and mosquitoes a pad of cotton-wool, moistened with the extract and applied to the spot will soon cause the pain and swelling to subside.

Diluted with warm water, the extract is used for inflammation of the eyelids.

¶ *Dosage.* Liquor Hamamelidis, $\frac{1}{2}$ to 3 drachms (a distillate of the fresh leaves). Used also with equal parts of glycerine as injection for piles.

Liquid extract, 5 to 15 minims (preparation of the dried leaves made with alcohol) externally for varicose veins. Injection for piles, 2 to 5 minims.

Hamamelin, $\frac{1}{4}$ to 2 grains, in pill (powdered extractive from the bark). 1 to 3 grains with cacao butter is useful for piles.

Tincture (from the bark), 30 to 60 minims. 1 drachm in 3 oz. cold water given as enema for piles. Lotion of 1 or 2 drachms with water to an ounce useful for bruises.

Ointment: employed externally for piles.

WOAD

Ivatis tinctoria (LINN.)
N.O. Cruciferæ

Synonyms. (*Anglo-Saxon*) Wad.
    (*French*) Guède
    (*Italian*) Guado
    (*Spanish and French*) Pastel
    (*Dutch*) Weat
Part Used. Leaves

Dyer's Woad, French *Guède* (supposed to be derived from Gaudum, now Gualdo, the name of a town in the Roman States, where it was extensively cultivated), was formerly much cultivated in Britain for the dye extracted from the leaves. It is now nearly superseded by indigo, but is still cultivated in the south of France and in Flanders, as its dye is said to improve the quality and colour of indigo, when mixed in certain proportions. Woad is cultivated to a small extent in Lincolnshire and Woad mills are still worked at Wisbech, but not for the dye itself, the produce *fixes* true indigo, and is also used to form a base, or mordant, for a black dye.

Woad belongs to a genus spread over Southern Europe and Western Asia, and from having been much cultivated in many parts of Asia and Europe, has become established in stony and waste places as far north as Sweden. It is found in many parts of Great Britain, but not fully naturalized, except near Tewkesbury, where, according to Hooker, it appears to be indigenous. At the earliest time in the history of Britain it must have been plentiful in the country, since Cæsar found the natives stained with it, but afterwards, probably from its extensive use, it became less common, and we find our Saxon forefathers importing Woad to dye their home-spun cloth. Their name for it was *Wad* or *Waad*, whence the English name woad.

¶ *Description.* Gerard tells us:

'Glaston or Guadon, Woad is about three feet high, with long, bluish-green leaves growing round and out of the stalk, growing smaller as they reach the top, when they branch out with small yellow flowers, which in turn produce seed like little black tongues. The root is white and single. The Wild Woad is similar except that the stalk is softer, smaller and browner, and the leaves and tongues narrower. Where Woad is cultivated in fields, the wild Woad grows. It flowers from June to September. Cæsar in his fifth book of the French wars mentions that the British stained themselves blue with woad. Pliny in his 22nd book, Chapter I, says the French call it *Glastum* and British women and girls colouring themselves with it went naked to some of their sacrifices.

'Garden Woad is dry but not sharp, Wild Woad is drier and sharper and biting. The decoction made of Woad is good for hardness of the spleen, also good for wounds and ulcers to those of strong constitution and those accustomed to much physical labour and coarse fare. It is used as a dye, profitable to some, hurtful to many.'

Culpepper says:

'Some people affirm the plant to be destructive to bees, and fluxes them, which if it be, I cannot help it. I should rather think, unless bees be contrary to other creatures, it possesses them with the contrary disease, the herb being exceeding dry and binding. . . . A plaister made thereof, and applied to the region of the spleen which lies on the left side, takes away the hardness and pains thereof. The ointment is excellently good for such ulcers as abound with moisture, and takes away the corroding and fretting humours: It cools inflammations, quenches St. Anthony's fire, and stays defluxion of the blood to any part of the body.'

He also says that the seeds, if chewed, turn the saliva blue.

¶ *Cultivation.* The cultivation of Woad was formerly carried on by people who devoted themselves entirely to it, and as crops of the plant are not successful for more than two years on the same piece of land, they never stayed long in one place, but hiring land in various districts, led a wandering life with their families and gained their living by their crops. Later, many farmers devoted a portion of their land to the growth of Woad, alternating the spots year after year.

Good loam soil is needed, land in good heart, repeatedly ploughed and harrowed from autumn till the following August, when the seeds are sown in drills, being thinned out by hoeing when about a fortnight old, to a distance of about 6 inches apart. In the spring, careful hoeing to remove weeds is necessary. The first crop can be gathered as soon as the leaves are fully grown, while perfectly green. The leaves are picked off when the plant is coming into flower. If the land be good and the crop well husbanded, it will produce three or more gatherings, repeated at intervals of a few weeks, but the first two gatherings are the best. An acre of land will produce a ton of Woad, and in good seasons, a ton and a half. If the land in which the seed is sown should have been in culture before for other crops, it will require dressing before it is sown – about twenty loads of stable manure to the acre being laid on and ploughed in with the last ploughing before the seeds are sown, this being enough to keep the ground in heart till the final crop of Woad is gathered.

¶ *Treatment of the Crop.* The leaves are dried a little in the sun, then ground in a mill to a pasty mass, which is formed into heaps exposed to the air but protected from rain, until it ferments. A crust which forms over it is carefully prevented from breaking, and when fermentation is complete, usually in about a fortnight, the mass is again mixed up and formed into cakes. Before being used by the dyer, these cakes have to be again broken up, moistened and subjected to further fermentation. Much of the quality of the dye is said to depend on the way in which this operation is performed.

The colour is brought out by mixing an infusion of the Woad thus prepared with limewater.

The best Woad used to be worth £20 or more a ton, till its price declined on the introduction of indigo, to which it is inferior in richness of colour, but is more permanent.

It is stated, also, that Woad leaves, covered with boiling water, weighted down for half an hour and the water poured off, treated with caustic potash and subsequently with hydrochloric acid, yield a good indigo dye. If the time of infusion be increased, greens and browns are obtained.

How the Ancients prepared the blue dye is not known.

¶ *Medicinal Action and Uses.* The herb is so astringent, that it is not fit to be given internally as a medicine, and has only been used medicinally as a plaster, applied to the region of the spleen, and as an ointment for ulcers, inflammation and to stanch bleeding.

Ivatis indigotica is cultivated as a tinctorial plant in the north of China, where it is called Tein-ching. It is a small, half-shrubby plant, with a decumbent stem, bearing at its extremity several long drooping racemes of small yellow flowers, and smooth black fiddle-shaped pods about ½ inch long. The lower leaves are rather fleshy, on long stalks, oval, lance-shaped, and pointed, with the edges slightly toothed, the upper ones very much narrower and smaller. In the north of China, this plant takes the place of the indigo of the south, and its colouring matter is obtained by a process closely analogous to that employed in the preparation of indigo, but instead of being thoroughly inspissated so as to form solid cakes, it is used by the Chinese dyers in a semi-liquid or pasty state. It is commonly employed for dyeing cotton cloth, to which it imparts a dark-blue colour.

WOOD ANEMONE. *See* ANEMONE

WOOD BETONY. *See* BETONY

WOODRUFF, SWEET

Asperula odorata (LINN.)
N.O. Rubiaceæ

Synonyms. (*Old English*) Wuderove. Wood-rova
(*Old French*) Muge-de-boys
Part Used. Herb

The Sweet Woodruff, a favourite little plant growing in woods and on shaded hedgebanks, may be readily recognized by its small white flowers (in bloom in May and June) set on a tender stalk, with narrow, bright-green leaves growing beneath them in successive, star-like whorls, just as in Clivers or Goosegrass, about eight leaves to every whorl. Unlike the latter, however, its stems are erect and smooth: they rarely exceed a foot in height, their average being 8 or 9 inches. The plant is perennial, with creeping, slender root-stock.

Being a lover of woods and shady places, its deep-green foliage develops best in the half-shade, where the sunlight penetrates with difficulty. Should the branches over-shadowing it be cut away, and the full light fall upon it, it loses its colour and rapidly becomes much paler.

When the seed is quite ripe and dry, it is a rough little ball covered thickly with flexible, hooked bristles, white below, but black-tipped, and these catch on to the fur and feathers of any animal or bird that pushes through the undergrowth, and thus the seed is dispersed.

The name of the plant appears in the thirteenth century as 'Wuderove,' and later as 'Wood-rove' – the *rove* being derived, it is said, from the French *rovelle*, a wheel, in allusion to the spoke-like arrangement of the leaves in whorls. In old French works it appears as *Muge-de-boys*, musk of the woods.

Some of the old herbalists spelt the name Woodruff with an array of double consonants: Woodderowffe. Later this spelling was written in a rhyme, which children were fond of repeating:

WOODDE,
ROWFFE.

¶ *Cultivation.* As a rule, the plant is not cultivated, but collected from the woods, but it might be grown under orchard trees and can be propagated, (1) by seeds, sown as soon as ripe, in prepared beds of good soil, in the end of July or beginning of August, (2) by division of roots during the spring and early summer, just after flowering. Plant in moist, partially shaded ground, 1 foot apart.

¶ *Chemical Constituents.* The agreeable odour of Sweet Woodruff is due to a crystalline chemical principle called Coumarin, which is used in perfumery, not only on account of its own fragrance, but for its property of fixing other odours. It is the odorous principle also present in melilot, tonka beans, and various other plants belonging to the orders Leguminosæ, Graminæ and Orchidaceæ. It is employed in pharmacy to disguise disagreeable odours, especially that of iodoform, for which purpose 1 part of coumarin is used to 50 parts of iodoform. The plant further contains citric, malic and rubichloric acids, together with some tannic acid.

The powdered leaves are mixed with fancy snuffs, because of their enduring fragrance, and also put into *potpourri.*

WOOD SAGE. *See* SAGE

WOOD SANICLE. *See* SANICLE

WOOD SORREL. *See* SORREL

WORMSEED, AMERICAN

¶ *Medicinal Action and Uses.* Woodruff was much used as a medicine in the Middle Ages.

The fresh leaves, bruised and applied to cuts and wounds, were said to have a healing effect, and formerly a strong decoction of the fresh herb was used as a cordial and stomachic. It is also said to be useful for removing biliary obstructions of the liver.

The plant when newly gathered has but little odour, but when dried, has a most refreshing scent of new-mown hay, which is retained for years. Gerard tells us:

'The flowers are of a very sweet smell as is the rest of the herb, which, being made up into garlands or bundles, and hanged up in houses in the heat of summer, doth very well attemper the air, cool and make fresh the place, to the delight and comfort of such as are therein. It is reported to be put into wine, to make a man merry, and to be good for the heart and liver, it prevaileth in wounds, as *Cruciata* and other vulnerary herbs do.'

In Germany, one of the favourite hock-cups is still made by steeping the fresh sprigs in Rhine wine. This forms a specially delightful drink, known as *Maibowle*, and drunk on the first of May.

The dried herb may be kept among linen, like lavender, to preserve it from insects. In the Middle Ages it used to be hung and strewed in churches, and on St. Barnabas Day and on St. Peter's, bunches of box, Woodruff, lavender and roses found a place there. It was also used for stuffing beds.

Chenopodium anthelminticum (BERT.)
N.O. Chenopodiaceæ

Synonyms. Chenopodium Ambrosioides (Linn.). Mexican Tea. Jesuit's Tea. Herba Sancti Mariæ
Part Used. Seeds
Habitat. Indigenous to Mexico and South America, Missouri, New England, and eastern United States

The American Wormseed plant (*Chenopodium ambrosioides*, Linn.), and still more a variety of it, *C. ambrosioides*, var. *anthelminticum* (Bert), furnishes the important drug Chenopodium.

It is indigenous to Mexico and South America, but has become thoroughly naturalized as far north as Missouri and New England, where it grows about dwellings and in manured soils. It is now found in almost all parts of the eastern United States, a coarse,

perennial weed of the roadside and waste places, smoothish, more or less viscid-glandular, the stout, erect, angular and grooved stem growing to a height of about 2 feet.

¶ *Description.* The leaves are slightly petioled, oblong-lanceolate, toothed, the upper ones entire and tapering at both ends. The small, very numerous flowers are yellowish-green in colour and occur in numerous small clusters, or globular spikes, arranged in the axils of slender, lateral, leafy branches. The calyx is five-cleft, the lobes ovate, pointed. Stamens five, ovary covered on the top with small, oblong, stalked glands; styles, two to three. The fruit is perfectly enclosed in the calyx, obtusely angled, the seed smooth and shining, the embryo forming about three-quarters of a ring around the mealy albumen.

The drug consists of these small, irregular, globular fruits, not larger than the head of a pin. They are very light and of a greenish-yellow or brown colour. On rubbing the fruit, the membraneous pericarp is removed and the single, small, brownish-black seed is exposed.

The odour of the fruit is strong, resembling somewhat that of eucalyptus; the taste, pungent and bitter.

The fruit of *C. ambrosioides*, var. *anthelminticum* is even more aromatic.

Both varieties of the plant flower from July to September and the fruits ripen successively through the autumn and are collected in October.

The whole herb has a strong, peculiar, somewhat aromatic odour, which is due to the presence of a volatile oil and is retained on drying. The leaves have been used in place of tea in Mexico.

The American aborigines used the whole herb in decoction in painful menstruation, but its principal use has been – both leaves and seeds – as a vermifuge, and it is to-day considered one of the best expellents of lumbricoids.

Though all parts of the plant possess anthelmintic properties, the fruits and the oil extracted from them are alone employed, being official in the United States Pharmacopœia. It was long customary for the seeds to be administered in the form of a powder, or an electuary, but although the activity of the seed is unquestioned, it has now been entirely displaced in America by the volatile oil obtained by distillation from the crushed fruits, to which the medicinal importance of the fruit is due.

The oil was first isolated in 1895 by a German pharmacist who lived in Brazil, where the seeds had long been used as a vermifuge.

Most of this oil is distilled in Maryland, and since Baltimore is the commercial centre of that state, this oil is commonly known as Baltimore oil, in distinction from Western Missouri oil, which has at times played a rôle in the market. The plant is now cultivated in large quantities near Baltimore.

¶ *Constituents of the Oil.* American Wormseed oil, known as Chenopodium oil, is colourless or yellowish, when freshly distilled, becoming deeper yellow and even brownish by use. It has a peculiar, penetrating, somewhat camphoraceous odour (the peculiar odour of the plant), and a pungent, bitter taste.

The yield of oil from the crushed fruits is 0·6 to 1·0 per cent.

Its chief constituent is Ascaridole, to the high percentage of 60 to 70 per cent., an unstable substance, allied to cineal, readily decomposed on heating, with the production of a hydrocarbon. It also contains *p*-cymene, *a*-perpinene, probably dihydro-*p*-cymene and possibly sylvestrene. Betzine and choline have also been reported.

According to the researches of De Langen, Flue and Welhuizen, of the Dutch-Indian Medical Service, in 1919, the oil contains Glycol and Safrol, and these authors ascribe the powerful effect of the oil to the combination of Ascaridole and Safrol.

The characters of the oil are:

Specific gravity, 0·950 to 0·990.

Optical rotation, − 5° to 10°.

Refraction index, 1·4723 to 1·4726.

Saponification number, 246 to 280.

Soluble in three volumes of 70 per cent. alcohol.

Adulteration with American turpentine oil causes lowering of the specific gravity and insolubility in alcohol.

The fresh plant yields the alkaloid Chenopodine, a white tasteless and odourless crystalline powder, soluble in 11 parts of cold water, 3 of boiling water and 20 per cent. of alcohol.

¶ *Medicinal Action and Uses.* Chenopodium, being a very active anthelmintic, is frequently used for the expulsion of lumbricoid (round) worms, especially in children. Because of its efficacy, ease of administration and low toxicity, it is perhaps the most valuable of all the vermifuge remedies.

The bruised fruit may be given in doses of 20 grains, in the form of an electuary.

A fluid extract is prepared, of which the dose is ½ to 1 drachm.

The expressed juice of the fresh plant is also employed, in tablespoonful doses. A decoction made by boiling 1 oz. of the fresh plant with 1 pint of milk or water has sometimes been given in doses of a wineglassful.

The volatile oil is now much used, the dose of which, for a child, is from 5 to 10 minims.

The drug should be given in one full dose, fasting, and then be followed, in about two hours, by an active purgative, such as castor oil. When the purge has acted, the patient can take food. The treatment should be repeated ten days later. In view of the uncertain ascaridole contents of some samples, small doses should be given at first.

Toxic symptoms are transient dizziness and vomiting.

The oil has been recommended in the treatment of malaria, chorea, hysteria and other nervous diseases.

The plant has been employed, under the name of *Herba Sancti Mariæ*, in pectoral complaints, as an expectorant, in catarrh and asthma.

Although oil of Chenopodium has been official in the United States Pharmacopœia for many years, it does not appear to have received official recognition elsewhere. It owes its modern popularity to the investigations of Brüning, who repeatedly drew attention to it (see *Zeitschrift für exot. Path.*, 1906).

In 1912 two Dutch physicians, both working in Delhi (Dutch East Indies), stated that this essential oil is the most effective remedy against *ankylostomiasis*, the Hookworm disease. Originally, this disease was exclusively a tropical and subtropical one, but about thirty years ago, it appeared in mineworkers in Europe north of the Alps.

The Hookworm, which causes the disease, is called *Ankylostos duodenale*, the male of which attains a length of 10 mm., the female 14 mm. The living hookworm is flesh-coloured, the dead one has a grey or white colour. At the foot of the hook-formed teeth, glands, each consisting of a single cell, pour their contents into the wounds which the worm makes in the mucous membrane of the intestinal canal and into the blood-vessels by means of the teeth. It is supposed that the phenomena of the disease must be attributed to the mechanical changes brought about by the hookworm, as well as to a poisonous substance secreted by the worm. The worm deposits its eggs in the intestinal canal of its host. Together with the fæces, these eggs leave the body of the host. At a temperature of 25° to 30° C., the larva develops, and after two changes of skin, enters into the body of the new host by means of vegetables, drinking-water, or through the skin.

Several medicaments have been tried against the hookworm; thymol had appeared to be the only remedy that had been used with some success, but it is much surpassed by Chenopodium oil, which gives better results than eucalyptus, betanaphthol, or thymol.

The use of this oil commenced when thymol was not available during the early days of the Great War. It proved to be satisfactory in every way and is the drug commonly used in Ceylon since 1917. Statistics indicate that in three treatments, about 95 per cent. of the worms are removed from the body. It has also been used in Fiji and has proved an anthelmintic of great potency. It is said there that over 80 per cent. of the worms are expelled after a single dose.

The maximum individual dose would appear to be 1 c.c., but it is best given in three cacheta of 0·5 c.c. each, at two-hourly intervals, followed three hours later by a saline purge of 1 oz. of magnesium sulphate.

The observances of the two Dutch physicians Schüffner and Vervoort have been confirmed by other medical men, and at present, Chenopodium oil has become the specific remedy against the Hookworm disease.

It is, however, a dangerous remedy in the hands of the layman on account of its activity, for unfortunately, the oil as it appears in commerce contains markedly varying quantities of the active principle Ascaridole, and the amount lessens with keeping, making it desirable that dealers should always mention the Ascaridole percentage of the oil they are selling and the date of distillation. The freshly-distilled oil in cases of overdoses has been known to cause symptoms of poisoning. Ascaridole, extracted and administered in place of the whole oil, is effective, and the use of it eliminates uncertainty of the strength of a dose of the oil, but it is relatively costly.

Carbon tetrachloride, recently introduced as a remedy for Hookworm, has proved most efficient. It is the cheapest of all advocated treatments, but the dose of 3 mils., at present given, sometimes proves dangerous and would appear to require reduction. A combination of this drug with Ascaridole is being now tested.

Chenopodium oil has also been shown to be of great service against the tapeworm and is employed in veterinary practice in a worm mixture for dogs, combined with oil of turpentine, oil of aniseed, castor oil and olive oil.

Since this oil has proved so important, steps have been taken to cultivate the plant in the Dutch East Indies, and these endeavours have met with great success, and manufacture of the oil in Netherlands India is now being extensively carried on.

¶ *Other Species.*

From *C. glaucum* (Linn.), the Oak-leaved Goosefoot of the United States, a medicinal tincture is made, which is used for expelling round-worms. There exists some doubt as to whether the properties of the tincture are not also due in part to the aphis that infests the plant.

This species is also a native of Great Britain. The European and Asiatic *C. Botrys*, Jerusalem Oak, or Feather Geranium, is considered an expectorant in France.

See ARRACHS, BEETS, CHENOPODIUMS, GOOSEFOOT, GLASSWORTS, QUINOA SPINACH.

WORMSEED, LEVANT

Artemisia cina (BERG.)
N.O. Compositæ

Synonyms. Sea Wormwood. Santonica. Semen Sanctum. Semen Cinæ. Semen Contra. Semen Santonici. Artemesia Lercheana. Artemisia maritima, var. Stechmanniana. Artemisia maritima, var. pauciflora. Artemesia Chamæmelifolia

(*Italian*) Semenzina

Part Used. Seeds

The Levant Wormseed, largely imported into Britain, is derived from a variety of the Sea Wormwood. Several species of Wormwood are mentioned by Dioscorides as being effective as a vermifuge, one of which was reported as growing in the country of the Santones in Gaul. Its ancient reputation has been maintained in modern times, for the universally employed vermifuge Santonin (the very name derived from classic days) is produced from Santonica – popularly called Wormseed – which consists of the minute, dried, unexpanded flower-heads of a Russian variety of the Sea Wormwood (*Artemisia maritima*, var. *Stechmanniana*, Bess.). This variety, which some botanists consider to be a distinct species, under the name of *A. Cina* (Berg.), or *A. chamæmelifolia* (Vill.), grows in profusion in Siberia, Turkestan and Chinese Mongolia. The greater part of the Wormseed is used in Turkestan, where it grows in enormous quantities in the desert of the Kirghiz, especially near the town of Chimkent, where a factory has been erected in which large quantities of Santonin are produced from the Wormseed collected in the vicinity, not more than 10 per cent. of the drug being now exported in the crude state, in which condition it is known in this country as Levant Wormseed. The plant is low and shrubby, throwing up a number of erect stems on which the little greenish-yellow, oblong flower-heads are borne. Each head is about ⅛ inch long and 1/16 inch in diameter, and contains three to five minute, tubular flowers. In July and August, before the flowers expand, they are stripped from the stems and dried, being brought into Chimkent by the Kirghiz and other tribes.

Wormseed has long been used as an anthelmintic. Tragus, in 1531, in Brunfels' *Herbal*, mentions Wormseed as being imported by way of Genoa; it was employed in Italy under the name of Semenzina (diminutive of *Semenza*, seed), in the belief that it consisted of small seeds. From this word is derived the name of *Semen cinæ*, by which the drug is often known: *Semen contra* (another of its names) is an abbreviation of *Semen contra vermes*. The drug at first sight appears to consist of a number of small brownish, ridged seeds, and it is not till they are closely examined that their true nature becomes apparent.

The drug exhales when crushed an agreeable aromatic odour, and possesses a bitter, aromatic camphoraceous taste. As imported, it frequently contains considerable fragments of the leaves and slender flower-stalks.

¶ *Constituents.* The chief constituent of Wormseed is a crystalline principle, Santonin, to which the anthelmintic property of the drug is due. Santonin attains its maximum 2·3 to 3·6 per cent. in July and August; after the flowerheads have expanded, it rapidly diminishes in quantity. It is extracted from the flower-heads by treating them with Milk of Lime, the Santonin being converted into soluble calcium santonate. It occurs in colourless, shining, flat prisms, without odour and almost tasteless at first, but afterwards developing a bitter taste. It is sparingly soluble in water, but soluble in alcohol and ether.

Wormseed also contains a crystalline substance, Artemisin, and a yellow volatile oil consisting of Cineol, to which its odour is due.

¶ *Medicinal Action and Uses.* Wormseed is one of the oldest and most common anthelmintics, especially for children. In domestic practice the seeds are used powdered, combined with honey or treacle, the dose of the seeds taken thus in substance being 10 to 30 grains. The seeds have also been employed in infusion or decoction, but in these forms their bitterness is a strong objection. As a general rule, however, the crude drug Wormseed is seldom administered, its active constituent Santonin being employed. It acts as a direct poison to parasites, and is used as a remedy for round-worms, which it rapidly expels; it has also an effect on thread-worms to a lesser degree, but has no action on tape-worms. It is usually administered as a powder or in lozenges, not in solution, and is often given with calomel, or compound powder of scammony.

¶ *Preparations.* Santonin, 2 to 5 grains. Santonin lozenges, B.P.

Several cases are on record of fatal poisoning by Santonin, and Santonin rendered yellow by exposure to direct sunlight is sometimes preferred, it being stated to be less poisonous. It is known as yellow Santonin, or Photosantonin.

Even small doses of Santonin will produce remarkable effects on the vision, appreciation of colour being so disturbed that objects appear to have a yellowish tinge, which is sometimes preceded by a faint colour. Santonin may also cause headache, nausea and vomiting, and in large doses, epileptiform convulsions.

See MUGWORT, WORMWOOD.

WORMWOODS

N.O. Compositæ

The Wormwoods are members of the great family of Compositæ and belong to the genus *Artemisia*, a group consisting of 180 species, of which we have four growing wild in England, the Common Wormwood, Mugwort, Sea Wormwood and Field Wormwood. In addition, as garden plants, though not native, Tarragon (*A. dracunculus*) claims a place in every herb-garden, and Southernwood (*A. abrotanum*), an old-fashioned favourite, is found in many borders, whilst others, such as *A. sericea*, *A. cana* and *A. alpina*, form pretty rockwork shrubs.

The whole family is remarkable for the extreme bitterness of all parts of the plant: 'as bitter as Wormwood' is a very Ancient proverb.

In some of the Western states of North America there are large tracts almost entirely destitute of other vegetation than certain kinds of *Artemisia*, which cover vast plains. The plants are of no use as forage: and the few wild animals that feed on them are said to have, when eaten, a bitter taste. The Artemisias also abound in the arid soil of the Tartarean steppes and in other similar situations.

The genus is named *Artemisia* from Artemis, the Greek name for Diana. In an early translation of the *Herbarium* of Apuleius we find:

'Of these worts that we name Artemisia, it is said that Diana did find them and delivered their powers and leechdom to Chiron the Centaur, who first from these Worts set forth a leechdom, and he named these worts from the name of Diana, Artemis, that is Artemisias.'

WORMWOOD, COMMON

Artemisia Absinthium (LINN.)
N.O. Compositæ

Synonym. Green Ginger
Part Used. Whole Herb
Habitat. Europe, Siberia, and United States of America

The Common Wormwood held a high reputation in medicine among the Ancients. Tusser (1577), in *July's Husbandry*, says:

'While Wormwood hath seed get a handful or twaine
To save against March, to make flea to refraine:
Where chamber is sweeped and Wormwood is strowne,
What saver is better (if physick be true)
For places infected than Wormwood and Rue?
It is a comfort for hart and the braine,
And therefore to have it it is not in vaine.'

Besides being strewn in chambers as Tusser recommended, it used to be laid among stuffs and furs to keep away moths and insects.

According to the Ancients, Wormwood counteracted the effects of poisoning by hemlock, toadstools and the biting of the sea-dragon. The plant was of some importance among the Mexicans, who celebrated their great festival of the Goddess of Salt by a ceremonial dance of women, who wore on their heads garlands of Wormwood.

With the exception of Rue, Wormwood is the bitterest herb known, but it is very wholesome and used to be in much request by brewers for use instead of hops. The leaves resist putrefaction, and have been on that account a principal ingredient in antiseptic fomentations.

An Old Love Charm

'On St. Luke's Day, take marigold flowers, a sprig of marjoram, thyme, and a little *Wormwood*; dry them before a fire, rub them

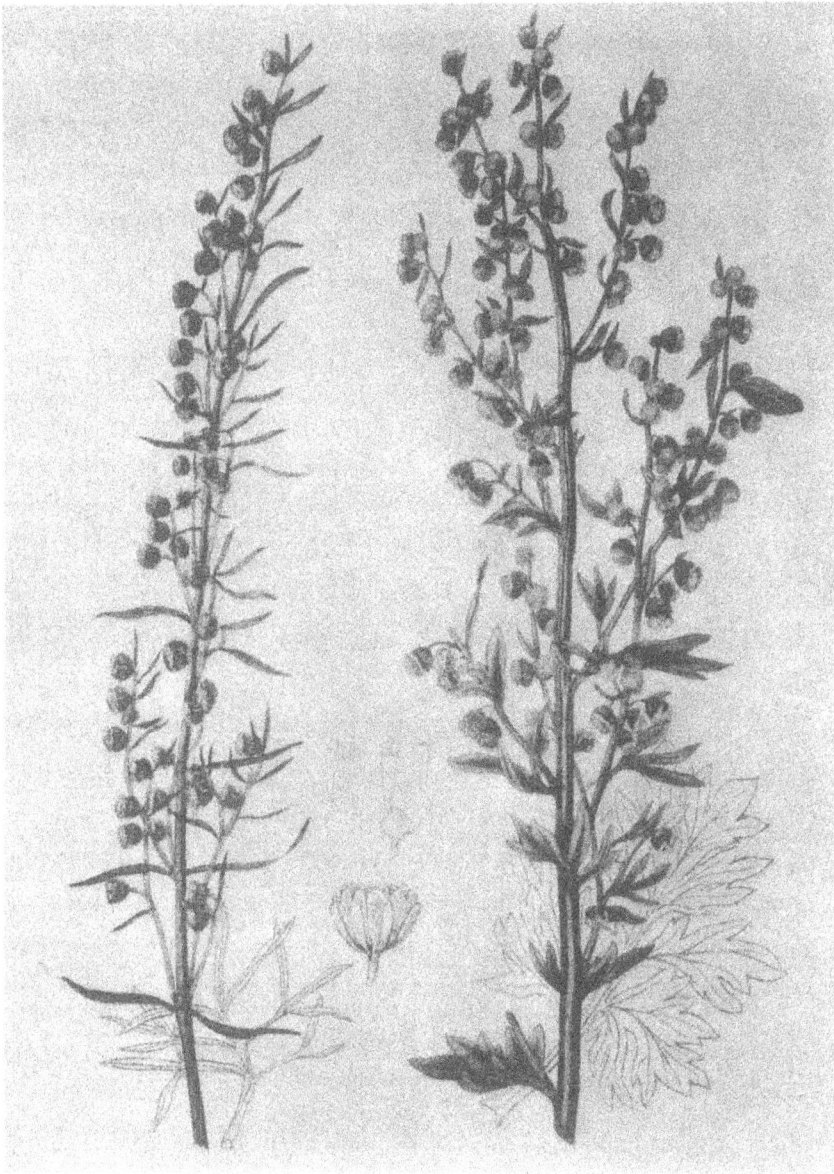

LEVANT WORMSEED AND LEVANT WORMWOOD
Artemisia Cina and *Artemisia Absinthium*

ZEDOARY
Curcuma Zedoaria

to powder; then sift it through a fine piece of lawn, and simmer it over a slow fire, adding a small quantity of virgin honey, and vinegar. Anoint yourself with this when you go to bed, saying the following lines three times, and you will dream of your partner "that is to be":

"St. Luke, St. Luke, be kind to me,
In dreams let me my true-love see." '

Culpepper, writing of the three Wormwoods most in use, the Common Wormwood, Sea Wormwood and Roman Wormwood, tells us: 'Each kind has its particular virtues' . . . the Common Wormwood is 'the strongest,' the Sea Wormwood, 'the second in bitterness,' whereas the Roman Wormwood, 'to be found in botanic gardens' – the first two being wild – 'joins a great deal of aromatic flavour with but little bitterness.'

The Common Wormwood grows on roadsides and waste places, and is found over the greater part of Europe and Siberia, having been formerly much cultivated for its qualities. In Britain, it appears to be truly indigenous near the sea and locally in many other parts of England and Scotland, from Forfar southwards. In Ireland it is a doubtful native. It has become naturalized in the United States.

¶ *Description.* The root is perennial, and from it arise branched, firm, leafy stems, sometimes almost woody at the base. The flowering stem is 2 to 2½ feet high and whitish, being closely covered with fine silky hairs. The leaves, which are also whitish on both sides from the same reason, are about 3 inches long by 1½ broad, cut into deeply and repeatedly (about three times pinnatifid), the segments being narrow (linear) and blunt. The leaf-stalks are slightly winged at the margin. The small, nearly globular flowerheads are arranged in an erect, leafy panicle, the leaves on the flower-stalks being reduced to three, or even one linear segment, and the little flowers themselves being pendulous and of a greenish-yellow tint. They bloom from July to October. The ripe fruits are not crowned by a tuft of hairs, or pappus, as in the majority of the Compositæ family.

The leaves and flowers are very bitter, with a characteristic odour, resembling that of thujone. The root has a warm and aromatic taste.

¶ *Cultivation.* Wormwood likes a shady situation, and is easily propagated by division of roots in the autumn, by cuttings, or by seeds sown in the autumn soon after they are ripe. No further care is needed than to keep free from weeds. Plant about 2 feet apart each way.

¶ *Parts Used.* The whole herb – leaves and tops – gathered in July and August, when the plant is in flower and dried.

Collect only on a dry day, after the sun has dried off the dew. Cut off the upper green portion and reject the lower parts of the stems, together with any discoloured or insect-eaten leaves. Tie loosely in bunches of uniform size and length, about six stalks to a bunch, and spread out in shape of a fan, so that the air can get to all parts. Hang over strings, in the open, on a fine, sunny, warm day, but in half-shade, otherwise the leaves will become tindery; the drying must not be done in full sunlight, or the aromatic properties will be partly lost. Aromatic herbs should be dried at a temperature of about 70°. If no sun is available, the bunches may be hung over strings in a covered shed, or disused greenhouse, or in a sunny warm attic, provided there is ample ventilation, so that the moist heated air may escape. The room may also be heated with a coke or anthracite stove, care being taken that the window is kept open during the day. If after some days the leaves are crisp and the stalks still damp, hang the bunches over a stove, when the stalks will quickly finish drying. Uniformity in size in the bunches is important, as it facilitates packing. When the drying process is completed, pack away at once in airtight boxes, as otherwise the herbs will absorb about 12 per cent. moisture from the air. If sold to the wholesale druggists in powdered form, rub through a sieve as soon as thoroughly dry, before the bunches have had time to absorb any moisture, and pack in tins or bottles at once.

¶ *Constituents.* The chief constituent is a volatile oil, of which the herb yields in distillation from 0·5 to 1·0 per cent. It is usually dark green, or sometimes blue in colour, and has a strong odour and bitter, acrid taste. The oil contains thujone (absinthol or tenacetone), thujyl alcohol (both free and combined with acetic, isovalerianic, succine and malic acids), cadinene, phellandrene and pinene. The herb also contains the bitter glucoside *absinthin*, absinthic acid, together with tannin, resin, starch, nitrate of potash and other salts.

¶ *Medicinal Action and Uses.* Tonic, stomachic, febrifuge, anthelmintic.

A nervine tonic, particularly helpful against the falling sickness and for flatulence. It is a good remedy for enfeebled digestion and debility.

¶ *Preparations*. Fluid extract, ½ to 1 drachm. Wormwood Tea, made from 1 oz. of the herb, infused for 10 to 12 minutes in 1 pint of boiling water, and taken in wineglassful doses, will relieve melancholia and help to dispel the yellow hue of jaundice from the skin, as well as being a good stomachic, and with the addition of fixed alkaline salt, produced from the burnt plant, is a powerful diuretic in some dropsical cases. The ashes yield a purer alkaline salt than most other vegetables, except Beanstalks and Broom.

The juice of the larger leaves which grow from the root before the stalk appears has been used as a remedy for jaundice and dropsy, but it is intensely nauseous. A light infusion of the tops of the plant, used fresh, is excellent for all disorders of the stomach, creating an appetite, promoting digestion and preventing sickness after meals, but it is said to produce the contrary effect if made too strong.

The flowers, dried and powdered, are most effectual as a vermifuge, and used to be considered excellent in agues. The essential oil of the herb is used as a worm-expeller, the spirituous extract being preferable to that distilled in water. The leaves give out nearly the whole of their smell and taste both to spirit and water, but the cold water infusions are the least offensive.

The intensely bitter, tonic and stimulant qualities have caused Wormwood not only to be an ingredient in medicinal preparations, but also to be used in various liqueurs, of which absinthe is the chief, the basis of absinthe being absinthol, extracted from Wormwood. Wormwood, as employed in making this liqueur, bears also the name 'Wermuth' – preserver of the mind – from its medicinal virtues as a nervine and mental restorative. If not taken habitually, it soothes spinal irritability and gives tone to persons of a highly nervous temperament. Suitable allowances of the diluted liqueur will promote salutary perspiration and may be given as a vermifuge. Inferior absinthe is generally adulterated with copper, which produces the characteristic green colour.

The drug, *absinthium*, is rarely employed, but it might be of value in nervous diseases such as neurasthenia, as it stimulates the cerebral hemispheres, and is a direct stimulant of the cortex cerebri. When taken to excess it produces giddiness and attacks of epileptiform convulsions. Absinthium occurs in the British Pharmacopœia in the form of extract, infusion and tincture, and is directed to be extracted also from *A. maritima*, the Sea Wormwood, which possesses the same virtues in a less degree, and is often more used as a stomachic than the Common Wormwood. Commercially this often goes under the name of Roman Wormwood, though that name really belongs to *A. Pontica*. All three species were used, as in Culpepper's time.

Dr. John Hill (1772) recommends Common Wormwood in many forms. He says:

'The Leaves have been commonly used, but the flowery tops are the right part. These, made into a light infusion, strengthen digestion, correct acidities, and supply the place of gall, where, as in many constitutions, that is deficient. One ounce of the Flowers and Buds should be put into an earthen vessel, and a pint and a half of boiling water poured on them, and thus to stand all night. In the morning the clear liquor with two spoonfuls of wine should be taken at three draughts, an hour and a half distance from one another. Whoever will do this regularly for a week, will have no sickness after meals, will feel none of that fulness so frequent from indigestion, and wind will be no more troublesome; if afterwards, he will take but a fourth part of this each day, the benefit will be lasting.'

He further tells us that if an ounce of these flowers be put into a pint of brandy and let to stand six weeks, the resultant tincture will in a great measure prevent the increase of gravel – and give great relief in gout. 'The celebrated Baron Haller has found vast benefit by this; and myself have very happily followed his example.'

WORMWOOD, ROMAN

Artemesia Pontica
N.O. Compositæ

Part Used. Herb

Roman Wormwood (*Artemesia Pontica*) is not indigenous to this country, being a native of Southern Europe. It grows about the same height as the Common Wormwood, but has smaller and more finely cut leaves, the segments being narrower, the upper leaves more resembling those of Southernwood; the leaves are white with fine hairs on both upper and under surfaces. The flowers, which blossom in July, are numerous, at the tops of the branches, and are darker and much smaller than those of Common Wormwood.

This is the most delicate though the least strong of the Wormwoods; the aromatic flavour with which its bitterness is mixed causes it to be employed in making the liqueur *Vermuth*.

Medicinally, the fresh tops are used, and also the whole herb, dried. Much of the *A. Pontica* in commerce is *A. maritima*.

Culpepper considered the Roman Wormwood 'excellent to strengthen the stomach.' Also that 'the juice of the fresh tops is good against obstructions of the liver and spleen. ... An infusion of the flowering tops strengthens digestion. A tincture is good

against gravel and gives great relief in the gout.'

Dr. John Hill says of this plant that it is the 'most delicate, but of least strength. The Wormwood wine, so famous with the Germans, is made with Roman Wormwood, put into the juice and work'd with it; it is a strong and an excellent wine, not unpleasant, yet of such efficacy to give an appetite that the Germans drink a glass with every other mouthful, and that way eat for hours together, without sickness or indigestion.'

WORMWOOD, SEA

Artemesia maritima
N.O. Compositæ

Synonym. Old Woman
Parts Used. Young flowering tops and shoots
Habitat. In Britain it is found as far as Wigton on the West and Aberdeen on the East; also in north-east Ireland and in the Channel Islands

The Sea Wormwood, in its many variations of form, has an extremely wide distribution in the northern hemisphere of the Old World, occurring mostly in saltish soils. It is found in the salt marshes of the British Isles, on the coasts of the Baltic, of France and the Mediterranean, and on saline soils in Hungary; thence it extends eastwards, covering immense tracts in Southern Russia, the region of the Caspian and Central Siberia to Chinese Mongolia.

¶ *Description.* It somewhat resembles *Artemesia Absinthium*, but is smaller. The stems rise about a foot or 18 inches in height. The leaves are twice pinnatifid, with narrow, linear segments, and, like the whole plant, are covered on both sides with a white cottony down. The small, oblong flower-heads – each containing three to six tubular florets – are of a yellowish or brownish tint; they are produced in August and September, and are arranged in racemes, sometimes drooping, sometimes erect.

Popularly this species is called 'Old Woman,' in distinction to 'Old Man' or Southernwood, which it somewhat resembles, though it is more delicate-looking and lacks the peculiar refreshing scent of 'Old Man.'

Dr. Hill says of this species:

'This is a very noble bitter: its peculiar province is to give an appetite, as that of the Common Wormwood is to assist digestion; the flowery tops and the young shoots possess the virtue: the older Leaves and the Stalk should be thrown away as useless. ... The apothecaries put three times as much sugar as of the ingredient in their Conserves; but the virtue is lost in the sweetness, those will not keep so well that have less sugar, but 'tis easy to make them fresh as they are wanted.'

The plant abounds in salt marshes in which cattle have been observed to fatten

quickly, and thus the herb has acquired the reputation of being beneficial to them, but they do not eat it generally, and the richness of maritime pasturage must be regarded as the true reason of their improvement under such circumstances.

¶ *Part Used.* The flowering tops and young shoots are used, collected and dried in the same manner as Wormwood.

¶ *Medicinal Action and Uses.* The plant possesses the same properties as the other Wormwoods, but is less powerful. It is a bitter tonic and aromatic.

Although it is not now employed in regular medical practice, it is often made use of by country people for intermittent fever, and for various other medicinal purposes instead of the true Wormwood.

Thornton, in his *Family Herbal*, tells us that

'beat up with thrice its weight of fine sugar, it is made up into a conserve ordered by the London College, and may be taken where the other preparations disgust too much.'

It acts as a tonic and is good in worm cases, and Culpepper gives the following uses for it:

'Boiling water poured upon it produces an excellent stomachic infusion, but the best way is taking it in a tincture made with brandy. Hysteric complaints have been completely cured by the constant use of this tincture. In the scurvy and in the hypochondriacal disorders of studious, sedentary men, few things have a greater effect: for these it is best in strong infusion. The whole blood and all the juices of the body are effected by taking this herb. It is often used in medicine instead of the Roman Wormwood, though it falls far short of it in virtue.'

See MUGWORT, SOUTHERNWOOD, WORMSEED (LEVANT).

WOUNDWORT, HEDGE

Stachys sylvatica (LINN.)
N.O. Labiatæ

Part Used. Herb

The Hedge Stachys, or Hedge Woundwort, the most frequent of the *Stachys*, is a coarse, hairy, malodorous plant, common in woods and hedges. It has thick, creeping roots that throw up tall stems, 2 or 3 feet high. Like the rest of the genus and labiate plants in general, these are quadrangular, but instead of being hollow (like the Deadnettles) they are filled with pith and solid; they are very hairy and often more or less red in colour.

The stem branches a good deal, though the upright character of the plant is preserved, the branches being very similar in character to the main stem and issuing from it in pairs, opposite to each other, at the same spot from which the leaf-stalks arise, the leaves being thrown off from the stem in pairs, each at right angles to the pair above and below it. The blades of the leaves are heart-shaped, similar in form to those of the nettle, with bold, saw-like teeth to the margins, and are on rather long footstalks.

The flowers grow in rings or whorls upon the stem, as in the other species of *Stachys*, each ring having narrow, leafy bracts beneath it, and being separated from the other by an intervening space of stem, the whole forming a long, terminal spike. There are rarely more than six flowers in each whorl. The lower lip of each flower is entire, beautifully variegated with white upon the dull crimson-purple ground and with its sides folded back. The upper lip is also entire and very convex, slightly viscid to the touch. The four stamens are beneath the protecting hood formed by the upper part of the flower, two of them longer than the others, their anthers first dull violet, then becoming black and containing pure white pollen. When in seed, the calyx teeth become rigid, and as the calyx tube dries and contracts, the four little nutlets enclosed are shot out. The corolla tube is often half filled with honey, and the mouth of the tube is provided with stiff white hairs to keep insect visitors to the centre of the channel, this flower laying itself out to be fertilized by hive bees, humble bees and long-tongued flies, who settle on the lower lip, and as they creep up the channel of the petal tube, get dusted with the pollen from the stamens in the hooded petal.

An old authority tells us that this herb 'stamped with vinegar and applied in manner of a pultis, taketh away wens and hard swellings, and inflammation of the kernels under the eares and jawes,' and also that the distilled water of the flowers 'is used to make the heart merry, to make a good colour in the face, and to make the vitall spirits more fresh and lively.'

It is said that a yellow dye can be obtained from the plant, and it has been suggested that the very tough fibres of its stem might be utilized commercially; it has also been classed among the Woundworts good for stanching blood. Referring to its pungent fœtid smell when rubbed, Green, in his *Universal Herbal* (1832), considers that 'being one of those that powerfully affect the nerves, it might prove no contemptible stimulant if judiciously used.' He informs us also that toads are thought to be fond of living under its shade, and that though sheep and goats eat it, cows and hogs refuse it.

WOUNDWORT, MARSH

Stachys palustris (LINN.)
N.O. Labiatæ

Synonyms. All-Heal. Panay. Opopanewort. Clown's Woundwort. Rusticum Vulna Herba. Downy Woundwort

Part Used. Herb

The Marsh Woundwort is common in marshy meadows and by the sides of rivers and ditches in most parts of Great Britain.

¶ *Description.* From its root-stock, which is perennial, with numerous, white, fleshy, subterranean stolons, which creep in all directions, it throws up stout stems, 2 or 3 feet high, quadrangular, having many pairs of rather elongated, oblong leaves, tapering to a point and usually clasping the stem at the base. The light purple labiate flowers are arranged in a long spike terminating the stem, usually with only six flowers in each whorl. The long-stalked leaves that spring directly from the root, as in the Wood Betony, have mostly faded off by the time the flowers appear in late summer. The whole plant is very hairy.

This plant had formerly a great reputation as a vulnerary, being strongly recommended by Gerard in his *Herbal*. He tells us that once being in Kent, visiting a patient, he accidentally heard of a countryman who had cut himself severely with a scythe, and had bound a quantity of this herb, bruised with grease and 'laid upon in manner of a poultice' over the wound, which healed in a week, though it would 'have required forty daies with balsam itself.' Gerard continues:

'I saw the wound and offered to heal the same for charietie, which he refused, saying I could not heal it so well as himself – a clownish answer, I confesse, without any thanks for my good-will: whereupon I have named it "Clown's Woundwort."'

Parkinson gives the same origin of the name.

Gerard himself, according to his own account, afterwards 'cured many grievous wounds, and some mortale with the same herbe.' The plant was regarded as a valuable remedy in such cases long before Gerard's time, having long borne the names, among country people, All-heal and Woundwort. The Welsh have an ancient name for it bearing the same signification.

It has edible roots. These are tuberous and attain a considerable size; when boiled they form a wholesome and nutritious food, rather agreeable in flavour. The young shoots may likewise be eaten cooked like Asparagus, but though pleasant in taste they have a disagreeable smell.

In modern herbal medicine this plant (which is collected in July, when just coming into flower and dried in the same manner as Wood Betony) is employed for its antiseptic and antispasmodic properties. It relieves gout, cramp and pains in the joints and vertigo. The bruised leaves, which have an unpleasant odour and an astringent taste, when applied to a wound will stop bleeding and heal the wound, as is claimed for them by old tradition, and the fresh juice is made into a syrup and taken internally to stop hæmorrhages, dysentery, etc.

See BETONY, WOOD.

YAM, WILD

Dioscorea Villosa (LINN.)
N.O. Dioscoreaceæ

Synonyms. Dioscorea. Colic Root. Rheumatism Root. Wilde Yamwurzel
Part Used. Dried rhizome
Habitat. Southern United States and Canada

¶ *Description.* There are upwards of 150 varieties of Dioscorea, many, like the potato, being edible. An Indo-Chinese species is used as a dye in Southern China. *Dioscorea Villosa* is a perennial, twining plant, with long, knotty, matted, contorted, ligneous root-stocks. The root is long, branched, crooked, and woody, the taste being insipid, afterwards acrid, and having no odour. It is usually sold in pieces of various lengths, which are difficult to pulverize, as the root flattens out when this is attempted. The therapeutical value is lost after the first year, so that it should be freshly gathered and carefully dried each year.

¶ *Constituents.* Much saponin has been found in the roots, and a substance improperly called *dioscorein*, obtained by precipitating the tincture with water.

¶ *Medicinal Action and Uses.* Antispasmodic. Perhaps the best relief and promptest cure for bilious colic, especially helpful in the nausea of pregnant women. Valuable also in painful cholera morbus with cramps, neuralgic affections, spasmodic hiccough and spasmodic asthma.

¶ *Dosage.* ½ to 1 drachm of fluid extract. Dioscorein, ¼ to 4 grains.

¶ *Poisonous, if any, with Antidotes.* An alkaloid separated from the Javanese *D. hirsuta* has been found to be a convulsive poison, resembling picrotoxin, but much feebler.

YARROW

Achillea millefolium (LINN.)
N.O. Compositæ

Synonyms. Milfoil. Old Man's Pepper. Soldier's Woundwort. Knight's Milfoil. Herbe Militaris. Thousand Weed. Nose Bleed. Carpenter's Weed. Bloodwort. Staunchweed. Sanguinary. Devil's Nettle. Devil's Plaything. Bad Man's Plaything. Yarroway.
(*Saxon*) Gearwe
(*Dutch*) Yerw
(*Swedish*) Field Hop
Part Used. Whole Herb
Habitat. Yarrow grows everywhere, in the grass, in meadows, pastures, and by the roadside. As it creeps greatly by its roots and multiplies by seeds it becomes a troublesome weed in gardens, into which it is seldom admitted in this country, though it is cultivated in the gardens of Madeira

The name *Yarrow* is a corruption of the Anglo-Saxon name for the plant – *gearwe*; the Dutch, *yerw*.

¶ *Description.* The stem is angular and rough, the leaves alternate, 3 to 4 inches long and 1 inch broad, clasping the stem at the base, bipinnatifid, the segments very finely cut, giving the leaves a feathery appearance.

It flowers from June to September, the flowers, white or pale lilac, being like minute daisies, in flattened, terminal, loose heads, or cymes. The whole plant is more or less hairy, with white, silky appressed hairs.

Yarrow was formerly much esteemed as a vulnerary, and its old names of Soldier's Wound Wort and Knight's Milfoil testify to this. The Highlanders still make an ointment from it, which they apply to wounds, and Milfoil tea is held in much repute in the Orkneys for dispelling melancholy. Gerard tells us it is the same plant with which Achilles stanched the bleeding wounds of his soldiers, hence the name of the genus, *Achillea*. Others say that it was discovered by a certain Achilles, Chiron's disciple. It was called by the Ancients, the *Herba Militaris*, the military herb.

Its specific name, *millefolium*, is derived from the many segments of its foliage, hence also its popular name, Milfoil and Thousand Weed. Another popular name for it is Nosebleed, from its property of stanching bleeding of the nose, though another reason given for this name is that the leaf, being rolled up and applied to the nostrils, causes a bleeding from the nose, more or less copious, which will thus afford relief to headache. Parkinson tells us that 'if it be put into the nose, assuredly it will stay the bleeding of it' – so it seems to act either way.

It was one of the herbs dedicated to the Evil One, in earlier days, being sometimes known as Devil's Nettle, Devil's Plaything, Bad Man's Plaything, and was used for divination in spells.

Yarrow, in the eastern counties, is termed *Yarroway*, and there is a curious mode of divination with its serrated leaf, with which the inside of the nose is tickled while the following lines are spoken. If the operation causes the nose to bleed, it is a certain omen of success:

'Yarroway, Yarroway, bear a white blow,
If my love love me, my nose will bleed now.'

An ounce of Yarrow sewed up in flannel and placed under the pillow before going to bed, having repeated the following words, brought a vision of the future husband or wife:

'Thou pretty herb of Venus' tree,
    Thy true name it is Yarrow;
Now who my bosom friend must be,
    Pray tell thou me to-morrow.'
        (Halliwell's *Popular Rhymes*, etc.)

It has been employed as snuff, and is also called Old Man's Pepper, on account of the pungency of its foliage. Both flowers and leaves have a bitterish, astringent, pungent taste.

In the seventeenth century it was an ingredient of salads.

¶ *Parts Used*. The whole plant, stems, leaves and flowers, collected in the wild state, in August, when in flower.

¶ *Constituents*. A dark green, volatile oil, a peculiar principle, *achillein*, and achilleic acid, which is said to be identical with aconitic acid, also resin, tannin, gum and earthy ash, consisting of nitrates, phosphates and chlorides of potash and lime.

¶ *Medicinal Action and Uses*. Diaphoretic, astringent, tonic, stimulant and mild aromatic.

Yarrow Tea is a good remedy for severe colds, being most useful in the commencement of fevers, and in cases of obstructed perspiration. The infusion is made with 1 oz. of dried herb to 1 pint of boiling water, drunk warm, in wineglassful doses. It may be sweetened with sugar, honey or treacle, adding a little Cayenne Pepper, and to each dose, a teaspoonful of Composition Essence. It opens the pores freely and purifies the blood, and is recommended in the early stages of children's colds, and in measles and other eruptive diseases.

A decoction of the whole plant is employed for bleeding piles, and is good for kidney disorders. It has the reputation also of being a preventative of baldness, if the head be washed with it.

¶ *Preparations*. Fluid extract, ½ to 1 drachm. An ointment made by the Highlanders of Scotland of the fresh herb is good for piles, and is also considered good against the scab in sheep.

An essential oil has been extracted from the flowers, but is not now used.

Linnæus recommended the bruised herb, fresh, as an excellent vulnerary and styptic. It is employed in Norway for the cure of rheumatism, and the fresh leaves chewed are said to cure toothache.

In Sweden it is called 'Field Hop' and has been used in the manufacture of beer. Linnæus considered beer thus brewed more intoxicating than when hops were used.

It is said to have a similar use in Africa.

Culpepper spoke of Yarrow as a profitable herb in cramps, and Parkinson recommends a decoction to be drunk warm for ague.

The medicinal values of the Yarrow and the Sneezewort (*A. millefolium* and *A. ptar-*

mica), once famous in physic, were discarded officially in 1781.

Woolly Yellow Yarrow (*A. tomentosa*) is very rare, and a doubtful native; its leaves are divided and woolly, the flowers bright yellow.

YELLOW DOCK. *See* DOCKS

YELLOW FLAG. *See* IRISES

YELLOW PARILLA. *See* PARILLA

YERBA REUMA

Frankenia grandifloria (CHAM. and SCHLECHT)
N.O. Frankeniaceæ

Synonyms. Frankenia. Flux Herb
Part Used. Herb
Habitat. California, Nevada, Arizona and Northern Mexico

¶ *Description*. A small, shrubby plant, with a prostrate, much-branched stem, about 6 inches long, growing in sandy places. It is salty to the taste, leaving an astringent after-taste. It has no odour.

¶ *Constituents*. It contains about 6 per cent. of tannin.

¶ *Medicinal Action and Uses*. Astringent. The herb is used as a remedy in catarrhal affections, especially of the nose and genito-urinary tract.

When diluted with from two to five times its volume of water, it may be used as an injection or spray.

It may also be taken internally.

¶ *Dosage*. Of fluid extract, 10 to 20 minims.

YERBA SANTA

Eriodictyon glutinosum (BENTH.)
N.O. Hydrophyllaceæ

Synonyms. Mountain Balm. Consumptive's Weed. Gum Bush. Bear's Weed. Holy or Sacred Herb. Eriodictyon Californicum (Hook and Arn.)
Part Used. Dried leaves
Habitat. California, Northern Mexico

¶ *Description*. A low, shrubby evergreen plant, 2 to 4 feet high, found growing abundantly in clumps on dry hills in California and Northern Mexico. The stem is smooth, usually branched near the ground, and covered with a peculiar glutinous resin, which covers all the upper side of the plant. Leaves, thick and leathery, smooth, of a yellowish colour, their upper side coated with a brownish varnish-like resin, the under surface being yellowish-white reticulated and tomentose, with a prominent midrib, alternate, attached by short petioles, at acute angle with the base; shape, elliptical, narrow, 2 to 5 inches long, ¾ inch wide, acute and tapering to a short leaf-stalk at the base. The margin of the leaf, dentate, unequal, bluntly undulate. The flowers, bluish, in terminal clusters of six to ten, in a one-sided raceme, the corolla funnel-like, calyx sparsely hirsute.

¶ *Constituents*. The chief constituents are five phenolic bodies, eriodictyol, homœriodictyol, chrysocriol, zanthœridol and eridonel. Free formic and other acids, glycerides of fatty acids; a yellow volatile oil; a phytosterol, a quantity of resin, some glucose. Taste, balsamic and sweetish, afterwards acrid, but not bitter, recalls Dulcamara and creates a flow of saliva. Odour, aromatic. The leaves are brittle when dry, but flexible in a warm, moist atmosphere. *Eriodictyon Californicum* is official in the United States Dispensary. Alcohol is the best agent for the fluid extract of the dried plant.

¶ *Medicinal Action and Uses*. Recommended for bronchial and laryngeal troubles and in chronic pulmonary affections, in the treatment of asthma and hay-fever in combination with *Grindelia robusta*. Likewise advised for hæmorrhoids and chronic catarrh of the bladder. Much used in California as a bitter tonic and a stimulating balsamic expectorant and is a most useful vehicle to disguise the unpleasant taste of quinine. Male fern and Hydrastis. In asthma, the leaves are often smoked. Aromatic syrup is the best vehicle for quinine.

¶ *Dosage*. 15 to 60 grains.

¶ *Other Species*. *E. tomentosum*, often found growing next to *E. Californicum*, especially in South California, but is easily distinguished from *E. Californicum*, being a larger shrub, and having a dense coat of short, villous hairs, colouring with age, whity-rusty; corolla, salver-shaped; leaves oval or oblong, and obtuse.

(*POISON*)
YEW [1]

Taxus Baccata
N.O. Taxaceæ and Coniferæ

Poisonous Parts. Leaves, seed and fruit
Habitat. Europe, North Africa, Western Asia

¶ *Description*. A tree 40 to 50 feet high, forming with age a very stout trunk covered with red-brown, peeling bark and topped with a rounded or wide-spreading head of branches; leaves spirally attached to twigs, but by twisting of the stalks brought more or less into two opposed ranks, dark, glossy, almost black-green above, grey, pale-green or yellowish beneath, ½ to 1½ inches long, $\frac{1}{8}$ to $\frac{1}{12}$ inch wide. Flowers unisexual, with the sexes invariably on different trees, produced in spring from the leaf axils of the preceding summer's twigs. Male, a globose cluster of stamens; female, an ovule surrounded by small bracts, the so-called fruit bright red, sometimes yellow, juicy and encloses the seed.

No tree is more associated with the history and legends of Great Britain than the Yew. Before Christianity was introduced it was a sacred tree favoured by the Druids, who built their temples near these trees – a custom followed by the early Christians. The association of the tree with places of worship still prevails.

Many cases of poisoning amongst cattle have resulted from eating parts of the Yew.

¶ *Constituents*. The fruit and seeds seem to be the most poisonous parts of the tree. An alkaloid taxine has been obtained from the seeds; this is a poisonous, white, crystalline powder, only slightly soluble in water; another principle, Milossin, has also been found.

¶ *Uses*. The wood was formerly much valued in archery for the making of long bows. The wood is said to resist the action of water and is very hard, and, before the use of iron became general, was greatly valued.

ZEDOARY

Curcuma Zedoaria (ROSCOE)
N.O. Zingiberaceæ

Synonyms. Turmeric. Zitterwurzel
Part Used. Dried rhizome
Habitat. East Indies and Cochin-China

¶ *Description*. There are two kinds of Zedoary, the long and the round, distinguished by the names of *radix zedoaria longæ* (Curcuma Zerumbet, the Long Zedoary of the shops) and *radix zedoaria rotundæ*. The long is in slices, or oval fingers; the round in transverse, rounded sections, twisted and wrinkled, greyish-brown in colour, hairy, rough, and with few root scars. The odour is camphoraceous, and the taste warm, aromatic, and slightly bitter, resembling ginger. The five commercial varieties come from China, Bengal, Madras, Java and Cochin-China, and vary in size and colour. When chewed they turn the saliva yellow. The powder is coloured brown-red by alkalis and boric acid. The Zerumbet has been erroneously confused with the round Zedoary.

Curcuma Starch, or East Indian Arrow-root, is prepared from the rhizomes of *Curcuma angustifolia*.

Some varieties of Zedoary are used as an ingredient in condiments and curries.

¶ *Constituents*. A volatile oil, when distilled with water, fixed oil, pungent resin, curcumin (an orange-yellow, tasteless, resinous principle), starch, mucilage, and an alkaloid.

¶ *Medicinal Action and Uses*. Aromatic, stimulant. Useful in flatulent colic and debility of the digestive organs, though it is rarely employed, as ginger gives the same, or better results. It is used as an ingredient in bitter tincture of Zedoary, antiperiodic pills (with and without aloes) bitter tincture, antiperiodic tincture (with and without alocs).

¶ *Dosages*. From 10 grains to ½ drachm. Fluid extract, 10 to 30 drops. Infusion of ½ oz. to a pint of boiling water, 1 tablespoonful.

---

[1] In homœopathy a tincture of the young shoots and also of the berries is used in a variety of diseases: cystitis, eruptions, headache and neuralgia, affections of the heart and kidneys, dimness of vision, and gout and rheumatism. – EDITOR.